FIFTH EDITION

Investments

FIFTH EDITION
Investments

FRANK K. REILLY
Bernard J. Hank Professor
University of Notre Dame

EDGAR A. NORTON
Illinois State University

The Dryden Press
Harcourt Brace College Publishers
Fort Worth   Philadelphia   San Diego   New York   Orlando   Austin   San Antonio
Toronto   Montreal   London   Sydney   Tokyo

Executive Editor   Mike Reynolds
Market Strategist   Charlie Watson
Developmental Editor   Terri House
Project Editor   Elaine Richards
Art Director   Scott Baker
Production Manager   Anne Dunigan

Cover credit: Wendy Grossman

ISBN: 0-03-022343-1
Library of Congress Catalog Card Number: 98-85990

Address for Domestic Orders
The Dryden Press, 6277 Sea Harbor Drive, Orlando, FL 32887-6777
800-782-4479

Address for International Orders
International Customer Service
The Dryden Press, 6277 Sea Harbor Drive, Orlando, FL 32887-6777
407-345-3800
(fax) 407-345-4060
(e-mail) hbintl@harcourtbrace.com

Address for Editorial Correspondence
The Dryden Press, 301 Commerce Street, Suite 3700, Fort Worth, TX 76102

Web Site Address
http://www.hbcollege.com

THE DRYDEN PRESS, DRYDEN, and the DP LOGO are registered trademarks of
Harcourt Brace & Company.

Printed in the United States of America

 9 0 1 2 3 4 5 6 7   0 3 2   9 8 7 6 5 4 3

The Dryden Press
Harcourt Brace College Publishers

To my best friend and wife, Therese,
and our greatest gifts and sources of happiness,
Frank K. III, Charlotte, and Lauren,
Clarence R. II, Therese B. and Anita,
Edgar B., Michele, Kayleigh, and Madison J.T.
-F.K.R.

To those who are special to me:
Mom, Dad, and Joy,
my wife, Becky, and her parents,
and my gifts from God: Matthew and Amy.
-E.A.N.

THE DRYDEN PRESS SERIES IN FINANCE

PREFACE

The pleasure of authoring a textbook comes from writing about a subject that you enjoy and find exciting. As authors, we hope that we can pass on to the reader not only knowledge but also the excitement that we feel for the subject. In addition, writing about investments brings an added stimulant because the subject can affect the reader during his or her entire business career and beyond. We hope what readers derive from this course will help them enjoy better lives because they will have learned how to manage their resources properly.

The purpose of this book is to help you understand how to manage your money so that you will derive the maximum benefit from what you earn. To accomplish this purpose, you need to learn about the investment alternatives that are available today and, more importantly, to develop a way of analyzing and thinking about investments that will remain with you in the years ahead when new and different investment opportunities become available.

Because of its dual purpose, the book mixes description and theory. The descriptive material discusses available investment instruments and considers the purpose and operation of capital markets in the United States and around the world. The theoretical portion details how you should evaluate current investments and future opportunities so that you can construct a portfolio of investments that will satisfy your risk–return objectives.

Preparing this fifth edition has been challenging for two reasons. First, many changes have occurred in the securities markets during the last few years in terms of theory, financial instruments, and trading practices. Second, as mentioned in prior editions, capital markets continue to become global, and new markets are being created around the world. Consequently, very early in the book (in Chapter 3) we present the compelling case for global investing. Subsequently, to ensure that you are prepared to function in this new global environment, almost every chapter discusses how investment practice or theory is influenced by the globalization of investments and capital markets. This completely integrated treatment is to ensure that you leave this course with a global mindset on investments that will serve you during the 21st century.

INTENDED MARKET

This book is addressed to both graduate and undergraduate students who want an in-depth discussion of investments and portfolio management. The presentation of the material is intended to be rigorous without being overly quantitative. A proper discussion of the modern developments in investments and portfolio theory must be rigorous. The summary results of numerous empirical studies reflect our personal belief that it is essential for theories to be exposed to the real world and be judged on the basis of how well they help us understand and explain reality.

MAJOR CHANGES AND ADDITIONS IN THE FIFTH EDITION

The order of the chapters in this edition has been rearranged to better reflect how many users teach the subject of investments, particularly equity analysis. Chapters relevant to stock analysis now follow each other sequentially (Chapters 9 through 14). After equity analysis is covered, bond valuation is discussed (Chapters 15 and 16) in a manner which builds upon earlier chapters which covered security valuation, financial statement analysis, and economic analysis. Subsequent chapters discuss basic and advanced derivatives (Chapters 17 and 18) and portfolio management issues (Chapters 19 through 22).

To reflect the growing use of the World Wide Web as a learning tool and a source of information, each chapter contains an annotated list of Web sites which relate to the chapter's topic. Students will want to "surf the net" using these applications to gain further insight into the practice of investments and the textbook discussions.

A consistent industry and company example is used in the equity valuation-oriented chapters. We review the financial statements of Walgreens, analyze influences on the retail drug store industry and the firm, and estimate the intrinsic value of Walgreens stock.

The text has been thoroughly updated. In addition to chapter revisions, this edition includes several new questions and problems, many from Chartered Financial Analyst exams. About half the chapters include "A Word From the Street," which features a comment from leading practitioners on how they use and apply the material from the chapter. By chapter, some specific changes include the following:

Chapter 2	Reflects the Tax Reform Act of 1997 and includes a discussion of regular IRAs and Roth IRAs. The need for investor education is stressed, including the need for diversification among those in employer-sponsored retirement programs. Tax, cultural, and regulatory factors are seen to cause asset allocation differences across countries.
Chapter 3	Increased description of international bond markets and an additional discussion of real estate instruments, such as REITs and CREFs.
Chapter 4	Our coverage of securities markets includes the AMEX/NASDAQ merger and other updates concerning domestic and foreign exchanges.
Chapter 5	We discuss the Brinson Partners Global Security Market Index. The chapter features a full update on bond market indexes and includes a summary description of dozens of indexes from around the world.
Chapter 6	Two new companies, Coca-Cola and Exxon, are used to explain the concepts of portfolio theory.
Chapter 8	Contains updated information and references on efficient markets tests, including the use of the BV/MV ratio as a determinant of return potential. Discusses the anomaly literature and its implications for security analysis and portfolio management.
Chapter 9	Analyzes the financial statements of Walgreens, a firm which we continue to analyze in subsequent equity analysis chapters. The discussion of business risk has been simplified. Analysis of debt ratios includes examples with lease payments.
Chapter 10	The chapter has been rewritten in order to highlight the two general approaches toward valuation: discounted cash flow (such as the dividend discount model) and relative valuation (such as P/E and P/B, among others).
Chapter 11	The chapter's presentation of international influences has been streamlined and simplified. The chapter's discussion includes the changes in the

composition of the index of leading economic indicators. The IMKAV principle (Identify and Monitor Key Assumptions and Variables) is well-illustrated by a comparison of forecasts and supporting reasons of leading practitioners in recent years.

Chapter 12   Factors influencing industry performance (demographics, societal values, regulation, Porter's competitive forces, etc.) are discussed in the context of the retail drug industry. The concept of theme investing is introduced in this chapter. The section on global industry analysis is shortened and focuses on the retail drug sector industry.

Chapter 13   The company analysis chapter is updated to show, with detailed examples, the process of applying discounted cash flow and relative valuation techniques to determine the fundamental value of Walgreens stock.

Chapter 14   The "extreme" levels of some indicators are updated to reflect recent market conditions. The chapter includes expanded coverage of moving averages.

Chapter 15   Our discussion of influences and trends in the global bond market includes the U.S. Treasury's inflation-protected bonds and recent innovations in the bond market toward 50- and 100-year maturity bonds.

Chapter 16   Improvements include distinguishing between nominal and effective yields and their effect on bond price calculations. In addition, we emphasize the interaction between the expectations and liquidity preference theories when explaining the term structure of interest rates.

Chapter 17   The introduction to derivatives chapter presents a clearer discussion of options, payoff profiles, and the differences between forwards, futures, and options. New contracts, including the "mini" S&P 500, are introduced. The sections on option pricing influences, put-call parity, and synthetic securities have been rewritten.

Chapter 18   The advanced derivatives chapter has been shortened while continuing to stress the basics of options on futures, warrants, and convertible securities.

Chapter 19   The chapter includes new sections on style investing and its applications in equity portfolio management. In addition, we discuss the characteristics that a good "value" manager should possess and how they differ from the characteristics of a good "growth" manager.

Chapter 20   This chapter includes a new section on style investing and its applications to fixed income portfolio management.

Chapter 21   The investment company chapter includes a number of updates and new discussions including: the trend away from new closed-end fund offerings; the sources of return and risk differences among money-market funds; new innovations in the mutual fund industry, including life-stage funds and mutual fund "supermarkets;" and different classes of mutual fund shares. We discuss the investor's need to consider the tax-efficiency of their investment strategy and fund selection. The chapter updates the discussion of the academic debate on whether investors can identify mutual funds that can outperform passive benchmarks consistently.

Chapter 22   We examine the implications of style investing by focusing on the importance of identifying appropriate benchmarks. We review two methods for determining a portfolio's style exposure: returns-based analysis and characteristic analysis. The mathematically oriented discussion of time-weighted and dollar-weighted rates of return has been moved to an appendix.

SUPPLEMENTS

The *Instructor's Manual/Test Bank*, prepared by Jeanette Diamond of the University of Nebraska–Omaha, contains the following aids for each chapter: an overview of the chapter; answers to all of the questions and problems; and a test bank of multiple-choice questions. A set of approximately 75 transparency masters is also available to instructors to facilitate the inclusion of key figures and illustrations from the book in classroom lectures.

A *Computerized Test Bank*, available in Windows format, is also free to instructors and contains all the test questions found in the printed *Test Bank*. The computerized test bank program, ExaMaster+™, has many features that facilitate exam preparation: random question selection; key-word searches; adding and editing test items; conversion of multiple-choice questions into short-answer questions; and creation of customized exams by question scrambling.

Spreadsheet Templates in Microsoft Excel are available for students. Students can enter data or information on the various templates related to the concepts and techniques in the text and the calculations are performed.

Lecture Presentation Software has been developed to cover all the essential concepts in each chapter. These slides, created in Microsoft PowerPoint, are designed to enhance the lecture experience.

A *Web Page* can be accessed through www.dryden.com that will provide up-to-date teaching and learning aids for instructors and students.

The Dryden Press will provide complimentary supplements or supplement packages to those adopters qualified under our adoption policy. Please contact your local sales representative to learn how you may qualify.

ACKNOWLEDGMENTS

So many people have helped us in so many ways that we hesitate to list them, fearing we may miss someone. Accepting this risk, we will begin with the University of Notre Dame and Illinois State University for their direct support. Professor Reilly would also like to thank the Bernard J. Hank family, who have endowed the Chair that helped bring him back to Notre Dame and has provided support for his work.

We would like to thank the following reviewers for this edition:

Susan Coleman, *University of Hartford*
John A. MacDonald, *Clarkson University*
Jeffrey A. Manzi, *Ohio University*
Francis J. McGrath, *Iona College*
Raj A. Padmaraj, *Bowling Green State University*
Murli Rajan, *University of Scranton*
Ata Yesilyaprak, *Alcorn State University*

We were fortunate to have the following excellent reviewers for earlier editions:

Robert Angell, *East Carolina University*
George Aragon, *Boston College*
Brian Belt, *University of Missouri–Kansas City*
Omar M. Benkato, *Ball State University*
Arand Bhattacharya, *University of Cincinnati*
Carol Billingham, *Central Michigan University*
Susan Block, *University of California–Santa Barbara*
Gerald A. Blum, *Babson College*

Robert J. Brown, *Harrisburg, Pennsylvania*
Dosoung Choi, *University of Tennessee*
John Clinebell, *University of Northern Colorado*
James P. D'Mello, *Western Michigan University*
Eugene F. Drzycimski, *University of Wisconsin–Oshkosh*
John Dunkelberg, *Wake Forest University*
Eric Emory, *Sacred Heart University*
Thomas Eyssell, *University of Missouri–St. Louis*
James Feller, *Middle Tennessee State University*
Eurico Ferreira, *Clemson University*
Michael Ferri, *John Carroll University*
Joseph E. Finnerty, *University of Illinois*
Harry Friedman, *New York University*
R. H. Gilmer, *University of Mississippi*
Stephen Goldstein, *University of South Carolina*
Steven Goldstein, *Robinson-Humphrey/American Express*
Keshav Gupta, *Oklahoma State University*
Sally A. Hamilton, *Santa Clara University*
Ronald Hoffmeister, *Arizona State University*
Ron Hutchins, *Eastern Michigan University*
A. James Ifflander, *Arizona State University*
Stan Jacobs, *Central Washington University*
Kwang Jun, *Michigan State University*
George Kelley, *Erie Community College*
Ladd Kochman, *Kennesaw State College*
Jaroslaw Komarynsky, *Northern Illinois University*
Tim Krehbiel, *Oklahoma State University*
Danny Litt, *Century Software Systems/UCLA*
Miles Livingston, *University of Florida*
Christopher Ma, *Texas Tech University*
Stephen Mann, *University of South Carolina*
Jeffrey A. Manzi, *Ohio University*
George Mason, *University of Hartford*
John Matthys, *DePaul University*
Michael McBain, *Marquette University*
Dennis McConnell, *University of Maine*
Jeanette Medewitz, *University of Nebraska–Omaha*
Jacob Michaelsen, *University of California–Santa Cruz*
Nicholas Michas, *Northern Illinois University*
Edward M. Miller, *University of New Orleans*
Lalatendu Misra, *University of Texas–San Antonio*
Michael Murray, *LaCrosse, Wisconsin*
John Peavy, *Southern Methodist University*
George Philippatos, *University of Tennessee*
Aaron L. Phillips, *The American University*
George Pinches, *University of Kansas*
Rose Prasad, *Central Michigan University*
George A. Racette, *University of Oregon*
Bruce Robin, *Old Dominion University*
James Rosenfeld, *Emory University*
Stanley D. Ryals, *Investment Counsel, Inc.*
Katrina F. Sherrerd, *Association of Investment Management and Research*
Frederic Shipley, *DePaul University*
Douglas Southard, *Virginia Polytechnic Institute*
Harold Stevenson, *Arizona State University*
Kishore Tandon, *City University of New York–Baruch College*
Donald Thompson, *Georgia State University*

David E. Upton, *Virginia Commonwealth University*
E. Theodore Veit, *Rollins College*
Bruce Wardrep, *East Carolina University*
Rolf Wubbels, *New York University*

Valuable comments and suggestions have come from former graduate students at the University of Illinois: Paul Fellows, University of Iowa; Wenchi Kao, DePaul University; and David Wright, University of Wisconsin–Parkside. Once more, we were blessed with bright, dedicated research assistants when we needed them the most. This includes Kieren McCabe and Paul Rainey, who were careful, dependable, and creative.

Current and former colleagues have been very helpful: Rob Battalio, Yu-Chi Chang, Michael Hemler, Bill Nichols, Juan Rivera, and Norlin Rueschhoff, University of Notre Dame; C. F. Lee, Rutgers University; and John M. Wachowicz, University of Tennessee. As always, some of the best insights and most stimulating comments come during runs with a very good friend, Jim Gentry of the University of Illinois.

We are convinced that professors who want to write a book that is academically respectable, relevant, as well as realistic require help from the "real world." We have been fortunate to develop relationships with a number of individuals (including a growing number of former students) whom we consider our contacts with reality.

We especially want to thank Robert Conway of Goldman Sachs & Company for suggesting several years ago that the book should reflect the rapidly evolving global market. This was very important advice and it has had a profound effect on this book over time.

The following individuals have graciously provided important insights and material:

Sharon Athey, *Brown Brothers Harriman*
Joseph C. Bencivenga, *Bankers Trust*
Lowell Benson, *Robert A. Murray Partners*
David G. Booth, *Dimensional Fund Advisors, Inc.*
Gary Brinson, *Brinson Partners, Inc.*
Charles K. Brown, *Goldman Sachs & Co.*
Roy Burry, *Kidder, Peabody & Co.*
Abby Joseph Cohen, *Goldman Sachs & Co.*
Thomas Coleman, *Adler, Coleman and Co. (NYSE)*
Robert Conway, *Goldman Sachs & Co.*
Robert J. Davis, *Crimson Capital Co.*
Robert J. Davis, Jr., *Goldman Sachs & Co.*
Philip Delaney, Jr., *Northern Trust Bank*
Steven Einhorn, *Goldman Sachs & Co.*
Sam Eisenstadt, *Value Line*
Frank Fabozzi, *Yale University*
Kenneth Fisher, *Forbes*
John J. Flanagan, Jr., *Lawrence, O'Donnell, Marcus & Co.*
Martin S. Fridson, *Merrill Lynch Pierce Fenner & Smith*
Richard A. Grasso, *New York Stock Exchange, Inc.*
William J. Hank, *Moore Financial Corporation*
Lea B. Hansen, *Grunwich Associates*
Joanne Hill, *Goldman Sachs & Co.*
John W. Jordan II, *The Jordan Company*
Andrew Kalotay, *Kalotay Associates*
Luke Knecht, *RCM Capital Management*
Mark Kritzman, *Windham Capital Management*
C. Prewitt Lane, *ICH Companies*
Martin Leibowitz, *TIAA-CREF*
Douglas R. Lempereur, *Templeton Investment Counsel, Inc.*
Robert Levine, *Nomura Securities*

Scott Lummer, *Ibbotson Associates*
Richard McCabe, *Merrill Lynch Pierce Fenner & Smith*
Michael McCowin, *Wisconsin Investment Board*
Terrence J. McGlinn, *McGlinn Capital Markets*
Scott Malpass, *University of Notre Dame*
John Maginn, *Mutual of Omaha*
Joseph McAlinden, *Morgan Stanley Dean Witter*
Kenneth R. Mayer, *Lincoln Capital Management*
Salvatore Muoio, *SM Investors, LP*
Robert G. Murray, *First Interstate Bank of Oregon*
Ian Rossa O'Reilly, *Wood Gundy, Inc.*
Philip J. Purcell III, *Morgan Stanley Dean Witter*
Jack Pycik, *Consultant*
Chet Ragavan, *Merrill Lynch Pierce Fenner & Smith*
John C. Rudolf, *Summit Capital Management*
Guy Rutherford, *Morgan Stanley Dean Witter*
Stanley Ryals, *Investment Counsel, Inc.*
Ron Ryan, *Ryan Labs, Inc.*
Sean St. Clair
Brian Singer, *Brinson Partners*
William Smith, *Morgan Stanley Dean Witter*
James Stork, *Duff & Phelps*
Masao Takamori, *Tokyo Stock Exchange*
Anthony Vignola, *Kidder, Peabody & Co.*
William M. Wadden, *Stein, Roe & Farnham*
Sushil Wadhwani, *Goldman Sachs & Co.*
Jeffrey M. Weingarten, *Goldman Sachs & Co.*
Robert Wilmouth, *National Futures Association*
Richard S. Wilson, *Ryan Labs, Inc.*

We continue to benefit from the help and consideration of the dedicated people who are or have been associated with the Institute of Chartered Financial Analysts, which is now a part of the Association for Investment Management and Research: Tom Bowman, Whit Broome, Bob Johnson, Bob Luck, Pete Morley, Sue Martin, Katie Sherrerd, Clay Singleton and Donald Tuttle.

Professor Reilly would like to thank his assistant, Cheri Gray, who had the unenviable task of keeping his office and his life in some sort of order during this project. Elaine Richards, project editor, and Kathy Dennis, associate project editor, put up with both of our schedules and brought the book from messy manuscript and sloppy exhibits to bound volume.

As always, our greatest gratitude is to our families—past, present, and future. Our parents gave us life and helped us understand love and how to give it. Most important are our wives who provide love, understanding, and support throughout the day and night. We thank God for our children and grandchildren who ensure that our lives are full of love, laughs, and excitement.

FRANK K. REILLY
Notre Dame, Indiana
EDGAR A. NORTON
Normal, Illinois
November 1998

ABOUT THE AUTHORS

FRANK K. REILLY is the Bernard J. Hank Professor of Business Administration, and former dean of the College of Business Administration at the University of Notre Dame. Holding degrees from the University of Notre Dame (B.B.A.), Northwestern University (M.B.A.), and the University of Chicago (Ph.D.), Professor Reilly has taught at the University of Illinois, the University of Kansas, and the University of Wyoming in addition to the University of Notre Dame. He has several years of experience as a senior securities analyst, as well as experience in stock and bond trading. A Chartered Financial Analyst (CFA), he has been a member of the Council of Examiners, the Council on Education and Research, the grading committee, and is currently on the Board of Trustees of the Institute of Chartered Financial Analysts and Chairman of the Board of the Association of Investment Management and Research. Professor Reilly has been president of the Financial Management Association, the Midwest Business Administration Association, the Eastern Finance Association, the Academy of Financial Services, and the Midwest Finance Association. He is or has been on the board of directors of the First Interstate Bank of Wisconsin, Norwest Bank of Indiana, the Investment Analysts Society of Chicago, Brinson Global Funds, Fort Dearborn Income Securities, Greenwood Trust Co., NIBCO, Inc., International Board of Certified Financial Planners, Battery Park Funds, Inc., Morgan Stanley Dean Witter Trust FSB, and the Association for Investment Management and Research.

As the author of more than 100 articles, monographs, and papers, his work has appeared in numerous publications including *Journal of Finance, Journal of Financial and Quantitative Analysis, Journal of Accounting Research, Financial Management, Financial Analysts Journal, Journal of Fixed Income,* and *Journal of Portfolio Management.* In addition to *Investments,* Fifth Edition, Professor Reilly is the co-author of another textbook, *Investment Analysis and Portfolio Management,* Fifth Edition (The Dryden Press, 1997) with Keith C. Brown.

Professor Reilly was named on the list of *Outstanding Educators in America* and has received the University of Illinois Alumni Association Graduate Teaching Award, the Outstanding Educator Award from the M.B.A. class at the University of Illinois, and the Outstanding Teacher Award from the M.B.A. class at Notre Dame. He also received the C. Stewart Sheppard Award from the Association of Investment Management and Research (AIMR) for his contribution to the educational mission of the Association. He is editor of *Readings and Issues in Investments, Ethics and the Investment Industry,* and *High Yield Bonds: Analysis and Risk Assessment,* and is or has been a member of the editorial boards of *Financial Management, The Financial Review, International Review of Economics and Finance, The Financial Services Review, The Journal of Applied Business Research, Journal of Financial Education, Quarterly Review of Economics and Finance,* and the *European Journal of Finance.* He is included in *Who's Who in Finance and Industry, Who's Who in America, Who's Who in American Education,* and *Who's Who in the World.*

EDGAR A. NORTON is professor of finance and associate dean for the College of Business at Illinois State University. He holds a double major in computer science and economics from Rensselaer Polytechnic Institute, where he graduated magna cum laude. Professor Norton received his M.S. and Ph.D. from the University of Illinois at Urbana-Champaign. A Chartered Financial Analyst (CFA), he regularly receives certificates of achievement, signifying his continual development in the field of investments. Professor Norton has served as a grader for Chartered Financial Analyst exams and has served as a curriculum consultant for the Chartered Financial Analyst equity specialization program. He has taught at Fairleigh Dickinson University, Liberty University and Northwest Missouri State University.

Professor Norton has authored or co-authored more than 30 papers that have been published in journals and conference proceedings, as well as presented at international, national, and regional conferences. His papers have been published in journals such as *Financial Review, Academy of Management Executive, Journal of the Midwest Finance Association, Journal of Business Venturing, Journal of Business Ethics, Journal of Small Business Finance, Journal of Business Research, Small Business Economics,* and *Journal of Small Business Management.* He co-authored a paper that received an Award of Excellence at the 36th International Council of Small Business World Conference, held in Vienna, Austria. He is a co-author of *Economic Justice in Perspective: A Book of Readings.* Professor Norton has been listed in *Who's Who in the East, Who's Who in American Education,* and *Who's Who Among Young American Professionals.*

Most students take this course because they want to learn to invest excess earnings. In addition, some may consider the investments field as an area for future employment. Over the years, many students have asked us, "What are the job opportunities in the investments area?" Here is a brief discussion of some specific investment-related positions with various financial institutions.

1. **Registered Representative with a Brokerage Firm.** Also referred to as a *broker,* the registered representative is involved in the sale of stocks, bonds, options, commodities, and other investment instruments to individuals or institutions. If you decide to buy or sell stock, you call your broker at the investment firm where you have an account, and he or she arranges the purchase or sale. If you are a regular customer, your broker may call you and suggest that you buy or sell some stock; if you agree, he or she will arrange it. It typically takes several years for a broker to build a clientele, but once this is done, the profession can be very exciting and financially rewarding—for the broker as well as for the clients.

2. **Investment Analysis: Brokerage Firms and/or Investment Bankers.** This field involves analysis of alternative industries, the companies in the industry, and their securities as support for registered representatives. For example, as an employee for Merrill Lynch, Pierce, Fenner & Smith, you might make an analysis of the computer industry and all the major companies in the industry and then prepare a report. This report would be used by the registered representatives at Merrill Lynch offices all over the country.

    Alternatively, if your firm is an investment banking firm that underwrites new stock or bond issues, you may analyze the industry and companies within the industry regarding a potential securities issue your firm will underwrite in order to determine its needs and to provide suggestions regarding the characteristics of the issue. In addition, investment bankers are heavily involved in finding merger partners for their clients and helping negotiate terms. As an analyst you would help answer these questions: how much is the potential merger firm worth, and what are reasonable terms?

3. **Investment Analysis: Banks.** Banks require investment analysis in two major areas—loans and trust departments. Obviously, a firm that is being considered for a commercial loan must be analyzed to find out why the firm needs money, how much money the firm needs, and when and how it will be able to repay the loan.

    Bank trust departments manage trust accounts for individuals and pension funds for companies. The capital is invested in various combinations of stocks and bonds. Again, banks need analysts to examine various industries and individual companies and to recommend securities that should be bought, sold, or held in the trust accounts.

4. **Investment Analysis: Money Managers and Mutual Funds.** Both groups manage large portfolios of stocks, bonds, and other assets for clients. Money managers manage pension funds, university endowment funds, and individual accounts (over $1 million)

for wealthy individuals. As an investment analyst, you would examine various industries and the companies within them and make recommendations regarding which stocks and bonds should be included in various portfolios.

In mutual funds (also referred to as *investment companies*), investors pool their money and acquire a portfolio of stocks and/or bonds. The investment company that manages the portfolio will hire analysts to examine industries and companies and to help them select stocks and bonds for various funds that can range from Treasury bonds to high-yield bonds to growth stocks.

5. **Investment Analysis: Insurance Companies.** Insurance companies typically have large investment portfolios that they manage in order to derive returns for policyholders. Although the asset mix of the portfolios differs depending upon the type of insurance (life versus property and casualty), the normal emphasis is on fixed-income securities.

6. **Portfolio Managers.** The financial firms mentioned previously (banks, investment counselors, mutual funds, insurance companies) employ portfolio managers in addition to analysts. The portfolio managers are responsible for gathering information and recommendations from the analysts. On the basis of the information, the recommendations, and the overall needs of the portfolio, they make final decisions about the securities in the portfolio.

7. **Financial Planners.** Because most individuals do not have the time or the desire to learn about stocks, bonds, and all the other components of a properly constructed portfolio, recent years have brought significant growth in the number of individuals and firms that provide assistance in personal financial planning. Based upon what a client tells a financial planner about his or her current assets, goals, needs, and constraints, the financial planner provides a blueprint of how that client should invest and in what financial instruments. The point is, financial planning firms need employees to help create appropriate financial plans for clients, analyze individual securities, and construct and monitor portfolios that fulfill the clients' financial plans.

SOME FACTORS TO CONSIDER

Many firms hire only investment analysts who have had three or four years of experience. How do you get the experience if nobody will hire you for that first job? It is necessary to contact a large number of firms in the field and show a willingness to apply yourself. Even if you get a job as an analyst, your beginning salary will probably be low compared to those for other jobs. Most investment firms believe that the first few years are almost entirely a training program, which is very costly to the firm. The good news is that once you get the initial position and the necessary experience, the long-run earnings potential for an experienced analyst or portfolio manager is substantial.

For some analyst jobs, firms typically hire individuals with graduate degrees. Often firms also hire undergraduates and encourage them to pursue graduate degrees in evening programs.

Almost anyone considering a career in investment analysis or portfolio management should attempt to become a Chartered Financial Analyst (CFA). This is a professional designation similar to the CPA in accounting. The designation is very well regarded by financial institutions around the world. The program and its requirements are described in an appendix at the back of the book.

Alternatively, individuals interested in being a financial planner should consider becoming a Certified Financial Planner (CFP), which is likewise a professional designation which indicates you passed a rigorous test in the area and have agreed to abide by a set of ethical standards.

BRIEF CONTENTS

CONTENTS

THE INVESTMENT
BACKGROUND

THE CHAPTERS IN THIS SECTION WILL PROVIDE A BACK-ground for your study of investments by answering the following questions:

- Why do people invest?
- How do you measure the returns and risks for alternative investments?
- What factors should you consider when you make asset allocation decisions?
- What investments are available?
- How do securities markets function?
- How and why are securities markets in the United States and around the world changing?
- What are the major uses of security market indexes?
- How can you evaluate the market behavior of common stocks and bonds?
- What factors cause differences among stock-and-bond market indexes?

In the first chapter we consider why an individual would invest, how to measure the rates of return and risk for alternative investments, and what factors determine an investor's required rate of return on an investment. The latter point will be important in subsequent analyses when we work to understand investor behavior, the markets for alternative securities, and the valuation of various investments.

Because the ultimate decision facing an investor is the makeup of his or her portfolio, Chapter 2 deals with the all-important asset allocation decision. This includes specific steps in the portfolio management process and factors that influence the makeup of an investor's portfolio over his or her life cycle.

To minimize risk, investment theory asserts the need to diversify. Chapter 3 begins our exploration of invest-ments available to investors, by making an overpowering case for investing globally rather than limiting choices to only U.S. securities. Building on this premise, we discuss several investment instruments found in global markets. We conclude the chapter with a review of the historical rates of return and measures of risk for a number of alternative asset groups.

In Chapter 4 we examine how markets work in general, and then specifically focus on the purpose and function of primary and secondary bond and stock markets. During the 1980s and 1990s, significant changes have occurred in the operation of the securities market, including a trend toward a global market. After discussing these changes, the globalization of existing markets, and the rapid development of new capital markets around the world, we speculate about how global markets will continue to expand available investment alternatives.

Investors, market analysts, and financial theorists often gauge the behavior of securities markets by evaluating changes in various market indexes and evaluate portfolio performance by comparing a portfolio's results to an appropriate benchmark. In Chapter 5 we examine and compare a number of stock-market and bond-market indexes that can be used for these purposes for the domestic and global markets.

This initial section provides the framework for you to understand various securities, how to allocate among alternative asset classes, the markets where they are bought and sold, the indexes that reflect their performance, and how you might manage a collection of investments in a portfolio. Specific portfolio management techniques are de-scribed in later chapters.

1

The Investment Setting

In this chapter we will answer the following questions:

♦ Why do individuals invest?

♦ What is an investment?

♦ How do investors measure the rate of return on an investment?

♦ How do investors measure the risk related to alternative investments?

♦ What factors contribute to the rates of return that investors require on alternative investments?

♦ What macroeconomic and microeconomic factors contribute to *changes* in the required rates of return for individual investments and investments in general?

This initial chapter discusses several topics basic to the subsequent chapters. We begin by defining the term *investment* and discussing the returns and risks related to investments. This leads to a presentation of how to measure the expected and historical rates of returns for an individual asset or a portfolio of assets. In addition, we consider how to measure risk not only for an individual investment, but also for an investment that is part of a portfolio.

The third section of the chapter discusses the factors that determine the required rate of return for an individual investment. The factors discussed are those that contribute to an asset's *total* risk. Because most investors have a portfolio of investments, it is necessary to consider how to measure the risk of an asset when it is a part of a large portfolio of assets. The risk that prevails when an asset is part of a portfolio is referred to as its *systematic* risk.

The final section deals with what causes *changes* in an asset's required rate of return over time. Changes occur because of both macroeconomic events that affect all investment assets and microeconomic events that affect the specific asset.   ♦

WHAT IS AN INVESTMENT?

For most of your life, you will be earning and spending money. Rarely, though, will your current money income exactly balance with your consumption desires. Sometimes you may have more money than you want to spend; at other times you may want to purchase more than you can afford. These imbalances will lead you either to borrow or to save to maximize the long-run benefits from your income.

When current income exceeds current consumption desires, people tend to save the excess. They can do any of several things with these savings. One possibility is to put the money under a mattress or bury it in the backyard until some future time when consumption desires exceed current income. When they retrieve their savings from the mattress or backyard, they have the same amount they saved.

Another possibility is that they can give up the immediate possession of these savings for a future larger amount of money that will be available for future consumption. This tradeoff of *present* consumption for a higher level of *future* consumption is the reason for saving. What you do with the savings to make them increase over time is *investment*.[1]

Those who give up immediate possession of savings (that is, defer consumption) expect to receive in the future a greater amount than they gave up. Conversely, those who consume more than their current income (that is, borrow) must be willing to pay back in the future more than they borrowed.

The rate of exchange between *future consumption* (future dollars) and *current consumption* (current dollars) is the *pure rate of interest*. Both people's willingness to pay this difference for borrowed funds and their desire to receive a surplus on their savings give rise to an interest rate referred to as the *pure time value of money*. This interest rate is established in the capital market by a comparison of the supply of excess income available (savings) to be invested and the demand for excess consumption (borrowing) at a given time. If you can exchange $100 of certain income today for $104 of certain income 1 year from today, then the pure rate of exchange on a risk-free investment (that is, the time value of money) is said to be 4 percent (104/100 − 1).

The investor who gives up $100 today expects to consume $104 of goods and services in the future. This assumes that the general price level in the economy stays the same. This price stability has rarely been the case during the past several decades when inflation rates have varied from 1.1 percent in 1986 to 13.3 percent in 1979, with an average of about 5.5 percent a year from 1970 to 1998. If investors expect a change in prices, they will require a higher rate of return to compensate for it. For example, if an investor expects a rise in prices (that is, he or she expects inflation) at the rate of 2 percent during the period of investment, he or she will increase the required interest rate by 2 percent. In our example, the investor would require $106 in the future to defer the $100 of consumption during an inflationary period (a 6 percent nominal interest rate will be required instead of 4 percent).

Further, if the future payment from the investment is not certain, the investor will demand an interest rate that exceeds the pure time value of money plus the inflation rate. The uncertainty of the payments from an investment is the *investment risk*. The additional return added to the nominal interest rate is called a *risk premium*. In our previous example, the investor would require more than $106 one year from today to compensate for the uncertainty. As an example, if the required amount were $110, $4, or 4 percent, would be considered a risk premium.

---

[1]In contrast, when current income is less than current consumption desires, people borrow to make up the difference. Although we will discuss borrowing on several occasions, the major emphasis of this text is how to invest savings.

Investment Defined

From our discussion we can specify a formal definition of investment. Specifically, an **investment** is the current commitment of dollars for a period of time in order to derive future payments that will compensate the investor for (1) the time the funds are committed, (2) the expected rate of inflation, and (3) the uncertainty of the future payments. The "investor" can be an individual, a government, a pension fund, or a corporation. Similarly, this definition includes all types of investments, including investments by corporations in plant and equipment and investments by individuals in stocks, bonds, commodities, or real estate. This text emphasizes investments by individual investors. In all cases the investor is trading a *known* dollar amount today for some *expected* future stream of payments that will be greater than the current outlay.

At this point, we have answered the questions about why people invest and what they want from their investments. They invest to earn a return from savings due to their deferred consumption. They want a rate of return that compensates them for the time, the expected rate of inflation, and the uncertainty of the return. This return, the investor's **required rate of return**, is discussed throughout this book. A central question of this book is how investors select investments that will give them their required rates of return.

The next section of this chapter describes how to measure the expected or historical rate of return on an investment and also how to quantify the uncertainty of expected returns. You need to understand these techniques for measuring the rate of return and the uncertainty of these returns to evaluate the suitability of a particular investment. Although our emphasis will be on financial assets such as bonds and stocks, we will refer to other assets such as art and antiques. Chapter 3 discusses the range of financial assets and also considers some nonfinancial assets.

MEASURES OF RETURN AND RISK

The purpose of this book is to help you understand how to choose among alternative investment assets. This selection process requires that you estimate and evaluate the expected risk–return tradeoffs for the alternative investments available. Therefore, you must understand how to measure the rate of return and the risk involved in an investment accurately. To meet this need, in this section we examine ways to quantify return and risk. The presentation will consider how to measure both *historical* and *expected* rates of return and risk.

We consider historical measures of return and risk because this book and other publications provide numerous examples of historical average rates of return and risk measures for various assets, and understanding these presentations is important. In addition, these historical results are often used by investors when attempting to estimate the *expected* rates of return and risk for an asset class.

The first measure is the historical rate of return on an individual investment over the time period the investment is held (that is, its holding period). Next, we consider how to measure the *average* historical rate of return for an individual investment over a number of time periods. The third subsection considers the average rate of return for a *portfolio* of investments.

Given the measures of historical rates of return, we will present the traditional measures of risk for a historical time series of returns (that is, the variance and standard deviation).

Following the presentation of measures of historical rates of return and risk, we turn to estimating the *expected* rate of return for an investment. Obviously, such an estimate contains a great deal of uncertainty, and we present measures of this uncertainty or risk.

Measures of Historical Rates of Return

When you are evaluating alternative investments for inclusion in your portfolio, you will often be comparing investments with widely different prices or lives. As an example, you might want to compare a $10 stock that pays no dividends to a stock selling for $150 that pays dividends of $5 a year. To properly evaluate these two investments, you must accurately compare their historical rates of returns. A proper measurement of the rates of return is the purpose of this section.

When we invest, we defer current consumption in order to add to our wealth so that we can consume more in the future. Therefore, when we talk about a return on an investment, we are concerned with the *change in wealth* resulting from this investment. This change in wealth can be due either to cash inflows such as interest or dividends, or caused by a change in the price of the asset (positive or negative).

If you commit $200 to an investment at the beginning of the year and you get back $220 at the end of the year, what is your return for the period? The period during which you own an investment is called its *holding period*, and the return for that period is the **holding period return (HPR)**. In this example, the HPR is 1.10, calculated as follows:

1.1
$$HPR = \frac{\text{Ending Value of Investment}}{\text{Beginning Value of Investment}}$$
$$= \frac{\$220}{\$200} = 1.10$$

This value will always be zero or greater, that is, it can never be a negative value. A value greater than 1.0 reflects an increase in your wealth, which means that you received a positive rate of return during the period. A value less than 1.0 means that you suffered a decline in wealth, which indicates that you had a negative return during the period. An HPR of zero indicates that you lost all of your money.

Although HPR helps us express the change in value of an investment, investors generally evaluate returns in *percentage terms on an annual basis*. This conversion to annual percentage rates makes it easier to directly compare alternative investments that have markedly different characteristics. The first step in converting an HPR to an annual percentage rate is to derive a percentage return, referred to as the **holding period yield (HPY)**. The HPY is equal to the HPR minus 1.

1.2
$$HPY = HPR - 1$$

In our example:

$$HPY = 1.10 - 1 = 0.10$$
$$= 10\%$$

To derive an *annual* HPY, you compute an *annual* HPR and subtract 1. Annual HPR is found by:

1.3
$$\text{Annual HPR} = HPR^{1/n}$$

where:

n = **number of years the investment is held**

Consider an investment that cost $250 and is worth $350 after being held for two years:

$$\text{HPR} = \frac{\text{Ending Value of Investment}}{\text{Beginning Value of Investment}} = \frac{\$350}{\$250}$$

$$= 1.40$$

$$\text{Annual HPR} = 1.40^{1/n}$$

$$= 1.40^{1/2}$$

$$= 1.1832$$

$$\text{Annual HPY} = 1.1832 - 1 = 0.1832$$

$$= 18.32\%$$

In contrast, consider an investment of $100 held for only six months that earned a return of $12:

$$\text{HPR} = \frac{\$112}{\$100} = 1.12 \ (n = .5)$$

$$\text{Annual HPR} = 1.12^{1/.5}$$

$$= 1.12^2$$

$$= 1.2544$$

$$\text{Annual HPY} = 1.2544 - 1 = 0.2544$$

$$= 25.44\%$$

Note that we made some implicit assumptions when converting the HPY to an annual basis. This annualized holding period yield computation assumes a constant annual yield for each year. In the two-year investment, we assumed an 18.32 percent rate of return each year, compounded. In the partial year HPR that was annualized, we assumed that the return is compounded for the whole year. That is, we assumed that the rate of return earned during the first part of the year is likewise earned on the value at the end of the first six months. The 12 percent rate of return for the initial six months compounds to 25.44 percent for the full year.[2]

Remember one final point: The ending value of the investment can be the result of a change in price for the investment alone (for example, a stock going from $20 a share to $22 a share), income from the investment alone, or a combination of price change and income. Ending value includes the value of everything related to the investment.

Computing Mean Historical Returns

Now that we have calculated the HPY for a single investment for a single year, we want to consider **mean rates of return** for a single investment and for a portfolio of investments. Over a number of years, a single investment will likely give high rates of return during some years and low rates of return, or possibly negative rates of return, during others. Your analysis should consider each of these returns, but you also want a summary figure that indicates this investment's typical experience, or the rate of return you should expect to receive if you owned this investment over an extended period of time. You can derive such a summary figure by computing the mean rate of return for this investment over some period of time.

Alternatively, you might want to evaluate a portfolio of investments that might include similar investments (for example, all stocks, or all bonds) or a combination of investments (for example, stocks, bonds, and real estate). In this instance, you would calculate the mean rate of return for this portfolio of investments for an individual year or for a number of years.

---

[2]To check that you understand the calculations, determine the annual HPY for a three-year HPR of 1.50. (Answer: 14.47 percent.) Compute the annual HPY for a three-month HPR of 1.06. (Answer: 26.25 percent.)

Single Investment   Given a set of annual rates of return (HPYs) for an individual invest-ment, there are two summary measures of return performance. The first is the arithmetic mean return, the second the geometric mean return. To find the **arithmetic mean (AM)**, the sum (Σ) of annual holding period yields is divided by the number of years (n) as follows:

1.4
$$AM = \Sigma HPY/n$$

where:

ΣHPY = the sum of annual holding period yields

An alternative computation, the **geometric mean (GM)**, is the nth root of the product of the HPRs for n years.

1.5
$$GM = \left[\pi\, HPR\right]^{1/n} - 1$$

where:

π = the product of the annual holding period returns as follows:

$$(HPR_1) \times (HPR_2) \ldots (HPR_n)$$

To illustrate these alternatives, consider an investment with the following data:

Year	Beginning Value	Ending Value	HPR	HPY
1	100.0	115.0	1.15	0.15
2	115.0	138.0	1.20	0.20
3	138.0	110.4	0.80	−0.20

$$AM = [(.15) + (.20) + (-.20)]/3$$
$$= 0.15/3$$
$$= 0.05 = 5\%$$

$$GM = [(1.15) \times (1.20) \times (0.80)]^{1/3} - 1$$
$$= (1.104)^{1/3} - 1$$
$$= 1.03353 - 1$$
$$= 0.03353 = 3.353\%$$

Investors are typically concerned with long-term performance when comparing alternative investments. GM is considered a superior measure of the long-term mean rate of return because it indicates the compound annual rate of return based on the ending value of the investment versus its beginning value.[3] Specifically, using the prior example, if we compounded 3.353 percent for three years, $(1.03353)^3$, we would get an ending wealth value of 1.104.

Although the arithmetic average provides a good indication of the expected rate of return for an investment during a future individual year, it is biased upward if you are attempting to measure an asset's long-term performance. This is obvious for a volatile security. Consider, for example, a security that increases in price from $50 to $100 during year 1 and drops back to $50 during year 2. The annual HPYs would be:

---

[3]Note that the GM is the same whether you compute the geometric mean of the individual annual holding period yields or the annual HPY for a three-year period, comparing the ending value to the beginning value, as discussed earlier under annual HPY for a multiperiod case.

Year	Beginning Value	Ending Value	HPR	HPY
1	50	100	2.00	1.00
2	100	50	0.50	−0.50

This would give an arithmetic mean rate of return of:

$$[(1.00) + (-0.50)]/2 = 50/2$$
$$= 0.25 = 25\%$$

This investment brought no change in wealth and therefore no return, yet the arithmetic mean rate of return is computed to be 25 percent.

The geometric mean rate of return would be:

$$(2.00 \times 0.50)^{1/2} - 1 = (1.00)^{1/2} - 1$$
$$= 1.00 - 1 = 0\%$$

This answer of a 0 percent rate of return accurately measures the fact that there was no change in wealth from this investment.

When rates of return are the same for all years, the geometric mean will be equal to the arithmetic mean. If the rates of return vary over the years, the geometric mean will always be lower than the arithmetic mean. The difference between the two mean values will depend on the year-to-year changes in the rates of return. Larger annual changes in the rates of return, that is, more volatility, will result in a greater difference between the alternative mean values.

An awareness of both methods of computing mean rates of return is important because published accounts of investment performance or descriptions of financial research will use both the AM and the GM as measures of average historical returns. We will also use both throughout this book. Currently most studies dealing with long-run historical rates of return include both arithmetic and geometric mean rates of return.

A Portfolio of Investments   The mean historical rate of return (HPY) for a portfolio of investments is measured as the weighted average of the HPYs for the individual investments in the portfolio, or the overall change in value of the original portfolio. The weights used in computing the averages are the relative *beginning* market values for each investment; this is referred to as dollar-weighted or value-weighted mean rate of return. This technique is demonstrated by the examples in Table 1.1. As shown, the HPY is the same (9.5 percent) whether you compute the weighted average return using the beginning market value weights or if you compute the overall change in the total value of the portfolio.

Although the analysis of historical performance is useful, selecting investments for your portfolio requires you to predict the rates of return you *expect* to prevail. The next section discusses how you would derive such estimates of expected rates of return. We recognize the great uncertainty regarding these future expectations, and we will discuss how one measures this uncertainty, which is referred to as the risk of an investment.

Calculating Expected Rates of Return

Risk is the uncertainty that an investment will earn its expected rate of return. In the examples in the prior section, we examined *realized* historical rates of return. In contrast, an investor who is evaluating a future investment alternative expects or anticipates a certain rate of return. The investor might say that he or she *expects* the investment will provide a rate of return of 10 percent, but this is actually the investor's most likely estimate, also

Table 1.1 *Computation of Holding Period Yield for a Portfolio*

Investment	Number of Shares	Beginning Price	Beginning Market Value	Ending Price	Ending Market Value	HPR	HPY	Market Weight	Weighted HPY
A	100,000	$10	$ 1,000,000	$12	$ 1,200,000	1.20	20%	0.05	0.01
B	200,000	20	4,000,000	21	4,200,000	1.05	5	0.20	0.01
C	500,000	30	15,000,000	33	16,500,000	1.10	10	0.75	0.075
Total			$20,000,000		$21,900,000				.095

$$HPR = \frac{21,900,000}{20,000,000} = 1.095$$

$$HPY = 1.095 - 1 = .095$$
$$= 9.5\%$$

referred to as a *point estimate*. Pressed further, the investor would probably acknowledge the uncertainty of this point estimate return and admit the possibility that, under certain conditions, the annual rate of return on this investment might go as low as -10 percent or as high as 25 percent. The point is, the specification of a larger range of possible returns from an investment reflects the investor's uncertainty regarding what the actual return will be. Therefore, a larger range of expected returns makes the investment riskier.

An investor determines how certain the expected rate of return on an investment is by analyzing estimates of expected returns. To do this, the investor assigns probability values to all *possible* returns. These probability values range from zero, which means no chance of the return, to one, which indicates complete certainty that the investment will provide the specified rate of return. These probabilities are typically subjective estimates based on the historical performance of the investment or similar investments modified by the investor's expectations for the future. As an example, an investor may know that about 30 percent of the time the rate of return on this particular investment was 10 percent. Using this information along with future expectations regarding the economy, one can derive an estimate of what might happen in the future.

The *expected* return from an investment is defined as:

$$\text{Expected Return} = \sum_{i=1}^{n} (\text{Probability of Return}) \times (\text{Possible Return})$$

1.6
$$E(R_i) = [(P_1)(R_1) + (P_2)(R_2) + (P_3)(R_3) + \ldots + (P_n R_n)]$$
$$E(R_i) = \sum_{i=1}^{n} (P_i)(R_i)$$

Let us begin our analysis of the effect of risk with an example of perfect certainty wherein the investor is absolutely certain of a return of 5 percent. Figure 1.1 illustrates this situation.

Perfect certainty allows only one possible return, and the probability of receiving that return is 1.0. Few investments provide certain returns. In the case of perfect certainty, there is only one value for $P_i R_i$:

$$E(R_i) = (1.0)(0.05) = 0.05$$

In an alternative scenario, suppose an investor believed an investment could provide several different rates of return depending on different possible economic conditions. As an example, in a strong economic environment with high corporate profits and little or no inflation, the investor might expect the rate of return on common stocks during the

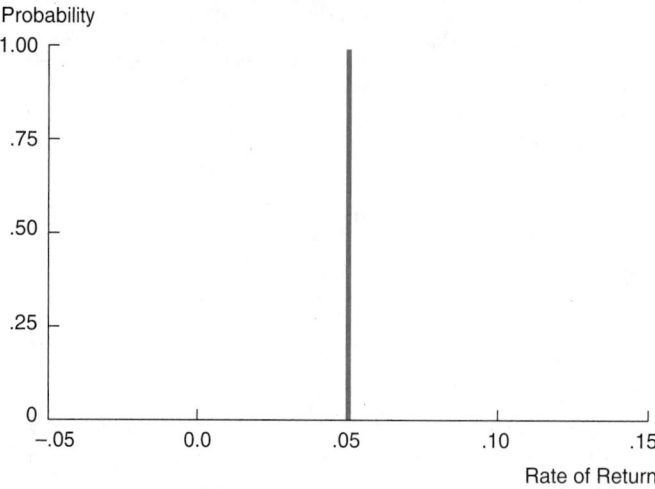

Figure 1.1   *Probability Distribution for Risk-Free Investment*

next year to reach as high as 20 percent. In contrast, if there is an economic decline with a higher-than-average rate of inflation, the investor might expect the rate of return on common stocks during the next year to be −20 percent. Finally, with no major change in the economic environment, the rate of return during next year would probably approach the long-run average of 10 percent.

The investor might estimate probabilities for each of these economic scenarios based on past experience and the current outlook as follows:

Economic Conditions	Probability	Rate of Return
Strong economy, no inflation	0.15	0.20
Weak economy, above-average inflation	0.15	−0.20
No major change in economy	0.70	0.10

This set of potential outcomes can be visualized as shown in Figure 1.2.

The computation of the expected rate of return $[E(R_i)]$ is as follows:

$$E(R_i) = [(0.15)(0.20)] + [(0.15)(-0.20)] + [(0.70)(0.10)]$$
$$= 0.07$$

Obviously, the investor is less certain about the expected return from this investment than about the return from the prior investment with its single possible return.

A third example is an investment with ten possible outcomes ranging from −40 percent to 50 percent with the same probability for each rate of return. A graph of this set of expectations would appear as shown in Figure 1.3.

In this case, there are numerous outcomes from a wide range of possibilities. The expected rate of return $[E(R_i)]$ for this investment would be:

$$E(R_i) = (0.10)(-0.40) + (0.10)(-0.30) + (0.10)(-0.20) + (0.10)(-0.10) + (0.10)(0.0)$$
$$+ (0.10)(0.10) + (0.10)(0.20) + (0.10)(0.30) + (0.10)(0.40) + (0.10)(0.50)$$
$$= (-0.04) + (-0.03) + (-0.02) + (-0.01) + (0.00) + (0.01) + (0.02) + (0.03)$$
$$+ (0.04) + (0.05)$$
$$= 0.05$$

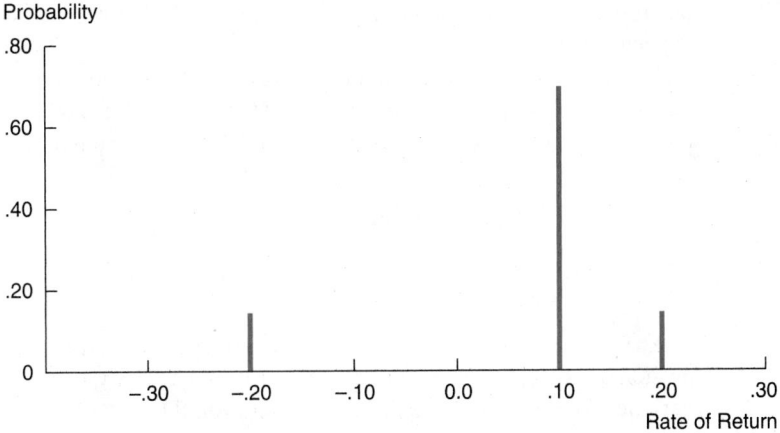

Figure 1.2 *Probability Distribution for Risky Investment with Three Possible Rates of Return*

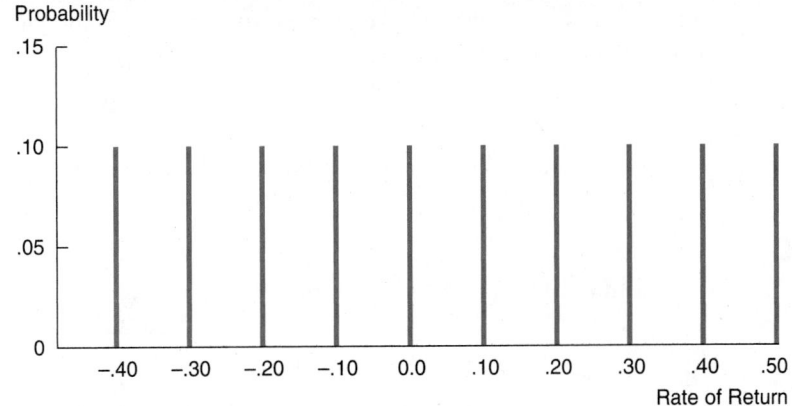

Figure 1.3 *Probability Distribution for Risky Investment with Ten Possible Rates of Return*

The *expected* rate of return for this investment is the same as the certain return discussed in the first example, but in this case, the investor is highly uncertain about the *actual* rate of return. This would be considered a risky investment because of that uncertainty. We would anticipate that an investor faced with the choice between this risky investment and the certain (risk-free) case would select the certain alternative. This expectation is based on the belief that most investors are **risk averse**, which means that if everything else is the same, they will select the investment that offers greater certainty.

Measuring the Risk of Expected Rates of Return

We have shown that we can calculate the expected rate of return and evaluate the uncertainty, or risk, of an investment by identifying the range of possible returns from that investment and assigning each possible return a weight based on the probability that it will occur. Although the graphs help us visualize the dispersion of possible returns, most investors want to quantify this dispersion using statistical techniques. These statistical measures

allow you to compare the return and risk measures for alternative investments directly. Two possible measures of risk (uncertainty) have received support in theoretical work on portfolio theory: the *variance* and the *standard deviation* of the estimated distribution of expected returns.

In this section, we demonstrate how variance and standard deviation measure the dispersion of possible rates of return around the expected rate of return. We will work with the examples discussed earlier. The formula for variance is as follows:

1.7

$$\text{Variance } (\sigma^2) = \sum_{i=1}^{n} (\text{Probability}) \times \left(\begin{array}{c} \text{Possible} \\ \text{Return} \end{array} - \begin{array}{c} \text{Expected} \\ \text{Return} \end{array} \right)^2$$

$$= \sum_{i=1}^{n} (P_i)[R_i - E(R_i)]^2$$

Variance   The larger the **variance** for an expected rate of return, the greater the dispersion of expected returns and the greater the uncertainty, or risk, of the investment. The variance for the perfect-certainty example would be:

$$(\sigma^2) = \sum_{i=1}^{n} P_i[R_i - E(R_i)]^2$$
$$= 1.0(0.05 - 0.05)^2 = 1.0(0.0) = 0$$

Note that in perfect certainty, there is *no variance of return* because there is no deviation from expectations, and therefore *no risk*, or *uncertainty*. The variance for the second example would be:

$$(\sigma^2) = \sum_{i=1}^{n} P_i[R_i - E(R_i)]^2$$
$$= [(0.15)(0.20 - 0.07)^2 + (0.15)(-0.20 - 0.07)^2 + (0.70)(0.10 - 0.07)^2]$$
$$= [0.010935 + 0.002535 + 0.00063]$$
$$= .0141$$

Standard Deviation   The **standard deviation** is the square root of the variance:

1.8

$$\text{Standard Deviation} = \sqrt{\sum_{i=1}^{n} P_i[R_i - E(R_i)]^2}$$

For the second example, the standard deviation would be:

$$\sigma = \sqrt{0.0141}$$
$$= 0.11874$$

A Relative Measure of Risk   In some cases, an unadjusted variance or standard deviation can be misleading. If conditions are not similar, that is, if there are major differences in the expected rates of return, it is necessary to use a measure of *relative variability* to indicate risk per unit of expected return. A widely used relative measure of risk is the **coefficient of variation** calculated as follows:

1.9

$$\frac{\text{Coefficient of}}{\text{Variation (CV)}} = \frac{\text{Standard Deviation of Returns}}{\text{Expected Rate of Return}}$$

$$= \frac{\sigma_i}{E(R)}$$

The CV for the example above would be:

$$CV = \frac{0.11874}{0.07000}$$
$$= 1.696$$

This measure of relative variability and risk is used by financial analysts to compare alternative investments with widely different rates of return and standard deviations of returns. As an illustration, consider the following two investments:

	Investment A	Investment B
Expected return	.07	.12
Standard deviation	.05	.07

Comparing absolute measures of risk, investment B appears to be riskier because it has a standard deviation of 7 percent versus 5 percent for investment A. In contrast, the CV figures show that investment B has less risk per unit of expected return as follows:

$$CV_A = \frac{0.05}{0.07} = 0.714$$

$$CV_B = \frac{0.07}{0.12} = 0.583$$

Risk Measures for Historical Returns

To measure the risk for a series of historical rates of returns, we use the same measures as for expected returns (variance and standard deviation) except that we consider the historical holding period yields (HPY) as follows:

1.10
$$\sigma^2 = \sum_{i=1}^{n}[HPY_i - E(HPY)]^2/n$$

where:

σ^2 = **the variance of the series**
HPY_i = **the holding period yield during period** i
$E(HPY)$ = **the expected value of the holding period yield that is equal to the arithmetic mean of the series**
n = **the number of observations**

The standard deviation is the square root of the variance. Both measures indicate how much the individual observations over time deviated from the expected value of the series. An example computation is contained in the appendix to this chapter. As we will see in subsequent chapters where we present historical rates of return for alternative asset classes, presenting the standard deviation as a measure of risk for the series or asset class is fairly common.

DETERMINANTS OF REQUIRED RATES OF RETURN

In this section we continue our consideration of factors that you must consider when selecting securities for an investment portfolio. You will recall that this selection process involves finding securities that provide a rate of return that compensates you for the time value of money during the period of investment, the expected rate of inflation during the period, and the risk involved.

Table 1.2 *Promised Yields on Alternative Bonds*

Type of Bond	1990	1991	1992	1993	1994	1995	1996	1997
U.S. Government 3-month Treasury bills	7.50%	5.38%	3.43%	3.00%	4.25%	5.49%	5.01%	5.06%
U.S. Government long-term bonds	8.74	8.16	7.52	6.59	7.41	6.93	6.80	6.67
Aaa corporate bonds	9.32	8.77	8.14	7.77	7.97	7.59	7.37	7.27
Baa corporate bonds	10.36	9.80	8.98	7.93	8.63	7.83	8.05	7.87

Source: *Federal Reserve Bulletin,* various issues.

The summation of these three components is called the *required rate of return*. This is the minimum rate of return that you should accept from an investment to compensate you for deferring consumption. Because of the importance of the required rate of return to the total investment selection process, this section contains a discussion of the three components and what influences each of them.

The analysis and estimation of the required rate of return is complicated by the behavior of market rates over time. First, a wide range of rates are available for alternative investments at any time. Second, the rates of return on specific assets change dramatically over time. Third, the difference between the rates available (that is, the spread) on different assets change over time.

The yield data in Table 1.2 for alternative bonds demonstrates these three characteristics. First, even though all of these securities have promised returns based upon bond contracts, the promised annual yields during any year differ substantially. As an example, during 1991 the average yields on alternative assets ranged from 5.38 percent on T-bills to 9.80 percent for Baa corporate bonds. Second, the changes in yields for a specific asset are shown by the three-month Treasury bill rate that went from 7.50 percent in 1990 down to 3.00 percent in 1993. Third, an example of a change in the difference between yields over time (referred to as a spread) is shown by the Baa–Aaa spread.[4] The yield spread in 1991 was 103 basis points (9.80–8.77), but was only 24 basis points in 1995 (7.83–7.59). (A basis point is .01 percent.)

Because differences in yields result from the riskiness of each investment, you must understand the risk factors that affect the required rates of return and include them in your assessment of investment opportunities. Because the required returns on all investments change over time, and because large differences separate individual investments, you need to be aware of the several components that determine the required rate of return, starting with the risk-free rate. The discussion in this chapter considers the three components of the required return and briefly discusses what affects these components. The presentation in Chapter 10 on valuation theory will discuss the factors that affect these components in greater detail.

The Real Risk-Free Rate

The **real risk-free rate (RFR)** is the basic interest rate, assuming no inflation and no uncertainty about future flows. An investor in an inflation-free economy who knew with certainty what cash flows he or she would receive at what time would demand the real risk-free rate on an investment. Earlier we called this the *pure time value of money*, because

---

[4]Bonds are rated by rating agencies based upon the credit risk of the securities, that is, the probability of default. Aaa is the top rating Moody's (a prominent rating service) gives to bonds with almost no probability of default. (Only U.S. Treasury bonds are considered to be of higher quality.) Baa is a lower rating Moody's gives to bonds of generally high quality that have some possibility of default under adverse economic conditions.

the only sacrifice the investor made was deferring the use of the money for a period of time. This real risk-free rate of interest is the price charged for the exchange between current goods and future goods.

Two factors, one subjective and one objective, influence this exchange price. The subjective factor is the time preference of individuals for the consumption of income. When individuals give up $100 of consumption this year, how much consumption do they want a year from now to compensate for that sacrifice? The strength of the human desire for current consumption influences the rate of compensation required. Time preferences vary among individuals, and the market creates a composite rate that includes the preferences of all investors. This composite rate changes gradually over time because it is influenced by all the investors in the economy, whose changes in preferences may offset one another.

The objective factor that influences the real risk-free rate is the set of investment opportunities available in the economy. The investment opportunities are determined in turn by the long-run real growth rate of the economy. A rapidly growing economy produces more and better opportunities to invest funds and experience positive rates of return. A change in the economy's long-run real growth rate causes a change in all investment opportunities and a change in the required rates of return on all investments. Just as investors supplying capital should demand a higher rate of return when growth is higher, those looking for funds to invest should be willing and able to pay a higher rate because of the higher growth rate. Thus, a *positive* relationship exists between the real growth rate in the economy and the real RFR.

Factors Influencing the Nominal Risk-Free Rate

Earlier, we observed that an investor would be willing to forgo current consumption in order to increase future consumption at a rate of exchange called the *risk-free rate of interest*. This rate of exchange was measured in real terms because the investor wanted to increase the actual consumption of actual goods and services rather than consuming the same amount that had come to cost more money. Therefore, when we discuss rates of interest, we need to differentiate between real rates of interest that adjust for changes in the general price level, as opposed to *nominal* rates of interest that are stated in money terms. That is, nominal rates of interest are determined by real rates of interest, plus factors that will affect the nominal rate of interest that prevails in the market, such as the expected rate of inflation and the monetary environment. It is important to understand these factors.

As noted earlier, the variables that determine the real risk-free rate change only gradually over the long term. Therefore, you might expect the required rate on a risk-free investment to be quite stable over time. As discussed in connection with Table 1.2, rates on three-month T-bills were *not* stable over the period from 1991 to 1997. This is demonstrated with additional observations in Table 1.3, which contains yields on T-bills for the period 1978 to 1997.

Investors view T-bills as a prime example of a default-free investment because the government has unlimited ability to derive income from taxes or to create money from which to pay interest. Therefore, rates on T-bills should change only gradually. In fact, the data show a highly erratic pattern. Specifically, there was an increase from 7 percent to more than 14 percent in 1981 before declining to less than 6 percent in 1986 and 3.33 percent in 1993. In sum, T-bill rates almost doubled in three years and then declined by almost 60 percent in five years. Clearly, the nominal rate of interest on a default-free investment is *not* stable in the long run or the short run, even though the underlying determinants of the real RFR are quite stable. The point is, two other factors influence the *nominal*

Table 1.3   *Three-Month Treasury Bill Yields and Rates of Inflation*

Year	3-Month T-Bills	Rate of Inflation	Year	3-Month T-bills	Rate of Inflation
1978	7.19%	7.70%	1998	6.67%	4.42%
1979	10.07	11.30	1989	8.11	4.65
1980	11.43	7.70	1990	7.50	6.11
1981	14.03	10.40	1991	5.38	3.06
1982	10.61	6.10	1992	3.43	2.90
1983	8.61	3.20	1993	3.33	2.75
1984	9.52	4.00	1994	4.25	2.67
1985	7.48	3.80	1995	5.49	2.54
1986	5.98	1.10	1996	5.01	3.32
1987	5.78	4.40	1997	5.06	1.70

Source: *Federal Reserve Bulletin,* various issues; *Economic Report of the President,* various issues.

risk-free rate: (1) the relative ease or tightness in the capital markets, and (2) the expected rate of inflation.

Conditions in the Capital Market   You will recall from prior courses in economics and finance that the purpose of capital markets is to bring together investors who want to invest savings with companies or governments who need capital to expand or to finance budget deficits. The cost of funds at any time (the interest rate) is the price that equates the current supply and demand for capital. A change in the relative ease or tightness in the capital market is a short-run phenomenon caused by a temporary disequilibrium in the supply and demand of capital.

As an example, disequilibrium could be caused by an unexpected change in monetary policy (for example, a change in the growth rate of the money supply) or fiscal policy (for example, a change in the federal deficit). Such a change in monetary policy or fiscal policy will produce a change in the nominal risk-free rate of interest, but the change should be short-lived because in the longer run, the higher or lower interest rates will affect capital supply and demand. As an example, a decrease in the growth rate of the money supply (a tightening in monetary policy) will reduce the supply of capital and increase interest rates. In turn, this increase in rates (for example, the price of money) will cause an increase in savings and a decrease in the demand for capital by corporations or individuals. These changes will bring rates back to the long-run equilibrium, which is based on the long-run growth rate of the economy.

Expected Rate of Inflation   Previously, it was noted that if investors expected the price level to increase during the investment period, they would require the rate of return to include compensation for the expected rate of inflation. Assume that you require a 4 percent real rate of return on a risk-free investment, but you expect prices to increase by 3 percent during the investment period. In this case, you should increase your required rate of return by this expected rate of inflation to about 7 percent [(1.04 × 1.03) − 1]. If you do not increase your required return, the $104 you receive at the end of the year will represent a real return of only 1 percent, not 4 percent. Because prices have increased by 3 percent during the year, what previously cost $100 now costs $103, so you can consume only about 1 percent more at the end of the year [($104/103) − 1]. If you had required a 7.12 percent nominal return, your real consumption could have increased by 4 percent [($107.12/103) − 1]. Therefore, an investor's nominal required rate of return in current dollars on a risk-free investment should be:

1.11   Nominal RFR = (1 + Real RFR) × (1 + Expected Rate of Inflation) − 1

Rearranging the formula, you can calculate the real risk-free rate of return on an investment as follows:

1.12 $$\text{Real RFR} = \left[\frac{(1 + \text{Nominal Risk-Free Rate of Return})}{(1 + \text{Rate of Inflation})}\right] - 1$$

To see how this works, assume that the nominal return on U.S. government T-bills was 9 percent during a given year, when the rate of inflation was 5 percent. In this instance, the real risk-free rate of return on these T-bills was 3.8 percent, as follows:

$$\text{Real RFR} = [(1 + 0.09)/(1 + 0.05)] - 1$$
$$= 1.038 - 1$$
$$= 0.038 = 3.8\%$$

This discussion makes it clear that the nominal rate of interest on a risk-free investment is not a good estimate of the real RFR, because the nominal rate can change dramatically in the short run in reaction to temporary ease or tightness in the capital market or because of changes in the expected rate of inflation. The significant changes in the average yield on T-bills shown in Table 1.3 were caused by the large changes in the rates of inflation during this period, also shown in Table 1.3.

The Common Effect   All the factors discussed thus far regarding the required rate of return affect all investments equally. Whether the investment is in stocks, bonds, real estate, or machine tools, if the expected rate of inflation increases from 2 percent to 6 percent, the investor's required return for *all* investments should increase by 4 percent. Similarly, if a decline in the expected real growth rate of the economy causes a decline in the real RFR of 1 percent, the required return on all investments should decline by 1 percent.

Risk Premium

A risk-free investment was defined as one for which the investor is certain of the amount and timing of the expected returns. The returns from most investments do not fit this pattern. An investor typically is not completely certain of the income to be received or when it will be received. Investments can range in uncertainty from basically risk-free securities such as T-bills to highly speculative investments such as the common stock of small companies engaged in high-risk enterprises.

Most investors require higher rates of return on investments to compensate for any uncertainty. This increase in the required rate of return over the nominal risk-free rate is the **risk premium**. Although the required risk premium represents a composite of all uncertainty, it is possible to consider several fundamental sources of uncertainty. In this section we identify and discuss briefly the major sources, including: (1) business risk, (2) financial risk (leverage), (3) liquidity risk, (4) exchange rate risk, and (5) country risk.

Business risk is the uncertainty of income flows caused by the nature of a firm's business. The less certain the income flows of the firm, the less certain the income flows to the investor. Therefore, the investor will demand a risk premium that is based on the uncertainty caused by the basic business of the firm. As an example, a retail food company would typically experience stable sales and earnings growth over time and would have low business risk compared to a firm in the auto industry, where sales and earnings fluctuate substantially over the business cycle, implying high business risk.

Financial risk is the uncertainty introduced by the method by which the firm finances its investments. If a firm uses only common stock to finance investments, it incurs only

business risk. If a firm borrows money to finance investments, it must pay fixed financing charges (in the form of interest to creditors) prior to providing income to the common stockholders, so the uncertainty of returns to the equity investor increases. This increase in uncertainty because of fixed-cost financing is called *financial risk* or *financial leverage*, and causes an increase in the stock's risk premium.[5]

Liquidity risk is the uncertainty introduced by the secondary market for an investment.[6] When an investor acquires an asset, he or she expects that the investment will mature (as with a bond) or that it will be salable to someone else. In either case, the investor expects to be able to convert the security into cash and use the proceeds for current consumption or other investments. The more difficult it is to make this conversion, the greater the liquidity risk. An investor must consider two questions about liquidity when assessing the liquidity risk of an investment: (1) How long will it take to convert the investment into cash? (2) How certain is the price to be received? Similar uncertainty faces an investor who wants to acquire an asset: How long will it take to acquire the asset? How uncertain is the price to be paid?

Uncertainty regarding how fast an investment can be bought or sold, or the existence of uncertainty about its price, increases liquidity risk. A U.S. government Treasury bill has almost no liquidity risk because it can be bought or sold in minutes at a price almost identical to the quoted price. In contrast, examples of illiquid investments include a work of art, an antique, or a parcel of real estate in a remote area. Such an investment may require a long time to find a buyer, and the selling price could vary substantially from expectations. Investors will increase their required rates of return to compensate for liquidity risk. This could also be a significant consideration when investing in foreign securities depending on the country and the liquidity of its stock and bond markets.

Exchange rate risk is the uncertainty of returns to an investor who acquires securities denominated in a currency different from his or her own. The likelihood of incurring this risk is becoming greater as investors buy and sell assets around the world, as opposed to only assets within their own countries. A U.S. investor who buys Japanese stock denominated in yen must consider not only the uncertainty of the return in yen, but also any change in the exchange value of the yen relative to the U.S. dollar. That is, in addition to the foreign firm's business and financial risk and the security's liquidity risk, the investor must consider the additional uncertainty of the return when it is converted from yen to U.S. dollars.

As an example of exchange rate risk, assume that you buy 100 shares of Mitsubishi Electric at 1,050 yen when the exchange rate is 115 yen to the dollar. The dollar cost of this investment would be about $9.13 per share (1,050/115). A year later you sell the 100 shares at 1,200 yen when the exchange rate is 130 yen to the dollar. When you calculate the HPY in yen, you find the stock has increased in value by about 14 percent (1,200/1,050), but this is the HPY for a Japanese investor. A U.S. investor receives a much lower rate of return because during this time period the yen has weakened relative to the dollar by about 13 percent (that is, it requires more yen to buy a dollar—130 versus 115). At the new exchange rate, the stock is worth $9.23 per share (1,200/130). Therefore, the return to you as a U.S. investor would be only about 1 percent ($9.23/$9.13) versus 14 percent for the Japanese investor. The difference in return for the Japanese investor and U.S. investor is because of the decline in the value of the yen relative to the dollar. Clearly, the exchange rate could have gone in the other direction, the dollar weakening against the yen. In this case, as a U.S. investor you would have experienced the 14 percent return measured in yen, as well as a gain from the exchange rate change.

[5]For a discussion of financial leverage, see Eugene F. Brigham, *Fundamentals of Financial Management*, 8th ed. (Hinsdale, Ill.: The Dryden Press, 1998), 221–225.

[6]You will recall from prior courses that the overall capital market is composed of the primary market and the secondary market. Securities are initially sold in the primary market and all subsequent transactions take place in the secondary market. These concepts are discussed in Chapter 4.

The more volatile the exchange rate between two countries, the less certain you would be regarding the exchange rate, the greater the exchange rate risk, and the larger would be the exchange rate risk premium you would require.[7]

There can also be exchange rate risk for a U.S. firm that is extensively multinational in terms of sales and components (costs). As will be discussed, this risk can generally be hedged at a cost.

Country risk, also called *political risk*, is the uncertainty of returns caused by the possibility of a major change in the political or economic environment of a country. The United States is acknowledged to have the smallest country risk in the world because its political and economic systems are the most stable. Nations with high country risk include Russia, because of the health problems of Yeltsin and the several changes in the government hierarchy and its currency during 1998, and Indonesia, where there were student demonstrations, major riots and fires prior to the resignation of President Suharto in May 1998. In both instances the stock markets experienced significant declines surrounding these events.[8] Individuals who invest in countries that have unstable political–economic systems must add a country risk premium when determining their required rates of return.

When investing globally (which will be emphasized throughout the book), investors must consider these additional uncertainties. How liquid are the secondary markets for stocks and bonds in the country? Are any of the country's securities traded on major stock exchanges in the United States, London, Tokyo, or Germany? What will happen to exchange rates during the investment period? What is the probability of a political or economic change that will adversely affect your rate of return? Exchange rate risk and country risk differ among countries. A good measure of exchange rate risk would be the absolute variability of the exchange rate relative to a composite exchange rate. The analysis of country risk is much more subjective and must be based on the history and current environment of the country.

This discussion of risk components can be considered a security's *fundamental risk* because it deals with the intrinsic factors that should affect a security's standard deviation of returns over time. In subsequent discussion, the standard deviation of returns is referred to as a measure of *total risk*.

$$\text{Risk Premium} = f(\text{Business Risk, Financial Risk, Liquidity Risk,}$$
$$\text{Exchange Rate Risk, Country Risk})$$

Risk Premium and Portfolio Theory

An alternative view of risk has been derived from extensive work in portfolio theory and capital market theory by Markowitz, Sharpe, and others.[9] These theories are dealt with in greater detail in Chapters 6 and 7, but their impact on the risk premium should be mentioned briefly at this point. This prior work by Markowitz and Sharpe indicated that investors should use an *external market* measure of risk. Under a specified set of assumptions, all

[7]An article that examines the pricing of exchange rate risk in the U.S. market is Philippe Jorion, "The Pricing of Exchange Rate Risk in the Stock Market," *Journal of Financial and Quantitative Analysis 26*, no. 3 (September 1991): 363–376.

[8]Carlotta Gall, "Moscow Stock Market Falls by 11.8%," *Financial Times* (May 19, 1998):1; "Russian Contagion Hits Neighbours," *Financial Times* (May 29, 1998): p. 17; John Thornhill, "Russian Stocks Fall 10% over Lack of Support from IMF," *Financial Times* (June 2, 1998): p. 1; Robert Chote, "Indonesia Risks Further Unrest as Debt Talks Falter," *Financial Times* (May 11, 1998), p. 1; Sander Thoenes, " Suharto Cuts Visit as Riots Shake Jakarta," *Financial Times* (May 14, 1998), p. 12; Sander Thoenes, "Economy Hit As Jakarta Is Paralysed," *Financial Times* (May 15, 1998), p. 17.

[9]These works include Harry Markowitz, "Portfolio Selection," *Journal of Finance 7*, no. 1 (March 1952): 77–91; Harry Markowitz, *Portfolio Selection—Efficient Diversification of Investments* (New Haven, Conn.: Yale University Press, 1959); and William F. Sharpe, "Capital Asset Prices: A Theory of Market Equilibrium Under Conditions of Risk," *Journal of Finance* 19, no. 3 (September 1964): 425–442.

rational, profit-maximizing investors want to hold a completely diversified market portfolio of risky assets, and they borrow or lend to arrive at a risk level that is consistent with their risk preferences. Under these conditions, the relevant risk measure for an individual asset is its *comovement with the market portfolio*. This comovement, which is measured by an asset's covariance with the market portfolio, is referred to as an asset's **systematic risk,** the portion of an individual asset's total variance attributable to the variability of the total market portfolio. In addition, individual assets have variance unrelated to the market portfolio (that is, nonmarket variance) that is due to unique features. This nonmarket variance is called *unsystematic risk* and it is generally considered unimportant because it is eliminated in a large, diversified portfolio. Therefore, under these assumptions, *the risk premium for an individual earning asset is a function of the asset's systematic risk with the aggregate market portfolio of risky assets.* The measure of an asset's systematic risk is referred to as its *beta:*

$$\text{Risk Premium} = f(\text{Systematic Market Risk})$$

Fundamental Risk versus Systematic Risk

Some might expect a conflict between the market measure of risk (systematic risk) and the fundamental determinants of risk (business risk, and so on). A number of studies have examined the relationship between the market measure of risk (systematic risk) and accounting variables used to measure the fundamental risk factors such as business risk, financial risk, and liquidity risk. The authors have generally concluded that *a significant relationship exists between the market measure of risk and the fundamental measures of risk.*[10] Therefore, the two measures of risk can be complementary. This consistency seems reasonable because, in a properly functioning capital market, the market measure of the risk should reflect the fundamental risk characteristics of the asset. As an example, you would expect a firm that has high business risk and financial risk to have an above average beta. At the same time, as we will discuss in Chapter 7, a firm that has a high level of fundamental risk and a large standard deviation can have a lower level of systematic risk because its variability of earnings and stock price is not related to the aggregate economy or the aggregate market. Therefore, one can specify the risk premium for an asset as:

$$\text{Risk Premium} = f(\text{Business Risk, Financial Risk, Liquidity Risk, Exchange}$$
$$\text{Rate Risk, Country Risk})$$
$$\text{or}$$
$$\text{Risk Premium} = f(\text{Systematic Market Risk})$$

Summary of Required Rate of Return

The overall required rate of return on alternative investments is determined by three variables: (1) the economy's real RFR, which is influenced by the investment opportunities in the economy (that is, the long-run real growth rate); (2) variables that influence the nominal RFR, which include short-run ease or tightness in the capital market and the expected rate of inflation. (Notably, these variables, which determine the nominal RFR, are the same for all investments); and (3) the risk premium on the investment. In turn, this

---

[10]A brief review of some of the earlier studies is contained in Donald J. Thompson II, "Sources of Systematic Risk in Common Stocks," *Journal of Business* 49, no. 2 (April 1976): 173–188. There is a further discussion of specific variables in Chapter 9.

risk premium can be related to fundamental factors including business risk, financial risk, liquidity risk, exchange rate risk, and country risk, or it can be a function of systematic market risk (beta).

Measures and Sources of Risk   In this chapter we have examined both measures and sources of risk arising from an investment. The *measures* of risk for an investment are:

♦ Variance of rates of return
♦ Standard deviation of rates of return
♦ Coefficient of variation of rates of return (standard deviation/means)
♦ Covariance of returns with the market portfolio (beta)

The *sources* of risk are:

♦ Business risk
♦ Financial risk
♦ Liquidity risk
♦ Exchange rate risk
♦ Country risk

RELATIONSHIP BETWEEN RISK AND RETURN

Previously, we showed how to measure the risk and rates of return for alternative investments, and we discussed what determines the rates of return that investors require. This section discusses the risk–return combinations that might be available at a point in time and illustrates the factors that cause *changes* in these combinations.

Figure 1.4 graphs the expected relationship between risk and return. It shows that investors increase their required rates of return as perceived risk (uncertainty) increases. The line that reflects the combination of risk and return available on alternative investments is referred to as the **security market line (SML)**. The SML reflects the risk–return combinations available for all risky assets in the capital market at a given time. Investors would select investments that are consistent with their risk preferences; some would consider only low-risk investments, whereas others welcome high-risk investments.

Figure 1.4   *Relationship between Risk and Return*

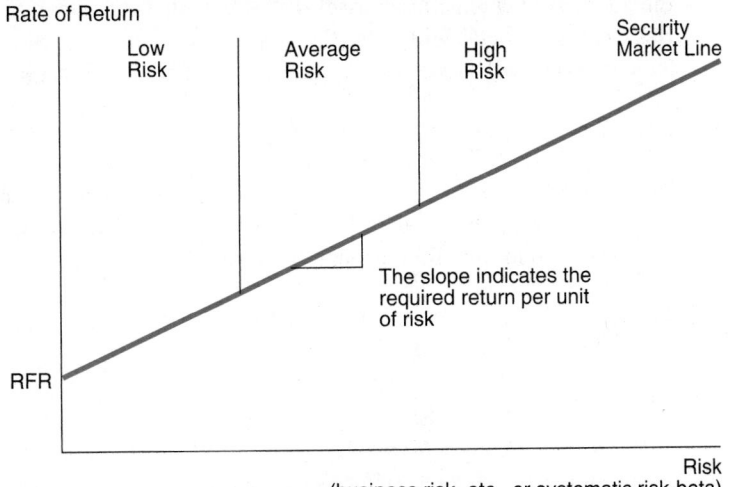

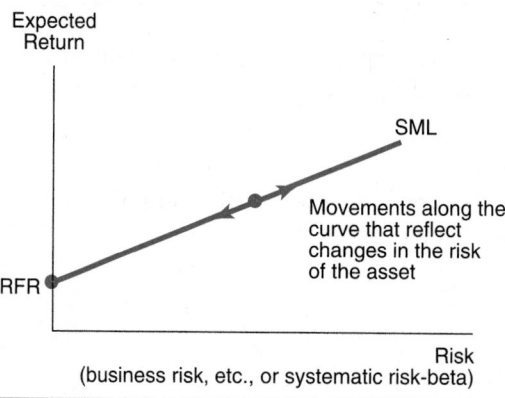

Beginning with an initial security market line, three changes can occur. First, individual investments can change positions on the SML because of changes in the perceived risk of the investments. Second, the slope of the SML can change because of a change in the attitudes of investors toward risk; that is, investors can change the returns they require per unit of risk. Third, the SML can experience a parallel shift due to a change in the real RFR or the expected rate of inflation—that is, a change in the nominal RFR. These three possibilities are discussed in this section.

Movements along the SML

Investors place alternative investments somewhere along the SML based on their perceptions of the risk of the investment. Obviously, if an investment's risk changes due to a change in one of its risk sources (business risk, and such), it will move along the security market line. For example, if a firm increases its financial risk by selling a large bond issue that increases its financial leverage, investors will perceive its common stock as riskier and the stock will move up the SML to a higher risk position. Investors will then require a higher rate of return. As the common stock becomes riskier, it changes its position on the SML. Any change in an asset that affects its fundamental risk factors or its market risk (that is, its beta) will cause the asset to move *along* the SML as shown in Figure 1.5. Note that the SML does not change, only the position of assets on the SML.

Changes in the Slope of the SML

The slope of the security market line indicates the return per unit of risk required by all investors. Assuming a straight line, it is possible to select any point on the SML and compute a risk premium (RP) through the equation:

1.13
$$RP_i = R_i - RFR$$

where:

RP_i = **risk premium for asset *i***
R_i = **the expected return for asset *i***
RFR = **the expected return on a risk-free asset**

Figure 1.6 *Plot of Moody's Corporate Bond Yield Spreads (Baa–Aaa): Monthly 1966–1996*

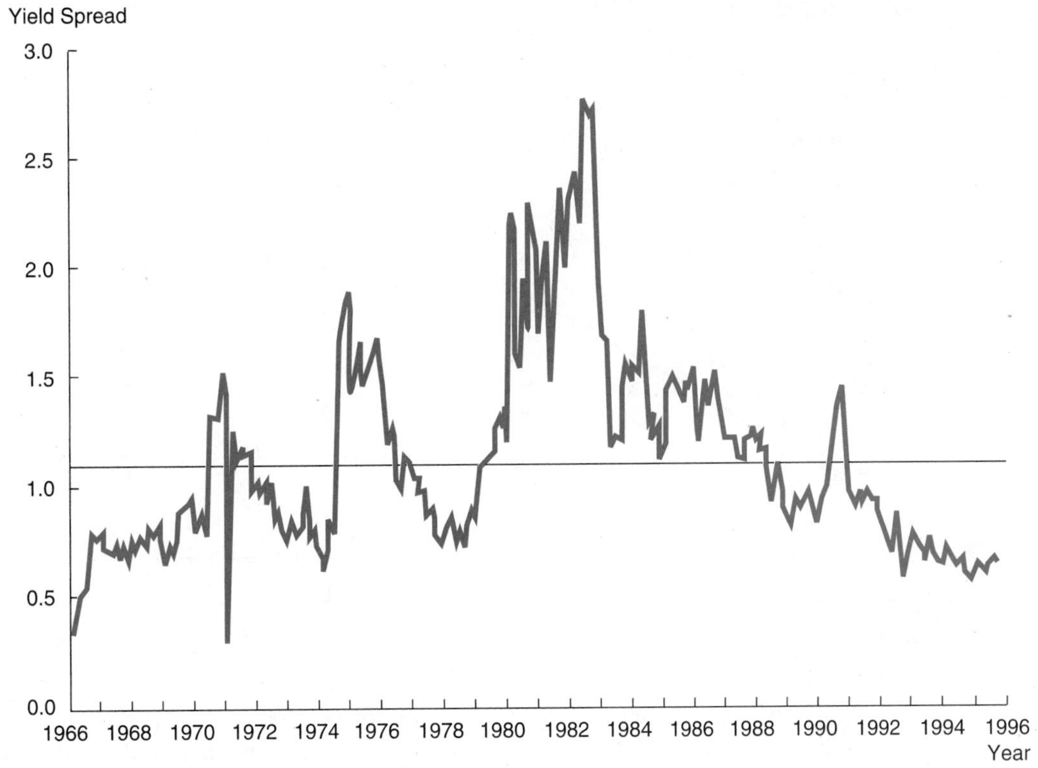

If a point on the SML is identified as the portfolio that contains all the risky assets in the market (referred to as the *market portfolio*), it is possible to compute a market risk premium as follows:

1.14
$$RP_m = R_m - RFR$$

where:

RP_m = **the risk premium on the market portfolio**
R_m = **the expected return on the market portfolio**
RFR = **the expected return on a risk-free asset**

This market risk premium is *not constant* because the slope of the security market line changes over time. Although we do not understand completely what causes these changes in the slope, we do know that there are changes in the *yield* differences between assets with different levels of risk even though the inherent risk differences are relatively constant.

These differences in yields are referred to as **yield spreads**, and these spreads change over time. As an example, if the yield on a portfolio of Aaa-rated bonds is 7.50 percent and the yield on a portfolio of Baa-rated bonds is 9.00 percent, we would say that the yield spread is 1.50 percent. This 1.50 percent is referred to as a risk premium because the Baa-rated bond is considered to have higher credit risk, that is, greater probability of default. This Baa−Aaa spread is *not* constant over time. For an example of changes in a yield spread, note the substantial difference in yields on Aaa-rated bonds and Baa-rated bonds shown in Figure 1.6.

Figure 1.7   *Change in Market Risk Premium*

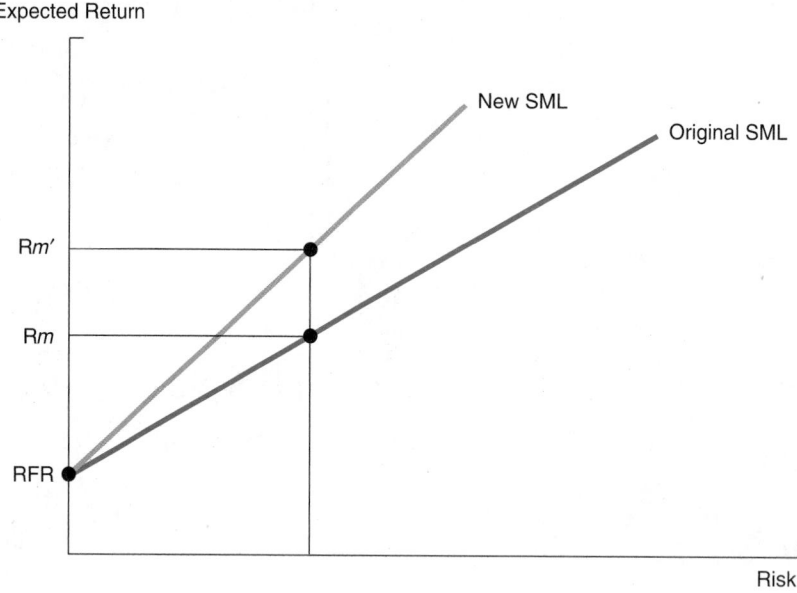

Although the underlying risk factors for the portfolio of bonds in the Aaa-rated bond index and the Baa-rated bond index would probably not change dramatically over time, it is clear from the time-series plot in Figure 1.6 that the difference in yields has experienced changes of more than 100 basis points (1 percent) in a short period of time (for example, see the increase in 1974 to 1975 and the dramatic decline in 1983 to 1984). Such a significant change in the yield spread during a period where there is no change in the risk characteristics of Baa bonds relative to Aaa bonds would imply a change in the market risk premium. Specifically, although the risk levels of the bonds remain relatively constant, investors have changed the yield spreads they demand to accept this relatively constant difference in risk.

This change in the risk premium implies a change in the slope of the security market line. Such a change is shown in Figure 1.7. The figure assumes an increase in the market risk premium, which means an increase in the slope of the market line. Such a change in the slope of the SML (the risk premium) will affect the required rate of return for all risky assets. Irrespective of where an investment is on the original SML, its required rate of return will increase, although its individual risk characteristics remain unchanged.

Changes in Capital Market Conditions or Expected Inflation

The graph in Figure 1.8 shows what happens to the SML when there are changes in one of the following factors: (1) expected real growth in the economy, (2) capital market conditions, or (3) the expected rate of inflation. For example, an increase in expected real growth, temporary tightness in the capital market, or an increase in the expected rate of inflation will cause the SML to experience a parallel shift upward. The parallel shift occurs because changes in expected real growth, in market conditions, or a change in the expected rate of inflation affect all investments no matter what their levels of risk.

Figure 1.8   *Capital Market Conditions, Expected Inflation, and the Security Market Line*

Expected Return

New SML

Original SML

RFR*

RFR

Risk

Summary of Changes in the Required Rate of Return

The relationship between risk and the required rate of return for an investment can change in three ways:

1. A movement *along* the SML demonstrates a change in the risk characteristics of a specific investment, such as a change in its business risk, its financial risk, or its systematic risk (its beta). This change affects only the individual investment.
2. A change in the *slope* of the SML occurs in response to a change in the attitudes of investors toward risk. Such a change demonstrates that investors want either higher or lower rates of return for the same risk. This is also described as a change in the market risk premium (R_m − RFR). A change in the risk premium will affect all risky investments.
3. A *shift* in the security market line reflects a change in expected real growth, in market conditions, such as ease or tightness of money, or a change in the expected rate of inflation. Again, such a change will affect all investments.

Investments Online

There are a great many Internet sites which seek to assist the beginning or novice investor. Because they cover the basics, have helpful links to other internet sites, and sometimes allow users to calculate items of interest (rates of return, the size of an investment necessary to meet a certain goal, and so on), these sites are useful for the experienced investor, too.

Investments Online *(cont.)*

www.financenter.com

Financenter has nearly everything for personal financial decisions. It includes insights about buying or selling a home or car, using a credit line, and information helpful for making insurance and investing decisions. It includes a "smart calculator" to help investors, both novice and experienced, answer a variety of questions.

www.investorama.com

This site allows you to obtain information on stocks, including stock price and mutual fund quotes. It contains links to over 6000 finance-related sites in 70 different categories. In addition, this site has links to the home pages of over 4000 public companies, where you can obtain current company information and financial statements. For the beginner, this site has several tutorials on investing.

www.moneyadvisor.com

Some financial decisions involve qualitative factors as investors or borrowers weigh one choice against another. Other decisions are more quantitative in nature, and some are a mix of both. To help you with decisions in the latter two categories, this Web site features a calculator feature to help make decisions such as whether to buy or lease a car. Other calculations and information can answer questions about loans, mortgages, insurance, tax, college and other saving goals. The site also includes several "just for fun" calculations. By answering several questions you can compute your body mass ratio and compare it to the ideal; you can also estimate your life expectancy.

www.investorguide.com

This is another site offering a plethora of information that is useful to both the novice and seasoned investor. It contains links to pages with market summaries, news research, and much more. It offers users a glossary of investment terms and 1000 questions and answers on a variety of topics. Basic investment education issues are taught here, and users can learn more through links to discussion groups, investment strategies, and many other topics. There are links to a number of personal financial help pages, including sites dealing with buying a home or car, retirement, loans, and insurance. It offers links to a number of calculator functions to help users make financial decisions.

Some other sites that may be of interest:

www.finweb.com   electronic publishing, databases, working papers, links to other Web sites

www.cob.ohio-state.edu/dept/fin/osudata.htm   links to numerous finance sites

www.aaii.org   home page for the American Association of Individual Investors, a group dealing with investor education.

Many representatives of the financial press have Internet sites:

www.wsj.com   The *Wall Street Journal*

www.ft.com   *Financial Times*

www.fortune.com   *Fortune* magazine

www.money.com   *Money* magazine

www.forbes.com   *Forbes* magazine

www.worth.com   *Worth* magazine

www.barrons.com   *Barron's* newspaper

SUMMARY

The purpose of this chapter is to provide background that can be used in subsequent chapters. To achieve that goal, we covered several topics:

♦ We discussed why individuals save part of their income and why they decide to invest their savings. We defined *investment* as the current commitment of these savings for a period of time to derive a rate of return that compensates for the time involved, the expected rate of inflation, and the uncertainty.

♦ We examined ways to quantify historical return and risk to help analyze alternative investment opportunities. We considered two measures of mean return (arithmetic and geometric) and applied these to a historical series for an individual investment and to a portfolio of investments during a period of time.

♦ We considered the concept of uncertainty and alternative measures of risk (the variance, standard deviation, and a relative measure of risk—the coefficient of variation).

♦ Prior to discussing the determinants of the required rate of return for an investment, we noted that the estimation of the required rate of return is complicated because the rates on individual investments change over time, because there is a wide range of rates of return available on alternative investments, and because the differences between required returns on alternative investments (for example, the yield spreads) likewise change over time.

♦ We examined the specific factors that determine the required rate of return: (a) the real risk-free rate, which is based on the real rate of growth in the economy, (b) the nominal risk-free rate, which is influenced by capital market conditions and the expected rate of inflation, and (c) a risk premium, which is a function of fundamental factors such as business risk, or the systematic risk of the asset relative to the market portfolio (that is, its beta).

♦ We discussed the risk–return combinations available on alternative investments at a point in time (illustrated by the SML) and the three factors that can cause changes in this relationship. First, a change in the inherent risk of an investment (that is, its fundamental risk or market risk) will cause a movement along the SML. Second, a change in investors' attitudes toward risk will cause a change in the required return per unit of risk, that is, a change in the market risk premium. Such a change will cause a change in the slope of the SML. Finally, a change in expected real growth, in capital market conditions, or in the expected rate of inflation will cause a parallel shift of the SML.

Based on this understanding of the investment environment, you are prepared to consider the asset allocation decision. This is the subject of Chapter 2.

Questions

1. Discuss the overall purpose people have for investing. Define investment.
2. As a student, are you saving or borrowing? Why?
3. Divide a person's life from ages twenty to seventy into ten-year segments and discuss the likely saving or borrowing patterns during each of these periods.
4. Discuss why you would expect the saving–borrowing pattern to differ by occupation (for example, for a doctor versus a plumber).
5. The *Wall Street Journal* reported that the yield on common stocks is about 4 percent, whereas a study at the University of Chicago contends that the annual rate of return on common stocks since 1926 has averaged about 10 percent. Reconcile these statements.
6. Some financial theorists consider the variance of the distribution of expected rates of return to be a good measure of uncertainty. Discuss the reasoning behind this measure of risk and its purpose.

7. Discuss the three components of an investor's required rate of return on an investment.
8. Discuss the two major factors that determine the market nominal risk-free rate (RFR). Explain which of these factors would be more volatile over the business cycle.
9. Briefly discuss the five fundamental factors that influence the risk premium of an investment.
10. You own stock in the Gentry Company, and you read in the financial press that a recent bond offering has raised the firm's debt/equity ratio from 35 percent to 55 percent. Discuss the effect of this change on the variability of the firm's net income stream, other factors being constant. Discuss how this change would affect your required rate of return on the common stock of the Gentry Company.
11. Draw a properly labeled graph of the security market line (SML) and indicate where you would expect the following investments to fall along that line. Discuss your reasoning.
    a. Common stock of large firms
    b. U.S. government bonds
    c. United Kingdom government bonds
    d. Low-grade corporate bonds
    e. Common stock of a Japanese firm
12. Explain why you would change your nominal required rate of return if you expected the rate of inflation to go from zero (no inflation) to 7 percent. Give an example of what would happen if you did not change your required rate of return under these conditions.
13. Assume the long-run growth rate of the economy increased by 1 percent and the expected rate of inflation increased by 4 percent. What would happen to the required rates of return on government bonds and common stocks? Show graphically how the effects of these changes would differ between these alternative investments.
14. You see in the *Wall Street Journal* that the yield spread between Baa corporate bonds and Aaa corporate bonds has gone from 350 basis points (3.5 percent) to 200 basis points (2 percent). Show graphically the effect of this change in yield spread on the SML and discuss its effect on the required rate of return for common stocks.
15. Give an example of a liquid investment and an illiquid investment. Discuss why you consider each of them to be liquid or illiquid.

Problems

1. On February 1, you bought some stock for $34 a share and a year later you sold it for $39 a share. During the year you received a cash dividend of $1.50 a share. Compute your HPR and HPY on this stock investment.
2. On August 15, you purchased some stock at $65 a share and a year later you sold it for $61 a share. During the year, you received dividends of $3 a share. Compute your HPR and HPY on this investment.
3. At the beginning of last year you invested $4,000 in 80 shares of the Chang Corporation. During the year Chang paid dividends of $5 per share. At the end of the year you sold the 80 shares for $59 a share. Compute your total HPY on these shares and indicate how much was due to the price change and how much was due to the dividend income.
4. The rates of return computed in Problems 1, 2, and 3 are nominal rates of return. Assuming that the rate of inflation during the year was 4 percent, compute the real rates of return on these investments. Compute the real rates of return if the rate of inflation were 8 percent.
5. During the past 5 years, you owned two stocks that had the following annual rates of return:

Year	Stock T	Stock B
1	0.19	0.08
2	0.08	0.03
3	−0.12	−0.09
4	−0.03	0.02
5	0.15	0.04

a. Compute the arithmetic mean annual rate of return for each stock. Which is most desirable by this measure?

b. Compute the standard deviation of the annual rate of return for each stock. (Use Chapter 1 Appendix if necessary.) By this measure, which is the preferable stock?

c. Compute the coefficient of variation for each stock. (Use the Chapter 1 Appendix if necessary.) By this relative measure of risk, which stock is preferable?

d. Compute the geometric mean rate of return for each stock. Discuss the difference between the arithmetic mean return and the geometric mean return for each stock. Relate the differences in the mean returns to the standard deviation of the return for each stock.

6. You are considering acquiring shares of common stock in the Madison Beer Corporation. Your rate of return expectations are as follows:

Possible Rate of Return	Probability
−0.10	0.30
0.00	0.10
0.10	0.30
0.25	0.30

Compute the expected return $[E(R_i)]$ on this investment.

7. A stockbroker calls you and suggests that you invest in the Fast and Powerful Computer Company. After analyzing the firm's annual report and other material, you believe that the distribution of rates of return is as follows:

Possible Rate of Return	Probability
−0.60	0.05
−0.30	0.20
−0.10	0.10
0.20	0.30
0.40	0.20
0.80	0.15

Compute the expected return $[E(R_i)]$ on this stock.

8. Without any formal computations, do you consider Madison Beer in Problem 6 or Fast and Powerful Computer in Problem 7 to present greater risk? Discuss your reasoning.

9. During the past year, you had a portfolio that contained U.S. government T-bills, long-term government bonds, and common stocks. The rates of return on each of them were as follows:

U.S. government T-bills	5.50%
U.S. government long-term bonds	7.50
U.S. common stocks	11.60

During the year, the consumer price index, which measures the rate of inflation, went from 160 to 172 (1982–1984 = 100). Compute the rate of inflation during this year. Compute the real rates of return on each of the investments in your portfolio based on the inflation rate.

10. You read in *Business Week* that a panel of economists has estimated that the long-run real growth rate of the U.S. economy over the next five-year period will average 3 percent. In addition, a bank newsletter estimates that the average annual rate of inflation during this five-year period will be about 4 percent. What nominal rate of return would you expect on U.S. government T-bills during this period?

11. What would your required rate of return be on common stocks if you wanted a 5 percent risk premium to own common stocks given what you know from Problem 10? If common stock investors became more risk averse, what would happen to the required rate of return on common stocks? What would be the impact on stock prices?

12. Assume that the consensus required rate of return on common stocks is 14 percent. In addition, you read in *Fortune* that the expected rate of inflation is 5 percent and the estimated long-term real growth rate of the economy is 3 percent. What interest rate would you expect on U.S. government T-bills? What is the approximate risk premium for common stocks implied by these data?

References

Fama, Eugene F., and Merton H. Miller. *The Theory of Finance*. New York: Holt, Rinehart and Winston, 1972.

Fisher, Irving. *The Theory of Interest*. New York: Macmillan, 1930; reprinted by Augustus M. Kelley, 1961.

GLOSSARY

Arithmetic mean (AM) A measure of mean return equal to the sum of annual holding period yields divided by the number of years.

Business risk Uncertainty due to the nature of a firm's business that affects the variability of sales and earnings.

Coefficient of variation (CV) A measure of relative variability that indicates risk per unit of return. It is equal to: standard deviation divided by the mean value. When used in investments, it is equal to: standard deviation of returns divided by the expected rate of return.

Country risk Uncertainty due to the possibility of major political or economic change in the country where an investment is located. Also called *political risk*.

Exchange rate risk Uncertainty due to the denomination of an investment in a currency other than that of the investor's own country.

Financial risk Uncertainty due to the method by which a firm finances its investments.

Geometric mean (GM) The *n*th root of the product of the annual holding period returns for *n* years minus 1.

Holding period return (HPR) The total return from an investment, including all sources of income, for a given period of time. A value of 1.0 indicates no gain or loss.

Holding period yield (HPY) The total return from an investment for a given period of time stated as a percentage.

Investment The current commitment of dollars for a period of time in order to derive future payments that will compensate the investor for the time the funds are committed, the expected rate of inflation, and the uncertainty of future payments.

Liquidity risk Uncertainty due to the ability to buy or sell an investment in the secondary market.

Mean rate of return The average of an investment's returns over an extended period of time.

Real risk-free rate (RFR) The basic interest rate with no accommodation for inflation or uncertainty. The pure time value of money.

Required rate of return The return that compensates investors for their time, the expected rate of inflation, and the uncertainty of the return.

Risk The uncertainty that an investment will earn its expected rate of return.

Risk averse The assumption about investors that they will choose the least risky alternative, all else being equal.

Risk premium (RP) The increase over the nominal risk-free rate that investors demand as compensation for an investment's uncertainty.

Security market line (SML) The line that reflects the combination of risk and return of alternative investments.

Standard deviation A measure of variability equal to the square root of the variance.

Systematic risk The portion of an individual asset's total variance that is attributable to the variability of the total market portfolio.

Variance A measure of variability equal to the sum of the squares of a return's deviation from the mean, divided by *n*.

Yield spread The difference between yields of investments at a point in time.

APPENDIX 1   *Computation of Variance and Standard Deviation*

Variance and standard deviation are measures of how actual values differ from the expected values (arithmetic mean) for a given series of values. In this case, we want to measure how rates of return differ from the arithmetic mean value of a series. There are other measures of dispersion, but variance and standard deviation are the best known because they are used in statistics and probability theory. Variance is defined as:

$$\text{Variance } (\sigma^2) = \sum_{i=1}^{n} (\text{Probability})(\text{Possible Return} - \text{Expected Return})^2$$

$$= \sum_{i=1}^{n} (P_i)[R_i - E(R_i)]^2$$

Consider the following example, as discussed in the chapter:

Probability of Possible Return (P_i)	Possible Return (R_i)	$P_i R_i$
0.15	0.20	0.03
0.15	−0.20	−0.03
0.70	0.10	0.07
		$\Sigma = 0.07$

This gives an expected return [$E(R_i)$] of 7 percent. The dispersion of this distribution as measured by variance is:

Probability (P_i)	Return (R_i)	$R_i - E(R_i)$	$[R_i - E(R_i)]^2$	$P_i[R_i - E(R_i)]^2$
0.15	0.20	0.13	0.0169	0.002535
0.15	−0.20	−0.27	0.0729	0.010935
0.70	0.10	0.03	0.0009	0.000630
				$\Sigma = 0.014100$

The variance (σ^2) is equal to 0.0141. The standard deviation is equal to the square root of the variance:

$$\text{Standard Deviation } (\sigma) = \sqrt{\sum_{i=1}^{n} P_i[R_i - E(R_i)]^2}$$

Consequently, the standard deviation for the preceding example would be:

$$\sigma_i = \sqrt{0.0141} = 0.11874$$

In this example, the standard deviation is approximately 11.87 percent. Therefore, you could describe this distribution as having an expected value of 7 percent and a standard deviation of 11.87 percent.

In many instances, you might want to compute the variance or standard deviation for a historical series in order to evaluate the past performance of the investment. Assume that you are given the following information on annual rates of return (HPY) for common stocks listed on the New York Stock Exchange (NYSE):

Year	Annual Rate of Return
19_5	0.07
19_6	0.11
19_7	−0.04
19_8	0.12
19_9	−0.06

In this case, we are not examining expected rates of return, but actual returns. Therefore, we assume equal probabilities, and the expected value (in this case the mean value, R) of the series is the sum of the individual observations in the series divided by the number of observations, or 0.04 (0.20/5). The variances and standard deviations are:

Year	R_i	$R_i - \bar{R}$	$(R_i - \bar{R})2$	
19_5	0.07	0.03	0.0009	$\sigma^2 = 0.0286/5$
19_6	0.11	0.07	0.0049	$= 0.00572$
19_7	−0.04	−0.08	0.0064	
19_8	0.12	0.08	0.0064	$\sigma = \sqrt{0.00572}$
19_9	−0.06	−0.10	0.0110	$= 0.0756$
			$\Sigma = 0.0286$	

We can interpret the performance of NYSE common stocks during this period of time by saying that the average rate of return was 4 percent and the standard deviation of annual rates of return was 7.56 percent.

Coefficient of Variation

In some instances you might want to compare the dispersion of two different series. The variance or standard deviation are *absolute* measures of dispersion. That is, they can be influenced by the magnitude of the original numbers. To compare series with greatly different values, you need a *relative* measure of dispersion. A measure of relative dispersion is the coefficient of variation, which is defined as:

$$\text{Coefficient of Variation (CV)} = \frac{\text{Standard Deviation of Returns}}{\text{Expected Rate of Return}}$$

A larger value indicates greater dispersion relative to the arithmetic mean of the series. For the previous example, the CV would be:

$$CV_1 = \frac{0.0756}{0.0400} = 1.89$$

It is possible to compare this value to a similar figure having a markedly different distribution. As an example, assume you wanted to compare this investment to another investment that had an average rate of return of 10 percent and a standard deviation of 9 percent. The standard deviations alone tell you that the second series has greater dispersion (9 percent versus 7.56 percent) and might be considered to have higher risk. In fact, the relative dispersion for this second investment is much less.

$$CV_1 = \frac{0.0756}{0.0400} = 1.89$$

$$CV_2 = \frac{0.0900}{0.1000} = 0.90$$

Considering the relative dispersion and the total distribution, most investors would probably prefer the second investment.

Problems

1. Your rate of return expectations for the common stock of Gray Disc Company during the next year are:

Possible Rate of Return	Probability
−0.10	0.25
0.00	0.15
0.10	0.35
0.25	0.25

    a. Compute the expected return $[E(R_i)]$ on this investment, the variance of this return (σ^2), and its standard deviation (σ).
    b. Under what conditions can the standard deviation be used to measure the relative risk of two investments?
    c. Under what conditions must the coefficient of variation be used to measure the relative risk of two investments?

2. Your rate of return expectations for the stock of Kayleigh Computer Company during the next year are:

Possible Rate of Return	Probability
−0.60	0.15
−0.30	0.10
−0.10	0.05
0.20	0.40
0.40	0.20
0.80	0.10

    a. Compute the expected return $[E(R_i)]$ on this stock, the variance (σ^2) of this return, and its standard deviation (σ).
    b. On the basis of expected return $[E(R_i)]$ alone, discuss whether Gray Disc or Kayleigh Computer is preferable.
    c. On the basis of standard deviation (σ) alone, discuss whether Gray Disc or Kayleigh Computer is preferable.
    d. Compute the coefficients of variation (CVs) for Gray Disc and Kayleigh Computer and discuss which stock return series has the greater relative dispersion.

3. The following are annual rates of return for U.S. government T-bills and United Kingdom common stocks.

Year	U.S. Government T-Bills	United Kingdom Common Stock
19_5	.063	.150
19_6	.081	−.043
19_7	.076	.374
19_8	.090	.192
19_9	.085	−.106

    a. Compute the arithmetic mean rate of return and standard deviation of rates of return for the two series.
    b. Discuss these two alternative investments in terms of their arithmetic average rates of return, their absolute risk, and their relative risk.
    c. Compute the geometric mean rate of return for each of these investments. Compare the arithmetic mean return and geometric mean return for each investment and discuss this difference between mean returns as related to the standard deviation of each series.

The Asset Allocation Decision

In this chapter we will answer the following questions:

♦ What is asset allocation?

♦ What are the four steps in the portfolio management process?

♦ What is the role of asset allocation in investment planning?

♦ Why is a policy statement important to the planning process?

♦ What objectives and constraints should be detailed in a policy statement?

♦ How and why do investment goals change over a person's lifetime and circumstances?

♦ Why is investment education necessary?

♦ Why do asset allocation strategies differ across national boundaries?

The previous chapter informed us that *risk drives return*. Therefore, the practice of investing funds and managing portfolios should focus primarily on managing risk rather than on managing returns.

This chapter examines some of the practical implications of risk management in the context of asset allocation. **Asset allocation** is the process of deciding how to distribute an investor's wealth among different countries and asset classes for investment purposes. An **asset class** is comprised of securities that have similar characteristics, attributes, and risk/return relationships. A broad asset class such as "bonds" can be divided into smaller asset classes, such as Treasury bonds, corporate bonds, and high-yield bonds. We will see that, in the long run, the highest compounded returns will most likely accrue to those investors with larger exposures to risky assets. We will also see that although there are no shortcuts or guarantees to investment success, maintaining a reasonable and disciplined approach to investing will increase the likelihood of investment success over time.   ♦

The asset allocation decision is not an isolated choice; rather, it is a component of a portfolio management process. In this chapter we present an overview of the four-step portfolio management process. As we will see, the first step in the process is to develop an investment policy statement, or plan, that will guide all future decisions. Much of an asset allocation strategy depends on the investor's policy statement. The policy statement includes the investor's goals or objectives, constraints, and investment guidelines.

What we mean by an "investor" can range from an individual to trustees overseeing a corporation's multi-billion-dollar pension fund, a university endowment, or invested premiums for an insurance company. Regardless of who the investor is or how simple or complex their investment needs, he or she should develop a policy statement prior to making long-term investment decisions. Although to help illustrate this process most of our examples will be in the context of an individual investor, the concepts we introduce here—investment objectives, constraints, benchmarks, and so on—apply to any investor, individual or institutional. We'll review historical data to show the importance of the asset allocation decision and discuss the need for investor education, an important issue for individuals as well as companies who offer retirement or other savings plans to their employees. The chapter concludes by examining asset allocation strategies across national borders to show the effect of market environment and culture on investing patterns; what is appropriate for a U.S.-based investor is not necessarily appropriate for a non-U.S.-based investor.

INDIVIDUAL INVESTOR LIFE CYCLE

Financial plans and investment needs are as different as each individual. Investment needs change over a person's life cycle. How individuals structure their financial plan should be related to their age, financial status, future plans, and needs.

The Preliminaries

Before embarking on an investment program, we need to make sure other needs are satisfied. No serious investment plan should be started until a potential investor has adequate income to cover living expenses and has a safety net should the unexpected occur.

Insurance   Life insurance should be a component of any financial plan. Life insurance protects loved ones against financial hardship should death occur before our financial goals are met. The death benefit paid by the insurance company can help pay medical bills and funeral expenses and provide a lump sum of cash the family can use to maintain their lifestyle, retire debt, or invest for future needs (for example, children's education, spouse retirement). One of the first steps in developing a financial plan is to purchase adequate life insurance coverage; experts suggest life insurance coverage should be seven to ten times an individual's annual salary.

Insurance can serve more immediate purposes as well, including as a means to meet long-term goals such as retirement planning. On reaching retirement age, you can receive the cash or surrender value of your life insurance policy and use the proceeds to supplement your retirement life-style or for estate planning purposes.

You can choose among several basic life insurance contracts. *Term life insurance* provides only a death benefit; the premium to purchase the insurance changes every renewal period. Term insurance is the least expensive life insurance to purchase, although the premium will rise as you age to reflect the increased probability of death. *Universal* and *variable life policies,* although technically different from each other, are similar in that they each provide both a death benefit and a savings plan to the insured. The premium

paid on such policies exceeds the cost to the insurance company of providing the death benefit alone; the excess premium is invested in a number of investment vehicles chosen by the insured. The policy's cash value grows over time, in part based on the size of the excess premium and in part on the performance of the underlying investment funds. Insurance companies may restrict the ability to withdraw funds from these policies before the policyholder reaches a certain age.

Insurance coverage also provides protection against other uncertainties. Health insurance helps to pay medical bills. Disability insurance provides continuing income should you become unable to work. Automobile and home (or rental) insurance provide protection against accidents and damage to cars or residences.

Although nobody ever expects to use their insurance coverage, a first step in a sound financial plan is to have adequate coverage "just in case." Lack of insurance coverage can ruin the best planned investment program.

Cash Reserve   Emergencies, job layoffs and unforseen expenses happen, and good investment opportunities emerge. It is important to have a cash reserve to help meet these occasions. In addition to providing a safety cushion, a cash reserve reduces the likelihood of being forced to sell investments at inopportune times to cover unexpected expenses. Most experts recommend a cash reserve of about six months' worth of living expenses. Calling it a "cash" reserve does not mean the funds should be in cash; rather, the funds should be in investments you can easily convert to cash with little chance of a loss in value. Money market mutual funds and bank accounts are appropriate vehicles for the cash reserve.

Similar to the financial plan, an investor's insurance and cash reserve needs will change over his or her life. We've already mentioned how a retired person may "cash out" a life insurance policy to supplement income. The need for disability insurance declines when a person retires. In contrast, other insurance such as supplemental Medicare coverage or nursing home insurance may become more important.

Life Cycle Investment Strategies

Assuming the basic insurance and cash reserve needs are met, individuals can start a serious investment program with their savings. Because of changes in their net worth and risk tolerance, individuals' investment strategies will change over their lifetime. Below we review various phases in the investment life cycle. Although each individual's needs and preferences are different, some general traits affect most investors over the life cycle. Let's look at the four life cycle phases as shown in Figure 2.1.

Accumulation Phase   Individuals in the early-to-middle years of their working careers are in the **accumulation phase**. As the name implies, they are attempting to accumulate assets to satisfy fairly immediate needs (for example, a down payment for a house) or longer-term goals (children's college education, retirement). Typically, their net worth is small, and debt from car loans or their own past college loans may be heavy. As a result of their typically long investment time horizon and their earning ability, individuals in the accumulation phase are willing to make moderately high-risk investments in the hopes of making above-average nominal returns over time.

Consolidation Phase   Individuals in the **consolidation phase** are typically past the midpoint of their careers, have paid off much or all of their outstanding debts, and perhaps have paid, or have the assets to pay, their children's college bills. Earnings exceed expenses, so the excess can be invested to provide for future retirement or estate planning needs. The typical investment horizon is still long (twenty to thirty years), so moderate-risk investments remain attractive. They have some concern about capital preservation, as they do not want to take large risks that may put their current nest egg in jeopardy.

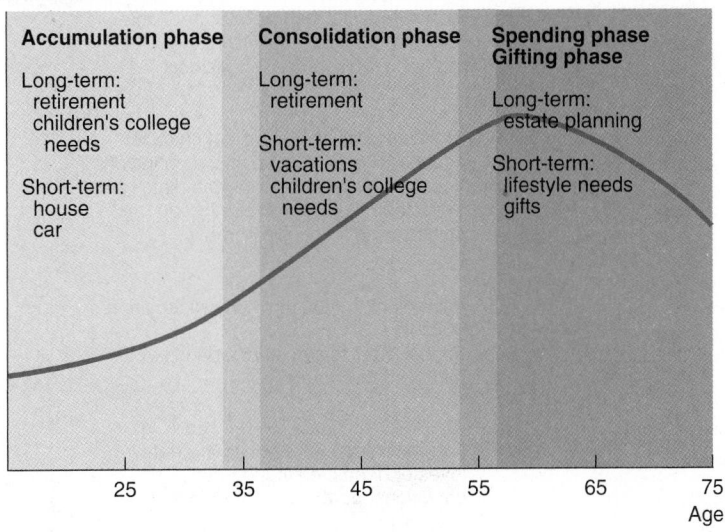

Figure 2.1   *Rise and Fall of Personal Net Worth over a Lifetime*

Spending Phase   The **spending phase** typically begins when individuals retire. Living expenses are covered by social security income and income from prior investments, including employer pension plans. Because their earning years have concluded (although some retirees take part-time positions or do consulting work), they seek greater protection of their capital. At the same time, they must balance their desire to preserve the nominal value of their savings with the need to protect themselves against a decline in the *real* value of their savings due to inflation. The average sixty-five-year-old person in the United States has a life expectancy of about twenty years. Thus, although their overall portfolio may be less risky than in the consolidation phase, they still need to have some risky growth investments, such as common stocks, for inflation protection.

Gifting Phase   The **gifting phase** is similar to, and may be concurrent with, the spending phase. In this stage, individuals believe they have sufficient income and assets to cover their expenses while maintaining a reserve for uncertainties. Excess assets can provide financial assistance to relatives or friends, establish charitable trusts, or fund trusts that provide an estate planning tool to minimize estate taxes.

Life Cycle Investment Goals

During the investment life cycle, individuals have a variety of financial goals. **Near-term, high-priority goals** are shorter-term financial objectives that individuals set to fund purchases that are personally important to them, such as accumulating funds to make a house down payment, buy a new car, or take a trip. Parents with teenage children may have a near-term, high-priority goal to accumulate funds to help pay college expenses. Because of the emotional importance of these goals and their short time horizon, high-risk investments are not usually considered suitable for achieving them.

Long-term, high-priority goals typically include some form of financial independence, such as the ability to retire at a certain age. Because of their long-term nature, higher-risk investments can help meet these objectives.

Figure 2.2   *The Portfolio Management Process*

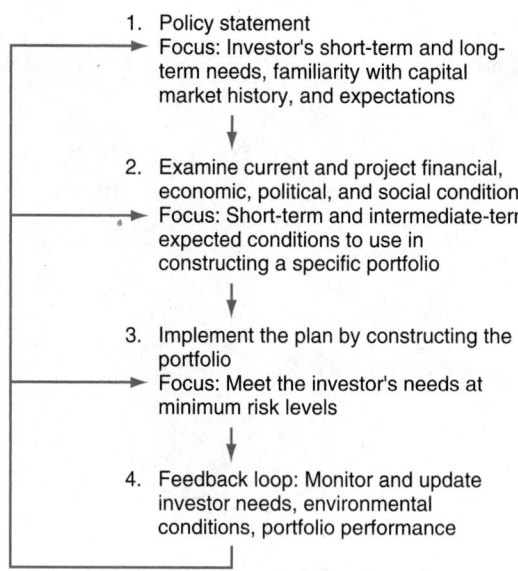

1. Policy statement
   Focus: Investor's short-term and long-term needs, familiarity with capital market history, and expectations

2. Examine current and project financial, economic, political, and social conditions
   Focus: Short-term and intermediate-term expected conditions to use in constructing a specific portfolio

3. Implement the plan by constructing the portfolio
   Focus: Meet the investor's needs at minimum risk levels

4. Feedback loop: Monitor and update investor needs, environmental conditions, portfolio performance

Lower-priority goals are just that—it might be nice to meet these objectives, but it is not critical. Examples include the ability to purchase a new car every few years, redecorate the home with expensive furnishings, or take a long, luxurious vacation.

A well-developed policy statement considers these needs over an investor's lifetime. The following sections detail the process for managing a portfolio, constructing an investment policy, and monitoring its applicability to the investor over time.

THE PORTFOLIO MANAGEMENT PROCESS

The process of managing an investment portfolio never stops. Once the funds are initially invested according to the plan, the real work begins in monitoring and updating the status of the portfolio and the investor's needs.

The first step in the portfolio management process, as seen in Figure 2.2, is for the investor, either alone or with the assistance of an investment adviser, to construct a **policy statement**. The policy statement is a road map; in it investors specify the types of risks they are willing to take and their investment goals and constraints. All investment decisions are based on the policy statement to ensure they are appropriate for the investor. We will examine the process of constructing a policy statement later in this chapter. Because investor needs change over time, the policy statement must be periodically reviewed and updated.

The process of investing seeks to peer into the future and determine strategies that offer the best possibility of meeting the policy statement guidelines. In the second step of the portfolio management process, the investor should study current financial and economic conditions and forecast future trends. The investor's needs, as reflected in the policy statement, and financial market expectations will jointly determine investment strategy. Economies are dynamic; they are affected by numerous industry struggles, politics, and changing demographics and social attitudes. Thus, the portfolio will require constant

monitoring and updating to reflect changes in financial market expectations. We take a closer look at the process of evaluating and forecasting economic trends in Chapter 11.

The third step of the portfolio management process is to construct the portfolio. With the investor's policy statement and financial market forecasts as input, the investor and any advisers determine how to allocate available funds across different countries, asset classes, and securities. This involves constructing a portfolio that will minimize the investor's risks while meeting the needs specified in the policy statement. Financial theory frequently assists portfolio construction, as we will discuss in Part 2. Some of the practical aspects of selecting investments for inclusion in a portfolio are discussed in Parts 4 and 5.

The fourth step in the portfolio management process is the continual monitoring of the investor's needs and capital market conditions. When necessary, the policy statement is updated and the investment strategy is modified accordingly. A component of the monitoring process is to evaluate a portfolio's performance and compare results to the expectations and the requirements listed in the policy statement. The evaluation of portfolio performance is discussed in Chapter 22.

THE NEED FOR A POLICY STATEMENT

As we noted above, a policy statement is a road map that guides the investment process. Constructing a policy statement is an invaluable planning tool that will help the investor understand his or her own needs better as well as assist an adviser or portfolio manager in managing a client's funds. While it does not guarantee investment success, a policy statement will provide discipline for the investment process and reduce the possibility of making hasty, inappropriate decisions. There are two important reasons for constructing a policy statement: First, it helps the investor decide on realistic investment goals after learning about the financial markets and the risks of investing. Second, it creates a standard by which to judge the performance of the portfolio manager.

Understand and Articulate Realistic Investor Goals

When asked what their investment goal is, people often say, "to make a lot of money," or some similar response. Such a goal has two drawbacks: first, it may not be appropriate for the investor, and second, it is too open-ended to provide guidance for specific investments and time frames. Such an objective is well suited for someone going to the racetrack or buying lottery tickets, but it is inappropriate for someone investing funds in financial and real assets.

An important purpose of writing a policy statement is to help investors understand their own needs, objectives, and investment constraints. A policy statement is a means for investors to learn about financial markets and the risks of investing. This will help prevent them from making inappropriate investment decisions in the future and will increase the possibility that they will satisfy their specific, measurable financial goals.

Thus, the policy statement helps the investor to specify realistic goals and become more informed about the risks and costs of investing. Market values of assets, whether they be stocks, bonds, or real estate, can fluctuate dramatically. For example, during the October 1987 crash, the Dow Jones Industrial Average (DJIA) fell more than 500 points (more than 20 percent) in one day; during the October 1989 minicrash, the DJIA fell 150 points in one day. The 554 point drop in the Dow in October 1997 was "only" a 7 percent decline, because the Dow was at a much higher level than in the late 1980s. A review of market history shows that it is not unusual for asset prices to decline by 10 percent to 20 percent or more of their value over several months. Investors will typically focus on

a single statistic, such as an 11 percent average annual rate of return on stocks, and expect the market to rise 11 percent every year. Such thinking ignores the risk of stock investing. Part of the process of developing a policy statement is for the investor to become familiar with the risks of investing, because we know that a strong positive relationship exists between risk and return.

One expert in the field recommends that investors should think about the following set of questions and explain their answers as part of the process of constructing a policy statement:

1. What are the real risks of an adverse financial outcome, especially in the short run?
2. What probable emotional reactions will I have to an adverse financial outcome?
3. How knowledgeable am I about investments and markets?
4. What other capital or income sources do I have? How important is this particular portfolio to my overall financial position?
5. What, if any, legal restrictions may affect my investment needs?
6. What, if any, unanticipated consequences of interim fluctuations in portfolio value might affect my investment policy?

Adapted from Charles D. Ellis, *Investment Policy: How to Win the Loser's Game* (Homewood, Ill. Dow Jones–Irwin, 1985), 25–26.

In summary, constructing a policy statement is mainly the investor's responsibility. It is a process whereby investors articulate their realistic needs and goals and become familiar with financial markets and investing risks. Without this information, investors cannot adequately communicate their needs to the portfolio manager. Without this input from investors, the portfolio manager cannot construct a portfolio that will satisfy clients' needs; the result will most likely be future aggravation and dissatisfaction.

Standards for Evaluating Portfolio Performance

The policy statement also assists in judging the performance of the portfolio manager. Performance cannot be judged without an objective standard; the policy statement provides that objective standard. The portfolio's performance should be compared to guidelines specified in the policy statement, not on the portfolio's overall return. For example, if an investor has a low tolerance for risky investments, the portfolio manager should not be fired simply because the portfolio does not perform as well as the risky S&P 500 stock index. Because risk drives returns, the investor's lower-risk investments, as specified in the investor's policy statement, will probably earn lower returns than if all the investor's funds were placed in the stock market.

Many times the policy statement will include a **benchmark portfolio,** or comparison standard. The risk of the benchmark, and the assets included in the benchmark, should agree with the client's risk preferences and investment needs. In turn, the investment performance of the portfolio manager should be compared to this benchmark portfolio. For example, an investor who specifies low-risk investments in the policy statement should compare the portfolio manager's performance against a low-risk benchmark portfolio. Likewise, an investor seeking high-risk, high-return investments should compare the portfolio's performance against a high-risk benchmark.

Because it sets an objective performance standard, the policy statement acts as a starting point for periodic portfolio review and client communication with managers. Questions concerning portfolio performance or the manager's faithfulness to the policy can

be addressed in the context of the written policy guidelines. Managers should mainly be judged by whether they consistently followed the client's policy guidelines. The portfolio manager who makes unilateral deviations from policy is not working in the best interests of the client. Therefore, even deviations that result in higher portfolio returns can and should be grounds for the manager's dismissal.

Thus, we see the importance of the client constructing the policy statement: the client must first understand his or her own needs before communicating them to the portfolio manager. In turn, the portfolio manager must implement the client's desires by following the investment guidelines. As long as policy is followed, shortfalls in performance should not be a major concern. Remember that the policy statement is designed to impose an investment discipline on the client and portfolio manager. As noted in questions 1 and 6 on page 42, clients must enter the investment arena with their eyes open. The less knowledgeable they are, the more likely clients are to inappropriately judge the performance of the portfolio manager.

Other Benefits

A sound policy statement helps to protect the client against a portfolio manager's inappropriate investments or unethical behavior. Without clear, written guidance, some managers may try to make themselves look good by investing in high-risk investments, hoping to earn a quick return. Not only are actions counter to the investor's specified needs and risk preferences inappropriate, high-risk investment strategies can end up losing money and causing the investor large, unexpected losses. Though legal recourse is a possibility against such action, writing a clear and unambiguous policy statement should safeguard against such unethical manager performance.

Just because one manager currently manages your account does not mean that person will always manage your funds. As with other positions, your portfolio manager may be promoted or dismissed or may take a better job. Therefore, after a while your funds may come under the management of an individual you do not know and who does not know you. To prevent costly delays during this transition, you can ensure that the new manager "hits the ground running" with a clearly written policy statement. A policy statement should prevent delays in monitoring and rebalancing your portfolio and help create a seamless transition from one money manager to another.

To sum up, a clearly written policy statement helps avoid future potential problems. When the client specifies needs and desires, the portfolio manager can more effectively construct an appropriate portfolio. The policy statement acts as an objective performance measure for portfolio performance, helps guard against ethical lapses by the portfolio manager, and aids in the transition between money managers. Therefore, the first step before beginning any investment program, whether it is for an individual or a multi-billion-dollar pension fund, is to construct a policy statement.

An appropriate policy statement should satisfactorily answer the following questions:

1. Is the policy carefully designed to meet the specific needs and objectives of this particular investor? (Cookie-cutter or one-size-fits-all policy statements are generally inappropriate.)
2. Is the policy written so clearly and explicitly that a competent stranger could manage the portfolio in conformance with the client's needs? In case of a manager transition, could the new manager use this policy to handle your portfolio in accordance to your needs?

3. Would the client have been able to remain committed to the policies during the capital market experiences of the past sixty to seventy years? That is, does the client fully understand investment risks and the need for a disciplined approach to the investment process?
4. Would the portfolio manager have been able to maintain fidelity to the policy over the same period? (Discipline is a two-way street; we do not want the portfolio manager to change strategies because of a disappointing market.)
5. Would the policy, if implemented, achieve the client's objectives? (Bottom line: would the policy have worked to meet the client's needs?)

Adapted from Charles D. Ellis, *Investment Policy: How to Win the Loser's Game* (Homewood, Ill.: Dow Jones–Irwin, 1985), 62.

INPUT TO THE POLICY STATEMENT

Before an investor and adviser can construct a policy statement, they need to have an open and frank exchange of information, ideas, fears, and goals. To build a framework for this information-gathering process, the client and adviser need to discuss the client's investment objectives and constraints. Let us illustrate this framework by discussing the investment objectives and constraints that may confront "typical" twenty-five-year-old and sixty-five-year-old investors.

Investment Objectives

The investor's **objectives** are his or her investment goals expressed in terms of both risk and returns. The relationship between risk and returns requires that goals not be expressed only in terms of returns. Expressing goals only in terms of returns can lead to inappropriate and even unethical investment practices by the portfolio manager, such as the use of high-risk investment strategies or account "churning," which involves moving quickly in and out of investments in an attempt to buy low and sell high.

For example, a person may have a stated return goal such as "double my investment in five years." Before such a statement becomes part of the policy statement, the client must become fully informed of investment risks associated with such a goal, including the possibility of loss. *A careful analysis of the client's risk tolerance should precede any discussion of return objectives.* It makes little sense for a person who is risk averse to invest funds in high-risk assets. Investment firms survey clients to gauge their risk tolerance. For example, starting in 1990 Merrill Lynch has asked its clients to place themselves in one of the four categories in Figure 2.3. Sometimes investment magazines or books contain tests that individuals can take to help them evaluate their risk tolerance (see Figure 2.4).

Risk tolerance is more than a function of an individual's psychological makeup; it is affected by other factors, including a person's current insurance coverage and cash reserves, as we discussed. Risk tolerance is affected by an individual's family situation (for example, marital status and the number and ages of children) and by age. We know that older persons generally have shorter investment time frames within which to make up any losses; they also have years of experience, including living through various market gyrations and "corrections" (a euphemism for downtrends or crashes) that younger people have not experienced or whose effect they do not fully appreciate. Risk tolerance is also influenced by one's current net worth and income expectations. All else being equal, individuals with higher incomes have a greater propensity to undertake risk, because their incomes can help cover any shortfall. Likewise, individuals with larger net

Figure 2.3	*Initial Risk Categories and Suggested Initial Asset Allocations for Merrill Lynch Clients*

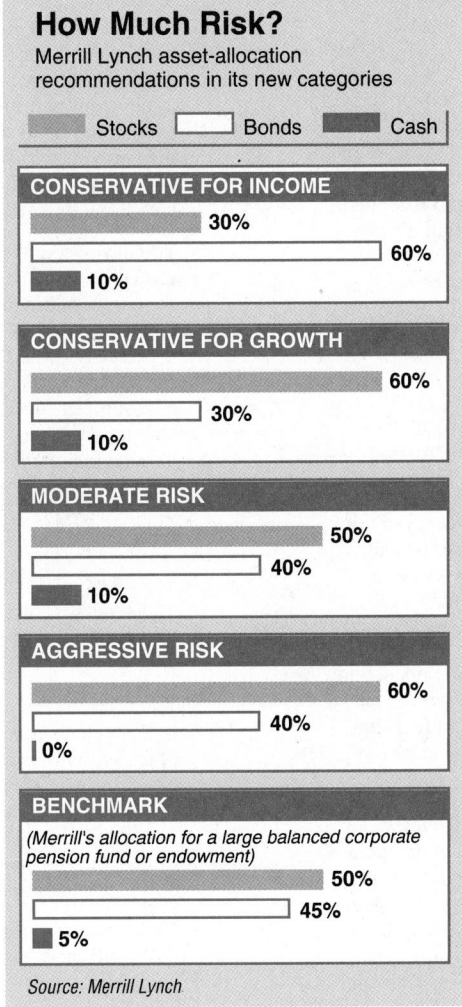

Source: Merrill Lynch

worths can afford to place some assets in risky investments while the remaining assets provide a cushion against losses.

A person's return objective may be stated in terms of an absolute or relative percentage return, but it may also be stated in terms of a general goal, such as capital preservation, current income, capital appreciation, or total return.

Capital preservation means the investors want to minimize their risk of loss, usually in real terms: they seek to maintain the purchasing power of their investment. In other words, the return needs to be no less than the rate of inflation. Generally, this is a strategy for strongly risk-averse investors or for funds soon to be needed, say, next year's tuition payment or a down payment on a house.

Capital appreciation is an appropriate objective when the investors want the portfolio to grow in real terms over time to meet some future need. Under this strategy, growth

Figure 2.4   *How Much Risk Is Right for You?*

You ve heard the expression no pain, no gain ? In the investment world, the comparable phrase would be no risk, no reward.

How you feel about risking your money will drive many of your investment decisions. The risk-comfort scale extends from very conservative (you don t want to risk losing a penny regardless of how little your money earns) to very aggressive (you re willing to risk much of your money for the possibility that it will grow tremendously). As you might guess, most investors tolerance for risk falls somewhere in between.

If you re unsure of what your level of risk tolerance is, this quiz should help.

1. You win $300 in an office football pool. You:
   a) spend it on groceries b) purchase lottery tickets
   c) put it in a money market account d) buy some stock.

2. Two weeks after buying 100 shares of a $20 stock, the price jumps to over $30. You decide to: a) buy more stock; its obviously a winner b) sell it and take your profits c) sell half to recoup some costs and hold the rest d) sit tight and wait for it to advance even more.

3. On days when the stock market jumps way up, you:
   a) wish you had invested more b) call your financial adviser and ask for recommendations c) feel glad you re not in the market because it fluctuates too much d) pay little attention.

4. You re planning a vacation trip and can either lock in a fixed room-and-meals rate of $150 per day or book standby and pay anywhere from $100 to $300 per day. You: a) take the fixed-rate deal b) talk to people who have been there about the availability of last-minute accommodations c) book stand-by and also arrange vacation insurance because you re leery of the tour operator d) take your chances with stand-by.

5. The owner of your apartment building is converting the units to condominiums. You can buy your unit for $75,000 or an option on for $15,000. (Units have recently sold for close to $100,000, and prices seem to be going up.) For financing, you ll have to borrow the down payment and pay mortgage and condo fees higher than your present rent. You: a) buy your unit b) buy your unit and look for another to buy c) sell the option and arrange to rent the unit yourself d) sell the option and move out because you think the conversion will attract couples with small children.

6. You have been working three years for a rapidly growing company. As an executive, you are offered the option of buying up to 2% of company stock 2,000 shares at $10 a share. Although the company is privately owned (its stock does not trade on the open market), its majority owner has made handsome profits selling three other businesses and intends to sell this one eventually. You: a) purchase all the shares you can and tell the owner you would invest more if allowed b) purchase all the shares c) purchase half the shares d) purchase a small amount of shares.

7. You go to a casino for the first time. You choose to:
   a) play quarter slot machines b) $5 minimum-bet roulette c) dollar slot machine d) $25 minimum-bet blackjack.

8. You want to take someone out for a special dinner in a city that s new to you. How do you pick a place? a) read restaurant reviews in the local newspaper b) ask co-workers if they know of a suitable place c) call the only other person you know in this city, who eats out a lot but only recently moved there d) visit the city sometime before your dinner to check out the restaurants yourself.

9. The expression that best describes your lifestyle is:
   a) no guts, no glory b) just do it! c) look before you leap d) all good things come to those who wait.

10. Your attitude toward money is best described as:
    a) a dollar saved is a dollar earned b) you ve got to spend money to make money c) cash and carry only d) whenever possible, use other people s money.

SCORING SYSTEM: Score your answers this way: 1) a-1, b-4, c-2, d-3 2) a-4, b-1, c-3, d-2 3) a-3, b-4, c-2, d-1 4) a-2, b-3 c-1, d-4 5) a-3, b-4, c-2, d-1 6) a-4, b-3, c-2, d-1 7) a-1, b-3, c-2, d-4 8) a-2, b-3, c-4, d-1 9) a-4, b-3, c-2, d-1 10) a-2, b-3,c-1, d-4.

What your total score indicates:

■ 10-17: You re not willing to take chances with your money, even though it means you can t make big gains.

■ 18-25: You re semi-conservative, willing to take a small chance with enough information.

■ 24-32: You re semi-aggressive, willing to take chances if you think the odds of earning more are in your favor.

■ 33-40: You re aggressive, looking for every opportunity to make your money grow, even though in some cases the odds may be quite long. You view money as a tool to make more money.

mainly occurs through capital gains, that is, buying assets at a low price and selling them later at a higher price. This is an aggressive strategy for investors willing to take on risk to meet their objective. Generally longer-term investors seeking to build a retirement or college education fund may have this goal.

When **current income** is the return objective, the investors want the portfolio to concentrate on generating income rather than capital gains. This strategy sometimes suits investors who want to supplement their earnings with income generated by their portfolio to meet their living expenses. Retirees may favor this objective for part of their portfolio to help generate spendable funds.

The objective for the **total return** strategy is similar to that of capital appreciation; namely, the investors want the portfolio to grow over time to meet a future need. Whereas the capital appreciation strategy seeks to do this primarily through capital gains, the total return strategy seeks to increase portfolio value by both capital gains and reinvesting current income. Because the total return strategy has both income and capital gains components, its risk exposure lies between that of the current income and capital appreciation strategies.

Investment Objective: Twenty-five-year-old   What is an appropriate investment objective for our typical twenty-five-year-old investor? Let's assume he holds a steady job, is a valued employee, has adequate insurance coverage and enough money in the bank to provide a cash reserve. Let's also assume that his current long-term, high-priority investment goal is to build a retirement fund. Depending on his risk preferences, he can select a strategy carrying moderate to high amounts of risk because the income stream from his job will probably grow over time. Further, given his young age and income growth potential, a low-risk strategy such as capital preservation or current income is inappropriate for his retirement fund goal; a total return or capital appreciation objective would be most appropriate. Here's a possible objective statement:

> Invest funds in a variety of moderate to higher risk investments. The average risk of the equity portfolio should exceed that of a broad stock market index such as the NYSE stock index. Equity exposure should range from 80 percent to 95 percent of the total portfolio. Remaining funds should be invested in short- and intermediate-term notes and bonds.

Investment Objective: Sixty-five-year-old   Assume our typical sixty-five-year-old investor likewise has adequate insurance coverage and a cash reserve. Let's also assume she is retiring this year. This individual will want less risk exposure than the twenty-five-year-old investor, because her earning power from employment will soon be ending; she will not be able to recover any investment losses by saving more out of her paycheck. Depending on her income from social security and a pension plan, she may need some current income from her retirement portfolio to meet living expenses. Given that she can be expected to live an average of another twenty years, she will need protection against inflation. A risk-averse investor will choose a combination of current income and capital preservation strategy; a more risk-tolerant investor will choose a combination of current income and total return in an attempt to have principal growth outpace inflation. Here's an example of such an objective statement:

> Invest in stock and bond investments to meet income needs (from bond income and stock dividends) and to provide for real growth (from equities). Fixed income securities should comprise 60–70 percent of the total portfolio; of this, 10–20 percent should be invested in short-term securities for extra liquidity and safety. The remaining 30–40 percent of the portfolio should be invested in high-quality stocks whose risk is approximate to those of the S&P 500 index.

More detailed analyses for our twenty-five-year-old and our sixty-five-year-old would make more specific assumptions about the risk tolerance of each, as well as clearly enumerate their investment goals, return objectives, the funds they each have to invest at the present, and the funds they each expect to have to invest over time.

Investment Constraints

In addition to the investment objective that sets limits on risk and return, certain other constraints also affect the investment plan. Investment constraints include liquidity needs, an investment time horizon, tax factors, legal and regulatory constraints, and unique needs and preferences.

Liquidity Needs   An asset is **liquid** if it can be quickly converted to cash at a price close to fair market value. Generally, assets are more liquid if many traders are interested in a fairly standardized product. Treasury bills are a highly liquid security; real estate and venture capital are not.

Investors may have liquidity needs that the investment plan must take into consideration. For example, although an investor may have a primary long-term goal, several near-term goals may also require available funds. Wealthy individuals with sizable tax obligations need adequate liquidity to pay their taxes without upsetting their investment plan. Some saving for retirement may need funds for shorter-term purposes such as buying a car, a house, or making college tuition payments.

Our typical twenty-five-year-old investor probably has little need for liquidity as he focuses on his long-term retirement fund goal. This constraint may change, however, should he face a period of unemployment or should near-term goals, such as honeymoon expenses or a house down payment, enter the picture. Should any changes occur, the investor needs to revise his policy statement and financial plans accordingly.

Our soon-to-be-retired sixty-five-year-old investor has a greater need for liquidity than the younger investor. Although she may receive regular checks from her pension plan and social security, it is not likely that they will equal her working paycheck. She will want some of her portfolio in liquid securities to meet unexpected expenses or bills.

Time Horizon   Time horizon as an investment constraint briefly entered our earlier discussion of near-term and long-term high-priority goals. A close (but not perfect) relationship exists between an investor's time horizon, liquidity needs, and ability to handle risk. Investors with long investment horizons generally require less liquidity and can tolerate greater portfolio risk: less liquidity because the funds are not usually needed for many years; greater risk tolerance because any shortfalls or losses can be overcome by returns earned in subsequent years.

Investors with shorter time horizons generally favor less risky investments because losses are harder to overcome during a short time frame.

Because of life expectancies, our twenty-five-year-old investor has a longer investment time horizon than our sixty-five-year-old investor. But, as discussed earlier, this does not mean the sixty-five-year-old should put all her money in short-term CDs; she needs the inflation protection that long-term investments such as common stock can provide. Still, because of the time horizon constraint, the twenty-five-year-old will probably have a greater proportion of his portfolio in equities including stocks in small firms or international firms than the sixty-five-year-old.

Tax Concerns   Investment planning is complicated by the tax code; taxes complicate the situation even more if international investments are part of the portfolio. Taxable income from interest, dividends, or rents is taxable at the investor's marginal tax rate. The marginal tax rate is the proportion of the next one dollar in income paid as taxes. Table 2.1 shows the marginal tax rates for different levels of taxable income. As of 1997, the top federal marginal tax rate was 39.6 percent. State taxes make the tax bite even higher.

Capital gains or losses arise from asset price changes. They are taxed differently than income. Income is taxed when it is received; capital gains or losses are taxed only when the asset is sold and the gain or loss is realized. **Unrealized capital gains** reflect the price

Table 2.1   *Individual Marginal Tax Rates, 1997*

	Taxable Income	Tax	Percent on Excess
Married Filing Jointly	$ 0	$ 0.00	15%
	41,200	6,180.00	28
	99,600	22,532.00	31
	151,750	38,698.50	36
	271,050	81,646.50	39.6
Single	$ 0	$ 0.00	15%
	24,650	3,697.50	28
	59,750	13,525.50	31
	124,650	33,644.50	36
	271,050	86,348.50	39.6
Head of Household	$ 0	$ 0.00	15%
	33,050	4,957.50	28
	85,350	19,601.50	31
	138,200	35,985.00	36
	271,050	83,811.00	39.6
Married Filing Separately	$ 0	$ 0.00	15%
	20,600	3,090.00	28
	49,800	11,266.00	31
	75,875	19,349.25	36
	135,525	40,823.25	39.6

appreciation of currently held assets that have *not* been sold; the tax liability on unrealized capital gains can be deferred indefinitely. Capital gains only become taxable after the asset has been sold for a price higher than its cost or **basis**. If appreciated assets are passed on to an heir upon the investor's death, the basis of the assets is considered to be their value on the date of the holder's death. The heirs can then sell the assets and not pay capital gains tax. **Realized capital gains** occur when an appreciated asset has been sold; taxes are due on the realized capital gains only.

Capital gains taxes are paid on realized capital gains. The Tax Reform Act of 1997 lowered the top capital gain tax rate to 20 percent for assets held longer than eighteen months. For taxpayers in the 15 percent tax bracket (single filers earning less than $24,650 or married joint filers earning less than $41,200) the capital gains tax rate is only 10 percent.

Beginning in the year 2001, another change in the capital gains regulations will occur. Profits on assets purchased after the year 2000 and held for at least five years will be only 18 percent. For filers in the 15 percent income tax bracket, the capital gains tax rate will fall to 8 percent on assets held longer than five years if the asset is sold in the year 2001 or later.[1] Two things are certain; the 1997 tax changes will increase recordkeeping requirements and they will keep tax advisers busy.

Sometimes we make a trade-off between taxes and diversification needs. If entrepreneurs concentrate much of their wealth in equity holdings of their firm, or if employees purchase substantial amounts of their employer's stock through payroll deduction plans during their working life, their portfolios may contain a large amount of unrealized capital gains. In addition, the risk position of such a portfolio may be quite high, because it is concentrated in a single company. The decision to sell some of the company stock in order to diversify the portfolio's risk by reinvesting the proceeds in other assets must be balanced against the resulting tax liability.

[1]Christopher Georges, "Congress Clears Tax, Budget Bills," *Wall Street Journal,* August 1, 1997, pp. A2, A11.

Some find the difference between average and marginal income tax rates confusing. The **marginal tax rate** is the part of each additional dollar in income that is paid as tax. Thus, a married person, filing jointly, with an income of $50,000 will have a marginal tax rate of 28 percent. The 28 percent marginal tax rate should be used to determine after-tax returns on investments.

The **average tax rate** is simply a person's total tax payment divided by their total income. It represents the average tax paid on each dollar the person earned. From Table 2.1, a married person, filing jointly, will pay $8,644 in tax on a $50,000 income [$6,180 plus .28($50,000 − $41,200)]. His or her average tax rate is $8,644/$50,000 or 17.29 percent.

Note that the average tax rate is a weighted average of the person's marginal tax rates paid on each dollar of income. The first $41,200 of income has a marginal tax rate of 15 percent; the next $8,800 has a 28 percent marginal tax rate:

$$\frac{\$41,200}{\$50,000} \times .15 + \frac{\$8,800}{\$50,000} \times .28 = .1729, \text{ or the average tax rate of } 17.29\%$$

Another tax factor is that some sources of income are exempt from federal and state taxes. Interest on federal securities, such as Treasury bills, notes, and bonds, is exempt from state taxes. Interest on municipal bonds (bonds issued by a state or other local governing body) are exempt from federal taxes. Further, if the investor purchases municipal bonds issued by a local governing body of the state in which they live, the interest is exempt from both state and federal income tax. Thus, high-income individuals have an incentive to purchase municipal bonds to reduce their tax liabilities.

The after-tax return on a taxable investment is:

$$\text{After-Tax Return} = \text{Pre-Tax Return} (1 - \text{Marginal Tax Rate})$$

Thus, the after-tax return on a taxable investment should be compared to that on municipals before deciding which should be purchased by a tax-paying investor. Alternatively, a municipal's equivalent taxable yield can be computed. The equivalent taxable yield is what a taxable bond investment would have to offer to produce the same after-tax return as the municipal. It is given by:

$$\text{Equivalent Taxable Yield} = \frac{\text{municipal yield}}{1 - \text{marginal tax rate}}$$

To illustrate, if an investor is in the 28 percent marginal tax bracket, a taxable investment yield of 8 percent has an after-tax yield of 8 percent × (1 − .28) or 5.76 percent; an equivalent-risk municipal security offering a yield greater than 5.76 percent offers the investor greater after-tax returns. On the other hand, a municipal bond yielding 6 percent has an equivalent taxable yield of 6%/(1 − .28) = 8.33%; to earn more money after taxes, an equivalent-risk taxable investment has to offer a return greater than 8.33 percent.

Other means to reduce tax liabilities are available to the investor. Contributions to an IRA (individual retirement account) may qualify as a tax deduction if certain income limits are met. In any case, the investment returns of the IRA investment, including any income, are deferred until the funds are withdrawn from the account. Any funds withdrawn from an IRA are taxable as current income, regardless of whether growth in the IRA occurs as a result of capital gains, income, or both. The benefits of deferring taxes can dramatically compound over time. Figure 2.5 illustrates how $1000 invested in an IRA at a tax-deferred rate of 8 percent grows compared to funds invested in a taxable investment that

Figure 2.5   *Effect of Tax Deferral on Investor Wealth over Time*

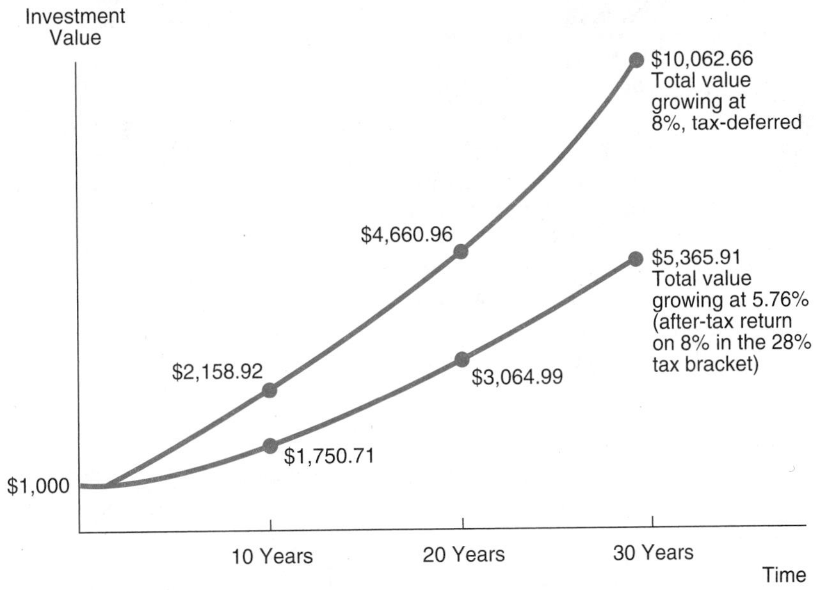

Investment
Value

$10,062.66
Total value
growing at
8%, tax-deferred

$4,660.96

$5,365.91
Total value
growing at 5.76%
(after-tax return
on 8% in the 28%
tax bracket)

$2,158.92

$3,064.99

$1,750.71

$1,000

10 Years   20 Years   30 Years

Time

returns (from bond income) 8 percent pre-tax. For an investor in the 28 percent bracket, this investment grows at an after-tax rate of 5.76 percent. After thirty years, the value of the tax-deferred investment has grown to nearly twice as large as the taxable investment.

Tax-deductible contributions of up to $2,000 to a regular IRA are subject to income and other limitations. The Tax Reform Act of 1997 created the Roth IRA. The Roth IRA contribution, although not tax deductible, allows up to $2,000 to be invested each year; the returns on this investment will grow on a tax-deferred basis and can be withdrawn, tax-free, if the funds are invested for at least five years and are withdrawn after the investor reaches age 59½.[2] The Roth IRA is subject to limitations based on the investor's annual income, but the income ceiling is much higher than the regular IRA. For example, for joint filers, the income ceiling for a regular IRA is $80,000; for the Roth IRA, the income ceiling is $160,000. Only $2,000 each year ($4,000 for couples) can be invested in a Roth IRA each year. Individuals can put money into both a regular IRA and a Roth IRA each year—but the annual contribution for both can not exceed $2,000.[3]

For money you intend to invest in some type of IRA, the advantage of the Roth IRA's tax-free withdrawals will outweigh the tax-deduction benefit from the regular IRA—unless you expect your tax rate when the funds are withdrawn to be substantially less than when you initially invest the funds. Let's illustrate this with a hypothetical example.

Suppose you are considering investing $2,000 in either a regular or Roth IRA account. Let's assume your current marginal tax rate is 28 percent and that, over your twenty-year time horizon, your $2,000 investment will grow to $20,000, tax-deferred in either account; this represents an average annual return of 12.2 percent.

---

[2] Earlier tax-free withdrawals are possible if the funds are to be used for educational purposes or first-time home purchases.

[3] For additional insights, see Jonathan Clements, "Jam Today or Jam Tomorrow? Roth IRA Will Show Many Investors It Pays to Wait," *Wall Street Journal*, September 16, 1997, p. C1.

Table 2.2   *Comparing the Regular versus Roth IRA Returns*

	REGULAR IRA	ROTH IRA
Invested funds:	$2,000 + $560 tax savings on the tax-deductive IRA investment	$2,000 (no tax deduction)
Time Horizon:	20 years	20 years
Rate of return assumption:	12.2 percent tax-deferred on the IRA investment; 8.8 percent on invested tax savings (represents the after-tax return on 12.2 percent)	12.2 percent tax-deferred on the IRA investment
Funds available after 20 years (taxes ignored)	$20,000 (pre-tax) from IRA investment; $3,025 (after-tax) from invested tax savings	$20,000 from IRA investment
Funds available after 20 years, 15 percent marginal tax rate at retirement	$20,000 less tax (.15 × $20,000) plus $3,025 from invested tax savings equals **$20,025**	**$20,000**
Funds available after 20 years, 28 percent marginal tax rate at retirement	$20,000 less tax (.28 × $20,000) plus $3,025 from invested tax savings equals **$17,425**	**$20,000**
Funds available after 20 years, 40 percent marginal tax rate at retirement	$20,000 less tax (.40 × $20,000) plus $3,025 from invested tax savings equals **$15,025**	**$20,000**

In a Roth IRA no tax is deducted when the $2,000 is invested; but in a regular IRA, the $2,000 investment is tax-deductible and will lower your tax bill by $560 (0.28 × $2,000). Thus, in a Roth IRA, only $2,000 is assumed to be invested; for a regular IRA, both the $2,000 and the $560 tax saving are assumed to be invested. We will assume the $560 is invested at an after-tax rate of 12.2% × (1 − .28) = 8.8 percent. After twenty years, this amount will grow to $3,025. Table 2.2 shows the calculations.

Table 2.2 shows that, unless the investor believes her tax bracket will be lower *and she invests the regular IRA tax savings*, the Roth IRA will give her more after-tax dollars at the end of the assumed twenty-year time horizon.

Tax questions can puzzle the most astute minds. For example, depending on one's situation, it may be best to hold stock in taxable, rather than in tax-deferred accounts such as IRAs, company retirement plans, and variable annuities. The main reason is, earnings on such tax-deferred accounts are taxed as ordinary income when the funds are withdrawn. Even if most of the growth in a tax-deferred equity investment arises from capital gains, the withdrawals will be taxed at the higher ordinary income tax rate. Stocks held in taxable accounts will likely have large capital gains tax liability over the years; thus, after the 1997 Tax Reform Act's slashing of realized capital gains tax rates, taxable equity accounts may offer better after-tax return potential than tax deferred investments. This will not be true in all cases; needless to say, any analysis must consider each investor's return, time horizon, and tax assumptions.[4]

Other tax-deferred investments include cash values of life insurance contracts; they accumulate tax-free until the funds are withdrawn. Employers may offer employees 401(k) or 403(b) plans, which allow the employee to reduce taxable income by making tax-deferred investments; many times employee contributions are matched by employer donations (up to a specified limit), thus allowing the employees to double their investment with little risk!

[4]Ellen E. Schultz, "Stock Funds May Be Wrong for Your IRA," *Wall Street Journal,* January 4, 1996, pp. C1, 21.

Our typical twenty-five-year-old investor probably is in a fairly low tax bracket, so detailed tax planning will not be a major concern, and tax-exempt income, such as that available from municipals, will also not be a concern. Nonetheless, he should still invest as much as possible into tax-deferred plans such as an IRA or 401(k). The drawback to such investments, however, is that early withdrawals (before age 59½) are taxable and subject to an additional 10 percent early withdrawal tax. Should the liquidity constraint of these plans be too restrictive, the young investor should probably consider total return- or capital-appreciation–oriented mutual funds as a means to gain diversification and meet his objectives.

Our sixty-five-year-old retiree may face a different situation. If she is in a high tax bracket prior to retiring—and therefore has sought tax-exempt income and tax-deferred investments—her situation may change shortly after retirement. Without large regular paychecks, the need for tax-deferred investments or tax-exempt income becomes less. Taxable income may now offer higher after-tax yields than tax-exempt municipals due to the investor's lower tax bracket. Should her employer's stock be a large component of her retirement account, careful decisions must be made regarding the need to diversify versus the cost of realizing large capital gains (in her lower tax bracket).

Legal and Regulatory Factors   As we will examine more closely in Chapter 4, the investment process and the financial markets are highly regulated and subject to numerous laws. At times, these legal and regulatory factors constrain the investment strategies of individuals and institutions.

In our discussion about taxes, we mentioned one such constraint: funds removed from a regular IRA account or 401(k) plan before age 59½ are taxable and subject to an additional 10 percent withdrawal penalty. You may also be familiar with the tag line in many bank CD advertisements—"substantial interest penalty upon early withdrawal." Regulations and rules such as these may make such investments unattractive for investors with substantial liquidity needs in their portfolios.

Regulations can also constrain the investment choices available to someone in a **fiduciary** role. A fiduciary, or trustee, supervises an investment portfolio of a third party, such as a trust account or discretionary account.[5] The fiduciary must make investment decisions in accordance with the owner's wishes; a properly written policy statement assists this process. In addition, trustees of a trust account must meet the "prudent man" standard, which means that they must invest and manage the funds as a prudent person would manage their own affairs. Notably, the prudent-man standard is based on the composition of the entire portfolio, not each individual asset in the portfolio.[6]

All investors must respect some laws, such as insider trading prohibitions. As we will discuss in Chapter 4, insider trading involves the purchase and sale of securities on the basis of important information that is not publicly known. Typically, the people possessing such private or inside information are the firm's managers, who have a fiduciary duty to their shareholders. Security transactions based on access to inside information violates the fiduciary trust the shareholders have placed with management, because the managers seek personal financial gain from their privileged position as agents for the shareholders.

For our typical twenty-five-year-old investor, legal and regulatory matters will be of little concern, with the possible exception of insider trading laws and the penalties associated with early withdrawal of funds from tax-deferred retirement accounts. Should he seek a financial adviser to assist him in constructing a financial plan, the financial adviser would have to obey the regulations pertinent to a client–adviser relationship.

---

[5] A discretionary account is one in which the fiduciary, many times a financial planner or stock broker, has the authority to purchase and sell assets in the owner's portfolio without first receiving the owner's approval.

[6] As we will discuss in Chapter 6, it is sometimes wise to hold assets that are individually risky in the context of a well-diversified portfolio, even if the investor is strongly risk averse.

Similar concerns confront our sixty-five-year-old investor. In addition, as a retiree if she wants to do some estate planning and set up trust accounts, she should seek legal and tax advice to ensure her plans are properly implemented.

Unique Needs and Preferences   This category covers the individual and sometimes idiosyncratic concerns of each investor. Some investors may want to exclude certain investments from their portfolio solely on the basis of personal preference or for social consciousness reasons. For example, they may request that no firms that manufacture or sell tobacco, alcohol, pornography, or environmentally harmful products be included in their portfolio. More than $162 billion was invested by year-end 1995 by groups and individuals using specific written screening criteria for socially conscious investments.

Another example of a personal constraint is the time and expertise a person has for managing their portfolio. Busy executives may prefer to relax during nonworking hours and let a trusted adviser manage their investments. Retirees, on the other hand, may have the time but believe they lack the expertise to choose and monitor investments, so they may also seek professional advice.

Some of the points we previously raised in discussing the other constraints can also be considered as unique needs and preferences. For example, consider the entrepreneur or businessperson with a large portion of his wealth—and emotion—tied up in his firm's stock. Though it may be financially prudent to sell some of the firm's stock and reinvest the proceeds for diversification purposes, it may be hard for the individual to approve such a strategy due to emotional ties to the firm. Further, if the stock holdings are in a private company, it may be difficult to find a buyer except if shares are sold at a discount from their fair market value.

Because each investor is unique, the implications of this final constraint differ for each person; there is no "typical" twenty-five-year-old or sixty-five-year-old investor. Each individual will have to decide—and then communicate specific goals in a well-constructed policy statement.

Institutional investors (endowments, pension funds, and the like) need to have investment policy statements, too. Factors considered by institutional investors when developing policy statements are found in the appendix.

Constructing the Policy Statement

A policy statement may not have separate headings for each, but should incorporate the investor's objectives (risk and return) and constraints (liquidity, time horizon, tax factors, legal and regulatory constraints, and unique needs and preferences). The policy statement allows the investor to determine what factors are personally important that should be reflected in the investment plan. Communicating these needs, goals, or aspirations to the investment adviser gives the adviser a better chance of constructing an investment strategy that will satisfy the investor's objectives and constraints. But each investor needs to take that first important step of the investment process and develop a financial plan to guide investments even if he or she does not consult with an adviser. To do without a plan or to plan poorly is to place the success of the financial plan in jeopardy.

Surveys show that fewer than 40 percent of employees who participate in their firm's retirement savings plan have a good understanding of the value of diversification, the harmful effect of inflation on one's savings, or the relationship between risk and return. With the youngest of the so-called baby-boomers in their forties, the market for financial planning services and education is a growth industry.

Participants in employer-sponsored retirement plans have invested an average of 42 percent of their retirement funds in their employer's stock. Having so much money invested in one asset violates diversification principles. To put this in context, most mutual funds

are limited to having no more than 5 percent of their assets in any one company's stock; a firm's pension plan can invest no more than 10 percent of their funds in the firm's stock. Thus, individuals are unfortunately doing what government regulations prevent many institutional investors from doing.[7] Other studies point out that the average stock allocation in retirement plans is lower than it should be to allow for growth of principal over time.

Investors are, in general, neglecting that important first step to achieve financial success: they are not planning for the future. Studies of retirement plans show that Americans are not saving enough to finance their retirement years and they are not planning sufficiently for what will happen to their savings after they retire.[8] Americans are saving at about one-half the rate needed to finance their retirement. This poor savings rate, coupled with lack of diversification and lack of equity growth potential in their portfolios, can lead to disappointments in one's retirement years.

THE IMPORTANCE OF ASSET ALLOCATION

A major reason why investors develop policy statements is to determine an overall investment strategy. Though a policy statement does not indicate which specific securities to purchase and when they should be sold, it should provide guidelines as to the asset classes to include and the relative proportions of the investor's funds to invest in each class. How the investor divides funds into different asset classes is the process of asset allocation. Rather than present strict percentages, asset allocation is usually expressed in ranges. This allows the investment manager some freedom, based on his or her reading of capital market trends, to invest toward the upper or lower end of the ranges. For example, suppose a policy statement requires that common stocks be 60 percent to 80 percent of the value of the portfolio and that bonds should be 20 percent to 40 percent of the portfolio's value. Should a manager be particularly bullish about stocks, he will increase the allocation of stocks toward the 80 percent upper end of the equity range and decrease bonds toward the 20 percent lower end of the bond range. Should he be more optimistic about bonds, that manager may shift the allocation closer to 40 percent of the funds invested in bonds with the remainder in equities.

A review of historical data and empirical studies indicates the importance of the asset allocation decision and the investment policy statement process. In general, four decisions are made when constructing an investment strategy:

♦ What asset classes to consider for investment;
♦ What normal or policy weights to assign to each eligible asset class;
♦ The allowable allocation ranges based on policy weights;
♦ What specific securities to purchase for the portfolio.

Studies on investment performance over time have come to a surprising conclusion: 85 percent to 95 percent of overall investment returns arise from the first and second decisions, the long-term asset allocation decisions. Thus, searching for a good stockpicker to manage your money but overlooking the need for an asset allocation policy is similar to overlooking the forest because you see only the trees. Good investment managers may

---

[7]Ellen R. Schultz, "Workers Put Too Much in Their Employer's Stock," *Wall Street Journal,* September 13, 1996, pp. C1, C25.

[8]Andy Pasztor, "Middle-Aged, Elderly Have Fewer Assets Than Expected," *Wall Street Journal,* July 25, 1995, p. B1; Jonathan Clements, "Retirement Honing: How Much Should You Have Saved for a Comfortable Life?," *Wall Street Journal,* January 28, 1997, p. C1; Jonathan Clements, "Squeezing the Right Amount from a Retirement Stash," *Wall Street Journal,* February 25, 1997, p. C1; Jonathan Clements, "Curb Your Spending, Boost Your Saving and Watch Retirement Nest Egg Grow," *Wall Street Journal,* September 2, 1997, p. C1.

Figure 2.6 *The Effect of Taxes and Inflation on Investment Returns, 1926–1997*

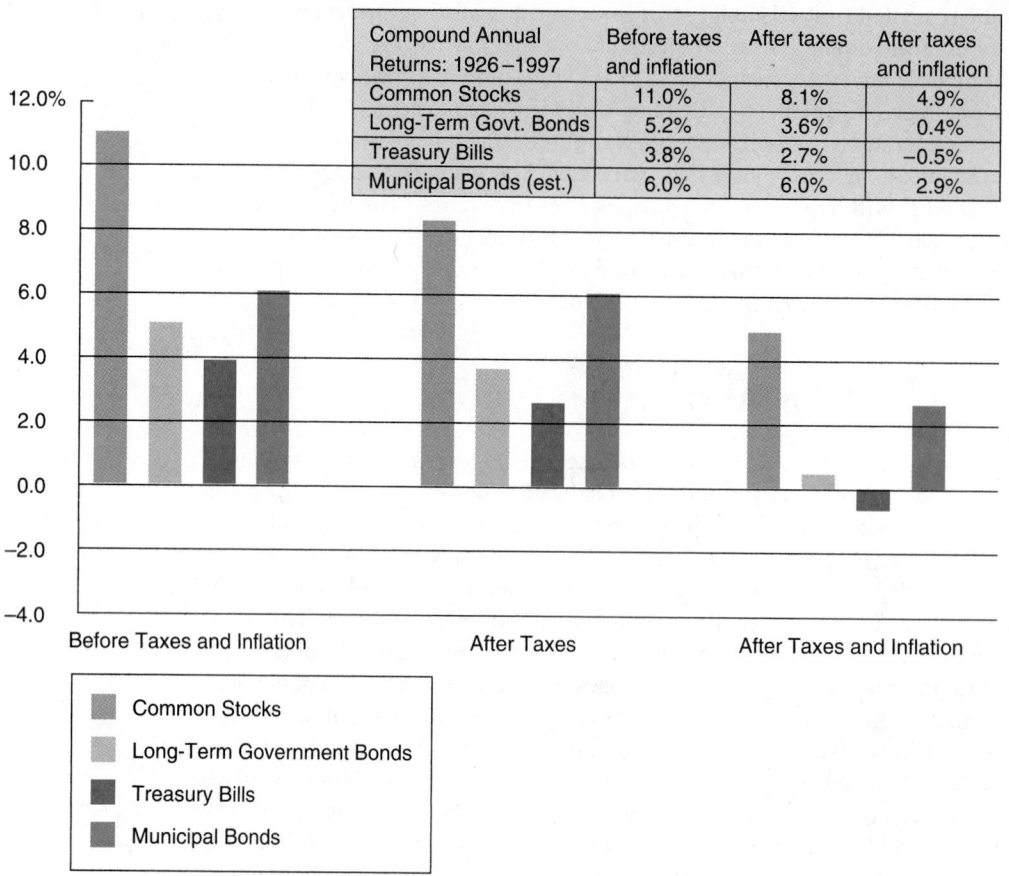

Compound Annual Returns: 1926–1997	Before taxes and inflation	After taxes	After taxes and inflation
Common Stocks	11.0%	8.1%	4.9%
Long-Term Govt. Bonds	5.2%	3.6%	0.4%
Treasury Bills	3.8%	2.7%	−0.5%
Municipal Bonds (est.)	6.0%	6.0%	2.9%

Source: *Stocks, Bonds, Bills, and Inflation,* Ibbotson Associates, Chicago, IL 1998 and author calculations.

add some value to portfolio performance, but the major source of investment return—and risk—over time is the asset allocation decision. A well-constructed policy statement can go a long way toward ensuring that an appropriate asset allocation decision is implemented. Although our data review will focus primarily on U.S. securities, in Chapter 3 we will present a strong case for global asset allocation.

Real Investment Returns after Taxes and Costs

Figure 2.6 provides additional historical perspectives on returns. It indicates how an investment of $1 would have grown over the 1926 to 1997 period. It also examines, using fairly conservative assumptions, how investment returns are affected by taxes and inflation.

Focusing first on stocks, funds invested in 1926 in the S&P 500 would have averaged an 11.0 percent annual return by the end of 1997. Unfortunately, this return is unrealistic because if the funds really were invested over time, taxes would have to be paid and inflation would erode the real purchasing power of the invested funds.

Except for tax-exempt investors and tax-deferred accounts, annual tax payments reduce investment returns. Incorporating taxes into the analysis lowers the after-tax average annual return of a stock investment to 8.1 percent.

But the major reduction in the value of our investment is caused by inflation. The real after-tax average annual return on a stock over this time frame was only 4.9 percent, which is quite a bit less than our initial unadjusted 11.0 percent return!

This example shows the long-run impact of taxes and inflation on the real value of a stock portfolio. For bonds and bills, however, the results in Figure 2.6 show something even more surprising. After adjusting for taxes, long-term bonds barely maintained their purchasing power; T-bills *lost* value in real terms. One dollar invested in long-term government bonds in 1926 gave the investor an annual average after-tax real return of 0.4 percent. An investment in Treasury bills lost an average of 0.5 percent after taxes and inflation. Municipal bonds, because of the protection they offer from taxes, earned an average annual real return of over 2 percent during this time.

The results of this historical analysis imply that, for taxable investments, the only way to maintain purchasing power over time when investing in financial assets is to invest in common stocks. An asset allocation decision for a taxable portfolio that does not include a substantial commitment to common stocks may make it difficult for the portfolio to maintain real value over time.[9]

Returns and Risks of Different Asset Classes

By focusing on returns we have ignored its partner—risk. Assets with higher long-term returns have these returns to compensate for their risk. Table 2.3 illustrates returns (unadjusted for costs and taxes) for several asset classes over time. As expected, the higher returns available from equities come at the cost of higher risk. This is precisely why investors need a policy statement and why the investor and manager must understand the capital markets and have a disciplined approach to investing. Safe Treasury bills will sometimes outperform equities, and, because of their higher risk, common stocks sometimes lose significant value. These are times when undisciplined and uneducated investors sell their stocks at a loss and vow never to invest in equities again. In contrast, these are times when disciplined investors stick to their investment plan and position their portfolio for the next bull market.[10] By holding on to their stocks and perhaps purchasing more at depressed prices, the equity portion of the portfolio will experience a substantial increase in the future.

The asset allocation decision determines to a great extent both the returns and the volatility of the portfolio. Table 2.3 indicates that stocks are riskier than bonds or T-bills. Figure 2.7 and Table 2.4 illustrate the year-by-year volatility of stock returns and show that stocks have sometimes earned returns lower than those of T-bills for extended periods of time. Sticking with an investment policy and riding out the difficult times can earn attractive long-term rates of return.[11]

One popular way to measure risk is to examine the variability of returns over time by computing a standard deviation or variance of annual rates of return for an asset class. This measure indicates that stocks are risky and T-bills are not. Another intriguing measure of risk is the probability of *not* meeting your investment return objective. From this perspective, if the investor has a long time horizon, the risk of equities is small and that of T-bills is large because of their differences in expected returns.

[9]Of course other equity-oriented investments, such as venture capital or real estate, may also provide inflation protection after adjusting for portfolio costs and taxes. Studies of the performance of the new inflation-protected Treasury securities may show their usefulness in protecting investors from inflation as well.

[10]Newton's law of gravity seems to work two ways in financial markets. What goes up must come down; it also appears over time that what goes down may come back up. Contrarian investors and some "value" investors use this concept to try to outperform the indexes over time.

[11]The added benefits of diversification—combining different asset classes in the portfolio—may reduce overall portfolio risk without harming potential return. The topic of diversification is discussed in Chapter 6.

Table 2.3   *Historical Average Annual Returns and Return Variability, 1926–1997*

	Geometric Mean	Arithmetic Mean	Standard Deviation	Distribution
Large company stocks	11.0%	13.0%	20.3%	
Small company stocks	12.7	17.7	33.9	
Long-term corporate bonds	5.7	6.1	8.7	
Long-term government bonds	5.2	5.6	9.2	
Intermediate-term government bonds	5.3	5.4	5.7	
U.S. Treasury bills	3.8	3.8	3.2	
Inflation	3.1	3.2	4.5	

*The 1933 Small Company Stock Total Return was 142.9 percent.

−90%   0%   90%

Source: © *Stocks, Bonds, Bills, and Inflation 1998 Yearbook,* ™ Ibbotson Associates, Chicago (annually updates work by Roger G. Ibbotson and Rex A. Sinquefield). Used with permission. All rights reserved.

Table 2.4   *Over Long Time Periods, Equities Offer Higher Returns*

Stocks far outperformed Treasury bills during the thirty years through 1997, but stocks often did worse than T-bills when held for shorter periods during those thirty years.

	Compound Annual Total Return*
S&P 500 Stock Index	12.7%
Treasury Bills	6.8

Length of Holding Period (calendar years)	Percentage of Periods That Stocks Trailed Bills
1	37%
5	23
10	17
20	0

*Price change plus reinvested income

Source: Author calculatons. Data from *Stocks, Bonds, Bills, and Inflation,* Ibbotson Associates, Chicago, IL 1998.

Figure 2.7   *Equity Risk: Long-Term and Short-Term Perspectives*

Historically, the S&P 500 Has Posted Healthy Gains. . .

Total returns, by decade, including share price gains and reinvested dividends, in percent

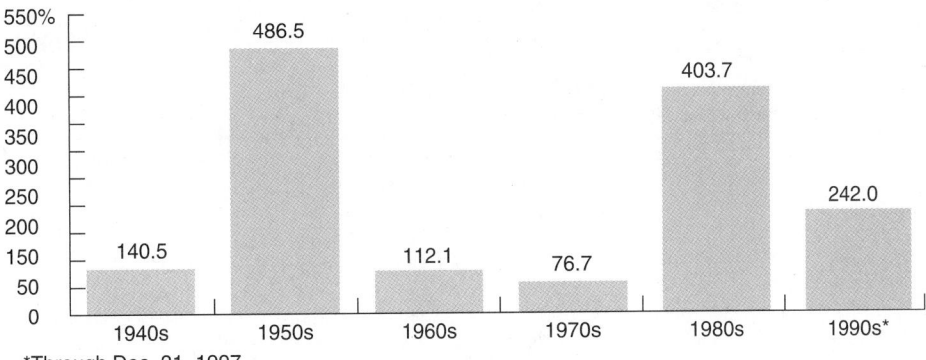

*Through Dec. 31, 1997

. . .But Getting There Can Be Rough

Annual total returns including share price gains and reinvested dividends, in percent

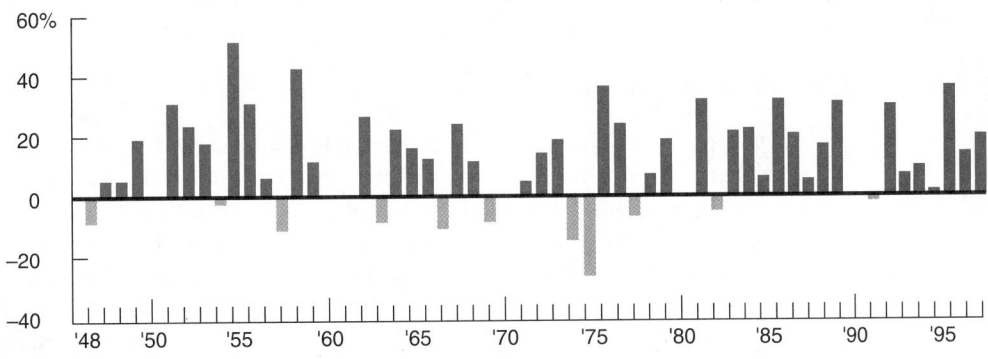

Sources: "Why It's Risky Not to Invest More in Stocks," *Wall Street Journal*, February 11, 1992, C1, and Ibbotson Associates, Inc. Updated by authors, using Ibbotson Associates data.

Focusing solely on return variability as a measure of risk ignores a significant risk for income-oriented investors, such as retirees or endowment funds. "Safe," income-oriented investments such as Treasury bills or certificates of deposit suffer from *reinvestment risk,* that is, the risk that interim cash flows or the principal paid at maturity will be reinvested in a lower-yielding security. The year of 1992 was particularly hard on investors in "safe" T-bills, because their T-bill income fell 37 percent from 1991 levels due to lower interest rates. Table 2.5 compares the variability of income payouts from common stocks (measured by the dividends from the S&P 500), and T-bills. Over the 1926 to 1997 time frame, dividend income from stocks rose fifty-seven times compared to forty-one times for T-bills. The income from stocks fell only eleven times, while T-bill rollovers resulted in an income loss twenty-eight times. The worst one-year drop in stock income, 39.0 percent in 1932, was not as severe as the largest decline, 76.6 percent, in T-bill income, which occurred in 1940. In addition, the growth rate of income from stocks far outpaced that of inflation and the growth of income from T-bills. During the 1926 through 1997 period, stock dividends rose more than 1,800 percent, inflation rose 700 percent, and T-bill income rose only 60 percent. When one considers the growth in principal that stocks offer,

Table 2.5 *Comparison of Income Payouts from Common Stocks and Treasury Bills, 1926–1997*

During the past seventy-one years, stocks have been a more reliable source of income than either bonds or Treasury bills. The figures below presume that each year an investor spent all dividend and interest income kicked off by the securities, but left the capital intact.

	Years When Payout Rose	Years When Payout Fell	Worst One-Year Drop in Income	1926 TO 1997 Change in Value of Income	Change in Value of Principal
Stocks	57	13	−39%	1,824.6%	5,152.4%
20-Year Treasury bonds	39	32	−9.5	78	−9.4
5-Year Treasury bonds	41	30	−36.9	62.4	25.7
Treasury bills	42	29	−76.6	60.9	—

Table data source: Ibbotson Associates, Inc.

Source: "T-Bill Trauma and the Meaning of Risk," *Wall Street Journal,* February 12, 1993, p. C1. Reprinted with permission of the *Wall Street Journal.* ©1993 Dow Jones and Co., Inc. All rights reserved. Updated by the authors, using Ibbotson data.

we see that "conservative," income-oriented T-bill investors are in fact exposed to substantial amounts of risk.

Asset Allocation Summary

A carefully constructed policy statement determines the types of assets that should be included in a portfolio. The asset allocation decision, not the selection of specific stocks and bonds, determines most of the portfolio's returns over time. Although seemingly risky, investors seeking capital appreciation, income, or even capital preservation over long time periods will do well to include a sizable allocation to the equity portion in their portfolio. As reviewed in this section, a strategy's risk may depend on the investor's goals and time horizon. At times, investing in T-bills may be a riskier strategy than investing in common stocks due to reinvestment risks and the risk of not meeting long-term investment return goals.

ASSET ALLOCATION AND CULTURAL DIFFERENCES

Thus far our analysis has focused on U.S. investors. Non-U.S. investors make their asset allocation decisions in much the same manner. But because they face different social, economic, political, and tax environments, their allocation decisions differ from those of U.S. investors. Figure 2.8 shows the portfolio mixes of institutional investors in the United States, United Kingdom, Germany, and Japan. In the United States, equities (both foreign and domestic) comprise about 45 percent of invested assets. In the United Kingdom, equities make up 72 percent of assets; in Germany, equities are only 11 percent of the portfolio; in Japan, equities are 24 percent of assets.

National differences can explain much of the divergent portfolio strategies. Of these four nations, the average age of the population is the highest in Germany and Japan and lowest in the United States and the United Kingdom, which helps explain the greater use of equities in the latter countries. Government privatization programs during the 1980s in the United Kingdom encouraged equity ownership among individual and institutional investors. In Germany, regulations prevent insurance firms from having more than 20 percent of their assets in equities. Both Germany and Japan have banking sec-

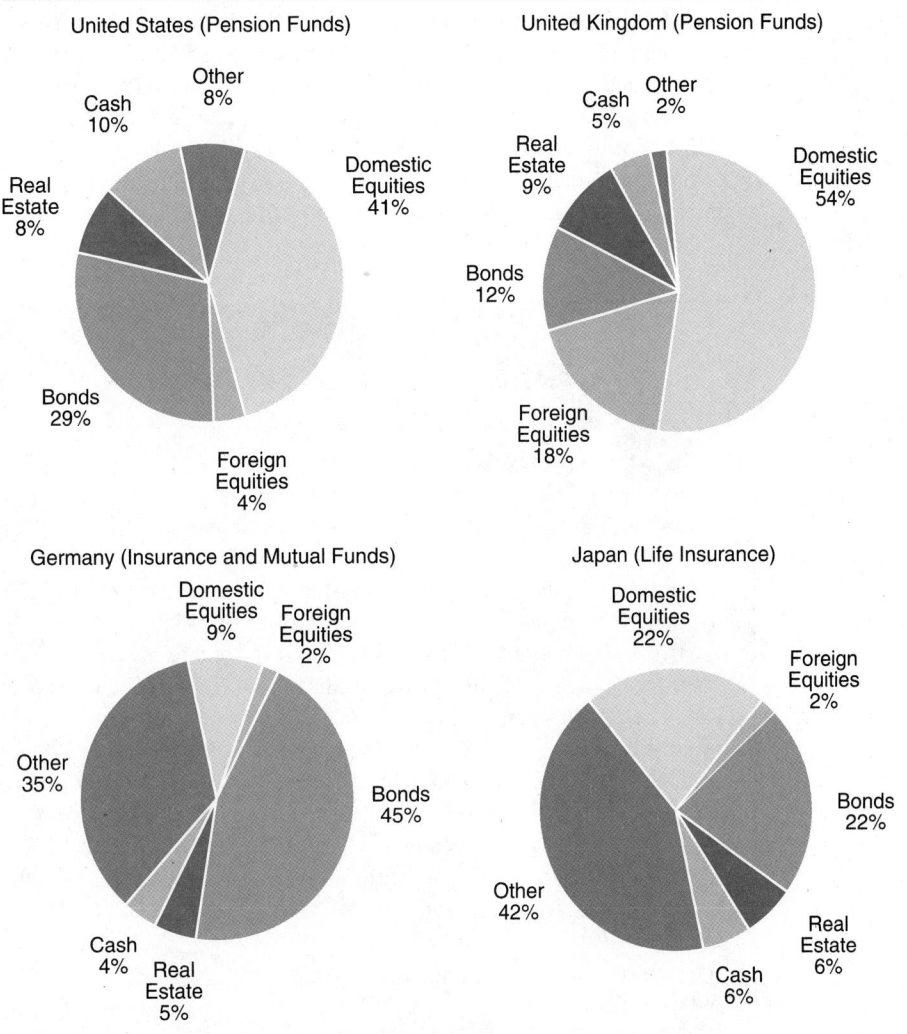

Figure 2.8   *Portfolio Mixes, Various Countries, 1990–1991*

tors that invest privately in firms and whose officers sit on corporate boards. Since 1960, in the United Kingdom cost of living has increased at a rate more than 4.5 times that of Germany; this inflationary bias in the United Kingdom economy favors equities in U.K. asset allocations.

The need to invest in equities for portfolio growth is less in Germany, where workers receive generous state pensions. Germans tend to show a cultural aversion to the stock market: Many Germans are risk-averse and consider stock investing a form of gambling. Although this attitude is showing signs of change, the German stock market is rather illiquid, with only a handful of stocks accounting for 50 percent of total stock trading volume.[12]

---

[12]Peter Gumbel, "The Hard Sell: Getting Germans to Invest in Stocks," *Wall Street Journal,* August 4, 1995, p. A2.

Other OECD (Organization for Economic Cooperation and Development) countries place regulatory restrictions on institutional investors. For example, pension funds in Austria must have at least 50 percent of their assets in bank deposits or schilling-denominated bonds. Belgium limits pension funds to a minimum 15 percent investment in government bonds. Finland places a 5 percent limit on investments outside its borders by pension funds, and French pension funds must invest a minimum of 34 percent in public debt instruments.[13]

Asset allocation policy and strategy are determined in the context of an investor's objectives and constraints. Among the factors that explain differences in investor behavior across countries, however, we must look at their political and economic environment.

Investments Online

Many inputs go into an investment policy statement as an investor maps out his or her objectives and constraints. Some inputs and helpful information are available in the following Web sites. Many of the sites mentioned in Chapter 1 contain important information and insights about asset allocation decisions, as well.

www.ssa.gov   Expected retirement funds from Social Security can be obtained by using the Social Security Administration's Web site.

www.ibbotson.com   Much of the data in this chapter's charts and tables came from Ibbotson's published sources. Many professional financial planners make use of Ibbotson's data and education resources.

www.mfea.com   This is the home page of the Mutual Fund Education Alliance. It contains much useful information that is relevant here and to Chapter 21, Portfolio Management Using Investment Companies. This site covers key investing concepts and has a discussion of risk versus reward. What is most relevant here is a page within the Web site: **www.mfea.com/planidx.html** presents a risk-tolerance quiz for investors.

Other interesting sites include:

www.asec.com   Home page of the American Saving Education Council

www.cccsedu.org/home.html   Home page of the Consumer Credit Counseling Service. It contains insights on managing and getting out of debt, money management, education issues, and a "fritter finder," which helps users find out where all their income goes.

Many professional organizations have Web sites for use by their members, those interested in seeking professional finance designations, and those interested in seeking advice from a professional financial adviser. These sites include:

www.aimr.org   Association for Investment Management and Research home page. AIMR awards the CFA (Chartered Financial Analyst) designation. This site provides information about the CFA designation, AIMR publications, investor education, and various Internet resources.

www.iafp.org   International Association for Financial Planning home page contains links of use to consumers (financial planning topics, careers, how to select a financial planner), and professionals (by way of links to other sites dealing with the association, governments, investor relations, law, taxes, and so on).

---

[13]Joel Chernoff, "OECD Eyes Pension Rules," *Pensions and Investments,* December 23, 1996, pp. 2, 34.

Investments Online *(cont.)*

www.amercoll.edu   This is the Web site for The American College, which is the training arm of the insurance industry. The American College offers the CLU and ChFC designations, which are typically earned by insurance professionals.

www.icfp.org   The home page for the Institute for Certified Financial Planners. The site offers features and topics of interest to financial planners, including information on earning the CFP designation and receiving the *Journal of Financial Planning.*

www.napfa.org   This is the home page for the National Association of Personal Financial Advisors. This is the trade group for fee-only financial planners. Fee-only planners do not sell products on commission, or, should they recommend a commission-generating product, they pass the commission on to the investor. This site features press releases, finding a fee-only planner in your area, a list of financial resources on the Web and position openings in the financial planning field.

SUMMARY

♦ The chapter has reviewed the importance of developing an investment policy statement prior to implementing a serious investment plan. By forcing investors to examine their needs, risk tolerance, and familiarity with the capital markets, chances improve for correctly identifying appropriate investor objectives and constraints. Investment plans are enhanced by the accurate formulation of a policy statement.

♦ We also reviewed the importance of the asset allocation decision in determining long-run portfolio investment returns and risks. Because the asset allocation decision follows setting the objectives and constraints, it is clear that the success of the investment program depends on the first step, the construction of the policy statement.

♦ Investors have many opportunities to invest in both domestic and international assets. The next chapter reviews investment choices and makes a strong case for including global assets in the asset allocation decision.

Questions

1. "Young people with little wealth should not invest money in risky assets such as the stock market, because they can't afford to lose what little money they have." Do you agree or disagree with this statement? Why?

2. Your healthy sixty-three-year-old neighbor is about to retire and comes to you for advice. From talking with her, you find out she was planning on taking all the money out of her company's retirement plan and investing it in bond mutual funds and money market funds. What advice should you give her?

3. Discuss how an individual's investment strategy may change as he or she goes through the accumulation, consolidation, spending, and gifting phases of life.

4. Why is a policy statement important?

5. Use the questionnaire in the "How much risk is right for you?" box (see p. 46) to determine your risk tolerance. Use this information to help write a policy statement for yourself.

6. Your forty-five-year-old uncle is twenty years away from retirement; your thirty-five-year-old older sister is about thirty years away from retirement. How might their investment policy statements differ?

7. What information is necessary before a financial planner can assist a person in constructing an investment policy statement?

8. Use the Internet to find the home pages for some financial planning firms. What strategies do they emphasize? What do they say about their asset allocation strategy? What are their firms' emphases: value investing, international diversification, principal preservation, retirement and estate planning, and such?

9. CFA Examination Level III (1993)

   Mr. Franklin is seventy years of age, in excellent health, pursues a simple but active lifestyle, and has no children. He has interest in a private company for $90 million and has decided that a medical research foundation will receive half of the proceeds now; it will also be the primary beneficiary of his estate upon his death. Mr. Franklin is committed to the foundation's well-being because he believes strongly that, through it, a cure will be found for the disease that killed his wife. He now realizes that an appropriate investment policy and asset allocations are required if his goals are to be met through investment of his considerable assets. Currently, the following assets are available for use in building an appropriate portfolio:

$45.0 million cash (from sale of the private company interest, net of pending $45 million gift to the foundation)	
10.0 million stocks and bonds ($5 million each)	
9.0 million warehouse property (now fully leased)	
1.0 million Franklin residence	
$65.0 million total available assets	

   A. Formulate and justify an investment policy statement setting forth the appropriate guidelines within which future investment actions should take place. Your policy statement must encompass all relevant objective and constraint considerations.

   B. Recommend and justify a long-term asset allocation that is consistent with the investment policy statement you created in Part A above. Briefly explain the key assumptions you made in generating your allocation.

Problems

1. Suppose your first job pays you $28,000 annually. What percentage should your cash reserve contain? How much life insurance should you carry if you are unmarried? If you are married with two young children?

2. What is the marginal tax rate for a couple, filing jointly, if their taxable income is $20,000? $40,000? $60,000? What is their tax bill for each of these income levels? What is the average tax rate for each of these income levels?

3. What is the marginal tax rate for a single individual if his taxable income is $20,000? $40,000? $60,000? What is his tax bill for each of these income levels? What is his average tax rate for each of these income levels?

4. a. Someone in the 36 percent tax bracket can earn 9 percent annually on her investments in a tax-exempt IRA account. What will be the value of a one-time $10,000 investment in five years? Ten years? Twenty years?

   b. Suppose the above 9 percent return is taxable rather than tax-deferred and the taxes are paid annually. What will be the after-tax value of her $10,000 investment after five, ten, and twenty years?

5. a. Someone in the 15 percent tax bracket can earn 10 percent on his investments in a tax-exempt IRA account. What will be the value of a $10,000 investment in five years? Ten years? Twenty years?

   b. Suppose the above 10 percent return is taxable rather than tax-deferred. What will be the after-tax value of his $10,000 investment after five, ten, and twenty years?

References

Bhatia, Sanjiv, ed. *Managing Assets for Individual Investors* (Charlottesville, VA: Association for Investment Management and Research, 1995).

Ellis, Charles D. *Investment Policy: How to Win the Loser's Game*. Homewood, Ill: Dow Jones–Irwin, 1985.

Peavy, John. *Cases in Portfolio Management*. Charlottesville, VA: Association for Investment Management and Research, 1990.

Peavy, John W., ed. *Investment Counsel for Private Clients* (Charlottesville, VA: Association for Investment Management and Research, 1993).

GLOSSARY

Accumulation phase   Phase in the investment life cycle during which individuals in the early-to-middle years of their working career attempt to accumulate assets to satisfy short-term needs and longer-term goals.

Actuarial rate of return   The discount rate used to find the present value of a defined benefit pension plan's future obligations and thus determine the size of the firm's annual contribution to the plan.

Asset allocation   The process of deciding how to distribute an investor's wealth among different asset classes for investment purposes.

Asset class   A collection of securities that have similar characteristics, attributes, and risk/return relationships.

Basis of an asset   For tax purposes, the cost of an asset.

Benchmark portfolio   A comparison standard of risk and assets included in the policy statement and similar to the investor's risk preference and investment needs, which can be used to evaluate the investment performance of the portfolio manager.

Capital appreciation   A return objective in which the investor seeks to increase the portfolio value, primarily through capital gains, over time to meet a future need; generally a goal of an investor willing to take on risk to meet a goal.

Capital preservation   A return objective in which the investor seeks to minimize the risk of loss; generally a goal of the risk-averse investor.

Consolidation phase   Phase in the investment life cycle during which individuals who are typically past the midpoint of their career have earnings that exceed expenses and invest them for future retirement or estate planning needs.

Current income   A return objective in which the investor seeks to generate income rather than capital gains; generally a goal of an investor who wants to supplement earnings with income to meet living expenses.

Fiduciary   A person who supervises or oversees the investment portfolio of a third party, such as in a trust account, and makes investment decisions in accordance with the owner's wishes.

Gifting phase   Phase in the investment life cycle during which individuals use excess assets to financially assist relatives or friends, establish charitable trusts, or construct trusts to minimize estate taxes.

Liquid   Term used to describe an asset that can be quickly converted to cash at a price close to fair market value.

Long-term, high-priority goal   A long-term financial investment goal of personal importance that typically includes achieving financial independence, such as being able to retire at a certain age.

Lower-priority goal   A financial investment goal of lesser personal importance, such as taking a luxurious vacation or buying a car every few years.

Near-term, high-priority goal   A short-term financial investment goal of personal importance, such as accumulating funds for making a house down payment or buying a car.

Objectives   The investor's goals expressed in terms of risk and return and included in the policy statement.

Overfunded plan   A defined benefit pension plan in which the present value of the pension liabilities is less than the plan's assets.

Personal trust   An amount of money set aside by a grantor and often managed by a third party, the trustee; often constructed so one party receives income from the trust's investments and another party receives the residual value of the trust after the income beneficiary's death.

Policy statement   A statement in which the investor specifies investment goals, constraints, and risk preferences.

Realized capital gains   Capital gains that result when an appreciated asset has been sold; realized capital gains are taxable.

Spending phase   Phase in the investment life cycle during which individuals' earning years end as they retire. They pay for expenses with income from social security and prior investments and invest to protect against inflation.

Total return   A return objective in which the investor wants to increase the portfolio value to meet a future need by both capital gains and current income reinvestment.

Underfunded plan   A defined benefit pension plan in which the present value of the fund's liabilities to employees exceeds the value of the fund's assets.

Unrealized capital gains   Capital gains that reflect the price appreciation of currently held unsold assets; taxes on unrealized capital gains can be deferred indefinitely.

A P P E N D I X   2   *Objectives and Constraints of Institutional Investors*

Institutional investors manage large amounts of funds in the course of their business. They include mutual funds, pension funds, insurance firms, endowments, and banks. In this section we review the characteristics of various institutional investors and discuss their typical investment objectives and constraints.

Mutual Funds

A mutual fund pools together sums of money from investors, which are then invested in financial assets. Each mutual fund has its own investment objective, such as capital appreciation, high current income, or money market income. A mutual fund will state its investment objective, and investors, as part of their own investment strategies, choose the funds in which to invest. Two basic constraints face mutual funds: those created by law to protect mutual fund investors, and those that represent choices made by the mutual fund's managers. Some of these constraints will be discussed in the mutual fund's prospectus, which must be given to all prospective investors before they purchase shares in a mutual fund. Mutual funds will be discussed in more detail in Chapter 21.

Pension Funds

Pension funds are a major component of retirement planning for individuals. As of March 1997, U.S. pension assets were nearly $6.4 trillion. Basically, a firm's pension fund receives contributions from the firm, its employees, or both. The funds are invested with the purpose of giving workers either a lump sum payment or the promise of an income stream after their retirement. **Defined benefit pension plans** promise to pay retirees a specific income stream after retirement. The size of the benefit is usually based on factors that include the worker's salary or time of service, or both. The company contributes a certain amount each year to the pension plan; the size of the contribution depends on assumptions concerning future salary increases and the rate of return to be earned on the plan's assets. Under a defined benefit plan, the company carries the risk of paying the future pension benefit to retirees; should investment performance be poor, or should the company be unable to make adequate contributions to the plan, the shortfall must be made up in future years. "Poor" investment performance means the actual return on the plan's assets fell below the assumed **actuarial rate of return**. The actuarial rate is the discount rate used to find the present value of the plan's future obligations and thus determines the size of the firm's annual contribution to the pension plan.

Defined contribution pension plans do not promise set benefits; rather, employees' benefits depend on the size of the contributions made to the pension fund and the returns

earned on the fund's investments. Thus, the plan's risk is borne by the employees. Unlike a defined benefit plan, employees' retirement income is not an obligation of the firm.

A pension plan's objectives and constraints depend on whether the plan is a *defined benefit plan* or a *defined contribution plan.* We review each separately below.

Defined Benefit   The plan's risk tolerance depends on the plan's funding status and its actuarial rate. For **underfunded plans** (where the present value of the fund's liabilities to employees exceeds the value of the funds' assets), a more conservative approach toward risk is taken to ensure that the funding gap is closed over time. This may entail a strategy whereby the firm makes larger plan contributions and assumes a lower actuarial rate. **Overfunded plans** (where the present value of the pension liabilities is less than the plan's assets), allow a more aggressive investment strategy in which the firm reduces its contributions and increases the risk exposure of the plan. The return objective is to meet the plan's actuarial rate of return, which is set by actuaries who estimate future pension obligations based on assumptions about future salary increases, current salaries, retirement patterns, worker life expectancies, and the firm's benefit formula. The actuarial rate also helps determine the size of the firm's plan contributions over time.

The liquidity constraint on defined benefit funds is mainly a function of the average age of employees. A younger employee base means less liquidity is needed; an older employee base generally means more liquidity is needed to pay current pension obligations to retirees. The time horizon constraint is also affected by the average age of employees, although some experts recommend using a five to ten year horizon for planning purposes. Taxes are not a major concern to the plan, because pension plans are exempt from paying tax on investment returns. The major legal constraint is that the plan must be run in accordance with ERISA, the Employee Retirement and Income Security Act, and investments must satisfy the "prudent man" standard when evaluated in the context of the overall pension plan's portfolio.

Defined Contribution   As the individual worker decides how his contributions to the plan are to be invested, the objectives and constraints for defined contribution plans depend on the individual. Because the worker carries the risk of inadequate retirement funding rather than the firm, defined contribution plans are generally more conservatively invested (some suggest that employees tend to be too conservative). If, however, the plan is considered more of an estate planning tool for a wealthy founder or officer of the firm, a higher risk tolerance and return objective is appropriate because most of the plan's assets will ultimately be owned by the individual's heirs.

The liquidity and time horizon needs for the plan differ depending on the average age of the employees and the degree of employee turnover within the firm. Similar to defined benefit plans, defined contribution plans are tax-exempt and are governed by the provisions of ERISA.

Endowment Funds

Endowment funds arise from contributions made to charitable or educational institutions. Rather than immediately spending the funds, the organization invests the money for the purpose of providing a future stream of income to the organization. The investment policy of an endowment fund is the result of a "tension" between the organization's need for current income and the desire to plan for a growing stream of income in the future to protect against inflation.

To meet the institution's operating budget needs, the fund's return objective is often set by adding the spending rate (the amount taken out of the funds each year) and the expected inflation rate. Funds that have more risk-tolerant trustees may have a higher spending rate than those overseen by more risk-averse trustees. Because a total return approach usually

serves to meet the return objective over time, the organization is generally withdrawing both income and capital gain returns to meet budgeted needs. The risk tolerance of an endowment fund is largely affected by the collective risk tolerance of the organization's trustees.

Due to the fund's long-term time horizon, liquidity requirements are minor except for the need to spend part of the endowment each year and maintain a cash reserve for emergencies. Many endowments are tax-exempt, although income from some private foundations can be taxed at either a 1 percent or 2 percent rate. Short-term capital gains are taxable, but long-term capital gains are not. Regulatory and legal constraints arise on the state level, where most endowments are regulated. Unique needs and preferences may affect investment strategies, especially among college or religious endowments, which sometimes have strong preferences about social investing issues.

Insurance Companies

The investment objectives and constraints for an insurance company depend on whether it is a life insurance company or a nonlife (such as a property and casualty) insurance firm.

Life Insurance Companies   Except for firms dealing only in term life insurance, life insurance firms collect premiums during a person's lifetime that must be invested until a death benefit is paid to the insurance contract's beneficiaries. At any time the insured can turn in his policy and receive its cash surrender value. Discussing investment policy for an insurance firm is also complicated by the insurance industry's proliferation of insurance and quasi-investment products.

Basically, an insurance company wants to earn a positive "spread," which is the difference between the rate of return on investment minus the rate of return it credits its various policyholders. This concept is similar to a defined-benefit pension fund that tries to earn a rate of return in excess of its actuarial rate. If the spread is positive, the insurance firm's surplus reserve account rises; if not, the surplus account declines by an amount reflecting the negative spread. A growing surplus is an important competitive tool for life insurance companies. Attractive investment returns allow the company to advertise better policy returns than those of their competitors. A growing surplus also allows the firm to offer new products and expand insurance volume.

Because life insurance companies are quasi-trust funds for savings, fiduciary principles limit the risk tolerance of the invested funds. The National Association of Insurance Commissioners (NAIC) establishes risk categories for bonds and stocks; companies with excessive investments in higher-risk categories must set aside extra funds in a mandatory securities valuation reserve (MSVR) to protect policyholders against losses.

Insurance companies' liquidity needs have increased over the years due to increases in policy surrenders and product-mix changes. A company's time horizon depends upon its specific product mix. Life insurance policies require longer-term investments, whereas guaranteed insurance contracts (GICs) and shorter-term annuities require shorter investment time horizons.

Tax rules changed considerably for insurance firms in the 1980s. For tax purposes, investment returns are divided into two components: first, the policyholder's share, which is the return portion covering the actuarially assumed rate of return needed to fund reserves; and second, the balance that is transferred to reserves. Unlike pensions and endowments, life insurance firms pay income and capital gains taxes at the corporate tax rates on this second component of return.

Except for the NAIC, most insurance regulation is on the state level. Regulators oversee the eligible asset classes and the reserves (MSVR) necessary for each asset class, and enforce the "prudent man" investment standard. Audits ensure that various accounting rules and investment regulations are followed.

Nonlife Insurance Companies   Cash outflows are somewhat predictable for life insurance firms, based on their mortality tables. In contrast, the cash flow required by major accidents, disasters, and lawsuit settlements are not as predictable for nonlife insurance firms.

Due to their fiduciary responsibility to claimants, risk exposures are low to moderate. Depending on the specific company and competitive pressures, premiums may be affected both by the probability of a claim and the investment returns earned by the firm. Typically, casualty insurance firms invest their insurance reserves in bonds for safety purposes and to provide needed income to pay claims; capital and surplus funds are invested in equities for their growth potential. As with life insurers, property and casualty firms have a stronger competitive position when their surplus accounts are larger than competitors'. Many insurers now focus on a total return objective as a means to increase their surplus accounts over time.

Because of uncertain claim patterns, liquidity is a concern for property and casualty insurers who also want liquidity so they can switch between taxable and tax-exempt investments as their underwriting activities generate losses and profits. The time horizon for investments is typically shorter than that of life insurers, although many invest in long-term bonds to earn the higher yields available on these instruments. Investing strategy for the firm's surplus account focuses on long-term growth.

Regulation of property and casualty firms is more permissive than for life insurers. Similar to life companies, states regulate classes and quality of investments for a certain percentage of the firm's assets. But beyond this restriction, insurers can invest in many different types and qualities of instruments, except that some states limit the proportion of real estate assets.

Banks

Pension funds, endowments, and insurance firms obtain virtually free funds for investment purposes. Not so with banks. To have funds to lend, they must attract investors in a competitive interest rate environment. They compete against other banks and also against companies that offer other investment vehicles, from bonds to common stocks. A bank's success relies primarily on its ability to generate returns in excess of its funding costs.

A bank tries to maintain a positive difference between its cost of funds and its returns on assets. If banks anticipate falling interest rates, they will try to invest in longer-term assets to lock in the returns while seeking short-term deposits, whose interest cost is expected to fall over time. When banks expect rising rates they will try to lock in longer-term deposits with fixed-interest costs, while investing funds short term to capture rising interest rates. The risk of such strategies is that losses may occur should a bank incorrectly forecast the direction of interest rates. The aggressiveness of a bank's strategy will be related to the size of its capital ratio and the oversight of regulators.

Banks need substantial liquidity to meet withdrawals and loan demand. A bank has two forms of liquidity. Internal liquidity is provided by a bank's investment portfolio that includes highly liquid assets that can be sold to raise cash. A bank has external liquidity if it can borrow funds in the federal funds markets (where banks lend reserves to other banks), from the Federal Reserve Bank's discount window, or by selling certificates of deposit at attractive rates.

Banks have a short time horizon for several reasons. First, they have a strong need for liquidity. Second, because they want to maintain an adequate interest revenue–interest expense spread, they generally focus on shorter-term investments to avoid interest rate risk and to avoid getting "locked in" to a long-term revenue source. Third, because banks

typically offer short-term deposit accounts (demand deposits, NOW accounts, and such.), they need to match the maturity of their assets and liabilities to avoid taking undue risks.[14]

Banks are heavily regulated by numerous state and federal agencies. The Federal Reserve Board, the Comptroller of the Currency, and the Federal Deposit Insurance Corporation all oversee various components of bank operations. The Glass-Steagall Act restricts the equity investments that banks can make. Unique situations that affect each bank's investment policy depend on their size, market, and management skills in matching asset and liability sensitivity to interest rates. For example, a bank in a small community may have many customers who deposit their money with it for the sake of convenience. A bank in a more populated area will find its deposit flows are more sensitive to interest rates and competition from nearby banks.

Institutional Investor Summary

Among the great variety of institutions, each institution has its "typical" investment objectives and constraints. This discussion has given us a flavor of the differences that exist between types of institutions and some of the major issues confronting them. Notably, just as with individual investors, "cookie-cutter" policy statements are inappropriate for institutional investors. The specific objectives, constraints, and investment strategies must be determined on a case-by-case basis.

---

[14]An asset/liability mismatch caused the ultimate downfall of savings and loan associations. They attracted short-term liabilities (deposit accounts) and invested in long-term assets (mortgages). When interest rates became more volatile in the early 1980s and short-term rates increased dramatically, S&Ls suffered large losses.

CHAPTER

3

Selecting Investments in a Global Market

This chapter answers the following questions:

♦ Why should investors have a global perspective regarding their investments?

♦ What has happened to the relative size of U.S. and foreign stock and bond markets?

♦ What are the differences in the rates of return on U.S. and foreign securities markets?

♦ How can changes in currency exchange rates affect the returns that U.S. investors experience on foreign securities?

♦ Is there additional advantage to diversifying in international markets beyond the benefits of domestic diversification?

♦ What alternative securities are available? What are their cash flow and risk properties?

♦ What are the historical return and risk characteristics of the major investment instruments?

♦ What is the relationship among the returns for foreign and domestic investment instruments? What is the implication of these relationships for portfolio diversification?

Individuals are willing to defer current consumption for many reasons. Some save for their children's college tuition or their own; others wish to accumulate down payments for a home, car, or boat; others want to amass adequate retirement funds for the future. Whatever the reason for an investment program, the techniques we used in Chapter 1 to measure risk and return will help you evaluate alternative investments.   ♦

But what are those alternatives? Thus far, we have said little about the investment opportunities available in financial markets. In this chapter, we address this issue by surveying investment alternatives. This is essential background for making the asset allocation decision discussed in Chapter 2 and for later chapters where we analyze several individual investments such as bonds, common stock, and other securities. It is also important when we consider how to construct and evaluate portfolios of investments.

As an investor in the 21st century, you have an array of investment choices unavailable a few decades ago. Together, the dynamism of financial markets, technological advances, and new regulations have resulted in numerous new investment instruments and expanded trading opportunities.[1] Improvements in communications and relaxation of international regulations have made it easier for investors to trade in both domestic and global markets. Telecommunications networks enable U.S. brokers to reach security exchanges in London, Tokyo, and other European and Asian cities as easily as those in New York, Chicago, and other U.S. cities. The competitive environment in the brokerage industry and the deregulation of the banking sector have made it possible for more financial institutions to compete for investor dollars. This has spawned investment vehicles with a variety of maturities, risk–return characteristics, and cash flow patterns. In this chapter we examine some of these choices.

As an investor, you need to understand the differences among investments so you can build a properly diversified **portfolio** that conforms to your objectives. That is, you should seek to acquire a group of investments with different patterns of returns over time. If chosen carefully, such portfolios minimize risk for a given level of return because low or negative rates of return on some investments during a period of time are offset by above-average returns on others. The goal is to build a balanced portfolio of investments with relatively stable overall rates of return. A major goal of this text is to help you understand and evaluate the risk–return characteristics of investment portfolios. An appreciation of alternative security types is the starting point for this analysis.

This chapter is divided into three main sections. As noted earlier, investors can choose securities from financial markets around the world. Therefore, in the first section we look at a combination of reasons why investors *should* include foreign as well as domestic securities in their portfolios. Taken together, these reasons provide a compelling case for global investing. We continue the investigation of where to invest in Chapter 4 when we examine securities markets around the world in more detail.

In the second section of this chapter, we discuss securities in domestic and global markets, describing their main features and cash flow patterns. From this discussion, you will see that the varying risk–return characteristics of alternative investments suit the preferences of different investors. Some securities are more appropriate for individuals, whereas others are better suited for financial institutions such as insurance companies and pension funds.

The third and final section contains an assessment of the historical risk and return performance of several investment instruments from around the world and examines the relationship among the returns for many of these securities. An understanding of these relationships will provide further support for global investing.

THE CASE FOR GLOBAL INVESTMENTS

Twenty years ago, the bulk of investments available to individual investors consisted of stocks and bonds sold on U.S. securities markets. Now, however, a call to your broker gives

---

[1]For an excellent discussion of the reasons for the development of numerous financial innovations and the effect of these innovations on world capital markets, see Merton H. Miller, *Financial Innovations and Market Volatility* (Cambridge, MA: Blackwell Publishers, 1991).

you access to a wide range of securities sold throughout the world. Currently, you can purchase stock in General Motors or Toyota, U.S. Treasury bonds or Japanese government bonds, a mutual fund that invests in U.S. biotechnology companies, a global growth stock fund or a German stock fund, or options on a U.S. stock index along with innumerable other investments.

Several changes have caused this explosion of investment opportunities. For one, the growth and development of numerous foreign financial markets such as those in Japan, the United Kingdom, and Germany, as well as in emerging markets such as China, have made these markets accessible and viable for investors around the world. Numerous U.S. investment firms have recognized this opportunity and established and expanded facilities in these countries. This expansion was aided by major advances in telecommunications technology that made it possible to maintain constant contact with offices and financial markets around the world. In addition to the efforts by U.S. firms, foreign firms and investors undertook counterbalancing initiatives with wealth derived from oil sales and from foreign exchange provided by surpluses in balances of payments. As a result, investors and investment firms from around the world found it desirable and possible to trade securities worldwide. Thus, investment alternatives are available from the traditional U.S. financial markets and from security markets around the world.[2]

Three interrelated reasons U.S. investors should think of constructing global investment portfolios can be summarized as follows:

1. When investors compare the absolute and relative sizes of U.S. and foreign markets for stocks and bonds, they see that ignoring foreign markets reduces their choices to less than 50 percent of available investment opportunities. Because more opportunities broaden your range of risk–return choices, it makes sense to evaluate foreign securities when selecting investments and building a portfolio.
2. The rates of return available on non-U.S. securities often have substantially exceeded those for only U.S. securities. The higher returns on non-U.S. *equities* can be justified by the higher growth rates for the countries where they are issued. These superior results have continued to prevail even when the returns were risk-adjusted.
3. One of the major tenets of investment theory is that investors should diversify their portfolio. Because the relevant factor when diversifying a portfolio is low correlation between asset returns, diversification with uncorrelated foreign securities can help to substantially reduce portfolio risk.

In this section, we analyze these reasons to demonstrate the advantages to a growing role of foreign financial markets for U.S. investors and to assess the benefits and risks of trading in these markets.

Relative Size of U.S. Financial Markets

Prior to 1970, the securities traded in the U.S. stock and bond markets comprised about 65 percent of all the securities available in world capital markets. Therefore, a U.S. investor selecting securities strictly from U.S. markets had a fairly complete set of investments available. Under these conditions, most U.S. investors probably believed it not worth the time and effort to expand their investment universe to include the limited investments available in foreign markets. That situation has changed dramatically over the past thirty years. Currently, investors who ignore foreign markets limit their investment choices substantially.

---

[2]In this regard, see Scott E. Pardee, "Internationalization of Financial Markets," *Federal Reserve Bank of Kansas City, Economic Review* (February 1987): 3–7.

Figure 3.1   *Total Investable Capital Market*

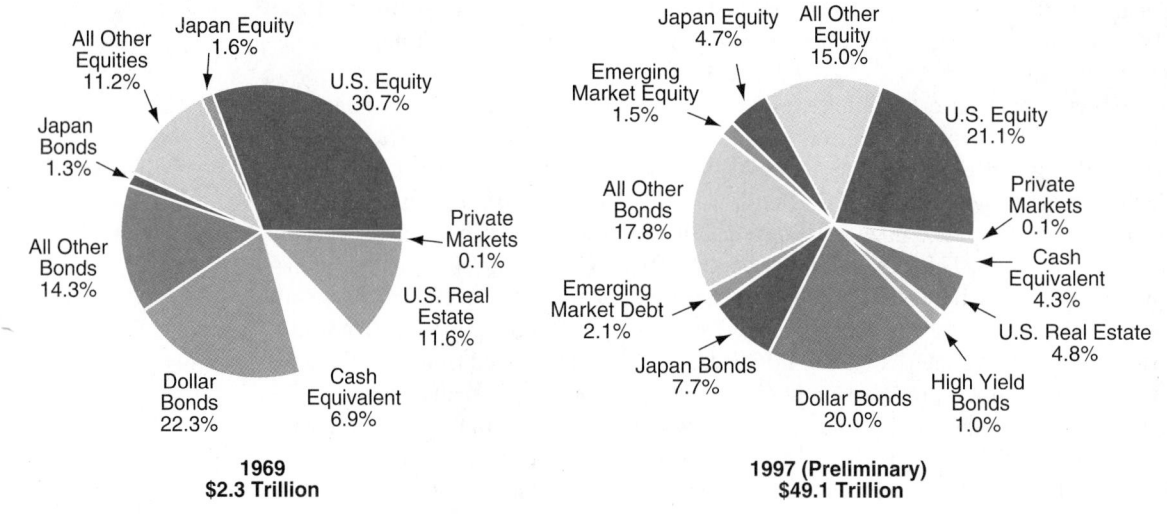

1969
$2.3 Trillion

1997 (Preliminary)
$49.1 Trillion

Source: Brinson Partners, Inc., Chicago, IL.

Figure 3.1 shows the breakdown of securities available in world capital markets in 1969 and 1997. Not only has the overall value of all securities increased dramatically (from $2.3 trillion to $49 trillion), but the composition has also changed. Concentrating on proportions of bond and equity investments, the figure shows that U.S. dollar bond and equity securities made up 53 percent of the total value of all securities in 1969 versus 28.4 percent for nondollar bonds and equity. By 1997, U.S. bonds and equities accounted for 42.1 percent of the total securities market versus 48.8 percent for nondollar bonds and stocks. These data indicate that if you consider only the stock and bond market, the U.S. proportion of this combined market has declined from 63 percent of the total in 1969 to about 46 percent in 1997.

The point is, the U.S. security markets now include a smaller proportion of the total world capital market, and it is likely that this trend will continue. The faster economic growth of many other countries compared to the United States will require foreign governments and individual companies to issue debt and equity securities to finance this growth. Therefore, U.S. investors should consider investing in foreign securities because of the growing importance of these foreign securities in world capital markets. Not investing in foreign stocks and bonds means you are ignoring almost 54 percent of the securities that are available to you.

Rates of Return on U.S. and Foreign Securities

An examination of the rates of return on U.S. and foreign securities not only demonstrates that many non-U.S. securities provide superior rates of return, but also shows the impact of the exchange rate risk discussed in Chapter 1.

Global Bond Market Returns   Table 3.1 reports annual compound rates of return for several major international bond markets for 1987–1996. The *domestic return* is the rate of return an investor within the country would earn. In contrast, the return in U.S. dollars is what a U.S. investor would earn after adjusting for changes in the currency exchange rates during the period.

Table 3.1 *International Bond Market Compound Annual Rates of Return: 1987–1996*

	COMPONENTS OF RETURN		
	Total Domestic Return	**Total Return in U.S. $**	**Exchange Rate Effect**
Canada	10.89	10.98	0.01
France	10.52	12.73	2.00
Germany	7.41	9.79	2.22
Japan	6.49	9.90	3.20
United Kingdom	11.30	12.91	1.45
United States	8.10	8.10	—

Source: Frank K. Reilly and David J. Wright, "Global Bond Markets: Benchmarks and Risk–Return Performance" (May, 1997). Based on data from Merrill Lynch Bond Indexes.

An analysis of the domestic returns in Table 3.1 indicates that the performance of the U.S. bond market ranked fourth out of the six countries. When the impact of exchange rates is considered, the U.S. experience was the lowest out of six. The difference in performance for domestic versus U.S. dollar returns means that the exchange rate effect for a U.S. investor who invested in foreign bonds was always positive (that is, the U.S. dollar was weak) and added to the domestic performance.

As an example, the domestic return on Japanese bonds was 6.49 percent compared with the return for U.S. bonds of 8.10 percent. The Japanese foreign exchange effect was 3.20 percent, which increased the return on Japanese bonds converted to U.S. dollars to 9.90 percent, which was above the return for U.S. bonds. The point is, a U.S. investor in non-U.S. bonds from several countries could experience rates of return close to or above those of U.S. investors who limited themselves to the U.S. bond market.

Global Equity Market Returns   Table 3.2 shows the compound growth rate of prices in local currencies and in U.S. dollars for twelve major equity markets, four areas of the world, and the total world for the period from 1986 to 1997. The performance in local currency indicated that the U.S. market was ranked seventh of the total seventeen countries and areas or was the seventh of twelve countries. The performance results in U.S. dollars indicate that the currency effect was positive for investors in ten of the eleven foreign countries (the U.S. dollar was weak relative to these currencies). The currency effect only hurt the U.S. dollar returns for Sweden. Overall, in U.S. dollar returns, the U.S. market was ranked fifteenth of the seventeen countries and areas or eleventh of twelve countries.

Like the bond market performance, these results for equity markets around the world indicate that investors who limited themselves to the U.S. market experienced rates of return below those in many other countries. This is true for comparisons that considered both domestic returns and rates of return adjusted for exchange rates.

Individual Country Risk and Return

As shown, most countries experienced higher compound returns on bonds and stocks than the United States. A natural question is whether these superior rate of return results are attributable to higher levels of risk for securities in these countries.

Table 3.3 contains the returns and risk measures for six major bond markets in local currency and U.S. dollars, along with a composite ratio of return per unit of risk. The results in local currency are similar to the rate of return results—the U.S. bond market ranked fourth of the six countries. The results when returns and risk are measured in U.S. dollars were quite different. Specifically, although the return always increased because of the

Table 3.2 FT-Actuaries World Equity Total Return Performance: Average Yearly Returns in Local Currency and U.S. Dollars, 1986–1997

| | LOCAL CURRENCY | | U.S. DOLLARS | |
	Percent	Rank[a]	Percent	Rank[a]
Australia	15.5	7 (6)	16.2	10 (8)
Canada	11.1	13 (10)	11.1	15 (11)
France	15.4	8 (7)	17.4	5 (5)
Germany	11.0	14 (11)	13.7	13 (10)
Italy	13.9	11 (9)	13.8	12 (9)
Japan	4.8	17 (12)	9.4	17 (12)
Netherlands	16.9	3 (3)	19.3	3 (3)
Spain	21.7	2 (2)	22.0	1 (1)
Sweden	22.1	1 (1)	21.6	2 (2)
Switzerland	14.0	10 (8)	16.8	6 (6)
United Kingdom	16.6	5 (5)	18.0	4 (4)
United States	16.7	4 (4)	16.7	7 (7)
Europe	14.8	9	16.5	8
Pacific Basin	5.7	16	9.9	16
Europe and Pacific	10.0	15	13.1	14
North America	16.4	6	16.4	9
World	12.4	12	14.1	11

[a]Based on rank within seventeen countries and areas (rank for only the twelve countries). (T) indicates a tie in the ranking.

Table 3.3 International Bond Market Return–Risk Results: Local Currency and U.S. Dollars, 1987–1996

| | LOCAL CURRENCY | | | U.S. DOLLARS | | |
Country	Return	Risk	Return/Risk	Return	Risk	Return/Risk
Canada	10.89	6.58	1.66	10.98	9.08	1.21
France	10.52	4.26	2.47	12.73	10.94	1.16
Germany	7.41	3.18	2.33	9.79	11.74	0.83
Japan	6.49	4.91	1.32	9.90	14.08	0.70
United Kingdom	11.30	6.49	1.74	12.91	13.60	0.95
United States	8.10	4.77	1.70	8.10	4.77	1.70

weak dollar, the risk measures typically increased dramatically (that is, the average risk for the five non-U.S. countries went from 5.08 percent to 11.89 percent). As a result, the returns per unit of risk declined significantly and the U.S. performance ranked first. Beyond the impact on the relative results in U.S. dollars, these significant increases in the volatility for returns of foreign stocks in U.S. dollars are evidence of the exchange rate risk discussed in Chapter 1.

Figure 3.2 contains the scatter plot of local currency equity returns (the compound growth rate of price) and risk for the 12 individual countries, four regions of the world, and the total world for 1986 to 1997. The risk measure is the standard deviation of daily returns as discussed in Chapter 1. Notably, the U.S. market experienced one of the lowest risk values. The return-to-risk position above the line of best fit indicates that the U.S. performance in local currency was tied for first out of seventeen, mainly because of the low measure of risk. The results in U.S. dollars in Figure 3.3 show similar risk results. Measuring return and risk in U.S. dollars, the U.S. return/risk performance is ranked third of 17.

Figure 3.2   *Annual Rates of Return and Risk for Major Stock Markets in Local Currency: 1986–1997*

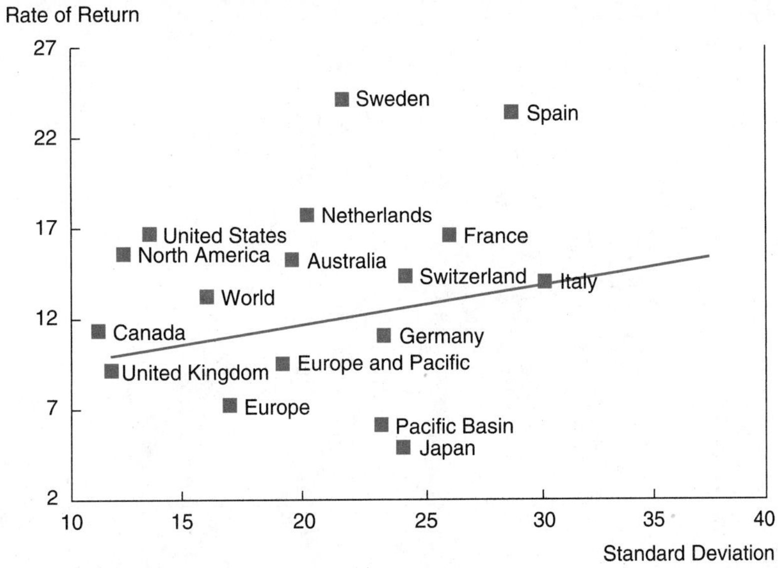

While most countries or areas experienced higher returns in U.S. dollars, the risk measures increased substantially due to the exchange rate risk.

Risk of Combined Country Investments

Thus far, we have discussed the risk and return results for individual countries. In Chapter 1, we considered the idea of combining a number of assets into a portfolio and noted that investors should create diversified portfolios to reduce the variability of the returns over time. We discussed how proper diversification reduces the variability (our measure of risk) of the portfolio because alternative investments have different patterns of returns over time. Specifically, when the rates of return on some investments are negative or below average, other investments in the portfolio will be experiencing above-average rates of return. Therefore, if a portfolio is properly diversified, it should provide a more stable rate of return for the total portfolio (that is, it will have a lower standard deviation and therefore less risk). Although we will discuss and demonstrate portfolio theory in detail in Chapter 6, we need to consider the concept at this point to fully understand the benefits of global investing.

The way to measure whether two investments will contribute to diversifying a portfolio is to compute the correlation coefficient between their rates of return over time. Correlation coefficients can range from +1.00 to −1.00. A correlation of +1.00 means that the rates of return for these two investments move exactly together. Combining investments that move together in a portfolio would not help diversify the portfolio because they have identical rate-of-return patterns over time. In contrast, a correlation coefficient of −1.00 means that the rates of return for two investments move exactly opposite to each other. When one investment is experiencing above-average rates of return, the other is suffering through similar below-average rates of return. Combining two investments with large negative correlation in a portfolio would contribute much to diversification because it would stabilize the rates of return over time, reducing the standard deviation of the

Figure 3.3   *Annual Rates of Return and Risk for Major Stock Markets in U.S. Dollars: 1986–1997*

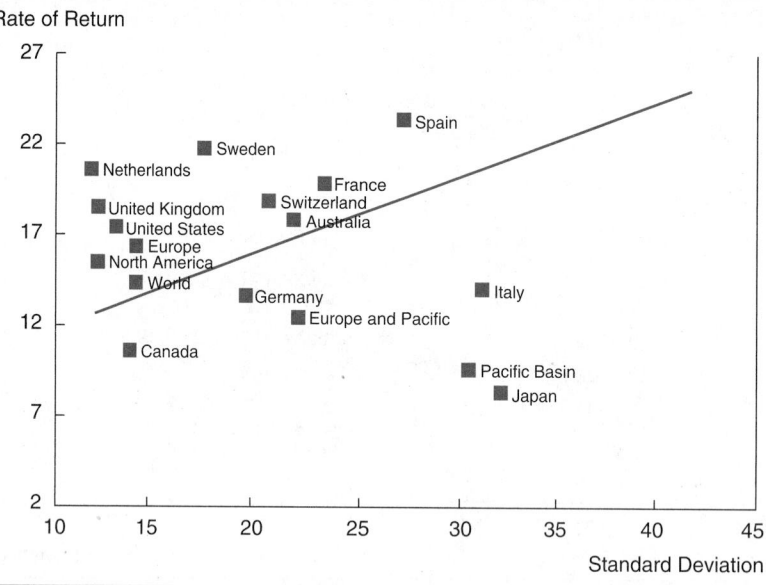

Table 3.4   *Correlation Coefficients between Rates of Return on Bonds in the United States and Major Foreign Markets: 1987–1996 (Monthly Data)*

	Domestic Returns	**Returns in U.S. Dollars**
Canada	0.72	0.57
France	0.47	0.32
Germany	0.44	0.27
Japan	0.34	0.15
United Kingdom	0.40	0.23

Source: Frank K. Reilly and David J. Wright, "Global Bond Markets: Alternative Benchmarks and Risk–Return Performance" (May, 1997).

portfolio rates of return and hence the risk of the portfolio. Therefore, if you want to diversify your portfolio and reduce your risk, you want an investment that has either *low positive* correlation, *zero* correlation, or, ideally, *negative correlation* with the other investments in your portfolio. With this in mind, the following discussion considers the correlations of returns among U.S. bonds and stocks with the returns on foreign bonds and stocks.

Global Bond Portfolio Risk   Table 3.4 lists the correlation coefficients between rates of return for bonds in the United States and bonds in major foreign markets in domestic and U.S. dollar terms from 1987 to 1996. Notice that only one correlation between domestic rates of return is above 0.50. For a U.S. investor, the important correlations are between the rates of return in U.S. dollars. In this case, all the correlations between returns in U.S. dollars are substantially lower than the correlations among domestic returns and there is only one correlation above 0.32. Notably, while the individual volatilities increased substantially when returns were converted to U.S. dollars, the correlations among returns in U.S. dollars declined.

These low positive correlations among returns in U.S. dollars mean that U.S. investors have substantial opportunities for risk reduction through global diversification of bond portfolios. A U.S. investor who bought bonds in any market except Canada would substantially reduce the standard deviation of the well-diversified portfolio.

Why do these correlation coefficients for returns between U.S. bonds and those of various foreign countries differ? That is, why is the U.S.–Canada correlation 0.57 whereas the U.S.–Japan correlation is only 0.15? The answer is because the international trade patterns, economic growth, fiscal policies, and monetary policies of the countries differ. We do not have an integrated world economy, but rather a collection of economies that are related to one another in different ways, As an example, the U.S. and Canadian economies are closely related because of their geographic proximity, similar domestic economic policies, and the extensive trade between them. Each is the other's largest trading partner. In ·contrast, the United States has less trade with Japan and the fiscal and monetary policies of the two countries differ dramatically.

A country between these extremes is France. The United States has a significant trade relationship with France, but each has a fairly independent set of economic policies. Therefore, the U.S.–France correlation falls between those with Canada and Japan. The point is, macroeconomic differences cause the correlation of bond returns between the United States and each country to likewise differ. These differing correlations make it worthwhile to diversify with foreign bonds, and the different correlations indicate which countries will provide the greatest reduction in the standard deviation (risk) of returns for a U.S. investor.

Also, *the correlation of returns between a single pair of countries changes over time* because the factors influencing the correlations such as international trade, economic growth, fiscal policy, and monetary policy change over time. A change in any of these variables will produce a change in how the economies are related and in the relationship between returns on bonds. As an example, the correlation between bond returns in the United States and Japan before 1980 was quite low, reflecting limited trade and independent economic policies. During the 1980s and 1990s international trade between the two countries increased substantially and so did the correlation between returns on bonds.

Figure 3.4 shows what happens to the risk–return tradeoff when we combine U.S. and foreign bonds. A comparison of a completely non-U.S. portfolio (100 percent foreign) and a 100 percent U.S. portfolio indicates that the non-U.S. portfolio has both a higher rate of return and a higher standard deviation of returns than the U.S. portfolio. Combining the two portfolios in different proportions provides an interesting set of points.

As we will discuss in Chapter 6, the expected rate of return is a weighted average of the two portfolios. In contrast, the risk (standard deviation) of the combination is *not* a weighted average, but also depends on the correlation between the two portfolios. In this example, the risk levels of the combined portfolios decline below those of the individual portfolios. Therefore, by adding non-correlated foreign bonds to a portfolio of U.S. bonds, a U.S. investor is able to not only increase the expected rate of return, but also reduce the risk of a bond portfolio.

Global Equity Portfolio Risk   The correlation of world equity markets resembles that for bonds. Table 3.5 lists the correlation coefficients between monthly equity returns of each country and the U.S. market (in both domestic and U.S. dollars) for the 12-year period from 1986 to 1997. Most of the correlations between local currency returns (seven of eleven) top 0.50. The correlations among rates of return adjusted for exchange rates were always lower; only four of the eleven correlations between U.S. dollar returns exceed 0.50, and the average correlation was only 0.47.

These relatively small positive correlations between U.S. stocks and foreign stocks have similar implications to those derived for bonds. Investors can reduce the overall risk of their stock portfolios by including foreign stocks.

Figure 3.4 *Risk–Return Trade-Off for International Bond Portfolios*

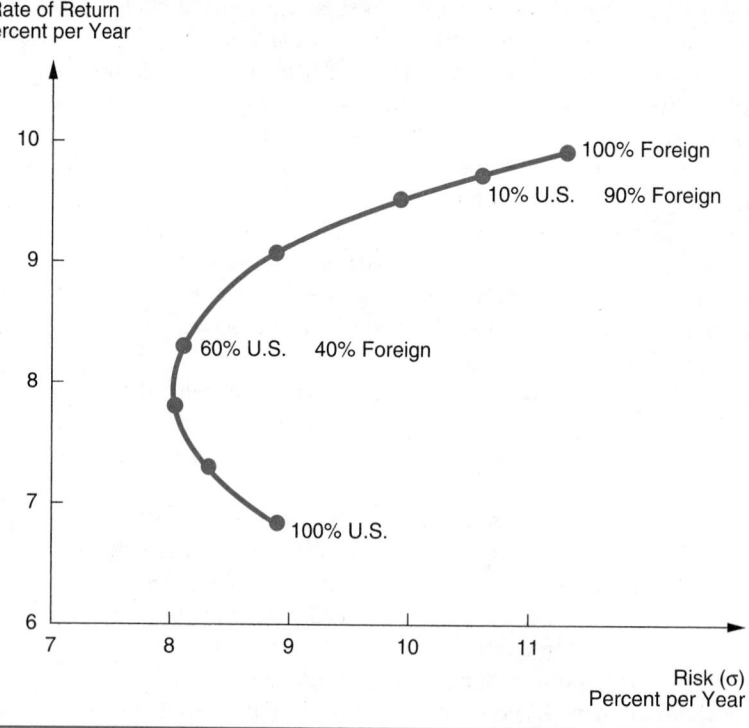

Source: Kenneth Cholerton, Pierre Piergerits, and Bruno Solnik, "Why Invest in Foreign Currency Bonds?" *Journal of Portfolio Management* 12, no. 4 (Summer 1986) pp. 4–8. This copyrighted material is reprinted with permission from *Journal of Portfolio Management*, a publication of Institutional Investor, Inc., 488 Madison Avenue, NY, NY 10022.

Table 3.5 *Correlation Coefficients between Total Returns on Common Stocks in the United States and Major Foreign Stock Markets: 1986–1997 (Monthly Data)*

	Local Currency Total Returns	**U.S. Dollar Total Returns**
Australia	0.53	0.43
Canada	0.75	0.73
France	0.57	0.47
Germany	0.49	0.39
Italy	0.33	0.26
Japan	0.35	0.23
Netherlands	0.69	0.62
Spain	0.55	0.47
Sweden	0.48	0.45
Switzerland	0.64	0.52
United Kingdom	0.74	0.62

Source: Computed by authors using FT/S&P-AWI Total Return Indexes. Supplied by Goldman Sachs & Co.

Figure 3.5 demonstrates the impact of international equity diversification. These curves demonstrate that as you increase the number of randomly selected securities in a portfolio, the standard deviation will decline due to the benefits of diversification *within your own country*. This is referred to as domestic diversification. After a certain number

Figure 3.5   *Risk Reduction through National and International Diversification*

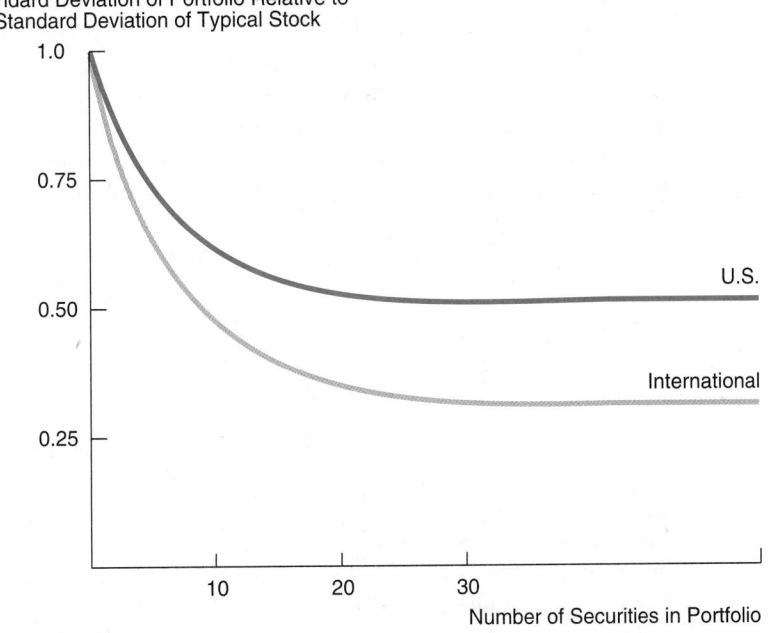

Standard Deviation of Portfolio Relative to
Standard Deviation of Typical Stock

U.S.

International

Number of Securities in Portfolio

Source: B. H. Solnik, "Why Not Diversify Internationally Rather than Domestically?" *Financial Analysts Journal* (July–August 1974): 48–54. Reprinted by permission of the *Financial Analysts Journal*.

of securities (thirty to forty), the curve will flatten out at a risk level that reflects the basic market risk for the domestic economy. The lower curve illustrates the benefits of international diversification. This curve demonstrates that adding foreign securities to a U.S. portfolio to create a global portfolio enables an investor to experience lower overall risk because the non-U.S. securities are not correlated with our economy or our stock market, allowing the investor to eliminate some of the basic market risks of the U.S. economy.

To see how this works, consider, for example, the effect of inflation and interest rates on all U.S. securities. As discussed in Chapter 1, all U.S. securities will be affected by these variables. In contrast, a Japanese stock is mainly affected by what happens in the Japanese economy and will typically not be affected by changes in U.S. variables. Thus, adding Japanese, German, and French stocks to a U.S. stock portfolio reduces the portfolio risk of the global portfolio to a level that reflects only worldwide systematic factors.

Summary on Global Investing   At this point, we have considered the relative size of the market for non-U.S. bonds and stocks and found that it has grown in size and importance, becoming too big to ignore. We have also examined the rates of return for foreign bond and stock investments and determined that, in most instances, their rates of return per unit of risk were superior to those in the U.S. market. Finally, we discussed constructing a portfolio of investments and the importance of diversification in reducing the variability of returns over time, which reduces the risk of the portfolio. It was noted that in order to have successful diversification an investor should combine investments with low positive or negative correlations between rates of return. An analysis of the correlation between rates of return on U.S. and foreign bonds and stocks indicated a consistent pattern of low positive correlations. Therefore, the existence of relatively high rates of return on foreign securities combined with low correlation coefficients indicates that

adding foreign stocks and bonds to a U.S. portfolio *will almost certainly reduce the risk of the portfolio and can possibly increase its average return.*

As promised, several rather compelling reasons exist for adding foreign securities to a U.S. portfolio. Therefore, developing a global investment perspective is important because such an approach has been shown to be justified, and because this current trend in the investment world will continue in the future. Implementing this new global investment perspective will not be easy because it requires an understanding of new terms, instruments (such as Eurobonds), and institutions (such as non-U.S. stock and bond markets). Still, the effort is justified because you are developing a set of skills and a way of thinking that will serve you always.

The next section presents an overview of investment alternatives from around the world, beginning with fixed-income investments and progressing through numerous alternatives.

GLOBAL INVESTMENT CHOICES

This section provides an important foundation for subsequent chapters in which we describe techniques to value individual investments and combine alternative investments into properly diversified portfolios that conform to your risk-return objectives. In this section, we briefly describe the numerous investment alternatives available and provide a brief overview of each. The purpose of this survey is to briefly introduce each of these investment alternatives so you can appreciate the full spectrum of alternatives.

The investments are divided by asset classes. Specifically, in the first subsection, we describe fixed-income investments, including bonds and preferred stocks. In the second subsection, we discuss equity investments, and the third subsection contains a discussion of special equity instruments such as warrants and options, which have characteristics of both fixed-income and equity instruments. In subsection four, we consider futures contracts that allow for a wide range of return–risk profiles. The fifth subsection considers investment companies.

All these investments are called *financial assets* because their payoffs are in money. In contrast, *real assets* such as real estate, are discussed in the sixth subsection. We conclude with assets that are considered *low liquidity investments* because of the relative difficulty in buying and selling them. This includes art, antiques, coins, stamps, and precious gems.

The final section of the chapter describes the historical return and risk patterns for many individual investment alternatives and the correlations among the returns for these investments. This additional background and perspective will help you evaluate individual investments in order to build a properly diversified portfolio of investments from around the world.

Fixed Income Investments

Fixed income investments have a contractually mandated payment schedule. Their investment contracts promise specific payments at predetermined times, although the legal force behind the promise varies and this affects their risks and required returns. At one extreme, if the issuing firm does not make its payment at the appointed time, creditors can declare the issuing firm bankrupt. In other cases (for example, income bonds), the issuing firm must make payments only if it earns profits. In yet other instances (for example, preferred stock), the issuing firm does not have to make payments unless its board of directors votes to do so.

Investors who acquire fixed-income securities (except preferred stock) are really lenders to the issuers. Specifically, you lend some amount of money, the *principal*, to the

borrower. In return, the borrower promises to make periodic interest payments and to pay back the principal at the maturity of the loan.

Savings Accounts   You might not think of savings accounts as fixed-income investments, yet an individual who deposits funds in a savings account at a bank or savings and loan association (S&L) is really lending money to the institution and, as a result, earning a fixed payment. These investments are generally considered to be convenient, liquid, and low-risk because almost all are insured. Consequently, their rates of return are generally low compared with other alternatives. Several versions of these accounts have been developed to appeal to investors with differing objectives.

The passbook savings account has no minimum balance, and funds may be withdrawn at any time with little loss of interest. Due to its flexibility, the promised interest on passbook accounts is relatively low.

For investors with larger amounts of funds who are willing to give up liquidity, banks and S&Ls developed **certificates of deposit (CDs)**, which require minimum deposits (typically $500) and have fixed durations (usually three months, six months, one year, two years). The promised rates on CDs are higher than those for passbook savings, and the rate increases with the size and the duration of the deposit. An investor who wants to cash in a CD prior to its stated expiration date must pay a heavy penalty in the form of a much lower interest rate.

Investors with large sums of money ($10,000 or more) can invest in Treasury bills (T-bills)—short-term obligations (maturing in three to twelve months) of the U.S. government. To compete against T-bills, banks and S&Ls issue money market certificates, which require minimum investments of $10,000 and have minimum maturities of six months. The promised rate on these certificates fluctuates at some premium over the weekly rate on six-month T-bills. Investors can redeem these certificates only at the bank of issue, and they incur penalties if they withdraw their funds before maturity.

Capital Market Instruments   **Capital market investments** are fixed-income obligations that trade in the secondary market, which means you can buy and sell them to other individuals or institutions. Capital market instruments fall into four categories: (1) U.S. Treasury securities, (2) U.S. government agency securities, (3) municipal bonds, and (4) corporate bonds.

U.S. Treasury Securities

All government securities issued by the U.S. Treasury are fixed-income instruments. They may be bills, notes, or bonds depending on their times to maturity. Specifically, bills mature in one year or less, notes in over one to ten years, and bonds in more than ten years from time of issue. U.S. government obligations are essentially free of credit risk because there is little chance of default and they are highly liquid.

U.S. Government Agency Securities

Agency securities are sold by various agencies of the government to support specific programs, but they are not direct obligations of the Treasury. Examples of agencies that issue these bonds include the Federal National Mortgage Association (FNMA or Fannie Mae), which sells bonds and uses the proceeds to purchase mortgages from insurance companies or savings and loans; and the Federal Home Loan Bank (FHLB), which sells bonds and loans the money to its twelve banks, which in turn provide credit to savings and loans and other mortgage-granting institutions. Other agencies are the Government National Mortgage Association (GNMA or Ginnie Mae), Banks for Cooperatives, Federal Land Banks (FLBs), and the Federal Housing Administration (FHA).

Although the securities issued by federal agencies are not direct obligations of the government, they are virtually default-free because it is inconceivable that the government would

allow them to default. Also they are fairly liquid. Because they are not officially guaranteed by the Treasury, they are not considered riskless. Also, because they are not as liquid as Treasury bonds, they typically provide slightly higher returns than Treasury issues.

Municipal Bonds

Municipal bonds are issued by local government entities as either general obligation or revenue bonds. General obligation bonds (GOs) are backed by the full taxing power of the municipality, whereas revenue bonds pay the interest from revenue generated by specific projects (the revenue to pay the interest on sewer bonds comes from water taxes).

Municipal bonds differ from other fixed-income securities because they are tax-exempt. The interest earned from them is exempt from taxation by the federal government and by the state that issued the bond, provided the investor is a resident of that state. For this reason, municipal bonds are popular with investors in high tax brackets. For an investor having a marginal tax rate of 35 percent, a regular bond with an interest rate of 8 percent yields a net return after taxes of only 5.20 percent [$0.08 \times (1 - 0.35)$]. Such an investor would prefer a tax-free bond of equal risk with a 6 percent yield. This allows municipal bonds to offer yields that are lower than yields on comparable taxable bonds, generally by about 25 to 30 percent.

Corporate Bonds

Corporate bonds are fixed-income securities issued by industrial corporations, public utility corporations, or railroads to raise funds to invest in plant, equipment, or working capital. They can be broken down by issuer, in terms of credit quality (measured by the ratings assigned by an agency on the basis of probability of default), in terms of maturity (short term, intermediate term, or long term), or based on some component of the indenture (sinking fund or call feature).

All bonds include an **indenture**, which is the legal agreement that lists the obligations of the issuer to the bondholder, including the payment schedule and features such as call provisions and sinking funds. **Call provisions** specify when a firm can issue a call for the bonds prior to their maturity, at which time current bondholders must submit the bonds to the issuing firm, which redeems them (that is, pays back the principal and a small premium). A **sinking fund** provision specifies payments the issuer must make to redeem a given percentage of the outstanding issue prior to maturity.

Corporate bonds fall into various categories based on their contractual promises to investors. They will be discussed in order of their seniority.

Senior secured bonds are the most senior bonds in a firm's capital structure and have the lowest risk of distress or default. They include various secured issues that differ based on the assets that are pledged. **Mortgage bonds** are backed by liens on specific assets such as land and buildings. In the case of bankruptcy, the proceeds from the sale of these assets are used to pay off the mortgage bondholders. **Collateral trust bonds** are a form of mortgage bond except that the assets backing the bonds are financial assets such as stocks, notes, and other high-quality bonds. Finally, **equipment trust certificates** are mortgage bonds that are secured by specific pieces of transportation equipment such as locomotives and box cars for a railroad and airplanes for an airline.

Debentures are promises to pay interest and principal, but they pledge no specific assets (referred to as *collateral*) in case the firm does not fulfill its promise. This means that the bondholder depends on the success of the borrower to make the promised payment. Debenture owners usually have first call on the firm's earnings and any assets that are not already pledged by the firm as backing for senior secured bonds. If the issuer does not make an interest payment, the debenture owners can declare the firm bankrupt and claim any unpledged assets to pay off the bonds.

Subordinated bonds are similar to debentures, but in the case of default, subordinated bondholders have claim to the assets of the firm only after the firm has satisfied the claims of all senior secured and debenture bondholders. That is, the claims of subordinated bondholders are subordinate to those of other bondholders. Within this general category of subordinated issues, you can find senior subordinated, subordinated, and junior subordinated bonds. Junior subordinated bonds have the weakest claim of all bondholders.

Income bonds stipulate interest payment schedules, but the interest is due and payable only if the issuers earn the income to make the payment by stipulated dates. If the company does not earn the required amount, it does not have to make the interest payment and it cannot be declared bankrupt. Instead, the interest payment is considered in arrears and, if subsequently earned, it must be paid off. Because the issuing firm is not legally bound to make its interest payments except when the firm earns it, an income bond is not considered as safe as a debenture or a mortgage bond, so income bonds offer higher returns to compensate investors for the added risk. Although there are a limited number of corporate income bonds, these income bonds are fairly popular with municipalities because municipal revenue bonds are basically income bonds.

Convertible bonds have the interest and principal characteristics of other bonds, with the added feature that the bondholder has the option to turn them back to the firm in exchange for its common stock. For example, a firm could issue a $1,000 face-value bond and stipulate that owners of the bond could turn the bond in to the issuing corporation and convert it into forty shares of the firm's common stock. These bonds appeal to investors because they combine the features of a fixed-income security with the option of conversion into the common stock of the firm, should the firm prosper.

Because of their desirability, convertible bonds generally pay lower interest rates than nonconvertible debentures of comparable risk. The difference in the required interest rate increases with the growth potential of the company because this increases the value of the option to convert the bonds into common stock. These bonds are almost always subordinated to the nonconvertible debt of the firm, so they are considered to have higher credit risk and are rated lower.

An alternative to convertible bonds is a debenture with warrants attached. A **warrant** allows the bondholder to purchase the firm's common stock from the firm at a specified price for a given time period. The specified purchase price for the stock set in the warrant is typically above the price of the stock at the time the firm issues the bond but below the expected future stock price. The warrant makes the debenture more desirable, which lowers its required yield. The warrant also provides the firm with future common stock capital when the holder exercises the warrant and buys the stock from the firm.

Unlike the typical bond that pays interest every six months and its face value at maturity, a **zero coupon bond** promises no interest payments during the life of the bond but only the payment of the principal at maturity. Therefore, the purchase price of the bond is the present value of the principal payment at the required rate of return. For example, the price of a zero coupon bond that promises to pay $10,000 in five years with a required rate of return of 8 percent is $6,756. To find this, assuming semiannual compounding (which is the norm), use the present value factor for ten periods at 4 percent, which is 0.6756.

Preferred Stock

Preferred stock is classified as a fixed-income security because its yearly payment is stipulated as either a coupon (for example, 5 percent of the face value) or a stated dollar amount (for example, $5 preferred). Preferred stock differs from bonds because its payment is a dividend and therefore not legally binding. For each period, the firm's board of directors must vote to pay it, similar to a common stock dividend. Even if the firm earned enough money to pay the preferred stock dividend, the board of directors could theoretically vote

to withhold it. Because most preferred stock is cumulative, the unpaid dividends would accumulate to be paid in full at a later time.

Although preferred dividends are not legally binding as the interest payments on a bond are, they are considered *practically* binding because of the credit implications of a missed dividend. Because corporations can exclude 80 percent of intercompany dividends from taxable income, preferred stocks have become attractive investments for financial corporations. For example, a corporation that owns preferred stock of another firm and receives $100 in dividends can exclude 80 percent of this amount and pay taxes on only 20 percent of it ($20). Assuming a 40 percent tax rate, the tax would only be $8 or 8 percent versus 40 percent on other investment income. Due to this tax benefit, the yield on high-grade preferred stock is typically lower than that on high-grade bonds.

International Bond Investing

As noted earlier, more than half of all fixed-income securities available to U.S. investors are issued by firms in countries outside the United States. Investors identify these securities in different ways: by the country or city of the issuer (for example, United States, United Kingdom, Japan); by the location of the primary trading market (for example, United States, London); by the home country of the major buyers; and by the currency in which the securities are denominated (for example, dollars, yens, pounds sterling). We identify foreign bonds by their country of origin and include these other differences in each description.

A **Eurobond** is an international bond denominated in a currency not native to the country where it is issued. Specific kinds of Eurobonds include Eurodollar bonds, Euroyen bonds, Eurodeutschemark bonds, and Eurosterling bonds. A Eurodollar bond is denominated in U.S. dollars and sold outside the United States to non-U.S. investors. A specific example would be a U.S. dollar bond issued by General Motors and sold in London. Eurobonds are typically issued in Europe, with the major concentration in London.

Eurobonds can also be denominated in yen or deutsche marks. For example, Nippon Steel can issue Euroyen bonds for sale in London. Also, if it appears that investors are looking for foreign currency bonds, a U.S. corporation can issue a Euroyen bond in London.

Yankee bonds are sold in the United States, denominated in U.S. dollars, but issued by foreign corporations or governments. This allows a U.S. citizen to buy the bond of a foreign firm or government but receive all payments in U.S. dollars, eliminating exchange rate risk.

An example would be a U.S. dollar–denominated bond issued by British Airways.[3] Similar bonds are issued in other countries, including the Bulldog Market, which involves British sterling–denominated bonds issued in the United Kingdom by non-British firms, or the Samurai Market, which involves yen-denominated bonds issued in Japan by non-Japanese firms.

International domestic bonds are sold by an issuer within its own country in that country's currency. An example would be a bond sold by Nippon Steel in Japan denominated in yen. A U.S. investor acquiring such a bond would receive maximum diversification, but would incur exchange rate risk.

Equity Instruments

This section describes several equity instruments, which differ from fixed-income securities because their returns are not contractual. As a result, you can receive returns that are much better or much worse than what you would receive on a bond. We begin with

---

[3]For a discussion of the growth of this market related to stocks, see Michael Siconolf, "Foreign Firms Step Up Offerings in U.S." *Wall Street Journal*, June 1, 1992, C1, C2.

common stock, the most popular equity instrument and probably the most popular investment instrument.

Common stock represents *ownership* of a firm. Owners of the common stock of a firm share in the company's successes and problems. If, like Wal-Mart Stores, McDonald's, Microsoft, or Intel, the company prospers, the investor receives high rates of return and can become wealthy. In contrast, the investor can lose money if the firm does not do well or even goes bankrupt, as the once formidable Penn Central, W. T. Grant, and Interstate Department Stores all did. In these instances, the firm is forced to liquidate its assets and pay off all its creditors. Notably, the firm's preferred stockholders and common stock owners receive what is left. Investing in common stock entails all the advantages and disadvantages of ownership and is a relatively risky investment compared with fixed-income securities.

Common Stock Classifications   When considering an investment in common stock, people tend to divide the vast universe of stocks into categories based on general business lines and by industry within these business lines. The division gives classifications for industrial firms, utilities, transportation firms, and financial institutions. Within each of these business lines are industries. The most diverse group—the industrial group—includes such industries as automobiles, industrial machinery, chemicals, and beverages. Utilities include electrical power companies, gas suppliers, and the water industry. Transportation includes airlines, trucking firms, and railroads. Financial institutions include banks, savings and loans, insurance companies and investment firms.

An alternative classification scheme might separate domestic (U.S.) and foreign common stocks. We avoid this division because the business line–industry breakdown is more appropriate and useful when constructing a diversified portfolio of global common stock investments. With a global capital market, the focus of analysis should include all the companies in an industry viewed in a global setting. For example, when considering the automobile industry, it is necessary to go beyond pure U.S. auto firms like General Motors and Ford, and consider auto firms from throughout the world such as Honda Motors, Porsche, Daimler-Chrysler, Nissan, and Fiat.

Therefore, our subsequent discussion on foreign equities concentrates on how you buy and sell these securities because this procedural information has often been a major impediment. Many investors may recognize the desirability of investing in foreign common stock because of the risk and return characteristics, but they may be intimidated by the logistics of the transaction. The purpose of the next section is to alleviate this concern by explaining the alternatives available.

Acquiring Foreign Equities   Currently, there are several ways to acquire foreign common stock:

1. Purchase or sale of American Depository Receipts (ADRs)
2. Purchase or sale of American shares
3. Direct purchase or sale of foreign shares listed on a U.S. or foreign stock exchange
4. Purchase or sale of international or global mutual funds

Purchase or Sale of American Depository Receipts

The easiest way to acquire foreign shares directly is through **American Depository Receipts (ADRs)**. These are certificates of ownership issued by a U.S. bank that represent indirect ownership of a certain number of shares of a specific foreign firm on deposit in a bank in the firm's home country. ADRs are a convenient way to own foreign shares because the investor buys and sells them in U.S. dollars and receives all dividends in U.S. dollars. This means that the price and returns reflect both the domestic returns for the stock and the exchange rate effect. Also, the price of an ADR can reflect the fact that it represents multiple shares—for example, an ADR can be for five or ten shares of the foreign stock. ADRs can be issued at the discretion of a bank based on the demand

for the stock. The shareholder absorbs the additional handling costs of an ADR through higher transfer expenses, which are deducted from dividend payments.

ADRs are quite popular in the United States because of their diversification benefits.[4] By the end of 1997, 356 foreign companies had stocks listed on the New York Stock Exchange (NYSE) and more than 288 of these were available through ADRs, including all the stock listed from Japan, the United Kingdom, Australia, Mexico, and the Netherlands. In addition, 84 foreign firms are listed on the American Stock Exchange (AMEX) with most of the non-Canadian stocks available through ADRs.

Purchase or Sale of American Shares

American shares are securities issued in the United States by a transfer agent acting on behalf of a foreign firm. Because of the added effort and expense incurred by the foreign firm, a limited number of American shares are available.

Direct Purchase or Sale of Foreign Shares

The most difficult and complicated foreign equity transaction takes place in the country where the firm is located because it must be carried out in the foreign currency and the shares must then be transferred to the United States. This routine can be cumbersome. A second alternative is a transaction on a foreign stock exchange outside the country where the securities originated. For example, if you acquired shares of a French auto company listed on the London Stock Exchange (LSE), the shares would be denominated in pounds and the transfer would be swift, assuming your broker has a membership on the LSE.

Finally, you could purchase foreign stocks listed on the NYSE or AMEX. This is similar to buying a U.S. stock, but only a limited number of foreign firms qualify for—and are willing to accept—the cost of listing. Still, this number is growing. At the end of 1997, more than 83 foreign firms (mostly Canadian) were directly listed on the NYSE, in addition to the firms that were available through ADRs. Also, many foreign firms are traded on the National Association of Securities Dealers Automatic Quotations (NASDAQ) system.

Purchase or Sale of International or Global Mutual Funds

Numerous investment companies invest all or a portion of their funds in stocks of firms outside the United States. The alternatives range from *global funds*, which invest in both U.S. stocks and foreign stocks, to *international funds*, which invest almost wholly outside the United States. In turn, international funds can: (1) diversify across many countries, (2) concentrate in a segment of the world (for example, Europe, South America, the Pacific basin), (3) concentrate in a specific country (for example, the Japan Fund, the Germany Fund, the Italy Fund, or the Korea Fund), or (4) concentrate in types of markets (for example, emerging markets, which would include stocks from countries such as Thailand, Indonesia, India, and China). A mutual fund is a convenient path to global investing, particularly for a small investor, because the purchase or sale of one of these funds is similar to a transaction for a comparable U.S. mutual fund.[5]

Special Equity Instruments: Options

In addition to common stock investments, it is also possible to invest in equity-derivative securities, which are securities that have a claim on the common stock of a firm. This would

[4]For evidence of this, see Dennis T. Officer and Ronald Hoffmeister, "ADRs: A Substitute for the Real Thing?" *Journal of Portfolio Management* 13, no. 2 (Winter 1987): 61–65; and Mahmoud Wahab and Amit Khandwala, "Why Not Diversify Internationally with ADRs?" *Journal of Portfolio Management* 19, no. 2 (Winter 1993): 75–82.
[5]Mutual funds in general and those related to global investing will be discussed in Chapter 21.

include **options**—rights to buy or sell common stock at a specified price for a stated period of time. The two kinds of option instruments are (1) warrants and (2) puts and calls.

Warrants   As mentioned earlier, a warrant is an option issued by a corporation that gives the holder the right to acquire a firm's common stock from the company at a specified price within a designated time period. The warrant does not constitute ownership of the stock, only the option to buy the stock.

Puts and Calls   A **call option** is similar to a warrant because it is an option to buy the common stock of a company within a certain period at a specified price called the *striking price*. A call option differs from a warrant because it is not issued by the company but by another investor who is willing to assume the other side of the transaction. Options also are typically valid for a shorter time period than warrants. Call options are generally valid for less than a year, whereas warrants extend more than five years. The holder of a **put option** has the right to sell a given stock at a specified price during a designated time period. Puts are useful to investors who expect a stock price to decline during the specified period or investors who own the stock and want protection from a price decline.

Futures Contracts

Another instrument that provides an alternative to the purchase of an investment is a **futures contract**. This agreement provides for the future exchange of a particular asset at a specified delivery date (usually within nine months) in exchange for a specified payment at the time of delivery. Although the full payment is not made until the delivery date, a good faith deposit, the *margin*, is made to protect the seller. This is typically about 10 percent of the value of the contract.

The bulk of trading on the commodity exchanges is in futures contracts. The current price of the futures contract is determined by the participants' beliefs about the future for the commodity. For example, in July of a given year, a trader could speculate on the Chicago Board of Trade for wheat in September, December, March, and May of the next year. If the investor expected the price of a commodity to rise, he or she could buy a futures contract on one of the commodity exchanges for later sale. If the investor expected the price to fall, he or she could sell a futures contract on an exchange with the expectation of buying similar contracts later when the price had declined to cover the sale.

Several differences exist between investing in an asset through a futures contract and investing in the asset itself. One is the use of borrowed funds to finance the futures purchase, which increases the volatility of returns. Because an investor puts up only a small portion of the total value of the futures contract (10 to 15 percent), when the price of the commodity changes, the change in the total value of the contract is large compared to the amount invested. Another unique aspect is the term of the investment: Although stocks can have infinite maturities, futures contracts typically expire in less than a year.

Financial Futures   In addition to futures contracts on commodities, a recent innovation has been the development of futures contracts on financial instruments such as T-bills, Treasury bonds, and Eurobonds. For example, it is possible to buy or sell a futures contract that promises future delivery of $100,000 of Treasury bonds at a set price and yield. The major exchanges for financial futures are the Chicago Mercantile Exchange (CME) and the Chicago Board of Trade (CBOT). These futures contracts allow individual investors, bond portfolio managers, and corporate financial managers to protect themselves against volatile interest rates. Certain currency futures allow individual investors or portfolio managers to speculate on or to protect against changes in currency exchange rates. Finally, futures contracts pertain to stock market series such as the

S&P (Standard & Poor's) 500, the *Value Line* Index, and the Nikkei Average on the Tokyo Stock Exchange.

Investment Companies

The investment alternatives described so far are individual securities that can be acquired from a government entity, a corporation, or another individual. However, rather than directly buying an individual stock or bond issued by one of these sources, you may choose to acquire these investments indirectly by buying shares in an investment company, also called a *mutual fund*, that owns a portfolio of individual stocks, bonds, or a combination of the two. Specifically, an **investment company** sells shares in itself and uses the proceeds of this sale to acquire bonds, stocks, or other investment instruments. As a result, an investor who acquires shares in an investment company is a partial owner of the investment company's portfolio of stocks or bonds. We distinguish investment companies by the types of investment instruments they acquire. Discussions of some of the major types follow.

Money Market Funds   **Money market funds** are investment companies that acquire high-quality, short-term investments (referred to as *money market* instruments) such as T-bills, high-grade commercial paper (public short-term loans) from various corporations, and large CDs from the major money center banks. The yields on the money market portfolios always surpass those on normal bank CDs because the investment by the money market fund is larger and the fund can commit to longer maturities than the typical individual. In addition, the returns on commercial paper are above the prime rate. The typical minimum initial investment in a money market fund is $1,000, it charges no sales commission, and minimum additions are $250 to $500. You can always withdraw funds from your money market fund without penalty (typically by writing a check on the account), and you receive interest to the day of withdrawal.

Individuals tend to use money market funds as alternatives to bank savings accounts because they are generally quite safe (although they are not insured, they typically limit their investments to high-quality, short-term investments), they provide yields above what is available on most savings accounts, and the funds are readily available. Therefore, you might use one of these funds to accumulate funds to pay tuition or for a down payment on a car. Because of relatively high yields and extreme flexibility and liquidity, the total value of these funds reached more than $1 trillion in 1997.

Bond Funds   Bond funds generally invest in various long-term government, corporate, or municipal bonds. They differ by the type and quality of the bonds included in the portfolio as assessed by various rating services. Specifically, the bond funds range from those that invest only in risk-free government bonds and high-grade corporate bonds to those that concentrate in lower-rated corporate or municipal bonds, called *high-yield bonds* or *junk bonds*. The expected rate of return from various bond funds will differ, with the low-risk government bond funds paying the lowest returns and the high-yield bond funds expected to pay the highest returns.

Common Stock Funds   Numerous common stock funds invest to achieve stated investment objectives, which can include aggressive growth, income, precious metal investments, and international stocks. Such funds offer smaller investors the benefits of diversification and professional management. To meet the diverse needs of investors, numerous funds have been created that concentrate in one industry or sector of the economy such as chemicals, electric utilities, health, housing, and technology. These funds are diversified within a sector or an industry, but are not diversified across the total market. Investors who participate in a sector or an industry fund bear more risk than investors in a total

market fund because the sector funds will tend to fluctuate more than an aggregate market fund that is diversified across all sectors. Also, international funds that invest outside the United States and global funds that invest in the United States and in other countries offer opportunities for global investing by individual investors.[6]

Balanced Funds   Balanced funds invest in a combination of bonds and stocks of various sorts depending on their stated objectives.

Real Estate

Like commodities, most investors view real estate as an interesting and profitable investment alternative but believe that it is only available to a small group of experts with a lot of capital to invest. In reality, some feasible real estate investments require no detailed expertise or large capital commitments. We will begin by considering low-capital alternatives.

Real Estate Investment Trusts (REITS)   A **real estate investment trust** is an investment fund designed to invest in various real estate properties. It is similar to a stock or bond mutual fund, except that the money provided by the investors is invested in property and buildings rather than in stocks and bonds. There are several types of REITs.

Construction and development trusts lend the money required by builders during the initial construction of a building. Mortgage trusts provide the long-term financing for properties. Specifically, they acquire long-term mortgages on properties once construction is completed. Equity trusts own various income-producing properties such as office buildings, shopping centers, or apartment houses. Therefore, an investor who buys shares in an equity real estate investment trust is buying part of a portfolio of income-producing properties.

REITs have experienced periods of great popularity and significant depression in line with changes in the aggregate economy and the money market. Although they are subject to cyclical risks depending on the economic environment, they offer small investors a way to participate in real estate investments.[7]

Direct Real Estate Investment   The most common type of direct real estate investment is the purchase of a home, which is the largest investment most people ever make. Today, according to the Federal Home Loan Bank, the average cost of a single family house exceeds $100,000. The purchase of a home is considered an investment because the buyer pays a sum of money either all at once or over a number of years through a mortgage. For most people, those unable to pay cash for a house, the financial commitment includes a down payment (typically 10 to 20 percent of the purchase price) and specific mortgage payments over a twenty to thirty-year period that include reducing the loan's principal and paying interest on the outstanding balance. Subsequently, a homeowner hopes to sell the house for its cost plus a gain.

Raw Land

Another direct real estate investment is the purchase of raw land with the intention of selling it in the future at a profit. During the time you own the land, you have negative cash flows caused by mortgage payments, property maintenance, and taxes. An obvious risk is the possible difficulty of selling it for an uncertain price. Raw land generally has low liquidity

---

[6]For a study that examines the diversification of individual country funds, see Warren Bailey and Joseph Lim, "Evaluating the Diversification Benefits of the New Country Funds," *Journal of Portfolio Management* 18, no. 3 (Spring 1992): 74–80.

[7]See Eric S. Hardy, "The Ground Floor," *Forbes*, August 14, 1995, 185; and Susan E. Kuhn, "Real Estate: A Smart Alternative to Stocks," *Fortune*, May 27, 1996, 186.

compared to most stocks and bonds. An alternative to buying and selling the raw land is the development of the land into a housing project or a shopping mall.

Land Development

Typically, land development involves buying raw land, dividing it into individual lots, and building houses on it. Alternatively, buying land and building a shopping mall would also be considered land development. This is a feasible form of investment, but requires a substantial commitment of capital, time, and expertise. Although the risks can be high because of the commitment of time and capital, the rates of return from a successful housing or commercial development can be significant.[8]

Rental Property

Many investors with an interest in real estate investing acquire apartment buildings or houses with low down payments, with the intention of deriving enough income from the rents to pay the expenses of the structure, including the mortgage payments. For the first few years following the purchase, the investor generally has no reported income from the building because of tax-deductible expenses including the interest component of the mortgage payment and depreciation on the structure. Subsequently, rental property provides a cash flow and an opportunity to profit from the sale of the property.[9]

Low-Liquidity Investments

Most of the investment alternatives we have described are traded on securities markets. Except for real estate, most of these securities have good liquidity. Although many investors view the investments we discuss in this section as alternatives to financial investments, financial institutions do not typically acquire them because they are considered to be fairly illiquid and have high transaction costs compared to stocks and bonds. Many of these assets are sold at auctions, causing expected prices to vary substantially. In addition, transaction costs are high because there is generally no national market for these investments, so local dealers must be compensated for the added carrying costs and the cost of searching for buyers or sellers. Given these liquidity risk considerations, many financial theorists view the following low-liquidity investments more as hobbies than investments, even though studies have indicated that some of these assets have experienced substantial rates of return.

Antiques   The investors who earn the greatest returns from antiques are dealers who acquire them at estate sales or auctions to refurbish and sell at a profit. If we gauge the value of antiques based on prices established at large public auctions, it appears that many serious collectors enjoy substantial rates of return. In contrast, the average investor who owns a few pieces to decorate his or her home finds such returns elusive. The high transaction costs and illiquidity of antiques may erode any profit that the individual may earn when selling these pieces. The subsequent discussion of rates of return on various assets will provide some evidence on the returns.

Art   The entertainment sections of newspapers or the personal finance sections of magazines often carry stories of the results of major art auctions, such as when Van Gogh's *Irises* and *Sunflowers* sold for $59 million and $36 million, respectively.

---

[8]For a review of studies that have examined returns on real estate, see William Goetzmann and Roger Ibbotson, "The Performance of Real Estate as an Asset Class," *Journal of Applied Corporate Finance* 3, no. 1 (Spring 1990): 65–76; C. F. Myer and James Webb, "Return Properties of Equity REITs, Common Stocks, and Commercial Real Estate: A Comparison," *Journal of Real Estate Research* 8, no. 1 (1993): 87–106; and Stephen Ross and Randall Zisler, "Risk and Return in Real Estate," *Journal of Real Estate Financial Economics* 4, no. 2 (1991): 175–190. For an analysis of the diversification possibilities, see Susan Hudson-Wilson and Bernard L. Elbaum, "Diversification Benefits for Investors in Real Estate," *Journal of Portfolio Management* 21, no. 3 (Spring 1995): 92–99.

[9]For a discussion of this alternative, see Diane Harris, "An Investment for Rent," *Money*, April 1984, 87–90.

Obviously, these examples and others indicate that some paintings have increased significantly in value and thereby generated large rates of return for their owners. However, investing in art typically requires substantial knowledge of art and the art world, a large amount of capital to acquire the work of well-known artists, patience, and an ability to absorb high transaction costs. For investors who enjoy fine art and have the resources, these can be satisfying investments, but for most small investors, this is a difficult area in which to get returns that compensate for the uncertainty and illiquidity. This was especially true between 1989 and 1994 when there was a bear market in art.[10]

Coins and Stamps   Many individuals enjoy collecting coins or stamps as a hobby and as an investment. The market for coins and stamps is fragmented compared to the stock market, but it is more liquid than the market for art and antiques. Indeed, the volume of coins and stamps traded has prompted the publication of weekly and monthly price lists.[11] An investor can get a widely recognized grading specification on a coin or stamp and, once graded, a coin or stamp can usually be sold quickly through a dealer.[12] It is important to recognize that the difference between the bid price the dealer will pay to buy the stamp or coin and the asking or selling price the investor must pay the dealer is going to be fairly large compared to the difference between the bid and ask prices on stocks and bonds.

Diamonds   Diamonds can be and have been good investments during many periods. Still, investors who purchase diamonds must realize that: (1) diamonds can be highly illiquid, (2) the grading process that determines their quality is quite subjective, (3) most investment-grade gems require substantial investments, and (4) they generate no positive cash flow during the holding period until the stone is sold. In fact, during the holding period the investor must cover costs of insurance and storage. Finally, there are appraisal costs before selling.[13]

In this section, we have described the most common investment alternatives to introduce you to the range of investments available. We will discuss many of these in more detail when we consider how you evaluate them for investment purposes. You should keep in mind that new investment alternatives are constantly being created and developed. You can keep abreast of these by reading business newspapers and magazines.

In our final section, we will present some data on historical rates of return and risk measures for several of these investments to provide background on their historical return–risk performance. This should give you some feel for the returns and risk characteristics you might expect in the future.

HISTORICAL RISK/RETURNS ON ALTERNATIVE INVESTMENTS

How do investors weigh the costs and benefits of owning investments and make decisions to build portfolios that will provide the best risk–return combinations? To help individual

---

[10]For a discussion of art sold at auction, see Alexandra Peers, "With Spring Auction, Shaky Art Market Faces Flood of Less-than-Stellar Works," *Wall Street Journal*, April 29, 1992, C1, C16; and "Market Is Picture of Optimism in Flux," *Wall Street Journal*, April 26, 1996, C1.

[11]A weekly publication for coins is *Coin World*, published by Amos Press, Inc., 911 Vandermark Rd., Sidney, OH 45367. There are several monthly coin magazines, including *Coinage*, published by Behn-Miller Publications, Inc., Encino, CA. Amos Press also publishes several stamp magazines, including *Linn's Stamp News* and *Scott Stamp Monthly*. These magazines provide current prices for coins and stamps.

[12]For an article that describes the alternative grading services, see Diana Henriques, "Don't Take Any Wooden Nickels," *Barron's*, June 19, 1989, 16, 18, 20, 32. For an analysis of commemorative coins, see R. W. Bradford, "How to Lose a Mint," *Barron's*, March 6, 1989, 54, 55.

[13]For a discussion of problems and opportunities, see "When to Put Your Money into Gems," *Business Week*, March 16, 1981, 158–161.

or institutional investors answer this question, financial theorists have examined extensive data and attempted to provide information on the return and risk characteristics of various investments.

Many theorists have studied the historical rates of return on common stocks, and a growing interest in bonds has caused investigators to assess their performance as well. Because inflation has been so pervasive, many studies include both nominal and real rates of return on investments. Still other investigators have examined the performance of such assets as real estate, foreign stocks, art, antiques, and commodities. This section reviews some of the major studies that provide background on the rates of return and risk for these investment alternatives. This should help you to make decisions on the alternatives you might want to examine when building your investment portfolio and the allocation to the various asset classes.

Stocks, Bonds, and T-Bills

A set of studies by Ibbotson and Sinquefield (I&S) examined historical nominal and real rates of return for seven major classes of assets in the United States: (1) large-company common stocks, (2) small-capitalization common stocks,[14] (3) long-term U.S. government bonds, (4) long-term corporate bonds, (5) intermediate-term U.S. government bonds, (6) U.S. Treasury bills, and (7) consumer goods (a measure of inflation).[15] For each asset, the authors calculated total rates of return before taxes or transaction costs.

These investigators computed geometric and arithmetic mean rates of return and computed nine series derived from the basic series. Four of these series were net returns reflecting different premiums: (1) a *risk premium*, which I&S defined as the difference in the rate of return that investors receive from investing in large company common stocks (as represented by the stocks in the S&P 500 Index that is described in Chapter 5) rather than in risk-free U.S. Treasury bills; (2) a *small-stock premium*, which they defined as the return on small-capitalization stocks minus the return on large-company stocks; (3) a *horizon premium*, which they defined as the difference in the rate of return received from investing in long-term government bonds rather than short-term U.S. Treasury bills; and (4) a *default premium*, which they defined as the difference between the rates of return on long-term risky corporate bonds and long-term risk-free government bonds. I&S also computed the real inflation-adjusted rates of return for common stocks, small-capitalization stocks, Treasury bills, long-term government bonds, intermediate-term government bonds, and long-term corporate bonds.

A summary of the rates of return, risk premiums, and standard deviations for the basic and derived series appears in Table 3.6. As discussed in Chapter 1, the geometric means of the rates of return are always lower than the arithmetic means of the rates of return, and the difference between these two mean values increases with the standard deviation of returns.

During the period from 1926 to 1997, large-company common stocks returned 11.0 percent a year, compounded annually. To compare this to other investments, the results

---

[14]Small-capitalization stocks were broken out as a separate class of asset because several studies have shown that firms with relatively small capitalization (stock with low market value) have experienced rates of return and risk significantly different from those of stocks in general. Therefore, they were considered a unique asset class. We will discuss these studies in Chapter 7, which deals with the efficient markets hypothesis. The large company stock returns are based upon the S&P Composite Index of 500 stocks—the S&P 500.

[15]The original study was Roger G. Ibbotson and Rex A. Sinquefield, "Stocks, Bonds, Bills, and Inflation: Year-by-Year Historical Returns (1926–1974)," *Journal of Business* 49, no. 1 (January 1976): 11–47. Although this study was updated in several monographs, the current update is contained in *Stocks, Bonds, Bills, and Inflation: 1998 Yearbook* (Chicago: Ibbotson Associates, 1998). A seventh asset class (intermediate-term U.S. Government bonds) was not part of the original studies but was added during the past decade.

Table 3.6   *Basic and Derived Series: Historical Highlights (1926–1997)*

Series	Annual Geometric Mean Rate of Return	Arithmetic Mean of Annual Returns	Standard Deviation of Annual Returns
Large company stocks	11.0%	13.0%	20.3%
Small capitalization stocks	12.7	17.7	33.9
Long-term corporate bonds	5.7	6.1	8.7
Long-term government bonds	5.2	5.6	9.2
Intermediate-term government bonds	5.3	5.4	5.7
U.S. Treasury bills	3.8	3.8	3.2
Consumer price index	3.1	3.2	4.5
Equity risk premium	6.9	8.9	20.4
Small stock premium	1.6	3.1	18.2
Default premium	0.4	0.4	3.0
Horizon premium	1.5	1.7	8.6
Large company stock—inflation adjusted	7.7	9.7	20.5
Small capitalization stock—inflation adjusted	9.3	14.2	33.3
Long-term corporate bonds—inflation adjusted	2.6	3.0	10.0
Long-term government bonds—inflation adjusted	2.1	2.6	10.5
Intermediate-term government bonds—inflation adjusted	2.1	2.3	7.0
U.S. Treasury bills—inflation adjusted	0.6	0.7	4.2

Source: © *Stocks, Bonds, Bills, and Inflation: 1998 Yearbook™*, Ibbotson Associates, Chicago (annually updates work by Roger G. Ibbotson and Rex A. Sinquefield). Used with permission. All rights reserved.

show that common stock experienced a risk premium of 6.9 percent and inflation-adjusted real returns of 7.7 percent per year. In contrast to all common stocks, the small-capitalization stocks (which are represented by the smallest 20 percent of stocks listed on the NYSE measured by market value) experienced a geometric mean return of 12.7 percent, which was a premium compared to all common stocks of 1.6 percent.

Although common stocks and small-capitalization stocks experienced higher rates of return than the other asset groups, their returns were also more volatile as measured by the standard deviations of annual returns.

Long-term U.S. government bonds experienced a 5.2 percent annual return, a real return of 2.1 percent, and a horizon premium (compared to Treasury bills) of 1.5 percent. Although the returns on these bonds were lower than those on stocks, they were also far less volatile.

The annual compound rate of return on long-term corporate bonds was 5.7 percent, the default premium compared to U.S. government bonds was 0.4 percent, and the inflation-adjusted return was 2.6 percent. Although corporate bonds provided a higher return, as one would expect, the volatility of corporate bonds was slightly lower than that experienced by long-term government bonds.

The nominal return on U.S. Treasury bills was 3.8 percent a year, whereas the inflation-adjusted return was 0.6 percent. The standard deviation of nominal returns for T-bills was the lowest of the series examined, which reflects the low risk of these securities and is consistent with the lowest rate of return.

This study reported the rates of return, return premiums, and risk measures on various asset groups in the United States. As noted, the rates of return were generally consistent with the uncertainty (risk) of annual returns as measured by the standard deviations of annual returns.

World Portfolio Performance

Expanding this analysis from domestic to global securities, Ibbotson, Siegel, and Love examined the performance of numerous assets, not only in the United States, but around the

world.[16] Specifically, for the period from 1960 to 1984 they constructed a value-weighted portfolio of stocks, bonds, cash (the equivalent of U.S. T-bills), real estate, and precious metals from the United States, Northern and Western Europe, Japan, Hong Kong, Singapore, Canada, and Australia. They computed annual returns, risk measures, and correlations among the returns for alternative assets. Table 3.7 shows the geometric and arithmetic average annual rates of return and the standard deviations of returns for that period.

Asset Return and Risk   The results in Table 3.7 generally confirm the expected relationship between annual rates of return and the risk of these securities. The riskier assets—those that had higher standard deviations—experienced the highest returns. For example, silver had the highest arithmetic mean rate of return (20.51 percent) but also the largest standard deviation (75.34 percent), whereas risk-free U.S. cash equivalents (T-bills) had low returns (6.49 percent) and the smallest standard deviation (3.22 percent). The data amassed by Ibbotson et al. could be used to assess the relative risk of assets in a portfolio, as well as risk and return values for each asset.

Relative Asset Risk   Calculating the coefficients of variation (CVs), which measure relative variability, Ibbotson et al. found a wide range of values. The lowest CVs were experienced by the cash equivalents (T-bills) and real estate investments. Silver had the highest CV value because of its large standard deviation, and corporate bonds the next highest because of a relatively small mean return. The CVs for stocks ranged from 1.46 to 2.04, with U.S. stocks about in the middle (1.66). Finally, the world market portfolios had rather low CVs (0.62 and 0.68), demonstrating the benefits of global diversification.

Correlations between Asset Returns   Table 3.8 is a correlation matrix of selected U.S. and world assets. The first column shows that U.S. equities have a reasonably high correlation with European equities (0.640) and other foreign equities (0.807), but low correlation with Asian equities (0.237). Also, U.S. equities show a negative correlation with U.S. government bonds (−0.006), farm real estate (−0.171), and gold (−0.088). You will recall from our earlier discussion that you can use this information to build a diversified portfolio by combining those assets with low positive or negative correlations.

Art and Antiques

Unlike financial securities, where the results of transactions are reported daily, art and antique markets are fragmented and lack any formal transaction reporting system. This makes it difficult to gather data. The best-known series that attempt to provide information about the changing value of art and antiques were developed by Sotheby's, a major art auction firm. These value indexes cover thirteen areas of art and antiques and a weighted aggregate series that is a combination of the thirteen.

Reilly examined these series for the period from 1975 to 1991 and computed rates of return, measures of risk, and the correlations among the various art and antique series.[17] Figure 3.6 shows these data and compares them with returns for one-year Treasury bonds, the Lehman Brothers Government/Corporate Bond Index, the Standard & Poor's 500 Stock Index, and the annual inflation rate.

These results vary to such a degree that it is impossible to generalize about the performance of art and antiques. As shown, the average annual compound rates of return (measured by the geometric means) ranged from a high of 16.8 percent (modern paintings) to a low of 9.99 percent (English silver). Similarly, the standard deviations varied from

[16]Roger G. Ibbotson, Laurence B. Siegel, and Kathryn S. Love, "World Wealth: Market Values and Returns," *Journal of Portfolio Management* 12, no. 1 (Fall 1985): 4–23.

[17]Frank K. Reilly, "Risk and Return on Art and Antiques: The Sotheby's Indexes," Eastern Finance Association Meeting, April 1987. The results reported are a summary of the study results and have been updated through September 1991.

Table 3.7	*World Capital Market: Total Annual Returns (1960–1984)*			
	Geometric Mean	Arithmetic Mean	Standard Deviation[a]	Coefficient of Variation[b]
Equities				
United States	8.81%	10.20%	16.89%	1.66
Foreign				
Europe	7.83	8.94	15.58	1.74
Asia	15.14	18.42	30.74	1.67
Other	8.14	10.21	20.88	2.04
Equities total	9.08	10.21	15.28	1.46
Bonds				
United States				
Corporate[c]	5.35	5.75	9.63	1.67
Government	5.91	6.10	6.43	1.05
United States total	5.70	5.93	7.16	1.21
Foreign				
Corporate domestic	8.35	8.58	7.26	0.85
Government domestic	5.79	6.04	7.41	1.23
Crossborder	7.51	7.66	5.76	0.75
Foreign total	6.80	7.01	6.88	0.98
Bonds total	6.36	6.50	5.56	0.86
Cash equivalents				
United States	6.49	6.54	3.22	0.49
Foreign	6.00	6.23	7.10	1.14
Cash total	6.38	6.42	2.92	0.45
Real estate[d]				
Business	8.49	8.57	4.16	0.49
Residential	8.86	8.93	3.77	0.42
Farms	11.86	12.13	7.88	0.65
Real estate total	9.44	9.49	3.45	0.36
Metals				
Silver	9.14	20.51	75.34	3.67
Gold	9.08	12.62	29.87	2.37
Metals total	9.11	12.63	29.69	2.35
U.S. market wealth portfolio	8.63	8.74	5.06	0.58
Foreign market wealth portfolio	7.76	8.09	8.48	1.05
World market wealth portfolio				
Excluding metals	8.34	8.47	5.24	0.62
Including metals	8.39	8.54	5.80	0.68
U.S. inflation rate	5.24	5.30	3.60	0.68

[a]Standard deviation from arithmetic mean.

[b]Coefficient of variation equals standard deviation/arithmetic mean.

[c]Including preferred stock.

[d]United States only.

Source: *Journal of Portfolio Management* 12, no. 1 (Fall 1985) pp. 4–23. This copyrighted material is reprinted with permission from *Journal of Portfolio Management*, a publication of Institutional Investor, Inc., 488 Madison Avenue, NY, NY 10022.

21.67 percent (Impressionist–Post Impressionist paintings) to 8.74 percent (American furniture). The relative risk measures (the coefficients of variation) varied from a high of 1.33 (continental silver) to a low value of 0.71 (English furniture). The annual rankings likewise changed over time.

Although there was a wide range of mean returns and risk, the risk–return plot in the figure indicates a fairly consistent relationship between risk and return during this sixteen-year

Table 3.8   *Correlation Matrix of World Capital Market Security Returns*

	U.S. Equities	U.S. Market Portfolio	World Market Including Metals
U.S. equities	1.000	0.917	0.757
Europe equities	0.640	0.605	0.706
Asia equities	0.237	0.209	0.351
Other equities	0.807	0.754	0.753
Foreign total: equities	0.672	0.626	0.732
World total: equities	0.964	0.886	0.805
U.S. corporate bonds and preferred stock	0.323	0.393	0.207
U.S. government bonds	−0.006	0.152	−0.023
U.S. total: bonds	0.166	0.284	0.093
Foreign domestic corporation bonds	0.050	0.153	0.380
Foreign domestic government bonds	−0.024	0.171	0.426
Foreign total: bonds	0.052	0.191	0.429
World total: bonds	0.124	0.172	0.389
U.S. cash equivalents (T-bills)	0.079	0.130	−0.004
Foreign cash equivalents	−0.386	−0.233	0.105
World total: cash equivalents	−0.238	0.103	0.046
Business real estate	0.164	0.394	0.390
Residential real estate	0.125	0.442	0.552
Farm real estate	−0.171	−0.019	0.133
U.S. total: real estate	0.054	0.371	0.531
Gold	−0.088	0.104	0.427
Silver	0.116	0.291	0.283
World total: metals	−0.086	0.111	0.427
U.S. market wealth portfolio	0.917	1.000	0.873
Foreign market wealth portfolio	0.510	0.533	0.727
World market wealth portfolio (excluding metals)	0.861	0.925	0.924
World market wealth portfolio (including metals)	0.757	0.873	1.000

Source: *Journal of Portfolio Management* 12, no. 1 (Fall 1985) pp. 19–21. This copyrighted material is reprinted with permission from the *Journal of Portfolio Management*, a publication of Institutional Investor, Inc., 488 Madison Avenue, NY, NY 10022.

period. Comparing the art and antique results to the bond and stock indexes indicates that the stocks and bonds experienced results in the middle of the art and antique series.

Analysis of the correlation matrix of these assets in Table 3.9 using annual rates of return reveals several important relationships. First, the correlations among alternative antique and art categories (for example, paintings and furniture) vary substantially from above 0.90 to negative correlations. Second, the correlations between rates of return on art/antiques and bonds are generally negative. Third, the correlations of art/antiques with stocks are typically small positive values. Finally, the correlation of art and antiques with percentage changes in the CPI (the rate of inflation) indicates that several of the categories have been fairly good inflation hedges since they were positively correlated with inflation (for example, Chinese ceramics), and they were clearly superior inflation hedges compared to long bonds and common stocks.[18] This would suggest that a properly diversified portfolio of art, antiques, stocks, and bonds might provide a fairly low-risk portfolio. It is important to reiterate the earlier observation that most art and antiques are considered to be quite illiquid and the transaction costs are fairly high compared to the financial assets we have discussed.

[18]These results for stocks are consistent with several prior studies that likewise found a negative relationship between inflation and rates of return on stocks, which indicates that common stocks have generally been poor inflation hedges. In this regard, see Eugene F. Fama, "Stock Returns, Real Activity, Inflation and Money," *American Economic Review* 71, no. 2 (June 1991): 545–565; and Jeffrey Jaffe and Gershon Mandelker, "The 'Fisher Effect' for Risky Assets: An Empirical Investigation," *Journal of Finance* 31, no. 2 (June 1976): 447–458.

Figure 3.6 *Geometric Mean Rates of Return and Standard Deviation for Sotheby's Indexes, S&P 500, Bond Market Series, One-Year Bonds, and Inflation: 1976–1991*

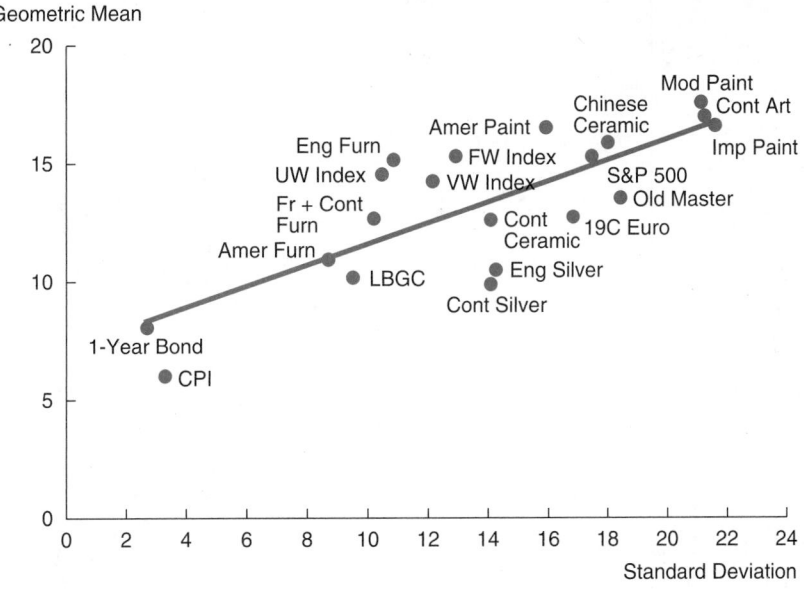

Source: Adapted from Frank K. Reilly, "Risk and Return on Art and Antiques: The Sotheby's Indexes," Eastern Finance Association Meeting, May 1987. (Updated through September 1991.)

Real Estate

Somewhat similar to art and antiques, returns on real estate are difficult to derive because of the limited number of transactions and the lack of a national source of data for the transactions that allows one to accurately compute rates of return. In the study by Goetzmann and Ibbotson, the authors gathered data on commercial real estate through REITs and Commingled Real Estate Funds (CREFs) and estimated returns on residential real estate from a series created by Case and Shiller.[19] The summary of the real estate returns compared to various stock, bond, and an inflation series is contained in Table 3.10. As shown, the two commercial real estate series reflected strikingly different results. The CREFs had lower returns and low volatility, while the REIT index had higher returns and risk. Notably, the REIT returns were higher than those of common stocks, but the risk measure for real estate was lower (there was a small difference in the time period). The residential real estate series reflected lower returns and low risk. The longer-term results indicate that all the real estate series experience lower returns than common stock, but they also had much lower risk.

Table 3.11 shows the correlations among annual returns for the various asset groups. The results indicate a relatively low positive correlation between commercial real estate and stocks. In contrast, there was negative correlation between stocks and residential real estate and farm real estate. This negative relationship with real estate was also true for

[19]William N. Goetzmann and Roger G. Ibbotson, "The Performance of Real Estate as an Asset Class," *Journal of Applied Corporate Finance* 3, no 1 (Spring 1990): 65–76; Carl Case and Robert Shiller, "Price of Single Family Homes Since 1970: New Indexes for Four Cities," National Bureau of Economic Research, Inc., Working Paper No. 2393 (1987).

Table 3.9 *Correlation Coefficients Among Annual Rates of Return for Art, Antiques, Stocks, Bonds, and Inflation: 1976–1991 (September Year End)*

	Old Mast.	19C Euro.	Impr. Pt.-Im.	Mod. Paint.	Cont. Art	Amer. Paint.	Cont. Ceram.	Chin. Ceram.	Engl. Silver	Cont. Silver	Ameri. Furn.	Fr. & Cont. Furn.	Engl. Furn.	Fix Wt. Index	Unwtd. Index	Pr. W. Index	1-yr. T Bond	LBGC Bond	S&P 500	CPI
Old masters paintings	*																			
Nineteenth-century European paintings	0.948	*																		
Impressionist–Post Impressionist paintings	0.442	0.467	*																	
Modern paintings	0.403	0.473	0.969	*																
Continental art	0.780	0.652	0.566	0.476	*															
American paintings	0.599	0.515	0.464	0.386	0.674	*														
Continental ceramics	0.589	0.584	0.200	0.191	0.227	0.498	*													
Chinese ceramics	0.447	0.419	0.279	0.267	0.279	0.561	0.708	*												
English silver	0.394	0.497	0.117	0.186	0.057	-0.012	0.295	0.098	*											
Continental silver	0.628	0.709	0.354	0.404	0.301	0.054	0.600	0.270	0.729	*										
American furniture	-0.176	-0.204	0.185	0.165	-0.071	0.012	-0.251	-0.167	0.122	-0.168	*									
French and continental furniture	0.648	0.755	0.116	0.192	0.310	0.143	0.622	0.459	0.541	0.764	-0.379	*								
English furniture	0.234	0.328	0.548	0.605	-0.016	0.433	0.471	0.449	0.105	0.222	0.043	0.178	*							
Fixed-weight index	0.817	0.835	0.851	0.838	0.727	0.637	0.536	0.525	0.359	0.622	0.001	0.525	0.550	*						
Unweighted index	0.859	0.872	0.740	0.731	0.700	0.677	0.666	0.611	0.450	0.686	-0.017	0.620	0.540	0.977	*					
Price-weighted index	0.828	0.826	0.791	0.776	0.733	0.723	0.610	0.593	0.397	0.611	0.000	0.536	0.555	0.984	0.990	*				
One-year Treasury bond	-0.331	-0.376	-0.089	-0.131	0.159	-0.109	-0.570	-0.269	-0.103	-0.302	0.130	-0.248	-0.612	-0.269	-0.309	-0.258	*			
LBGC bond index	-0.169	-0.182	-0.280	-0.308	-0.173	-0.308	-0.422	-0.318	0.052	-0.210	-0.159	-0.328	-0.351	-0.322	-0.366	-0.359	-0.080	*		
S&P 500	0.038	-0.026	-0.082	-0.134	-0.097	-0.127	-0.041	-0.015	-0.031	-0.058	0.144	-0.113	-0.030	-0.075	-0.080	-0.121	-0.224	0.127	*	
Consumer Price Index	0.008	0.010	0.064	0.056	0.161	0.283	0.290	0.462	0.127	0.085	0.118	0.338	-0.024	0.141	0.224	0.227	0.496	-0.647	-0.322	*

Source: Frank K. Reilly, "Risk and Return on Art and Antiques," July 1992.

Table 3.10 *Summary Statistics of Commercial and Residential Real Estate Series Compared to Stocks, Bonds, T-Bills, and Inflation*

Series	Date	Geometric Mean	Arithm. Mean	Standard Deviation
Annual Returns 1969–1987				
CREF (Comm.)	1969–87	10.8%	10.9%	2.6%
REIT (Comm.)	1972–87	14.2	15.7	15.4
C&S (Res.)	1970–86	8.5	8.6	3.0
S&P (Stocks)	1969–87	9,2	10.5	18.2
LTG (Bonds)	1969–87	7.7	8.4	13.2
TBILL (Bills)	1969–87	7.6	7.6	1.4
CPI (Infl.)	1969–87	6.4	6.4	1.8
Annual Returns over the Long Term				
I&S (Comm.)	1960–87	8.9%	9.1%	5.0%
CPIHOME (Res.)	1947–86	8.1	8.2	5.2
USDA (Farm)	1947–87	9.6	9.9	8.2
S&P (Stocks)	1947–87	11.4	12.6	16.3
LTG (Bonds)	1947–87	4.2	4.6	9.8
TBILL (Bills)	1947–87	4.9	4.7	3.3
CPI (Infl.)	1947–87	4.5	4.6	3.9

Source: William N. Goetzmann and Roger G. Ibbotson, "The Performance of Real Estate as an Asset Class," *Journal of Applied Corporate Finance* 3, no. 1 (Spring 1990): 65–76. Reprinted with permission.

Table 3.11 *Correlations of Annual Real Estate Returns with the Returns on Other Asset Classes*

	I&S	CREF	CPI Home	C&S	Farm	S&P	20-Yr. Gvt.	1-Yr. Gvt.	Infl.
I&S	1								
CREF	0.79	1							
CPI Home	0.52	0.12	1						
C&S	0.26	0.16	0.82	1					
Farm	0.06	−0.06	0.51	0.49	1				
S&P	0.16	0.25	−0.13	−0.20	−0.10	1			
20-Yr. Gvt.	−0.04	0.01	−0.22	−0.54	−0.44	0.11	1		
1-Yr. Gvt.	0.53	0.42	0.13	−0.56	−0.32	−0.07	0.48	1	
Infl.	0.70	0.35	0.77	0.56	0.49	−0.02	−0.17	0.26	1

Note: Correlation coefficient for each pair of asset classes uses the maximum number of observations, that is, the minimum length of the two series in the pair.

Source: William N. Goetzmann and Roger G. Ibbotson, "The Performance of Real Estate as an Asset Class," *Journal of Applied Corporate Finance* 3, no. 1 (Spring 1990): 65–76. Reprinted with permission.

twenty-year government bonds. Several studies that considered international commercial real estate and REITs indicated the returns were correlated with stock prices, but also provided significant diversification.[20]

These results imply that returns on real estate are equal to or slightly lower than common stocks, but real estate possesses favorable risk results. Specifically, real estate had much lower standard deviations as unique assets, and either low positive or negative correlations with other asset classes in a portfolio context.

[20]P. A. Eichholtz, "Does International Diversification Work Better for Real Estate than for Stocks and Bonds?" *Financial Analysts Journal* 52, no. 1 (January–February 1996): 56–62; S. R. Mull and L. A. Soenen, "U.S. REITs as an Asset Class in International Investment Portfolios," *Financial Analysts Journal* 53, no. 2 (March–April 1997): 55–61; and D. C. Quan and S. Titman, "Commercial Real Estate Prices and Stock Market Returns: An International Analysis," *Financial Analysts Journal* 53, no. 3 (May–June 1997): 21–34.

Investments Online

As this chapter describes, the variety of financial products is huge and potentially confusing to the novice (not to mention the experienced professional). Two good rules of investing are (1) stick to your risk tolerance; many people will try to sell instruments which may not be appropriate for the typical individual investor and (2) don't invest in something if you don't understand it. Web sites mentioned in Chapters 1 and 2 provide useful information on a variety of investments. Below we list a few others that may be of interest.

www.wiso.gwdg.de/ifbg/finance.html
This site modestly labels itself as "Finance on the WWW." It contains an international selection of guides, sites, and general information. Among other features, it contains links to bond, stock, mutual fund, futures and options, exchange rates, financial services, and personal finance sites. For the more sophisticated user, links exist to sites that deal with investment research, law and finance, technical analysis, fundamental analysis, and portfolio analysis (topics that are discussed in future chapters!).

www.global-investor.com
This site contains information on ADRs, global financial information, and allows users to follow the performance of the world's major markets. It provides a number of links to global, regional, and country markets.

www.nfsn.com
The home page of the National Financial Services Network offers information on personal and commercial financial products and services, in addition to news, interest rate updates, and stock price quotes.

www.emgmkts.com
The Emerging Markets Companion home page contains information on emerging markets in Asia, Latin America, Africa, and Eastern Europe. Available information and links includes news, prices, market information, and research.

www.datastream.com
Datastream's home page provides financial information services to the global securities industry. It includes end-of-day price quotes for over 32,000 stocks traded around the world, information on stock market indexes, exchange rates, and bond indexes.

Other sites of interest include:

www.euro.net/innovation/Finance_Base/Fin_encyc.html
This site contains an international financial encyclopedia of investing terms, instruments, and companies.

www.sothebys.com
Home page of Sotheby's Inc., the auction house. This site contains auction updates and information on collectibles, Internet resources, and featured upcoming sales.

Figure 3.7 *Alternative Investments — Risk and Return Characteristics*

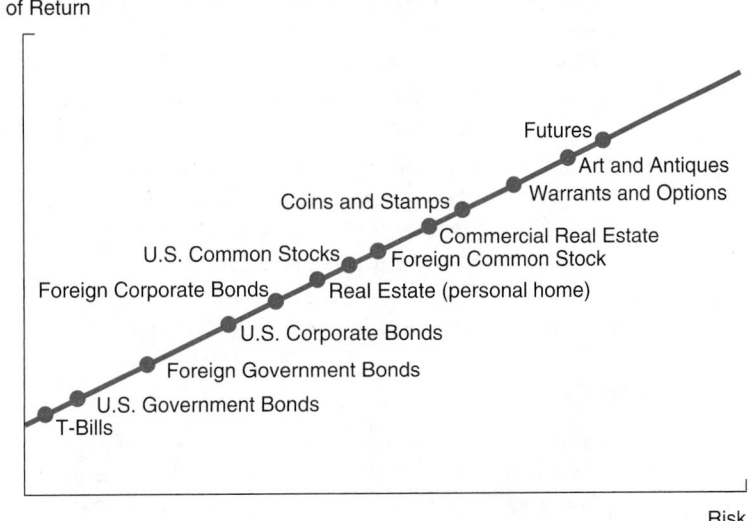

SUMMARY

♦ Investors who want the broadest range of choices in investments must consider foreign stocks and bonds in addition to domestic financial assets. Many foreign securities offer investors higher risk-adjusted returns than domestic securities. In addition, the low positive or negative correlations between foreign and U.S. securities makes them ideal for building a diversified portfolio.

♦ Figure 3.7 summarizes the risk and return characteristics of the investment alternatives described in this chapter. Some of the differences are due to unique factors that we discussed. Foreign bonds are considered riskier than domestic bonds because of the unavoidable uncertainty due to exchange rate risk and country risk. The same is true for foreign and domestic common stocks. Investments such as art, antiques, coins, and stamps require heavy liquidity risk premiums. You should divide consideration of real estate investments between your personal home, on which you do not expect as high a return because of nonmonetary factors, and commercial real estate, which requires a much higher rate of return due to cash flow uncertainty and illiquidity.

♦ Studies on the historical rates of return for common stocks and other investment alternatives (including bonds, commodities, real estate, foreign securities, and art and antiques) point toward two generalizations.[21]

1. A positive relationship typically holds between the rate of return earned on an asset and the variability of its historical rate of return. This is expected in a world of risk-averse investors who require higher rates of return to compensate for more uncertainty.

2. The correlation among rates of return for selected alternative investments is typically quite low, especially for U.S. and foreign stocks and bonds and between these financial assets and real assets, as represented by art, antiques, and real estate. This confirms the advantage of diversification among investments from around the world.

---

[21]An excellent discussion of global investing and extensive analysis of returns and risks for alternative asset classes is Roger G. Ibbotson and Gary P. Brinson, *Global Investing* (New York: McGraw-Hill, 1993).

♦ In addition to describing many direct investments, such as stocks and bonds, we also discussed investment companies that allow investors to buy investments indirectly. These can be important to investors who want to take advantage of professional management but also want instant diversification with a limited amount of funds. With $10,000, you may not be able to buy many individual stocks or bonds, but you could acquire shares in a mutual fund, which would give you a share of a diversified portfolio that might contain 100 to 150 different U.S. and international stocks or bonds.

♦ Now that we know the range of domestic and foreign investment alternatives, our next task is to learn about the markets in which they are bought and sold. That is the objective of the next chapter. The discussion in Chapter 4 will help us understand how markets match buyers and sellers of investments. Later chapters will describe how investors evaluate the risk and return characteristics of alternative investments to build diversified portfolios that are consistent with their objectives.

Questions

1. What are the advantages of investing in the common stock rather than the corporate bonds of a company? Compare the certainty of returns for a bond with those for a common stock. Draw a line graph to demonstrate the pattern of returns you would envision for each of these assets over time.
2. Discuss three factors that cause U.S. investors to consider including global securities in their portfolios.
3. Discuss why international diversification reduces portfolio risk. Specifically, why would you expect low correlation in the rates of return for domestic and foreign securities?
4. Discuss why you would expect a *difference* in the correlation of returns between securities from the United States and from alternative countries (for example, Japan, Canada, South Africa).
5. Discuss whether you would expect any *change* in the correlations between U.S. stocks and the stocks for different countries. For example, discuss whether you would expect the correlation between U.S. and Japanese stock returns to change over time.
6. When you invest in Japanese or German bonds, what major additional risks must you consider besides yield changes within the country?
7. Some investors believe that international investing introduces additional risks. Discuss these risks and how they can affect your return. Give an example.
8. What alternatives to direct investment in foreign stocks are available to investors?
9. You are a wealthy individual in a high tax bracket. Why might you consider investing in a municipal bond rather than a straight corporate bond, even though the promised yield on the municipal bond is lower?
10. You can acquire convertible bonds from a rapidly growing company or from a utility. Speculate on which convertible bond would have the lower yield and discuss the reason for this difference.
11. Compare the liquidity of an investment in raw land with that of an investment in common stock. Be specific as to why and how they differ. (Hint: Begin by defining *liquidity*.)
12. What are stock warrants and call options? How do they differ?
13. Discuss why financial analysts consider antiques and art to be illiquid investments. Why do they consider coins and stamps to be more liquid than antiques and art? What must an investor typically do to sell a collection of art and antiques? Briefly contrast this procedure to the sale of a portfolio of stocks that are listed on the New York Stock Exchange.
14. You have a fairly large portfolio of U.S. stocks and bonds. You meet a financial planner at a social gathering who suggests that you diversify your portfolio by investing in gold. Discuss whether the correlation results in Table 3.8 support this suggestion.
15. You are an avid collector/investor of American paintings. Based on the information in Figure 3.6, describe your risk–return results during the period from 1976 to 1991 compared to U.S. common stocks.
16. *CFA Examination 1 (1993)*
    Chris Smith of XYZ Pension Plan has historically invested in the stocks of only U.S. domiciled companies. Recently, he has decided to add international exposure to the plan portfolio.

   a. Identify and briefly discuss *three* potential problems that Smith may confront in selecting international stocks that he did not face in choosing U.S. stocks.

17. *CFA Examination III (1993)*

TMP has been experiencing increasing demand from its institutional clients for information and assistance related to international investment management. Recognizing that this is an area of growing importance, the firm has hired an experienced analyst/portfolio manager specializing in international equities and market strategy. His first assignment is to represent TMP before a client company's investment committee to discuss the possibility of changing their present "U.S. securities-only" investment approach to one including international investments. He is told that the committee wants a presentation that fully and objectively examines the basic, substantive considerations on which the committee should focus its attention, including both theory and evidence. The company's pension plan has no legal or other barriers to adoption of an international approach, no non-U.S. pension liabilities currently exist.

   a. Identify and briefly discuss *three* reasons for adding international securities to the pension portfolio and *three* problems associated with such an approach.

   b. Assume that the committee has adopted a policy to include international securities in its pension portfolio. Identify and briefly discuss *three* additional *policy-level* investment decisions the committee must make *before* management selection and actual implementation can begin.

Problems

1. Calculate the current horizon (maturity) premium on U.S. government securities based on data in the *Wall Street Journal*. The long-term security should have a maturity of at least twenty years.

2. Using a source of international statistics, compare the percentage change in the following economic data for Japan, Germany, Canada, and the United States for a recent year. What were the differences, and which country or countries differed most from the United States?

   a. Aggregate output (GDP)

   b. Inflation

   c. Money supply growth

3. Using a recent edition of *Barron's*, examine the weekly percentage change in the stock price indexes for Japan, Germany, Italy, and the United States. For each of three weeks, which foreign series moved most closely with the U.S. series? Which series diverged most from the U.S. series? Discuss these results as they relate to international diversification.

4. Using published sources (for example, The *Wall Street Journal, Barron's, Federal Reserve Bulletin*), look up the exchange rate for U.S. dollars with Japanese yen for each of the past ten years (you can use an average for the year or a specific time period each year). Based on these exchange rates, compute and discuss the yearly exchange rate effect on an investment in Japanese stocks by a U.S. investor. Discuss the impact of this exchange rate effect on the risk of Japanese stocks for a U.S. investor.

5. *CFA Examination* (Adapted)

The following information is available concerning the historical risk and return relationships in the U.S. capital markets:

U.S. Capital Markets Total Annual Returns, 1960–1984

Investment Category	Arithmetic Mean	Geometric Mean	Standard Deviation of Return[a]
Common stocks	10.28%	8.81%	16.9%
Treasury bills	6.54	6.49	3.2
Long-term government bonds	6.10	5.91	6.4
Long-term corporate bonds	5.75	5.35	9.6
Real estate	9.49	9.44	3.5

[a]Based on arithmetic mean.

Source: Adapted from R. G. Ibbotson, Laurence B. Siegel, and Kathryn S. Love, "World Wealth: Market Values and Returns," *Journal of Portfolio Management* 12, no. 1 (Fall 1985): 4–23.

a. Explain why the geometric and arithmetic mean returns are not equal and whether one or the other may be more useful for investment decision making. [5 minutes]
b. For the time period indicated, rank these investments on a risk-adjusted basis from most to least desirable. Explain your rationale. [6 minutes]
c. Assume the returns in these series are normally distributed.
  1. Calculate the range of returns that an investor would have expected to achieve 95 percent of the time from holding common stocks. [4 minutes]
  2. Suppose an investor holds real estate for this time period. Determine the probability of at least breaking even on this investment. [5 minutes]
d. Assume you are holding a portfolio composed entirely of real estate. Discuss the justification, if any, for adopting a mixed asset portfolio by adding long-term government bonds. [5 minutes]

6. You are given the following long-run annual rates of return for alternative investment instruments:

U.S. Government T-bills	4.50%
Large cap common stock	12.50
Long-term corporate bonds	5.80
Long-term government bonds	5.10
Small capitalization common stock	14.60

a. On the basis of these returns, compute the following:
  1. The common-stock risk premium
  2. The small-firm stock–risk premium
  3. The horizon (maturity) premium
  4. The default premium
b. The annual rate of inflation during this period was 4 percent. Compute the real rate of return on these investment alternatives.

References

Elton, Edwin J., and Martin J. Gruber, eds. *Japanese Capital Markets*. New York: Harper & Row Publishers, 1990.

European Bond Commission. *The European Bond Markets*. Chicago: Probus Publishing, 1989.

Fabozzi, Frank J., ed. *The Japanese Bond Markets*. Chicago: Probus Publishing, 1990.

Fisher, Lawrence, and James H. Lorie. *A Half Century of Returns on Stocks and Bonds*. Chicago: University of Chicago Graduate School of Business, 1977.

Grabbe, J. Orlin. *International Financial Markets*. New York: Elsevier Science Publishing, 1986.

Hamao, Yasushi. "Japanese Stocks, Bonds, Inflation, 1973–1987." *Journal of Portfolio Management* 16, no. 2 (Winter 1989).

Ibbotson, Roger G., and Gary P. Brinson. *Global Investing*. New York: McGraw-Hill, 1993.

Lessard, Donald R. "International Diversification." In *The Financial Analyst's Handbook*, 2d ed., edited by Sumner N. Levine. Homewood, IL: Dow Jones–Irwin, 1988.

Malvey, Jack. "Global Corporate Bond Portfolio Management," in *The Handbook of Fixed Income Securities*, 5th ed., edited by Frank J. Fabozzi. Chicago, IL: Irwin Professional Publishing, 1997.

Murphy, Brian, David Won, and Deepak Gulrajani. "Valuation and Risk Analysis of International Bonds." In *The Handbook of Fixed-Income Securities*, 4th ed., edited by Frank J. Fabozzi and T. Dessa Fabozzi. Burr Ridge, IL: Irwin Professional Publishing, 1995.

Reilly, Frank K., and David J. Wright. "Global Bond Markets: An Analysis of Alternative Benchmarks and Risk–Return Performance." Midwest Finance Association Meeting (March 1995).

Rosenberg, Michael R. " International Fixed-Income Investing: Theory and Practice." In *The Handbook of Fixed-Income Securities,* 5th ed., edited by Frank J. Fabozzi. Chicago, IL: Irwin Professional Publishing, 1997.

Siegel, Laurence B., and Paul D. Kaplan. "Stocks, Bonds, Bills, and Inflation Around the World." In *Managing Institutional Assets*, edited by Frank J. Fabozzi. New York: Harper & Row, 1990.

Solnik, Bruno. *International Investments*. 3d ed. Reading, MA: Addison-Wesley Publishing, 1995.

Steward, Christopher, and Adam Greshin, "International Bond Markets and Instruments." In *The Handbook of Fixed-Income Securities,* 5th ed., edited by Frank J. Fabozzi. Chicago, IL: Irwin Professional Publishing, 1997.

Van der Does, Rein W. "Investing in Foreign Securities." In *The Financial Analyst's Handbook*, 2d ed., edited by Sumner N. Levine. Homewood, IL: Dow Jones–Irwin, 1988.

Wilson, Richard S., and Frank J. Fabozzi. *The New Corporate Bond Market.* Chicago: Probus Publishing, 1990.

GLOSSARY

American Depository Receipts (ADRs)   Certificates of ownership issued by a U.S. bank that represent indirect ownership of a certain number of shares of a specific foreign firm. Shares are held on deposit in a bank in the firm's home country.

Call options   Options to buy a firm's common stock within a certain period at a specified price called the *striking price.*

Call provisions   Specifies when and how a firm can issue a call for bonds outstanding prior to their maturity.

Capital market instruments   Fixed-income investments that trade in the secondary market.

Certificates of deposit (CDs)   Instruments issued by banks and S&Ls that require minimum deposits for specified terms and that pay higher rates of interest than deposit accounts.

Collateral trust bonds   A mortgage bond wherein the assets backing the bond are financial assets like stocks and bonds.

Common stock   An equity investment that represents ownership of a firm, with full participation in its success or failure. The firm's directors must approve dividend payments.

Convertible bonds   A bond with the added feature that the bondholder has the option to turn the bond back to the firm in exchange for a specified number of common shares of the firm.

Debentures   Bonds that promise payments of interest and principal but pledge no specific assets. Holders have first claim on the issuer's income and unpledged assets.

Equipment trust certificates   Mortgage bonds that are secured by specific pieces of transportation equipment like boxcars and planes.

Eurobonds   Bonds denominated in a currency not native to the country in which they are issued.

Fixed-income investments   Loans with contractually mandated payment schedules from investors to firms or governments.

Futures contract   An agreement that provides for the future exchange of a particular asset at a specified delivery date in exchange for a specified payment at the time of delivery.

Income bonds   Debentures that stipulate interest payments only if the issuer earns the income to make the payments by specified dates.

Indenture   The legal agreement that lists the obligations of the issuer of a bond to the bondholder including payment schedules, call provisions, and sinking funds.

International domestic bonds   Bonds issued by a foreign firm, denominated in the firm's native currency, and sold within its own country.

Investment company   A firm that sells shares of the company and uses the proceeds to buy stock, bonds, or other financial instruments.

Money market funds   Investment companies that hold portfolios of high-quality, short-term securities like T-bills. High liquidity and superior returns make them a good alternative to bank savings accounts.

Mortgage bonds   Bonds that pledge specific assets such as buildings and equipment. The proceeds from the sale of these assets are used to pay off bondholders in case of bankruptcy.

Options   The right to buy or sell a firm's common stock at a specified price for a stated period of time.

Portfolio   A group of investment. Ideally, the investments should have different patterns of returns over time.

Preferred stock   An equity investment that stipulates that dividend payment either as a coupon or a stated dollar amount. The firms directors may withhold payments.

Put options   Options to sell a firm's common stock within a certain period at a specified price.

Real estate investment trusts (REITs)   Investment funds that hold portfolios of real estate investment.

Senior secured bonds   The most senior bonds in a firm's capital structure. They have a first claim on specific assets of the firm in case of bankruptcy.

Sinking fund   A provision that specifies payments the issuer must make to redeem a given percentage of an outstanding bond issue prior to maturity.

Subordinated bonds   Debentures that, in case of default, entitle holders to claims on the issuer's assets only after the claims of holders of senior debentures and mortgage bonds are satisfied.

Warrant An instrument that allows the holder to purchase a specified number of shares of the firm's common stock from the firm at a specified price for a given period of time.

Yankee bonds Bonds sold in the United States and denominated in U.S. dollars but issued by a foreign firm or government.

Zero coupon bond A bond sold at a discount from par value that promises no interest payment during the life of the bond, only the payment of the par value (principal) at maturity.

APPENDIX 3 — *Covariance and Correlation*

Covariance

Because most students have been exposed to the concepts of covariance and correlation, the following discussion is set forth in intuitive terms with examples to help the reader recall the concepts.[1]

Covariance is an absolute measure of the extent to which two sets of numbers move together over time, that is, how often they move up or down together. In this regard, move together means they are generally above their means or below their means at the same time. Covariance between i and j is defined as:

$$COV_{ij} = \frac{\Sigma(i - \bar{i})(j - \bar{j})}{N}$$

If we define $(i - \bar{i})$ as i' and $(j - \bar{j})$ as j', then

$$COV_{ij} = \frac{\Sigma i' j'}{N}$$

Obviously, if both numbers are consistently above or below their individual means at the same time, their products will be positive, and the average will be a large positive value. In contrast, if the i value is below its mean when the j value is above its mean or vice versa, their products will be large negative values, giving negative covariance.

Table 3A.1 should make this clear. In this example, the two series generally moved together, so they showed positive covariance. As noted, this is an *absolute* measure of their relationship and, therefore, can range from $+\infty$ to $-\infty$. Note that the covariance of a variable with itself is its *variance*.

Correlation

To obtain a relative measure of a given relationship, we use the correlation coefficient (r_{ij}), which is a measure of the relationship:

$$r_{ij} = \frac{COV_{ij}}{\sigma_i \sigma_j}$$

You will recall from your introductory statistics course that:

---

[1] A more detailed, rigorous treatment of the subject can be found in any standard statistics text, including S. Christian Albright, *Statistics for Business and Economics* (New York: Macmillan, 1987), 63–67.

Table 3A.1 *Calculation of Covariance*

Observation	i	j	$i - \bar{i}$	$j - \bar{j}$	$i'j'$
1	3	8	-4	-4	16
2	6	10	-1	-2	2
3	8	14	$+1$	$+2$	2
4	5	12	-2	0	0
5	9	13	$+2$	$+1$	2
6	11	15	$+4$	$+3$	12
Σ	42	72			34
Mean	7	12			
Cov_{ij}	$= \dfrac{34}{6} = +5.67$				

Table 3A.2 *Calculation of Correlation Coefficient*

Observation	$i - \bar{i}\,^a$	$(i - \bar{i})^2$	$j - \bar{j}\,^a$	$(j - \bar{j})^2$
1	-4	16	-4	16
2	-1	1	-2	4
3	$+1$	1	$+2$	4
4	-2	4	0	0
5	$+2$	4	$+1$	1
6	$+4$	16	$+3$	9
		42		34

$$\sigma_i^2 = 42/6 = 7.00 \qquad\qquad \sigma_j^2 = 34/6 = 5.67$$

$$\sigma_I = \sqrt{7.00} = 2.65 \qquad\qquad \sigma_j = \sqrt{5.67} = 2.38$$

$$r_{ij} = \text{Cov}_{ij}/\sigma_i\sigma_j = \frac{5.67}{(2.65)(2.38)} = \frac{5.67}{6.31} = 0.898$$

$$\sigma_i = \sqrt{\frac{\Sigma(i - \bar{i})^2}{N}}$$

If the two series move completely together, then the covariance would equal $\sigma_i\sigma_j$ and:

$$\frac{\text{COV}_{ij}}{\sigma_i\sigma_j} = 1.0$$

The correlation coefficient would equal unity in this case, and we would say the two series are perfectly correlated. Because we know that:

$$r_{ij} = \frac{\text{COV}_{ij}}{\sigma_i\sigma_j}$$

we also know that $\text{COV}_{ij} = r_{ij}\sigma_i\sigma_j$. This relationship may be useful when computing the standard deviation of a portfolio, because in many instances the relationship between two securities is stated in terms of the correlation coefficient rather than the covariance.

Continuing the example given in Table 3A.1, the standard deviations are computed in Table 3A.2, as is the correlation between i and j. As shown, the two standard deviations

are rather large and similar, but not exactly the same. Finally, when the positive covariance is normalized by the product of the two standard deviations, the results indicate a correlation coefficient of 0.898, which is obviously quite large and close to 1.00. Apparently, these two series are highly related.

Problems

1. As a new analyst, you have calculated the following annual rates of return for both Lauren Corporation and Kayleigh Industries.

Year	Lauren's Rate of Return	Kayleigh's Rate of Return
1995	5	5
1996	12	15
1997	−11	5
1998	10	7
1999	12	−10

Your manager suggests that because these companies produce similar products, you should continue your analysis by computing their covariance. Show all calculations.

2. You decide to go an extra step by calculating the coefficient of correlation using the data provided in Problem 1 above. Prepare a table showing your calculations and explain how to interpret the results. Would the combination of Lauren and Kayleigh be good for diversification?

Organization and Functioning of Securities Markets

This chapter answers the following questions:

♦ What is the purpose and function of a market?

♦ What are the characteristics that determine the quality of a market?

♦ What is the difference between a primary and secondary capital market and how do these markets support each other?

♦ What are the national exchanges and how are the major securities markets around the world becoming linked (what is meant by "passing the book")?

♦ What are regional stock exchanges and over-the-counter (OTC) markets?

♦ What are the alternative market-making arrangements available on the exchanges and the OTC market?

♦ What are the major types of orders available to investors and market makers?

♦ What are the major functions of the specialist on the NYSE and how does the specialist differ from the central market maker on other exchanges?

♦ What are the major factors that have caused significant changes in markets around the world during the past 15 years?

♦ What are some of the major changes in world capital markets expected over the next decade?

The stock market, the Dow Jones Industrials, and the bond market are part of our everyday experience. Each evening on the television news broadcasts we find out how stocks and bonds fared; each morning we read in our daily newspapers about expectations for a market rally or decline. Yet most people have an imperfect understanding of how domestic and world capital markets actually function. To be a successful investor in a global environment, you must know what financial markets are available around the world and how they operate.   ♦

In Chapter 1, we considered why individuals invest and what determines their required rate of return on investments. In Chapter 2, we discussed the life cycle for investors and the alternative asset allocation decisions by investors during different phases. In Chapter 3, we learned about the numerous alternative investments available and why we should diversify with securities from around the world. This chapter takes a broad view of securities markets and provides a detailed discussion of how major stock markets function. We conclude with a consideration of how global securities markets are changing.

We begin with a discussion of securities markets and the characteristics of a good market. Two components of the capital markets are described: primary and secondary. Our main emphasis in this chapter is on the secondary stock market. We consider the national stock exchanges around the world and how these markets, separated by geography and by time zones, are becoming linked into a twenty-four-hour market. We also consider regional stock markets and the over-the-counter market and provide a detailed analysis of how alternative exchange markets operate. The final section considers numerous historical changes in financial markets since the mid-1970s, additional current changes, and significant changes expected into the next century. These numerous changes in our securities markets will have a profound effect on what investments are available to you from around the world and how you buy and sell them.

WHAT IS A MARKET?

This section provides the necessary background for understanding different securities markets around the world and the changes that are occurring. The first part considers the general concept of a market and its function. The second part describes the characteristics that determine how well a particular market will fulfill its function. The third part of the section describes primary and secondary capital markets and how they interact and depend on one another.

A **market** is the means through which buyers and sellers are brought together to aid in the transfer of goods and/or services. Several aspects of this general definition seem worthy of emphasis. First, a market need not have a physical location. It is only necessary that the buyers and sellers can communicate regarding the relevant aspects of the transaction.

Second, the market does not necessarily own the goods or services involved. When we discuss what is required for a good market, you will note that ownership is not involved; the important criterion is the smooth, cheap transfer of goods and services. In most financial markets, those who establish and administer the market do not own the assets. They simply provide a physical location or an electronic system that allows potential buyers and sellers to interact, and they help the market function by providing information and facilities to aid in the transfer of ownership.

Finally, a market can deal in any variety of goods and services. For any commodity or service with a diverse clientele, a market should evolve to aid in the transfer of that commodity or service. Both buyers and sellers will benefit from the existence of a market. Basically, we take markets for granted because they are vital to a smooth-operating economy. Still, it is important to recognize that the quality of alternative markets can differ.

Characteristics of a Good Market

Throughout this book, we will discuss markets for different investments such as stocks, bonds, options, and futures in the United States and throughout the world. We will refer to these markets using various terms of quality such as strong, active, liquid, or illiquid.

There are many financial markets, but they are not all equal—some are active and liquid, others are relatively illiquid, and inefficient in their operations. To appreciate these discussions, you should be aware of the characteristics that investors look for when evaluating the quality of a market. In this section, we describe those characteristics.

One enters a market to buy or sell a good or service quickly at a price justified by the prevailing supply and demand. To determine the appropriate price, participants must have timely and accurate information on the volume and prices of past transactions and on all currently outstanding bids and offers. Therefore, one attribute of a good market is *availability of information.*

Another prime requirement is **liquidity**, the ability to buy or sell an asset quickly and at a known price—that is, a price not substantially different from the prices for prior transactions, assuming no new information is available. An asset's likelihood of being sold quickly, sometimes referred to as its *marketability,* is a necessary, but not a sufficient, condition for liquidity. The expected price should also be fairly certain, based on the recent history of transaction prices and current bid-ask quotes.[1]

A component of liquidity is **price continuity**, which means that prices do not change much from one transaction to the next unless substantial new information becomes available. Suppose no new information is forthcoming, and the last transaction was at a price of $20; if the next trade were at $20\frac{1}{8}$, the market would be considered reasonably continuous.[2] A continuous market without large price changes between trades is a characteristic of a liquid market.

A market with price continuity requires *depth,* which means that numerous potential buyers and sellers must be willing to trade at prices above and below the current market price. These buyers and sellers enter the market in response to changes in supply and demand or both and thereby prevent drastic price changes. In summary, liquidity requires marketability and price continuity, which, in turn, require depth.

Another factor contributing to a good market is the **transaction cost**. Lower costs (as a percent of the value of the trade) make for a more efficient market. An individual comparing the cost of a transaction between markets would choose a market that charges 2 percent of the value of the trade compared with one that charges 5 percent. Most microeconomic textbooks define an efficient market as one in which the cost of the transaction is minimal. This attribute is referred to as *internal efficiency.*

Finally, a buyer or seller wants the prevailing market price to adequately reflect all the information available regarding supply and demand factors in the market. If such conditions change as a result of new information, the price should change accordingly. Therefore, participants want prices to adjust quickly to new information regarding supply or demand, which means that prices reflect all available information about the asset. This attribute is referred to as **external efficiency or informational efficiency**. This attribute is discussed extensively in Chapter 8.

In summary, a good market for goods and services has the following characteristics:

1. Timely and accurate information is available on the price and volume of past transactions.
2. It is liquid, meaning an asset can be bought or sold quickly at a price close to the prices for previous transactions (has price continuity), assuming no new information has been received. In turn, price continuity requires depth.

---

[1]For a more formal discussion of liquidity and the effects of different market systems, see Sanford J. Grossman and Merton H. Miller, "Liquidity and Market Structure," *Journal of Finance* 43, no. 3 (July 1988): 617–633; and Puneet Handa and Robert A. Schwartz, "How Best to Supply Liquidity to a Securities Market," *Journal of Portfolio Management* 22, no. 2 (Winter 1996): 44–51.

[2]You should be aware that common stocks are sold in increments of sixteenths of a dollar, or $0.0625. Therefore, $20\frac{1}{16}$ means the stock sold at $20.0625 per share.

3. Transactions entail low costs, including the cost of reaching the market, the actual brokerage costs, and the cost of transferring the asset.
4. Prices rapidly adjust to new information so the prevailing price is fair since it reflects all available information regarding the asset.

Organization of the Securities Market

Before discussing the specific operation of the securities market, you need to understand its overall organization. The principal distinction is between **primary markets**, where new securities are sold, and **secondary markets**, where outstanding securities are bought and sold. Each of these markets is further divided based on the economic unit that issued the security. The following discussion considers each of these major segments of the securities market with an emphasis on the individuals involved and the functions they perform.

PRIMARY CAPITAL MARKETS

The primary market is where new issues of bonds, preferred stock, or common stock are sold by government units, municipalities, or companies to acquire new capital.[3]

Government Bond Issues

All U.S. government bond issues are subdivided into three segments based on their original maturities. **Treasury bills** are negotiable, non-interest-bearing securities with original maturities of one year or less. They are currently issued for three months, six months, or one year. **Treasury notes** have original maturities of two to ten years, and they have generally been issued with two-, three-, four-, five-, seven-, and ten-year terms. Finally, **Treasury bonds** have original maturities of more than ten years.

To sell bills, notes, and bonds, the Treasury relies on Federal Reserve System auctions. In an auction held each week, institutions and some individuals submit bids for T-bills at prices below par that imply specific yields. (The bidding process and pricing are discussed in detail in Chapter 15.)

Treasury notes and bonds are likewise sold at auction by the Federal Reserve, but the bids state yields rather than prices. That is, the Treasury specifies how much it wants and when the notes or bonds will mature. After receiving the competitive bid yields and quantity, the Treasury determines the stop-out yield bid (the highest yield it will accept) based on the bids received and how much it wants to borrow. The Fed also receives many noncompetitive bids from investors who are willing to pay the average price of the accepted competitive tenders. All noncompetitive bids are accepted.

Municipal Bond Issues

New municipal bond issues are sold by one of three methods: competitive bid, negotiation, or private placement. Competitive bid sales typically involve sealed bids. The bond issue is sold to the bidding syndicate of underwriters that submits the bid with the lowest interest cost in accordance with the stipulations set forth by the issuer. Negotiated sales involve contractual arrangements between underwriters and issuers wherein the

---

[3]For an excellent set of studies related to the primary market, see Michael C. Jensen and Clifford W. Smith, Jr., eds., "Symposium on Investment Banking and the Capital Acquisition Process," *Journal of Financial Economics* 15, no. 1/2 (January–February 1986).

underwriter helps the issuer prepare the bond issue and set the price and has the exclusive right to sell the issue. Private placements involve the sale of a bond issue by the issuer directly to an investor or a small group of investors (usually institutions).

Note that two of the three methods require an *underwriting* function. Specifically, in a competitive bid or a negotiated transaction, the investment banker typically underwrites the issue, which means the firm purchases the entire issue at a specified price, relieving the issuer from the risk and responsibility of selling and distributing the bonds. Subsequently, the underwriter sells the issue to the investing public. For municipal bonds, this underwriting function is performed by both investment banking firms and commercial banks.

The underwriting function can involve three services: origination, risk-bearing, and distribution. Origination involves the design of the bond issue and initial planning. To fulfill the risk-bearing function, the underwriter acquires the total issue at a price dictated by the competitive bid or through negotiation and accepts the responsibility and risk of reselling it for more than the purchase price. Distribution means selling it to investors, typically with the help of a selling syndicate that includes other investment banking firms or commercial banks.

In a negotiated bid, the underwriter will carry out all three services. In a competitive bid, the issuer specifies the amount, maturities, coupons, and call features of the issue and the competing syndicates submit a bid for the entire issue that reflects the yields they estimate for the bonds. The issuer may have received advice from an investment firm on the desirable characteristics for a forthcoming issue. but this advice would have been on a fee basis and would not necessarily involve the ultimate underwriter who is responsible for risk-bearing and distribution. Finally, a private placement involves no risk-bearing, but an investment banker could assist in locating potential buyers and negotiating the characteristics of the issue.

Municipal bonds are either general obligation (GO) bonds that are backed by the full taxing power of the municipality, or revenue bonds that are dependent on the revenues from a specific project that was funded by an issue such as a toll road, a hospital, or a sewage system. Commercial banks dominate the management of GO bond sales, and investment banking firms dominate revenue bond sales.

The municipal bond market has experienced two major trends during the past decade. First, it has shifted toward negotiated bond issues versus competitive bids. Currently, about 75 percent of issues are negotiated deals. Second, the market has shifted toward revenue bonds, wherein almost 70 percent of the market is revenue issues. These two trends are related because revenue issues tend to be negotiated underwritings. Although many states require that GO bond issues be sold through competitive bidding, they seldom impose such a requirement on revenue issues.[4]

Corporate Bond and Stock Issues

Corporate securities include bond and stock issues. Corporate bond issues are almost always sold through a negotiated arrangement with an investment banking firm that maintains a relationship with the issuing firm. In a global capital market that involves an explosion of new instruments, the origination function is becoming more important because the corporate chief financial officer (CFO) will probably not be completely familiar with the availability and issuing requirements of many new instruments and the alternative capital markets around the world. Investment banking firms compete for underwriting business by creating new instruments that appeal to existing investors and by

---

[4]For a further discussion, see David S. Kidwell and Eric H. Sorensen, "Investment Banking and the Underwriting of New Municipal Issues," in *The Municipal Bond Handbook,* ed. by F. J. Fabozzi, S. G. Feldstein, I. M. Pollack, and F. G. Zarb (Homewood, IL: Dow Jones–Irwin, 1983).

advising issuers regarding desirable countries and currencies. As a result, the expertise of the investment banker can help reduce the issuer's cost of new capital.

Once a stock or bond issue is specified, the underwriter will put together a syndicate of other major underwriters and a selling group for its distribution. For common stock, *new issues* are typically divided into two groups. The first and largest group is *seasoned* new issues that are offered by companies that have outstanding stock with existing public markets. For example, in 1995 General Motors sold a new issue of common stock. General Motors common stock already had a large and active market, and the company decided to issue new shares, which increased the number of outstanding shares, to acquire new equity capital.

The second major category of new stock issues is referred to as **initial public offerings (IPOs)**, wherein a company decides to sell common stock to the public for the first time. At the time of an IPO offering, there is no existing public market for the stock, that is, the company has been closely held. An example would be an IPO by Polo Ralph Lauren in June, 1997, at $26 per share. The company is a leading manufacturer and distributor of men's clothing. The purpose of the offering was to get additional capital to expand its operations.

New issues (seasoned or IPOs) are typically underwritten by investment bankers, who acquire the total issue from the company and sell the securities to interested investors. The underwriter gives advice to the corporation on the general characteristics of the issue, its pricing, and the timing of the offering. The underwriter also accepts the risk of selling the new issue after acquiring it from the corporation.[5]

Relationships with Investment Bankers   The underwriting of corporate issues typically takes one of three forms: negotiated, competitive bids, or best-efforts arrangements. As noted, negotiated underwritings are the most common, and the procedure is the same as for municipal issues.

A corporation may also specify the type of securities to be offered (common stock, preferred stock, or bonds) and then solicit competitive bids from investment banking firms. This is rare for industrial firms but is typical for utilities, which may be required to sell the issue via a competitive bid by state laws. Although competitive bids typically reduce the cost of an issue, it also brings fewer services from the investment banker. The banker gives less advice but still accepts the risk-bearing function by underwriting the issue and fulfills the distribution function.

Alternatively, an investment banker can agree to support an issue and sell it on a *best-efforts basis.* This is usually done with speculative new issues. In this arrangement, the investment banker does not underwrite the issue because it does not buy any securities. The stock is owned by the company, and the investment banker acts *as a broker* to sell whatever it can at a stipulated price. The investment banker earns a lower commission on such an issue than on an underwritten issue. With any of these arrangements, the lead investment banker will typically form an underwriting syndicate of other investment bankers to spread the risk and also help in the sales. In addition, if the issue is large, the lead underwriter and underwriting syndicate will form a selling group of smaller firms to help in the distribution.

Introduction of Rule 415   The typical practice of negotiated arrangements involving numerous investment banking firms in syndicates and selling groups has changed with the introduction of Rule 415, which allows large firms to register security issues and sell them piecemeal during the following two years. These issues are referred to as *shelf reg-*

[5]For an extended discussion of the underwriting process, see Richard A. Brealey and Stewart C. Myers, *Principles of Corporate Finance,* 4th ed. (New York: McGraw-Hill, 1991), Chapter 15.

istrations because, after they are registered, the issues lie on the shelf and can be taken down and sold on short notice whenever it suits the issuing firm. As an example, General Electric could register an issue of 5 million shares of common stock during 1999 and sell a million shares in early 1999, another million shares late in 1999, 2 million shares in early 2000, and the rest in late 2000.

Each offering can be made with little notice or paperwork by one underwriter or several. In fact, because relatively few shares may be involved, the lead underwriter often handles the whole deal without a syndicate or uses only one or two other firms. This arrangement has benefited large corporations because it provides great flexibility, reduces registration fees and expenses, and allows firms issuing securities to request competitive bids from several investment banking firms.

On the other hand, some observers fear that shelf registrations do not allow investors enough time to examine the current status of the firm issuing the securities. Also, the follow-up offerings reduce the participation of small underwriters because the underwriting syndicates are smaller and selling groups are almost nonexistent. Shelf registrations have typically been used for the sale of straight debentures rather than common stock or convertible issues.[6]

Private Placements and Rule 144A

Rather than a public sale using one of these arrangements, primary offerings can be sold privately. In such an arrangement, referred to as a **private placement**, the firm designs an issue with the assistance of an investment banker and sells it to a small group of institutions. The firm enjoys lower issuing costs because it does not need to prepare the extensive registration statement required for a public offering. The institution that buys the issue typically benefits because the issuing firm passes some of these cost savings on to the investor as a higher return. In fact, the institution should require a higher return because of the absence of any secondary market for these securities, which implies higher liquidity risk.

The private placement market has been changed dramatically by the introduction of Rule 144A by the SEC. This rule allows corporations—including non-U.S. firms—to place securities privately with large, sophisticated institutional investors without extensive registration documents. The SEC intends to provide more financing alternatives for U.S. and non-U.S. firms and possibly increase the number, size, and liquidity of private placements.[7]

SECONDARY FINANCIAL MARKETS

In this section, we consider the purpose and importance of secondary markets and provide an overview of the secondary markets for bonds, financial futures, and stocks. Next, we consider national stock markets around the world. Finally, we will discuss regional and over-the-counter stock markets and provide a detailed presentation on the functioning of stock exchanges.

Secondary markets permit trading in outstanding issues; that is, stocks or bonds already sold to the public are traded between current and potential owners. The proceeds

---

[6]For further discussion of Rule 415, see Beth McGoldrick, "Life with Rule 415," *Institutional Investor* 17, no. 2 (February 1983): 129–133; and Robert J. Rogowski and Eric H. Sorensen, "Deregulation in Investment Banking: Shelf Registration, Structure and Performance," *Finance Management* 14, no. 1 (Spring 1985): 5–15.

[7]For a discussion of the rule and private placements, see Michael Siconolfi and Kevin Salwen, "SEC Ready to Ease Private-Placement Rules," *Wall Street Journal,* April 13, 1990, C1, C5. For a discussion of some reactions to Rule 144A, see John W. Milligan, "Two Cheers for 144A," *Institutional Investor* 24, no. 9 (July 1990): 117–119; and Sara Hanks, "SEC Ruling Creates a New Market," *Wall Street Journal,* May 16, 1990, A12.

from a sale in the secondary market do not go to the issuing unit (the government, municipality, or company), but rather to the current owner of the security.

Why Secondary Markets Are Important

Before discussing the various segments of the secondary market, we must consider its overall importance. Because the secondary market involves the trading of securities initially sold in the primary market, *it provides liquidity to the individuals who acquired these securities*. After acquiring securities in the primary market, investors want to sell them again to acquire other securities, buy a house, or go on a vacation. The primary market benefits greatly from the liquidity provided by the secondary market because investors would hesitate to acquire securities in the primary market if they thought they could not subsequently sell them in the secondary market. That is, without an active secondary market, potential issuers of stocks or bonds would have to provide a much higher rate of return to compensate investors for the substantial liquidity risk.

Secondary markets are also important to issuers because the prevailing market price of the securities is determined by transactions in the secondary market. New issues of outstanding stocks or bonds to be sold in the primary market are based on prices and yields in the secondary market. As a result, capital costs for the government, municipalities, and corporations are determined by investor expectations and actions that are reflected in market prices prevailing in the secondary market.[8] Even nonpublic IPOs are priced based on the prices and values of comparable stocks or bonds in the public secondary market.

Secondary Bond Markets

The secondary market for bonds distinguishes among those issued by the federal government, municipalities, or corporations.

Secondary Markets for U.S. Government and Municipal Bonds   U.S. government bonds are traded by bond dealers that specialize in either Treasury bonds or agency bonds. Treasury issues are bought or sold through a set of thirty-five primary dealers, including large banks in New York and Chicago and some of the large investment banking firms (for example, Merrill Lynch, First Boston, Morgan Stanley). These institutions and other firms also make markets for government agency issues, but there is no formal set of dealers for agency securities.[9]

The major market makers in the secondary municipal bond market are banks and investment firms. Banks are active in municipal bond trading because they are involved in the underwriting of general obligation issues and they commit large parts of their investment portfolios to these securities. Also, many large investment firms have municipal bond departments that are active in underwriting and trading these issues.

Secondary Corporate Bond Markets   The secondary market for corporate bonds has two major segments: security exchanges and an over-the-counter (OTC) market. The

---

[8]In the literature on market microstructure, it is noted that the secondary markets also have an effect on market efficiency, the volatility of security prices, and the serial correlation in security returns. In this regard, see F. D. Foster and S. Viswanathan, "The Effects of Public Information and Competition on Trading Volume and Price Volatility," *Review of Financial Studies* 6, no. 1 (Spring 1993): 23–56; C. N. Jones, G. Kaul, and M. L. Lipson, "Information, Trading and Volatility," *Journal of Financial Economics* 36, no. 1 (August 1994): 127–154; H. Bessembinder, Kalok Chan, and P. J. Sequin, "An Empirical Examination of Information Differences of Opinion, and Trading Activity," *Journal of Financial Economics* 40, no. 1 (January 1996): 105–134.

[9]For a discussion of non-U.S. bond markets, see European Bond Commission, *The European Bond Markets* (Chicago: Probus Publishing, 1989); and Frank J. Fabozzi, ed., *The Japanese Bond Market* (Chicago: Probus Publishing, 1990).

major exchange for corporate bonds is the New York Stock Exchange Fixed Income Market. By the end of 1997, more than 1,200 corporate bond issues were listed on this exchange with a combined par value of about $265 billion and a combined market value of approximately $270 billion.[10] On a typical day, there are about 1,600 trades with a total volume of about $31 million. Notably, currently all the trading on the NYSE's bond market is done through its *Automated Bond System (ABS),* which is a fully automated trading and information system that allow subscribing firms to enter and execute bond orders through terminals in their offices.[11] Users receive immediate execution reports and locked-in compared trades. In addition, 92 issues are listed on the American Stock Exchange (AMEX) with par value of over $11 billion, a total market value of almost $10 billion, and typical daily trading volume in excess of $1.4 million.

All corporate bonds not listed on one of the exchanges are traded over-the-counter by dealers who buy and sell for their own accounts. In sharp contrast to what occurs for stocks where most of the trading takes place on the national exchanges such as the NYSE, in the United States about 90 percent of *corporate bond trades occur on the OTC market.* Virtually all large trades are carried out on the OTC market, even for the bonds that are listed on an exchange. The fact is, the NYSE bond market is considered the "odd-lot" market for bonds. As such, the prices reported on the exchanges are generally considered to be inexact estimates of prices associated with large transactions.[12]

The major bond dealers are the large investment banking firms that underwrite the issues such as Merrill Lynch, Goldman Sachs, Salomon Brothers, Lehman Brothers, Kidder Peabody, and Morgan Stanley Dean Witter. Because of the limited trading in corporate bonds compared to the fairly active trading in government bonds, corporate bond dealers do not carry extensive inventories of specific issues. Instead, they hold a limited number of bonds desired by their clients, and when someone wants to do a trade, they work more like brokers than dealers.

Financial Futures

In addition to the market for the bonds, recently a market has developed for futures contracts related to these bonds. These contracts allow the holder to buy or sell a specified amount of a given bond issue at a stipulated price. The two major futures exchanges are the Chicago Board of Trade (CBOT) and the Chicago Mercantile Exchange (CME). These futures contracts and the futures market are discussed in Chapter 17.

Secondary Equity Markets

The secondary equity market is usually broken down into three major segments: (1) the major national stock exchanges, including the New York, the American, the Tokyo, and the London stock exchanges; (2) regional stock exchanges in such cities as Chicago, San Francisco, Boston, Osaka and Nagoya in Japan, and Dublin in Ireland; and (3) the over-the-counter (OTC) market, which involves trading in stocks not listed on an organized exchange.

---

[10]*NYSE Fact Book* (New York: NYSE, 1998), 82. If you include U.S. government issues and non-U.S. issues of companies, banks, and governments, there are almost 2,100 issues with a par value and market value of more than $2,700 billion.

[11]Gregory Zuckerman, "Electronic Trading in Bond Market Is Slow to Catch on," *Wall Street Journal* (June 3, 1998), p. C1.

[12]For an empirical analysis of the differences, see Arthur D. Warga, "Corporate Bond Price Discrepancies in the Dealer and Exchange Markets," *Journal of Fixed Income* 1, no. 3 (December 1991): 7–16.

The first two segments, referred to as *listed securities exchanges,* differ only in size and geographic emphasis. Both are composed of formal organizations with specific members and specific securities (stocks or bonds) that have qualified for listing. Although the exchanges typically consider similar factors when evaluating firms that apply for listing, the level of requirement differs (the national exchanges have more stringent requirements). Also, the prices of securities listed on alternative stock exchanges are determined using several different trading (pricing) systems that will be discussed in the next section.

Securities Exchanges As indicated, the secondary stock market is composed of three segments: national stock exchanges, regional stock exchanges, and the over-the-counter market. We will discuss each of these separately because they differ in importance within countries and they have different trading systems. As an investor interested in trading global securities, you should be aware of these differences. Following a brief discussion of alternative trading systems and a consideration of call versus continuous markets, we describe the three segments of the equity market. We begin with a discussion of the major national stock exchanges in the world because they typically are the dominant markets within a country. The next section will consider regional stock exchanges, and then we discuss the over-the-counter stock market.

Alternative trading systems Although stock exchanges are similar in that only qualified stocks can be traded by individuals who are members of the exchange, they can differ in their *trading systems.* There are two major trading systems, and an exchange can use one of these or a combination of them. One is a *pure auction market,* in which interested buyers and sellers submit bid and ask prices for a given stock to a central location where the orders are matched by a broker who does not own the stock, but who acts as a facilitating agent. Participants refer to this system as *price-driven* because shares of stock are sold to the investor with the highest bid price and bought from the seller with the lowest offering price.

The other major trading system is a *dealer market* where individual dealers provide liquidity by buying and selling the shares of stock for themselves. Therefore, in such a market, investors wanting to buy or sell shares of a stock must go to a dealer. Ideally, dealers will compete against each other to provide the highest bid prices when you are selling and the lowest asking price when you are buying stock. When we discuss the various exchanges, we will indicate the trading system used.

Call versus continuous markets Beyond the alternative trading systems for equities, the operation of exchanges can differ in terms of when and how the stocks are traded.

In **call markets**, trading for individual stocks takes place at specified times. The intent is to gather all the bids and asks for the stock and attempt to arrive at a single price where the quantity demanded is as close as possible to the quantity supplied. This trading arrangement is generally used during the early stages of development of an exchange when there are few stocks listed or a small number of active investors–traders. If you envision an exchange with only a few stocks listed and a few traders, you would call the roll of stocks and ask for interest in one stock at a time. After determining all the available buy and sell orders, exchange officials attempt to arrive at a single price that will satisfy *most* of the orders, and all orders are transacted at this one price.

Notably, call markets also are used at the opening for stocks on the NYSE if there is an overnight buildup of buy and sell orders, in which case the opening price can differ from the prior day's closing price. Also, this concept is used if trading is suspended during the day because of some significant new information. In either case, the specialist or market maker would attempt to derive a new equilibrium price using a call-market approach that would reflect the imbalance and take care of most of the orders. For example, assume a stock had been trading at about $42 per share and some significant, new, positive information was released overnight or during the day. If it was overnight

it would affect the opening; if it happened during the day it would affect the price established after trading was suspended. If the buy orders were three or four times as numerous as the sell orders, the price based on the call market might be $44, which is the specialists' estimate of a new equilibrium price that reflects the supply–demand caused by the new information. It is contended that this temporary use of the call-market mechanism contributes to a more orderly market and less volatility in such instances because it attempts to avoid major up and down price swings.

In a **continuous market**, trades occur at any time the market is open. Stocks in this continuous market are priced either by auction or by dealers. If it is a dealer market, dealers are willing to make a market in the stock, which means that they are willing to buy or sell for their own account at a specified bid and ask price. If it is an auction market, enough buyers and sellers are trading to allow the market to be continuous, that is, when you come to buy stock, there is another investor available and willing to sell stock. A compromise between a pure dealer market and a pure auction market is a combination wherein the market is basically an auction market, but there exists an intermediary who is willing to act as a dealer if the pure auction market does not have enough activity. These dealers provide temporary liquidity to ensure that the market will be liquid as well as continuous.

The Chapter 4 Appendix contains two tables that list the characteristics of stock exchanges around the world and indicate whether the exchange provides a continuous market, a call-market mechanism, or a mixture of the two. Notably, although many exchanges are considered continuous, they also employ a call-market mechanism on specific occasions such as at the open and during trading suspensions. The NYSE is such a market.

National Stock Exchanges   Two U.S. securities exchanges are generally considered national in scope: the New York Stock Exchange (NYSE) and the American Stock Exchange (AMEX). Outside the United States, each country typically has one national exchange, such as the Tokyo Stock Exchange (TSE), the London Exchange, the Frankfurt Stock Exchange, and the Paris Bourse. These exchanges are considered national because of the large number of listed securities, the prestige of the firms listed, the wide geographic dispersion of the listed firms, and the diverse clientele of buyers and sellers who use the market.

New York Stock Exchange (NYSE)   The New York Stock Exchange (NYSE), the largest organized securities market in the United States, was established in 1817 as the New York Stock and Exchange Board. The Exchange dates its founding to when the famous Buttonwood Agreement was signed in May 1792 by twenty-four brokers.[13] The name was changed to the New York Stock Exchange in 1863.

At the end of 1997, approximately 3,200 companies had stock issues listed on the NYSE, for a total of 3,670 stock issues (common and preferred) with a total market value of more than $8.0 trillion. The specific listing requirements for the NYSE as of 1997 appear in Table 4.1.

The average number of shares traded daily on the NYSE has increased steadily and substantially, as shown in Table 4.2. Prior to the 1960s, the daily volume averaged less than 3 million shares, compared with current average daily volume in excess of 526 million shares and record volume over 1.2 billion shares on October 28, 1997.

The NYSE has dominated the other exchanges in the United States in trading volume. During the past decade, the NYSE has consistently accounted for about 80 percent of all shares traded on U.S. listed exchanges, as compared with about 10 percent for the American Stock Exchange and about 10 percent for all regional exchanges combined. Because share prices on the NYSE tend to be higher than those on the AMEX, the dollar value

---

[13]The NYSE considers the signing of this agreement the birth of the Exchange and celebrated its 200th birthday during 1992. For a pictorial history, see *Life,* collectors' edition, Spring 1992.

Table 4.1   Listing Requirements for Stocks on the NYSE and the AMEX

	NYSE	AMEX
Pretax income last year[a]	$ 2,500,000	$ 750,000 latest year or two of last three years
Pretax income last two years	2,000,000	
Net tangible assets	18,000,000	4,000,000
Shares publicly held	1,100,000	500,000
Market value of publicly held shares[b]	18,000,000	3,000,000[c]
Minimum number of holders of round lots (100 shares or more)	2,000	800

[a]For AMEX, this is *net* income last year.
[b]This minimum required market value varies over time, depending on the value of the NYSE Common Stock Index. For specifics, see the *1998 NYSE Fact Book*, 31–34.
[c]The AMEX only has one minimum.

Sources: *NYSE Fact Book* (New York: NYSE, 1998); and *AMEX Fact Book* (New York: AMEX, 1998). Reprinted by permission.

Table 4.2   Average Daily Reported Share Volume Traded on Selected Stock Markets (× 1,000)

Year	NYSE	AMEX	NASDAQ	TSE
1955	2,578	912	N.A.	8,000
1960	3,042	1,113	N.A.	90,000
1965	6,176	2,120	N.A.	116,000
1970	11,564	3,319	N.A.	144,000
1975	18,551	2,138	5,500	183,000
1980	44,871	6,427	26,500	359,000
1985	109,169	8,337	82,100	428,000
1990	156,777	13,158	131,900	500,000
1991	178,917	13,309	163,300	380,000
1992	202,266	14,157	190,800	269,000
1993	264,519	18,111	263,000	353,000
1994	291,357	17,945	295,100	342,200
1995	346,101	20,128	401,400	369,600
1996	411,953	22,158	543,700	405,500
1997	526,925	24,389	585,000(e)	420,000(e)

N.A. = not available. (e) = estimate.

Sources: *NYSE Fact Book* (New York: NYSE, various issues); *AMEX Fact Book* (New York: AMEX, various issues); *Tokyo Stock Exchange Fact Book* (Tokyo: TSE, various issues). Reprinted with permission.

of trading on the NYSE has averaged about 85 percent of the total value of U.S. trades, compared with less than 5 percent for the AMEX and a little over 10 percent for the regional exchanges.[14]

The volume of trading and relative stature of the NYSE is reflected in the price of a membership on the exchange (referred to as a seat). As shown in Table 4.3, the price of membership has fluctuated in line with trading volume and other factors that influence the profitability of membership.

American Stock Exchange (AMEX)   The American Stock Exchange (AMEX) was begun by a group who traded unlisted shares at the corner of Wall and Hanover Streets in New York. It was originally called the Outdoor Curb Market. In 1910, it established formal trading rules and changed its name to the New York Curb Market Association.

---

[14]For a breakdown of shares traded and their value, see Securities and Exchange Commission, *Annual Report* (Washington, DC: U.S. Government Printing Office, annual); and *NYSE Fact Book* (New York: NYSE, annual). For a discussion of trading volume and membership prices, see Anita Rashavan, "Stock Boom Doesn't Spur Bull Market in Seats," *Wall Street Journal*, March 24, 1993, C1, C25; and Greg Ip, "Prices Soften for Exchange Seats," *Wall Street Journal*, May 27, 1998, C1, C17.

Table 4.3 *Membership Prices on the NYSE and the AMEX ($000)*

	NYSE High	NYSE Low	AMEX High	AMEX Low		NYSE High	NYSE Low	AMEX High	AMEX Low
1925	$150	$ 99	$ 38	$ 9	1985	$ 480	$ 310	$160	$115
1935	140	65	33	12	1990	430	250	170	84
1945	95	49	32	12	1991	440	345	120	80
1955	90	49	22	12	1992	600	410	110	76
1960	162	135	60	51	1993	775	500	163	92
1965	250	190	80	55	1994	830	760	205	155
1970	320	130	185	70	1995	1,050	785	152	105
1975	138	55	72	34	1996	1,450	1,225	210	150
1980	275	175	252	95	1997	1,750	1,175	420	200

Sources: *NYSE Fact Book* (New York: NYSE, various issues); *AMEX Fact Book* (New York: AMEX, various issues). Reprinted by permission of the New York Stock Exchange and the American Stock Exchange.

The members moved inside a building in 1921 and continued to trade mainly in unlisted stocks (stocks not listed on one of the registered exchanges) until 1946, when its volume in listed stocks finally outnumbered that in unlisted stocks. The current name was adopted in 1953.

The AMEX is a national exchange, distinct from the NYSE because, except for a short period in the late 1970s, no stocks have been listed on both the NYSE and AMEX at the same time. The AMEX has emphasized foreign securities, listing 64 foreign issues in 1997. Trading in these issues constituted about 13 percent of total volume.[15] Warrants were listed on the AMEX for a number of years before the NYSE listed them.

The AMEX has become a major options exchange since January 1975 when it began listing options on stocks. Since then it has added options on interest rates and stock indexes, which are discussed in Chapter 17.

At the end of 1997, 829 stock issues were listed on the AMEX.[16] As shown in Table 4.2, average daily trading volume has fluctuated substantially over time, growing overall from below 500,000 shares to more than 24 million shares per day in 1997. Because of the differences between the NYSE and the AMEX, most large brokerage firms are members of both exchanges. An evolving merger of the AMEX, NASDAQ, and the Philadelphia Stock Exchange is considered with the OCT presentation.

Tokyo Stock Exchange (TSE)   Of the eight stock exchanges in Japan, those in Tokyo, Osaka, and Nagoya are the largest. The TSE dominates its country's market much as the NYSE does the United States. Specifically, about 87 percent of trades in volume and 83 percent of value occur on the TSE. The market value of stocks listed on the TSE surpassed the NYSE during 1987 but fell below it when the Japanese stock market declined following its peak in December 1989.

The Tokyo Stock Exchange Co., Ltd., established in 1878, was replaced in 1943 by the Japan Securities Exchange, a quasi-governmental organization that absorbed all existing exchanges in Japan. The Japan Securities Exchange was dissolved in 1947, and the Tokyo Stock Exchange in its present form was established in 1949. The trading mechanism is a price-driven system wherein an investor submits bid and ask prices for stocks. At the end of 1997, there were about 1,700 companies listed with a total market value of 300.2 trillion yen (this equals about 2.4 trillion dollars at an exchange rate of 125 yen to the dollar). As shown in Table 4.2, average daily share volume has increased by more than

[15]*AMEX Fact Book* (New York: AMEX, 1998).

[16]The requirements for listing on the AMEX appear in Table 4.1.

ten times, from 90 million shares per day in 1960 to a peak of over 1 billion shares in 1988 prior to a decline to about 400 million shares in 1997. The value of shares traded in U.S. dollars has increased by almost fifty times from 1960 to 1997 because of the substantial increase in the prices of the shares and the rising value of the yen.

Both domestic and foreign stocks are listed on the Tokyo Exchange. The domestic stocks are further divided between the First and Second Sections. The First Section contains about 1,200 stocks and the Second Section about 450 stocks. The 150 most active stocks on the First Section are traded on the trading floor. Trading in all other domestic stocks and all foreign stocks is conducted by computer. From on-line terminals in their offices, member firms enter buy and sell orders that are received at the exchange. A clerk employed by a *Saitori* member, the TSE member firm responsible for this function, matches buy and sell orders for each stock on the electronic book-entry display screen and returns confirmations to the trading parties. The same information is also recorded on the trade-report printer and displayed on all stock-quote screens on the trading floor.

Besides domestic stocks, foreign company stocks are listed and traded on the TSE foreign stock market, which was opened in December 1973. Only a limited number of foreign companies were listed before 1985, but by the end of 1997, the TSE listed 77 foreign companies. The value of daily average trading in foreign stocks has fluctuated dramatically. It was highly active in 1987 and 1989 (over 11 billion yen), but has been declining steadily since 1989.

London Stock Exchange (LSE)   The largest established securities market in the United Kingdom, generally referred to as "The Stock Exchange," is the London Stock Exchange. Since 1973, it has served as the stock exchange of Great Britain and Ireland, with operating units in London, Dublin, and six other cities. Both listed securities (bonds and equities) and unlisted securities are traded on the LSE. The listed equity segment involves more than 2,600 companies (2,700 security issues) with a market value in excess of 374 billion pounds (approximately $561 billion at an exchange rate of $1.50/pound). Of the 2,600 companies listed on the LSE, about 600 are foreign firms—the largest number on any exchange.

The stocks listed on the LSE are divided into three groups: Alpha, Beta, and Gamma. The Alpha stocks are the 65 most actively traded stocks, and the Betas are the 500 next most active stocks. In Alpha and Beta stocks, market makers are required to offer firm bid–ask quotes to all members of the exchange. For the rest of the stocks (Gamma stocks), market quotations are only indicative and must be confirmed before a trade. All equity trades must be reported to the Stock Exchange Automated Quotation (SEAQ) system within minutes, although only trades in Alpha stocks are reported in full on the trading screen.

The pricing system on the LSE is done by competing dealers who communicate via computers in offices away from the stock exchange. This system is similar to the NASDAQ system used in the OTC market in the United States, which is described in the next section.

Other national exchanges   Other national exchanges are located in Frankfurt, Toronto, and Paris.[17] In addition, the International Federation of Stock Exchanges was established in 1961. Members include thirty-five exchanges or national associations of stock exchanges in twenty-nine countries. Located in Paris, the federation's twenty-nine full members and six associate members meet every autumn to promote closer collaboration among themselves and to promote the development of securities markets.[18]

---

[17]In an attempt to attain global recognition and economies of scale, Germany's three major exchanges merged in 1995. See Andrew Fisher, "Top Three German Exchanges to Merge," *Financial Times,* May 9, 1995. Also, the Paris exchange has gone to electronic trading and a continuous market. A discussion of changes due to the European Union is contained in Barry Riley, "Aim for Bourse without Borders," *Financial Times* (May 18, 1998), p. 15.

[18]For further discussions of equity markets around the world, see David Smyth, *Worldly Wise Investor* (New York: Franklin Watts, 1988); *The Spicer and Oppenheim Guide to Securities Markets around the World* (New York: John Wiley & Sons, 1988); and Bryan de Caires, ed., *Kidder Peabody Guide to International Capital Markets* (London: Euromoney Publications, 1988). An appendix at the end of this chapter summarizes information about stock exchanges around the world in both developed markets and emerging markets.

New exchanges are constantly being established in many emerging countries around the world. Almost all of these countries have exceptionally large needs for capital to finance private growth as well as the necessary infrastructure projects to support growth (such as roads, housing, sewage systems). As noted earlier, it is recognized that operational, liquid secondary equity markets are mandatory if a country aims to take advantage of international sources of capital. For example, stock markets were established between 1991 and 1993 in Russia and Poland, in China (Shanghai and Shenzchen) in 1986, and in Hungary (Budapest) in 1990. More recent exchanges were created in Peru and Sri Lanka.

As an indication of growth in the area, the International Finance Corporation (IFC), a subsidiary of the World Bank, began creating stock indexes for emerging markets in the early 1980s. By 1997, they had created stock market indexes for twenty-six major emerging markets with prices beginning in 1975, and subsequent stock indexes for 47 markets. For example, their database during 1997 went from 72 to 80 countries.[19]

The global twenty-four-hour market   Our discussion of the global securities market will tend to emphasize the three markets in New York, London, and Tokyo because of their relative size and importance, and because they represent the major segments of a worldwide tewnty-four-hour stock market. You will often hear about a continuous market where investment firms "pass the book" around the world. This means the major active market in securities moves around the globe as trading hours for these three markets begin and end. Consider the individual trading hours for each of the three exchanges, translated into a twenty-four-hour eastern standard time (EST) clock:

	Local Time (24-hr. Notations)	24-Hour EST
New York Stock Exchange	0930–1600	0930–1600
Tokyo Stock Exchange	0900–1100	2300–0100
	1300–1500	0300–0500
London Stock Exchange	0815–1615	0215–1015

Imagine trading starting in New York at 0930 and going until 1600 in the afternoon, being picked up by Tokyo late in the evening and going until 0500 in the morning, and continuing in London (with some overlap) until it begins in New York again (with some overlap) at 0930. Alternatively, it is possible to envision trading as beginning in Tokyo at 2300 hours and continuing until 0500, when it moves to London, then ends the day in New York. This latter model seems the most relevant because the first question a London trader asks in the morning is "What happened in Tokyo?" and the U.S. trader asks "What happened in Tokyo and what *is* happening in London?" The point is, the markets operate almost continuously and are related in their response to economic events. Therefore, as an investor you are not dealing with three separate and distinct exchanges, but with one interrelated world market.[20] Clearly, this interrelationship is growing daily because of numerous multiple listings where stocks are listed on several exchanges around the world (such as the NYSE and TSE) and the availability of sophisticated telecommunications.

---

[19]The primary source of information and data on these markets is the annual *Emerging Stock Markets Fact Book* (Washington, DC: International Finance Corporation).

[20]For an example of global trading, see "How Merrill Lynch Moves Its Stock Deals All Around the World," *Wall Street Journal,* November 9, 1987, 1, 19; and *Opportunity and Risk in the 24-Hour Global Marketplace* (New York: Coopers & Lybrand, 1987). In response to this trend toward global trading, the International Organization of Securities Commissions (IOSCO) has been established. For a discussion of it, see David Lascelles, "Calls to Bring Watchdogs into Line," *Financial Times,* August 14, 1989, 10.

REGIONAL EXCHANGES AND THE OVER-THE-COUNTER MARKET

Within most countries, regional stock exchanges compete with and supplement the national exchanges by providing secondary markets for the stocks of smaller companies. Beyond these exchanges, trading off the exchange (the over-the-counter [OTC] market) includes all stocks not listed on one of the formal exchanges. The size and significance of the regional exchanges versus the OTC market and the relative impact of these two sectors on the overall secondary stock markets vary among countries. In the first part of this section, we will discuss the rationale for and operation of regional stock exchanges. The second part of the section describes the OTC market, including heavy emphasis on the OTC market in the United States where it is a large and growing part of the total secondary stock market.

Regional Securities Exchanges   Regional exchanges typically have the same operating procedures as the national exchanges in the same countries, but they differ in their listing requirements and the geographic distributions of the listed firms. Regional stock exchanges exist for two main reasons: First, they provide trading facilities for local companies not large enough to qualify for listing on one of the national exchanges. Their listing requirements are typically less stringent than those of the national exchanges, as presented in Table 4.1.

Second, regional exchanges in some countries list firms that also list on one of the national exchanges to give local brokers who are not members of a national exchange access to these securities. As an example, American Telephone & Telegraph and General Motors are listed on both the NYSE and several regional exchanges. This dual listing or the use of unlisted trading privileges (UTP) allows a local brokerage firm that is not large enough to purchase a membership on the NYSE to buy and sell shares of a dual-listed stock (such as General Motors) without going through the NYSE and giving up part of the commission. The regional exchanges in the United States are:

♦ Chicago Stock Exchange
♦ Pacific Stock Exchange (San Francisco–Los Angeles)
♦ Philadelphia Exchange (merger proposed with AMEX/NASDAQ)
♦ Boston Stock Exchange
♦ Cincinnati Stock Exchange

The Chicago, Pacific, and PBW exchanges account for about 90 percent of all regional exchange volume. In turn, total regional exchange volume is 9 to 10 percent of total exchange volume in the United States.

In Japan, seven regional stock exchanges supplement the Tokyo Stock Exchange. The exchange in Osaka accounts for about 10 percent and that in Nagoya for about 2.3 percent of the total volume. The remaining exchanges in Kyoto, Hiroshima, Fukuoto, Niigata, and Sapporo together account for less than 1 percent of volume.

The United Kingdom has one stock exchange in London with operating units in seven cities, including Dublin, Belfast, Birmingham, Manchester, Bristol, Liverpool, and Glasgow. Germany has eight stock exchanges, including its national exchange in Frankfurt where approximately 50 percent of the trading occurs. There are regional exchanges in Düsseldorf, Munich, Hamburg, Berlin, Stuttgart, Hanover, and Bremen.[21]

Without belaboring the point, each country typically has one national exchange that accounts for the majority of trading and several regional exchanges that have less strin-

---

[21]As noted, the largest three exchanges have merged, which has created an exchange encompassing more than 80 percent of total volume. Recently a similar idea has been proposed in the U.S. Greg Ip, "Superregional Exchange is a Bold Idea," *Wall Street Journal,* July 15, 1998, C1, C18.

Table 4.4   *Number of Companies and Issues Trading on NASDAQ: 1980–1997*

Year	Number of Companies	Number of Issues
1980	2,894	3,050
1985	4,136	4,784
1990	4,132	4,706
1991	4,094	4,684
1992	4,113	4,764
1993	4,611	5,393
1994	4,902	5,761
1995	5,122	5,955
1996	5,556	6,384
1997	5,487	6,208

Source: *NASDAQ Fact Book* (Washington, DC: National Association of Securities Dealers, 1998), 5.

gent listing requirements to allow trading in smaller firms. Recently, several national exchanges have created second-tier markets that are divisions of the national exchanges to allow smaller firms to be traded as part of the national exchanges.[22] In general, the fortunes of the regional exchanges have fluctuated substantially over time, based on interest in small, young firms and institutional interest in dual-listed stocks.

Over-the-Counter (OTC) Market   The over-the-counter (OTC) market includes trading in all stocks not listed on one of the exchanges. It can also include trading in listed stocks, which is referred to as the *third market,* and is discussed in the following section. The OTC market is not a formal organization with membership requirements or a specific list of stocks deemed eligible for trading.[23] In theory, any security can be traded on the OTC market as long as a registered dealer is willing to make a market in the security (willing to buy and sell shares of the stock).

Size of the OTC market   The U.S. OTC market is the largest segment of the U.S. secondary market in terms of the number of issues traded. It is also the most diverse in terms of quality. As noted earlier, about 3,500 issues are traded on the NYSE and about 900 issues on the AMEX. In contrast, almost 5,000 issues are actively traded on the OTC market's NASDAQ National Market System (NMS).[24] Another 1,000 stocks are traded on the NASDAQ system independent of the NMS. Finally, 1,000 OTC stocks are regularly quoted in the *Wall Street Journal* but not in the NASDAQ system. Therefore, a total of almost 7,000 issues are traded on the OTC market—substantially more than on the NYSE and AMEX combined.

Table 4.4 sets forth the growth in the number of companies and issues on NASDAQ. The growth in average daily trading is shown in Table 4.2 relative to some national exchanges. As of the end of 1997, 470 issues on NASDAQ were either foreign stocks or American Depository Receipts (ADRs). Trading in foreign stocks and ADRs represented over 5 percent of total NASDAQ share volume in 1997. About 300 of these issues trade on both NASDAQ and a foreign exchange such as Toronto. In 1988, NASDAQ developed a link with the Singapore Stock Exchange that allows twenty-four-hour trading from NASDAQ in New York to Singapore to a NASDAQ/London link and back to New York.

---

[22]An example of these second-tier markets is the Second Section on the TSE and the Unlisted Stock Market (USM) on the LSE. In both cases, the exchange is attempting to provide trading facilities for smaller firms without changing their listing requirements for the national exchange.

[23]The requirements of trading on different segments of the OTC trading system will be discussed later in this section.

[24]NASDAQ is an acronym for National Association of Securities Dealers Automated Quotations. The system is discussed in detail in a later section. To be traded on the NMS, a firm must have a certain size and trading activity and at least four market makers. A specification of requirements for various components of the NASDAQ system is contained in Table 4.5.

Although the OTC market has the greatest number of issues, the NYSE has a larger total value of trading. In 1997 the approximate value of equity trading on the NYSE was about $5,700 billion, and NASDAQ was about $3,500 billion. Notably, the NASDAQ value exceeded what transpired on the LSE ($700 billion) and on the TSE ($873 billion).

There is tremendous diversity in the OTC market because it imposes no minimum requirements. Stocks that trade on the OTC range from those of small, unprofitable companies to large, extremely profitable firms (such as Microsoft, Intel). On the upper end, all U.S. government bonds are traded on the OTC market as are the majority of bank and insurance stocks. Finally, about 100 exchange-listed stocks are traded on the OTC—the third market.

Merger of AMEX, NASDAQ, and Philadelphia Exchange In March, 1998, it was announced that the AMEX would be merged into the NASDAQ organization to create a combination auction exchange and dealer market. The merger was approved by both boards and was to be completed by the end of 1998. In June 1998 the Philadelphia Stock Exchange agreed to join the NASDAQ and the AMEX. This was followed by proposals for alliances between the London and Frankfurt Exchanges and then the Chicago Board Options Exchange and Pacific Exchange.[25]

Operation of the OTC As noted, any stock can be traded on the OTC as long as someone indicates a willingness to make a market whereby the party buys or sells for his or her own account acting as a dealer.[26] This differs from most transactions on the listed exchanges, where some members keep the book and as brokers attempt to match buy and sell orders. Therefore, the OTC market is referred to as a *negotiated market,* in which investors directly negotiate with dealers.

Unlisted Securities Market (USM) The Unlisted Securities Market (USM) was started by the LSE in 1980 to handle smaller companies that lack sufficiently long trading records for full listing. The USM was established and supervised by the LSE. Because of low volume the market was disbanded in 1993. The stocks on this market either were listed on the main exchange (LSE) or became part of a bulletin board market without market makers.[27]

The NASDAQ System *The National Association of Securities Dealers Automated Quotation (NASDAQ)* system is an automated, electronic quotation system for the vast OTC market. Any number of dealers can elect to make markets in an OTC stock. The actual number depends on the activity in the stock. The average number of market makers for all stocks on the NASDAQ system was 10.7 in 1997, according to the *NASDAQ Fact Book.*

NASDAQ makes all dealer quotes available immediately. The broker can check the quotation machine and call the dealer with the best market, verify that the quote has not changed, and make the sale or purchase. The NASDAQ system has three levels to serve firms with different needs and interests.

Level 1 provides a single median representative quote for the stocks on NASDAQ. This quote system is for firms that want current quotes on OTC stocks but do not consistently buy or sell OTC stocks for their customers and are not market makers. This composite quote changes constantly to adjust for any changes by individual market makers.

Level 2 provides instantaneous current quotations on NASDAQ stocks by all market makers in a stock. This quotation system is for firms that consistently trade OTC stocks.

---

[25]Greg Ip, "AMEX/NASDAQ Merger to Trigger an Electronic Facelift," *Wall Street Journal,* June 3, 1998, C1, C25; Greg Ip, "Philadelphia Exchange to Join NASDAQ, AMEX," *Wall Street Journal,* June 10, 1998, C1, C23, and Greg Ip, "Mergers of Markets May Mean Trading Will Be Cheaper, Speedier, and Easier," *Wall Street Journal,* July 14, 1998, C1, C13.

[26]*Dealer* and *market maker* are synonymous.

[27]The bulletin board would be a broker market.

Given an order to buy or sell, brokers check the quotation machine, call the market maker with the best market for their purposes (highest bid if they are selling, lowest offer if buying), and consummate the deal.

Level 3 is for OTC market makers. Such firms want Level 2, but they also need the capability to change their own quotations, which Level 3 provides.

Listing requirements for NASDAQ   Quotes and trading volume for the OTC market are reported in two lists: a National Market System (NMS) list and a regular NASDAQ list. As of 1998, there were four sets of listing requirements. The first, for initial listing on any NASDAQ system, is the least stringent. The second is for automatic (mandatory) inclusion on the NASDAQ/NMS system. For stocks on this system, reports include up-to-the-minute volume and last-sale information for the competing market makers as well as end-of-the-day information on total volume and high, low, and closing prices. In addition, two sets of criteria govern voluntary participation on the NMS by companies with different characteristics. Alternative 1 accommodates companies with limited assets or net worth but substantial earnings; Alternative 2 is for large companies that are not necessarily as profitable. The four sets of criteria are set forth in Table 4.5.

A sample trade   Assume you are considering the purchase of 100 shares of Intel. Although Intel is large enough and profitable enough to be listed on a national exchange, the company has never applied for listing because it enjoys an active market on the OTC. (It is one of the volume leaders with daily volume typically above 1 million shares and often in excess of 5 million shares.) When you contact your broker, he or she will consult the NASDAQ electronic quotation machine to determine the current dealer quotations for INTC, the trading symbol for Intel.[28] The quote machine will show that about 35 dealers are making a market in INTC. An example of differing quotations might be as follows:

Dealer	Bid	Ask
1	$85\frac{1}{2}$	$85\frac{3}{4}$
2	$85\frac{3}{8}$	$85\frac{5}{8}$
3	$85\frac{1}{4}$	$85\frac{5}{8}$
4	$85\frac{3}{8}$	$85\frac{3}{4}$

Assuming these are the best markets available from the total group, your broker would call either Dealer 2 or Dealer 3 because they have the lowest offering prices. After verifying the quote, your broker would give one of these dealers an order to buy 100 shares of INTC at $85\frac{5}{8}$ ($85.625 a share). Because your firm was not a market maker in the stock, the firm would act as a broker and charge you $8,562.50 plus a commission for the trade. If your firm had been a market maker in INTC, with an asking price of $85\frac{5}{8}$, the firm would have sold the stock to you at $85\frac{5}{8}$ net (without commission). If you had been interested in selling 100 shares of Intel instead of buying, the broker would have contacted Dealer 1, who made the highest bid.

Changing dealer inventory   Let us consider the price quotations by an OTC dealer who wants to change his or her inventory on a given stock. For example, assume Dealer 4, with a current quote of $85\frac{3}{8}$ bid–$85\frac{3}{4}$ ask, decides to increase his or her holdings of INTC. The NASDAQ quotes indicate that the highest bid is currently $85\frac{1}{2}$. Increasing the bid to $85\frac{1}{2}$ would bring some of the business currently going to Dealer 1. Taking a more aggressive action, the dealer might raise the bid to $85\frac{5}{8}$ and buy all the stock offered, including some from Dealers 2 and 3, who are offering it at $85\frac{5}{8}$. In this example, the dealer raises the bid

---

[28]Trading symbols are one- to four-letter codes used to designate stocks. Whenever a trade is reported on a stock ticker, the trading symbol appears with the figures. Many symbols are obvious, such as GM (General Motors), F (Ford Motors), GE (General Electric), and T (American Telephone & Telegraph).

Table 4.5A   *NASDAQ National Market Quantitative Standards*

Standard	Alternative 1	Initial NASDAQ National Market Listing Alternative 2	Continued NASDAQ National Market Inclusion
Registration under Section 12(g) of the Securities Exchange Act of 1934 or Equivalent	Yes	Yes	Yes
Net Tangible Assets[a]	$4 million	$12 million	$1 million[b]
Net Income (In Last Fiscal Year or Two of Last Three Fiscal Years)	$400,000	—	—
Pretax Income (In Last Fiscal Year or Two of Last Three Fiscal Years)	$750,000	—	—
Public Float (Shares)[c]	500,000	1 million	200,000
Operating History	—	3 years	—
Market Value of Float	$3 million	$15 million	$1 million
Minimum Bid Per Share	$5	$3	$1[d]
Shareholders			
—if between 0.5 and 1 million shares publicly held	800	400	400[e] —
—if more than 1 million shares publicly held	400	400	—
—if more than 0.5 million shares publicly held and average daily volume in excess of 2,000 shares	400	400	—
Number of Market Makers	2	2	2

a. "Net Tangible Assets" means total assets (excluding goodwill) minus total liabilities.

b. Continued NASDAQ National Market inclusion requires net tangible assets of at least $2 million if the issuer has sustained losses from continuing operations and/or net losses in two of its three most recent fiscal years or $4 million if the issuer has sustained losses from the continuing operations and/or net losses in three of its four most recent fiscal years.

c. Public float is defined as shares that are not "held directly or indirectly by any officer or director of the issuer and by any person who is the beneficial owner of more than 10 percent of the total shares outstanding. . . ."

d. Or, in alternative, market value of public float of $3 million and $4 million of net tangible assets.

e. Or 300 shareholders of round lots.

Table 4.5B   *Quantitative Standards for Domestic Stocks in the NASDAQ SmallCap Market*

Initial Listing		Continued Listing	
Registration under Section 12(g) of The Securities Exchange Act of 1934 or Equivalent	Yes	Registration under Section 12(g) of The Securities Exchange Act of 1934 or Equivalent	Yes
Total Assets	$4 million	Total Assets	$2 million
Capital and Surplus	$2 million	Capital and Surplus	$1 million
Public Float (Shares)	100,000	Public Float (Shares)	100,000
Market Value of Public Float	$1 million	Market Value of Public Float	$200,000[a]
Market Makers	2[a]	Market Makers	2[a]
Bid Price Per Share	$3	Bid Price Per Share	$1[a,b]
Shareholders	300	Shareholders	300

Note: All amendments to entry and maintenance requirements also apply to non-Canadian foreign and American Depositary Receipts, except for amended entry and maintenance requirements for price per share and market value of public float.

a. A deficiency in the maintenance criteria for market value of public float, market makers, and bid price will be determined if the issuer fails any of these requirements for 10 consecutive days. If failure of any of the 10-day tests occur, the issuer will be notified promptly and will be given 30 calendar days to comply with the market-maker criteria and 90 calendar days to comply with the bid price or market value of public float requirements.

b. The rule allows issuers that fail to meet the minimum bid price requirement to continue to qualify if they continue to meet the $1 million market value of public float and $2 million in capital and surplus requirements.

Source: *The NASDAQ Stock Market Fact Book* (Washington, DC, 1997), pp. 51, 212.

price but does not change the asking price, which was above those of Dealers 2 and 3. This dealer will buy stock but probably will not sell any. A dealer who had excess stock would keep the bid below the market (lower than $85\frac{1}{2}$) and reduce the asking price to $85\frac{5}{8}$ or less. Dealers constantly change their bid and ask prices or both, depending on their current inventories or changes in the outlook based on new information for the stock.[29]

Third Market   As mentioned, the term **third market** describes over-the-counter trading of shares listed on an exchange. Although most transactions in listed stocks take place on an exchange, an investment firm that is not a member of an exchange can make a market in a listed stock. Most of the trading on the third market is in well-known stocks such as AT&T, IBM, and Xerox. The success or failure of the third market depends on whether the OTC market in these stocks is as good as the exchange market and whether the relative cost of the OTC transaction compares favorably with the cost on the exchange. This market is critical during the relatively few periods when trading is not available on the NYSE either because trading is suspended or the exchange is closed.[30]

Fourth Market   The term **fourth market** describes direct trading of securities between two parties with no broker intermediary. In almost all cases, both parties involved are institutions. When you think about it, a direct transaction is really not that unusual. If you own 100 shares of AT&T Corp. and decide to sell it, there is nothing wrong with simply offering it to your friends or associates at a mutually agreeable price (for example, based on exchange transactions) and making the transaction directly.

Investors typically buy or sell stock through brokers because it is faster and easier. Also, you would expect to get a better price for your stock because the broker has a good chance of finding the best buyer. You are willing to pay a commission for these liquidity services. The fourth market evolved because of the substantial fees charged by brokers to institutions with large orders. At some point, it becomes worthwhile for institutions to attempt to deal directly with each other and bypass the brokerage fees. Assume an institution decides to sell 100,000 shares of AT&T, which is selling for about $65 per share, for a total value of $6.5 million. The average commission on such a transaction prior to the advent of negotiated rates in 1975 was about 1 percent of the value of the trade, or about $65,000. This cost made it attractive for a selling institution to spend some time and effort finding another institution interested in increasing its holdings of AT&T and negotiating a direct sale. Currently, such transactions cost about 5 cents per share, which implies a cost of $5,000 for the 100,000 share transactions. This is lower, but still not trivial. Because of the diverse nature of the fourth market and the lack of reporting requirements, no data are available regarding its specific size or growth.

DETAILED ANALYSIS OF EXCHANGE MARKETS

The importance of listed exchange markets requires that we discuss them at some length. In this section, we discuss several types of membership on the exchanges, the major types of orders, and the role and function of exchange market makers—a critical component of a good exchange market.

---

[29]Some studies have examined the determinants of dealers' bid–ask spreads, including H. R. Stoll, "Inferring the Components of the Bid–Ask Spread: Theory and Empirical Tests," *Journal of Finance* 44, no. 1 (March 1989): 115–134.

[30]Craig Torres, "Third Market Trading Crowds Stock Exchanges," *Wall Street Journal,* March 8, 1990, C1, C9. For an analysis of the effect of this trading, see Robert H. Battalio, "Third-Market Broker-Dealers: Cost Competitors or Cream Skimmers," *Journal of Finance* 52, no. 1 (March 1997), 341–352.

Exchange Membership

Listed U.S. securities exchanges typically offer four major categories of membership: (1) specialist, (2) commission broker, (3) floor broker, and (4) registered trader. Specialists (or exchange market makers), who constitute about 25 percent of the total membership on exchanges, will be discussed after a description of types of orders.

Commission brokers are employees of a member firm who buy or sell for the customers of the firm. When you place an order to buy or sell stock through a brokerage firm that is a member of the exchange, in many instances the firm contacts its commission broker on the floor of the exchange. That broker goes to the appropriate post on the floor and buys or sells the stock as instructed.

Floor brokers are independent members of an exchange who act as brokers for other members. As an example, when commission brokers for Merrill Lynch become too busy to handle all of their orders, they will ask one of the floor brokers to help them. At one time, these people were referred to as *$2 brokers* because that is what they received for each order. Currently, they receive about $4 per 100-share order.[31]

Registered traders are allowed to use their memberships to buy and sell for their own accounts. They therefore save commissions on their own trading, and observers believe they have an advantage because they are on the trading floor. The exchanges and others are willing to allow these advantages because these traders provide the market with added liquidity, but regulations limit how they trade and how many registered traders can be in a trading crowd around a specialist's booth at any time. In recent years, registered traders have become **registered competitive market makers (RCMMs)**, who have specific trading obligations set by the exchange. Their activity is reported as part of the specialist group.[32]

Types of Orders

It is important to understand the different types of orders entered by investors and the specialist as a dealer.

Market Orders   The most frequent type of order is a **market order**, an order to buy or sell a stock at the best current price. An investor who enters a market sell order indicates a willingness to sell immediately at the highest bid available at the time the order reaches the specialist on the exchange or an OTC dealer. A market buy order indicates that the investor is willing to pay the lowest offering price available at the time the order reaches the floor of the exchange or an OTC dealer. Market orders provide immediate liquidity for someone willing to accept the prevailing market price.

Assume you are interested in General Electric (GE) and you call your broker to find out the current "market" on the stock. The quotation machine indicates that the prevailing market is 75 bid–75¼ ask. This means that the highest current bid on the books of the specialist is 75; that is, $75 is the most that anyone has offered to pay for GE. The lowest offer is 75¼; that is, the lowest price anyone is willing to accept to sell the stock. If you placed a market buy order for 100 shares, you would buy 100 shares at $75.25 a

---

[31]These brokers received some unwanted notoriety in 1998: Dean Starkman and Patrick McGeehan, "Floor Brokers on Big Board Charged in Scheme," *Wall Street Journal,* February 26, 1998, C1, C21; and Suzanna McGee, " '$2 Brokers' Worried About Notoriety from Charges of Illegal Trading Scheme," *Wall Street Journal,* March 5, 1998, C1, C22.

[32]Prior to the late 1970s, there also were odd-lot dealers who bought and sold to individuals with orders for less than round lots (usually 100 shares). Currently, this function is handled by either the specialist or some large brokerage firm.

share (the lowest ask price) for a total cost of $7,525 plus commission. If you submitted a market sell order for 100 shares, you would sell the shares at $75 each and receive $7,500 less commission.

Limit Orders The individual placing a **limit order** specifies the buy or sell price. You might submit a bid to purchase 100 shares of Coca-Cola stock at $65 a share when the current market is 70 bid–70$\frac{1}{4}$ ask, with the expectation that the stock will decline to $65 in the near future.

You must also indicate how long the limit order will be outstanding. Alternative time specifications are basically boundless. A limit order can be instantaneous ("fill or kill," meaning fill the order instantly or cancel it). It can also be good for part of a day, a full day, several days, a week, or a month. It can also be open-ended, or good until canceled (GTC).

Rather than wait for a given price on a stock, your broker will give the limit order to the specialist, who will put it in a limit-order book and act as the broker's representative. When and if the market reaches the limit-order price, the specialist will execute the order and inform your broker. The specialist receives a small part of the commission for rendering this service.

Short Sales Most investors purchase stock ("go long") expecting to derive their return from an increase in value. If you believe that a stock is overpriced, however, and want to take advantage of an expected decline in the price, you can sell the stock short. A **short sale** is the sale of stock that you do not own with the intent of purchasing it back later at a lower price. Specifically, you would borrow the stock from another investor through your broker, sell it in the market, and subsequently replace it at (you hope) a price lower than the price at which you sold it. The investor who lent the stock has the proceeds of the sale as collateral. In turn, this investor can invest these funds in short-term, risk-free securities. Although a short sale has no time limit, the lender of the shares can decide to sell the shares, in which case your broker must find another investor willing to lend the shares.[33]

Three technical points affect short sales. First, a short sale can be made only on an *uptick trade,* meaning the price of the short sale must be higher than the last trade price. This is because the exchanges do not want traders to force a profit on a short sale by pushing the price down through continually selling short. Therefore, the transaction price for a short sale must be an uptick or, without any change in price, the previous price must have been higher than its previous price (a zero uptick). For an example of a zero uptick, consider the following set of transaction prices: 42, 42$\frac{1}{4}$, 42$\frac{1}{4}$. You could sell short at 42$\frac{1}{4}$ even though it is no change from the previous trade at 42$\frac{1}{4}$ because that trade was an uptick trade.

The second technical point concerns dividends. The short seller must pay any dividends due to the investor who lent the stock. The purchaser of the short-sale stock receives the dividend from the corporation, so the short seller must pay a similar dividend to the lender.

A final point is that short sellers must post the same margin as an investor who had acquired stock. This margin can be in any unrestricted securities owned by the short seller.

Special Orders In addition to these general orders, there are several special types of orders. A *stop loss order* is a conditional market order whereby the investor directs the sale of a stock if it drops to a given price. Assume you buy a stock at 50 and expect it to go up. If you are wrong, you want to limit your losses. To protect yourself, you could put

[33]For a discussion of profitable short-selling results, see Gary Putka, "Fortune Smiles on Short Side of Market," *Wall Street Journal,* October 27, 1987, 5; negative results are highlighted in William Power, "Short Sellers Take It on the Chin Again," *Wall Street Journal,* June 29, 1993, C1, C2; and William Power, "Short Sellers Set to Catch Tumbling Overvalued Stocks," *Wall Street Journal,* December 28, 1993, C1, C2. For a further discussion of short-selling events, see Carol J. Loomis, "Short Sellers and the Seamy Side of Wall Street," *Fortune,* July 22, 1996, pp. 66–72; and Gary Weiss, "The Secret World of Short Sellers," *Business Week,* August 5, 1996, pp. 62–68.

Figure 4.1   *Borrowing against Stocks—Amount of Margin Credit Extended by Brokers and Dealers at End of Month ($ Billions)*

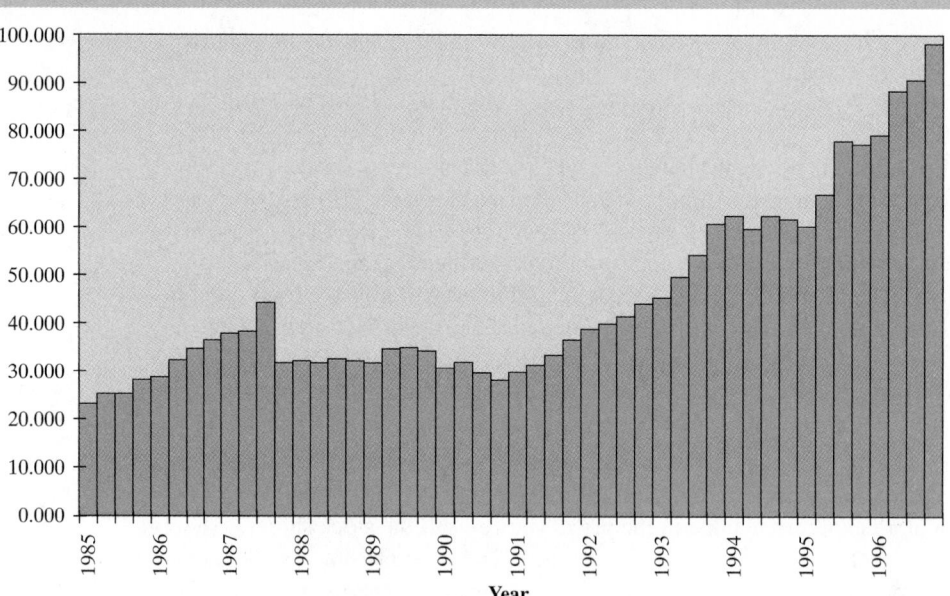

in a stop loss order at 45. In this case, if the stock dropped to 45, your stop loss order would become a market sell order, and the stock would be sold at the prevailing market price. The stop loss order does not guarantee that you will get the $45; you can get a little bit more or a little bit less. Because of the possibility of market disruption caused by a large number of stop loss orders, exchanges have, on occasion, canceled all such orders on certain stocks and not allowed brokers to accept further stop loss orders on those issues.

A related type of stop loss tactic for short sales is a *stop buy order.* An investor who has sold stock short and wants to minimize any loss if the stock begins to increase in value would enter this conditional buy order at a price above that at which the investor sold the stock short. Assume you sold a stock short at 50, expecting it to decline to 40. To protect yourself from an increase, you could put in a stop buy order to purchase the stock using a market buy order if it reached a price of 55. This conditional buy order would hopefully limit any loss on the short sale to approximately $5 a share.

Margin Transactions   On any type of order, an investor can pay for the stock with cash or borrow part of the cost, leveraging the transaction. Leverage is accomplished by buying on **margin,** which means the investor pays for the stock with some cash and borrows the rest through the broker, putting up the stock for collateral.

As shown in Figure 4.1, the dollar amount of margin credit extended by members of the NYSE has increased consistently since 1991 and reached record levels in 1997. The interest rate charged on these loans by the investment firms is typically 1.50 percent above the rate charged by the bank making the loan. The bank rate, referred to as the *call money rate,* is generally about 1 percent below the prime rate. For example, in August 1998, the prime rate was 8.50 percent, and the call money rate was 7.25 percent.

Federal Reserve Board Regulations T and U determine the maximum proportion of any transaction that can be borrowed. These regulations were enacted during the 1930s because of the contention that the excessive credit extended for stock acquisition con-

tributed to the stock market collapse of 1929. Since the enactment of the regulations, this *margin requirement* (the proportion of total transaction value that must be paid in cash) has varied from 40 percent (allowing loans of 60 percent of the value) to 100 percent (allowing no borrowing). As of September 1998, the initial margin requirement specified by the Federal Reserve was 50 percent, although individual investment firms can require higher rates.

After the initial purchase, changes in the market price of the stock will cause changes in the *investor's equity,* which is equal to the market value of the collateral stock minus the amount borrowed. Obviously, if the stock price increases, the investor's equity as a proportion of the total market value of the stock increases, that is, the investor's margin will exceed the initial margin requirement.

Assume you acquired 200 shares of a $50 stock for a total cost of $10,000. A 50 percent initial margin requirement allowed you to borrow $5,000, making your initial equity $5,000. If the stock price increases by 20 percent to $60 a share, the total market value of your position is $12,000, and your equity is now $7,000, or 58 percent ($7,000/$12,000). In contrast, if the stock price declines by 20 percent to $40 a share, the total market value would be $8,000, and your investor's equity would be $3,000, or 37.5 percent ($3,000/$8,000).

This example demonstrates that buying on margin provides all the advantages and the disadvantages of leverage. Lower margin requirements allow you to borrow more, increasing the percentage of gain or loss on your investment when the stock price increases or decreases. The leverage factor equals 1/percent margin. Thus, as in the example, if the margin is 50 percent, the leverage factor is 2, that is, 1/.50. Therefore, when the rate of return on the stock is plus or minus 10 percent, the return on your equity is plus or minus 20 percent. If the margin declines to 33 percent, you can borrow more (67 percent), and the leverage factor is 3(1/.33). When you acquire stock or other investments on margin, you are increasing the financial risk of the investment beyond the risk inherent in the security itself. You should increase your required rate of return accordingly.[34]

The following example shows how borrowing by using margin affects the distribution of your returns before commissions and interest on the loan. When the stock increased by 20 percent, your return on the investment was as follows:

1.   The market value of the stock is $12,000, which leaves you with $7,000 after you pay off the loan.
2.   The return on your $5,000 investment is:

$$\frac{7,000}{5,000} - 1 = 1.40 - 1$$

$$= 0.40 = 40\%$$

In contrast, if the stock declined by 20 percent to $40 a share, your return would be as follows:

1.   The market value of the stock is $8,000, which leaves you with $3,000 after you pay off the loan.
2.   The return on your $5,000 investment is:

[34]For a discussion of margin calls following market declines in 1987 and 1990, see Karen Slater, "Margin Calls Create Dilemma for Investors," *Wall Street Journal,* October 23, 1987, 21; William Power, "Stocks' Drop Spurs Margin Calls Less Severe than in Earlier Falls," *Wall Street Journal,* August 15, 1990, C1. For a discussion of the investment environment in 1993, see Michael Siconolfi, "Does Margin-Loan Binge Signal Stock-Market Top?" *Wall Street Journal,* April 23, 1993, C1, C16.

$$\frac{3{,}000}{5{,}000} - 1 = 0.60 - 1$$

$$= -0.40 = -40\%$$

You should also recognize that this symmetrical increase in gains and losses is only true prior to commissions and interest. Obviously, if we assume a 6 percent interest on the borrowed funds (which would be $5,000 \times .06 = 300) and a $100 commission on the transaction, the results would indicate a lower increase and a larger negative return as follows:

$$20\% \text{ increase:} \frac{\$12{,}000 - \$5{,}000 - \$300 - \$100}{5{,}000} - 1$$

$$= \frac{6{,}600}{5{,}000} = -1$$

$$= 0.32 = 32\%$$

$$20\% \text{ decline:} \frac{\$8{,}000 - \$5{,}000 - \$300 - \$100}{5{,}000} - 1$$

$$= \frac{2{,}600}{5{,}000} = -1$$

$$= -0.48 = -48\%$$

In addition to the initial margin requirement, another important concept is the **maintenance margin**, which is the required proportion of your equity to the total value of the stock; the maintenance margin protects the broker if the stock price declines. At present, the minimum maintenance margin specified by the Federal Reserve is 25 percent, but, again, individual brokerage firms can dictate higher margins for their customers. If the stock price declines to the point where your equity drops below 25 percent of the total value of the position, the account is considered undermargined, and you will receive a **margin call** to provide more equity. If you do not respond with the required funds in time, the stock will be sold to pay off the loan. The time allowed to meet a margin call varies between investment firms and is affected by margin conditions. Under volatile conditions, the time allowed to respond to a margin call can be shortened drastically.

Given a maintenance margin of 25 percent, when you buy on margin you must consider how far the stock price can fall before you receive a margin call. The computation for our example is as follows: If the price of the stock is P and you own 200 shares, the value of the position is 200P and the equity in the account is $200P - $5,000$. The percentage margin is $(200P - 5{,}000)/200P$. To determine the price, P, that is equal to 25 percent (0.25), we use the equation:

$$\frac{200P - \$5{,}000}{200P} = 0.25$$

$$200P - 5{,}000 = 50P$$
$$P = \$33.33$$

Therefore, when the stock is at $33.33, the equity value is exactly 25 percent; so if the stock goes below $33.33, the investor will receive a margin call.

To continue the previous example, if the stock declines to $30 a share, its total market value would be $6,000 and your equity would be $1,000, which is only about 17 percent of the total value ($1,000/$6,000). You would receive a margin call for approximately

$667, which would give you equity of $1,667, or 25 percent of the total value of the account ($1,667/$6,667).[35]

Exchange Market Makers

Now that we have discussed the overall structure of the exchange markets and the orders that are used to buy and sell stocks, we can discuss the role and function of the market makers on the exchange. These people and the role they play differ among exchanges. For example, on U.S. exchanges these people are called *specialists;* on the TSE they are a combination of the *Saitori* and regular members. Most exchanges do not have a single market maker but have competing dealers. On exchanges that have central market makers, these individuals are critical to the smooth and efficient functioning of these markets.

As noted, a major requirement for a good market is liquidity, which depends on how the market makers do their job. Our initial discussion centers on the specialist's role in U.S. markets, followed by a consideration of comparable roles on exchanges in other countries.

U.S. Markets   The specialist is a member of the exchange who applies to the exchange to be assigned stocks to handle.[36] The typical specialist will handle about fifteen stocks. The capital requirement for specialists changed in April 1988 in response to the October 1987 market crash. Specifically, the minimum capital required of each specialist unit was raised to $1 million or the value of 15,000 shares of each stock assigned, whichever is greater.

Functions of the specialist   Specialists have two major functions. First, they serve as *brokers* to match buy and sell orders and to handle special limit orders placed with member brokers. An individual broker who receives a limit order (or stop loss or stop buy order) leaves it with the specialist, who executes it when the specified price occurs. For this service, the specialist receives a portion of the broker's commission on the trade.

The second major function of a specialist is to act as a *dealer* to maintain a fair and orderly market by providing liquidity when the normal flow of orders is not adequate. In this capacity, the specialist must buy and sell for his or her own account (like an OTC dealer) when public supply or demand is insufficient to provide a continuous, liquid market.

Consider the following example. If a stock is currently selling for about $40 per share, the current bid and ask in an auction market (without the intervention of the specialist) might be a 40 bid–41 ask. Under such conditions, random market buy and sell orders might cause the stock price to fluctuate between 40 and 41 constantly—a movement of 2.5 percent between trades. Most investors would probably consider such a price pattern too volatile; the market would not be considered continuous. Under such conditions, the specialist is expected to provide "bridge liquidity" by entering alternative bids and asks or both to narrow the spread and improve the stock's price continuity. In this example, the specialist could enter a bid of $40\frac{1}{2}$ or $40\frac{3}{4}$ or an ask of $40\frac{1}{2}$ or $40\frac{1}{4}$ to narrow the spread to one-half or one-quarter point.

Specialists can enter either side of the market, depending on several factors, including the trend of the market. They are expected to buy or sell against the market when prices are clearly moving in one direction. Specifically, they are required to buy stock for

[35]For a further discussion, see Georgette Jasen, "Cheap Margin Loans Are Tempting, but Beware," *Wall Street Journal,* April 23, 1993, C1, C21.

[36]Each stock is assigned to one specialist. Most specialists are part of a unit that can be a formal organization of specialists (a specialist firm) or a set of independent specialists who join together to spread the work load and the risk of the stocks assigned to the unit. At the end of 1997, a total of 479 individual specialists made up 53 specialist units (about 9 specialists per unit).

their own inventories when there is an excess of sell orders and the market is definitely declining. Alternatively, they must sell stock from their inventories or sell it short to accommodate an excess of buy orders when the market is rising. Specialists are not expected to prevent prices from rising or declining, but only to ensure that the prices change in an orderly fashion (that is, to maintain price continuity). Evidence that they have fulfilled this requirement is that during recent years NYSE stocks traded unchanged from, or within one-eighth point of, the price of the previous trade about 95 percent of the time.

Another factor affecting a specialists' decision on how to narrow the spread is their current inventory position in the stock. For example, if they have large inventories of a given stock, all other factors being equal, they would probably enter on the ask (sell) side to reduce these heavy inventories. In contrast, specialists who have little or no inventory of shares because they had been selling from their inventories, or selling short, would tend toward the bid (buy) side of the market to rebuild their inventories or close out their short positions.

Finally, the position of the limit order book will influence how they act. Numerous limit buy orders (bids) close to the current market and few limit sell orders (asks) might indicate a tendency toward higher prices because demand is apparently heavy and supply is limited. Under such conditions, a specialist who is not bound by one of the other factors would probably opt to accumulate stock in anticipation of a price increase. The specialists on the NYSE have historically participated as dealers in 10 to 12 percent of all trades.

Specialist income   The specialist derives income from the broker and the dealer functions. The actual breakdown between the two sources depends on the specific stock. In an actively traded stock such as IBM, a specialist has little need to act as a dealer because the substantial public interest in the stock creates a tight market (that is, a small bid–ask spread). In such a case, the main source of income would come from maintaining the limit orders for the stock. The income derived from acting as a broker for a stock such as IBM can be substantial and it is basically without risk.

In contrast, a stock with low trading volume and substantial price volatility would probably have a fairly wide bid–ask spread, and the specialist would have to be an active dealer. The specialist's income from such a stock would depend on his or her ability to trade it profitably. Specialists have a major advantage when trading because of their limit order books. Officially, only specialists are supposed to see the limit order book, which means that they would have a monopoly on very important information regarding the current supply and demand for a stock. The fact is that currently the specialists routinely share the limit order book with other brokers, so it is not a competitive advantage.[37]

Most specialists attempt to balance their portfolios between strong broker stocks that provide steady, riskless income and stocks that require active dealer roles. Notably, following the October 1987 market crash, specialists were required to increase their capital positions substantially, which would reduce their return on investment.[38]

---

[37]For evidence that the specialists do not fare too badly when they trade against the market, see Frank K. Reilly and Eugene F. Drzycimski, "The Stock Exchange Specialist and the Market Impact of Major World Events," *Financial Analysts Journal* 31, no. 4 (July–August 1975): 27–32. Also, if a major imbalance in trading arises due to new information, the specialist can request a temporary suspension of trading. For an analysis of what occurs during these trading suspensions, see Michael H. Hopewell and Arthur L. Schwartz, Jr., "Temporary Trading Suspensions in Individual NYSE Securities," *Journal of Finance* 33, no. 5 (December 1978): 1355–1373; and Frank J. Fabozzi and Christopher K. Ma, "The Over-the-Counter Market and New York Stock Exchange Trading Halts," *The Financial Review* 23, no. 4 (November 1988): 427–437. An example of a dramatic halt is discussed in Martha Brannigan, "Shares of Policy Management Nose-Dive 43%," *Wall Street Journal*, April 7, 1993, A4.

[38]For a discussion of the problems facing specialists, see Edward A. Wyatt, "Eye of the Hurricane," *Barron's*, February 19, 1990, 28. For a rigorous analysis of specialist trading, see Ananth Madhaven and George Sofianos, "An Empirical Analysis of NYSE Specialist Trading," *Journal of Financial Economics* 48, no. 2 (May 1998): 189–210.

Tokyo Stock Exchange (TSE)   As of 1997, the TSE has a total of 124 "regular members" (100 Japanese members and 24 foreign members) and 1 *Saitori* member (4 *Saitori* firms merged during 1992). For each membership, the firm is allowed several people on the floor of the exchange, depending on its trading volume and capital position (the average number of employees on the floor is 20 per firm for a regular member and about 300 employees for the *Saitori* member). The employees of a regular member are called *trading clerks,* and the employees of the *Saitori* member are called *intermediary clerks.*

Regular members buy and sell securities on the TSE either as agents or principals (brokers or dealers). *Saitori* members specialize in acting as intermediaries (brokers) for transactions among regular members, and they maintain the books for limit orders. (Stop loss and stop buy orders as well as short selling are not allowed.) Therefore, *Saitori* members have some of the characteristics of the U.S. exchange specialists, because they match buy and sell orders for customers, handle limit orders, and are not allowed to deal with public customers. They *differ* from the U.S. exchange specialists because they do not act as dealers to maintain an orderly market. Only regular members are allowed to buy and sell for their own accounts. Therefore, the TSE is a two-way, continuous auction, order-driven market where buy and sell orders directly interact with one another with the *Saitori* acting as the auctioneer (intermediary) between firms submitting the orders.

Also, although there are about 1,700 listed domestic stocks and 100 foreign stocks on the First Section, only the largest 150 stocks are traded on the floor of the exchange. Trading on the floor is enhanced by an electronic system called the Floor Order Routing and Execution System (FORES). This system is designed to: (1) automate order routing for small orders, (2) replace manual order books with electronic order books that can execute orders, and (3) computerize the reporting and confirmation process. All other stocks on the TSE are traded through a computer system called CORES, which stands for Computer-assisted Order Routing and Execution System. With CORES, after an order is entered into the central processing unit, it becomes part of an electronic "book," which is monitored by a S*aitori* member who matches all buy and sell orders on the computer in accordance with trading rules. The system also automatically executes all orders for transactions at the last sale price and provides a narrow bid–ask spread within which orders are executed.

TSE membership is available to corporations licensed by the Minister of Finance. Member applicants may request any of four licenses: (1) to trade securities as a dealer, (2) to trade as a broker, (3) to underwrite new securities on secondary offerings, or (4) to handle retail distribution of new or outstanding securities. A firm may have more than one license, but cannot act as a principal and agent in the same transaction. The minimum capital requirements for these licenses vary from 200 million to 3 billion yen ($2 million to $30 million) depending on the type of license.

Although Japan's securities laws allow foreign securities firms to obtain membership on the exchanges, the individual exchanges determine whether membership will be granted. Twenty-four foreign firms have become members of the TSE since 1986.[39]

London Stock Exchange (LSE)   Historically, members on the LSE were either brokers who could trade shares on behalf of customers, or jobbers who bought and sold shares as principals. Following a major deregulation (the "Big Bang") on October 27, 1986,

---

[39]Some observers have questioned the pure economics of these memberships, but the firms have defended them as a means of becoming a part of the Japanese financial community. In this regard, see Kathryn Graven, "Tokyo Stock Exchange's Broker-Fees Cut Is Seen Trimming Foreign Firms' Profits," *Wall Street Journal,* October 2, 1987, 17; and Marcus W. Brauchli, "U.S. Brokerage Firms Operating in Japan Have Mixed Results," *Wall Street Journal,* August 16, 1989, A1, A8.

brokers are allowed to make markets in various equities and gilts (British government bonds) and jobbers can deal with non-stock-exchange members, including the public and institutions.

Membership in the LSE is granted based on experience and competence, and there are no citizenship or residency requirements. Currently, more than 5,000 individual memberships are held by 214 broker firms and 22 jobbers. Although individuals gain membership, the operational unit is a firm that pays membership fees based on the number of exchange-approved members it employs during its first year of membership. Subsequently, a member firm pays an annual charge equal to 1 percent of its gross revenues.

CHANGES IN THE SECURITIES MARKETS

Since 1965, numerous changes have emerged prompted by the significant growth of trading by large financial institutions such as banks, insurance companies, pension funds, and investment companies because the trading requirements of these institutions differ from those of individual investors. Additional changes have transpired because of capital market globalization. In this section, we point out these changes and discuss why they occurred, consider their impact on the market, and speculate about future changes.

Evidence and Effect of Institutionalization

The growing influence of large financial institutions is shown by data on block trades (transactions involving at least 10,000 shares) and the size of trades in Table 4.6.

Financial institutions are the main source of large block trades, and the number of block trades on the NYSE has grown steadily from a daily average of 9 in 1965 to over 11,000 a day in 1997. On average, such trades constitute more than half of all the volume on the exchange. Institutional involvement is also reflected in the average size of trades, which has grown consistently from about 200 shares in 1965 to about 1,300 shares per trade in 1997.[40]

Several major effects of this institutionalization of the market have been identified:

1. Negotiated (competitive) commission rates
2. The influence of block trades
3. The impact on stock price volatility
4. The development of a National Market System (NMS)

In the following sections, we discuss how each of these effects has affected the operation of the U.S. securities market.

Negotiated Commission Rates

Background   When the NYSE was formally established in 1792, it was agreed that members would carry out all trades in designated stocks on the exchange, and that they would charge nonmembers on the basis of a *minimum commission schedule* that outlawed price cutting. The minimum commission schedule was initially developed to

---

[40]Although the influence of institutional trading is greatest on the NYSE, it is also a major factor on the AMEX, where block trades constituted about 43 percent of share volume in 1997, and on the NASDAQ-NMS, where block trades accounted for almost 50 percent of share volume in 1997. Evidence of continued institutional growth is that mutual fund sales in 1997 were a record $378 billion. See Robert McGough, "Stock Funds' Inflows Total $99 Billion in '96," *Wall Street Journal*, May 29, 1996, C1, C23.

Table 4.6 *Block Transactions[a] and Average Shares per Sale on the NYSE*

Year	Total Number of Block Transactions	Total Number of Shares in Block Trades (× 1,000)	Percentage of Reported Volume	Average Number of Block Transactions per Day	Average Shares per Sale
1965	2,171	48,262	3.1%	9	224
1970	17,217	450,908	15.4	68	388
1975	34,420	778,540	16.6	136	495
1980	133,597	3,311,132	29.2	528	872
1985	539,039	14,222,272	51.7	2,139	1,878
1986	665,587	17,811,335	49.9	2,631	1,881
1987	970,679	24,497,241	51.2	3,639	2,112
1988	768,419	22,270,680	54.5	3,037	2,303
1989	872,811	21,316,132	51.1	3,464	2,123
1990	843,365	19,681,849	49.6	3,333	2,082
1991	981,077	22,474,382	49.6	3,878	1,670
1992	1,134,832	26,069,383	50.7	4,468	1,684
1993	1,477,859	35,959,117	53.7	5,841	1,441
1994	1,654,505	40,757,770	55.5	6,565	1,495
1995	1,963,889	49,736,912	57.0	7,793	1,489
1996	2,348,457	58,510,323	55.9	9,246	1,392
1997	2,831,321	67,832,129	50.9	11,191	1,300

[a]Trades of 10,000 shares or more.

Source: *NYSE Fact Book* (New York: NYSE, various issues). Reprinted by permission.

compensate for handling small orders and made no allowance for the trading of large orders by institutions. As a result, institutional investors had to pay substantially more in commissions than the costs of the transactions justified.

The initial reaction to the excess commissions was "give-ups," whereby brokers agreed to pay part of their commissions (sometimes as much as 80 percent) to other investment firms designated by the institution making the trade that provided services to the institution. These commission transfers were referred to as *soft dollars*. Another response was the increased use of the third market, where commissions were not fixed as they were on the NYSE. The fixed commission structure also fostered the development and use of the fourth market.

Negotiated Commissions   In 1970, the SEC began a program of negotiated commissions on large transactions and finally allowed negotiated commissions on all transactions on May 1, 1975 ("May Day").

The effect on commissions charged has been dramatic. Currently, commissions for institutions are in the range of 5 to 10 cents per share regardless of the price of the stock, which implies a large discount on high-priced shares. Individuals also receive discounts from numerous competing discount brokers who charge a straight transaction fee and provide no research advice or safekeeping services. These discounts vary depending on the size of the trade. Discount brokerage firms advertise extensively the *Wall Street Journal* and *Barron's*.

The reduced commissions caused numerous mergers and liquidations by smaller investment firms after May Day. Also, with fixed minimum commissions, it was cheaper for most institutions to buy research using soft dollars than to do their own research. When competitive rates reduced excess commissions, the institutions switched to large brokerage firms that had good trading and research capabilities. As a result, many independent research firms either disbanded or merged with full-service brokerage firms.

Some observers expected regional exchanges to be adversely affected by competitive rates. Apparently, the unique trading capabilities on these exchanges prevented this because the relative trading on these exchanges has been maintained and increased.[41]

Total commissions paid have shown a significant decline, and the size and structure of the industry have changed as a result. Although independent research firms and the third market have contracted, regional stock exchanges have felt little impact.

The Impact of Block Trades

Because the increase in institutional development has caused an increase in the number and size of block trades, it is important to consider how block trades influence the market and understand how they trade.

Block Trades on the Exchanges   The increase in block trading by institutions has strained the specialist system, which had three problems with block trading: capital, commitment, and contacts (the "three Cs"). First, specialists did not have the capital needed to acquire blocks of 10,000 or 20,000 shares. Second, even when specialists had the capital, they may have been unwilling to commit the capital because of the large risks involved. Finally, because of Rule 113, specialists were not allowed to directly contact institutions to offer a block brought by another institution. Therefore, they were cut off from the major source of demand for blocks and were reluctant to take large positions in thinly traded stocks.

Block Houses   This lack of capital, commitment, and contacts by specialists on the exchange created a vacuum in block trading that resulted in the development of block houses. *Block houses* are investment firms (also referred to as *upstairs traders* because they are away from the exchange floor) that help institutions locate other institutions interested in buying or selling blocks of stock. A good block house has (1) the capital required to position a large block, (2) the willingness to commit this capital to a block transaction, and (3) contacts among institutions.

Example of a Block Trade   Assume a mutual fund decides to sell 50,000 of its 250,000 shares of Ford Motors. The fund decides to do it through Goldman Sachs & Company (GS&Co.), a large block house and lead underwriter for Ford that knows institutions interested in the stock. After being contacted by the fund, the traders at Goldman Sachs contact several institutions that own Ford to see if any of them want to add to their position and to determine their bids. Assume that the previous sale of Ford on the NYSE was at $46\frac{3}{4}$ and GS& Co. receives commitments from four different institutions for a total of 40,000 shares at an average price of $46\frac{5}{8}$. Goldman Sachs returns to the mutual fund and bids $46\frac{1}{2}$ minus a negotiated commission for the total 50,000 shares. Assuming the fund accepts the bid, Goldman Sachs now owns the block and immediately sells 40,000 shares to the four institutions that made prior commitments. It also "positions" 10,000 shares; that is, it owns the 10,000 shares and must eventually sell them at the best price possible. Because GS&Co. is a member of the NYSE, the block will be processed

[41]For a discussion of trading on regional exchanges and the third market, see J. L. Hamilton, "Off-Board Trading of NYSE-Listed Stocks: The Effects of Deregulation and the National Market System," *Journal of Finance* 42, no. 5 (December 1987): 1331–1346. Three papers examine the impact of regional exchanges and the practice of purchasing order flow that would normally go to the NYSE; see Robert H. Battalio, "Third Market Broker-Dealers: Cost Competitors or Cream Skimmers?" *Journal of Finance* 52, no. 1 (March 1997): 341–352; and Robert Battalio, Jason Greene, and Robert Jennings, "Do Competing Specialists and Preferencing Dealers Affect Market Quality?" University of Notre Dame Working Paper (December 1995); and David Easley, Nicholas Kiefer, and Maureen O'Hara, "Cream-Skimming or Profit Sharing? The Curious Role of Purchased Order Flow," *Journal of Finance* 51, no. 3 (July 1996): 811–833.

("crossed") on the exchange as one transaction of 50,000 shares at $46\frac{1}{2}$. The specialist on the NYSE might take some of the stock to fill limit orders on the book at prices between $46\frac{1}{2}$ and $46\frac{3}{4}$.

For working on this trade, GS&Co. receives a negotiated commission, but it has committed almost $470,000 to position the 10,000 shares. The major risk to GS&Co. is the possibility of a subsequent price change on the 10,000 shares. If it can sell the 10,000 shares for $46\frac{1}{2}$ or more, it will just about break even on the position and have the commission as income. If the price of the stock weakens, GS&Co. may have to sell the position at $46\frac{1}{4}$ and take a loss on it of about $2,500, offsetting the income from the commission.

This example indicates the importance of institutional contacts, capital to position a portion of the block, and willingness to commit that capital to the block trade. Without all three, the transaction would not take place.

Institutions and Stock Price Volatility

Some stock market observers speculate there should be a strong positive relationship between institutional trading and stock price volatility because institutions trade in large blocks, and it is contended that they tend to trade together. Empirical studies of the relationship between the proportion of trading by large financial institutions and stock price volatility have never supported the folklore.[42] In a capital market where trading is dominated by institutions, the best environment is one where all institutions are actively involved because they provide liquidity for one another and for noninstitutional investors.

National Market System (NMS)

The development of a National Market System (NMS) has been advocated by financial institutions because it is expected to provide greater efficiency, competition, and lower cost of transactions. Although there is no generally accepted definition of an NMS, four major characteristics are generally expected:

1. Centralized reporting of all transactions
2. Centralized quotation system
3. Centralized limit order book (CLOB)
4. Competition among all qualified market makers.

Centralized Reporting   Centralized reporting requires a composite tape to report all transactions in a stock regardless of where the transactions took place. On the tape you might see a trade in GM on the NYSE, another trade on the Chicago Exchange, and a third on the OTC. The intent is to provide on the tape full information of all completed trades.

As of June 1975, the NYSE began operating a central tape that includes all NYSE stocks traded on other exchanges and on the OTC. The volume of shares reported on the consolidated tape is shown in Table 4.7. The breakdown among the seven exchanges and two OTC markets appears in Table 4.8. Therefore, this component of a National Market System (NMS) is available for stocks listed on the NYSE. As shown, although the volume

---

[42]In this regard, see Frank K. Reilly and John M. Wachowicz, "How Institutional Trading Reduces Market Volatility," *Journal of Portfolio Management* 5, no. 2 (Winter 1979): 11–17; Neil Berkman, "Institutional Investors and the Stock Market," *New England Economic Review* (November–December 1977): 60–77; and Frank K. Reilly and David J. Wright, "Block Trades and Aggregate Stock Price Volatility," *Financial Analysts Journal* 40, no. 2 (March–April 1984): 54–60.

Table 4.7 *Consolidated Tape Volume (Thousands of Shares)*

1976	6,281,008	1990	48,188,072
1980	12,935,607	1991	55,294,725
1985	32,988,595	1992	63,064,667
1986	42,478,164	1993	81,926,892
1987	55,472,855	1994	88,870,770
1988	47,390,121	1995	106,554,583
1989	49,794,547	1996	126,340,065
		1997	159,451,717

Source: *NYSE Fact Book* (New York: NYSE, 1998): 26.

Table 4.8 *Exchanges and Markets Involved in Consolidated Tape with Percentage of Trades During 1997*

	Percentage		Percentage
AMEX	0.00%	NASD	10.49%
Boston	2.07	NYSE	74.43
Chicago	4.63	Pacific	4.14
Cincinnati	2.50	Philadelphia	1.74
Instinet	0.00		

Source: *NYSE Fact Book* (New York: NYSE, 1998): 25.

of trading is dispersed among the exchanges and the NASD, the NYSE is clearly dominant and has increased its share since a low point in 1992.[43]

Centralized Quotation System A centralized quotation system would list the quotes for a given stock (say, IBM) from all market makers on the national exchanges, the regional exchanges, and the OTC. With such a system, a broker who requested the current market quota for IBM would see all the prevailing quotes and should complete the trade on the market with the best quote.

Intermarket Trading System A centralized quotation system is currently available—the Intermarket Trading System (ITS), developed by the American, Boston, Chicago, New York, Pacific, and Philadelphia Stock Exchanges and the NASD. ITS consists of a central computer facility with interconnected terminals in the participating market centers. As shown in Table 4.9, the number of issues included, the volume of trading, and the size of trades have all grown substantially. Of the 4,535 issues included on the system in 1997, 3,711 were listed on the NYSE and 874 were listed on the AMEX.

With ITS, brokers and market makers in each market center indicate specific buying and selling commitments through a composite quotation display that shows the current quotes for each stock in every market center. A broker is expected to go to the best market to execute a customer's order by sending a message committing to a buy or sell at the price quoted. When this commitment is accepted, a message reports the transaction. The following example illustrates how ITS works.

A broker on the NYSE has a market order to sell 100 shares of IBM stock. Assuming the quotation display at the NYSE shows that the best current bid for IBM is on the Pacific

[43]For a discussion of these changes, see Craig Torres and William Power, "Big Board Is Losing Some of Its Influence Over Stock Trading," *Wall Street Journal,* April 17, 1990, A1, A6; Janet Bush, "Hoping for a New Broom at the NYSE," *Financial Times,* August 16, 1990, 13; William Power, "Big Board, at Age 200, Scrambles to Protect Grip on Stock Market," *Wall Street Journal,* May 13, 1992, A1, A8; Pat Widder, "NYSE in 200th Year as 'Way of Doing Business,'" *Chicago Tribune,* May 17, 1992, Section 7, pp. 1, 4; and Pat Widder, "NASDAQ Has Its Eyes Set on the Next 100 Years," *Chicago Tribune,* May 17, 1992, Section 7, pp. 1, 4.

Table 4.9 *Intermarket Trading System Activity*

Year	Issues Eligible	DAILY AVERAGE		Average Size of Trade
		Share Volume	Executed Trades	
1980	884	1,565,900	2,868	546
1985	1,288	5,669,400	5,867	966
1990	2,126	9,387,114	8,744	1,075
1991	2,306	10,408,566	9,971	1,044
1992	2,532	10,755,704	10,179	1,057
1993	2,922	11,488,147	10,567	1,087
1994	3,293	11,122,019	10,650	1,045
1995	3,542	12,185,064	10,911	1,117
1996	4,001	12,721,968	11,426	1,113
1997	4,535	15,429,377	14,057	1,098

Source: *NYSE Fact Book* (New York: NYSE, 1998): 26.

Stock Exchange (PSE), the broker will enter an order to sell 100 shares at the bid on the PSE. Within seconds, the commitment flashes on the computer screen and is printed out at the PSE specialist's post where it is executed against the PSE bid. The transaction is reported back to New York and on the consolidated tape. Both brokers receive immediate confirmation and the results are transmitted to the appropriate market centers at the end of each day. Thereafter, each broker completes his or her own clearance and settlement procedure.

The ITS system currently provides centralized quotations for stocks listed on the NYSE and specifies whether a bid or ask *away* from the NYSE market is superior to that *on* the NYSE. Note, however, that the system lacks several characteristics. It does not have the capability for automatic execution at the best market. Instead you must contact the market maker and indicate that you want to buy or sell, at which time the bid or ask may be withdrawn. Also, it is not mandatory that a broker go to the best market. Although the best price may be at another market center, a broker might consider it inconvenient to trade on that exchange if the price difference is not substantial. It is almost impossible to audit such actions. Still, even with these shortcomings, substantial technical and operational progress has occurred on a central quotation system.

Central Limit Order Book (CLOB)   Substantial controversy has surrounded the idea of a central limit order book (CLOB) that would contain all limit orders from all exchanges. Ideally, the CLOB would be visible to everyone, and all market makers and traders could fill orders on it. Currently, most limit orders are placed with specialists on the NYSE and filled when a transaction on the NYSE reaches the stipulated price. The NYSE specialist receives some part of the commission for rendering this service. The NYSE has opposed a CLOB because its specialists do not want to share this lucrative business. Although the technology for a CLOB is available, it is difficult to estimate when it will become a reality.

Competition Among Market Makers (Rule 390)   Market makers have always competed on the OTC market, but competition has been opposed by the NYSE. The argument in favor of competition among market makers is that it forces dealers to offer better bids and asks, or they will not do any business. Several studies have indicated that competition among a large number of dealers (as in the OTC market) results in a smaller spread. In contrast, the NYSE argues that a central auction market forces all orders to one central location where the orders are exposed to all interested participants and this central

auction results in the best market and execution, including many transactions at prices between the current bid and ask.

To help create a centralized market, the NYSE's Rule 390 requires members to obtain the permission of the exchange before carrying out a transaction in a listed stock off the exchange. This rule is intended to draw all volume to the NYSE so that the exchange can provide the most complete auction market. The exchange contends that Rule 390 is necessary to protect the auction market, arguing that its elimination would fragment the market, tempting members to trade off the exchange and to internalize many orders (that is, members would match orders from their own customers, which would keep these orders from exposure to the full auction market). Hamilton contends that the adverse effects of fragmentation are more than offset by the benefits of competition.[44] Progress in achieving this final phase of the NMS has been slow because of strong opposition by members of the investment community and caution by the SEC.

New Trading Systems

As daily trading volume has gone from about 5 million shares to more than 520 million shares, it has become necessary to introduce new technology into the trading process. Currently, the NYSE routinely handles days with volume over 400 million and had a record daily high of more than 1.2 billion in 1998. The following discussion considers some technological innovations that assist in the trading process.

Super Dot Super Dot is an electronic order-routing system through which member firms transmit market and limit orders in NYSE-listed securities directly to the posts where securities are traded or to the member firm's booth. After the order has been executed, a report of execution is returned directly to the member firm office over the same electronic circuit, and the execution is submitted directly to the comparison systems. Member firms can enter market orders up to 2,099 shares and limit orders in round or odd lots up to 30,099 shares. An estimated 85 percent of all market orders enter the NYSE through the Super Dot system.

Display Book The Display Book is an electronic workstation that keeps track of all limit orders and incoming market orders. This includes incoming Super Dot limit orders.

Opening Automated Report Service (OARS) OARS, the opening feature of the Super Dot system, accepts member firms' preopening market orders up to 30,099 shares. OARS automatically and continuously pairs buy and sell orders and presents the imbalance to the specialist prior to the opening of a stock. This system helps the specialist determine the opening price and the potential need for a preopening call market.

Market Order Processing Super Dot's postopening market order system is designed to accept member firms' postopening market orders up to 30,099 shares. The system provides rapid execution and reporting of market orders. During 1997, 92.4% of market orders were executed and reported in less than sixty seconds.

Limit Order Processing The limit order processing system electronically files orders to be executed when and if a specific price is reached. The system accepts limit orders up to 99,999 shares and electronically updates the Specialists' Display Book. Good-until-canceled orders that are not executed on the day of submission are automatically stored until executed or canceled.

[44]James L. Hamilton, "Marketplace Fragmentation Competition and the Efficiency of the Stock Exchange," *Journal of Finance* 34, no. 1 (March 1979): 171–187. For a more recent article, see Hans R. Stoll, "Organization of the Stock Market: Competition or Fragmentation," *Journal of Applied Corporate Finance* 5, no. 4 (Winter 1993): 89–93.

Global Market Changes

NYSE Off-Hours Trading   One of the major concerns of the NYSE is the continuing erosion of its market share for stocks listed on the NYSE due to global trading. Specifically, the share of trading of NYSE-listed stock has declined from about 80 to 85 percent during the early 1980s to about 75 percent in 1997. This reflects an increase in trading on regional exchanges and the third market, some increase in fourth-market trading, but mainly an increase in trading in foreign markets in London and Tokyo. The NYSE has attempted to respond to this by expanding its trading hours and listing more non-U.S. stocks. The expansion of hours was initiated in May 1991, when the SEC approved a two-year pilot program of two NYSE crossing sessions.

Crossing Session I (CSI) provides the opportunity to trade individual stocks at the NYSE closing prices after the regular session—from 4:15 P.M. to 5:00 P.M. In 1997, CSI averaged 358,000 shares per day and had a record of 14 million shares in September 1995. Crossing Session II (CSII) allows trading a collection of at least 15 NYSE stocks with a market value of at least $1 million. This session is from 4:00 P.M. to 5:15 P.M. During 1997, the average daily share volume during CSII was about 4.1 million shares.

Listing foreign stocks on the NYSE   A major goal and concern for the NYSE is the ability to list foreign stocks on the exchange. The NYSE chairman, Richard A. Grasso, has stated on several occasions that the exchange recognizes that much of the growth in the coming decades will be in foreign countries and their stocks. As a result, the exchange wants to list a number of these stocks. The problem is that current SEC regulations will not allow the NYSE to list these firms because they follow less-stringent foreign accounting and disclosure standards. Specifically, many foreign companies issue financial statements less frequently and with less information than what is required by the SEC. As a result, about 360 foreign firms currently have shares traded on the NYSE (mainly through ADRs), but it is contended that 2,000 to 3,000 foreign companies would qualify for listing on the NYSE except for the accounting rules. The exchange contends that unless the rules are adjusted and the NYSE is allowed to compete with other world exchanges (the LSE lists more than 600 foreign stocks), it will eventually become a regional exchange in the global market. The view of the SEC is that they have an obligation to ensure that investors receive adequate disclosure. This difference hopefully will be resolved during 1999 in favor of allowing additional foreign listings.[45] Even with the stringent requirements, stocks from more than sixty companies were listed during 1997.

London Stock Exchange   The London Stock Exchange initiated several major changes on October 27, 1986, in an event referred to as the *Big Bang*. As a result of this event, brokers can act as market makers, jobbers can deal with the public and with institutions, and all commissions are fully negotiable.

The gilt market was restructured to resemble the U.S. government securities market. The Bank of England approved a system whereby 27 primary dealers make markets in U.K. government securities and transact with a limited number of interdealer brokers. This new arrangement has created a more competitive environment.

Trades are reported on a system called *Stock Exchange Automated Quotations (SEAQ) International,* which is an electronic market-price information system similar to NAS-DAQ. In addition, real-time prices are being shared with the NYSE while the NASD provides certain U.S. OTC prices to the London market. Also, as discussed earlier, thirty-five

[45]The NYSE argument is supported in the following articles: William J. Baumol and Burton Malkiel, "Redundant Regulation of Foreign Security Trading and U.S. Competitiveness," *Journal of Applied Corporate Finance* 5, no. 4 (Winter 1993): 19–27; and Franklin Edwards, "Listing of Foreign Securities on U.S. Exchanges," *Journal of Applied Corporate Finance* 5, no. 4 (Winter 1993): 28–36.

U.S. OTC stocks are available for twenty-four-hour trading between New York, Tokyo, Singapore, and London.

Access to membership on the exchange has increased; foreign firms are admitted as members, and they can be wholly owned by non-U.K. firms. As a result, some U.S. banks have acquired British stockbrokers, and several major U.S. firms are now members of the exchange.

Effects of the Big Bang   Probably one of the most visually striking changes caused by the Big Bang occurred on the trading floor of the LSE. Prior to October 1986, the activity on the floor of the LSE was similar to that on the NYSE and the TSE—large numbers of people gathered around trading posts and moving between the phones and the posts. Currently, the exchange floor is completely deserted except for some traders in stock options. Once they introduced competitive market makers on the floor of the exchange, it was just as easy to buy and sell listed stocks away from the exchange using the quotes on SEAQ.

The rest of the Big Bang's effects can be summarized by the phrase "more business, less profit." Specifically, there is more activity throughout the system, but profit margins have declined or disappeared due to the intense competition. In the process, many firms have merged or been acquired by firms from the United States, Japan, or Germany that have been willing to accept lower returns to establish market presence.[46]

Tokyo Stock Exchange (TSE)   The TSE experienced a "big bang" during 1998 that introduced more competition in trading commissions and also encouraged competition among market participants.

By late 1997, twenty-five foreign firms were members of the TSE. Four Japanese investment firms dominate the Japanese financial market: Nomura, Daiwa, Nikko, and Yamaichi. The foreign firms were less aggressive between 1992 and 1997 because of the dramatic slowdown in the Japanese economy and its securities market.[47]

Paris Bourse   The monopoly on stock trading that was formerly held by the big brokerage houses has been opened up to French and foreign banks. As a result, some investment firms began to merge with banks to acquire the capital needed to trade in a world market. The Bourse has also introduced a continuous auction market rather than its previous call market.[48]

Frankfurt Stock Exchange   As noted earlier, the German stock market has merged the three largest stock exchanges to create a large high-technology exchange that is attempting to compete with the London Exchange for European business.[49]

Future Developments

In addition to the expected effects of the NMS and a global capital market, there are other changes that you should understand.

More Specialized Investment Companies   Although more individuals want to own stocks and bonds, they have increasingly acquired this ownership through investment

---

[46]Craig Forman, "Britain's Deregulation Leaves a Casualty Trail in Securities Industry," *Wall Street Journal,* October 14, 1987, 1, 18.

[47]For a discussion of the problems, see Robert Thomson, "New Plea to Japan to Reform Markets," *Financial Times,* February 5, 1993, 17; Gilliam Tett, "Tokyo Urged to Boost System of Regulation under Big Bang," *Financial Times,* April 15, 1998, 1; and James Kynge and John Ridding, "China Calls for Japan to Act as Asian Crises Bites," *Financial Times,* June 10, 1998, 1.

[48]Fiona Gleizes, "Paris Bourse Begins Its Own 'Big Bang' in Effort to Rival London's Exchange," *Wall Street Journal,* January 4, 1988, 15.

[49]Andrew Fisher, "Top Three German Exchanges to Merge," *Financial Times,* May 9, 1995.

companies because most individuals find it too difficult and time-consuming to do their own analysis. This increase in fund sales has caused an explosion of new funds (discussed in Chapters 3 and 21) that provide numerous opportunities to diversify in a wide range of asset classes.

This trend toward specialized funds will continue and could possibly include other investment alternatives such as stamps, coins, and art. Because of the lower liquidity of foreign securities, stamps, coins, and art, many of these new mutual funds will be closed-end and will be traded on an exchange. These closed-end funds and their surge in popularity are discussed in Chapter 21.

Changes in the Financial Services Industry   The financial services industry is experiencing a major change in makeup and operation. Prior to 1960, the securities industry was composed of specialty firms that concentrated in specific investments such as stocks, bonds, commodities, real estate, or insurance. A trend during the early 1980s focused on creating financial supermarkets that considered all of these investment alternatives around the world. Prime examples would be Merrill Lynch, which acquired insurance and real estate subsidiaries and Travelers Insurance that acquired Salomon Brothers and Smith Barney. A subset includes firms that are global in coverage, but limit their product line to mainstream investment instruments such as bonds, stocks, futures, and options. Firms in this category would include Merrill Lynch, Goldman Sachs, and recently merged Morgan Stanley Dean Witter, among others. At the other end of the spectrum, large banks such as Citicorp want to become involved in the investment banking business.

In contrast to financial supermarkets, some firms have decided not to be all things to all people. These firms are going the specialty, or "boutique," route, attempting to provide unique, superior financial products. Examples include discount brokers, investment firms that concentrate on institutional or individual investors, or firms that concentrate on an industry such as banking.

It appears we are moving toward a world with two major groups. Specifically, one group would include a few global investment firms that deal in almost all the asset classes available, while the second group would include numerous firms that provide specialized services in unique products.

Beyond these firm changes, the advances in technology continue to accelerate and promise to affect how the secondary market will be organized and operated.[50] Specifically, computerized trading has made tremendous inroads during the past five years and promises to introduce numerous additional changes into the twenty-first century in markets around the world. The twenty-four-hour market will require extensive computerized trading.

Investments Online

Many Internet sites deal with different aspects of investing. Earlier site suggestions led you to information and prices of securities traded both in the U.S. and around the globe. Here are some additional sites of interest:

---

[50]This includes the "Market 2000" report, prepared by the SEC, that is concerned with the organization and operation of securities markets in the United States. Notably, many emerging market exchanges are able to "leapfrog" to the latest technology. This also includes the technology innovations related to the merger of the NASD, the AMEX, and the Philadelphia Exchange discussed earlier. This is also discussed in Paula Dwyer, A. Osterland, K. Capell, and S. Reier, "The 21st Century Stock Market," *Business Week,* August 10, 1998: 66–72.

Investments Online *(cont.)*

www.quote.com
This site offers substantial market information, including price quotes on stocks, bonds, and options. Charts of price activity at 5-minute, 15-minute, daily, or weekly intervals are available. News sources at this site include Reuters, S&P News, and EDGAR Online (a Securities and Exchange Commission database). Various research sources are offered, including Lipper, Disclosure, Zacks, First Call, and Options Analytics.

www.sec.gov
The Web site of the SEC (Securities and Exchange Commission) offers news and information, investor assistance and complaint handling, SEC rules, enforcement, and data.

www.nyse.com
www.amex.com
www.nasdaq.com
The Web sites of the New York Stock Exchange, the American Stock Exchange, and the National Association of Securities Dealers Automated Quotation (NASDAQ) system offer information about the relevant market, price quotes, listings of firms, and investor services. The AMEX site includes price quotes for SPDRs (S&P Depository Receipts, which represent ownership in the S&P 500 index or the S&P Midcap 400 index) and WEBS (World Equity Benchmark Shares), which track the Morgan Stanley Capital International (MSCI) indexes of 17 different countries.

www.etrade.com
www.schwab.com
www.ml.com
Many brokerage houses have Web pages. These are three examples of such sites. E*Trade Securities is an example of an on-line brokerage firm which allows investors to trade securities over the Internet. Schwab is a discount broker, whereas Merrill Lynch is a full-service broker with a reputation for good research.

Summary

♦ The securities market is divided into primary and secondary markets. Secondary markets provide the liquidity that is critical for primary markets. The major segments of the secondary markets include listed exchanges (the NYSE, AMEX, TSE, LSE, and regional exchanges), the over-the-counter market, the third market, and the fourth market. Because you will want to invest across these secondary markets within a country as well as among countries, you need to understand how the markets differ and how they are similar.

♦ Many of the dramatic changes in our securities markets during the past thirty years are due to an increase in institutional trading and to rapidly evolving global markets. It is important to understand what has happened and why it happened because numerous changes have occurred—and many more are yet to come. You need to understand how these changes will affect your investment alternatives and opportunities. You must look not only for the best investment, but also for the best securities market. This discussion should provide the background to help you make that trading decision.

Questions

1. Define *market* and briefly discuss the characteristics of a good market.
2. You own 100 shares of General Electric stock and you want to sell it because you need the money to make a down payment on a stereo. Assume there is absolutely no secondary market system in common stocks. How would you go about selling the stock? Discuss what you would have to do to find a buyer, how long it might take, and the price you might receive.
3. Define *liquidity* and discuss the factors that contribute to it. Give examples of a liquid asset and an illiquid asset, and discuss why they are considered liquid and illiquid.
4. Define a primary and secondary market for securities and discuss how they differ. Discuss why the primary market is dependent on the secondary market.
5. Give an example of an initial public offering (IPO) in the primary market. Give an example of a seasoned equity issue in the primary market. Discuss which would involve greater risk to the buyer.
6. Find an advertisement for a recent primary offering in the *Wall Street Journal*. Based on the information in the ad, indicate the characteristics of the security sold and the major underwriters. How much new capital did the firm derive from the offering before paying commissions?
7. Briefly explain the difference between a competitive bid underwriting and a negotiated underwriting.
8. The figures in Table 4.3 reveal a major difference in the price paid for a membership (seat) on the NYSE compared with one on the AMEX. How would you explain this difference?
9. What are the major reasons for the existence of regional stock exchanges? Discuss how they differ from the national exchanges.
10. Which segment of the secondary stock market (listed exchanges or the OTC) is larger in terms of the number of issues? Which is larger in terms of the value of the issues traded?
11. Discuss the three levels of NASDAQ in terms of what each provides and who would subscribe to each.
12. a. Define the third market. Give an example of a third-market stock.
    b. Define the fourth market. Discuss why a financial institution would use the fourth market.
13. Briefly define each of the following terms and give an example:
    a. Market order
    b. Limit order
    c. Short sale
    d. Stop loss order
14. Briefly discuss the two major functions and sources of income for the NYSE specialist.
15. Describe the duties of the *Saitori* member on the TSE. Discuss how these duties differ from those of the NYSE specialist.
16. Discuss why the U.S. equity market has experienced major changes since 1965.
17. What were give-ups? What are "soft dollars"? Discuss why soft dollars and give-ups existed when there were fixed commissions.
18. The discussion of block trades noted that the specialist is hampered by the three Cs. Discuss each of the three Cs as it relates to block trading.
19. Describe block houses and explain why they evolved. Describe what is meant by *positioning* part of a block.
20. a. Describe the major attributes of the National Market System (NMS).
    b. Briefly describe the ITS and what it contributes to the NMS. Discuss the growth of the ITS.
21. The chapter includes a discussion of expected changes in world capital markets. Discuss one of the suggested changes in terms of what has been happening or discuss an evolving change that was not mentioned.

Problems

1. The initial margin requirement is 60 percent. You have $40,000 to invest in a stock selling for $80 a share. Ignoring taxes and commissions, show in detail the impact on your rate of return if the stock rises to $100 a share and if it declines to $40 a share assuming: (a) you pay cash for the stock, and (b) you buy it using maximum leverage.

2. Lauren has a margin account and deposits $50,000. Assuming the prevailing margin requirement is 40 percent, commissions are ignored, and The Gentry Shoe Corporation is selling at $35 per share:
   a. How many shares can Lauren purchase using the maximum allowable margin?
   b. What is Lauren's profit (loss) if the price of Gentry's stock
      1. rises to $45?
      2. falls to $25?
   c. If the maintenance margin is 30 percent, to what price can Gentry Shoe fall before Lauren will receive a margin call?
3. Suppose you buy a round lot of Maginn Industries stock on 55 percent margin when the stock is selling at $20 a share. The broker charges a 10 percent annual interest rate, and commissions are 3 percent of the total stock value on both the purchase and sale. A year later you receive a $0.50 per share dividend and sell the stock for 27. What is your rate of return on the investment?
4. You decide to sell short 100 shares of Charlotte Horse Farms when it is selling at its yearly high of 56. Your broker tells you that your margin requirement is 45 percent and that the commission on the purchase is $155. While you are short the stock, Charlotte pays a $2.50 per share dividend. At the end of 1 year, you buy 100 shares of Charlotte at 45 to close out your position and are charged a commission of $145 and 8 percent interest on the money borrowed. What is your rate of return on the investment?
5. You own 200 shares of Shamrock Enterprises that you bought at $25 a share. The stock is now selling for $45 a share.
   a. If you put in a stop loss order at $40, discuss your reasoning for this action.
   b. If the stock eventually declines in price to $30 a share, what would be your rate of return with and without the stop loss order?
6. Two years ago, you bought 300 shares of Kayleigh Milk Co. for $30 a share with a margin of 60 percent. Currently, the Kayleigh stock is selling for $45 a share. Assuming no dividends and ignoring commissions, (a) compute the annualized rate of return on this investment if you had paid cash and (b) your rate of return with the margin purchase.
7. The stock of the Michele Travel Co. is selling for $28 a share. You put in a limit buy order at $24 for one month. During the month, the stock price declines to $20, then jumps to $36. Ignoring commissions, what would have been your rate of return on this investment? What would be your rate of return if you had put in a market order? What if your limit order was at $18?

References

AMEX Fact Book. New York: AMEX, published annually.

Amihad, Y., T. Ho, and Robert Schwartz. *Market Making and the Changing Structure of the Securities Industry.* New York: Lexington-Heath, 1985.

Amihad, Y., and H. Mendelson. "Trading Mechanisms and Stock Returns: An Empirical Investigation." *Journal of Finance* 42, no. 3 (July 1987).

Beidleman, Carl, ed. *The Handbook of International Investing.* Chicago: Probus Publishing, 1987.

Blume, Marshall E., and Jeremy J. Siegel. "The Theory of Security Pricing and Market Structure." *Financial Markets, Institutions and Instruments* 1, no. 3 (1992). New York University Salomon Center.

Blume, Marshall E., and Michael Goldstein. "Quotes, Order Flow, and Price Discovery." *Journal of Finance* 52, no. 1 (March 1997).

Christie, William, and Paul Schultz. "Why Do NASDAQ Market-Makers Avoid Odd-Eighth Quotes?" *Journal of Finance* 49, no. 5 (December 1994).

Cohen, Kalman, Steven Maier, Robert Schwartz, and David Whitcomb. *The Microstructure of Securities Markets.* Englewood Cliffs, NJ: Prentice-Hall, 1986.

Dutts, Prajit, and Ananth Madhaven. "Competition and Collusion in Dealer Markets." *Journal of Finance* 52, no. 1 (March 1997).

Economides, Nicholas, and Robert A. Schwartz. "Electronic Call Market Trading." *Journal of Portfolio Management* 21, no. 3 (Spring 1995).

Grabbe, J. Orlin. *International Financial Markets.* New York: Elsevier, 1986.

Grossman, S. J., and Merton H. Miller. "Liquidity and Market Structure." *Journal of Finance* 43, no. 2 (June 1988).

Hasbrouck, Joel. "Assessing the Quality of a Security Market: A New Approach to Transaction-Cost Measurement." *Review of Financial Studies* 6, no. 1 (1993).

Huang, Roger, and Hans Stoll. "Dealer Versus Auction Markets: A Paired Comparison of Execution Costs on NASDAQ and the NYSE." *Journal of Financial Economics* 41, no. 3 (July 1996).

Ibbotson, Roger G., and Gary P. Brinson. *Global Investing.* New York: McGraw-Hill, 1993.

Kee, C. "Market Integration and Price Execution for NYSE-Listed Securities." *Journal of Finance* 48, no. 2 (June 1993).

Madhaven, Ananth. "Trading Mechanisms in Securities Markets." *Journal of Finance* 47, no. 2 (June 1992).

McInish, Thomas, and Robert A. Wood. "Hidden Limit Orders on the NYSE." *Journal of Portfolio Management* 21, no. 3 (Spring 1995).

NASDAQ Fact Book. Washington, DC: National Association of Securities Dealers, published annually.

Neal, Robert. "A Comparison of Transaction Cost Between Competitive Market Maker and Specialist Market Structures." *Journal of Business* 65, no. 3 (July 1992).

NYSE Fact Book. New York: NYSE, published annually.

Pagano, M. "Trading Volume and Asset Liquidity." *Quarterly Journal of Economics* 104, no. 2 (1989).

Petersen, M., and D. Fialkowski. "Posted versus Effective Spreads: Good Prices or Bad Quotes?" *Journal of Financial Economics* 35, no. 3 (June 1994).

Sherrerd, Katrina F., ed. *Execution Techniques, True Trading Costs, and the Microstructure of Markets.* Charlottesville, VA: Association for Investment Management and Research, 1993.

Sobel, Robert. *N.Y.S.E.: A History of the New York Stock Exchange, 1935–1975.* New York: Weybright and Talley, 1975.

Sobel, Robert. *The Curbstone Brokers: The Origins of the American Stock Exchange.* New York: Macmillan, 1970.

Solnik, Bruno. *International Investments.* 3d ed. Reading, MA: Addison-Wesley, 1995.

Stoll, Hans. *The Stock Exchange Specialist System: An Economic Analysis.* Monograph Series in Financial Economics 1985–2. New York University, 1985.

Stoll, Hans, and Robert Whaley. "Stock Market Structure and Volatility." *Review of Financial Studies* 3, no. 1 (1990).

Toyko Stock Exchange Fact Book. Tokyo: TSE, published annually.

U.S. Congress, Office of Technology Assessment. *Trading Around the Clock: Global Securities Markets and Information Technology—Background Paper,* OTA-BP-CIT-66. Washington, DC: U.S. Government Printing Office, July 1990.

Viner, Aron. *Inside Japanese Financial Markets.* Homewood, IL: Dow Jones–Irwin, 1988.

GLOSSARY

Call market   A market in which trading for individual stocks only takes place at specified times. All the bids and asks available at the time are combined and the market administrators specify a single price that will possibly clear the market at that time.

Commission brokers   Employees of a member firm who buy or sell for the customers of the firm.

Continuous market   A market where stocks are priced and traded continuously either by an auction process or by dealers during the time the market is open.

Floor brokers   Independent members of an exchange who act as brokers for other members.

Fourth market   Direct trading of securities between owners, usually institutions, without any broker intermediation.

Initial public offering (IPO)   A new issue by a firm that has no existing public market.

Limit order   An order that lasts for a specified time to buy or sell a security when and if it trades at a specified price.

Liquidity   The ability to buy or sell an asset quickly and at a price which is not substantially different from the prices of prior transactions.

Margin   The percent of cash a buyer pays for a security, borrowing the balance from the broker. This introduces leverage which increases the risk of the transaction.

Market   The means through which buyers and sellers are brought together to aid in the transfer of goods and/or services.

Market order   An order to buy or sell a security immediately at the best price available.

National Association of Securities Dealers Automated Quotation (NASDAQ) system   An electronic system for providing bid–ask quotes on OTC securities.

Price continuity   A feature of a liquid market in which prices change little from one transaction to the next due to the depth of the market.

Primary market   The market in which newly issued securities are sold by their issuers.

Private placement   A new issue sold directly to a small group of investors, usually institutions.

Registered competitive competitive market makers (RCMM)   Members of an exchange who are allowed to use their memberships to buy or sell for their own account within the specific trading obligations set down by the exchange.

Secondary market   The market in which outstanding securities are bought and sold by owners other than the issuers.

Short sale   The sale of borrowed stock with the intention of repurchasing it later at a lower price and earning the difference.

Third market   Over-the-counter trading of securities listed on an exchange.

Transaction cost   The cost of executing a trade. Low costs characterize an internally efficient market.

Treasury bill   A negotiable U.S. government security with a maturity of less than one year that pays no periodic interest but yields the difference between its par value and its discounted purchase price.

Treasury bond   A U.S. government security with a maturity of more than ten years that pays interest periodically.

Treasury note   A U.S. government security with maturities of one to ten years that pays interest periodically.

Characteristics of Developed and Developing Markets around the World

Table 4A   Developed Markets around the World

Country	Principal Exchange	Other Exchanges	Total Market Capitalization ($ Billions)	Available Market Capitalization ($ Billions)	Trading Volume ($ Billions)	Domestic Issues Listed	Total Issues Listed	Auction Mechanism	Official Specialists	Options/ Futures Trading	Price Limits	Principal Market Indexes
Australia	Sydney	5	82.3	53.5	39.3	N.A.	1,496	Continuous	No	Yes	None	All Ordinaries—324 issues
Austria	Vienna	—	18.7	8.3	37.2	125	176	Call	Yes	No	5%	GZ Aktienindex—25 issues
Belgium	Brussels	3	48.5	26.2	6.8	186	337	Mixed	No	Few	10%	Brussels Stock Exchange Index—186 issues
Canada	Toronto	4	186.8	124.5	71.3	N.A.	1,208	Continuous	Yes	Yes	None	TSE 300 Composite Index
Denmark	Copenhagen	—	29.7	22.2	11.1	N.A.	284	Mixed	No	No	None	Copenhagen Stock Exchange Index—38 issues
Finland	Helsinki	—	9.9	1.7	5.2	N.A.	125	Mixed	N.A.	N.A.	N.A.	KOP (Kansallis-Osake-Pannki) Price Index
France	Paris	6	256.5	137.2	129.0	463	663	Mixed	Yes	Yes	4%	CAC General Index—240 issues
Germany	Frankfurt	7	297.7	197.9	1,003.7	N.A.	355	Continuous	Yes	Options	None	DAX: FAZ (Frankfurter Allgemeine Zeitung)
Hong Kong	Hong Kong	—	67.7	37.1	34.6	N.A.	479	Continuous	No	Futures	None	Hang Seng Index—33 issues
Ireland	Dublin	—	8.4	6.4	5.5	N.A.	N.A.	Continuous	No	No	None	J&E Davy Total Market Index
Italy	Milan	9	137.0	73.2	42.6	N.A.	317	Mixed	No	No	10–20%	Banca Commerziale—209 issues
Japan	Tokyo	7	2,754.6	1,483.5	1,602.4	N.A.	1,576	Continuous	Yes	No	10% down	TOPIX—1,097 issues; TSE II—423 issues; Nikkei 225

Table 4A *Developed Markets around the World (concluded)*

Country	Principal Exchange	Other Exchanges	Total Market Capitalization ($ Billions)	Available Market Capitalization ($ Billions)	Trading Volume ($ Billions)	Domestic Issues Listed	Total Issues Listed	Auction Mechanism	Official Specialists	Options/ Futures Trading	Price Limits	Principal Market Indexes
Luxembourg	Luxembourg	—	1.5	0.9	0.1	61	247	Continuous	N.A.	N.A.	N.A.	Domestic Share Price Index—9 issues
Malaysia	Kuala Lumpur	—	199.3	95.0	126.4	430	478	Continuous	No	No	None	Kuala Lumpur Composite Index—83 issues
The Netherlands	Amsterdam	—	112.1	92.4	80.4	279	569	Continuous	Yes	Options	Variable	ANP—CBS General Index—51 issues
New Zealand	Wellington	—	6.7	5.3	2.0	295	451	Continuous	No	Futures	None	Barclay's International Price Index—40 issues
Norway	Oslo	9	18.4	7.9	14.1	N.A.	128	Call	No	No	None	Oslo Bors Stock Index—50 issues
Singapore	Singapore	—	28.6	15.6	8.2	N.A.	324	Continuous	No	No	None	Straits Times Index—30 issues; SES—32 issues
South Africa	Johannesburg	—	72.7	N.A.	8.2	N.A.	N.A.	Continuous	No	Options	None	JSE Actuaries Index—141 issues
Spain	Madrid	3	86.6	46.8	41.0	N.A.	368	Mixed	No	No	10%	Madrid Stock Exchange Index—72 issues
Sweden	Stockholm	—	59.0	24.6	15.8	N.A.	151	Mixed	No	Yes	None	Jacobson & Ponsbach—30 issues
Switzerland	Zurich	6	128.5	75.4	376.6	161	380	Mixed	No	Yes	5%	Société de Banque Suisse—90 issues
United Kingdom	London	5	756.2	671.1	280.7	1,911	2,577	Continuous	No	Yes	None	Financial Times (FT) Ordinaries—750 issues; FTSE 100; FT 33
United States	New York	6	9,431.1	8,950.3	5,778.7	N.A.	3,358	Continuous	Yes	Yes	None	S&P 500; Dow Jones Industrial Average; Wilshire 5000; Russell 3000

Notes: Market capitalizations (both total and available) are as of December 31, 1990, except for South African market capitalization, which is from 1988. Available differs from total market capitalization by subtracting cross holdings, closely held and government-owned shares, and takes into account restrictions on foreign ownership. Number of issues listed are from 1988 except for Malaysia, which is from 1994. Trading volume data are 1990 except for Switzerland, which are from 1988. Trading institutions data are from 1987. Market capitalizations (both total and available) for all countries except the United States and South Africa are from the Salomon-Russell Global Equity Indices. U.S. market capitalization (both total and available) is from the Frank Russell Company. All trading volume information (except for Switzerland) and Malaysian total issues listed are from the *Emerging Stock Markets Factbook: 1991*, International Finance Corp. 1991. Trading institutions information is from Richard Roll, "The International Crash of 1987," *Financial Analysts Journal*, September/October 1988. South African market capitalization, number of issues listed for all countries (except Malaysia), and Swiss trading volume are reproduced courtesy of Euromoney Books, extracted from *The G.T. Guide to World Equity Markets: 1989, 1988.*

Source: Roger G. Ibbotson and Gary P. Brinson, *Global Investing* (New York: McGraw-Hill, 1993): 109–111. Reproduced with permission of The McGraw-Hill Companies.

Table 4B *Emerging Markets around the World*

Country	Principal Exchange	Other Exchanges	Market Capitalization ($ Billions)	Trading Volume ($ Billions)	Total Issues Listed	Auction Mechanism	Principal Market Indexes
Argentina	Buenos Aires	4	36.9	11.4	156	N.A.	Buenos Aires Stock Exchange Index
Brazil	São Paulo	9	189.2	109.5	544	Continuous	BOVESPA Share Price Index—83 issues
Chile	Santiago	—	68.2	5.3	279	Mixed	IGPA Index—180 issues
China	Shanghai	1	43.5	97.5	291	Continuous	Shanghai Composite Index
Colombia	Bogotá	1	14.0	2.2	90	N.A.	Bogotá General Composite Index
Greece	Athens	—	14.9	5.1	216	Continuous	Athens Stock Exchange Industrial Price Index
India	Bombay	14	127.5	27.3	4,413	Continuous	Economic Times Index—72 issues
Indonesia	Jakarta	—	47.2	11.8	216	Mixed	Jakarta Stock Exchange Index
Israel	Tel Aviv	—	10.6	5.5	267	Call	General Share Index—all listed issues
Jordan	Amman	—	4.6	0.6	95	N.A.	Amman Financial Market Index
Mexico	Mexico City	—	130.2	83.0	206	Continuous	Bolsa de Valores Index—49 issues
Nigeria	Lagos	—	2.7	N.A.	177	Call	Nigerian Stock Exchange General Index
Pakistan	Karachi	—	12.2	3.2	724	Continuous	State Bank of Pakistan Index
Philippines	Makati	1	55.5	13.9	189	N.A.	Manila Commercial & Industrial Index—25 issues
Portugal	Lisbon	1	16.2	5.2	195	Call	Banco Totta e Acores Share Index—50 issues
South Korea	Seoul	—	191.8	286.0	699	Continuous	Korea Composite Stock Price Index
Taiwan	Taipei	—	247.3	711.0	313	Continuous	Taiwan Stock Exchange Index
Thailand	Bangkok	—	131.4	80.2	389	Continuous	Securities Exchange of Thailand Price Index
Turkey	Istanbul	—	21.6	21.7	176	Continuous	Istanbul Stock Exchange Index—50 issues
Venezuela	Caracas	1	4.1	0.9	90	Continuous	Indice de Capitalization de la BVC
Zimbabwe	N.A.	—	1.8	0.2	64	N.A.	Zimbabwe S.E. Industrial Index

Notes: Market capitalizations, trading volume, and total issues listed are as of 1994. Market capitalization, trading volume, and total issues listed for Brazil and São Paulo only. Trading volume for the Philippines is for both Manila and Makati. Total issues listed for India is Bombay only. Trading institutions information is from 1987 and 1988. Market capitalizations, trading volume, and total issues listed are from the *Emerging Stock Markets Factbook: 1995*, International Finance Corp., 1995. Trading institutions information is from Richard Roll, "The International Crash of 1987." *Financial Analysts Journal*, September/October 1988.

Source: Roger G. Ibbotson and Gary P. Brinson, *Global Investing* (New York: McGraw-Hill, 1993): 125–126. Reproduced with permission of The McGraw-Hill Companies.

CHAPTER

5

Security-Market Indicator Series

This chapter answers the following questions:

♦ What are some major uses of security-market indicator series (indexes)?

♦ What are the major characteristics that cause alternative indexes to differ?

♦ What are the major stock-market indexes in the United States and globally, and what are their characteristics?

♦ What are the major bond-market indexes for the United States and the world?

♦ What are some of the composite stock–bond market indexes?

♦ Where can you get historical and current data for all these indexes?

♦ What is the relationship among many of these indexes in the short run (monthly)? ♦

A fair statement regarding **security-market indicator series**—especially those outside the United States—is that everybody talks about them, but few people understand them. Even those investors familiar with widely publicized stock-market series, such as the Dow Jones Industrial Average (DJIA), usually know little about indexes for the U.S. bond market or for non-U.S. stock markets such as Tokyo or London.

Although portfolios are obviously composed of many different individual stocks, investors typically ask, "What happened to the market today?" The reason for this question is that if an investor owns more than a few stocks or bonds, it is cumbersome to follow each stock or bond individually to determine the composite performance of the portfolio. Also, there is an intuitive notion that most individual stocks or bonds move with the aggregate market. Therefore, if the overall market rose, an individual's portfolio probably also increased in value. To supply investors with a composite report on market

performance, some financial publications or investment firms have developed stock-market and bond-market indexes.[1]

The initial section discusses several ways that investors use market indicator series. An awareness of these significant functions should provide an incentive for becoming familiar with these series and indicates why we present a full chapter on this topic. The second section considers what characteristics cause alternative indexes to differ. In this chapter, we discuss numerous stock-market and bond-market indexes. You should understand their differences and why one of them is preferable for a given task because of its characteristics. The third section presents the most well-known U.S. and global stock market series separated into groups based on the weighting scheme used. The fourth section considers bond-market indexes, which is a relatively new topic, not because the bond market is new, but because the creation and maintenance of total return bond indexes are new. Again, we consider international bond indexes following the domestic indexes. In section five, we consider composite stock market–bond market series. Our final section examines how these indexes relate to each other over monthly intervals. This comparison demonstrates the important factors that cause high or low correlation among series. With this background, you should be able to make an intelligent choice of the indicator series that is best for you based upon how you want to use the index.

USES OF SECURITY-MARKET INDEXES

Security-market indexes have at least five specific uses. A primary application is to use the index values to compute total returns for an aggregate market or some component of a market over a specified time period and use the rates of return computed as a *benchmark* to judge the performance of individual portfolios. A basic assumption when evaluating portfolio performance is that any investor should be able to experience a rate of return comparable to the market return by randomly selecting a large number of stocks or bonds from the total market; hence, a superior portfolio manager should consistently do better than the market. Therefore, *an aggregate stock- or bond-market index can be used as a benchmark to judge the performance of professional money managers.* You should recall from our earlier discussion that you should also analyze the differential risk for the portfolios being judged as compared to the risk inherent in the benchmark.

Indicator series are also used to develop an index portfolio. As we will discuss later, it is difficult for most money managers to consistently outperform specified market indexes on a risk-adjusted basis over time. If this is true, an obvious alternative is to invest in a portfolio that will emulate this market portfolio. This notion led to the creation of *index funds,* whose purpose is to track the performance of the specified market series (index) over time, that is, derive similar rates of return.[2] The original index fund concept was related to common stocks. Subsequently, development of comprehensive, well-specified bond-market indexes and similar inferior performance relative to the bond market by most bond portfolio managers has led to a similar phenomenon in the fixed-income area (bond index funds).[3]

Securities analysts, portfolio managers, and others use security-market indexes to examine the factors that influence aggregate security price movements (that is, the indexes are

---

[1]Throughout this chapter and the book, we will use *indicator series* and *indexes* interchangeably, although *indicator series* is the more correct specification because it refers to a broad class of series; one popular type of series is an index, but there can be other types and many different indexes.

[2]For a discussion of developments in indexing, see "New Ways to Play the Indexing Game," *Institutional Investor* 22, no. 13 (November 1988): 92–98; and Edward A. Wyatt, "Avidly Average," *Barron's,* May 22, 1989, 17, 30.

[3]See Fran Hawthorne, "The Battle of the Bond Indexes," *Institutional Investor* 20, no. 4 (April 1986).

used to measure aggregate market movements). A similar use is to analyze the relationship among stock and bond returns of different countries. An example is the analysis of the relationship among U.S., Japanese, and German stock or bond returns.

Another group interested in an aggregate market series is "technicians," who believe past price changes can be used to predict future price movements. For example, to project future stock price movements, technicians would plot and analyze price and volume changes for a stock market series like the Dow Jones Industrial Average.

Finally, work in portfolio and capital market theory has implied that the relevant risk for an individual risky asset is its *systematic risk,* which is the relationship between the rates of return for a risky asset and the rates of return for a market portfolio of risky assets.[4] Therefore, it is necessary when computing the systematic risk for an individual risky asset (security) to relate its returns to the returns for an aggregate market index that is used as a proxy for the market portfolio of risky assets.

DIFFERENTIATING FACTORS IN CONSTRUCTING MARKET INDEXES

Because the indicator series are intended to reflect the overall movements of a group of securities, it is necessary to consider which factors are important in computing an index that is intended to represent a total population.

The Sample

The size of the sample, the breadth of the sample, and the source of the sample used to construct a series are all important.

A small percentage of the total population will provide valid indications of the behavior of the total population *if* the sample is properly selected. In fact, at some point the costs of taking a larger sample will almost certainly outweigh any benefits of increased size. The sample should be *representative* of the total population; otherwise, its size will be meaningless. A large biased sample is no better than a small biased sample. The sample can be generated by completely random selection or by a nonrandom selection technique that is designed to incorporate the characteristics of the desired population. Finally, the *source* of the sample is important if there are any differences between segments of the population, in which case samples from each segment are required.

Weighting Sample Members

Our second concern is with the weight given to each member in the sample. Three principal weighting schemes are used: (1) a price-weighted series, (2) a value-weighted series, and (3) an unweighted series, or what would be described as an equally weighted series.

Computational Procedure

Our final consideration is selecting the computational procedure. One alternative is to take a simple arithmetic average of the various members in the series. Another is to

---

[4]This concept and its justification are discussed in Chapters 6 and 7. Subsequently, we will consider the difficulty of finding an index that is an appropriate proxy for the market portfolio of risky assets.

compute an index and have all changes, whether in price or value, reported in terms of the basic index. Finally, some prefer using a geometric average of the components rather than an arithmetic average.

STOCK-MARKET INDICATOR SERIES

As mentioned in the introduction to this chapter, we hear a lot about what happens to the Dow Jones Industrial Average (DJIA) each day. In addition, you might also hear about other stock indexes, such as the NYSE Composite, the S&P 500 index, the AMEX index, or even the Nikkei Average. If you listen carefully, you will realize that these indexes change by differing amounts. Reasons for some differences are obvious, such as the DJIA versus the Nikkei Average, but others are not. This section will briefly review how the major series differ in terms of the characteristics discussed in the prior section. As a result, you should come to understand that the movements over time for alternative indexes *should* differ and you will understand why they differ.

The discussion of the indexes is organized by the weighting of the sample of stocks. We begin with the price-weighted series because some of the most popular indexes are in this category. The next group is the value-weighted series, which is the technique currently used for most indexes. Finally, we will examine the unweighted series.

Price-Weighted Series

A **price-weighted series** is an arithmetic average of current prices, which means that index movements are influenced by the differential prices of the components.

Dow Jones Industrial Average   The best-known price weighted series is also the oldest and certainly the most popular stock-market indicator series, the Dow Jones Industrial Average (DJIA). The DJIA is a price-weighted average of thirty large, well-known industrial stocks that are generally the leaders in their industry (blue chips) and are listed on the NYSE. The DJIA is computed by totaling the current prices of the 30 stocks and dividing the sum by a divisor that has been adjusted to take account of stock splits and changes in the sample over time.[5] The divisor is adjusted so the index value will be the same before and after the split. This is demonstrated in Table 5.1.

Table 5.1   *Example of Change in DJIA Divisor When a Sample Stock Splits*

	Before Split	After Three-for-One Split by Stock A	
	Prices	Prices	
A	30	10	
B	20	20	
C	10	10	
	60 ÷ 3 = 20	40 ÷ X = 20	X = 2 (New Divisor)

---

[5]A complete list of all events that have caused a change in the divisor since the DJIA went to thirty stocks on October 1, 1928, is contained in Phyllis S. Pierce, ed., *The Business One Irwin Investor's Handbook* (Burr Ridge, IL: Dow Jones Books, annual). Prior to 1992, it was the *Dow Jones Investor's Handbook*. In May 1996 the DJIA celebrated its 100th birthday, which was acknowledged with two special sections entitled "A Century of Investing" and "100 Years of the DJIA," *Wall Street Journal,* May 28, 1996.

		PERIOD T + 1	
	Period T	**Case A**	**Case B**
A	100	110	100
B	50	50	50
C	30	30	33
Sum	180	190	183
Divisor	3	3	3
Average	60	63.3	61
Percentage change		5.5	1.7

Table 5.2 *Demonstration of the Impact of Differently Priced Shares on a Price-Weighted Indicator Series*

$$\text{DJIA}_t = \sum_{i=1}^{30} p_{it}/D_{adj}$$

where:

DJIA_t = the value of the DJIA on day t

p_{it} = the closing price of stock i on day t

D_{adj} = the adjusted divisor on day t

In Table 5.1, three stocks are employed to demonstrate the procedure used to derive a new divisor for the DJIA when a stock splits. When stocks split, the divisor becomes smaller as shown. The cumulative effect of splits can be derived from the fact that the divisor was originally 30.0, but as of August 1998 it was 0.24275.

The adjusted divisor ensures that the new value for the series is the same as it would have been without the split. In this case, the pre-split index value was 20. Therefore, after the split, given the new sum of prices, the divisor is adjusted downward to maintain this value of 20. The divisor is also changed in the rare instances of a change in the sample makeup of the series.

Because the series is price weighted, a high-priced stock carries more weight than a low-priced stock, so, as shown in Table 5.2, a 10 percent change in a $100 stock ($10) will cause a larger change in the series than a 10 percent change in a $30 stock ($3). In Case A, when the $100 stock increases by 10 percent, the average rises by 5.5 percent; in Case B, when the $30 stock increases by 10 percent, the average rises by only 1.7 percent.

The DJIA has been criticized on several counts. First, the sample used for the series is limited. It is difficult to conceive that 30 nonrandomly selected blue-chip stocks can be representative of the 3,000 stocks listed on the NYSE. Beyond the limited number, the stocks included are the largest and most prestigious companies in various industries. Therefore, it is contended that the DJIA probably reflects price movements for large, mature, blue-chip firms rather than for the typical company listed on the NYSE. Several studies have pointed out that the DJIA has not been as volatile as other market indexes and that the long-run returns on the DJIA are not comparable to the other NYSE stock indexes.

In addition, because the DJIA is price weighted, when companies have a stock split, their prices decline, and therefore their weight in the DJIA is reduced—even though they may be large and important. Therefore, the weighting scheme causes a downward bias in the DJIA, because the stocks that have higher growth rates will have higher prices, and because such stocks tend to split, they will consistently lose weight within the index.[6]

---

[6]For discussions of these problems, see H. L. Butler, Jr., and J. D. Allen, "The Dow Jones Industrial Average Reexamined," *Financial Analysts Journal* 35, no. 6 (November–December 1979): 37–45. For several articles that consider the origin and performance of the DJIA during its 100 years, see "100 Years of the DJIA," section in the *Wall Street Journal,* May 28, 1996, R29–R56. For a recent discussion of differing results, see Greg Ip, "What's Behind the Trailing Performance of the Dow Industrials versus the S & P 500?" *Wall Street Journal,* August 20, 1998, C1, C17.

Regardless of the several criticisms made of the DJIA, a fairly close relationship exists between the *daily* percentage changes for the DJIA and comparable price changes for other NYSE indexes, as shown in a subsequent section of this chapter. Dow Jones also publishes an average of twenty stocks in the transportation industry and 15 utility stocks. Detailed reports of the averages are contained daily in the *Wall Street Journal* and weekly in *Barron's,* including hourly figures.

Nikkei-Dow Jones Average   Also referred to as the Nikkei Stock Average Index, the Nikkei-Dow Jones Average is an arithmetic average of prices for 225 stocks on the First Section of the Tokyo Stock Exchange (TSE). This is the best-known series in Japan, and it has been used to show stock price trends since the reopening of the TSE. Notably, it was formulated by Dow Jones and Company, and, similar to the DJIA, it is a price-weighted series, so a large price change for a small company will have the same impact as a similar price change of a large firm. It is also criticized because the 225 stocks that are included only comprise about 15 percent of all stocks on the First Section. The results for this index are reported daily in the *Wall Street Journal* and the *Financial Times* and weekly in *Barron's.*

Value-Weighted Series

A **value-weighted series** is generated by deriving the initial total market value of all stocks used in the series (Market Value = Number of Shares Outstanding × Current Market Price). This initial figure is typically established as the base and assigned an index value (the most popular beginning index value is 100, but it can vary—say, 10, 50). Subsequently, a new market value is computed for all securities in the index, and the current market value is compared to the initial "base" value to determine the percentage of change, which in turn is applied to the beginning index value.

$$\text{Index}_t = \frac{\Sigma P_t Q_t}{\Sigma P_b Q_b} \times \text{Beginning Index Value}$$

where:

Index$_t$ = index value on day *t*
  P$_t$ = ending prices for stocks on day *t*
  Q$_t$ = number of outstanding shares on day *t*
  P$_b$ = ending price for stocks on base day
  Q$_b$ = number of outstanding shares on base day

A simple example for a three-stock index is shown in Table 5.3. As you can see, there is an *automatic adjustment* for stock splits and other capital changes with a value-weighted index because the decrease in the stock price is offset by an increase in the number of shares outstanding.

In a value-weighted index, the importance of individual stocks in the sample depends on the market value of the stocks. Therefore, a specified percentage change in the value of a large company has a greater impact than a comparable percentage change for a small company. As shown in Table 5.4, if we assume that the only change is a 20 percent increase in the value of Stock A, which has a beginning value of $10 million, the ending index value would be $202 million, or an index of 101. In contrast, if only Stock C increases by 20 percent from $100 million, the ending value will be $220 million or an index value of 110. The point is, price changes for the large market value stocks in a value-weighted index will dominate changes in the index value over time.

Table 5.5 is a summary of the characteristics of the major price-weighted, market value-weighted, and equal-weighted stock price indexes for the United States and major

Table 5.3 Example of a Computation of a Value-Weighted Index

Stock	Share Price	Number of Shares	Market Value
December 31, 1998			
A	$10.00	1,000,000	$ 10,000,000
B	15.00	6,000,000	90,000,000
C	20.00	5,000,000	100,000,000
Total			$200,000,000
			Base Value Equal to an Index of 100
December 31, 1999			
A	$12.00	1,000,000	$ 12,000,000
B	10.00	12,000,000[a]	120,000,000
C	20.00	5,500,000[b]	110,000,000
Total			$242,000,000

$$\text{New Index Value} = \frac{\text{Current Market Value}}{\text{Base Value}} \times \text{Beginning Index Value}$$

$$= \frac{\$242,000,000}{\$200,000,000} \times 100$$

$$= 1.21 \times 100$$

$$= 121$$

[a]Stock split two-for-one during the year.
[b]Company paid a 10 percent stock dividend during the year.

Table 5.4 Demonstration of the Impact of Different Values on a Market Value–Weighted Stock Index

| | | DECEMBER 31, 1998 | | DECEMBER 31, 1999 | | | |
| | | | | CASE A | | CASE B | |
Stock	Number of Shares	Price	Value	Price	Value	Price	Value
A	1,000,000	$10.00	$ 10,000,000	$12.00	$ 12,000,000	$10.00	$ 10,000,000
B	6,000,000	15.00	90,000,000	15.00	90,000,000	15.00	90,000,000
C	5,000,000	20.00	100,000,000	20.00	100,000,000	24.00	120,000,000
			$200,000,000		$202,000,000		$220,000,000
Index Value			100.00		101.00		110.00

foreign countries. As shown, the major differences are the number of stocks in the index, but more important, the *source* of the sample (stocks from the NYSE, the OTC, the AMEX, or from a foreign country such as the United Kingdom or Japan).

Figure 5.1 shows the "Stock Market Data Bank" from the *Wall Street Journal* of June 11, 1998, which contains values for many of the U.S. stock indexes we have discussed. Figure 5.2 shows a similar table for alternative indexes created and maintained by the *Financial Times*.

Unweighted Price Indicator Series

In an **unweighted index**, all stocks carry equal weight regardless of their price or market value. A $20 stock is as important as a $40 stock, and the total market value of the company is unimportant. Such an index can be used by individuals who randomly select stock for their portfolio and invest the same dollar amount in each stock. One way to

Table 5.5 *Summary of Stock Market Indexes*

Name of Index	Weighting	Number of Stocks	Source of Stocks
Dow Jones Industrial Average	Price	30	NYSE
Nikkei-Dow Jones Average	Price	225	TSE
S&P 400 Industrial	Market value	400	NYSE, OTC
S&P Transportation	Market value	20	NYSE, OTC
S&P Utilities	Market value	40	NYSE, OTC
S&P Financials	Market value	40	NYSE, OTC
S&P 500 Composite	Market value	500	NYSE, OTC
NYSE			
Industrial	Market value	1,420	NYSE
Utility	Market value	227	NYSE
Transportation	Market value	48	NYSE
Financial	Market value	864	NYSE
Composite	Market value	2,559	NYSE
NASDAQ			
Composite	Market value	4,879	OTC
Industrial	Market value	3,019	OTC
Banks	Market value	320	OTC
Insurance	Market value	107	OTC
Other finance	Market value	646	OTC
Transportation	Market value	91	OTC
Telecommunications	Market value	141	OTC
AMEX Market Value	Market value	900	AMEX
Dow Jones Equity Market Index	Market value	2,300	NYSE, AMEX, OTC
Wilshire 5000 Equity Value	Market value	5,000	NYSE, AMEX, OTC
Russell Indexes			
3,000	Market value	3,000	NYSE, AMEX, OTC
1,000	Market value	1,000 largest	NYSE, AMEX, OTC
2,000	Market value	2,000 smallest	NYSE, AMEX, OTC
Financial Times Actuaries Index			
All Share	Market value	700	LSE
FT100	Market value	100 largest	LSE
Small Cap	Market value	250	LSE
Mid Cap	Market value	250	LSE
Combined	Market value	350	LSE
Tokyo Stock Exchange Price Index (TOPIX)	Market value	1,800	TSE
Value Line Averages			
Industrials	Equal (geometric average)	1,499	NYSE, AMEX, OTC
Utilities	Equal	177	NYSE, AMEX, OTC
Rails	Equal	19	NYSE, AMEX, OTC
Composite	Equal	1,695	NYSE, AMEX, OTC
Financial Times Ordinary Share Index	Equal (geometric average)	30	LSE
FT-Actuaries World Indexes	Market value	2,275	24 countries, 3 regions (returns in $, £, ¥, DM, and local currency)
Morgan Stanley Capital International (MSCI) Indexes	Market value	1,375	19 countries, 3 international, 38 international industries (returns in $ and local currency)
Dow Jones World Stock Index	Market value	2,200	13 countries, 3 regions, 120 industry groups (returns in $, £, ¥, DM, and local currency)
Euromoney—First Boston Global Stock Index	Market value	—	17 countries (returns in $ and local currency)
Salomon-Russell World Equity Index	Market value	Russell 1000 and S-R PMI of 600 non-U.S. stocks	22 countries (returns in $ and local currency)

Figure 5.1   *Stock Market Data Bank*

STOCK MARKET DATA BANK 6/10/98

MAJOR INDEXES

†12-MO HIGH	LOW		DAILY HIGH	LOW	CLOSE	NET CHG	% CHG	†12-MO CHG	% CHG	FROM 12/31	% CHG
DOW JONES AVERAGES											
9211.84	7161.15	30 Industrials	9096.00	8952.27	8971.70	– 78.22	– 0.86	+ 1395.87	+ 18.43	+ 1063.45	+ 13.45
3686.02	2676.49	20 Transportation	3503.19	3425.20	3440.34	– 21.37	– 0.62	+ 763.85	+ 28.54	+ 183.84	+ 5.65
292.64	220.56	15 Utilities	294.16	290.49	292.64	+ 1.66	+ 0.57	+ 72.08	+ 32.68	+ 19.57	+ 7.17
2960.79	2324.68	65 Composite	2908.06	2864.59	2871.21	– 16.41	– 0.57	+ 546.53	+ 23.51	+ 263.84	+ 10.12
1071.47	818.38	DJ Global-US	1062.83	1048.52	1050.42	– 6.18	– 0.58	+ 232.04	+ 28.35	+ 128.06	+ 13.69
NEW YORK STOCK EXCHANGE											
585.62	453.50	Composite	580.28	573.31	574.37	– 3.13	– 0.54	+ 120.87	+ 26.65	+ 63.18	+ 12.36
720.86	574.10	Industrials	717.41	707.92	709.06	– 5.11	– 0.72	+ 134.96	+ 23.51	+ 78.68	+ 12.48
388.87	278.03	Utilities	380.97	376.87	378.74	+ 0.43	+ 0.11	+ 100.71	+ 36.22	+ 43.55	+ 12.99
537.19	404.33	Transportation	509.79	501.69	503.19	– 4.54	– 0.89	+ 98.86	+ 24.45	+ 36.94	+ 7.92
576.63	416.22	Finance	559.37	553.81	555.06	– 1.53	– 0.27	+ 138.84	+ 33.36	+ 59.10	+ 11.92
STANDARD & POOR'S INDEXES											
1130.54	869.57	500 Index	1126.00	1110.27	1112.28	– 6.13	– 0.55	+ 242.71	+ 27.91	+ 141.85	+ 14.62
1311.46	1019.09	Industrials	1311.19	1291.84	1294.08	– 9.07	– 0.70	+ 271.57	+ 26.56	+ 172.70	+ 15.40
249.41	193.38	Utilities	247.46	243.63	246.12	+ 2.24	+ 0.92	+ 52.74	+ 27.27	+ 10.31	+ 4.37
380.67	283.10	400 MidCap	362.33	357.64	357.98	– 4.03	– 1.11	+ 74.88	+ 26.45	+ 24.61	+ 7.38
206.18	157.38	600 SmallCap	190.48	187.73	187.84	– 2.64	– 1.39	+ 30.46	+ 19.35	+ 6.68	+ 3.69
242.49	185.88	1500 Index	239.63	236.47	236.85	– 1.51	– 0.63	+ 50.97	+ 27.42	+ 28.05	+ 13.43
NASDAQ STOCK MARKET											
1917.61	1407.85	Composite	1800.76	1773.18	1773.25	– 27.51	– 1.53	+ 365.40	+ 25.95	+ 202.90	+ 12.92
1290.90	938.99	Nasdaq 100	1224.33	1199.11	1199.30	– 24.18	– 1.98	+ 250.30	+ 26.38	+ 208.50	+ 21.04
1414.11	1137.76	Industrials	1326.89	1310.91	1310.95	– 20.36	– 1.53	+ 173.19	+ 15.22	+ 89.92	+ 7.36
1945.34	1582.22	Insurance	1834.11	1806.83	1810.39	– 20.50	– 1.12	+ 228.17	+ 14.42	+ 12.44	+ 0.69
2297.71	1526.64	Banks	2144.48	2133.90	2136.04	– 14.72	– 0.68	+ 609.40	+ 39.92	+ 52.82	+ 2.54
831.58	584.92	Computer	765.10	748.98	748.98	– 14.83	– 1.94	+ 161.54	+ 27.50	+ 130.32	+ 21.06
395.37	245.77	Telecommunications	383.99	379.15	379.33	– 7.22	– 1.87	+ 133.56	+ 54.34	+ 72.73	+ 23.72
OTHERS											
753.67	616.10	Amex Composite	714.21	706.31	706.85	– 7.22	– 1.01	+ 84.18	+ 13.52	+ 22.24	+ 3.25
595.18	455.36	Russell 1000	588.89	581.14	582.20	– 3.58	– 0.61	+ 126.84	+ 27.85	+ 68.41	+ 13.31
491.41	387.62	Russell 2000	456.74	450.83	451.08	– 5.66	– 1.24	+ 63.46	+ 16.37	+ 14.06	+ 3.22
627.21	481.33	Russell 3000	616.76	608.95	609.95	– 4.10	– 0.67	+ 128.62	+ 26.72	+ 66.90	+ 12.32
508.39	413.06	Value-Line(geom.)	482.54	476.83	477.11	– 5.43	– 1.13	+ 64.05	+ 15.51	+ 22.76	+ 5.01
10782.75	8227.15	Wilshire 5000	...	...	10454.90	– 72.50	– 0.69	+ 2227.75	+ 27.08	+ 1156.71	+ 12.44

†-Based on comparable trading day in preceding year.

Source: *The Wall Street Journal*, June 11, 1998, C2.

visualize an unweighted series is to assume that equal dollar amounts are invested in each stock in the portfolio (for example, an equal $1,000 investment in each stock would work out to 50 shares of a $20 stock, 100 shares of a $10 stock, and 10 shares of a $100 stock). In fact, the actual movements in the index are typically based on *the arithmetic average of the percent changes in price or value for the stocks in the index.* The use of percentage price changes means that the price level or the market value of the stock does not make a difference—each percentage change has equal weight. This arithmetic average of percent changes procedure is used in academic studies when the authors specify equal weighting.

In contrast to computing an arithmetic average of percentage changes, both Value Line and the *Financial Times* Ordinary Share Index compute a *geometric* mean of the holding period returns *and* derive the holding period yield from this calculation. Table 5.6 contains an example of an arithmetic average and a geometric average. This demonstrates the downward bias of the geometric calculation. Specifically, the geometric mean of holding

Figure 5.2   Financial Times *Actuaries Shares Indices*

FTSE Actuaries Share Indices   **The UK Series**
Produced in conjunction with the Faculty and Institute of Actuaries

	Jun 8	Day's chge%	Jun 5	Jun 4	Year ago	Gross yield%	Net yield%	Net cover	P/E ratio	Xd adj. ytd	Total Return
FTSE 100	6037.8	+1.5	5947.3	5860.8	4686.7	2.73	2.31	2.02	22.64	78.04	2641.89
FTSE 250	5960.3	+0.4	5934.6	5921.6	4484.1	2.77	2.34	2.00	22.49	65.13	2554.03
FTSE 250 ex IT	6030.0	+0.4	6007.5	5997.4	4488.1	2.85	2.41	2.06	21.26	67.00	2593.55
FTSE 350	2935.8	+1.3	2897.7	2862.5	2265.2	2.74	2.31	2.02	22.61	36.79	2624.20
FTSE 350 ex IT	2939.4	+1.3	2900.9	2865.5	2264.6	2.75	2.33	2.03	22.36	37.12	1347.69
FTSE 350 Higher Yield	2842.1	+1.1	2811.4	2782.5	2198.3	3.74	3.20	1.88	17.76	47.17	2171.85
FTSE 350 Lower Yield	3032.6	+1.5	2988.6	2948.2	2338.2	2.01	1.67	2.21	28.22	28.47	2202.64
FTSE SmallCap	2782.68	+0.3	2775.34	2767.32	2279.49	2.96	2.40	1.52	27.81	27.48	2418.83
FTSE SmallCap ex IT	2790.31	+0.2	2785.25	2778.12	2262.11	3.15	2.55	1.57	25.28	28.82	2450.21
FTSE All-Share	2868.10	+1.2	2832.79	2800.01	2222.17	2.75	2.32	1.99	22.88	35.44	2601.62
FTSE All-Share ex IT	2874.23	+1.3	2838.37	2805.27	2221.12	2.77	2.34	2.00	22.50	35.92	1341.40

Source: *Financial Times*, June 9, 1998, p. 36.

Table 5.6   *Example of an Arithmetic and Geometric Mean of Percentage Changes*

	SHARE PRICE			
Stock	**T**	**T + 1**	**HPR**	**HPY**
X	10	12	1.20	0.20
Y	22	20	.91	−0.09
Z	44	47	1.07	0.07

$$\Pi = 1.20 \times .91 \times 1.07$$
$$= 1.168$$
Geometric mean $= 1.168^{1/3} = 1.0531$

$$\Sigma = 0.18$$
Arithmetic mean $= 0.18/3 = 0.06$
$$= 6\%$$

Index Value (T) $\times$ 1.0531 $=$ Index Value (T + 1)
Index Value (T) $\times$ 1.06 $=$ Index Value (T + 1)

period yields (HPY) shows an average change of only 5.3 percent versus the actual change in wealth of 6 percent.

Global Equity Indexes

As described in the Chapter 4 Appendix, there are stock-market indexes available for most individual foreign markets similar to those we described for Japan (the Nikkei and TOPIX) and the United Kingdom (the several *Financial Times* indexes) described in Table 5.5. While these local indexes are closely followed within each country, a problem arises in comparing the results implied by these indexes to one another because of a lack of consistency among them in sample selection, weighting, or computational procedure. To solve these comparability problems, several groups have computed a set of country stock indexes with consistent sample selection, weighting, and computational procedure. As a result, these indexes can be directly compared and combined to create various regional indexes (for example, Pacific Basin). We will describe the three major sets of global equity indexes.

FT/S&P-Actuaries World Indexes   The FT/S&P-Actuaries World Indexes are jointly compiled by The Financial Times Limited, Goldman Sachs & Company, and Standard & Poor's (the "compilers") in conjunction with the Institute of Actuaries and the Faculty of Actuaries. Approximately 2,461 equity securities in 30 countries are measured, covering at least 70 percent of the total value of all listed companies in each country. Actively traded medium and small capitalization stocks are included along

with major international equities. All securities included must allow direct holdings of shares by foreign nationals.

The indexes are market-value weighted and have a base date of December 31, 1986 = 100. The index results are reported in U.S. dollars, U.K. pound sterling, Japanese yen, German mark, and the local currency of the country. Performance results are calculated after the New York markets close and are published the following day in the *Financial Times* as shown in Table 5.7. In addition to the individual countries and the world index, there are several geographic subgroups, as shown in Table 5.7.

Morgan Stanley Capital International (MSCI) Indexes   The Morgan Stanley Capital International Indexes consist of three international, nineteen national, and thirty-eight international industry indexes. The indexes consider some 1,375 companies listed on stock exchanges in 19 countries with a combined market capitalization that represents approximately 60 percent of the aggregate market value of the stock exchanges of these countries. All the indexes are market-value weighted. Table 5.8 contains the countries included, the number of stocks, and market values for stocks in the various countries and groups.

In addition to reporting the indexes in U.S. dollars and the country's local currency, the following valuation information is available: (1) price-to-book value (P/BV) ratio, (2) price-to-cash earnings (earnings plus depreciation) (P/CE) ratio, (3) price-to-earnings (P/E) ratio, and (4) dividend yield (YLD). These ratios help in analyzing different valuation levels among countries and over time for specific countries.

Notably, the Morgan Stanley group index for Europe, Australia, and the Far East (EAFE) is being used as the basis for futures and options contracts on the Chicago Mercantile Exchange and the Chicago Board Options Exchange. Several of the MSCI country indexes, the EAFE index, and a world index are reported daily in the *Wall Street Journal,* as shown in Figure 5.3.

Dow Jones World Stock Index   In January 1993, Dow Jones introduced its World Stock Index. Composed of more than 2,200 companies worldwide and organized into 120 industry groups, the index includes twenty-eight countries representing more than 80 percent of the combined capitalization of these countries. In addition to the twenty-eight countries shown in Figure 5.4, the countries are grouped into three regions: Asia/Pacific, Europe/Africa, and the Americas. Finally, each country's index is calculated in its own currency as well as in the U.S. dollar, British pound, German mark, and Japanese yen. The index is reported daily in the *Wall Street Journal* (domestic), in the *Wall Street Journal Europe,* and in the *Asian Wall Street Journal.* It is published weekly in *Barron's.*[7]

Comparison of World Stock Indexes   As shown in Table 5.9, the correlations between the three series since December 31, 1991, when the DJ series became available, indicate that the results with the alternative world stock indexes are quite comparable.

BOND-MARKET INDICATOR SERIES[8]

Investors know little about the several bond-market series because these bond series are relatively new and not widely published. Knowledge regarding these bond series is becoming more important because of the growth of fixed-income mutual funds and the consequent need to have a reliable set of benchmarks to use in evaluating

---

[7]"Journal Launches Index Tracking World Stocks," *Wall Street Journal,* January 5, 1993, C1.

[8]The discussion in this section draws heavily from Frank K. Reilly, and David J. Wright, "Bond Market Indexes," *Handbook of Fixed Income Securities,* 5th ed., edited by Frank J. Fabozzi (Chicago: Irwin Professional Publishing, 1997).

Table 5.7 FT/S&P Actuaries World Indexes

FT/S&P ACTUARIES WORLD INDEXES

The FT/S&P Actuaries World Indexes are owned by FTSE International Limited, Goldman Sachs & Co. and Standard & Poor's. The indexes are compiled by FTSE International and Standard & Poor's in conjunction with the Faculty of Actuaries and the Institute of Actuaries. NetWest Securities, Ltd. was a co-founder of the indexes.

NATIONAL AND REGIONAL MARKETS Figures in parentheses show number of lines of stock	US Dollar Index	Day's Change %	FRIDAY JUNE 6 1996 Pound Sterling Index	Yen Index	DM Index	Local Currency Index	Local % chg on day	Gross Div. Yield	THURSDAY JUNE 4 1996 US Dollar Index	Pound Sterling Index	Yen Index	DM Index	Local Currency Index	DOLLAR INDEX 52 week High	52 week Low	Year ago (approx)
Australia (72)	185.52	-2.8	168.11	163.66	171.01	205.40	-0.7	3.86	190.85	172.26	166.76	174.99	206.75	243.87	185.52	232.17
Austria (23)	244.09	-0.4	221.18	215.33	225.00	224.87	0.1	1.51	245.01	221.14	214.09	224.66	224.52	253.73	181.60	195.63
Belgium (26)	363.74	1.0	329.60	320.88	335.30	328.04	1.6	2.24	359.98	324.92	314.55	330.08	322.95	363.74	234.33	247.38
Brazil (26)	228.65	1.6	207.19	201.71	210.77	484.89	1.6	2.11	225.13	203.20	196.72	206.43	477.06	322.44	184.94	264.69
Canada (120)	238.42	0.2	216.04	210.32	219.77	252.04	0.5	1.58	238.02	214.83	207.98	218.24	250.74	248.78	199.10	209.08
Denmark (34)	503.08	-0.5	455.87	443.80	463.74	462.15	0.0	1.31	505.68	456.43	441.87	463.67	462.15	521.81	375.32	381.46
Finland (28)	434.80	1.6	393.99	383.57	400.80	491.65	2.1	1.86	428.05	386.36	374.03	392.49	481.51	451.12	267.45	267.45
France (78)	335.41	0.8	303.93	295.89	309.18	312.81	1.4	1.88	332.57	300.18	290.60	304.94	308.52	335.41	217.48	220.52
Germany (58)	303.71	0.9	275.20	267.92	279.96	279.96	1.5	1.19	300.88	271.57	262.90	275.88	275.88	303.71	204.89	212.69
Greece (37)	297.72	-0.3	269.78	262.64	274.44	641.87	0.1	1.42	298.62	269.53	260.93	273.81	641.44	307.94	284.88	—
Hong Kong, China (66)	253.20	-0.4	229.44	223.37	233.40	251.92	-0.4	6.26	254.31	229.54	222.22	233.18	253.02	580.03	253.20	525.52
Indonesia (27)	32.46	1.5	29.42	28.64	29.92	232.01	1.5	3.05	31.99	28.88	27.96	29.34	228.65	254.90	27.26	239.69
Ireland (16)	514.79	0.8	466.47	454.13	474.53	509.78	1.4	1.91	510.62	460.89	446.18	468.20	503.00	560.44	341.21	341.21
Italy (54)	170.03	0.8	154.07	150.00	156.74	221.71	1.3	1.27	168.66	152.23	147.38	154.65	218.83	177.15	86.93	88.26
Japan (480)	89.67	-1.4	81.25	79.10	82.66	79.10	-0.5	1.00	90.97	82.11	79.49	83.41	79.49	141.12	88.52	134.05
Malaysia (106)	138.95	-2.5	125.91	122.58	128.09	213.28	-2.1	3.00	142.49	128.61	124.51	130.66	217.87	538.33	113.56	534.34
Mexico (29)	1484.03	0.8	1344.76	1309.17	1367.99	14206.33	0.3	1.71	1472.59	1329.15	1286.75	1350.25	14156.42	1901.98	1415.52	477.55
Netherlands (19)	526.88	0.3	477.43	464.80	485.68	480.58	0.8	1.92	525.28	474.11	458.99	481.64	476.51	532.74	376.29	376.29
New Zealand (14)	63.53	-3.2	57.57	56.04	58.56	65.71	-0.9	4.63	65.64	59.25	57.36	60.19	66.30	96.47	63.53	90.54
Norway (38)	317.58	2.1	287.78	280.16	292.75	321.03	2.4	1.96	311.00	280.71	271.75	285.16	313.65	374.64	310.69	310.69
Philippines (22)	85.69	-0.1	77.65	75.60	78.99	167.30	0.2	1.24	85.80	77.44	74.97	78.67	166.97	172.36	57.54	169.15
Portugal (18)	276.74	3.2	250.77	244.13	255.10	343.98	3.7	1.11	268.22	242.09	234.37	245.93	331.61	299.39	268.22	—
Singapore (42)	157.22	-2.4	142.46	138.69	144.92	123.04	-1.8	2.47	161.12	145.43	140.79	147.74	125.25	268.22	144.01	393.80
South Africa (42)	279.33	-1.1	253.11	246.42	257.49	313.60	-0.7	2.75	282.45	254.94	246.81	258.99	315.78	364.24	227.66	360.22
Spain (31)	393.39	1.2	356.48	347.04	362.63	448.68	1.7	1.71	388.64	350.79	339.60	356.36	441.01	398.54	236.28	252.22
Sweden (49)	607.27	2.3	550.28	535.72	559.79	700.80	3.0	1.67	593.69	535.86	518.76	544.37	680.45	615.21	439.98	453.30
Switzerland (30)	412.79	0.9	374.05	364.15	380.51	377.29	1.4	1.09	409.27	369.41	357.62	375.27	372.10	414.95	285.85	293.23
Thailand (38)	16.75	-0.5	15.18	14.77	15.44	28.14	0.4	9.54	16.84	15.20	14.71	15.44	28.03	69.09	13.10	64.39
United Kingdom (206)	384.05	1.0	348.01	338.80	354.02	348.01	1.4	2.84	380.42	343.36	332.41	348.81	343.36	401.84	294.50	294.50
USA (632)	454.42	1.7	411.78	400.88	418.89	454.42	1.7	1.41	446.96	403.42	390.55	409.82	446.96	462.18	341.93	341.93
Americas (807)	410.58	1.6	372.05	362.20	378.47	347.19	1.6	1.43	404.12	364.76	353.12	370.55	341.69	418.95	313.33	313.33
Europe (745)	366.16	0.9	331.80	323.02	337.53	345.25	1.4	1.96	362.75	327.41	316.97	332.61	340.37	367.09	259.30	259.30
Eurobloc (351)	106.31	0.9	108.26	111.51	105.94	105.95	1.4	1.61	105.40	106.91	109.51	104.48	104.49	106.34	100.00	—
Nordic (149)	525.00	1.7	475.73	463.14	483.95	529.57	2.3	1.67	516.13	465.96	450.99	473.25	517.54	536.56	388.51	390.11
Pacific Basin (867)	96.20	-1.5	87.17	84.86	88.68	85.34	-0.5	1.74	97.66	88.15	85.34	89.55	85.79	158.99	95.32	152.70
Euro-Pacific (1612)	208.72	0.3	189.13	184.13	192.40	183.45	0.9	1.90	208.15	187.88	181.88	190.86	181.82	216.04	172.03	197.19
North America (752)	440.57	1.6	399.23	388.66	406.12	440.81	1.6	1.42	433.62	391.38	378.90	397.60	433.79	448.61	333.87	333.87
Europe Ex. UK (539)	344.57	0.9	312.24	303.97	317.63	333.16	1.5	1.53	341.38	308.13	298.30	313.02	328.32	345.25	234.29	234.29
Europe Ex. Eurobloc (394)	99.59	1.0	101.42	104.46	99.24	100.67	1.5	2.31	98.58	100.00	102.43	97.72	99.20	100.97	96.35	—
Europe Ex. UK Ex. Eurobloc (188)	103.46	1.1	105.35	108.52	103.10	103.04	1.7	1.31	102.28	103.75	106.27	101.38	101.30	104.20	99.32	—
Pacific Ex. Japan (387)	160.55	-1.8	145.48	141.63	148.00	168.76	-0.7	4.63	163.45	147.53	142.83	149.88	170.00	318.98	160.55	313.24
World Ex. Eurobloc (2110)	97.68	1.0	88.51	86.17	90.04	98.69	1.2	1.66	96.70	87.29	84.50	88.67	97.47	100.18	96.07	—
World Ex. US (1829)	211.79	0.3	191.91	186.84	195.23	190.23	0.9	1.89	211.22	190.65	184.57	193.67	188.60	200.18	175.30	200.80
World Ex. UK (2255)	281.11	1.0	254.72	247.98	259.13	258.33	1.3	1.51	278.36	251.24	243.23	255.23	255.10	287.02	234.24	240.89
World Ex. Japan (1981)	389.14	1.2	352.62	343.29	358.71	382.83	1.5	1.72	384.35	346.91	335.85	352.42	377.30	394.39	302.94	302.94
The World Index (2461)	289.83	1.0	262.63	255.68	267.17	266.43	1.3	1.65	287.00	259.05	250.78	263.16	263.08	296.57	241.30	245.52

Source: *Financial Times*, June 9, 1998, 37.

Table 5.8 *Market Coverage of Morgan Stanley Capital International Indexes as of August 26, 1998*

	GDP EAFE	Weights[a] World	Companies in Index	U.S. $ Billion	Free EAFE[b]	World
Austria	1.5	0.9	20	24.1	0.4	0.2
Belgium	1.8	1.1	17	123.1	1.9	0.9
Denmark	1.3	0.8	22	64.1	1.0	0.5
Finland	1.0	0.6	20	70.0	1.1	0.5
France	10.7	6.5	67	639.2	9.9	4.6
Germany	16.2	9.9	62	728.9	11.3	5.3
Ireland	0.5	0.3	17	31.6	0.5	0.2
Italy	9.4	5.7	52	331.0	5.1	2.4
The Netherlands	2.7	1.7	23	369.4	5.7	2.7
Norway	1.2	0.7	30	30.5	0.5	0.2
Portugal	0.8	0.5	20	43.3	0.7	0.3
Spain	4.2	2.6	31	207.6	3.2	1.5
Sweden	1.7	1.0	38	197.2	3.0	1.4
Switzerland	2.1	1.3	32	523.3	8.1	3.8
United Kingdom	9.7	5.9	136	1,466.4	22.7	10.6
Europe	64.6	39.4	587	4,849.8	74.9	35.2
Australia	2.6	1.6	54	147.6	2.3	1.1
Hong Kong	1.2	0.8	34	114.0	1.8	0.8
Japan	29.9	18.3	308	1,292.7	20.0	9.4
Malaysia	0.5	0.3	72	23.3	0.4	0.2
New Zealand	0.5	0.3	9	12.7	0.2	0.1
Singapore	0.7	0.4	35	32.1	—	0.2
Singapore (free)	—	—	35	32.8	0.5	—
Pacific	35.4	21.6	512	1,622.3	—	11.8
Pacific (free)	—	—	512	1,623.0	25.1	—
Pacific Free ex Japan	—	—	204	330.3	5.1	—
EAFE	100.0	61.0	1,099	6,472.1	—	46.9
EAFE (free)	—	—	1,099	6,472.8	100.0	—
Canada	—	24	78	264.1	—	1.9
United States	—	36.6	383	7,059.9	—	51.2
The World Index	—	100.0	1,560	13,796.1	—	100.0
The World Index (free)	—	—	1,560	13,796.8	—	—
Nordic countries	5.1	3.1	110	361.8	—	2.6
Europe ex UK	54.9	33.5	451	3,383.3	—	24.5
Far East	32.3	19.7	449	1,462.0	—	10.6
Far East (free)	—	—	449	1,462.7	22.6	—
EASEA Index	70.1	42.7	791	5,179.4	—	37.5
North America	—	39.0	461	7,324.0	—	53.1
Kokusai Index	—	81.8	1,252	12,503.4	—	90.6

[a]GDP weight figures represent the initial weights applicable for the first month. They are used exclusively in the MSCI "GDP weighted" indexes.

[b]Free indicates that only stocks that can be acquired by foreign investors are included in the index. If the number of companies is the same and the value is different, it indicates that the stocks available to foreigners are priced differently from domestic shares.

Source: Morgan Stanley Capital International (New York: Morgan Stanley & Co., 1998).

Figure 5.3 *Listing of Morgan Stanley Capital International Stock Index Values for June 11, 1998*

Morgan Stanley Indexes

	JUNE 9	JUNE 8	% FROM 12/31/97
U.S.	1072.6	1069.1	+ 15.5
Britain	1792.1	1795.6	+ 16.8
Canada	862.5	864.3	+ 14.8
Japan	779.9	771.8	+ 1.4
France	1341.5	1342.5	+ 39.4
Germany	741.1	745.2	+ 33.4
Hong Kong	4510.8	4626.2	− 29.9
Switzerland	944.8	948.8	+ 22.3
Australia	524.5	528.0	+ 1.1
World Index	1081.3	1080.4	+ 15.5
EAFE MSCI-p	1373.9	1375.9	+ 15.6

As calculated by Morgan Stanley Capital International
Perspective, Geneva. Each index, calculated in local
currencies, is based on the close of 1969 equaling 100.

Source: *Wall Street Journal,* June 11, 1998, C12.

performance.[9] Also, because the performance of many fixed-income money managers has been unable to match that of the aggregate bond market, interest has been growing in bond index funds, which requires the development of an index to emulate.[10]

Notably, the creation and computation of bond-market indexes is more difficult than a stock-market series for several reasons. First, the universe of bonds is much broader than that of stocks, ranging from U.S. Treasury securities to bonds in default. Second, the universe of bonds is changing constantly because of numerous new issues, bond maturities, calls, and bond sinking funds. Third, the volatility of prices for individual bonds and bond portfolios changes because bond price volatility is affected by duration, which is likewise changing constantly because of changes in maturity, coupon, and market yield (see Chapter 16). Finally, significant problems can arise in correctly pricing the individual bond issues in an index (especially corporate and mortgage bonds) compared to the current and continuous transactions prices available for most stocks used in stock indexes.

The subsequent discussion will be divided into the following three subsections: (1) U.S. investment-grade bond indexes, including Treasuries; (2) U.S. high-yield bond indexes; and (3) global government bond indexes. Notably, all of these indexes indicate total rates of return for the portfolio of bonds, including price change, accrued interest, and coupon income reinvested. Also most of the indexes are market-value weighted using current prices and outstanding par values publicly held. Table 5.10 is a summary of the characteristics for the indexes available for these three segments of the bond market.

Investment-Grade Bond Indexes

As shown in Table 5.10, four investment firms have created and maintain indexes for Treasury bonds and other bonds considered investment grade, that is, the bonds are rated

---

[9]For a discussion of the evaluation of bond portfolios, see Gifford Fong, Charles Pearson, Oldrick Vasicek, and Theresa Conroy, "Fixed-Income Portfolio Performance: Analyzing Sources of Return," in *The Handbook of Fixed-Income Securities,* 3rd ed., ed. by Frank J. Fabozzi (Homewood, IL: Business One Irwin, 1991). For a discussion of benchmark selection, see Chris P. Dialynas, "The Active Decisions in the Selection of Passive Management and Performance Bogeys," and Daralyn B. Peifer, "A Sponsor's View of Benchmark Portfolios," in *The Handbook of Fixed-Income Securities,* 5th ed., edited by Frank J. Fabozzi (Chicago, IL: Irwin Professional Publishing, 1997).

[10]For a discussion of this phenomenon, see Fran Hawthorne, "The Battle of the Bond Indexes," *Institutional Investor* 20, no. 4 (April 1986); and Sharmin Mossavar-Rahmani, "Indexing Fixed Income Investments," in *The Handbook of Fixed-Income Securities,* 5th ed., edited by Frank J. Fabozzi (Chicago: Irwin Professional Publishing, 1997).

Figure 5.4   *Dow Jones World Stock Index Listing*

DOW JONES GLOBAL INDEXES

5:30 p.m., Wednesday, June 10, 1998

REGION/ COUNTRY	DJ GLOBAL INDEXES, LOCAL CURRENCY	PCT. CHG.	IN U.S. DOLLARS 5:30 P.M. INDEX	CHG.	PCT. CHG.	12-MO HIGH	12-MO LOW	12-MO CHG.	PCT. CHG.	FROM 12/31	PCT. CHG.
Americas			259.41	− 1.86	− 0.71	266.27	206.21	+ 53.20	+ 25.80	+ 29.17	+ 12.67
Brazil†	1111 − 4.23		371.39	− 16.40	− 4.23	595.18	340.28	− 129.57	− 25.87	− 72.02	− 16.24
Canada	216.60 − 1.34		170.72	− 3.14	− 1.81	181.01	144.54	+ 20.83	+ 13.89	+ 16.63	+ 10.79
Chile	191.51 − 1.62		157.62	− 2.59	− 1.62	234.77	153.34	− 70.36	− 30.86	− 25.53	− 13.94
Mexico	320.52 − 3.48		110.56	− 4.74	− 4.11	152.46	110.09	− 6.15	− 5.27	− 33.39	− 23.20
U.S.	1050.42 − 0.59		1050.42	− 6.18	− 0.58	1071.47	818.16	+ 232.26	+ 28.39	+ 128.09	+ 13.89
Venezuela	468.95 − 1.50		53.66	− 0.82	− 1.51	113.11	53.66	− 24.60	− 31.43	− 35.98	− 40.13
Latin America			176.39	− 6.81	− 3.72	259.69	175.20	− 48.82	− 21.68	− 41.42	− 19.02
Europe/Africa			238.70	− 2.25	− 0.93	241.80	173.48	+ 63.79	+ 36.47	+ 49.91	+ 26.43
Austria	156.84 − 1.93		132.53	− 3.90	− 2.86	141.18	102.77	+ 21.45	+ 19.31	+ 23.95	+ 22.06
Belgium	298.57 + 0.20		252.50	− 1.79	− 0.70	254.33	162.85	+ 75.44	+ 42.61	+ 74.66	+ 41.98
Denmark	247.24 − 0.13		213.95	− 2.21	− 1.02	217.28	155.99	+ 55.39	+ 34.94	+ 29.82	+ 16.19
Finland	624.00 + 0.03		473.60	− 4.37	− 0.91	494.22	297.78	+ 160.41	+ 51.22	+ 163.00	+ 52.48
France	255.90 + 0.04		220.12	− 1.91	− 0.86	222.03	143.85	+ 73.52	+ 50.14	+ 62.55	+ 39.69
Germany	311.21 + 0.42		262.46	− 1.11	− 0.42	264.41	170.33	+ 79.98	+ 43.83	+ 69.27	+ 35.85
Greece	427.43 − 1.66		245.85	− 7.41	− 2.93	260.01	137.69	+ 70.29	+ 40.03	+ 94.44	+ 62.37
Ireland	365.72 − 1.09		318.76	− 4.99	− 1.54	337.00	207.74	+ 111.02	+ 53.44	+ 75.63	+ 31.10
Italy	314.02 + 0.37		219.28	− 1.05	− 0.48	230.56	119.70	+ 99.57	+ 83.18	+ 63.59	+ 40.85
Netherlands	401.47 + 0.11		338.61	− 2.67	− 0.78	348.09	249.02	+ 89.30	+ 35.82	+ 72.32	+ 27.16
Norway	209.66 − 1.66		165.13	− 4.58	− 2.70	198.66	150.24	− 2.46	− 1.47	− 5.31	− 3.11
Portugal	442.23 0.00		325.07	− 2.78	− 0.85	361.91	189.20	+ 135.56	+ 71.53	+ 97.52	+ 42.85
South Africa	199.29 − 4.03		104.73	− 5.43	− 4.93	136.74	89.78	− 29.66	− 22.07	+ 1.61	+ 1.56
Spain	401.80 + 0.80		257.26	− 0.18	− 0.07	268.00	157.09	+ 84.76	+ 49.14	+ 74.51	+ 40.78
Sweden	435.41 − 1.23		302.79	− 7.70	− 2.48	312.17	223.96	+ 68.35	+ 29.15	+ 64.19	+ 26.90
Switzerland	428.63 − 0.79		391.53	− 5.17	− 1.30	400.81	275.25	+ 102.73	+ 35.57	+ 64.67	+ 19.78
United Kingdom	232.47 − 0.20		202.63	− 1.33	− 0.65	208.94	156.03	+ 44.44	+ 28.09	+ 27.51	+ 15.71
Europe/Africa (ex. South Africa)			246.30	− 2.07	− 0.83	249.19	176.77	+ 69.13	+ 39.02	+ 52.64	+ 27.18
Europe/Africa (ex. U.K. & S. Africa)			273.52	− 2.51	− 0.91	277.14	187.71	+ 83.58	+ 44.00	+ 67.21	+ 32.58
Asia/Pacific			69.98	− 1.64	− 2.29	119.95	69.98	− 47.41	− 40.39	− 9.17	− 11.59
Australia	154.06 − 1.15		119.07	− 2.95	− 2.42	163.33	119.07	− 36.05	− 23.24	− 14.72	− 11.00
Hong Kong	160.61 − 4.84		161.20	− 8.21	− 4.85	364.28	161.20	− 157.77	− 49.46	− 66.40	− 29.17
Indonesia	159.38 − 0.88		27.14	− 0.24	− 0.88	200.14	25.45	− 160.58	− 85.54	− 42.54	− 61.05
Japan	74.40 − 0.87		65.57	− 1.19	− 1.78	105.04	65.57	− 37.23	− 36.22	− 4.82	− 6.84
Malaysia	94.63 − 2.86		63.74	− 3.46	− 5.15	235.67	53.74	− 171.93	− 72.96	− 16.18	− 20.24
New Zealand	141.59 − 1.32		130.43	− 3.85	− 2.87	213.76	130.43	− 75.29	− 36.60	− 38.87	− 22.96
Philippines	182.52 + 0.13		118.40	− 1.92	− 1.60	272.76	82.69	− 144.34	− 54.94	+ 7.20	+ 6.48
Singapore	82.96 − 1.97		77.08	− 2.93	− 3.66	185.61	77.08	− 103.61	− 57.34	− 37.87	− 32.94
South Korea	54.80 − 4.88		29.85	− 1.50	− 4.78	104.87	23.31	− 69.25	− 69.88	+ 1.65	+ 5.83
Taiwan	166.63 − 3.30		123.25	− 4.87	− 3.80	225.92	123.25	− 62.29	− 33.57	− 29.82	− 19.48
Thailand	48.40 − 5.86		26.27	− 1.99	− 7.04	92.26	22.90	− 56.84	− 68.39	− 3.88	− 12.87
Asia/Pacific (ex. Japan)			106.06	− 4.03	− 3.66	217.72	106.06	− 103.85	− 49.47	− 30.26	− 22.20
World (ex. U.S.)			144.77	− 2.07	− 1.41	152.46	121.49	+ 0.52	+ 0.36	+ 15.15	+ 11.69
DJ WORLD STOCK INDEX			190.30	− 1.90	− 0.99	196.23	160.48	+ 22.01	+ 13.08	+ 21.61	+ 12.81

Indexes based on 6/30/S2=100 for U.S., 12/31/91=100 for World.
†Local currency index shown in 000s.

©1998 Dow Jones & Co. Inc., All Rights Reserved.

Source: *Wall Street Journal,* June 11, 1998, C12.

Table 5.9 *Correlations of Percent Price Changes of Alternative World Stock Indexes 12/31/91–12/31/97*

	U.S. Dollars
FT—MS:	.998
FT—DJ:	.997
MS—DJ:	.996

BBB or higher. As demonstrated in Reilly and Wright and shown in Chapter 4, the relationship among the returns for these bonds is strong (that is, correlations average about 0.95), regardless of the segment of the market. This implies that the returns for all these bonds are being driven by aggregate interest rates—that is, shifts in the government yield curve.

High-Yield Bond Indexes

One of the fastest-growing segments of the U.S. bond market during the past fifteen years has been the high-yield bond market, which includes bonds that are not investment grade—that is, they are rated BB, B, CCC, CC, and C. Because of this growth, four investment firms and two academicians created indexes related to this market. A summary of the characteristics for these indexes is included in Table 5.10. As shown in a study by Reilly and Wright, the relationship among the alternative high-yield bond indexes is weaker than among the investment-grade indexes, and this is especially true for the bonds rated CCC.[11]

Merrill Lynch Convertible Securities Indexes In March 1988, Merrill Lynch introduced a convertible bond index with data beginning in January 1987. This index includes 600 issues in three major subgroups: U.S. domestic convertible bonds, Eurodollar convertible bonds issued by U.S. corporations, and U.S. domestic convertible preferred stocks. The issues included must be public U.S. corporate issues, have a minimum par value of $25 million, and have a minimum maturity of one year.

Global Government Bond Market Indexes

Similar to the high-yield bond market, the global bond market has experienced significant growth in size and importance during the recent five-year period. Unlike the high-yield bond market, this global segment is completely dominated by government bonds because few non-U.S. countries have a corporate bond market, much less a high-yield corporate bond market. Once again, several major investment firms have responded to the needs of investors and money managers by creating indexes that reflect the performance for the global bond market, certain individual countries, and several regions. As shown in Table 5.10, the various indexes have several similar characteristics such as measuring total rates of return, using market-value weighting, and using trader pricing. At the same time, the total sample sizes differ as do numbers of countries included.

Reilly and Wright's analysis of performance in this market, shown in Chapter 3, indicates that the differences mentioned have caused some large differences in the long-term risk–return performance by the alternative indexes.[12] Also, the low correlation among

[11]Frank K. Reilly and David J. Wright, "An Analysis of High Yield Bond Benchmarks," *Journal of Fixed Income* 3, no. 4 (March 1994): 6–24. The uniqueness of CCC bonds is demonstrated in Frank K. Reilly and David J. Wright, "High-Yield Bonds and Segmentation in the Bond Market," mimeo (January 1998).

[12]Frank K. Reilly and David J. Wright, "Global Bond Markets: Alternative Benchmarks and Risk–Return Performance," mimeo (May 1997).

Table 5.10 Summary of Bond Market Indexes

Name of Index	Number of Issues	Maturity	Size of Issues	Weighting	Pricing	Reinvestment Assumption	Subindexes Available
U.S. Investment-Grade Bond Indexes							
Lehman Brothers	5,000+	Over 1 year	Over $100 million	Market value	Trader priced and model priced	No	Government, gov./corp., corporate, mortgage-backed, asset-backed
Merrill Lynch	5,000+	Over 1 year	Over $50 million	Market value	Trader priced and model priced	In specific bonds	Government, gov./corp., corporate, mortgage
Ryan Treasury	300+	Over 1 year	All Treasury	Market value and equal	Market priced	In specific bonds	Treasury
Salomon Brothers	5,000+	Over 1 year	Over $50 million	Market value	Trader priced	In one-month T-bill	Broad inv. grade, Treas.-agency, corporate, mortgage
U.S. High-Yield Bond Indexes							
Blume-Keim	233	Over 10 years	Over $25 million	Equal	Trader priced	Yes	Only composite
First Boston	423	All maturities	Over $75 million	Market value	Trader priced	Yes	Composite and by rating
Lehman Brothers	624	Over 1 year	Over $100 million	Market value	Trader priced	No	Composite and by rating
Merrill Lynch	735	Over 1 year	Over $25 million	Market value	Trader priced	Yes	Composite and by rating
Salomon Brothers	299	Over 7 years	Over $50 million	Market value	Trader priced	Yes	Composite and by rating
Global Government Bond Indexes (Initial Date of Index)							
Lehman Brothers (January 1987)	800	Over 1 year	Over $200 million	Market value	Trader priced	Yes	Composite and 13 countries, local and U.S. dollars
Merrill Lynch (December 1985)	9,736	Over 1 year	Over $50 million	Market value	Trader priced	Yes	Composite and 9 countries, local and U.S. dollars
J. P. Morgan (12/31/85)	445	Over 1 year	Over $100 million	Market value	Trader priced	Yes in index	Composite and 11 countries, local and U.S. dollars
Salomon Brothers (12/31/84)	400	Over 1 year	Over $250 million	Market value	Trader priced	Yes at local short-term rate	Composite and 14 countries, local and U.S. dollars

Source: Frank K. Reilly, Wenchi Kao, and David J. Wright, "Alternative Bond Market Indexes," *Financial Analysts Journal* 48, no. 3 (May–June, 1992): 14–58; Frank K. Reilly and David J. Wright, "An Analysis of High-Yield Bond Benchmarks," *Journal of Fixed Income* 3, no. 4 (March 1994): 6–24; and Frank K. Reilly and David J. Wright, "Global Bond Markets: Alternative Benchmarks and Risk–Return Performance," mimeo (May 1997).

the various countries is similar to stocks. Finally, there was a significant exchange rate effect on volatility and correlations.

COMPOSITE STOCK–BOND INDEXES

Beyond separate stock indexes and bond indexes for individual countries, a natural step is the development of a composite series that measures the performance of all securities in a given country. A composite series of stocks and bonds makes it possible to examine the benefits of diversifying with a combination of asset classes such as stocks and bonds in addition to diversifying within the asset classes of stocks or bonds.

Merrill Lynch–Wilshire U.S. Capital Markets Index (ML–WCMI)

A market-value-weighted index called Merrill Lynch–Wilshire Capital Markets Index (ML–WCMI) measures the total return performance of the combined U.S. taxable fixed-income and equity markets. It is basically a combination of the Merrill Lynch fixed-income indexes and the Wilshire 5000 common-stock index. As such, it tracks more than 10,000 stocks and bonds. The makeup of the index is as follows (as of December, 1997):

Security	$ in Billions	Percent of Total
Treasury bonds	$1,085	20.89%
Agency bonds	166	3.20
Mortgage bonds	467	8.99
Corporate bonds	453	8.72
OTC stocks	331	6.37
AMEX stocks	105	2.02
NYSE stocks	2,586	49.92
	$5,193	100.00%

Brinson Partners Global Security Market Index (GSMI)

The Brinson Partner GSMI series contains both U.S. stocks and bonds, but also includes non-U.S. equities and nondollar bonds as well as an allocation to cash. The specific breakdown is as follows (as of June, 1998):

	Percent
Equities	
U.S. large capitalization	35
U.S. small and mid-cap	15
Non-U.S.	17
Fixed Income	
U.S. domestic investment grade	18
International dollar bonds	2
Nondollar bonds	8
Cash	5
Total	100

Although related to the relative market values of these asset classes, the weights specified are not constantly adjusted. The construction of the GSMI used optimization techniques to identify the portfolio mix of available global asset classes that matches the risk level of a typical U.S. pension plan. The index is balanced to the policy weights monthly.

Because the GSMI contains both U.S. and international stocks and bonds, it is clearly the most diversified benchmark available with a weighting scheme that approaches

market values. As such, it is closest to the theoretically specified "market portfolio of risky assets" referred to in the CAPM literature.[13]

COMPARISON OF INDEXES OVER TIME

This section discusses price movements in the different series for various monthly or annual intervals.

Correlations among Monthly Equity Price Changes

Table 5.11 contains a matrix of the correlation coefficients of the monthly percentage of price changes for a set of U.S. and non-U.S. equity-market indexes during the 25-year period from 1972 to 1997.[14] Most of the correlation differences are attributable to sample differences, that is, differences in the firms listed on the alternative stock exchanges. Most of the major series—except the Nikkei Stock Average—are market-value-weighted indexes that include a large number of stocks. Therefore, the computational procedure is generally similar and the sample sizes are large or all-encompassing. Thus, the major difference between the indexes is that the stocks are from different segments of the U.S. stock market or from different countries.

There is a high positive correlation (0.92) between the alternative NYSE series (the S&P 500 and the NYSE composite). These indexes are also highly correlated with the Wilshire 5000 index that is value weighted, which means it is heavily influenced by the large NYSE stocks in the index.

In contrast, there are lower correlations between these NYSE series and the AMEX series (about 0.72) or the NASDAQ index (about 0.78). Further, the relationship between the Russell 2000 Index and the other U.S. series ranges from 0.73 to 0.91, which reflects the fact that the Russell 2000 series includes a sample of small-cap stocks from all exchanges.

The correlations among the U.S. series and those from Canada, the United Kingdom, Germany, and Japan support the case for global investing. The relationships among the two TSE series were correlated about 0.87 even though the sample sizes, weightings, and computations differ. These within-country results attest to the importance of the basic sample. In contrast, the U.S.–Canada and U.S.–U.K. correlations, which averaged about 0.73, and the U.S.–Japan correlations, which were about 0.30, confirm the benefits of global diversification because such low correlations reduce the variance of a portfolio.

Correlations among Monthly Bond Indexes

The correlations among the monthly bond return series in Table 5.12 consider a variety of bond series, including investment-grade bonds, U.S. high-yield bonds, and government bond indexes for several major non-U.S. countries (GE–Germany, JA–Japan, and UK–the United Kingdom). The correlations among the U.S. investment-grade–bond series ranged from 0.90 to 0.99, confirming that although the *level* of interest rates differs due to the

---

[13]This GSMI series is used in a study that examines the effect of alternative benchmarks on the estimate of the security market and estimates of individual stock betas. See Frank K. Reilly and Rashid A. Akhtar, "The Benchmark Error Problem with Global Capital Markets," *Journal of Portfolio Management* 22, no. 1 (Fall 1995). Brinson Partners has a Multiple Markets Index (MMI) that also contains venture capital and real estate. Because these assets are not actively traded, the value and rate of return estimates tend to be relatively stable, which reduces the standard deviation of the series.

[14]In earlier editions of the text, the correlations examined daily percentage price changes. The shift to monthly percentage price changes made it possible to consider a wider range of non-U.S. equity indexes. Notably, the monthly price change correlation results among U.S. indexes are similar to the daily results.

Table 5.11 *Correlation Coefficients among Monthly Percentage Price Changes in Alternative Equity Market Indicator Series: January 1972 (When Available) to December 1997*

	S&P 500	NYSE	AMEX	NASDAQ Industr.	Wilshire 5000	Russell 2000[a]	Toronto SE 300	Tokyo SE	Nikkei	FAZ[b]	FT All-Share[b]	M-S World	FT/S&P World[c]
S&P 500	—												
NYSE	0.919	—											
AMEX	0.719	0.801	—										
NASDAQ Ind.	0.783	0.881	0.824	—									
Wilshire 5000	0.906	0.987	0.817	0.906	—								
Russell 2000	0.731	0.848	0.764	0.913	0.870	—							
Toronto 300	0.687	0.761	0.768	0.740	0.768	0.723	—						
Tokyo SE	0.302	0.299	0.245	0.251	0.284	0.249	0.269	—					
Nikkei	0.358	0.350	0.280	0.308	0.335	0.325	0.293	0.872	—				
FAZ	0.501	0.534	0.381	0.404	0.515	0.440	0.452	0.279	0.330	—			
FT All-Share	0.615	0.712	0.591	0.620	0.693	0.618	0.627	0.266	0.379	0.514	—		
M-S World	0.763	0.821	0.658	0.704	0.808	0.669	0.714	0.588	0.631	0.525	0.651	—	
FT/S&P World	0.590	0.695	0.508	0.589	0.666	0.572	0.616	0.664	0.731	0.505	0.617	0.960	—

[a]Russell 2000 series starts in 1979.

[b]FAZ and FT All-Share series start in 1983.

[c]FT/S&P World Index series starts in 1986.

Table 5.12   *Correlations among Monthly Bond Returns for U.S. Investment-Grade Bonds, U.S. High-Yield Bonds, and Non-U.S. Government Bonds: 1985–1997*

	LBGC	LBG	LBC	LBM	LBA	MLHYM	SBGE	SBJA	SBUK
LBGC	—								
LBG	0.997	—							
LBC	0.976	0.958	—						
LBM	0.919	0.905	0.927	—					
LBA	0.995	0.990	0.978	0.952	—				
MLHYM	0.457	0.419	0.548	0.454	0.465	—			
SBGE	0.308	0.321	0.259	0.298	0.308	−0.031	—		
SBJA	0.183	0.196	0.159	0.142	0.178	0.043	0.486	—	
SBUK	0.280	0.297	0.227	0.235	0.276	−0.013	0.656	0.455	—

Table 5.13   *Mean and Standard Deviation of Annual Percentage Price Change for Stock Price Series 1972–1997*

	Geometric Mean	Arithmetic Mean	Standard Deviation	Coefficient of Variation
DJIA	8.79	10.09	16.70	1.66
S&P 400	9.29	10.58	16.44	1.55
S&P 500	9.06	10.35	16.49	1.59
AMEX Value Index	10.04	12.26	22.07	1.80
NASDAQ Comp.	11.89	13.94	20.81	1.49
Russell 2000[a]	15.61	17.00	18.05	1.06
Wilshire 5000	9.29	10.69	17.07	1.60
Toronto S.E. Comp.	11.32	12.54	16.52	1.32
FT All-Share	10.37	14.36	31.94	2.22
FAZ	7.58	10.16	24.27	2.39
Nikkei	6.97	9.74	25.77	2.65
Tokyo S.E. Index	6.86	9.84	27.15	2.76
MS World	8.58	9.82	16.19	1.65

[a]The Russell 2000 index was initiated in 1979.

risk premium, the overriding factors that determine the rates of return for investment-grade bonds over time are *systematic* interest rate variables.

The correlations among investment-grade bonds and HY bonds indicate significantly lower correlations (0.40 to 0.54), caused by definite equity characteristics of HY bonds.[15] Finally, the low and diverse relationships among U.S. investment-grade bonds and non-U.S. government bond series (0.14 to 0.33) reflect different interest-rate movements and exchange-rate effects (these non-U.S. government results are U.S. dollar returns). Again, these results support global diversification.

Mean Annual Stock Price Changes

The mean and standard deviation of annual percentage of price changes for the major stock indexes is contained in Table 5.13. One would expect differences among the price changes and measures of risk for the various series due to the different samples. For example, the NYSE series should have lower rates of return and risk measures than the AMEX and OTC series. The results generally confirm these expectations. For example, the Russell 2000 reflects the results for the small-capitalization segment of the U.S. stock

[15]For a detailed analysis of this point, see Frank K. Reilly and David J. Wright, "High Yield Bonds and Segmentation in the Bond Market," mimeo (January 1998).

Table 5.14 *Mean and Standard Deviation of Annual Rates of Return for Lehman Brothers Bond Indexes 1976–1997*

	Geometric Mean	Arithmetic Mean	Standard Deviation	Coefficient of Variation
Government/Corporate	9.68	9.95	8.04	0.81
Government	9.65	9.77	7.15	0.73
Corporate	10.17	10.60	10.25	0.97
Mortgage-Backed	9.94	10.35	10.07	0.97
Yankee	10.34	10.73	9.63	0.90
Aggregate	9.75	10.02	8.17	0.82

market. This series, which began in 1979, shows higher returns than the large-cap NYSE series during most individual years.

Regarding non-U.S. results, the Canadian results on the Toronto Exchange had higher average returns than the NYSE, and lower risk than the NASDAQ. The United Kingdom (that is, the FT All-Share) had higher returns than the NYSE indexes, but much larger variability, while Germany (the FAZ) had lower returns than the U.S., but similar volatility. Finally, the Japanese markets experienced lower returns and slightly lower volatility than the U.S. markets. Remember, these non-U.S. stock results reflect the domestic price changes and do not consider the exchange-rate effect.

These results for the Japanese market were significantly affected by poor results during 1990 to 1997. Because the Japanese stock market had relatively low correlation with alternative U.S. stock-market indexes (Table 5.11), it indicates that Japan would have been a prime source of diversification benefits even with the higher volatility.

Annual Bond Rates of Return

Table 5.14 shows the mean and standard deviation of annual total rates of return for the Lehman Brothers bond-market indexes.[16] You cannot directly compare the bond and stock results because the bond results are *total* rates of return versus annual percentage price change results for stocks (most of the stock series do not report dividend data).

The major comparison for the bond series should be among the average rates of return and the risk measures, because although the monthly rates of return are correlated, we would expect a difference in the level of return due to the differential risk premiums. The results generally confirm our expectations (that is, there typically are lower returns and risk measures for the government series followed by higher returns and risk for corporate and mortgage bonds.

Investments Online

We've seen several previous Web sites which offer online users a look at current market conditions in the form of a time-delayed market index (some sites offer real-time stock and

---

[16]Because of the high correlations among the monthly rates of return as shown in Table 5.12, the results for various bond-market segments (government, corporate, mortgages) are similar regardless of the source (Lehman Brothers, Merrill Lynch, Salomon Brothers, Ryan). Therefore, only the Lehman Brothers results are presented in Table 5.14.

SUMMARY

♦ Given the several uses of security-market indicator series, you should know how they are constructed and the differences among them. If you want to use one of the many series to learn how the "market" is doing, you should be aware of what market you are dealing with so you can select the appropriate index. As an example, are you only interested in the NYSE or do you also want to consider the AMEX and the OTC? Beyond the U.S. market, are you interested in Japanese or U.K. stocks, or do you want to examine the total world market?[17]

♦ Indexes are also used as benchmarks to evaluate portfolio performance. In this case, you must be sure the index (benchmark) is consistent with your investing universe. If you are investing worldwide, you should not judge your performance relative to the DJIA, which is limited to thirty U.S. blue-chip stocks. For a bond portfolio, the index should match your investment philosophy. Finally, if your portfolio contains both stocks and bonds, you must evaluate your performance against an appropriate combination of indexes.

♦ Whenever you invest, you examine numerous market indexes to tell you what has happened and how successful you have been. The selection of the appropriate indexes for information or evaluation will depend on how knowledgeable you are regarding the various series. The purpose of this chapter is to help you understand what to look for and how to make the right decision.

Questions

1. Discuss briefly several uses of security-market indicator series.
2. What major factors must be considered when constructing a market index? Put another way, what characteristics differentiate indexes?

---

[17]For a readable discussion on this topic, see Anne Merjos, "How's the Market Doing?" *Barron's,* August 20, 1990, 18–20, 27, 28. Chapter 22 includes an extensive discussion of the purpose and construction of benchmarks and considers the evaluation of portfolio performance.

3. Explain how a market indicator series is price weighted. In such a case, would you expect a $100 stock to be more important than a $25 stock? Why?

4. Explain how to compute a value-weighted series.

5. Explain how a price-weighted series and a value-weighted series adjust for stock splits.

6. Describe an unweighted price-indicator series and describe how you would construct such a series. Assume a 20 percent price change in GM ($40/share; 50 million shares outstanding) and Coors Brewing ($25/share and 15 million shares outstanding). Explain which stock's change will have the greater impact on this index.

7. If you correlated percentage changes in the Wilshire 5000 equity index with percentage changes in the NYSE composite, the AMEX index, and the NASDAQ composite index, would you expect a difference in the correlations? Why or why not?

8. There are high correlations among the monthly percentage price changes for the alternative NYSE indexes. Discuss the reason for this similarity: is it size of sample, source of sample, or method of computation?

9. Compare stock price indicator series for the three U.S. equity-market segments (NYSE, AMEX, OTC) for the period 1972 to 1997. Discuss whether the results in terms of average annual price change and risk (variability of price changes) were consistent with economic theory.

10. Discuss the relationship (correlations) between the two stock price indexes for the Tokyo Stock Exchange (TSE). Examine the correlations among the TSE series and two NYSE series. Explain why these relationships differ.

11. You learn that the Wilshire 5000 market value-weighted series increased by 16 percent during a specified period, whereas a Wilshire 5000 equal-weighted series increased by 23 percent during the same period. Discuss what this difference in results implies.

12. Why is it contended that bond-market indexes are more difficult to construct and maintain than stock-market index series?

13. The Wilshire 5000 market value-weighted index increased by 5 percent, whereas the Merrill Lynch–Wilshire Capital Markets Index increased by 15 percent during the same period. What does this difference in results imply?

14. The Russell 1000 increased by 8 percent during the past year, whereas the Russell 2000 increased by 15 percent. Discuss the implication of these results.

15. Based on what you know about the *Financial Times* (FT) World Index, the Morgan Stanley Capital International World Index, and the Dow Jones World Stock Index, what level of correlation would you expect among monthly rates of return? Discuss the reasons for your answer based on the factors that affect indexes.

Problems

1. You are given the following information regarding prices for a sample of stocks:

		PRICE	
Stock	Number of Shares	T	T + 1
A	1,000,000	60	80
B	10,000,000	20	35
C	30,000,000	18	25

 a. Construct a *price-weighted* series for these three stocks, and compute the percentage change in the series for the period from T to T + 1.

 b. Construct a *value-weighted* series for these three stocks, and compute the percentage change in the series for the period from T to T + 1.

 c. Briefly discuss the difference in the results for the two series.

2. a. Given the data in Problem 1, construct an equal-weighted series by assuming $1,000 is invested in each stock. What is the percentage change in wealth for this portfolio?

    b. Compute the percentage of price change for each of the stocks in Problem 1. Compute the arithmetic average of these percentage changes. Discuss how this answer compares to the answer in 2a.

    c. Compute the geometric average of the percentage changes in 2b. Discuss how this result compares to the answer in 2b.

3. For the past five trading days, on the basis of figures in the *Wall Street Journal,* compute the daily percentage price changes for the following stock indexes:
    a. DJIA
    b. S&P 400
    c. AMEX Market Value Series
    d. NASDAQ Industrial Index
    e. FT-100 Share Index
    f. Nikkei Stock Price Average

Discuss the difference in results for a and b, a and c, a and d, a and e, a and f, e and f. What do these differences imply regarding diversifying within the United States versus diversifying between countries?

4.

	PRICE			SHARES		
Company	A	B	C	A	B	C
Day 1	12	23	52	500	350	250
Day 2	10	22	55	500	350	250
Day 3	14	46	52	500	175[a]	250
Day 4	13	47	25	500	175	500[b]
Day 5	12	45	26	500	175	500

[a]Split at close of Day 2
[b]Split at close of Day 3

    a. Calculate a Dow Jones Industrial Average for Days 1 through 5.

    b. What effects have the splits had in determining the next day's index? (Hint: Think of the relative weighting of each stock.)

    c. From a copy of the *Wall Street Journal,* find the divisor that is currently being used in calculating the DJIA. (Normally this value can be found on pages C2 and C3.)

5. Utilizing the price and volume data in Problem 4,
    a. Calculate a Standard & Poor's Index for Days 1 through 5 using a beginning index value of 10.

    b. Identify what effects the splits had in determining the next day's index. (Hint: Think of the relative weighting of each stock.)

6. Based on the following stock price and shares outstanding information, compute the beginning and ending values for a price-weighted index and a market-value-weighted index.

	DECEMBER 31, 1998		DECEMBER 31, 1999	
	Price	Shares Outstanding	Price	Shares Outstanding
Stock K	20	100,000,000	32	100,000,000
Stock M	80	2,000,000	45	4,000,000[a]
Stock R	40	25,000,000	42	25,000,000

[a]Stock split two-for-one during the year

    a. Compute the percent change in the value of each index.

    b. Explain the difference in results between the two indexes.

    c. Compute the results for an unweighted index and discuss why these results differ from others.

7. a. Assume a base index value of 100 at the beginning of 1972. Using the returns in Table 5.13, what would be your ending index value if you owned the stocks in the Nikkei Average through 1997?

   b. In addition to knowing this domestic rate of return, you are told that the exchange rate at the beginning of 1972 was ¥200 to the dollar and it was ¥125 to the dollar at the end of 1997. Compute the compound return in U.S. dollars.

References

Fisher, Lawrence, and James H. Lorie. *A Half Century of Returns on Stocks and Bonds.* Chicago: University of Chicago Graduate School of Business, 1997.

Ibbotson Associates. *Stocks, Bonds, Bills and Inflation.* Chicago: Ibbotson Associates, annual.

Lorie, James H., Peter Dodd, and Mary Hamilton Kimpton. *The Stock Market: Theories and Evidence.* 2d ed. Homewood, IL: Richard D. Irwin, 1985.

Reilly, Frank K., and David J. Wright, "Bond Market Indexes," in *Handbook of Fixed Income Securities,* 5th ed., edited by Frank J. Fabozzi. Chicago, IL: Irwin Professional Publishing., 1997

GLOSSARY

Price-weighted series An indicator series calculated as an arithmetic average of the current prices of the sampled securities.

Security-market indicator series An index created as a statistical measure of the performance of an entire market or segment of a market based on a sample of securities from the market or segment of a market.

Value-weighted series An indicator series calculated as the total market value of the securities in the sample.

Unweighted index An indicator series affected equally by the performance of each security in the sample regardless of price or market value. Also referred to as an equal weighted series.

APPENDIX 5 *Foreign Stock-Market Indexes*

Index Name	Number of Stocks	Weights of Stocks	Calculation Method	History of Index
ATX-index (Vienna)	All stocks listed on the exchange	Market capitalization	Value weighted	Base year 1967, 1991 began including all stocks (Value = 100)
Swiss Market Index	18 stocks	Market capitalization	Value weighted	Base year 1988, stocks selected from the Basle, Geneva, and Zurich Exchanges (Value = 1500)
Stockholm General Index	All stocks (voting) listed on exchange	Market capitalization	Value weighted	Base year 1979, continuously updated (Value = 100)
Copenhagen Stock Exchange Share Price Index	All stocks traded	Market capitalization	Value weighted	Share price is based on average price of the day
Oslo SE Composite Index (Sweden)	25 companies			Base year 1972 (Value = 100)
Johannesburg Stock Exchange Actuaries Index	146 companies	Market capitalization	Value weighted	Base year 1959 (Value = 100)

Index Name	Number of Stocks	Weights of Stocks	Calculation Method	History of Index
Mexican Market Index	Variable number, based on capitalization and liquidity		Value weighted (adjustment for value of paid-out dividends)	Base year 1978, high dollar returns in recent years
Milan Stock Exchange MIB	Variable number, based on capitalization and liquidity		Weighted arithmetic average	Change base at beginning of each year (Value = 1000)
Belgium BEL-20 Stock Index	20 companies	Market capitalization	Value weighted	Base year 1991 (Value = 1000)
Madrid General Stock Index	92 stocks	Market capitalization	Value weighted	Change base at beginning of each year
Hang Seng Index (Hong Kong)	33 companies	Market capitalization	Value weighted	Started in 1969, accounts for 75 percent of total market
FT-Actuaries World Indexes	2,212 stocks	Market capitalization	Value weighted	Base year 1986
FT-SE 100 Index (London)	100 companies	Market capitalization	Value weighted	Base year 1983 (Value = 1000)
CAC General Share Index (French)	212 companies	Market capitalization	Value weighted	Base year 1981 (Value = 100)
Morgan Stanley World Index	1,482 stocks	Market capitalization	Value weighted	Base year 1970 (Value = 100)
Singapore Straits Times Industrial Index	30 stocks	Unweighted		
German Stock Market Index (DAX)	30 companies (Blue Chips)	Market capitalization	Value weighted	Base year 1987 (Value = 1000)
Frankfurter Allgemeine Zeitung Index (FAZ) (German)	100 companies (Blue Chips)	Market capitalization	Value weighted	Base year 1958 (Value = 100)
Australian Stock Exchange Share Price Indices	250 stocks (92 percent) of all shares listed	Market capitalization	Value weighted	Introduced in 1979
Dublin ISEQ Index	71 stocks (54 official, 17 unlisted. All stocks traded	Market capitalization	Value weighted	Base year 1988 (Value = 1000)
HEX Index (Helsinki)	Varies with different share price indexes	Market capitalization	Value weighted	Base changes every day
Jakarta Stock Exchange	All listed shares (148 currently)	Market capitalization	Value weighted	Base year 1982 (Value = 100)
Taiwan Stock Exchange Index	All ordinary stocks (listed for at least a month)	Market capitalization	Value weighted	Base year 1966 (Value = 100)
TSE 300 Composite Index (Toronto)	300 stocks (comprised of 14 subindexes)`	Market capitalization (adjusted for major shareholders)	Value weighted	Base year 1975 (Value = 1000)
KOSPI (Korean Composite Stock Price Index)	All common stocks listed on exchange	Market capitalization (adjusted for major shareholders)	Value weighted	Base year 1980 (Value = 100)

PART

2

DEVELOPMENTS IN INVESTMENT THEORY

THE CHAPTERS IN PART 1 PROVIDED BACKGROUND ON why individuals invest their funds and what they expect to derive from this activity. We also argued very strongly for a global investment program, described the major instruments and capital markets in a global investment environment, and showed the relationship among these instruments and markets.

At this point, we are ready to discuss how to analyze and value the various investment instruments. In turn, valuation requires the estimation of expected returns (cash flow) and determination of the risk involved in the securities. Before we can begin the analysis, we need to understand several major developments in investment theory that have influenced how we specify and measure risk in the valuation process. The purpose of the three chapters in this part is to provide this necessary background on risk and asset valuation.

Chapter 6 provides an introduction to portfolio theory which was developed by Harry Markowitz. This theory provided the first rigorous measure of risk for investors and showed how one selects alternative assets in order to diversify and to reduce the risk of a portfolio. Markowitz also derived a risk measure for individual securities within the context of an efficient portfolio.

Subsequent to the development of the Markowitz portfolio model, William Sharpe and several other academi-cians extended the Markowitz portfolio theory model into a general equilibrium asset pricing model that included an alternative risk measure of all risky assets. Chapter 7 contains a detailed discussion of these developments and an explanation of the relevant risk measure implied by this valuation model, referred to as the *capital asset pricing model* (CAPM). We introduce the CAPM at this early point in the book because the risk measure implied by this model has been used extensively in various valuation models.

Chapter 7 also contains a discussion of an alternative asset pricing model referred to as the *arbitrage pricing theory* (APT). This theory was developed by Steve Ross in response to criticisms of the CAPM because of its restrictive assumptions and the difficulty in testing it. The fundamental differences between the CAPM and the APT models is that APT requires fewer assumptions and is considered a multivariate risk model compared to the CAPM, which is a single risk variable model (beta).

Chapter 8 describes the concept of *efficient capital markets* (ECM), which hypothesizes that security prices reflect the effect of all information. This chapter considers why markets should be efficient, discusses how one goes about testing this hypothesis, describes the results of numerous tests, and discusses the implications of the diverse results for those engaged in technical and fundamental analysis, as well as portfolio management.

An Introduction to Portfolio Management

6

This chapter answers the following questions:

♦ What do we mean by *risk aversion* and what evidence indicates that investors are generally risk averse?

♦ What are the basic assumptions behind the Markowitz portfolio theory?

♦ What do we mean by *risk* and what are some of the alternative measures of risk used in investments?

♦ How do you compute the expected rate of return for an individual risky asset or a portfolio of assets?

♦ How do you compute the standard deviation of rates of return for an individual risky assets?

♦ What do we mean by the *covariance* between rates of return and how do you compute covariance?

♦ What is the relationship between covariance and correlation?

♦ What is the formula for the standard deviation for a portfolio of risky assets and how does it differ from the standard deviation of an individual risky asset?

♦ Given the formula for the standard deviation of a portfolio, why and how do you diversify a portfolio?

♦ What happens to the standard deviation of a portfolio when you change the correlation between the assets in the portfolio?

♦ What is the risk-return–efficient frontier of risky assets?

♦ Is it reasonable for alternative investors to select different portfolios from the portfolios on the efficient frontier?

♦ What determines which portfolio on the efficient frontier is selected by an individual investor?   ♦

One of the major advances in the investment field during the past few decades has been the recognition that the creation of an optimum investment portfolio is not simply a matter of combining a lot of unique individual securities that have desirable risk–return characteristics. Specifically, it has been shown that you must consider the relationship *among* the investments if you are going to build an optimum portfolio that will meet your investment objectives. The recognition of what is important in creating a portfolio was demonstrated in the derivation of portfolio theory.

This chapter explains portfolio theory step by step. It introduces you to the basic portfolio risk formula that you must understand when you are combining different assets. When you understand this formula and its implications, you will increase your understanding of not only why you should diversify your portfolio, but also *how* you should diversify. The subsequent chapter introduces asset pricing models and capital market theory with an emphasis on determining the appropriate risk measure for individual assets.

SOME BACKGROUND ASSUMPTIONS

Before presenting portfolio theory, we need to clarify some general assumptions of the theory. This includes not only what we mean by an *optimum portfolio,* but also what we mean by the terms *risk aversion* and *risk.*

One basic assumption of portfolio theory is that as an investor you want to maximize the returns from your investments for a given level of risk. To adequately deal with such an assumption, certain ground rules must be laid. First, your portfolio should *include all of your assets and liabilities,* not only your stocks or even your marketable securities, but also such items as your car, house, and less marketable investments such as coins, stamps, art, antiques, and furniture. The full spectrum of investments must be considered because the returns from all these investments interact, and *this relationship between the returns for assets in the portfolio is important.* Hence, a good portfolio is *not* simply a collection of individually good investments.

Risk Aversion

Portfolio theory also assumes that investors are basically **risk averse**, meaning that, given a choice between two assets with equal rates of return, they will select the asset with the lower level of risk. Evidence that most investors are risk averse is that they purchase various types of insurance, including life insurance, car insurance, and health insurance. Buying insurance basically involves an outlay of a given amount to guard against an uncertain, possibly larger outlay in the future. When you buy insurance, this implies that you are willing to pay the current known cost of the insurance policy to avoid the uncertainty of a potentially large future cost related to a car accident or a major illness. Further evidence of risk aversion is the difference in promised yield (the required rate of return) for different grades of bonds that supposedly have different degrees of credit risk. As you might know from reading about corporate bonds, the promised yield on bonds increases as you go from AAA (the lowest risk class) to AA to A, and so on. This increase in yields means that investors require a higher rate of return to accept higher risk.

This does not imply that everybody is risk averse, or that investors are completely risk averse regarding all financial commitments. The fact is, not everybody buys insurance for everything. Some people have no insurance against anything, either by choice or because they cannot afford it. In addition, some individuals buy insurance related to some risks such as auto accidents or illness, but they also buy lottery tickets and gamble at race tracks or in casinos, where it is known that the expected returns are negative, which means

that participants are willing to pay for the excitement of the risk involved. This combination of risk preference and risk aversion can be explained by an attitude toward risk that is not completely risk averse or risk preferring, but is a combination of the two that depends on the amount of money involved. Friedman and Savage speculate that this is the case for people who like to gamble for small amounts (in lotteries or nickel slot machines), but buy insurance to protect themselves against large losses such as fire or accidents.[1]

While recognizing such attitudes, our basic assumption is that most investors committing large sums of money to developing an investment portfolio are risk averse. Therefore, we expect a positive relationship between expected return and expected risk. Notably, this is also what we generally find in terms of historical results—that is, a positive relationship exists between the rates of return on various assets and their measures of risk as shown in Chapter 3.

Definition of Risk

Although there is a difference in the specific definitions of *risk* and *uncertainty,* for our purposes and in most financial literature the two terms are used interchangeably. In fact, one way to define risk is *the uncertainty of future outcomes.* An alternative definition might be *the probability of an adverse outcome.* Subsequently, in our discussion of portfolio theory, we will consider several measures of risk that are used when developing the theory.

Markowitz Portfolio Theory

In the 1950s and early 1960s, the investment community talked about risk, but there was no specific measure for the term. To build a portfolio model, however, investors had to quantify their risk variable. The basic portfolio model was developed by Harry Markowitz, who derived the expected rate of return for a portfolio of assets and an expected risk measure.[2] Markowitz showed that the variance of the rate of return was a meaningful measure of portfolio risk under a reasonable set of assumptions, and he derived the formula for computing the variance of a portfolio. This formula for the variance of a portfolio not only indicated the importance of diversifying your investments to reduce the total risk of a portfolio, but also showed *how* to effectively diversify. The Markowitz model is based on several assumptions regarding investor behavior:

1. Investors consider each investment alternative as being represented by a probability distribution of expected returns over some holding period.
2. Investors maximize one-period expected utility, and their utility curves demonstrate diminishing marginal utility of wealth.
3. Investors estimate the risk of the portfolio on the basis of the variability of expected returns.
4. Investors base decisions solely on expected return and risk, so their utility curves are a function of expected return and the expected variance (or standard deviation) of returns only.
5. For a given risk level, investors prefer higher returns to lower returns. Similarly, for a given level of expected return, investors prefer less risk to more risk.

[1]Milton Friedman and Leonard J. Savage, "The Utility Analysis of Choices Involving Risk," *Journal of Political Economy* 56, no. 3 (August 1948): 279–304.

[2]Harry Markowitz, "Portfolio Selection," *Journal of Finance* 7, no. 1 (March 1952): 77–91; and Harry Markowitz, *Portfolio Selection—Efficient Diversification of Investments* (New York: John Wiley & Sons, 1959).

Under these assumptions, *a single asset or portfolio of assets is considered to be efficient if no other asset or portfolio of assets offers higher expected return with the same (or lower) risk, or lower risk with the same (or higher) expected return.*

Alternative Measures of Risk

One of the best-known measures of risk is the *variance,* or *standard deviation of expected returns.*[3] It is a statistical measure of the dispersion of returns around the expected value whereby a larger variance or standard deviation indicates greater dispersion, all other factors being equal. The idea is that the more disperse the expected returns, the greater the uncertainty of those returns in any future period.

Another measure of risk is the *range of returns.* In this case, it is assumed that a larger range of expected returns, from the lowest to the highest return, means greater uncertainty and risk regarding future expected returns.

Instead of using measures that analyze all deviations from expectations, some observers believe that when you invest you should be concerned only with *returns below expectations,* which means that you only consider deviations below the mean value. A measure that only considers deviations below the mean is the *semivariance.* Extensions of the semivariance measure only computed expected returns *below zero* (that is, negative returns), or returns below some specific asset such as T-bills, the rate of inflation, or a benchmark. These measures of risk implicitly assume that investors want to *minimize the damage* from returns less than some target rate. Assuming that investors would welcome positive returns or returns above some target rate, the returns above expectations or a target rate are not considered when measuring risk.

Although there are numerous potential measures of risk, we will use the variance or standard deviation of returns because (1) this measure is somewhat intuitive, (2) it is a correct and widely recognized risk measure, and (3) it has been used in most of the theoretical asset pricing models.

Expected Rates of Return

The expected rate of return for *an individual investment* is computed as shown in Table 6.1. The expected return for an individual risky asset with the set of potential returns and an assumption of equal probabilities used in the example would be 11 percent.

The expected rate of return for a *portfolio* of investments is simply the weighted average of the expected rates of return for the individual investments in the portfolio. The weights are the proportion of total value for the investment.

The expected rate of return for a hypothetical portfolio with four risky assets is shown in Table 6.2. The expected return for this portfolio of investments would be 11.5 percent. The effect of adding or dropping any investment from the portfolio would be easy to determine because you would use the new weights based on value and the expected returns for each of the investments. This computation of the expected return for the portfolio $[E(R_{port})]$ can be generalized as follows:

$$E(R_{port}) = \sum_{i=1}^{n} W_i R_i$$

where:

W_i = **the percent of the portfolio in asset** *i*
R_i = **the expected rate of return for asset** *i.*

---

[3]We consider the variance and standard deviation as one measure of risk because the standard deviation is the square root of the variance.

Table 6.1	*Computation of Expected Return for an Individual Risky Asset*		

Probability	Possible Rate of Return (Percent)	Expected Return (Percent)
.25	.08	.0200
.25	.10	.0250
.25	.12	.0300
.25	.14	.0350
		E(R) = .1100

Table 6.2	*Computation of the Expected Return for a Portfolio of Risky Assets*		

Weight (W_i) (Percent of Portfolio)	Expected Security Return (R_i)	Expected Portfolio Return ($W_i \times R_i$)
.20	.10	.0200
.30	.11	.0330
.30	.12	.0360
.20	.13	.0260
		$E(R_{port})$ = .1150

Variance (Standard Deviation) of Returns for an Individual Investment

As noted, we will be using the variance or the standard deviation of returns as the measure of risk (recall that the standard deviation is the square root of the variance). Therefore, at this point, we will demonstrate how you would compute the standard deviation of returns for an individual investment. Subsequently, after discussing some other statistical concepts, we will consider the determination of the standard deviation for a *portfolio* of investments.

The variance, or standard deviation, is a measure of the variation of possible rates of return, R_i, from the expected rate of return $[E(R_i)]$ as follows:

$$\text{Variance } (\sigma^2) = \sum_{i=1}^{n} [R_i - E(R_i)]^2 P_i.$$

where P_i is the probability of the possible rate of return, R_i.

$$\text{Standard Deviation } (\sigma) = \sqrt{\sum_{i=1}^{n} [R_i - E(R_i)]^2 P_i.}$$

The computation of the variance and standard deviation of returns for the individual risky asset in Table 6.1 is set forth in Table 6.3.

Variance (Standard Deviation) of Returns for a Portfolio

Two basic concepts in statistics, covariance and correlation, must be understood before we discuss the formula for the variance of the rate of return for a portfolio.

Covariance of Returns   In this section, we discuss what the covariance of returns is intended to measure, give the formula for computing it, and present an example of the computation. Covariance is a measure of the degree to which two variables "move together" relative to their individual mean values over time. In portfolio analysis, we usually are concerned with the covariance of *rates of return* rather than prices or some other

Table 6.3   *Computation of the Variance for an Individual Risky Asset*

Possible Rate of Return (R_i)	Expected Return $E(R_i)$	$R_i - E(R_i)$	$[R_i - E(R_i)]^2$	P_i	$(R_i - E(R_i))^2 P_i$
.08	.11	.03	.0009	.25	.000225
.10	.11	.01	.0001	.25	.000025
.12	.11	.01	.0001	.25	.000025
.14	.11	.03	.0009	.25	.000225
					.000500

Variance (σ^2) = .00050
Standard Deviation (σ) = .02236

Table 6.4   *Computation of Monthly Rates of Return*

	Coca-Cola			Exxon		
Date	Closing Price	Dividend	Rate of return (%)	Closing Price	Dividend	Rate of return (%)
12/96	52.500			49.000		
1/97	58.000		10.48	51.813		5.74
2/97	61.000		5.17	50.125		−3.26
3/97	55.875	0.14	−8.17	53.875	0.41	8.30
4/97	63.500		13.65	56.750		5.34
5/97	68.375		7.68	59.250		4.41
6/97	68.000	0.14	−0.34	61.250	0.41	4.07
7/97	69.250		1.84	64.188		4.80
8/97	55.313		−20.13	61.188		−4.67
9/97	61.000	0.14	10.54	64.063	0.41	5.37
10/97	56.500		−7.38	61.438		−4.10
11/97	62.500		10.62	61.000		−0.71
12/97	66.688	0.15	6.94	61.188	0.41	0.98
		$E(R_{Coca-Cola})$ =	2.57		$E(R_{Exxon})$ =	2.19

variable.[4] A positive covariance means that the rates of return for two investments tend to move in the same direction relative to their individual means during the same time period. In contrast, a negative covariance indicates that the rates of return for two investments tend to move in different directions relative to their means during specified time intervals over time. The *magnitude* of the covariance depends on the variances of the individual return series, as well as on the relationship between the series.

Table 6.4 contains the monthly closing prices and dividends for Coca-Cola and Exxon. You can use these data to compute monthly rates of return for these two stocks during 1997. Figures 6.1 and 6.2 contain a time-series plot of the monthly rates of return for the two stocks during 1997. Although the rates of return for the two stocks moved together during some months, in other months they moved in opposite directions. The covariance statistic provides an *absolute* measure of how they moved together over time.

[4]Returns, of course, can be measured in a variety of ways, depending on the type of asset. You will recall that we defined returns (R_i) in Chapter 1 as:

$$R_i = \frac{EV - BV + CF}{BV}$$

where EV is ending value, BV is beginning value, and CF is the cash flow during the period.

Figure 6.1   *Time-Series Returns for Coca-Cola: 1997*

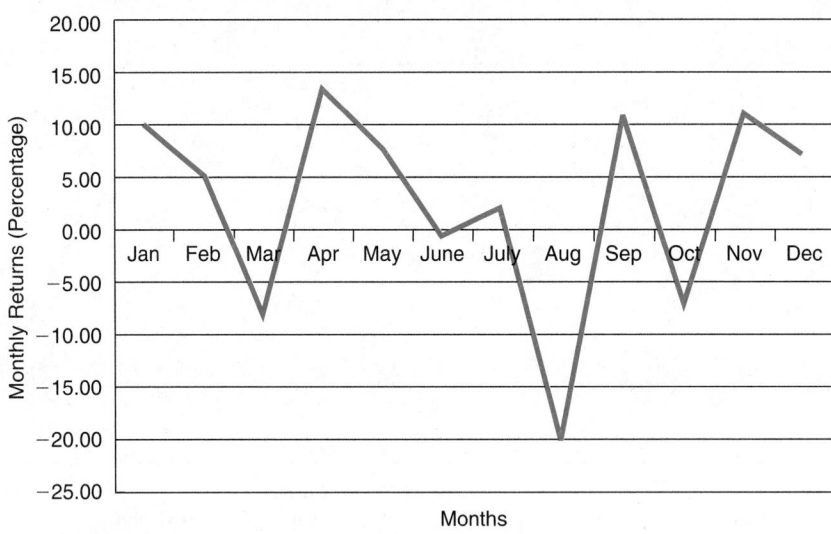

Figure 6.2   *Time-Series Returns for Exxon: 1997*

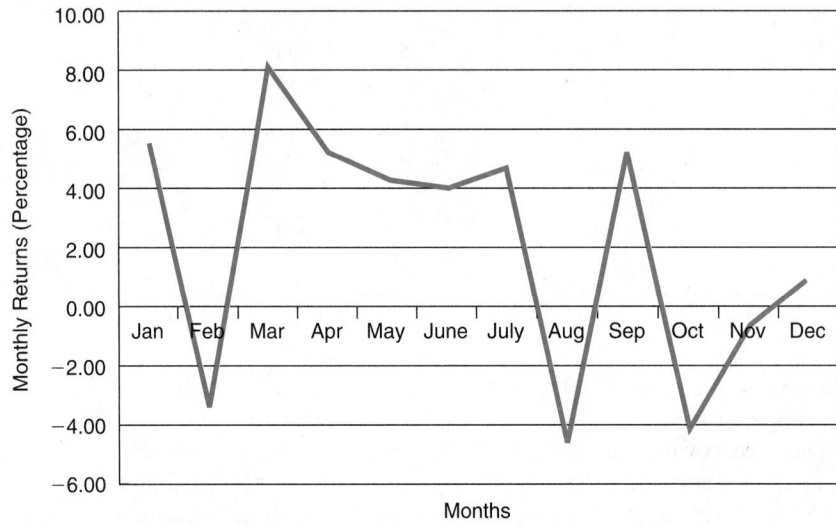

For two assets, i and j, the covariance of rates of return is defined as:

$$\text{Cov}_{ij} = E\{[R_i - E(R_i)][R_j - E(R_j)]\}.$$

When we apply this formula to the monthly rates of return for Coca-Cola and Exxon during 1997, it becomes:

$$\frac{1}{12}\sum_{i=1}^{12}[R_i - E(R_i)][R_j - E(R_j)].$$

As can be seen, if the rates of return for one stock are above (below) its mean rate of return during a given period, and the returns for the other stock are likewise above (below)

Table 6.5   *Computation of Covariance of Returns for Coca-Cola and Exxon: 1997*

| | Monthly Return (%) | | | | | |
Date	Coca-Cola (R_i)	Exxon (R_j)	Coca-Cola $R_i - E(R_i)$	Exxon $R_j - E(R_j)$	Coca-Cola $[R_i - E(R_i)]$	Exxon $\times$ $[R_j - E(R_j)]$
1/97	10.48	5.74	7.91	3.55		28.08
2/97	5.17	−3.26	2.60	−5.45		−14.17
3/97	−8.17	8.30	−10.74	6.11		−65.62
4/97	13.65	5.34	11.08	3.15		34.90
5/97	7.68	4.41	5.11	2.22		11.34
6/97	−0.34	4.07	−2.91	1.88		−5.47
7/97	1.84	4.80	−0.73	2.61		−1.91
8/97	−20.13	−4.67	−22.70	−6.86		155.72
9/97	10.54	5.37	7.97	3.18		25.35
10/97	−7.38	−4.10	−9.95	−6.29		62.59
11/97	10.62	−0.71	8.05	−2.90		−23.35
12/97	6.94	0.98	4.37	−1.21		−5.29
	$E(R_i) = 2.57$	$E(R_j) = 2.19$			Sum =	202.17

$$Cov_{ij} = 202.17/12 = 16.85$$

its mean rate of return during this same period, then the *product* of these deviations from the mean is positive. If this happens consistently, the covariance of returns between these two stocks will be some large positive value. If, however, the rate of return for one of the securities is above its mean return while the return on the other security is below its mean return, the product will be negative. If this contrary movement happened consistently, the covariance between the rates of return for the two stocks would be a large negative value.

Table 6.5 contains the monthly rates of return during 1997 for Coca-Cola and Exxon as computed in Table 6.4. One might expect the returns for the two stocks to have reasonably low covariance because of the differences in the products of these firms. The expected returns E(R) were the arithmetic mean of the monthly returns:

$$E(R_i) = \frac{1}{12} \sum_{i=1}^{12} R_{it}$$

and

$$E(R_j) = \frac{1}{12} \sum_{j=1}^{12} R_{jt}$$

All figures (except those in the last column) were rounded to the nearest hundredth of 1 percent. As shown in Table 6.4, the average monthly return was 2.57 percent for Coca-Cola and 2.19 percent for Exxon stock. The results in Table 6.5 show that the covariance between the rates of return for these two stocks was:

$$Cov_{ij} = \frac{1}{12} \times 202.17$$
$$= 16.85$$

Interpretation of a number such as 16.85 is difficult; is it high or low for covariance? We know the relationship between the two stocks is generally positive, but it is not possible to be more specific. Figure 6.3 contains a scatter diagram with paired values of R_{it} and R_{jt} plotted against each other. This plot demonstrates the linear nature and strength

Figure 6.3   *Scatter Plot of Monthly Returns for Coca-Cola and Exxon: 1997*

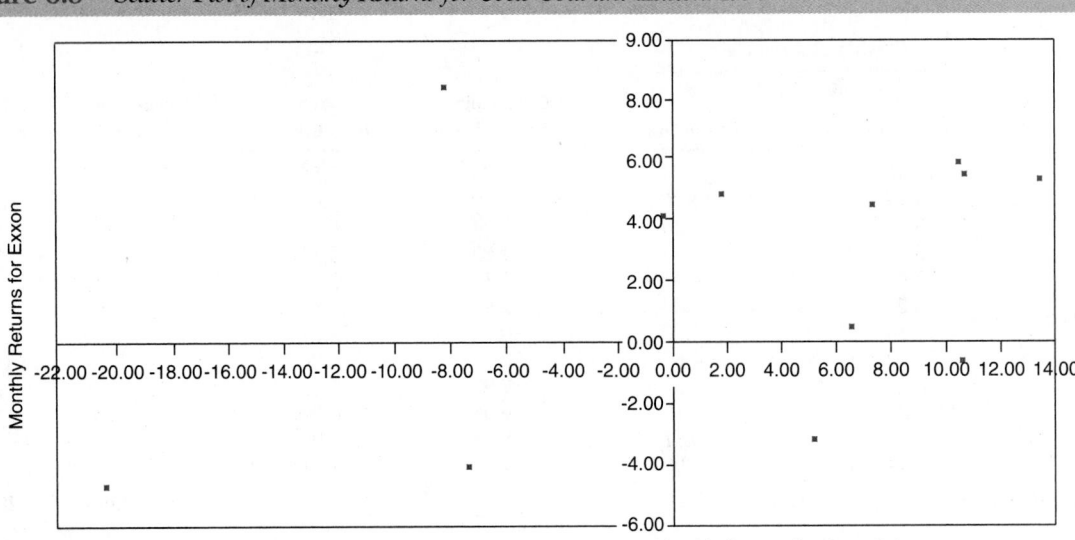

of the relationship and shows several instances during 1997 when Coca-Cola experienced negative returns relative to its mean return when Exxon had positive rates of return relative to its mean.

Covariance and Correlation   Covariance is affected by the variability of the two individual return series. Therefore, a number such as the 16.85 in our example might indicate a weak positive relationship if the two individual series were volatile, but would reflect a strong positive relationship if the two series were stable. Obviously, you want to "standardize" this covariance measure taking into consideration the variability of the two individual return series, as follows:

$$r_{ij} = \frac{Cov_{ij}}{\sigma_i \sigma_j}$$

where:

r_{ij} = **the correlation coefficient of returns**
σ_i = **the standard deviation of R_{it}**
σ_j = **the standard deviation of R_{jt}.**

Standardizing the covariance by the individual standard deviations yields the **correlation coefficient** (r_{ij}), which can vary only in the range −1 to +1. A value of +1 would indicate a perfect positive linear relationship between R_i and R_j, meaning the returns for the two stocks move together in a completely linear manner. A value of −1 indicates a perfect negative relationship between the two return series such that when one stock's rate of return is above its mean, the other stock's rate of return will be below its mean by the comparable amount.

To calculate this standardized measure of the relationship, you need to compute the standard deviation for the two individual return series. We already have the values for $R_{it} - E(R_i)$ and $R_{jt} - E(R_j)$ in Table 6.5. We can square each of these values and sum them as shown in Table 6.6 to calculate the variance of each return series.

Table 6.6 *Computation of Standard Deviation of Returns for Coca-Cola and Exxon: 1997*

Date	Coca-Cola		Exxon	
	$R_i - E(R_i)$	$[R_i - E(R_i)]^2$	$R_j - E(R_j)$	$[R_j - E(R_j)]^2$
1/97	7.90	62.45	3.55	12.60
2/97	2.60	6.75	−5.45	29.70
3/97	−10.75	115.48	6.11	37.33
4/97	11.07	122.60	3.15	9.92
5/97	5.10	26.04	2.22	4.93
6/97	−2.92	8.51	1.88	3.53
7/97	−0.74	0.54	2.61	6.81
8/97	−22.70	515.30	−6.86	47.06
9/97	7.96	63.39	3.18	10.11
10/97	−9.95	99.02	−6.29	39.56
11/97	8.05	64.73	−2.90	8.41
12/97	4.37	19.07	−1.21	1.46
		Sum = 1103.89		Sum = 211.42

Variance$_i$ = 1103.89/12 = 91.99   Variance$_j$ = 211.42/12 = 17.62

Standard Deviation$_i$ = $(91.99)^{1/2}$ = 9.59   Standard Deviation$_j$ = $(17.62)^{1/2}$ = 4.20

$$\sigma^2_i = \frac{1}{12}(1103.89) = 91.99$$

and

$$\sigma^2_j = \frac{1}{12}(211.42) = 17.62$$

The standard deviation for each series is the square root of the variance for each, as follows:

$$\sigma_i = \sqrt{91.99} = 9.59$$
$$\sigma_j = \sqrt{17.62} = 4.20$$

Thus, based on the covariance between the two series and the individual standard deviations, we can calculate the correlation coefficient between returns for Coca-Cola and Exxon as

$$r_{ij} = \frac{Cov_{ij}}{\sigma_i\sigma_j} = \frac{16.85}{(9.59)(4.20)} = \frac{16.85}{40.28} = 0.418$$

Obviously, this formula also implies that

$$Cov_{ij} = r_{ij}\sigma_i\sigma_j = (.418)(9.59)(4.20) = 16.85$$

Standard Deviation of a Portfolio

As noted, a correlation of +1.0 would indicate perfect positive correlation, and a value of −1.0 would mean that the returns moved in a completely opposite direction. A value of zero would mean that the returns had no linear relationship, that is, they were uncorrelated statistically. That does *not* mean that they are independent. The value of r_{ij} = 0.418

is significant but not high. This relatively low correlation is not unusual for stocks in diverse industries. Correlation between stocks of companies *within* some industries approach 0.85.

Portfolio Standard Deviation Formula   Now that we have discussed the concepts of covariance and correlation, we can consider the formula for computing the standard deviation of returns for a *portfolio* of assets, our measure of risk for a portfolio. As noted, Harry Markowitz derived the formula for computing the standard deviation of a portfolio of assets.[5]

In Table 6.2, we showed that the expected rate of return of the portfolio was the weighted average of the expected returns for the individual assets in the portfolio; the weights were the percentage of value of the portfolio. Under such conditions, we can easily see the impact adding or deleting an asset would have on the portfolio's expected return.

One might assume it is possible to derive the standard deviation of the portfolio in the same manner, that is, by computing the weighted average of the standard deviations for the individual assets. This would be a mistake. Markowitz derived the general formula for the standard deviation of a portfolio as follows:[6]

$$\sigma_{\text{port}} = \sqrt{\sum_{i=1}^{n} w_i^2 \sigma_i^2 + \sum_{i=1}^{n} \sum_{\substack{j=1 \\ i \neq j}}^{n} w_i w_j \text{Cov}_{ij}}$$

where:

σ_{port} = **the standard deviation of the portfolio**

w_i = **the weights of the individual assets in the portfolio, where weights are determined by the proportion of value in the portfolio**

σ_i^2 = **the variance of rates of return for asset i**

Cov_{ij} = **the covariance between the rates of return for assets i and j, where $\text{Cov}_{ij} = r_{ij}\sigma_i\sigma_j$**

This formula indicates that the standard deviation for a portfolio of assets is a function of the weighted average of the individual variances (where the weights are squared), *plus* the weighted covariances between all the assets in the portfolio. The standard deviation for a portfolio of assets encompasses not only the variances of the individual assets, but *also* includes the covariances between pairs of individual assets in the portfolio. Further, it can be shown that, in a portfolio with a large number of securities, this formula reduces to the sum of the weighted covariances.

Although most of the subsequent demonstration will consider portfolios with only two assets because it is possible to show the effect in two dimensions, we will demonstrate the computations for a three-asset portfolio. Still, it is important at this point to consider what happens in a large portfolio with many assets. Specifically, what happens to the portfolio's standard deviation when you add a new security to such a portfolio? As shown by the formula, we see two effects. The first is the asset's own variance of returns, and the second is the covariance between the returns of this new asset and the returns of *every other asset that is already in the portfolio*. The relative weight of these numerous covariances is substantially greater than the asset's unique variance, and the more assets in the portfolio, the more this is true. This means that the important factor to consider when adding an investment to a portfolio that contains a number of other investments is *not* the investment's own variance, but *its average covariance with all the other investments in the portfolio.*

---

[5]Markowitz, *Portfolio Selection.*

[6]For the detailed derivation of this formula, see Markowitz, *Portfolio Selection.*

In the following examples we will consider the simple case of a two-asset portfolio. We do these relatively simple calculations and provide graphs with two assets to demonstrate the impact of different covariances on the total risk (standard deviation) of the portfolio.

Demonstration of the Portfolio Standard Deviation Calculation   Because of the assumptions used in developing the Markowitz portfolio model, any asset or portfolio of assets can be described by two characteristics: the expected rate of return and the expected standard deviation of returns. Therefore, the following demonstrations can be applied to two *individual* assets with the indicated return–standard deviation character-istics and correlation coefficients, two *portfolios* of assets, or two *asset classes* with the indicated return–standard deviation characteristics and correlation coefficients.

Equal risk and return—changing correlations   Consider first the case in which both assets have the same expected return and expected standard deviation of return. As an example, let us assume

$$E(R_1) = .20$$
$$E(\sigma_1) = .10$$
$$E(R_2) = .20$$
$$E(\sigma_2) = .10.$$

To show the effect of different covariances, assume different levels of correlation between the two assets. Consider the following examples where the two assets have equal weights in the portfolio ($W_1 = .50$; $W_2 = .50$). Therefore, the only value that changes in each exam-ple is the correlation between the returns for the two assets.

Recall that

$$Cov_{ij} = r_{ij}\sigma_i\sigma_j.$$

Consider the following alternative correlation coefficients and the covariances they yield. The covariance will be equal to $r_{1,2}$ (.10)(.10) because both standard deviations are 0.10.

a. $r_{1,2} = 1.00$; $Cov_{1,2} = (1.00)(.10)(.10) = .01$
b. $r_{1,2} = .50$; $Cov_{1,2} = (0.50)(.10)(.10) = .005$
c. $r_{1,2} = .00$; $Cov_{1,2} = .000$
d. $r_{1,2} = -.50$; $Cov_{1,2} = -.005$
e. $r_{1,2} = -1.00$; $Cov_{1,2} = -.01.$

Now let us see what happens to the standard deviation of the portfolio under these five conditions. Recall that

$$\sigma_{port} = \sqrt{\sum_{i=1}^{n} w_i^2\sigma_i^2 + \sum_{i=1}^{n}\sum_{\substack{j=1 \\ i\neq j}}^{n} w_i w_j Cov_{ij}}$$

When this general formula is applied to a two-asset portfolio, it is

$$\sigma_{port} = \sqrt{w_1^2\sigma_1^2 + w_2^2\sigma_2^2 + 2w_1 w_2 r_{1,2}\sigma_1\sigma_2}$$

or

$$\sigma_{port} = \sqrt{w_1^2\sigma_1^2 + w_2^2\sigma_2^2 + 2w_1 w_2 Cov_{1,2}}.$$

Thus, in Case a,

$$\begin{aligned}
\sigma_{port\,(a)} &= \sqrt{(0.5)^2(0.10)^2 + (0.5)^2(0.10)^2 + 2(0.5)(0.5)(0.01)} \\
&= \sqrt{(0.25)(0.01) + (0.25)(0.01) + 2(0.25)(0.01)} \\
&= \sqrt{0.01} \\
&= 0.10.
\end{aligned}$$

In this case, where the returns for the two assets are perfectly positively correlated, the standard deviation for the portfolio is, in fact, the weighted average of the individual standard deviations. The important point is that we get no real benefit from combining two assets that are perfectly correlated; they are like one asset already because their returns move together.

Now consider Case b, where $r_{1,2}$ equals 0.50.

$$\begin{aligned}
\sigma_{port\,(b)} &= \sqrt{(0.5)^2(0.10)^2 + (0.5)^2(0.10)^2 + 2(0.5)(0.5)(0.005)} \\
&= \sqrt{(0.0025) + (0.0025) + 2(0.25)(0.005)} \\
&= \sqrt{0.0075} \\
&= 0.0866.
\end{aligned}$$

The only term that changed from Case a is the last term, $Cov_{1,2}$, which changed from 0.01 to 0.005. As a result, the standard deviation of the portfolio declined by about 13 percent, from 0.10 to 0.0866. Note that *the expected return did not change* because it is simply the weighted average of the individual expected returns; it is equal to 0.20 in both cases.

You should be able to confirm through your own calculations that the standard deviations for Portfolios c and d are as follows:

c.   .0707
d.   .05.

The final case where the correlation between the two assets is −1.00 indicates the ultimate benefits of diversification.

$$\begin{aligned}
\sigma_{port\,(e)} &= \sqrt{(0.5)^2(0.10)^2 + (0.5)^2(0.10)^2 + 2(0.5)(0.5)(-0.01)} \\
&= \sqrt{(0.0050) + (-0.0050)} \\
&= \sqrt{0} \\
&= 0.
\end{aligned}$$

Here, the negative covariance term exactly offsets the individual variance terms, leaving an overall standard deviation of the portfolio of zero. *This would be a risk-free portfolio.*

Figure 6.4 illustrates a graph of such a pattern. Perfect negative correlation gives a mean combined return for the two securities over time equal to the mean for each of them, so the returns for the portfolio show no variability. Any returns above and below the mean for each of the assets are *completely offset* by the return for the other asset, so there is *no variability* in total returns, that is, *no risk,* for the portfolio. This combination of two assets that are completely negatively correlated provides the maximum benefits of diversification—it completely eliminates risk.

The graph in Figure 6.5 shows the difference in the risk–return posture for these five cases. As noted, the only effect of the change in correlation is the change in the standard deviation of this two-asset portfolio. Combining assets that are not perfectly correlated

Figure 6.4   *Time Patterns of Returns for Two Assets with Perfect Negative Correlation*

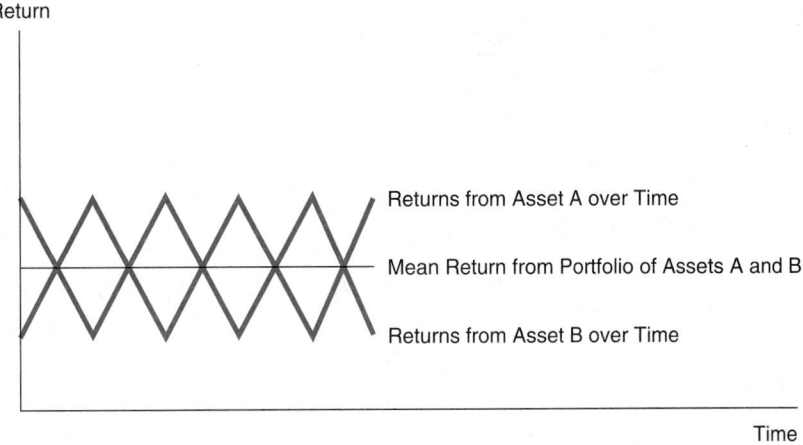

Figure 6.5   *Risk–Return Plot for Portfolios with Equal Returns and Standard Deviations but Different Correlations*

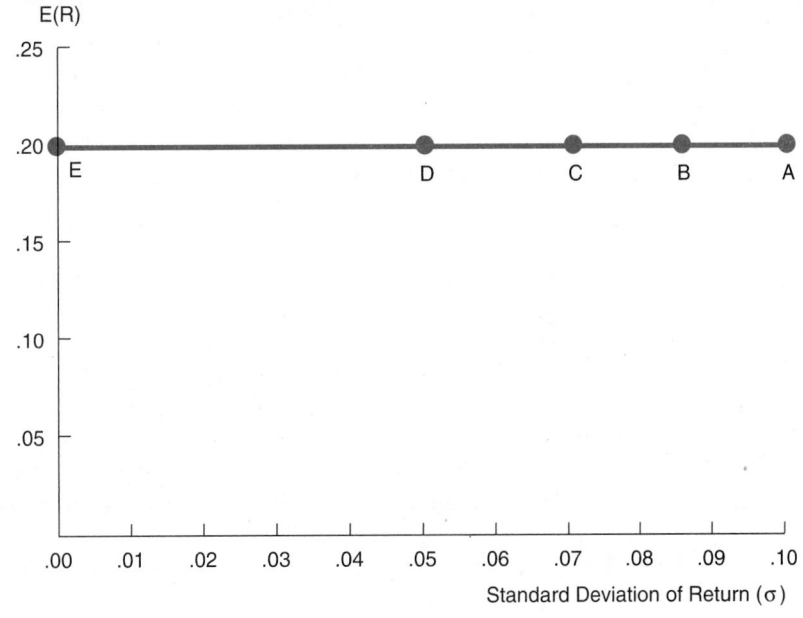

does *not* affect the expected return of the portfolio, but it *does* reduce the risk of the portfolio (as measured by its standard deviation). When we eventually reach the ultimate combination of perfect negative correlation, risk is eliminated.

Combining stocks with different returns and risk   The previous discussion indicated what happens when only the correlation coefficient (covariance) differs between the assets. We now consider two assets (or portfolios) with different expected rates of return

and individual standard deviations.[7] We will show what happens when we vary the correlations between them. We will assume two assets with the following characteristics:

Asset	$E(R_i)$	W_i	σ^2_i	σ_i
1	.10	.50	.0049	.07
2	.20	.50	.0100	.10

The previous set of correlation coefficients gives a different set of covariances because the standard deviations are different. For example, the covariance in Case b would be $(0.50)(.07)(.10) = .0035$.

Case	Correlation Coefficient	Covariance $(r_{ij}\sigma_i\sigma_j)$
a	+1.00	.0070
b	+0.50	.0035
c	0.00	.0000
d	−0.50	−.0035
e	−1.00	−.0070

Because we are assuming the same weights in all cases (50/50), the expected return in every instance will be

$$E(R_{port}) = 0.50(0.10) + 0.50(0.20)$$
$$= 0.15.$$

The standard deviation for Case a will be

$$\sigma_{port\,(a)} = \sqrt{(0.5)^2(0.07)^2 + (0.5)^2(0.10)^2 + 2(0.5)(0.5)(0.0070)}$$
$$= \sqrt{0.007225}$$
$$= 0.085.$$

Again, with perfect positive correlation, the standard deviation of the portfolio is the weighted average of the standard deviations of the individual assets:

$$(0.5)(0.07) + (0.5)(0.10) = 0.085.$$

As you might envision, changing the weights with perfect positive correlation causes the standard deviation for the portfolio to change in a linear fashion. This is an important point to remember when we discuss the capital asset pricing model (CAPM) in the next chapter.

For Cases b, c, d, and e, the standard deviation for the portfolio would be as follows:[8]

$$\sigma_{port\,(b)} = \sqrt{(0.001225) + (0.0025) + (0.5)(0.0035)}$$
$$= \sqrt{(0.005475}$$
$$= 0.07399$$
$$\sigma_{port\,(c)} = \sqrt{(0.001225) + (0.0025) + (0.5)(0.00)}$$
$$= 0.0610$$

---

[7]As noted, these could be two asset classes. For example, asset 1 could be low risk–return bonds and asset 2 could be higher return–higher risk stocks.

[8]In all the following examples we will skip some steps because you are now aware that only the last term changes. You are encouraged to work out the individual steps to ensure that you understand the computational procedure.

Figure 6.6   *Risk–Return Plot for Portfolios with Different Returns, Standard Deviations, and Correlations*

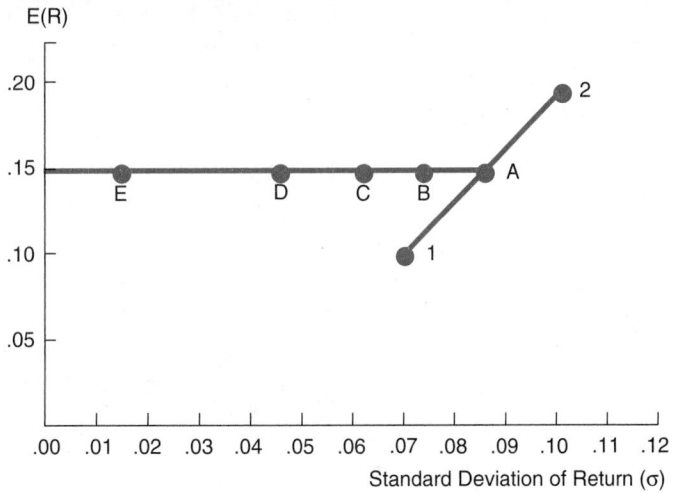

$$\sigma_{\text{port (d)}} = \sqrt{(0.001225) + (0.0025) + (0.5)(-0.0035)}$$
$$= 0.0444$$
$$\sigma_{\text{port (e)}} = \sqrt{(0.003725) + (0.5)(-0.0070)}$$
$$= 0.015.$$

Note that, in this example, with perfect negative correlation the standard deviation of the portfolio is not zero. This is because the different examples have equal weights, but the individual standard deviations are not equal.[9]

Figure 6.6 shows the results for the two individual assets and the portfolio of the two assets assuming the correlation coefficients vary as set forth in Cases a through e. As before, the expected return does not change because the proportions are always set at .50 − .50, so all the portfolios lie along the horizontal line at the return, R = .15.

Constant correlation with changing weights   If we changed the weights of the two assets while holding the correlation coefficient constant, we would derive a set of combinations that trace an ellipse starting at Asset 2, going through the .50 − .50 point, and ending at Asset 1. We can demonstrate this with Case c, in which the correlation coefficient of zero eases the computations. We begin with 100 percent in Asset 2 (Case f) and change the weights as follows, ending with 100 percent in Asset 1 (Case l):

Case	W_1	W_2	$E(R_i)$
f	.00	1.00	.20
g	.20	.80	.18
h	.40	.60	.16
i	.50	.50	.15
j	.60	.40	.14
k	.80	.20	.12
l	1.00	.00	.10

[9]The two appendixes to this chapter show proofs for equal weights with equal variances and solve for the appropriate weights to get zero standard deviation when standard deviations are not equal.

We already know the standard deviation (σ) for Portfolio i. In Cases f, g, h, j, k, and l, the standard deviations would be[10]

$$\begin{aligned}
\sigma_{\text{port (g)}} &= \sqrt{(0.20)^2(0.07)^2 + (0.80)^2(0.10)^2 + 2(0.20)(0.80)(0.00)} \\
&= \sqrt{(0.04)(0.0049) + (0.64)(0.01) + (0)} \\
&= \sqrt{0.006596} \\
&= 0.0812 \\
\sigma_{\text{port (h)}} &= \sqrt{(0.40)^2(0.07)^2 + (0.60)^2(0.10)^2 + 2(0.40)(0.60)(0.00)} \\
&= \sqrt{0.004384} \\
&= 0.0662 \\
\sigma_{\text{port (j)}} &= \sqrt{(0.60)^2(0.07)^2 + (0.40)^2(0.10)^2 + 2(0.60)(0.40)(0.00)} \\
&= \sqrt{0.003364} \\
&= 0.0580 \\
\sigma_{\text{port (k)}} &= \sqrt{(0.80)^2(0.07)^2 + (0.20)^2(0.10)^2 + 2(0.80)(0.20)(0.00)} \\
&= \sqrt{0.003536} \\
&= 0.0595.
\end{aligned}$$

These alternative weights with a constant correlation would yield the following risk–return combinations:

Case	W_1	W_2	$E(R_i)$	$E(\sigma_{\text{port}})$
f	0.00	1.00	0.20	0.1000
g	0.20	0.80	0.18	0.0812
h	0.40	0.60	0.16	0.0662
i	0.50	0.50	0.15	0.0610
j	0.60	0.40	0.14	0.0580
k	0.80	0.20	0.12	0.0595
l	1.00	0.00	0.10	0.0700

A graph of these combinations appears in Figure 6.7. You could derive a complete curve by simply varying the weighting by smaller increments.

A notable result is that with low, zero, or negative correlations, it is possible to derive portfolios that have *lower risk than either single asset*. In our set of examples where $r_{ij} = 0.00$, this occurs in cases h, i, j, and k. This ability to reduce risk is the essence of diversification. In turn, we see that the crucial factors that affect diversification are the correlation between assets and the weighting among them.

As shown in Figure 6.7, the curvature in the graph depends on the correlation between the two assets or portfolios. With $r_{ij} = +1.00$, the combinations lie along a straight line between the two assets. When $r_{ij} = 0.50$, the curve is to the right of our $r_{ij} = 0.00$ curve, while the $r_{ij} = -0.50$ is to the left. Finally, when $r_{ij} = -1.00$, the graph would be two straight lines that would touch at the vertical line (zero risk) with some combination. As discussed in Appendix B of this chapter, it is possible to solve for the specified set of weights that would give a portfolio with zero risk. In this case, it is $W_1 = 0.412$ and $W_2 = 0.588$.

A Three-Asset Portfolio

A demonstration of what occurs with a three-asset class portfolio is useful because it shows the dynamics of the portfolio process when we add additional assets to a portfolio. It also

---

[10]Again, you are encouraged to fill in the steps we skipped in the computations.

Figure 6.7   *Portfolio Risk–Return Plots for Different Weights When $r_{i,j}$ = +1.00; +0.50; 0.00; −0.50; −1.00*

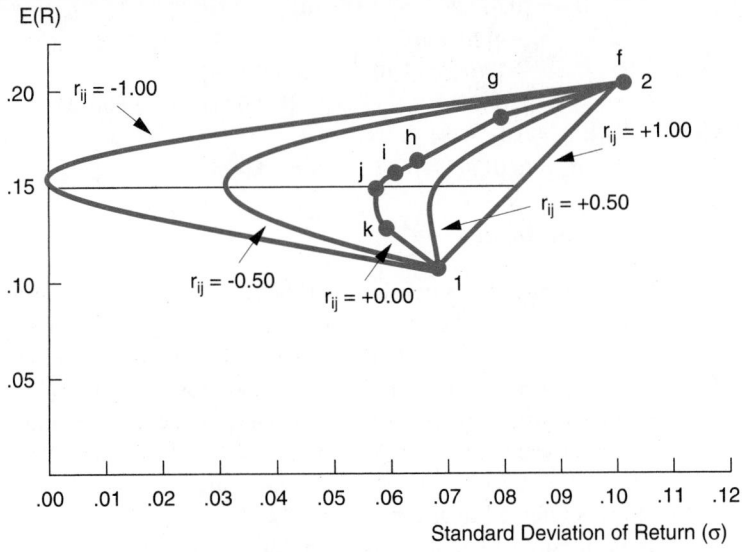

shows the rapid growth in the computations required, which is why we will stop at three assets.

In this example, we will combine three asset classes we have been discussing: stocks, bonds, and cash equivalents.[11] We will assume the following characteristics for these assets:

Asset Classes	$E(R_i)$	$E(\sigma_i)$	W_i
Stocks (S)	.12	.20	.60
Bonds (B)	.08	.10	.30
Cash equivalent (C)	.04	.03	.10

The correlations are as follows:

$$r_{S,B} = 0.25; r_{S,C} = -0.08; r_{B,C} = 0.15$$

Given the weights specified, the $E(R_p)$ is:

$$E(R_p) = (0.60)(0.12) + (0.30)(0.08) + (0.10)(0.04)$$
$$= (.072 + .024 + .004) = .100 = 10.00\%$$

When we apply the generalized formula to the expected standard deviation of a three-asset class, it is as follows:

$$\sigma_p^2 = [W_S^2\sigma_S^2 + W_B^2\sigma_B^2 + W_C^2\sigma_C^2] + [2\,W_S W_B \sigma_S \sigma_B r_{S,B} + 2W_S W_C \sigma_S \sigma_C r_{S,C} + 2W_B W_C \sigma_B \sigma_C r_{B,C}]$$

---

[11]The asset allocation articles regularly contained in *Wall Street Journal* generally refer to these three asset classes.

Using the characteristics specified, the standard deviation of this three-asset class portfolio (σ_p) would be:

$$
\begin{aligned}
\sigma_p^2 &= [0.6)^2(.20)^2 + (0.3)^2(.10)^2 + (0.1)^2(.03)^2] \\
&\quad + \{[2(0.6)(0.3)(0.20)(0.10)(0.25)] + [2(0.6)(0.1)(0.20)(0.03)(-0.08)] \\
&\quad + [2(0.3)(0.1)(0.10)(0.03)(0.15)]\} \\
&= [.015309] + \{[.0018] + [-.0000576] + [.000027]\} \\
&= 0.0170784 \\
\sigma_p &= (0.0170784)^{1/2} = .1306 = 13.06\%
\end{aligned}
$$

Estimation Issues

It is important to keep in mind that the results of this portfolio asset allocation depend on the accuracy of the statistical inputs. In the current instance, this means that for every asset (or asset class) being considered for inclusion in the portfolio, you must estimate its expected returns and standard deviation. In addition, the correlation coefficient among the entire set of assets must also be estimated. The number of correlation estimates can be significant—for example, for a portfolio of 100 securities, the number is 4,950 (that is, $99 + 98 + 97 + \ldots$). The potential source of error that arises from these approximations is referred to as *estimation risk*.

It is possible to reduce the number of correlation coefficients that must be estimated by assuming that stock returns can be described by a single index market model as follows:

$$R_i = a_i + b_i R_m + \epsilon_i$$

where:

b_i = the slope coefficient that relates the returns for security i to the returns for the aggregate stock market

R_m = the returns for the aggregate stock market

If all the securities are similarly related to the market and a b_i derived for each one, it can be shown that the correlation coefficient between two securities i and j is given as:

$$r_{ij} = b_i b_j \frac{\sigma_m^2}{\sigma_i \sigma_j}$$

where σ_m^2 = the variance of returns for the aggregate stock market.

This reduces the number of estimates from 4,950 to 100—that is, once you have derived a slope estimate (b_i) for each security, the correlation estimates can be computed. Keep in mind that this assumes that the single index market model provides a good estimate of security returns.

The Efficient Frontier

If we examined different two-asset combinations and derived the curves assuming all the possible weights, we would have a graph like that in Figure 6.8. The envelope curve that contains the best of all these possible combinations is referred to as the **efficient frontier**. Specifically, *the efficient frontier represents that set of portfolios that has the maximum rate of return for every given level of risk, or the minimum risk for every level of return.* An example of such a frontier is shown in Figure 6.9. Every portfolio that lies on the efficient frontier has either a higher rate of return for equal risk or lower risk for an equal rate of return than some portfolio beneath the frontier. Thus, we would say that Portfolio A *dominates*

Figure 6.8 *Numerous Portfolio Combinations of Available Assets*

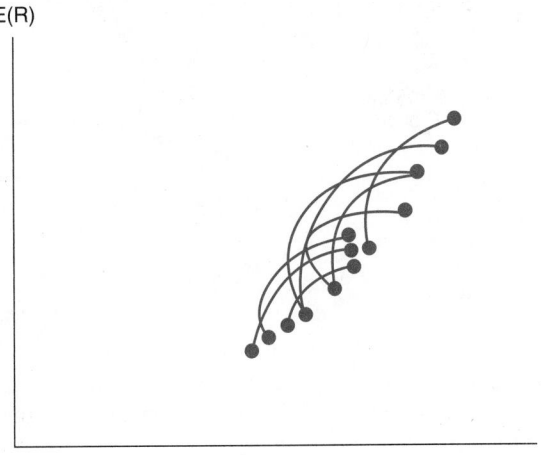

Portfolio C because it has an equal rate of return but substantially less risk. Similarly, Portfolio B dominates Portfolio C because it has equal risk but a higher expected rate of return. Because of the benefits of diversification among imperfectly correlated assets, we would expect the efficient frontier to be made up of *portfolios* of investments rather than individual securities. Two possible exceptions arise at the end points, which represent the asset with the highest return and that asset with the lowest risk.

As an investor, you will target a point along the efficient frontier based on your utility function and your attitude toward risk. No portfolio on the efficient frontier can dominate any other portfolio on the efficient frontier. All of these portfolios have different return and risk measures, with expected rates of return that increase with higher risk.

The Efficient Frontier and Investor Utility

The curve in Figure 6.9 shows that the slope of the efficient frontier curve decreases steadily as you move upward. This implies that adding equal increments of risk as you move up the efficient frontier gives you diminishing increments of expected return. To evaluate this slope, we calculate the slope of the efficient frontier as follows:

$$\frac{\Delta E(R_{port})}{\Delta E(\sigma_{port})}$$

An individual investor's utility curves specify the trade-offs he or she is willing to make between expected return and risk. In conjunction with the efficient frontier, these utility curves determine which *particular* portfolio on the efficient frontier best suits an individual investor. Two investors will choose the same portfolio from the efficient set only if their utility curves are identical.

Figure 6.10 shows two sets of utility curves along with an efficient frontier of investments. The curves labeled $U_1 U_2 U_3$ are for a strongly risk-averse investor. These utility curves are quite steep, indicating that the investor will not tolerate much additional risk to obtain additional returns. The investor is equally disposed toward any E(R), E(σ) combinations along a specific utility curve, such as U_1.

Figure 6.9   *Efficient Frontier for Alternative Portfolios*

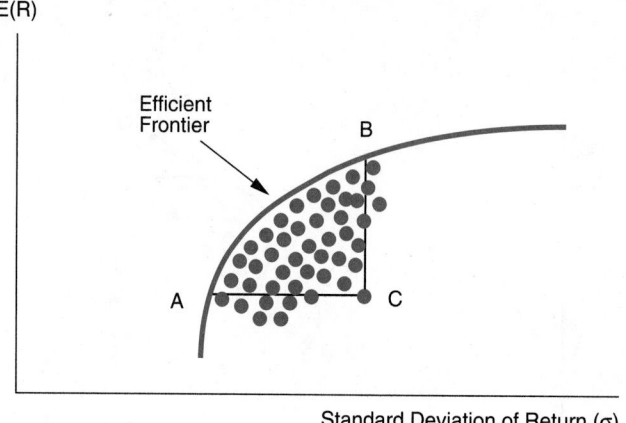

Figure 6.10   *Selecting an Optimal Risky Portfolio*

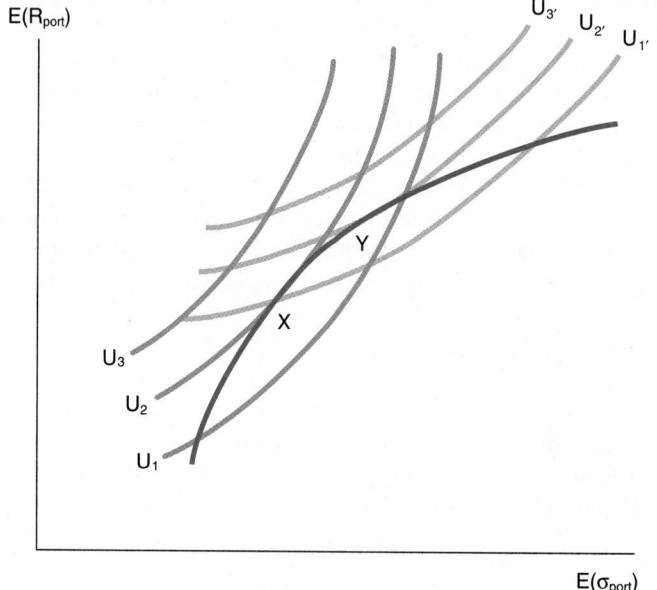

The curves labeled $U_{3'}$ $U_{2'}$ $U_{1'}$ characterize a less risk-averse investor. Such an investor is willing to tolerate a bit more risk to get a higher expected return.

The **optimal portfolio** is the efficient portfolio that has the highest utility for a given investor. It lies at *the point of tangency between the efficient frontier and the curve with the highest possible utility.* A conservative investor's highest utility is at point X in Figure 6.10, where the curve U_2 just touches the efficient frontier. A less risk-averse investor's highest utility occurs at point Y, which represents a portfolio with higher expected returns and higher risk than the portfolio at X.

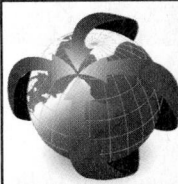

Investments Online

By seeking to operate on the efficient frontier, portfolio managers try to minimize risk for a certain level of return, or maximize return for a given level of risk. Software programs, called optimizers, are used by portfolio managers to determine the shape of the efficient frontier as well as to determine some of the portfolios which lie on it. Financial planners use information on past returns and manager performance, in addition to optimizers, to make recommendations to their clients. Some interesting Web sites for money managers include:

www.pionline.com

This is the home page for *Pensions and Investments*, a newspaper for money managers. Items on the home page include links to news of interest to managers, PIPER performance data on over 3,000 equity, fixed income, real estate, and global portfolios managed by over 1,100 management firms, research (with links to thousands of articles and listings), and other links to organizations such as central banks, consultants, and sellers of investment-related products. The performance section shows, among other items, returns, risk, and graphic analyses of over 60 PIPER style universes and over 90 benchmark portfolios.

www.investmentnews.com

Investment News is a sister publication to *Pensions and Investments*, with a focus toward the financial advisor. This site includes information on financial planning, the mutual fund industry, regulation, equity performance, and industry trends.

www.micropal.com

This site provides fund information for over 38,000 funds in 19 countries. Performance data is available over daily, weekly, and monthly intervals. Users can see performance by fund objective, read economic commentaries, and screen and sort the site's database.

www.riskview.com

The creators of this home page want to help people identify risk in their portfolios. It includes access to risk and return for about 3,000 equities from 29 countries. The site features historical return and volatility measures, risk–return analysis, and forecasts of future volatilities and correlations.

www.alternativeinvestment.com

The home page of Alternative Investment Corporation seeks to encourage investors to use convertible securities and "convertible arbitrage" in their portfolios (convertible arbitrage, as explained on this site, involves going long in a convertible security while shorting shares some of the underlying equity). It presents an interesting application of this chapter, since the firm attempts to identify investments with low correlations to the stock and bond markets in an effort to shift investors' efficient frontier outward. If a site visitor enters data from their current portfolio, an optimizer program will compute two portfolio solutions (maximum return for the portfolio's current risk, and minimum risk for the portfolio's current return).

SUMMARY

♦ The basic Markowitz portfolio model derived the expected rate of return for a portfolio of assets and a measure of expected risk, which is the standard deviation of expected rate of return. Markowitz shows that the expected rate of return of a portfolio is the weighted average of the expected return for the individual investments in the portfolio. The standard deviation of a portfolio is a function not only of the standard deviations for the individual investments, but *also* of the covariance between the rates of return for all the pairs of assets in the portfolio. In a large portfolio, these covariances are the important factors.

♦ Different weights or amounts of a portfolio held in various assets yield a curve of potential combinations. Correlation coefficients among assets are the critical factor you must consider when selecting investments because you can maintain your rate of return while reducing the risk level of your portfolio by combining assets or portfolios that have low positive or negative correlation.

♦ Assuming numerous assets and a multitude of combination curves, the efficient frontier is the envelope curve that encompasses all of the best combinations. It defines the set of portfolios that has the highest expected return for each given level of risk, or the minimum risk for each given level of return. From this set of dominant portfolios, you select the one that lies at the point of tangency between the efficient frontier and your highest utility curve. Because risk–return utility functions differ, your point of tangency and, therefore, your portfolio choice will probably differ from those of other investors.

♦ At this point, we understand that an optimum portfolio is a combination of investments, each having desirable individual risk–return characteristics that also fit together based on their correlations. This deeper understanding of portfolio theory should lead you to reflect back on our earlier discussion of global investing. Because many foreign stock and bond investments provide superior rates of return compared with U.S. securities *and* have low correlations with portfolios of U.S. stocks and bonds, including these foreign securities in your portfolio will help you to reduce the overall risk of your portfolio while possibly increasing your rate of return.

Questions

1. Why do most investors hold diversified portfolios?
2. What is covariance, and why is it important in portfolio theory?
3. Why do most assets of the same type show positive covariances of returns with each other? Would you expect positive covariances of returns between *different* types of assets such as returns on Treasury bills, General Electric common stock, and commercial real estate? Why or why not?
4. What is the relationship between covariance and the correlation coefficient?
5. Explain the shape of the efficient frontier.
6. Draw a properly labeled graph of the Markowitz efficient frontier. Describe the efficient frontier in exact terms. Discuss the concept of dominant portfolios and show an example of one on your graph.
7. Assume you want to run a computer program to derive the efficient frontier for your feasible set of stocks. What information must you input to the program?
8. Why are investors' utility curves important in portfolio theory?
9. Explain how a given investor chooses an optimal portfolio. Will this choice always be a diversified portfolio, or could it be a single asset? Explain your answer.
10. Assume that you and a business associate develop an efficient frontier for a set of investments. Why might the two of you select different portfolios on the frontier?

11   Draw a hypothetical graph of an efficient frontier of U.S. common stocks. On the same graph, draw an efficient frontier assuming the inclusion of U.S. bonds as well. Finally, on the same graph, draw an efficient frontier that includes U.S. common stocks, U.S. bonds, and stocks and bonds from around the world. Discuss the differences in these frontiers.

12. Stocks L, M, and N each have the same expected return and standard deviation. The correlation coefficients between each pair of these stocks are:

L and M correlation coefficient = +0.8
L and N correlation coefficient = +0.2
M and N correlation coefficient = −0.4

Given these correlations, a portfolio constructed of which pair of stocks will have the lowest standard deviation? Explain.

Problems

1.   Considering the world economic outlook for the coming year and estimates of sales and earning for the pharmaceutical industry, you expect the rate of return for Lauren Labs common stock to range between −20 percent and +40 percent with the following probabilities:

Probability	Possible Returns
0.10	−0.20
0.15	−0.05
0.20	0.10
0.25	0.15
0.20	0.20
0.10	0.40

Compute the expected rate of return $[E(R_i)]$ for Lauren Labs.

2.   Given the following market values of stocks in your portfolio and their expected rates of return, what is the expected rate of return for your common stock portfolio?

Stock	Market Value ($ Mil.)	$E(R_i)$
Phillips Petroleum	$15,000	0.14
Starbucks	17,000	−0.04
International Paper	32,000	0.18
Intel	23,000	0.16
Walgreens	7,000	0.12

3.   The following are the monthly rates of return for Madison Corp. and for General Electric during a six-month period.

Month	Madison Corp.	General Electric
1	−.04	.07
2	.06	−.02
3	−.07	−.10
4	.12	.15
5	−.02	−.06
6	.05	.02

Compute the following:
a.   Expected monthly rate of return $[E(R_i)]$ for each stock.
b.   Standard deviation of returns for each stock.

   c. Covariance between the rates of return.

   d. The correlation coefficient between the rates of return.

What level of correlation did you expect? How did your expectations compare with the computed correlation? Would these two stocks offer a good chance for diversification? Why or why not?

4. You are considering two assets with the following characteristics:

$$E(R_1) = .15 \qquad E(\sigma_1) = .10 \qquad W_1 = .5$$
$$E(R_2) = .20 \qquad E(\sigma_2) = .20 \qquad W_2 = .5$$

Compute the mean and standard deviation of two portfolios if $r_{1,2} = .40$ and $-.60$, respectively. Plot the two portfolios on a risk–return graph and briefly explain the results.

5. Given: $E(R_1) = .10$
$$E(R_2) = .15$$
$$E(\sigma_1) = .03$$
$$E(\sigma_2) = .05$$

Calculate the expected returns and expected standard deviations of a two-stock portfolio in which Stock 1 has a weight of 60 percent under the following conditions:

   a. $r_{1,2} = $ 1.00

   b. $r_{1,2} = $ .75

   c. $r_{1,2} = $ .25

   d. $r_{1,2} = $ .00

   e. $r_{1,2} = $ $-.25$

   f. $r_{1,2} = $ $-.75$

   g. $r_{1,2} = $ -1.00

6. Given: $E(R_1) = .12$
$$E(R_2) = .16$$
$$E(\sigma_1) = .04$$
$$E(\sigma_2) = .06$$

Calculate the expected returns and expected standard deviations of a two-stock portfolio having a correlation coeffcient of .70 under the following conditions:

   a. $w_1 = 1.00$

   b. $w_1 = $ .75

   c. $w_1 = $ .50

   d. $w_1 = $ .25

   e. $w_1 = $ .05

Plot the results on a return–risk graph. Without calculations, draw in what the curve would look like if the correlation coefficient had been 0.00; or if it had been -0.70.

7. The following are monthly percentage price changes for four market indexes:

Month	DJIA	S&P 400	AMEX	NIKKEI
1	.03	.02	.04	.04
2	.07	.06	.10	$-.02$
3	$-.02$	$-.01$	$-.04$	.07
4	.01	.03	.03	.02
5	.05	.04	.11	.02
6	$-.06$	$-.04$	$-.08$	.06

Compute the following:

   a. Expected monthly rate of return for each series.

   b. Standard deviation for each series.

   c. Covariance between the rates of return for the following indexes:

      DJIA—S&P 400

      S&P 400—AMEX

      S&P 400—NIKKEI

      AMEX—NIKKEI

d. The correlation coefficients for the same four combinations.
e. Using the answers from parts a, b, and d, calculate the expected return and standard deviation of a portfolio consisting of equal parts of (1) the S&P and the AMEX and (2) the S&P and the NIKKEI. Discuss the two portfolios.

8. The standard deviation of Shamrock Corp. stock is 19 percent. The standard deviation of David Co. stock is 14 percent. The covariance between these two stocks is 100. What is the correlation between Shamrock and David stock?

References

Elton, Edwin J., and Martin J. Gruber. *Modern Portfolio Theory and Investment Analysis.* 5th ed. New York: John Wiley & Sons, Inc., 1995.

Farrell, James L., Jr. *Portfolio Management: Theory and Application.* 2d ed. New York: McGraw-Hill, 1997.

Harrington, Diana R. *Modern Portfolio Theory, the Capital Asset Pricing Model, and Arbitrage Pricing Theory: A User's Guide.* 2d ed. Englewood Cliffs, NJ: Prentice-Hall, 1987.

Maginn, John L., and Donald L. Tuttle, eds. *Managing Investment Portfolios: A Dynamic Process.* 2d ed. Sponsored by The Institute of Chartered Financial Analysts. Boston, Warren, Gorham and Lamont, 1990.

Markowitz, Harry. "Portfolio Selection." *Journal of Finance* 7, no. 1 (March 1952).

Markowitz, Harry. *Portfolio Selection: Efficient Diversification of Investments.* New York: John Wiley & Sons, 1959.

GLOSSARY

Correlation coefficient A standardized measure of the relationship between two series that ranges from -1.00 to $+1.00$.

Covariance A measure of the degree to which two variables, such as rates of return for investment assets, move together over time relative to their individual mean returns.

Efficient frontier The curve that defines the set of portfolios with the maximum rate of return for every given level of risk, or the minimum risk for a given rate of return.

Optimal portfolio The efficient portfolio with the highest utility for a given investor, found by the point of tangency between the efficient frontier and the investor's highest utility curve.

APPENDIX 6   *A. Proof That Minimum Portfolio Variance Occurs with Equal Weights When Securities Have Equal Variance*

When $E(\sigma_1) = E(\sigma_2)$, we have:

$$
\begin{aligned}
E(\sigma^2_{port}) &= w_1^2 E(\sigma_1)^2 + (1 - w_1)^2 E(\sigma_1)^2 + 2w_1(1 - w_1)r_{1,2}E(\sigma_1)^2 \\
&= E(\sigma_1)^2[w_1^2 + 1 - 2w_1 + w_1^2 + 2w_1 r_{1,2} - 2w_1^2 r_{1,2}] \\
&= E(\sigma_1)^2[2w_1^2 + 1 - 2w_1 + 2w_1 r_{1,2} - 2w_1^2 r_{1,2}]
\end{aligned}
$$

For this to be a minimum,

$$
\frac{\partial E(\sigma^2_{port})}{\partial w_1} = 0 = E(\sigma_1)^2[4w_1 - 2 + 2r_{1,2} - 4w_1 r_{1,2}]
$$

Assuming $E(\sigma_1)^2 > 0$,

$$
\begin{aligned}
4w_1 - 2 + 2r_{1,2} - 4w_1 r_{1,2} &= 0 \\
4w_1(1 - r_{1,2}) - 2(1 - r_{1,2}) &= 0
\end{aligned}
$$

from which

$$w_1 = \frac{2(1 - r_{1,2})}{4(1 - r_{1,2})} = \frac{1}{2}$$

regardless of $r_{1,2}$. Thus, if $E(\sigma_1) = E(\sigma_2)$, $E(\sigma^2_{port})$ will *always* be minimized by choosing $w_1 = w_2 = \frac{1}{2}$, regardless of the value of $r_{1,2}$, except when $r_{1,2} = +1$ (in which case $E(\sigma_{port})$ = $E(\sigma_1) = E(\sigma_2)$. This can be verified by checking the second-order condition

$$\frac{\partial E(\sigma^2_{port})}{\partial w^2_1} > 0.$$

Problems

1. The following information applies to Questions 1a and 1b. The general equation for the weight of the first security to achieve minimum variance (in a two-stock portfolio) is given by

$$w_1 = \frac{E(\sigma_2)^2 - r_{1,2}\,E(\sigma_1)E(\sigma_2)}{E(\sigma_1)^2 + E(\sigma_2)^2 - 2r_{1,2}\,E(\sigma_1)E(\sigma_2)}.$$

   1a. Show that $w_1 = .5$ when $E(\sigma_1) = E(\sigma_2)$.

   1b. What is the weight of Security 1 that gives minimum portfolio variance when $r_{1,2} = .5$, $E(\sigma_1) = .04$, and $E(\sigma_2) = .06$?

B. Derivation of Weights That Will Give Zero Variance When Correlation Equals −1.00

$$E(\sigma^2_{port}) = w^2_1E(\sigma_1)^2 + (1 - w_1)^2E(\sigma_2)^2 + 2w_1(1 - w_1)r_{1,2}E(\sigma_1)E(\sigma_2)$$
$$= w^2_1E(\sigma_1)^2 + E(\sigma_2)^2 - 2w_1E(\sigma_2) + w^2_1E(\sigma_2)^2 + 2w_1r_{1,2}E(\sigma_1)E(\sigma_2) - 2w^2_1r_{1,2}E(\sigma_1)E(\sigma_2)$$

If $r_{1,2} = -1$, this can be rearranged and expressed as

$$E(\sigma^2_{port}) = w^2_1[E(\sigma_1)^2 + 2E(\sigma_1)E(\sigma_2) + E(\sigma_2)^2] - 2w[E(\sigma_2)^2 + E(\sigma_1)E(\sigma_2)] + E(\sigma_2)^2$$
$$= w^2_1[E(\sigma_1) + E(\sigma_2)]^2 - 2w_1E(\sigma_2)[E(\sigma_1) + E(\sigma_2)] + E(\sigma_2)^2$$
$$= \{w_1[E(\sigma_1) + E(\sigma_2)] - E(\sigma_2)\}^2$$

We want to find the weight, w_1, which will reduce $E(\sigma^2_{port})$ to *zero;* therefore,

$$w_1[E(\sigma_1) + E(\sigma_2)] - E(\sigma_2) = 0,$$

which yields

$$w_1 = \frac{E(\sigma_2)}{E(\sigma_1) + E(\sigma_2)}, \text{ and } w_2 = 1 - w_1 = \frac{E(\sigma_1)}{E(\sigma_1) + E(\sigma_2)}.$$

Problem

1. Given two assets with the following characteristics:

$E(R_1) = .12$	$E(\sigma_1) = .04$
$E(R_2) = .16$	$E(\sigma_2) = .06$

Assume that $r_{1,2} = -1.00$. What is the weight that would yield a zero variance for the portfolio?

CHAPTER

7

An Introduction to Asset Pricing Models

This chapter answers the following questions:

♦ What are the assumptions of the capital asset pricing model?
♦ What is a risk-free asset and what are its risk–return characteristics?
♦ What is the covariance and correlation between the risk-free asset and a risky asset or portfolio of risky assets?
♦ What is the expected return when you combine the risk-free asset and a portfolio of risky assets?
♦ What is the standard deviation when you combine the risk-free asset and a portfolio of risky assets?
♦ When you combine the risk-free asset and a portfolio of risky assets on the Markowitz efficient frontier, what does the set of possible portfolios look like?
♦ Given the initial set of portfolio possibilities with a risk-free asset, what happens when you add financial leverage (that is, borrow)?
♦ What is the market portfolio, what assets are included in this portfolio, and what are the relative weights for the alternative assets included?
♦ What is the capital market line (CML)?
♦ What do we mean by complete diversification?
♦ How do we measure diversification for an individual portfolio?
♦ What are systematic and unsystematic risk?
♦ Given the CML, what is the separation theorem?
♦ Given the CML, what is the relevant risk measure for an individual risky asset?
♦ What is the security market line (SML), and how does it differ from the CML?
♦ What is *beta*, and why is it referred to as a standardized measure of systematic risk?
♦ How can you use the SML to determine the expected (required) rate of return for a risky asset?

♦ Using the SML, what do we mean by an undervalued and overvalued security, and how do we determine whether an asset is undervalued or overvalued?

♦ What is an asset's characteristic line, and how do you compute the characteristic line for an asset?

♦ What is the impact on the characteristic line when you compute it using different return intervals (such as weekly versus monthly) and when you employ different proxies (that is, benchmarks) for the market portfolio (for example, the S&P 500 versus a global stock index)?

♦ What is the arbitrage pricing theory (APT) and how does it differ from the capital asset pricing model (CAPM) in terms of assumptions?

♦ How does the APT differ from the CAPM in terms of risk measures?   ♦

Following the development of portfolio theory by Markowitz, two major theories have been put forth that employ the theory to derive a model for the valuation of risky assets. In this chapter, we introduce these two models. The background on asset pricing models is important at this point in the book because the risk measures implied by these models are a necessary input for our subsequent discussion on the valuation of risky assets. The bulk of the presentation concerns capital market theory and the capital asset pricing model (CAPM) that was developed almost concurrently by three individuals. More recently, an alternative asset valuation model has been proposed, the arbitrage pricing theory (APT). This theory and the implied pricing model are likewise introduced and discussed.

CAPITAL MARKET THEORY: AN OVERVIEW

Because capital market theory builds on portfolio theory, this chapter begins where the discussion of the Markowitz efficient frontier ended. We assume that you have examined the set of risky assets and derived the aggregate efficient frontier. Further, we assume that you and all other investors want to maximize your utility in terms of risk and return, so you will choose portfolios of risky assets on the efficient frontier at points where your utility maps are tangent to the frontier as shown in Figure 6.10. When you make your investment decision in this manner, you are referred to as a *Markowitz efficient investor*.

Capital market theory extends portfolio theory and develops a model for pricing all risky assets. The final product, the *capital asset pricing model (CAPM)*, will allow you to determine the required rate of return for any risky asset.

We begin with the background of capital market theory that includes the underlying assumptions of the theory and a discussion of the factors that led to its development following the Markowitz portfolio theory. Principal among these factors was the analysis of the effect of assuming the existence of a risk-free asset. This is the subject of the next section.

We will see that assuming the existence of a risk-free rate has significant implications for the potential return and risk and alternative risk–return combinations. This discussion implies a central portfolio of risky assets on the efficient frontier, which we call the *market portfolio*. We discuss the market portfolio in the third section and what it implies regarding different types of risk.

The fourth section considers which types of risk are relevant to an investor who believes in capital market theory. Having defined a measure of risk, we consider how you determine your required rate of return on an investment. You can then compare this

required rate of return to your estimate of the asset's expected rate of return during your investment horizon to determine whether the asset is undervalued or overvalued. The section ends with a demonstration of how to calculate the risk measure implied by capital market theory.

The final section discusses an alternative asset pricing model, the arbitrage pricing theory (APT). This model requires fewer assumptions than the CAPM and contends that the required rate of return for a risky asset is a function of *multiple* factors. This is in contrast to the CAPM, which is a single-factor model, that is, it assumes that the risk of an asset is determined by a single variable, its beta. There is a brief demonstration of how to evaluate the risk of an asset and determine its required rate of return using the APT model.

Background for Capital Market Theory

When dealing with any theory in science, economics, or finance, it is necessary to articulate a set of assumptions that specify how the world is expected to act. This allows the theoretician to concentrate on developing a theory that explains how some facet of the world will respond to changes in the environment. In the first part of this section, we consider the main assumptions that underlie the development of capital market theory. The second part of the section considers the major assumptions that allowed theoreticians to extend the portfolio model's techniques for combining investments into an optimal portfolio to a model that explains how to determine the value of those investments (or other assets).

Assumptions of Capital Market Theory   Because capital market theory builds on the Markowitz portfolio model, it requires the same assumptions, along with some additional ones:

1. All investors are Markowitz efficient investors who want to target points on the efficient frontier. The exact location on the efficient frontier and, therefore, the specific portfolio selected, will depend on the individual investor's risk–return utility function.
2. Investors can borrow or lend any amount of money at the risk-free rate of return (RFR). Clearly, it is always possible to lend money at the nominal risk-free rate by buying risk-free securities such as government T-bills. It is not always possible to borrow at this risk-free rate, but we will see that assuming a higher borrowing rate does not change the general results.
3. All investors have homogeneous expectations; that is, they estimate identical probability distributions for future rates of return. Again, this assumption can be relaxed. As long as the differences in expectations are not vast, their effects are minor.
4. All investors have the same one-period time horizon such as one month, six months, or one year. The model will be developed for a single hypothetical period, and its results could be affected by a different assumption. A difference in the time horizon would require investors to derive risk measures and risk-free assets that are consistent with their investment horizons.
5. All investments are infinitely divisible, which means that it is possible to buy or sell fractional shares of any asset or portfolio. This assumption allows us to discuss investment alternatives as continuous curves. Changing it would have little impact on the theory.
6. There are no taxes or transaction costs involved in buying or selling assets. This is a reasonable assumption in many instances. Neither pension funds nor religious groups have to pay taxes, and the transaction costs for most financial institutions are less than 1 percent on most financial instruments. Again, relaxing this assumption modifies the results, but it does not change the basic thrust.
7. There is no inflation or any change in interest rates, or inflation is fully anticipated. This is a reasonable initial assumption, and it can be modified.

8. Capital markets are in equilibrium. This means that we begin with all investments properly priced in line with their risk levels.

You may consider some of these assumptions unrealistic and wonder how useful a theory we can derive with these assumptions. In this regard, two points are important. First, as mentioned, relaxing many of these assumptions would have only minor influence on the model and would not change its main implications or conclusions. Second, a theory should never be judged on the basis of its assumptions, but rather on how well it explains and helps us predict behavior in the real world. If this theory and the model it implies help us explain the rates of return on a wide variety of risky assets, it is useful, even if some of its assumptions are unrealistic. Such success implies that the questionable assumptions must be unimportant to the ultimate objective of the model, which is to explain the pricing and rates of return on assets.

Development of Capital Market Theory   The major factor that allowed portfolio theory to develop into capital market theory is the concept of a risk-free asset. Following the development of the Markowitz portfolio model, several authors considered the implications of assuming the existence of a **risk-free asset**, that is, an asset with *zero variance*. As we will show, such an asset would have zero correlation with all other risky assets and would provide the *risk-free rate of return (RFR)*. It would lie on the vertical axis of a portfolio graph.

This assumption allows us to derive a generalized theory of capital asset pricing under conditions of uncertainty from the Markowitz portfolio theory. This achievement is generally attributed to William Sharpe, for which he received the Nobel prize, but Lintner and Mossin derived similar theories independently.[1] Consequently, you may see references to the Sharpe-Lintner-Mossin (SLM) capital asset pricing model.

Risk-Free Asset

As noted, the assumption of a risk-free asset in the economy is critical to asset pricing theory. Therefore, this section explains the meaning of a risk-free asset and shows the effect on the risk and return measures when this risk-free asset is combined with a portfolio on the Markowitz efficient frontier.

We have defined a **risky asset** as one from which future returns are uncertain and we have measured this uncertainty by the variance, or standard deviation of returns. Because the expected return on a risk-free asset is entirely certain, the standard deviation of its return is zero ($\sigma_{RF} = 0$). The rate of return earned on such an asset should be the risk-free rate of return (RFR), which, as we discussed in Chapter 1, should equal the expected long-run growth rate of the economy with an adjustment for short-run liquidity. The next sections show what happens when we introduce this risk-free asset into the risky world of the Markowitz portfolio model.

Covariance with a Risk-Free Asset   Recall that the covariance between two sets of returns is

$$\text{Cov}_{ij} = \sum_{i=1}^{n} [R_i - E(R_i)][R_j - E(R_j)]/n.$$

---

[1]William F. Sharpe, "Capital Asset Prices: A Theory of Market Equilibrium Under Conditions of Risk," *Journal of Finance* 19, no. 3 (September 1964): 425–442; John Lintner, "Security Prices, Risk and Maximal Gains from Diversification," *Journal of Finance* 20, no. 4 (December 1965): 587–615; and J. Mossin, "Equilibrium in a Capital Asset Market," *Econometrica* 34, no. 4 (October 1966): 768–783.

Because the returns for the risk-free asset are certain, $\sigma_{RF} = 0$, which means $R_i = E(R_i)$ during all periods. Thus, $R_i - E(R_i)$ will also equal zero, and the product of this expression with any other expression will equal zero. Consequently, the covariance of the risk-free asset with any risky asset or portfolio of assets will always equal zero. Similarly, the correlation between any risky asset i, and the risk-free asset, RF, would be zero because it is equal to

$$r_{RFi} = \text{Cov}_{RFi}/\sigma_{RF}\sigma_j.$$

Combining a Risk-Free Asset with a Risky Portfolio   What happens to the average rate of return and the standard deviation of returns when you combine a risk-free asset with a portfolio of risky assets such as those that exist on the Markowitz efficient frontier?

Expected return   Like the expected return for a portfolio of two risky assets, the expected rate of return for a portfolio that includes a risk-free asset is the weighted average of the two returns:

$$E(R_{port}) = w_{RF}(RFR) + (1 - w_{RF})E(R_i)$$

where:

w_{RF} = **the proportion of the portfolio invested in the risk-free asset**
$E(R_i)$ = **the expected rate of return on risky Portfolio i.**

Standard deviation   Recall from Chapter 6 that the expected variance for a two-asset portfolio is

$$E(\sigma_{port}^2) = w_1^2\sigma_1^2 + w_2^2\sigma_2^2 + 2w_1 w_2 r_{1,2}\sigma_1\sigma_2.$$

Substituting the risk-free asset for Security 1, and the risky asset portfolio for Security 2, this formula would become

$$E(\sigma_{port}^2) = w_{RF}^2\sigma_{RF}^2 + (1 - w_{RF})^2\sigma_i^2 + 2w_{RF}(1 - w_{RF})r_{RFi}\sigma_{RF}\sigma_i.$$

We know that the variance of the risk-free asset is zero, that is, $\sigma_{RF}^2 = 0$. Because the correlation between the risk-free asset and any risky asset, i, is also zero, the factor r_{RFi} in the equation above also equals zero. Therefore, any component of the variance formula that has either of these terms will equal zero. When you make these adjustments, the formula becomes

$$E(\sigma_{port}^2) = (1 - w_{RF})^2\sigma_i^2$$

The standard deviation is

$$E(\sigma_{port}^2) = \sqrt{(1 - w_{RF})^2\sigma_i^2}$$
$$= (1 - w_{RF})\sigma_i$$

Therefore, the standard deviation of a portfolio that combines the risk-free asset with risky assets is *the linear proportion of the standard deviation of the risky asset portfolio.*

The risk–return combination   Because both the expected return *and* the standard deviation of return for such a portfolio are linear combinations, a graph of possible portfolio returns and risks looks like a straight line between the two assets. Figure 7.1 shows

Figure 7.1   *Portfolio Possibilities Combining the Risk-Free Asset and Risky Portfolios on the Efficient Frontier*

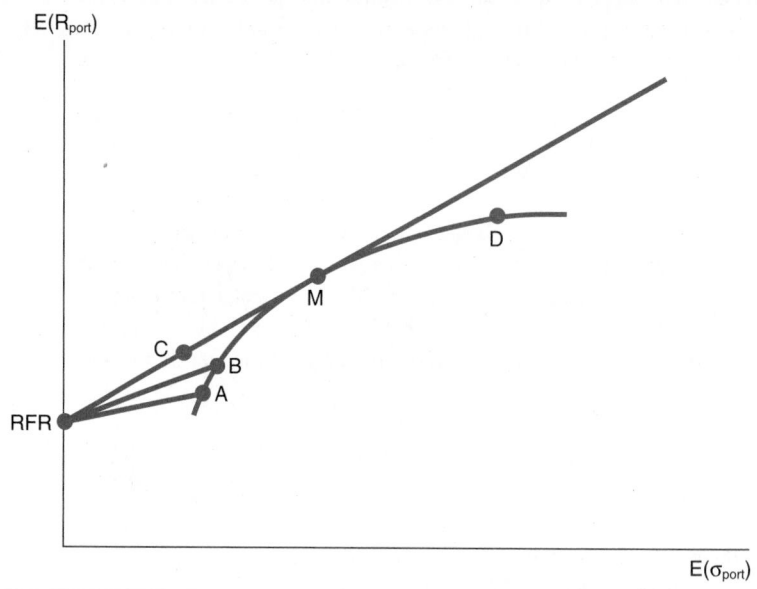

a graph depicting portfolio possibilities when a risk-free asset is combined with alternative risky portfolios on the Markowitz efficient frontier.

You can attain any point along the straight line RFR-A by investing some portion of your portfolio in the risk-free asset w_{RF} and the remainder $(1 - w_{RF})$ in the risky asset portfolio at Point A on the efficient frontier. This set of portfolio possibilities dominates all the risky asset portfolios on the efficient frontier below Point A because some portfolio along Line RFR-A has equal variance with a higher rate of return than the portfolio on the original efficient frontier. Likewise, you can attain any point along the Line RFR-B by investing in some combination of the risk-free asset and the risky asset portfolio at Point B. Again, these potential combinations dominate all portfolio possibilities on the original efficient frontier below Point B (including Line RFR-A).

You can draw further lines from the RFR to the efficient frontier at higher and higher points until you reach the point where the line is tangent to the frontier, which occurs in Figure 7.1 at Point M. The set of portfolio possibilities along Line RFR-M dominates *all* portfolios below Point M. For example, you could attain a risk and return combination between the RFR and Point M (Point C) by investing one-half of your portfolio in the risk-free asset (that is, lending money at the RFR) and the other half in the risky portfolio at Point M.

Risk–return possibilities with leverage   An investor may want to attain a higher expected return than is available at Point M in exchange for accepting higher risk. One alternative would be to invest in one of the risky asset portfolios on the efficient frontier beyond Point M such as the portfolio at Point D. A second alternative is to add *leverage* to the portfolio by *borrowing* money at the risk-free rate and investing the proceeds in the risky asset portfolio at Point M. What effect would this have on the return and risk for your portfolio?

If you borrow an amount equal to 50 percent of your original wealth at the risk-free rate, w_{RF} will not be a positive fraction, but rather a negative 50 percent ($w_{RF} = -.50$). The effect on the expected return for your portfolio is:

$$E(R_{port}) = w_{RF}(RFR) + (1 - w_{RF})E(R_M)$$
$$= -0.50(RFR) + [1 - (-0.50)]E(R_M)$$
$$= -0.50(RFR) + 1.50E(R_M).$$

The return will increase in a *linear* fashion along the Line RFR-M because the gross return increases by 50 percent, but you must pay interest at the RFR on the money borrowed. For example, assume that $E(RFR) = .06$ and $E(R_M) = .12$. The return on your leveraged portfolio would be:

$$E(R_{port}) = -0.50(0.06) + 1.5(0.12)$$
$$= -0.03 + 0.18$$
$$= 0.15.$$

The effect on the standard deviation of the leveraged portfolio is similar.

$$E(\sigma_{port}) = (1 - w_{RF})\sigma_M$$
$$= [1 - (-0.50)]\sigma_M = 1.50\sigma_M$$

where:

σ_M = **the standard deviation of the M portfolio.**

Therefore, *both return and risk increase in a linear fashion along the original Line RFR-M,* and this extension dominates everything below the line on the original efficient frontier. Thus, you have a new efficient frontier: the straight line from the *RFR* tangent to Point M. This line is referred to as the capital market line (CML) and is shown in Figure 7.2.

Our discussion of portfolio theory stated that, when two assets are perfectly correlated, the set of portfolio possibilities falls along a straight line. Therefore, because the CML is a straight line, it implies that all the portfolios on the CML are perfectly positively correlated. This positive correlation appeals to our intuition because all these portfolios on the CML combine the risky asset Portfolio M and the risk-free asset. You either invest part of your portfolio in the risk-free asset and the rest in the risky asset portfolio M, or

Figure 7.2   *Derivation of Capital Market Line Assuming Lending or Borrowing at the Risk-Free Rate*

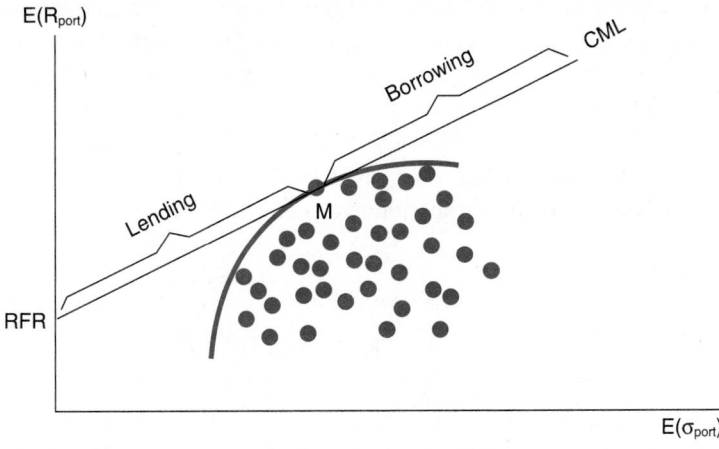

you borrow at the risk-free rate and invest these funds in the risky asset portfolio. In either case, all the variability comes from the risky asset M portfolio. The only difference between the alternative portfolios on the CML is the magnitude of the variability caused by the proportion of the risky asset portfolio in the total portfolio.

The Market Portfolio

Because Portfolio M lies at the point of tangency, it has the highest portfolio possibility line, and everybody will want to invest in Portfolio M and borrow or lend to be somewhere on the CML. This portfolio must, therefore, include *all risky assets*. If a risky asset were not in this portfolio in which everyone wants to invest, there would be no demand for it and therefore no value.

Because the market is in equilibrium, it is also necessary that all assets are included in this portfolio in *proportion to their market value*. If, for example, an asset accounts for a higher proportion of the M portfolio than its market value justifies, excess demand for this asset will increase its price until its relative market value becomes consistent with its proportion in the portfolio.

This portfolio that includes all risky assets is referred to as the **market portfolio**. It includes not only common stocks, but *all* risky assets, such as non-U.S. stocks, U.S. and non-U.S. bonds, options, real estate, coins, stamps, art, or antiques. Because the market portfolio contains all risky assets, it is a **completely diversified portfolio**, which means that all the risk unique to individual assets in the portfolio is diversified away. Specifically, the unique risk of any asset is offset by the unique variability of the other assets in the portfolio.

This unique (diversifiable) risk is also referred to as **unsystematic risk.** This implies that only **systematic risk**, which is defined as the variability in all risky assets caused by macroeconomic variables, remains in the market portfolio. This systematic risk, measured by the standard deviation of returns of the market portfolio, can change over time with changes in the macroeconomic variables that affect the valuation of all risky assets.[2] Examples of such macroeconomic variables would be variability of growth in the money supply, interest rate volatility, and variability in such factors as industrial production, corporate earnings, and cash flow.

How to Measure Diversification   All portfolios on the CML are perfectly positively correlated, which means that all portfolios on the CML are perfectly correlated with the completely diversified market Portfolio M. This implies a measure of complete diversification.[3] Specifically, a completely diversified portfolio would have a correlation with the market portfolio of +1.00. This is logical because complete diversification means the elimination of all the unsystematic or unique risk. Once you have eliminated all unsystematic risk, only systematic risk is left, which cannot be diversified away. Therefore, completely diversified portfolios would correlate perfectly with the market portfolio because it has only systematic risk.

Diversification and the Elimination of Unsystematic Risk   As discussed in Chapter 6, the purpose of diversification is to reduce the standard deviation of the total

---

[2]For an analysis of changes in stock price volatility, see G. William Schwert, "Why Does Stock Market Volatility Change over Time?" *Journal of Finance* 44, no. 5 (December 1989): 1115–1153; Peter S. Spiro, "The Impact of Interest Rate Changes on Stock Price Volatility," *Journal of Portfolio Management* 16, no. 2 (Winter 1990): 63–68; James M. Poterba and Lawrence H. Summers, "The Persistence of Volatility and Stock Market Fluctuations," *American Economic Review* 76, no. 4 (December 1981): 1142–1151; R. R. Officer, "The Variability of the Market Factor of the New York Stock Exchange," *Journal of Business* 46, no. 3 (July 1973): 434–453.

[3]James Lorie, "Diversification: Old and New," *Journal of Portfolio Management* 1, no. 2 (Winter 1975): 25–28.

Figure 7.3 *Number of Stocks in a Portfolio and the Standard Deviation of Portfolio Return*

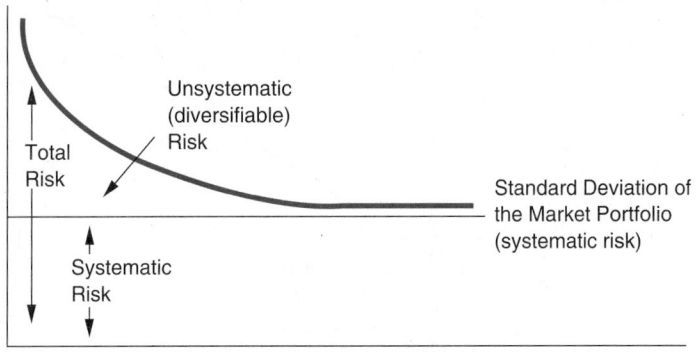

portfolio. This assumes imperfect correlations among securities.[4] Ideally, as you add securities, the average covariance for the portfolio declines. An important question is, about how many securities must be included to arrive at a completely diversified portfolio? To discover the answer, you must observe what happens as you increase the sample size of the portfolio by adding securities that have some positive correlation. The typical correlation among U.S. securities is about 0.5 to 0.6.

One set of studies examined the average standard deviation for numerous portfolios of randomly selected stocks of different sample sizes.[5] For example, Evans and Archer computed the standard deviation for portfolios of increasing numbers up to twenty stocks. The results indicated a large initial impact wherein the major benefits of diversification were achieved rather quickly. Specifically, about 90 percent of the maximum benefit of diversification was derived from portfolios of twelve to eighteen stocks. Figure 7.3 shows a graph of the effect.

A study by Statman compared the benefits of lower risk from diversification to the added transaction costs with more securities. It concluded that a well-diversified stock portfolio must include at least thirty stocks for a borrowing investor and forty stocks for a lending investor.[6]

By adding stocks to the portfolio that are not perfectly correlated with stocks in the portfolio, you can reduce the overall standard deviation of the portfolio, but you *cannot eliminate variability.* The standard deviation of your portfolio will eventually reach the level of the market portfolio, where you will have diversified away all unsystematic risk, but you still have market or systematic risk. You cannot eliminate the variability and uncertainty of macroeconomic factors that affect all risky assets. At the same time, you will recall from the discussion in Chapter 3 that you can attain a lower level of systematic risk by diversifying globally versus only investing in the United States because some of the systematic

---

[4]The discussion in Chapter 6 leads one to conclude that securities with negative correlation would be ideal. Although this is true in theory, it is difficult to find such assets in the real world.

[5]John L. Evans and Stephen H. Archer, "Diversification and the Reduction of Dispersion: An Empirical Analysis," *Journal of Finance* 23, no. 5 (December 1968): 761–767; Thomas M. Tole, "You Can't Diversify without Diversifying," *Journal of Portfolio Management* 8, no. 2 (Winter 1982): 5–11.

[6]Meir Statman, "How Many Stocks Make a Diversified Portfolio?" *Journal of Financial and Quantitative Analysis* 22, no. 3 (September 1987): 353–363.

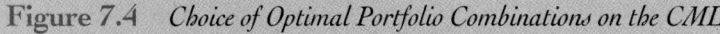

Figure 7.4   *Choice of Optimal Portfolio Combinations on the CML*

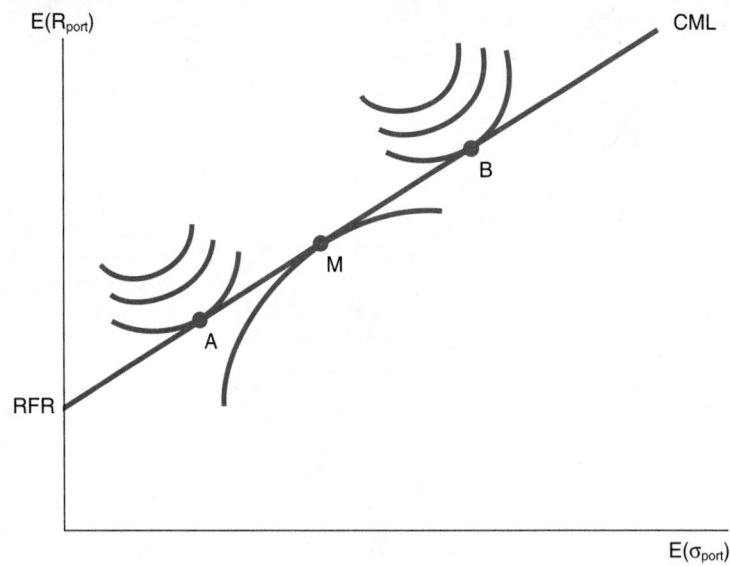

risk factors in the U.S. market (such as U.S. monetary policy) are not correlated with systematic risk variables in other countries such as Germany and Japan. As a result, if you diversify globally you eventually get down to a world systematic-risk level.

The CML and the Separation Theorem   The CML leads all investors to invest in the same risky asset portfolio, the M portfolio. Individual investors should only differ regarding their position on the CML, which depends on their risk preferences.

In turn, how they get to a point on the CML is based on their *financing decisions.* If you are relatively risk averse, you will lend some part of your portfolio at the RFR by buying some risk-free securities and investing the remainder in the market portfolio. For example, you might invest in the portfolio combination at Point A in Figure 7.4. In contrast, if you prefer more risk, you might borrow funds at the RFR and invest everything (all of your capital plus what you borrowed) in the market portfolio, building the portfolio at Point B. This financing decision provides more risk but greater returns than the market portfolio. As discussed earlier, because portfolios on the CML dominate other portfolio possibilities, the CML becomes the efficient frontier of portfolios, and investors decide where they want to be along this efficient frontier. Tobin called this division of the investment decision from the financing decision the **separation theorem**.[7] Specifically, to be somewhere on the CML efficient frontier, you initially decide to invest in the market portfolio M. This is your *investment* decision. Subsequently, based on your risk preferences, you make a separate *financing* decision either to borrow or to lend to attain your preferred point on the CML.

A Risk Measure for the CML   In this section, we show that the relevant risk measure for risky assets is *their covariance with the M portfolio,* which is referred to as their systematic risk. The importance of this covariance is apparent from two points of view.

---

[7]James Tobin, "Liquidity Preference as Behavior Towards Risk," *Review of Economic Studies* 25, no. 2 (February 1958): 65–85.

First, in discussing the Markowitz portfolio model, we noted that the relevant risk to consider when adding a security to a portfolio is *its average covariance with all other assets in the portfolio.* In this chapter, we have shown that *the only relevant portfolio is the M portfolio.* Together, these two findings mean that the only important consideration for any individual risky asset is its average covariance with all the risky assets in the M portfolio, or simply, *the asset's covariance with the market portfolio.* This covariance, then, is the relevant risk measure for an individual risky asset.

Second, because all individual risky assets are a part of the M portfolio, one can describe their rates of return in relation to the returns for the M portfolio using the following linear model:

$$R_{it} = a_i + b_i R_{Mt} + \epsilon$$

where:

$R_{i,t}$ = **return for asset i during period t**
a_i = **constant term for asset i**
b_i = **slope coefficient for asset i**
R_{Mt} = **return for the M portfolio during period t**
ϵ = **random error term.**

The variance of returns for a risky asset could be described as

$$\begin{aligned}
\text{Var}(R_{it}) &= \text{Var}(a_i + b_i R_{Mt} + \epsilon) \\
&= \text{Var}(a_i) + \text{Var}(b_i R_{Mt}) + \text{Var}(\epsilon) \\
&= 0 + \text{Var}(b_i R_{Mt}) + \text{Var}(\epsilon).
\end{aligned}$$

Note that $\text{Var}(b_i R_{Mt})$ is the variance of return for an asset related to the variance of the market return, or the *systematic variance or risk.* Also, $\text{Var}(\epsilon)$ is the residual variance of return for the individual asset that is not related to the market portfolio. This residual variance is the variability that we have referred to as the unsystematic or *unique risk or variance* because it arises from the unique features of the asset. Therefore:

$$\text{Var}(R_{i,t}) = \text{Systematic Variance} + \text{Unsystematic Variance}.$$

We know that a completely diversified portfolio such as the market portfolio has had all the unsystematic variance eliminated. Therefore, the unsystematic variance of an asset is not relevant to investors, because they can and do eliminate it when making an asset part of the market portfolio. Therefore, investors should not expect to receive added returns for assuming this unique risk. Only the systematic variance is relevant because it *cannot* be diversified away, because it is caused by macroeconomic factors that affect all risky assets.

THE CAPITAL ASSET PRICING MODEL: EXPECTED RETURN AND RISK

Up to this point, we have considered how investors make their portfolio decisions, including the significant effects of a risk-free asset. The existence of this risk-free asset resulted in the derivation of a capital market line (CML) that became the relevant efficient frontier. Because all investors want to be on the CML, an asset's covariance with the market portfolio of risky assets emerged as the relevant risk measure.

Figure 7.5 *Graph of Security Market Line*

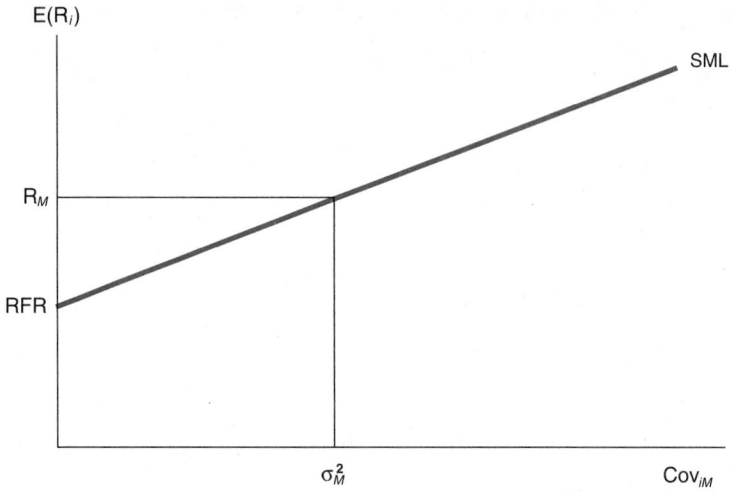

Now that we understand this relevant measure of risk, we can proceed to use it to determine an appropriate expected rate of return on a risky asset. This step takes us into the **capital asset pricing model (CAPM)**, which is a model that indicates what should be the expected or required rates of return on risky assets. This transition is important because it helps you to value an asset by providing an appropriate discount rate to use in any valuation model. Alternatively, if you have already estimated the rate of return that you think you will earn on an investment, you can compare this *estimated* rate of return to the *required* rate of return implied by the CAPM and determine whether the asset is undervalued, overvalued, or properly valued.

To accomplish the foregoing, we demonstrate the creation of a security market line (SML) that visually represents the relationship between risk and the expected or the required rate of return on an asset. The equation of this SML, together with estimates for the return on a risk-free asset and on the market portfolio, can generate expected or required rates of return for any asset based on its systematic risk. You compare this required rate of return to the rate of return you estimate that you earn on the investment to determine if the investment is undervalued or overvalued. After demonstrating this procedure, we finish the section with a demonstration of how to calculate the systematic risk variable for a risky asset.

The Security Market Line (SML)

We know that the relevant risk measure for an individual risky asset is its covariance with the market portfolio ($\text{Cov}_{i,M}$). Therefore, we draw the risk–return relationship as shown in Figure 7.5 with the systematic covariance variable ($\text{Cov}_{i,M}$) as the risk measure.

The return for the market portfolio (R_M) should be consistent with its own risk, which is the covariance of the market with itself. If you recall the formula for covariance, you will see that the covariance of any asset with itself is its variance, $\text{Cov}_{i,i} = \sigma_i^2$. In turn, the covariance of the market with itself is the variance of the market rate of return $\text{Cov}_{m,m} = \sigma_M^2$. Therefore, the equation for the risk–return line in Figure 7.5 is:

Figure 7.6   *Graph of SML with Normalized Systematic Risk*

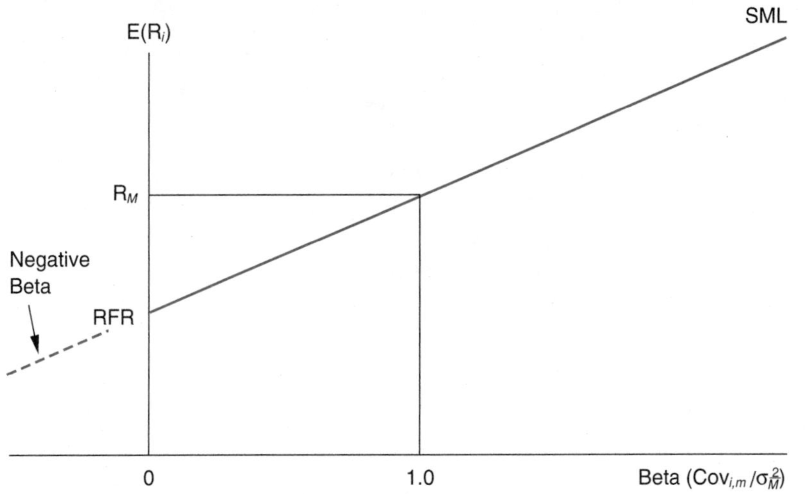

$$E(R_i) = RFR + \frac{R_M - RFR}{\sigma_M^2}(Cov_{i,M})$$

$$= RFR + \frac{Cov_{i,M}}{\sigma_M^2}(R_M - RFR).$$

Defining $Cov_{i,M}/\sigma_M^2$ as beta (β_i), this equation can be stated:

$$E(R_i) = RFR + \beta_i(R_M - RFR).$$

Beta can be viewed as a *standardized* measure of systematic risk. Specifically, we already know that the covariance of any asset *i* with the market portfolio (Cov_{iM}) is the relevant risk measure. Beta is a standardized measure of risk because it relates this covariance to the variance of the market portfolio. As a result, the market portfolio has a beta of 1. Therefore, if the β_i for an asset is above 1.0, the asset has higher normalized systematic risk than the market, which means that it is more volatile than the overall market portfolio.

Given this standardized measure of systematic risk, the SML graph can be expressed as shown in Figure 7.6. This is the same graph as in Figure 7.5, except there is a different measure of risk. Specifically, the graph in Figure 7.6 replaces the covariance of an asset's returns with the market portfolio as the risk measure with the standardized measure of systematic risk (beta), which is the covariance of an asset with the market portfolio divided by the variance of the market portfolio.

Determining the Expected Rate of Return for a Risky Asset   The equation above and the graph in Figure 7.6 tell us that the expected rate of return for a risky asset is determined by the RFR plus a risk premium for the individual asset. In turn, the risk premium is determined by the systematic risk of the asset (β_i), and the prevailing **market risk premium** (R_M − RFR). To demonstrate how you would compute the expected or required rates of return, consider the following example stocks assuming you have already computed betas:

Stock	Beta
A	0.70
B	1.00
C	1.15
D	1.40
E	−0.30

Assume that we expect the economy's RFR to be 6 percent (0.06) and the return on the market portfolio (R_M) to be 12 percent (0.12). This implies a market risk premium of 6 percent (0.06). With these inputs, the SML equation would yield the following expected (required) rates of return for these five stocks:

$$E(R_i) = RFR + \beta_i(R_M - RFR)$$
$$E(R_A) = 0.06 + 0.70\,(0.12 - 0.06)$$
$$= 0.102 = 10.2\%$$
$$E(R_B) = 0.06 + 1.00\,(0.12 - 0.06)$$
$$= 0.12 = 12\%$$
$$E(R_C) = 0.06 + 1.15\,(0.12 - 0.06)$$
$$= 0.129 = 12.9\%$$
$$E(R_D) = 0.06 + 1.40\,(0.12 - 0.06)$$
$$= 0.144 = 14.4\%$$
$$E(R_E) = 0.06 + (-0.30)\,(0.12 - 0.06)$$
$$= 0.06 - 0.018$$
$$= 0.042 = 4.2\%.$$

As stated, these are the expected (required) rates of return that these stocks should provide based on their systematic risks and the prevailing SML.

Stock A has lower risk than the aggregate market, so you should not expect (require) its return to be as high as the return on the market portfolio of risky assets. You should expect (require) Stock A to return 10.2 percent. Stock B has systematic risk equal to the market's (beta = 1.00), so its required rate of return should likewise be equal to the expected market return (12 percent). Stocks C and D have systematic risk greater than the market's so they should provide returns consistent with their risk. Finally, Stock E has a *negative* beta (which is quite rare in practice), so its required rate of return, if such a stock could be found, would be below the RFR.

In equilibrium, *all* assets and *all* portfolios of assets should plot on the SML. That is, all assets should be priced so that their **estimated rates of return**, which are the actual holding period rates of return that you anticipate, are consistent with their levels of systematic risk. Any security with an estimated rate of return that plots above the SML would be considered underpriced because it implies that you *estimated* you would receive a rate of return on the security that is above its *required* rate of return based on its systematic risk. In contrast, assets with estimated rates of return that plot below the SML would be considered overpriced. This position relative to the SML implies that your estimated rate of return is below what you should require based on the asset's systematic risk.

In an efficient market in equilibrium, you would not expect any assets to plot off the SML because, in equilibrium, all stocks should provide holding period returns that are equal to their required rates of return. Alternatively, a market that is "fairly efficient" but not completely efficient may misprice certain assets because not everyone will be aware of all the relevant information for an asset.

As we will discuss in Chapter 8 on the topic of efficient markets, a superior investor has the ability to derive value estimates for assets that are consistently superior to the

Table 7.1 *Price, Dividend, and Rate of Return Estimates*

Stock	Current Price (P_i)	Expected Price (P_{t+1})	Expected Dividend (D_{t+1})	Estimated Future Rate of Return (Percent)
A	25	27	0.50	10.0%
B	40	42	0.50	6.2
C	33	39	1.00	21.2
D	64	65	1.10	3.3
E	50	54	—	8.0

Table 7.2 *Comparison of Required Rate of Return to Estimated Rate of Return*

Stock	Beta	Required Return $E(R_i)$	Estimated Return	Estimated Return Minus $E(R_i)$	Evaluation
A	0.70	10.2	10.0	−0.2	Properly valued
B	1.00	12.0	6.2	−5.8	Overvalued
C	1.15	12.9	21.2	8.3	Undervalued
D	1.40	14.4	3.3	−11.1	Overvalued
E	−0.30	4.2	8.0	3.8	Undervalued

consensus market evaluation. As a result, such an investor will earn better rates of return than the average investor on a risk-adjusted basis.

Identifying Undervalued and Overvalued Assets Now that we understand how to compute the rate of return one should expect or require for a specific risky asset using the SML, we can compare this *required* rate of return to the asset's *estimated* rate of return over a specific investment horizon to determine whether it would be an appropriate investment. To make this comparison, you need an independent estimate of the return outlook for the security based on either fundamental or technical analysis techniques that will be discussed in subsequent chapters. Let us continue the example for the five assets discussed in the previous section.

Analysts in a major trust department have been following these five stocks. Based on extensive fundamental analysis, the analysts provide the price and dividend outlooks contained in Table 7.1. Given these projections, you can compute the estimated rates of return the analysts would anticipate during this holding period.

Table 7.2 summarizes the relationship between the required rate of return for each stock based on its systematic risk as computed earlier and its estimated rate of return (from Table 7.1) based on the current and future prices, and its dividend outlook.

Plotting these estimated rates of return and stock betas on the SML we specified earlier gives the graph shown in Figure 7.7. Stock A is almost exactly on the line, so it is considered properly valued because its estimated rate of return is almost equal to its required rate of return. Stocks B and D are considered overvalued because their estimated rates of return during the coming period are below what an investor should expect (require) for the risk involved. As a result, they plot below the SML. In contrast, Stocks C and E are expected to provide rates of return greater than we would require based on their systematic risk. Therefore, both stocks plot above the SML, indicating that they are undervalued stocks.

Assuming that you trusted your analyst to forecast estimated returns, you would take no action regarding Stock A, but you would buy Stocks C and E and sell Stocks B and D. You might even sell Stocks B and D short if you favored such aggressive tactics.

Figure 7.7   *Plot of Estimated Returns on SML Graph*

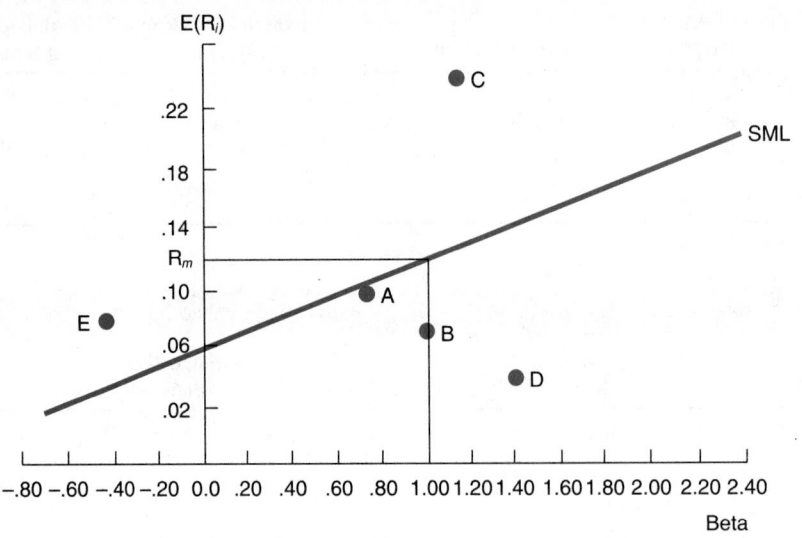

Calculating Systematic Risk: The Characteristic Line   The systematic risk input for an individual asset is derived from a regression model, referred to as the asset's **characteristic line** with the market portfolio:

$$R_{i,t} = \alpha_i + \beta_i R_{M,t} + \epsilon$$

where:

$R_{i,t}$ = **the rate of return for asset *i* during period *t***
$R_{M,t}$ = **the rate of return for the market portfolio M during period *t***
α_i = **the constant term, or intercept, of the regression, which equals $R_i - \beta_i R_M$**
β_i = **the systematic risk (beta) of asset *i* equal to $Cov_{i,M}/\sigma_M^2$**
ϵ = **the random error term.**

The characteristic line is the regression line of best fit through a scatter plot of rates of return for the individual risky asset and for the market portfolio of risky assets over some designated past period, as shown in Figure 7.8.

The impact of the time interval   In practice the number of observations and the time interval used in the regression vary. Value Line Investment Services derives characteristic lines for common stocks using weekly rates of return for the most recent five years (260 weekly observations). Merrill Lynch, Pierce, Fenner & Smith uses monthly rates of return for the most recent five years (sixty monthly observations). Because there is no theoretically correct time interval for analysis, we must make a trade-off between enough observations to eliminate the impact of random rates of return and an excessive length of time such as fifteen or twenty years over which the subject company may have changed dramatically. Remember that what you really want is the *expected* systematic risk for the potential investment. In this analysis, you are analyzing historical data to help you derive a reasonable expectation of systematic risk.

A couple of studies have considered the effect of the time interval used to compute betas (weekly versus monthly). Statman examined the relationship between Value Line (VL)

Figure 7.8 *Scatter Plot of Rates of Return*

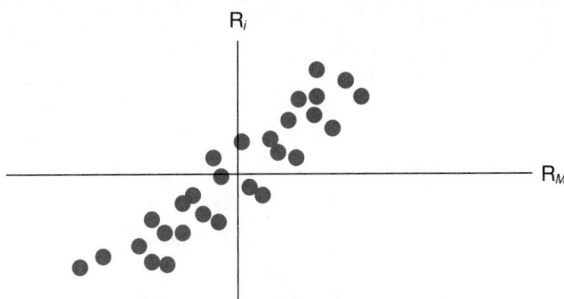

betas and Merrill Lynch (ML) betas and found a relatively weak relationship.[8] Reilly and Wright examined a larger sample and analyzed the differential effects of return computation, market index, and the time interval and likewise found a weak relationship between VL and ML betas.[9] They showed that the major cause of the significant differences in beta was the use of monthly versus weekly intervals.

They also found that the interval effect depended on the sizes of the firms. The shorter weekly interval caused a larger beta for large firms and a smaller beta for small firms. For example, from 1975 to 1979, the average beta for the smallest decile of firms using monthly data was 1.682, but the average beta for these small firms using weekly data was only 1.080. The authors concluded that the return time interval makes a difference, and the impact of the time interval increases as the size of the firm declines.

The effect of the market proxy   Another significant decision when computing an asset's characteristic line is which indicator series to use as a proxy for the market portfolio of all risky assets. Most investigators use the Standard & Poor's 500 Composite Index as a proxy for the market portfolio, because the stocks in this index encompass a large proportion of the total market value of U.S. stocks. Also, it is a value-weighted series, which is consistent with the theoretical market series. Still, this series only contains U.S. stocks, most of them listed on the NYSE. You will recall our earlier discussion where it was noted that the theoretically correct market portfolio of all risky assets should include U.S. stocks and bonds, non-U.S. stocks and bonds, real estate, coins, stamps, art, antiques, and any other marketable risky asset from around the world.[10]

Example Computations of a Characteristic Line   The following examples show how you would compute characteristic lines for Coca-Cola based on the monthly rates of return during 1997.[11] Twelve is not enough observations for statistical purposes,

[8]Meir Statman, "Betas Compared: Merrill Lynch vs. Value Line," *Journal of Portfolio Management* 7, no. 2 (Winter 1981): 41–44.

[9]Frank K. Reilly and David J. Wright, "A Comparison of Published Betas," *Journal of Portfolio Management* 14, no. 3 (Spring 1988): 64–69.

[10]Substantial discussion surrounds the market index used and its impact on the empirical results and usefulness of the CAPM. This concern is discussed further and demonstrated in the subsequent section on computing an asset's characteristic line. The effect of the market proxy is also considered when we discuss the arbitrage pricing theory (APT) in this chapter and in Chapter 22 when we discuss the evaluation of portfolio performance.

[11]These betas are computed using only monthly price changes for Coca-Cola, the S&P 500, and the M-S World Index (dividends are not included). This is done for simplicity but is also based on a study indicating that betas derived with and without dividends are correlated 0.99: William Sharpe and Guy M. Cooper, "Risk–Return Classes of New York Stock Exchange Common Stocks," *Financial Analysts Journal* 28, no. 2 (March–April 1972): 35–43.

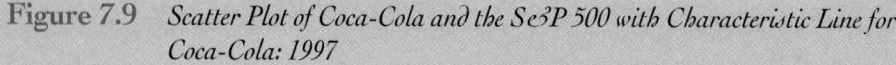

Figure 7.9   *Scatter Plot of Coca-Cola and the S&P 500 with Characteristic Line for Coca-Cola: 1997*

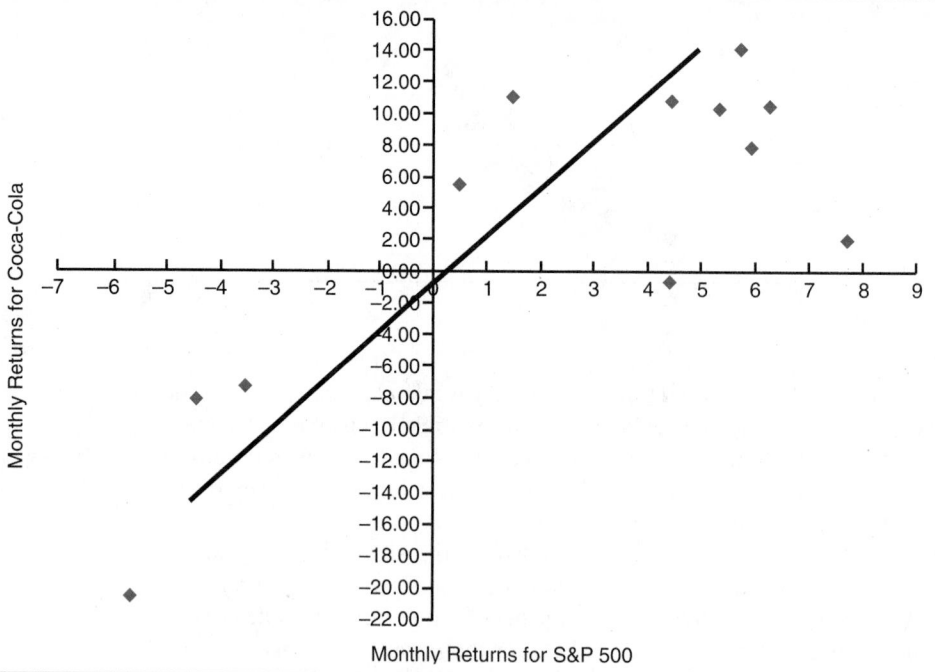

Monthly Returns for S&P 500

but it should provide a good example. We demonstrate the computations using two different proxies for the market portfolio. The first is the typical analysis in which the S&P 500 is used as the market proxy. The second example uses the Morgan Stanley (M-S) World Equity Index as the market proxy. This analysis allows us to demonstrate the effect of a more complete proxy of stocks.

The monthly price changes are computed using the closing prices for the last day of each month. These data for Coca-Cola, the S&P 500, and the M-S World Index are contained in Table 7.3. Figure 7.9 contains the scatter plot of the percentage price changes for Coca-Cola and the S&P 500. During this twelve-month period, Coca-Cola had returns that varied when compared with the aggregate market returns as proxied by the S&P 500. As a result, the covariance between Coca-Cola and the S&P 500 series was a fairly large positive value (34.98). The covariance divided by the variance of the S&P 500 market portfolio (21.16) indicates that Coca-Cola's beta relative to the S&P 500 was equal to 1.65. This analysis indicates that during this limited time period Coca-Cola was riskier than the aggregate market proxied by the S&P 500.

When we draw this characteristic line on Figure 7.9, the scatter plots are reasonably close to the characteristic line, which is consistent with the correlation coefficient of 0.74. The computation of the characteristic line for Coca-Cola using the M-S World Index as the proxy for the market is contained in Table 7.3, and the scatter plots are in Figure 7.10. At this point, it is important to consider what one might expect to be the relationship between the beta relative to the S&P 500 versus the betas with the M-S World Index. This requires a consideration of the two components in the computation of beta: (1) the covariance between the stock and the benchmark and (2) the variance of returns for the benchmark series. Notably, there is no obvious answer regarding what will happen for either

Table 7.3 *Computation of Beta of Coca-Cola with Selected Indexes*

	Index		Return			S&P 500 $R_{S\&P} - E(R_{S\&P})$ (1)	M-S World $R_{M-S} - E(R_{M-S})$ (2)	Coca-Cola $R_{KO} - E(R_{KO})$ (3)	(4)[a]	(5)[b]
Date	S&P 500	M-S World	S&P 500	M-S World	Coca-Cola					
12/96	740.74	820.40								
1/97	786.16	829.10	6.13	1.06	10.48	3.75	-0.07	7.66	28.73	-0.54
2/97	790.82	837.40	0.59	1.00	5.17	-1.79	-0.13	2.35	-4.21	-0.31
3/97	757.12	819.70	-4.26	-2.11	-8.40	-6.64	-3.24	-11.22	74.50	36.35
4/97	801.34	843.30	5.84	2.88	13.65	3.46	1.75	10.83	37.47	18.95
5/97	848.28	893.00	5.86	5.89	7.68	3.48	4.76	4.86	16.91	23.13
6/97	885.15	939.70	4.35	5.23	-0.55	1.97	4.10	-3.37	-6.64	-13.82
7/97	954.31	980.80	7.81	4.37	1.84	5.43	3.24	-0.98	-5.32	-3.18
8/97	899.47	980.80	-5.75	0.00	-20.13	-8.13	-1.13	-22.95	186.58	25.93
9/97	947.28	963.50	5.32	-1.76	10.28	2.94	-2.89	7.46	21.93	-21.56
10/97	914.62	911.60	-3.45	-5.39	-7.38	-5.83	-6.52	-10.20	59.47	66.50
11/97	955.40	926.50	4.46	1.63	10.62	2.08	0.50	7.80	16.22	3.90
12/97	970.84	933.60	1.62	0.77	10.62	-0.76	-0.36	7.80	-5.93	-2.81
Average			2.38	1.13	2.82			Total =	419.71	132.54
Standard Deviation			4.60	3.25	10.23					

$\text{Cov}_{KO,S\&P} = 419.71 / 12 = 34.98$ $\quad$ $\text{Var}_{S\&P} = \text{St.Dev}_{S\&P}^2 = 4.60^2 = 21.16$ $\quad$ $\text{Beta}_{KO,S\&P} = 34.98 / 21.16 = 1.65$ $\quad$ $\text{Alpha}_{KO,S\&P} = 2.82 - (1.65 * 2.38) = -1.11$

$\text{Cov}_{KO,M-S} = 132.54 / 12 = 11.05$ $\quad$ $\text{Var}_{M-S} = \text{St.Dev}_{M-S}^2 = 3.25^2 = 10.56$ $\quad$ $\text{Beta}_{KO,M-S} = 11.05 / 10.56 = 1.05$ $\quad$ $\text{Alpha}_{KO,M-S} = 2.82 - (1.05 * 1.13) = 1.63$

$\text{Correlation coef.}_{KO,S\&P} = 34.98 / (4.60 * 10.23) = 0.74$ $\quad$ $\text{Correlation coef.}_{KO,M-S} = 11.05 / (3.25 * 10.23) = 0.33$

[a] Column (4) is equal to column (1) multiplied by column (3).

[b] Column (5) is equal to column (2) multiplied by column (3).

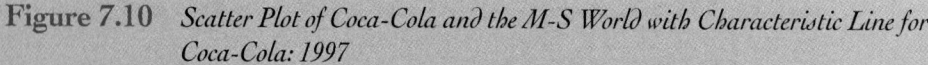

Figure 7.10   *Scatter Plot of Coca-Cola and the M-S World with Characteristic Line for Coca-Cola: 1997*

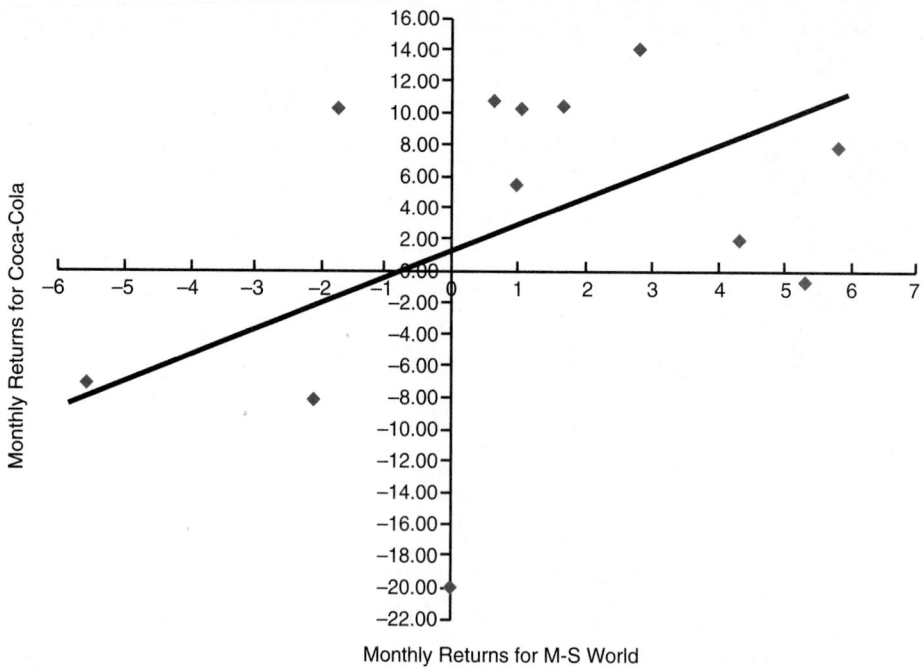

series because one would typically expect both components to change. Specifically, the covariance of Coca-Cola with the S&P 500 will probably be higher than with the other series because you are matching a U.S. stock with a U.S. market index rather than a world index. Thus, the covariance with the other indexes will generally be smaller. At the same time, the variance of returns for the world stock index should typically also be smaller than the variance for the S&P 500 because it is a more diversified stock portfolio.

Therefore, the direction of change for the beta will depend on the relative change in the two components. An empirical observation is that generally the beta is smaller with the world stock index because the covariance is definitely lower, but the variance is only slightly smaller.[12] The results of this example were consistent with expectations. The beta with the world stock index was smaller (1.05 vs. 1.65) because the covariance was much lower, whereas the variance of the market was marginally smaller (10.56 for the M-S series vs. 21.16 for the S&P 500).

The differences in beta were consistent with expectations. The fact that they differed is significant and reflects the potential problem that can occur in a global environment where it becomes difficult to select the appropriate proxy for the market portfolio.

ARBITRAGE PRICING THEORY (APT)

At this point, we have discussed the basic theory of the CAPM, the effects of changing some of its major assumptions, and its dependence on a market portfolio of all risky assets.

---

[12]For a demonstration of this effect for a large sample that confirms these expectations, see Frank K. Reilly and Rashid A. Akhtar, "The Benchmark Error Problem with Global Capital Markets," *Journal of Portfolio Management* 22, no. 1 (Fall 1995): 33–52.

In addition, the model assumes that investors have quadratic utility functions and that the distribution of security prices is normal—that is, symmetrically distributed, with a variance term that can be estimated.

Some tests of the CAPM indicate that the beta coefficients for individual securities are not stable, but the beta of portfolios generally were stable assuming long enough sample periods and adequate trading volume. Some studies have also supported a positive linear relationship between rates of return and systematic risk for portfolios of stock. In contrast, a set of papers by Roll criticized the usefulness of the model because of its dependence on a market portfolio of risky assets, and Roll contends that such a portfolio is not currently available.[13] Roll points out that when the CAPM is used to evaluate portfolio performance, it is necessary to select a proxy for the market portfolio as a benchmark for performance. It has been shown in the Reilly-Akhtar paper that the performance results can be changed substantially because of the market proxy used.

Given these questions, the academic community has considered an alternative asset pricing theory that is reasonably intuitive and requires only limited assumptions. This **arbitrage pricing theory (APT)**, developed by Ross in the early 1970s and initially published in 1976, has three major assumptions:[14]

1. Capital markets are perfectly competitive.
2. Investors always prefer more wealth to less wealth with certainty.
3. The stochastic process generating asset returns can be represented as a K factor model (to be described).

Equally important, the following major assumptions are *not* required: (1) quadratic utility function, (2) normally distributed security returns, and (3) a market portfolio that contains all risky assets and is mean-variance efficient. Obviously, if a theory without these assumptions is able to explain differential security prices, it would be considered a superior theory because it is simpler (that is, it requires fewer assumptions).

As noted, the theory assumes that the stochastic process generating asset returns can be represented as a K factor model of the form

$$R_i = E_i + b_{i1}\delta_1 + b_{i2}\delta_2 + \ldots + b_{ik}\delta_k + \epsilon_i \qquad \text{for } i = 1 \text{ to } N$$

where:

R_i = **return on asset i during a specified time period**
E_i = **expected return for asset i**
b_{ik} = **reaction in asset i's returns to movements in a common factor**
δ_k = **a common factor with a zero mean that influences the returns on all assets**
ϵ_i = **a unique effect on asset i's return that, by assumption, is completely diversifiable in large portfolios and has a mean of zero**
N = **number of assets.**

Two terms require elaboration: δ_k and b. As indicated, the δ_k terms are the *multiple* factors expected to have an impact on the returns of *all* assets. Examples of such factors might

[13]Richard Roll, "A Critique of the Asset Pricing Theory's Tests," *Journal of Financial Economics* 4, no. 4 (March 1977): 129–176; Richard Roll, "Ambiguity When Performance Is Measured by the Securities Market Line," *Journal of Finance* 33, no. 4 (September 1978): 1051–1069; and Richard Roll, "Performance Evaluation and Benchmark Error II," *Journal of Portfolio Management* 7, no. 2 (Winter 1981): 17–22.

[14]Stephen Ross, "The Arbitrage Theory of Capital Asset Pricing," *Journal of Economic Theory* 13, no. 2 (December 1976): 341–360; Stephen Ross, "Return, Risk, and Arbitrage," in *Risk and Return in Finance*, edited by I. Friend and J. Bicksler (Cambridge: Ballinger, 1977), 189–218.

include inflation, growth in GNP, major political upheavals, or changes in interest rates. The APT contends there are many such factors, in contrast to the CAPM, where it is contended that the only relevant variable is the covariance of the asset with the market portfolio, that is, its beta coefficient.

Given these common factors, the b_{ik} terms determine how each asset reacts to this common factor. To extend the earlier example, although all assets may be affected by growth in GNP, the effects will differ across assets. For example, stocks of cyclical firms that produce autos, steel, or heavy machinery will have larger b_{ik} terms for this common factor than noncyclical firms, such as grocery chains. Likewise, you will hear discussions about interest-sensitive stocks: all stocks are affected by changes in interest rates, but some stocks experience larger effects. It is possible to envision other examples of common factors such as inflation, exchange rates, interest rate spreads, and so on. Still, in the application of the theory, *the factors are not identified.* That is, when we discuss the empirical studies, three, four, or five factors that affect security returns will be identified, but *there is no indication of what these factors represent.*

Similar to the CAPM model, it is assumed that the unique effects (ϵ_i) are independent and will be diversified away in a large portfolio. The APT assumes that, in equilibrium, the return on a zero-investment, zero-systematic-risk portfolio is zero when the unique effects are diversified away. This assumption and some theory from linear algebra imply that the expected return on any asset i (E_i) can be expressed as

$$E_i = \lambda_0 + \lambda_1 b_{i1}, + \lambda_2 b_{i2} + \ldots + \lambda_k b_{ik}$$

where:

λ_0 = **the expected return on an asset with zero systematic risk where $\lambda_0 = E_0$**
λ_1 = **the risk premium related to each of the common factors—for example, the risk premium related to interest rate risk ($\lambda_i = E_i = E_0$)**
b_{ik} = **the pricing relationship between the risk premium and asset i—that is, how responsive asset i is to this common factor K.**

Consider the following example of two stocks and a two-factor model:

λ_1 = **changes in the rate of inflation. The risk premium related to this factor is 1 percent for every 1 percent change in the rate ($\lambda_1 = .01$)**
λ_2 = **percent growth in real GNP. The average risk premium related to this factor is 2 percent for every 1 percent change in the rate ($\lambda_2 = .02$)**
λ_0 = **the rate of return on a zero-systematic-risk asset (zero beta: $b_{0j} = 0$) is 3 percent ($\lambda_0 = .03$).**

The two assets (X, Y) have the following response coefficients to these factors:

b_{x1} = **the response of asset X to changes in the rate of inflation is 0.50 ($b_{x1} = .50$). This asset is not very responsive to changes in the rate of inflation**
b_{y1} = **the response of asset Y to changes in the rate of inflation is 2.00 ($b_{y1} = 2.00$)**
b_{x2} = **the response of asset X to changes in the growth rate of real GNP is 1.50 ($b_{x2} = 1.50$)**
b_{y2} = **the response of asset Y to changes in the growth rate of real GNP is 1.75 ($b_{y2} = 1.75$)**

These response coefficients indicate that if these are the major factors influencing asset returns, asset Y is a higher-risk asset, and therefore its expected (required) return should be greater, as shown below:

$$E_i = \lambda_0 + \lambda_1 b_{i1} + \lambda_2 b_{i2}$$
$$= .03 + (.01)b_{i1} + (.02)b_{i2}.$$

Therefore:

$$E_x = .03 + (.01)(0.50) + (.02)(1.50)$$
$$= .065 = 6.5\%$$
$$E_y = .03 + (.01)(2.00) + (.02)(1.75)$$
$$= .085 = 8.5\%.$$

If the prices of the assets do not reflect these returns, we would expect investors to enter into arbitrage arrangements whereby they would sell overpriced assets short and use the proceeds to purchase the underpriced assets until the relevant prices were corrected. Given these linear relationships, it should be possible to find an asset or a combination of assets with equal risk to the mispriced asset, yet a higher return.

Empirical Tests of the APT

Studies by Roll and Ross and by Chen have provided results that support the APT because the model was able to explain different rates of return, in some cases with results that were superior to those of the CAPM.[15] In contrast, results of Reinganum's study do not support the model because it did not explain small-firm results.[16] Finally, Dhrymes and Shanken both questioned the usefulness of the model because it was not possible to identify the factors. Under these conditions, they question whether the theory is testable.[17]

At this time, the theory is relatively new and will be subject to continued testing. The important points to remember are that the model requires fewer assumptions and considers multiple factors to explain the risk of an asset.

Investments Online

Asset pricing models show how risk measures or underlying return-generating factors will affect asset returns. Estimates from such models are usually proprietary and are available from providers only by buying their research. Of course, users can always purchase their raw data elsewhere (see some of our earlier Internet discussions) and develop their own estimates of beta and factor sensitivities.

www.valueline.com

The Value Line Investment Survey has been a long-time favorite of investors and many local and college/university libraries subscribe to it. It is a popular source of finding a stock's beta. Value Line Publishing, Inc.'s Web site contains useful information for the on-line researcher and student of investments. Its site features investment-related articles, a case study, business forecast, and a product directory, which lists the venerable investment survey as well as Value Line's mutual fund, options, and Value Screen products, and many others.

---

[15]Richard Roll and Stephen A. Ross, "An Empirical Investigation of the Arbitrage Pricing Theory," *Journal of Finance* 35, no. 5 (December 1980): 1073–1103; and Nai-fu Chen, "Some Empirical Tests of Theory of Arbitrage Pricing," *Journal of Finance* 18, no. 5 (December 1983): 1393–1414.

[16]Marc R. Reinganum, "The Arbitrage Pricing Theory: Some Empirical Results," *Journal of Finance* 36, no. 2 (May 1981): 313–321.

[17]Phoebus J. Dhrymes, "The Empirical Relevance of Arbitrage Pricing Models," *Journal of Portfolio Management* 10, no. 4 (Summer 1984): 35–44; Jay Shanken, "The Arbitrage Pricing Theory: Is It Testable?" *Journal of Finance* 37, no. 5 (December 1982): 1129–1140.

Investments Online *(cont.)*

www.barra.com

For subscribers, Barra's Web site offers a gold mine of data and analytical analysis. Links offer information on portfolio management, investment data, market indices, and research. Barra offers its clients data, software, consulting, as well as money management services for equity, fixed income, currency, and other global financial instruments. Barra estimates multiple factor models and their global and single country equity models provide risk analysis on over 25,000 globally traded securities, including predicted and historical beta values.

www.sharpe.stanford.edu/home.html

William F. Sharpe, the 1990 winner of the Nobel prize in Economics because of his development of the Capital Asset Pricing Model, has a home page on the Internet. Among other items, Web surfers can read drafts of a sophisticated textbook in progress, some of his published papers, and case studies he has written. Sharpe's site offers monthly returns data on a number of mutual funds, stock indices, and bond indices, and links to other finance sites.

SUMMARY

♦ The assumptions of capital market theory expand on those of the Markowitz portfolio model and include consideration of the risk-free rate of return. The correlation and covariance of any asset with a risk-free asset are zero, so that any combination of an asset or portfolio with the risk-free asset generates a linear return and risk function. Therefore, when you combine the risk-free asset with any risky asset on the Markowitz efficient frontier, you derive a set of straight-line portfolio possibilities.

♦ The dominant line is the one that is tangent to the efficient frontier. This dominant line is referred to as the *capital market line (CML),* and all investors should target points along this line depending on their risk preferences.

♦ Because all investors want to invest in the risky portfolio at the point of tangency, this portfolio—referred to as the market portfolio—must contain all risky assets in proportion to their relative market values. Moreover, the investment decision and the financing decision can be separated because, although everyone will want to invest in the market portfolio, investors will make different financing decisions about whether to lend or borrow based on their individual risk preferences.

♦ Given the CML and the dominance of the market portfolio, the relevant risk measure for an individual risky asset is its covariance with the market portfolio, that is, its *systematic risk.* When this covariance is standardized by the covariance for the market portfolio, we derive the well-known beta measure of systematic risk and a security market line (SML) that relates the expected or required rate of return for an asset to its beta. Because all individual securities and portfolios should plot on this SML, you can determine the expected (required) return on a security based on its systematic risk (its beta).

♦ Alternatively, assuming security markets are not always completely efficient, you can identify undervalued and overvalued securities by comparing your estimate of the rate of return to be earned on an investment to its expected (required) rate of return. The systematic risk variable (beta) for an individual risky asset is computed using a regression model that generates an equation referred to as the asset's *characteristic line.*

♦ We concluded the chapter with a discussion of an alternative asset pricing model—the arbitrage pricing theory (APT) model. This included a discussion of the necessary assumptions and the basics of the model as well as an example of its use. We also considered some of the tests of the model that have generated mixed results. Because of the mixed results and the importance of the topic, it is likely that testing of this model will continue.

Questions

1. Explain why the set of points between the risk-free asset and a portfolio on the Markowitz efficient frontier is a straight line.
2. Draw a graph that shows what happens to the Markowitz efficient frontier when you combine a risk-free asset with alternative risky asset portfolios on the Markowitz efficient frontier. Explain this graph.
3. Draw and explain why the line from the RFR that is tangent to the efficient frontier defines the dominant set of portfolio possibilities.
4. Discuss what risky assets are in Portfolio M and why they are in it.
5. Discuss leverage and its effect on the CML.
6. Discuss and justify a measure of diversification for a portfolio in terms of capital market theory.
7. What changes would you expect in the standard deviation for a portfolio of stocks between 4 and 10 stocks, between 10 and 20 stocks, and between 50 and 100 stocks?
8. Discuss why the investment and financing decisions are separate when you have a CML.
9. Given the CML, discuss and justify the relevant measure of risk for an individual security.
10. Capital market theory divides the variance of returns for a security into systematic variance and unsystematic or unique variance. Describe each of these terms.
11. The capital asset pricing model (CAPM) contends that there is systematic and unsystematic risk for an individual security. Which is the relevant risk variable and why is it relevant? Why is the other risk variable not relevant?
12. How does the SML differ from the CML?
13. *CFA Examination I (1993)*
    Identify and briefly discuss *three* criticisms of beta as used in the Capital Asset Pricing Model (CAPM). [6 minutes]
14. *CFA Examination I (1993)*
    Briefly explain whether investors should expect a higher return from holding Portfolio A versus Portfolio B under Capital Asset Pricing Theory (CAPM). Assume that both portfolios are fully diversified. [6 minutes]

	Portfolio A	Portfolio B
Systematic risk (beta)	1.0	1.0
Specific risk for each individual security	High	Low

15. *CFA Examination II (1994)*
    You have recently been appointed chief investment officer of a major charitable foundation. Its large endowment fund is currently invested in a broadly diversified portfolio of stocks (60 percent) and bonds (40 percent). The foundation's board of trustees is a group of prominent individuals whose knowledge of modern investment theory and practice is superficial. You decide a discussion of basic investment principles would be helpful.
    a. Explain the concepts of *specific risk, systematic risk, variance, covariance, standard deviation,* and *beta* as they relate to investment management. [12 minutes]
    You believe that the addition of other asset classes to the endowment portfolio would improve the portfolio by reducing risk and enhancing return. You are aware that depressed conditions in U.S. real estate markets are providing opportunities for property acquisition at levels of expected return that are unusually high by historical standards. You believe that an investment in U.S. real estate would be both appropriate and timely, and have decided to recommend a 20 percent position be established with funds taken equally from stocks and bonds.
    Preliminary discussions revealed that several trustees believe real estate is too risky to include in the portfolio. The Board Chairman, however, has scheduled a special meeting for

further discussion of the matter and has asked you to provide background information that will clarify the risk issue.

To assist you, the following expectational data have been developed:

Asset Class	Return	Standard Deviation	Correlation Matrix U.S. Stocks	U.S. Bonds	U.S. Real Estate	U.S. T-Bills
U.S. Stocks	12.0%	21.0%	1.00			
U.S. Bonds	8.0	10.5	0.14	1.00		
U.S. Real Estate	12.0	9.0	−0.04	−0.03	1.00	
U.S. Treasury Bills	4.0	0.0	−0.05	−0.03	0.25	1.00

b. Explain the effect on *both* portfolio risk *and* return that would result from the addition of U.S. real estate. Include in your answer *two* reasons for any change you expect in portfolio risk. (Note: It is *not* necessary to compute expected risk and return.) [8 minutes]

c. Your understanding of capital market theory causes you to doubt the validity of the expected return and risk for U.S. real estate. Justify your skepticism. [5 minutes]

Problems

1. Assume that you expect the economy's rate of inflation to be 3 percent, giving an RFR of 6 percent and a market return (R_M) of 12 percent.

a. Draw the SML under these assumptions.

b. Subsequently, you expect the rate of inflation to increase from 3 percent to 6 percent. What effect would this have on the RFR and the R_M? Draw another SML on the graph from Part a.

c. Draw an SML on the same graph to reflect an RFR of 9 percent and an R_M of 17 percent. How does this SML differ from that derived in Part b? Explain what has transpired.

2. You expect an RFR of 10 percent and the market return (R_M) of 14 percent. Compute the expected (required) return for the following stocks, and plot them on an SML graph.

Stock	Beta	$E(R_i)$
U	0.85	
N	1.25	
D	−0.20	

3. You ask a stockbroker what the firm's research department expects for these three stocks. The broker responds with the following information:

Stock	Current Price	Expected Price	Expected Dividend
U	22	24	0.75
N	48	51	2.00
D	37	40	1.25

Plot your estimated returns on the graph from Problem 2 and indicate what actions you would take with regard to these stocks. Discuss your decisions.

4. Select a stock from the NYSE and collect its month-end prices for the latest thirteen months to compute twelve monthly percentage of price changes ignoring dividends. Do the same for the S&P 500 series. Prepare a scatter plot of these series on a graph and draw a visual characteristic line of best fit (the line that minimizes the deviations from the line). Compute the slope of this line from the graph.

5. Given the returns derived in Problem 4, compute the beta coefficient using the formula and techniques employed in Table 7.3. How many negative products did you have for the covariance? How does this computed beta compare to the visual beta derived in Problem 4?

6. Look up the index values and compute the monthly rates of return for either the FT World Index or the Morgan Stanley World Index.

a. Compute the beta for your NYSE stock from Problem 4 using one of these world stock indexes as the proxy for the market portfolio.

b. How does this world beta compare to your S&P beta? Discuss the difference.

7. Look up this stock in *Value Line* and record the beta derived by *VL*. How does this *VL* beta compare to the beta you computed using the S&P 500? Discuss reasons why the betas might differ.

8. Select a stock that is listed on the AMEX and plot the returns during the past twelve months relative to the S&P 500. Compute the beta coefficient. Did you expect this stock to have a higher or lower beta than the NYSE stock? Explain your answer.

9. Given the returns for the AMEX stock in Problem 8, plot the stock returns relative to monthly rates of return for the AMEX Market Value Index and compute the beta coefficient. Does this beta differ from that derived in Problem 8? If so, how can you explain this? (Hint: Analyze the specific components of the formula for the beta coefficient. How did the components differ between Problems 8 and 9?)

10. Using the data from the prior questions, compute the beta coefficient for the AMEX Index relative to the S&P 500 Index. A priori, would you expect a beta less than or greater than 1.00? Discuss your expectations and the actual results.

11. Based on five years of monthly data, you derive the following information for the companies listed.

Company	a_i (Intercept)	σ_i	r_{iM}
Intel	0.22	12.10%	0.72
Chrysler	0.10	14.60	0.33
Anheuser Busch	0.17	7.60	0.55
Merck	0.05	10.20	0.60
S&P 500	0.00	5.50	1.00

a. Compute the beta coefficient for each stock.

b. Assuming a risk-free rate of 8 percent and an expected return for the market portfolio of 15 percent, compute the expected (required) return for all the stocks and plot them on the SML.

c. Plot the following estimated returns for the next year on the SML and indicate which stocks are undervalued or overvalued.

◆ Intel—20%
◆ Chrysler—15%
◆ Anheuser Busch—19%
◆ Merck—10%

12. Calculate the expected (required) return for each of the following stocks when the risk-free rate is .08 and you expect the market return to be .15.

Stock	Beta
A	1.72
B	1.14
C	0.76
D	0.44
E	0.03
F	−0.79

13. The following are the historic returns for the Anita Computer Company:

Year	Anita Computer	General Index
1	37	15
2	9	13
3	−11	14
4	8	−9
5	11	12
6	4	9

Based on this information, compute the following:

a. The correlation coefficient between Anita Computer and the General Index.

b. The standard deviation for the company and the index.

c. The beta for the Anita Computer Company.

14. *CFA Examination II (1995)*
    The following information describes the expected return and risk relationship for the stocks of two of WAH's competitors.

	Expected Return	**Standard Deviation**	**Beta**
Stock X	12.0%	20%	1.3
Stock Y	9.0	15	0.7
Market Index	10.0	12	1.0
Risk-free rate	5.0		

Using only the data shown above:

a. Draw and label a graph showing the Security Market Line and position stocks X and Y relative to it using the template provided in the answer book. [5 minutes]

b. Compute the alphas *both* for stock X *and* for stock Y. Show your work. [4 minutes]

c. Assume that the risk-free rate increases to 7 percent with the other data in the matrix above remaining unchanged. Select the stock providing the higher expected risk-adjusted return and justify your selection. Show your calculations.

References

Brinson, Gary P., Jeffrey J. Diermeier, and Gary Schlarbaum. "A Composite Portfolio Benchmark for Pension Plans." *Financial Analysts Journal* 42, no. 2 (March–April 1986).

Chen, F. N., Richard Roll, and Steve Ross. "Economic Forces and the Stock Market." *Journal of Business* (July 1986).

Hagin, Robert. *Modern Portfolio Theory.* Homewood, IL: Dow Jones–Irwin, 1979.

Handa, Puneet, S. P. Kothari, and Charles Wasley. "The Relation between the Return Interval and Betas: Implications of the Size Effect." *Journal of Financial Economics* 23, no. 1 (June 1989).

Hawawini, Gabriel A. "Why Beta Shifts as the Return Interval Changes." *Financial Analysts Journal* 39, no. 3 (May–June 1983).

Reilly, Frank K., and Rashid A. Akhtar. "The Benchmark Error Problem with Global Capital Markets." *Journal of Portfolio Management* 22, no. 1 (Fall 1995).

GLOSSARY

Arbitrage pricing theory (APT) A theory concerned with deriving the expected or required rates of return on risky assets based on the asset's systematic relationship to several risk factors. This multifactor model is in contrast to the single-factor CAPM.

Beta A standardized measure of systematic risk based upon an asset's covariance with the market portfolio.

Capital asset pricing model (CAPM) A theory concerned with deriving the expected or required rates of return on risky assets based on the assets' systematic risk levels.

Capital market line (CML) The line from the intercept point that represents the risk-free rate tangent to the original efficient frontier; it becomes the new efficient frontier.

Completely diversified portfolio A portfolio in which all unsystematic risk has been eliminated by diversification.

Estimated rate of return The rate of return an investor anticipates earning from a specific investment over a particular future holding period.

Market portfolio The portfolio that includes all risky assets with relative weights equal to their proportional market values.

Market risk premium The amount of return above the risk-free rate that investors expect from the market in general as compensation for systematic risk.

Risk-free asset An asset with returns that exhibit zero variance.

Risky asset An asset with uncertain future returns.

Separation theorem The proposition that the investment decision, which involves investing in the market portfolio on the capital market line, is separate from the financing decision, which targets a specific point on the CML based on the investor's risk preference.

Systematic risk The variability of returns that is due to macroeconomic factors that affect all risky assets. Because it affects all risky assets, it cannot be eliminated by diversification.

Unsystematic risk Risk that is unique to an asset, derived from its particular characteristics. It can be eliminated in a diversified portfolio.

CHAPTER

8

Efficient Capital Markets

In this chapter we will answer the following questions:

♦ What do we mean when we say that capital markets are efficient?

♦ Why *should* capital markets be efficient?

♦ What factors contribute to an efficient market?

♦ Given the overall efficient market hypothesis, what are the three subhypotheses and what are the implications of each of them?

♦ How do you test the weak-form efficient market hypothesis (EMH) and what are the results of the tests?

♦ How do you test the semistrong-form EMH and what are the test results?

♦ How do you test the strong-form EMH and what are the test results?

♦ For each set of tests, which results support the hypothesis and which results indicate an anomaly related to the hypothesis?

♦ What are the implications of the results for

♦ technical analysis?

♦ fundamental analysis?

♦ portfolio managers with superior analysts?

♦ portfolio managers with inferior analysts?

♦ What is the evidence related to the EMH for markets in foreign countries?

An **efficient capital market** is one in which security prices adjust rapidly to the arrival of new information and, therefore, the current prices of securities reflect all information about the security. Some of the most interesting and important academic research during the past twenty years has analyzed whether our capital markets are efficient. This

extensive research is important because its results have significant real-world implications for investors and portfolio managers. In addition, the efficiency of capital markets is one of the most controversial areas in investment research because opinions regarding the efficiency of capital markets differ widely.

Because of its importance and the controversy, you need to understand the meaning of the terms *efficient capital markets* and the *efficient market hypothesis (EMH)*. You should understand the analysis performed to test the EMH and the results of studies that either support or contradict the hypothesis. Finally, you should be aware of the implications of these results when you analyze alternative investments and work to construct a portfolio.

We are considering the topic of efficient capital markets at this point for two reasons. First, the discussions in previous chapters have given you an understanding of how the capital markets function, so now it seems natural to consider the efficiency of the market in terms of how prices react to new information. Second, the overall evidence on capital market efficiency is best described as mixed; some studies support the hypothesis and others do not. The implications of these diverse results are important for you as an investor involved in analyzing securities and working to build a portfolio.

This chapter contains four major sections. The first discusses why we would expect capital markets to be efficient and the factors that contribute to an efficient market where the prices of securities reflect available information.

The efficient market hypothesis has been divided into three subhypotheses to facilitate testing. The second section describes these three subhypotheses and the implications of each of them.

Section three is the largest section because it contains a discussion of the results of numerous studies. This review of the research reveals that a large body of evidence supports the EMH, but a growing number of other studies do not support the hypotheses.

The final section discusses what these results imply for an investor who uses either technical analysis or fundamental analysis or for a portfolio manager who has access to superior or inferior analysts. We conclude with a brief discussion of the evidence for markets in foreign countries.

WHY SHOULD CAPITAL MARKETS BE EFFICIENT?

As noted earlier, in an efficient capital market, security prices adjust rapidly to the infusion of new information, and, therefore, current security prices fully reflect all available information. To be absolutely correct, this is referred to as an **informationally efficient market**. Although the idea of an efficient capital market is relatively straightforward, we often fail to consider *why* capital markets *should* be efficient. What set of assumptions imply an efficient capital market?

An initial and important premise of an efficient market requires that *a large number of profit-maximizing participants analyze and value securities,* each independently of the others.

A second assumption is that *new information regarding securities comes to the market in a random fashion,* and the timing of one announcement is generally independent of others.

The third assumption is especially crucial: *profit-maximizing investors adjust security prices rapidly to reflect the effect of new information.* Although the price adjustment may be imperfect, it is unbiased. This means that sometimes the market will overadjust, and other times it will underadjust, but you cannot predict which will occur at any given time. Security prices adjust rapidly because of the many profit-maximizing investors competing against one another.

The combined effect of (1) information coming in a random, independent fashion and (2) numerous competing investors adjusting stock prices rapidly to reflect this new information means that one would expect price changes to be independent and random. You can see that the adjustment process requires a large number of investors following the movements of the security, analyzing the impact of new information on its value, and buying or selling the security until its price adjusts to reflect the new information. This scenario implies that informationally efficient markets require some minimum amount of trading and that more trading by numerous competing investors should cause a faster price adjustment, making the market more efficient. We will return to this need for trading and investor attention when we discuss some anomalies of the EMH.

Finally, because security prices adjust to all new information, these security prices should reflect all information that is publicly available at any point in time. Therefore, the security prices that prevail at any time should be an unbiased reflection of all currently available information, including the risk involved in owning the security. Therefore, in an efficient market *the expected returns implicit in the current price of the security should reflect its risk.*

ALTERNATIVE EFFICIENT MARKET HYPOTHESES

Most of the early work related to efficient capital markets was based on the *random walk hypothesis,* which contended that changes in stock prices occurred randomly. This early academic work contained extensive empirical analysis without much theory behind it. An article by Fama attempted to formalize the theory and organize the growing empirical evidence.[1] Fama presented the efficient market theory in terms of a *fair game model,* contending that investors can be confident that a current market price fully reflects all available information about a security and the expected return based upon this price is consistent with its risk.

Beyond articulating the efficient market (EM) theory in terms of a fair-game model, in his original article, Fama divided the overall efficient market hypothesis (EMH) and the empirical tests of the hypothesis into three subhypotheses depending on the information set involved: (1) weak-form EMH, (2) semistrong-form EMH, and (3) strong-form EMH.

In a 1991 review article, Fama again divided the empirical results into three groups, but shifted empirical results between the prior categories.[2] Basically, the weak-form category was broadened to include numerous studies previously considered in the semistrong-form category. Although there is logic in the new division, the initial division is believed more intuitive. Therefore, the following discussion uses the original categories but organizes the presentation of results using the new categories.

In the remainder of this section we describe the three hypotheses and the implications of each of them. In the following section, we briefly describe how researchers have tested these hypotheses and summarize the results of these tests.

Weak-Form Efficient Market Hypothesis

The **weak-form EMH** assumes that current stock prices fully reflect all *security-market information,* including the historical sequence of prices, rates of return, trading volume data,

[1]Eugene F. Fama, "Efficient Capital Markets: A Review of Theory and Empirical Work," *Journal of Finance* 25, no. 2 (May 1970): 383–417.

[2]Eugene F. Fama, "Efficient Capital Markets: II," *Journal of Finance* 46, no. 5 (December 1991): 1575–1617.

and other market-generated information, such as odd-lot transactions, block trades, and transactions by exchange specialists. Because it assumes that current market prices already reflect all past returns and any other security-market information, this hypothesis implies that past rates of return and other market data should have no relationship with future rates of return (that is, rates of return should be independent). Therefore, this hypothesis contends that you should gain little from using any trading rule that decides whether to buy or sell a security based on past rates of return or any other past market data.

Semistrong-Form Efficient Market Hypothesis

The **semistrong-form EMH** asserts that security prices adjust rapidly to the release of *all public information*; that is, current security prices fully reflect all public information. The semistrong hypothesis encompasses the weak-form hypothesis, because all the market information considered by the weak-form hypothesis, such as stock prices, rates of return, and trading volume, is public. Public information also includes all nonmarket information, such as earnings and dividend announcements, price-to-earnings (P/E) ratios, dividend–yield (D/P) ratios, book value–market value (BV/MV) ratios, stock splits, news about the economy, and political news. This hypothesis implies that investors who base their decisions on any important new information *after it is public* should not derive above-average risk-adjusted profits from their transactions, considering the cost of trading, because the security price already reflects all such new public information.

Strong-Form Efficient Market Hypothesis

The **strong-form EMH** contends that stock prices fully reflect *all information from public and private sources*. This means that no group of investors has monopolistic access to information relevant to the formation of prices. Therefore, this hypothesis contends that no group of investors should be able to consistently derive above-average risk-adjusted rates of return. The strong-form EMH encompasses both the weak-form and the semistrong-form EMH. Further, the strong-form EMH extends the assumption of efficient markets, in which prices adjust rapidly to the release of new public information, to assume perfect markets, in which all information is cost-free and available to everyone at the same time.

TESTS AND RESULTS OF EFFICIENT MARKET HYPOTHESES

Now that you understand the three components of the EMH and what each of them implies regarding the effect on security prices of different sets of information, we can consider how a person conducting research in this area tests to see whether the data support the hypotheses. Therefore, in this section we discuss the specific tests used to gauge support for the hypotheses and we summarize the results of these tests.

Like most hypotheses in finance and economics, the evidence on the EMH is mixed. Some studies have supported the hypotheses and indicate that capital markets are efficient. Results of other studies have revealed some **anomalies** related to these hypotheses, raising questions about support for them.

Weak-Form Hypothesis: Tests and Results

Researchers have formulated two groups of tests of the weak-form EMH. The first category involves statistical tests of independence between rates of return. The second

entails a comparison of risk–return results for trading rules that make investment decisions based on past market information relative to the results from a single buy-and-hold policy, which assumes that you buy stock at the beginning of a test period and hold it to the end.

Statistical Tests of Independence   As discussed earlier, the EMH contends that security returns over time should be independent of one another because new information comes to the market in a random, independent fashion, and security prices adjust rapidly to this new information. Two major statistical tests have been employed to verify this independence.

First, **autocorrelation tests** of independence measure the significance of positive or negative correlation in returns over time. Does the rate of return on day t correlate with the rate of return on day $t - 1$, $t - 2$, or $t - 3$?[3] Those who believe that capital markets are efficient would expect insignificant correlations for all such combinations.

Several researchers have examined the serial correlations among stock returns for several relatively short time horizons including one day, four days, nine days, and sixteen days. The results typically indicated insignificant correlation in stock returns over time. Some recent studies that considered portfolios of stocks of different market size have indicated that the autocorrelation is stronger for portfolios of small market size stocks. Therefore, although the older results tend to support the hypothesis, the more recent studies cast doubt on it for portfolios of small firms, although these results could be affected by nonsynchronous trading for small-firm stocks.

The second statistical test of independence is the **runs test**.[4] Given a series of price changes, each price change is either designated a plus ($+$) if it is an increase in price or minus ($-$) if it is a decrease in price. The result is a set of pluses and minuses as follows: $+++-+--++--++$. A run occurs when two consecutive changes are the same; two or more consecutive positive or negative price changes constitute one run. When the price changes in a different direction, such as when a negative price change is followed by a positive price change, the run ends and a new run may begin. To test for independence, you would compare the number of runs for a given series to the number in a table of expected values for the number of runs that should occur in a random series.

Studies that have examined stock price runs have confirmed the independence of stock price changes over time. The actual number of runs for stock price series consistently fell into the range expected for a random series. Therefore, these statistical tests of stocks on the NYSE and on the OTC market have likewise confirmed the independence of stock price changes over time.

Although short-horizon stock returns have generally supported the weak-form EMH, several studies that examined price changes for individual *transactions* on the NYSE found significant serial correlations. Notably, none of these studies attempted to show that the dependence of transaction price movements could be used to earn above-average risk-adjusted returns after considering the trading rule's substantial transaction costs.

Tests of Trading Rules   The second group of tests of the weak-form (EMH) were developed in response to the assertion that the prior statistical tests of independence were too rigid to identify the intricate price patterns examined by technical analysts. As we will discuss in Chapter 14, technical analysts do not expect a set number of positive or negative price changes as a signal of a move to a new equilibrium in the market. They typically look for a general consistency in the price trend over time. Such a trend might include

---

[3]For a discussion of tests of independence, see S. Christian Albright, *Statistics for Buisness and Economics* (New York: Macmillan Publishing, 1987), 515–517.

[4]For the details of a runs test, see Albright, *Statistics for Business and Economics,* 695–699.

both positive and negative changes. For this reason technical analysts believed that their trading rules were too sophisticated and complicated to be properly tested by rigid statistical tests.

In response to this objection, investigators attempted to examine alternative technical trading rules through simulation. Advocates of an efficient market hypothesized that investors could not derive abnormal profits above a buy-and-hold policy using any trading rule that depended solely on past market information about factors such as price, volume, odd-lot sales, or specialist activity.

The trading rule studies compared the risk–return results derived from trading-rule simulations, including transactions costs, to the results from a simple buy-and-hold policy. Three major pitfalls can negate the results of a trading rule study:

1. The investigator should *use only publicly available data* when implementing the trading rule. As an example, the trading activities of specialists as of December 31 may not be publicly available until February 1, so you should not factor in information about specialist trading activity until then.
2. When computing the returns from a trading rule, you should *include all transactions costs* involved in implementing the trading strategy because most trading rules involve many more transactions than a simple buy-and-hold policy.
3. You must *adjust the results for risk* because a trading rule might simply select a portfolio of high-risk securities that should experience higher returns.

Researchers have encountered two operational problems in carrying out these tests of specific trading rules. First, some trading rules require too much subjective interpretation of data to simulate mechanically. Second, the almost infinite number of potential trading rules makes it impossible to test all of them. As a result, only the better-known technical trading rules have been examined.

Another factor that you should recognize is that some studies have been somewhat biased. Specifically, the studies have been restricted to relatively simple trading rules, which many technicians contend are rather naïve. In addition, these studies typically employ readily available data from the NYSE, which is biased toward well-known, heavily traded stocks that certainly should trade in efficient markets. Recall that because markets should be more efficient with higher numbers of aggressive, profit-maximizing investors attempting to adjust stock prices to reflect new information, market efficiency depends on trading volume. Specifically, *more trading in a security should promote market efficiency.* Alternatively, for securities with relatively few stockholders and little trading activity, the market could be inefficient simply because fewer investors would be analyzing the effect of new information, and this limited interest would result in insufficient trading activity to move the price of the security quickly to a new equilibrium value that would reflect the new information. Therefore, using only active, heavily traded stocks when testing a trading rule could bias the results toward finding efficiency.

Results of Simulations of Specific Trading Rules   In the most popular trading technique, **filter rules**, an investor trades a stock when the price change exceeds a filter value set for it. As an example, an investor using a 5 percent filter would envision a positive breakout if the stock were to rise 5 percent from some base, suggesting that the stock price would continue to rise. A technician would acquire the stock to take advantage of the expected continued rise. In contrast, a 5 percent decline from some peak price would be considered a breakout on the downside, and the technician would expect a further price decline and would sell any holdings of the stock, and possibly even sell the stock short.

Studies of this trading rule have used a range of filters from 0.5 percent to 50 percent. The results indicated that small filters would yield above-average profits *before* taking

account of trading commissions. However, small filters generate numerous trades and, therefore, substantial trading costs. When these trading commissions were considered, all the trading profits turned to losses. Alternatively, trading using larger filters did not yield returns above those of a simple buy-and-hold policy.

Researchers have simulated other trading rules that used past market data other than stock prices.[5] Trading rules have been devised that use odd-lot figures, advanced-decline ratios, short sales, short positions, and specialist activities. These simulation tests have generated mixed results. Most of the early studies suggested that these trading rules generally would not outperform a buy-and-hold policy on a risk-adjusted basis after commissions, although several recent studies have indicated support for specific trading rules. Therefore, most evidence from simulations of specific trading rules indicates that most trading rules have not been able to beat a buy-and-hold policy. Therefore, these results generally support the weak-form EMH, but the results are not unanimous.

Semistrong-Form Hypothesis: Tests and Results

Recall that the semistrong-form EMH asserts that security prices adjust rapidly to the release of all public information; that is, security prices fully reflect all public information. Using the organization employed by Fama in his recent paper, studies that have tested the semistrong-form EMH can be divided into the following sets of studies:

1. Studies to predict future rates of return using available public information beyond pure market information such as prices and trading volume considered in the weak-form tests. These studies can involve either *time-series analysis* of returns or the *cross-section distribution* of returns for individual stocks. Advocates of the EMH would contend that it would not be possible to predict *future* returns using past returns or to predict the distribution of future returns using public information.
2. Event studies that examine how fast stock prices adjust to specific significant economic events. A corollary approach would be to test whether it is possible to invest in a security after the public announcement of a significant event and experience significant abnormal rates of return. Again, advocates of the EMH would expect security prices to adjust rapidly, such that it would not be possible for investors to experience superior risk-adjusted returns by investing after the public announcement and paying normal transactions costs.

Adjustment for Market Effects   For any of these tests, you need to adjust the security's rates of return for the rates of return of the overall market during the period considered. The point is, a 5 percent return in a stock during the period surrounding an announcement is meaningless until you know what the aggregate stock market did during the same period and how this stock normally acts under such conditions. If the market had experienced a 10 percent return during this period, the 5 percent return for the stock may be lower than expected.

Authors of studies undertaken prior to 1970 generally recognized the need to make such adjustments for market movements. They typically assumed that the individual stocks should experience returns equal to the aggregate stock market. This assumption meant that the market adjustment process simply entailed subtracting the market return from the return for the individual security to derive its **abnormal rate of return**, as follows:

---

[5]Many of these trading rules are discussed in Chapter 14 on technical analysis.

8.1
$$AR_{it} = R_{it} - R_{mt}$$

where:

AR_{it} = **abnormal rate of return on security *i* during period *t***
R_{it} = **rate of return on security *i* during period *t***
R_{mt} = **rate of return on a market index during period *t***

In the example where the stock experienced a 5 percent increase while the market increased 10 percent, the stock's abnormal return would be minus 5 percent.

Since the 1970s, many authors have adjusted the rates of return for securities by an amount different from the market rate of return, because they recognize that based on work with the CAPM, all stocks do not change by the same amount as the market. That is, as discussed in Chapter 7, some stocks are more volatile than the market, and some are less volatile. These possibilities mean that you must determine an **expected rate of return** for the stock based on the market rate of return *and* the stock's relationship with the market (its beta). As an example, suppose a stock is generally 20 percent more volatile than the market (that is, it has a beta of 1.20). In such a case, if the market experiences a 10 percent rate of return, you would expect this stock to experience a 12 percent rate of return. Therefore, you would determine the abnormal return by computing the difference between the stock's actual rate of return and its *expected rate of return* as follows:

8.2
$$AR_{it} = R_{it} - E(R_{it})$$

where:

$E(R_{it})$ = **the expected rate of return for stock *i* during period *t* based on the market rate of return and the stock's normal relationship with the market (its beta)**

Continuing with the example, if the stock that was expected to have a 12 percent return (based on a market return of 10 percent and a stock beta of 1.20) had only a 5 percent return, its abnormal rate of return during the period would be minus 7 percent. Over the normal long-run period, you would expect the abnormal returns for a stock to sum to zero. Specifically, during one period the returns may exceed expectations, and the next period they may fall short of expectations.

To summarize, there are two sets of tests of the semi-strong-form EMH. In the first set, investigators attempt to predict the time series of future rates of return for individual stocks or the aggregate market using public information. For example, is it possible to predict abnormal returns over time for the market based on specified values or changes in the aggregate dividend yield or the risk premium spread for bonds? Alternatively, analysts look for public information regarding individual stocks that will allow them to predict the cross-sectional distribution of risk-adjusted rates of return (that is, test whether it is possible to use variables such as the earnings–price ratio, market value size, book-value/market value ratio, or the dividend yield to predict which stocks will experience above-average or below-average risk-adjusted rates of return). In the second set of tests (**event studies**), they examine abnormal rates of return for the period immediately after an announcement of a significant economic event such as a stock split to determine whether an investor can derive above-average risk-adjusted rates of return by investing after the release of public information.

In both sets of tests, the emphasis is on the analysis of abnormal rates of return that deviate from long-term expectations, or returns that are adjusted for a stock's specific risk characteristics and overall market rates of return during the period.

Results of Return Prediction Studies   The *time-series tests* assume that in an efficient market the best estimate of *future* rates of return will be the long-run *historical* rates of return. The point of the tests is to determine whether any public information will provide superior estimates of returns for a short-run horizon (one to six months) or a long-run horizon (one to five years).

The results of these studies have indicated limited success in predicting short-horizon returns, but the analysis of long-horizon returns has been quite successful. After postulating that the aggregate dividend yield (D/P) was a proxy for the risk premium on stocks, they found a positive relationship between the D/P and future stock-market returns. Subsequent authors found that the predictive power increases with the horizon. Specifically, *long-run* returns on stocks can be predicted as long as you can predict aggregate output.

Several studies have considered the dividend yield, but also two variables related to the term structure of interest rates: (1) a *default spread,* which is the difference between the yields on lower-grade and Aaa-rated long-term corporate bonds (this spread has been used in earlier chapters of this book as a proxy for a market risk premium), and (2) the *term structure spread,* which is the difference between the long-term Aaa yield and the yield on one-month Treasury bills. It has been shown that these variables can be used to predict stock returns and bond returns. Similar variables in foreign countries have also been useful for predicting returns for foreign common stocks.

The reasoning for these empirical results is as follows: when the two most significant variables—the dividend yield (D/P) and the default spread—are high, it implies that investors are expecting or requiring a high return on stocks and bonds, and this occurs during poor economic environments, as reflected in the growth rate of output. A poor economic environment also implies a low wealth environment wherein investors perceive higher risk for investments. As a result, to invest and shift consumption from the present to the future investors will require a high rate of return. It is suggested that if you invest during this risk-averse period, your subsequent returns will be above normal.

Quarterly earnings reports   Studies that address quarterly reports are considered part of the times-series analysis. Specifically, these studies question whether it is possible to predict future returns for a stock based on publicly available quarterly earnings reports.

Numerous studies done in the early 1970s provided evidence against the semistrong EMH.[6] The typical test used in the early studies examined firms that experienced changes in quarterly earnings that differed from expectation by different amounts (for example, plus or minus 10, 20, 30, and 40 percent). The results generally indicated abnormal returns during the thirteen or twenty-six weeks following the announcement of a large unanticipated earnings change (referred to as an **earnings surprise**). These results suggest that the earnings surprise is *not* instantaneously reflected in security prices. Some debated whether the results were caused by market inefficiencies or a problem with the CAPM, but the consensus seems to favor the market inefficiency argument.

More recent earnings announcement studies have employed the concept of *standardized unexpected earnings (SUE).*[7] Rather than examine the percentage differences between actual and expected earnings, this technique normalizes the difference between actual

---

[6]Representative studies in the area are H. A. Latané, O. Maurice Joy, and Charles P. Jones, "Quarterly Data, Sort-Rank Routines, and Security Evaluation," *Journal of Business* 43, no. 4 (October 1970): 427–438; and C. Jones and R. Litzenberger, "Quarterly Earnings Reports and Intermediate Stock Price Trends," *Journal of Finance* 25, no. 1 (March 1970): 143–148.

[7]These include Henry A. Latané and Charles P. Jones, "Standardized Unexpected Earnings—A Progress Report," *Journal of Finance* 32, no. 5 (December 1977): 1457–1465; and Henry A. Latané and Charles Jones, "Standardized Unexpected Earnings: 1971–1977," *Journal of Finance* 34, no. 3 (June 1979): 717–724.

and expected earnings for the quarter by the standard error of estimate from the regression used to derive the expected earnings figure. Specifically, the SUE is

$$\frac{\text{Reported EPS}_t - \text{Predicted EPS}_t}{\substack{\text{Standard Error of Estimate for the} \\ \text{Estimating Regression Equation}}}$$

Therefore, the SUE indicates how many standard errors the reported EPS figure is above or below the predicted EPS figure. The typical categories are greater than 4.0, between 4.0 and 3.0, between 3.0 and 2.0, and so on, all the way to less than minus 4.0.

An extensive analysis by Rendleman, Jones, and Latané (RJL) using a large sample and daily returns provided evidence that large SUEs were accompanied by significant abnormal stock price changes.[8] RJL also examined the impact of different risk adjustments or no risk adjustment (implicitly assuming that the various SUE portfolios have comparable risk levels) and concluded that the results were not sensitive to the risk adjustments. The analysis of daily data from twenty days before a quarterly earnings announcement to ninety days after the announcement indicated that 31 percent of the total response in stock returns came before the announcement, 18 percent on the day of the announcement, and 51 percent afterward.

Several studies examined reasons for the earnings drift following earnings announcements and found that unexpected earnings explained more than 80 percent of the subsequent stock price drift for the total time period. Mendenhall and later Bernard and Thomas reviewed the prior studies and attempted to explain this pervasive drift.[9] Part of the reason for the stock price drift was the *earnings revisions* that followed the earnings surprises and contributed to the positive correlations of prices.

In summary, these results indicate that the market has not adjusted stock prices to reflect the release of quarterly earnings surprises as fast as expected by the semi-strong EMH. As a result, it appears that earnings surprises and earnings revisions can be used to predict returns for individual stocks. These results are evidence against the EMH.[10]

The final set of studies that attempted to predict rates of return are the *calendar studies.* These studies questioned whether some regularities in the rates of return during the calendar year would allow investors to predict returns on stocks. These studies include numerous studies on "The January Anomaly" and studies that consider a variety of other daily and weekly regularities.

The January anomaly Several years ago Branch proposed a unique trading rule for those interested in taking advantage of tax selling.[11] Investors (including institutions) tend to engage in tax selling toward the end of the year to establish losses on stocks that have declined. After the new year, the tendency is to reacquire these stocks or to buy other stocks that look attractive. This scenario would produce downward pressure on stock prices in

---

[8]Richard J. Rendleman, Jr., Charles P. Jones, and Henry A. Latané, "Empirical Anomalies Based on Unexpected Earnings and the Importance of Risk Adjustments," *Journal of Financial Economics* 10, no. 3 (November 1982): 269–287; and C. P. Jones, R. J. Rendleman, Jr., and H. A. Latané, "Earnings Announcements: Pre- and Post-Responses," *Journal of Portfolio Management* 11, no. 3 (Spring 1985): 28–32.

[9]Richard R. Mendenhall, "An Investigation of Anomalies Based on Unexpected Earnings" (Ph.D. dissertation, Indiana University, 1986); and Victor L. Bernard and Jacob K. Thomas, "Post-Earnings-Announcement Drift: Delayed Price Response or Risk Premium?" *Journal of Accounting Research* 27, Supplement (1989).

[10]Academic studies such as these that have indicated the importance of earnings surprises have led the *Wall Street Journal* to publish a section on "earnings surprises" in connection with regular quarterly earnings reports.

[11]Ben Branch, "A Tax Loss Trading Rule," *Journal of Business* 50, no. 2 (April 1977): 198–207. These results were generally confirmed in Ben Branch and Kyun Chun Chang, "Tax-Loss Trading—Is the Game Over or Have the Rules Changed?" *Financial Review* 20, no. 1 (February 1985): 55–69.

late November and December and positive pressure in early January. Those who believe in efficient markets would not expect such a seasonal pattern to persist; it should be eliminated by arbitrageurs who would buy in December and sell in early January.

A supporter of the hypothesis found that December trading volume was abnormally high for stocks that had declined during the previous year and that volume was abnormally low for stocks that had experienced large gains. Significant abnormal returns occurred during January for stocks that had experienced losses during the prior year.

This was confirmed by a price pattern on the last day of December and the first four days of January that showed that stocks with negative returns during the prior year had higher returns around January 1 and 2. Assuming a purchase at the high price for the second-to-last trading day and sales at the low price on the fourth day of the new year, and also adding commissions, there was no profit on the NYSE, but there was an excess return on the AMEX. It was concluded that because of transaction costs, arbitrageurs must not be eliminating the January tax-selling anomaly. Subsequent analysis showed that more than 50 percent of the January effect was concentrated in the first week of trading, particularly on the first day of the year.

Several studies provided support for a January effect inconsistent with the tax-selling hypothesis. Specifically, two studies examined what happened in foreign countries that did not have our tax laws or a December year-end. In both cases (in Canada and Australia) they found abnormal returns in January, but the results could not be explained by tax laws. Other phenomena about January were also found, including the fact that the classic relationship between risk and return is strongest during this month. Finally, there is a year-end trading volume bulge in late December that carries over to January.

In summary, the January anomaly is intriguing because it is so pervasive. Its relationship with the small-firm effect will be discussed in a subsequent section. This seasonal impact also influences trading volume, and a tax-loss explanation of this anomaly has received mixed support. Despite numerous studies, the January anomaly poses as many questions as it answers.[12]

Other calendar effects   Although not as significant as the January anomaly, several other "calendar" effects have been examined, including a monthly effect, a weekend/day-of-the-week effect, and an intraday effect. One study found a significant monthly effect wherein all the market's cumulative advance occurred during the first half of trading months.

An analysis of the weekend effect found that the mean return for Monday was significantly negative during five-year subperiods and a total period. In contrast, the average return for the other four days was positive. Another study found negative Monday results back to 1928 for individual exchange-listed stocks and for active OTC stocks. It was also found that the Monday effect is similar for different size firms that were exchange-traded or on the OTC.

A study decomposed the Monday effect that is typically measured from Friday close to Monday close into a *weekend effect* from Friday close to Monday open, and a *Monday trading effect* from Monday open to the Monday close. It was shown that the negative Monday effect found in prior studies actually occurs from the Friday close to the Monday open (that is, it is really the weekend effect). After adjusting for the weekend effect, the Monday trading effect was positive. Further, it was found that the Monday effect and the nontrading effect were on average positive in January and negative for all other months and the size effect only existed in January.

Two studies have examined this question using intraday observations. Given a total period 1963 to 1983 they found a change in the pattern of returns before and after 1974.

---

[12]An article that reviews these studies and others is Donald B. Keim, "The CAPM and Equity Return Regularities," *Financial Analysts Journal* 42, no. 3 (May–June 1986): 19–34.

During the period 1974 to 1983, the Monday effect was concentrated in the weekend effect. In contrast, before 1974 the Monday effect occurred during the Monday trading period. These two sets of results imply a shift in the timing of the weekend effect wherein the negative effect occurs during the weekend. Notably, the Monday trading effect has turned positive because the negative Monday morning effect is swamped by positive Monday afternoon returns.

Finally, study results indicated that for *large firms,* the negative Monday effect occurred before the market opened (it was a weekend effect), whereas for smaller firms most of the negative Monday effect occurred during the day on Monday (it was a Monday trading effect).

Predicting Cross-Sectional Returns   Assuming an efficient market, all securities should lie along a security-market line that relates the expected rate of return to an appropriate risk measure. Put another way, *all securities should have equal risk-adjusted returns* because security prices should reflect all public information that would influence the security's risk. Therefore, studies in this category attempt to determine if it is possible to predict the future distribution of risk-adjusted rates of return (that is, can you use public information to predict what stocks will enjoy above-average risk-adjusted returns and which will experience below-average risk-adjusted returns?).

These studies typically examine the usefulness of alternative measures of size or quality as a tool to rank stocks in terms of risk-adjusted returns. The reader should be forewarned that all of these tests involve *a joint hypothesis* because they consider not only the efficiency of the market, but also are dependent on the asset pricing model that provides the measure of risk used in the test. Specifically, if a test determines that it is possible to predict future differential risk-adjusted returns, these results could occur because the market is not efficient, *or* they could be because the measure of risk is faulty and, therefore, the measures of risk-adjusted returns are wrong.

Price-earnings ratios and returns   Several studies have tested the EMH by examining the relationship between the historical price-earnings (P/E) ratios for stocks and the returns on the stocks. Some have suggested that low P/E stocks will outperform high P/E stocks because growth companies enjoy high P/E ratios, but the market tends to overestimate the growth potential and thus overvalues these growth companies, while undervaluing low-growth firms with low P/E ratios. A relationship between the historical P/E ratios and subsequent risk-adjusted market performance would constitute evidence against the semistrong EMH, because it would imply that investors could use publicly available information regarding P/E ratios to predict future abnormal returns.

Researchers typically divided the stocks into five P/E classes and determined the risk and return for portfolios of high and low P/E ratio stocks. The average annual rates of return ranged from 9 percent for high P/E ratio stocks to 16 percent for the low P/E ratio group. An unexpected result was that the low P/E ratio group also had lower risk. Performance measures that consider both return and risk indicated that low P/E ratio stocks experienced superior risk-adjusted results relative to the market, whereas high P/E ratio stocks had significantly inferior risk-adjusted results.[13] Subsequent analysis indicated some influence from taxes and transaction costs, but it was concluded that publicly available P/E ratios possess valuable information regarding future returns. Obviously, these results are inconsistent with semistrong efficiency.

Another study examined P/E ratios with adjustments for firm size, industry effects, and infrequent trading and likewise found that the risk-adjusted returns for stocks in the lowest P/E ratio quintile were superior to those in the highest P/E ratio quintile.

---

[13]Composite performance measures are discussed in Chapter 22.

The size effect   Several authors have examined the impact of size (measured by total market value) on the risk-adjusted rates of return. All stocks on the NYSE or on the NYSE and the AMEX were ranked by market value and divided into ten equally weighted portfolios. The risk-adjusted returns for extended periods (twenty to thirty-five years) indicated that the small firms consistently experienced significantly larger risk-adjusted returns than the larger firms. It was contended that it was the size, not the P/E ratio, that caused the results discussed in the prior subsection, but this contention was disputed.

Recall that these studies on market efficiency are dual tests of the EMH *and* the CAPM. Abnormal returns may occur because the markets are inefficient, or because the market model is not properly specified and therefore provides incorrect estimates of risk and expected returns.

It was suggested that the riskiness of the small firms was improperly measured because small firms are traded less frequently. An earlier study had suggested an alternative way to measure beta for infrequently traded stocks. When this alternative technique was used, it confirmed that the small firms had much higher risk, but the tests of whether these larger betas could explain the large differences in rates of return indicated that the difference in beta did not account for the large difference in rates of return.

A study that examined the impact of transaction costs confirmed that total market value varies inversely with risk-adjusted returns, but also found a strong positive correlation between average price per share and market value; firms with small market value have low stock prices. Because transaction costs vary inversely with price per share, they must be considered when examining the small-firm effect. Transaction costs include both the dealer's bid–ask spread and the broker's commission, and it was shown that there was a significant difference in the percentage cost for large firms (2.71 percent) versus small firms (6.77 percent). This differential in transaction costs, with frequent trading, can have a significant impact on the results. Assuming daily transactions, the original small-firm effects are reversed, whereas with less trading, the original abnormal returns recur. The point is, size-effect studies must consider realistic transaction costs and specify holding period assumptions.

A size-effect study that investigated a buy-and-hold strategy for longer periods of time had results similar to an annual trading strategy. Two holding-period strategies were considered: a one-year holding period, with rebalancing every year, and a buy-and-hold strategy from 1963 through 1980. With *annual* rebalancing, the small-firm portfolio grew from one dollar in 1963 to more than forty-six dollars without commissions, whereas one dollar in the largest-firm portfolio grew to about four dollars. With *no* rebalancing, a dollar in the small-firm portfolio grew to about eleven dollars, whereas one dollar in the large-firm portfolio again grew to more than four dollars. Transaction costs were not considered with annual rebalancing because the differential returns were so large that no reasonable transaction costs could overcome this return superiority. In summary, the small firms outperformed the large firms after considering risk and transaction costs, assuming annual rebalancing.

Most studies on the size effect employed large databases and long time periods (thirty to fifty years) to show that this phenomenon has existed for many years. In contrast, a study that examined the performance over various intervals of time concluded that *the small-firm effect is not stable.* During some periods they found the negative relationship between size and return derived by others, but during others (such as, 1967 to 1975) they found a positive relationship where large firms outperformed the small firms. Notably, this positive relationship held during the following recent periods: 1984–87; 1989–90; and 1995–97. A study by Reinganum acknowledges this instability, but contends that the small-firm effect is still a long-run phenomenon.[14]

---

[14]Marc R. Reinganum, "A Revival of the Small Firm Effect," *Journal of Portfolio Management* 18, no. 3 (Spring 1992): 55–62.

Neglected firms and trading activity   Arbel and Strebel considered an additional influence beyond size—attention or neglect.[15] They measured attention in terms of the number of analysts who regularly follow a stock and divided the stocks into three groups: (1) highly followed, (2) moderately followed, and (3) neglected. They confirmed the small-firm effect but also found a neglected-firm effect caused by the lack of information and limited institutional interest. The neglected-firm concept applied across size classes. Contrary results are reported by Beard and Sias who found no evidence of a neglected firm premium after controlling for capitalization.[16]

Another study examined the impact of trading volume by considering the relationship between returns, market value, and trading activity. The results confirmed the relationship between size and rates of return and then considered the impact of trading volume as an alternative explanation because of a strong positive correlation between size and trading activity. A relationship between return and trading activity would justify the excess return for small stocks on the basis of a liquidity premium. The results indicated no significant difference between the mean returns of the highest and lowest trading activity portfolios. A test on firms with comparable trading activity confirmed the size effect. In summary, the size effect could not be explained by differential trading activity. A subsequent study hypothesized that firms with less information require higher returns. Using the period of listing as a proxy for information, they found a negative relationship between returns and the period of listing after adjusting for firm size and the January effect.

In summary, firm size has emerged as a major predictor of future returns and an anomaly in the efficient markets literature. There have been numerous attempts to explain the size anomaly in terms of superior risk measurements, transaction costs, analysts' attention, trading activity, and differential information. In general, no single study has been able to explain these unusual results. Apparently, the two strongest explanations are the risk measurements and the higher transaction costs. Depending on the frequency of trading, these two factors may account for much of the differential. These results indicate that the size effect must be considered in any event study that uses long intervals and contains a sample of firms with significantly different market values.

Book value–market value ratio   This ratio that relates the book value (BV) of a firm's equity to the market value (MV) of its equity was initially suggested by Rosenberg, Reid, and Lanstein as a predictor of stock returns.[17] They found a significant positive relationship between current values for this ratio and future stock returns and contended that such a relationship between available public information and future returns was evidence against the EMH.

The strongest support for the importance of this ratio was provided in a study by Fama and French that evaluated the joint effects of market beta, size, E/P ratio, leverage, and the BV/MV ratio (referred to as BE/ME) on the cross-section average returns on NYSE, AMEX, and NASDAQ stocks.[18] Whereas the analysis concentrates on the period 1963 to 1990, additional analysis considers earlier periods and subperiods within the total period. They analyzed the hypothesized positive relationship between beta and expected

---

[15]Avner Arbel and Paul Strebel, "Pay Attention to Neglected Firms!" *Journal of Portfolio Management* 9, no. 2 (Winter 1983): 37–42.

[16]Craig Beard and Richard Sias, "Is There a Neglected-Firm Effect?" *Financial Analysts Journal* 53, no. 5 (September–October 1997): 19–23.

[17]Barr Rosenberg, Kenneth Reid, and Ronald Lanstein, "Persuasive Evidence of Market Inefficiency," *Journal of Portfolio Management* 11, no. 3 (Spring 1985): 9–17. Many studies define this ratio as "book-to-market value" (BV/MV) because it implies a positive relationship, but most practitioners refer to it as the "price-to-book value" (P/B) ratio. Obviously the concept is the same, but the sign changes.

[18] Eugene F. Fama and Kenneth R. French, "The Cross-Section of Expected Stock Returns," *Journal of Finance* 47, no. 2 (June 1992): 427–465.

returns and found that this positive relationship found in empirical studies for the period pre-1969 disappeared during the period 1963 to 1990. In contrast, the negative relationship between size and average return was significant by itself and significant after inclusion of other variables.

In addition, they found a significant positive relationship between the BV/MV ratio and average return that persisted even when other variables are included. Most importantly, *both* size and the BV/MV ratio are significant when included together and they dominate other ratios. Specifically, although leverage and the E/P ratio were significant by themselves or when considered with size, they become insignificant when *both* size and the BV/MV ratio are considered.

A demonstration of the significance of both size and the BV/MV ratio can be seen from the results in Table 8.1, which shows the separate and combined effect of the two variables. As shown, going across the Small-ME (small size) row, BV/MV captures strong variation in average returns (0.70 to 1.92 percent). Alternatively, controlling for the BV/MV ratio leaves a size effect in average returns (the high BV/MV results decline from 1.92 to 1.18 percent when going from small to large). These positive results for the BV/MV ratio were replicated for returns on Japanese stocks.

In summary, the tests of publicly available ratios that can be used to predict the cross-section of expected returns for stocks have provided substantial evidence in conflict with the semistrong-form EMH. Significant results were found for E/P ratios, market value size, neglected firms, leverage, and BV/MV ratios. Although recent work has indicated that the optimal combination appears to be size and the BV/MV ratio, a new study by Jensen, Johnson and Mercer indicates that this combination only works during periods of expansive monetary policy.[19]

Results of Event Studies   The use of event studies to test the EMH has been a major growth sector during the past twenty years. Recall that the intent of these studies is to examine abnormal rates of return surrounding significant economic information. Those who advocate the EMH would expect returns to adjust quickly to announcements of new information such that it is not possible for investors to experience positive abnormal rates of return by acting after the announcement. Because of space constraints, we cannot consider the many studies but only summarize the results for some of the more popular events considered.

Because numerous studies have examined the price reaction to specific events, the discussion of results is organized by event or item of public information. Specifically, we will review the results of event studies that examined the price movements and profit potential surrounding stock splits, the sale of initial public offerings, exchange listings, unexpected world or economic events, and the announcements of significant accounting changes. We will see that the results for most of these studies have supported the semistrong-form EMH.

Stock split studies   One of the more popular economic events to examine is stock splits. Some believe that the prices of stocks that split will increase in value because the shares are priced lower, which increases demand for them. In contrast, advocates of efficient markets would not expect a change in value, reasoning that the firm has simply issued additional stock and nothing fundamentally affecting the value of the firm has occurred.

A well-known test of the semistrong hypothesis is the FFJR study, which hypothesized that stock splits alone should not cause higher rates of return because they add nothing to the value of a firm.[20] They expected no significant price change following a split because any relevant information (such as, earnings growth) that caused the split would have already been discounted.

---

[19]Gerald R. Jensen, Robert R. Johnson, and Jeffrey M. Mercer, "New Evidence on Size and Price-to-Book Effects in Stock Returns," *Financial Analysts Journal* 53 no. 6 (November–December 1997): 34–42.

[20]E. F. Fama, L. Fisher, M. Jensen, and R. Roll, "The Adjustment of Stock Prices to New Information," *International Economic Review* 10, no. 1 (February 1969): 1–21.

Table 8.1 *Average Monthly Returns on Portfolios Formed on Size and Book-to-Market Equity; Stocks Sorted by ME (Down) and then BE/ME (Across); July 1963 to December 1990*

In June of each year t, the NYSE, AMEX, and NASDAQ stocks that meet the CRSP-COMPUSTAT data requirements are allocated to ten size portfolios using the NYSE size (ME) breakpoints. The NYSE, AMEX, and NASDAQ stocks in each size decile are then sorted into ten BE/ME portfolios using the book-to-market ratios for year $t - 1$. BE/ME is the book value of common equity plus balance-sheet deferred taxes for fiscal year $t - 1$, over market equity for December of year $t - 1$. The equal-weighted monthly portfolio returns are then calculated for July of year t to June of year $t + 1$.

Average monthly return is the time-series average of the monthly equal-weighted portfolio returns (in percent).

The All column shows average returns for equal-weighted size decile portfolios. The All row shows average returns for equal-weighted portfolios of the stocks in each BE/ME group

BOOK-TO-MARKET PORTFOLIOS

	All	Low	2	3	4	5	6	7	8	9	High
All	1.23	0.64	0.98	1.06	1.17	1.24	1.26	1.39	1.40	1.50	1.63
Small-ME	1.47	0.70	1.14	1.20	1.43	1.56	1.51	1.70	1.71	1.82	1.92
ME-2	1.22	0.43	1.05	0.96	1.19	1.33	1.19	1.58	1.28	1.43	1.79
ME-3	1.22	0.56	0.88	1.23	0.95	1.36	1.30	1.30	1.40	1.54	1.60
ME-4	1.19	0.39	0.72	1.06	1.36	1.13	1.21	1.34	1.59	1.51	1.47
ME-5	1.24	0.88	0.65	1.08	1.47	1.13	1.43	1.44	1.26	1.52	1.49
ME-6	1.15	0.70	0.98	1.14	1.23	0.94	1.27	1.19	1.19	1.24	1.50
ME-7	1.07	0.95	1.00	0.99	0.83	0.99	1.13	0.99	1.16	1.10	1.47
ME-8	1.08	0.66	1.13	0.91	0.95	0.99	1.01	1.15	1.05	1.29	1.55
ME-9	0.95	0.44	0.89	0.92	1.00	1.05	0.93	0.82	1.11	1.04	1.22
Large-ME	0.89	0.93	0.88	0.84	0.71	0.79	0.83	0.81	0.96	0.97	1.18

Source: Eugene F. Fama and Kenneth French, "The Cross-Section of Expected Stock Returns," *Journal of Finance* 47, no. 2 (June 1992): 446.

The FFJR study analyzed abnormal price movements surrounding the time of the split and divided the sample into those stocks that split and did not raise their dividends, and those stocks that split and did raise their dividends. Both groups experienced positive abnormal price changes prior to the split. Stocks that split but did *not* increase their dividend experienced abnormal price *declines* following the split and within twelve months lost all their accumulated abnormal gains. In contrast, stocks that split and also increased their dividend experienced no abnormal returns after the split.

These results, which indicated that stock splits do not result in higher rates of return for stockholders after the split, support the semistrong EMH because they indicate that investors cannot gain from the information on a split after the public announcement. These results were confirmed by subsequent studies that examined monthly and daily returns around the announcement of the split. Another study reported positive results on the day of the announcement and subsequent days.

In summary, most studies found no short-run or long-run positive impact on security returns because of a stock split, although the results are not unanimous.

Initial public offerings During the past twenty years a number of closely held companies have gone public by selling some of their common stock. Determining the appropriate price for an initial public offer (IPO) is a difficult task. Because of uncertainty about the appropriate offering price and the risk involved in underwriting such issues, it has been the prevailing hypothesis that the underwriters would tend to underprice these new issues.[21]

[21]For a discussion of these reasons, see Frank K. Reilly and Kenneth Hatfield, "Investor Experience with New Stock Issues," *Financial Analysts Journal* 25, no. 5 (September–October 1969): 73–80.

Given this general expectation of underpricing, the studies in this area have generally considered three sets of questions: (1) How great is the underpricing on average, does the underpricing vary over time, and if so, why? (2) What factors cause different amounts of underpricing for alternative issues? (3) How fast does the market adjust the price for the underpricing?

The answer to the first question seems to be an average underpricing of about 15 percent, but it varies over time as shown by the results in Table 8.2.[22] Numerous factors have been suggested for the differential underpricing of alternative issues, but the major variables seem to be: various risk measures, the size of the firm, the prestige of the underwriter, and the status of the firm's accounting firms. Finally, on the question of direct interest to the EMH, the more recent results indicate that the price adjustment to the underpricing takes place within one day after the offering.[23] Therefore, it appears that some underpricing of the IPO occurs when it is offered, but the only ones who benefit from this underpricing are the few investors who receive allocations of the original issue—almost all subsequent purchases reflect the rapid price adjustment. The evidence indicates that investors who acquire the stock at these aftermarket adjusted prices do not experience abnormal rates of return. This rapid adjustment of the initial underpricing would support the semistrong EMH.

Exchange listing   Another significant economic event for a firm and its stock is the decision to become listed on a national exchange, especially the NYSE. Such a listing is expected to increase the market liquidity of the stock and add to its prestige. Two questions are important. First, does an exchange listing permanently increase the value of the firm? Second, can an investor derive abnormal returns from investing in the stock when a new listing is announced or around the time of the actual listing? Although the results differed slightly, the overall consensus is that listing on a national exchange causes no permanent change in the long-run value of a firm. The results about abnormal returns from investing in such stocks were mixed. All the studies agreed that: (1) the stocks' prices increased before any listing announcements, and (2) stock prices consistently declined after the actual listing. The crucial question is, what happens between the announcement of the application for listing and the actual listing (a period of four to six weeks)? Although the evidence varies, more recent studies point toward profit opportunities immediately after the announcement that a firm is applying for listing. There is also the possibility of excess returns from price declines after the actual listing.[24] Finally, studies that have examined the impact of listing on the risk of the securities found no significant change in systematic risk or the firm's cost of equity.

In summary, these studies on exchange listings indicate no long-run effects on value or risk. They do, however, give some evidence of short-run profit opportunities. This

[22]Example studies that measured these returns include Roger G. Ibbotson, "Price Performance of Common Stock New Issues," *Journal of Financial Economics* 2, no. 3 (September 1975): 235–272; Dennis E. Logue, "On the Pricing of Unseasoned New Issues, 1965–1969," *Journal of Financial and Quantitative Analysis* 8, no. 1 (January 1973): 91–103; Frank K. Reilly, "Further Evidence on Short-Run Results for New Issue Investors," *Journal of Financial and Quantitative Analysis* 8, no. 1 (January 1973): 83–90; Frank K. Reilly, "New Issues Revisited," *Financial Management* 6, no. 4 (Winter 1977): 28–42; and B. M. Neuberger and C. A. Lachapelle, "Unseasoned New Issue Price Performance on Three Tiers: 1975–1980," *Financial Management* 12, no. 3 (Autumn 1983): 23–28.

[23]In this regard, see Robert E. Miller and Frank K. Reilly, "An Examination of Mispricing, Returns, and Uncertainty for Initial Public Offerings," *Financial Management* 16, no. 2 (January 1987): 33–38; and Andrew J. Chalk and John W. Peavy, III, "Initial Public Offerings: Daily Returns, Offering Types, and the Price Effect," *Financial Analysts Journal* 43, no. 5 (September–October 1987): 65–69. For an excellent overall review of the research on this topic, see Roger G. Ibbotson, Jody L. Sindelar, and Jay R. Ritter, "The Market Problems with the Pricing of Initial Public Offerings," *Journal of Applied Corporate Finance* 7, no. 1 (Spring 1994): 66–74.

[24]See Gary Sanger and John McConnell, "Stock Exchange Listings Firm Value and Security Market Efficiency: The Impact of NASDAQ," *Journal of Financial and Quantitative Analysis* 21, no. 1 (March 1986): 1–25; John J. McConnell and Gary Sanger, "A Trading Strategy for New Listings on the NYSE," *Financial Analysts Journal* 40, no. 1 (January–February 1989): 38–39.

Table 8.2   *Number of Offerings, Average Initial Return, and Gross Proceeds of Initial Public Offerings in 1960–92*

Year	Number of Offerings[a]	Average Initial Return, %[b]	Gross Proceeds $ Millions[c]	Year	Number of Offerings[a]	Average Initial Return, %[b]	Gross Proceeds $ Millions[c]
1960	269	17.83	$ 553	1980	259	49.36	$ 1,404
1961	435	34.11	1,243	1981	438	16.76	3,200
1962	298	−1.61	431	1982	198	20.31	1,334
1963	83	3.93	246	1983	848	20.79	13,168
1964	97	5.32	380	1984	516	11.52	3,932
1965	146	12.75	409	1985	507	12.36	10,450
1966	85	7.06	275	1986	953	9.99	19,260
1967	100	37.67	641	1987	630	10.39	16,380
1968	368	55.86	1,205	1988	435	5.27	5,750
1969	780	12.53	2,605	1989	371	6.47	6,068
1970	358	−0.67	780	1990	276	9.47	4,519
1971	391	21.16	1,655	1991	367	11.83	16,420
1972	562	7.51	2,724	1992	509	10.90	23,990
1973	105	−17.82	330				
1974	9	−6.98	51				
1975	14	−1.86	264	1960-69	2,661	21.25	7,988
1976	34	2.90	237	1970-79	1,658	8.95	6,868
1977	40	21.02	151	1980-89	5,155	15.18	80,946
1978	42	25.66	247	1990-92	1,152	10.85	44,929
1979	103	24.61	429	Total	10,626	15.26	$140,731

[a]The number of offerings excludes Regulation A offerings (small issues, raising less than $1.5 million during the 1980s), real estate investment trusts (REITs) and closed-end funds. Data are from Roger G. Ibbotson and Jeffry F. Jaffe, "'Hot Issues' Markets," *Journal of Finance* (September 1975) for 1960–70; Jay R. Ritter, "The 'Hot Issues' Market of 1980," *Journal of Business* (April 1984) for 1971–82; *Going Public: The IPO Reporter* for 1983–84; and Investment Dealer's Digest Information Services and Security Data Company for 1985–92. Returns data for 1988–92 exclude best efforts offerings. If these are included, the average initial returns for these years would presumably be higher.

[b]Initial returns are computed as the percentage return from the offering price to the end-of-the-calendar month bid price, less the market return, for offerings in 1960–76. For 1977–92, initial returns are computed as the percentage return from the offering price to the end-of-the-first-day bid price, without adjusting for market movements. Data are from Ibbotson and Jaffe (op. cit.) for 1960–70, Ritter (op. cit.) for 1971–82, and prepared by the authors for 1983–92. Initial returns for 1988–92 were prepared with the assistance of Zhewei Ma.

[c]Gross proceeds data come from various issues of the *S.E.C. Monthly Statistical Bulletin* and *Going Public: The IPO Reporter* for 1960–87, and Securities Data Co. for 1988–92. Only the U.S. portion of international equity offerings is included in the gross proceeds figures.

Source: Roger G. Ibbotson, Jody L. Sindelar, and Jay R. Ritter, "The Market Problems with the Pricing of Initial Public Offerings," *Journal of Applied Corporate Finance* 7, no. 1 (Spring 1994): 69.

implies profit opportunities by investors using public information, which does not support the semistrong-form EMH.

    Unexpected world events and economic news   The results of several studies that examined the response of security prices to world or economic news have supported the semistrong-form EMH. An analysis of the reaction of stock prices to unexpected world events, such as the Eisenhower heart attack and the Kennedy assassination, found that prices adjusted to the news before the market opened or before it reopened after the announcement. A study that examined the response to announcements about money supply, inflation, real economic activity, and the discount rate found either no impact or an impact that did not persist beyond the announcement day. Finally, an analysis of hourly stock returns and trading volume response to surprise announcements about money supply, prices, industrial production, and the unemployment rate found that unexpected information about money supply and prices had an impact that was reflected in about one hour.

    Announcements of accounting changes   Numerous studies have analyzed the impact of announcements of accounting changes on stock prices. In efficient markets, security prices should react quickly and predictably to announcements of accounting changes. An

announcement of an accounting change that affects the economic value of the firm should cause a rapid change in stock prices. An accounting change that affects reported earnings, but has no economic significance, should not affect stock prices. As an example, consider what should happen when a firm changes its depreciation accounting method for reporting purposes from accelerated to straight-line. In this case, the firm should experience an increase in reported earnings, but this change has no economic consequence. An analysis of stock price movements surrounding this accounting change in depreciation method generally supported the EMH because there was no indication of positive price changes following the change, and there were some negative effects because it was postulated that firms making such an accounting change are typically performing poorly.

During periods of high inflation, many firms will change their inventory method from first-in, first-out (FIFO) to last-in, first-out (LIFO). Such a change causes a decline in reported earnings but benefits the firm because it reduces its taxable earnings and, therefore, tax expenses. Advocates of efficient markets would expect positive price changes from the tax savings and study results confirmed this expectation. Although reported earnings were lower than they would have been with FIFO, stock prices generally increased for firms that made such changes in their inventory methods. In this regard, there is some evidence that the U.S. market is more efficient than some foreign markets.

Therefore, these studies indicate that the securities markets react quite rapidly to accounting changes and also adjust security prices as one would expect on the basis of the true value (that is, analysts are able to pierce the accounting veil and value securities on the basis of economic events).[25]

Corporate events   An area that has received substantial analysis during the past few years is corporate finance events such as mergers and acquisitions, re-organization, and various security offerings (common stock, straight bonds, convertible bonds). Again there are two general questions of interest: (1) What is the market impact of these alternative events? (2) How fast does the market react to these events and adjust the security prices?

On the question of the reaction to corporate events, the answer is almost unanimous that stock prices react as one would expect based on the underlying economic impact of the action. An example would be the reaction to mergers where the stock of the firm being acquired increases in line with the premium offered by the acquiring firm, whereas the stock of the acquiring firm declines or experiences no change because of the concern that they overpaid for the firm. On the question of speed of reaction, the evidence indicates fairly rapid adjustment, with the time period shortening as shorter interval data is analyzed (using daily data, most studies find that the price adjustment is completed in about three days). Numerous studies related to financing decisions are reviewed by Smith.[26] The rapidly growing number of studies on corporate control that consider mergers and reorganizations are reviewed by Jensen and Warner.[27]

Summary on the Semistrong-Form EMH   Clearly, the evidence from tests of the semistrong EMH is mixed. The hypothesis receives strong and almost unanimous support from the numerous event studies on a range of events including stock splits, initial

---

[25]For an extensive review of studies directed to this contention, see William H. Beaver, *Financial Reporting: An Accounting Revolution* (Englewood Cliffs, N.J.: Prentice-Hall, Inc., 1981), especially Chapter 6; V. Bernard and J. Thomas, "Evidence That Stock Prices Do Not Fully Reflect the Implications of Current Earnings for Future Earnings," *Journal of Accounting and Economics* (December 1990): 305–341; and R. Holthausen and D. Larcker, "The Prediction of Stock Returns Using Financial Statement Information," *Journal of Accounting and Economics* (June/September 1992): 373–412.

[26]Clifford W. Smith, Jr., "Investment Banking and the Capital Acquisition Process," *Journal of Financial Economics* 15, no. 1–2 (January–February 1986): 3–29.

[27]Michael C. Jensen and Jerald B. Warner, "The Distribution of Power Among Corporate Managers, Shareholders, and Directors," *Journal of Financial Economics* 20, no. 1–2 (January–March 1988): 3–24.

public offerings, world events and economic news, accounting changes, and a variety of corporate finance events. About the only mixed results come from exchange listing studies.

In sharp contrast, the numerous studies on predicting rates of return over time or for a cross-section of stocks presented evidence that indicated markets were not semistrong efficient. This included time-series studies on dividend yields, risk premiums, calendar patterns, and quarterly earnings surprises. Equally pervasive were the anomalous results for cross-sectional predictors such as size, the BV/MV ratio (when there is expansive monetary policy), E/P ratios, and neglected firms.

Strong-Form Hypothesis: Tests and Results

The strong-form EMH contends that stock prices fully reflect *all information,* public and private. This implies that no group of investors has access to *private information* that will allow them to consistently experience above-average profits. This extremely rigid hypothesis requires not only that stock prices must adjust rapidly to new public information, but also that no group has access to private information.

Tests of the strong-form EMH have analyzed returns over time for different identifiable investment groups to determine whether any group consistently received above-average risk-adjusted returns. To consistently earn positive abnormal returns, the group must have access to important private information or an ability to act on public information before other investors. Such results would indicate that security prices were not adjusting rapidly to *all* new information.

Investigators interested in testing this form of the EMH have analyzed the performance of four major groups of investors. First, several researchers have analyzed the returns experienced by *corporate insiders* from their stock trading. Another group of studies analyzed the returns available to *stock exchange specialists.* The third group of tests examined the ability of the group of *security analysts* at Value Line and elsewhere to select stocks that outperform the market. Finally, studies have examined the overall performance of *professional money managers.* The analysis of money managers' performance typically emphasized the risk-adjusted returns experienced by mutual funds because of the availability of data. Recently, these tests have been replicated for pension plans and endowment funds.

Corporate Insider Trading   Corporate insiders are required to report to the SEC each month on their transactions (purchases or sales) in the stock of the firm for which they are insiders. Insiders include major corporate officers, members of the board of directors, and owners of 10 percent or more of any equity class of securities. About six weeks after the reporting period, this insider trading information is made public by the SEC. These insider trading data have been used to identify how corporate insiders have traded and determine whether they bought on balance before abnormally good price movements and sold on balance before poor market periods for their stock.[28] The results of these studies have generally indicated that corporate insiders consistently enjoyed above-average profits especially on purchase transactions. This implies that many insiders had private information from which they derived above-average returns on their company stock.

---

[28]Early studies on this topic include James H. Lorie and Victor Niederhoffer, "Predictive and Statistical Properties of Insider Trading," *Journal of Law and Economics* 11 (April 1968): 35–53; and Joseph E. Finnerty, "Insiders Activity and Inside Information: A Multivariate Analysis," *Journal of Financial and Quantitative Analysis* 11, no. 2 (June 1976): 205–215. Recent studies include M. Chowdhury, J. S. Howe and J. C. Lin, "The Relation Between Aggregate Insider Transactions and Stock Market Returns," *Journal of Financial and Quantitative Analysis* 28, no. 3 (September 1993); 431–437, and R. R. Pettit and P. C. Venkatesh, "Insider Trading and Long-Run Return Performance," *Financial Management* 24, no. 2 (Summer 1995): 88–103.

In addition, a study found that *public* investors who consistently traded with the insiders based on announced insider transactions would have enjoyed excess risk-adjusted returns (after commissions), although a subsequent study concluded that the market had eliminated this inefficiency. Specifically, a recent study found that the realizable return to investors who attempt to act on insider reports was not positive after considering total transaction costs. Other studies contended that you can substantially increase the returns from using insider trading information by combining it with key financial ratios and you should consider what group of insiders (board chair, officers, directors versus other insiders) is doing the buying and selling.

Overall, these results provide mixed support for the EMH. Although several studies indicate the ability for insiders to experience abnormal profits, several recent studies indicate it is not possible for the noninsider to use this information to receive excess returns. Also, it is not possible to use *aggregate* insider trading activity as a guide to market timing. Notably, because of investor interest in these data as a result of academic research, the *Wall Street Journal* currently publishes a monthly column entitled "Inside Track" that discusses the largest insider transactions.

Stock Exchange Specialists   Several studies examining the function of stock exchange specialists have determined that specialists have monopolistic access to certain important information about unfilled limit orders. One would expect specialists to derive above-average returns from this information. This expectation is generally supported by the data. It appears that specialists generally make money because they typically sell shares at higher prices than their purchase price. Also, they apparently make money when they buy or sell after unexpected announcements and when they trade in large blocks of stock.

An SEC study in the early 1970s examined the rates of return earned on capital by the specialists and found that these rates of return were substantially above normal, which would not support the strong-form EMH. In fairness to current specialists, the environment in the late 1990s differs substantially from that in the early 1970s. Recent results indicate that specialists are experiencing much lower rates of return following the introduction of competitive rates and other trading practices that have reduced specialists' fees.

Security Analysts   Several tests have considered whether it is possible to identify a set of analysts who have the ability to select undervalued stocks. The analysis involves determining whether, after a stock selection by an analyst is made known, a significant abnormal return is available to those who follow their recommendation. These studies and those that discuss performance by money managers are more realistic and relevant than those that considered corporate insiders and stock exchange specialists because these analysts and money managers are full-time investment professionals with no obvious advantage except emphasis and training. If anyone should be able to select undervalued stocks, it should be these "pros." The first group of tests examine Value Line rankings, followed by an analysis of how investors react to revelations of recommendations by individual analysts.

The Value Line enigma   Value Line (VL) is a large well-known advisory service that publishes financial information on approximately 1,700 stocks. Included in its report is a timing rank, which indicates Value Line's expectation regarding a firm's common stock performance over the coming twelve months. A rank of 1 is the most favorable performance and 5 the worst. This ranking system, initiated in April 1965, assigns numbers based on four factors:

1. An earnings and price rank of each security relative to all others
2. A price momentum factor
3. Year-to-year relative changes in quarterly earnings
4. A quarterly earnings "surprise" factor (actual quarterly earnings compared with VL estimated earnings)

The firms are ranked based on a composite score for each firm. The top and bottom 100 are ranked 1 and 5, respectively, the next 300 from the top and bottom are ranked 2 and 4, and the rest (approximately 900) are ranked 3. Rankings are assigned every week based on the latest data. Notably, all the data used to derive the four factors are public information.

The preliminary ranking is made every Wednesday, and the final ranking is sent to the printer on Friday. (Typically five or six changes occur between Wednesday and Friday due to unusual new information.) The new rankings are ready to be distributed on the following Wednesday, and Value Line attempts a staggered mailing so that everyone should receive the weekly *Survey* on Friday.

Several years after the ranking was started, Value Line indicated that the performance of the stocks in the various ranks differed substantically. Specifically, Value Line contended that the stocks rated 1 substantially outperformed the market, and the stocks rated 5 seriously underperformed the market (the performance figures did not include dividend income but also did not charge commissions).

Black tested the Value Line system over the period 1965 to 1970 by constructing portfolios grouped by rank and revised the portfolios monthly.[29] He concluded that rank-1 firms outperformed rank-5 firms by 20 percent per year on a risk-adjusted basis and that even with round-trip transaction costs of 2 percent, the net rate of return for a long position in rank-1 stocks would have been positive. A subsequent study examined the top one hundred stocks in rank and concluded that if you consistently owned these stocks and adjusted your portfolio weekly, the returns would be superior *before* transaction costs but not after. Alternatively, if you assumed annual portfolio revisions, the strategy generated abnormal returns after transaction costs. Abnormal returns were consistent with the rankings, but only the returns for rank 5 were significantly negative, implying that VL has the ability to select underperformers. An analysis of a strategy of buying upgraded stocks and selling short those downgraded indicated significant negative abnormal returns for down-ranked stocks, but only limited significance for stocks that were upgraded. Finally, although the negative abnormal returns for the rank-5 portfolios were *statistically* significant, the trading rules were not profitable after transaction costs.

Another study found that although all rank changes affect stock prices, the most significant impact occurs when stocks go from rank 2 to 1. Other changes in rank were followed by statistically significant changes that were much smaller than for a move from 2 to 1. It appears that the price movements require three days, if Thursday is considered as Day 0 because some people might receive the *Value Line Survey* on Thursday. Clearly after Monday, there is no significant impact. Also, smaller firms experienced a larger reaction to changes in rank and the change requires several days. However, acting on the rank change from 2 to 1 for the smallest firms would not be profitable due to the large transaction costs of small firms. Therefore, although evidence shows that VL rank changes provide information content and that the price adjustment is not instantaneous, the absolute price change is *not* large enough to generate excess returns after transaction costs.

A study examined the relationship between the VL recommendation and firm size to see if the VL record is because of the firm size phenomenon. The overall results imply no relationship between the VL rankings and size.

An analysis of the daily price changes around the release of initial reviews and consequent new rankings of stocks indicated that there were no significant abnormal returns for stocks assigned any other ranking than 1. This implies that these other rankings contain little information. Notably, there were no significant price changes after Day + 1.

---

[29]Fischer Black, "Yes, Virginia, There Is Hope: Tests of the Value Line Ranking System," *Financial Analysts Journal* 29, no. 5 (September–October 1973): 10–14.

It is concluded that some of the rankings (mainly rank 1) contain information, but the market is fairly efficient in adjusting to it.

Finally, as noted previously, one of the four factors considered when ranking firms is quarterly earnings "surprises," and it appears that this is an important factor. Because of this impact, Affleck-Graves and Mendenhall contend that the longer-term abnormal returns from the VL ranking are caused by the quarterly postearnings announcement drift discussed earlier.[30] Put another way, the authors contend that this VL anomaly is caused by the quarterly earnings anomaly.

In summary, the several studies on the Value Line engima indicate that there is information in the VL rankings (especially either rank 1 or 5) and in changes in the rankings (especially going from 2 to 1). Further, most of the recent evidence indicates that the market is fairly efficient, because the abnormal adjustments appear to be complete by Day + 2. An analysis of study results over time indicates a faster adjustment to the rankings during recent years. Also, despite statistically significant price changes, mounting evidence indicates that it is not possible to derive abnormal returns from these announcements after considering realistic transaction costs. Some of the strongest evidence in this regard is the fact that Value Line's Centurion Fund, which concentrates on rank-1 stocks, has consistently underperformed the market over the past decade.

Analysts' recommendations   There is evidence in favor of the existence of superior analysts who apparently possess private information. This evidence is provided in two studies where the authors found that the prices of stocks mentioned in the *Wall Street Journal* column "Heard on the Street" experience a significant change on the day that the column appears. A recent study by Womach found that analysts appear to have both market timing and stock-picking ability, especially in connection with sell recomendations that are relatively rare.[31]

Performance of Professional Money Managers   The studies of professional money managers are more realistic and widely applicable than the analysis of insiders and specialists because money managers typically do not have monopolistic access to important new information. Still, they are highly trained professionals who work full-time at investment management. Therefore, if any "normal" set of investors should be able to derive above-average profits, it should be this group. Also, if any noninsider should be able to derive inside information, professional money managers should, because they conduct extensive management interviews.

Most studies on the performance of money managers have examined mutual funds because performance data is readily available on them. Only recently have data been available for bank trust departments, insurance companies, and investment advisers. The original mutual fund studies indicated that most funds were unable to match the performance of a buy-and-hold policy.[32] When risk-adjusted returns were examined *without* considering commission costs, slightly more than half of the money managers did better than the overall market. When commission costs, load fees, and management costs were considered, approximately two-thirds of the mutual funds did *not* match aggregate market performance. It was also found that funds were inconsistent in their performance.

More recent studies have generally provided similar results on performance. Notably, one study found that funds during the period 1965 to 1984 were able to beat the market after research and transaction costs but, a subsequent study using more extensive risk

[30]John Affleck-Graves and Richard R. Mendenhall, "The Relation Between the Value Line Enigma and Post-Earnings-Announcement Drift," *Journal of Financial Economics* 31, no. 1 (February 1992): 75–96.

[31]Kent L. Womach, "Do Brokerage Analysts' Recommendations Have Investment Value?" *Journal of Finance* 51, no. 1 (March 1996): 137–167.

[32]These studies and others on this topic are reviewed in Chapter 21.

Table 8.3   *Annualized Rates of Return during Alternative Periods Ending December 31, 1997*

	1 Year	2 Years	4 Years	6 Years	8 Years	10 Years
U.S. Equity Broad Universe Medians						
Equity accounts	30.6	26.6	21.5	18.1	17.0	18.3
Equity pooled accounts	30.5	26.4	21.6	17.4	16.2	17.5
Equity-oriented separate accounts	30.7	26.8	21.4	18.3	17.3	18.5
Special equity pooled accounts	25.9	22.6	18.2	18.8	17.9	19.5
Mutual Fund Universe Medians						
Balanced mutual funds	20.2	16.8	13.5	12.0	12.4	13.0
Equity mutual funds	26.3	22.8	18.2	16.1	15.1	16.2
U.S. Equity Style Universe Medians						
Growth equity accounts	31.3	26.3	20.8	16.4	18.0	19.2
Small capitalization accounts	25.5	24.4	19.4	19.6	18.0	19.7
Value equity accounts	30.4	26.7	21.6	19.4	18.0	18.2
Market-oriented accounts	31.0	26.7	21.6	19.4	16.7	18.2
S&P 500 Index	33.4	28.2	23.0	18.3	17.3	18.6
Number of Universes with Returns above the S&P 500	0	0	0	5	6	7

Source: Frank Russell Company, Tacoma, WA. Reprinted by permission.

measurement refuted these results. Therefore, the vast majority of money manager studies support the EMH because the results indicate mutual fund managers generally cannot beat a buy-and-hold policy.

As noted, recently it has been possible to get performance data for pension plans and endowment funds. Given this data, several studies have documented that the performances of pension plans did not match that of the aggregate market. Another study documented that the performance of endowment funds was likewise not able to beat a buy-and-hold policy.

The figures in Table 8.3 provide a rough demonstration of these results for recent periods. These data are collected by Frank Russell Analytical Services as part of its performance evaluation service. Table 8.3 contains the median rates of return for several investment groups compared to the Standard & Poor's 500 Index.[33]

Looking at the long-term, ten-year results, the first set of universes are banks that experienced returns above the Standard & Poor's 500 during the long-term periods (6-8-10 years), but not the recent periods. The mutual funds never had superior results. Finally, the four equity style universes typically did better. In summary, seven of the ten universes beat the market for the 10 year period. Notably, these results are *not* adjusted for risk. Interestingly, these results are generally not consistent with the mutual fund results and would not support the strong-form EMH.

Conclusions Regarding the Strong-Form EMH   The tests of the strong-form EMH generated mixed results, but the bulk of relevant evidence supported the hypothesis. The results for two unique groups of investors (corporate insiders and stock exchange specialists) did not support the hypothesis because both groups apparently have monopolistic access to important information and use it to derive above-average returns.

Tests to determine whether there are any analysts with private information concentrated on the Value Line rankings and publications of analysts' recommendations. The results for Value Line rankings have changed over time and currently tend toward support for the EMH. Specifically, the adjustment to rankings and ranking changes is fairly rapid, and

---

[33]The results for these individual accounts have an upward bias because they consider only accounts retained (for example, if a firm or bank does a poor job on an account and the client leaves, those results would not be included).

it appears that trading is not profitable after transactions costs. Also, there is a question whether the Value Line anomaly is really due to the quarterly earnings surprise anomaly. Alternatively, individual analysts recommendations seem to contain significant information.

Finally, the performance by professional money managers generally provided support for the strong-form EMH. The vast majority of money manager performance studies have indicated that the investments by these highly trained, full-time investors could not consistently out-perform a simple buy-and-hold policy on a risk-adjusted basis. This has been true for mutual funds, pension plans, and endowment funds. Because money managers are similar to most investors who do not have consistent access to inside information, these latter results are considered more relevant to the hypothesis. Therefore, it appears that there is overall support for the strong-form EMH as applied to most investors.

IMPLICATIONS OF EFFICIENT CAPITAL MARKETS

Having reviewed the results of numerous studies related to different facets of the EMH, the important question is what does this mean to individual investors, financial analysts, portfolio managers and institutions. Overall, the results of numerous studies indicate that the capital markets are efficient as related to numerous sets of information. At the same time, research has uncovered a substantial number of instances where the market apparently fails to adjust rapidly to public information. Given these mixed results regarding the existence of efficient capital markets, it is important to consider the implications of this contrasting evidence of market efficiency.

The following discussion considers the implications of both sets of evidence. Specifically given results that support the EMH, we consider what techniques will not work and what you do if you can't beat the market. In contrast, because of the evidence that fails to support the EMH, we discuss what information should be considered when attempting to derive superior investment results.

Efficient Markets and Technical Analysis

The assumptions of technical analysis directly oppose the notion of efficient markets. A basic premise of technical analysis is that stock prices move in trends that persist.[34] Technicians believe that when new information comes to the market, it is not immediately available to everyone but is typically disseminated from the informed professional to the aggressive investing public and then to the great bulk of investors. Also, technicians contend that investors do not analyze information and act immediately. This process takes time. Therefore, they hypothesize that stock prices move to a new equilibrium after the release of new information in a gradual manner, which causes trends in stock price movements that persist for certain periods.

Technical analysts believe that nimble traders can develop systems to detect the beginning of a movement to a new equilibrium (called a "breakout"). Hence, they hope to buy or sell the stock immediately after its breakout to take advantage of the subsequent price adjustment.

The belief in this pattern of price adjustment directly contradicts advocates of the EMH who believe that security prices adjust to new information very rapidly. These EMH advocates do not contend, however, that prices adjust perfectly, which implies a chance of

---

[34]Chapter 14 contains an extensive discussion of technical analysis.

overadjustment or underadjustment. Still, because it is uncertain whether the market will over- or underadjust at any time, you cannot derive abnormal profits from adjustment errors.

If the capital market is weak-form efficient as indicated by most of the results and prices fully reflect all relevant market information, no technical trading system that depends only on past trading data can have any value. By the time the information is public, the price adjustment has taken place. Therefore, a purchase or sale using a technical trading rule should not generate abnormal returns after taking account of risk and transaction costs.

Efficient Markets and Fundamental Analysis

As you know from our prior discussion, fundamental analysts believe that, at any time, there is a basic intrinsic value for the aggregate stock market, various industries, or individual securities and that these values depend on underlying economic factors. Therefore, investors should determine the intrinsic value of an investment asset at a point in time by examining the variables that determine value such as current and future earnings, interest rates, and risk variables. If the prevailing market price differs from the estimated intrinsic value by enough to cover transaction costs, you should take appropriate action: You buy if the market price is substantially below intrinsic value and sell if it is above. Investors who engage in fundamental analysis believe that occasionally market price and intrinsic value differ, but eventually investors recognize the discrepancy and correct it.

If you can do a superior job of *estimating* intrinsic value, you can consistently make superior market timing (asset allocation) decisions or acquire undervalued securities and generate above-average returns. Fundamental analysis involves aggregate market analysis, industry analysis, company analysis, and portfolio management. The divergent results from the EMH research has important implications for all of these components.

Aggregate Market Analysis with Efficient Capital Markets   Chapters 9 and 11 make a strong case that intrinsic value analysis should begin with aggregate market analysis. Still, the EMH implies that if you examine only *past* economic events, it is unlikely that you will be able to outperform a buy-and-hold policy because the market rapidly adjusts to known economic events. Evidence suggests that the market experiences long-run price movements, but to take advantage of these movements in an efficient market, you must do a superior job of *estimating* the relevant variables that cause these long-run movements. Put another way, if you only use *historical* data to estimate future values and invest on the basis of these estimates, you will *not* experience superior risk-adjusted returns.

Industry and Company Analysis with Efficient Capital Markets   As discussed in Chapter 12, the wide distribution of returns from different industries and companies clearly justifies industry and company analysis. Again, the EMH does not contradict the potential value of such analyses but implies that you need to (1) understand the relevant variables that affect rates of return, and (2) do a superior job of *estimating* movements in these relevant valuation variables. To demonstrate this, Malkiel and Cragg developed a model that did an excellent job of explaining past stock price movements using historical data. When this evaluation model was employed to project *future* stock price changes using *past* company data, however, the results were consistently inferior to a buy-and-hold policy.[35] This implies that, even with a good valuation model, you cannot select stocks that will provide superior returns using only past data as inputs.

[35]Burton G. Malkiel and John G. Cragg, "Expectations and the Structure of Share Prices," *American Economic Review* 60, no. 4 (September 1970): 601–617.

Another study showed that the crucial difference between the stocks that enjoyed the best and worst price performance during a given year was the relationship between expected earnings of professional analysts and actual earnings (that is, it was earnings surprises). Specifically, stock prices increased if actual earnings substantially exceeded expected earnings, and stock prices fell if actual earnings did not reach expected levels. Thus, if you can do a superior job of projecting earnings and your expectations *differ from the consensus,* you will probably have a superior stock selection record. Put another way, *you must be able to predict earnings surprises.*[36]

The quest to be a superior analyst holds some good news and some suggestions. The good news is related to the strong-form tests that indicated the likely existence of superior analysts. It was shown that the rankings by Value Line contained information value, even though it might not be possible to profit from the work of these analysts after transaction costs. Also, the price adjustments to the publication of analyst recommendations also points to the existence of superior analysts. The point is, there are some superior analysts, but a limited number, and it is not an easy task to be among this select group. Most notably, to be a superior analyst you must do a superior job of *estimating* the relevant valuation variables and *predicting earning surprises.*

The suggestions for those involved in fundamental analysis are based on the studies that considered the cross-section of future returns. As noted, these studies indicated that E/P ratios, size, and the BV/MV ratios were able to differentiate future return patterns with size and the BV/MV ratio appearing to be the optimal combination. Therefore, these factors should be considered when selecting a universe or analyzing firms. In addition, the evidence suggests that neglected firms should be given extra consideration.

How to Evaluate Analysts or Investors   If you want to determine if an individual is a superior analyst or investor, you should examine the performance of numerous securities that this analyst or investor recommends over time in relation to the performance of a set of randomly selected stocks of the same risk class. The stock selections of a superior analyst or investor should *consistently* outperform the randomly selected stocks. The consistency requirement is crucial because you would expect a portfolio developed by random selection to outperform the market about half the time.

Conclusions about Fundamental Analysis   A text on investments can indicate the relevant variables that you should analyze and describe the important analysis techniques, but actually estimating the relevant variables is as much an art and a product of hard work as it is a science. If the estimates could be done on the basis of some mechanical formula, you could program a computer to do it, and there would be no need for analysts. Therefore, the superior analyst or successful investor must understand what variables are relevant to the valuation process and have the ability to do a superior job of *estimating* these variables. Alternatively, one could be superior if he or she has the ability to interpret the impact or estimate the effect of some public information better than others.

Efficient Markets and Portfolio Management

As noted, studies have indicated that professional money managers cannot beat a buy-and-hold policy on a risk-adjusted basis. One explanation for this generally inferior performance is that there are no superior analysts and the cost of research and trading forces the results of merely adequate analysis into the inferior category. Another explanation, which is favored by the author and has some empirical support from the Value Line and

---

[36]This is a major point made in H. Russell Fogler, "A Modern Theory of Security Analysis," *Journal of Portfolio Management* 19, no. 3 (Spring 1993): 6–14.

analyst recommendation results, is that money management firms employ both superior and inferior analysts and the gains from the recommendations by the few superior analysts are offset by the costs and the poor results derived from the recommendations of the inferior analysts.

This raises the question, should a portfolio be managed actively or passively? The point of the following discussion is that the decision of how one manages the portfolio (actively or passively) should depend on whether the manager has access to superior analysts. A portfolio manager with superior analysts or an investor who believes that he or she has the time and expertise to be a superior investor can manage a portfolio actively by attempting to time major market trends or looking for undervalued securities and trading accordingly. In contrast, without access to superior analysts or the time and ability to be a superior investor, you should manage passively and assume that all securities are properly priced based on their levels of risk.

Portfolio Management with Superior Analysts   A portfolio manager with access to superior analysts who have unique insights and analytical ability should follow their recommendations. The superior analysts should make investment recommendations for a certain proportion of the portfolio, and the portfolio manager should ensure that the risk preferences of the client are maintained.

Also, the superior analysts should be encouraged to concentrate their efforts in mid-cap stocks that possess the liquidity required by institutional portfolio managers, but because they do not receive the attention given the top-tier stocks, the markets for these neglected stocks may be less efficient than the market for large well-known stocks.

Recall that capital markets are expected to be efficient because many investors receive new information and analyze its effect on security values. If the number of analysts following a stock differ, one could conceive of differences in the efficiency of the markets. New information on top-tier stocks is well publicized and rigorously analyzed so the price of these securities should adjust rapidly to reflect the new information. In contrast, middle-tier firms receive less publicity and fewer analysts follow these firms, so prices might be expected to adjust less rapidly to new information. Therefore, the possibility of finding temporarily undervalued securities among these neglected stocks are greater. Again, in line with the cross-section study results, these superior analysts should pay particular attention to the BV/MV ratio, to the size of stocks being analyzed, and to the monetary policy environment.[37]

Portfolio Management without Superior Analysts   If you do not have access to superior analysts, your procedure should be as follows. First, you should *measure your risk preferences* or those of your clients. Then build a portfolio to match this risk level by investing a certain proportion of the portfolio in risky assets and the rest in a risk-free asset as discussed in Chapter 7.

You must *completely diversify* the risky asset portfolio on a global basis so it moves consistently with the world market. In this context, proper diversification means eliminating all unsystematic (unique) variability. In our prior discussion, we estimated the number of securities needed to gain most of the benefits (more than 90 percent) of a completely diversified portfolio at about fifteen to twenty securities. More than one hundred stocks are required for complete diversification. To decide how many securities to actually include in your global portfolio, you must balance the added benefits of complete worldwide diversification against the costs of research for the additional stocks.

---

[37]The evidence is in Eugene F. Fama and Kenneth French, "The Cross-Section of Expected Stock Returns," *Journal of Finance* 47, no. 2 (June 1992): 427–465.

Finally, you should *minimize transaction costs.* Assuming that the portfolio is completely diversified and is structured for the desired risk level, excessive transaction costs that do not generate added returns will detract from your expected rate of return. Three factors are involved in minimizing total transaction costs.

1. Minimize taxes. Methods of accomplishing this objective vary, but it should receive prime consideration.
2. Reduce trading turnover. Trade only to liquidate part of the portfolio or to maintain a given risk level.
3. When you trade, minimize liquidity costs by trading relatively liquid stocks. To accomplish this, submit limit orders to buy or sell several stocks at prices that approximate the specialist's quote. That is, you would put in limit orders to buy stock at the bid price or sell at the ask price. The stock bought or sold first is the most liquid one; all other orders should be withdrawn.

In summary, if you lack access to superior analysts, you should do the following:

1. Determine and quantify your risk preferences.
2. Construct the appropriate portfolio by dividing the total portfolio between risk-free assets and a risky asset portfolio.
3. Diversify completely on a global basis to eliminate all unsystematic risk.
4. Maintain the specified risk level by rebalancing when necessary.
5. Minimize total transaction costs.

The Rationale and Use of Index Funds   As the prior discussion indicates, efficient capital markets and a lack of superior analysts imply that many portfolios should be managed passively so that their performance matches that of the aggregate market, minimizing the costs of research and trading. In response to this desire, several institutions have introduced *market funds,* also referred to as *index funds,* which are security portfolios designed to duplicate the composition, and therefore the performance, of a selected market index series.

Three major investment services started equity index funds in the early 1970s: American National Bank and Trust Company of Chicago; Batterymarch Financial Management Corporation of Boston; and Wells Fargo Investment Advisors, a division of Wells Fargo Bank in San Francisco. All these firms designed equity portfolios to match the performance of the S&P 500 Index. Analysis by the author has documented that the correlation of quarterly rates of return for the index funds and the S&P 500 from 1975 to 1995 exceeded .98. This shows that these index funds generally fulfill their stated goal of matching market performance.

Although these initial funds were available only to institutional investors, at least five index mutual funds are currently available to individuals. In addition, this concept has been extended to other areas of investments. Index bond funds attempt to emulate the bond-market indexes discussed in Chapter 5. Also, some index funds focus on specific segments of the market such as international-bond-index funds, international-stock-index funds that target specific countries, and index funds that target small-capitalization stocks in the United States and Japan.[38] The point is, when portfolio managers decide that they want a given asset class in their portfolio, they often look for index funds to fulfill this need. The use of index funds to get representation may be easier and less costly in terms of research and commissions, and it may provide the same or better performance than what is available from active portfolio management.

---

[38]For a discussion of some of these indexes, see James A. White, "The Index Boom: It's No Longer Just the S&P 500 Stock Index," *Wall Street Journal,* May 19, 1991, C1, C3.

Efficiency in European Equity Markets

With rare exception, the discussion in this chapter has addressed the efficiency of U.S. markets. The growing importance of world markets raises a natural question about the efficiency of securities markets outside the United States. Numerous studies have dealt with this set of questions, and a discussion of them would substantially lengthen the chapter. Fortunately, a monograph by Hawawini contains a review of numerous studies that examined the behavior of European stock prices and evaluated the efficiency of European equity markets.[39] The monograph lists more than 280 studies covering fourteen Western European countries from Austria to the United Kingdom classified by country and within each country into five categories:

1. Market model, beta estimation, and diversification
2. Capital asset pricing model and arbitrage pricing model
3. Weak-form test of market efficiency
4. Semistrong-form tests of market efficiency
5. Strong-form tests of market efficiency

Hawawini offers the following overall conclusion after acknowledging that European markets are smaller and less active than U.S. markets.

> Our review of the literature indicates that despite the peculiarities of European equity markets, the behavior of European stock prices is, with few exceptions, surprisingly similar to that of U.S. common stocks. That is true even for countries with extremely narrow equity markets such as Finland. The view that most European equity markets, particularly those of smaller countries, are informationally inefficient does not seem to be borne out by the data. We will see that most of the results of empirical tests performed on European common stock prices are generally in line with those reported by researchers who used U.S. data.

This implies that when one considers securities outside the United States, it is appropriate to assume a level of efficiency similar to that for U.S. markets.

Investments Online

Capital market prices reflect current news items fairly quickly. On the other hand, a portfolio manager should not ignore news just because prices adjust quickly. News provides information he/she can use to structure portfolios and allows the managers to update potential future scenarios.

A number of news sources are available on the Internet. Some of them, such as **www.bloomberg.com, www.ft.com,** and **www.wsj.com,** were listed in previous chapters. Other sites include:

www.pointcast.com The Web site of Pointcast. This system allows you to have news sent directly to your PC, at no charge.

www.cnnfn.com The financial network site for the Cable News Network (CNN). The CNN Web site is **www.cnn.com.**

www.cnbc.com The Web site of the CNBC cable TV station.

www.abcnews.com, www.cbsnews.com, and **www.nbcnews.com** are the URLs for news from ABC, CBS, and NBC. The NBC site is the home page of the MSNBC station.

---

[39]Gabriel Hawawini, *European Equity Markets: Price Behavior and Efficiency,* Monograph 1984-4/5, Monograph Series in Finance and Economics, Salomon Brothers Center for the Study of Financial Institutions, Graduate School of Business, New York University, 1984.

SUMMARY

- The efficiency of capital markets has implications for the investment analysis and management of your portfolio. Capital markets should be efficient because numerous rational, profit-maximizing investors react quickly to the release of new information. Assuming prices reflect new information, they are unbiased estimates of the securities' true, intrinsic value, and there should be a consistent relationship between the return on an investment and its risk.

- The voluminous research on the EMH has been divided into three segments that have been tested separately. The weak-form EMH states that stock prices fully reflect all market information, so any trading rule that uses past market data to predict future returns should have no value. The results of most studies consistently supported this hypothesis.

- The semistrong-form EMH asserts that security prices adjust rapidly to the release of all public information. The tests of this hypothesis either examine the opportunities to predict future rates of return (either a time series or a cross-section), or they involve event studies in which investigators analyzed whether investors could derive above-average returns from trading on the basis of public information. The test results for this hypothesis were clearly mixed. On the one hand, the results for almost all the event studies related to economic events such as stock splits, initial public offerings, and accounting changes consistently supported the semistrong hypothesis. In contrast, several studies that examined the ability to predict rates of return on the basis of unexpected quarterly earnings, P/E ratios, size, neglected stocks, and the BV/MV ratio, as well as several calendar effects generally did not support the hypothesis.

- The strong-form EMH states that security prices reflect all information. This implies that nobody has private information, so no group should be able to derive above-average returns consistently. Studies that examined the results for corporate insiders and stock exchange specialists do not support the strong-form hypothesis. An analysis of individual analysts as represented by Value Line or by recommendations published in the *Wall Street Journal* give mixed results. The results indicated that the Value Line rankings have significant information but it may not be possible to profit from it, whereas the recommendations by analysts indicated the existence of private information. In contrast, the performance by professional money managers supported the EMH because their risk-adjusted investment performance (whether mutual funds, pension funds, or endowment funds) was typically inferior to results achieved with buy-and-hold-policies.

- The EMH indicates that technical analysis should be of no value. All forms of fundamental analysis are useful, but they are difficult to implement, because they require the ability *to estimate future values* for relevant economic variables. Superior analysis is possible but difficult because it requires superior projections. Those who manage portfolios should constantly evaluate investment advice to determine whether it is superior.

- Without access to superior analytical advice, you should run your portfolio like an index fund. In contrast, those with superior analytical ability should be allowed to make decisions, but they should concentrate their efforts on mid-cap firms and neglected firms where there is a higher probability of discovering misvalued stocks. The analysis should be particularly concerned with a firm's BV/MV ratio and its size.

- This chapter contains some good news and some bad news. The good news is that the practice of investment analysis and portfolio management is not an art that has been lost to the great computer in the sky. Viable professions still await those willing to extend the effort and able to accept the pressures. The bad news is that many bright, hardworking people with extensive resources make the game tough. In fact, those competitors have created a fairly efficient capital market in which it is extremely difficult for most analysts and portfolio managers to achieve superior results.

Questions

1. Discuss the rationale for expecting an efficient capital market. What factor would you look for to differentiate the market efficiency for two alternative stocks?
2. Define and discuss the weak-form EMH. Describe the two sets of tests used to examine the weak-form EMH.
3. Define and discuss the semistrong-form EMH. Describe the two sets of tests used to examine the semistrong-form EMH.
4. What is meant by the term *abnormal rate of return*?
5. Describe how you would compute the abnormal rate of return for a stock for a period surrounding an economic event. Give a brief example for a stock with a beta of 1.40.
6. Assume you want to test the EMH by comparing alternative trading rules to a buy-and-hold policy. Discuss the three common mistakes that can bias the results against the EMH.
7. Describe the results of a study that supported the semistrong-form EMH. Discuss the nature of the test and specifically why the results support the hypothesis.
8. Describe the results of a study that did *not* support the semistrong-form EMH. Discuss the nature of the test and specifically why the results did not support the hypothesis.
9. For many of the EMH tests, it is really a test of a "joint hypothesis." Discuss what is meant by this concept and, in instance, what are the joint hypotheses being tested?
10. Define and discuss the strong-form EMH. Why do some observers contend that the strong-form hypothesis really requires a perfect market in addition to an efficient market? Be specific.
11. Discuss how you would test the strong-form EMH. Why are these tests relevant? Give a brief example.
12. Describe the results of a study that did *not* support the strong-form EMH. Discuss the test involved and specifically why the results reported did not support the hypothesis.
13. Describe the results of a study that supported the strong-form EMH. Discuss the test involved and specifically why these results support the hypothesis.
14. What does the EMH imply for the use of technical analysis?
15. What does the EMH imply for fundamental analysis? Discuss specifically what it does not imply.
16. In a world of efficient capital markets, what do you have to do to be a superior analyst? How would you test whether an analyst were superior?
17. What advice would you give to your superior analysts in terms of the set of firms to analyze and variables that should be considered in the analysis? Discuss your reasoning for this advice.
18. How should a portfolio manager without any superior analysts run his or her portfolio?
19. Describe the goals of an index fund. Discuss the contention that index funds are the ultimate answer in a world with efficient capital markets.
20. At a social gathering you meet the portfolio manager for the trust department of a local bank. He confides to you that he has been following the recommendations of the department's six analysts for an extended period and has found that two are superior, two are average, and two are clearly inferior. What would you recommend that he do to run his portfolio?
21. Discuss your reaction to Hawawini's summary of findings related to the EMH for the European equity markets. Were you surprised?
22. Describe a test of the weak-form EMH for the Japanese stock market and indicate where you would get the required data.
23. *CFA Examination I (1992)*
    a. List and briefly define the *three* forms of the Efficient Market Hypothesis. [6 minutes]
    b. Discuss the role of a portfolio manager in a perfectly efficient market. [9 minutes]
24. *CFA Examination II (1993)*
    Tom Max, TMP's quantitative analyst, has developed a portfolio construction model about which he is excited. To create the model, Max made a list of the stocks currently in the S&P 500 Stock Index and obtained annual operating cash flow, price, and total return data for each issue for the past five years. As of each year-end, this universe was divided into five equal-weighted portfolios of one hundred issues each, with selection based solely on the price/cash flow rankings of the individual stocks. Each portfolio's average annual return was then calculated.

    During this five-year period, the linked returns from the portfolios with the lowest price/cash flow ratio generated an annualized total return of 19.0 percent, or 3.1 percentage

points better than the 15.9 percent return on the S&P 500 Stock Index. Max also noted that the lowest price–cash-flow portfolio had a below-market beta of 0.91 over this same time span.

   a. Briefly comment on Max's use of the beta measure as an indicator of portfolio risk in light of recent academic tests of its explanatory power with respect to stock returns. [5 minutes]

   b. You are familiar with the literature on market anomalies and inefficiencies. Against this background, discuss Max's use of a single-factor model (price–cash flow) in his research. [8 minutes]

   c. Identify and briefly describe *four* specific concerns about Max's test procedures and model design. (The issues already discussed in your answers to Parts a and b above may *not* be used in answering Part c.) [12 minutes]

25. *CFA Examination III (1995)*

   a. Briefly explain the concept of the *efficient market hypothesis* (EMH) and each of its three forms— *weak, semistrong, and strong*—and briefly discuss the degree to which existing empirical evidence supports each of the three forms of the EMH. [8 minutes]

   b. Briefly discuss the implications of the efficient market hypothesis for investment policy as it applies to:

    (i) technical analysis in the form of charting, and

    (ii) fundamental analysis. [4 minutes]

   c. Briefly explain *two* major roles or responsibilities of portfolio managers in an efficient market environment. [4 minutes]

   d. Briefly discuss whether active asset allocation among countries could consistently outperform a world market index. Include a discussion of the implications of *integration versus segmentation* of international financial markets as it pertains to portfolio diversification, but ignore the issue of stock selection. [6 minutes]

Problems

1. Compute the abnormal rates of return for the following stocks during period t (ignore differential systematic risk):

Stock	R_{it}	R_{mt}
B	11.5%	4.0%
F	10.0	8.5
T	14.0	9.6
C	12.0	15.3
E	15.9	12.4

R_{it} = return for stock i during period t

R_{mt} = return for the aggregate market during period t

2. Compute the abnormal rates of return for the five stocks in Problem 1 assuming the following systematic risk measures (betas):

Stock	i
B	0.95
F	1.25
T	1.45
C	0.70
E	−0.30

3. Compare the abnormal returns in Problems 1 and 2 and discuss the reason for the difference in each case.

4. You are given the following data regarding the performance of a group of stocks recommended by an analyst and set of stocks with matching betas:

Stock	Beginning Price	Ending Price	Dividend
C	43	47	1.50
C-match	22	24	1.00
R	75	73	2.00
R-match	42	38	1.00
L	28	34	1.25
L-match	18	16	1.00
W	52	57	2.00
W-match	38	44	1.50
S	63	68	1.75
S-match	32	34	1.00

Based on the composite results for these stocks (assume equal weights), would you judge this individual to be a superior analyst? Discuss your reasoning.

5. Look up the daily trading volume for the following stocks during a recent five-day period.

♦ Merck
♦ Anheuser Busch
♦ Intel
♦ McDonald's
♦ General Electric

Randomly select five stocks from the NYSE and examine their daily trading volume for the same five days.

a. What are the average daily volumes for the two samples?
b. Would you expect this difference to have an impact on the efficiency of the markets for the two samples? Why or why not?

References

Affleck-Graves, John, and Richard R. Mendenhall. "The Relation Between the Value Line Enigma and Post-Earnings-Announcement Drift." *Journal of Financial Economics* 21, no. 1 (February 1992).

Ball, Ray. "The Theory of Stock Market Efficiency: Accomplishments and Limitations." *Journal of Applied Corporate Finance* 8, no. 1 (Spring, 1995).

Balvers, Ronald J., Thomas F. Cosimano, and Bill McDonald. "Predicting Stock Returns in an Efficient Market." *Journal of Finance* 45, no. 4 (September 1990).

Banz, R. W. "The Relationship Between Return and Market Value of Common Stocks." *Journal of Financial Economics* 9, no. 1 (March 1981).

Barry, Christopher B., and Stephen J. Brown. "Differential Information and the Small Firm Effect." *Journal of Financial Economics* 13, no. 2 (June 1984).

Basu, Senjoy. "Investment Performance of Common Stocks in Relation to Their Price-Earnings Ratios: A Test of the Efficient Market Hypothesis." *Journal of Finance* 32, no. 3 (June 1977).

Beatty, Randolph, and Jay Ritter. "Investments Banking, Reputation, and the Underpricing of Initial Public Offerings." *Journal of Financial Economics* 15, no.1 (March 1986).

Berkowitz, Stephen A., Louis D. Finney, and Dennis Logue. *The Investment Performance of Corporate Pension Plans.* New York: Quorum Books, 1988.

Bernard, Victor. "Capital Markets Research in Accounting During the 1980's: A Critical Review," in *The State of Accounting Research as We Enter the 1990's,* Thomas J. Frecka, Ed. (Urbana: University of Illinois Press, 1989).

Bernard, Victor L., and Jacob K. Thomas. "Post-Earnings–Announcements Drift: Delayed Price Response or Risk Premium?" *Journal of Accounting Research* 27, Supplement (1989).

Fama, Eugene F. "Efficient Capital Market: II." *Journal of Finance* 46, no. 5 (December 1991).

Harvey, Campbell. "The World Price of Covariance Risk." *Journal of Finance* 46, no.1 (March 1991).

Hawawini, Gabriel. *European Equity Markets: Price Behavior and Efficiency,* Monograph 1984-4/5. Monograph Series in Finance and Economics, Salomon Brothers Center for the Study of Financial Institutions, Graduate School of Business, New York University, 1984.

Huberman, Gur, and Shmuel Kandel. "Market Efficiency and Value Line's Record." *Journal of Business* 63, no. 2 (April 1990).

Ibbotson, Roger G., Jody Sindelar, and Jay R. Ritter. "Initial Public Offerings." *Journal of Applied Corporate Finance* 1, no. 3 (Summer 1988).

Jain, Prom C. "Response of Hourly Stock Prices and Trading Volume to Economic News." *Journal of Business* 61, no. 2 (April 1988).

Keim, Donald B. "Size-Related Anomalies and Stock Return Seasonality." *Journal of Financial Economics* 12, no. 1 (June 1983).

Keim, Donald B., and Robert F. Stambaugh. "Predicting Returns in Stock and Bond Markets." *Journal of Financial Economics* 17, no. 2 (December 1986).

Lev, Baruch. "On the Usefulness of Earnings and Earning Research: Lessons and Directions from Two Decades of Empirical Research," *Journal of Accounting Research* (Supplement, 1989).

Malkiel, Burton G. *A Random Walk Down Wall Street.* New York: Norton, 1995.

Miller, Robert E., and Frank K. Reilly. "Examination of Mispricing, Returns, and Uncertainty for Initial Public Offerings." *Financial Management* 16, no. 2 (January 1987).

Ou, J. and S. Penman, "Financial Statement Analysis and the Prediction of Stock Returns." *Journal of Accounting and Economics* (November 1989).

Reilly, Frank K., and Eugene F. Drzycimski. "Short-Run Profits from Stock Splits." *Financial Management* 10, no. 3 (Summer 1981).

Seyhun, H. Nejat. "Insider Profits, Costs of Trading, and Market Efficiency." *Journal of Financial Economics* 16, no. 2 (June 1986).

GLOSSARY

Abnormal rate of return   The amount by which a security's return differs from the market's expected rate of return based on the market's rate of return and the security's relationship with the market.

Anomalies   Security price relationships that appear to contradict a well-regarded hypothesis; in this case, the efficient market hypothesis.

Autocorrelation test   A test of the weak-form efficient market hypothesis that compares security price changes over time to check for predictable correlation patterns.

Earnings surprise   A company announcement of earnings that differ from analysts' prevailing expectations.

Efficient capital market   A market in which security prices rapidly reflect all information about securities.

Event study   Research that examines the reaction of a security's price to a specific company or world event or news announcement.

Expected rate of return   The return that analysts' calculations suggest a security should provide, based on the market's rate of return during the period and the security's relationship to the market.

Filter rule   A trading rule that recommends security transactions when price changes exceed a previously determined percentage.

Informationally efficient market   A more technical term for an efficient capital market that emphasizes the role of information.

Runs test   A test of the weak-form efficient market hypothesis that checks for trends that persist longer in terms of positive or negative price changes than one would expect for a random series.

Semistrong-form efficient market hypothesis   The belief that security prices fully reflect all publicly available information, including information from security transactions and company, economic, and political news.

Strong-form efficient market hypothesis   The belief that security prices fully reflect all information from both public and private sources.

Trading rule   A formula for deciding on current transactions based on historical data.

Weak-form efficient market hypothesis   The belief that security prices fully reflect all security market information.

P A R T

VALUATION PRINCIPLES AND PRACTICES

BASED UPON THE CHAPTERS IN THE FIRST TWO PARTS, you know the purpose of investing and the importance of an appropriate asset allocation decision. You also know about the numerous investment instruments available on a global basis, and you have the background regarding the institutional characteristics of the capital markets. In addition, you are aware of the major developments in investment theory as they relate to portfolio theory, capital asset pricing, and efficient capital markets. Therefore, at this point you are in a position to consider the theory and practice of estimating the value of various securities, which is the heart of investing and leads to the construction of a portfolio that is consistent with your risk-return objectives. You will recall that the investment decision is based on a comparison of an asset's intrinsic value and its market price.

The major source of information regarding a stock or bond is the corporation's financial statements. Chapter 9 considers what financial statements are available and what information they provide, followed by an extended discussion of the financial ratios used to answer several questions about a firm's liquidity, its operating performance, its risk profile, and its growth potential.

In Chapter 10, we emphasize a top-down, three-step valuation process that considers market analysis, then industry analysis, and finally company and stock valuation. As part of this, we consider the basic principles of valuation and apply these principles to the valuation of bonds, preferred stock, and common stock. Because of the complexity and importance of valuing common stock, we consider two general approaches to this task: (1) discounted cash-flow valuation techniques, and (2) several relative valuation techniques such as price-to-earnings or price-to-book value. We conclude by reviewing the basic factors that determine the required rate of return for an investment and the growth rate of earnings and dividends for domestic and international firms.

Chapter 11 deals with a major question for the global investor—how to allocate assets across countries based on the state of their economies and the outlook for their security markets. We examine some specific tools used in this analysis. Additionally, within each country it is necessary to make a further allocation among available asset classes including stocks, bonds, and cash.

Analysis of Financial Statements

This chapter answers the following questions:

♦ What are the major financial statements provided by firms and what specific information does each of them contain?

♦ Why do we use financial ratios to examine the performance of a firm, and why is it important to examine performance relative to the economy and a firm's industry?

♦ What are the major categories for financial ratios and what questions are answered by the ratios in these categories?

♦ What specific ratios help determine a firm's internal liquidity, operating performance, risk profile, growth potential, and external liquidity?

♦ How can the DuPont analysis help evaluate a firm's return on equity over time?

♦ What are some of the major differences between U.S. and non-U.S. financial statements and how do these differences affect the financial ratios?

♦ What is a "quality" balance sheet or income statement?

♦ Why is financial statement analysis done if markets are efficient and forward-looking?

♦ What major financial ratios help analysts in the following areas: stock valuation, estimating and evaluating systematic risk, predicting the credit ratings on bonds, and predicting bankruptcy?

Financial statements are the main source of information for major investment decisions, including whether to lend money to a firm (invest in its bonds), to acquire an ownership stake in a firm (buy its preferred or common stock), or to buy warrants or options on a firm's stock. In this chapter, we first introduce a corporation's major financial statements

and discuss why and how financial ratios are useful. In subsequent sections, we provide example computations of ratios that reflect internal liquidity, operating performance, risk analysis, growth analysis, and external liquidity. Because analysts deal with foreign stocks and bonds, we also discuss factors that affect the analysis of foreign financial statements. In the final section, we address four major areas in investments where financial ratios have been effectively employed.

Our example company in this chapter is Walgreen Company, the largest retail drugstore chain in the United States. It operates 2,358 drugstores in 34 states and Puerto Rico. General merchandise accounts for 25 percent of total sales and pharmacy generates 44 percent.

MAJOR FINANCIAL STATEMENTS

Financial statements are intended to provide information on the resources available to management, how these resources were financed, and what the firm accomplished with them. Corporate shareholder annual and quarterly reports include three required financial statements: the balance sheet, the income statement, and the statement of cash flows. In addition, reports that must be filed with the Securities and Exchange Commission (SEC), for example, the 10-K and 10-Q reports, carry detailed information about the firm such as information on loan agreements and data on product line and subsidiary performance. Information from the basic financial statements can be used to calculate financial ratios and to analyze the operations of the firm to determine what factors influence a firm's earnings and cash flows.

Generally Accepted Accounting Principles

Among the input used to construct the financial statements are **generally accepted accounting principles (GAAP)**, which are formulated by the Financial Accounting Standards Board (FASB). The FASB recognizes that it would be improper for all companies to use identical and restrictive accounting principles. Some flexibility and choice are needed because industries and firms within industries differ in their operating environments. Therefore, the FASB allows companies some flexibility to choose among appropriate GAAP for their use. This flexibility allows the firm's managers to choose accounting standards that best reflect company practice. On the negative side, this flexibility can allow firms to appear healthier than they really are. Given this possibility, the financial analyst must rigorously analyze the available financial information to separate those firms that *appear* attractive from those that actually are in good financial shape.

Fortunately, the FASB requires that financial statements include footnotes that inform analysts regarding which accounting principles were used by the firm. Because accounting principles frequently differ among firms, the footnote information assists the financial analyst in adjusting the financial statements of companies so the analyst can better compare "apples with apples."

Balance Sheet

The **balance sheet** shows what resources (assets) the firm controls and how it has financed these assets. Specifically, it indicates the current and fixed assets available to the firm *at a point in time* (the end of the fiscal year or the end of a quarter). In most cases, the firm owns these assets, but some firms lease assets on a long-term basis. How the firm has financed the acquisition of these assets is indicated by its mixture of current liabilities

Table 9.1   *Walgreen Company and Subsidiaries Consolidated Balance Sheet ($ Millions)*
Years Ended August 31, 1995, 1996, and 1997

	1997	1996	1995
Assets			
Current Assets			
Cash and cash equivalents	$ 73	$ 9	$ 22
Trade accounts receivable—net of allowances	376	288	246
Inventories	1,733	1,632	1,454
Other current assets	144	90	91
Total Current Assets	2,326	2,019	1,813
Property, plant, and equipment	2,502	2,108	1,831
Less accumulated depreciation	748	659	582
Property—Net	1,754	1,448	1,249
Other non-current assets	125	166	191
Total assets	4,207	3,634	3,253
Liabilities and Shareholders' Equity			
Current Liabilities			
Short-term debt	$ 0	$ 0	$ 0
Current portion of long-term debt	0	0	0
Trade accounts payable	813	692	606
Accrued expenses and other liabilities	554	467	448
Income taxes payable	72	23	23
Total Current Liabilities	1,439	1,182	1,078
Long-term Debt	0	0	0
Other Non-current Liabilities	282	263	240
Deferred Income Taxes	113	145	142
Preferred Stock, $.25 par value, authorized 8,000,000 shares; none issued	—	—	—
Common Shareholders' Equity			
Common stock, $.3125 par value, authorized 800 million shares; issued and outstanding 246,141,072 in 1996 and 1995	77	77	77
Retained earnings	2,266	1,966	1,716
Total Common Shareholders' Equity	2,373	2,043	1,793
Total Liabilities and Common Shareholders' Equity	$4,207	$3,634	$3,253

Source: Walgreen annual reports.

(accounts payable or short-term borrowing), long-term liabilities (fixed debt), and own-ers' equity (preferred stock, common stock, and retained earnings).

The balance sheet for Walgreen in Table 9.1 represents the *stock* of assets and its financing mix as of the end of Walgreen's fiscal year, August 31, 1995, 1996, and 1997.

Income Statement

The **income statement** contains information on the profitability of the firm during some *period of time* (a quarter or a year). In contrast to the balance sheet, which indicates the firm's financial position at a fixed point in time, the income statement indicates the *flow* of sales, expenses, and earnings during a period of time. The income statement for Walgreen for the years 1995, 1996, and 1997 appears in Table 9.2. We concentrate on earnings from operations after tax as the relevant net earnings figure. In the case of Walgreen, this is the same as net income; the firm has no nonrecurring or unusual income or expense items.

Table 9.2   *Walgreen Company and Subsidiaries Consolidated Statement of Income ($ Millions, Except Per Share Data). Years Ended August 31, 1995, 1996, and 1997*

	1997	1996	1995
Net sales	$ 13,363	$ 11,778	$ 10,395
Cost of goods sold	9,682	8,515	7,482
Gross profit	3,681	3,264	2,913
Selling, general and administrative expenses	2,973	2,660	2,393
Operating profit (EBIT)	708	604	520
Interest Income	6	5	5
Interest Expense	2	2	1
Operating income before income taxes	712	607	524
Provision for income taxes	276	235	203
Operating income after taxes	436	372	321
Reported net income	436	372	321
Reported net income available for Common	436	372	321
Per Common Share			
Operating income after taxes	$ 0.88	$ 0.75	$ 0.65
Reported net income	$ 0.88	$ 0.75	$ 0.65
Dividends declared	$ 0.24	$ 0.22	$ 0.20
Average Number of Common Shares Outstanding ('000)	493,790	495,664	493,524

Source: Walgreen annual reports.

Statement of Cash Flows

Based upon our earlier discussion on valuation, you know that cash flows are a critical input. In response to a growing interest in this data, accountants now require firms to provide such information. The **statement of cash flows** integrates the information on the balance sheet and income statement. For a given period, it shows the effects on the firm's cash flow of income flows (based on the most recent year's income statement) and changes in various items on the balance sheet (based on the two most recent annual balance sheets). The result is a set of cash flow values that you can use to estimate the value of a firm and evaluate the risk and return of the firm's bonds and stock.

The statement of cash flows has three sections: cash flows from operating activities, cash flows from investing activities, and cash flows from financing activities. The sum total of the cash flows from the three sections is the net change in the cash position of the firm. This bottom-line number should equal the difference in the cash balance between the ending and beginning balance sheets. The statements of cash flow for Walgreen for 1995, 1996, and 1997 appear in Table 9.3.

Cash Flow from Operating Activities   This section lists the sources and uses of cash that arise from the normal operations of a firm. In general , the net cash flow from operations is computed as the net income reported on the income statement including changes in net working capital items (ie, receivables, inventories, and so on) plus adjustments for noncash revenues and expenses (such as depreciation), or:

$$\text{Cash Flow from Operating Activities} = \text{Net Income} + \text{Noncash Revenue and Expenses} + \text{Changes in Net Working Capital Items}$$

Consistent with our discussion above, the cash account is not included in the calculations of cash flow from operations. Notably, Walgreen has been able to generate consistently large and growing cash flows from operations after accounting for consistent increases in receivables and inventory.

Table 9.3 *Walgreen Company and Subsidiaries Consolidated Statement of Cash Flows ($ Millions) Years Ended August 31, 1995, 1996, and 1997*

	1997	1996	1995
Cash Flow from Operating Activities:			
Net Income	$ 436	$ 372	$ 321
Adjustments to reconcile net income to net cash provided by operating activities:			
Cumulative effect of accounting changes	0	0	0
Depreciation and amortization	164	147	132
Deferred income taxes and other items	8	3	(7)
Other	8	5	3
Changes in operating assets and liabilities (used in) provided from continuing operations:			
(Increase) decrease in trade accounts receivable	(74)	(60)	(36)
(Increase) decrease in inventories	(101)	(178)	(191)
(Increase) decrease in other current assets	0	1	(8)
Increase (decrease) in trade accounts payable	121	85	73
Accrued expenses and other liabilities	73	42	42
Income taxes	12	(9)	1
Insurance reserve	0	3	15
Net Cash Provided by Operating Activities	$ 650	$ 411	$ 345
Cash Flow from Investing Activities:			
Additions to property, plant, and equipment	$ (485)	$ (365)	$ (310)
Net borrowing against corporate-owned life insurance	16	47	(34)
Net proceeds from marketable securities	0	0	30
Disposition of property and equipment	15	18	15
Net Cash Used in Investing Activities	$ (486)	$ (299)	$ (299)
Cash Flow from Financing Activities:			
Cash dividends	$ (116)	$ (105)	$ (93)
Cost of employee stock purchase and option plans	(18)	(13)	(6)
Proceeds from employee stock plans	35	(7)	4
Payments of long-term obligations	(1)	0	(7)
Net Cash Used in Financing Activities	$ (100)	$ (125)	$ (102)
Net increase (decrease) in cash and cash equivalents	64	(13)	(56)
Cash and cash equivalents—beginning of year	9	22	78
Cash and cash equivalents—end of year	73	9	22

Source: Walgreen annual reports.

Cash Flows from Investing Activities   A firm makes investments in both its own noncurrent and fixed assets, and the equity of other firms (which may be subsidiaries or joint ventures of the parent firm. They are listed in the "investment" account of the balance sheet). Increases and decreases in these non-current accounts are considered investment activities. The cash flow from investing activities is the change in gross plant and equipment plus the change in the investment account. The changes are added if they represent a source of funds; otherwise they are subtracted. The dollar changes in these accounts are computed using the firm's two most recent balance sheets. Most firms experience negative cash flows from investments due to capital expenditures. Walgreen results likewise reflect large negative values due to significant capital expenditures.

Cash Flows from Financing Activities   Cash flow from financing activities is computed as financing sources minus financing uses. Inflows are created by actions increasing notes payable and long-term liability and equity accounts, such as bond and stock issues. Financing uses (outflows) include decreases in such accounts (that is, the pay down

of liability accounts or the repurchase of common shares). Dividend payments to equityholders are likewise a financing cash outflow.

The sum total of the cash flows from operating, investing, and financing activities is the net increase or decrease in the firm's cash. The statement of cash flows provides some of the cash flow detail that is lacking in the balance sheet and income statement.

Alternative Measures of Cash Flow

There are several cash flow measures an analyst can use to determine the underlying health of the corporation.

Cash Flow from Operations   This includes the traditional measure of cash flow, which is equal to net income plus depreciation expense and deferred taxes. But as we have just seen, it is also necessary to adjust for changes in operating (current) assets and liabilities that either use or provide cash. For example, an increase in accounts receivable implies that either the firm is using cash to support this increase or the firm did not collect all the sales reported. In contrast, an increase in a current liability account such as accounts payable means that the firm acquired some assets but has not paid for them, which is a source (increase) of cash flow (that is, the firm's suppliers are implicitly providing financing to the firm). These changes in operating assets or liabilities can add to or subtract from the cash flow estimated from the traditional measure of cash flow: net income plus noncash expenses. The table below compares the cash flow from operations figures (Table 9.3) to the traditional cash flow figures for Walgreen from 1995 to 1997:

	Traditional Cash Flow Equals Net Income + Depreciation + Change in Def. Taxes	Cash Flow from Operations from Statement of Cash Flows
1997	568	650
1996	522	411
1995	456	345

In two of the three years the cash flow from operations was less than the traditional cash flow estimate because of the several adjustments needed to arrive at cash flow from options. Therefore, using this more exact measure of cash flow, the Walgreen ratios would not have been as strong. For many firms this is fairly typical because the effect of working capital changes is often a large negative cash flow due to necessary increases in receivables or inventory (especially for high-growth companies).

Free Cash Flow   Free cash flow modifies cash flow from operations to recognize that some investing and financing activities are critical to the firm. It is assumed that these expenditures must be made before a firm can use its cash flow for other purposes such as reducing debt outstanding or repurchasing common stock. The two additional expenditures considered are: (1) capital expenditures (an investing expenditure) and (2) dividends (a financing activity). These two items are subtracted from cash flow from operations as follows (some only subtract capital expenditures):

	Cash Flow from Operations	− Capital Expenditures	− Dividends	= Free Cash Flow
1997	650	485	116	49
1996	411	365	105	(59)
1995	345	310	93	(58)

For firms involved in leveraged buyouts, this free cash flow number is critical because the new owners typically want to use the free cash flow as funds available for retiring

outstanding debt. It is not unusual for a firm's free cash flow to be a negative value. The free cash flow for Walgreen has been negative because of fairly heavy capital expenditures and larger dividends. Notably, this free cash flow value or a variation of it without dividends will be used in the subsequent cash flow valuation models.

Purpose of Financial Statement Analysis

Financial statement analysis seeks to evaluate management performance in several important areas, including profitability, efficiency, and risk. Although we will necessarily analyze historical data, the ultimate goal is to provide insights that will help you to *project* future management performance, including pro forma balance sheets, income statements, cash flows, and risk. It is the firm's expected future performance that determines whether you should lend money to a firm or invest in it.

ANALYSIS OF FINANCIAL RATIOS

Analysts use financial ratios because numbers in isolation typically convey little meaning. Knowing that a firm earned a net income of $100,000 is less informative than also knowing the sales figure that generated this income ($1 million or $10 million) and the assets or capital committed to the enterprise. Thus, ratios are intended to provide meaningful *relationships* between individual values in the financial statements.

Because the major financial statements report numerous individual items, it is possible to produce numerous potential ratios, many of which will have little value. Therefore, you want to limit your examination to the most relevant ratios and categorize them into groups that provide information on important economic characteristics of the firm. It is also important to recognize the need for relative analysis.

Importance of Relative Financial Ratios

Just as a single number from a financial statement is of little use, an individual financial ratio has little value except in relation to comparable ratios for other entities. That is, *only relative financial ratios are relevant.* The important comparisons examine a firm's performance relative to

♦ The aggregate economy
♦ Its industry or industries
♦ Its major competitors within the industry
♦ Its past performance (time-series analysis)

The comparison to the aggregate economy is important because almost all firms are influenced by the economy's expansions and contractions (recessions) in the business cycle. It is unreasonable to expect an increase in the profit margin for a firm during a recession; a stable margin might be encouraging under such conditions. In contrast, a small increase in a firm's profit margin during a major business expansion may be a sign of weakness. Comparing a firm's financial ratios relative to a similar set of ratios for the economy will help you to understand how a firm reacts to the business cycle and will help you *estimate* the future performance of the firm during subsequent business cycles.

Probably the most popular comparison relates a firm's performance to that of its industry. Different industries affect the firms within them differently, but this relationship is always significant. The industry effect is strongest for industries with homogeneous products such as steel, rubber, glass, and wood products, because all firms within these

industries experience coincidental shifts in demand. In addition, these firms employ fairly similar technology and production processes. For example, even the best-managed steel firm experiences a decline in sales and profit margins during a recession. In such a case, the relevant question might be, how did the firm perform relative to other steel firms? As part of this, you should examine an industry's performance relative to aggregate economic activity to understand how the industry responds to the business cycle.

Data for industry average and median financial ratios are published by a number of organizations such as Dun & Bradstreet *(Industry Norms and Key Business Ratios);* Robert Morris Associates *(Annual Statement Studies);* Standard and Poor's *(Analysts Handbook);* and the Federal Trade Commission *(Quarterly Financial Report for Manufacturing, Mining and Trade Corporations).* These sources are available at most libraries.

When comparing a firm's financial ratios to industry ratios, you may not feel comfortable using the average (mean) industry value when there is wide nonsymmetric dispersion of individual firm ratios within the industry. This specific problem can be addressed by using industry median ratios (one-half of firms in the industry have ratios above the median value; one-half have ratios below it). An interquartile range for the ratio may also be helpful.

Alternatively, you may believe that the firm being analyzed is not typical—(that is, it has a unique component. Under these conditions, a **cross-sectional analysis** may be appropriate, in which you compare the firm to a subset of firms within the industry that are comparable in size or characteristics. As an example, within the computer industry, you might want to compare IBM to firms such as Apple rather than industry average data, which include numerous small firms that produce unique products or services.

Another practical problem with comparing a firm's ratios to an industry average is that many large firms are multi-product and multi-industry in nature. Inappropriate comparisons can arise when a multi-industry firm is evaluated against the ratios from a single industry. Two approaches can help mitigate this problem. The first method is to use cross-sectional analysis by comparing the firm against a rival that operates in many of the same markets. The second method is to construct composite industry average ratios for the firm. To do this, the firm's annual report or 10-K filing is used to identify each industry in which the firm operates and the proportion of total firm sales derived from each industry. Composite industry average ratios are constructed by computing weighted average ratios based on the proportion of firm sales derived from each industry.

You also should examine a firm's relative performance over time to determine whether it is progressing or declining. This **time-series analysis** is helpful when estimating future performance. For example, some may want to calculate the average of a ratio for a five- or ten-year period without considering the trend. This can result in misleading conclusions. For example, an average rate of return of 10 percent can be based on rates of return that have increased from 5 percent to 15 percent over time, or it can be based on a series that begins at 15 percent and declines to 5 percent. Obviously, the difference in the trend for these series would have a major impact on your estimate for the future.

COMPUTATION OF FINANCIAL RATIOS

We divide the financial ratios into six major categories that will help us understand the important economic characteristics of a firm. In this section, we focus on describing the various ratios and computing them using Walgreen's data. Comparative analysis of Walgreen's ratios with the economy and industry will be discussed in a later section. The six categories are

1. Common size statements
2. Internal liquidity (solvency)

3. Operating performance
    a. Operating efficiency
    b. Operating profitability
4. Risk analysis
    a. Business risk
    b. Financial risk
5. Growth analysis
6. External liquidity (marketability)

Common Size Statements

Common size statements "normalize" balance sheet and income statement items to allow easier comparison of different-size firms. A common size balance sheet expresses all balance sheet accounts as a *percentage of total assets.* A common size income statement expresses all income statement items as a *percentage of sales.* Table 9.4 is the common size balance sheet for Walgreen, and Table 9.5 contains the common size income statement. Common size ratios are useful to quickly compare two different-size firms and to examine trends over time within a single firm. Common size statements also give an analyst insight into the structure of a firm's financial statements, that is, the percentage of sales consumed by production costs or interest expense, the proportion of assets that are liquid, or the proportion of liabilities that are short-term obligations. For example, for Walgreen the common size balance sheet shows a small decline in the ratio of current assets and an increase in the proportion of net property. Alternatively, the common size income statement in Table 9.5 shows Walgreen's cost of goods sold was quite stable from 1993 to 1997 in proportion to sales. This combined with a lower ratio for selling, general and administrative expenses means the firm has experienced a consistent increase in its operating profit margin before and after taxes.

EVALUATING INTERNAL LIQUIDITY

Internal liquidity (solvency) ratios indicate the ability of the firm to meet future short-term financial obligations. They compare near-term financial obligations such as accounts payable or notes payable with current assets or cash flows that will be available to meet these obligations.

Internal Liquidity Ratios

Current Ratio   Clearly the best-known liquidity measure is the current ratio, which examines the relationship between current assets and current liabilities as follows:

$$\text{Current Ratio} = \frac{\text{Current Assets}}{\text{Current Liabilities}}$$

For Walgreen, the current ratios were (all ratios are in thousands of dollars)

$$1997: \frac{2,326}{1,439} = 1.62$$

$$1996: \frac{2,019}{1,182} = 1.71$$

$$1995: \frac{1,813}{1,078} = 1.68$$

Table 9.4	*Walgreen Company and Subsidiaries Common Size Balance Sheet** *Years Ended August 31, 1993, 1994, 1995, 1996, and 1997*				

	1997	1996	1995	1994	1993
Assets					
Current Assets					
Cash and cash equivalents	0.02%	0.24%	0.68%	2.68%	3.61%
Trade accounts receivable—net of allowances	8.94	7.94	7.57	6.67	5.50
Inventories	41.19	44.91	44.70	43.43	43.15
Other current assets	3.42	2.47	2.79	3.68	4.28
Total Current Assets	55.29	55.57	55.74	57.51	57.71
Property, plant, and equipment	59.47	58.00	56.29	54.91	54.45
Less accumulated depreciation	17.78	18.14	17.89	17.59	17.87
Property—Net	41.69	39.86	38.40	37.32	36.58
Other non-current assets	3.02	4.58	5.86	5.17	5.71
Total assets	100.00%	100.00%	100.00%	100.00%	100.00%
Liabilities and Shareholders' Equity					
Current Liabilities					
Short-term debt	0.00%	0.00%	0.00%	0.00%	0.00%
Current portion of long-term debt	0.00	0.00	0.00	0.00	0.00
Trade accounts payable	19.32	19.04	18.64	18.32	16.85
Accrued expenses and other liabilities	13.17	12.86	13.78	17.03	17.14
Income taxes payable	1.71	0.63	0.72	0.77	0.86
Total Current Liabilities	34.20	32.53	33.14	0.36	34.85
Long-Term Debt	0.00	0.00	0.00	0.00	0.00
Other Noncurrent Liabilities	6.70	7.25	7.38	3.81	3.93
Deferred Income Taxes	2.69	4.00	4.37	5.97	6.84
Preferred Stock, $.25 par value, authorized 8,000,000 shares; none issued	—	—	—	—	—
Common Shareholders' Equity					
Common stock, $.15625 par value, authorized 1,600 million shares; issued and outstanding 493,789,966 in 1997 and 492,282,144 in 1996 and 1995	2.54	2.12	2.36	2.64	3.03
Retained Earnings	53.86	54.11	52.75	51.46	51.35
Total Common Shareholders' Equity	56.40	56.23	55.11	54.10	54.38
Total Liabilities and Common Shareholders' Equity	100.00%	100.00%	100.00%	100.00%	100.00%

*Percentages may not add to 100.0% due to rounding.

These current ratios experienced a small decline during the three years and are consistent with the "typical" current ratio. As always, it is important to compare these values with similar figures for the firm's industry and the aggregate market. If the ratios differ from the industry results, it is necessary to determine what causes the difference and what might explain it. This comparative analysis is considered in a subsequent section.

Quick Ratio   Some observers believe you should not consider total current assets when gauging the ability of the firm to meet current obligations because inventories and some other assets included in current assets might not be very liquid. As an alternative, they prefer the quick ratio, which relates current liabilities to only relatively liquid current assets (cash items and accounts receivable) as follows:

Table 9.5   *Walgreen Company and Subsidiaries Common Size Income Statement** *
Years Ended August 31, 1993, 1994, 1995, 1996, and 1997

	1997	%	1996	%	1995	%	1994	%	1993	%
Net sales	13,363	100.00	11,778	100.00	10,395	100.00	9,235	100.00	8,295	100.00
Cost of goods sold	9,682	72.45	8,515	72.29	7,482	71.98	6,614	71.62	5,959	71.84
Gross profit	3,681	27.55	3,264	27.71	2,913	28.02	2,621	28.38	2,336	28.16
Selling, general and administrative expenses	2,973	22.25	2,660	22.58	2,393	23.02	2,165	23.44	1,930	23.26
Operating profit	708	5.30	604	5.13	520	5.00	456	4.93	406	4.90
Interest Income	6	0.01	5	0.04	5	0.05	5	0.06	7	0.08
Interest Expense	2	0.00	2	0.02	1	0.01	3	0.03	6	0.08
Operating income before income taxes	712	5.33	607	5.15	524	5.04	458	4.96	400	4.82
Provision for income taxes	276	2.07	235	2.00	203	1.95	176	1.91	154	1.86
Operating income after taxes	436	3.26	372	3.16	321	3.09	282	3.05	245	2.96
Reported net income	436	3.26	372	3.16	321	3.09	282	3.05	222	2.67
Operating income after taxes available for Common	436	3.26	372	3.16	321	3.09	282	3.05	222	2.67
Reported net income available for Common	436	3.26	372	3.16	321	3.09	282	3.05	222	2.67

*Percentages may not add to 100.0% due to rounding.

$$\text{Quick Ratio} = \frac{\text{Cash} + \text{Marketable Securities} + \text{Receivables}}{\text{Current Liabilities}}$$

This ratio is intended to indicate the amount of highly liquid assets available to pay near-term liabilities. Walgreens' quick ratios were

$$1997: \frac{449}{1,439} = 0.31$$

$$1996: \frac{297}{1,182} = 0.25$$

$$1995: \frac{268}{1,078} = 0.25$$

These quick ratios for Walgreen were below the norm and were fairly constant over the three years. As before, you should compare these values relative to what happened in the industry and the economy. When possible, you would want to question management regarding the reason for these relatively low liquidity ratios.

Cash Ratio   The most conservative liquidity ratio is the cash ratio, which relates the firm's cash and short-term marketable securities to its current liabilities as follows:

$$\text{Cash Ratio} = \frac{\text{Cash and Marketable Securities}}{\text{Current Liabilities}}$$

Walgreen's cash ratios were

$$1997: \frac{73}{1,439} = 0.05$$

$$1996: \frac{9}{1,182} = 0.01$$

$$1995: \frac{22}{1,078} = 0.02$$

The cash ratios during these three years have been quite low and they would be cause for concern except that the firm has strong lines of credit at various banks. Still, as an investor you would want to know the reason for these low levels.

Receivables Turnover   In addition to examining liquid assets relative to near-term liabilities, it is useful to analyze the quality (liquidity) of the accounts receivable. One way to do this is to calculate how often the firm's receivables turn over, which implies an average collection period. The faster these accounts are paid, the sooner the firm gets the funds that can be used to pay off its own current liabilities. Receivables turnover is computed as follows:

$$\text{Receivables Turnover} = \frac{\text{Net Annual Sales}}{\text{Average Receivables}}$$

Analysts typically derive the average receivables figure from the beginning receivables figure plus the ending value divided by two. Walgreen receivables turnover ratios were

$$1997: \frac{13,363}{(376 + 288)/2} = 40.2 \text{ times}$$

$$1996: \frac{11,778}{(288 + 246)/2} = 44.1 \text{ times}$$

It is not possible to compute a turnover value for 1995 because the tables used do not include a beginning receivables figure for 1995 (that is, we lack the ending receivables figure for 1994).

Given these annual receivables turnover figures, you can compute an average collection period as follows:

$$\text{Average Receivable Collection Period} = \frac{365}{\text{Annual Turnover}}$$

$$1997: \frac{365}{40.2} = 9.1 \text{ days}$$

$$1996: \frac{365}{44.1} = 8.3 \text{ days}$$

These results indicate that Walgreen currently collects its accounts receivable in about nine days on average, and this collection record is fairly stable. To determine whether these account collection numbers are good or bad, they should be related to the firm's credit policy and to comparable numbers for other firms in the industry. Such an analysis would indicate similar collection periods for other drugstore chains since this is basically a cash business.

The receivables turnover is one of the ratios where *you do not want to deviate too much from the norm.* In an industry where the norm is forty days, a collection period of 80 days

would indicate slow-paying customers, which increases the capital tied up in receivables and the possibility of bad debts. You would want the firm to be somewhat below the norm (35 days versus 40 days), but a figure *substantially below* the norm, such as 20 days, might indicate overly stringent credit terms relative to your competition, which could be detrimental to sales.

Inventory Turnover   Another current asset that should be examined in terms of its liquidity is inventory—the firm's inventory turnover and the implied processing time. Inventory turnover can be calculated relative to sales or cost of goods sold. The preferred turnover ratio is relative to cost of goods sold (CGS) because CGS does not include the profit implied in sales. For Walgreen the turnover ratios are as follows:

$$1997: \frac{9,682}{(1,733 + 1,632)/2} = 5.7 \text{ times}$$

$$1996: \frac{8,514}{(1,632 + 1,454)/2} = 5.5 \text{ times}$$

Given the turnover values, you can compute the average inventory processing time as follows:

$$\text{Average Inventory Processing Period} = \frac{365}{\text{Annual Turnover}}$$

$$1997: \frac{365}{5.7} = 64 \text{ days}$$

$$1996: \frac{365}{5.5} = 66 \text{ days}$$

Although this seems like a low turnover figure, it is encouraging that the inventory processing period is declining. Still, it is always essential to examine this figure relative to an industry norm. Notably, it will be affected by the products carried by the chain—for instance, if the chain adds high profit margin items such as cosmetics and liquor, these products may have a lower turnover.

As with receivables, you don't want an extremely low turnover value and long processing time because this implies that capital is being tied up in inventory and could signal obsolete inventory. Alternatively, an abnormally high inventory turnover and a short processing time could mean inadequate inventory that could lead to outages and slow delivery to customers, which would adversely affect sales.

Cash Conversion Cycle   An alternative measure of overall internal liquidity is the cash conversion cycle, which combines information from the receivables turnover, the inventory turnover, and the accounts payable turnover. The point is, cash is tied up in assets for a certain number of days. Specifically, cash is committed to receivables for the collection period and is tied up for a number of days in inventory—the inventory process period. At the same time, the firm receives an offset to this capital commitment from its own suppliers who provide interest-free loans to the firm by carrying the firm's payables (the payables' payment period is equal to 365/the payables' turnover ratio). In turn, the payables turnover ratio is equal to:

$$\text{Payables Turnover Ratio} = \frac{\text{Cost of Goods Sold}}{\text{Average Trade Payables}}$$

$$1997: \frac{9,682}{(813 + 692)/2} = 12.9 \text{ times}$$

$$1996: \frac{8{,}514}{(692 + 606)/2} = 13.1 \text{ times}$$

$$\text{Payables Payment Period} = \frac{365}{\text{Payables Turnover}}$$

$$1997: \frac{365}{12.9} = 28 \text{ days}$$

$$1996: \frac{365}{13.1} = 28 \text{ days}$$

Therefore the cash conversion cycle equals:

Year	Receivables Days	+	Inventory Processing Days	−	Payables Payment Period	=	Cash Conversion Cycle
1997	9		64		28		45 days
1996	8		66		28		46 days

Walgreen has improved (reduced) its inventory processing days, but is paying its bills at about the same speed, which has caused a small decline in its cash conversion cycle. Although the overall cash conversion cycle appears to be quite good (about 45 days), as always you should examine the firm's long-term trend and compare it to other drugstore chains.

EVALUATING OPERATING PERFORMANCE

The ratios that indicate how well the management is operating the business can be divided into two subcategories: (1) operating efficiency ratios and (2) operating profitability ratios. Efficiency ratios examine how the management uses its assets and capital, measured in terms of the dollars of sales generated by various asset or capital categories. Profitability ratios analyze the profits as a percentage of sales and as a percentage of the assets and capital employed.

Operating Efficiency Ratios

Total Asset Turnover   The total asset turnover ratio indicates the effectiveness of the firm's use of its total asset base (net assets equals gross assets minus depreciation on fixed assets). It is computed as follows:

$$\text{Total Asset Turnover} = \frac{\text{Net Sales}}{\text{Average Total Net Assets}}$$

Walgreen's total asset turnover values were

$$1997: \frac{13{,}363}{(4{,}207 + 3{,}634)/2} = 3.4 \text{ times}$$

$$1996: \frac{11{,}778}{(3{,}634 + 3{,}253)/2} = 3.4 \text{ times}$$

You must compare this ratio to that of other firms in an industry because it varies substantially between industries. For example, total asset turnover ratios range from about 1 for large capital-intensive industries (steel, autos, and other heavy manufacturing

companies) to over 10 for some retailing operations. It also can be affected by the use of leased facilities.

Again, you should consider a *range* of turnover values. It is poor management to have an exceedingly high asset turnover relative to your industry because this might imply too few assets for the potential business (sales) or the use of outdated, fully depreciated assets. It is equally poor management to have a too low relative asset turnover because this implies tying up capital in an excess of assets relative to the needs of the firm.

Beyond the analysis of the total asset base, it is insightful to examine the utilization of some specific assets such as inventories and fixed assets. Because we have already examined the receivables and inventory turnover as part of our liquidity analysis, we will examine the fixed asset ratio.

Net Fixed Asset Turnover   The net fixed asset turnover ratio reflects the firm's utilization of fixed assets. It is computed as follows:

$$\text{Fixed Asset Turnover} = \frac{\text{Net Sales}}{\text{Average Net Fixed Assets}}$$

Walgreen's fixed asset turnover ratios were

$$1997: \frac{13,363}{(1,754 + 1,448)/2} = 8.3 \text{ times}$$

$$1996: \frac{11,778}{(1,448 + 1,249)/2} = 8.7 \text{ times}$$

These turnover ratios must be compared with those of firms in the same industry and should consider the impact of leased assets. Also remember that an abnormally low turnover implies capital tied up in excessive fixed assets, while an abnormally high asset turnover ratio can indicate the use of old, fully depreciated equipment that may be obsolete.

Equity Turnover   In addition to specific asset turnover ratios, it is useful to examine the turnover for alternative capital components. An important one, equity turnover, is computed as follows:

$$\text{Equity Turnover} = \frac{\text{Net Sales}}{\text{Average Equity}}$$

Equity includes preferred and common stock, paid-in capital, and total retained earnings.[1] The difference between this ratio and total asset turnover is that it excludes current liabilities and long-term debt. Therefore, when examining this series, it is important to consider the firm's capital ratios because the firm can increase its equity turnover ratio by increasing its proportion of debt capital (that is, a higher debt/equity ratio).

Walgreen's equity turnover ratios were

$$1997: \frac{13,363}{(2,373 + 2,043)/2} = 6.0 \text{ times}$$

$$1996: \frac{11,778}{(2,043 + 1,793)/2} = 6.1 \text{ times}$$

---

[1]Some investors prefer to only consider *owner's* equity, which would not include preferred stock.

Walgreen has experienced a fairly consistent increase in this ratio during the past several years. In our later analysis of sustainable growth, we examine the variables that affect the equity turnover ratio to understand what caused any changes.

Given some understanding of the firm's record of operating efficiency, as shown by its ability to generate sales from its assets and capital, the next step is to examine its profitability in relation to its sales and capital.

Operating Profitability Ratios

The ratios in this category indicate two facets of profitability: (1) the rate of profit on sales (profit margin) and (2) the percentage return on capital employed.

Gross Profit Margin   Gross profit equals net sales minus the cost of goods sold. The gross profit margin is computed as

$$\text{Gross Profit Margin} = \frac{\text{Gross Profit}}{\text{Net Sales}}$$

The gross profit margins for Walgreen were

$$1997: \frac{3{,}681}{13{,}363} = 27.6\%$$

$$1996: \frac{3{,}264}{11{,}778} = 27.7\%$$

$$1995: \frac{2{,}913}{10{,}395} = 28.0\%$$

This ratio indicates the basic cost structure of the firm. An analysis over time relative to a comparable industry figure shows the firm's relative cost–price position. Walgreen experienced basically no change in this margin during 1997. As always, it is important to compare these margins with industry statistics.

Operating Profit Margin   Operating profit is gross profit minus sales, general, and administrative (SG & A) expenses. The operating profit margin equals

$$\text{Operating Profit Margin} = \frac{\text{Operating Profit}}{\text{Net Sales}}$$

For Walgreen the operating profit margins were

$$1997: \frac{708}{13{,}363} = 5.3\%$$

$$1996: \frac{604}{11{,}778} = 5.1\%$$

$$1995: \frac{520}{10{,}395} = 5.0\%$$

The variability of the operating profit margin over time is a prime indicator of the business risk for a firm. For Walgreen, this margin has increased slightly over time.

There are two additional deductions from operating profit—interest expense and net foreign exchange loss. This indicates operating income before income taxes.

In some instances, investors add back depreciation expense and compute a profit margin that consists of earnings before interest, taxes, and depreciation (EBITD). This alternative operating profit margin reflects all controllable expenses and is used as a proxy for pre-tax cash flow. It can provide great insights regarding the profit performance of heavy manufacturing firms with large depreciation charges. It also can indicate earnings available to pay fixed financing costs. This latter use will be discussed in the section on financial risk.

Net Profit Margin   This margin relates net income to sales. In the case of Walgreen, this is the same as operating income after taxes because the firm does not have any significant nonoperating adjustments, including the cumulative effect of accounting changes. The net income used is earnings after taxes but before dividends on preferred and common stock. For most firms this margin is equal to

$$\text{Net Profit Margin} = \frac{\text{Net Income}}{\text{Net Sales}}$$

As noted, Walgreen's net profit margin is based on income after taxes as follows:

$$1997: \frac{436}{13{,}363} = 3.3\%$$

$$1996: \frac{372}{11{,}778} = 3.2\%$$

$$1995: \frac{321}{10{,}395} = 3.1\%$$

This ratio should be computed based on sales and earnings from *continuing* operations because our analysis seeks to derive insights about *future* expectations. Therefore, results for continuing operations are relevant rather than the profit or loss that considers earnings from discontinued operations or the gain or loss from the sale of these operations.

Common Size Income Statement   Beyond these ratios, an additional technique for analyzing operating profitability is a common size income statement, which lists all expense and income items as a percentage of sales. Analyzing this statement for several years (five at least) will provide useful insights regarding the trends in cost figures and profit margins.

Table 9.5 shows a common size statement for Walgreen for five years. These statements were discussed earlier where the stability in the percentage of cost of goods was highlighted and the small decline in SG & A expenses caused an increase in the net margin.

Beyond the analysis of earnings on sales, the ultimate measure of the success of management is the profits earned on the assets or the capital committed to the enterprise. Several ratios help us evaluate this important relationship.

Return on Total Capital   The return on total capital ratio relates the firm's earnings to all the capital involved in the enterprise (debt, preferred stock, and common stock). Therefore, the earnings figure used is the net income from continuing operations (before any dividends) *plus* the interest paid on debt.

$$\text{Return on Total Capital} = \frac{\text{Net Income} + \text{Interest Expense}}{\text{Average Total Capital}}$$

Walgreen incurred interest expense for long- and short-term debt. The gross interest expense value used in this ratio differs from the "net" interest expense item in the income statement, which is measured as gross interest expense minus interest income.

Walgreen's rate of return on total capital was

$$1997: \frac{436 + 2}{(4,207 + 3,634)/2} = 11.2\%$$

$$1996: \frac{372 + 2}{(3,634 + 3,253)/2} = 10.9\%$$

This ratio indicates the firm's return on all the capital it employed. It should be compared with the ratio for other firms in the industry and the economy. If this rate of return does not match the perceived risk of the firm, one might question if the entity should continue to exist because the capital involved in the enterprise could be used more productively elsewhere in the economy. For Walgreen, the results indicate stable results with an increase during the last several years.

Return on Owner's Equity   The return on owner's equity (ROE) ratio is extremely important to the owner of the enterprise (the common stockholder) because it indicates the rate of return that management has earned on the capital provided by the owner after accounting for payments to all other capital suppliers. If you consider all equity (including preferred stock), this return would equal

$$\text{Return on Total Equity} = \frac{\text{Net Income}}{\text{Average Total Equity}}$$

If an investor is concerned only with owner's equity (the common-shareholder's equity), the ratio would be calculated

$$\text{Return on Owner's Equity} = \frac{\text{Net Income} - \text{Preferred Dividend}}{\text{Average Common Equity}}$$

Walgreen generated return on owner's equity of

$$1997: \frac{436 - 0}{(2,373 + 2,043)/2} = 19.8\%$$

$$1996: \frac{372 - 0}{(2,043 + 1,793)/2} = 19.4\%$$

This ratio reflects the rate of return on the equity capital provided by the owners. It should correspond to the firm's overall business risk, but it also should reflect the financial risk assumed by the common stockholder because of the prior claims of the firm's bondholders.

The DuPont System   The importance of ROE as an indicator of performance makes it desirable to divide the ratio into several components that provide insights into the causes of a firm's ROE or any changes in it. This breakdown of ROE into component ratios is generally referred to as the **DuPont System**. To begin, the return on equity (ROE) ratio can be broken down into two ratios that we have discussed—net profit margin and equity turnover.

$$\text{ROE} = \frac{\text{Net Income}}{\text{Common Equity}} = \frac{\text{Net Income}}{\text{Net Sales}} \times \frac{\text{Net Sales}}{\text{Common Equity}}$$

This breakdown is an identity because we have both multiplied and divided by net sales. To maintain the identity, the common equity value used is the year-end figure rather than the average of the beginning and ending value. This identity reveals that ROE equals the net profit margin times the equity turnover, which implies that a firm can improve its return on equity by *either* using its equity more efficiently (increasing its equity turnover) or by becoming more profitable (increasing its net profit margin).

As noted previously, a firm's equity turnover is affected by its capital structure. Specifically, a firm can increase its equity turnover by employing a higher proportion of debt capital. We can see this effect by considering the following relationship:

$$\frac{\text{Net Sales}}{\text{Equity}} = \frac{\text{Net Sales}}{\text{Total Assets}} \times \frac{\text{Total Assets}}{\text{Equity}}$$

Similar to the prior breakdown, this is an identity because we have both multiplied and divided the equity turnover ratio by total assets. This equation indicates that the equity turnover ratio equals the firm's *total asset turnover* (a measure of efficiency) times the ratio of total assets to equity, which is a measure of financial leverage. Specifically, this latter ratio of total assets to equity indicates the proportion of total assets financed with debt. *All assets have to be financed by either equity or some form of debt* (either current liabilities or long-term debt). Therefore, the higher the ratio of assets to equity, the higher the proportion of debt to equity. A total asset/equity ratio of 2, for example, indicates that for every two dollars of assets there is a dollar of equity, which means the firm financed one-half of its assets with equity. This implies that it financed the other half with debt. A total asset/equity ratio of 3 indicates that only one-third of total assets was financed with equity, so two-thirds must have been financed with debt. This breakdown of the equity turnover ratio implies that a firm can increase its equity turnover either by increasing its total asset turnover (becoming more efficient) or by increasing its financial leverage ratio (financing assets with a higher proportion of debt capital). This financial leverage ratio is also referred to as the financial leverage multiplier whereby the first two ratios equal return on total assets (ROTA) and ROTA times the financial leverage multiplier equals ROE.

Combining these two breakdowns, we see that a firm's ROE is composed of three ratios as follows:

$$\frac{\text{Net Income}}{\text{Common Equity}} = \frac{\text{Net Income}}{\text{Net Sales}} \times \frac{\text{Net Sales}}{\text{Total Assets}} \times \frac{\text{Total Assets}}{\text{Common Equity}}$$

$$= \frac{\text{Profit}}{\text{Margin}} \times \frac{\text{Total Asset}}{\text{Turnover}} \times \frac{\text{Financial}}{\text{Leverage}}$$

As an example of this important set of relationships, the figures in Table 9.6 indicate what has happened to the ROE for Walgreen and the components of its ROE during the sixteen-year period from 1982 to 1997. As noted, these ratio values employ year-end balance sheet figures (assets and equity) rather than the average of beginning and ending data.

The DuPont results in Table 9.6 indicate several significant trends:

1. The overall ROE experienced significant stability with a beginning value of 18.73 and an ending value of 18.35.
2. The asset turnover ratio was likewise stable with a total range of 3.06 to 3.31.
3. The profit margin series experienced a stable increase from 2.75 to 3.26.

Table 9.6 *Components of Return on Total Equity for Walgreen Company*[a]

Year	(1) Sales/Total Assets	(2) Net Profit Margin (%)	(3)[b] Return on Total Assets	(4) Total Assets/ Equity	(5)[c] Return on Equity (%)
1982	3.31	2.75	9.09	2.06	18.73
1983	3.29	2.96	9.72	2.04	19.84
1984	3.26	3.11	10.16	2.03	20.60
1985	3.29	2.98	9.79	2.00	19.58
1986	3.06	2.82	8.62	2.16	18.64
1987	3.14	2.42	7.60	2.19	16.63
1988	3.23	2.64	8.54	2.12	18.12
1989	3.20	2.87	9.18	2.04	18.74
1990	3.16	2.89	9.12	2.02	18.42
1991	3.21	2.90	9.31	1.94	18.04
1992	3.15	2.95	9.30	1.92	17.90
1993	3.27	2.67	8.74	1.84	16.07
1994	3.17	3.05	9.69	1.85	17.91
1995[d]	3.20	3.09	9.86	1.81	17.89
1996[d]	3.24	3.16	10.23	1.78	18.19
1997[d]	3.18	3.26	10.37	1.77	18.35

[a]Ratios use year-end data for total assets and common equity rather than averages of the year.

[b]Column (3) is equal to column (1) times column (2).

[c]Column (5) is equal to column (3) times column (4).

[d]ROE is calculated using operating income after taxes.

4. The product of the total asset turnover and the net profit margin is equal to return on total assets (ROTA), which experienced an overall increase from 9.09 percent to 10.37 percent.
5. The financial leverage multiplier (total assets/equity) experienced a steady decline from 2.06 to 1.77. Notably, most of this debt is trade credit which is non-interest bearing. The fact is, the firm has almost no interest-bearing debt, except for the long-term leases on drugstores to be considered in the financial risk section.
6. Finally, as a result of the increasing ROTA and the declining financial leverage, the firm's ROE has been quite constant overall beginning at 18.73 and ending at 18.35.

An Extended DuPont System[2] Beyond the original DuPont System, some analysts have suggested using an extended DuPont System, which provides additional insights into the effect of financial leverage on the firm and also pinpoints the effect of income taxes on the firm's ROE. Because both financial leverage and tax rates have changed dramatically over the past decade, these additional insights are important.

In the prior presentation, we started with the ROE and divided it into components. In contrast, we now begin with the operating profit margin (EBIT divided by sales) and introduce additional ratios to derive an ROE value. Combining the operating profit margin and the total asset turnover ratio yields the following:

$$\frac{EBIT}{Net\ Sales} \times \frac{Net\ Sales}{Total\ Assets} = \frac{EBIT}{Total\ Assets}$$

[2]The original DuPont System was the three-component breakdown discussed in the prior section. Because this analysis also involves the components of ROE, some still refer to its as the DuPont System. In our presentation, we refer to it as the extended DuPont System to differentiate it from the original three component system.

This ratio is the operating profit return on total assets. To consider the negative effects of financial leverage, we examine the effect of interest expense as a percentage of total assets:

$$\frac{EBIT}{Total\ Assets} - \frac{Interest\ Expense}{Total\ Assets} = \frac{Net\ Before\ Tax}{Total\ Assets}$$

We consider the positive effect of financial leverage with the financial leverage multiplier as follows:

$$\frac{Net\ Before\ Tax\ (NBT)}{Total\ Assets} \times \frac{Total\ Assets}{Common\ Equity} = \frac{Net\ Before\ Tax\ (NBT)}{Common\ Equity}$$

This indicates the pretax return on equity. To arrive at ROE, we must consider the tax rate effect. We do this by multiplying the pretax ROE by a tax retention rate as follows:

$$\frac{Net\ Before\ Tax}{Common\ Equity} \times \left(100\% - \frac{Income\ Taxes}{Net\ Before\ Tax}\right) = \frac{Net\ Income}{Common\ Equity}$$

In summary, we have the following five components:

1. $\dfrac{EBIT}{Sales}$ = Operating Profit Margin

2. $\dfrac{Sales}{Total\ Assets}$ = Total Asset Turnover

3. $\dfrac{Interest\ Expense}{Total\ Assets}$ = Interest Expense Rate

4. $\dfrac{Total\ Assets}{Common\ Equity}$ = Financial Leverage Multiplier

5. $\left(100\% - \dfrac{Income\ Taxes}{Net\ Before\ Tax}\right)$ = Tax Retention Rate

To demonstrate the use of this extended DuPont System, Table 9.7 contains the calculations using the five components for the years 1982 through 1997. The first column indicates that the firm's operating profit margin peaked in 1985 and has subsequently generally declined. We know from the prior discussion that the firm's total asset turnover (column 2) has been fairly constant overall. As a result, operating return on assets has looked good. As discussed, because of almost no interest-bearing debt, column 4 shows a small negative impact of leverage.

Column 5 reflects the firm's operating performance before the positive impact of financing (the leverage multiplier) and any impact of taxes. These results show strong performance by the firm overall. Column 6 reflects the steady decline in financial leverage. Column 8 shows the effect of lower tax rates and thus a higher overall tax retention rate that increased from the mid-50 percent range to the low 60 percent rate. In summary, this breakdown should likewise help you to understand *what* happened to a firm's ROE as well as *why* it happened. The intent is to determine what happened to the firm's internal operating results, its financial leverage, and what was the effect of external government tax policy.

RISK ANALYSIS

Risk analysis examines the uncertainty of income flows for the total firm and for the individual sources of capital (that is, debt, preferred stock, and common stock). The typical

Table 9.7 Extended DuPont System Analysis for Walgreen: 1982–1997[a]

Year	(1) EBIT/Sales (Percent)	(2) Sales/Total Assets (Times)	(3) EBIT/Total Assets (Percent)[b]	(4) Interest Expense/Total Assets (Percent)	(5) Net Before Tax/Total Assets (Percent)[c]	(6) Total Assets/Common Equity (Times)	(7) Net Before Tax/Common Equity (Percent)[d]	(8) Tax Retention Rate	(9) Return on Equity (Percent)[e]
1982	4.32	3.31	14.30	(0.85)	15.15	2.06	31.20	0.60	18.75
1983	5.16	3.29	17.00	0.25	16.75	2.04	34.20	0.56	19.30
1984	5.57	3.26	18.20	(0.24)	18.44	2.03	37.40	0.55	20.65
1985	5.63	3.29	18.50	0.43	18.07	2.00	36.10	0.54	19.57
1986	5.37	3.06	16.40	0.74	15.66	2.16	33.90	0.55	18.63
1987	4.92	3.14	15.50	1.22	14.28	2.19	31.30	0.53	16.69
1988	4.59	3.23	14.80	1.01	13.79	2.12	29.30	0.62	18.10
1989	4.71	3.20	15.10	0.57	14.53	2.04	29.70	0.63	18.79
1990	4.70	3.16	14.90	0.17	14.73	2.02	29.80	0.62	18.52
1991	4.77	3.21	15.30	0.44	14.86	1.94	28.80	0.63	18.00
1992	4.80	3.15	15.10	0.23	14.87	1.92	28.60	0.62	17.87
1993	4.90	3.31	16.20	0.26	15.94	1.82	29.00	0.61	17.80
1994	4.93	3.21	15.90	(0.10)	16.00	1.83	29.20	0.62	17.96
1995[f]	5.00	3.20	15.99	0.04	15.95	1.81	28.90	0.61	17.70
1996[f]	5.13	3.24	16.62	0.06	16.56	1.78	29.50	0.61	18.07
1997[f]	5.30	3.17	16.83	0.05	16.92	1.77	30.00	0.61	18.30

[a]The percents in this table may not be the same as in Table 9.5 due to rounding.

[b]Column (3) is equal to column (1) times column (2).

[c]Column (5) is equal to column (3) times column (4).

[d]Column (7) is equal to column (5) times column (6).

[e]Column (9) is equal to column (7) times column (8).

[f]ROE is calculated using operating income after taxes.

approach examines the major factors that cause a firm's income flows to vary. More volatile income flows mean greater risk (uncertainty) facing the investor.

The total risk of the firm has two components: business risk and financial risk. The next section discusses the concept of business risk: how you measure it, what causes it, and how you measure its individual causes. The following section discusses financial risk and describes the ratios by which you measure it.

Business Risk[3]

Recall that business risk is the uncertainty of income caused by the firm's industry. In turn, this uncertainty is due to the firm's variability of sales caused by its products, customers, and the way it produces its products. Specifically, a firm's earnings vary over time because its sales and production costs vary. As an example, the earnings for a steel firm will probably vary more than those of a grocery chain because (1) over the business cycle, steel sales are more volatile than grocery sales and (2) the steel firm's large fixed production costs make its earnings vary more than its sales.

Business risk is generally measured by the variability of the firm's operating income over time which is measured by the standard deviation of the historical operating earnings series.

Besides measuring overall business risk, we can examine the two factors that contribute to the variability of operating earnings: sales variability and operating leverage.

Sales Variability   Sales variability is the prime determinant of earnings variability. Operating earnings must be as volatile as sales. Notably, the variability of sales is largely outside the control of management. Specifically, although the variability of sales is affected by a firm's advertising and pricing policy, the major cause is its industry. For example, sales for a firm in a cyclical industry, such as automobiles or steel, will be volatile over the business cycle compared to sales of a firm in a noncyclical industry, such as retail food or hospital supplies.

Operating Leverage   The variability of a firm's operating earnings also depends on its mixture of production costs. Total production costs of a firm with no *fixed* production costs would vary directly with sales, and operating profits would be a constant proportion of sales. The firm's operating profit margin would be constant and its operating profits would have the same relative volatility as its sales. Realistically, firms always have some fixed production costs (buildings, machinery, or relatively permanent personnel and such). Fixed production costs cause operating profits to vary more than sales over the business cycle. During slow periods, profits decline by a larger percentage than sales. In contrast, during an economic expansion, profits will increase by a larger percentage than sales.

The employment of fixed production costs is referred to as **operating leverage**. Clearly, greater operating leverage makes the operating earnings series more volatile relative to the sales series.[4]

Financial Risk

Financial risk, you will recall, is the additional uncertainty of returns to equity holders due to a firm's use of fixed obligation debt securities. This financial uncertainty is in addi-

---

[3]For a further discussion on this general topic, see Eugene Brigham and Louis C. Gapenski, *Financial Management: Theory and Practice,* 8th ed. (Fort Worth, TX: Dryden, 1997), Chapters 6 and 10. For a detailed discussion of the computations, see Frank K. Reilly and Keith Brown, *Investment Analysis and Portfolio Management,* 5th ed. (Fort Worth, TX: Dryden, 1997).

[4]For a further treatment of this area, see James C. Van Horne, *Financial Management and Policy,* 9th ed. (Englewood Cliffs, NJ: Prentice-Hall, 1993), Chapter 27, and C.F. Lee, Joseph E. Finnerty and Edgar A. Norton, *Foundations of Financial Management* (St. Paul, MN: West Publishing Co., 1997), Chapter 5.

tion to the firm's business risk. When a firm sells bonds to raise capital, the interest payments on this capital precede the computation of common stock earnings, and these interest payments are fixed obligations. As with operating leverage, during good times the earnings available for common stock will experience a larger percentage increase than operating earnings, whereas during a business decline the earnings available to stockholders will decline by a larger percentage than operating earnings because of these fixed financial costs. Also, as a firm increases its debt financing with fixed contractual obligations, it increases its financial risk and the possibility of default and bankruptcy.

Two sets of financial ratios help measure financial risk. The first set are balance sheet ratios that indicate the proportion of capital derived from debt securities compared to equity capital (preferred and common stock). The second set of ratios considers the earnings or the cash flow available to pay fixed financial charges.

Proportion of Debt (Balance Sheet) Ratios The proportion of debt ratios indicate what proportion of the firm's capital is derived from debt compared to other sources of capital such as preferred stock, common stock, and retained earnings. A higher proportion of debt capital compared to equity capital makes earnings more volatile and increases the probability that a firm will be unable to meet the required interest payments and will default on the debt. Therefore, higher proportion of debt ratios indicate greater financial risk.

The acceptable level of financial risk for a firm depends on its business risk. If the firm has low business risk, investors are willing to accept higher financial risk. For example, retail food companies typically have rather stable operating earnings over time and therefore relatively *low* business risk, which means that they can have *higher* financial risk.

Debt–equity ratio The debt–equity ratio is equal to

$$\text{Debt–Equity Ratio} = \frac{\text{Total Long-Term Debt}}{\text{Total Equity}}$$

The debt figure includes all long-term fixed obligations, including subordinated convertible bonds. The equity typically is the book value of equity and includes preferred stock, common stock, and retained earnings. Some analysts prefer to exclude preferred stock and consider only common equity. Total equity is preferable if some of the firms being analyzed have preferred stock. Alternatively, if the preferred stock dividend is considered an interest payment, you might want to compute a ratio of debt plus preferred stock relative to common equity.

Two sets of debt ratios can be computed: *with and without deferred taxes.* Most balance sheets include an accumulated deferred tax figure, which comes just below long-term debt and other liabilities on the balance sheet. There is some controversy regarding whether you should treat these deferred taxes as a liability or as part of permanent capital. Some argue that if the deferred tax has accumulated because of the difference in accelerated and straight-line depreciation, this liability may never be paid. That is, as long as the firm continues to grow and add new assets, this total deferred tax account continues to grow and is never paid off. Alternatively, if the deferred tax account is because of differences in the recognition of income on long-term contracts such as government contracts, there will be a reversal, and this liability must eventually be paid. To resolve this question, you must determine the reason for the deferred tax account and examine its long-term trend.[5]

[5]For a further discussion of this, see Gerald I. White, Ashwinpaul C. Sondhi, and Dov Fried, *The Analysis and Use of Financial Statements*, 2nd. ed. (New York: Wiley, 1997), 1017–18.

Walgreen's deferred tax account arose because of a depreciation difference, and it has typically grown over time. The following ratios are computed with the conservative assumption that includes deferred taxes as a long-term liability. The debt–equity ratios for Walgreen were

Including Deferred Taxes as Long-Term Debt

$$1997: \frac{395}{2,373} = 16.65\%$$

$$1996: \frac{408}{2,043} = 39.94\%$$

$$1995: \frac{382}{1,793} = 42.61\%$$

These ratios indicate a relatively small and declining debt burden for the firm over the three-year period.

Long-term debt/total capital ratio The debt–total capital ratio indicates the proportion of long-term capital derived from long-term debt capital. It is computed as

$$\text{L.T. Debt/Total L.T. Capital Ratio} = \frac{\text{Total Long-Term Debt}}{\text{Total Long-Term Capital}}$$

The long-term capital would include all long-term debt, any preferred stock, and total equity. The debt–total capital ratios for Walgreen were

Including Deferred Taxes as Long-Term Debt

$$1997: \frac{395}{2,768} = 14.27\%$$

$$1996: \frac{408}{2,451} = 16.65\%$$

$$1995: \frac{382}{2,175} = 17.56\%$$

Again, this ratio indicates a decrease in the firm's financial risk for the same reason as before (a large increase in equity capital).

Total debt ratios In some cases, it is useful to compare total debt (current liabilities plus long-term liabilities) to total capital (total debt plus total equity). This is especially revealing for a firm that derives substantial capital from short-term borrowing. The total debt–total capital ratios for Walgreen were

Including Deferred Taxes as Long-Term Debt

$$1997: \frac{1,834}{4,207} = 43.6\%$$

$$1996: \frac{1,591}{3,634} = 43.8\%$$

$$1995: \frac{1,460}{3,253} = 44.9\%$$

This ratio indicates that about 44 percent of Walgreen's assets are currently financed with debt. These ratios should be compared with those of other companies in the industry to evaluate their consistency with the business risk of this industry. Such a comparison also would indicate how much higher this total debt ratio can go.

Although this ratio indicates a relatively low proportion of total debt, some observers would consider it too conservative because it includes accounts payable and accrued expenses, which are *noninterest-bearing debt.* In the case of Walgreen, if this noninterest debt along with deferred taxes is excluded from debt and from total capital the ratio declines to a low proportion as follows:

$$\text{Total Interest-Bearing Debt/Total Capital} = \frac{\text{Total Interest Debt}}{\text{Total Capital-Non-Int. Liab.}}$$

$$1997: \frac{282}{2,655} = 10.6\%$$

$$1996: \frac{263}{2,307} = 11.4\%$$

$$1995: \frac{240}{2,033} = 11.8\%$$

Earnings or Cash Flow Ratios   In addition to ratios that indicate the proportion of debt on the balance sheet, investors use ratios that relate the *flow* of earnings or cash that is available to meet the required interest and lease payments. A higher ratio of earnings or cash flow relative to fixed financial charges indicates lower financial risk.

Interest coverage   Interest coverage is computed as follows:

$$\text{Interest Coverage} = \frac{\text{Income Before Interest and Taxes (EBIT)}}{\text{Debt Interest Charges}}$$

$$= \frac{\text{Net Income + Income Taxes + Interest Expense}}{\text{Interest Expense}}$$

This ratio indicates how many times the fixed interest charges are earned, based on the earnings available to pay these expenses.[6] Alternatively, one minus the reciprocal of the coverage ratio indicates how far earnings could decline before it would be impossible to pay the interest charges from current earnings. For example, a coverage ratio of 5 means that earnings could decline by 80 percent (1 minus 1/5), and the firm could still pay its fixed financial charges. Walgreen's interest coverage ratios (using the gross interest expense) were

$$1997: \frac{436 + 2 + 276}{2} = 357 \text{ times}$$

$$1996: \frac{372 + 2 + 235}{2} = 273 \text{ times}$$

$$1995: \frac{321 + 1 + 203}{1} = 411 \text{ times}$$

---

[6]The net income figure used in the analysis is the operating income after taxes because, once again, it is important to exclude earnings and cash flows that are considered nonrecurring and only consider those that should be available in the future (that is, those from ongoing operations).

The ratios are extremely high and reflect almost no public interest-bearing debt.

Although Walgreen has little public interest-bearing debt, similar to many retail firms the company stores generally operate in leased premises. Specifically, original non-cancellable lease terms typically range from ten to twenty years and may contain escalation clauses and typically provide for contingent rentals based upon sales. For Walgreen, the minimum lease payment plus contingent rental for each year 1995–97 were as follows (in millions):

1997—389
1996—351
1995—311

The rules of thumb used by bond-rating agencies is to assume that one-third of the lease payment is the interest component. Therefore, if we add this to the interest expense figures used in prior ratios, the coverage ratios become

$$\text{Interest Coverage} = \frac{\text{EBIT}}{\text{Interest Expense} + \frac{1}{3}\text{Lease Payments}}$$

$$1997: \frac{714}{2 + (389/3)} = \frac{714}{132} = 5 \text{ times}$$

$$1996: \frac{609}{2 + (351/3)} = \frac{609}{119} = 5 \text{ times}$$

$$1995: \frac{525}{1 + (311/3)} = \frac{525}{105} = 5 \text{ times}$$

The trend of Walgreen's coverage ratios has been consistent with the overall trend in the proportion of debt ratios. The proportion of debt ratios and the cash flow ratios do not always give consistent results because the proportion of debt ratios are not sensitive to changes in earnings and cash flow or to changes in the interest rates on the debt. For example, if interest rates increase or if the firm replaces old debt with new debt that has a higher interest rate, no change would occur in the proportion of debt ratios, but the interest coverage ratio would decline. Also, the interest coverage ratio is sensitive to an increase or decrease in earnings. Therefore, the results using balance sheet ratios and coverage ratios can differ.

Total fixed charge coverages   You might want to determine how well earnings cover *total* fixed financial charges including any noncancellable lease payments and any preferred dividends paid out of earnings *after* taxes. If you want to consider preferred dividends, you must determine the pretax earnings needed to meet these preferred dividend payments, as follows:

$$\frac{\text{Fixed Charge Coverage}}{} = \frac{\text{Income Before Interest, Taxes, and Lease Payments}}{\text{Debt Interest} + \text{Lease Payments} + (\text{Preferred Dividend}/[1 - \text{Tax Rate}])}$$

Cash Flow Ratios

As an alternative to these earnings coverage ratios, analysts employ several cash flow ratios that relate the cash flow available from operations to either interest expense, total fixed charges, or the face value of outstanding debt. The first set of cash flow to interest expense or total fixed charges are an extension of the earnings coverage ratios. The second set of cash flow ratios are unique because they relate the *flow* of earnings and noncash expenses

against the *stock* of outstanding debt. These cash flow-to-outstanding-debt ratios have been significant variables in numerous studies concerned with predicting bankruptcies and bond ratings.[7]

Cash flow–coverage ratio   These ratios are an alternative to the earnings coverage ratio. The motivation is that a firm's earnings and cash flow typically will differ substantially (these differences have been noted and will be considered in a subsequent section). To have ratios that can be compared to similar values for the industry and the aggregate market, the cash flow value used is the "traditional" measure of cash flow, which is equal to net income plus depreciation expense plus the change in deferred taxes (if there was an increase in deferred taxes) for the period (the depreciation expense and deferred tax values are typically given in the cash flow statements in the footnotes or in both).

$$1997: \frac{436 + 164 + (-32)}{2} = 284 \text{ times}$$

$$1996: \frac{372 + 147 + 3}{2} = 261 \text{ times}$$

$$1995: \frac{321 + 132 + 4}{1} = 456 \text{ times}$$

To compute a cash-flow coverage ratio comparable to the earnings coverage ratio, it is necessary to add back the interest charges to this cash flow value because interest expense was deducted to arrive at net income. In addition, we also consider one-third of lease payments as an interest component. Given these adjustments, the cash-flow coverage ratios equal

$$\text{Cash Flow Coverage} = \frac{\text{Traditional Cash Flow} + \text{Int. Expenses} + \frac{1}{3} \text{Lease Payments}}{\text{Int. Expense plus } \frac{1}{3} \text{Lease Payments}}$$

$$1997: \frac{568 + 2 + 130}{132} = 5.3 \text{ times}$$

$$1996: \frac{522 + 2 + 117}{119} = 5.4 \text{ times}$$

$$1995: \frac{456 + 1 + 104}{105} = 5.3 \text{ times}$$

Cash flow–long-term debt ratio   Beyond relating cash flow to the required interest expense, several studies have used a ratio that relates cash flow to a firm's outstanding debt as a predictor of bankruptcy and found that this ratio was an excellent explanatory variable in these studies (as noted, they are listed in the references). The cash flow figure used in most studies is the traditional measure used in the prior cash flow coverage ratios. Therefore, the ratios would be computed as

$$\text{Cash Flow/LT Debt} = \frac{\text{Net Income} + \text{Depreciation Expense} + \text{Change in Deferred Tax}}{\text{Book Value of Long-Term Debt}}$$

For Walgreen these ratios were computed based on operating earnings after taxes plus the depreciation expense and deferred taxes reported in the footnotes. Again, we computed these ratios with deferred taxes as follows:

---

[7]A list of studies in which ratios or cash flow variables are used to predict bankruptcies or bond ratings is included in the reference section.

$$\text{Including Deferred Taxes} \atop \text{as Long-Term Debt}$$

$$1997: \frac{436 + 164 + (-32)}{395} = 144\%$$

$$1996: \frac{372 + 147 + 3}{408} = 128\%$$

$$1995: \frac{321 + 132 + 4}{382} = 119\%$$

Cash flow–total debt ratio   Investors also should consider the relationship of cash flow to total debt to check that a firm has not had a significant increase in its short-term borrowing. For Walgreen, these ratios were

$$\text{Including Deferred Taxes} \atop \text{as Long-Term Debt}$$

$$1997: \frac{568}{1,834} = 31.0\%$$

$$1996: \frac{522}{1,591} = 32.8\%$$

$$1995: \frac{456}{1,460} = 31.2\%$$

When you compare these ratios to those with only long-term debt, they reflect the firm's proportion of short-term debt due to short-term borrowing and trade accounts payable. As before, some analysts would exclude accounts payable because they are noninterest-bearing. As before, it is important to compare these flow ratios with similar ratios for other companies in the industry and with the overall economy to gauge the firm's relative performance.

Alternative measures of cash flow   As noted, these cash flow ratios used the traditional measure of cash flow. The requirement that companies must prepare and report the statement of cash flows to stockholders has raised interest in other, more exact measures of cash flow. The first is the *cash flow from operations,* which is taken directly from the statement of cash flows. A second measure is *free cash flow,* which is a modification of the cash flow from operations discussed earlier. The table below summarizes the values derived earlier in the chapter.

Year	Traditional Cash Flow	Cash Flow from Operations	Free Cash Flow Before Div.	Free Cash Flow After Div.
1997	568	650	165	49
1996	522	411	46	(59)
1995	456	345	35	(58)

ANALYSIS OF GROWTH POTENTIAL

Importance of Growth Analysis

The analysis of **sustainable growth potential** examines ratios that indicate how fast a firm should grow. Analysis of a firm's growth potential is important for both lenders and owners. Owners know that the value of the firm depends on its future growth in earnings and dividends. In the following chapter, we discuss various valuation models, which determine

the value of the firm based on alternative cash flows, your required rate of return for the stock, and the firm's expected growth rate of cash flows.

Creditors also are interested in a firm's growth potential because the firm's future success is the major determinant of its ability to pay obligations, and the firm's future success is influenced by its growth. Some financial ratios used in credit analysis measure the book value of a firm's assets relative to its financial obligations. The rationale for this ratio is that it assumes that the firm can sell these assets and use the proceeds to pay off the loan in case of default. Selling assets in a forced liquidation will typically yield only about ten to fifteen cents on the dollar. Currently, most analysts recognize that the more relevant analysis measures the ability of the firm to pay off its obligations as an ongoing enterprise, and its growth potential indicates its future status as an ongoing enterprise.

Determinants of Growth

The growth of business, like the growth on any economic entity including the aggregate economy, depends on

1. The amount of resources retained and reinvested in the entity
2. The rate of return earned on the resources retained

The more a firm reinvests, the greater its potential for growth. Alternatively, for a given level of reinvestment, a firm will grow faster if it earns a higher rate of return on the resources reinvested. Therefore, the growth of equity earnings is a function of two variables: (1) the percentage of net earnings retained (the firm's retention rate) and (2) the rate of return earned on the firm's equity capital (the firm's ROE).

$$g = \text{Percentage of Earnings Retained} \times \text{Return on Equity}$$
$$= \text{RR} \times \text{ROE}$$

where:

g = **potential growth rate**
RR = **the retention rate of earnings**
ROE = **the firm's return on equity**

The retention rate is a decision by the board of directors based on the investment opportunities available to the firm. Theory suggests that the firm should retain earnings and reinvest them as long as the expected rate of return on the investment exceeds the firm's cost of capital.

As discussed earlier in the chapter, the firm's ROE is a function of three components:

♦ Net profit margin
♦ Total asset turnover
♦ Financial leverage (total assets/equity)

Therefore, a firm can increase its ROE by increasing its profit margin, by becoming more efficient (increasing its total asset turnover), or by increasing its financial leverage and financial risk. As discussed, you should examine and estimate each of the components when estimating the ROE for a firm.

The growth potential analysis for Walgreen begins with the retention rate (RR):

$$\text{Retention Rate} = 1 - \frac{\text{Dividends Declared}}{\text{Operating Income after Taxes}}$$

Walgreen RR figures were

$$1997: 1 - \frac{.24}{.88} = 0.73$$

$$1996: 1 - \frac{.22}{.75} = 0.71$$

$$1995: 1 - \frac{.20}{.65} = 0.69$$

These results shown in Table 9.8 indicate that the retention rate for Walgreen has been extremely stable during the sixteen-year period at about 70 percent.

Table 9.6 contains the three components of ROE for the period 1982–97. Table 9.8 contains the two factors that determine a firm's growth potential and the implied growth rate during the past sixteen years. Overall, Walgreen has experienced a slight decline in its growth potential from about 14 percent in the early years to 12–13 percent recently.

Table 9.8 reinforces our understanding of the importance of the firm's ROE. Walgreens' retention rate was quite stable throughout the period, implying that the firm's ROE determined its growth rate. This analysis indicates that the important consideration is the long-run outlook for the components of sustainable growth. As an investor, you need to *project* changes in each of the components of ROE and employ these projections to estimate an ROE to use in the growth model along with an estimate of the firm's long-run retention rate. We will come back to these concepts on numerous occasions when valuing the market, industries, and individual firms, especially growth companies where the ROEs are notably high and vulnerable to competition.

EXTERNAL MARKET LIQUIDITY

Market Liquidity Defined

In Chapter 8 we discussed market liquidity as the ability to buy or sell an asset quickly with little price change from a prior transaction assuming no new information. AT&T and IBM are examples of liquid common stocks because you can sell them quickly with little price change from the prior trade. You might be able to sell an illiquid stock quickly, but the price would be significantly different from the prior price. Alternatively, the broker might be able to get a specified price, but could take several days doing so.

Determinants of Market Liquidity

Investors should know the liquidity characteristics of securities they currently own or may buy because liquidity can be important if they want to change the composition of their portfolios. Although the major determinants of market liquidity are reflected in market trading data, several internal corporate variables are good proxies for these market variables. The most important determinant of external market liquidity is the number of shares or the dollar value of shares traded (the dollar value adjusts for different price levels). More trading activity indicates a greater probability that you can find someone to take the other side of a desired transaction. Another measure of market liquidity is the bid–ask spread (a smaller spread indicates greater liquidity). Fortunately, certain internal corporate variables correlate highly with these market trading variables:

Table 9.8 *Walgreen Company Components of Growth and the Implied Sustainable Growth Rate*

Year	(1) Retention Rate[a]	(2) Return on Equity[b]	(3)[c] Sustainable Growth Rate
1982	0.72	18.73	13.49
1983	0.74	19.84	14.68
1984	0.74	20.60	15.24
1985	0.71	19.58	13.90
1986	0.70	18.64	13.05
1987	0.68	16.63	11.31
1988	0.71	18.12	12.87
1989	0.73	18.74	13.68
1990	0.72	18.42	13.26
1991	0.71	18.04	12.81
1992	0.71	17.90	12.71
1993	0.67	16.07	10.77
1994	0.70	17.91	12.54
1995	0.69	17.89	12.52
1996	0.71	18.19	12.91
1997	0.73	18.35	13.40

[a]Operating income after taxes is used to calculate retention rate.

[b]From Table 9.6.

[c]Column (3) is equal to column (1) times column (2).

1. Total market value of outstanding securities (number of common shares outstanding times the market price per share)
2. Number of security owners

Numerous studies have shown that the main determinant of the bid–ask spread (besides price) is the dollar value of trading.[8] In turn, the value of trading correlates highly with the market value of the outstanding securities and the number of security holders. This relationship holds because with more shares outstanding, there will be more stockholders to buy or sell at any time for a variety of purposes. Numerous buyers and sellers provide liquidity.

You can estimate the market value of Walgreen's outstanding stock as the average number of shares outstanding during the year (adjusted for stock splits) times the average market price for the year (equal to the high price plus the low price divided by two) as follows:[9]

$$1997: 493,789,966 \times [(30+16)/2] = \$11.36 \text{ billion}$$
$$1996: 492,282,144 \times [(18+12)/2] = \$7.38 \text{ billion}$$
$$1995: 492,282,144 \times [(13+10)/2] = \$5.66 \text{ billion}$$

These market values would place Walgreen in the large-capitalization category, which usually begins at about $5 billion. Walgreen's stockholders number 43,000, including more than 600 institutions that own approximately 51 percent of the outstanding stock.

A final measure, **trading turnover** (the percentage of outstanding shares traded during a period of time), also indicates trading activity. During calendar year 1997, about 296 million shares of Walgreen were traded, which indicates turnover of approximately 60 percent (296 million/494 million). This compares with the average turnover for the NYSE

[8]Studies on this topic were discussed in Chapter 4.

[9]These values are for the Walgreen fiscal year. Stock prices are rounded to the nearest whole dollar.

of about 50 percent. These large values for market value, the number of stockholders and institutional holders, and the high trading turnover indicate a highly liquid market in the common stock of Walgreen. That is, Walgreen has extremely low external liquidity risk.

COMPARATIVE ANALYSIS OF RATIOS

We have discussed the importance of comparative analysis, but so far we have concentrated on the selection and computation of specific ratios. Table 9.9 contains most of the ratios discussed for Walgreen, the Retail Drug Store Industry (as derived from the S&P *Analysts Handbook*), and the S&P 400 Index. The three-year comparison should provide some insights, although you typically would want to examine data for a five- to ten-year period. It is necessary to do the comparison for the period 1994–96 because industry and market data from Standard and Poor's were not available for 1997 until late in 1998.

Internal Liquidity

The three basic ratios (current ratio, quick ratio, and cash ratio) provided mixed results regarding liquidity for Walgreen relative to the industry and market. The current ratio is above the industry and market. The firm's receivables turnover has increased and its collection period is so fast that the collection period is substantially less than the S&P 400 and the retail drug store industry (eight days versus forty and ninety in 1996). Because it has declined steadily, the difference is probably because of its basic credit policy.

Overall, the comparisons indicate reasonably strong internal liquidity. An additional positive factor is the firm's ability to sell high-grade commercial paper and the existence of several major bank credit lines.

Operating Performance

This segment of the analysis considers efficiency ratios (turnovers) and profitability ratios. Given the nature of the analysis, the major comparison is relative to the industry. Walgreen's turnover ratios were substantially above the retail drug industry. Specifically, during 1994 to 1996, all the turnover ratios for Walgreen (except for working capital turnover) exceeded comparable industry turnovers.

This was offset partially by profitability from sales, which was only adequate. Operating and net profit margins were consistently below the aggregate market and industry.

The profit performance related to invested capital was historically strong. The retail drug store industry return on total capital was consistently above the S&P 400, and Walgreen was above the retail drug store industry in 1995 and 1996. The drug store industry experienced ROEs substantially above the market, and Walgreen attained higher ROEs than its industry in 1996.

Financial Risk

Walgreen's financial risk ratios, measured in terms of proportion of debt, were consistently below those of the industry and the market, indicating a low financial risk posture. Similarly the financial risk flow ratios for Walgreen were substantially above the market and its industry. These comparisons confirm that Walgreen has not increased its very low financial risk position during the past several years. Note that the financial risk ratios in Table 9.9 assume that deferred taxes are long-term debt, a conservative assumption for a firm with a strong growth pattern like Walgreen.

Table 9.9 *Summary of Financial Ratios for Walgreen, S&P Retail Drug Stores, S&P 400 Index: 1994–96*

	1996			1995			1994		
	Walgreen	Drug Stores	S&P 400	Walgreen	Drug Stores	S&P 400	Walgreen	Drug Stores	S&P 400
Internal Liquidity									
Current ratio	1.71	1.20	1.38	1.68	1.20	1.24	1.59	1.20	1.25
Quick ratio	0.25	0.70	0.96	0.25	0.60	0.85	0.29	0.70	0.85
Cash ratio	0.01	0.17	0.18	0.02	0.15	0.16	0.10	0.16	0.16
Receivables turnover	44.06	9.00	4.07	47.25	11.94	4.23	55.42	11.89	4.07
Average collection period	8.28	40.56	89.60	7.73	30.56	86.26	6.59	30.70	89.79
Working capital/sales	0.07	0.05	12.26	0.07	0.04	8.43	0.07	0.04	8.45
Operation Performance									
Total asset turnover	3.42	1.39	0.90	3.37	1.49	0.90	3.39	1.48	0.90
Inventory turnover (sales)[a]	7.63	6.74	9.50	8.49	8.82	9.60	7.83	9.13	9.30
Working capital turnover	14.07	18.59	8.16	14.14	27.00	11.86	15.37	25.77	11.83
Net fixed asset turnover	8.73	3.00	2.78	8.91	3.96	2.77	9.18	4.02	2.69
Equity turnover	6.14	3.61	3.33	6.18	4.67	3.29	6.26	4.38	3.13
Profitability									
Gross profit margin	27.71	—	—	28.02	—	—	28.38	—	—
Operating profit margin[b]	5.13	14.56	14.86	5.00	12.68	13.61	4.93	12.66	13.08
Net profit margin[b]	3.16	5.13	5.35	3.09	4.96	3.73	3.05	4.99	3.24
Return on total capital[b]	10.96	7.72	6.96	10.45	9.80	5.76	19.27	10.20	5.61
Return on owner's equity[b]	19.38	18.53	17.80	19.06	23.20	12.28	19.10	21.82	10.14
Financial Risk									
Debt–equity ratio[c]	7.11	84.79	130.20	7.94	107.23	136.30	11.03	91.15	122.62
Long-term debt/long-term capital[c]	6.64	44.95	56.56	7.35	50.50	57.68	9.94	46.80	55.08
Total debt/total capital[c]	6.64	60.72	69.96	7.35	64.93	72.00	9.94	63.19	70.30
Interest coverage[b]	273.78	6.41	4.70	441.12	6.17	3.40	178.27	5.97	2.90
Cash flow/long-term debt[b,c]	809.91	39.87	25.07	1232.78	36.22	21.48	330.38	37.33	22.52
Cash flow/total debt[b,c]	809.91	19.15	14.01	1232.78	18.15	11.39	330.38	18.42	11.67
Growth Analysis[d]									
Retention rate[b]	0.71	0.56	0.61	0.70	0.56	0.42	0.70	0.56	0.33
Return on equity[b]:	18.20	20.78	17.14	17.90	24.31	12.86	17.92	21.54	9.79
Total asset turnover	3.42	1.39	0.91	3.37	1.49	0.92	3.17	1.48	0.94
Total assets/equity	1.78	2.91	3.51	1.81	3.30	3.76	1.85	2.92	3.50
Net profit margin[b]	3.16	5.13	5.35	3.09	4.96	3.73	3.05	4.99	3.24
Sustainable growth rate[b]	12.86	11.58	10.47	12.53	13.66	5.40	12.57	11.98	3.23

[a]Computed using sales since cost of sales not available for industry and S&P 400.

[b]Calculated using operating income after taxes.

[c]Ratios include deferred taxes and long-term debt.

[d]Calculated using year-end data.

Table 9.10 *Comparative Balance Sheet Formats*

United Kingdom

Net assets employed
    Fixed assets
    Subsidiaries
    Associated companies
    Current assets
    Less: current liabilities
    Less: deferred liabilities
Assets represented by:
    Share capital
    Reserves

Canada

Assets
    Current assets
    Investments
    Fixed assets
    Other assets
Liabilities and shareholders' equity
    Current liabilities
    Long-term debt
    Deferred income taxes
    Shareholders' equity

Australia

Share capital and reserves and liabilities
    Share capital and reserves
    Long-term debt and deferred income taxes
    Current liabilities
Assets
    Fixed assets
    Investments
    Current assets

Germany

Assets
    Outstanding payments on subscribed share capital
    Fixed assets and investments
    Revolving assets
    Deferred charges and prepaid expenses
    Accumulated net loss (of period)
Liabilities and shareholders' equity
    Share capital
    Open reserves
    Adjustments to assets
    Reserves for estimated liabilities and accrued expenses
    Deferred income
    Accumulated net profit (of period)

Source: *Professional Accounting in 30 Countries,* pp. 51, 125–126, 169, 629, 746–749. Copyright © 1975 by the American Institute of Certified Public Accountants, Inc. Reprinted by permission of the AICPA.

Growth Analysis

Walgreen has generally maintained a sustainable growth rate similar to its industry, and both Walgreen and the industry have outperformed the aggregate market. The major factor causing a difference in growth for the firm and its industry is a slightly lower ROE, but the retention rate for Walgreen was consistently higher.

In sum, Walgreen has adequate liquidity, a good operating record, and low financial risk even when you consider the leases on stores. Your success as an investor depends on how well you use these historical numbers to derive meaningful *estimates* of future performance and then use these estimates in a valuation model.

ANALYSIS OF NON-U.S. FINANCIAL STATEMENTS

As noted previously, your portfolio should encompass other economies and markets, numerous global industries, and many foreign firms in these global industries. You should recognize, however, that non-U.S. financial statements will differ widely from those in this chapter and a typical accounting course. Accounting conventions differ substantially among countries. Although it is impossible to discuss alternative accounting conventions in detail, we will consider some of the major differences in format and principle.

Accounting Statement Format Differences

Table 9.10 contains examples of balance sheet formats for several countries and indicates some major differences in accounts and the order of presentation. As an example, in the

Table 9.11 *Comparative Income Statement Formats*

United Kingdom

Group turnover
Profit before taxation and extraordinary items
    Less: Taxation based on profit for the year
Profit after taxation and before extraordinary items
    Less: Extraordinary items
Profits attributable to shareholders of parent company

Japan

Sales
    Less: Cost of goods sold
Gross profit on sales
    Less: Selling and administrative expenses
Operating income
    Add: Nonoperating revenue
Gross profit for the period
    Less: Nonoperating expenses
Net income for the period

Australia

Sales and revenue
    Less: Cost of sales
Operating profit
    Add: Income from investments
    Less: Interest to other persons
Pretax profit
    Less: Provision for income tax
Net profit before extraordinary items
    Less: Extraordinary items
Net profit after extraordinary items
Unappropriated profits, previous year
Prior year adjustments
Transfer from general reserve
Available for appropriation
Dividends
Transfer to general reserve
Transfer to capital profits reserve
Unappropriated profits, end of year

Germany

Net sales
Increase or decrease of finished and unfinished products
Other manufacturing costs for fixed assets
Total output
Raw materials and supplies, purchased goods consumed in sale
Gross profit
Income from profit transfer agreements
Income from trade investments
Income from other long-term investments
Other interest and similar income
Income from retirement and appraisal of fixed assets
Income from the cancellation of lump allowances
Income from the cancellation of overstated reserves
Other income, including extraordinary in the sum of DM
Income from loss transfer agreements
Total income
Wages and salaries
Social taxes
Expenses for pension plans and relief
Depreciation and amortization of fixed assets and investments
Depreciation and amortization of finance investments
Losses by deduction or on retirement of current assets
Losses on retirement of fixed assets and investments
Interest and similar expenses
Taxes on income and net assets
Other expenses
Profits transferable to parent company under profit transfer
    agreement
Profit or loss for the period
Profit or loss brought forward from preceding year
Release of reserves
Amounts appropriated to reserves out of profit of period
Accumulated net profit or loss

Source: *Professional Accounting in 30 Countries,* pp. 52, 350, 351, 630, 750, 753. Copyright © 1975 by the American Institute of Certified Public Accountants, Inc. Reprinted by permission of the AICPA.

United Kingdom fixed assets are presented above current assets, and current liabilities are automatically subtracted from current assets. In Australia, capital accounts are presented initially, and the current assets are placed below long-term assets. The balance sheet items are similar to those in the United States, but almost exactly opposite in presentation. Clearly, the accounts and presentation in Canada are similar to those in the United States. Germany's accounts also are similar except that they have numerous reserve accounts on the liability side. Besides finding similarities to the U.S. firms, you need to consider the techniques used to derive individual items.

    The comparative income statement formats in Table 9.11 show that the U.K. statements have much less detail than U.S. statements. This limits your ability to analyze trends in expense items. Although Japanese statements are fairly similar to those of the United States, you should be aware of nonoperating income and expense items. These can be

substantial because Japanese firms typically have heavy investments in the common stock of suppliers and customers as a sign of goodwill. The income and gains (or losses) from these equity holdings can be a substantial permanent component of a firm's net income.

The Australian statements, like the British, combine numerous expense items and include several items concerned with the distribution of the net income. Finally, income statements from Germany are highly detailed and contain many unusual income and expense items. These details provide numerous opportunities to control the profit or loss for the period.

Differences in Accounting Principles

Beyond the differences in the presentation format, numerous differences appear in the accounting principles used to arrive at the income, expense, and balance sheet items. Choi and Bavishi compared accounting standards for ten countries and highlighted the differences.[10] Table 9.12 synthesizes the differences in thirty-two specific items. Following a discussion of several major areas, the authors conclude

> Perhaps the major conclusion drawn from analyzing the annual reports of the world's leading industrial firms is that fundamental differences in accounting practices between each of ten countries examined are not as extensive as was initially feared. Major differences observed relate to accounting for goodwill, deferred taxes, long-term leases, discretionary reserves, and foreign-currency translation. Having observed this comforting fact, the user must be cautioned against assuming that consistency and harmonization exist among the annual reports of all foreign companies.[11]

International Ratio Analysis

The tendency is to analyze accounting statements using financial ratios similar to those discussed in this chapter. Although this is certainly legitimate, it is important to recognize that the representative ratio values and trends may differ among countries because of local accounting practices and business norms. Choi et al. compared a common set of ratios for a sample of companies in the United States, Japan, and Korea.[12] Table 9.13 compares the mean values for these ratios and the differences among them. These ratios differ substantially for all manufacturing as well as for specific important industries (chemical, textiles, and transportation). Following an extensive discussion of the ratios, the authors conclude

> On the basis of these findings, institutional, cultural, political and tax considerations in Japan and Korea do indeed cause their accounting ratios to differ from U.S. norms without necessarily reflecting better or worse financial risk and return characteristics being measured. . . .
>
> A major conclusion of our study is that accounting measurements reflected in corporate financial reports represent, in one sense, merely "numbers" that have limited meaning and significance in and of themselves. Meaning and significance come from and depend upon an

---

[10]Frederick D. S. Choi and Vinod B. Bavishi, "Diversity in Multinational Accounting," *Financial Executive* 50, no. 7 (August 1982): 36–39. This table also is presented and discussed in Frederick D. S. Choi and Gerhard G. Mueller, *International Accounting* (Englewood Cliffs, NJ: Prentice-Hall, 1984), 72–76.

[11]Choi and Bavishi, "Diversity in Multinational Accounting," 39. Another comparison of accounting standards for the United States, the United Kingdom, the European Economic Community, and Canada is contained in Thomas G. Evans, Martin E. Taylor, and Oscar Holzmann, *International Accounting and Reporting* (New York: Macmillan, 1985), 106–113.

[12]Frederick D. S. Choi, Hisaaki Hino, Sang Kee Min, Sang Oh Nam, Junichi Ujiie, and Arthur J. Stonehill, "Analyzing Foreign Financial Statements: The Use and Misuse of International Ratio Analysis," *Journal of International Business Studies* (Spring–Summer 1983): 113–131, reprinted in Frederick D. S. Choi and Gerhard G. Mueller, *Frontiers of International Accounting: An Anthology* (Ann Arbor, MI: UMI Research Press, 1985).

understanding of the environmental context from which the numbers are drawn as well as the relationship between the numbers and the underlying economic phenomena that are the real items of interest.[13]

THE QUALITY OF FINANCIAL STATEMENTS

Analysts sometimes speak of the quality of a firm's earnings, or the quality of a firm's balance sheet. In general, quality financial statements are a good reflection of reality; accounting tricks and one-time changes are not used to make the firm appear stronger than it really is. Some factors that lead to lower-quality financial statements were mentioned previously when we discussed ratio analysis. Other quality influences are discussed below.

Balance Sheet

A high-quality balance sheet typically has a conservative use of debt or leverage. Therefore, the potential of financial distress resulting from the need to service debt is quite low. Little use of debt also implies the firm has unused borrowing capacity; should an attractive investment opportunity arise, the firm can draw on that unused capacity to invest wisely for the shareholders' benefit.

A quality balance sheet contains assets with a market value greater than their book value. The capability of management and the existence of intangible assets such as goodwill, trademarks, or patents will make the market value of the firm's assets exceed their book values. In general, as a result of inflation and historical cost accounting, we might expect the market value of assets to exceed their book values. Some situations in which the opposite may occur include the use of outdated, technologically inferior assets; unwanted or out-of-fashion inventory; and the presence of nonperforming assets on the firm's books (an example would be a bank that has not written off nonperforming loans).

The presence of off-balance-sheet liabilities also harms the quality of a balance sheet. Such liabilities may include joint ventures and loan commitments or guarantees to subsidiaries.

Income Statement

High-quality earnings are *repeatable* earnings. For example, they arise from sales among customers who are expected to do repeat business with the firm and from costs that are not artificially low as a result of unusual and short-lived input price reductions. One-time and nonrecurring items, such as accounting changes, mergers, and asset sales, should be ignored when examining earnings. Unexpected exchange rate fluctuations that work in the firm's favor to raise revenues or reduce costs should also be viewed as nonrecurring.

High-quality earnings result from the use of conservative accounting principles that do not result in overstated revenues and understated costs. The closer the earnings are to cash, the higher the quality of the income statement. Suppose a firm sells furniture "on time" by allowing customers to make monthly payments. A higher-quality income statement will recognize revenue using the "installment" principle; that is, as the cash is collected each month, in turn, annual sales will reflect only the cash collected from sales during the year. A lower-quality income statement will recognize 100 percent of the revenue from a sale at the time of sale, even though payments may stretch well into next year.

---

[13]Choi et al., "Analyzing Foreign Financial Statements," 131.

Table 9.12 *Synthesis of Accounting Differences*

Accounting Principles	United States	Australia	Canada	France	Germany	Japan	The Netherlands	Sweden	Switzerland	United Kingdom
1. Marketable securities recorded at the lower of cost or market?	Yes	Yes	Yes	Yes	Yes	Yes	Yes	Yes	Yes	Yes
2. Provision for uncorrectable accounts made?	Yes	Yes	Yes	No	Yes	Yes	Yes	Yes	Yes	Yes
3. Inventory costed using FIFO?	Mixed	Yes	Mixed	Mixed	Yes	Mixed	Mixed	Yes	Yes	Yes
4. Manufacturing overhead allocated to year-end inventory?	Yes	Yes	Yes	Yes	Yes	Yes	Yes	Yes	No	Yes
5. Inventory valued at the lower of cost or market?	Yes	Yes	Yes	Yes	Yes	Yes	Yes	Yes	Yes	Yes
6. Accounting for long-term investments: less than 20 percent ownership: cost method?	Yes	Yes	Yes	Yes*	Yes	Yes	No(K)	Yes	Yes	Yes
7. Accounting for long-term investments: 21–50 percent ownership: equity method?	Yes	No(G)	Yes	Yes*	No(B)	No(B)	Yes	No(B)	No(B)	Yes
8. Accounting for long-term investments: more than 50 percent ownership: full consolidation?	Yes	Yes	Yes	Yes*	Yes	Yes	Yes	Yes	Yes	Yes
9. Both domestic and foreign subsidiaries consolidated?	Yes	Yes	Yes	Yes	No**	Yes	Yes	Yes	Yes	Yes
10. Acquisitions accounted for under the pooling-of-interest method?	Yes	No(C)	No(C)	No(C)	No(C)	No(C)	No(C)	No(C)	No(C)	No(C)
11. Intangible assets: goodwill amortized?	Yes	Yes	Yes	Yes	No	Yes	Mixed	Yes	No**	No**
12. Intangible assets: other than goodwill amortized?	Yes	Yes	Yes	Yes	Yes	Yes	Yes	Yes	No**	No**
13. Long-term debt includes maturities longer than one year?	Yes	Yes	Yes	Yes	Yes	Yes	Yes	Yes	Yes	Yes
14. Discount/premium on long-term debt amortized?	Yes	Yes	Yes	No	No(D)	Yes	Yes	No	No	No
15. Deferred taxes recorded when accounting income is not equal to taxable income?	Yes	Yes	Yes	Yes	Yes	Yes	Yes	No	No	Yes
16. Financial leases (long-term) capitalized?	Yes	No	Yes	No	No	No	No	No	No	No
17. Company pension fund contribution provided regularly?	Yes	Yes	Yes	Yes	Yes	Yes	Yes	Yes	Yes	Yes
18. Total pension fund assets and liabilities excluded from company's financial statement?	Yes	Yes	Yes	Yes	No	Yes	Yes	No	No	Yes
19. Research and development expensed?	Yes	Yes	Yes	Yes	Yes	Yes	Yes	Yes	Yes	Yes
20. Treasury stock deducted from owner's equity?	Yes	NF	Yes	Yes	No	Yes	Mixed	NF	NF	NF
21. Gains or losses on treasury stock taken to owner's equity?	Yes	NF	Yes	Yes	No	No**	Mixed	NF	NF	NF

(continued)

Table 9.12 (concluded)

Accounting Principles	United States	Australia	Canada	France	Germany	Japan	The Netherlands	Sweden	Switzerland	United Kingdom
22. No general purpose (purely discretionary) reserves allowed?	Yes	Yes	Yes	No	No	No	No	No	No	Yes
23. Dismissal indemnities accounted for on a pay-as-you-go basis?	Yes	Yes	Yes	Yes	Yes	Yes	NF	Yes	NF	Yes
24. Minority interest excluded from consolidated income?	Yes	Yes	Yes	Yes	No	Yes	Yes	Yes	Yes	Yes
25. Minority interest excluded from consolidated owner's equity?	Yes	Yes	Yes	Yes	No	Yes	Yes	Yes	Yes	Yes
26. Are intercompany sales or profits eliminated on consolidation?	Yes	Yes	Yes	Yes	Yes	Yes	Yes	Yes	Yes	Yes
27. Basic financial statements reflect a historical cost valuation (no price level adjustment)?	Yes	No	Yes	No	Yes	Yes	No	No	No	No
28. Supplementary inflation-adjusted financial statements provided?	Yes	No**	No**	No	No	No	No**	No	No**	Yes
29. Straight-line depreciation adhered to?	Yes	Yes	Yes	Mixed	Mixed	Mixed	Yes	Yes	Yes	Yes
30. No expense depreciation permitted?	Yes	No	Yes	No	Yes	Yes	No	No	No	No
31. Temporal method of foreign currency translation employed?	Yes	Mixed	Yes	No(E)	No(E)	Mixed	No(E)	No(L)	No(E)	No(E)
32. Currency translation gains or losses reflected in current income?	Yes	Mixed	Yes	Mixed	Mixed	Mixed	No(J)	Mixed	No(H)	No

Key
Yes—Predominant practice.
Yes*—Minor modifications, but still predominant practice.
No**—Minority practice.
No—Accounting principle in question is not adhered to.
NF—Not found.
Mixed—Alternative practices followed with no majority.
B—Cost method is used.
C—Purchase method is used.
D—Long-term debt includes maturities longer than four years.

E—Current rate method of foreign-currency translation.
F—Weighted average is used.
G—Cost or equity.
H—Translation gains and losses are deferred.
I—Market is used.
J—Owner's equity.
K—Equity.
L—Monetary/Nonmonetary.

Source: "Diversity in Multinational Accounting" by Frederick D. S. Choi and Vinod B. Bavishi. Reprinted with permission from *Financial Executive*, August 1982, copyright © 1982 by Financial Executives Institute, 10 Madison Avenue, P.O. Box 1938, Morristown, NJ 07962-1938.

Table 9.13   *Mean Differences in Aggregate Financial Ratios: United States, Japan, Korea (Unadjusted)*

Enterprise Category	Current Ratio	Quick Ratio	Debt Ratio	Times Interest Earned	Inventory Turnover
All Manufacturing					
Japan (976)	1.15	0.80	0.84	1.60	5.00
Korea (354)	1.13	0.46	0.78	1.80	6.60
United States (902)	1.94	1.10	0.47	6.50	6.80
Difference (U.S.–Japan)	40%	26%	(77%)	75%	26%
Difference (U.S.–Korea)	42%	58%	(66%)	73%	2%
Chemicals					
Japan (129)	1.30	0.99	0.79	1.80	7.10
Korea (54)	1.40	0.70	0.59	2.40	7.10
United States (n.a.)	2.20	1.30	0.45	6.50	6.50
Difference (U.S.–Japan)	42%	22%	(74%)	72%	(8%)
Difference (U.S.–Korea)	36%	45%	(31%)	62%	(9%)
Textiles					
Japan (81)	1.00	0.77	0.81	1.10	6.20
Korea (34)	1.00	0.37	0.83	1.30	4.90
United States (n.a.)	2.30	1.20	0.48	4.30	6.50
Difference (U.S.–Japan)	55%	38%	(70%)	74%	5%
Difference (U.S.–Korea)	55%	70%	(74%)	70%	24%
Transportation					
Japan (85)	1.20	0.86	0.83	1.90	3.90
Korea (14)	0.95	0.40	0.91	1.90	18.60
United States (n.a.)	1.60	0.74	0.52	8.70	5.60
Difference (U.S.–Japan)	21%	(16%)	(61%)	78%	28%
Difference (U.S.–Korea)	40%	46%	(75%)	77%	(234%)

THE VALUE OF FINANCIAL STATEMENT ANALYSIS

Financial statements, by their nature, are backward-looking. They report the firm's assets, liabilities, and equity as of a certain (past) date; they report a firm's revenues, expenses, or cash flows over some (past) time period. An efficient capital market will have already incorporated this past information into security prices; so it may seem, at first glance, that analysis of a firm's financial statements and ratios is a waste of the analyst's time.

The fact is, the opposite is true. Analysis of financial statements allows the analyst to gain knowledge of a firm's operating and financial structure. This, in turn, assists the analyst in determining the effects of *future* events on the firm's cash flows. Likely future scenarios can be analyzed and a knowledge of the firm's operating and financial leverage can help the analyst gauge the risk and expected cash flows of the firm. Combining knowledge of the firm's strategy, operating, and financial leverage and possible macro- and microeconomic scenarios is necessary to determine an appropriate market price for the firm's stock. Combining what is known about the firm, based on the analysis of historical data, with potential future scenarios allows analysts to evaluate the risks facing the firm and then to develop an expected return forecast based on these risks. The final outcome of the process, as future chapters will detail, is the market's determination of the firm's current value which is compared to its security price.

Table 9.13   *(concluded)*

Enterprise Category	Average Collection Period	Fixed Asset Turnover	Total Asset Turnover	Profit Margin	Return on Total Assets	Return on Net Worth
All Manufacturing						
Japan (976)	86	3.10	0.93	.013	0.12	.071
Korea (354)	33	2.80	1.20	.023	.028	.131
United States (902)	43	3.90	1.40	.054	.074	.013
Difference (U.S.–Japan)	(102%)	22%	32%	26%	84%	49%
Difference (U.S.–Korea)	24%	29%	9%	57%	62%	6%
Chemicals						
Japan (129)	88	2.80	0.90	.015	.014	.065
Korea (54)	33	1.60	0.90	.044	.040	.100
United States (n.a.)	50	2.80	1.10	.073	.081	.148
Difference (U.S.–Japan)	(75%)	0%	19%	79%	83%	52%
Difference (U.S.–Korea)	34%	44%	19%	39%	50%	32%
Textiles						
Japan (81)	66	3.50	0.92	.003	.003	.017
Korea (34)	30	2.20	1.00	.010	.011	.064
United States (n.a.)	48	5.80	1.80	.027	.049	.094
Difference (U.S.–Japan)	(39%)	40%	50%	87%	93%	82%
Difference (U.S.–Korea)	36%	63%	44%	62%	78%	32%
Transportation						
Japan (85)	116	4.50	0.90	.017	.015	.092
Korea (14)	18	1.10	0.80	.026	.021	.221
United States (n.a.)	31	6.50	1.60	.049	.078	.161
Difference (U.S.–Japan)	278%	30%	44%	65%	80%	43%
Difference (U.S.–Korea)	40%	84%	50%	47%	73%	(37%)

Note: Parentheses indicate foreign ratios greater than U.S. ratios.

Source: Frederick D. S. Choi, Hisaaki Hino, Sang Kee Min, Sang Oh Nam, Junichi Ujiie, and Arthur J. Stonehill, "Analyzing Foreign Financial Statements: The Use and Misuse of International Ratio Analysis," *Journal of International Business Studies* (Spring–Summer 1983): 113–131.

USES OF FINANCIAL RATIOS

We have discussed the role of financial ratios in measuring firm performance and risk. Financial ratios have been used in four major areas in investments (1) stock valuation, (2) the identification of internal corporate variables that affect a stock's systematic risk (beta), (3) assigning credit quality ratings on bonds, and (4) predicting insolvency (bankruptcy) of firms. In this section, we discuss how ratios have been used in each of these four areas and the specific ratios found to be most useful.

Stock Valuation Models

As will be discussed in the following chapter most valuation models attempt to derive a value based upon one of several present value of cash flow models or an appropriate relative valuation ratio for a stock. As we will discuss in Chapters 10 and 13, all the valuation models are influenced by the expected growth rate of earnings, cash flows, dividends and the required rate of return on the stock. Clearly, financial ratios can help in making both estimates. The estimate of the growth rate employs the ratios discussed in the potential growth rate section—the retention rate and the return on equity.

When estimating the required rate of return on an investment (k), you will recall from Chapter 1 that it depends on the risk premium for the security, which is a function of business risk, financial risk, and liquidity risk. Business risk typically is measured in terms of earnings variability, financial risk is identified by either the debt proportion ratios or the flow ratios (that is, the interest coverage ratios or the cash flow ratios), and insights regarding a stock's liquidity risk can be derived from the external liquidity measures discussed.

The typical empirical valuation model has examined a cross section of companies and used a multiple regression model that relates the price–earnings ratios for the sample firms to some of the following corporate variables (the averages generally consider the past five or ten years):[14]

Financial Ratios
1. Average debt/equity
2. Average interest coverage
3. Average dividend payout
4. Average return on equity
5. Average market price to book value

Variability Measures
1. Coefficient of variation of operating earnings
2. Systematic risk (beta)

Nonratio Variables
1. Average growth rate of earnings

Financial Ratios and Systematic Risk

As discussed in Chapter 7, the capital asset pricing model (CAPM) asserts that the relevant risk variable for an asset should be its systematic risk, which is its beta coefficient related to the market portfolio of all risky assets. In efficient markets, a relationship should exist between internal corporate risk variables and market-determined risk variables such as beta. Numerous studies have tested this relationship by examining internal corporate variables intended to reflect business risk and financial risk.[15] Some of the significant variables (usually five-year averages) included were

Financial Ratios
1. Dividend payout
2. Total debt/total assets
3. Cash flow/total debt
4. Interest coverage
5. Working capital/total assets
6. Current ratio

Variability Measures
1. Variance of operating earnings
2. Coefficient of variation of operating earnings
3. Coefficient of variation of operating profit margins
4. Operating earnings beta (company earnings related to aggregate earnings)

[14]A list of studies in this area appears in the reference section at the end of the chapter.
[15]A list of studies in this area appears in the reference section at the end of the chapter.

Nonratio Variables
1. Asset size
2. Market value of stock outstanding

Financial Ratios and Bond Ratings

As will be discussed in Chapter 15, four financial services assign quality ratings to bonds on the basis of the issuing company's ability to meet all its obligations related to the bond. An AAA or Aaa rating indicates high quality and almost no chance of default, whereas a C rating indicates the bond is already in default. Studies have used financial ratios to predict the rating to be assigned to a bond.[16] The major financial variables considered (again, typically five-year averages) were as follows:

Financial Ratios
1. Long-term debt/total assets
2. Total debt/total capital
3. Net income plus depreciation (cash flow)/long-term senior debt
4. Cash flow/total debt
5. Net income plus interest/interest expense (fixed charge coverage)
6. Market value of stock/par value of bonds
7. Net operating profit/sales
8. Net income/total assets
9. Working capital/sales
10. Sales/net worth (equity turnover)

Variability Measures
1. Coefficient of variation (CV) of net earnings
2. Coefficient of variation of return on assets

Nonratio Variables
1. Subordination of the issue
2. Size of the firm (total assets)
3. Issue size
4. Par value of all publicly traded bonds of the firm

Financial Ratios and Insolvency (Bankruptcy)

Analysts have always been interested in using financial ratios to identify which firms might default on a loan or declare bankruptcy. Several studies have attempted to identify a set of ratios for this purpose.[17] The typical study examines a sample of firms that have declared bankruptcy against a matched sample of firms in the same industry and of comparable size that have not failed. The analysis involves examining a number of financial ratios expected to reflect declining liquidity for several years (usually five years) prior to the declaration of bankruptcy. The goal is to determine which ratios or set of ratios provide the best predictions of bankruptcy. Some of the models have been able to properly classify more than 80 percent of the firms one year prior to failure, and some achieve high

---

[16]A list of studies in this area appears in the reference section at the end of the chapter.

[17]A list of studies on this topic appears in the reference section at the end of the chapter. The five ratios designated by an asterisk (*) are the ratios used in the well-known Altman Z-score model following. Edward I. Altman, "Financial Ratios, Discriminant Analysis and the Prediction of Corporate Bankruptcy," *Journal of Finance* 23, no. 4 (September 1968): 589–609.

classification results three to five years before failure. The financial ratios typically included in successful models were [18]

Financial Ratios
1. Cash flow/total debt
2. Cash flow/long-term debt
3. Sales/total assets*
4. Net income/total assets
5. EBIT/total assets*
6. Total debt/total assets
7. Market value of stock/book value of debt*
8. Working capital/total assets*
9. Retained earnings/total assets*
10. Current ratio
11. Cash/current liabilities
12. Working capital/sales

Limitations of Financial Ratios

We must reinforce the earlier point that you should always consider *relative* financial ratios. In addition, you should be aware of other questions and limitations of financial ratios:

1. Are alternative firms' accounting treatment comparable? As you know from prior accounting courses, there are several generally accepted methods for treating various accounting items, and the alternatives can cause a difference in results for the same event. Therefore, you should check on the accounting treatment of significant items and adjust the values for major differences. This becomes a critical consideration when dealing with non-U.S. firms.
2. How homogeneous is the firm? Many companies have several divisions that operate in different industries. This may make it difficult to derive comparable industry ratios.
3. Are the implied results consistent? It is important to develop a total profile of the firm and not depend on only one set of ratios (for example, internal liquidity ratios). As an example, a firm may be having short-term liquidity problems but be profitable, and the profitability will eventually alleviate the short-run liquidity problems.
4. Is the ratio within a reasonable range for the industry? As noted on several occasions, you typically want a *range* of values for the ratio because a value that is either too high or too low for the industry can be a cause for concern.

Investments Online

Many publicly traded companies have Web sites which, among other pieces of information, contain financial information. Sometimes complete copies of the firm's annual report and SEC filings are on their home page. Since the focus of this chapter has been Walgreen's financial statements, here are some relevant sites:

---

[18]In addition to the several studies that have used financial ratios to predict bond ratings and failures, other studies have also used cash flow variables or a combination of financial ratios and cash flow variables for these predictions, and the results have been quite successful. These studies are listed in the reference section at the end of the chapter.

www.walgreens.com/hm.html   Walgreen's home page, with financial information available through links from this page.

At least three of Walgreen's competitors have Web sites featuring financial information. These include:

www.cvs.com   The home page for CVS Pharmacy

www.riteaid.com   Rite Aid Corporation's home page

www.longs.com   The Web site for Longs Drug Stores.

Commercially oriented and government-sponsored databases are available through the Web, too:

www.sec.gov/edgarhp.htm

This is the Web address for gaining entrance into the SEC's EDGAR (electronic data gathering, analysis, and retrieval database). Most firm's SEC filings are accessible through EDGAR, including filings for executive compensation, 10-K, and 10-Q forms for over 8500 firms.

www.hoovers.com

Hoovers Online is a commercial source of company-specific information, including financial statements and stock performance. Some data are available for free, including a company profile, news, stock price and chart of recent stock price performance. It contains links to a number of sources, including the firm's annual report, SEC filings, and earnings per share estimates by Zacks.

www.dnb.com

Dun & Bradstreet is a well-known gatherer of financial information. Corporations make use of its business credit reporting services. D&B publishes industry average financial ratios which are useful in equity and fixed income analysis.

SUMMARY

♦ The overall purpose of financial statement analysis is to help you make decisions on investing in a firm's bonds or stocks. Financial ratios should be examined relative to the economy, the firm's industry, the firm's main competitors, and the firm's past relative ratios.

♦ The specific ratios can be divided into five categories, depending on the purpose of the analysis: internal liquidity, operating performance, risk analysis, growth analysis, and external market liquidity. When analyzing the financial statements for non-U.S. firms, you must consider differences in format and in accounting principles. These differences will cause different values for specific ratios in alternative countries. Four major uses of financial ratios are (1) stock valuation, (2) the identification of internal corporate variables affecting a stock's systematic risk (beta), (3) assigning credit quality ratings on bonds, and (4) predicting insolvency (bankruptcy).

♦ A final caveat: you can envision a large number of potential financial ratios through which to examine almost every possible relationship. The trick is not to come up with more ratios, but to attempt to limit the number of ratios so you can examine them in a meaningful way. This entails an analysis of the ratios over time relative to the economy, the industry, or the past. Any additional effort should be spent on deriving

better comparisons for a limited number of ratios that provide insights into the questions of interest to you (for example, the firm's future operating performance or its financial risk).

Questions

1. Discuss briefly two decisions that require the analysis of financial statements.
2. Why do analysts use financial ratios rather than the absolute numbers? Give an example.
3. Besides comparing a company's performance to its total industry, discuss what other comparisons should be considered *within* the industry.
4. How might a jewelry store and a grocery store differ in terms of asset turnover and profit margin? Would you expect their return on total assets to differ assuming equal business risk? Discuss.
5. Describe the components of business risk, and discuss how the components affect the variability of operating earnings.
6. Would you expect a steel company or a retail food chain to have greater business risk? Discuss this expectation in terms of the components of business risk.
7. When examining a firm's financial structure, would you be concerned with the firm's business risk? Why or why not?
8. How does the fixed charge coverage ratio differ from the total debt to total asset ratio? If they gave conflicting signals regarding financial risk, which would you prefer and why?
9. Give an example of how a cash flow ratio might differ from a proportion of debt ratio. Assuming these ratios differ for a firm (for example, the cash flow ratios indicate high financial risk, while the proportion of debt ratio indicates low risk), which ratios would you follow? Justify your choice.
10. Why is the analysis of growth potential important to the common stockholder? Why is it important to the debt-investor?
11. Discuss the general factors that determine the rate of growth of *any* economic unit.
12. A firm is earning 24 percent on equity and has low risk. Discuss why you would expect it to have a high or low retention rate.
13. The Orange Company earned 18 percent on equity, whereas the Blue Company earned only 14 percent on equity. Does this mean that Orange will grow faster than Blue? Explain.
14. In terms of the factors that determine market liquidity, why do investors consider real estate to be a relatively illiquid asset?
15. Discuss some internal company factors that would indicate a firm's market liquidity.
16. Select one of the limitations of ratio analysis and indicate why you believe it is a major limitation.

Problems

1. The Shamrock Vegetable Company has the following results:

Net sales	$6,000,000
Net total assets	4,000,000
Depreciation	160,000
Net income	400,000
Long-term debt	2,000,000
Equity	1,160,000
Dividends	160,000

   a. Compute Shamrock's ROE directly. Confirm this using the three components.

b. Using the ROE computed in Part a, what is the expected sustainable growth rate for Shamrock?

c. Assuming the firm's net profit margin went to .04, what would happen to Shamrock's ROE?

d. Using the ROE in Part c, what is the expected sustainable growth rate? What if dividends were only $40,000?

2. Three companies have the following results during the recent period.

	K	L	M
Net profit margin	.04	.06	.10
Total assets turnover	2.20	2.00	1.40
Total assets/equity	2.40	2.20	1.50

a. Derive for each its return on equity based on the three DuPont components.

b. Given the following earnings and dividends, compute the sustainable growth rate for each firm.

Earnings/share	2.75	3.00	4.50
Dividends/share	1.25	1.00	1.00

3. Given the following balance sheet, fill in the ratio values for 1999 and discuss how these results compare with both the industry average and Eddies' past performance.

Eddies Enterprises
Consolidated Balance Sheet
Years Ended December 31, 1998 and 1999

Assets (Dollars in Thousands)

	1999	1998
Cash	$ 100	$ 90
Receivables	220	170
Inventories	330	230
Total current assets	650	490
Property, plant, and equipment	1,850	1,650
Depreciation	350	225
Net properties	1,500	1,425
Intangibles	150	150
Total assets	2,300	2,065

Liabilities and Shareholders' Equity

	1999	1998
Accounts payable	$ 85	$ 105
Short-term bank notes	125	110
Current portion of long-term debt	75	—
Accruals	65	85
Total current liabilities	350	300
Long-term debt	625	540
Deferred taxes	100	80
Preferred stock (10%, $100 par)	150	150
Common stock ($2 par, 100,000 issued)	200	200
Additional paid-in capital	325	325
Retained earnings	550	470
Common shareholders' equity	1,075	995
Total liabilities and shareholders' equity	2,300	2,065

Eddies Enterprises
Consolidated Statement of Income
Years Ended December 31, 1998 and 1999
(Dollars in Thousands)

	1999	1998
Net sales	$3,500	$2,990
Cost of goods sold	2,135	1,823
Selling, general, and administrative expenses	1,107	974
Operating profit	258	193
Net interest expense	62	54
Income from operations	195	139
Income taxes	66	47
Net income	129	91
Preferred dividends	15	15
Net income available for common shares	114	76
Dividends declared	40	30

	Eddies (1999)	Eddies' Average	Industry Average
Current ratio	_____	2.000	2.200
Quick ratio	_____	1.000	1.100
Receivables turnover	_____	18.000	18.000
Average collection period	_____	20.000	21.000
Total asset turnover	_____	1.500	1.400
Inventory turnover	_____	11.000	12.500
Fixed-asset turnover	_____	2.500	2.400
Equity turnover	_____	3.200	3.000
Gross profit margin	_____	.400	.350
Operating profit margin	_____	8.000	7.500
Return on capital	_____	.107	.120
Return on equity	_____	.118	.126
Return on common equity	_____	.128	.135
Debt/equity ratio	_____	.600	.500
Debt/total capital ratio	_____	.400	.370
Interest coverage	_____	4.000	4.500
Fixed charge coverage	_____	3.000	4.000
Cash flow/long-term debt	_____	.400	.450
Cash flow/total debt	_____	.250	.300
Retention rate	_____	.350	.400

4. *CFA Examination I (1990)*
   (Question 4 is composed of two parts, for a total of twenty minutes.)
   The DuPont formula defines the net return on shareholders' equity as a function of the following components:

   ◆ operating margin
   ◆ asset turnover
   ◆ interest burden
   ◆ financial leverage
   ◆ income tax rate

   Using *only* the data in the table shown below:
   a. Calculate *each* of the *five* components listed above for 1985 *and* 1989, and calculate the
      return on equity (ROE) for 1985 *and* 1989, using all of the *five* components. Show cal-
      culations. [15 minutes]

b. Briefly discuss the impact of the changes in asset turnover *and* financial leverage on the change in ROE from 1985 to 1989. [5 minutes]

	1985	1989
Income Statement Data		
Revenues	$542	$979
Operating income	38	76
Depreciation and amortization	3	9
Interest expense	3	0
Pretax income	32	67
Income taxes	13	37
Net income after tax	19	30
Balance Sheet Data		
Fixed assets	$ 41	$ 70
Total assets	245	291
Working capital	123	157
Total debt	16	0
Total shareholders' equity	159	220

References

General

Beaver, William H. *Financial Reporting: An Accounting Revolution.* Englewood Cliffs, NJ: Prentice-Hall, 1989.

Bernstein, Leopold A. *Financial Statement Analysis: Theory, Application, and Interpretation.* 5th ed. Homewood, IL: Richard D. Irwin, 1995.

Chen, Kung H., and Thomas A. Shimerda. "An Empirical Analysis of Useful Financial Ratios." *Financial Management* 10, no. 1 (Spring 1981).

Foster, George. *Financial Statement Analysis.* 2nd ed. Englewood Cliffs, NJ: Prentice-Hall, 1978.

Frecka, Thomas J., and Cheng F. Lee. "Generalized Financial Ratio Adjustment Processes and Their Implications." *Journal of Accounting Research* 27, no. 1 (Spring 1983).

Gombola, Michael J., and Edward Ketz. "Financial Ratio Patterns in Retail and Manufacturing Organizations." *Financial Management* 12, no. 2 (Summer 1983).

Heckel, Kenneth S., and Joshua Livnat. *Cash Flow and Security Analysis.* 2nd ed. Burr Ridge, IL: Business One Irwin, 1996.

Helfert, Erich A. *Techniques of Financial Analysis.* 6th ed. Homewood, IL: Richard D. Irwin, 1987.

Higgins, Robert C. *Analysis for Financial Management,* 4th ed. (Chicago: Irwin, 1995)

Johnson, W. Bruce. "The Cross-Sectional Stability of Financial Ratio Patterns." *Journal of Financial and Quantitative Analysis* 14, no. 5 (December 1979).

Lev, Baruch, and S. Ramu Thiagarajan. "Fundamental Information Analysis." *Journal of Accounting Research* 37, no. 2 (Autumn 1993).

White, Gerald I., Ashwinpaul Sondhi, and Dov Fried. *The Analysis and Use of Financial Statements,* 2nd ed. New York: Wiley, 1998.

Analysis of International Financial Statements

Arpan, Jeffrey S., and Lee H. Rodebaugh. *International Accounting and Multinational Enterprises.* New York: Wiley, 1981.

Choi, Frederick D. S., ed. *Multinational Accounting: A Research Framework for the Eighties.* Ann Arbor, MI: UMI Research Press, 1981.

Choi, Frederick D. S., and Vinod B. Bavishi. "Diversity in Multinational Accounting." *Financial Executive* 50, no. 7 (August 1982).

Choi, Frederick D. S., H. Hino, S. K. Min, S. O. Nam, J. Ujiie, and A. I. Stonehill. "Analyzing Foreign Financial Statements: The Use and Misuse of International Ratio Analysis." *Journal of International Business Studies* (Spring–Summer 1983).

Choi, Frederick D. S., and Gerhard G. Mueller. *International Accounting.* Englewood Cliffs, NJ: Prentice-Hall, 1984.

Choi, Frederick D. S., and Gerhard G. Mueller. *Frontiers of International Accounting: An Anthology.* Ann Arbor, MI: UMI Research Press, 1985.

Evans, Thomas G., Martin E. Taylor, and Oscar Holzmann. *International Accounting and Reporting.* New York: Macmillan, 1985.

Fitzgerald, R., A. Stickler, and T. Watts. *International Survey of Accounting Principles and Practices.* Scarborough, Ontario: Price Waterhouse International, 1979.

Gray, S. J., J. C. Shaw, and L. B. McSweeney. "Accounting Standards and Multinational Corporations." *Journal of International Business Studies* 12, no. 1 (Spring–Summer 1981).

Nair, R. D., and Werner G. Frank. "The Impact of Disclosure and Measurement Practices in International Accounting Classifications." *Accounting Review* 55, no. 3 (July 1980).

Financial Ratios and Stock Valuation Models

Babcock, Guilford. "The Concept of Sustainable Growth." *Financial Analysts Journal* 26, no. 3 (May–June 1970).

Beaver, William, and Dale Morse. "What Determines Price–Earnings Ratios?" *Financial Analysts Journal* 34, no. 4 (July–August 1978).

Copeland, Tom, Tim Koller and Jack Murrin. *Valuation: Measuring and Managing the Value of Companies,* 2nd ed. (New York: John Wiley & Co., 1996)

Damodaran, Aswath. *Damodaran on Valuation* (New York: John Wiley & Co., 1994).

Estep, Tony. "Security Analysis and Stock Selection: Turning Financial Information into Return Forecasts." *Financial Analysts Journal* 43, no. 4 (July–August 1987).

Fairfield, Patricia M. "P/E, P/B and the Present Value of Future Dividends." *Financial Analysts Journal* 50, no. 4 (July–August 1994).

Farrell, James L. "The Dividend Discount Model: A Primer." *Financial Analysts Journal* 41, no. 6 (November–December 1985).

Malkiel, Burton G., and John G. Cragg. "Expectations and the Structure of Share Prices." *American Economic Review* 60, no. 4 (September 1970).

Palepu, Krishna G., Victor L. Bernard, and Paul M. Healy. *Business Analysis and Valuation* (Cincinnati, OH: South-Western Publishing Co., 1996).

Wilcox, Jarrod W. "The P/B-ROE Valuation Model." *Financial Analysts Journal* 40, no. 1 (January–February 1984).

Financial Ratios and Systematic Risk (Beta)

Beaver, William H., Paul Kettler, and Myron Scholes. "The Association Between Market-Determined and Accounting-Determined Risk Measures." *Accounting Review* 45, no. 4 (October 1970).

Gahlon, James M., and James A. Gentry. "On the Relationship Between Systematic Risk and the Degrees of Operating and Financial Leverage." *Financial Management* 11, no. 2 (Summer 1982).

Mandelker, Gerson M., and S. Ghon Rhee. "The Impact of the Degrees of Operating and Financial Leverage on the Systematic Risk of Common Stock." *Journal of Financial and Quantitative Analysis* 19, no. 1 (March 1984).

Rosenberg, Barr. "Prediction of Common Stock Investment Risk." *Journal of Portfolio Management* 11, no. 1 (Fall 1984).

Rosenberg, Barr. "Prediction of Common Stock Betas." *Journal of Portfolio Management* 11, no. 2 (Winter 1985).

Thompson, Donald J., II. "Sources of Systematic Risk in Common Stocks." *Journal of Business* 49, No. 2 (April 1976).

Financial Ratios and Bond Ratings

Ang, James S., and A. Kiritkumar. "Bond Rating Methods: Comparison and Validation." *Journal of Finance* 30, no. 2 (May 1975).

Fisher, Lawrence. "Determinants of Risk Premiums on Corporate Bonds." *Journal of Political Economy* 67, no. 3 (June 1959).

Gentry, James A., David T. Whitford, and Paul Newbold. "Predicting Industrial Bond Ratings with a Probit Model and Funds Flow Components." *Financial Review* 23, no. 3 (August 1988).

Kaplan, Robert S., and Gabriel Urwitz. "Statistical Models of Bond Ratings: A Methodological Inquiry." *Journal of Business* 52, no. 2 (April 1979).

Pinches, George E., and Kent A. Mingo. "The Role of Subordination and Industrial Bond Ratings." *Journal of Finance* 30, no. 1 (March 1975).

Standard and Poor's Corporation. "Corporation Bond Ratings: An Overview." 1978.

Financial Ratios and Corporate Bankruptcy

Altman, Edward I. "Financial Ratios, Discriminant Analysis, and the Prediction of Corporate Bankruptcy." *Journal of Finance* 23, no. 4 (September 1968).

Altman, Edward I. *Corporate Financial Distress and Bankruptcy.* 2nd ed. New York: Wiley, 1993.

Altman, Edward I., Robert G. Haldeman, and P. Narayanan. "Zeta Analysis: A New Model to Identify Bankruptcy Risk of Corporations." *Journal of Banking and Finance* 1, no. 2 (June 1977).

Aziz, A., and G. H. Lawson. "Cash Flow Reporting and Financial Distress Models: Testing of Hypothesis." *Financial Management* 18, no. 1 (Spring 1989).

Beaver, William H. "Financial Ratios as Predictors of Failure." *Empirical Research in Accounting: Selected Studies,* 1966, supplement to vol. 4 *Journal of Accounting Research.*

Beaver, William H. "Market Prices, Financial Ratios, and the Prediction of Failure." *Journal of Accounting Research* 6, no. 2 (Autumn 1968).

Beaver, William H. "Alternative Accounting Measures as Predictors of Failure." *Accounting Review* 43, no. 1 (January 1968).

Casey, Cornelius, and Norman Bartczak. "Using Operating Cash Flow Data to Predict Financial Distress: Some Extensions." *Journal of Accounting Research* 23, no. 1 (Spring 1985).

Collins, R. B. "An Empirical Comparison of Bankruptcy Prediction Models." *Financial Management* 9, no. 2 (Summer 1980).

Dumbolena, I. G., and J. M. Shulman. "A Primary Rule for Detecting Bankruptcy: Watch the Cash." *Financial Analysts Journal* 44, no. 5 (September–October 1988).

Gentry, James A., Paul Newbold, and David T. Whitford. "Classifying Bankrupt Firms with Funds Flow Components." *Journal of Accounting Research* 23, no. 1 (Spring 1985).

Gentry, James A., Paul Newbold, and David T. Whitford. "Predicting Bankruptcy: If Cash Flow's Not the Bottom Line, What Is?" *Financial Analysts Journal* 41, no. 5 (September–October 1985).

Gombola, M. F., M. E. Haskins, J. E. Katz, and D. D. Williams. "Cash Flow in Bankruptcy Prediction." *Financial Management* 16, no. 4 (Winter 1987).

Largay, J. A., and C. P. Stickney. "Cash Flows Ratio Analysis and the W. T. Grant Company Bankruptcy." *Financial Analysts Journal* 36, no. 4 (July–August 1980).

Menash, Yaw M. "The Differential Bankruptcy Predictive Ability of Specific Price Level Adjustments: Some Empirical Evidence." *Accounting Review* 58, no. 2 (April 1983).

Ohlson, J. A. "Financial Ratios and the Probabalistic Prediction of Bankruptcy." *Journal of Accounting Research* 18, no. 2 (Spring 1980).

Reilly, Frank K. "Using Cash Flows and Financial Ratios to Predict Bankruptcies." In *Analyzing Investment Opportunities in Distressed and Bankrupt Companies.* Charlottesville, VA: The Institute of Chartered Financial Analysts, 1991.

Wilcox, Jarrod W. "A Prediction of Business Failure Using Accounting Data." *Empirical Research in Accounting: Selected Studies,* 1973, supplement to vol. 11 *Journal of Accounting Research.*

Glossary

Balance sheet   A financial statement that shows what assets the firm controls at a fixed point in time and how it has financed these assets.

Business risk   The variability of operating income arising from the characteristics of the firm's industry. Two sources of business risk are sales variability and operating leverage.

Common size statements   The normalization of balance sheet and income statement items to allow for easier comparison of different-size firms.

Cross-sectional analysis   An examination of a firm's performance in comparison to other firms in the industry with similar characteristics to the firm being studied.

DuPont analysis   A method of examining ROE by breaking it down into three component parts.

Financial risk   The variability of future income arising from the firm's fixed financing costs, for example, interest payments. The effect of fixed financial costs is to magnify the effect of changes in operating profit on net income or earnings per share.

Free cash flow   This cash flow measure equals cash flow from operations minus capital expenditures and dividends.

Generally accepted accounting principles (GAAP)   Accounting principles formulated by the Financial Accounting Standards Board and used to construct financial statements.

Income statement   A financial statement that shows the flow of the firm's sales, expenses, and earnings over a period of time.

Internal growth rate   A measure of how quickly the firm can increase its sales and assets without external financing.

Internal liquidity (solvency) ratios   Relationships between items of financial data that indicate the firm's ability to meet short-term financial obligations.

Operating efficiency ratios   Ratios that measure a firm's utilization of its assets and capital.

Operating leverage   The use of fixed-production costs in the firm's operating cost structure. The effect of fixed costs is to magnify the effect of a change in sales on operating profits.

Operating profitability ratios   Ratios that measure the ability of the firm to earn returns on sales.

Quality financial statements   A term analysts use to describe financial statements that are conservative and a good reflection of reality.

Statement of cash flows   A financial statement that shows the effects on the firm's cash flow of income flows and changes in its balance sheet.

Sustainable growth rate   A measure of how fast a firm can grow using internal equity and debt financing to keep the capital structure constant over time.

Time-series analysis   An examination of a firm's performance data over a period of time.

Trading turnover   The percentage of outstanding shares traded during a period of time.

CHAPTER

10

An Introduction to Security Valuation

This chapter answers the following questions:

♦ What are the two major approaches to the investment process?
♦ What are the specifics and logic of the top-down (three-step) approach and what is the empirical evidence related to its viability?
♦ When valuing an asset, what are the required inputs?
♦ After you have valued an asset, what is the investment decision process?
♦ How do you determine the value of bonds?
♦ How do you determine the value of preferred stock?
♦ What are the two primary approaches to the valuation of common stock?
♦ How do you apply the discounted cash flow valuation approach and what are the major discounted cash flow valuation techniques?
♦ What is the dividend discount model (DDM) and what is its logic?
♦ What is the effect of the assumptions of the DDM when valuing a growth company?
♦ How do you apply the DDM to the valuation of a firm that is expected to experience temporary supernormal growth?
♦ How do you apply the relative valuation approach to valuation and what are the major relative valuation ratios used?
♦ How can you use the DDM to develop an earnings multiplier model?
♦ What does the DDM model imply are the factors that determine a stock's P/E ratio?
♦ How do you estimate the major inputs to the stock valuation models: (1) the required rate of return and (2) the expected growth rate of earnings and dividends?
♦ What additional factors must be considered when estimating the required rate of return and growth rate for a foreign security?   ♦

At the start of this book, we defined an investment as a commitment of funds for a period of time to derive a rate of return that would compensate the investor for the time during which the funds are invested, for the expected rate of inflation during the investment horizon, and for the uncertainty involved. From this definition, we know that the first step in making an investment is determining your required rate of return.

Once you have determined this rate, some investment alternatives such as savings accounts and T-bills are fairly easy to evaluate because they provide stated cash flows. Most investments have expected cash flows and a stated market price (for example, common stock), and you must evaluate the investment to determine if its market price is consistent with your required return. To do this, you must estimate the value of the security based on its expected cash flows and your required rate of return. This is the process of estimating the value of an asset. After you have completed estimating a security's intrinsic value, you compare this estimated intrinsic value to the prevailing market price to decide whether you want to buy the security or not.

This **investment decision process** is similar to the process you follow when deciding on a corporate investment or when shopping for clothes, a stereo, or a car. In each case, you examine the item and decide how much it is worth to you (its value). If the price equals its estimated value or less, you would buy it. The same technique applies to securities except that the determination of a security's value is more formal.

We start our investigation of security valuation by discussing the **valuation process**. There are two general approaches to the valuation process: (1) the top-down, three-step approach or (2) the bottom-up, stock valuation, stockpicking approach. Both of these approaches can be implemented by either fundamentalists or technicians. The difference between the two approaches is the perceived importance of economic and industry influence on individual firms and stocks.

Advocates of the top-down, three-step approach believe that both the economy/market and the industry effect have a significant impact on the total returns for individual stocks. In contrast, those who employ the bottom-up, stockpicking approach contend that it is possible to find stocks that are undervalued relative to their market price, and these stocks will provide superior returns *regardless* of the market and industry outlook.

Both of these approaches have numerous supporters, and advocates of both approaches have been quite successful.[1] In this book, we advocate and present the top-down, three-step approach because of its logic and empirical support. Although we believe that a portfolio manager or an investor can be successful using the bottom-up approach, we believe that it is more difficult to be successful because these stockpickers are ignoring substantial information from the market and the firms' industry.

Although we know that the value of a security is determined by its quality and profit potential, we also believe that the economic environment and the performance of a firm's industry influence the value of a security and its rate of return. Because of the importance of these economic and industry factors, we present an overview of the valuation process that describes these influences and explains how they can be incorporated into the analysis of security value. Subsequently, we describe the theory of value and emphasize the factors that affect the value of securities.

Next, we apply these valuation concepts to the valuation of different assets—bonds, preferred stock, and common stock. In this section, we show how the valuation models help investors calculate how much they should pay for these assets. In the final section, we emphasize the estimation of the variables that affect value (the required rate of

---

[1]For the history and selection process of a legendary stockpicker, see Robert G. Hagstrom, Jr., *The Warren Buffett Way* (New York: Wiley, 1994), or Roger Lowenstein, *Buffett: The Making of an American Capitalist* (New York: Random House, 1995).

return and the expected rate of growth). We conclude with a discussion of additional factors that must be considered when we extend our analysis to the valuation of international securities.

AN OVERVIEW OF THE VALUATION PROCESS

Psychologists suggest that the success or failure of an individual can be caused as much by environment as by genetic gifts. Extending this idea to the valuation of securities means we should consider the economic environment during the valuation process. Regardless of the qualities or capabilities of a firm and its management, the economic environment will have a major influence on the success of a firm and the realized rate of return on the investment.

As an example, assume you own shares of the strongest and most successful firm producing home furnishings. If you own the shares during a strong economic expansion, the sales and earnings of the firm will increase and your rate of return on the stock should be quite high. In contrast, if you own the same stock during a major economic recession, the sales and earnings of this firm would probably experience a decline and the price of its stock would be stable or decline. Therefore, when assessing the future value of a security, it is necessary to analyze the outlook for the aggregate economy, the security markets, and the firm's specific industry.

The valuation process is like the chicken-and-egg dilemma. Do you start by analyzing the macroeconomy and various industries before individual stocks, or do you begin with individual securities and gradually combine these firms into industries and the industries into the entire economy? For reasons discussed in the next section, we contend that the discussion should begin with an analysis of aggregate economies and overall securities markets and progress to different industries with a global perspective. Only after a thorough analysis of a global industry are you in a position to properly evaluate the securities issued by individual firms within the better industries. Thus, we recommend a three-step, top-down valuation process in which you first examine the influence of the general economy on all firms and the security markets, then analyze the prospects for various global industries in this economic environment, and finally turn to the analysis of individual firms in the industries and to the common stock of these firms. Figure 10.1 indicates the procedure recommended.

WHY A THREE-STEP VALUATION PROCESS?

Monetary and fiscal policy measures enacted by various agencies of national governments influence the aggregate economies of those countries. The resulting economic conditions influence all industries and companies within the economies.

General Economic Influences

Fiscal policy initiatives such as tax credits or tax cuts can encourage spending, whereas additional taxes on income, gasoline, cigarettes, and liquor can discourage spending. Increases or decreases in government spending on defense, on unemployment insurance or retraining programs, or on highways also influence the general economy. All such policies influence the business environment for firms that rely directly on those expenditures. In addition, we know that government spending has a strong *multiplier effect*. For example, increases in road building increase the demand for earthmoving equipment and

Figure 10.1   *Overview of the Investment Process*

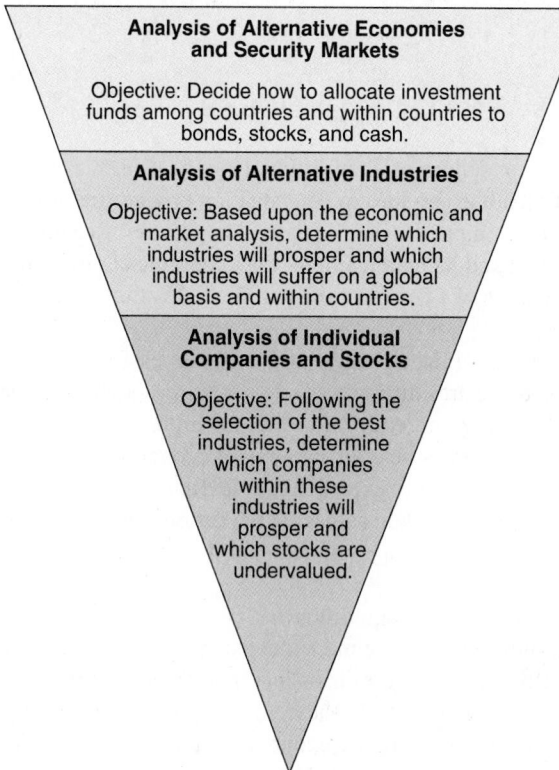

concrete materials. As a result, in addition to construction workers, the employees in those industries that supply the equipment and materials have more to spend on consumer goods, which raises the demand for consumer goods, which affects another set of suppliers.

Monetary policy produces similar economic changes. A restrictive monetary policy that reduces the growth rate of the money supply reduces the supply of funds for working capital and expansion for all businesses. Alternatively, a restrictive monetary policy that targets interest rates would raise market interest rates and therefore firms' costs, and make it more expensive for individuals to finance home mortgages and the purchase of other durable goods such as autos and appliances. Monetary policy therefore affects all segments of an economy and that economy's relationship with other economies.

Any economic analysis requires the consideration of inflation. As we have discussed, inflation causes differences between real and nominal interest rates and changes the spending and savings behavior of consumers and corporations. In addition, unexpected changes in the rate of inflation make it difficult for firms to plan, which inhibits growth and innovation. Beyond the impact on the domestic economy, differential inflation and interest rates influence the trade balance between countries and the exchange rate for currencies.

In addition to monetary and fiscal policy actions, events such as war, political upheavals in foreign countries, or international monetary devaluations produce changes in the business environment that add to the uncertainty of sales and earnings expectations and therefore the risk premium required by investors. For example, the political uncertainty in Russia during 1995–1998 caused a significant increase in the risk premium for investors in Russia and a subsequent reduction in investment and spending in Russia. In

contrast, the end of apartheid in South Africa and its open election in 1994 were viewed as a positive event and led to a significant increase in economic activity in the country. Similarly, the peace accord in Northern Ireland caused a major influx of investment dollars.

In short, it is difficult to conceive of any industry or company that can avoid the impact of macroeconomic developments that affect the total economy. Because aggregate economic events have a profound effect on all industries and companies within these industries, these macroeconomic factors should be considered before industries are analyzed.

Taking a global portfolio perspective, the asset allocation for a country within a global portfolio will be affected by its economic outlook. If a recession is imminent in a country, you would expect a negative impact on its security prices. Because of these economic expectations, investors would be apprehensive about investing in most industries in the country. Given these expectations, the best investment decision would probably be a smaller allocation to the country. Specifically, the country will be **underweighted** in portfolios relative to its weight based on its market value. Further, given these pessimistic expectations, any funds invested in the country would be directed to low-risk sectors of the economy.

In contrast, optimistic economic and stock market outlooks for a given country should lead an investor to increase the overall allocation to this country (**overweight** the country compared to its weights determined by its relative market value). After allocating funds among countries, the investor looks for outstanding industries in each country. This search for the best industries is enhanced by the economic analysis because the future performance of an industry depends on the country's economic outlook *and* the industry's expected relationship to the economy.

Industry Influences

The second step in the valuation process is to identify those industries that will prosper or suffer in the long run or during the expected aggregate near-term economic environment. Examples of conditions that affect specific industries are strikes within a major producing country, import or export quotas or taxes, a worldwide shortage or an excess supply of a resource, or government-imposed regulations on an industry.

You should remember that alternative industries react to economic changes at different points in the business cycle. For example, firms typically increase capital expenditures when they are operating at full capacity at the peak of the economic cycle. Therefore, industries that provide plant and equipment will typically be affected toward the end of a cycle. In addition, alternative industries have different responses to the business cycle. As an example, cyclical industries such as steel or autos typically do much better than the aggregate economy during expansions, but they suffer more during contractions. In contrast, noncyclical industries such as retail food would not experience a significant decline during a recession, but also would not experience a strong increase during an economic expansion.

Another factor that will have a differential effect on industries is demographics. For example, it is widely recognized that the U.S. population is weighted toward "baby boomers" entering their mid-50s and a large surge in senior citizens over age sixty-five. These two groups have heavy demand for second homes and hospital care and the industries related to these segments.

Firms that sell in international markets can benefit or suffer as foreign economies shift. An industry with a substantial worldwide market might experience low demand in its domestic market, but benefit from growing demand in its international market. As an example, much of the growth for Coca-Cola and Pepsi and the fast-food chains such as McDonald's and Burger King has come from international expansion in Europe and the Far East.

In general, an industry's prospects within the global business environment will determine how well or poorly an individual firm will fare, so industry analysis should precede company analysis. Few companies perform well in a poor industry, so even the best company in a poor industry is a bad prospect for investment. For example, poor sales and earnings in the farm equipment industry during the late 1980s had a negative impact on Deere and Co., a well-managed firm and probably the best firm in its industry. Though Deere performed better than other firms in the industry (some went bankrupt), its earnings and stock performance still fell far short of its past performance, and the company did poorly compared to firms in most other industries.

Company Analysis

After determining that an industry's outlook is good, an investor can analyze and compare individual firms' performance within the entire industry using financial ratios and cash flow values. As we discussed in Chapter 9, many ratios for firms are valid only when they are compared to the performance of their industries.

You undertake company analysis to identify the best company in a promising industry. This involves examining a firm's past performance, but more important, its future prospects. After you understand the firm and its outlook, you can determine its value. In the final step, you compare this estimated value to the firm's market price and decide whether its stock or bonds are good investments.

Your final goal is to select the best stock or bonds within a desirable industry and include it in your portfolio based on its relationship (correlation) with all other assets in your portfolio. As we will discuss in more detail in Chapter 13, the best stock for investment purposes may not necessarily be issued by the best company because the stock of the finest company in an industry may be overpriced, which would cause it to be a poor investment. You cannot know whether a security is undervalued or overvalued until you have analyzed the company, estimated its intrinsic value, and compared your estimated value to the market price of the stock.

Does the Three-Step Process Work?

Although you might agree with the logic of the three-step investment process, you might wonder how well this process works in selecting investments. Several academic studies have supported this technique. First, studies indicated that most changes in an individual firm's *earnings* could be attributed to changes in aggregate corporate earnings and changes in the firm's industry, with the aggregate earnings changes being more important. Although the relative influence of the general economy and the industry on a firm's earnings varied among individual firms, the results consistently demonstrated that the economic environment had a significant effect on firm earnings.

Second, several studies have found a relationship between aggregate stock prices and various economic series such as employment, income, or production. These results supported the view that a relationship exists between stock prices and economic expansions and contractions.[2]

Third, an analysis of the relationship between *rates of return* for the aggregate stock market, alternative industries, and individual stocks showed that most of the changes in rates of return for individual stocks could be explained by changes in the rates of return

---

[2]For a further discussion of this and empirical support, see Geoffrey Moore and John P. Cullity, "Security Markets and Business Cycles" in *The Financial Analysts Handbook*, 2nd ed., ed. Sumner N. Levine (Homewood, IL: Dow Jones–Irwin, 1988).

for the aggregate stock market and the stock's industry. Although the importance of the market effect tended to decline over time and the significance of the industry effect varied among industries, the combined market–industry effect on an individual stock's rate of return was still important.[3]

These results from academic studies support the use of the three-step investment process. This investment decision approach is consistent with the discussion in Chapter 2, which contended that the most important decision is the asset allocation decision.[4] The asset allocation specifies: (1) what proportion of your portfolio will be invested in various nations' economies; (2) within each country, how you will divide your assets among stocks, bonds, or other assets; and (3) your industry selections, based on which industries are expected to prosper in the projected economic environment. We provide an example of global asset allocation in Chapter 11.

Now that we have described and justified the three-step process, we need to consider the theory of valuation. The application of this theory allows us to compute estimated values for the market, for alternative industries, and for individual firms and stocks. Finally, we compare these estimated values to current market prices and decide whether we want to make particular investments.

THEORY OF VALUATION

You may recall from your studies in accounting, economics, or corporate finance that the value of an asset is the present value of its expected returns. Specifically, you expect an asset to provide a stream of returns during the period of time you own it. To convert this estimated stream of returns to a value for the security, you must discount this stream at your required rate of return. This process of valuation requires estimates of (1) the stream of expected returns and (2) the required rate of return on the investment.

Stream of Expected Returns

An estimate of the expected returns from an investment encompasses not only the size but also the form, time pattern, and the uncertainty of returns, which affect the required rate of return.

Form of Returns   The returns from an investment can take many forms, including earnings, cash flows, dividends, interest payments, or capital gains (increases in value) during a period. We will consider several alternative valuation techniques that use different forms of returns. As an example, one common stock valuation model applies a multiplier to a firm's earnings, whereas another valuation model computes the present value of a firm's operating cash flows, and a third model estimates the present value of dividend payments. Returns or cash flows can come in many forms, and you must consider all of them to evaluate an investment accurately.

---

[3]For an analysis, see Stephen L. Meyers, "A Re-Examination of Market and Industry Factors in Stock Price Behavior," *Journal of Finance* 28, no. 3 (June 1973): 695–705.

[4]Authors who examine this question generally refer to it as market timing. Studies on this topic include Robert F. Vandell and Jerry L. Stevens, "Evidence of Superior Performance from Timing," *Journal of Portfolio Management* 15, no. 3 (Spring 1989): 38–42; and Jerry Wagner, Steve Shellans, and Richard Paul, "Market Timing Works Where It Matters Most . . . in the Real World," *Journal of Portfolio Management* 18, no. 4 (Summer 1992): 86–90. The classic study that established the importance of asset allocation is Gary P. Brinson, L. R. Hood, and G. L. Beebower, "Determinants of Portfolio Performance," *Financial Analysts Journal* 42, no. 4 (July–August 1986): 35–43; followed by Gary P. Brinson, Brian D. Singer, and G. L. Beebower, "Determinants of Portfolio Performance II: An Update," *Financial Analysts Journal* 47, no. 3 (May–June 1991): 40–48.

Time Pattern and Growth Rate of Returns   You cannot calculate an accurate value for a security unless you can estimate when you will receive the returns or cash flows. Because money has a time value, you must know the time pattern and growth rate of returns from an investment. This knowledge will make it possible to properly value the stream of returns relative to alternative investments with a different time pattern and growth rate of returns.

Required Rate of Return

Uncertainty of Returns   You will recall from Chapter 1 that the required rate of return on an investment is determined by (1) the economy's real risk-free rate of return, plus (2) the expected rate of inflation during the holding period, plus (3) a risk premium that is determined by the uncertainty of returns. All investments are affected by the risk-free rate and the expected rate of inflation because these two variables determine the nominal risk-free rate. Therefore, the factor that causes a difference in required rates of return is the risk premium for alternative investments. In turn, this risk premium depends on the uncertainty of returns on the assets.

We can identify the sources of the uncertainty of returns by the internal characteristics of assets or by market-determined factors. Earlier, we subdivided the internal characteristics into business risk (BR), financial risk (FR), liquidity risk (LR), exchange rate risk (ERR), and country risk (CR). The market-determined risk measures are the systematic risk of the asset, its beta, or its multiple APT factors.

Investment Decision Process: A Comparison of Estimated Values and Market Prices

To ensure that you receive your required return on an investment, you must estimate the intrinsic value of the investment at your required rate of return, and then compare this estimated intrinsic value to the prevailing market price. You should not buy an investment if its market price exceeds your estimated value because the difference will prevent you from receiving your required rate of return on the investment. In contrast, if the estimated value of the investment exceeds the market price, you should buy the investment. In summary:

If Estimated Value > Market Price, Buy

If Estimated Value < Market Price, Don't Buy

For example, assume you read about a firm that produces athletic shoes and that its stock is listed on the NYSE. Using one of the valuation models we will discuss, and making estimates of earnings and growth based on the company's annual report and other information, you estimate the company's stock value using your required rate of return as twenty dollars a share. After estimating this value, you look in the paper and see that the stock is currently being traded at fifteen dollars a share. You would want to buy this stock because you think it is worth twenty dollars a share and you can buy it for fifteen dollars a share. In contrast, if the current market price were twenty-five dollars a share, you would not want to buy the stock.

The theory of value provides a common framework for the valuation of all investments. Different applications of this theory generate different estimated values for alternative investments because of the different payment streams and characteristics of the securities. The interest and principal payments on a bond differ substantially from the expected dividends and future selling price for a common stock. The initial discussion that follows applies the discounted cash flow method to bonds, preferred stock, and common stock. This presentation demonstrates that the same basic model is useful across a range of investments. Sub-

sequently, because of the difficulty in estimating the value of common stock, we consider two general approaches and numerous techniques to the valuation of stock.

VALUATION OF ALTERNATIVE INVESTMENTS

Valuation of Bonds

Calculating the value of bonds is relatively easy because the size and time pattern of cash flows from the bond over its life are known. A bond typically promises

1. Interest payments every six months equal to one-half the coupon rate times the face value of the bond.
2. The payment of the principal on the bond's maturity date.

As an example, in 2000 a $10,000 bond due in 2015 with a 10 percent coupon will pay $500 every six months for its fifteen-year life. In addition, the bond issuer promises to pay the $10,000 principal at maturity in 2015. Therefore, assuming the bond issuer does not default, the investor knows what payments (cash flows) will be made and when they will be made.

Applying the valuation theory, which states that the value of any asset is the present value of its cash flows, the value of the bond is the present value of the interest payments, which we can think of as an annuity of $500 every six months for fifteen years, and the present value of the principal payment, which in this case is the present value of $10,000 in fifteen years. The only unknown for this asset (assuming the borrower does not default) is the rate of return you should use to discount the expected stream of returns (cash flows). If the prevailing nominal risk-free rate is 9 percent, and the investor requires a 1 percent risk premium on this bond because there is some probability of default, the required rate of return would be 10 percent.

The present value of the interest payments is an annuity for thirty periods (fifteen years every six months) at one-half the required return (5 percent):[5]

$$\$500 \times 15.3725 = \$7,686$$
(present value of interest payments at 10 percent)

The present value of the principal is likewise discounted at 5 percent for thirty periods:[6]

$$\$10,000 \times .2314 = \$2,314$$
(present value of the principal payment at 10 percent)

This can be summarized as follows:

Present value of interest payments $500 × 15.3725   = $ 7,686
Present value of principal payment $10,000 × .2314 =   2,314
Total value of bond at 10 percent   = $10,000

This is the amount that an investor should be willing to pay for this bond, assuming that the required rate of return on a bond of this risk class is 10 percent. If the market price

---

[5]The annuity factors and present value factors are contained in Appendix C at the end of the book.
[6]If we used annual compounding, this would be 0.239 rather than 0.2314. We use semiannual compounding because it is consistent with the interest payments and is used in practice.

of the bond is above this value, the investor should not buy it because the promised yield to maturity will be less than the investor's required rate of return.

Alternatively, assuming an investor requires a 12 percent return on this bond, its value would be:

$$\$500 \times 13.7648 = \$6,882$$
$$\$10,000 \times .1741 = \underline{1,741}$$
$$\text{Total value of bond at 12 percent} = \overline{\$8,623}$$

This example shows that if you want a higher rate of return, you will not pay as much for an asset; that is, a given stream of cash flows has a lower value to you. As before, you would compare this computed value to the market price of the bond to determine whether you should invest in it.[7]

Valuation of Preferred Stock

The owner of a preferred stock receives a promise to pay a stated dividend, usually each quarter, for an infinite period. Preferred stock is a **perpetuity** because it has no maturity. As was true with a bond, stated payments are made on specified dates although the issuer of this stock lacks the same legal obligation to pay investors as bonds do. Payments are made only after the firm meets its bond interest payments. Because this increases the uncertainty of returns, investors should require a higher rate of return on a firm's preferred stock than on its bonds. Although this differential in required return should exist in theory, it generally does not exist in practice because of the tax treatment accorded dividends paid to corporations. As described in Chapter 3, 80 percent of intercompany preferred dividends are tax-exempt, making the effective tax rate on them about 6.8 percent, assuming a corporate tax rate of 34 percent. This tax advantage stimulates the demand for preferred stocks by corporations and, because of this demand, the yield on them has generally been below that on the highest-grade corporate bonds.

Because preferred stock is a perpetuity, its value is simply the stated annual dividend divided by the required rate of return on preferred stock (k_p) as follows:

$$V = \frac{\text{Dividend}}{k_p}$$

Assume a preferred stock has a $100 par value and a dividend of $8 a year. Because of the expected rate of inflation, the uncertainty of the dividend payment, and the tax advantage to you as a corporate investor, your required rate of return on this stock is 9 percent. Therefore, the value of this preferred stock to you is

$$V = \frac{\$8}{.09}$$

$$= \$88.89.$$

Given this estimated value, you would inquire about the current market price to decide whether you would want to buy this preferred stock. If the current market price is ninety-five dollars, you would decide against a purchase, whereas if it is eighty dollars,

---

[7]To test your mastery of bond valuation, check that if the required rate of return were 8 percent, the value of this bond would be $11,729.

you would buy the stock. Also, given the market price of preferred stock, you can derive its promised yield. Assuming a current market price of eighty-five dollars, the promised yield would be

$$k_p = \frac{\text{Dividend}}{\text{Price}} = \frac{\$8}{\$85.00} = .0941.$$

Approaches to the Valuation of Common Stock

Because of the complexity and importance of valuing common stock, various techniques for accomplishing this task have been devised over time. These techniques fall into one of two general approaches: (1) the discounted cash-flow valuation techniques, where the value of the stock is estimated based upon the present value of some measure of cash flow including dividends, operating cash flow, and free cash flow; and (2) the relative valuation techniques, where the value of a stock is estimated based upon its price relative to variables considered to be significant to valuation such as earnings, cash flow, book value, or sales. Figure 10.2 provides a visual presentation of the alternative approaches and specific techniques.

An important point is that *both of these approaches and all of these valuation techniques have several common factors*. First, all of them are significantly affected by the investor's *required rate of return* on the stock because this rate becomes the discount rate. Second, all of them are affected by *the estimated growth rate of the variable* used in the valuation technique, for example, dividends, earnings, cash flow, or sales. As noted in the efficient-market discussion, both of these critical variables must be *estimated*. As a result, different analysts using the same valuation techniques will derive different estimates of value for a stock because they have different estimates for these critical variable inputs.

The following discussion of equity valuation techniques considers the specific models and the theoretical and practical strengths and weakness of each of them.

Discounted Cash-Flow Valuation Techniques

All of these valuation techniques are based on the basic valuation model, which asserts that the value of an asset is the present value of its expected future cash flows as follows:

$$V_j = \sum^{t=n} \frac{CF_t}{(1 + k)^t}$$

Where:

V_j = **value of stock j**
n = **life of the asset**
CF_t = **cash flow in period t**
k = **the discount rate that is equal to the investors' required rate of return for asset j, which is determined by the uncertainty (risk) of the stock's cash flows.**

As noted, the specific cash flows used will differ between techniques. They range from dividends (the best-known model) to operating cash flow and free cash flow. We begin with a fairly detailed presentation of the present-value-of-dividend model, referred to as the dividend discount model (DDM), because it is intuitively appealing and is the best-known model. Also, its general approach is similar to the approach used for implementing other discounted cash-flow models.

Figure 10.2 *Common Stock Valuation Approaches and Specific Techniques*

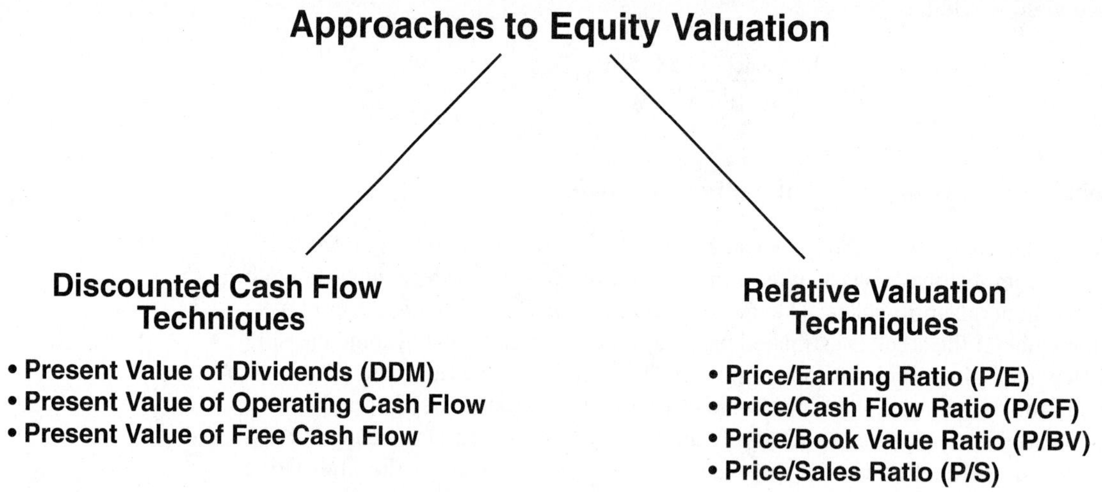

Approaches to Equity Valuation

Discounted Cash Flow Techniques

- Present Value of Dividends (DDM)
- Present Value of Operating Cash Flow
- Present Value of Free Cash Flow

Relative Valuation Techniques

- Price/Earning Ratio (P/E)
- Price/Cash Flow Ratio (P/CF)
- Price/Book Value Ratio (P/BV)
- Price/Sales Ratio (P/S)

The Dividend Discount Model (DDM)   The **dividend discount model** assumes that the value of a share of common stock is the present value of all future dividends as follows:[8]

$$V_j = \frac{D_1}{(1+k)} + \frac{D_2}{(1+k)^2} + \frac{D_3}{(1+k)^3}$$
$$+ \ldots + \frac{D_\infty}{(1+k)^\infty}$$
$$= \sum_{}^{n} \frac{D_t}{(1+k)^t}$$

where:

V_j = value of common stock j
D_t = dividend during period t
k = required rate of return on stock j.

An obvious question is, what happens when the stock is not held for an infinite period? A sale of the stock at the end of Year 2 would imply the following formula:

$$V_j = \frac{D_1}{(1+k)} + \frac{D_2}{(1+k)^2} + \frac{SP_{j2}}{(1+k)^2}.$$

The value is equal to the two dividend payments during Years 1 and 2 plus the sale price (*SP*) for stock *j* at the end of Year 2. The expected selling price of stock *j* at the end of Year 2 (SP_{j2}) is simply the value of all remaining dividend payments.

---

[8]This model was initially set forth in J. B. Williams, *The Theory of Investment Value* (Cambridge, MA: Harvard, 1938). It was subsequently reintroduced and expanded by Myron J. Gordon, *The Investment, Financing, and Valuation of the Corporation* (Homewood, IL: Irwin, 1962).

$$SP_{j2} = \frac{D_3}{(1+k)} + \frac{D_4}{(1+k)^2} + \ldots + \frac{D_\infty}{(1+k)^\infty}$$

If SP_{j2} is discounted back to the present by $1/(1+k)^2$, this equation becomes

$$PV(SP_{j2}) = \frac{\dfrac{D_3}{(1+k)} + \dfrac{D_4}{(1+k)^2} + \ldots + \dfrac{D_\infty}{(1+k)^\infty}}{(1+k)^2}$$

$$= \frac{D_3}{(1+k)^3} + \frac{D_4}{(1+k)^4} + \ldots + \frac{D_\infty}{(1+k)^\infty}$$

which is simply an extension of the original equation. Whenever the stock is sold, its value (that is, the sale price at that time) will be the present value of all future dividends. When this ending value is discounted back to the present, you are back to the original dividend discount model.

What about stocks that pay no dividends? Again, the concept is the same, except that some of the early dividend payments are zero. Notably, there are expectations that *at some point* the firm will start paying dividends. If investors lacked such an expectation, nobody would be willing to buy the security. It would have zero value. A firm with a non-dividend-paying stock is reinvesting its capital rather than paying current dividends so that its earnings and dividend stream will be larger and grow faster in the future. In this case, we would apply the DDM as:

$$V_j = \frac{D_1}{(1+k)} + \frac{D_2}{(1+k)^2} + \frac{D_3}{(1+k)^3}$$

$$+ \ldots + \frac{D_\infty}{(1+k)^\infty}$$

where:

$D_1 = 0$

$D_2 = 0.$

The investor expects that when the firm starts paying dividends in Period 3, it will be a large initial amount and dividends will grow faster than those of a comparable stock that had paid out dividends. The stock has value because of these *future* dividends. We will apply this model to several cases having different holding periods that will show you how it works.

One-year holding period   Assume an investor wants to buy the stock, hold it for one year, and then sell it. To determine the value of the stock—that is, how much the investor should pay for it—using the DDM, we must estimate the dividend to be received during the period, the expected sale price at the end of the holding period, and the investor's required rate of return.

To estimate the dividend for the coming year, adjust the current dividend for expectations regarding the change in the dividend during the year. Assume the company we are analyzing earned $2.50 a share last year and paid a dividend of $1 a share. Assume further the firm has been fairly consistent in maintaining this 40 percent payout over time. The consensus of financial analysts is that the firm will earn about $2.75 during the coming year and will raise its dividend to $1.10 per share.

A crucial estimate is the expected selling price for the stock a year from now. You can estimate this expected selling price by either of two alternative procedures. In the first, you can apply the dividend discount model where you estimate the specific dividend payments for a number of years into the future and calculate the value from these estimates. In the second, the earnings multiplier model, you multiply the future expected earnings

for the stock by an earnings multiple, which you likewise estimate, to find an expected sale price. We will discuss this model in a later section of the chapter. For now, assume you prefer the DDM. Applying this model, you project the sales price of this stock a year from now to be twenty-two dollars.

Finally, you must determine the required rate of return. As discussed before, the nominal risk-free rate is determined by the real risk-free rate and the expected rate of inflation. A good proxy for this rate is the promised yield on one-year government bonds because your investment horizon (expected holding period) is one year. You estimate the stock's risk premium by comparing its risk level to the risk of other potential investments. In later chapters, we discuss how you can estimate this risk. For the moment, assume that one-year government bonds are yielding 10 percent, and you believe that a 4 percent risk premium over the yield of these bonds is appropriate for this stock. Thus, you specify a required rate of return of 14 percent.

In summary, you have estimated the dividend at $1.10 (payable at year-end), an ending sale price of $22, and a required rate of return at 14 percent. Given these inputs, you would estimate the value of this stock as follows:

$$V_1 = \frac{\$1.10}{(1 + .14)} + \frac{\$22.00}{(1 + .14)}$$

$$= \frac{1.10}{1.14} + \frac{22.00}{1.14}$$

$$= .96 + 19.30$$

$$= \$20.26.$$

Note that we have not mentioned the current market price of the stock. This is because the market price is not relevant to you as an investor except as a comparison to the independently derived value based on your estimates of the relevant variables. Once we have calculated the stock's value as $20.26, we can compare it to the market price and apply the investment decision rule: If the stock's market price is more than $20.26, do not buy; if it is equal to or less than $20.26, buy.

Multiple-year holding period   If you anticipate holding the stock for several years and then selling it, the valuation estimate is harder. You must forecast several future dividend payments and estimate the sale price of the stock several years in the future.

The difficulty with estimating future dividend payments is that the future stream can have numerous forms. The exact estimate of the future dividends depends on two projections. The first is your outlook for earnings growth because earnings are the source of dividends. The second projection is the firm's dividend policy, which can take several forms. A firm can have a constant percent payout of earnings each year, which implies a change in dividend each year, or the firm could follow a step pattern in which it increases the dividend rate by a constant dollar amount each year or every two or three years. The easiest dividend policy to analyze is one where the firm enjoys a constant growth rate in earnings and maintains a constant dividend payout. This set of assumptions implies that the dividend stream will experience a constant growth rate that is equal to the earnings growth rate.

Assume the expected holding period is three years, and you estimate the following dividend payments at the end of each year:

Year 1	$1.10/share
Year 2	$1.20/share
Year 3	$1.35/share

The next estimate is the expected sale price (*SP*) for the stock three years in the future. Again, if we use the DDM for this estimate, you would need to project the dividend growth

pattern for this stock beginning three years from now. Assume an estimated sale price using the DDM of thirty-four dollars.

The final estimate is the required rate of return on this stock during this period. Assuming the 14 percent required rate is still appropriate, the value of this stock is

$$V = \frac{1.10}{(1 + .14)^1} + \frac{1.20}{(1 + .14)^2} + \frac{1.35}{(1 + .14)^3} + \frac{34.00}{(1 + .14)^3}$$

$$= \frac{1.10}{(1.14)} + \frac{1.20}{(1.30)} + \frac{1.35}{(1.4815)} + \frac{34.00}{(1.4815)}$$

$$= .96 + .92 + .91 + 22.95$$

$$= \$25.74.$$

Again, to make an investment decision you would compare this estimated value for the stock to its current market price to determine whether you should buy.

At this point, you should recognize that the valuation procedure discussed here is similar to that used in corporate finance when making investment decisions, except that the cash flows are from dividends instead of returns to an investment project. Also, rather than estimating the scrap value or salvage value of a corporate asset, we are estimating the ending sale price for the stock. Finally, rather than discounting cash flows using the firm's cost of capital, we use the individual's required rate of return. In both cases, we are looking for excess present value, which means that the present value of expected cash inflows—that is, the estimated intrinsic value of the asset—exceeds the present value of cash outflows, which is the market price of the asset.

Infinite period model   We can extend the multiperiod model by extending our estimates of dividends five, ten, or fifteen years into the future. The benefits derived from these extensions would be minimal, however, and you would quickly become bored with this exercise. Instead, we will move to the infinite period dividend discount model, which assumes investors estimate future dividend payments for an infinite number of periods.

Needless to say, this is a formidable task! We must make some simplifying assumptions about this future stream of dividends to make the task viable. The easiest assumption is that *the future dividend stream will grow at a constant rate for an infinite period.* This is a rather heroic assumption in many instances, but where it does hold, we can use the model to value individual stocks as well as the aggregate market and alternative industries. This model is generalized as follows:

$$V_j = \frac{D_0(1 + g)}{(1 + k)} + \frac{D_0(1 + g)^2}{(1 + k)^2} + \ldots + \frac{D_0(1 + g)^n}{(1 + k)^n}$$

where:

V_j = **the value of stock** j
D_0 = **the dividend payment in the current period**
 g = **the constant growth rate of dividends**
 k = **the required rate of return on stock** j
 n = **the number of periods, which we assume to be infinite.**

In the appendix to this chapter, we show that with certain assumptions, this infinite period constant growth rate model can be simplified to the following expression:

$$V_j = \frac{D_1}{k - g}.$$

You will probably recognize this formula as one that is widely used in corporate finance to estimate the cost of equity capital for the firm.

To use this model, you must estimate (1) the required rate of return (k) and (2) the expected growth rate of dividends (g). After estimating g, it is a simple matter to estimate D_1, because it is the current dividend (D_0) times $(1 + g)$.

Consider the example of a stock with a current dividend of $1 a share, which you expect to rise to $1.09 next year. You believe that, over the long run, this company's earnings and dividends will continue to grow at 9 percent; therefore, your estimate of g is 0.09. For the long run, you expect the rate of inflation to decline, so you set your long-run required rate of return on this stock at 13 percent; your estimate of k is 0.13. To summarize the relevant estimates:

$$g = .09$$
$$k = .13$$
$$D_1 = 1.09 \ (\$1.00 \times 1.09)$$
$$V = \frac{1.09}{.13 - .09}$$
$$= \frac{1.09}{.04}$$
$$= \$27.25.$$

A small change in any of the original estimates will have a large impact on V as shown by the following examples:

1. $g = .09; k = .14; D_1 = \$1.09.$ (We assume an increase in k.)

$$V = \frac{\$1.09}{.14 - .09}$$
$$= \frac{\$1.09}{.05}$$
$$= \$21.80$$

2. $g = .10; k = .13; D_1 = \$1.10.$ (We assume an increase in g.)

$$V = \frac{\$1.10}{.13 - .10}$$
$$= \frac{\$1.10}{.03}$$
$$= \$36.67$$

These examples show that as small a change as 1 percent in either g or k produces a large difference in the estimated value of the stock. The crucial relationship that determines the value of the stock is the *spread between the required rate of return (k) and the expected growth rate of dividends (g)*. Anything that causes a decline in the spread will cause an increase in the computed value, whereas any increase in the spread will decrease the computed value.

Infinite Period DDM and Growth Companies

As noted in the appendix, the infinite period DDM has the following assumptions:

1. Dividends grow at a constant rate.

2. The constant growth rate will continue for an infinite period.
3. The required rate of return *(k) is greater than the infinite growth rate (g).* If it is not, the model gives meaningless results because the denominator becomes negative.

What is the effect of these assumptions if you want to use this model to value the stock of growth companies such as Intel, Merck, Microsoft, McDonald's, and Wal-Mart? **Growth companies** are firms that have the opportunities and abilities to earn rates of return on investments that are consistently above their required rates of return.[9] To exploit these outstanding investment opportunities, these firms generally retain a high percentage of earnings for reinvestment, and their earnings grow faster than those of the typical firm. You will recall from the discussion in Chapter 9 that a firm's substainable growth is a function of its retention rate and its return on equity (ROE). Notably, as discussed below, the earnings growth pattern for these growth companies is inconsistent with the assumptions of the infinite period DDM.

First, the infinite period DDM assumes dividends will grow at a constant rate for an infinite period. This assumption seldom holds for companies currently growing at above average rates. As an example, Intel and Wal-Mart have both grown at rates in excess of 30 percent a year for several years. It is unlikely that they can maintain such extreme rates of growth and the ROEs implied by this growth for an infinite period in an economy where other firms will compete with them for these high rates of return.

Second, during the periods when these firms experience abnormally high rates of growth, their rates of growth probably exceed their required rates of return. There is *no* automatic relationship between growth and risk; a high-growth company is not necessarily a high-risk company. In fact, a firm growing at a high constant rate would have lower risk (less uncertainty) than a low-growth firm with an unstable earnings pattern.

In summary, some firms experience periods of abnormally high rates of growth for some finite periods of time. The infinite-period DDM cannot be used to value these true growth firms because these high-growth conditions are temporary and therefore inconsistent with the assumptions of the model. In the following section we discuss how to supplement the DDM to value a firm with temporary supernormal growth. In Chapter 13 we will discuss additional models used for estimating the stock values of growth companies.

Valuation with Temporary Supernormal Growth

Thus far, we have considered how to value a firm with different growth rates for short periods of time (one to three years) and how to value a stock with a model that assumes a constant growth rate for an infinite period. We also noted that the assumptions of the model make it impossible to use the infinite period constant growth model to value true growth companies. A company cannot permanently maintain a growth rate higher than its required rate of return, because competition will eventually enter this apparently lucrative business, which will reduce the firm's profit margins and therefore its ROE and growth rate. Therefore, after a few years of exceptional growth—i.e., a period of temporary supernormal growth—a firm's growth rate is expected to decline and eventually its growth rate will stabilize at a level consistent with the assumptions of the infinite-period DDM.

To determine the value of a temporary supernormal growth company, you must combine the previous models. In analyzing the initial years of exceptional growth, you

---

[9]Growth companies are discussed in Ezra Salomon, *The Theory of Financial Management* (New York: Columbia University Press, 1963), and Merton Miller and Franco Modigliani, "Dividend Policy, Growth, and the Valuation of Shares," *Journal of Business* 34, no. 4 (October 1961): 411–433. Models to value growth companies are discussed in Chapter 13.

examine each year individually. If the company is expected to have two or three stages of supernormal growth, you must examine each year during these stages of growth. When the firm's growth rate stabilizes at a rate below the required rate of return, you can compute the remaining value of the firm assuming constant growth using the DDM and discount this lump-sum constant growth value back to the present. The technique should become clear as you work through the following example.

The Bourke Company has a current dividend (D_0) of two dollars a share. The following are the expected annual growth rates for dividends.

Year	Dividend Growth Rate
1–3:	25%
4–6:	20
7–9:	15
10 on:	9

The required rate of return for the stock is 14 percent. Therefore, the value equation becomes

$$V_i = \frac{2.00\,(1.25)}{1.14} + \frac{2.00\,(1.25)^2}{(1.14)^2} + \frac{2.00\,(1.25)^3}{(1.14)^3}$$

$$+ \frac{2.00\,(1.25)^3\,(1.20)}{(1.14)^4} + \frac{2.00\,(1.25)^3\,(1.20)^2}{(1.14)^5}$$

$$+ \frac{2.00\,(1.25)^3\,(1.20)^3}{(1.14)^6} + \frac{2.00\,(1.25)^3\,(1.20)^3\,(1.15)}{(1.14)^7}$$

$$+ \frac{2.00\,(1.25)^3\,(1.20)^3\,(1.15)^2}{(1.14)^8} + \frac{2.00\,(1.25)^3\,(1.20)^3\,(1.15)^3}{(1.14)^9}$$

$$+ \frac{\dfrac{2.00\,(1.25)^3\,(1.20)^3\,(1.15)^3\,(1.09)}{(.14-.09)}}{(1.14)^9}$$

The computations in Table 10.1 indicate that the total value of the stock is $94.36. As before, you would compare this estimate of intrinsic value to the market price of the stock when deciding whether to purchase the stock. The difficult part of the valuation is estimating the supernormal growth rates and determining *how long* each of the growth rates will last.

To summarize this section the initial present value of cash flow stock valuation model considered was the dividend discount model (DDM). We noted that the infinite period DDM cannot be applied to the valuation of stock for growth companies because the flow of earnings for the growth company is inconsistent with the assumptions of the infinite period constant growth DDM model. We were able to modify the DDM model to evaluate companies with temporary supernormal growth. In the following sections we discuss the other present value of cash flow techniques assuming a similar set of scenarios.

Present Value of Operating Cash Flows

In this model, you are deriving the value of the total firm because you are discounting the total operating cash flows prior to the payment of interest to the debt-holders. Therefore, once you estimate the value of the total firm, you must subtract the value of debt to arrive at an estimate of the value of the firm's equity. The total value is equal to:

Table 10.1 *Computation of Value for the Stock of a Company with Temporary Supernormal Growth*

Year	Dividend	Discount Factor (14 percent)	Present Value
1	$ 2.50	0.8772	$ 2.193
2	3.12	0.7695	2.401
3	3.91	0.6750	2.639
4	4.69	0.5921	2.777
5	5.63	0.5194	2.924
6	6.76	0.4556	3.080
7	7.77	0.3996	3.105
8	8.94	0.3506	3.134
9	10.28	0.3075[b]	3.161
10	11.21		
	$224.20[a]	0.3075[b]	68.941
		Total value =	$94.355

[a]Value of dividend stream for Year 10 and all future dividends (that is, $11.21/(0.14 − 0.09) = $224.20).

[b]The discount factor is the ninth-year factor because the valuation of the remaining stream is made at the end of Year 9 to reflect the dividend in Year 10 and all future dividends.

$$V_{Fj} = {}^{t=n}\!\!\sum \frac{OCF_t}{(1 + WACC_j)^t}$$

Where:

V_{Fj} = value of firm j

n = number of periods assumed to be infinite

OCF_t = the firm's operating cash flow in period t. The specification of operating cash flow will be discussed in Chapter 13.

$WACC_j$ = firm j's weighted average cost of capital to be discussed in Chapter 13.

Similar to the process with the DDM, it is possible to envision this as a model that requires estimates for an infinite period. If you are dealing with a mature firm whereby its operating cash flows have reached a stage of stable growth, you can adapt the infinite period constant growth DDM model as follows:

$$V_{Fj} = \frac{OCF_t}{WACC_j - g_{OCF}}$$

where:

g_{OCF} = long-term constant growth of operating cash flow.

Alternatively, assuming that the firm is expected to experience several different rates of growth for OCF, these estimates can be divided into three or four stages, as demonstrated with the temporary supernormal dividend growth model. As with the dividend model, the analyst must estimate the *rate* of growth and the *duration* of growth for each of these periods of growth as follows:

Year	OCF Growth Rate
1–4	20%
5–7	16
8–10	12
11 on	7

Therefore, the calculations would estimate the specific OCFs for each year through Year 10 based on the expected growth rates, but you would use the infinite-growth model estimate when the growth rate reached stability after Year 10. As noted, after determining the value of the total firm V_{Fj}, you must subtract the value of all nonequity items including accounts payable, total interest-bearing debt, deferred taxes, and preferred stock to arrive at the estimated value of the firm's equity. This calculation will be demonstrated in Chapter 13.

Present Value of Free Cash Flows to Equity

The third discounted cash flow technique deals with "free" cash flows to equity derived *after* operating cash flows have been adjusted for debt payments (interest and principle) and after capital expenditures necessary to maintain the firm's asset base. Also, these cash flows precede dividend payments to the common stockholder. Such cash flows are referred to as "free" because they follow all obligations to other capital suppliers (debt and preferred stock) and consider the funds needed to maintain the firm's asset base.

Notably, because these are cash flows available to equity owners, the discount rate used is the firm's cost of equity (k) rather than the firm's WACC.

$$V_{sj} = \sum^{t=n} \frac{FCF_t}{(1 + k_j)^t}$$

where:

V_{sj} = **Value of the stock of firm** *j*
n = **number of periods assumed to be infinite**
FCF_t = **the firm's free cash flow in period** *t*. **The specification of free cash flow will be discussed in Chapter 13.**

Again, how an analyst would implement this general model depends upon the firm's position in its life cycle—that is, if the firm is expected to experience stable growth, analysts will use the infinite-growth model, whereas if it is expected to experience a period of temporary supernormal growth, analysts should use the multistage-growth model similar to the process used with dividends and for operating cash flow.

Relative Valuation Techniques

In contrast to the various discounted cash flow techniques that attempt to estimate a specific value for a stock based on its specific growth rates and its discount rate, the relative valuation techniques implicitly contend that it is possible to determine the value of a firm's stock by comparing it to similar stocks on the basis of several relative ratios that compare a firm's stock price to relevant variables that affect a stock's value such as earnings, cash flow, book value, and sales. Therefore, in this section we discuss the following relative-valuation ratios: (1) price/earnings (P/E), (2) price/cash flow (P/CF), (3) price/book value (P/BV), and price/sales (P/S). We begin with the P/E ratio, also referred to as the earnings multiplier model, because it is the most popular relative-valuation ratio and because we will show that the P/E ratio can be directly related back to the DDM in a manner that indicates the variables that affect the P/E ratio.

Earnings Multiplier Model

As noted, many investors prefer to estimate the value of common stock using an **earnings multiplier model**. The reasoning for this approach recalls the basic concept that the

value of any investment is the present value of future returns. In the case of common stocks, the returns that investors are entitled to receive are the net earnings of the firm. Therefore, one way investors can derive value is by determining how many dollars they are willing to pay for a dollar of expected earnings (typically represented by the estimated earnings during the following twelve-month period). For example, if investors are willing to pay ten times expected earnings, they would value a stock they expect to earn two dollars a share during the following year at twenty dollars. You can compute the prevailing earnings multiplier, also referred to as the **price/earnings (P/E) ratio**, as follows:

$$\text{Earnings Multiplier} = \text{Price/Earnings Ratio}$$
$$= \frac{\text{Current Market Price}}{\text{Expected Twelve-Month Earnings}}.$$

This computation of the current earnings multiplier (P/E ratio) indicates the prevailing attitude of investors toward a stock's value. Investors must decide if they agree with the prevailing P/E ratio (that is, is the earnings multiplier too high or too low?) based upon how it compares to the P/E ratio for similar firms and stocks.

To answer this question, we must consider what influences the earnings multiplier (P/E ratio) over time. For example, over time the aggregate stock market P/E ratio, as represented by the S&P 400 Index, has varied from about six times earnings to about twenty-five times earnings.[10] The infinite-period dividend discount model can be used to indicate the variables that should determine the value of the P/E ratio as follows:[11]

$$P_i = \frac{D_1}{k - g}$$

If we divide both sides of the equation by E_1 (expected earnings during the next twelve months), the result is

$$\frac{P_i}{E_1} = \frac{D_1/E_1}{k - g}$$

Thus, the P/E ratio is determined by

1. The *expected* dividend payout ratio (dividends divided by earnings).
2. The required rate of return on the stock (k).
3. The *expected* growth rate of dividends for the stock (g).

As an example, if we assume a stock has an expected dividend payout of 50 percent, a required rate of return of 12 percent, and an expected growth rate for dividends of 8 percent, this would imply the following:

$$D/E = .50; k = .12; g = .08$$
$$P/E = \frac{.50}{.12 - .08}$$
$$= .50/.04$$
$$= 12.5.$$

---

[10]When computing historical P/E ratios, the practice is to use earnings for the past twelve months rather than expected earnings. Although this will influence the level, it demonstrates the changes in the P/E ratio over time. Although it is appropriate to use historical P/E ratios for past comparison, we strongly believe that investment decisions should emphasize future P/E ratios that use *expected* earnings.

[11]In this formulation of the model we use P rather than V (that is, the value is stated as the estimated price of the stock).

Again, a small change in either or both k or g will have a large impact on the earnings multiplier, as shown in the following two examples.

1. D/E = .50; k = .13; g = .08. (In this example, we assume an increase in k.)

$$P/E = \frac{.50}{.13 - .08}$$

$$= \frac{.50}{.05}$$

$$= 10$$

2. D/E = .50; k = .12; g =.09. (In this example, we assume an increase in g and the original k.)

$$P/E = \frac{.50}{.12 - .09}$$

$$= \frac{.50}{.03}$$

$$= 16.7$$

3. D/E = .50; k = .11; g = .09. (In this example, we assume a fairly optimistic scenario where k declines to 11 percent and there is an increase in the expected growth rate of dividends to 9 percent).

$$P/E = \frac{.50}{.11 - .09}$$

$$= \frac{.50}{.02}$$

$$= 25$$

As before, *the spread between k and g is the main determinant of the size of the P/E ratio.* Although the dividend payout ratio has an impact, we are generally referring to a firm's long-run target payout, which is typically rather stable with little effect on year-to-year changes in the P/E ratio (earnings multiplier).

After estimating the earnings multiple, you would apply it to your estimate of earnings for the next year (E_1) to arrive at an estimated value. In turn, E_1 is based on the earnings for the current year (E_0) and your expected growth rate of earnings. Using these two estimates, you would compute an estimated value of the stock and compare this to its market price.

Consider the following estimates for an example firm:

$$D/E = .50$$
$$k = .12$$
$$g = .09$$
$$E_0 = \$2.00$$

Using these estimates, you would compute an earnings multiple of:

$$P/E = \frac{.50}{.12 - .09} = \frac{.50}{.03} = 16.7$$

Given current earnings (E_0) of \$2.00 and a g of 9 percent, you would expect E_1 to be \$2.18. Therefore, you would estimate the value (price) of the stock as

$$V = 16.7 \times \$2.18$$
$$= \$36.41$$

As before, you would compare this estimated value of the stock to its current market price to decide whether you should invest in it.

The Price-Cash Flow Ratio

The growth in popularity of this relative valuation technique can be traced to some concern with the propensity of some firms to manipulate earnings per share, whereas cash flow values are generally less prone to manipulation. Also, as noted, cash flow values are important in fundamental valuation and they are critical when doing credit analysis. The price to cash-flow ratio is computed as follows:

$$P/CF_j = \frac{P_t}{CF_{t+1}}$$

where:

P/CF_j = the price/cash flow ratio for firm j.
P_t = the price of the stock in period t.
CF_{t+1} = the expected cash flow per share for firm j.

Regarding what variables affect this ratio, the factors are similar to the P/E ratio. Specifically, the main variables should be the expected growth rate of the cash flow variable used and the risk of the stock as indicated by the uncertainty or variability of the cash flow series over time. The specific cash flow variable used will vary depending upon the nature of the company and industry and which cash flow specification (for example, operating cash flow or free cash flow) is the best measure of performance for this industry. An appropriate ratio can also be affected by the firm's capital structure.

The Price-Book Value Ratio

This ratio has been widely used by analysts in the banking industry as a measure of relative value. The book values of banks are considered good indicators of value because most bank assets are liquid assets such as bonds and commercial loans. This ratio gained in popularity and credibility based upon a study by Fama and French that indicated a significant inverse relationship between P/BV ratios and excess rates of return for a cross section of stocks.[12] The P/BV ratio is specified as follows:

$$P/BV_j = \frac{P_t}{BV_t}$$

where:

P/BV_j = the price/book value ratio for firm j.
P_t = the price of the stock in period t.
BV_t = the end of year book value per share for firm j.

---

[12] Eugene Fama and Kenneth French, "The Cross Section of Expected Returns," *Journal of Finance* 47, no. 2 (June 1992).

As with other ratios, it is important to match the price with the estimated book value that is expected to prevail at the end of the year. The difficulty is that this future book value may not be generally available.

The Price-Sales Ratio

The price/sales ratio has experienced a volatile history. Historically, it was a favorite of Phillip Fisher, a well-known money manager in the late 1950s,[13] his son, and others. Recently it has been suggested as a useful ratio by Martin Leibowitz, a widely admired stock and bond portfolio manager.[14] These advocates consider this ratio meaningful and useful for two reasons. First, they believe that strong and consistent sales growth is a requirement for a growth company. Although they note the importance of an above-average profit margin, the growth process must begin with sales. Second, given all the data in the balance sheet and income statement, sales information is subject to less manipulation than any other data item. The specific P/S ratio is:

$$\frac{P}{S_j} = \frac{P_t}{S_t}$$

where:

$\dfrac{P}{S_j}$ = the price to sales ratio for firm j.

P_t = the price of the stock in period t.
S_t = the expected sales per share for firm j.

Again, it is important to match the stock price with the firm's expected sales per share, which may be difficult to derive for a large cross section of stocks. Two caveats are relevant to the price to sales ratio. First, it is important to recognize that this particular relative valuation ratio can vary dramatically by industry. For example, the sales per share for retail firms such as Kroger or Wal-Mart are typically much higher than sales per share for computer or microchip firms. The reason for this difference is related to the second consideration, the profit margin on sales. The point is, retail food stores have high sales per share, which will cause a low P/S ratio, which is considered good until one realizes that these firms have low net profit margins. Therefore, you want to carry out your relative comparison using the P/S ratio between firms in the same or similar industries.

ESTIMATING THE INPUTS: THE REQUIRED RATE OF RETURN AND THE EXPECTED GROWTH RATE OF VALUATION VARIABLES

This section deals with estimating two inputs that are critical to the valuation process irrespective of which approach or technique is being used: the required rate of return (k) and the expected growth rate of earnings and valuation variables—i.e., earnings, cash flow, and dividends.

---

[13]Phillip A. Fisher, *Common Stock and Uncommon Profits,* Rev. ed. (Woodside, CA: PSR Publications, 1984); Kenneth L. Fisher, *Super Stocks* (Homewood, IL: Dow Jones–Irwin, 1984); and A. J. Senchak, Jr. and John D. Martin, "The Relative Performance of the PSR and PER Investment Strategies," *Financial Analysts Journal* 43, no. 2 (March–April, 1987): 46–56.

[14]Martin L. Leibowitz, *Sales Driven Franchise Value* (Charlottesville, VA: The Research Foundation of the Institute of Chartered Financial Analysts, 1997).

We will review these factors and discuss how the estimation of these variables differs for domestic versus foreign securities. Although the valuation procedure is the same for securities around the world, k and g differ among countries. Therefore, we will review the components of the required rate of return for U.S. securities and then consider the components for foreign securities. Following this, we will turn to the estimation of the growth rate of earnings, cash flow, and dividends for domestic stocks and then discuss estimating growth for foreign stocks.

Required Rate of Return (k)

This discussion is a brief review of the determinants of the nominal required rate of return on an investment including a consideration of factors for non-U.S. markets. As noted above, it is necessary to estimate the investor's required rate of return on an investment irrespective of which approach is used or which of the techniques is applied. This required rate of return will be the discount rate for most cash flow models and will affect all of the the relative-valuation techniques. The only instance of a difference in the discount rate is between the present value of dividends and the present value of free cash flow techniques, which use the required rate of return on equity (k), and the present value of operating cash flow technique, which uses the weighted-average cost of capital (WACC). Even in this latter instance, the cost of equity is a critical input to estimating the firm's WACC.

Recall that three factors influence an investor's required rate of return:

1. The economy's real risk-free rate (RRFR)
2. The expected rate of inflation (I)
3. A risk premium (RP)

The Economy's Real Risk-Free Rate   This is the absolute minimum rate that an investor should require. It depends on the real growth rate of this economy because capital invested should grow at least as fast as the economy. It is recognized that this rate can be affected for short periods of time by temporary tightness or ease in the capital markets.

The Expected Rate of Inflation   Investors are interested in real rates of return that will allow them to increase their rate of consumption. Therefore, if investors expect a given rate of inflation, they should increase their required nominal risk-free rate of return (NRFR) to reflect any expected inflation as follows:

$$NRFR = [1 + RRFR][1 + E(I)] - 1$$

where:

$E(I)$ = **expected rate of inflation.**

The two factors that determine the NRFR affect all investments, from U.S. government securities to highly speculative land deals. Investors who hope to calculate security values accurately must carefully estimate the expected rate of inflation. Not only does it affect all investments, but its extreme volatility makes its estimation difficult.

The Risk Premium   The risk premium causes differences in the required rates of return among alternative investments that range from government bonds to corporate bonds to common stocks. The RP also explains the difference in the expected return among securities of the same type. For example, this is the reason corporate bonds with different ratings of Aaa, Aa, or A have different yields, and why different common stocks have widely varying earnings multipliers despite similar growth expectations.

In Chapter 1, we noted that investors demand a risk premium because of the uncertainty of returns expected from an investment. A measure of this uncertainty of returns

Figure 10.3 *Time-Series Plot of Lehman Brothers Corporate Bond Yield Spreads (Baa–Aaa): Monthly 1973–1998*

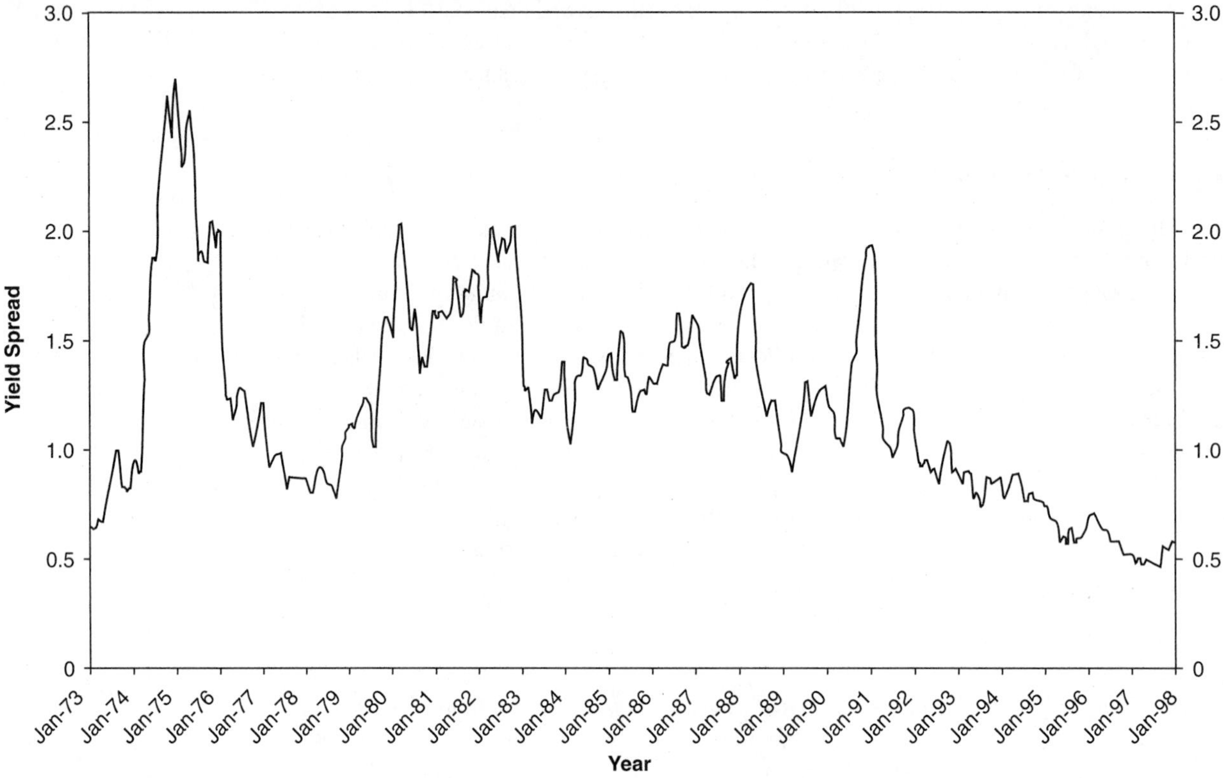

Source: Lehman Brothers

was the dispersion of expected returns. We suggested several internal factors that influence a firm's variability of returns, such as its business risk, financial risk, and liquidity risk. We noted that foreign investments bring additional risk factors, including exchange rate risk and country (political) risk.

Changes in the risk premium Because different securities have different patterns of returns and different guarantees to investors, we expect their risk premiums to differ. In addition, the risk premiums for the same securities can *change over time*. For example, Figure 10.3 shows the spread between the yields to maturity for Aaa-rated corporate bonds and Baa-rated corporate bonds from 1973 to 1998. This yield spread, or difference in yield, is a measure of the risk premium for investing in higher-risk bonds (Baa) compared to low risk bonds (Aaa). As shown, the yield spread varied from about .40 percent to 2.69 percent (from less than one-half of 1 percent to almost 3 percent).

Figure 10.4 contains a plot of the *ratio* of the yields for the same period, which indicates the percentage risk premium of Baa bonds compared to Aaa bonds. You might expect a larger difference in yield between Baa and Aaa bonds if Aaa bonds are yielding 12 percent rather than 6 percent. The yield ratio in Figure 10.4 adjusts for this size difference. This shows that even adjusting for the yield level difference, the percent risk premium varies from about 1.06 to 1.31—a 6 percent premium to a 31 percent premium over the base yield on Aaa bonds. This change in risk premium over time occurs because either investors perceive a change in the level of risk of Baa bonds compared to Aaa bonds, or

Figure 10.4   *Time-Series Plot of the Ratio of Lehman Brothers Corporate Bond Yields (Baa–Aaa): Monthly 1973–1998*

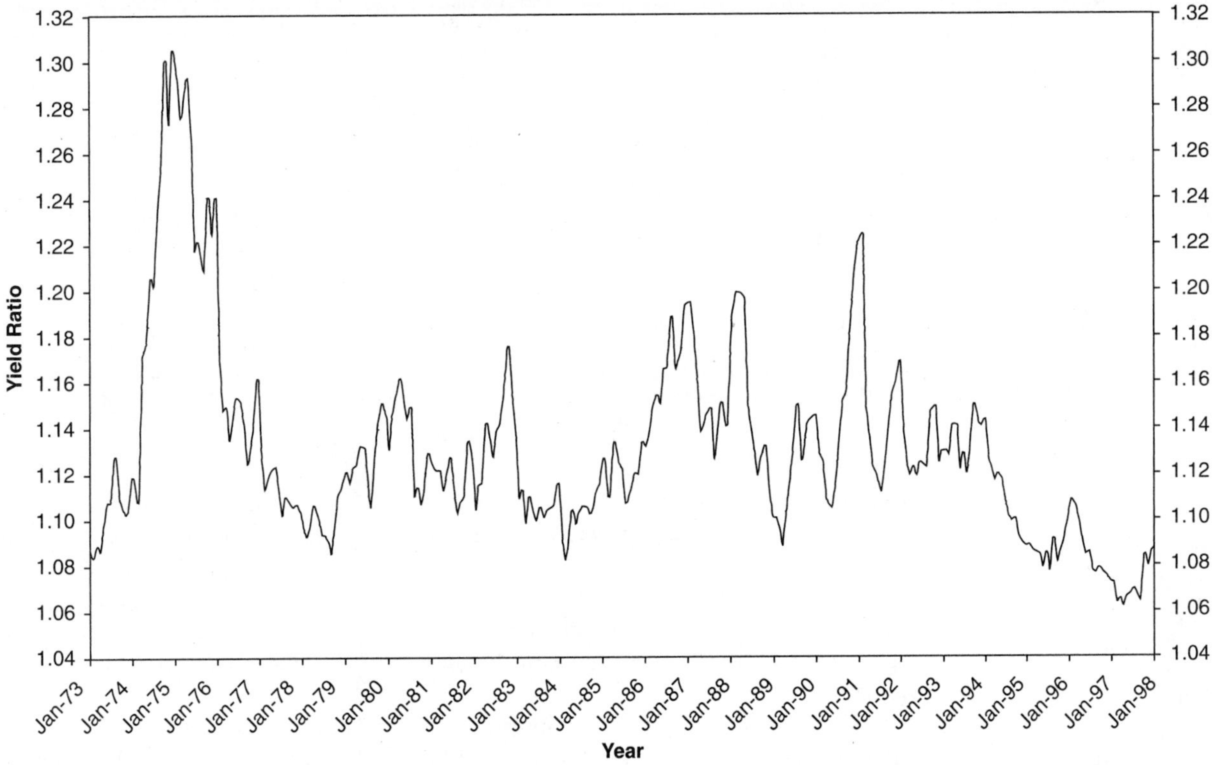

Source: Lehman Brothers

there is a change in the amount of return that investors require to accept the same level of risk. In either case, this change in the risk premium for a set of assets implies a change in the slope of the security market line (SML). This change in the slope of the SML was demonstrated in Chapter 1.

Estimating the Required Return for Foreign Securities

Our discussion of the required rate of return for investments has been limited to the domestic market. Although the basic valuation model and its variables are the same around the world, there are significant differences in the specific variables. This section points out where these differences occur.

Foreign Real RFR   Because the RRFR in other countries should be determined by the real growth rate within the particular economy, the estimated rate can vary substantially among countries due to differences in an economy's real growth rate. An example of differences in the real growth rate of gross domestic product (GDP) can be seen in Table 10.2. There is a range of estimates for 1999 of 1.7 percent (that is, 1.2 percent for Japan compared with 2.9 percent for the United States). This difference in the growth rates of real GDP implies a substantial difference in the RRFR for these countries.

Inflation Rate   To estimate the NRFR for a country, you must also estimate its expected rate of inflation and adjust the NRFR for this expectation. Again, this rate of

Table 10.2   *Growth of Real GDP (Percentage Changes from Previous Year)*

Period	United States	Japan	Germany	France	United Kingdom	Italy
1987	3.7%	4.6%	1.7%	1.9%	4.5%	3.0%
1988	4.4	5.8	3.6	3.4	4.6	4.2
1989	2.5	4.8	4.0	3.6	1.9	3.2
1990	0.8	5.6	4.6	2.5	1.0	1.9
1991	0.1	3.6	3.3	1.2	−1.2	1.5
1992	2.1	1.5	1.5	1.2	−0.5	1.0
1993	3.0	0.1	−1.9	−0.7	1.9	−0.4
1994	3.5	0.5	2.9	2.8	4.0	2.1
1995	2.0	0.9	1.9	2.2	2.5	3.0
1996	2.8	3.9	1.4	1.6	2.5	0.7
1997	3.8	0.9	2.2	2.3	3.1	1.5
1998[e]	3.5	−0.1	2.7	3.0	2.0	2.3
1999[e]	2.9	1.2	2.8	2.7	2.0	2.4

Source: "World Investment Strategy Highlights" (London: Goldman, Sachs International Ltd., June 1998). Reprinted by permission of Goldman, Sachs & Co.

inflation typically varies substantially among countries. The price change data in Table 10.3 show that the expected rate of inflation during 1999 varied from 0.2 percent in Japan to 3.2 percent in the United Kingdom. Assuming equal growth, this implies a difference in the nominal required rate of return between these two countries of 3.0 percent. Such a difference in *k* can have a substantial impact on estimated values as demonstrated earlier. Again, you must make a separate estimate for each individual country in which you are evaluating securities.

To demonstrate the combined impact of differences in real growth and expected inflation, Table 10.4 shows the results of the following computation for the six countries based on the 1999 estimates:

$$\text{NRFR} = (1 + \text{Real Growth}) \times (1 + \text{Expected Inflation}) - 1$$

Given the differences between countries in the two components, the range in the NRFR of 4.0 percent is not surprising (5.4 percent for the United States versus 1.4 percent for Japan). As demonstrated earlier, such a difference in *k* for an investment will have a significant impact on its value.

Risk Premium   You must also derive a risk premium for the investments in each country. Again, the five risk components differ substantially between countries: business risk, financial risk, liquidity risk, exchange rate risk, and country risk. *Business risk* can vary because it is a function of the variability of economic activity within a country and of the operating leverage used by firms within the country. Firms in different countries assume significantly different *financial risk* as well. For example, Japanese firms use substantially more financial leverage than U.S. or U.K. firms. Regarding *liquidity risk,* the U.S. capital markets are acknowledged to be the most liquid in the world, with Japan and the U.K. being close behind. In contrast, some emerging markets are quite illiquid and investors should add a significant liquidity risk premium.

When investing globally, you also must estimate *exchange rate risk,* which is the additional uncertainty of returns caused by changes in the exchange rates for the currency of another country. This uncertainty can be small for a U.S. investor in a country such as Hong Kong because the currency is pegged to the U.S. dollar. In contrast, in some countries, substantial volatility in the exchange rate over time can mean significant differences in

Table 10.3 *Changes in Consumer or Retail Prices*
(Percentage Changes from Previous Year)

Period	United States	Japan	Germany	France	United Kingdom	Italy
1987	3.7%	0.1%	0.3%	3.3%	4.1%	4.6%
1988	4.1	0.7	1.3	2.7	4.9	5.0
1989	4.8	2.3	2.8	3.4	7.8	6.6
1990	5.4	3.0	2.7	3.4	9.5	6.1
1991	4.7	3.2	3.5	3.1	6.0	6.0
1992	3.0	1.7	4.0	2.8	3.7	5.2
1993	3.0	1.3	4.2	2.1	1.6	4.2
1994	2.6	0.7	2.7	2.1	2.4	3.9
1995	2.8	0.0	1.8	1.6	2.8	5.4
1996	2.9	0.1	1.5	2.0	3.0	3.9
1997	2.3	1.7	1.8	1.2	2.8	1.7
1998(e)	1.6	0.5	1.2	1.1	2.9	1.9
1999(e)	2.4	0.2	2.0	1.4	3.2	2.1

Source: "World Investment Strategy Highlights" (London: Goldman, Sachs International Ltd., June 1998). Reprinted by permission of Goldman, Sachs & Co.

Table 10.4 *Estimates of 1999 Nominal RFR for Major Countries*

Country	Real Growth in GDP[a]	Expected Inflation[b]	Nominal RFR
United States	2.9%	2.4%	5.4%
Japan	1.2	0.2	1.4
Germany	2.8	2.0	4.9
France	2.7	1.4	4.1
United Kingdom	2.0	3.2	5.3
Italy	2.4	2.1	4.5

[a]Taken from Table 10.2
[b]Taken from Table 10.3

Source: Reprinted by permission of Goldman, Sachs & Co.

the domestic return for the country and return in U.S. dollars.[15] The level of volatility for the exchange rate differs between countries. The greater the uncertainty regarding future changes in the exchange rate the larger the exchange rate risk for the country.[16]

Recall that country risk arises from unexpected events in a country such as upheavals in its political or economic environment. Recent examples of political and economic disruptions have occurred in Russia when Yeltsin engineered a significant change in his staff during 1998 and subsequently there was substantial uncertainty about the potential devaluation of the ruble. The result was a stock market decline of over 60% between January and August, 1998. Another example was the unrest in Indonesia during 1998 that led to riots and the eventual resignation of President Suharto. Such political unrest or a change in the economic environment creates uncertainties that increase the risk of investments in these countries. Before investing in such countries, investors must evaluate the additional returns they should require to accept this increased uncertainty.

---

[15]Although we generally refer to these as domestic and U.S. dollar returns, you will also see references to *hedged* returns (for example, domestic) and *unhedged* returns (returns in U.S. dollars). In some cases, the hedged returns will adjust for the cost of hedging.

[16]For a thorough analysis of exchange rate determination and forecasting models, see Michael Rosenberg, *Currency Forecasting* (Burr Ridge, IL: Irwin Professional Publishing, 1996).

Thus, when estimating required rates of return on foreign investments, you must evaluate these differences in fundamental risk factors and assign a unique risk premium for each country.

Expected Growth Rate of Dividends

After arriving at a required rate of return, the investor must estimate the growth rate of cash flows, earnings, and dividends because the alternative valuation models for common stock depend heavily on good estimates of growth (g) for these variables. The procedure we describe here is similar to the presentation in Chapter 9, where we used financial ratios to measure a firm's growth potential.

The growth rate of dividends is determined by the growth rate of earnings and the proportion of earnings paid out in dividends (the payout ratio). Over the short run, dividends can grow faster or slower than earnings if the firm changes its payout ratio. Specifically, if a firm's earnings grow at 6 percent a year and it pays out exactly 50 percent of earnings in dividends, then the firm's dividends will likewise grow at 6 percent a year. Alternatively, if a firm's earnings grow at 6 percent a year and the firm increases its payout, then during the period when the payout ratio increases, dividends will grow faster than earnings. In contrast, if the firm reduces its payout ratio, dividends will grow slower than earnings for a period of time. Because there is a limit to how long this difference in growth rates can continue, most investors assume that the long-run dividend payout ratio is fairly stable. Therefore, analysis of the growth rate of dividends typically concentrates on an analysis of the growth rate of equity earnings. Also, as will be shown in Chapter 13, these earnings are also the major factor driving the operating or the free cash flows for the firm.

When a firm retains earnings and acquires additional assets, if it earns some positive rate of return on these additional assets, the total earnings of the firm will increase because its asset base is larger. How rapidly earnings increase depends on (1) the proportion of earnings it retains and reinvests in new assets and (2) the rate of return it earns on these new assets. Specifically, the growth rate (g) of equity earnings (that is, earnings per share) without any external financing is equal to the percentage of net earnings retained (the retention rate, which equals 1 − the payout ratio) times the rate of return on equity capital.

$$g = (\text{Retention Rate}) \times (\text{Return on Equity})$$
$$= \text{RR} \times \text{ROE}$$

Therefore, a firm can increase its growth rate by increasing its retention rate (reducing its payout ratio) and investing these added funds at its historic ROE. Alternatively, the firm can maintain its retention rate but increase its ROE. For example, if a firm retains 50 percent of net earnings and consistently has an ROE of 10 percent, its net earnings will grow at the rate of 5 percent a year, as follows:

$$g = \text{RR} \times \text{ROE}$$
$$= .50 \times .10$$
$$= .05.$$

If, however, the firm increases its retention rate to 75 percent and invests these additional funds in internal projects that earn 10 percent, its growth rate will increase to 7.5 percent, as follows:

$$g = .75 \times .10$$
$$= .075.$$

If, instead, the firm continues to reinvest 50 percent of its earnings, but derives a higher rate of return on these investments, say 15 percent, it can likewise increase its growth rate, as follows:

$$g = .50 \times .15$$
$$= .075.$$

Breakdown of ROE   Although the retention rate is a management decision, changes in the firm's ROE result from changes in its operating performance or its financial leverage. As discussed in Chapter 9, we can divide the ROE ratio into three components:

$$\text{ROE} = \frac{\text{Net Income}}{\text{Sales}} \times \frac{\text{Sales}}{\text{Total Assets}} \times \frac{\text{Total Assets}}{\text{Equity}}$$

$$= \frac{\text{Profit}}{\text{Margin}} \times \frac{\text{Total Asset}}{\text{Turnover}} \times \frac{\text{Financial}}{\text{Leverage}}$$

This breakdown allows us to consider the three factors that determine a firm's ROE.[17] Because it is a multiplicative relationship, an increase in any of the three ratios will cause an increase in ROE. Two of the three ratios reflect operating performance and one indicates a firm's financing decision.

The first operating ratio, net profit margin, indicates the firm's profitability on sales. This ratio changes over time for some companies and is highly sensitive to the business cycle. For growth companies, this is one of the first ratios to decline as increased competition forces price cutting, thus reducing profit margins. Also, during recessions profit margins decline because of price cutting or because of higher percentages of fixed costs due to lower sales.

The second component, total asset turnover, is the ultimate indicator of operating efficiency and reflects the asset and capital requirements of the business. Although this ratio varies dramatically by industry, within an industry it is an excellent indicator of management's operating efficiency.

The final component, total assets/equity, does not measure operating performance, but rather financial leverage. Specifically, it indicates how management has decided to finance the firm. This management decision regarding the financing of assets has financial risk implications for the stockholder.

Knowing this breakdown of ROE, you must examine past results and expectations for a firm and develop *estimates* of the three components and therefore an estimate of a firm's ROE. This estimate of ROE combined with the firm's retention rate will indicate its future growth potential. This breakdown of ROE will be employed extensively in the market-industry-company analysis chapters.

Estimating Dividend Growth for Foreign Stocks

The underlying factors that determine the growth rates for foreign stocks are similar to those for U.S. stocks, but the value of the equation's components may differ substantially from what is common in the United States. The differences in the retention rate or the

---

[17]You will recall from Chapter 9 (Table 9.8) that it is possible to employ an extended DuPont system that involves eight ratios. For purposes of this discussion, the three ratios indicate the significant differences among countries.

components of ROE result from differences in accounting practices as well as alternative management performance or philosophy.

Retention Rates   The retention rates for foreign corporations differ within countries, but differences also exist among countries due to differences in the country's investment opportunities. As an example, firms in Japan have a higher retention rate than firms in the United States, whereas the rate of retention in France is much lower. Therefore, you need to examine the retention rates for a number of firms in a country as a background for estimating the standard rate within a country.

Net Profit Margin   The net profit margin of foreign firms can differ because of different accounting conventions between countries. Foreign accounting rules may allow firms to recognize revenue and allocate expenses differently from U.S. firms. For example, German firms are allowed to build up large reserves for various reasons. As a result, they report low earnings for tax purposes. Also, different foreign depreciation practices require adjustment of earnings and cash flows.

Total Asset Turnover   Total asset turnover can likewise differ among countries because of different accounting conventions on the reporting of asset value at cost or market values. For example, in Japan a large part of the market values for some firms comes from their real estate holdings and their common stock investments in other firms. These assets are reported at cost, which typically has substantially understated their true value. This also means that the total asset turnover ratio for these firms is substantially overstated.

Total Asset/Equity Ratio   This ratio, a measure of financial leverage, differs among countries because of differences in economic environments, tax laws, management philosophies regarding corporate debt, and accounting conventions. In several countries, the attitude toward debt is much more liberal than in the United States. A prime example is Japan, where debt as a percentage of total assets is almost 50 percent higher than a similar ratio in the United States. Notably, most corporate debt in Japan entails borrowing from banks at fairly low rates of interest. Balance sheet debt ratios may be higher in Japan than in the United States or other countries, but because of the lower interest rates in Japan, the fixed-charge coverage ratios such as the times interest earned ratio might be similar to those in other countries. The point is, it is important to consider the several cash flow financial risk ratios along with the balance sheet debt ratios.

Consequently, when analyzing a foreign stock market or an individual foreign stock, when you estimate the growth rate for earnings and dividends you must consider the three components of the ROE just as you would for a U.S. stock. You must recognize that the financial ratios for foreign firms can differ from those of U.S. firms, as discussed in Chap-

ter 9. Subsequent chapters on valuation applied to the aggregate market, various industries, and companies contain examples of these differences.

SUMMARY

♦ As an investor, you want to select investments that will provide a rate of return that compensates you for your time, the expected rate of inflation, and the risk involved. To help you find these investments, this chapter considers the theory of valuation by which you derive the value of an investment using your required rate of return. We consider the two investment decision processes, which are the top-down, three-step approach and the bottom-up, stockpicking approach. We argue that a preferable approach is the top-down approach in which you initially consider the aggregate economy and market, then examine alternative industries, and finally analyze individual firms and their stocks.

♦ We apply the valuation theory to a range of investments including bonds, preferred stock, and common stock. Because the valuation of common stock is more complex and difficult, we suggest two alternative approaches (the present value of cash flows and the relative valuation approach) and several techniques for these approaches. Notably, we do *not* consider these competitive approaches, but suggest that *both* approaches should be used. Although we use several different valuation models, the investment decision rule is always the same: if the estimated value of the investment is greater than the market price, you should buy the investment; if the estimated value of an investment is less than its market price, you should not invest in it.

♦ We conclude with a review of factors that you need to consider when estimating the value of stock with either approach—your required rate of return on an investment and the growth rate of earnings, cash flow, and dividends. Finally, we consider some unique factors that affect the application of these valuation models to foreign stocks.

Questions

1. Discuss the difference between the top-down and bottom-up approaches. What is the major assumption that causes the difference in these two approaches?
2. What is the benefit of analyzing the market and alternative industries before individual securities?
3. Discuss why you would not expect all industries to have a similar relationship to the economy. Give an example of two industries that have different relationships to the economy.
4. Discuss why estimating the value for a bond is easier than estimating the value for common stock.
5. Would you expect the required rate of return for a U.S. investor in U.S. common stocks to be the same as the required rate of return on Japanese common stocks? What factors would determine the required rate of return for stocks in these countries?
6. Would you expect the nominal RFR in the United States to be the same as in Germany? Discuss your reasoning.
7. Would you expect the risk premium for an investment in an Indonesian stock to be the same as a stock from the United Kingdom? Discuss your reasoning.
8. Would you expect the risk premium for an investment in a stock from Singapore to be the same as a stock from the United States? Discuss your reasoning.

Problems

1. What is the value to you of a 14 percent coupon bond with a par value of $ 10,000 that matures in 10 years if you want a 12 percent return? Use semiannual compounding.
2. What would the value of the bond in Problem 1 be if you wanted a 16 percent rate of return?

3. The preferred stock of the Clarence Biotechnology Company has a par value of $100 and a $9 dividend rate. You require an 11 percent rate of return on this stock. What is the maximum price you would pay for it? Would you buy it at a market price of $96?

4. The Baron Basketball Company (BBC) earned $10 a share last year and paid a dividend of $6 a share. Next year, you expect BBC to earn $11 and continue its payout ratio. Assume that you expect to sell the stock for $132 a year from now. If you require 14 percent on this stock, how much would you be willing to pay for it?

5. Given the expected earnings and dividend payments in Problem 4, if you expected a selling price of $110 and required a 10 percent return on this investment, how much would you pay for the BBC stock?

6. Over the long run, you expect dividends for BBC to grow at 8 percent and you require 12 percent on the stock. Using the infinite period DDM, how much would you pay for this stock?

7. Based on new information regarding the popularity of basketball, you revise your growth estimate for BBC to 10 percent. What is the maximum P/E ratio you will apply to BBC, and what is the maximum price you will pay for the stock?

8. The Shamrock Dogfood Company (SDC) has consistently paid out 40 percent of its earnings in dividends. The company's return on equity is 16 percent. What would you estimate as its dividend growth rate?

9. Given the low risk in dog food, your required rate of return on SDC is 13 percent. What P/E ratio would you apply to the firm's earnings?

10. What P/E ratio would you apply if you learned that SDC had decided to increase its payout to 50 percent?

11. Discuss three ways a firm can increase its ROE. Make up an example to illustrate your discussion.

12. It is widely known that grocery chains have low profit margins—on average they earn about 1 percent on sales. How would you explain the fact that their ROE is about 12 percent? Does this seem logical?

13. Compute a recent five-year average of the following ratios for three companies of your choice (attempt to select diverse firms):
    a. Retention rate
    b. Net profit margin
    c. Equity turnover
    d. Total asset turnover
    e. Total assets/equity.
    Based on these ratios, explain which firm should have the highest growth rate of earnings.

14. You have been reading about the Pear Computer Company (PCC), which currently retains 90 percent of its earnings ($5 a share this year). It earns an ROE of almost 40 percent. Assuming a required rate of return of 16 percent, how much would you pay for PCC on the basis of the earnings multiplier model? Discuss your answer. What would you pay for Pear Computer if its retention rate was 60 percent and its ROE was 19 percent? Show your work.

15. Gentry Can Company's (GCC) latest annual dividend of $1.25 a share was paid yesterday and maintained its historic 7 percent annual rate of growth. You plan to purchase the stock today because you believe that the dividend growth rate will increase to 8 percent for the next three years and the selling price of the stock will be $40 per share at the end of that time.
    a. How much should you be willing to pay for the GCC stock if you require a 14 percent return?
    b. What is the maximum price you should be willing to pay for the GCC stock if you believe that the 8 percent growth rate can be maintained indefinitely and you require a 14 percent return?
    c. If the 8 percent rate of growth is achieved, what will the price be at the end of Year 3, assuming the conditions in Problem 15b?

16. In the *Federal Reserve Bulletin,* find the average yield of AAA and BBB bonds for a recent month. Compute the risk premium (in basis points) and the percentage risk premium on BBB bonds relative to AAA bonds. Discuss how these values compare to those shown in Figures 10.3 and 10.4.

References

Bhatia, Sanjiv, ed. *Global Equity Investing.* Proceedings of a seminar by the Association of Investment Management and Research. Charlottesville, VA: AIMR, December 1, 1995.

Billingsley, Randall, ed. *Corporate Financial Decision Making and Equity Analysis.* Proceedings of a seminar by the Association of Investment Management and Research. Charlottesville, VA: AIMR, January 18, 1995.

Copeland, T. E., Tim Koller, and Jack Murrin, *Valuation: Measuring and Managing the Value of Companies,* Second Edition (New York: Wiley, 1996).

Damodaran, Aswath, *Damodaran on Valuation* (New York: Wiley, 1994).

Farrell, James L. "The Dividend Discount Model: A Primer." *Financial Analysts Journal* 41, no. 6 (November–December 1985).

Fogler, H. Russell, ed. *Blending Quantitative and Traditional Equity Analysis.* Proceedings of a seminar by the Association of Investment Management and Research. Charlottesville, VA: AIMR, March 31, 1994.

Gastineau, Gary L,, and Sanjiv Bhatia, eds. *Risk Management.* Proceedings of a seminar by the Association of Investment Management and Research. Charlottesville, VA: AIMR, October 10, 1995.

Levine, Sumner N., ed. *The Financial Analysts Handbook.* 2nd ed. Homewood, IL: Dow Jones–Irwin, 1988.

Palepu, Krishna, Victor Bernard, and Paul Healy, *Business Analysis and Valuation* (Cincinnati, OH: Southwestern Publishing, 1996).

Sharpe, William, and Katrina Sherrerd, eds. *Quantifying the Market Risk Premium Phenomenon for Investment Decision Making.* Proceedings of a seminar by the Association of Investment Management and Research. Charlottesville, VA: AIMR, September 26, 1989.

Shaked, Israel. "International Equity Markets and the Investment Horizon." *Journal of Portfolio Management* 11, no. 2 (Winter 1985).

Squires, Jan, ed. *Value and Growth Styles in Equity Investing.* Proceedings of a seminar by the Association of Investment Management and Research. Charlottesville, VA: AIMR, February 15, 1995.

Squires, Jan, ed. *Equity Research and Valuation Techniques.* Proceedings of a seminar by the Association of Investment Management and Research. Charlottesville, VA: AIMR, December 9, 1997.

Vandell, Robert F., and Jerry L. Stevens. "Evidence of Superior Performance from Timing." *Journal of Portfolio Management* 15, no. 3 (Spring 1989).

Wagner, Jerry, Steven Shellans, and Richard Paul. "Market Timing Works Where It Matters Most . . . in the Real World." *Journal of Portfolio Management* 18, no. 4 (Summer 1992).

GLOSSARY

Dividend discount model (DDM) A technique for estimating the value of a stock issue as the present value of all future dividends.

Earnings multiplier model A technique for estimating the value of a stock issue as a multiple of its earnings per share.

Growth company A firm that has the opportunity to earn returns on investments that are consistently above its required rate of return.

Investment decision process Estimation of value for comparison with market price to determine whether or not to invest.

Overweighted A condition in which a portfolio, for whatever reason, includes more of a class of securities than the relative market value alone would justify.

Perpetuity An investment without any maturity date. It provides returns to its owner idefinitely.

Price/earnings (P/E) ratio The number by which earnings per share is multiplied to estimate a stock's value; also called the *earnings multiplier.*

Underweighted A condition in which a portfolio, for whatever reason, includes less of a class of securitites than the relative market value alone would justify.

Valuation process Part of the investment decision process in which you estimate the value of a security.

APPENDIX 10

Derivation of Constant Growth Dividend Discount Model (DDM)

The basic model is

$$P_0 = \frac{D_1}{(1+k)^1} + \frac{D_2}{(1+k)^2} + \frac{D_3}{(1+k)^3} + \ldots + \frac{D_n}{(1+k)^n}$$

where

P_0 = **current price**
D_i = **expected dividend in period** i
k = **required rate of return on asset** j.

If growth rate (g) is constant,

$$P_0 = \frac{D_0(1+g)^1}{(1+k)^1} + \frac{D_0(1+g)^2}{(1+k)^2} + \ldots + \frac{D_0(1+g)^n}{(1+k)^n}.$$

This can be written

$$P_0 = D_0\left[\frac{(1+g)}{(1+k)} + \frac{(1+g)^2}{(1+k)^2} + \frac{(1+g)^3}{(1+k)^3} + \ldots + \frac{(1+g)^n}{(1+k)^2}\right].$$

Multiply both sides of the equation by $\frac{1+k}{1+g}$:

$$\left[\frac{(1+g)}{(1+k)}\right]P_0 = D_0\left[1 + \frac{(1+g)}{(1+k)} + \frac{(1+g)^2}{(1+k)^2} + \ldots + \frac{(1+g)^{n-1}}{(1+k)^{n-1}}\right].$$

Subtract the previous equation from this equation:

$$\left[\frac{(1+k)}{(1+g)} - 1\right]P_0 = D_0\left[1 - \frac{(1+g)^n}{(1+k)^n}\right]$$

$$\left[\frac{(1+k)-(1+g)}{(1+g)}\right]P_0 = D_0\left[1 - \frac{(1+g)^n}{(1+k)^n}\right].$$

Assuming k > g, as N → ∞, the term in brackets on the right side of the equation goes to 1, leaving:

$$\left[\frac{(1+k)-(1+g)}{(1+g)}\right]P_0 = D_0.$$

This simplifies to

$$\left[\frac{(1+k-1-g)}{(1+g)}\right]P_0 = D_0,$$

which equals

$$\left[\frac{k-g}{(1+g)}\right]P_0 = D_0.$$

This equals

$$(k-g)P_0 = D_0(1+g)$$

since

$$D_0(1+g) = D_1,$$

so:

$$(k-g)P_0 = D_1$$

$$P_0 = \frac{D_1}{k-g}.$$

Remember, this model assumes

♦ A constant growth rate
♦ An infinite time period
♦ The required return on the investment (k) is greater than the expected growth rate (g).

CHAPTER

11

Economic and Market Analysis

In this chapter we will answer the following questions:

- How does economic analysis relate to what we already know about efficient markets, valuation, and financial statement analysis?
- What are the components of gross domestic product (GDP)?
- What causes changes in these components over time?
- How do monetary and fiscal policy affect the economy?
- How do international economic factors affect the U.S. economy?
- What are the major determinants of an economy's long-term growth?
- What are the primary influences affecting the short-term growth of an economy?
- What indicators can be used to forecast economic variables?
- What are the risks in constructing an economic forecast?
- What is expectational analysis?
- How can economic analysis assist in the construction of global multi-asset portfolios? ◆

Analysis of the economy—where we are and where we are headed—should be the first component of security analysis. By studying the big picture of the national and international economy, we can better identify factors and trends that will affect industries and firms in the future and make security buy-and-sell decisions accordingly.

Economic analysis may appear difficult because leading economists may disagree on some points of economic theory and policy prescriptions. Still, there is enough agreement to aid those who wish to buy and sell securities and manage portfolios. This chapter avoids discussion of theory and focuses instead mainly on the practice of economic forecasting and its role in portfolio management and security selection.

370

RELATING ECONOMIC ANALYSIS TO EFFICIENT MARKETS, VALUATION, AND FINANCIAL STATEMENTS

Efficient Markets

Our discussion of efficient capital markets in Chapter 8 may lead some to believe that attempts to outperform the market indexes on a risk-adjusted basis is an exercise in futility. Notably, although more pension funds are "indexing" their investments, more academic and practitioner studies are finding anomalies related to the efficient market hypothesis (EMH). Perhaps we can produce superior risk-adjusted performance by focusing our analysis on some of the apparent anomalies discovered through research on efficient markets. Smaller firms, firms with low P/E ratios, firms with low MV/BV ratios, firms with earnings surprises, and neglected firms not heavily scrutinized by Wall Street analysts may give amateur investors or analysts a chance to concentrate their research efforts and outperform the market indexes.

Economic analysis provides an overview of what may happen in the domestic and international economic arena to identify future trends or themes. An investor who focuses research efforts on attractive industry sectors and firms with the above-mentioned characteristics, might possibly identify attractive securities to purchase.

Another implication of the EMH is that the market consensus for expectations about the economy, firms, and interest rate trends is incorporated into asset prices. *Therefore, for an analyst to experience above-average risk-adjusted returns, he or she must have well-reasoned expectations that differ from the market consensus, and must usually be correct.* Perhaps a disciplined approach to analyzing information—an approach that removes the emotions that sometimes blind proper decision making—might lead to superior returns. We discuss this method later in the chapter.

Valuation

The discussion of security valuation in Chapter 10 indicated that the basic influences affecting the prices of stocks, bonds, and other assets were: expected cash flows, market interest rates, and risk premiums. Therefore, useful economic analysis should provide insights regarding cash flow trends, interest rate trends, and risk premium analysis. This may involve analysis of the economy's expected growth, inflation, demographic shifts, and the political environment.

Financial Statements

In Chapter 9 we saw how analyzing financial statements can indicate a firm's strengths and weaknesses. By combining this information with an economic forecast, an analyst gains perspective on what the future may hold for a particular firm and its bond- and stockholders.[1] For example, a forecast of a percentage change in a firm's sales, coupled with the analyst's knowledge of the firm's operating and financial leverage, results in a forecast of net income and earnings per share.

Chapter 8, on efficient capital markets, provided a dose of reality to show that identifying undervalued securities is not easy. At the same time, the chapters on security valuation, financial statement analysis, and this chapter on economic analysis give us the

---

[1] For empirical evidence linking economic and accounting information to excess stock returns, see Baruch Lev and S. Ramu Thiagarajan, "Fundamental Information Analysis," *Journal of Accounting Research* vol. 37 no. 2 (Autumn 1993), pp. 190–215.

basic tools we need to attempt to identify mispriced securities. Part 4 uses these tools to analyze equities; Part 5 uses these tools to examine fixed-income securities.

GENERIC APPROACHES TO SECURITY ANALYSIS

Emphasizing History

Two basic approaches are useful in evaluating securities. One approach is generally backward-looking. Specifically, investors select securities for purchase or sale by examining past data, trends, and relationships and by assuming the future will be an extension of the past. Advocates of this approach may attempt to exploit market anomalies by using quantitative screens to construct portfolios (for example, buy only low P/E stocks or only stocks with small market capitalizations), or they may use technical analysis, which we will discuss in some detail in Chapter 14.

Focusing on the Future

The second approach is forward-looking. In this approach, although proponents might use some historical information, they focus mainly on determining likely future trends and investing accordingly. These investors may take either a top-down or a bottom-up approach to investing.

Top-Down Approach   This text advocates the top-down approach. As described in Chapter 10, in the **top-down approach** an investor first reviews a country's macroeconomy and forecasts likely trends. From this analysis arise implications for different industries and economic sectors. By combining both the economic and industry analysis, firms are analyzed with an eye to identifying as purchase candidates those best positioned to take advantage of the expected economic and industry trends; those firms that will suffer in the expected economic/industry environment are sell candidates.

Bottom-Up Approach   As the name implies, the **bottom-up approach** to investment analysis focuses mainly on microeconomic (firm-specific) factors that will lead to firm success. An integral part of this type of analysis is putting together a rationale or "story" that explains the analyst's views on why the firm is poised for future success irrespective of the economic/industry environment. Rather than dealing with trends in the economy, the "story" will focus on firm- and industry-specific factors that increase the likelihood of investor success. Whereas the "top-downers" examine both macro and micro elements that affect the future of a firm, the "bottom-uppers" focus mainly on the micro elements.

Both top-downers and bottom-uppers can claim many investment success stories. We choose to focus on top-down analysis because it places more structure on the investment analysis process and assists investors in identifying relationships, themes, and assumptions between the economy, industry, and company. Over time, investment analysts develop their own modifications and styles for analyzing firms. There are probably as many different analytical techniques and preferences as there are investment professionals. We believe our focus on the top-down approach will best serve your future needs and experiences. In the following section we begin our discussion of the top-down approach by briefly reviewing some basic economic concepts.

A QUICK REVIEW OF ECONOMIC CONCEPTS

A discussion of the macroeconomy usually has at least two components: (1) the national economy and (2) how the international economy affects the national economy.

Domestic Economic Activity

Economic forecasters attempt to determine trends in major economic variables such as gross domestic product (GDP), inflation, and interest rates. We discuss methods of forecasting inflation and interest rates later in this chapter; first we focus on GDP.

Gross domestic product (GDP) is the sum total of the goods and services produced within a nation's borders in a year. To be useful to investment analysts, GDP estimates need to be broken down into their components, so analysts can derive sector and industry growth forecasts. Such a component analysis is important, as economic variables such as income, interest rates, and exchange rates have differential effects on the components of GDP.

GDP has five major components: consumption spending, investment spending, government expenditures, goods and services produced domestically for export, and the production of goods and services consumed in the process of distributing imports to the domestic consumer.

Consumption spending is the purchases of households and consumers and comprises about two-thirds of GDP. Changes in consumption spending are affected by changes in income, consumer sentiment, and taxes. *Investment spending* is mainly comprised of investment by businesses in their assets. It is affected by factors such as expectations of future sales and interest rates. *Government spending* includes government budget plans. *Export and import activity* encompasses spending relevant to the shipment of goods into or out of the domestic economy and is affected by exchange rates and the strength or weakness of both the United States' and other countries' economies.

Figure 11.1 illustrates changes in the composition of GDP since 1985. This graph plots the main components of GDP spending (consumption, investment, government, and net exports) as a percentage of total GDP each year. During 1985 to 1996, consumption spending generally rose, although it was flat in the late 1980s and fell slightly in 1995. In 1996, consumption spending was nearly 68 percent of GDP. Investment spending fell by more than 14 percent (from 9.01 percent of GDP to 7.7 percent of GDP) between 1986 and 1991 before recovering in 1992. Government spending fluctuated slightly, but started a downward trend as percent of GDP in 1991. Net exports have been negative, showing the U.S. economy's proclivity for spending more on imports than it sells in overseas markets. The dollar level of GDP in 1996 was more than $7.4 trillion.

Such general trends can be used to make forecasts about industry spending. More importantly, these components of GDP can be broken down into smaller sectors to provide additional detail on growth prospects in individual sectors and industries. For example, consumption spending has three main components: spending on consumer durable goods (such as refrigerators, autos, and televisions), consumer nondurables (such as food and pharmaceuticals), and services. Spending on consumer durables is sensitive to the stage of the business cycle, expectations, and income. Consumer nondurables, by their nature, are less sensitive to these influences.

Figure 11.2 illustrates the changing proportions of consumption spending over time. The graph shows spending on the three main components of consumption spending (consumer durables, consumer nondurables, and services) expressed as a percentage of GDP. Durable goods spending is the smallest of the three and ranged from 7.69 percent (in 1991) to 9.02 percent (in 1986) during 1985 through 1996. Notably, in 1996 each percentage point of GDP equaled more than $74 billion, which means that small percentage changes can have large impacts on durable goods industry sales. Nondurable-goods spending was generally on a downward trend between 1985 and 1996, finishing at 20.3 percent of GDP. Services spending, on the other hand, grew as a component of GDP, rising nearly every year since 1985 to a level equal to 39.24 percent of GDP in 1996.

Figure 11.1   *Percentage of GDP Components Relative to Total GDP: Consumption, Investment, Government, and Net Export Spending, 1985–1996*

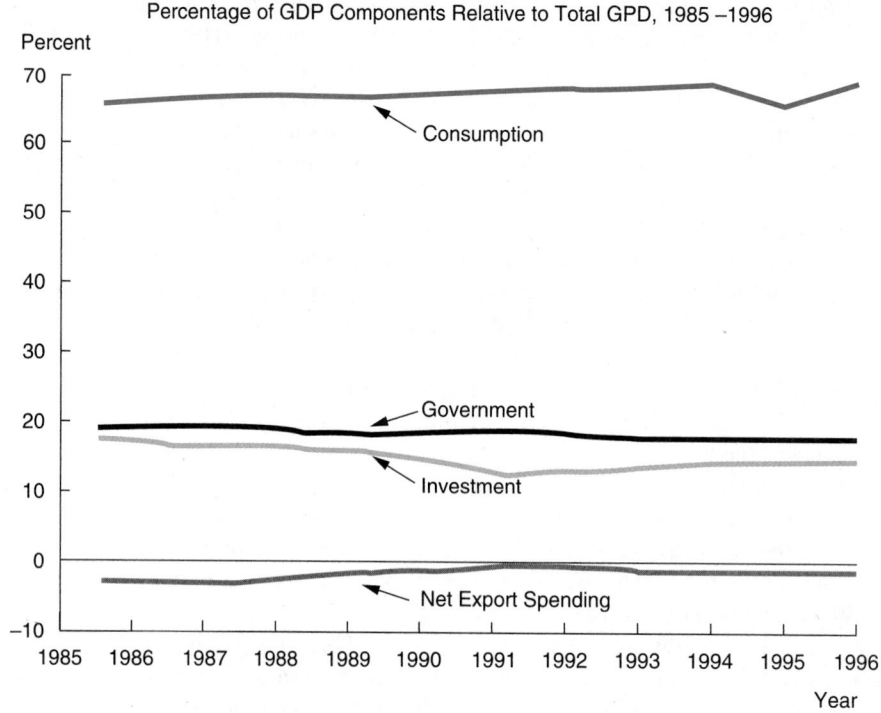

Percentage of GDP Components Relative to Total GPD, 1985 –1996

Source: Computed from *Economic Report of the President,* Washington, D.C., U.S. Government Printing Office, 1997.

The importance of the components of spending is seen in the period of economic growth that started in 1991 and was continuing as of this writing. Growth in spending for durable goods has far exceeded nondurable spending in the 1990s.[2] Sectors such as computers, autos, and housing have enjoyed strong growth whereas nondurable goods sectors, such as restaurants, retailers, and apparel makers have not. About 50 percent of the growth in real GDP during the 1990s is attributable to durable goods; in previous periods of economic growth, the durable goods sector accounted for only 20–30 percent of growth.

Investment spending also has several elements. It includes nonresidential investment spending on buildings and equipment used in the course of business as well as residential investing, such as home purchases, which are sensitive to demographic influences as well as income and interest rate levels. Another component of investment spending is business inventory investment. Unlike the first two elements, this one can be positive or negative, depending on whether businesses are adding to their inventories or facing inventory reductions. Also, whereas most residential and nonresidential spending is planned, this is not always the case with inventory investment. Specifically, inventory investment may rise because business production plans assumed sales would be higher than what occurred. Alternatively, inventory investment may decline because actual sales were higher than businesses expected.

---

[2]Fred R. Bleakley, "Some Invitations for Economic Party Haven't Arrived," *Wall Street Journal*, July 28, 1997, pp. A2, A4.

Figure 11.2   *Percentage of Consumption Spending Components Relative to Total GDP: Durable Goods, Nondurable Goods, and Service, 1985–1996*

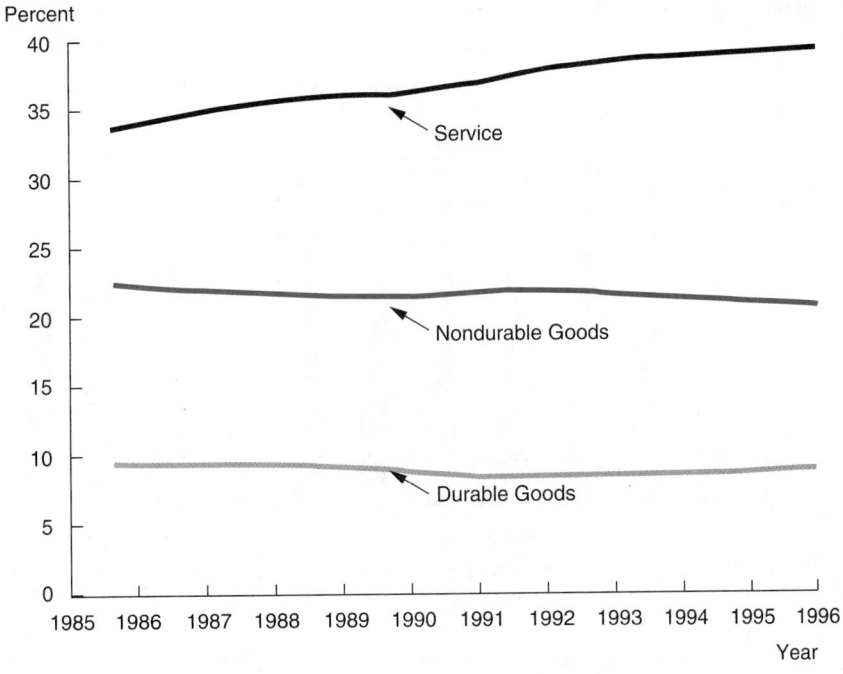

Source: Computed from *Economic Report of the President,* Washington, D.C., U.S. Government Printing Office, 1997.

Figure 11.3 shows how the components of investment spending changed as a percentage of GDP during the 1985–1996 period. The largest investment component, nonresidential investment spending, fell during much of this time before it started to rise in 1993. Another drop is apparent in the percentage of GDP spent on residential housing from 1985 to 1991, although it has risen since then. Business inventory investment as a percentage of GDP was rather small. Inventory investment generally fell during the 1985 to 1991 period, possibly because of movements by corporate America toward better inventory management and JIT (just-in-time) inventory control systems. Inventory growth since the early 1990s has occurred due to the robust economy after the 1991 recession.

Government spending also has several components: federal, state, and local. Federal spending can also be divided into various elements, including defense and nondefense spending.

Figure 11.4 shows the year-to-year percentage changes in consumption, investment, and government spending. Although the 1985–1996 time frame was generally one of economic growth, it did feature a short recession in 1991 and, as a result of six increases in interest rates by the Federal Reserve, an economic slowdown in 1994. Nonetheless, consumption spending grew at annual rates ranging from 3.5 percent to 7.3 percent during this time. Investment spending fell nearly 8 percent during the 1991 recession, but bounced back to grow 7.4 percent during 1992, 10 percent in 1993, and more than 16 percent during 1994. Government spending growth slowed during this time, 5–7 percent annually down to 3–4 percent annually. Even during a time of relative economic stability, variable growth rates reflect changes in the economy and investment opportunities.

Thus, developing an estimate for GDP is important, but for investment analysis it is also important to develop forecasts for each component of GDP. Forecasting that GDP

Figure 11.3   *Percentage of Investment Spending Components Relative to Total GDP: Nonresidential, Residential, and Business Inventory Investment, 1985–1996*

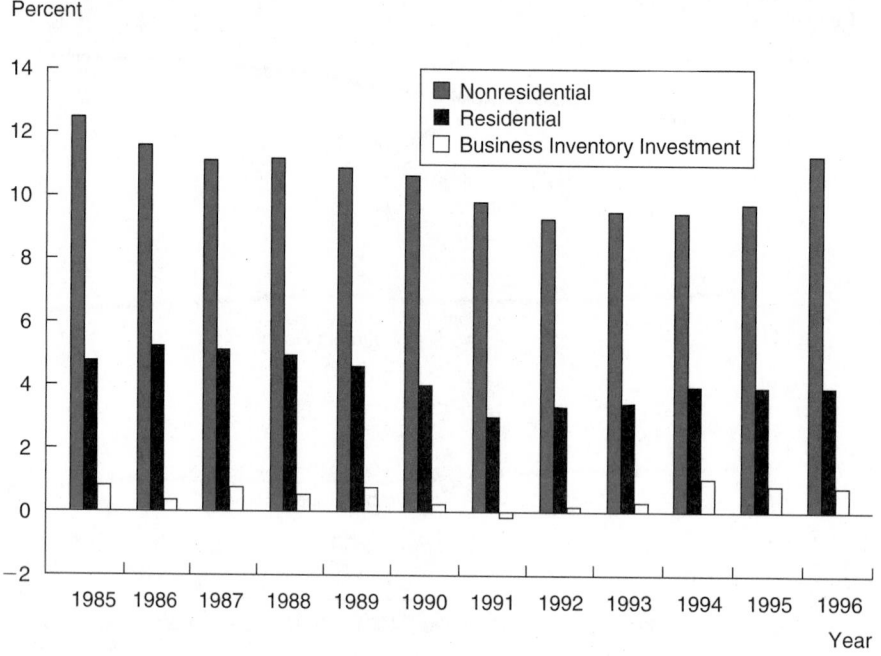

Source: Computed from *Economic Report of the President,* Washington, D.C., U.S. Government Printing Office, 1997.

will grow by 5 percent is important information, but for investment purposes it would be more valuable to know if the main impetus for that growth would be due to, for example, consumer spending in the durable goods market, residential construction, or businesses building their inventories. Knowing the source of the growth will identify industries or sectors deserving of closer scrutiny for possible investment.

As security analysts are trying to find undervalued securities or sectors, the information contained in a sector forecast is valuable. Presumably higher growth sectors will have faster earnings and cash flow growth than other sectors. Higher forecasted cash-flow levels and lower risk perceptions of such sectors may lead analysts to believe their stock prices or bond credit quality will have greater appreciation potential than other sectors. Of course, if the market has already anticipated this growth, stock P/E ratios and prices may reflect this optimism.

Domestic Economic Policies

The federal government and Federal Reserve use fiscal and monetary policy tools in their attempts to guide the economy. By their effects on the interest rate and economic growth, monetary and fiscal policy can affect financial market behavior and price levels.

Monetary policy involves the use of the power of the Federal Reserve Board (referred to as the Fed) to affect the money supply and aggregate economic activity. Many economists believe that the growth rate of the money supply has broad implications for future economic growth and future levels of inflation. As a consequence, most investment managers are interested in changes in the growth rate of the money supply and the current status of monetary policy. Many analysts are "Fed watchers," who seek to glean

Figure 11.4   *Year-to-Year Changes in Percentage Growth: Consumption, Investment, and Government Spending, 1986–1996*

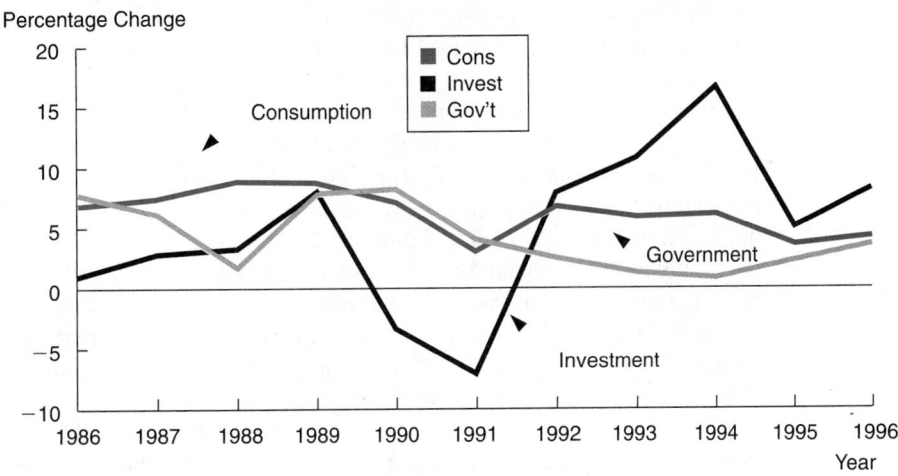

Source: Computed from *Economic Report of the President,* Washington, D.C., U.S. Government Printing Office, 1997.

information from Fed pronouncements and data that may indicate potential future changes in money supply growth, interest rates, and the inflation rate.

The Federal Reserve Board has three basic instruments with which it can administer its monetary policy:

1. open market operations, in which it purchases or sells government securities
2. determination of the discount rate (the interest rate banks pay when they borrow from the Fed)
3. the setting of reserve requirements for banks

Open market operations are the most frequently used tool of monetary policy. The term *open market* simply means the Fed will buy or sell securities (usually Treasury bills) from any market participant, rather than, for example, dealing only with the U.S. Treasury. You will recall from your macroeconomics course that when the Fed purchases government securities in the open market, it is trading dollars for securities. The dollars will be deposited in the seller's bank, which will increase the loanable reserves of the bank. Subsequently, through a multiplier process, deposits (and the money supply) in the U.S. banking system will rise. Sales of securities by the Fed have the opposite effect; they reduce the level of loanable funds, deposits, and money supply in the banking system. Financial and market analysts eagerly watch money supply figures, reported weekly in the financial press, for insight into the Fed's policy and its desire to either slow down or speed up the economy.

In addition to the weekly money supply figures, another useful indicator of monetary policy is the amount of **free reserves** available to the banking system; it is reported in the *Wall Street Journal* every Friday. The amount of free reserves is equal to the excess reserves of the banking system less bank borrowing from the Fed.[3] Because free reserves are

---

[3]Excess reserves equal total bank reserves (coin, currency, and deposits at the Fed) less the bank's required reserves. Banks must keep a specified fraction of their deposits on hand as required reserves. The Fed sets reserve requirement percentages.

generally positive when the Fed is purchasing securities in the open market, positive free reserves are considered an indicator of an expansionary monetary policy. This may indicate the Fed's desire to assist economic growth, maintain or expand liquidity, or maintain or lower interest rates. Negative free reserves, sometimes called *net borrowed reserves,* indicate a contractionary monetary policy, which the Fed may create to slow down the economy, ease inflationary pressures, or raise interest rates.

The effect of open market operations may also be evaluated through changes in the **federal funds rate,** the interest rate that banks charge each other for short-term interbank loans. But such attempts at estimating Federal Reserve policy are sometimes futile, as the Fed can only affect the supply of loanable reserves via open market operations; it cannot affect demand. As with any other price, the federal funds rate is a function of both the supply and the demand for short-term loans by banks. Many Fed watchers predict monetary policy and future interest rate trends by observing the federal funds rate.

The Fed rarely uses its powers to adjust the **reserve requirement** (the ratio of required reserves to total deposits at a bank). The reason for this is the money multiplier effect: small changes in the reserve ratio can have very large influences on money supply. The Fed occasionally adjusts the **discount rate** (the interest rate at which banks can borrow from the Fed) to implement monetary policy and transmit signals regarding future policy.

Many economists point to monetary policy as having a major effect on the economy and financial markets. A tight money policy by the Fed in the late 1920s and during much of the 1930s likely exacerbated, if not helped cause, the Great Depression. A markedly loose monetary policy with high money-supply growth rates in the late 1970s led to years of double-digit inflation in the United States. On a positive note, moves by the Fed to focus on money supply growth helped to end the era of double-digit inflation and created a period of disinflation, or lowering inflation, in the 1980s. In the 1990s, the Federal Reserve, led by Alan Greenspan, helped stimulate and extend an economic expansion by keeping inflation under control without restricting monetary policy so much that it would cause a recession.

Fiscal policy involves the use of government spending and taxing powers to influence the economy. Both tax laws and government expenditures affect the disposable incomes of consumers and corporations as well as the level of aggregate demand in the economy. Many analysts believe that efforts to reduce the federal budget deficit in the 1990s helped contribute to lower interest rates and a rising stock market. Some believe that capital gains tax cuts help stimulate investment in equities due to higher expected after-tax returns.

Fiscal policy can play a role in maintaining stable economic growth, according to some economists. For example, in a recession, aggregate demand for goods and services is less than aggregate supply. As a result, workers are laid off, production is reduced in an effort to reduce inventories, and capital investment projects are delayed. Expansionary fiscal policy in the form of increases in government spending or tax reductions may have the effect of increasing consumer and business income, which leads to an increase in aggregate demand and spending. The Fed can assist the process so that both expansionary monetary and fiscal policy work together to contribute to an economic recovery. Generally, a growing economy is associated with higher corporate earnings; if P/E ratios are stable or increasing, too, stock prices will rise.

When the economy is "heating up" or expanding too quickly, inflation may result. In this situation, the increase in demand is greater than the ability of firms to produce enough output, so we have "too much money chasing too few goods," which leads to higher prices—that is, inflation. Although many argue that the Fed can best control inflation by slowing the growth rate of the money supply, others argue for lower levels of government spending and higher taxes or both to reduce aggregate spending in an overheated economy. A coordinated effort will have the greatest effect.

The Global Economy

With the development of global trade and finance, analysts developing forecasts must consider the effects of international factors on domestic economies. Because many firms are affected by worldwide competition, top-down analysis in many instances must begin with an examination of *global* economic growth rather than domestic growth alone.

Global influences can have numerous effects on domestic economies. The health of foreign economies affects domestic industries and U.S. exports. If foreign economies are enjoying growth, U.S. exports will likely rise and export-based firms will prosper. These same industries will face a slowdown if foreign economies are in recession.

Movements toward freer trade, with the elimination of tariffs, quotas, and other trade restraints between countries, is generally a positive sign for economic growth. Although some domestic industries may do better than others in the short run, in general free trade helps expand markets and contributes to economic growth.

Trade is affected by changes in exchange rates. Thus, an analysis of global industries needs to review national growth forecasts as well as exchange rate trends. An **exchange rate** is the price of one currency in terms of another currency, such as ¥110/$ (110 yen to the dollar) or DM 1.50/$ (1.50 deutsche mark to the dollar). Should the U.S. dollar strengthen against a foreign currency (meaning one U.S. dollar can purchase more foreign currency units), imports from that nation may rise, because the goods from that country become cheaper in U.S.-dollar terms. For example, if we assume an exchange rate of 105 yen to the dollar, a car that costs ¥2,100,000 in Japan will cost $20,000 in the United States. Should the dollar strengthen to 110 yen to the dollar, this same car will sell for about $19,091. A strengthening dollar helps make imports less expensive in U.S.-dollar terms; insomuch as this increases demand for imported goods, competing domestic sectors may suffer. Also, because it basically reduces import prices, a strengthening U.S. dollar may ease U.S. inflation rates.

Notice the mirror effect here: as one currency gets stronger, the other currency necessarily becomes weaker. For example, if the dollar is gaining strength against the yen, it takes more yen to purchase one U.S. dollar; therefore, the prices of U.S.-manufactured goods in Japan will become more expensive for the Japanese consumer, even if their price in U.S.-dollar terms remains constant. If U.S. producers do not reduce their prices when the yen weakens relative to the U.S. dollar, it will become more difficult to sell U.S. goods in Japan; Japan will import less and the United States will export less.

Influences Affecting Exchange Rates   Several factors that cause exchange rates to fluctuate over time include differences in interest rates, inflation rates, and national income growth between countries. Central bank intervention and trade barriers also influence exchange rates.

Consider domestic investors for a moment: they want protection against inflation. Generally, in what is called the *Fisher effect,* expectations of higher inflation lead to increase in nominal interest rates. With a 4 percent inflation, investors may be happy with a 7 percent return, giving them a 3 percent real return, or a 3 percent increase in real purchasing power. If inflation rises to 6 percent, investors will require a 9 percent return in order to receive the same 3 percent increase in real purchasing power from their investment.

The Fisher effect (ignoring compounding) is summarized in the equation:

$$\text{real interest rate} = \text{nominal or observed interest rate} - \text{expected inflation}$$

or

$$\text{nominal interest rate} = \text{real interest rate} + \text{expected inflation}$$

From an international perspective, global investors want protection from fluctuating exchange rates. Fluctuations in exchange rates will affect investors' returns. An adverse move in exchange rates can lower the return received by the investor, even turning it into a loss.

For example, suppose the exchange rate between the United States and Canada is US$1 = Can$1.25. An investor takes US$100, exchanges it into Can$125, and invests it in Canadian securities. She earns 10 percent on her selections, so her Can$125 investment has grown to Can$137.50. But, if the U.S. dollar strengthened by 10 percent against the Canadian dollar over the course of the year, now one U.S. dollar can purchase 1.375 Canadian dollars. Converting her Canadian dollars back into U.S. dollars, she receives Can$137.5 × US$1/Can$1.375, or US$100. Her profits have been nullified by the affects of a stronger home currency.

The U.S. investor's 10 percent Canadian return, minus the 10 percent increase in the value of the U.S. dollar, resulted in a net domestic return of zero percent.

Investors will use an international variation of the Fisher effect when considering overseas investments to seek protection from expected exchange rate changes. A simple relationship to use is:

11.1a $$\text{Return in terms of the home currency} = \text{Return in the foreign currency} - \text{percentage change in the home currency's exchange rate}$$

or, rearranging,

11.1b $$\text{Return in the foreign currency} = \text{Domestic expected return} + \text{expected change in the home currency's exchange rate}$$

If, for example, investors expect their home currency to strengthen, they will add the expected percentage change in the exchange rate to their expected domestic return to determine the required return on overseas investments. Domestic investors will not invest overseas unless the expected overseas returns meet or exceed this required return.

Let's look at an example from the perspective of an overseas investor investing in the United States. Suppose a Japanese investor can earn 4 percent on bonds in Japan. Because of concerns about the U.S. trade deficit, suppose the U.S. dollar is expected to fall 5 percent in value against the Japanese yen next year. What return is required from U.S. bonds before our Japanese investor will want to buy them?

To equal the 4 percent domestic return on bonds, the Japanese investor will need a 9 percent return on his U.S. investment to compensate for the expected stronger yen (or the weaker dollar). We see this below using equation 11.1a:

$$\text{Domestic return} = \text{Overseas return} - \text{percentage change in the home currency's exchange rate}$$

$$\text{4 percent (Japan domestic return)} = \text{U.S. return} - (+5 \text{ percent expected strengthening in the yen})$$

Solving for the U.S. return, the Japanese investor will require a 9 percent return on his U.S. investment.

Should the U.S. dollar be expected to fall 7 percent, the Japanese investor will require a U.S. interest rate of 11 percent in order to entice him to invest in U.S. securities. Thus a falling dollar is expected to put upward pressure on U.S. interest rates and make borrowing more expensive for the U.S. government, corporations, and individuals. Exchange rate fluctuations can affect U.S. interest rates, from rates paid on Treasury bills to home mortgages!

Figure 11.5   *Relationship between Interest Rates and Exchange Rates, 1982–1988*

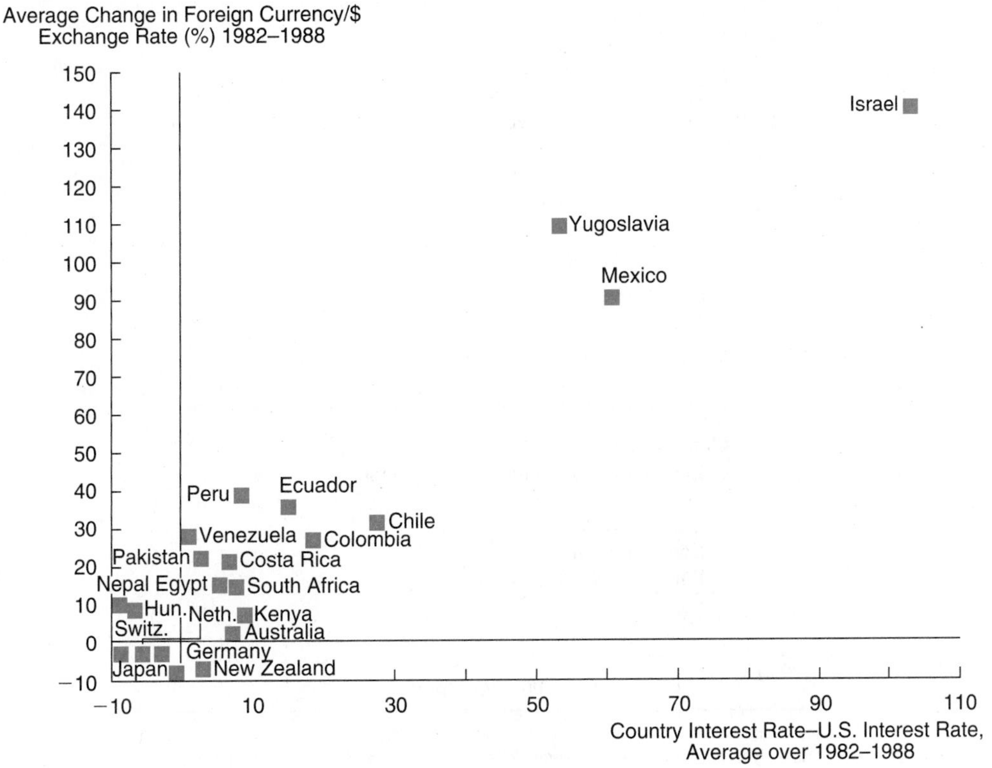

Average Change in Foreign Currency/$
Exchange Rate (%) 1982–1988

Source: Alan C. Shapiro, *Multinational Financial Management,* 4th ed. (Needham Heights, MA: Allyn and Bacon, 1992), p. 167.

According to this perspective, called *interest rate parity,* countries with weakening currencies will have higher domestic interest rates. Figure 11.5 shows that this hypothesized relationship between interest rates and exchange rate changes is true from the perspective of many different countries. Countries whose interest rates exceeded those in the U.S. generally had currencies whose value fell against the dollar; countries with interest rates below those in the U.S. had currencies which generally strengthened against the dollar.

As this section illustrates, an analysis of exchange rates and foreign economic trends is important in evaluating the domestic economy as well as global industries and firms.

INFLUENCES ON THE ECONOMY AND SECURITY MARKETS

Following this review of economics, we can discuss factors that affect future real economic growth, that is, the growth in output that occurs after the effects of inflation are removed. This section discusses factors that influence long-term and short-term growth expectations.

Influences on Long-Term Expectations

The long-term growth path of the economy is determined by supply factors. Growth will be constrained in the long run by limits in technology, the size and training of the labor force, and the availability of adequate resources and incentives to expand.

Table 11.1 *Foundations of Long-Term Growth Expectations*

Labor Effect
Population
Labor participation rate
   Labor force
     Percentage employed
       Workforce
         Hours worked per employee
           Total hours worked
           Business training
           Education

Capital Effect
   Capital stock (net)
     Capital employed
     Technology/R&D
     Capacity utilization

Contributing Factors
   Economic mix (manufacturing versus service)
   Peace expectations
   Energy availability
   Economic stability
   Foreign competition
   Incentives
     Regulation
     Tax mix
     Government share of output

Source: First Chicago Investment Advisors, as reported in Jeffrey J. Diermeier, "Capital Market Expectations: The Macro Factors," in John L. Maginn and Donald L. Tuttle, ed., *Managing Investment Portfolios: A Dynamic Process,* 2d ed. (Boston: Warren, Gorham, and Lamont, 1990), pp. 5–32.

Table 11.1 lists factors that affect long-term growth expectations. Positive or negative changes in these factors may lead to changes in future economic growth.

Another, perhaps simpler, way of viewing growth prospects is to focus on specific components of real output, as seen in Equation 11.2:

11.2
$$\text{Real Output} = \text{Population} \times \text{Labor Force Participation Rate} \\ \times \text{Average Number of Hours Worked per Week} \\ \times \text{Labor Productivity}$$

Population multiplied by the proportion of the population that is in the labor force equals the number of workers in the U.S. economy; multiplying this by the average number of hours worked per week gives the total number of man-hours of labor effort over a week's time. Labor productivity is defined as output per man-hour; thus, total man-hours of labor multiplied by output per man-hour results in economic output.

When focusing on long-term economic growth, we are not interested in the *levels* of the variables on the right-hand side of Equation 11.2, but in their *changes* over time. It is the changes, or growth, of the population, labor force participation, the workweek, and labor productivity that will lead to *growth* in real output over time. The factors in Table 11.1 under the headings "Capital Effect" and "Contributing Factors," in addition to labor force education and training, will affect labor productivity over time. This discussion makes it clear that demographic changes and technological improvements have a major effect on an economy's growth trends.

From a strict life-cycle perspective, we would expect growth to be generally slower in the developed European, Asian, and North American economies and faster in the developing (emerging) economies such as Eastern Europe, Africa, Central and South America, and the Pacific Rim. Sectors serving higher-growth global industries and higher-growth economies should benefit in the years ahead. Free trade will spur economic growth by allowing developed nations to meet the economic needs of developing nations.

Analysts' assumptions about labor, capital, and contributing factors can be useful in evaluating economic growth prospects. Politics, regulation, societal influences and demographics will affect these components of long-term growth.

Influences on Short-Term Expectations

In contrast to long-term expectations, mainly driven by supply factors, short-term expectations about the economy are mainly caused by demand factors. Fluctuations in demand relative to long-term supply constraints create fluctuations in real GDP, which are known as business cycles. When demand exceeds supply, inflation results; when demand is less than supply, rising unemployment and recession may occur. Short-term economic forecasting should focus on sources of demand as a means to predict future trends in economic variables. The following discussion considers several of the sources of demand.

Monetary Policy and Liquidity   Businesses need access to funds in order to borrow, raise capital, and invest in their assets. Likewise, individuals need access to funds to borrow to purchase homes, cars, and other high-priced durable goods. If monetary policy is too tight and banks have few excess reserves to lend, sources of capital become scarce and economic activity will slow or decline. Lack of liquidity can also occur if bank regulators are overly critical of bank lending practices. In such a case they may require banks to acquire more capital to support their lending activities.

Although liquidity is good for the economy, excess liquidity can be harmful. In a classic case of "too much money chasing too few goods," excessive money supply growth can lead to inflation, higher interest rates, and higher risk premiums due to the resulting uncertainty that inflation creates among consumers and business managers.

Inflation   Although inflation is mainly a monetary phenomenon, at times outside shocks to the system, such as raw material shortages, can cause increases, albeit temporary, in the inflation rate. Inflation usually occurs when short-term economic demand exceeds the long-term supply constraint. As such, inflation is typically seen as a sign that the end of an economic expansion is near. In terms of valuing financial assets, inflation reduces the real purchasing power of fixed-income securities. Also, it adds a layer of uncertainty to future business and investment decisions, which increases risk premiums. Studies have shown that as inflation increases costs to businesses, they are generally unable to pass all the cost increases through to the consumer, thereby squeezing their profit margins and leading to real declines in profitability. It is not surprising that many studies find negative correlations between a country's inflation rate and its short-term stock market returns.[4] Perhaps most important, an increase in the expected rate of inflation will cause nominal interest rates to rise, as predicted by the Fisher effect. Inflation in the United States may raise the price of our exports, thus reducing overseas sales while making imports appear more price competitive. Thus, inflation may create some job dislocations in export-sensitive industries and cause the value of the U.S. dollar to weaken in exchange markets.

---

[4]See, for example, Claude B. Erb, Campbell R. Harvey, and Tadas E. Viskanta, "Inflation and World Equity Selection," *Financial Analysts Journal,* Nov./Dec. 1995: 28–42, and the references therein.

Interest Rates   Interest rates are the price of credit. In general, increases in interest rates, whether caused by inflation, Fed policy, rising risk premiums, or other factors, will lead to reduced borrowing and an economic slowdown. Rising interest rates lead to declines in bond prices and typically lead to falling stock prices for several reasons. As noted in Chapter 1, when interest rates rise, investors' required rate of return on stocks will rise as well, causing prices to fall. Rising interest rates also make bond yields look more attractive relative to stock dividend yields.

International Influences   Rapid real growth overseas can create surges in demand for U.S. exports, leading to growth in export-sensitive industries and overall GDP. In contrast, the erection of trade barriers, quotas, nationalistic fervor, and currency restrictions can hinder the free flow of currency, goods, and services and harm the export sector of the U.S. economy. Although some attempts at policy coordination have been made by the G-7 nations, most coordination has focused on strengthening or weakening the exchange rates of some of its members, most notably those of the United States and Japan. The business cycles of the developed, the developing, and the less-developed nations do not rise and fall together. Therefore, a strong U.S. economy can at times assist economies experiencing a recession by importing their products, and vice versa.

Consumer Sentiment   As previously noted, consumer spending comprises about two-thirds of GDP. Some of this spending provides the basics of food, clothing, shelter, and medical care and is only slightly sensitive to consumer attitudes. Still, it makes intuitive sense that an optimistic consumer is willing to spend more than a pessimistic one. Optimistic consumer sentiment may lead consumers to make a long-delayed purchase of durable goods or to be more free with their dollars at gift-giving or vacation time. Such variations in consumer sentiment will lead to alternating periods of sales growth and decline for consumer-oriented industries, particularly manufacturers of consumer durables. It is also known that risk premiums, which are influenced by consumer and investor attitudes, change over the course of the business cycle. As a result, consumer sentiment can be expected to affect *both* cash flows (that is, higher or lower sales and operating incomes), as well as the required risk premiums on financial market investments.

Real Effects   Real effects differ from financial or monetary effects in that they influence the operations and manufacture of goods and services. Some economic theorists argue, unlike the monetarists and Keynesians, that economic fluctuations can be traced to random real shocks in the economy. Examples of real shocks include major political occurrences such as embargoes, declarations of war and peace, technological advances, tax code changes, and extended labor strikes. Although the effect of these shocks can concentrate in one industry or sector, multiplier effects can spread their expansionary or recessionary effects throughout the economy. Whether they are or are not the ultimate cause of business cycles is the subject for another course; what is important for investment purposes is that unforeseen shocks to the system can affect short-term expectations and lead to unexpected changes in demand relative to long-run supply. This effect, besides affecting investment cash flows in specific sectors, can also have market-wide influences on cash flows, inflation, interest rate levels, and economy-wide risk premiums.

Fiscal Policy   Fiscal policy affects short-run demand. Government spending can directly affect economic sectors and geographic regions. All else constant, some economists believe larger-than-expected increases in government spending will increase short-run demand; slower-than-expected increases may harm short-run demand.[5] Tax

---

[5]Because the federal budget always rises, it seems more appropriate to discuss lower-than-expected increases rather than spending reductions in the context of overall fiscal policy.

changes influence incentives to save, work, and invest, and may therefore affect both short-term expectations as well as long-term supply. Some economists think that decreases in the federal budget deficit reduce interest rates by lowering public-sector borrowing demand.

Summary of Short-Term Influences   A variety of expectations in the short-run affect demand. Increases and decreases in demand, relative to long-term constrained supply growth, result in business cycles and concomitant fluctuations in cash flows, interest rates, and risk premiums. As part of the top-down investment approach, analysts should examine short-term demand trends and influences. These influences can then be evaluated to estimate their influence on different economic sectors, industries, and investments. As the prior discussion shows, a variety of demand influences exist, including monetary and fiscal policy, real growth effects, changes in inflation and interest rates, consumer expectations, and international events. These can have a significant short-term impact on the U.S. economy. In the next section we discuss practical tools of use in forecasting short-term economic trends.

FORECASTING TOOLS

Despite some of the practical difficulties in preparing consistently accurate forecasts, the macroeconomic environment cannot be ignored by investment analysts. Fortunately, some general economic signals provide us with insights regarding future economic trends without requiring us to be experts in economics. In this section we discuss basic tools and relationships used by many economists. Our focus is the United States, but the concepts apply to any nation's economy. Forecasting should be an element of any valuation and investment action. A structured approach to estimating future trends provides expectations about future cash flow growth, interest rates, and risk premiums and helps us make anticipatory, rather than reactive, investment decisions.

As a cautionary warning, analysts should not focus only on economic trends. A comprehensive top-down forecasting process should consider a firm and its industry's total environment. This includes, but is not limited to, the effects of changing technology on the firm and its industry; changes in social trends; political and regulatory environments; and the effects on the firm and its industry of an increasingly global marketplace. We discuss these effects in Chapter 12, Industry Analysis.

Inflation Indicators

Portfolio managers want to predict inflation trends for two reasons. First, inflation generally rises before the onset of an economic downturn. Secondly, inflation is a great destroyer of wealth. Principal and fixed-income streams lose purchasing power and value as the price level rises. Should indicators predict an increase in inflation, investors must adjust their portfolios to better protect their wealth. Fortunately, we have several indicators of future inflation trends.

One indicator is actions by the Federal Reserve. Rapid growth in the money supply is often a precursor to inflation; slow money-supply growth typically means inflation should not be a concern. The determination of rapid or slow growth, which is referred to as easy or tight monetary policy, is a relative judgment that depends upon the rate of growth of the money supply *relative* to the real rate of growth of the economy—that is, you want the money supply to grow about as fast as other factors of production (for example, 3 percent real growth). Analysts like to keep an eye on the rate of growth of money supply measures such as M2 and changes in free reserves as indicators of current and future

money supply growth. Both of these quantities are published weekly in *The Wall Street Journal.*

Another indicator is commodity prices; adherents of cost-push or demand-pull inflation view commodity prices as the first indicator of inflation trends. Commodities used in these indexes include agricultural products such as wheat, beans, livestock, and sugar as well as minerals such as aluminum and copper. Several raw materials price indexes have gained popularity as inflation indicators. The *Journal of Commerce* publishes a price index of eighteen industrial-use raw materials, such as aluminum and lead. The Commodity Research Bureau compiles indexes of commodity spot and futures market prices for foretelling price trends in commodities although they are biased toward the grain markets. The Goldman Sachs Commodity Index also can be used to gauge future price trends; its drawback is that nearly 50 percent of the index is affected by oil prices. Some investors believe gold and other precious metals are good hedges against inflation, and so they purchase these commodities if inflation fears rise. Thus, some analysts watch gold prices to gain insight into the market's perceptions about future inflation. Other analysts observe price trends on national stock exchanges that have numerous natural resource and mineral stocks. Examples would include South Africa, Toronto, and the Australian stock markets.

Depending on an analyst's belief about market efficiency, the stock and bond market may provide additional inflation indicators. If interest rates follow the Fisher effect, increases in short-term T-bill rates should be a precursor of inflation. Differences between interest rates on Treasury securities and the relatively new inflation-indexed notes issued by the Treasury can provide an indication of the market's expectations about future inflation. Another inflation indicator might be rising stock prices for firms that benefit from higher inflation, such as oil exploration firms and mining firms. Obviously, these increases should be accompanied by price increases for the commodities involved.

Professional economists may also be a source of expertise on inflation trends. The Philadelphia Federal Reserve Bank publishes the Livingston surveys wherein economists are asked to forecast future inflation. Twice a year, in January and July, the *Wall Street Journal* publishes its own survey of economists who likewise forecast future price levels.

As a final indicator, the Center for International Business Cycle Research has developed a leading index of inflation. Components of this index include the proportion of the population that is employed, the growth rates of business, consumer and federal government debt, and changes in industrial commodity prices.

Monetary Indicators

Monetary indicators are important to observe for several reasons. First, as mentioned above, they are a predictor of future inflation. Second, they indicate trends in liquidity in the economy.

As noted earlier, Federal Reserve actions can have a significant impact on the trend of economic activity. It is important when we use this analysis to make investment decisions to note how the Fed's actions compare to financial market expectations; if the Fed's actions are unexpectedly too lax or too severe (that is, they are a surprise), interest rates and stock prices may respond sharply.

An example of this was the Fed's four increases in the federal funds rate in the first half of 1994. The first announcement took the markets by surprise; stock prices fell and bond yields rose as investors feared the specter of inflation previously seen only by the Fed. After calming the markets by arguing that it was merely shifting monetary policy from a "stimulative" to a "neutral" mode, little market reaction followed the Fed's second increase in the federal funds rate in March. After an unexpected third rate hike in April

Table 11.2	*Economic Series Included in the Conference Board Index of Leading Economic Indicators*

1. Average weekly hours of manufacturing workers
2. Average weekly initial claims for unemployment insurance
3. Real value of manufacturers' new orders for consumer goods and materials
4. Index of consumer expectations
5. Index of 500 common stock prices
6. Manufacturers new orders, nondefense capital goods in 1992 dollars
7. Index of new private housing starts authorized by local building permits
8. Vendor performance (the percentage of companies receiving delivery later than the industry average)
9. Real money supply, M2
10. Interest rate spread, ten-year Treasury bonds less federal funds rate

1994, the stock market fell. It rallied after the fourth increase in May because the market believed that was the final rate hike for the time being. But this expectation was incorrect, as the Fed raised interest rates two more times before the end of 1994.

Differences between Long-Term and Short-Term Interest Rates

Studies have found that tracking the difference between long-term and short-term interest rates on government securities (referred to as a maturity spread) is a useful predictor of the trend of economic activity. Usually, long-term interest rates exceed short-term rates for reasons we will discuss in Chapter 16. Alternatively, analysts believe that a larger-than-usual positive difference between, say, a ten-year Treasury bond and a three-month Treasury bill indicates an increase in economic activity in the next twelve to eighteen months. In contrast, no difference or a negative difference between the ten-year and three-month interest rate, it is contended, foretells an economic recession. Between 1955 and 1998 the United States went through seven recessions; all seven followed an interest rate differential between long-term and short-term bonds that was zero or negative. When this maturity spread became positive again, economic growth followed.

Cyclical Economic Indicators

Leading indicators are a set of economic variables whose values reach peaks and troughs before aggregate economic activity (as measured by real GDP) does. For example, the housing industry serves as such a leading indicator, as well as other heavy durable industries (such as furniture and autos). Generally, if the housing market picks up, it is expected that after a short lag the general economy will follow, because the increase in demand for housing will stimulate increased demand for construction materials, workers, and durables to furnish the home. The lag arises because of the time lapse between the first evidence of increased housing demand (that is, an increase in housing starts) and a noticeable effect on overall economic activity.

The Conference Board publishes a series of economic data on ten leading economic indicators (LEI) in the business cycle as listed in Table 11.2. Figure 11.6 shows how the **index of leading economic indicators** typically turns down before a recession and turns upward before the beginning of an economic expansion. It can, however, give uncertain signals; as Figure 11.6 also shows, sometimes the index declines and no recession follows.

For example, in the case of the 1990–91 recession, the index of leading economic indicators hit its peak six months before the recession was deemed to officially have begun.

Figure 11.6 *Graph of Leading, Coincident, and Lagging Economic Indicators and the U.S. Business Cycle*

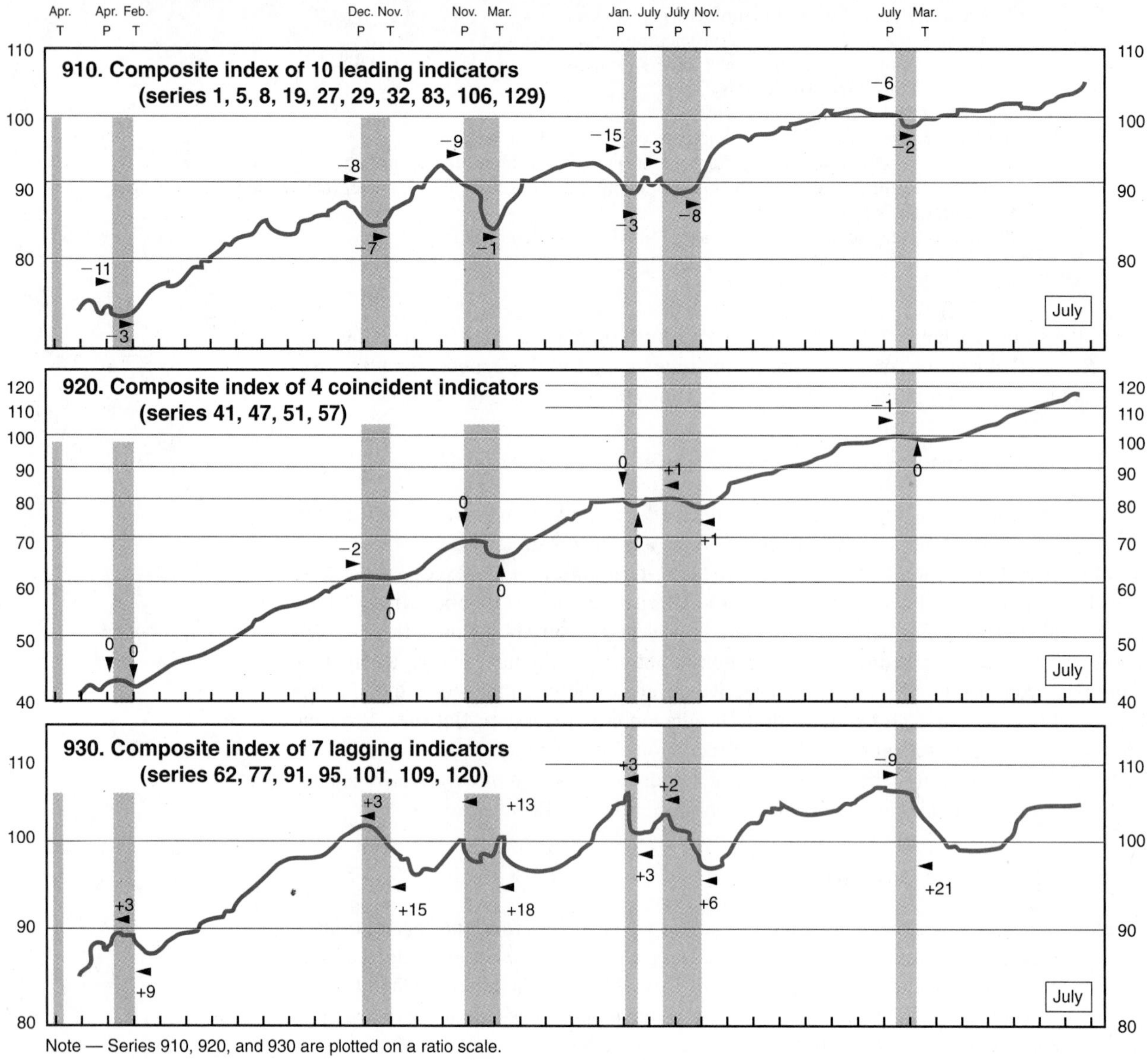

Note — Series 910, 920, and 930 are plotted on a ratio scale.

Note: Numbers and arrows indicate length of leads and lags in months from business cycle turning dates.
Source: *Business Cycle Indicators,* The Conference Board, New York, NY, September 1997, p. 5.

Because each indicator measures a different facet of the economy, they do not necessarily move up or down together. Figure 11.7 shows five of the ten indicators in the LEI to illustrate this point.

The leading-indicator approach to forecasting requires no assumptions about what causes economic behavior. Instead, it is an empirical process that relies on statistically detected patterns among economic variables, which are then used to forecast turning points in overall economic activity. Ongoing analysis of the LEI's components leads to changes in the index over time. In 1996, the LEI was reduced from eleven indicators to ten as two indicators were dropped (unfilled manufacturer orders and changes in sensitive materials

Figure 11.7   *Graph of Five Leading Economic Indicators*

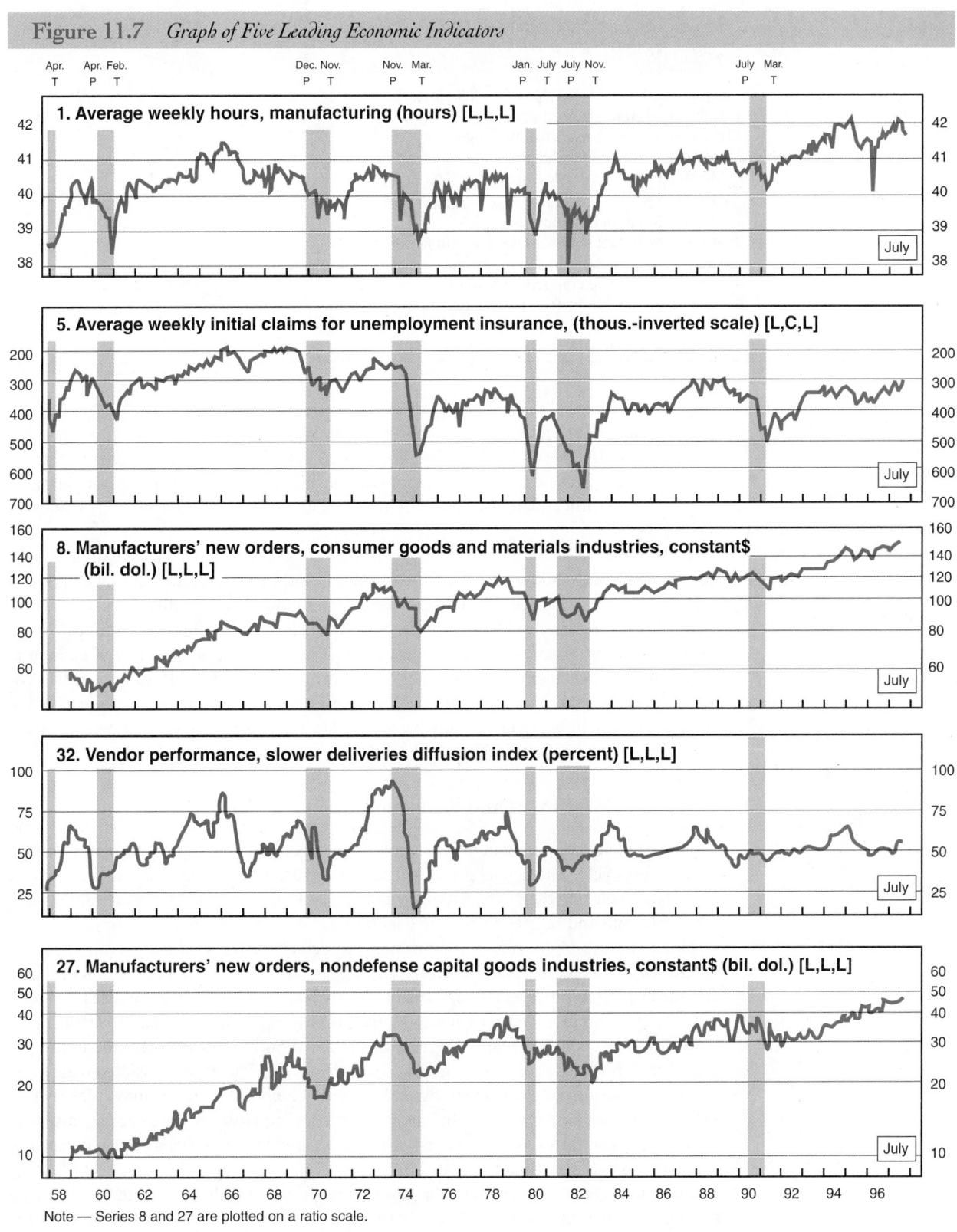

Note — Series 8 and 27 are plotted on a ratio scale.

Source: *Business Cycle Indicators,* The Conference Board, New York, NY, September 1997, p. 7.

Table 11.3 *Economic Series Included in the Conference Board Coincident and Lagging Economic Indicator Indexes*

Economic variables included in the Coincident Index:
1. Number of employees on nonagricultural payrolls
2. Personal income less transfer payments, expressed in 1992 dollars
3. Index of industrial production
4. Manufacturing and trade sales, expressed in 1992 dollars

Economic variables included in the Lagging Index:
1. Average duration of unemployment
2. Ratio of manufacturing and trade inventories to sales
3. Percentage change in the labor cost per unit of output in manufacturing
4. Average prime rate charged by banks
5. Commercial and industrial loans outstanding
6. Ratio of consumer installment credit outstanding to personal income
7. Change in the consumer price index (inflation rate) for services.

prices) and one was added: the interest rate spread between long-term and short-term rates. Because it relies on historical relationships to determine the series included, it sometimes gives incorrect signals. Nor does a relationship exist between changes in the leading economic indicator index and the strength and duration of business expansions or recessions.

The leading index helps us to see where we are going; the **coincident index of economic indicators** shows where we are. Similar to the LEI, the coincident index is comprised of economic series whose trends have been found to change direction at about the same time the business cycle hits a peak or trough. The **lagging index of economic indicators** discloses where the economy has been. It is composed of a variety of economic series, such as the unemployment rate, whose values follow the pattern of general economic activity, but with a lag of several months. The economic variables comprising the coincident and lagging indicators are listed in Table 11.3. The behavior of these composite indexes over time is seen in Figure 11.6.

Surveys of Sentiment and Expectations

Consumer expectations seem to play a role as the economy approaches turning points in the business cycle. The University of Michigan Consumer Sentiment Index queries a sample of households on their expectations over the next year. The index acts as a leading indicator by rising and falling before the general level of economic activity does.

Other surveys of consumer and business expectations focus on the overall economy and some focus on areas such as firms' capital spending or inventory investment plans. By subscribing to proprietary services or closely following the financial media, investment analysts can monitor how consumers and the business community feel about the economy and their spending plans. In general, the more optimistic they are, the better the prospects for increases in spending and economic growth. The more pessimistic they are, the worse the prospects for spending and growth. The problem with survey data is that individuals' and firms' reported plans may not come to fruition. Just because a survey reports that manufacturing firms expect to increase capital spending by a certain percentage does not mean they will actually do so.

Economic statistics released by the government provide another source of helpful information about current economic trends, particularly concerning various economic sectors. Every Monday the *Wall Street Journal* publishes a short commentary called "Tracking the

Figure 11.8 *Announcement Dates for Important Economic Data*

Tracking the Economy

INDICATOR	PERIOD COVERED	SCHEDULED RELEASE	PREVIOUS ACTUAL	TECHNICAL DATA CONSENSUS FORECAST
Purchasing Mgrs. Survey	January	Monday	53.1	52.8
Personal Income	December	Monday	+0.8%	+0.2%
Personal Spending	December	Monday	+0.4%	+0.5%
Construction spending	December	Monday	-0.9%	+0.8%
New Homes sales	December	Tuesday	830,000	818,000
Leading Indicators	December	Tuesday	+0.1%	+0.1%
Factory Orders	December	Thursday	+2.5%	-3.3%
Initial Jobless Claims	Week to Jan 31	Thursday	300,000	310,000
Money Supplies: M2	Week to Jan. 26	Thursday	+18.3 Billion	+11.0 Billion
Nonfarm Payrolls	January	Friday	+370,000	+263,000
Unemployment Rate	January	Friday	4.7%	4.7%
Consumer Borrowing	December	Friday	-$4.2 billion	+3.8 billion

Source: Technical Data

Source: The *Wall Street Journal,* February 2, 1998, p. A6. Reprinted by permission of the *Wall Street Journal,* © 1998 Dow Jones & Company, Inc. All Rights Reserved Worldwide.

Economy." The feature reports statistics to be released during the coming week (for example, housing starts, agricultural production, GDP), their previous values, and their consensus forecasts. Figure 11.8 gives an example of this feature.

Exchange Rates

Techniques for forecasting exchange rates are a matter of some controversy. Methods vary from rather naive models that assume future exchange rates will not change from current levels to models that use sophisticated econometric techniques. One simple technique that has performed well in tests when compared to more complex models is to assume future exchange rates will equal the rate quoted in the forward markets.[6]

Econometric Modeling

These are the most sophisticated of the forecasting tools. Based upon economic theory and mathematics, an **econometric model** specifies the statistical relationships between

[6]A forward rate contract is an agreement between two parties to exchange currencies at a predetermined exchange rate at a specific future time. Forward rate contracts are frequently used in international trade and finance to reduce the risk of fluctuating exchange rates. We will examine forward contracts in Chapter 17.

economic variables. The number of equations in econometric models range from a few to several hundred.

The more complex models allow computers to simulate the behavior of economic and industry variables for years into the future. They can be used to estimate the impact of virtually any important economic occurrence, including oil price changes, the effects of removing trade barriers, and currency devaluations. Econometric models also are useful in generating country market and asset class forecasts, which in turn can be used to allocate assets in a global portfolio.

The Nature of Effective Economic Forecasts[7]

With so many forecasting tools and so many well-trained and intelligent economists, why are forecasts often incorrect or unsuccessful in identifying profitable investment strategies?

Risks in Economic Forecasting

Several reasons may explain this anomaly. The first we can label "group think." Recall that in our initial discussion of the secret of successful investing we mentioned that in order to earn above-average, risk-adjusted returns, our expectations (forecast) *must differ* from the market consensus, and our forecast must *be correct* more often than it is incorrect. Unfortunately, human psychology being what it is, it is difficult to stray from the consensus opinion of other professionals. An old investment adage saying that "nobody ever got fired for having IBM in their portfolio" was probably true, despite the fact IBM stock hit its all-time high back in the early 1970s before it was finally eclipsed in the 1990s! By keeping economic forecasts "close" to that of other economists, analysts can more easily deflect criticism if their estimates are incorrect. Just as another old adage about safety in numbers was true thousands of years ago in a hunting and gathering society, so it is true today for economists on Wall Street.

Another reason is that too many analysts are shortsighted. They assume the future will be like the recent past—which is a great way to miss turning points and profit opportunities in the economy and financial markets. Too many analysts in the 1970s were stuck in the 1960s' growth mindset; too many analysts in the 1980s were still concerned about 1970s inflation; too many analysts in the late 1980s had forgotten about risk and were spoiled by declining interest rates and rising stock prices. The crash of October 1987 and the mini-crash of October 1989 helped to refresh their memories about risk! The bull markets of the 1990s have climbed a wall of fear as investors looked at higher and higher valuations and feared another 1987-like crash. What happens in the future will be based on *future* events (recall the discussion in an earlier chapter on systematic and unsystematic risk), not from simple extrapolations of the past.

Third, economists and other forecasters are overwhelmed by the quantity of statistical data available. Poor forecasting may be a problem of not seeing the forest because the trees are in the way. Also, problems can arise with government-issued data, which is often preliminary in nature and later updated or revised.

Fourth, rather than seek common threads of agreement as proposed in this chapter, some economists become involved in supporting their particular school of thought, whether it be Keynesian, monetarist, or supply-sider. Strict Keynesians did a poor forecast of the effect

---

[7]Our discussion in this section is based on D. Bostian, "The Nature of Effective Forecasts," in H. Kent Baker, ed., *Improving the Investment Decision Process—Better Use of Economic Inputs in Securities Analysis and Portfolio Management* (Charlottesville, Va.: Association for Investment Management and Research, 1992).

of the tax cuts in the early 1980s; monetarists incorrectly warned of rising inflation in the late 1980s; and supply-siders' predictions of shrinking budget deficits in the 1980s did not pan out. The complex econometric models previously discussed all have their biases related to these theories. Because the probability is high that none of these theories is a totally accurate description of reality, econometric forecasts will necessarily contain some error. Finally, economic forecasts are based on the forecaster's assumptions regarding what the Fed, Congress, and other countries' leaders will do. Monetary policy, fiscal policy, and political factors are difficult to predict.

A Possible Solution

To help increase the usefulness of economic forecasts, some of the subjective human element must be removed. We do *not* suggest a totally quantitative approach because that is what gets the econometricians in trouble. Some human input is necessary to modify forecasts based on experience and to include new information. The point is, we need a more *disciplined* approach to economic forecasting, a model that can be used throughout the entire economy–industry–firm, top-down analytic approach.

The underlying concept is that our forecasting and analytical process should take into account (1) the current environment, (2) the analyst's assumptions behind his or her estimates, and (3) a procedure for monitoring data and events to identify changes in the environment or violations of the analyst's assumptions. This process is called **expectational analysis**. The key thought behind expectational analysis is to *Identify and Monitor Key Assumptions and Variables (IMKAV)* throughout the top-down approach.

For example, the first step in the top-down analysis is to forecast broad economic, political, and demographic trends. It can involve any of the techniques we have discussed or other more sophisticated methods such as econometric analysis or scenario analysis. During this process, the analyst will have to make certain assumptions about monetary and fiscal policy, important political initiatives, and relationships with trading partners, among other items. At the end of this process, the analyst should have estimates of important economic variables and have identified what key assumptions he or she has made and what important variables or events must be monitored over time due to their importance to the forecast.

Business periodicals will occasionally have articles that report on investment professionals' outlooks and what future events might cause them to change their forecast. In one such article published at the beginning of 1994,[8] several investment strategists and research directors of major Wall Street investment houses discussed events that could cause the then-rising stock market to decline. Among the events mentioned were further unsettling developments regarding President Clinton and the possibility of a Whitewater scandal; turmoil caused by reemerging Communists in the former Soviet Union; a jump in inflation and oil prices; increases in interest rates; and unfavorable changes in global economic policy (specific examples included the German Bundesbank's refusal to lower interest rates and the Japanese government's decision not to further stimulate their economy). Notably, these investors were watching a number of political, domestic, and global economic influences as they tracked the market. With the benefit of hindsight, we know by the end of 1994 only the fear of higher interest rates became a reality. The Fed's decision to raise short-term interest rates shortly after this article appeared resulted in declines in the stock and bond markets; in the month of March 1994 alone, the S&P 500 stock index fell more than 4 percent.

---

[8]Steven E. Levingston, "Strategists Ponder Shocks That Could Kill Bull Run," *Wall Street Journal,* January 10, 1994, pp. C1, C2.

The second step of the top-down analysis is to relate the macroeconomic forecast to sectors of the economy. That is, how will the components of GDP (consumption, investment, government spending, and net exports) and their subcomponents change? What is different (or similar) about this time period from previous periods during this stage of the business cycle, or during this period of rising (or falling) inflation (or interest rates, or consumer expectations, etc.)? The analyst should identify key assumptions driving the analysis and monitor the important variables over time.

Third, the macro and sector forecast are related to specific industries as we will discuss in Chapter 12. Here, microeconomics and industry competition must be related to the economic analysis. Price elasticities, competitive positioning, and technological trends must be examined in the context of the assumed macroenvironment. The industry analyst must identify both macro and micro trends and influences that are especially relevant to his or her industry specialization and monitor them over time.

Finally, economic and industry analysis are applied to the individual firm, as we will examine in Chapter 13. As in the prior stages, the analyst needs to identify key assumptions in the top-down approach that are most important to support his or her recommendations concerning individual firms. These important economic–industry–firm assumptions must be monitored for changes that may affect the recommendation.[9]

Illustrations of IMKAV   Occasionally the *Wall Street Journal* and other business periodicals review the state of the economy and expectations for future stock market performance. Many times they present two or more perspectives on the current state of the economy and stock market. Reading these different perspectives provides examples that allow us to identify the forecaster's key assumptions and insights. So doing gives insight into possible investment sectors to consider. Also, it gives information concerning what news events investors should monitor to determine if the forecaster's assumptions are holding true or are being violated. Table 11.4 features some examples of market strategists' perceptions of the stock market in recent years.

Each analyst's forecast in Table 11.4 was based on his or her reading and analysis of economic data and trends. Part of their thinking may be colored by their economic beliefs (Keynesian, monetarist, supply-sider, or eclectic) or by the emphases they each placed on different aspects of the data. Regardless of how they did it, each forecast reflects each analyst's assumptions and key variables that they—and those reading the analyses—would want to monitor. For the record, the optimistic perspective proved to be the correct one in the mid-1990s, as concerns about higher inflation, higher interest rates, slower corporate profit growth, and declining exports did not come to pass, and the stock market enjoyed some of its best consecutive year performance ever.

Conclusion on IMKAV   Although the analysis can involve quantitative models,[10] the analyst's expertise is involved in identifying the important driving variables behind his or her analysis and in knowing what questions to ask and what numbers and events to watch closely. A disciplined approach such as expectational IMKAV analysis can help mitigate some of the practical problems such as "group think" and simple extrapolation that arise in forecasting. In addition, it forces some discipline on the investment analy-

---

[9]Viewers of "Wall $treet Week with Louis Rukeyser" on PBS will be familiar with IMKAV analysis, although it is not mentioned by name during the broadcast. Frequently, after guests discuss securities that they recommend for purchase, one of the panelists asks what would change their mind about their selections. This is IMKAV analysis—knowing why an asset is recommended for purchase and knowing what may change your opinion about its attractiveness.

[10]For a more quantitative review of links between the economy, stock market, and industries, see Frank K. Reilly and Keith C. Brown, *Investment Analysis and Portfolio Management,* 5th ed. (Fort Worth, Tex.: Dryden Press, 1997).

Table 11.4 *Economic Assumptions to Monitor*

Bearish	Bullish
1995[11]	
Economic outlook	
Expected higher inflation, fueled by wage increases, high-capacity utilization. Corporate profits had peaked.	Strong dollar would attract investors to the U.S. stock market. No fears of inflation because 1) producers were not passing higher material costs to consumers; 2) inflation was falling globally and productivity was rising; 3) Fed would keep inflation in check. Corporate profits would continue to rise.
Investment suggestions	
Buy stocks in firms with "low expectations," as bad economic news would not hurt these firms as much as those riding a wave of optimism.	Buy cyclical firms and firms in interest-rate sensitive sectors such as banking, insurance, and financial services.
Mid-1996[12]	
Economic outlook	
Fear of higher inflation because of 1) higher unit-labor costs due to strong economy; 2) low unemployment. Interest rates would rise because of higher inflation and because of greater borrowing demand by firms trying to meet product demand.	Inflation was not a foreseeable problem because the federal budget deficit was falling and the Federal Reserve had made fighting inflation a priority. Corporate profits would remain stable, then rise as strong economic growth overseas fueled demand for U.S. products.
Investment suggestions	
High valuation levels (P/E, price/book) would fall; invest in sectors with lower valuation levels, such as small capitalization stocks.	Growth stocks, stocks with substantial sales and earnings arising from global markets; Cyclical stocks attractive at this stage, too.
Late 1996[13]	
Economic outlook	
Inflation would rise, fueled by wage increases. Corporate profits had peaked as opportunity for lower inflation and the earnings benefits of downsizing were over and a strong dollar would hurt exports and overseas profits for U.S. firms. Interest rates would rise because of strong growth and demand.	Similar concerns as the bearish perspective, but belief that they would occur later, not sooner. Still saw opportunity for lower inflation and interest rates (due to the falling deficit and Fed's watch over inflation) and higher corporate profits.
Investment suggestions	
Invest in commodities and energy, and other inflation-sensitive sectors.	Technology and financial services were sectors with strong earnings growth likely to exceed that of the economy.
Mid-1997[14]	
Economic outlook	
Concerns of market liquidity disappear as investors try to exit the market all at once after a substantial market correction; Market valuation measures extremely high by historical standards. Investors ignore risk and their reaction in a sell-off of stocks is a concern.	Inflation is under control; interest rates steady or dropping; corporate profits continue to rise. The market is fairly priced; market valuations appear high only if we ignore the current environment of low interest rates.
Investment suggestions	
Underweight stocks; prefer bonds or short-term instruments.	Smaller capitalization stocks (their valuations aren't as high as large company stocks) and some cyclicals, such as autos, airlines, and some retailers; technology and financial services sectors.

---

[11]Dave Kansas, "Two Strategists Evaluate Stocks, Get Differing Results," *Wall Street Journal,* February 13, 1995, pp. C1, C2.
[12]John R. Dorfman, "Two Strategists Expect 1,000-Point Move In the Market, but in Different Directions," *Wall Street Journal,* July 31, 1996, pp. C1, C2.
[13]Suzanne McGee, "Bull vs. Bear: What's Ahead for Stocks in 1997," *Wall Street Journal,* December 2, 1996, pp. C1, C2.
[14]Suzanne McGee, "Today's Market Is Different, but So Are Risks," *Wall Street Journal,* August 25, 1997, pp. C1, C13; E. S. Browning, "Wall Street Gurus See Few Signs of 1987," *Wall Street Journal,* August 25, 1997, pp. C1, C2.

sis process by removing some of the emotion from buy-and-sell decisions; if an assumption is violated, the recommendation needs to be re-examined, regardless of what you may believe about the stock's attractiveness.

Such an approach helps identify when to sell stocks currently in the portfolio. Should key assumptions be violated, or key variables differ from what was forecast, it may be time to sell the position.[15]

APPLICATIONS OF ECONOMIC ANALYSIS TO ASSET ALLOCATION

The topic of economic analysis has implications for portfolio construction. The results of economic analysis can affect the composition of a global portfolio.

Asset Allocation across Countries

The techniques for analyzing an economy discussed in this chapter are not specific for the United States. Although U.S. economic data may be more plentiful, available, and timely than that from other countries, that should not hinder our analysis. Recognizing these problems will merely affect our perceptions of country risk and our need to closely monitor key assumptions and variables.

Global investors seek above-average, risk-adjusted returns regardless of their location. A disciplined investment approach can overcome such challenges as trends toward globalization of commerce, financial markets, and industry competition. Previously we discussed the diversification benefits of global investing and the opportunities for enhanced returns. Top-down analysis focuses on the global economy and macroeconomic factors favoring or hindering growth in different economies. Economies expected to grow faster than the average with above-average profit growth may be candidates for overweighting (as compared to the EAFE index) in a portfolio, assuming no severe currency blockages, restrictive tax laws, or other impediments and risk factors.

Allocation across Asset Classes[16]

In the Chapter 6 discussion of portfolio theory, we learned that the total risk of a portfolio is affected not only by variance of individual assets in the portfolio, but also by covariances between assets. We saw that portfolio variance is a weighted average of the asset covariances and that diversification will substantially reduce portfolio risk when the covariance or correlation between asset classes is not strongly positive.

For simplicity, let's assume there are only two asset classes, stocks and bonds, where stocks have higher expected returns and higher variances than bonds. If the returns of stocks and bonds are highly correlated, adding bonds to a portfolio of stocks may reduce return proportionately more than it reduces risk, thus leading to an inefficient portfolio. Should the returns between stocks and bonds have a low correlation, adding bonds to a stock port-

---

[15]As it focuses on expectations, IMKAV is relevant both to top-down and bottom-up analysts. Bottom-up analysts focus mainly on microeconomic, firm-specific factors that make a security an attractive purchase candidate (that is, it has a good story behind it). Bottom-up analysts would emphasize assumptions and key microeconomic variables; top-downers would examine both macro and micro factors. Nonetheless, both sets of analysts need to identify and monitor key assumptions and variables important to the investment decision.

[16]This discussion is based on P. Bernstein, "From Forecast to Portfolio Construction," in H. Kent Baker, ed., *Improving the Investment Decision Process—Better Use of Economic Inputs in Securities Analysis and Portfolio Management* (Charlottesville, Va.: Association for Investment Management and Research, 1992).

Figure 11.9 *Correlation of Stock and Bond Returns: S&P 500 vs. Intermediate-Term Government Bonds*

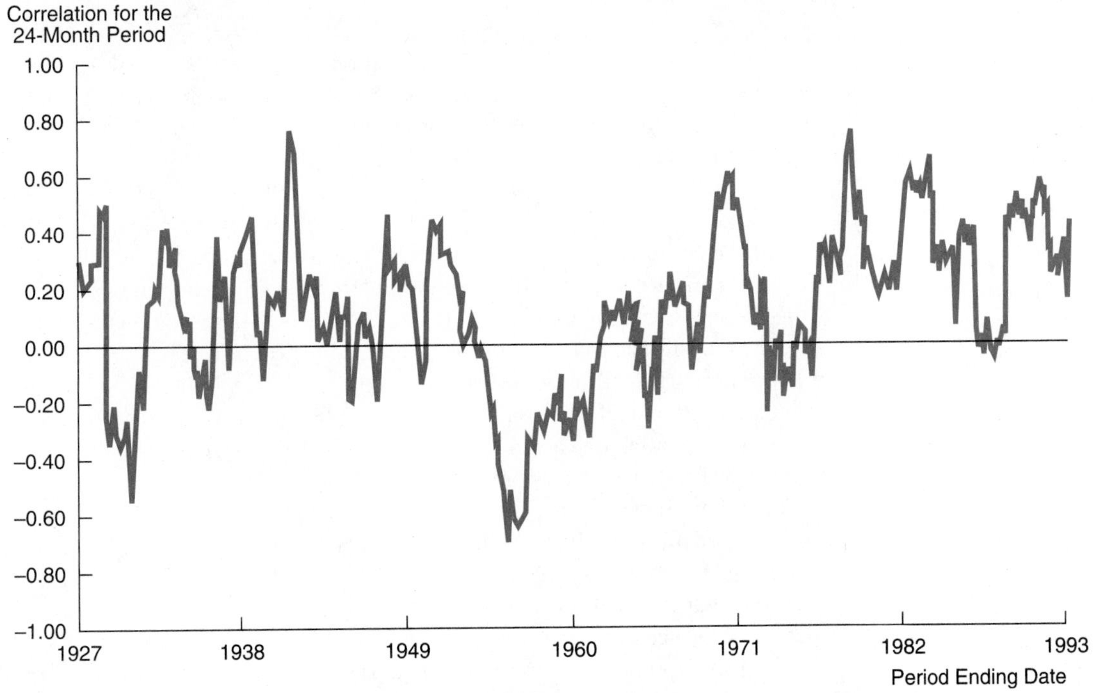

Source: © *Stocks, Bonds, Bills and Inflation* 1994 Yearbook™, Ibbotson Associates, Chicago (annually updates work by Roger G. Ibbotson and Rex A. Sinquefield). Used with permission.

folio will reduce the returns for the portfolio, but will also reduce risk by a proportionately larger amount, maintaining an efficient portfolio. If the correlation between stocks and bonds changes over time, the portfolio manager must forecast the correlation between stocks and bonds when allocating assets to maintain an efficient portfolio across time.

Analysis of historical stock and bond returns does indeed show that their correlation varies over time. As shown in Figure 11.9 during the period 1927–93, the twenty-four-month moving correlation between stock and bond returns has fluctuated between -.60 and +.80. Apparently, the use of a model to forecast future stock-to-bond correlation (as well as correlations between other pairs of assets) would be an important portfolio management tool.

In addition to correlation forecasting, other asset allocation tools exist that rely upon economic data. For example, studies have shown that the equity-risk premium is larger (meaning that stocks offer attractive expected returns) when real, inflation-adjusted bond returns are low. And when do fixed, nominal bond returns result in poor real returns? When inflation is high. Over time, numerous studies have shown that stocks have typically fallen during high inflation (that is, stocks are a poor inflation hedge). A portfolio manager who can do well at forecasting inflation trends can increase and decrease the allocation to stocks and bonds in his or her portfolio to take advantage of these relationships.

In addition to providing information regarding the industries or sectors in which to invest, economic analysis can provide the portfolio manager with other insights as well. Analysis-based models can relate economic expectations to global investing and to asset allocation.

Investments Online

The Internet contains a great many sources for economic and financial market information. Many banks, research firms, investment banks, stock brokerages, and government agencies feature data, analysis, or commentaries on their Web sites. Here are a few of the many Web resources you may wish to examine:

www.ms.com
The home page of Morgan Stanley includes the Global Economic Forum. The Forum is a compilation of reports filed by fifteen economists located around the world. The Forum is updated daily, and prior reports are available in an archive. This site features daily updates of the MSCI indexes of international markets and links to Morgan Stanley Dean Witter Equity Research pages.

www.dri.mcgraw-hill.com/index.htm
Standard & Poor's DRI subsidiary home page features links to S&P resources. Items of interest include a weekly analysis of international and U.S. economic news as well as current economic data.

www.yardeni.com
Edward Yardeni is the chief economist of Deutsche Morgan Grenfell (DMG). His home page contains links to market information, country information (including emerging markets), a weekly economic briefing, and studies of longer-term trends that affect the economy and financial markets. His site features a number of pull-down slides that provide links to Federal Reserve and U.S. Treasury information, as well as information about demographics, consumers, and marketing.

www.whitehouse.gov/fsbr/esbr.html
This is the Economics Statistics Briefing Room of the White House Web site. It includes links to data produced by certain federal agencies.

www.bog.frb.fed.us
The home page of the Board of Governors of the Federal Reserve System. This site features data and information on Fed-related activities, including research, money supply trends, board actions, consumer information, and reports to Congress. The site includes links to each of the twelve regional Federal Reserve Banks and to some foreign central banks. The Philadelphia Fed's site includes access to the Livingston Surveys and Surveys of Professional Forecasters; both provide professional economists' judgments about future economic trends. The URL is **www.phil.frb.org/econ/index.html**
Other sites of interest include:

www.worldbank.org Home page of the World Bank features data and articles.
www.bankamerica.com/econ_indicator/econ_indicator.html From the Web site of the Bank of America, this page features U.S. and global economic reviews, outlooks, and investment strategies.
www.stockinfo.standardpoor.com Another Standard & Poor site for their Equity Investor Service; it contains current headlines, weekly features, S&P stock reports, and information on the S&P stock indexes.
www.treasury.boi.ie Home page for the Bank of Ireland; offers economic updates.
www.infoweb.or.jp/dkb/welcom-e.html Home page for Dai-Ichi Kangyo Bank, Ltd; has links to information about the Japanese economy.
www.indobiz.com/index.htm Web site for Indonesia Business Center On-Line.

SUMMARY

♦ Economic analysis should focus on giving the analyst insight into the determinants of asset value, namely, the level of interest rates, asset risk premiums, and asset cash flow. In efficient markets, it will be difficult to find assets with intrinsic values different from their current market prices. A successful analyst must have insights that differ from the market consensus, and the analyst must be right often enough to outperform the market on a risk-adjusted basis over time.

♦ This chapter has reviewed concepts and tools analysts use to identify long-term and short-term trends in the economy, which they then relate to industry and firm conditions in top-down analysis. Forecasting techniques were reviewed. These tools will work best when combined with human judgment and experience in a disciplined process that identifies and monitors the analyst's key assumptions and variables over time. This will help the analyst determine when to sell currently owned securities and when securities previously shunned should be considered for purchase.

♦ The chapter also discussed the use of economic analysis in making portfolio asset allocation decisions. The forecasting tools discussed in this chapter are applicable to all countries, not just the United States. We saw that global investors will shift assets in and out of countries that offer attractive, risk-adjusted returns and growth opportunities. Asset allocation among asset classes can lead to superior returns over time if the analyst is successful in identifying and forecasting economic variables that influence asset class correlations and risk premiums.

Questions

1. How can what we've learned about efficient markets, valuation, and financial statement analysis assist the process of analyzing stocks using the top-down approach?
2. Why is it important to develop sectoral forecasts of GDP?
3. Describe how exchange rate changes affect U.S. exports, imports, and interest rates.
4. What factors affect exchange rates over time?
5. What is the expected effect on U.S. dollar exchange rates of each of the following events?
   a. The U.S. inflation rate increases relative to the rates of other economies.
   b. German interest rates rise.
   c. The Fed moves to increase interest rates.
   d. The United States goes into a recession.
   e. The Fed purchases U.S. dollars in the currency market.
6. Describe how monetary policy and fiscal policy affect the economy.
7. What factors influence long-term expectations of economic growth? Explain their effect on the economy.
8. What factors influence short-term expectations of economic growth? Explain their effect on the economy.
9. Describe the various indicators of inflation trends. How do they differ from one another?
10. Define leading, coincident, and lagging economic indicators. Give an example of an economic series in each category and discuss why you think the series belongs in that particular category.
11. It is fairly easy to determine the effect of a change in interest rates on the price of a bond. In contrast, some observers contend that it is harder to estimate the effect of a change in interest rates on common stocks. Discuss this contention.
12. What are the risks of forecasting the economy?
13. What is expectational analysis?

Problems

1. What is the expected level of U.S. interest rates based on the following conditions?

a. Expected change in exchange rate is 4 percent; foreign interest rate is 9 percent.

b. Expected change in exchange rate is -4 percent; foreign interest rate is 9 percent.

c. Expected change in exchange rate is 2.5 percent; foreign interest rate is 18 percent.

d. Expected change in exchange rate is -1.3 percent; foreign interest rate is 5 percent.

2. The current rate of inflation is 3 percent and long-term bonds are yielding 8 percent. You estimate that the rate of inflation will increase to 6 percent. What do you expect to happen to long-term bond yields? Compute the effect of this change in inflation on the price of a fifteen-year, 8 percent coupon bond.

3. You are told an investment firm projects a 10 percent return next year for U.S. stocks while German stocks are expected to give investors a 13 percent return.

a. Assuming that all risks except exchange rate risk are equal and that you expect the DM/U.S. dollar exchange rate to go from 1.50 to 1.30 during the year, discuss where you would invest and why.

b. Discuss where you would invest and why if you expected the exchange rate to go from 1.50 to 1.90.

4. Prepare a table showing the percentage change for each of the past ten years in (a) the Consumer Price Index (all items), (b) nominal GDP, (c) real GDP (in constant dollars), and (d) the GDP deflator. Discuss how much of nominal growth was caused by *real* growth and how much was caused by inflation. Is the outlook for next year any different from last year? Discuss.

5. *CFA Examination I (June 1983)*

Assume you are a fundamental research analyst following the automobile industry for a large brokerage firm. Identify and briefly explain the relevance of *three* major economic time series, economic indicators, or economic data items that would be significant to automotive industry and company research.

6. World Stock Market Indexes are published weekly in *Barron's* in the section labeled "Market Laboratory/ Stocks." Consult the latest available issue of this publication and the issue one year earlier to find the following information.

a. Show the closing value of each index on each date relative to the yearly high for each year.

b. Name the countries with markets in downtrends. Name those in uptrends.

c. For the two time periods, calculate the year's change relative to the beginning price. Based on this and the range of annual values, which markets seem the most volatile?

7. Using a source of financial data such as *Barron's* or the *Wall Street Journal:*

a. Plot the weekly percentage changes in the S&P 400 index (*y*-axis) versus comparable weekly percentage changes in the M2 money supply figures (*x*-axis) for the past ten weeks. Do you see a positive, negative, or zero correlation? (Monetary aggregates will lag the stock-market aggregates.)

b. Examine the trend in money rates (for example, federal funds, ninety-day T-bills, etc.) over the past ten weeks. Is there a correlation between these money rates? Estimate the correlation between the individual money rates and percentage changes in M1 money supply.

c. Examine the relationship between the weekly percentage changes in the S&P 400 Index and the DJIA for the past ten weeks. Plot the weekly percentage changes in each index using S&P as the *x*-axis and DJIA as the *y*-axis. Discuss your results as they relate to diversification. Do a similar comparison for the S&P 400 and the Nikkei Index and discuss these results.

References

Baker, H. Kent. ed. *Improving the Investment Decision Process—Better Use of Economic Inputs in Securities Analysis and Portfolio Management.* Charlottesville, Va.: Association for Investment Management and Research, 1992.

Diermeier, Jeffrey J. "Capital Market Expectations: The Macro Factors." In *Managing Investment Portfolios: A Dynamic Process,* 2d ed., edited by John L. Maginn and Donald L. Tuttle. Boston: Warren, Gorham, and Lamont, 1990.

Lehmann, Michael. *The Business One–Irwin Guide to Reading the Wall Street Journal.* 4th ed. Homewood, Ill.: Business One–Irwin, 1993.

Reilly, Frank, and Keith C. Brown. *Investment Analysis and Portfolio Management.* 5th ed. Fort Worth, Tex.: HBJ-Dryden Press, 1997.

Sherrerd, Katrina, F., ed. *Economic Analysis for Investment Professionals.* Charlottesville, Va.: Association for Investment Management and Research, 1997.

GLOSSARY

Bottom-up approach A forward-looking approach to evaluating securities in which trends are forecast based on an analysis of microeconomic, or firm-specific, factors.

Coincident index of economic indicators An indicator series that consists of a set of economic variables whose values reach peaks and troughs at about the same time as the aggregate economy.

Discount rate The interest rate at which banks can borrow from the Federal Reserve Board.

Econometric model A statistical estimation of mathematical relationships between economic variables as posited by economic theory.

Exchange rate The price of one nation's currency in terms of another nation's currency.

Expectational analysis A forecasting approach that includes an analysis of the current environment, the analyst's assumptions, and a procedure for monitoring data and events to identify changes in the environment or violations of the analyst's assumptions.

Federal funds rate The interest rate banks charge each other for short-term loans.

Fiscal policy The use of government spending and taxing powers.

Free reserves The amount of reserves available to the banking system; it is equal to the excess reserves of the banking system less bank borrowing from the Federal Reserve Board.

Gross domestic product (GDP) The sum total of the goods and services produced within a nation's borders. The five major components of GDP are consumption spending, investment spending, government expenditures, export production, and import production.

Lagging index of economic indicators An indicator series consisting of a set of economic variables whose values reach peaks and troughs after the aggregate economy.

Index of leading economic indicators An indicator series consisting of a set of economic variables whose values reach peaks and troughs in advance of the aggregate economy.

Monetary policy The use of the Federal Reserve Board's power to affect the money supply and aggregate economic activity.

Open market operations The most frequently used tool of monetary policy in which the Federal Reserve Board buys or sells securities from any market participant.

Reserve requirement The ratio of required reserves to total deposits at a bank.

Top-down approach A forward-looking approach to evaluating securities in which trends are forecast based on an analysis of macroeconomic factors.

APPENDIX 11 *Sources of Economic and Market Information*

In this appendix we review data sources useful in estimating overall economic changes for the United States and other major countries. We also review sources of information about securities markets.

U.S. Government Sources

It should come as no surprise that the main source of information on the U.S. economy is the federal government, which issues a variety of publications on the topic.

Federal Reserve Bulletin is a monthly publication issued by the Board of Governors of the Federal Reserve System. It is the primary source for almost all monetary data, including monetary aggregates; factors affecting member bank reserves; member bank reserve requirements; Federal Reserve open market transactions; and loans and investments of all commercial banks. In addition, it contains figures on financial markets, including interest rates and some stock-market statistics; data for corporate finance, including profits,

assets, and liabilities of corporations; extensive nonfinancial statistics on output, the labor force, and the GNP; and a major section on international finance.

Survey of Current Business is a monthly publication issued by the U.S. Department of Commerce that gives details on national income and production figures. It is probably the best source for current, detailed information on all segments of the gross domestic product (GDP) and national income. It also contains industrial production data for numerous segments of the economy. The *Survey* is an excellent secondary source for labor statistics (employment and wages), interest rates, and statistics on foreign economic development. It also contains data regarding the leading, coincident, and lagging economic series published by the Department of Commerce. These series are considered important by those who attempt to project peaks and troughs in the business cycle.

Economic Indicators is a monthly publication prepared for the Joint Economic Committee by the Council of Economic Advisers. It contains monthly and annual data on output, income, spending, employment, production, prices, money and credit, federal finance, and international economies.

The *Quarterly Financial Report (QFR)* is prepared by the Federal Trade Commission and contains aggregate statistics on the financial position of U.S. corporations. Based on an extensive quarterly sample survey, the *QFR* presents estimated statements of income and retained earnings, balance sheets, and related financial and operating ratios for all manufacturing corporations. The publication also includes data on mining and trade corporations. The statistical data are classified by industry and, within the manufacturing group, by size.

Business Statistics is a biennial supplement to the *Survey of Current Business,* which contains extensive historical data for approximately 2,500 series contained in the survey. The historical section contains monthly data for the past four or five years, quarterly data for the previous ten years, and annual data back to 1947, if available. A notable feature is a section of explanatory notes for each series that describes the series and indicates the original source for the data.

Historical Chart Book is an annual supplement to the *Federal Reserve Bulletin* that contains long-range financial and business series. It includes an excellent section on the various series that indicates the source of the data.

Each January, the president of the United States prepares the *Economic Report of the President,* which he transmits to the Congress. The report indicates what has transpired during the past year and discusses the current environment and what the president considers the major economic problems to face the country during the coming year. This publication also contains an extensive document entitled "The Annual Report of the Council of Economic Advisers," which generally runs more than 150 pages and contains a detailed discussion of developments in the domestic and international economies gathered by the council (the group that advises the president on economic policy). An appendix contains statistical tables relating to income, employment, and production. The tables typically provide annual data from the 1940s and in some instances from 1929.

Statistical Abstract of the United States, published annually since 1878, is the standard summary of statistics on the social, political, and economic organization of the United States. Prepared by the Bureau of the Census, it is designed to serve as a convenient statistical reference and as a guide to other statistical publications and sources. This volume, which currently runs more than 900 pages, includes data from many statistical publications, both government and private.

Bank Publications

In addition to government material, much data and comments on the economy are published by various banks. These generally appear monthly and are free of charge. They can be categorized as publications of the Federal Reserve Banks or of commercial banks.

Publications of Federal Reserve Banks

The Federal Reserve System is divided into twelve Federal Reserve districts; each of the Federal Reserve district banks has a research department that issues periodic reports. Although the various bank publications differ, all district banks publish monthly reviews, which are available to interested parties. These reviews typically contain one or several articles as well as regional economic statistics. A major exception is the St. Louis Federal Reserve Bank, which publishes in addition to its monthly review weekly, monthly, and quarterly statistical releases that contain extensive national and international data.

Publications of Commercial Banks

Various large banks prepare monthly letters available to interested individuals. These letters generally contain a comment on the current and future outlook of the economy and specific industries or segments of the economy.

Non-U.S. Economic Data

In addition to data on the U.S. economy, data on other countries in which you might consider investing are also important to acquire. Some of the available sources follow.

The *Economic Intelligence Unit* (EIU) publishes 83 separate quarterly reviews and an annual supplement covering the economic and business conditions and outlook for 160 countries. For each country the reviews consider the economy, trade and finance, trends in investment and consumer spending, along with comments on its political environment. Tables contain data on economic activity and foreign trade.

The EIU also publishes *European Trends,* which discusses the aggregate economic environment for the overall European community and the world.

The Organization for Economic Cooperation and Development (OECD) publishes semiannual surveys showing recent trends and policies and assessing short-term prospects for each country. An annual volume, *Historical Statistics,* contains annual percent change data for the most recent twenty years.

The *Economist* prepares country reports that contain extensive economic and demographic statistics on more than 100 countries around the world. Of greater importance is a detailed discussion that critically analyzes the current economic and political environment in the country and considers the future outlook. You may subscribe to reports for a selected list of countries or for all of them. The reports are updated twice yearly.

Worldwide Economic Indicators is an annual book published by the Business International Corporation that contains data for 131 countries on population, GDP by activity, wages and prices, foreign trade, and a number of specific items for the most recent four years.

Demographic Yearbook, published by the United Nations, contains statistics on population, births, deaths, life expectancy, marriages, and divorces for approximately 240 countries.

International Marketing Data and Statistics, published by Euromonitor Publications Ltd. of London, is an annual guide that contains data for 132 non-European countries on population, employment, production, trade, the economy, and other economic data.

United Nations Statistical Yearbook is a basic reference book that contains extensive economic statistics on all UN countries (population, construction, industrial production, and so on).

Eurostatistics, a monthly publication of the *Statistical Office of the European Communities (Luxembourg),* contains statistics for short-term economic analysis in ten European community countries and the United States. It generally includes data for six years on industrial production, employment and unemployment, external trade, prices, wages, and finance.

U.S. International Trade Administration, International Economic Indicators, is a quarterly publication of the U.S. Government Printing Office that contains comparative economic indicators and trends in the United States and its seven principal industrial competitors: France, Germany, Italy, Netherlands, United Kingdom, Japan, and Canada. The data are organized in five parts: general indicators, trade indicators, price indicators, finance indicators, and labor indicators. Notably, the sources for the data are contained at the back of the booklet.

International Financial Statistics, a monthly publication (with a yearbook issue) of the International Monetary Fund, is an essential source of current financial statistics such as exchange rates, fund position, international liquidity, money and banking statistics, interest rates (including LIBOR), prices, and production.

International Monetary Fund, Balance of Payments Yearbook is a two-part publication. The first part contains detailed balance-of-payments figures for more than 110 countries, and the second part contains world totals for balance-of-payments components and aggregates.

United Nations, Yearbook of International Trade Statistics is an annual report on import statistics over a four-year period for each of 166 countries. The commodity figures for each country are given by commodity code.

United Nations Yearbook of National Accounts Statistics is a comprehensive source of national account data that contains detailed statistics for 155 countries on domestic product and consumption expenditures, national income, and disposable income for a twelve-year period.

Also, some individual countries publish national income studies with detailed breakdowns as well as annual statistical reports that contain the more important statistics and include bibliographical sources for the tables. Examples include Brazil, Great Britain, Japan, and Switzerland.

Similar to the United States, major banks in various countries publish bulletins or letters that contain statistical reviews for the individual countries. Examples include:

♦ *Bank of Canada Review* (monthly)
♦ *Bank of England* (quarterly)
♦ *Bank of Japan* (monthly)
♦ *National Bank of Belgium* (monthly)
♦ *Deutsche Bundesbank* (monthly)

Weekly Security-Market Publications

For those wanting more up-to-date information on current economic and market trends, consider the following publications.

Barron's is a weekly publication of Dow Jones and Company that typically contains about six articles on topics of interest to investors and the most complete weekly listing of prices and quotes for all U.S. financial markets. It provides weekly data on individual stocks and the latest information on earnings and dividends as well as quotes on commodities, stock options, and financial futures. Finally, toward the back (typically the last four pages) is an extensive statistical section with detailed information on the U.S. securities market for the past week. Also included is a fairly extensive set of world security-market indicator series and interest rates around the world as well as an "International Trader" section that discusses price movements in the major global stock markets.

Asian Wall Street Journal is a weekly publication of *The Wall Street Journal* that concentrates on the Asian region. It includes detailed economic news and stock and bond quotes related to this area of the global market.

Credit Markets is a weekly newspaper by the publishers of the *Bond Buyer*. It provides a longer-term overview of the major news items that affect the aggregate Treasury and corporate bond market and also individual bonds. It includes an extensive statistical section listing bond calls, redemptions, the long-term future underwriting calendar, along with several security-market series.

Banking World is a weekly newspaper from the publishers of *American Banker*. It contains a summary of all the major news stories from Washington, the Federal Reserve, and all sectors of the financial services industry as well as news on marketing, technology, federal and state regulations, and specific financial firms.

Financial Services Week is a weekly publication from Fairchild Publications that is billed as "The Financial Planner's Newspaper." It contains articles on the overall stock and bond market, insurance, and special features such as "Planning for Dentists" and "Baby Boomers and Financial Services." It also includes consideration of tax changes and other legislation of importance to those involved in personal financial planning.

International Financing Review is a weekly magazine that contains stories and data regarding international investment banking firms and the international securities markets. *IFR* emphasizes fixed-income securities, global economies, and politics and is published by IFR Publishing, Ltd.

Equities International, another weekly magazine produced by IFR Publishing, deals with global markets but concentrates on equity instruments such as common stock, warrants, convertibles, options, and futures. The emphasis is on major trends and events in countries around the world. *EI* features a complete listing of stock market indexes for major global markets.

Euro Week, billed as "The Euromarket's First Newspaper," contains discussions related to notes, bonds, and stocks throughout Europe as well as longer articles on major news items in individual countries. A capital markets guide provides information on forthcoming securities issues. Also included is a listing of market indexes for various countries and a listing every quarter of the top investment banking firms in various categories (Eurobonds, Euro-equities) based on the value of the issues underwritten.

Daily Security-Market Publications

The *Wall Street Journal,* a daily national business newspaper published five days weekly by Dow Jones and Company, contains complete listings for the NYSE, the AMEX, the NASDAQ-OTC market, U.S. bond markets, options markets, and commodities quotations. It also includes a limited number of quotes for foreign stocks and a few non-U.S. stock market indicator series. It is recognized worldwide as a prime source of financial and business information for the United States.

Investors Daily, billed as "America's Business Newspaper," was initiated in 1984 as competition to the *Wall Street Journal.* It provides much of the same information but also attempts to provide added information related to stock prices, earnings, and trading volume. An extensive set of U.S. general market indexes, including several unique to it, are included. It contains little, however, on non-U.S. markets.

The *Financial Times* is published five times weekly in London with issues printed in New York and Los Angeles. Although it could be considered a British version of the *Wall Street Journal,* it is actually much more because it has a true *world* perspective on the financial news. It does an outstanding job of reporting financial news related not only to England, but also discusses the U.S. economy and security markets including extensive stock and bond quotes and security-market indicator series. It also contains news and data for Japan and other countries. Most important, however, is its global perspective in discussing and interpreting the news, which is critical to those involved in global investing.

A WORD FROM THE STREET

BY ANTHONY J. VIGNOLA

 The financial markets are conduits for processing and responding to many sources of information. With the increased globalization of investing and the advance of technology and communication, financial markets contain a heightened sensitivity and quickened response time to financial and economic data. Although great interest exists in company- and industry-specific data, the financial markets are more concerned with the economic data that have implications for all companies and are relevant to the overall state of the economy. Most companies still depend heavily on the state of the economic cycle and the direction of interest rates for their underlying source of profitability. Cyclical forces and the business cycle remain powerful forces that are major determinants of corporate profits and also major factors behind the flow of funds, inflation, and interest rates.

Weekly, monthly, and quarterly economic statistics are released by a variety of government and industry sources. These data provide insights into the performance of the economy and the direction of interest rates. Hardly a day passes without the release of some form of economic data that provides information about the pulse of the economy. The Federal Reserve and various government agencies are the main sources of economic data. Although the Federal Reserve is noted for its monetary and banking statistics, it is also a source of other views about the state of the economy, which are critical because the Fed uses that information to determine the course of monetary policy.

The quarterly rate of GDP growth is the most important and comprehensive assessment of the state of the economy, although it does not receive the attention that other statistics receive because most of its components are already known. Information about various sectors of the economy is released throughout each month. Frequently, the release time during a month is key to the weight attached to a particular economic statistic because a more complete picture of the performance of the economy is unveiled. In fact, each monthly economic statistic is a building block for the data that ultimately determine the level of GDP.

Anthony J. Vignola is managing director and chief economist of The Economics Group at Kidder, Peabody, Inc. He joined Kidder in 1981 and prior to becoming chief economist, was director of fixed income and economic research. He is the senior economic spokesman for Kidder, Peabody. Prior to joining Kidder, Peabody, Vignola worked at the U.S. Treasury Department in Washington in the Office of Secretary where he served as a financial economist specializing in Treasury debt management and domestic finance. Vignola currently writes a weekly report on the economy.

The *Bond Buyer* is a daily newspaper (five days a week) that concentrates on news and quotes related to the overall bond market, with special emphasis on the municipal bond market—its masthead reads, "The Authority on Municipal Bonds Since 1891." Besides news stories on events that affect bonds, the *Bond Buyer* includes extensive listings of new and forthcoming bond sales, bond calls and redemptions, and information on bond ratings. There are also numerous market indicator series reported with the emphasis on fixed-income series.

The *American Banker* is referred to as "The Daily Financial Services Newspaper." It contains articles of interest to bankers and others involved in the financial services industry on topics such as legislation and general news of the industry and major banks. Also included is a brief summary of the financial markets related to Treasuries, financial futures, and mortgage securities.

PART

4

EQUITY ANALYSIS

IN PART 3 WE CONSIDERED THE BASIC VALUATION PRINCI-ples and practices that apply to all securities and how the economic environment affects asset valuation. Financial statement analysis is an important component of both fixed income and equity analysis. In Part 4 we continue with an in-depth perspective of equity analysis by reviewing fundamental and technical methods of analyzing stocks. In Part 5 we will apply these same valuation principles and practices to the analysis of bonds.

We recall from the discussion in Chapter 10 that successful investing requires several steps, beginning with a valuation of the aggregate economy and market, progressing through the examination of various industries, and finally involving the analysis of individual companies and their securities. The globalization of the capital markets has definitely complicated this process; it is now necessary to consider several economies and markets on a worldwide basis followed by the analysis of world industries as contrasted to only the U.S. component of an industry. Of course, the number and complexity of companies to be analyzed in an industry is likewise increased.

Having discussed economic analysis in Chapter 11, we begin this part of the book with a discussion of industry analysis. Chapter 12 begins with a review of research related to industry analysis, which provides an incentive for carrying out such research. Subsequently we discuss the impact of cyclical and structural change on industries.

Porter's well-known framework for studying industries is reviewed, as are the insights available to us from analyzing the industry life cycle.

Chapter 13 on company analysis begins with a discussion of the difference between a company and its stock. It is pointed out that in many instances the common stock of a very fine company may not be a good investment, which is why we emphasize that company analysis and stock selection are two separate but dependent activities. An important component of company analysis is to examine the firm's strategy and competitive advantages in the context of the previously accomplished economic and industry analysis. Once again, a framework refined by Porter is used as a means to review the firm's strategy and earnings potential. The chapter extensively examines various methods used by analysts to estimate a firm's earnings and the intrinsic value of its stock price using both absolute and relative valuation methods.

The final chapter in this section, Chapter 14, deals with technical analysis, an alternative to the fundamental approach discussed in the prior chapters. Rather than attempting to estimate value based upon numerous external variables, the technical analyst contends that the market is its own best estimator. Therefore, he or she believes that it is possible to project future stock price movements based on past stock price changes or other stock market data. Various techniques used by technical analysts for U.S. and world markets are discussed and demonstrated.

CHAPTER 12

Industry Analysis

In this chapter we will answer the following questions:

♦ What differences occur between the returns for various industries during specific time periods and what is the implication of these differences?

♦ Are the returns for industries consistent over time, and what does this imply regarding industry analysis?

♦ Is performance for firms within an industry consistent, and what does this imply for industry analysis?

♦ Does risk differ among industries and what does this imply for industry analysis?

♦ What happens to risk for individual industries over time, and what does this imply for industry analysis?

♦ Why must an analyst review both cyclical change and structural change when analyzing an industry?

♦ What are the industrial life cycle and its stages, and how does the life cycle stage affect an industry's sales and earnings estimate?

♦ What are the five basic competitive forces that determine the intensity of competition in an industry and, thus, its rate of return on capital?

♦ What are some of the unique factors that must be considered in global industry analysis? ♦

When asked about his or her job, a securities analyst will typically reply that he or she is an oil analyst, a retail analyst, or a computer analyst. A widely read trade publication, *Institutional Investor,* selects an All-American analyst team each year based on industry groups. Investment managers talk about being in or out of the metals, the autos, or the

utilities. The reason for this constant reference to industry groups is that most professional investors are extremely conscious of differences among alternative industries and organize their analyses and portfolio decisions according to industry groups.

As we first saw in Chapter 10, the process of analyzing equity securities has three steps. In the top-down approach, the overall macroeconomy, including relevant international influences, is reviewed first. From this analysis, sectors and industries that may be expected to perform well are identified for closer analysis. In the third and final step, individual companies and their stocks are reviewed for possible purchase or sale. We discussed the process of analyzing the macroeconomy in Chapter 11. This chapter reviews industry analysis, and the following chapter examines company and stock analysis.

We know the three major determinants of an asset's price are cash flows, market interest rates, and risk. Market interest rates are largely determined by overall economic conditions, and all assets take the market rate as "given." What makes a particular required rate of return differ from another is the risk premium. Thus, our discussion of industry analysis will focus on analyzing cash flows and risk. The level of market interest rates should already have been estimated from our economic analysis.

Why Do Industry Analysis?

An **industry** is a set of businesses that produce similar products used by customers for similar purposes. We can define an industry broadly or narrowly, depending upon the purposes of the analysis. The "computer industry" includes a variety of specialty areas: software, hardware, peripheral devices, as well as personal computers, servers, and mainframe computers. An overly broad definition will not meet our practical needs of analysis—how can one analyst keep up with all the manufacturers and technologies of the above-mentioned products? The federal government's Standard Industrial Classification (SIC) code system assigns numbers to industries, ranging from a single-digit for broad classifications ("agriculture", for example) to seven-digit specific products. For practical purposes, most industry analysis is done at the two-, three, or four-digit SIC level. Besides government classifications, the Dow Jones Industry Groups are an example of another industry categorization which is popular in the investment community. A listing of these industry groups is shown in Figure 12.1.

Investment practitioners perform industry analysis because they believe it helps them isolate profitable investment opportunities. We likewise have recommended it as part of our three-step, top-down plan for valuing individual companies and selecting stocks for inclusion in our portfolio. What exactly do we learn from an industry analysis? Can we spot trends in industries that make them good investments? Studies of these questions have indicated unique patterns over time in the rates of return and risk measures in different industries. In this section we survey the results of studies that addressed these questions.

In the research we describe, investigators asked a set of questions designed to pinpoint the benefits and limitations of industry analysis. In particular, they wanted answers to the following set of questions:

♦ Is there a difference between the returns for alternative industries during specific time periods?
♦ Will an industry that performs well in one period continue to perform well in the future? That is, can we use past relationships between the market and an industry to predict future trends for the industry?
♦ Do firms within an industry show consistent performance over time?

Several studies also considered questions related to risk:

Figure 12.1   Dow Jones Industry Groups

Best Performers	% CHANGE 12/31/96 TO 12/31/97	COMPOUND ANN. CHG. 6/30/82 TO 12/31/97
Securities brokers	+80.05%	+20.98%
Broadcasting	+75.12	N.A.
Savings & loans	+72.62	+17.94
Advertising	+67.13	+21.01
Eastern states banks	+59.55	+17.81
Airlines	+57.80	+14.10
Home construction	+55.11	+16.23
Trucking	+54.76	+ 7.65
Oil-field equipment	+54.48	+ 8.68
Central states banks	+53.63	+20.71
Pharmaceuticals	+53.08	+20.42
Apparel retailers	+52.51	+20.68
Drug retailers	+51.39	+21.99
Entertainment	+50.25	+11.19
Transportation equip.	+49.83	+12.00
Office equipment	+48.14	+14.91
Adv. medical devices	+47.35	+21.95
Consumer services	+46.80	+16.14

Worst Performers	% CHANGE 12/31/96 TO 12/31/97	COMPOUND ANN. CHG. 6/30/82 TO 12/29/97
Footwear	−33.44%	N.A.
Precious metals	−30.78	+ 3.99%
Nonferrous (excl. alum.)	−28.75	+ 6.77
Heavy construction	−25.46	+ 6.50
Coal	−16.63	+ 6.45
Casinos	−11.49	+18.34
Health care	− 6.85	+14.37
Steel	− 6.12	+ 2.91
Mining	− 2.70	+ 8.51
Restaurants	+ 2.71	+16.72
Forest products	+ 4.03	+10.02
Aerospace & defense	+ 4.39	+18.12
Industrial tech.	+ 4.57	+ 9.72
Secondary oil cos.	+ 4.67	+ 6.43
Pollution control	+ 5.93	+13.93
Paper products	+ 6.43	+12.55
Semiconductors	+ 6.58	+22.67
Housewares, durables	+ 7.46	N.A.

N.A. Not available; groups were formed after 6/30/82 base

Source: *Wall Street Journal,* January 2, 1998, p. 36.

♦ Are there risk differences between different industries?
♦ Does the risk for individual industries vary or does it remain relatively constant over time?

We consider the results of these studies and come to some general conclusions about the value of industry analysis. This assessment helps us interpret the results of our industry valuation in the next section.

Cross-Sectional Industry Performance

To find out if the rates of return among different industries varied during a given time period, researchers would compare the performance of various industries. Similar performances during specific time periods for the different industries would indicate that industry analysis is unnecessary. As an example, suppose during 1998 the NYSE Index rose approximately 8 percent. If the returns for all industries were grouped between 7 and 9 percent, and if this result persisted in future periods, you might question whether it was worthwhile to conduct an industry analysis to find an industry that would return 9 percent when random selection would provide about 8 percent (the average return).

Studies of the annual industry performance have found that different industries have consistently shown *wide dispersion* in their rates of return. To illustrate, Table 12.1 shows the disparity in industry performance during 1997.

Table 12.1 *Best- and Worst-Performing Industry Groups, 1997*

1997 Dow Jones U.S. Industry Group Performance

Industry Group	Close on 12/31/96	Close on 12/31/97	% Change	Industry Group	Close on 12/31/96	Close on 12/31/97	% Change
BASIC MATERIALS	615.06	680.77	+10.68	Oil-majors	542.32	641.73	+18.33
Aluminum	486.69	524.11	+ 7.69	Oil-secondary	251.45	262.63	+ 4.45
Other non-ferrous	387.50	276.10	−28.75	Oilfield equip/svcs	234.79	363.39	+54.77
Chemicals	840.70	1009.76	+20.11	Pipelines	446.98	510.20	+14.14
Chem-Commodity	901.22	1111.51	+23.33	FINANCIAL	810.66	1203.36	+48.44
Chem-Specialty	763.80	862.26	+12.89	Banks, money ctr.	636.50	833.20	+30.90
Forest products	423.25	439.54	+ 3.85	Banks, regional	892.88	1362.97	+52.65
Mining, diversified	346.18	337.00	− 2.65	Banks-Central	1173.89	1852.06	+57.77
Paper products	588.26	625.48	+ 6.33	Banks-East	797.08	1269.45	+59.26
Precious metals	265.66	183.46	−30.94	Banks-South	754.03	1093.22	+44.98
Steel	166.06	155.96	− 6.08	Banks-West	1164.58	1658.41	+42.40
CONGLOMERATE	1222.07	1794.92	+46.88	Financial services	910.86	1444.29	+58.56
CONSUMER,CYCL	712.53	961.83	+34.99	Insurance, all	763.44	1098.94	+43.95
Advertising	1150.31	1922.34	+67.11	Ins-Full line	456.72	619.34	+35.61
Airlines	487.85	773.04	+58.46	Ins-Life	1071.01	1559.29	+45.59
Apparel	1377.77	1146.57	−16.78	Property/Casualty	995.22	1451.52	+45.85
Clothing/Fabrics	817.18	884.25	+ 8.21	Real estate	504.14	578.28	+14.71
Footwear	2287.83	1521.07	−33.52	Savings & loans	754.49	1292.02	+71.24
Auto manufac.	514.29	654.01	+27.17	Securities brokers	1064.74	1916.62	+80.01
Auto part & equip	492.72	617.09	+25.24	INDUSTRIAL	581.66	700.74	+20.47
Casinos	1546.69	1360.70	−12.03	Air Freight	396.13	537.62	+35.72
Home construction	669.68	1030.05	+53.54	Building Materials	739.42	893.03	+20.77
Home furnishing	397.74	519.20	+30.81	Containers/pkging	938.73	1049.28	+11.78
Lodging	781.28	1086.46	+39.06	Elec comp/equip	579.99	701.37	+20.93
Media	788.10	1226.83	+55.67	Factory equipment	338.75	411.60	+21.51
Broadcasting	820.51	1437.03	+75.14	Heavy construction	356.42	265.59	−25.48
Publishing	726.35	1052.00	+44.83	Heavy machinery	427.74	539.21	+26.06
Recreation Prods.	527.18	684.50	+29.84	Industrial services	511.84	603.89	+17.98
Entertainment	344.89	518.19	+50.25	Industrial, divers	624.32	807.25	+29.30
Other Rec Prod	588.95	718.92	+22.07	Marine transport	606.23	717.99	+18.44
Toys	690.43	899.95	+30.35	Pollution control	713.23	755.86	+ 5.98
Restaurants	1068.10	1099.36	+ 2.93	Railroads	876.01	968.27	+10.53
Retailers, apparel	1208.81	1843.51	+52.51	Transport equip	386.22	579.67	+50.09
Retailers, broadline	775.88	1121.76	+44.58	Trucking	202.98	313.73	+54.56
Retailers, drug	1438.70	2180.17	+51.54	TECHNOLOGY	730.24	891.62	+22.10
Retailers, specialty	734.41	1074.12	+46.26	Aerospace/Defense	1274.58	1322.67	+ 3.77
Consumer, Non-Cycl	1287.85	1738.25	+34.97	Communications tech	748.55	850.47	+13.62
Beverages, distill.	773.08	876.65	+13.40	Comptrs-w/IBM	364.76	514.75	+41.12
Beverages, soft drinks	2497.15	3293.61	+31.90	Comptrs-wo/IBM	621.87	887.96	+42.79
Consumer services	692.77	1017.93	+46.94	Diversified tech	583.20	654.41	+12.21
Cosmetics	1559.60	1946.95	+24.84	Industrial tech	402.40	421.13	+ 4.65
Food	1284.92	1723.54	+34.14	Medical/ Bio tech	1528.51	1967.83	+28.74
Food retailers	963.03	1289.89	+33.94	Advcd Med Devices	1469.23	2168.19	+47.57
Health care	863.32	802.31	− 7.07	Biotechnology	1592.84	1723.70	+ 8.22
Household prods.	1638.02	2219.85	+35.52	Office equipment	582.74	862.49	+48.01
House-Durable	1170.34	1251.21	+ 6.91	Semiconductor	2231.67	2375.96	+ 6.47
House-Non-Durable	1648.83	2284.91	+38.58	Software	7173.33	9373.56	+30.67
Medical supplies	930.71	1087.19	+16.81	UTILITIES	359.53	473.01	+31.56
Pharmaceuticals	1165.11	1782.21	+52.97	Telephone	545.38	758.43	+39.07
Tobacco	1423.25	1693.50	+18.99	Electric	247.02	295.90	+19.79
ENERGY	442.36	533.72	+20.65	Gas	229.81	277.43	+20.72
Coal	315.84	263.66	−16.52	Water	630.11	833.65	+32.30
Oil drilling	302.46	413.74	+36.79	DJ GLOBAL-U.S.	700.37	922.34	+31.69

Source: January 2, 1998, *Wall Street Journal*, p. R2.

In 1997, the securities brokerage industry fared the best, earning a return of 80.05 percent. The footwear industry performed the worst, falling in value by more than 33 percent. Some themes are evident in the lists of best and worst performers. Financial services, energy-dependent, and consumer-related industries were prevalent among the top performers. Commodities (metals, coal, and mining) industries were among the poor performers. Expectations of weak export sales, a result of economic turmoil in Asia in 1997, affected the stock price performance of a variety of Asian exporting industries, including technology, steel, and heavy construction.

These results imply that industry analysis is important and necessary to uncover performance differences that will help identify both unprofitable and profitable opportunities.

Industry Performance over Time

In another group of investigations, researchers tried to determine whether industries that perform well in one time period would continue to perform well in subsequent time periods or at least outperform the aggregate market in the later time period. In this case, investigators found almost *no association* in industry performance year to year or over sequential rising or falling markets.

These studies imply that past performance alone does not help you project future industry performance. The results do not, however, negate the usefulness of industry analysis. They simply confirm that investors must project future industry performance on the basis of future estimates of the relevant variables.

Performance of the Companies within an Industry

Other studies were designed to determine whether companies within an industry perform consistently. If all the firms within an industry performed consistently during a specified time period, investors would not need company analysis. In such a case, industry analysis alone would be enough because once you selected a profitable industry, you would know that all the stocks in that industry would do well.

These studies have typically found *wide dispersion* in performance among individual companies in most industries. An alternative measure is to examine industry influence on returns for individual stocks. Such analyses have found evidence of industry influence in specific industries such as oil or autos, but most stocks showed little or no industry effects, and industry impact has declined over time.[1]

Is industry analysis useless because not all firms in an industry move together? No. Even for industries that lack strong industry influence, industry analysis is valuable, selecting a superior company from a good industry is much easier than finding a good company in an unhealthy industry. By selecting the best stocks within an industry with good expectations, you avoid the risk that your analysis and selection of a good company will be offset by poor industry performance.

Differences in Industry Risk

Although studies have focused on industry rates of return, few of them have examined industry risk measures. One study of industry risk investigated two questions: (1) Did risk differ among industries during a given time period? (2) Were industry risk measures sta-

---

[1]For example, see Stephen L. Meyers, "A Re-Examination of Market and Industry Factors in Stock Price Behavior," *Journal of Finance* 28, no. 3 (June 1973): 695–705; and Miles Livingston, "Industry Movements of Common Stocks," *Journal of Finance* 32, no. 2 (June 1977): 861–874.

ble over time?[2] The study found a *wide range of risk* among different industries, and the spreads between risk levels typically widened during rising and falling markets. On a positive note, an analysis of the risk measures over time indicated that they were *reasonably stable* over time.

We can interpret these findings as follows: although risk measures for different industries showed substantial cross-sectional dispersion, individual industries' risk measures are stable over time. This means that the analysis of industry risk is necessary, but that historical analysis can aid attempts to estimate the future risk for an industry.

Summary of Research on Industry Analysis

Earlier we noted that several studies have sought answers to questions dealing with industry analysis. The conclusions of the studies are:

♦ During any time period, industry returns vary within a wide range, which means that industry analysis can be useful in the process of targeting investments.
♦ The rates of return for individual industries vary over time, so we cannot simply extrapolate past industry performance into the future.
♦ The rates of return of firms within industries also vary, so company analysis is a necessary follow-up to industry analysis.
♦ During any time period, different industries' risk levels vary within wide ranges, so we must examine and estimate the risk factors for alternative industries, as well as returns.
♦ Risk measures for individual industries remain fairly constant over time, so historical risk analysis can be useful when estimating future risk for an individual industry.

The results imply that industry analysis is necessary, both to avoid losses and to find better industries and, subsequently, to select individual stocks that provide superior risk–return opportunities for investors.

LINKS BETWEEN THE ECONOMY AND INDUSTRY SECTORS

Economic trends can and do affect industry performance. To track the relationships between an analyst's economic expectations and expected industry performance, we will use the IMKAV analysis from Chapter 11. By identifying and monitoring key assumptions and variables, we can monitor the economy and gauge the implications of new information on our original economic outlook and industry analysis. Recall that in order to do better than the market averages on a risk-adjusted basis we must have forecasts that differ from the market consensus *and* we must be correct more often than not.

Economic trends can take two basic forms: **cyclical changes** in the economy arise from the ups and downs of the business cycle, and **structural changes** lack a cyclical pattern. Structural changes occur when the economy is undergoing a major change in organization or in how it functions. As a result, excess labor or capital may exist in some sectors whereas shortages of labor and capital exist elsewhere. The "downsizing" of corporate America during the 1990s, transitions from socialist to market economies in Eastern Europe, and the transition in the United States from a manufacturing to a service economy are all

---

[2]Frank K. Reilly and Eugene Drzycimski, "Alternative Industry Performance and Risk," *Journal of Financial and Quantitative Analysis* 9, no. 3 (June 1974): 423–446.

Figure 12.2   *The Stock Market and the Business Cycle*

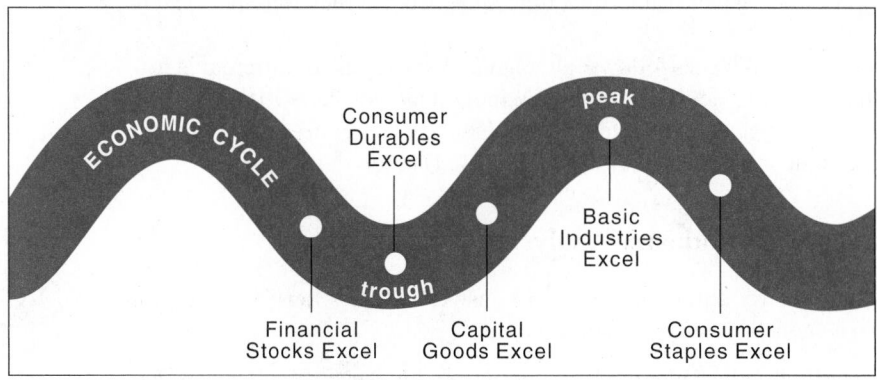

examples of structural change. Industry analysts must examine structural changes for the implications they hold for the industry under review. We will discuss frameworks for analyzing structural changes later in the chapter.

Concerning the effects of business cycles on industry analysis, there is a "folklore" on Wall Street that industry performance is related to the stage of the business cycle. What makes industry analysis challenging is that although the folklore may be true on average, every business cycle is different and those who look only at history are in danger of missing the current and evolving trends that will determine future market performance.

Switching from one industry group to another over the course of a business cycle is known as a *rotation strategy*. When trying to determine which industry groups will benefit from the next stage of the cycle, investors can apply Chapter 11's expectational analysis wherein they identify and monitor key assumptions and variables related to economic trends and industry characteristics.

By looking ahead to the next stage of the business cycle, investors try to purchase industry groups' stocks at current prices in order to take advantage of future sales and earnings growth.

Figure 12.2 presents a stylized graphic of which industry groups typically perform well in the different stages of the business cycle. Toward the end of a recession, financial stocks begin to rise in value as investors begin to anticipate the end of the recession. They anticipate that banks' earnings will rise as both the economy and loan demand recover. Brokerage houses may also be attractive investments; their sales and earnings will rise as investors trade securities and as businesses sell debt and equity during the economic recovery. These industry selections assume that the recession will end shortly, followed by positive economic news including increases in loan demand, housing construction, and security offerings.

Once the economy hits bottom and begins its recovery, consumer durable stocks typically make attractive investments. Such stocks include industries that produce expensive consumer items, such as cars, personal computers, refrigerators, lawn tractors, and snow blowers. These industries are attractive investments because a reviving economy will increase consumer confidence and personal income. Pent-up demand for expensive consumer purchases delayed during the recession, may be fulfilled during the coming recovery.

Once businesses finally recognize the economy is recovering and current levels of consumer spending are sustainable, they begin to think about modernizing, renovating, or pur-

chasing new equipment to satisfy rising demand, lower costs, expanding markets, or provide better service to customers. Thus, capital goods industries become attractive investments. Examples of capital goods industries include heavy equipment manufacturers, machine and tool die makers, and airplane manufacturers.

Cyclical industries include capital goods and consumer durables whose sales rise and fall along with general economic activity. Cyclical industries are attractive investments during the early stages of an economic recovery because of their high degree of operating leverage, which means that they benefit greatly from the sales increases during an economic expansion.[3] Industries with high financial leverage (that is, higher industry debt ratios), such as banks, likewise benefit from rising sales or loan volume.[4]

Traditionally, toward the business cycle peak, the rate of inflation increases as demand starts to outstrip supply. Basic materials industries, which transform raw materials into finished products, become investor favorites. These industries include the oil, gold, aluminum, and timber industries. Because inflation has little influence on the cost of extracting or finishing these products, the higher prices allow these industries to experience higher profit margins.

During a recession, some industry sectors typically do better than others. Consumer staples, such as pharmaceuticals, food, and beverages, tend to perform better than other sectors during a recession because, although spending may drop in other areas, people still spend money on these necessities. As a result, these "defensive" industries generally maintain their values during market declines.

If a weak domestic economy means a weak currency, industries with large export components may benefit because their goods become more cost competitive in overseas markets. The most attractive industries will be those with large markets in growing economies.

We have identified certain industries that typically make attractive investments over the course of the business cycle. Generally, investors should not invest with the current economic situation in mind because the efficient market has already incorporated current economic news into security prices. Rather, investors must forecast important economic variables three to six months in the future and invest accordingly while monitoring their key assumptions and variables. The following subsection considers several important economic variables and discusses how changes in these variables may affect different industries.

Inflation

Higher inflation is generally perceived as deleterious to the stock market, because it causes higher market interest rates, it increases uncertainty about future prices and costs (leading to higher risk perceptions), and it harms firms that cannot pass their cost increases on to consumers. Although a firm's nominal-cash flows may increase, its real-cash flows may fall if revenue increases fail to keep up with cost increases and rising fixed-asset prices. Although these adverse effects are true for most industries, some industry groups benefit from inflation. Firms in natural resource industries benefit *if* their production costs do not rise with inflation, because their oil, mineral, or metal output will likely sell at higher prices. Industries that have high operating and financial leverage may

---

[3]Operating leverage arises from the existence of fixed costs in a firm's operating structure. Industries with large fixed expenses, such as rent or lease payments, depreciation, or take-or-pay contracts will have high degrees of operating leverage. This means a small percentage change in sales can result in a large percentage change in operating income.

[4]Financial leverage arises from fixed financial costs (that is, interest expense) in a firm's capital structure. Industries that have extensive debt financing (such as banks or utilities) will have net income, which is sensitive to small changes in operating income.

benefit because many of their costs are fixed in nominal (current dollar) terms whereas revenues increase in line with inflation. Industries with high financial leverage also gain because their debts are repaid in cheaper dollars.

Interest Rates

Banks generally benefit from volatile interest rates,[5] because stable interest rates lead to heavy competitive pressures that squeeze their interest margins. Alternatively, interest rates moving upward or downward typically result in higher interest margins and profits. Because high interest rates harm the construction industry, they generally help industries that supply the do-it-yourselfer. High interest rates also benefit those whose income is dependent on interest income from bank CDs—for example, retirees.

International Economics

Both domestic and overseas events may cause the value of the U.S. dollar to fluctuate. A weaker U.S. dollar helps U.S. industries because their exports become comparatively cheaper in overseas markets while the goods of foreign competitors become more expensive in the United States. A stronger dollar has an opposite effect. Economic growth in world regions or specific countries benefits industries that have a large presence in those areas. The creation of free-trade zones, such as the European Community and the North American Free Trade Zone, assist industries that produce goods and services that previously faced quotas or tariffs in partner countries.

Consumer Sentiment

Because it comprises about two-thirds of GDP, consumption spending has a large impact on the economy. Optimistic consumers will be more willing to spend and borrow money for expensive goods, such as houses, cars, new clothes, and furniture. The performance of consumer cyclical industries such as these will be affected by changes in consumer sentiment, and consumers' willingness and ability to borrow and spend money.

Inputs

Inputs to production processes can also affect the investment attractiveness of an industry. Manufacturers using minerals, oil, or other raw materials as input to the production process generally perform better when the input is relatively abundant (and less expensive). Changing demographics over time may expose some industries to a shortage of entry-level workers or highly trained personnel. Companies in industries able to work around such shortages will have a competitive advantage over their rivals who cannot.

STRUCTURAL INFLUENCES ON THE ECONOMY AND INDUSTRY

Influences other than the economy are part of the business environment. Social trends, changes in technology, as well as political and regulatory environments all play a role in affecting the cash flow and risk prospects of different industries.

---

[5]Alfred C. Morley, ed., *The Financial Services Industry—Banks, Thrifts, Insurance Companies, and Securities Firms* (Charlottesville, Va: Association of Investment Management and Research, 1992).

Social Influences

Societal changes affect the economy and relevant industries in various ways. Changes in the composition of the population, lifestyle choices, and social values can lead to the rise and fall of industries, products, and corporate strategies irrespective of overall economic growth.

Demographics   In the past fifty years the United States has had a baby boom, a baby bust, and is now enjoying a baby boomlet as members of the baby boom generation (those born between the end of World War II and the early 1960s) have children. The influx of the baby boom and "the graying of the baby boom" has had a large impact on U.S. consumption, from advertising strategies to house construction to concerns over social security and health care. The study of demographics includes much more than population growth and age distributions. Demographics also includes the geographical distribution of people, the changing ethnic mix in a society, and changes in income distribution. Corporate marketing strategists and Wall Street industry analysts need to observe demographic trends and determine their effect on different industries and firms.

In the 1990s, the fastest-growing age groups in the United States will be those in their forties, fifties, teens, and over seventy; among the declining groups will be those between ages eighteen and twenty-four. By the year 2000, more than one in eight Americans will be sixty-five years of age or older. The changing age profile of Americans has implications for resource availability, namely, a possible shortage of entry-level workers leading to an increase in labor costs. It may also be difficult to find qualified persons to replace the retiring baby boomers. The "graying" of the U.S. population also affects U.S. savings patterns, as people in the forty-to-sixty age bracket usually save more than younger people. These trends may bode well for the financial services industry, which offers assistance to those who want to invest their savings. Alternatively, a declining population of entry-level workers and a greater propensity for older Americans to save may have a negative impact on some industries such as the retailing industry. For these same reasons, the consumption spending and retail sectors in Japan are not expected to do well in the 1990s either because the fastest-growing segment of Japan's population will be those over age fifty.

Lifestyles   Lifestyles deal with how people live, work, form households, consume, enjoy leisure, and educate themselves. Consumer behavior is affected by trends and fads. The rise and fall of jeans, "designer" jeans, chinos, and other styles in clothes illustrates the sensitivity of some markets to changes in consumer tastes. The increase in divorce rates, dual-career families, population shifts away from cities, and computer-based education and entertainment have influenced numerous industries, including housing, automobiles, convenience and catalog shopping, services, and home entertainment. From an international perspective, some U.S.-brand goods—from blue jeans to movies—have a high demand overseas. They are perceived to be more "in style" and perhaps higher quality than items produced domestically. Sales in several industries have benefited from this exercise of consumer choice overseas.

Social Values   Returns to nature, environmental consciousness, civil rights, the changing role of women in U.S. society during the past thirty years, growing concern over use of alcohol and tobacco—all reflect changing social values in the United States. Changes in society's values and outlook on issues can lead to changes in labor force participation, education, and consumption patterns. These, in turn, may have a positive or negative effect on different industries and sectors of the economy.

The Importance of Social Influences—An Example from the Retailing Industry   Changes in retail sales over time and across regions in the United States is mainly explained by two influences: population and per capita income. Still, this provides

little guidance to an analyst studying the retail apparel sector or the drug store industry. Studies have found that different social factors influence the sales of the various subsectors of the aggregate retail industry.[6] For example, unmarried young singles were found to spend more money in furniture stores and restaurants and less at drug stores. "Full-nesters"— households with children—spend more money in virtually all store categories when compared to other households, except for restaurants, where spending was less. The degree of mobility within a region, measured by relative automobile ownership, was statistically related to higher levels of spending in apparel, department, general merchandise, and variety stores; it had no impact on furniture store and drug store sales.

Such variables deal with the demand side of retailing. Studies have also found supply-side influences on retail spending per household. Factors such as assortment, service quality, and service quantity have been found to lead to higher retailing expenditures, although the size of the effect differs between the type of retailing establishment.

Industry analysts need to do these types of studies that examine demand and supply influences on industries and industry segments. Such studies provide greater insight into what influences sales, costs, or profits, and increases the ability of the analyst to forecast the effect of future economic and structural influences on the industry. Sources of information for such studies include surveys, trade association conferences and publications, and academic studies.

Technology

Trends in technology can affect both the industry product and the manufacturing and delivery processes. For example, demand has fallen for carburetors on cars because of electronic fuel-injection technology. The engineering process has changed because of the advent of computer-aided design and computer-aided manufacturing. Perpetual improvement of designs in the semiconductor and microprocessor industry has made that industry a difficult one to evaluate. Innovations in process technology allowed steel minimills to grow at the expense of large steel producers. Advances in technology allow some plant sites and buildings to generate their own electricity, bypassing their need for power from the local electric utility. Trucks have reduced railroads' market share in the long-distance carrier industry, and planes, not trains, now mainly carry people long distances. The "information superhighway" is becoming a reality and may lead to linkages between telecommunications and cable TV systems. Changes in technology have spurred capital spending in technological equipment as firms try to use microprocessors and software as a means to gain competitive advantages.

The retailing industry is a user of new technology. Some forecasters envision "relationship merchandising," in which customer databases will allow closer links between retail stores and customer needs.[7] Rather than doing market research to focus on aggregate consumer trends, specialized retailers can offer products that particular consumer segments desire in the locations that consumers prefer. Technology may allow retailers to become more organizationally decentralized and geographically diversified.

Major retailers already use a great deal of technology. Bar code scanning speeds the checkout process and allows the firm to track inventory. Use of customer credit cards allows

[6]Charles A. Ingene, "Using Economic Data in Retail Industry Analysis," in *The Retail Industry—General Merchandisers and Discounters, Specialty Merchandisers, Apparel Specialty, and Food/Drug Retailers,* ed. Charles A. Ingene (Charlottesville, Va.: Association for Investment Management and Research, 1993), pp. 18–25.

[7]Carl E. Steidtmann, "General Trends in Retailing," in *The Retail Industry—General Merchandisers and Discounters, Specialty Merchandisers, Apparel Specialty, and Food/Drug Retailers,* ed. Charles A. Ingene (Charlottesville, Va.: Association for Investment Management and Research, 1993), pp. 6–9.

firms to track customer purchases and send custom-made sales announcements. Electronic data interchange (EDI) allows the retailer to electronically communicate with suppliers to order new inventory and pay accounts payable. Electronic funds transfer allows retailers to move funds quickly and easily between local banks and headquarters.

Politics and Regulations

Because political change reflects social values, today's social trend may be tomorrow's law, regulation, or tax. The industry analyst needs to project and assess political changes relevant to the industry under study.

Some regulations and laws are based on economic reasoning. Due to utilities' positions as natural monopolies, their rates must be reviewed and approved by a regulatory body.[8] Some regulation involves social ends. For example, the Food and Drug Administration protects consumers by reviewing new drugs. Public and worker safety concerns spurred creation of the Consumer Product Safety Commission, Environmental Protection Agency, and laws such as OSHA. Well-meaning, overzealous regulators or politicians may try to "micromanage" an industry with the results of increasing firms' costs and restricting entry into the industry.

Some regulations arise because of concerns about fairness. Tax increases on higher incomes affect profitable firms and individuals. The oil windfall-profits tax that was instituted during the 1973 oil crisis taxed oil companies to reduce the benefit they would receive from selling oil at OPEC's higher prices.

Regulatory changes have affected numerous industries. The Depository Institution Deregulation and Monetary Control Act (DIDMCA) of 1980 transformed the savings and loan industry; the Financial Institutions Reform, Recovery and Enforcement Act of 1989 (FIRREA) was intended to reverse some of the excesses caused by the DIDMCA. Changing regulations and technology are bringing the various aspects of the financial services industry—banking, insurance, investment banking, and investment services— together.

Regulations and laws affect international commerce. International tax laws, tariffs, quotas, embargoes, and other trade barriers may affect different industries in various ways.

The retail industry is affected by several political and regulatory factors. First is the minimum-wage law, which specifies the minimum wage that can be paid to workers. A second factor is the uncertain result of health-care reform debate. Employer-paid health insurance would dramatically affect the labor costs of labor-intensive service industries such as retailing. Third, because goods must first be delivered to the stores, regulations that affect the cost of shipping by airplane, ship, or truck will affect retailers' costs. Finally, trends toward open international markets can assist retailers, because the elimination or reduction of tariffs and quotas will allow retailers to offer imported goods at lower prices. The removal of such barriers would also assist them in expanding their international marketing.

Workers want to have health insurance as an employment benefit. The rise of managed-care plans has occurred as employers sought to control ever-rising health-care costs. This resulted in declining profit margins in the retail drugstore sector, as managed-care plans

[8]Technology can change natural monopolies. We mentioned earlier how some firms are generating their own electrical power. Advancing technology resulted in AT&T losing its monopoly in the early 1980s. An antitrust suit filed against IBM in the 1960s was subsequently thrown out because changing computer technology and growing competition made such a suit moot. As another example of technology change leading to regulatory change, by the mid- and late-1990s, several states were allowing electric utilities, once considered a natural monopoly, to compete for customers in test markets.

with negotiation power over prescription prices replaced individuals as the real customer of drugstores. Two-thirds of pharmacy prescription sales arise from managed-care plans. More and more the corner drugstore proprietorship is being replaced by larger chain drugstores whose volume purchasing power and scale economies allows them to offer lower prescription prices to managed-care plans.

Theme Investing

Related to economic and structural analysis is the concept of theme investing. Theme investing is used by both top-down and bottom-up investors, although the top-down structure of the economy-industry-company analysis provides a framework for identifying and developing themes. **Theme investing** tries to identify megatrends, that is, economic, demographic, social, technological, and political trends that should persist long enough to have a major influence on industry and corporate profits in clearly defined "theme" areas. As we approach the year 2000, many publications will no doubt report their lists of investment themes for the new millennium. Some possibilities include:[9]

♦ Technology—a broad arena involving globalization, telecommunications, computers, information access
♦ Aging population—will affect financial services, leisure and tourism, health care
♦ Freer trade and developing-country growth—new markets, transportation systems, value of a company's "brand" recognition.

Identification of themes provide insight into industry analysis and the subsequent analysis of individual firms for investment purposes.

IMKAV

Economic influences on industries are important, but so are the social, technological, political, and regulatory factors discussed above. Similar to economic analysis, analysis of trends and patterns in these structural factors should include the identification and monitoring of key assumptions and variables (see the discussion of IMKAV analysis in Chapter 11). Over time, analysts should identify and monitor

♦ the current and emerging trends and patterns affecting an industry,
♦ the indicators of trends and patterns,
♦ the historical development of the trends and patterns, and
♦ the momentum toward change in these trends and patterns.

COMPETITIVE STRUCTURE OF AN INDUSTRY

In addition to macroeconomic and structural influences on an industry, microeconomic factors affect industry structure and competition. For example, monopolistic industries tend to be regulated; oligopolistic industries may be characterized by either tough competitive actions or a "live and let live" managerial philosophy; competitive industries are dynamic and are the toughest to evaluate. Competition in an oligopoly or competitive industry can be either price-based or non-price-based. Price competition occurs when

---

[9]Adapted from "Investment Strategy," a presentation by Robert J. Farrell, Senior Investment Adviser, Merrill Lynch, at the New York Society of Security Analysts, August 14, 1997.

Figure 12.3 *Forces Driving Industry Competition*

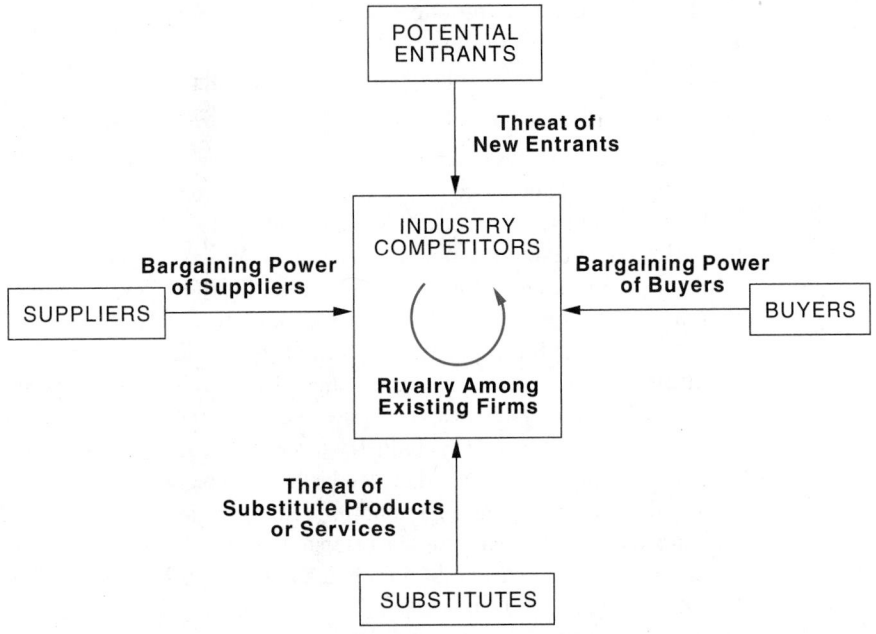

Source: Adapted and reprinted with the permission of The Free Press, a division of Simon & Schuster, from *Competitive Strategy: Techniques for Analyzing Industries and Competitors* by Michael E. Porter. Copyright © 1980 by The Free Press.

industry rivals attempt to gain market share by reducing prices. Non-price-based competition occurs when rivals use advertising, quality claims, warranties, service, and convenience in an attempt to differentiate themselves from the competition and to attract customers.

Porter's Competitive Forces

Porter's concept of **competitive strategy** is the search by a firm for a favorable competitive position in an industry.[10] To create a profitable competitive strategy, a firm must first examine the basic competitive structure of its industry; the potential profitability of a firm is heavily influenced by the inherent profitability of its industry. Hence, industry analysts need to determine the competitive structure of their industry and examine the factors that determine the relative competitive position of firms within the industry. In this section we consider the factors that determine the competitive structure of an industry. Our discussion of company analysis in Chapter 13 will cover the factors that determine the relative competitive position of a firm within its industry.

Porter believes that the **competitive environment** of an industry, or the intensity of competition among the firms in that industry, determines the ability of the firms to sustain above-average rates of return on invested capital. As seen in Figure 12.3, he suggests that five competitive forces determine the intensity of competition:

---

[10]Michael E. Porter, *Competitive Strategy: Techniques for Analyzing Industries and Competitors* (New York: Free Press, 1980); Michael Porter, "Industry Structure and Competitive Strategy; Keys to Profitability," *Financial Analysts Journal* 36, no. 4 (July–August 1980); and Michael Porter, *Competitive Advantage: Creating and Sustaining Superior Performance* (New York: Free Press, 1985).

1. Rivalry among existing competitors
2. Threat of new entrants
3. Threat of substitute products
4. Bargaining power of buyers
5. Bargaining power of suppliers

The relative effect of each of these five factors can vary dramatically among industries.

Rivalry among Existing Competitors You must examine in each industry the levels of price and non-price competition over time to judge if rivalry among firms is currently intense and growing, or if it is polite and stable. Rivalry increases when many firms of relatively equal size compete in an industry. When estimating the number and size of firms, be sure to include foreign competitors. Further, slow growth causes competitors to fight for market share and increases competition. High fixed costs stimulate the desire to operate at full capacity, which can lead to price cutting and greater competition. Finally, look for exit barriers, such as specialized facilities or labor agreements that will keep firms in an industry despite below-average or negative rates of return.

The retail drugstore (RDS) industry has enjoyed sales gains but with fewer competitors and lower profit margins. Managed health-care plans have been a driving force behind this trend. Stores are using segmentation strategies, are trying to increase customer service, are increasing their product offerings in an attempt to diversify from the low-margin prescription market. Major chains in the RDS industry include Walgreens, Rite Aid, Eckerd, CVS, and Longs.

Threat of New Entrants Although an industry may have few competitors, you must determine the likelihood of firms entering the industry and increasing competition. High barriers to entry, such as low current prices relative to costs, keep the threat of new entrants low. Other barriers to entry include the need to invest large financial resources to compete effectively in the industry. Also, substantial economies of scale give a current industry member an advantage over a new firm. New entrants might be discouraged if success in the industry requires extensive distribution channels that are hard to build because of exclusive distribution contracts. Similarly, high costs of switching products or brands (for example, changing a computer or telephone system) keep competition low. Finally, government policy can restrict entry by imposing licensing requirements or limiting access to materials (for example, lumber, coal). Lacking these barriers, competitors might easily enter an industry, increasing the competition and driving down potential rates of return.

The RDS industry is facing competition from other retailers who have pharmacies in their stores or who sell over-the-counter products, such as supermarkets and retail stores such as Wal-Mart. Another new entrant are firms involved in the mail-order prescription business. Although many chains do this as well, newcomers such as Veterans Administration and American Association of Retired Persons (AARP) together account for more than one-half of all mail-order prescriptions.

Threat of Substitute Products Substitute products limit the profit potential of an industry because they limit the prices that firms can charge. Although almost everything has a substitute, you must determine how close the substitute is in price and function to an industry's product. As an example, the threat of substitute glass containers hurt the metal container industry. Glass containers kept declining in price, forcing metal container prices and profits down. In the food industry, consumers constantly substitute between beef, pork, chicken, and fish. The role of technology cannot be ignored; technological progress drives the development of substitute products over time.

The threat of substitute products is not a major concern for the RDS industry; prescription medications are regulated by the U.S. Food and Drug Administration. That

industry's concern is rather new delivery systems that improve consumer convenience. Supermarkets, other retail stores, and mail order have grown as substitute delivery systems to offer consumers many ways to purchase the items they need.

Buyer Bargaining Power   Buyers can influence industry profitability when they bid down prices or demand higher quality or more services by bargaining among competitors. Buyers become powerful when they purchase a large volume relative to the sales of a supplier. The most vulnerable firm is a one-customer firm that supplies a single large manufacturer, as is common for auto-parts manufacturers or software developers. Buyers will be more conscious of the costs of items that represent a significant percentage of the firm's total costs or if the buying firm is feeling cost pressure from its customers. Also, buyers who know a lot about the costs of supplying an industry will bargain more intensely, such as the case when the buying firm supplies some of its own needs and also buys from outside. Buyers can affect an industry's competitive structure if they decide to vertically integrate and start supplying the product in-house rather than purchase it from an existing vendor.

In the RDS industry, managed-care providers wield the buyer bargaining power. As third-party payers, their prescription-drug reimbursement rate policies have cut into RDS prescription sales profits. The industry is reacting to this by seeking to diversify their product base to lessen the impact of large managed-care providers on overall industry sales.

Supplier Bargaining Power   Suppliers can alter future industry returns if they increase prices or reduce the quality or services they provide. Suppliers are more powerful if they are few and more concentrated than the industry to which they sell, and if they supply critical input to several industries, for which few if any substitutes exist. In this instance the suppliers are free to change prices and the services they supply to the firms in an industry. When analyzing supplier bargaining power, be sure to consider labor's power within each industry. Similar to buyer bargaining power, a supplier can change the competitive structure of an industry by deciding to vertically integrate forward in order to produce the final product.

The suppliers of the RDS industry's mainstay products are pharmaceutical firms. RDS firms have historically been price-takers; they have tried to cut costs and increase efficiencies to maintain profitability as pharmaceutical prices rose while managed-care reimbursements fell. Some drugstores have sought legal remedy by filing lawsuits against several pharmaceutical firms, alleging illegal discriminatory pricing. Thus, at this writing, legal pressure is being used to try to ease supplier pricing pressure.

To summarize, an investor can analyze these competitive forces to determine the intensity of the competition in an industry and assess its long-run profit potential. Analysts should examine each of these factors for every industry and develop a relative competitive profile. It is important to update this analysis of an industry's competitive environment over time because an industry's competitive structure can and will change over time.

Strategic Groups

Not all industries are comprised of homogeneous firms serving homogeneous consumers. Many industries are segmented, with firms competing against some, but not necessarily all, firms in an industry. A **strategic group** is a group of firms in an industry that follow similar strategies in their product or market approaches. For example, the retail industry is a broad industry comprised of several strategic groups. Department stores are one group, specialty retailers are another. Tool manufacturers may have one strategic group competing in the broad consumer category, the "do-it-yourselfer," whereas another group may focus on the needs of the professional tradesperson. Analysis of strategic groups is important when analyzing individual firms and their strategies.

Even a segment as seemingly specialized as the retail drugstore industry has strategic distinctions. Conventional drugstores (Walgreens, Osco) typically sell health and beauty aids, general merchandise, cards, and gift wrap at the front of the store and have the pharmacy in the rear of the store. Bantam drugstores (CVS) have smaller floor spaces than the conventionals and are more focused, emphasizing prescriptions and health and beauty aids. Deep-discounter (Phar-Mor, Drug Emporium) are larger than conventionals, provide a lower level of service, and are not as conveniently located, all as a means to lower their costs and their prices. Other formats include express drugstores (some locations of Walgreens and Rite-Aid), which feature little more than a pharmacy and some high-turnover items such as aspirin and cough syrup, and super drugstores (Longs), which are a cross between a conventional drugstore and a deep-discounter.

Industry Life Cycle

Another tool to help predict industry sales is to view the industry over time and divide its development into stages similar to those experienced by humans as they move from birth to adolescence, adulthood, middle age, and old age. The number of stages in this **industry life-cycle analysis** can vary based on how much detail you want. A five-stage model would include the following:

1. Pioneering development
2. Rapidly accelerating industry growth
3. Mature industry growth
4. Stabilization and market maturity
5. Deceleration of growth and decline

Figure 12.4 shows the growth path of sales during each stage. The vertical scale reflects sales levels, whereas the horizontal scale represents different time periods. To estimate industry sales, you must predict the length of time for each stage. This requires answers to such questions as How long will an industry grow at an accelerating rate (Stage 2)? How long will it be in a mature growth phase (Stage 3) before its sales growth stabilizes (Stage 4) and then declines (Stage 5)?

Besides sales estimates, this analysis of an industry's life cycle can also provide some insights into risk, profit margins, and earnings growth, although the profit measures do not necessarily parallel the sales growth. The profit margin series typically peaks early in the total cycle and then levels off and declines as competition is attracted by the early success of the industry.

To illustrate the contribution of life-cycle stages to sales estimates, we will briefly describe these stages and their identifiable characteristics. The current growth stage of an industry can be determined by comparing its characteristics to the following factors.

Pioneering Development   This stage begins following some type of marketing or technological breakthrough. During this start-up stage, the industry experiences modest sales growth and small or negative profit margins and profits. The market for the industry's product or service during this time is small, and firms incur major development costs. Cash flow is usually negative as cash is reinvested to finance growth, and outside financing sources usually are tapped to finance growth. Because of an uncertain industry future and the competition to come, it is difficult to identify "winners" at this stage. An example of an industry in the pioneering stage is interactive cable. At the present time, only a small percentage of U.S. homes are wired for interactive cable, and company alliances are just forming to try to exploit this technology in the marketplace.

Rapid Accelerating Growth   During this stage, a market develops for the product or service and demand becomes substantial. The limited number of firms in the indus-

Figure 12.4 *Life Cycle of an Industry*

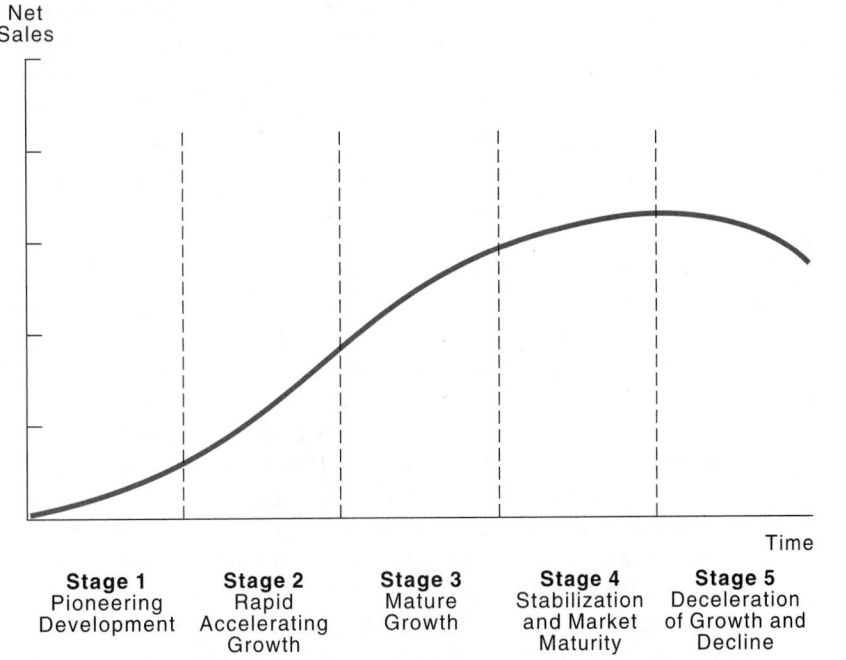

Net
Sales

Time

Stage 1	**Stage 2**	**Stage 3**	**Stage 4**	**Stage 5**
Pioneering	Rapid	Mature	Stabilization	Deceleration
Development	Accelerating	Growth	and Market	of Growth and
	Growth		Maturity	Decline

try face little competition, and individual firms can experience substantial backlogs. The profit margins are high. The high profit levels attract new entrants; in the following competitive battle some firms will ultimately be forced to exit the industry. Over time, the industry builds its productive capacity as existing firms and new entrants attempt to meet excess demand. High sales growth and high profit margins that increase as firms become more efficient cause industry and firm profits to explode. During this phase profits can grow from the low earnings base at more than 100 percent per year because of the rapid growth of sales and net profit margins. Some stable leading firms emerge as industry leaders, both in terms of product offerings and market share. These firms may be attractive for investment purposes—if their shares are not overpriced. Some firms may begin to pay small cash dividends. The biotechnology and the Internet information search industries are examples of industries in this stage.

Mature Growth   The success in Stage 2 has satisfied most of the demand for the industry goods or service. The large sales base may keep future sales growth above normal, but it no longer accelerates. As an example, if the overall economy is growing at 5 percent, sales for this industry might grow at a stabilizing rate of 10 to 15 percent a year. Also, the rapid growth of sales and the high historic profit margins continue to attract competitors to the industry; profit margins will stabilize and begin to decline to normal levels. Dividends rise from the low levels in Stage 2. Examples of industries at this life-cycle stage include the personal computer industry and retail store segments that specialize in certain goods, such as office supplies or materials for the "do-it-yourselfer."

Stabilization and Market Maturity   During this stage, which is probably the longest phase, the industry growth rate matches the growth rate of the aggregate economy or the segment of the economy of which the industry is a part. The market for the industry's product is saturated. During this stage, investors can estimate growth easily because sales correlate highly with an economic series (such as consumption expenditures).

Although sales grow in line with the economy, profit growth varies by industry and by individual firms within the industry because management ability to control costs differs among companies. Competition produces tight profit margins and the rates of return on capital (for example, return on assets, return on equity) eventually are equal to or slightly below the competitive level. More generous dividends are paid as firms in the industry may have difficulty finding attractive reinvestment opportunities. Examples include the supermarket industry and the U.S. cola segment of the soft-drink industry.

Deceleration of Growth, Decline   At this stage of maturity, the industry's sales growth declines because of shifts in demand or growth of substitutes. Profit margins continue to be squeezed, and some firms experience low profits or even losses. Firms that remain profitable may show low rates of return on capital, and investors begin thinking about alternative uses for the capital tied up in this industry. Examples of industries in this life-cycle stage are the mainframe computer industry and the U.S. cigarette industry; one has experienced declining growth over time because of changes in technology; the other because of a changing social and political climate.

These descriptions of the life-cycle stages are general, but still helpful in identifying where an industry currently is in its life cycle. Based on these guidelines, analysts can estimate potential sales growth for the industry.

The industry life cycle can be invigorated in any stage by product innovations that attract new consumers to use the product or that convince existing consumers to buy the new product. Traditional roller skates have been replaced by in-line skate models. Bicycles have been redesigned to be lighter and more durable. The game industry has been invigorated by the advent of computerized, high-quality graphic entertainment systems. Once found only in athletic clubs, smaller, durable home gyms and exercise equipment are now found in many homes.

Table 12.2 illustrates the predictions—sometimes contradictory—of industry life-cycle theories and strategy, competition, and performance. Here, only four stages are presented; for purposes of this table, Stages 3 (mature growth) and 4 (stabilization and market maturity) have been combined into a single stage: maturity. By identifying buyer behavior patterns, marketing strategies, the status of manufacturing and distribution, and industry margins, industry analysts can determine the relevant stage of an industry's life cycle.

CONDUCTING AN INDUSTRY ANALYSIS[11]

Paralysis of analysis is a common problem in analyzing the competitive structure of an industry. An abundance of data confronts the analyst, from published sources or industry participants.

Table 12.3 presents a framework for assembling and organizing industry data. By organizing raw data in this way, the analyst can develop a comprehensive picture of the industry and perform economic, life-cycle, and competitive analyses of it.

To create an initial overview, the analyst must first determine who is in the industry under study. Usually, identifying the leading competitors is easy, and additional research of news articles and trade publications will uncover others. Search for prior industry studies written by academics, consulting groups, or industry trade groups. The annual reports of firms in the industry are also required reading. Reviewing the prose of the reports for the past ten to fifteen years, including management's analysis of the year's results, can be enlightening.

During this process a more detailed data-gathering project should begin. Library articles can reveal important information about an industry, and the article references may dis-

---

[11]This section is based on Michael Porter, *Competitive Strategy* (New York: Free Press, 1980), pp. 368–382.

Table 12.2   *Predictions about Market Behavior and Competition over the Industry Life Cycle*

	Introduction	Growth	Maturity	Decline
Buyers and Buyer Behavior	High income purchases Buyer inertia Buyers must be convinced to try the product	Widening buyer group Consumer will accept uneven quality	Mass market Saturation Repeat buying Choosing among brands is the rule	Customers are sophisticated buyers of the product
Products and Product Change	Poor quality Product design and development key Many different product variations; no standards Frequent design changes Basic product designs	Products have technical and performance differentiation Reliability key for complex products Competitive product improvements Good quality	Superior quality Less product differentiation Standardization Less rapid product changes—more minor annual model changes Trade-ins become significant	Little product differentiation Spotty product quality
Marketing	Very high advertising/sales (a/s) Creaming price strategy High marketing costs	High advertising, but lower percent of sales than introductory Most promotion of ethical drugs Advertising and distribution key for nontechnical products	Market segmentation Efforts to extend life cycle Broaden line Service and deals more prevalent Packaging important Advertising competition Lower a/s	Low a/s and other marketing
Manufacturing and Distribution	Overcapacity Short production runs High skilled-labor content High production costs Specialized channels	Undercapacity Shift toward mass production Scramble for distribution Mass channels	Some overcapacity Optimum capacity Increasing stability of manufacturing process Lower labor skills Long production runs with stable techniques Distribution channels pare down their lines to improve their margins High physical distribution costs due to broad lines Mass channels	Substantial overcapacity Mass production Specialty channels
R&D	Changing production techniques			

close valuable sources. Other valuable sources of industry information include trade associations, trade magazines, the business press, corporate SEC filings, and industry-average data, available from Dun and Bradstreet, the *IRS Corporation Source Book of Statistics of Income,* and publications from the Bureau of Census (such as the *Census of Manufactures* or the *Census of Retail Trade*) and the Bureau of Labor Statistics (such as their *Wholesale Price Index*). Web browsers and Internet-based research from reliable sources offer additional opportunities to research industry and competitor characteristics.

Among the most valuable information sources are field interviews with industry management, members of sales forces, customers, suppliers, union leaders, technical

Table 12.2 *Predictions about Market Behavior and Competition over the Industry Life Cycle (continued)*

	Introduction	Growth	Maturity	Decline
Foreign Trade	Some exports	Significant exports Few imports	Falling exports Significant imports	No exports Significant imports
Overall Strategy	Best period to increase market share R&D, engineering are key functions	Practical to change price or quality image Marketing the key function	Bad time to increase market share Particularly if low-share company Having competitive costs becomes key Bad time to change price image or quality image "Marketing effectiveness" key	Cost control key
Competition	Few companies	Entry Many competitors Lots of mergers and casualties	Price competition Shakeout Increase in private brands Cyclicality sets in	Exits Fewer competitors
Risk	High risk	Risks can be taken here because growth covers them up	Cyclicality sets in	
Margins and Profits	High prices and margins Low profits Price elasticity to individual seller not as great as in maturity	High profits Highest profits Fairly high prices Lower prices than introductory phase Recession resistant High P/E's Good acquisition climate	Falling prices Lower profits Lower margins Lower dealer margins Increased stability of market shares and price structure Poor acquisition climate—tough to sell companies Lowest prices and margins	Low prices and margins Falling prices Prices might rise in late decline

Source: Adapted and reprinted with the permission of The Free Press, a division of Simon & Schuster, from *Competitive Strategy: Techniques for Analyzing Industries and Competitors* by Michael E. Porter, pp. 159–161. Copyright © 1980 by The Free Press.

consultants, and trade association officials. Sometimes they may offer contradictory perspectives, and the analyst must cross-check references and sources and construct a consistent evaluation.

We have discussed several ways of analyzing industries. Each analyst will develop his or her own preferences based upon experiences and research strengths. The Chapter 12 appendix presents another framework for analyzing industries used by a practicing analyst.

Only a few publications offer extensive information on a wide range of industries. The major source of data on various industries are industry publications and trade association magazines.

Industry Publications

Standard & Poor's Industry Survey is a two-volume reference work divided into thirty-four segments dealing with sixty-nine major domestic industries. Coverage in each area is divided into a basic analysis and a current analysis. The basic analysis examines the

Table 12.3 *Data Needs for an Industry Analysis*

Data Categories	Compilation
Product lines	By company
Buyers and their behavior	By year
Complementary products	By functional area
Substitute products	
Growth	
Rate	
Pattern (seasonal, cyclical)	
Determinants	
Technology of production and distribution	
Cost structure	
Economies of scale	
Value added	
Logistics	
Labor	
Marketing and selling	
Market segmentation	
Marketing practices	
Suppliers	
Distribution channels (if indirect)	
Innovation	
Types	
Sources	
Rate	
Economies of scale	
Competitors—strategy, goals, strengths and weaknesses, assumptions	
Social, political, legal environment	
Macroeconomic environment	

Source: Adapted and reprinted with the permission of The Free Press, a division of Simon & Schuster, from *Competitive Strategy: Techniques for Analyzing Industries and Competitors* by Michael E. Porter, p. 370. Copyright © 1980 by The Free Press.

long-term prospects for a particular industry based on an analysis of historical trends and problems. Major segments of the industry are spotlighted, and a comparative analysis of the principal companies in the industry is included. The current analysis discusses recent developments and provides statistics for an industry and specific companies along with appraisals of the industry's investment outlook.

Standard & Poor's Analysts Handbook contains selected income account and balance sheet items along with related financial ratios for the Standard & Poor's industry groups. (It is typically not available until about seven months after year-end.) These fundamental income and balance-sheet series allow comparisons of the major factors bearing on group stock price movements.

Value Line Industry Survey is an integral part of the *Value Line Investment Survey*. The reports for the 1,700 companies included are divided into 91 industries and updated by industry. In the binder containing these reports, the industry evaluation precedes the individual company reports. The industry report contains summary statistics for the industry on assets, earnings, and important ratios similar to what is included for companies. An industry stock price index is included, as well as a table that provides comparative data for all the individual companies in the industry on timeliness rank, safety rank, and financial strength. The discussion considers the major factors affecting the industry and concludes with an investment recommendation for the industry.

Table 12.4 *Industry References for the Retail Industry*

Publication	Frequency of Publication	Publisher	Content
Chain Drug Review	Bimonthly	Racher Press, Inc. 220 Fifth Avenue New York, NY 10001 (212) 213-6000	Events and trends pertinent to growth and development of the chain drugstore industry.
Chain Store Age Executive	Monthly	Lebhar-Friedman, Inc. 425 Park Avenue New York, NY 10022 (212) 756-5252	Merchandising information, operating techniques, training material and industry news for headquarters executives and store managers.
Current Business Reports: Annual Retail Trade	Annually	U.S. Bureau of Census Dept. of Commerce Washington, DC 20233 (301) 763-5294	Text tables and charts providing estimates of annual sales, year-end inventories and accounts receivable. By kind of business for retail trade.
DNR	Daily	Fairchild Publications 7 W. 34th Street New York, NY 10001 (609) 461-6248	*Daily News Record* has articles on men's wear and accessories.
Discount Merchandiser	Monthly	Macfadden Publishing, Inc. 233 Park Avenue S. New York, NY 10003 (212) 979-4680	Magazine covers trends in the discount and mass retailing industry.
Discount Store News	Biweekly	Lebhar-Friedman, Inc. 425 Park Avenue New York, NY 10022 (212) 756-5100	Newspaper covers industry and related stories.
Drug Store News	Bimonthly	Lebhar-Friedman, Inc. 425 Park Avenue New York, NY 10022 (212) 756-5220	National news and features of the drugstore industry.
MMR	Biweekly	Racher Press, Inc. 220 Fifth Avenue New York, NY 10001 (212) 213-6000	*Mass Market Retailers* features stories on mass merchandisers, drug chains, and supermarkets.
Progressive Grocer	Monthly	Maclean Hunter Media 263 Tresser Blvd. Stamford, CT 06901 (203) 325-3500	Magazine includes articles about trends in the industry, companies, and statistics.
Stores	Monthly	National Retail Federation, Inc. 325 7th St., NW Washington, DC 20004	Magazine with trends pertinent to retailing.
Supermarket Business	Monthly	Hawfrey Communications, Inc. 1086 Teaneck Rd. Teaneck, NJ 07666 (201) 833-1900	Magazine publishes articles on current issues in the supermarket industry.
Supermarket News	Weekly	Fairchild Publications 7 W. 34th Street New York, NY 10001 (800) 247-2160	Newspaper covers industry in general, with financial highlights and weekly chronology of major companies.
Women's Wear Daily	Daily	Fairchild Publications 7 W. 34th Street New York, NY 10001 (800) 289-0273	Retail trade publication covering women's and children's apparel, accessories, and cosmetics.

Source: Karen J. Sack, CFA, "Basic Analysis: Retailing," in *Standard & Poor's Industry Surveys,* May 9, 1996, p. R100.

Industry Magazines

The magazines published for various industries are an excellent source of data and general information. Some industries have several publications (for example, the computer industry has spawned at least five such magazines). Examples of industry publications include the following:

- *Computers*
- *Real Estate Today*
- *Chemical Week*
- *Modern Plastics*
- *Paper Trade Journal*
- *Automotive News*

A comprehensive list of retail industry magazines and newsletters is found in Table 12.4.

Trade Associations

Trade associations are organizations set up by those involved in an industry or a general area of business to provide information for education, advertising, lobbying for legislation, and problem solving. Trade associations typically gather extensive statistics for their industry. Examples of such organizations include the following:[12]

- Iron and Steel Institute
- American Railroad Association
- National Consumer Finance Association
- Institute of Life Insurance
- American Bankers Association
- Machine Tool Association

Global Industry Analysis

Because numerous firms are active in foreign markets and foreign sales are a growing portion of total sales for many firms, we must expand industry analysis to include the effects of foreign firms on global trade and industry returns. To see this, consider the auto industry. Besides Chrysler, Ford, and General Motors, it includes numerous firms from Japan, Germany, Italy, and Korea, among other countries. Thus, the analysis described earlier needs to include additional global factors. The degree to which this complicates the analysis depends upon the industry. Global analysis of the manufacturing-based auto industry will be much more complicated than the service-based retail drugstore industry, in which competition is much more localized. The biggest benefit of global analysis on the RDS industry is likely to relate to supplier bargaining power, as the global pharmaceutical industry sells its products to the RDS industry. Competition among competing prescription pharmaceutical products may lead competing suppliers to offer lower prices.

SUMMARY

- Several studies have examined industry performance and risk. They have found wide dispersion in the performance of different industries during specified time periods, imply-

---

[12]For a more extensive list, see *Encyclopedia of Associations* (Detroit: Gale Research Company, 1977) and *The World Guide to Trade Associations* (New York: R. R. Bowker, 1986).

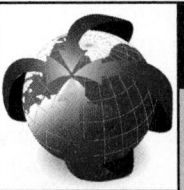

ing that industry analysis can help identify superior investments. They also showed inconsistent industry performance over time, implying that looking only at past performance of an industry has little value in projecting future performance. Also, the performance by firms within industries is typically inconsistent. Following the industry analysis, you must analyze individual companies in that industry.

♦ The analysis of industry risk indicated wide dispersion in the measures of risk for different industries, but a fair amount of consistency in the risk measure over time for individual industries. These results imply that risk analysis and measurement are useful in selecting industries and that past risk measures may be of some value.

♦ Industries are affected by economic events and trends. The rise and fall of the business cycle will make some industries look alternatively attractive and unattractive for investment purposes. Fluctuations in economic variables such as inflation, interest rates, or exchange rates may affect the investment potential of an industry irrespective of the stage of the business cycle.

♦ Other structural influences affect industries. Changing social factors, such as demographics, lifestyles, and values, may affect industries over and above the effect of the

business cycle. Similarly, changing technology and political and regulatory environments can also affect industry prospects. Throughout the process of industry analysis, the analyst needs to identify and monitor the key assumptions and variables that drive the forecast.

♦ An important part of industry analysis is the examination of five factors that determine the competitive environment in an industry, which in turn affects its long-run profitability. Strategic groups also play a role in affecting industry strategy and profitability. The stage of an industry's life cycle may affect investors' desires to invest at the current time.

♦ Global industry analysis must evaluate the effects not only of world supply, demand, and cost components for an industry, but also the impact of exchange rates on the total industry and the firms within it.

Questions

1. Briefly describe the results of studies that examined the performance of different industries during specific time periods and discuss their implications for industry analysis.
2. Briefly describe the results of the studies that examined industry performance over time and discuss their implications for industry analysis. Do these results complicate or simplify industry analysis?
3. Assume that all the firms in a particular industry have consistently experienced rates of return similar to the results for the industry. Discuss what this implies regarding the importance of industry and company analysis for this industry.
4. Some observers have contended that differences in the performance of various firms within an industry limit the usefulness of industry analysis. Discuss this contention.
5. Several studies have examined the difference in risk for alternative industries during a specified time period. Describe the results of these studies and discuss their implications for industry analysis.
6. What were the results when risk was examined for different industries during successive time periods? Discuss the implication of these results for industry analysis.
7. How do cyclical changes in the economy differ from structural changes? How do each affect industry analysis?
8. Discuss some examples of structural changes that may affect an industry.
9. You believe the current recession is about to end. How would you adjust an equity portfolio to take advantage of your forecast?
10. As a stock portfolio manager, you believe the current growth phase of the business cycle will persist for the next year. A friend of yours who manages a portfolio at a rival firm believes the economic cycle has peaked and a recession will soon begin. How might the composition of your portfolios differ from each other?
11. Identify an industry that is likely to do well and one that is likely to do poorly in each of the following situations:
    a. rising inflation
    b. health-care reform places price controls on the pharmaceutical industry
    c. interest rates decline
    d. the dollar strengthens against other currencies
    e. oil prices rise
    f. because of the aging of the baby boomers, the average age of the U.S. population is rising
12. How do demographics, lifestyles, and social values affect industry analysis?
13. Assume that you are analyzing an industry in the fourth stage of the industrial life cycle. How would you react if your industry-economic analysis predicted that sales per share for this industry would increase by 20 percent? Discuss your reasoning.
14. Discuss at what stage in the industrial life cycle you would like to discover a firm and justify your decision.
15. How does a strategic group differ from an industry?

16. Discuss an example of the impact of one of the five competitive forces on an industry's profitability.

CFA: 1998 Level I Sample Exam
17. Which of the following are characteristics of the maturity stage of the industry life cycle:
a. slowly growing sales
b. a highly competitive environment
c. many new competitors enter the market
d. price tends to be a major competitive weapon
e. technological advances occur

Problems

1. Select three industries from the *S&P Analysts Handbook* with different demand factors. For each industry indicate what economic series you would use to help you predict the growth for the industry. Discuss why the economic series selected is relevant for this industry.
2. Prepare a scatter plot for one of the industries in Problem 1 of industry sales per share and observations from the economic series you suggested for this industry. Do this for the most recent ten years using information available in the *Analysts Handbook.* Based on the results of the scatter plot, discuss whether the economic series was closely related to this industry's sales.
3. Using the *S&P Analysts Handbook,* calculate the means for the following variables of the S&P 400 and the industry of your choice during the past ten years:
a. Price/earnings multiplier
b. Retention rate
c. Return on equity
d. Equity turnover
e. Net profit margin
Note: Each of these entries is a ratio, so take care when averaging. Briefly comment on how your industry and the S&P 400 differ for each of the variables.
4. Where is your industry in its industrial life cycle? Justify your answer.
5. Evaluate your industry in terms of the five factors that determine an industry's competitive structure. Discuss your expectations for this industry's long-run profitability.
6. Industry information can be found in Barron's *Market Laboratory/Economic Indicators.* Using issues over the past six months, plot the trend for
a. Auto production
b. Auto inventories (domestic and imports)
c. Newsprint production
d. Newsprint inventories
e. Business inventories
What tentative conclusions do these data support regarding the current economic environment?

References

Fahey, Liam, and V. K. Narayanan. *Macroenvironmental Analysis for Strategic Management.* St. Paul, Minn.: West Publishing Company, 1986.

Ingene, Charles A., ed. *The Retail Industry—General Merchandisers and Discounters, Specialty Merchandisers, Apparel Specialty, and Food/Drug Retailers.* Charlottesville, Va.: Association for Investment Management and Research, 1993.

Morley, Alfred C., ed. *The Financial Services Industry—Banks, Thrifts, Insurance Companies, and Securities Firms.* Charlottesville, Va.: Association of Investment Management and Research, 1992.

Porter, Michael E. *Competitive Strategy: Techniques for Analyzing Industries and Competitors.* New York: Free Press, 1980.

Porter, Michael E. *Competitive Advantage: Creating and Sustaining Superior Performance.* New York: Free Press, 1985.

GLOSSARY

Competitive environment The level of intensity of competition among firms in an industry, determined by an examination of five competitive forces.

Competitive strategy The search by a firm for a favorable competitive position within an industry, which affects evaluation of the industry's prospects.

Cyclical change A type of economic trend resulting from the ups and downs of the business cycle.

Industry A set of businesses producing similar products used by customers for similar purposes.

Industry life-cycle analysis An analysis that focuses on the industry's stage of development.

Strategic group A group of firms in an industry that follows similar strategies in their product or market approaches.

Structural change A type of economic trend resulting from a major organizational change in the economy or in how it functions.

Theme investing An investment strategy that tries to identify megatrends, that is, economic, demographic, social, technological, and political trends that should persist long enough to have a major influence on industry and corporate profits in clearly defined areas.

A P P E N D I X 12 *Preparing an Industry Analysis*

What Is an Industry?[13]

Identifying a company's industry can be difficult in today's business world. Although airlines, railroads, and utilities may be easy to categorize, what about manufacturing companies with three different divisions and none of them dominant? Perhaps the best way to test whether or not a company fits into an industry grouping is to compare the operating results for the company and an industry. For our purposes, an industry is a group of companies with similar demand, supply, and operating characteristics.

The following is a set of guidelines for preparing an industry appraisal, including the topics to consider and some specific items to include.

Characteristics to Study

1. Price history reveals valuable long-term relationships
    a. Price–earnings ratios
    b. Common stock yields
    c. Price–book value ratios
    d. Price–cash flow ratios
2. Operating data shows comparisons of
    a. Return on total investment (ROI)
    b. Return on equity (ROE)
    c. Sales growth
    d. Trends in operating profit margin
    e. Evaluation of stage in industry life cycle
    f. Book value growth
    g. Earnings per share growth
    h. Profit margin trends
    i. Evaluation of exchange-rate risk from foreign sales

---

[13]Reprinted and adapted with permission of Stanley D. Ryals, CFA; Investment Council, Inc., La Crescenta, CA 91214.

A WORD FROM THE STREET

BY ROSSA O'REILLY, CFA

Investment analysts attempt to gain as many perspectives as possible on the outlook for an industry. In a "top-down" approach, they use macroeconomic analysis to assess the prospects for the industry in the context of expected trends in the overall economy and the cyclical and secular shifts in the composition of economic activity. In a "bottom-up" approach, they examine demand and supply factors specific to the industry. Changes in demographics, technology, and consumer tastes are important considerations in both analytical approaches. In addition, they consider studies of statistical relationships between industry trends and other economic variables.

Numerous economic, industry, and business publications are utilized as sources of information and numerous contacts are made with industry associations and individual companies, as well as their competitors, suppliers, and customers.

Analysts develop reasonably reliable forecasts using numerous approaches with a view to arriving at a range of projections. Analysts compare their projections with those of others, partly to study differences in methodology and conclusions, but also to identify differences between an analyst's forecast and consensus views. These differences are extremely important in uncovering investment opportunities because, in order to provide superior investment performance, a forecast must be both *correct* and *sufficiently different* from the consensus expectation currently reflected in the price of publicly traded securities.

Rossa O'Reilly, CFA, has been an investment analyst for twenty-six years, specializing in financial services, real estate, and corporate conglomerates. He has served on numerous professional association boards and accounting standard-setting bodies in the United States and Canada. Currently, O'Reilly is on the board of the Association of Investment Management and Research (AIMR) and on the Board of Trustees of the Institute of Chartered Financial Analysts.

---

3. Comparative results of industries show
    a. Effects of business cycles on each industry group
    b. Secular trends affecting results
    c. Industry growth compared to other industries
    d. Regulatory changes
    e. Importance of overseas operations

Factors in Industry Analysis
Markets for Products

1. Trends in the markets for the industry's major products, historical and projected
2. Industry growth relative to GDP or other relevant economic series; possible changes from past trends
3. Shares of market for major products among domestic and global producers; changes in market shares in recent years; outlook
4. Effect of imports on industry markets; share of market taken by imports; price and margin changes caused by imports
5. Effect of exports on their markets; trends in export prices and units exported; historical trends and expectations for the exchange rates in major non-U.S. countries

Financial Performance

1. Capitalization ratios; ability to raise new capital; earnings retention rate; financial leverage
2. Ratio of fixed assets to capital invested; depreciation policies; capital turnover

3. Return on total capital; return on equity capital; components of ROE
4. Return on foreign investments; need for foreign capital

Operations

1. Degrees of integration; cost advantages of integration; major supply contracts
2. Operating rates as a percentage of capacity; backlogs; new order trends
3. Trends of industry consolidation
4. Trends in industry competition
5. New product development; research and development expenditures in dollars and as a percentage of sales
6. Diversification; comparability of product lines

Management

1. Management depth and ability to develop from within; board of directors; organizational structure
2. Flexibility to deal with product demand changes; ability to identify and eliminate losing operations
3. Record and outlook of labor relations
4. Dividend progression

Sources of Industry Information

1. Independent industry journals
2. Industry and trade associations
3. Government reports and statistics
4. Independent research organizations
5. Brokerage house research

CHAPTER

13

Company Analysis and Stock Selection

In this chapter we will answer the following questions:

♦ Why is it important to differentiate between company analysis and stock analysis?

♦ What is the difference between a growth company and a growth stock?

♦ How do we apply the two valuation approaches and the several valuation techniques to Walgreens?

♦ What techniques serve to estimate the inputs to alternative valuation models?

♦ What techniques aid estimating company sales?

♦ How do we estimate the profit margins and earnings per share for a company?

♦ What procedures and factors do we consider when estimating the earnings multiplier for a firm?

♦ What two specific competitive strategies can a firm use to cope with the competitive environment in its industry?

♦ When should we consider selling a stock?   ♦

At this point you have made two decisions about your investment in equity markets. First, after analyzing the economy and stock markets for several countries, you have decided that you should invest some portion of your portfolio in common stocks. Second, after analyzing various industries, you have identified those that appear to offer above-average risk-adjusted performance over your investment horizon. You must now answer the final question in the fundamental analysis procedure: Which are the best companies within these desirable industries and are their stocks underpriced? Specifically, is the intrinsic value of the stock above its market value, or is the expected rate of return on the stock equal to or greater than its required rate of return?

We begin this chapter with a discussion of the difference between company analysis and stock selection. Company analysis should occur in the context of the prevailing eco-

nomic and industry conditions. We discuss some competitive strategies that can help firms maximize returns in an industry's competitive environment. We demonstrate cash flow models and relative valuation ratios that can be used to identify undervalued stocks. Cash flow and earnings-oriented models are suggested as ways to determine a stock's intrinsic value. We also review factors that will help you determine when to sell a stock that you currently own and discuss the pressures and influences that affect professional stock analysts. We conclude with an example of the analysis of foreign stocks.

This chapter discusses a number of methods used by practicing analysts to estimate intrinsic values.

COMPANY ANALYSIS VERSUS THE SELECTION OF STOCK

This chapter is titled "Company Analysis and Stock Selection" to convey the idea that the common stocks of good companies are not necessarily good investments. As a final step of the analysis, you must compare the intrinsic value of a stock to its market value to determine if it should be purchased. The point is, the stock of a wonderful firm with superior management and strong performance measured by sales and earnings growth can be priced so high that the true value of the stock is below its current market price. In contrast, the stock of a company with less success based on its sales and earnings growth may have a stock market price that is below its intrinsic value. In this case, although the company is not as good, its stock could be the better investment.

The classic confusion in this regard concerns growth companies versus growth stocks. The stock of a growth company is not necessarily a growth stock. Recognition of this difference is important for successful investing.

Growth Companies and Growth Stocks

Growth companies have historically been defined as companies that consistently experience above-average increases in sales and earnings. This definition has some limitations because many firms could qualify due to certain accounting procedures, mergers, or other external events.

In contrast, financial theorists define a growth company as a firm with the management ability and the opportunities to make investments that yield rates of return greater than the firm's required rate of return.[1] You will recall from financial management courses that this required rate of return is the firm's weighted average cost of capital (WACC). As an example, a growth company might be able to acquire capital at an average cost of 10 percent and yet have the management ability and the opportunity to invest those funds at rates of return of 15 to 20 percent. As a result of these investment opportunities, the firm's sales and earnings grow faster than those of similar risk firms and the overall economy. In addition, a growth company that has above-average investment opportunities should, and typically does, retain a large portion of its earnings to fund these superior investment projects.

Growth stocks are not necessarily shares in growth companies. A **growth stock** is a stock with a higher rate of return than other stocks in the market with similar risk characteristics. The stock achieves this superior risk-adjusted rate of return because at some point in time the market undervalued it compared to other stocks. Although the stock

---

[1]Ezra Solomon, *The Theory of Financial Management* (New York: Columbia University Press, 1963), 55–68; and Merton Miller and Franco Modigliani, "Dividend Policy, Growth and the Valuation of Shares," *Journal of Business* 34, no.4 (October 1961): 411–433.

market adjusts stock prices relatively quickly and accurately to reflect new information, available information is not always perfect or complete. Therefore, imperfect or incomplete information may cause a given stock to be undervalued or overvalued at a point in time.[2]

If the stock is undervalued, its price should eventually increase to reflect its true fundamental value when the correct information becomes available. During this period of price adjustment, the stock's realized return will exceed the required return for a stock with its risk, and during this period of adjustment it will be considered a growth stock. Growth stocks are not necessarily limited to growth companies. A future growth stock can be issued by any type of company, the stock need only be undervalued by the market.

The fact is, if investors recognize a growth company and discount its future earnings stream properly, the current market price of the growth company's stock will reflect its future earnings stream. Those who acquire the stock of a growth company at this correct market price will receive a rate of return consistent with the risk of the stock, even when the superior earnings growth is attained. In many instances overeager investors tend to inflate the price of a growth company's stock. Investors who pay the inflated price will earn a rate of return below the risk-adjusted required rate of return, despite the fact that the growth company fulfills its bright prospects. Several studies that have examined the stock price performance for samples of growth companies have found that their stocks performed poorly—that is, the stocks of growth companies have generally *not* been growth stocks.[3]

Defensive Companies and Stocks

Defensive companies are those whose future earnings are likely to withstand an economic downturn. One would expect them to have relatively low business risk and not excessive financial risk. Typical examples are public utilities or grocery chains—firms that supply basic consumer necessities.

There are two closely related concepts of a **defensive stock**. First, a defensive stock's rate of return is not expected to decline during an overall market decline, or decline less than the overall market. Second, our CAPM discussion indicated that an asset's relevant risk is its covariance with the market portfolio of risky assets, that is, an asset's systematic risk. A stock with low or negative systematic risk (a small positive or negative beta) may be considered a defensive stock according to this theory because its returns are unlikely to be harmed significantly in a bear market.

Cyclical Companies and Stocks

A **cyclical company**'s sales and earnings will be heavily influenced by aggregate business activity. Examples would be firms in the steel, auto, or heavy machinery industries. Such companies will do well during economic expansions and poorly during economic contractions. This volatile earnings pattern is typically a function of the firm's business risk and can be compounded by financial risk.

A **cyclical stock** will experience changes in its rates of return greater than changes in overall market rates of return. In terms of the CAPM, these would be stocks that have high

---

[2]An analyst is more likely to find such stocks outside the top tier of companies, because these top-tier stocks are scrutinized by numerous analysts; in other words, look for "neglected" stocks.

[3]Michael Solt and Meir Statman, "Good Companies, Bad Stocks," *Journal of Portfolio Management* 15, no. 4 (Summer 1989): 39–44 and Hersh Shafrin and Meir Statman, "Making Sense of Beta, Size, and Book-to-Market," *Journal of Portfolio Management* 21, no. 2 (Winter 1995): 26–34. Similar results for "excellent" companies are discussed in Michelle Clayman, "In Search of Excellence: The Investor's Viewpoint," *Financial Analysts Journal* 43, no. 3 (May–June 1987): 54–63 and in Michelle Clayman, "Excellence Revisited," *Financial Analysts Journal* 50, no. 3 (May–June 1994): 61–65.

betas. The stock of a cyclical company, however, is not necessarily cyclical. A cyclical stock is the stock of any company that has returns that are more volatile than the over-all market—that is, high-beta stocks.

Speculative Companies and Stocks

A **speculative company** is one whose assets involve great risk, but that also has a possibility of great gain. A good example of a speculative firm is one involved in oil exploration.

A **speculative stock** possesses a high probability of low or negative rates of return and a low probability of normal or high rates of return. Specifically, a speculative stock is one that is overpriced, leading to a high probability that during the future period when the market adjusts the stock price to its true value, it will experience either low or possibly negative rates of return. Such an expectation might be the case for an excellent growth company whose stock is selling at an extremely high price/earnings ratio.

Value versus Growth Investing

Some analysts also divide stocks into "growth" stocks and "value" stocks. As we discussed above, growth stocks are companies that will have positive earnings surprises and above-average risk adjusted rates of return because the stocks are undervalued. If the ana-lyst does a good job in identifying such companies, investors in these stocks will reap the benefits of seeing their stock prices rise after other investors identify their earnings growth potential. **Value stocks** are those that appear to be undervalued for reasons beside earn-ings growth potential. Value stocks are usually identified by analysts as having low P/E ratios or low ratios of price to book value. Cycles appear over time during which value stocks sometimes outperform growth stocks; at other times growth stocks outperform value stocks. Figure 13.1 shows the recent performance of a growth and value stock index for the period 1993–1997. During this period it appears value stocks were the better invest-ment choice.

The major point of this section is that you must examine a company to determine its characteristics and derive an estimate of the value of its stock. Subsequently, you com-pare this derived, intrinsic value of the stock to its current market price to determine whether you should acquire it. Specifically, based on a comparison of the stock's estimated intrinsic value and its market price, will the stock provide a rate of return equal to or greater than what is consistent with its risk?

ECONOMIC, INDUSTRY, AND STRUCTURAL LINKS TO COMPANY ANALYSIS

The analysis of companies and their stocks is the final step in the top-down approach to investing. Rather than selecting stocks on the basis of company-specific factors (as with bottom-up analysis), top-down analysts review the current state and future outlook for domestic and international sectors of the economy. On the basis of this macroeconomic analysis they identify industries that are expected to offer attractive returns in the expected future environment. Following these earlier macro analyses we turn our atten-tion to the process of analyzing firms in the selected industries. Because market inter-est rates are not affected by individual companies, our analysis concentrates on the remaining two determinants of a stock's intrinsic value: growth of the firm's expected cash flows and its risk.

Figure 13.1   *Comparison of the Performance of the Russell 3000 Value and Growth Stock Indexes: 1993–1997*

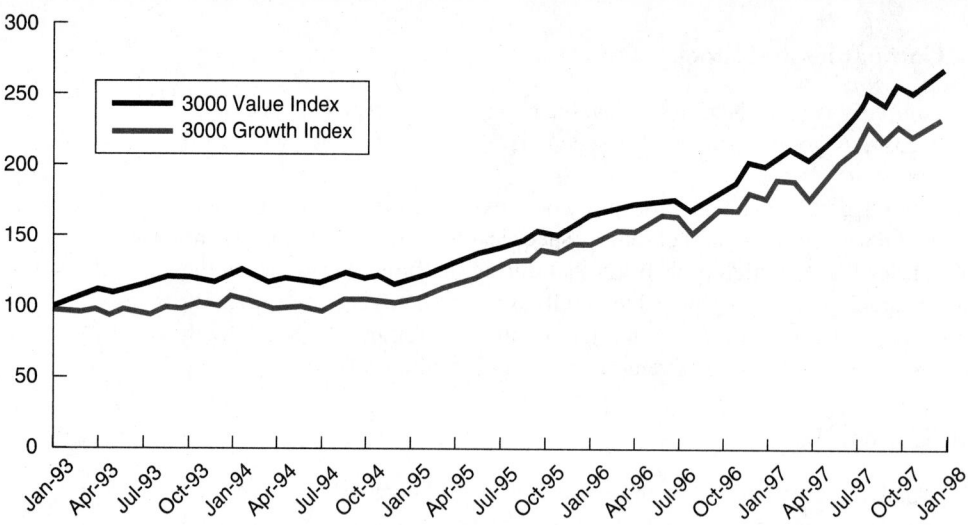

Source: Frank Russell & Co.

Economic and Industry Influences

If economic trends are favorable for an industry, the company analysis should focus on firms in that industry that are well positioned to benefit from the economic trends. For example, the expectation of lower interest rates and economic growth in the European community may be beneficial to such industries as heavy equipment, durable goods and automotive. But for investment purposes the most attractive firms in those industries will be those that already possess strong trading links and customer bases in Europe. In contrast, a firm that derives most of its revenue from U.S. domestic sales may not be as attractive a purchase candidate.

Firms with sales or earnings particularly sensitive to macroeconomic variables should also be considered. For example, although auto sales are related to the business cycle and consumer sentiment, sales of high-margin luxury and sports cars are even more sensitive to these factors. Thus, expectations of rapid economic growth may be beneficial to all auto manufacturers, but especially to those that sell to the high end of the market. If the U.S. dollar is strengthening against European currencies but declining against Pacific Rim currencies, it will benefit U.S. firms that export their goods to Asia rather than those that sell their goods in Europe.

As part of the analysis, research analysts will have to be familiar with the cash flow and risk attributes of the firms they are studying. In times of economic or industry growth, the most attractive candidates for purchase may not be the financially strong market leaders. Rather, the marginal firms in the industry or firms with high levels of operating leverage and financial leverage may benefit substantially. A modest percentage increase in revenue can be magnified into a much larger percentage rise in earnings and cash flow for the highly leveraged firm. The point is that all firms in an industry are not identical. They will have varying sensitivities to economic variables, such as economic growth, interest rates, input costs, and exchange rates, and will have different competitive strategies as we will discuss later. Because each firm is different, an investor must examine each firm to determine the best candidates for purchase under current and expected economic conditions.

Although our discussion has assumed that all firms in an industry will benefit from future economic trends, this is not necessarily the case. Sometimes, although poor economic news implies tough times for an industry, certain firms in that industry may remain attractive investments. Firms that have positioned themselves in anticipation of difficult economic times, or that have a well-diversified international revenue base, may do well while their rivals suffer from an economic recession. Such firms can become attractive when investors become overly pessimistic about an industry's prospects and heavy selling leads to inappropriate stock price declines in the industry.

Structural Influences

In addition to economic variables, other trends such as social trends, technology, and political and regulatory influences can have a major effect on some firms in an industry. Some firms in the industry can try to take advantage of demographic changes, shifts in consumer tastes and life-styles, or invest in technology as part of a strategy to lower costs and better serve their customers. Such firms may be able to grow and succeed despite unfavorable industry or economic conditions. For example, Wal-Mart became the nation's leading retailer in the 1990s because it benefited from smart management. The geographic location of many of its stores allowed it to benefit from rising regional population and lower labor costs. Its strategy that emphasized everyday low prices was appealing to consumers who had become concerned about the price and value of purchases. Wal-Mart's technologically advanced inventory and ordering systems, and the logistics of its distribution system, gave the retailer an advantage over less technically progressive rivals.

During the initial stage of an industry's life cycle the original firms in the industry can refine their technologies and move down the learning curve. Subsequent followers may also benefit from these initial actions. By watching the initial entrants, followers can learn from the leaders' mistakes and take the market lead away from them. Investors need to be aware of such strategies so they can evaluate companies and their stocks accordingly.

Political and regulatory events can create opportunities in an industry even when economic influences appear weak. Deregulation in trucking, airlines, and the financial services industries in the 1980s led to the creation of new companies and innovative strategies that returned continuing value to shareholders. A possible overhaul of the U.S. health care system led to a decline in the stock prices of many drug stocks in 1993, while hospital management stocks rose in value. If the saying "it's always darkest before dawn" has any truth to it, sharp price declines following bad industry news may be a good buying opportunity for investors with good analytical skills and cool heads. Some stocks may deserve lower prices following some political or regulatory events; but if the market also sends down the stock prices of good companies or companies with smaller exposures to the bad news, then an astute analyst may be able to identify buying opportunities of underpriced stocks within an industry.

The bottom line is that, although the economy plays a major role in determining overall market trends, and industry groups display sensitivity to economic variables, other structural changes may counterbalance the economic effects, or company management may be able to minimize the impact of economic events on a company. Analysts who are familiar with industry trends and company strategies can issue well reasoned buy-and-sell recommendations irrespective of the economic forecast. In the next section we review some models and factors that analysts should use when examining companies.

COMPANY ANALYSIS

This section, "Company Analysis," groups various analysis components for discussion. "Firm Competitive Strategies" contains a continuation of the Porter discussion of an industry's

competitive environment, and a later subsection discusses the basic SWOT analysis, where the objective is to articulate a firm's strengths, weaknesses, opportunities and threats. These two analyses should provide a complete understanding of a firm's overall *strategic* approach. Given this background, you are in a position to tackle the fundamental valuation models using the analytical tools provided in Chapter 9, "Analysis of Financial Statement," and Chapter 10, "Introduction to Security Valuation." In the rest of Chapter 13 we discuss estimating intrinsic value by implementing the two valuation approaches: (1) the present value of cash flows, and (2) relative valuation techniques. After applying the several valuation techniques to Walgreens, we discuss the significance of site visits to companies, how to prepare for an interview with management, and suggestions on when an investor should consider selling an asset. We also discuss external factors that can affect analysts' earnings and valuation estimate and decision making. We conclude the chapter with a discussion of unique considerations regarding evaluation of international companies and their stocks.

Firm Competitive Strategies

In describing competition within industries we identified five competitive forces that could affect the competitive structure and profit potential of an industry. They are: (1) current rivalry, (2) threat of new entrants, (3) potential substitutes, (4) bargaining power of suppliers, and (5) bargaining power of buyers. After you have determined the competitive structure of an industry, you should attempt to identify the specific competitive strategy employed by each firm and evaluate these strategies in terms of the overall competitive structure of the industry. As before, the analyst should identify and monitor the key assumptions and variables that affect the firm's attractiveness as a purchase candidate.

A company's competitive strategy can either be *defensive* or *offensive*. A **defensive competitive strategy** involves positioning the firm so that its capabilities provide the best means to deflect the effect of the competitive forces in the industry. Examples may include investing in fixed assets and technology to lower production costs or creating a strong brand image with increased advertising expenditures.

An **offensive competitive strategy** is one in which the firm attempts to use its strengths to affect the competitive forces in the industry and, in so doing, improves the firm's relative position in the industry. For example, Microsoft's domination in personal computer software is due to its ability to preempt rivals and to affiliate early in the product life cycle with IBM by becoming the writer of operating system software for a large portion of the PC market. Similarly, Wal-Mart used its buying power to obtain price concessions from its suppliers. This cost advantage, coupled with a superior delivery system to its stores, allowed Wal-Mart to grow against larger competitors until it became the leading U.S. retailer. Another example would be a firm that expands its scale of production in order to deter potential entrants.

As an investor, you must understand the alternatives available, determine each firm's strategy, judge whether the firm's strategy is reasonable for its industry, and finally, evaluate how successful the firm is in implementing its strategy.

In the following sections, we discuss analyzing a firm's competitive position and strategy. The analyst must decide whether the firm's management is correctly positioning the firm to take advantage of industry and economic conditions. The analyst's opinion about management's decisions should ultimately be reflected in the analyst's estimates of the firm's growth, dividends, earnings, and stock price.

Porter suggests two major competitive strategies: low-cost leadership and differentiation.[4] These two competitive strategies dictate how a firm has decided to cope with the

---

[4]Michael E. Porter, *Competitive Strategy: Techniques for Analyzing Industries and Companies* (New York: The Free Press, 1980); Michael E. Porter, *Competitive Advantage: Creating and Sustaining Superior Performance* (New York: The Free Press, 1985).

five competitive conditions that define an industry's environment. The strategies available and the ways of implementing them differ within each industry.

Low-Cost Strategy

The firm that pursues the low-cost strategy is determined to become *the* low-cost producer and, hence, the cost leader in its industry. Cost advantages vary by industry and might include economies of scale, proprietary technology, or preferential access to raw materials. In order to benefit from cost leadership, the firm must command prices near the industry average, which means that it must differentiate itself about as well as other firms. If the firm discounts price too much, it could erode the superior rates of return available because of its low cost. During the early 1990s, Wal-Mart was considered a low-cost source. The firm achieved this by volume purchasing of merchandise and lower-cost operations. As a result, the firm charged less, but still enjoyed higher profit margins and returns on capital than many of its competitors.

Differentiation Strategy

With the differentiation strategy, a firm seeks to identify itself as unique in its industry in an area that is important to buyers. Again, the possibilities for differentiation vary widely by industry. A company can attempt to differentiate itself based on its distribution system (selling in stores, by mail order, or door-to-door), or some unique marketing approach. A firm employing the differentiation strategy will enjoy above-average rates of return only if the price premium attributable to its differentiation exceeds the extra cost of being unique. Therefore, when you analyze a firm using this strategy, you must determine whether the differentiating factor is truly unique, whether it is sustainable, its cost, and if the price premium derived from the uniqueness is greater than its cost (is the firm experiencing above average rates of return?).

Focusing a Strategy

Whichever strategy it selects, a firm must determine where it will focus this strategy. Specifically, a firm must select segments in the industry and tailor its strategy to serve these specific groups. For example, a low-cost strategy would typically exploit cost advantages for certain segments of the industry, such as being the low-cost producer for the expensive segment of the market. Similarly, a differentiation focus would target the special needs of buyers in specific segments. For example, in the athletic shoe market, companies have attempted to develop shoes for unique sport segments such as tennis, basketball, aerobics, or walkers and hikers, rather than offering only shoes for runners. Firms thought that participants in these activities needed shoes with characteristics different from those desired by joggers. Equally important, they believed that these athletes would be willing to pay a premium for these special shoes. Again, you must ascertain if special possibilities exist, if they are being served by another firm, and if they can be priced to generate abnormal returns to the firm. Table 13.1 details some of Porter's ideas for the skills, resources, and company organizational requirements needed to successfully develop a cost leadership or differentiation strategy.

Next, you must determine which strategy the firm is pursuing and its success. Also, can the strategy be sustained? Further, you should evaluate a firm's competitive strategy over time, because strategies need to change as an industry evolves; different strategies work during different phases of an industry's life cycle. For example, differentiation strategies may work for an industry's firms during the growth stages. When the industry is in the mature stage, firms may try to lower their costs.

Table 13.1   *Skills, Resources, and Organizational Requirements Needed to Successfully Apply Cost Leadership and Differentiation Strategies*

Generic Strategy	Commonly Required Skills and Resources	Common Organizational Requirements
Overall cost leadership	Sustained capital investment and access to capital Process engineering skills Intense supervision of labor Products designed for ease in manufacture Low-cost distribution system	Tight cost control Frequent, detailed control reports Structured organization and responsibilities Incentives based on meeting strict quantitative targets
Differentiation	Strong marketing abilities Product engineering Creative flair Strong capability in basic research Corporate reputation for quality or technological leadership Long tradition in the industry or unique combination of skills drawn from other businesses Strong cooperation from channels	Strong coordination among functions in R&D, product development, and marketing Subjective measurement and incentives instead of quantitative measures Amenities to attract highly skilled labor, scientists, or creative people

Source: Adapted/reprinted with the permission of The Free Press, a division of Simon & Schuster from *Competitive Strategy: Techniques for Analyzing Industries and Competitors* by Michael E. Porter, pp. 40–41. Copyright © 1980 by The Free Press.

Through the analysis process, the analyst identifies what the company does well, what it doesn't do well, and where the firm is vulnerable to the five competitive forces. Some call this process developing a company's "story." This evaluation enables the analyst to determine the outlook and risks facing the firm. In summary, the industry's competitive forces and the firm's strategy for dealing with them is the key to determining the firm's long-run cash flows and risks of doing business.

Another framework for examining a firm's competitive position and its strategy is the SWOT analysis, the subject of the following section.

SWOT Analysis

SWOT analysis involves an examination of a firm's *Strengths*, *Weaknesses*, *Opportunities*, and *Threats*. It should help you evaluate a firm's strategies to exploit its competitive advantages or defend against its weaknesses. Strengths and weaknesses involve identifying the firm's own (internal) abilities, or lack thereof. Opportunities and threats include external situations, such as: competitive forces, discovery and development of new technologies, government regulations, domestic and international economic trends.

The *strengths* of a company give the firm a comparative advantage in the marketplace. Perceived strengths can include good customer service, high-quality products, strong brand image, customer loyalty, innovative R&D, market leadership, or strong financial resources. To remain strengths, they must continue to be developed, maintained, and defended through prudent capital investment policies.

Weaknesses result when competitors have potentially exploitable advantages over the firm. Once weaknesses are identified, the firm can select strategies to mitigate or correct the weaknesses. For example, a firm that is only a domestic producer in a global market can make investments that will allow it to export or produce its product overseas. Another example would be a firm with poor financial resources that would form joint ventures with financially stronger firms.

Opportunities, or environmental factors that favor the firm, can include a growing market for the firm's products, shrinking competition, favorable exchange rate shifts, a financial community that has confidence in the firm's future, or identification of a new market or product segment.

Threats are environmental factors that can hinder the firm in achieving its goals. Examples would include a slowing domestic economy (or sluggish overseas economies for exporters), an increase in industry competition, threats of entry, buyers or suppliers seeking to increase their bargaining power, or new technology that can hurt the industry's position. By recognizing and understanding opportunities and threats, an investor can make informed decisions about how the firm can exploit opportunities and mitigate threats.

Some Lessons from Lynch

Peter Lynch, the former portfolio manager of Fidelity Investments' highly successful Magellan Fund, looks for the following attributes when he analyzes firms.[5]

Favorable Attributes of Firms   The following attributes of firms may result in favorable stock market performance:

1. The firm's product is not faddish; it is one that consumers will continue to purchase over time. Investors should seek long-term investments by trying to recognize value in companies and stocks before others do.
2. The company should have some comparative competitive advantage over its rivals, otherwise its advantage and profits will disappear over time.
3. The firm's industry or product has the potential for market stability, because it has little or no need to innovate, create product improvements, or fear that it may lose a technological advantage. Market stability means less potential for entry. The remaining points imply little need for costly investments or R&D.
4. The firm can benefit from cost reductions, for example a computer manufacturer that uses technology provided by suppliers competing to deliver a faster and less-expensive machine or computer chip.
5. Firms that buy back their shares or have management (insiders) buying shares show that the firm and its insiders are putting their money into the firm.

Categorizing Companies   Lynch recommends placing firms into one of six categories. Firms in each category possess different characteristics, so investors need to focus on different firm attributes to determine if the firm is an attractive investment. The six categories are:

1. *Slow growers.* These firms are at or near the top of the industry or product life cycle. They typically pay a regular dividend due to few attractive internal investments. The investor should focus on potentially profitable new products or markets that will allow the firm to experience rising earnings and dividends.
2. *Stalwart.* Stalwarts are expected to have faster earnings growth, but their consistent growth, priced into the stock price, makes large stock price changes unlikely. Investors should focus on the firm's current P/E ratio versus its historical relationships with the industry and market. Investors also should look for anything that might increase the stalwart's earnings growth rate.
3. *Fast growers.* These are smaller, aggressive firms with high earnings growth potential (say, 20 percent to 25 percent per year). Fast growers don't have to be in a

---

[5]See two of his books: Peter Lynch, *One Up on Wall Street* (New York: Simon & Schuster, 1989); and Peter Lynch, *Beating the Street* (New York: Simon & Schuster, 1993).

fast-growing industry but may achieve growth by building on their competitive advantage and taking market share away from established rivals. These firms are risky because their stock prices tumble at the first sign of negative earnings surprises. Investors need to concentrate on *how the firm will sustain its growth rate.* How does current expansion compare to past growth? How is growth being financed? Is the firm maintaining its cash flow growth?

4. *Cyclicals.* These are firms whose sales and profits rise and fall with the business cycle. Investors need to focus on economic forecasts and the firm's internal conditions.

5. *Turnarounds.* These are firms with internal weaknesses but external opportunities that may allow them to recover from difficult times. Because of typically high leverage and investor pessimism, these firms are risky investments but they can be rewarding. Investors need to study public announcements on the firm's plans to correct its problems. Discussions with the firm's suppliers and customers can provide information about the success of the turnaround plan.

6. *Asset plays.* These are firms with valuable assets that are hidden on the balance sheet. Such assets may include valuable land holdings, film libraries, trademarks, cable TV subscribers, or patents. Investors attempt to value the firm's major divisions on a "stand alone" basis and then compare this intrinsic total value to the firm's per share value in the market.

Investors should make use of research on the competitive forces in an industry, a firm's responses to those forces, SWOT analysis, and Lynch's suggestions.

Remember the Financial Statements

Chapter 9 gave us insight into how we can uncover important information about a firm's cash flows and risk profile from its financial statements. Quarterly financial statements from U.S. firms allow the analyst to keep current on revenues, expenses, earnings, and cash flow trends within the firm. DuPont analysis helps pinpoint why a firm's profitability has changed. Operating performance and risk analysis can determine if the firm's operating and financial position is strengthening or worsening. Footnotes to the financial statements often reveal more useful information than the reported numbers do, including changes in accounting principles.

As noted in Chapter 9, return on assets (ROA) equals the product of the net profit margin and the total asset turnover ratio:

$$\text{ROA} = \frac{\text{Net Income}}{\text{Sales}} \times \frac{\text{Sales}}{\text{Total Assets}}$$

This ratio indicates the firm's strategic success. As noted, firms can have one of two generic strategies: cost leadership or product differentiation. ROA should be rising or keeping pace with the firm's competitors if the firm is successfully pursuing either of these strategies, but how ROA rises will depend on the firm's strategy. ROA should rise with a successful cost leadership strategy because of the firm's increasing operating efficiency. An example is a rising total asset turnover ratio as the firm expands into new markets, increasing its market share, or by using its assets more efficiently.

With a successful product-differentiation strategy, ROA will rise because of a rising profit margin. The firm can charge a premium price for its product, control costs, or dispose of less profitable operations.[6]

[6] Thomas I. Selling and Clyde P Stickney, "The Effects of Business Environment and Strategy on a Firm's Rate of Return on Assets," *Financial Analysts Journal* (January–February 1989): 43–52, 68.

ESTIMATING INTRINSIC VALUE

Now that the analysis of the economy, structural forces, the industry, a company, and its competitors is completed, it is time to estimate the intrinsic value of the firm's common stock. If the intrinsic value estimate exceeds the stock's current market price, the stock should be purchased. If the current market price exceeds our intrinsic value estimate, we should avoid the stock.

As noted in Chapter 10, analysts use two general approaches to valuation. The techniques that serve each of these approaches are listed below:

A. Present value of cash flows
    1. Present value of dividends (DDM)
    2. Present value of free cash flow to equity
    3. Present value of free cash flow

B. Relative valuation techniques
    1. Price/earnings ratio (P/E)
    2. Price/cash flow ratios (P/CF)
    3. Price/book value ratios (P/BV)
    4. Price/sales ratio (P/S)

The remainder of this section contains a brief presentation for each of these techniques as applied to Walgreens. The initial presentation considers the present value of cash flow (PVCF) models. Table 13.2 contains historical data for Walgreens related to variables required for the present value of cash flows models.

Present Value of Dividends

We learned in Chapter 10 that determining the present value of future dividends is a difficult task. Therefore, analysts apply one or more simplifying assumptions to dividend discount models (DDMs). The typical assumption is that the stock's dividends will grow at a constant rate over time. Although unrealistic for fast-growing or cyclical firms, DDMs may be appropriate for some mature slow-growing firms. More complex DDMs exist for more complicated growth forecasts. These include two-stage growth models (a period of fast growth followed by a period of constant growth) and three-stage growth models (a period of fast growth followed by a period of diminishing growth rates followed by a period of constant growth).[7]

For simplicity, we will initially discuss the constant dividend growth model. We saw in Chapter 10 that when dividends grow at a constant rate, a stock's price should equal next year's dividend, D_1, divided by the difference between investors' required rate of return on the stock (k) and the dividend growth rate (g):

$$\text{Intrinsic Value} = D_1 / (k - g)$$

With constant dividend growth, next year's dividend should equal the current dividend, D_0, increased by the constant dividend growth rate: $D_1 = D_0 (1 + g)$. Because the current dividend is known, to estimate intrinsic value we need only estimate two parameters: the dividend growth rate and investors' required rate of return.

---

[7]These were discussed in Chapter 10. For a detailed discussion of growth duration models, see Frank K. Reilly and Keith Brown, *Investment Analysis and Portfolio Management,* 5th ed. (Fort Worth, Tex.: Dryden Press, 1997).

Table 13.2 Input Data for Alternative Present Value of Cash Flow Models
(Dollars in Millions, except per share data)

Year	Dividend Per Share	Net Income	Depreciation Expense	Capital Spending	Change in Working Capital	Principal Repayment	New Debt Issues	FCFE	EBIT	Tax Rate	FCFF	1-Tax Rate	Time
1983	0.04	70.00	25.00	−71.00	−15.00	−3.00	0.00	6.00	146.76	0.45	20.26	0.55	1
1984	0.05	85.00	29.00	−68.00	−56.00	−3.00	0.00	−13.00	181.04	0.45	5.45	0.55	2
1985	0.06	94.00	34.00	−97.00	−61.00	−3.00	20.00	−13.00	209.33	0.46	−10.91	0.54	3
1986	0.06	103.00	44.00	−156.00	−72.00	−5.00	92.00	6.00	229.27	0.45	−57.17	0.55	4
1987	0.07	104.00	54.00	−122.00	−118.00	−4.00	5.00	−81.00	242.53	0.46	−55.98	0.54	5
1988	0.08	129.00	59.00	−114.00	49.00	−4.00	31.00	150.00	262.81	0.38	156.21	0.62	6
1989	0.09	154.00	64.00	−121.00	−97.00	−4.00	0.00	−4.00	300.78	0.37	35.84	0.63	7
1990	0.10	175.00	70.00	−192.00	−69.00	−4.00	0.00	−20.00	343.72	0.38	23.06	0.62	8
1991	0.12	195.00	84.00	−202.00	−129.00	−24.00	0.00	−76.00	381.32	0.38	−8.68	0.63	9
1992	0.13	221.00	92.00	−145.00	−32.00	−6.00	0.00	130.00	428.92	0.37	183.53	0.63	10
1993	0.15	245.00	105.00	−185.00	−28.00	−112.00	0.00	25.00	483.18	0.39	188.69	0.61	11
1994	0.17	282.00	118.00	−290.00	−58.00	−6.00	0.00	46.00	550.42	0.38	108.90	0.62	12
1995	0.20	321.00	132.00	−310.00	−104.00	−7.00	0.00	32.00	628.63	0.39	103.10	0.61	13
1996	0.22	372.00	147.00	−364.00	−116.00	0.00	2.00	41.00	724.83	0.39	111.21	0.61	14
1997	0.24	436.00	164.00	−485.00	34.00	−1.00	0.00	148.00	842.37	0.39	228.83	0.61	15

	Dividend Per Share						FCFE	EBIT		FCFF	
Annual Compound Growth Rate 83-97	13.65%						25.73%			18.90%	
Annual Compound Growth Rate 87-97	13.11%						6.60%	13.25%		21.00%	
Compound Sales Growth Rate 87-97	12.05%										
Compound Book Value per Share Growth Rate 87-97	14.34%										
ROE	19.00%										
Cost of Equity	11.00%										

Growth Rate Estimates   If the stock has had fairly constant dividend growth over the past five to ten years, one estimate of the constant growth rate is to use the actual growth of dividends over this time period. The average compound rate of growth is found by computing

$$\text{Average Dividend Growth Rate} = \sqrt[n]{\frac{D_n}{D_0}} - 1$$

In the case of Walgreens, the 1987 dividend (D_0) was $0.07 a share and the 1997 dividend (D_{10}) was $0.24 a share. The average dividend growth rate was

$$\sqrt[10]{\frac{\$0.24}{\$0.07}} - 1 = 0.1311.$$

or 13.11 percent. Clearly, it is inappropriate to blindly plug historical growth rates into our formulas because if we do, we've wasted our time analyzing economic, structural, industry, and company influences. Our analysis may have indicated that growth is expected to increase or decrease due to factors such as changes in government programs, demographic shifts, or changes in product mix. The historical growth rate may need to be raised or lowered to incorporate our prior findings.

In Chapter 9, we learned other ways to compute growth. The sustainable growth rate

$$RR \times ROE$$

assumes the firm will maintain a constant debt/equity ratio as it finances asset growth. We know that ROA can be expressed as the product of the firm's net profit margin and total asset turnover; ROE is the product of the net profit margin, total asset turnover, and the financial leverage multiplier. Thus, a firm's future growth rate and its components can be compared to its competitors, its industry, and the market. Although there is not necessarily a close relationship between the year-to-year growth in a firm's assets and its dividend cash flows, these calculations provide insight that, along with the rest of the top-down analysis, can assist the analyst in determining whether dividend growth may rise or fall in the future. For Walgreen, the sustainable growth rate calculation using 1997 data is[8]

$$g = RR \times ROE = 0.73 \times .198$$
$$= .1445 = 14.45\%$$

The dividend growth rate will be influenced by the age of the industry life cycle, structural changes, and economic trends. Economic–industry–firm analysis provides valuable information regarding future trends in dividend growth. Analysts who ask questions during interviews about management's plans to expand the firm, diversify into new areas, or change dividend policy can gather useful information about the firm's dividend policy. Averaging the historical growth rate of dividends (13.11 percent) and the implied sustainable growth estimate above of 14.45 percent, indicates a value of 13.78 percent. For simplicity we will use 14 percent for the estimated g.

Required Rate of Return Estimate   We know an investor's required rate of return has two basic components: the nominal risk-free interest rate and a risk premium. If the

---

[8]This sustainable growth rate value differs from the one in Chapter 9 because this calculation uses year-end values for ROE, while in Chapter 9 the equity value is an average of the beginning and ending values.

A WORD FROM THE STREET

BY ROY D. BURRY, CFA

 Investment decision making based primarily on individual company fundamentals combines an in-depth analysis of those critical variables driving the firm's stock and their comparison to the consensus views currently determining market price. Most often, the primary critical variable is anticipated earnings per share performance and expected growth. However, a host of other factors can also play important roles in consensus formation. These include dividend yield, financial condition, business risk, and numerous exogenous factors that affect a company beyond the firm's financial statements.

The low cost of portfolio indexing and the high cost of fundamental analysis performed on individual companies and industries require the security analyst to isolate those instances where the consensus presently determining market price is incorrect. The analyst, therefore, must not research an individual company and its stock in isolation but relative to generally held expectations that determine the valuations accorded the equities of well-researched concerns. This speaks to the competitive nature of the investment process, especially the analysis of companies and stocks, wherein the objective is to uncover mispriced securities that will provide excess risk-adjusted rates of return. It is this objective that represents the overriding justification for fundamental research.

Roy D. Burry, CFA, is currently with Oppenheimer & Co., Inc. Consistently ranked highly on the *Institutional Investor* All-American Research Team and in the Greenwich Research Associates survey, he has followed nine consumer-related industries and currently covers the beverage and tobacco groups. He is a member of the New York Society of Security Analysts, the Consumer Analysts Group, the Financial Analysts Federation, and was a member of the Council of Examiners that prepares the CFA Exam.

market is efficient, over time the return earned by investors should compensate them for the risk of the investment.

Notably, we must estimate *future* risk premiums to determine the stock's current intrinsic value. Estimates of the nominal risk-free interest rate are available from the initial analysis of the economy during the top-down approach. The risk premium of the firm must rely on other information derived from the top-down company analysis, including evaluation of the financial statements and capital market relationships.

In Chapter 9, we examined ratios that measure several aspects of the risk of a firm and its stock. Business risk, financial risk, liquidity risk, exchange rate risk, and country risk are types of risk to be reviewed in the context of our economy–industry–firm analysis. These measures can be compared against the firm's major competitors, its industry, and the overall market. This comparison will tell the analyst if the firm should have a higher or lower risk premium than other firms in the industry, the overall market, or the firm's historical risk premium. Accounting-based risk measures use historical data, whereas investment analysis requires an estimate of the future. Investors need to incorporate into the risk analysis any information uncovered during the top-down process that would lead to higher or lower risk estimates.

For a market-based risk estimate, the firm's characteristic line is estimated by regressing market returns on the stock's returns. We know the slope of this regression line is the stock's beta, or measure of systematic risk. Estimates of next year's risk-free rate and market return and an estimate of the stock's beta help estimate next year's required rate of return:

$$R_{stock} = E(RFR) + \beta_{stock}[E(R_{market}) - E(RFR)]$$

Again, this estimate of beta begins with historical market information. Because beta is affected by changes in a firm's business and financial risks, as well as other influences,

an investor should increase or lower the historical beta estimate based upon an analysis of the firm's future.

To demonstrate the estimate of the required rate of return equation for Walgreens we make several assumptions regarding components of the security market line (SML) discussed in Chapter 7. First is the prevailing nominal risk-free rate (RFR), which is estimated at about 6.5 percent—the current yield to maturity for the intermediate-term government bond. The expected equity market rate of return (R_{MKt}) depends on the expected market risk premium on stocks. There is substantial controversy on the appropriate estimate for the equity market risk premium—that is, the estimates range from a high of about 8 percent (the arithmetic mean of the actual risk premium since 1926) to a low of about 3 percent, which is the risk premium suggested in several academic studies. The authors reject both of these extreme values and suggest using a 5 percent risk premium (.05) The final estimate is the firm's systematic risk value (beta), which is typically derived based upon the following regression model (the characteristic line) noted in Chapter 7.

$$R_{WAG} = \alpha + \beta_{WAG} R_{Mkt}$$

where:

R_{WAG} = **Monthly rate of return for Walgreens**
α = **constant term**
β_{WAG} = **Beta coefficient for Walgreens**
  equal to $\dfrac{Cov_{W,m}}{\sigma_m^2}$

R_{Mkt} = **Monthly rate of returns for a market proxy—typically the S&P 500 Index**

When this regression was run using monthly rates of return during the five-year period 1993–1997 (sixty observations), the beta coefficient was estimated at 0.90.

Putting together the RFR of .065 and the market risk premium of .05 implies an expected market return (R_{Mkt}) of .115. This combined with the Walgreens beta of 0.90 indicates the following expected rate of return for Walgreens:

$$
\begin{aligned}
E(R) &= RFR + \beta_i(R_{Mkt} - RFR) \\
&= .065 + 0.90(.115 - .065) \\
&= .065 + 0.90 (.05) \\
&= .065 + .045 \\
&= .11 = 11.0\%
\end{aligned}
$$

The Present Value of Dividends Model (DDM)   At this point, the analyst would face a problem: the intent was to use the basic DDM that assumed a constant growth rate for an infinite period. You will recall that the model also required that k > g (the required rate of return is larger than the expected growth rate), which is not true in this case because k = 11 percent and g = 14 percent (see Table 13.2). Therefore, the analyst must employ a two- or three-stage growth model. Because of the fairly large difference in the current growth rate of 14 percent and the long-run constant growth rate of 8 percent, it seems reasonable to use a three-stage model that includes a gradual transition period. We assume that the growth periods are as follows:

g_1 = **five years (growing at 14 percent a year)**
g_2 = **six years (during this period it is assumed that the growth rate declines 1 percent per year for six years)**

Therefore, beginning with 1997, when dividends were $0.24, the future dividend payments will be as follows (the growth rate is in parenthesis):

High-Growth Period		Declining-Growth Period	
1998 (14%)	0.27	2003 (13%)	0.52
1999 (14%)	0.31	2004 (12%)	0.58
2000 (14%)	0.36	2005 (11%)	0.65
2001 (14%)	0.41	2006 (10%)	0.71
2002 (14%)	0.46	2007 (9%)	0.78
		2008 (8%)	0.84

Constant Growth Period:

$$P_{2008} = \frac{0.84(1 + .08)}{.11 - .08} = \frac{0.91}{.03} = \$30.33$$

The total value of the stock is the sum of the three present value streams discounted at 11 percent:

1. Present value of high-growth period	$ 1.30
2. Present value of declining-growth period	1.66
3. Present value of constant-growth period	9.62
Total Present Value of Dividends	$12.58

The estimated value based on the DDM is substantially lower than the market price in mid-1998 of about $40.00. This estimated value also implies a low P/E ratio based upon expected earnings in 1999 of about $1.18 per share (that is, about 10.7 times earnings) compared to the prevailing market P/E of more than 22 times 1999 earnings. In a subsequent section on relative valuation techniques, we compare the Walgreens P/E ratio to that of its industry and the market.

Present Value of Free Cash Flow to Equity   As noted in Chapter 10, this technique resembles a present value of earnings concept except that it considers the capital expenditures required to maintain and grow the firm and the change in working capital required for a growing firm (that is, an increase in accounts receivable and inventory). The specific definition of free cash flow to equity (FCFE) is:

Net Income + Depreciation Expense − Capital
Expenditures − Δ in Working Capital − Principal
Debt Repayments + New Debt Issues

This technique attempts to determine the free cash flow that is available to the stockholders after payments to all other capital suppliers and after providing for the continued growth of the firm. As noted in Chapter 10, given the current FCFE values, the alternative forms of the model are similar to those available for the DDM, which in turn depends on the firm's growth prospects. Specifically, if the firm is in its mature constant growth phase, it is possible to use a model similar to the reduced form DDM:

$$Value = \frac{FCFE_1}{k - g_{FCFE}}$$

where:

$FCFE_1$ = **the expected free cash flow to equity in period 1**
  k = **the required rate of return on equity for the firm**
  g_{FCFE} = **the expected constant growth rate of free cash flow to equity for the firm**

We already know from the prior dividend model that the firm's earnings are growing at a rate (about 14 percent) that exceeds the required rate of return. In the case of FCFE, it is necessary to consider the effect of capital expenditures relative to depreciation and changes in working capital as well as debt repayments and new-debt issues. The historical data in Table 13.2 shows that the FCFE series has had a volatile history with a growth rate exceeding 20 percent during the fourteen-year period. Such volatility makes it appropriate to use a more conservative 14 percent growth rate consistent with the growth of Walgreens sales and book value. Therefore, the following example again uses a three-stage growth model with characteristics similar to the dividend growth model.

g_1 = 14 percent for five years
g_2 = a constantly declining growth rate to 8 percent over six years
k = 11 percent cost of equity

The specific estimate of annual FCFE in $ million beginning with the actual 1997 value of $148 million are as follows:

High Growth		Declining Growth	
1998 (14%)	$169	2003 (13%)	$322
1999 (14%)	192	2004 (12%)	361
2000 (14%)	219	2005 (11%)	400
2001 (14%)	250	2006 (10%)	440
2002 (14%)	285	2007 (9%)	480
		2008 (8%)	518

$$\text{Constant Growth Period Value} = \frac{560}{.11 - .08} = \$18{,}667$$

The total value of the stock is the sum of the three present value streams discounted at 11 percent:

	($Mil)
1. Present value of high-growth cash flows	$ 802
2. Present value of declining-growth cash flows	1,025
3. Present value of constant-growth cash flows	5,923
Total present value of FCFE	$7,750

The outstanding shares in 1998 were approximately 494 million. Therefore, the per share value based upon the present value of FCFE is $15.69. Again, this estimated value is substantially lower than the prevailing market price of about $40. This value implies a P/E ratio of about 13.3 times estimated 1999 earnings of $1.18 per share.

Present Value of Operating Free Cash Flow   This is also referred to as *free cash flow to the firm* by Damodaran and *the entity DCF model* by Copeland, Koller, and Murrin.[9] The object is to determine a value for the total firm and subtract the value of the firm's debt obligations to arrive at a value for the firm's equity. Notably, in this valuation technique, we discount the firm's operating free cash flow to the firm (FCFF) at the firm's weighted average cost of capital (WACC) rather than its cost of equity.

---

[9]Aswath Damodaran, *Damodaran on Valuation* (New York: Wiley, 1994), Chapter 8, and Tom Copeland, Tim Koller, and Jack Murrin, *Valuation: Measuring and Managing the Value of Companies,* 2nd ed. (New York: Wiley, 1996), Chapter 5.

Operating free cash flow or *free cash flow to the firm* is equal to

$$\text{EBIT} (1 - \text{Tax Rate}) + \text{Depreciation Expense}$$
$$- \text{Capital Spending} - \Delta \text{ in Working Capital}$$
$$- \Delta \text{ in other assets}$$

This is the cash flow generated by a company's operations and available to all who have provided capital to the firm—both equity and debt. As noted, because it is the cash flow from *all capital suppliers,* it is discounted at the firm's WACC.

Again, the alternative specifications of this operating FCF model are similar to the DDM—that is, the specification depends upon the firm's growth prospects. Assuming an expectation of constant growth, you can use the reduced-form model

$$\textit{Firm Value} = \frac{FCFF_1}{WACC - g_{FCFF}} \text{ or } \frac{Oper.\,FCF_1}{WACC - g_{OFCF}}$$

where:

$FCFF_1$ = **the free cash flow for the firm in period 1**
Oper. FCF_1 = **the firm's operating free cash flow in period 1**
WACC = the firm's weighted average cost of capital
g_{FCFF} = **the constant growth rate of free cash flow for the firm**
g_{OFCF} = **the constant growth rate of operating free cash flow.**

As noted in Table 13.2, the compound annual growth rate for operating free cash flow (also referred to as free cash flow to the firm) during the fourteen-year period was 18.90%. An alternative measure of growth is the growth implied by the equation:

$$g = (RR)(ROIC)$$

where:

RR = the average retention rate
ROIC = EBIT (1 − Tax Rate) /Total Capital

For Walgreens, the recent retention rate is about 73 percent and the ROIC is equal to

$$ROIC = \frac{EBIT(1 - Tax\,Rate)}{Total\,Capital} = \frac{514}{2,800} = .1836\%$$
$$= 18.36\%$$

Therefore,

$$g = (.73)(.1836)$$
$$= .1340 = 13.40\%$$

The average of the two growth estimates (18.90% and 13.40%) is 16.15%. In the subsequent valuation calculation we will begin with a consecutive growth estimate for FCFF of 15%. The firm's weighted average cost of capital (WACC) is

$$WACC = W_E k + W_D i$$

where:

W_E = **the proportion of equity in total capital**
k = the after-tax cost of equity (from the SML)

W_D = the proportion of debt in total capital[10]
   i = the after-tax cost of debt[11]

For Walgreens,

$$W_E = 70; k = .11; W_D = 30\%; i = (.07)(1 - .39)$$
$$= .043$$

Thus,

$$\text{WACC} = (.70)(.11) + (.30)(.043)$$
$$= .077 + .013 = .09 = 9\%$$

Again, because the expected growth rate of operating free cash flow is greater than the firm's WACC, we cannot use the reduced-form model that assumes constant growth at this relatively high rate for an infinite period. Therefore, the following demonstration will employ the three-stage growth model with growth duration assumptions similar to the prior examples.

Given these inputs for recent growth and the firm's WACC, the growth estimates for a three-stage growth model are

g_1 = **15 percent for five years**
g_2 = **a constantly declining rate to 7 percent over six years.**[12]

The specific estimates for future operating FCF (or FCFF) are as follows beginning from the 1997 value of $229 million.

High-Growth Periods		P.V. at 9%	Declining-Growth Periods		P.V. at 9%
1998	$263	$ 241	2003	$524	$ 312
1999	303	255	2004	589	322
2000	348	269	2005	654	328
2001	401	284	2006	717	330
2002	461	300	2007	777	328
		$1,349	2008	831	332
					$1,942

$$Constant\ Growth = \frac{Oper.\ FCF_{2009}}{.09 - .07} = \frac{889}{.02} = \$44,450$$

Thus, the total value of the firm is:

	($Mil)
1. Present value of high-growth cash flows	$1,349
2. Present value of declining-growth cash flows	1,942
3. Present value of constant-growth cash flows	17,224
Total present value of operating FCF	$20,515

---

[10]The proportion of debt capital used in the WACC estimate is based on book value weights that consider the value of capitalized lease payments as debt.

[11]For this estimate we use the prevailing interest rate on corporate AA-rated bonds (7%), and Walgreens' recent tax rate of 39%.

[12]This 7% long-run growth rate assumption implies that we do not believe that FCFF can grow as fast as FCFE. Given a beginning growth rate of 15% and a long-run rate of 7% means that the growth rate will decline by .0133 per year.

Recall that the value of equity is the total value of the firm (PV of operating FCF) minus the current market value of debt, which is the present value of debt payments at the firm's cost of debt (.07). The values are as follows:

Total present value of operating FCF	$20,515
Minus: value of debt*	4,110
value of equity	16,405
Number of common shares	494 million
Value of equity per share	33.21

Again, this estimated value compares to the recent market value of about forty dollars. The $33.21 value implies a P/E of about 28 times estimated 1999 earnings of $1.18 per share.

To summarize, the valuations derived from the present value of cash flow techniques are as follows:

Present value of dividends	$12.58
Present value of FCFE	$15.69
Present value of operating FCF (Also, the PV of FCFF)	$33.21

All of these prices must be compared to the prevailing market price of forty dollars to determine the investment decision.

Relative Valuation Techniques

In this section, we present the data required to compute the several relative valuation ratios and demonstrate the use of these relative valuation techniques for Walgreens compared to the retail drugstore industry and the S&P 400 industrial index.

Table 13.3 contains the basic data required to compute the relative valuation ratios, and Table 13.4 contains the four sets of relative valuation ratios for Walgreens, its industry, and the aggregate market. This table also contains a comparison of the company ratios to similar ratios for the company's industry and the market. Such a comparison helps the analyst determine change in the relative valuation ratio over time and consider if the current valuation ratio for the company (Walgreens) is reasonable based on the financial characteristics of the firm versus its industry and the market. To aid in the analysis, four graphs contain the time series of the relative valuation ratios for the company, its industry, and the market. Four additional graphs show the relationship between the relative valuation ratios: for the company compared to its industry, and for the company compared to the stock market.

Price-Earnings Ratio

This is the most widely used and well-documented relative valuation ratio. We saw in Chapter 10 that the P/E ratio can be derived from the DDM as follows:

$$P/E_1 = \frac{D_1/E_1}{k - g}$$

---

*This includes the present value of minimum lease payments discounted at the firm's cost of debt (7 percent).

Table 13.3 Inputs for Relative Valuation Techniques: Walgreens, Retail Drugstore, S&P 400 Index 1977–1996

	Walgreens					Retail Drugstore					S&P 400 Index				
Year	Mean Price	EPS	Cash Flow P/S	Book Value P/S	Sales P/S	Mean Price	EPS	Cash Flow P/S	Book Value P/S	Sales P/S	Mean Price	EPS	Cash Flow P/S	Book Value P/S	Sales P/S
1977	0.52	0.07	0.06	0.33	3.84	18.93	1.79	2.20	9.35	43.99	109.40	11.45	19.94	82.21	224.24
1978	0.73	0.10	0.08	0.36	4.34	22.20	2.01	2.50	10.93	49.87	107.12	13.04	22.65	89.34	251.32
1979	0.92	0.14	0.10	0.41	4.93	22.38	2.55	3.26	13.95	73.39	115.79	16.29	27.06	98.71	292.38
1980	1.06	0.16	0.11	0.46	6.18	24.57	2.94	3.78	16.11	84.82	136.03	16.12	28.45	108.33	327.36
1981	1.46	0.18	0.13	0.53	7.03	34.62	3.29	4.31	18.45	95.50	141.48	16.74	30.52	116.06	344.31
1982	2.52	0.23	0.32	1.23	7.76	41.58	3.76	4.79	20.74	109.22	136.87	13.20	28.46	118.60	333.86
1983	4.15	0.29	0.58	2.15	9.53	56.70	4.50	5.90	23.34	118.85	174.90	14.77	30.41	122.32	334.07
1984	4.61	0.33	0.45	1.69	11.07	58.30	4.10	5.81	24.21	135.15	179.62	18.11	34.40	123.99	379.70
1985	6.47	0.38	0.52	1.96	12.76	68.28	4.22	6.24	26.82	153.30	208.99	15.28	33.44	125.89	398.42
1986	8.69	0.42	0.65	2.45	14.80	83.78	4.90	6.99	27.73	157.74	253.83	14.53	33.91	124.87	387.76
1987	8.74	0.42	0.64	2.54	17.28	98.93	5.53	8.16	30.79	191.72	324.30	20.28	40.46	134.19	430.35
1988	8.13	0.52	0.77	2.92	19.70	93.05	6.30	9.40	34.25	217.80	302.63	26.59	50.13	139.50	486.92
1989	10.00	0.63	0.90	3.33	21.71	107.46	6.69	10.07	38.31	239.68	364.58	26.83	50.02	145.34	541.38
1990	11.63	0.71	1.03	3.98	24.40	114.53	7.67	11.82	43.65	265.77	392.12	24.77	51.04	152.71	594.55
1991	15.88	0.79	1.14	4.39	27.18	139.70	8.26	12.29	50.94	283.50	428.81	16.91	44.41	157.05	586.86
1992	18.75	0.89	1.56	5.01	30.16	159.62	8.96	13.34	56.97	309.78	493.33	19.05	48.50	142.46	601.39
1993	19.82	0.90	1.75	5.60	33.47	162.19	7.09	11.84	60.04	329.20	520.21	21.93	50.61	136.91	603.62
1994	20.24	1.14	2.00	6.39	37.26	162.67	10.51	15.83	63.62	363.71	536.52	32.83	62.43	150.70	626.26
1995	26.55	1.30	2.26	7.28	41.94	215.26	11.76	17.77	68.93	413.52	638.97	35.44	68.51	163.94	676.62
1996	36.38	1.50	2.59	8.30	47.40	283.01	13.92	18.82	71.26	434.15	795.01	41.15	77.56	168.04	701.91
Mean	10.36	0.56	0.88	3.07	19.14	98.39	6.04	8.76	35.52	203.53	318.03	20.77	41.65	130.06	456.16

P/S = per share

Table 13.4 Relative Valuation Variables: Walgreens, Retail Drugstore, S&P 400 Index 1977–1996

Year	Price/Earnings Ratio					Price/Cash Flow Ratio					Price/Book Value					Price/Sales Ratio				
	Walgreens	Retail Drug	Ratio Co/Ind	S&P 400	Ratio Co/Mkt	Walgreens	Retail Drug	Ratio Co/Ind	S&P 400	Ratio Co/Mkt	Walgreens	Retail Drug	Ratio Co/Ind	S&P 400	Ratio Co/Mkt	Walgreens	Retail Drug	Ratio Co/Ind	S&P 400	Ratio Co/Mkt
1977	7.17	10.58	0.68	9.55	0.75	8.97	8.60	1.04	5.49	1.63	1.57	2.02	0.78	1.33	1.18	0.14	0.43	0.31	0.49	0.28
1978	7.07	11.05	0.64	8.21	0.86	9.08	8.88	1.02	4.73	1.92	2.02	2.03	0.99	1.20	1.68	0.17	0.45	0.38	0.43	0.39
1979	6.50	8.78	0.74	7.11	0.91	9.46	6.87	1.38	4.28	2.21	2.25	1.60	1.40	1.17	1.92	0.19	0.30	0.61	0.40	0.47
1980	6.60	8.36	0.79	8.44	0.78	9.61	6.50	1.48	4.78	2.01	2.27	1.53	1.49	1.26	1.81	0.17	0.29	0.59	0.42	0.41
1981	8.27	10.52	0.79	8.45	0.98	11.64	8.03	1.45	4.64	2.51	2.75	1.88	1.46	1.22	2.25	0.21	0.36	0.57	0.41	0.51
1982	10.85	11.06	0.98	10.37	1.05	8.00	8.68	0.92	4.81	1.66	2.06	2.00	1.03	1.15	1.78	0.32	0.38	0.85	0.41	0.79
1983	14.56	12.60	1.16	11.84	1.23	7.18	9.61	0.75	5.75	1.25	1.93	2.43	0.79	1.43	1.35	0.44	0.48	0.91	0.52	0.83
1984	13.86	14.22	0.97	9.92	1.40	10.26	10.03	1.02	5.22	1.97	2.73	2.31	1.18	1.45	1.89	0.42	0.43	0.97	0.47	0.88
1985	16.91	16.18	1.05	13.68	1.24	12.32	10.94	1.13	6.25	1.97	3.30	2.55	1.30	1.66	1.99	0.51	0.45	1.14	0.52	0.97
1986	20.68	17.10	1.21	17.42	1.19	13.28	11.99	1.11	7.49	1.77	3.54	3.02	1.17	2.03	1.74	0.59	0.53	1.11	0.65	0.90
1987	20.80	17.89	1.16	20.68	1.01	13.60	12.12	1.12	8.02	1.70	3.44	3.21	1.07	2.42	1.42	0.51	0.52	0.98	0.75	0.67
1988	15.63	14.77	1.06	11.35	1.38	10.54	9.90	1.06	6.04	1.75	2.78	2.72	1.03	2.17	1.28	0.41	0.43	0.97	0.62	0.66
1989	15.87	16.06	0.99	13.79	1.15	11.15	10.67	1.04	7.29	1.53	3.00	2.81	1.07	2.51	1.20	0.46	0.45	1.03	0.67	0.68
1990	16.37	14.93	1.10	15.83	1.03	11.31	9.69	1.17	7.68	1.47	2.92	2.62	1.11	2.57	1.14	0.48	0.43	1.11	0.66	0.72
1991	20.09	16.91	1.19	25.65	0.79	13.98	11.37	1.23	9.66	1.45	3.61	2.74	1.32	2.73	1.32	0.58	0.49	1.19	0.73	0.80
1992	21.07	17.81	1.18	25.90	0.81	11.90	11.97	1.00	10.17	1.18	3.74	2.80	1.34	3.46	1.08	0.62	0.52	1.21	0.82	0.76
1993	22.02	22.88	0.96	23.72	0.93	11.32	13.70	0.83	10.28	1.10	3.54	2.70	1.31	3.80	0.93	0.59	0.49	1.20	0.86	0.69
1994	17.75	15.48	1.15	16.21	1.10	10.12	10.28	0.98	8.47	1.19	3.17	2.56	1.24	3.55	0.89	0.54	0.45	1.21	0.86	0.63
1995	20.42	18.15	1.13	17.50	1.17	11.75	12.11	0.97	9.33	1.26	3.65	3.12	1.17	3.90	0.94	0.63	0.52	1.22	0.94	0.67
1996	24.25	20.33	1.19	19.32	1.26	14.05	15.04	0.93	10.25	1.37	4.38	3.97	1.10	4.73	0.93	0.77	0.65	1.18	1.13	0.68
Mean	15.34	14.78	1.01	14.75	1.05	10.98	10.35	1.08	7.03	1.64	2.93	2.53	1.17	2.29	1.44	0.44	0.45	0.94	0.64	0.67

Figure 13.2 *Time-Series Plot of Mean Price/Earnings Ratios for Walgreens, RSD Industry, and S&P 400*

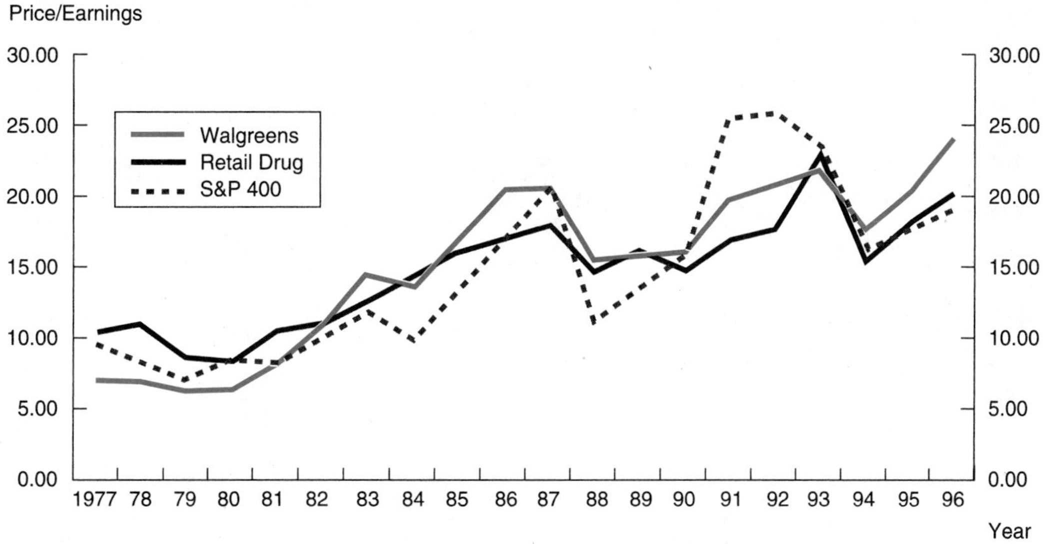

This formulation indicates that the P/E ratio is affected by two major variables:

1. the firm's required rate of return on its equity (k)
2. the firm's expected growth rate of dividends (g).

Therefore, the object of the analysis is to relate the firm's risk and expected growth to that of its industry and the market and determine if the firm's earnings multiple should be less than or greater than its industry and the market multiple.

Figure 13.2 contains the three time-series of P/E multiples for 1977–96. The P/E ratio used is equal to the mean price during Year t (the mean price equals the average of the high and low price during the year), divided by the earnings per share during Year t. This is referred to as the historical P/E ratio. All three series show an overall rising trend beginning at about ten times earnings and ending at over twenty times earnings. Notably, Walgreens' P/E ratio was initially below its industry and the market, but was above both series at the end in 1996. Specifically, as shown in Figure 13.3, the Co/Ind ratio of P/E ratios went from about 0.68 (that is, Walgreens' P/E was about 70 percent of the value of the industry P/E) to about 1.19 (Walgreens' P/E ratio was about 19 percent greater than the industry P/E ratio). Similarly, the Co/Mkt ratio of P/Es went from about 0.75 to 1.26. The question an analyst must ask is whether Walgreens' relative risk and its expected growth rate justifies this premium P/E ratio.

Price/Cash Flow Ratio

As noted in Chapter 10, the price/cash flow ratio has grown in prominence and use because many observers contend that a firm's cash flow is less subject to manipulation than its earnings per share and because cash flows are widely used in the present value of cash flow models discussed earlier. An important question is, which of the several cash flow specifications should an analyst employ? In this analysis, we use the "traditional" cash flow measure equal to net income plus the major noncash expense (depreciation) because

Figure 13.3 *Time-Series Plot of Relative Price/Earnings Ratios for Walgreens/Industry and Walgreens/Market*

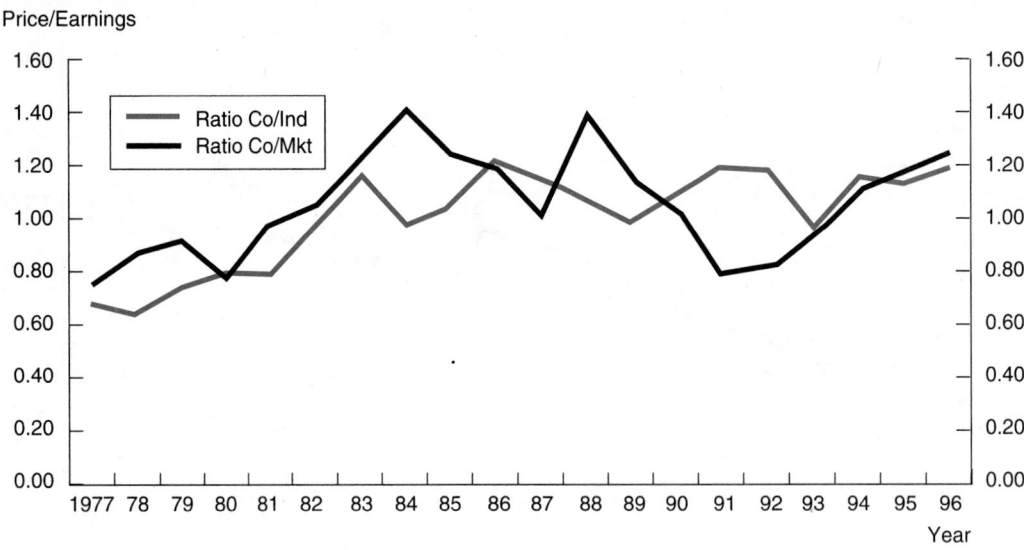

this cash flow measure can be derived for both the retail drugstore industry and the market. Although it is certainly possible to employ any of the other cash flow measures discussed, a demonstration using this measure should provide a valid comparison for learning purposes.

The time-series graph of the P/CF ratios in Figure 13.4 show a general increase for Walgreens and its industry from about 9 times in 1977 to almost 15 times in 1996, while the market P/CF ratio went from 6 times to 11 times. Notably, although the absolute values of the ratios increased, the graphs in Figure 13.5 show that Walgreens P/CF ratios relative to its industry experienced an overall decline from 1.04 and a high of 1.48 to an ending relative ratio of 0.93. Similarly, the Co/Mkt comparison started at 1.63, reached a high of 2.50 and ended at 1.37. This indicates an overall increase in the P/CF ratio, but a *decline* in the P/CF ratio relative to the firms' industry and the overall market. In this case, the question becomes what has happened to the firm's growth rate of cash flow and the risk of these cash flows that would justify this decline in the relative P/CF ratio.

Price/Book Value Ratio

The price-to-book value ratio (P/BV) has gained prominence because of the studies by Fama and French and several subsequent authors.[13] The rationale is that book value can be a reasonable measure of value for firms. Also, individual firms that have consistent accounting practice (for example, firms in the same industry), can be meaningfully compared. Notably, this measure can apply to firms with negative earnings or even negative cash flows. You should not attempt to compare this ratio for firms with different levels of hard assets—that is, don't compare a heavy industrial firm to a service firm.

[13]Eugene F. Fama and Kenneth R. French, "The Cross Section of Expected Stock Returns," *Journal of Finance* 47, no. 2 (June 1992): 427–450; Barr Rosenberg, Kenneth Raid, and Ronald Lanstein, "Persuasive Evidence of Market Inefficiency," *Journal of Portfolio Management* 11, no. 3 (Spring 1985): 9–17; and Patricia Fairfield, "P/E, P/B and the Present Value of Future Dividends," *Financial Analysts Journal* 50, no. 4 (July–August 1994): 23–31.

Figure 13.4 Time-Series Plot of Price/Cash Flow Ratios for Walgreens, RSD Industry, and S&P 400

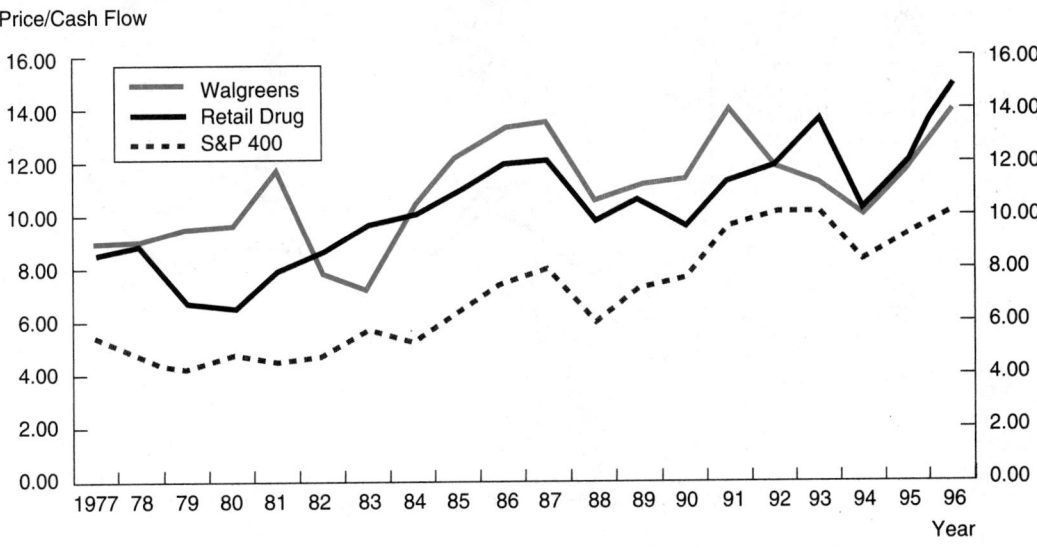

Figure 13.5 Time-Series Plot of Relative Price/Cash Flow Ratios of Walgreens/Industry and Walgreens/Market

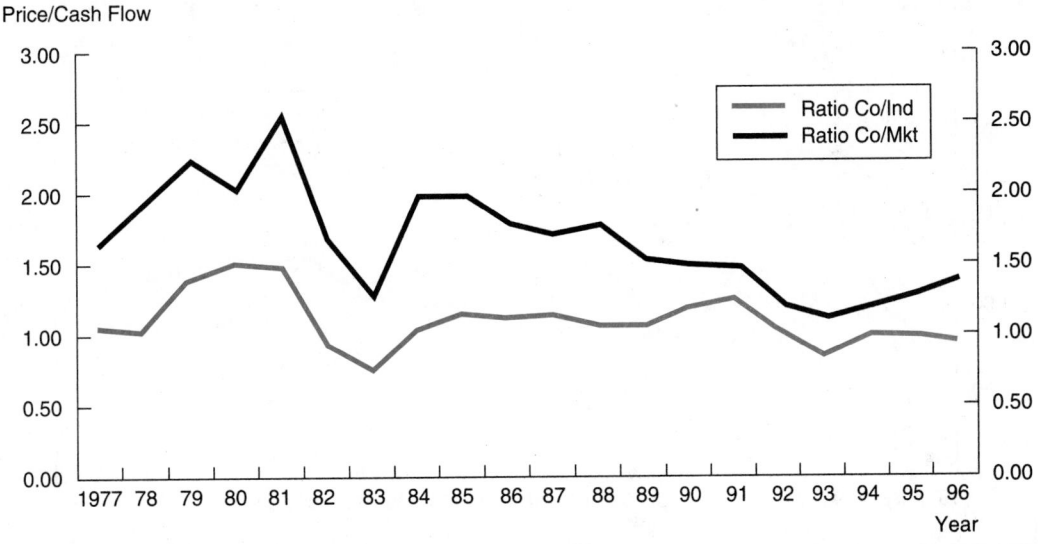

The annual P/BV ratios for Walgreens, its industry, and the market are in Table 13.4, along with the ratio of the company P/BV ratio relative to its industry and the market ratio. In this instance, the major valuable that should cause a difference in the P/BV ratio is the firm's ROE relative to its cost of capital (its WACC). Assuming that most firms in an industry have comparable WACCs, the major differential should be the firm's ROE because the larger the ROE–WACC difference, the greater the justified P/BV ratio.

Figure 13.6 *Time-Series Plot of Price/Book Value Ratios for Walgreens, RSD Industry, and S&P 400*

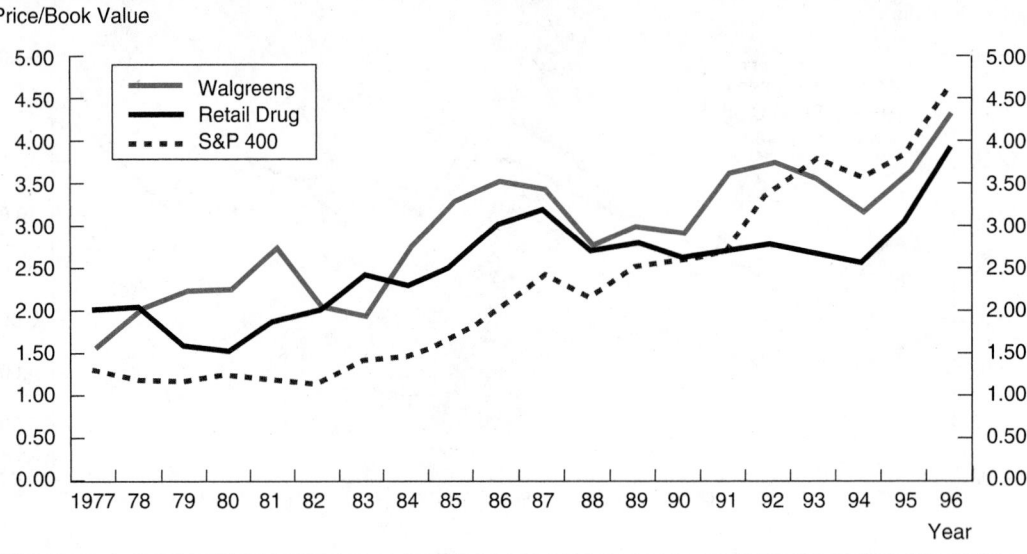

Figure 13.7 *Time-Series Plot of Relative Price/Book Value Ratios for Walgreens/Industry and Walgreens/Market*

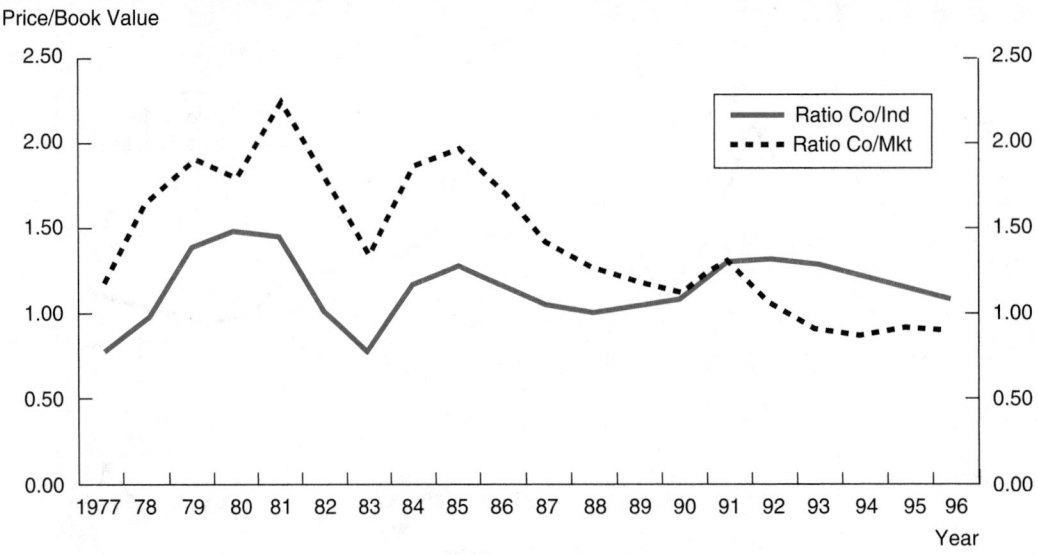

As shown in Figure 13.6, the P/BV ratios for the three components have increased from about 1.5–2.00 to 4.0–4.5. As shown in Figure 13.7, Walgreens has experienced a larger increase in its P/BV ratio than its industry as indicated by its Co/Ind ratio that has gone from about 0.80 to about 1.10. In contrast, the Co/Mkt ratio for Walgreens has *declined* from about 1.30 to about 0.90 at the end of the period. This latter trend is interesting in that the ROE for Walgreens has consistently been greater than for the S&P 400. One must

question whether this declining trend is because the beginning relationship was too high or because of a differential change in the WACC for Walgreens versus the market.

Price-to-Sales Ratio

The price-to-sales ratio (P/S) has had a long but generally neglected existence followed by a recent reawakening. In the late 1950s, Phillip Fisher in his classic book suggested this ratio as a valuable tool when considering investments, including growth stocks.[14] Subsequently, his son, Kenneth Fisher used the ratio as a major stock selection variable in his widely read book.[15] Recently, P/S has been suggested as a valuable tool in a monograph by award-winning author Martin Leibowitz, and the ratio was espoused by O'Shaughnessy in his book that compared several stock selection techniques.[16] Leibowitz makes the point that sales growth drives all subsequent earnings and cash flow, while those who are concerned with accounting manipulation point out that sales is one of the purest numbers available. As noted in Chapter 10, this ratio is equal to the P/E ratio times the net profit margin (Earnings/Sales), which implies that it is heavily influenced by the profit margin of the entity being analyzed.

As shown in Table 13.4 and Figure 13.8, the P/S ratio for Walgreens has experienced a significant increase from 0.14 to 0.77, compared to a moderate increase by its industry (0.43 to 0.65), and a healthy increase by the market (from 0.49 to 1.13). This substantial relative performance by Walgreens is reflected in Figure 13.9, which shows the plot of relative ratios wherein the Co/Ind ratio increased notably from 0.31 to 1.18, while the Co/Mkt ratio went from 0.28 to 0.68. Similar to prior comparisons, the question the analyst must ask is whether the growth of sales, the risk related to the sales growth and the profit margin of Walgreens can justify a higher P/S ratio than its industry.

Summary of Relative Valuation Ratios

Notably, the four individual relative valuation variables increased across the board—all four relative valuation ratios increased during the twenty-year period for the firm, its industry, and the aggregate stock market. The widespread increases suggest that the relative valuation ratio changes are caused by changes in some aggregate economic variables such as economic growth and economic risk factors. Interestingly, Dudley and McKelvey from Goldman Sachs & Co. argued that the U.S. economy has experienced several significant changes during the past two decades that have caused an important change in the nature and length of our economic expansions and contractions.[17]

In addition to these overall increases for all three segments (firm, industry, and market), Walgreens has generally experienced a larger increase than its industry in terms of its P/E ratio, P/BV ratio, and P/S ratio, while lagging in terms of its P/CF ratio. Compared to the market, the firm's P/E ratio and P/S ratio increased more than the market, while its P/CF ratio and its P/BV ratios increased less than the market. Assuming that an investor wants to use these ratios to determine relative value or to make an investment decision, he or she must examine the basic valuation factors to explain the differentials.

[14]Phillip A. Fisher, *Common Stocks and Uncommon Profits* (Woodside, CA: PSR Publications, 1958, 1960 rev. ed., 1984).

[15]Kenneth L. Fisher, *Super Stocks* (Woodside, CA: Business Classics, 1984).

[16]Martin L. Leibowitz, *Sales-Driven Franchise Value* (Charlottesville, VA: The Research Foundation of the Institute of Chartered Financial Analysis, 1997) and James P. O'Shaughnessy, *What Works on Wall Street* (New York: McGraw-Hill, 1997).

[17]William C. Dudley and Edward F. McKelvey, "The Brave New Business Cycle," (New York: Goldman Sachs & Co., October 1997).

Figure 13.8   *Time-Series Plot of Price/Sales Ratios for Walgreens, RSD Industry, and
Se3P 400*

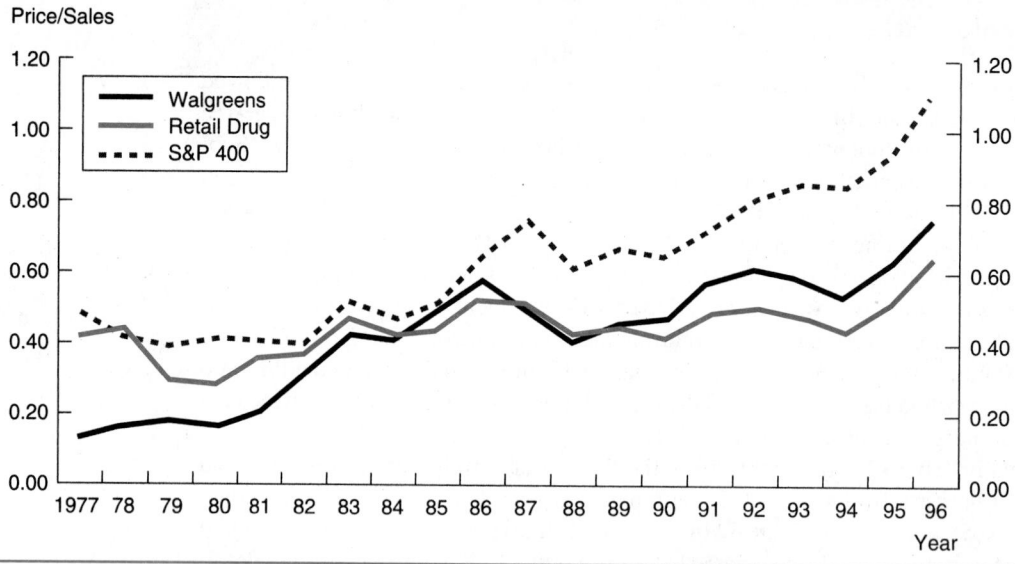

Figure 13.9   *Time-Series Plot of Relative Price/Sales Ratios for Walgreens/Industry and
Walgreens/Market*

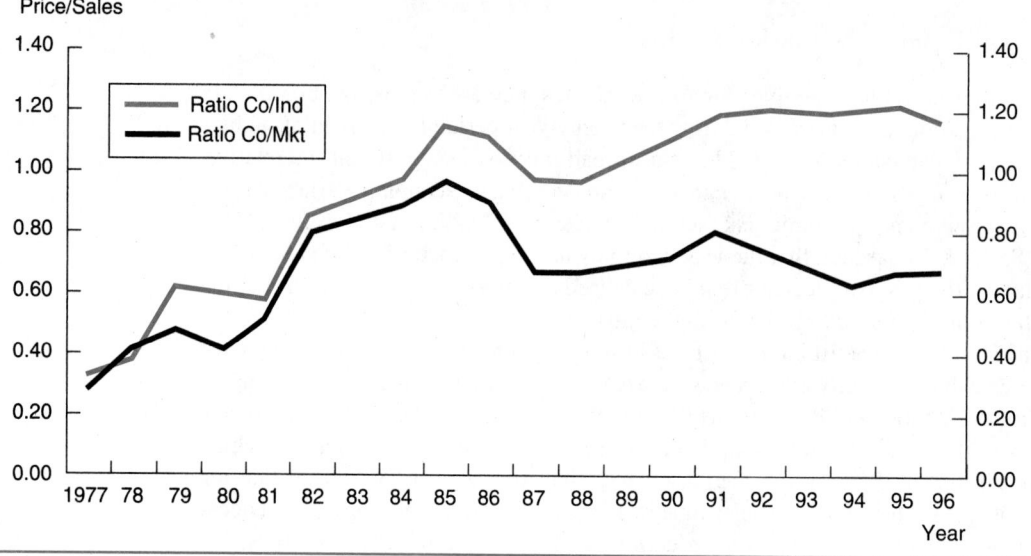

Specific Valuation with the P/E Ratio

In addition to judging the relative valuation for a firm by comparing several ratios, analysts also use the P/E ratio to determine a specific value for a firm. Such a valuation is
relatively common and requires the analyst to estimate next year's earnings per share (EPS)
and the firm's earnings multiple (P/E ratio). Because we have already discussed P/E ratio

analysis, this section considers several methods for estimating EPS that use both statistical and judgmental approaches.

Earnings Per Share Estimates   There are several approaches to estimating earnings per share (EPS). Earnings estimates can be derived using statistical or judgmental analyses. Studies have found that earnings usually have time-series properties, meaning that future earnings levels have a statistical relationship with prior earnings.

Using statistical methods to estimate earnings is as much an art as a science. The analyst must determine the independent variables that appear in the model, the estimation technique to use, and the historical time period over which the relationship is to be estimated.

Judgmental forecasts depend on subjective evaluation of many factors rather than a mathematical formula. Most analyst forecasts are judgmental in nature, although many are the result of both statistical and judgmental analysis. A statistical relationship may give the analyst a base estimate, which the analyst then adjusts up or down based upon his knowledge of quantitative and qualitative influences affecting the firm. Use of the judgmental approach has an advantage over the statistical method because the human mind can implicitly consider the data developed from the economy–industry–firm analysis and adjust the estimate accordingly. It is almost impossible to develop statistical models that include the effects of industry life cycle changes. competitive forces, and alternative strategies. A judgmental model requires the analyst to be knowledgeable about key assumptions and variables driving the estimate.

Earnings estimates can have a top-down orientation, a bottom-up orientation, or a mixture of both. A top-down forecast relates (statistically or judgmentally) the sensitivity of earnings to macroeconomic and industry variables. By forecasting these variables and knowing the earnings' sensitivity to them, an earnings estimate is forecast.

A bottom-up forecast focuses on earnings' sensitivity to firm-specific variables, such as sales growth and changes in the operating profit margin or tax rate. Estimates of future values for these firm variables, coupled with knowledge of profits' sensitivity to them, results in an earnings forecast. Should firm sales be related to economic and industry events, it is easy to combine the top-down and bottom-up approaches to estimate earnings.

Time Series   Typically, the time-series approach relates earnings per share in time period t to earnings in earlier time periods. The model states that current earnings are statistically related to prior period's earnings. Once this time-series model is estimated, earnings for time period $t + 1$ are forecast by inserting the current and prior period's earnings. The analyst may judgmentally adjust the resulting estimate to reflect the forecast of economic, industry, and firm-specific factors.

Sales–Profit Margin Approach   This method is a direct approach to estimating net income and EPS. Under this technique, a sales forecast is multiplied by a net profit margin (NI/Sales) estimate, resulting in a net income forecast. Earnings per share is then computed as the net income forecast divided by the number of shares outstanding:

$$EPS = \frac{\text{Sales Forecast} \times \text{Net Profit Margin}}{\text{Number of Shares Outstanding}}$$

$$= \frac{\text{Net Income}}{\text{Number of Shares}}$$

The sales forecast can be developed using a number of statistical and judgmental tools. Past sales trends or growth rates can be extrapolated into the future; sales can be estimated from a regression relationship relating firm sales to industry or economic variables; market share forecasts can be combined with industry sales forecasts to develop the firm's sales

forecast. If the firm is in the retail industry, sales can be estimated by multiplying the fore-casted number of stores next year by the expected average sales volume per store. The results of any of these analyses can be adjusted judgmentally using the analyst's insights from the economic–industry–firm analysis.

Net profit margins can be affected by various factors. The firm's internal performance should be reviewed, including general company trends and consideration of any problems that might affect future performance. The firm's operating and financial leverage should be estimated to show the relationship between sales changes and profit variability. The firm's profit margins should be reviewed historically against the industry's margins to deter-mine if past firm performance is attributable to its industry or is unique to the firm. As always, this history-oriented analysis must be supplemented with the analyst's fore-casts of future economic, industry, and firm developments.

Purely Judgmental Approaches to Estimating Earnings   The above methods could use statistical, judgmental, or both methods to estimate earnings. Here we present two purely judgmental analyses of earnings estimation.

Last year's income statement plus judgmental evaluations   Starting with last year's income statement and a brief review of historical changes and expected future develop-ments leads to an earnings forecast. As always, analysts need to identify and monitor the key assumptions and variables that are driving expected firm sales and profitability.

For example, the analyst may start with the sales revenue of the most recent year. A historical review will inform the analyst of the average sales growth rate during some recent period—say, the past ten years. The maximum and minimum sales growth rates are determined along with a review of economic, industry, and firm influences. This will allow the analyst to explain the proximate cause for good and poor sales growth rates. Reasons may include economic expansion or recession or new product introductions by the firm or its competitors. With these bounds of sales growth, the analyst subjectively evaluates favorable and unfavorable influences expected to affect the firm, its industry, and the econ-omy in the coming year. This analysis will lead to a sales growth forecast for the com-ing year.

The operating profit margin can likewise be evaluated beginning with the historical average and its upper and lower range. The analyst subjectively evaluates positive and neg-ative factors affecting the firm's costs and its pricing strategy that may affect the oper-ating profit margin. The operating profit margin times the sales forecast gives the analyst an estimate of the firm's operating income.

The difference between the firm's operating income and net income will reflect the firm's other income, its interest expense, and taxes. Based upon reading the footnotes and talk-ing with management, the analyst can estimate changes in other income sources (such as income from subsidiaries or marketable securities). Interest expense will be affected by the firm's debt and changes in interest rates. Expectations about future firm financing can be estimated by forecasting the firm's free cash flow in the coming year; negative cash flow means the firm may have to raise capital. The firm's tax obligation can be estimated by using corporate tax tables along with any expected changes in tax rates. Operating income, plus other income, less interest expense and taxes equals the analyst's estimate of net income.

An estimate of the number of shares outstanding over the coming year is based upon the firm's plans to issue equity, to force conversion of convertible bonds or preferred stock, or to repurchase stock. The earnings per share estimate will equal the analyst's judgmental estimate of net income divided by the estimate of shares outstanding.

The analyst may also want to use a scenario analysis to estimate expected earnings per share. Possible sales growth rates can be combined with alternative operating profit mar-gins in pessimistic, neutral, and optimistic scenarios. By assigning probabilities to each scenario, an expected earnings per share estimate can be calculated.

By comparing quarterly results to the analysts' estimate for the quarter, the analyst can evaluate the accuracy of his or her estimates. The quarterly financial reports, and subsequent discussions with industry experts and the firm's investor relations personnel allow analysts to incorporate new information into their forecast.

Using the consensus of analysts' earnings estimates   Zacks and IBES are two Wall Street research firms that systematically collect analysts' earnings estimates. Although specific analysts are not identified, Zacks and IBES report the average of the earnings per share estimates from analysts that cover the firm as well as the variance of the estimates from the consensus. It is assumed that these earnings estimates are reflected in the stock's current price.

Some analysts use the consensus estimate and work their way up a firm's income statement to check its reasonableness. If they believe the consensus estimate reflects overly optimistic (or pessimistic) expectations, they will flag the stock for further analysis.

For example, multiplying a firm's IBES consensus earnings estimate by the number of shares outstanding indicates a net income forecast.[18] Combining this with an estimate of the firm's average tax rate allows us to forecast the firm's earnings before tax. Interest expense can be approximated using the prior year's numbers and expected financing changes based on news releases by the firm or the previous year's free cash flow analysis. Adding interest expense to pretax earnings gives the IBES consensus estimate of operating income.

This is compared to the previous year's actual operating income. If the percentage difference can't be explained by reasonable sales growth or operating profit margin changes, the IBES earnings consensus may be in error, reflecting extreme optimism or pessimism by analysts. The analyst may then decide the firm is a candidate for sale (if the IBES consensus is too optimistic) or for purchase (if the IBES consensus is too pessimistic). The reason is, if the IBES consensus is incorrect, the resulting earnings surprise will lead to a large change in the stock's price as discussed in Chapter 8.

Site Visits and the Art of the Interview

Brokerage house analysts and portfolio managers have access to persons that the typical small investor does not. Analysts frequently contact corporate personnel by telephone, at formal presentations, or during plant site visits. Though insider trading laws restrict the analyst's ability to obtain material nonpublic information, these visits facilitate dialog between the corporation and the investor community. The analyst can gather information about the firm's plans and strategies, which helps the analyst understand the firm's prospects as an investment.

Interviewing is an art. The analyst wants information about the firm, and top management wants to put the firm in the best light possible. Thus, the analyst must be prepared to focus the interview on management's plans, strategies, and concerns. Management will typically indicate that earnings estimates may be "too high," "too low," or "about right." Discussions of new products under development are also valuable. Analysts try to gauge the sensitivity of the firms revenues, costs, and earnings to different scenarios by asking "what if" questions.

Analysts have frequent telephone contact with the firm's investor relations (IR) department who want analysts to know about company pronouncements. Notably, they will try to put as good a "spin" as possible on negative news events.

---

[18]A discussion of this method is found in Lawrence J. Haverty, Jr., "Interpreting the Retail Numbers," in *The Retail Industry: General Merchandisers and Discounters, Specialty Merchandisers, Apparel Specialty, and Food/Drug Retailers,* ed. Charles A. Ingene (Charlottesville, Va.: Association for Investment Management and Research, 1993), 75–80.

The chief financial officer and chief executive officer of the firm also meet with security analysts and discuss the firm's planning process and major issues confronting the industry. Subsequently, management is interested in the analyst's report because it should represent a fair, informed, and independent appraisal of the firm.

The analyst should talk to people other than top managers. Talking to middle managers or factory workers during a plant tour, visiting stores, and talking with customers provides insights beyond those of management. The firm's major customers can provide information regarding product quality and customer satisfaction. The firm's suppliers can furnish information about rising or falling supply orders and the timeliness of payments.

Making the Investment Decision

The investment decision can take either of two forms:

1. If your estimate of the stock's intrinsic value is equal to or greater than the current market price of the investment, buy the stock.
2. Using your estimate of the stock's future intrinsic value and (based upon one of the future relative valuation ratios) if you bought the stock at the current market price and held the investment during the future period, which is typically assumed to be a year. If this expected rate of return is equal to or greater than your required rate of return, buy the stock; if the expected return is below your required rate of return, do not buy it.

We will now apply these two forms of the investment decision. For the sake of illustration, suppose we estimate a stock's intrinsic value using the present value of FCF to be forty dollars a share.

Comparing the Estimated Value to the Current Market Price   Because the estimated intrinsic value is a present value we would compare the current market price of the stock to this estimated value. For example, if the stock was currently priced at thirty dollars a share, you would buy it; if it were currently priced at $45 a share, you would not buy it.

Calculating the Expected Rate of Return on a Stock   Assuming you estimated the stock's intrinsic value and dividend for the next year using the estimated P/E ratio and EPS estimates, you can estimate the expected rate of return, E(R), from investing in the stock:

$$E(R) = \frac{\text{Intrinsic Value} - \text{Current Price} + \text{Dividend}}{\text{Current Price}}$$

In our example, $40 is the estimated intrinsic value and $0.60 is the dividend. Assume the current market price is $35. Thus,

$$E(R) = \frac{\$40 - \$35 + \$0.60}{\$35} = 0.16 \text{ or } 16\%$$

Based on a required return of 11 percent, we would buy this stock because its expected rate of return is larger than our required rate of return.

The use of several valuation techniques may result in several different estimates of the stock's intrinsic value, which means several expected rates of return can be computed. As an investor you can either select the most reasonable estimate of intrinsic value and use this and the corresponding expected rate of return to make the investment decision, or you can compare this *expected* rate of return to your *required* rate of return.

If the intrinsic value estimates consistently generate expected returns below your required rate of return, you might want to compute the intrinsic value that would provide the desired return as follows:

Minimum Necessary Intrinsic Value = Current Price (1 + Required Return) − Dividend

The question then becomes: Is there any reasonable combination of expected growth and required rate of return estimate that would provide such an intrinsic value? You must decide if the economic, industry, and firm analysis can support such a conjecture.

Portfolio Asset Allocations   Note that in the context of a global portfolio, an expected return for a market that is below the investor's required return does *not* indicate no investment in that country's market. Rather, because of the benefits of diversification and because of the possibility the analysis may be incorrect, some funds will still be invested in the market. The portfolio manager would probably choose to *underweight* that country's market in the portfolio. For example, if the U.S. stock market comprised 40 percent of the weight of a global stock market index, a pessimistic appraisal of the near-term performance of the U.S. stock market may cause a portfolio manager to allocate only 30 percent or 35 percent of funds to the U.S. equity market. Funds would then be available to *overweight* those countries' markets that the analysis indicates have expected returns that exceeded their required returns.

Similar analysis can be done using industry sectors within a nation's stock market. In this case, intrinsic values and dividend payments from an industry index are used to estimate the expected return from an industry. Within a nation's equity market, industries offering expected returns above their required returns will be overweighted; industries offering expected returns below their required returns will be underweighted.[19]

WHEN TO SELL

Our analysis has focused on determining if a stock should be purchased. In fact, when we make a purchase, a subsequent question gains prominence: When should the stock be sold? Many times holding onto a stock too long leads to a return below expectations or less than what was available earlier. When stocks decline in value immediately following a portfolio manager's purchase, is this a further buying opportunity, or does the decline indicate that the stock analysis was incorrect?

The answer to when to sell a stock is contained in the same collection of research that convinced the analyst to purchase the stock in the first place. The analyst should have identified the key assumptions and variables driving the expectations for the stock. Analysis of the stock doesn't end when intrinsic value is computed and the research report is written. Once the key value drivers are identified, the analyst must continually monitor and update his or her knowledge base about the firm. Once the key assumptions and variables appear to have weakened, it is time to reevaluate, and possibly sell, the stock holding.

The stock should also be closely evaluated when the current price approaches the intrinsic value estimate. When the stock become fairly priced, it may be time to sell it and reinvest the funds in other underpriced stocks. In short, if the "story" for buying the stock still appears to be true, continue to hold it. If the "story" changes, it may be time to sell the stock. If you know why you bought the stock, you'll be able to recognize when to sell it.

---

[19]For detailed examples of the use of dividend discount models and earnings multiplier models in the context of market analysis and industry analysis, see Frank K. Reilly and Keith Brown, *Investment Analysis and Portfolio Management,* 5th ed. (Fort Worth, Tex.: Dryden, 1997).

INFLUENCES ON ANALYSTS

Stock analysts and portfolio managers are, for the most part, highly trained individuals who possess expertise in financial analysis and background in their industry. A computer hardware analyst knows as much about industry trends and new product offerings as any industry insider. A pharmaceutical analyst is able to independently determine the market potential of drugs undergoing testing and the FDA approval process. So why don't more brokerage house customers and portfolio managers who receive the analysts' expert advice achieve investment success? The following subsections discuss several factors that make it difficult to do consistently well.

Efficient Markets

As noted in Chapter 8, the efficient market is difficult to outsmart, especially for actively traded and frequently analyzed companies. Information about the economy, a firm's industry, and the firm itself are reviewed by numerous bright analysts, investors, and portfolio managers. Because of the market's ability to review and absorb information, stock prices generally approximate fair market value. Investors look for situations where stocks may not be fairly valued. Notably, with many market players, it is difficult to successfully, frequently, and consistently find undervalued shares. The analyst's best place to seek attractive stocks is not among well-known companies and actively traded stocks, because they are analyzed by dozens of Wall Street researchers. Stocks with smaller market capitalizations, those not covered by many analysts, or those whose shares are mainly held by individual investors may be the best places to search for inefficiencies. Smaller capitalization stocks sometimes are too small for time-constrained analysts or too small for purchase by institutional investors.[20] The price of stocks not researched by many analysts ("neglected stocks") may not reflect all relevant information.[21]

Paralysis of Analysis

Analysts spend most of their time in a relentless search for one more contact or one more piece of information that can keep the analyst's mind off the final output—that is, their stock recommendation. Analysts need to develop a systematic approach for gathering, monitoring, and reviewing relevant information about economic trends, industry competitive forces, and company strategy. Otherwise they become too busy collecting data, searching for all the answers. The analyst must evaluate the information as a whole to discern patterns that indicate the intrinsic value of the stock. Rather than searching for one more piece of information, analysts should evaluate what they already know about the stock's prospects.

Because markets are generally efficient, the consensus view about the firm is already reflected in its stock price. To earn above-average returns, the analyst must have expectations that differ from the consensus *and* the analyst must be correct. Thus, the analyst may want to concentrate on identifying what is wrong with the market consensus, or what surprises may upset the market consensus—that is, *estimate earning surprises.*

---

[20]According to SEC regulations, mutual funds cannot own more than 10 percent of a firm's shares. For some large funds, this constraint will make the resulting investment too small to have any significant impact on fund returns, so they do not bother to consider such stocks for purchase.

[21]Information on the number of analysts covering a stock is available from research firms such as IBES and Zacks.

Table 13.5	*Earnings and Dividends per Share for Major European Chemical Firms*				
		Earnings per Share			
Company	**Currency**	**1998E**	**1999E**	**Dividends Per Share (1999E)**	**Dividend Payout (1999)**
BASF	DM	5.0	4.9	2.0	.408
Bayer	DM	4.4	4.7	2.1	.447
Ciba	Sfr	8.9	10.4	2.5	.240
AKZO	DFL	26.0	27.8	9.5	.342
DSM	DFL	26.5	22.0	10.0	.455
L'Air Liquide	FFr	47.4	52.2	18.9	.362
BOC	BP	53.5	61.7	33.0	.535
AGA	SKr	5.1	6.0	3.4	.567

[a]Before extraordinary items.

E = Estimate.

Source: Charles K. Brown, Peter Clark, and Mark Tracey, "The Major European Chemicals/Pharma Groups—Testing Times (London: Goldman Sachs International Ltd., February 1993). Copyright 1993 by Goldman Sachs.

Forces Pulling on the Analyst

Although such linkages should not exist, at times communication occurs between a firm's investment banking and stock analysis division. If the investment bankers assist a firm in a stock or bond offering, it will be difficult for an analyst to issue a negative evaluation of the company. Advisory fees have been lost because of a negative stock recommendation. Despite attempts to ensure the independence of stock analysts, at times firm politics may get in the way.

The analyst is in frequent contact with the top officers of the company he analyzes. Although there are guidelines about receiving gifts and favors, it is sometimes difficult to separate personal friendship and impersonal corporate relationships. Corporate officials may try to convince the analyst that his pessimistic report is in error or glosses over recent positive developments. To mitigate these problems, an analyst should call the company's investor relations department immediately *after* changing a recommendation to explain his perspective. The analyst needs to maintain independence and have confidence in his or her analysis.

GLOBAL COMPANY ANALYSIS

One of our goals in this book is to demonstrate investment techniques that can be applied to foreign markets, industries, and companies. A major problem of global analysis is getting the data required for the analysis.

In this section, we will examine an analysis of the European chemical industry. The objective is to see how to select individual companies and specific stocks for your investment portfolio. We will work with tables assembled by Goldman Sachs. The tables contain data on several companies.

Earnings per Share Analysis

Table 13.5 contains estimated earnings per share values for the major firms for 1998 and 1999 as of 1998. This two-period comparison shows the outlook for these firms. Most estimates indicate a mixed pattern of growth among the firms for 1999. The dividend data indicate a range of payouts (that is, about 24 to 56 percent).

Table 13.6 Common Stock Statistics for Major European Chemical Firms

Company	P/E			P/CF			P/E Relative[4]			EV/EBITDA[5]			EV/EBIT			Gross Dividend Yield (%)		
	1997	1998E	1999E	1997	1998E	1999E	1997	1998E	1999E	1997	1998E	1999E	1997	1998E	1999E	1997	1998E	1999E
Commodity																		
BASF	16.3	16.0	16.4	6.8	7.0	7.0	0.75	0.66	0.78	6.5	6.6	6.5	10.6	11.2	11.3	3.6	3.6	3.6
DSM	7.1	7.8	9.3	3.5	3.7	4.0	0.38	0.34	0.46	3.3	2.9	3.0	5.8	5.1	5.8	4.9	4.9	4.9
EVC	17.2	nm	15.8	3.5	2.9	2.7	0.91	nm	0.78	4.5	3.2	3.2	26.5	9.5	11.1	7.7	7.7	7.7
Kemira	12.6	12.4	11.1	5.0	5.0	4.5	0.84	0.64	0.67	5.7	5.6	5.3	10.5	10.2	9.4	3.7	4.0	4.2
Solvay	18.1	18.4	17.9	6.2	7.0	6.7	1.20	0.91	0.95	6.5	6.3	6.1	12.5	12.2	11.9	2.9	2.9	2.9
Hybrid																		
Akzo Nobel	18.7	16.3	15.2	10.7	9.2	8.8	0.99	0.72	0.75	8.8	8.1	7.8	13.6	12.1	11.5	2.0	2.1	2.2
Albright & Wilson*	13.4	12.5	11.2	9.6	7.8	7.2	0.78	0.63	0.61	7.8			10.4			3.9	4.1	4.3
Bayer	19.5	17.9	16.6	8.8	8.7	8.1	0.89	0.74	0.79	8.2	7.8	7.2	12.9	11.9	10.9	3.4	3.6	3.8
Degussa [2]*	23.9	21.6	19.0	9.1	8.3	7.6	1.09	0.89	0.90	10.4			20.3			2.0	2.2	2.4
Hoechst	23.7	23.7	17.9	8.3	10.7	9.2	1.08	0.98	0.85	8.7	10.0	8.9	16.6	19.4	15.3	2.9	3.1	3.3
ICI	36.7	26.1	19.1	18.0	13.0	10.9	2.14	1.30	1.04	12	12	11	20.4	16.9	14.7	2.6	2.8	2.9
Rhône-Poulenc	31.1	27.2	23.0	10.7	11.9	11.4	1.44	1.07	1.05	9.9	9.0	8.6	17.0	15.0	13.3	1.8	1.9	2.2
Specialty																		
AGA	27.7	24.3	20.8	10.7	9.8	8.7	1.76	1.47	1.49	10.0	8.7	7.7	19.3	16.3	13.8	2.4	2.6	2.7
Air Liquide	27.6	24.6	22.4	13.1	11.5	10.5	1.28	0.97	1.02	10.9	9.3	8.4	17.4	15.0	13.5	2.0	2.2	2.4
BOC[2]	16.4	18.2	15.8	9.0	9.6	8.2	0.99	0.94	0.84	7.7	8.2	7.5	11.6	13.1	11.9	3.0	3.2	3.4
BTP[1]*	25.7	23.2	20.7	18.4	16.7	14.7	1.49	1.16	1.13	14.0			17.4			2.3	2.4	2.5
Ciba Specialty Chem.	22.7	21.4	18.3	13.5	12.0	10.7	0.94	0.70	0.69	11.7	8.9	7.9	16.9	12.6	10.8	1.1	1.1	1.3
Clariant	29.0	22.0	18.4	12.8	11.4	10.4	1.20	0.72	0.70	10.5	9.7	9.1	16.1	14.2	12.8	0.8	1.1	1.4
Croda*	22.4	21.6	20.2	15.4	13.1	11.7	0.81	0.80	0.80	11.4			15.8			2.2	2.3	2.5
Elementis*	17.9	14.0	10.8	14.4	24.9	30.3	1.00	0.81	0.82	7.5			11.4			2.3		
Henkel	27.8	24.1	21.0	11.3	10.7	9.8	1.27	0.99	0.99	9.4	8.9	8.5	18.3	16.5	15.1	1.4	1.6	1.9
Inspec*	13.9	16.0	14.7	5.2	9.7	8.9	0.81	0.80	0.80	9.6			12.4			2.2	2.3	2.5
Laporte*	17.2	16.3	15.1	7.5	12.1	11.1	1.11	0.91	0.77	9.9			12.6			3.0	3.2	3.4
SKW Trostberg[3]*	17.8	17.1	13.7	6.2	5.7	5.3	0.81	0.70	0.65	8.2			15.6			2.8	3.1	3.2
Yule Catto*	16.9	15.1	13.1	18.8	12.0	11.0	0.99	0.88	0.76	21.7			26.2			2.4	2.7	2.9

(1) March year end, (2) September year end. *Company not covered, consensus estimates provided by I/B/E/S.

(3) 1997 figures are estimates, (4) relative to local market, (5) EV = market cap + net debt + minorities (+ pension liabilities for German companies)

Source: Jackie Ashurst, Charles K. Brown, G. Haire, M. Tracey, J. A. Murphy, and J. Henderson, "The Major European Chemicals/Pharma Groups" (London: Goldman Sachs International Ltd., May 1998). Copyright 1998 by Goldman Sachs.

Table 13.7   *Share Price Performance for Major European Chemical Firms*

%	Absolute			Relative to FT-A Europe			Relative to local market		
	1 Month	3 Month	12 Month	1 Month	3 Month	12 Month	1 Month	3 Month	12 Month
BASF	−2.6	25.0	17.4	−2.7	9.0	−18.3	−3.0	7.3	−21.7
DSM	−1.6	7.1	5.2	−1.8	−6.6	−26.8	−2.8	−11.3	−30.6
EVC	−6.7	8.3	−30.0	−6.9	−5.5	−51.3	−7.8	−10.2	−53.8
Kemira	−0.5	12.6	21.4	−0.7	−1.8	−15.5	−10.1	−16.3	−27.4
Solvay	0.7	19.1	30.1	0.5	3.9	−9.4	−0.8	1.7	−6.5
Commodity Average	**−2.1**	**14.4**	**8.8**	**−2.3**	**−0.2**	**−24.2**	**−4.9**	**−5.8**	**−28.0**
Akzo Nobel	2.9	13.1	62.8	2.7	−1.4	13.4	1.7	−6.3	7.5
Albright & Wilson	1.4	27.9	18.5	1.2	11.6	−17.5	1.4	17.2	−8.0
Bayer	−5.1	2.7	17.4	−5.3	−10.5	−18.3	−5.6	−11.8	−21.7
Degussa	−5.8	8.8	36.4	−6.0	−5.1	−5.1	−6.3	−6.5	−9.1
Hoechst	−0.2	3.0	10.2	−0.4	−10.2	−23.3	−0.7	−11.5	−26.5
ICI	7.9	15.7	57.2	7.7	0.9	9.5	7.9	6.0	22.1
Rhône-Poulenc	7.5	15.5	65.9	7.3	0.7	15.5	4.3	−6.9	8.8
Hybrid Average	**1.1**	**19.6**	**39.1**	**0.9**	**4.3**	**−3.1**	**0.4**	**4.5**	**−1.8**
AGA	13.1	24.4	19.1	12.9	8.5	−17.1	11.9	8.3	−10.1
Air Liquide	3.5	25.2	33.5	3.2	9.2	−7.1	0.3	1.0	−12.5
BOC	3.5	4.4	0.3	3.3	−9.0	−30.2	3.5	−4.4	−22.1
BTP	32.0	47.6	94.9	31.8	28.7	35.7	32.0	35.2	51.3
Ciba Specialty Chemicals	−2.1	12.4	44.5	−2.3	−2.0	0.6	−2.7	1.5	−5.8
Clariant	2.7	18.6	104.4	2.5	3.4	42.3	2.0	7.1	33.2
Croda	13.2	28.7	55.5	13.0	12.2	8.3	13.2	17.9	20.7
Elementis	14.6	30.0	49.1	14.3	13.3	3.8	14.5	19.0	15.8
Henkel	2.2	24.7	56.8	2.0	8.8	9.2	1.7	7.1	4.6
Inspec	27.0	49.5	58.0	26.8	30.4	10.0	27.0	36.9	22.6
Laporte	9.3	28.9	35.9	9.1	12.4	−5.4	9.3	18.0	5.5
SKW Trostberg	−6.2	3.2	9.6	−6.4	−10.0	−23.7	−6.6	−11.3	−26.9
Yule Catto	15.3	19.0	18.7	15.1	3.8	−17.4	15.3	9.0	−7.9
Specialty Average	**9.9**	**24.3**	**44.6**	**9.6**	**8.4**	**0.7**	**9.3**	**11.2**	**5.3**

Source: Jackie Ashurst, Charles K. Brown, G. Haire, M. Tracey, J. A. Murphy, and J. Henderson, "The Major European Chemicals/Pharma Groups" (London: Goldman Sachs International Ltd., May 1998). Copyright 1998 by Goldman Sachs.

Common Stock Statistics

Given the prior analysis, Table 13.6 contains measures of stock performance and relative value for the firms in the industry. The absolute P/E ratios show the differences in the earnings multipliers among countries. The table contains interesting information on the individual stock P/E ratios relative to the average P/E ratio in the local market. As an example, Bayer's P/E ratio for 1999 is 16.6, which is only 89 percent of the average of all stocks in Germany. In contrast Air Liquide has a P/E ratio of 22.4, which is 102 percent of the average for stocks in France. This shows that two stocks in the same industry could have different relative valuations in different countries due to variations in accounting conventions or social attitudes. Such a difference in measures of relative valuation among countries should decline in the future as international accounting standards become more prevalent and global capital markets become more integrated.

The price/cash flow ratios likewise reflect major differences in relative valuation among countries. Again, these differences could be due to differences in real value or differences in accounting practices.

Table 13.8 *Company and Stock Price Data for Bayer*

Bayer   **Market Performer**

Price:	DM	78.75	Net Debt:	DMm	2,818	Price Target:	DM85
Market Value:	DMbn	57.3	Minorities[1]:	DMm	9581	Rel. to Germany 1 Month:	−5.6%
12 Month Range:	DM	85.5-57.1	Ent. Value:	DMbn	69.7	3 Months:	−11.8%
FT/S&P Germany:		266.9	No Shares:	m	727	12 Months:	−21.7%

Year to December:	Sales DMm	Pre-Tax Profit DMm	DVFA EPS DM	Net Div DM	CFPS DM	P/E	P/E Rel	P/CF	Gross Yield %
1996	48,608	4,464	3.8	1.70	8.0	20.5	0.75	9.9	3.1
1997	55,005	5,108	4.0	1.90	8.9	19.5	0.89	8.8	3.4
1998E	56,780	5,525	4.4	2.00	9.1	17.9	0.74	8.7	3.6
1999E	60,000	6,020	4.7	2.10	9.7	16.6	0.79	8.1	3.8

Options/Convertibles/Warrants: O/C/W   Ticker. BAYG.F
Listed ADRs: No. Non listed BAYRY, 1:1   (1) Includes pension liabilities

Source: Jackie Ashurst, Charles K. Brown, G. Haire, M. Tracey, J. A. Murphy, and J. Henderson, "The Major European Chemicals/Pharma Groups" (London: Goldman Sachs International Ltd., May 1998). Copyright 1998 by Goldman Sachs.

Share Price Performance

Table 13.7 compares the stock price changes for the major chemical firms. The results indicate large differences in absolute and relative stock performances. This comparison is very interesting because it demonstrates the effect of diversification when making foreign investments. The results deteriorated when they are compared to the S&P 500, both the FT-A Europe Index and to each stock's local market index. In summary, during this particular period both the FT-Europe and most local markets were strong, which hurt these relative comparisons.

Individual Company Analysis

The report concludes with a summary of the strengths and potential problems of each individual company. Table 13.8 summarizes the operating and stock results for Bayer, a German firm considered to be one of the world's leading chemical companies. The analysts' discussion that accompanies the business sector analysis in Table 13.9 that breaks down sales by product sector and indicates the percent of profit and profit margin for each sector. In addition, there is a geographic breakdown that highlights the firm's global expansion.

Based upon the sales, earnings, and valuation outlook for the firm, the analyst refers to the stock as a "market performer" which implies that it is expected to experience a return consistent with the aggregate European markets. Also, a stock price chart for Bayer (Figure 13.10) shows the absolute and relative movements for the firm's stock. As shown, although the stock price increased, it clearly underperformed the aggregate German market represented by the DAX 30 index.

SUMMARY

◆ This chapter demonstrated how you complete the fundamental analysis process by analyzing a company and deciding whether or not you should buy its stock. This requires a separate analysis of a company and its stock. A wonderful firm can have an overpriced stock, or a mediocre firm can have an underpriced stock.

Table 13.9 *Analysis of Sales, Profits, and Profit Margin by Business Sector and Geography for Bayer*

Bayer Business Sector Analysis 1997

	Sales		Trading Profit		Margin
	DMm	%	DMm	%	%
Health Care	13,635	25	1,871	34	13.7
Agriculture	5,697	10	945	17	16.6
Polymers	16,798	31	1,540	28	9.2
Chemicals	10,762	20	591	11	5.5
Agfa Group	8,113	15	481	9	5.9
Total	**55,005**	**100**	**5,428**	**100**	**9.9**

Bayer Geographical Analysis 1997

	Sales		Operating Profit		Margin
	DMm	%	DMm	%	%
Europe	25,961	47	3,542	65	13.6
North America	14,943	27	1,394	26	9.3
Latin America	4,425	8	155	3	3.5
Others	9,676	18	337	6	3.5
Total	**55,005**	**100**	**5,428**	**100**	**9.9**

Source: Jackie Ashurst, Charles K. Brown, G. Haire, M. Tracey, J. A. Murphy, and J. Henderson, "The Major European Chemicals/Pharma Groups" (London: Goldman Sachs International Ltd., May 1998). Copyright 1998 by Goldman Sachs.

Figure 13.10 *Bayer Price Performance 1996–1998*

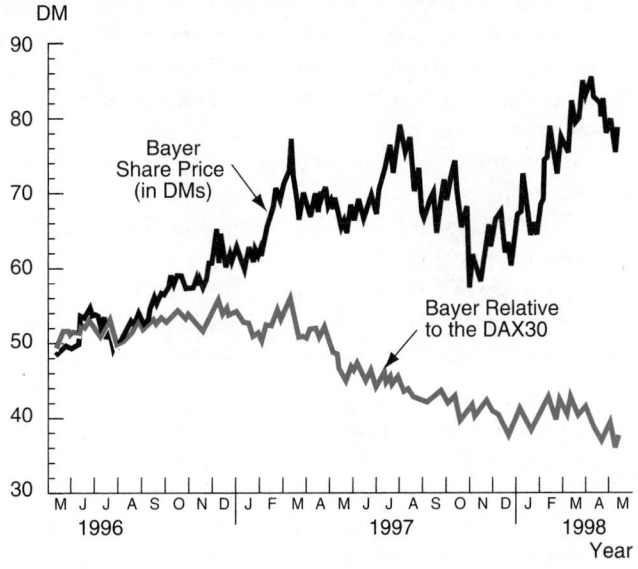

Source: Jackie Ashurst, Charles K. Brown, G. Haire, M. Tracey, J. A. Murphy, and J. Henderson, "The Major European Chemicals/Pharma Groups" (London: Goldman Sachs International Ltd., May 1998). Copyright 1998 by Goldman Sachs.

Investments Online

Many helpful sites have been reviewed in prior chapters, for example, examining individual firm sites and the SEC's EDGAR database for firm-specific information. Investment bank and brokerage house sites may also prove valuable, though they may expect payment for access to their published research on different firms. Still, many sites exist that allow users to examine free information and investing tips:

www.better-investing.com The home page for the National Association of Investment Clubs offers company information and investing ideas in addition to resources for those interested in setting up their own investment club.

www.fool.com This is the home page for the Motley Fool; despite its name, it is a well-known and popular site for investors to visit. It is chock-full of data, articles, educational resources, news, and investing ideas.

www.cfonews.com Corporate Financials Online provides links to news about selected publicly traded firms.

www.ibes.com The home page for the Institutional Brokers Estimate System. IBES maintains a database of analysts' earnings expectations on a variety of stocks. The database contains earnings per share estimates from 800 brokers on 17,000 stocks in 47 countries. The site offers free reports on a selected number of firms.

www.zacks.com This is the Web site for Zacks Investment Research. When the user types in a ticker symbol, Zacks provides links to a company profile, financials, analysts' consensus earnings estimates, and the number of analysts recommending strong buy, moderate buy, hold, moderate sell, and strong sell. Links allow the user to order brokerage reports. The site provides aggregate earnings growth estimates for the S&P 500, the market, and various economic sectors.

www.valueline.com This site was mentioned in an earlier chapter. The Value Line Investment Survey is a favorite source of information for many investors.

www.investorweb.com/default.asp This site provides links to investment newsletters, educational features, company links, and news.

investor.msn.com The home page of Microsoft Investor allows users to track investments, follow the market, read daily editorial and market summaries, and obtain company profiles.

www.marketedge.com MarketEdge, part of the Thomson Investors Network, has company stock reports for over 7,000 firms which are updated twice a month. Paying customers can select possible investments by screening stocks on 18 different variables.

www.nyssa.org The home page of the New York Society of Security Analysts includes many financial Web links and sources of market and company information.

♦ We reviewed how company analysis follows from our earlier research on economic, structural, and industry influences. We also discussed the strategic alternatives available to firms in response to different competitive pressures in their industries. The alternative strategies include low-cost leadership or differentiation, which should be focused toward alternative segments of the market. SWOT analysis helps an analyst assess a firm's internal strengths and weaknesses and its external opportunities and threats. Peter

Lynch suggests categorizing firms into six categories to help focus the analyst's research thrust. A careful review of the firm's financial statements gives insight into the firm's future potential. Interviews of top and middle managers, sales representatives, and customers can also provide valuable information.

♦ Estimating a stock's intrinsic value can follow one of two approaches (present value of cash flow or relative valuation ratios) and any of several techniques available for these approaches. We reviewed and demonstrated how to estimate the major inputs to these techniques and the results when they are applied to Walgreens. Following this demonstration, we discussed how one makes the investment decision, and we considered when it is appropriate to sell a stock in your portfolio.

♦ Analysts have a difficult job. The efficient market makes it difficult to find truly underpriced securities. The quantity of information available for an analyst to review can be overwhelming.

♦ We continued our example of global analysis by reviewing the company analysis related to the European chemical industry. This demonstration showed the importance of differential demand and cost factors among countries, the significance of different accounting conventions, and the impact of exchange rate differences.

Questions

1. Define a growth company and a speculative stock.
2. Give an example of a growth company and discuss why you identify it as such.
3. Give an example of a cyclical stock and discuss why you have designated it as such. Is it issued by a cyclical company?
4. A biotechnology firm is growing at a compound rate of more than 21 percent a year. (Its ROE is over 30 percent, and it retains about 70 percent of its earnings.) The stock of this company is priced at about sixty-five times next year's earnings. Discuss whether you consider this a growth company and a growth stock.
5. Select a company and indicate what economic series might be highly correlated with the firm's sales. Discuss why this is a relevant series.
6. Select a company and, based on reading its annual report and other public information, discuss its competitive strategy (low-cost producer or differentiation). Is the firm successful in implementing this strategy?
7. Discuss a company known to be a low-cost producer in its industry and consider what makes it possible for the firm to be a cost leader. Do the same for a firm known for differentiating.
8. Why is it not feasible to use the reduced form dividend discount model in the valuation of true growth companies?
9. You are told that a growth company has a P/E ratio of 10 times and a growth rate of 15 percent compared to the aggregate market, which has a growth rate of 8 percent and a P/E ratio of 11 times. What does this comparison imply regarding the growth company? What else do you need to know to properly compare the growth company to the aggregate market?
10. How is a domestic firm with 100 percent of its sales from the United States affected by fluctuating exchange rates?
11. Select a company and discuss the economic and structural influences that are affecting it.
12. Choose a firm and discuss its strengths and opportunities. How might the firm best address its weaknesses and threats?
13. How do Lynch's six categories assist the process of company analysis?
14. How might an analyst determine the value for a firm that pays no dividends and is expected to operate at a loss next year?
15. Explain the difference between statistical and judgmental forecasts of earnings. Give two examples of each.

16. How can an investor determine when it might be time to sell an investment?
17. Is being an accurate estimator of earnings a guarantee for success in stock investing? Why or why not?

Problems

1. Select two stocks in an industry of your choice and perform a common size income statement analysis over a two-year period.
   a. Discuss which firm is more cost effective.
   b. Discuss the relative year-to-year changes in gross profit margin, operating profit margin, and net profit margin for each company.
2. Select a company and examine its operating profit margin relative to the operating margin for its industry during the most recent ten-year period. Discuss the annual results in terms of levels and percentage changes.
3. Select any industry except chemicals and provide general background information on two non-U.S. companies from public sources. This background information should include their products, overall size (sales and assets), growth during the past five years (sales and earnings), ROE during the past two years, current stock prices, and P/E ratio.
4. Given Hitech's beta of 1.75 and a risk-free rate of 9 percent, what is the expected rate of return assuming
   a. A 15 percent market return?
   b. A 10 percent market return?
5. Select three companies from any industry.
   a. Compute their P/E ratios using last year's average price (high plus low/2) and earnings.
   b. Compute their growth rate of earnings over the last five years.
   c. Look up the most recent beta reported in *Value Line.*
   d. Discuss the relationships between P/E, growth, and risk.
6. *CFA Examination II (June 1981)*
   The value of an asset is the present value of the expected returns from the asset during the holding period. An investment will provide a stream of returns during this period, and it is necessary to discount this stream of returns at an appropriate rate to determine the asset's present value. A dividend valuation model such as the following is frequently used.

$$P_i = D_1/(k_i - g_i)$$

   where:

   P_i = **current price of common stock**
   D_1 = **expected dividend in next period**
   k_i = **required rate of return on stock** *i*
   g_i = **expected constant growth rate of dividends for stock** *i*

   a. Identify the three factors that must be estimated for any valuation model, and explain why these estimates are more difficult to derive for common stocks than for bonds. (9 minutes)
   b. Explain the principal problem involved in using a dividend valuation model to value
      (1) Companies whose operations are closely correlated with economic cycles.
      (2) Companies that are of giant size and are maturing.
      (3) Companies that are of small size and are growing rapidly.
      Assume all companies pay dividends. (6 minutes)
7. NDU, Inc. has paid annual dividends in the past six years of $0.40, 0.45, 0.50, 0.57, 0.65, and 0.75. What is the average growth rate of its dividends? What influences might cause an analyst to believe that the growth rate may rise in the future? What influences might cause an analyst to believe the growth rate may fall in the future?

8. The firm from problem 7, NDU, Inc., has a beta of 1.35. The expected market return is 14 percent and the risk-free rate is 4.5 percent. If an analyst believes that NDU's dividend growth will slow to 5 percent in the future, what is his estimate for the stock's intrinsic value?

9. Another analyst believes NDU's future constant dividend rate will be 6 percent. What is her estimate for NDU's intrinsic value?

10. Tuttle Inc. is expected to pay a $1 dividend next year; you've estimated its intrinsic value to be $10 a share. You require a 12 percent return on stock market investments with Tuttle's level of risk. If the current price of Tuttle was $9 a share, would you purchase it? What if the current price were $9.50? $10.00?

11. Using data and information sources such as *Value Line* and Standard & Poor's *Analysts Handbook* and *Industry Surveys,* apply two or more techniques to estimate a selected firms' earnings. If you had to choose a single dollar amount for the earnings estimate, what would it be? Explain why.

References

Association for Investment Management and Research and the Security Analysts Association of Japan. *Equity Securities Analysis and Evaluaton.* Charlottesville, Va.: Association for Investment Management and Research, 1993.

Copeland, Tom, Tim Koller, and Jack Murrin. *Valuation: Measuring and Managing the Value of Companies* (New York: Wiley, 1996).

Damodaran, Aswath. *Damodaran on Valuation* (New York: Wiley, 1994).

Lynch, Peter. *One Up on Wall Street.* New York: Simon & Schuster, 1989.

Pike, William H. *Why Stocks Go Up (and down).* Homewood, Ill.: Dow Jones–Irwin, 1983.

Porter, Michael E. *Competitive Advantage: Creating and Sustaining Superior Performance.* New York: The Free Press, 1985.

Squires, Jan R., ed. *Equity Research and Valuation Techniques* (Charlottesville, Va.: Association for Investment Management and Research, 1998).

GLOSSARY

Cyclical company   A firm whose earnings rise and fall with general economic activity.

Cyclical stock   A stock with a high beta; its gains typically exceed those of a rising market and its losses typically exceed those of a falling market.

Defensive company   Firms whose future earnings are likely to withstand an economic downturn.

Defensive stock   A stock whose return is not expected to decline as much as that of the overall market during a bear market.

Defensive strategy   A competitive strategy in which the firm positions itself so its capabilities provide the best means to deflect the effect of industry competitive forces.

Growth company   A company that consistently has the opportunities and ability to invest in projects that provide rates of return that exceed the firm's cost of capital. Because of these investment opportunities, it retains a high proportion of earnings, and its earnings grow faster than those of average firms.

Growth stock   A stock issue that generates a higher rate of return than other stocks in the market with similar risk characteristics.

Offensive strategy   A competitive strategy in which the firm uses its strengths to affect the competitive forces in the industry.

Speculative company   A firm with a great degree of business or financial risk, or both, with commensurate high earnings potential.

Speculative stock   A stock that appears highly overpriced compared to its reasonable valuation.

SWOT analysis   An examination of a firm's internal strengths and weaknesses and its external opportunities and threats.

Value stocks   Stocks that appear undervalued for reasons beside earnings growth potential. These stocks are usually identified based on low P/E ratios or low price-to-book ratios.

APPENDIX 13   *Information Sources for Company Analysis*

Extensive material is available on individual firms' stocks and bonds. Sources of these publications include individual companies; commercial publishing firms, which produce a vast array of material; reports provided by investment firms; and several investment magazines, which discuss the overall financial markets and provide opinions on individual companies and their stocks or bonds. We will discuss each of these sources and specific publications. Keep in mind that many of the sources described in the economy and industry analysis chapters also include discussions of individual stocks or bonds.

COMPANY-GENERATED INFORMATION

An obvious source of information about a company is the company itself. Indeed, some small firms may have no other source of information because trading activity in their stock is insufficient to justify inclusion in publications of commercial services or brokerage firms.

Annual Reports

Every firm with publicly traded stock must prepare and distribute to its stockholders an annual report of financial operations and current financial position. In addition to basic information, most reports discuss what happened during the year and outline future prospects. Most firms also publish quarterly financial reports that include brief income statements for the interim period and, sometimes, a balance sheet. These reports can be obtained directly from the company. To find an address for a company, you should consult Volume 1 of *Standard & Poor's Register of Corporations, Directors, and Executives,* which contains an alphabetical listing, by business name of approximately 37,000 corporations.

Security Prospectus

When a firm wants to sell securities (bonds, preferred stock, or common stock) in the primary market to raise new capital, the Securities and Exchange Commission (SEC) requires that it file a registration statement describing the securities being offered. It must provide extensive financial information beyond what is required in an annual report as well as nonfinancial information on its operations and personnel. A condensed version of the registration statement, referred to as a *prospectus,* is published by the underwriting firm and contains most of the relevant information. Copies of a prospectus for a current offering can be obtained from the underwriter or from the company. Investment banking firms will often advertise offerings in publications such as the *Wall Street Journal, Barron's,* or the *Financial Times.*

Required SEC Reports

In addition to registration statements, the SEC requires three *periodic* statements from publicly held firms. First, the 8-K form is filed each month, reporting any action that affects the debt, equity, amount of capital assets, voting rights, or other changes that might have a significant impact on the stock.

Second, the 9-K form is an unaudited report filed every six months that contains revenues, expenses, gross sales, and special items. It typically contains more extensive information than the quarterly statement.

Finally, the 10-K form is an annual version of the 9-K but is even more comprehensive. The SEC requires that firms indicate in their annual reports that a copy of their 10-K is available from the company upon request without charge.

COMMERCIAL PUBLICATIONS

Numerous advisory services supply information on the aggregate market and individual stocks. A partial list follows.

Standard & Poor's Publications

Standard & Poor's Corporation Records is a set of seven volumes. The first six contain basic information on all types of corporations (industrial, financial) arranged alphabetically. The volumes are in binders and are updated throughout the year. The seventh volume is a daily news volume that contains recent data on all companies listed in all the volumes.

Standard & Poor's Stock Reports are comprehensive two-page reports on numerous companies with stocks listed on the NYSE, AMEX, and traded over the counter. They include the near term sales and earnings outlook, recent developments, key income statement and balance sheet items, and a chart of stock price movements. They are in bound volumes by exchange and are revised every three to four months.

Standard & Poor's Stock Guide is a monthly publication that contains, in compact form, pertinent financial data on more than 5,000 common and preferred stocks. A separate section covers more than 400 mutual fund issues. For each stock, the guide contains information on price ranges (historical and recent), dividends, earnings, financial position, institutional holdings, and a ranking for earning and dividend stability. It is a useful quick reference for almost all actively traded stocks.

Standard & Poor's Bond Guide is a monthly publication that contains the most pertinent comparative financial and statistical information on a broad list of bonds including domestic and foreign bonds (about 3,900 issues), 200 foreign government bonds, and about 650 convertible bonds.

The Outlook is a weekly publication of Standard & Poor's Corporation that advises investors about the general market environment and specific groups of stocks or industries (for example, high-dividend stocks, stocks with low price-to-earnings ratios, high-yielding bonds, stocks likely to increase their dividends). Weekly stock index figures for eighty-eight industry groups and other market statistics are included.

Daily Stock Price Records is published quarterly by Standard & Poor's, with individual volumes for the NYSE, the AMEX, and the OTC market. Each quarterly book is divided into two parts. Part 1, "Major Technical Indicators of the Stock Market," is devoted to market indicators widely followed as technical guides to the stock market and includes price indicator series, volume series, and data on odd lots and short sales. Part 2, "Daily and Weekly Stock Action," gives daily high, low, close, and volume information as well as monthly data on short interest for individual stocks, insider trading information, a 200-day moving average of prices, and a weekly relative strength series. The books for the NYSE and AMEX are available from 1962 on; the OTC books begin in 1968.

Moody's Publications

Moody's Industrial Manual resembles the Standard & Poor's records service except it is organized by type of corporation (industrial, utility, and so on). The two-volume service is published once a year and covers industrial companies listed on the NYSE, the AMEX, and regional exchanges. One section concentrates on international industrial firms. Like all Moody's manuals, a news report volume covers events that occurred after publication of the basic manual.

Moody's OTC Industrial Manual is similar to the *Moody's Industrial Manual* of listed firms but is limited to stocks traded on the OTC market.

Moody's has manuals for various industries as well. *Moody's Public Utility Manual* provides information on public utilities, including electric and gas, gas transmission, telephone, and water companies. *Moody's Transportation Manual* covers the transportation industry, including railroads, airlines, steamship companies, electric railway, bus and truck lines, oil pipe lines, bridge companies, and automobile and truck leasing companies. *Moody's Bank and Finance Manual* covers the field of financial services represented by banks, savings and loan associations, credit agencies of the U.S. government, all phases of the insurance industry, investment companies, real estate firms, real estate investment trusts, and miscellaneous financial enterprises.

Moody's Municipal and Government Manual contains data on the U.S. government, all the states, state agencies, and more than 13,500 municipalities. It also includes some excellent information and data on foreign governments and international organizations.

Moody's International Manual provides financial information on about 3,000 major foreign corporations.

Value Line Publications

The *Value Line Investment Survey* is published in two parts. Volume I contains basic historic information on about 1,700 companies including a number of analytical measures of earnings stability, growth rates, a common stock safety factor, and a timing factor rating. Various studies have examined the usefulness of the timing factor ratings for investment purposes. The results of these studies were discussed in the efficient markets chapter.

The *Investment Survey* also includes extensive two-year *projections* for the given firms and three-year *estimates* of performance. As an example, in early 1998 it included an earnings projection for 1998, 1999, and 2000–2002. The second volume includes a weekly service that provides general investment advice and recommends individual stocks for purchase or sale.

The *Value Line OTC Special Situations Service* is published twenty-four times a year. It serves the experienced investor who is willing to accept high risk in the hope of realizing exceptional capital gains. Each issue discusses past recommendations and presents eight to ten new stocks for consideration.

BROKERAGE FIRM REPORTS

Besides the products of these information firms, many brokerage firms prepare reports on individual companies and their securities. Some of these reports are rather objective and contain only basic information, but others make specific recommendations.

COMPUTERIZED DATA SOURCES

In addition to the numerous published sources of data, some financial service firms have developed computerized data sources. Space limitations restrict the discussion to major sources.

Compustat is a computerized bank of financial data developed by Standard & Poor's and currently handled by a subsidiary, Investors Management Services. The Compustat tapes contain twenty years of data for approximately 2,220 listed industrial companies, 1,000 OTC companies, 175 utilities, 120 banks, and 500 Canadian firms. Quarterly

tapes contain twenty years of quarterly financial data for more than 2,000 industrial firms and twelve years of quarterly data for banks and utilities. The financial data on the annual tapes include almost every possible item from each firm's balance sheet and income statement as well as stock-market data (stock prices and trading volume).

Value Line Data Base contains historical annual and quarterly financial and market data for 1,600 industrial and finance companies beginning in 1954. It also provides quarterly data from 1963. In addition to historical data, it gives estimates of dividends and earnings for the coming year and the Value Line opinion regarding stock price stability and investment timing.

Compact Disclosure is a database on a compact disk with information on more than 4,000 public companies filing with the SEC. It is available from Disclosure Information Group of Bethesda, Maryland.

University of Chicago Stock Price Tapes is a set of monthly and daily stock price tapes developed by the Center for Research in Security Prices (CRSP) at the University of Chicago Graduate School of Business. The monthly tapes contain month-end prices from January 1926 to the present (updated annually) for every stock listed on the NYSE. Stock prices are adjusted for all stock splits, dividends, and any other capital changes. They added monthly AMEX data beginning from July 1962 to the NYSE monthly file to create the current NYSE/AMEX monthly file with information on approximately 6,100 securities.

The daily stock price tape contains the daily high, low, close, and volume figures since July 1962 for every stock listed on the NYSE and AMEX (approximately 5,600 securities). In 1988 the CRSP developed its NASDAQ historical data file with daily price quotes, volume, and information about capitalization and distributions to shareholders for more than 9,600 common stocks traded on the NASDAQ system since December 14, 1972. These tapes are updated at the end of each calendar year and supplied to subscribers each spring.

The *Media General Data Bank,* compiled by Media General Financial Services, Inc., includes current price and volume data plus major corporate financial data on 2,000 major companies. In addition, it contains ten years of daily price and volume information on more than 8,000 issues of approximately 4,000 firms on the NYSE, the AMEX, and the OTC market. Finally, it includes price and volume data on several major market indexes.

ISL Daily Stock Price Tapes are prepared by Interactive Data Corporation. They contain the same information as the *Daily Stock Price Records,* published by Standard & Poor's.

CHAPTER

14

Technical Analysis[1]

This chapter answers the following questions:

♦ How does technical analysis differ from fundamental analysis?

♦ What are the underlying assumptions of technical analysis?

♦ What major assumption causes a difference between technical analysis and the efficient market hypothesis?

♦ What are the major advantages of technical analysis compared to fundamental analysis?

♦ What are the major challenges to the assumptions of technical analysis and its rules?

♦ What is the logic for the major contrary opinion rules used by technicians?

♦ What are some of the significant rules used by technicians who want to follow the smart money and what is the logic of those rules?

♦ What is the breadth of market measures and what are they intended to indicate?

♦ What are the three types of price movements postulated in the Dow Theory and how are they used by a technician?

♦ Why do technicians consider the volume of trading important and how do they use it in their analysis?

♦ What are support and resistance levels, when do they occur, and how are they used by technicians?

♦ What is the purpose of moving average lines and how does the technician use one or several of them to detect major changes in trends?

---

[1]Richard T. McCabe, Chief Market Analyst at Merrill Lynch Capital Markets provided helpful comments and material for this chapter.

♦ What is the rationale behind the relative strength line for an industry or a stock and how is it interpreted?

♦ How are bar charts different from point-and-figure charts?

♦ What are some uses of technical analysis in foreign security markets?

♦ How is technical analysis used when analyzing bond markets?   ♦

The market reacted yesterday to the report of a large increase in the short interest on the NYSE.

Although the market declined today, it was not considered bearish because of the light volume.

The market declined today after three days of increases due to profit taking by investors.

These and similar statements appear daily in the financial news. All of them have as their rationale one of numerous technical trading rules. Technical analysts develop technical trading rules from observations of past price movements of the stock market and individual stocks. The philosophy behind technical analysis is in sharp contrast to the efficient market hypothesis that we studied, which contends that past performance has no influence on future performance or market values. It also differs from what we learned about fundamental analysis, which involves making investment decisions based on the examination of the economy, an industry, and company variables that lead to an estimate of value for an investment, which is then compared to the prevailing market price of the investment. In contrast to the efficient market hypothesis or fundamental analysis, **technical analysis** involves the examination of past market data such as prices and the volume of trading, which leads to an estimate of future price trends and, therefore, an investment decision. Whereas fundamental analysts use economic data that are usually separate from the stock or bond market, the technical analyst believes that using data *from the market itself* is a good idea because "the market is its own best predictor." Therefore, technical analysis is an alternative method of making the investment decision and answering the questions: What securities should an investor buy or sell? When should these investments be made?

Technical analysts see no need to study the multitude of economic, industry, and company variables to arrive at an estimate of future value because they believe that past price movements will signal future price movements. Technicians also believe that a change in the price trend may predict a forthcoming change in the fundamental variables such as earnings and risk earlier that the change is perceived or anticipated by most fundamental analysts. Are technicians correct? Many investors using these techniques claim to have experienced superior rates of return on many investments. In addition, many newsletter writers base their recommendations on technical analysis. Finally, even the major investment firms that employ many fundamental analysts also employ technical analysts to provide investment advice. Numerous investment professionals as well as individual investors believe in and use technical trading rules to make their investment decisions. Therefore, whether you are a fan of technical analysis or an advocate of the efficient market hypothesis, you should still have an understanding of the basic philosophy and reasoning behind these technical approaches. To help you understand technical analysis, we begin this chapter with an examination of the basic philosophy underlying all technical approaches to market analysis and company analysis. Subsequently, we consider the advantages and potential problems with the technical approach. Finally, we present and discuss alternative technical trading rules applicable to both the U.S. market and foreign securities markets.

UNDERLYING ASSUMPTIONS OF TECHNICAL ANALYSIS

Technical analysts base trading decisions on examinations of prior price and volume data to determine past market trends from which they predict future behavior for the market as a whole and for individual securities. Several assumptions lead to this view of price movements.

1. The market value of any good or service is determined solely by the interaction of supply and demand.
2. Supply and demand are governed by numerous factors, both rational and irrational. Included in these factors are those economic variables relied on by the fundamental analyst as well as opinions, moods, and guesses. The market weighs all these factors continually and automatically.
3. Disregarding minor fluctuations, *the prices for individual securities and the overall value of the market tend to move in trends, which persist for appreciable lengths of time.*
4   Prevailing trends change in reaction to shifts in supply and demand relationships. These shifts, no matter why they occur, *can be detected sooner or later in the action of the market itself.*[2]

Certain aspects of these assumptions are controversial, leading fundamental analysts and advocates of efficient markets to question their validity. Those aspects are emphasized above.

The first two assumptions are almost universally accepted by technicians and non-technicians alike. Almost anyone who has had a basic course in economics would agree that, at any point in time, the price of a security (or any good or service) is determined by the interaction of supply and demand. In addition, most observers would acknowledge that supply and demand are governed by many variables. The only difference in opinion might concern the influence of the irrational factors. A technical analyst might expect the irrational influence to persist for some time, whereas other market analysts would expect only a short-run effect with rational beliefs prevailing over the long run. Certainly, everyone would agree that the market continually weighs all these factors.

A stronger difference of opinion arises over the technical analysts' third assumption about the *speed of adjustment* of stock prices to changes in supply and demand. Technical analysts expect stock prices to move in trends that persist for long periods because they believe that new information that affects supply and demand does not come to the market at one point in time, but rather enters the market *over a period of time.* This pattern of information access occurs because of different sources of information or because certain investors receive the information or perceive fundamental changes earlier than others. As various groups ranging from insiders to well-informed professionals to the average investor receive the information and buy or sell a security accordingly, its price moves gradually toward the new equilibrium. Therefore, technicians do not expect the price adjustment to be as abrupt as fundamental analysts and efficient market supporters do, but expect a *gradual price adjustment* to reflect the gradual flow of information.

Figure 14.1 shows this process. The figure shows that new information causes a decrease in the equilibrium price for a security, but the price adjustment is not rapid. It occurs as a trend that persists until the stock reaches its new equilibrium. Technical analysts look for the beginning of a movement from one equilibrium value to a new equilibrium value. Technical analysts do not attempt to predict the new equilibrium value. They look for the start of a change so that they can get on the bandwagon early and benefit from the move to the new equilibrium by buying if the trend is up or selling if the trend is down. Obviously, rapid adjustment of prices as expected by those who espouse an efficient mar-

---

[2]These assumptions are summarized in Robert A. Levy, "Conceptual Foundations of Technical Analysis," *Financial Analysts Journal* 22, no. 4 (July–August 1966): 83.

Figure 14.1   *Technicians' View of Price Adjustment to New Information*

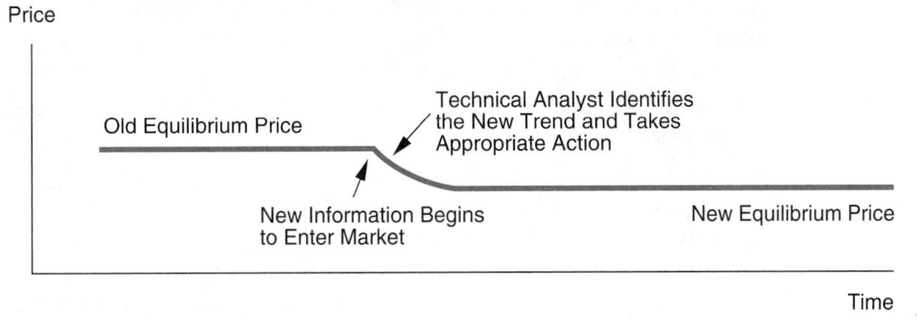

ket would keep the ride on the bandwagon so short that investors could not get onboard and benefit from the ride.

ADVANTAGES OF TECHNICAL ANALYSIS

Although technicians understand the logic of fundamental analysis, technical analysts see benefits in their approach compared to fundamental analysis. Most technical analysts admit that a fundamental analyst with good information, good analytical ability, and a keen sense of information's impact on the market should achieve above average returns. However, this statement requires qualification. According to technical analysts, it is important to recognize that the fundamental analysts can experience superior returns *only* if they obtain new information before other investors and process it *correctly* and *quickly*. Technical analysts do not believe the vast majority of investors can consistently get new information before other investors and consistently process it correctly and quickly.

In addition, technical analysts claim that a major advantage of their method is that *it is not heavily dependent on financial accounting statements*—the major source of information about the past performance of a firm or industry. As you know from Chapters 12 and 13, the fundamental analyst evaluates such statements to help project future return and risk characteristics for industries and individual securities. The technician points out several major problems with accounting statements:

1. They lack a great deal of information needed by security analysts, such as details on sales and general expenses or information related to sales, earnings, and capital utilized by product line and customers.
2. According to GAAP (Generally Accepted Accounting Principles), corporations may choose among several procedures for reporting expenses, assets, or liabilities, and these alternative procedures can produce vastly different values for expenses, income, return on assets, and return on equity. As a result, an investor can have trouble comparing the statements of two firms in the same industry, much less firms in different industries.
3. Many psychological factors and other nonquantifiable variables do not appear in financial statements. Examples include employee training and loyalty, customer goodwill, and general investor attitude toward an industry. Investor attitudes could become important when investors become concerned about the risk from restrictions or taxes on products such as tobacco or alcohol or when firms do business in countries that have significant political risk.

Therefore, because technicians are suspicious of financial statements, they consider it advantageous not to depend on them. As we will show, most of the data used by technicians, such as security prices, volume of trading, and other trading information, are derived from the stock market itself.

Also, a fundamental analyst must process new information correctly and *quickly* to derive a new intrinsic value for the stock or bond before the other investors can. Technicians, on the other hand, need only quickly recognize a movement to a new equilibrium value *for whatever reason*—that is, they need not know about an event and determine the effect of the event on the value of the firm and its stock.

Finally, assume a fundamental analyst determines that a given security is under- or overvalued a long time before other investors. He or she still must determine when to make the purchase or sale. Ideally, the highest rate of return would come from making the transaction just before the change in market value occurs. For example, assume that based on your analysis in February, you expect a firm to report substantially higher earnings in June. Although you could buy the stock in February, you would be better off waiting until about May to buy the stock so your funds would not be tied up for an extra three months, but you may be reticent to wait that long. Because most technicians do not invest until the move to the new equilibrium is underway, they contend that they are more likely to experience ideal timing compared to the fundamental analyst.

CHALLENGES TO TECHNICAL ANALYSIS

Those who question the value of technical analysis for investment decisions question the usefulness of this technique in two areas. First, they challenge some of its basic assumptions. Second, they challenge some of its specific trading rules and their long-run usefulness. In this section, we consider both of these challenges.

Challenges to Technical Analysis Assumptions

The major challenge to technical analysis is based on the results of empirical tests of the efficient market hypothesis (EMH). As discussed in Chapter 8, for technical trading rules to generate superior risk-adjusted returns after taking account of transactions costs, the market would have to be slow to adjust prices to the arrival of new information, that is, it would have to be inefficient. (This is referred to as the weak-form efficient market hypothesis.) The two sets of tests of the weak-form EMH are: (1) the statistical analysis of prices to determine if prices moved in trends or were a random walk, and (2) the analysis of specific trading rules to determine if their use could beat a buy-and-hold policy after considering transactions costs and risk. Almost all the studies testing the weak-form efficient market hypothesis using statistical analysis have found that prices do not move in trends based on statistical tests of autocorrelation and runs. These results support the efficient market hypothesis.

Regarding the analysis of specific trading rules, as discussed in Chapter 8, numerous technical trading rules exist that have not been or cannot be tested. Still, the vast majority of the results for the trading rules tested support the hypothesis.

Challenges to Technical Trading Rules

An obvious challenge to technical analysis is that the past price patterns or relationships between specific market variables and stock prices may not be repeated. As a result, a technique that previously worked might miss subsequent market turns. This possibility

leads most technicians to follow several trading rules and to seek a consensus of all of them to predict the future market pattern.

Other critics contend that many price patterns become self-fulfilling prophecies. For example, assume that many analysts expect a stock selling at $40 a share to go to $50 or more if it should rise above its current pattern and "break through" its channel at $45. As soon as it reaches $45, enough technicians will buy to cause the price to rise to $50, exactly as predicted. In fact, some technicians may place a limit order to buy the stock at such a breakout point. Under such conditions, the increase will probably be only temporary and the price will return to its true equilibrium.

Another problem with technical analysis is that the success of a particular trading rule will encourage many investors to adopt it. It is contended that this popularity and the result-ing competition eventually neutralize the value of the technique. If numerous investors focus on a specific technical trading rule, some of them will attempt to anticipate what will happen prior to the completed price pattern and either ruin the expected historical price pattern or eliminate profits for most users of the trading rule by causing the price to change faster than expected. For example, suppose it becomes known that technicians who invest on the basis of the amount of short selling have been enjoying high rates of return. Based on this knowledge, other technicians will likely start using these data and thus accelerate the stock price pattern following changes in the amount of short selling. As a result, the trading rule that provided high rates of return previously may no longer be profitable after the first few investors react.

Further, as we will see when we examine specific trading rules, *they all require a great deal of subjective judgment.* Two technical analysts looking at the same price pattern may arrive at widely different interpretations of what has happened and, therefore, will come to different investment decisions. This implies that the use of various techniques is nei-ther completely mechanical nor obvious. Finally, as we will discuss in connection with several trading rules, *the standard values that signal investment decisions can change over time.* Therefore, technical analysts must adjust the specified values that trigger investment decisions over time to conform to the new environment. In other cases, trading rules are abandoned because it appears they no longer work.

TECHNICAL TRADING RULES AND INDICATORS

To help you understand the specific technical trading rules, Figure 14.2 shows a typical stock price cycle that could be an example for the overall stock market or for an individual stock. The graph shows a peak and trough, along with a rising trend channel, a flat trend channel, a declining trend channel, and indications of when a technical analyst would ide-ally want to trade.

The graph begins with the end of a declining (bear) market that finishes in a **trough** followed by an upward trend that breaks through the **declining trend channel**. Confir-mation that the trend has reversed would be a buy signal. The technical analyst would buy stocks in general or an individual stock that showed this pattern.

The analyst would then look for the development of a **rising trend channel**. As long as the stock price stayed in this rising channel, the technician would hold the stock(s) for the upward ride. Ideally, you want to sell at the **peak** of the cycle, but you cannot iden-tify a peak until after the trend changes.

If the stock (or the market) begins trading in a flat pattern, it will necessarily break out of its rising trend channel. At this point, some technical analysts would sell, but most would hold to see if the stock experiences a period of consolidation and then breaks out of the **flat trend channel** on the upside and begins rising again. Alternatively, if the stock

Figure 14.2   *Typical Stock Market Cycle*

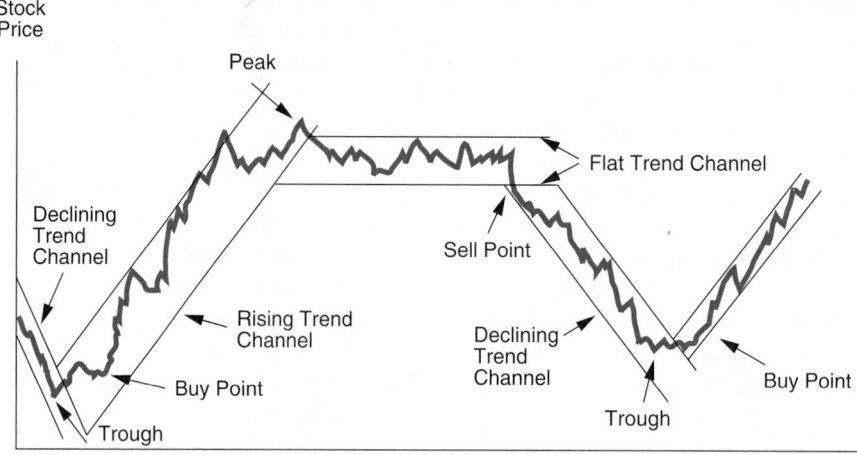

were to break out of the channel on the downside, the technician would take this as a sell signal and would expect a declining trend channel. The next buy signal would come after the trough when the price breaks out of the declining channel and establishes a rising trend. Subsequently, we will consider strategies to detect these changes in trend and the importance of volume in this analysis.

There are numerous technical trading rules and a range of interpretations for each of them, Almost all technical analysts watch many alternative rules and decide on a buy or sell decision based on a *consensus* of the signals because complete agreement of all the rules is rare. This section discusses most of the well-known techniques. The presentation on domestic indicators is divided into four sections based on the attitudes of technical analysts. The first group includes trading rules used by analysts who like to trade against the crowd using contrary-opinion signals. The second group of rules attempts to emulate astute investors, that is, the smart money. The next section includes technical indicators that are very popular but not easily classified. The fourth section covers pure price and volume techniques, including the famous Dow Theory. The final sections describe how these technical trading rules have been applied to foreign securities markets and bond markets.

Contrary-Opinion Rules

Many technical analysts rely on technical trading rules developed from the premise that the majority of investors are wrong as the market approaches peaks and troughs. Therefore, these technicians try to determine when the majority of investors is either strongly bullish or bearish and then trade in the opposite direction.[3]

Mutual Fund Cash Positions   Mutual funds hold some part of their portfolio in cash for one of several reasons. The most obvious reason is that they need cash to liquidate shares that fundholders sell back to the fund. Another reason is that the money from new

---

[3]Prior editions of this book included the percentage of odd-lot purchases and sales or odd-lot short sales as a percentage of total odd-lot sales as contrary-opinion rules. These are no longer included because odd-lot volume now accounts for a small proportion of total trading volume and is no longer considered a valid indication of small investor sentiment.

investments in the mutual fund may not have been invested. A third reason might be the portfolio manager's bearish outlook for the market, inspiring an asset allocation decision to increase the fund's defensive cash position.

Mutual funds' ratios of cash as a percentage of the total assets in their portfolios (the *cash ratio* or *liquid asset ratio*) are reported in the press, including monthly figures in *Barron's*.[4] This percentage of cash has varied in recent years from a low point of about 7 percent to a high point near 13 percent, although the range has increased during the past several years and there appears to be a rising trend to the series.

Contrary-opinion technicians consider the mutual funds a good proxy for the institutional investor. They also believe that mutual funds usually are wrong at peaks and troughs. Thus, they expect mutual funds to have a high percentage of cash near the trough of a market cycle, implying that they are bearish exactly at the time that they should be fully invested to take advantage of the impending market rise. At the market peak, technicians expect mutual funds to be almost fully invested with a low percentage of cash. This would indicate a bullish outlook by the mutual funds when they should be selling stocks and realizing gains for some part of their portfolios. Therefore, contrary-opinion technicians would watch for the mutual fund cash position to approach one of the extremes and act contrary to the mutual funds. Specifically, they would tend to buy when the cash ratio approaches 13 percent and to sell when the cash ratio approaches 7 percent.

Figure 14.3 contains a time-series plot of the Dow Jones Industrial Average (DJIA) and the mutual fund cash ratio. It shows apparent bullish signals in 1970, in late 1974, in 1982, and in late 1990 near market troughs. Bearish signals appeared in 1971, 1972 to 1973, and 1976 prior to market peaks. The cash ratio has been falling since the summer of 1993 and as of July 1998 was the lowest it had been since 1976.

A high mutual fund cash position also can be considered as a bullish indicator because of potential buying power. Whether the cash balances have built up because of stock sales completed as part of a selling program or because investors have been buying mutual funds (as in 1996 and 1997), technicians believe these cash funds will eventually be invested and will cause stock prices to increase. This "liquidity" concept was widely discussed as a major cause of the market rise in 1997 and 1998. Alternatively, a low cash ratio would mean that the institutions have bought heavily and are left with little potential buying power. Obviously, the low cash position in July 1998 would not be a positive market factor.

A couple of studies have examined this mutual fund cash ratio and its components as a predictor of market cycles. They concluded that the mutual fund liquid asset ratio was not as strong a predictor of market cycles as suggested by technical analysts.[5]

Credit Balances in Brokerage Accounts   Credit balances result when investors sell stocks and leave the proceeds with their brokers, expecting to reinvest them shortly. The amounts are reported by the SEC and the NYSE in *Barron's*. Because technical analysts view these credit balances as pools of potential purchasing power, they interpret a decline in these balances as bearish because it indicates lower purchasing power as the market approaches a peak. Alternatively, technicians view a buildup of credit balances as an increase in buying power and a bullish signal.

Note that the data used to interpret the market environment are stated in terms of an increase or decline in the credit balance series rather than comparing these balances to

[4]*Barron's* is a prime source for numerous technical indicators. For a readable discussion of relevant data and their use, see Martin E. Zweig, *Understanding Technical Forecasting* (New York: Dow Jones & Co., 1987).

[5]Paul H. Massey, "The Mutual Fund Liquidity Ratio: A Trap for the Unwary," *Journal of Portfolio Management* 5, no. 2 (Winter 1979): 18–21; and R. David Ranson and William G. Shipman, "Institutional Buying Power and the Stock Market," *Financial Analysts Journal* 37, no. 5 (September–October 1981): 62–68.

Figure 14.3   *Time-Series Plot of Dow Jones Industrial Average and Mutual Fund Cash-to-Asset Ratio (Cash/Total Assets)*

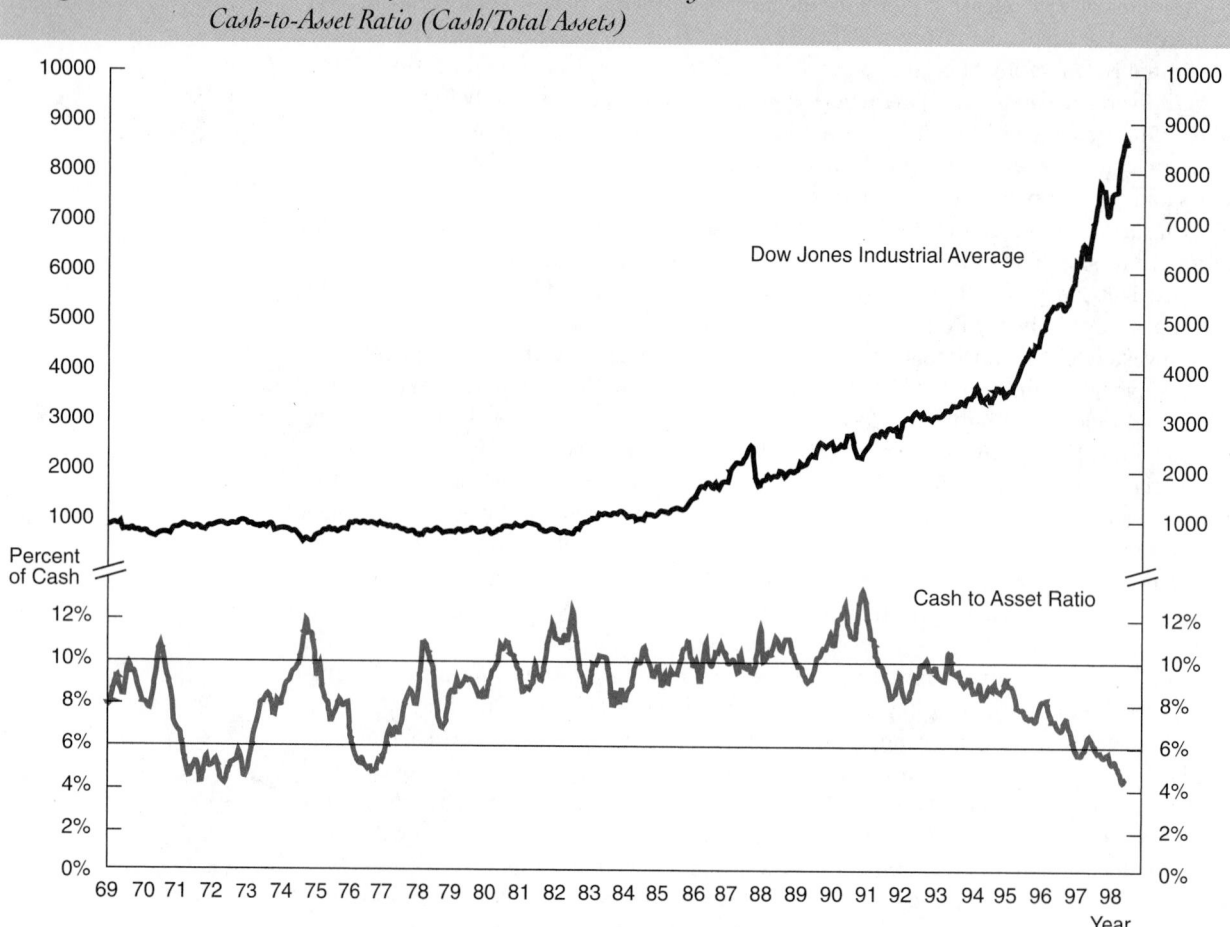

Source: *Where the Indicators Stand* (New York: Merrill Lynch, July 1998) Reprinted by permission of Merrill Lynch.

some other series. This assumption of an absolute trend could make interpretation difficult as market levels change.

Investment Advisory Opinions   Many technicians believe that if a large proportion of investment advisory services have a bearish attitude, this signals the approach of a market trough and the onset of a bull market. It is reasoned that because most advisory services tend to be trend followers, the number of bears usually is greatest when market bottoms are approaching. They develop this trading rule from the ratio of the number of advisory services that are bearish as a percentage of the number of services expressing an opinion.[6] A "bearish sentiment index" of 60 percent indicates a pervasive bearish attitude by advisory services, and contrarians would consider this a bullish indicator. In contrast, a decline of this bearish sentiment index to below 20 percent indicates a pervasive bullish attitude by advisory services, which technicians would interpret as a bearish sign.

---

[6]This ratio is compiled by Investors Intelligence, Larchmont, NY 10538. Richard McCabe at Merrill Lynch uses this series as one of his "Investor Sentiment Indicators."

Figure 14.4   *Time-Series Plot of Dow Jones Industrial Average and the Bullish and Bearish Sentiment Indexes*

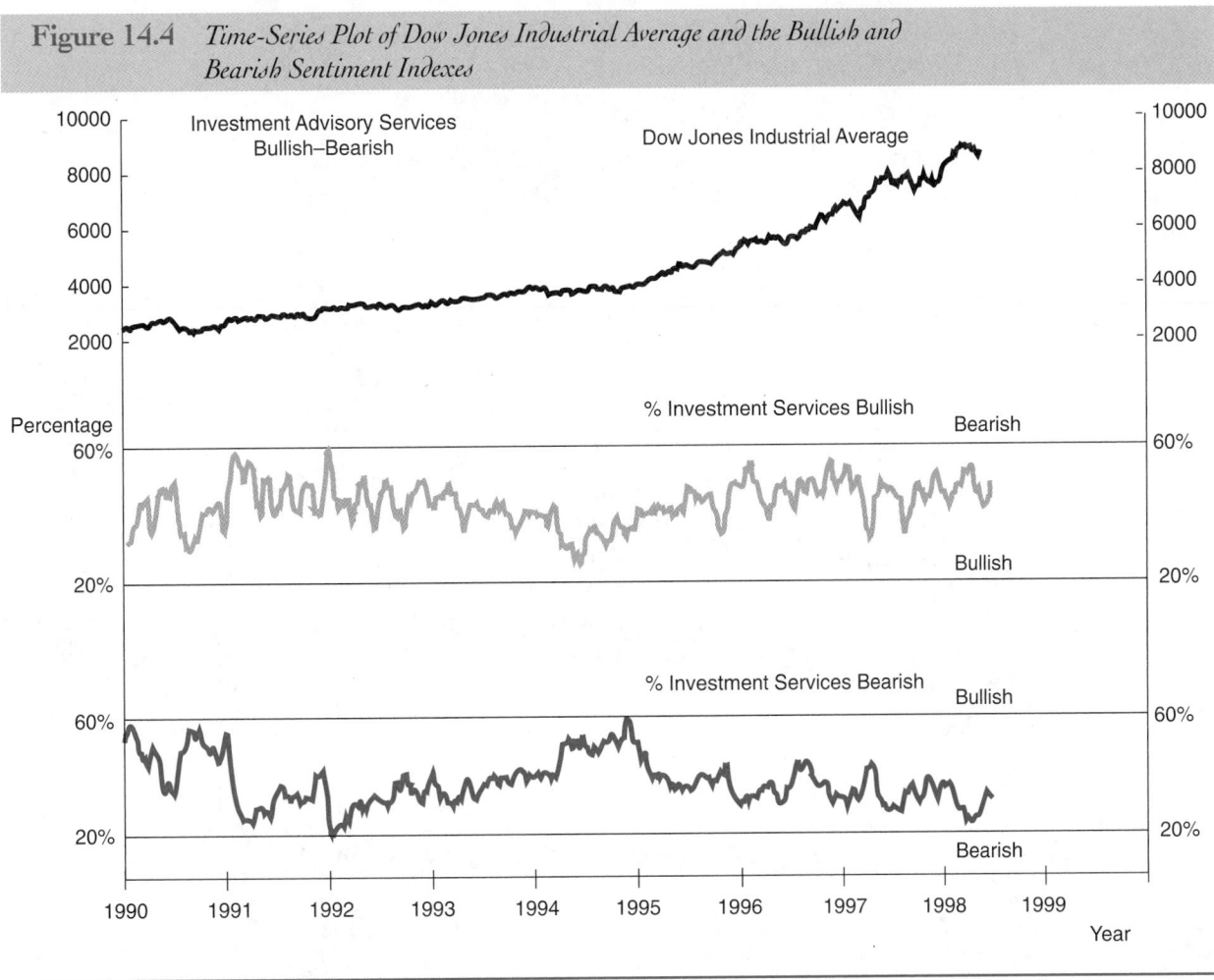

Source: "Where the Indicators Stand" (New York: Merrill Lynch, July, 1998). Source of data: Investor Intelligence, Larchmont NY 10538.

Figure 14.4 shows a time-series plot of the DJIA and both the bearish sentiment index and the bullish sentiment index. As of mid-1998, both indexes had moved toward the bearish boundary values, but subsequently moved back to the neutral territory.

OTC Versus NYSE Volume   This ratio of trading volume has historically been considered a measure of speculative activity. Prior to the 1970s, the accepted measure of speculative trading activity was the ratio of AMEX volume to NYSE volume. This ratio is no longer considered useful because the ratio of AMEX to NYSE volume has gone from about 50 percent in the 1950s and 1960s to about 10 percent or less currently. Instead, technicians currently use the ratio of OTC volume on the NASDAQ system to NYSE volume as a measure of speculative trading. Speculative trading typically peaks at market peaks. Figure 14.5 contains a time-series plot of the NASDAQ Composite Average and the OTC/NYSE volume ratio.

Notably, beyond changing from using AMEX volume to OTC volume, the interpretation of the ratio has changed—that is, the decision rules have changed. Specifically, in 1990 the

Figure 14.5 *Time-Series Plot of NASDAQ Composite Average and the Ratio of OTC Volume to NYSE Volume (Three-Week Average)*

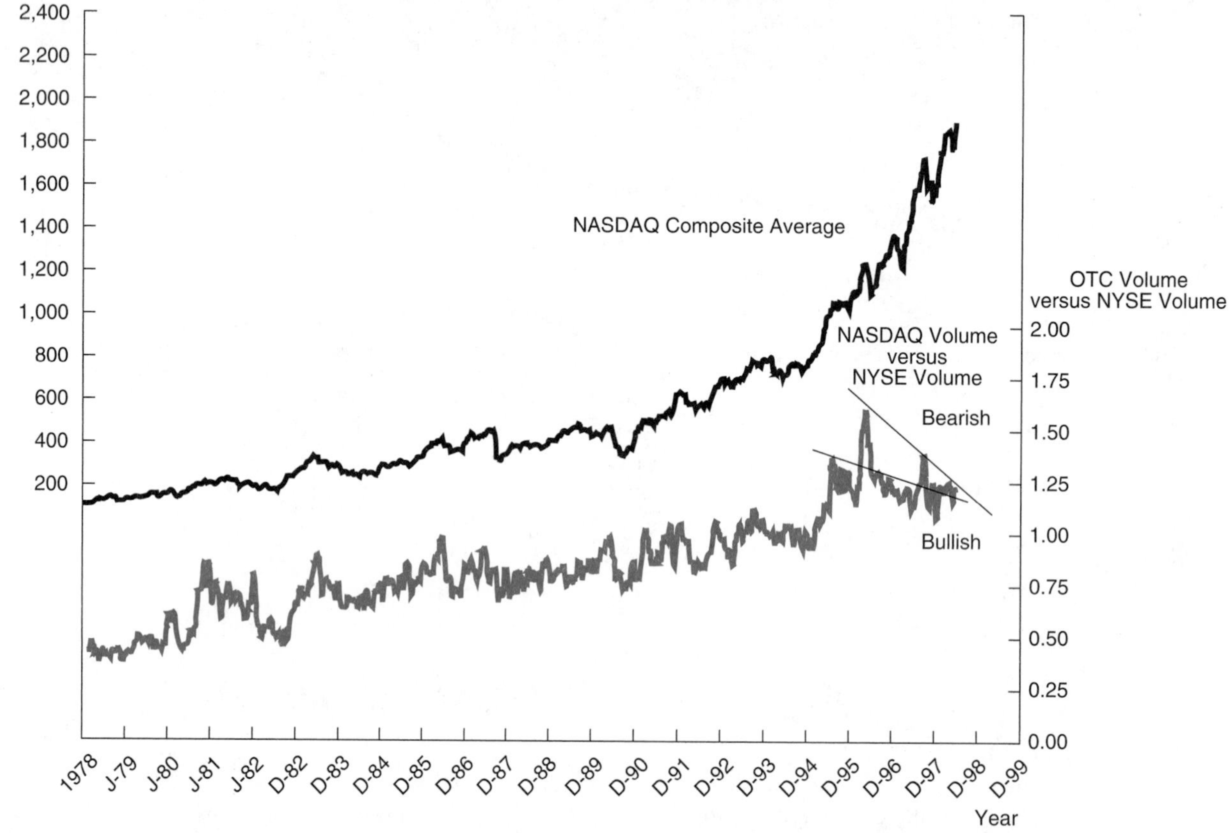

Source: *Where the Indicators Stand* (New York: Merrill Lynch, July 1998).

decision rules were 90 percent (this indicated heavy speculative trading) and 70 percent (this indicated low speculative trading and an over-sold market). The decision rules were changed to 100 percent and 80 percent in 1994 and to 112 percent and 87 percent in 1996. The source of this rising drift in the decision rules was faster growth in the number of stocks listed on the OTC, rapid growth in OTC trading volume over the year, and dominance of the OTC market by a few large-cap stocks. In 1998, it was decided to drop the percent values and detect excess speculative activity by using the *direction* of the volume ratio as a guide. As shown in Figure 14.5, as of mid-1998, the ratio was falling, which is a positive indicator.

The Chicago Board Options Exchange (CBOE) Put/Call Ratio The CBOE equity (only) put/call ratio is a relatively new tool of contrary-opinion technicians. They use put options, which give the holder the right to sell stock at a specified price for a given time period, as signals of a bearish attitude. The technicians reason that a higher put/call ratio indicates a more pervasive bearish attitude, which they consider a bullish indicator.

As shown in Figure 14.6, this ratio fluctuates between .50 and .30. It typically has been substantially less than 1 because investors tend to be bullish and avoid selling short or buying puts. The current decision rule states that a put/call ratio above .50—fifty puts are

Figure 14.6   *Time-Series Plot of Dow Jones Industrial Average and the CBOE Equity (Only) Put/Call Ratio (Five-Day Average)*

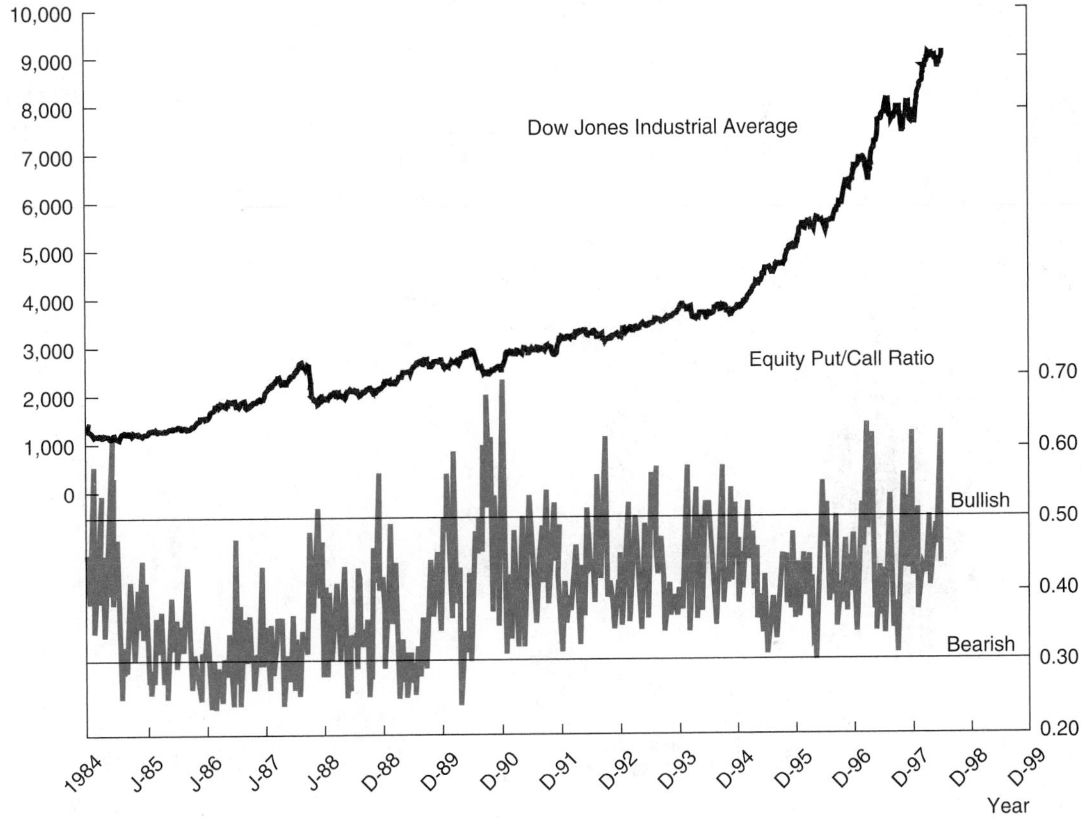

Source: *Where the Indicators Stand* (New York: Merrill Lynch, July, 1998)

traded for every one hundred calls—is considered bullish, while a relatively low put/call ratio of .30 or less is considered a bearish sign. The value of the ratio in mid-1998 was rated positive because it had been above .50.

Futures Traders Bullish on Stock Index Futures   Another relatively new measure used by contrary-opinion technicians is the percentage of speculators in stock index futures who are bullish. Specifically, an advisory service (Market Vane) surveys other firms that provide advisory services for the futures market along with individual traders involved in the futures market to determine whether these futures traders are bearish or bullish regarding stocks. A plot of the series in Figure 14.7 indicates that these technicians would consider it a bearish sign when more than 70 percent of the speculators are bullish, and it is bullish if the portion of bullish speculators declines to 30 percent or lower. Again, as of mid-1998 the series was within the specified boundaries indicating a neutral environment.

As you can see, technicians who seek to be contrary to the market have several series that provide measures of how the majority of investors are investing. They then take the opposite action. They generally would follow several of these series to provide a consensus regarding investors' attitudes.

Figure 14.7   *Time-Series Plot of Dow Jones Industrial Average and Percentage of Futures Traders Bullish on Stock Index Futures*

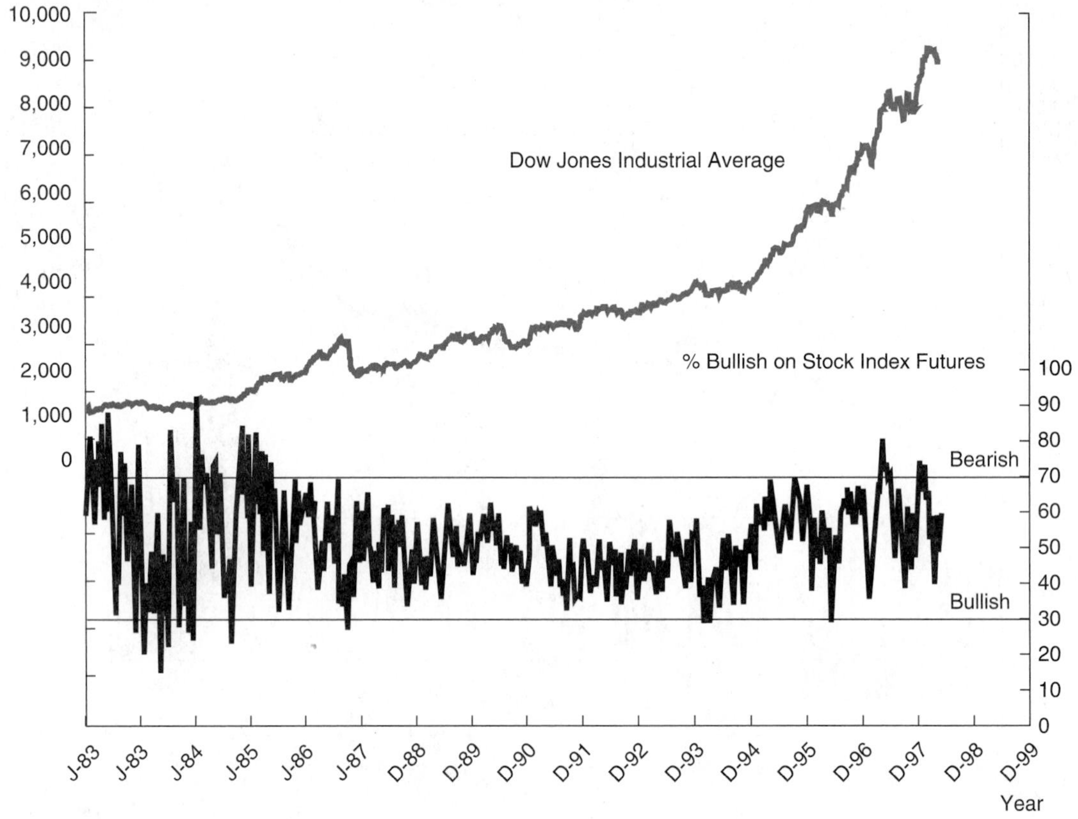

Source: *Where the Indicators Stand* (New York: Merrill Lynch, July 1998), Data Courtesy of Market Vane.

Follow the Smart Money

Some technical analysts have created a set of indicators that they expect to indicate the behavior of smart, sophisticated investors and create rules to follow them. In this section, we discuss some of the more popular indicators of what smart investors are doing.

The Confidence Index   Published by *Barron's,* the Confidence Index is the ratio of *Barron's* average yield on ten top-grade corporate bonds to the yield on the Dow Jones average of forty bonds. This index measures the difference in yield spread between high-grade bonds and a large cross section of bonds.[7] Because the yields on high-grade bonds always should be lower than those on a large cross section of bonds, this ratio should never exceed 100. It approaches 100 as the spread between the two sets of bonds gets smaller.

Technicians believe the ratio is a bullish indicator because, during periods of high confidence, investors are willing to invest more in lower-quality bonds for the added yield.

---

[7]Historical data for this series are contained in the *Dow Jones Investor's Handbook* (Princeton, NJ: Dow Jones Books, annual). Current figures appear in *Barron's.*

This investment attitude should cause a decrease in the average yield for the large cross section of bonds relative to the yield on high-grade bonds. Therefore, this ratio of yields, which is the Confidence Index, will increase. In contrast, when investors are pessimistic, they avoid investing in low-quality bonds and increase their investments in high-grade bonds. This shift in investment preference increases the yield spread between high-grade and average bonds, which causes the Confidence Index to decline.

Unfortunately, this interpretation of bond investor behavior is almost solely demand-oriented. Specifically, it assumes that changes in the yield spread are caused almost exclusively by changes in investor demand for different quality bonds. In fact, the yield differences have frequently changed because the supply of bonds in one of the groups increased. For example, a large issue of high-grade AT&T bonds could cause a temporary increase in yields on all high-grade bonds, which would reduce the yield spread and cause an increase in the Confidence Index without any change in investors' attitudes. Such a change in the supply of bonds can cause the series to generate a false signal of a change in confidence.

Advocates of the index believe that it reflects investor attitudes toward financial assets. Several studies have found that this index has been of little use in predicting stock price movements.

T-Bill–Eurodollar Yield Spread   An alternative measure of investor attitude or confidence on a global basis is the spread between T-bill yields and Eurodollar rates. It is reasoned that, at times of international crisis, this spread widens as money flows to safehaven U.S. T-bills, which causes a decline in this ratio. The stock market has tended to reach a trough shortly thereafter.

Short Sales by Specialists   Data for total short sales on the NYSE, along with those for the specialist on the exchange, appear weekly in *Barron's*. It should be no surprise after our discussion in Chapter 4 that technicians who want to follow smart money watch the specialist. Specialists regularly engage in short selling as a part of their market-making function, but they can exercise discretion in this area when they feel strongly about expected market changes.

The normal ratio of specialists' short sales to total short sales has been approximately 40 percent.[8] Technicians view a decline in this ratio below 30 percent as a bullish sign because it means that specialists are attempting to minimize their participation in short sales. A ratio above 50 percent is a bearish sign.

Note two points about this ratio. First, do not expect it to be a long-run indicator; the nature of the specialists' portfolio probably will limit it to short-run movements. Second, there is a two-week lag in reporting these data.

Although a graph of the specialist short-sales ratio indicated some support for the ratio as a buying signal, when used as a trading rule it provided insignificant excess returns.[9]

Debit Balances in Brokerage Accounts (Margin Debt)   Debit balances in brokerage accounts represent borrowing (margin debt) by knowledgeable investors from their brokers. These balances indicate the attitude of a sophisticated group of investors who engage in margin transactions. Therefore, an increase in debit balances by this astute group would be a bullish sign. In contrast, a decline in debit balances would indicate selling as these sophisticated investors liquidate their positions and could indicate less capital available for investing. In either case, this would be a bearish indicator.

---

[8]Notably, during the early 1970s the norm for this short sale ratio was about 55 percent, and it became about 45 percent pre-1981. Therefore, this is an example of another technique for which the decision ratio has changed over time.

[9]Frank K. Reilly and David Whitford, "A Test of the Specialists' Short Sale Ratio," *Journal of Portfolio Management* 8, no. 2 (Winter 1982): 12–18.

Monthly data on margin debt is reported in *Barron's.* Unfortunately, this series does not include borrowing by investors from other sources such as banks. Also, because it is an absolute value, technicians would look for changes in the trend of borrowing.

Other Market Environment Indicators

In this section, we discuss several indicators that show overall market sentiment and that are used to make investment decisions related to the aggregate market.

Breadth of Market   Breadth of market measures the number of issues that have increased each day and the number of issues that have declined. It helps explain the cause of a change of direction in a composite market series such as the DJIA or the S&P 400 Index. As discussed in Chapter 5, the major stock-market series are heavily influenced by the stocks of large firms because most indexes are value-weighted. As a result, it is possible for a stock-market series to increase, but the majority of the individual issues will not. This divergence between the value for the aggregate index and its components is a problem because it means that most stocks are not participating in the rising market. Such a situation can be detected by examining the advance–decline figures for all stocks on the exchange, along with the overall market index.

A useful way to specify the advance–decline series for analysis is to create a cumulative series of net advances or net declines. Each day major newspapers publish figures on the number of issues on the NYSE that advanced, declined, or were unchanged The figures for a five-day sample, as would be reported in *Barron's,* are shown in Table 14.1. These figures, along with changes in the DJIA at the bottom of the table, indicate to a technician a strong market advance because the DJIA was increasing and the net advance figure was strong, indicating that the market increase was broadly based and extended to most individual stocks. Even the results on Day 3, when the market declined eight points, were somewhat encouraging. Although the market was down, it was a slight net decline and the individual stocks were split just about 50–50, which points toward a fairly even environment.

An alternative specification of the advance–decline series, a **diffusion index,** shows the daily total of stocks advancing plus one-half the number unchanged, divided by the total number of issues traded. To smooth the series, Merrill Lynch computes a five-week moving average of these daily figures as shown in Figure 14.8.

Crossings from below to above 50 indicate the market's intermediate-term trend if the moving average series has turned from down to up. This advance–decline series also is used to measure intermediate trends and to signal overbought levels if it reaches very high levels of 56 to 60 or the market is considered oversold when it gets down to 40–44.

Table 14.1   *Daily Advances and Declines on the New York Stock Exchange*

Day	1	2	3	4	5
Issues traded	2,608	2,641	2,659	2,651	2,612
Advances	1,710	1,650	1,108	1,661	1,725
Declines	609	650	1,149	633	594
Unchanged	289	341	402	357	293
Net advances (advances minus declines)	+1,101	+1,000	−41	+1,028	+1,131
Cumulative net advances	+1,101	+2,101	+2,060	+3,088	+4,219
Changes in DJIA	+20.47	+13.99	−8.18	+9.16	+15.56

Sources: New York Stock Exchange and *Barron's.*

Figure 14.8   *Time-Series Plot of Dow Jones Industrial Average and Five-Week Moving Average of the Advance–Decline Diffusion Index*

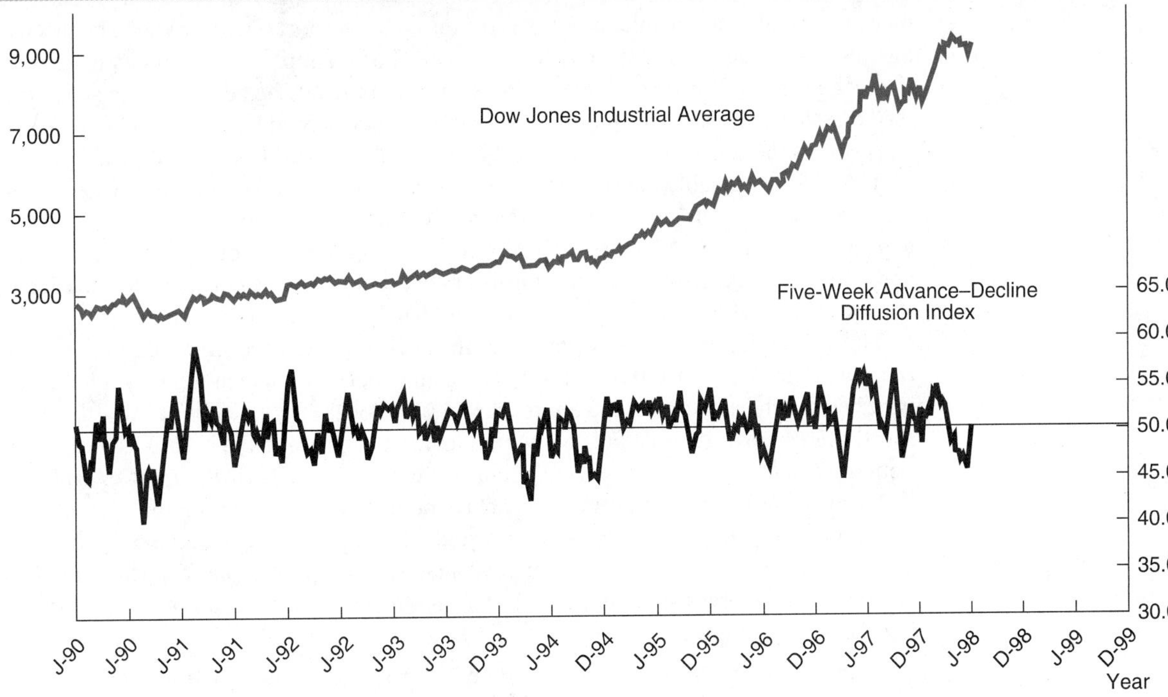

Source: *Where the Indicators Stand* (New York: Merrill Lynch, July 1998).

As of mid-1998, the diffusion indicator had turned up from the intermediate oversold level of 45 and was looking positive. The usefulness of the advance–decline series is supposedly greatest at market peaks and troughs when the composite value-weighted market series might be moving either up or down, but the majority of individual stocks might be moving in the opposite direction. As an example, near a peak, the DJIA would be increasing, but the net advance–decline ratio would become negative, the cumulative advance–decline series would level off and decline and the diffusion index would go below 50 percent. The *divergence* between the trend for the market index and the various advance–decline series would signal a market peak.

In contrast, as the market approached a trough, the composite market index would be declining, but the daily advance–decline ratio would become positive, the cumulative advance–decline index would turn up and the diffusion index would rise above 50 percent before the aggregate market index increased.[10] In summary, a technician would look for the advance–decline series to indicate a change in trend before the composite stock-market series.[11]

---

[10]Ideally the performance of the series should work at both peaks and troughs. In fact, it appears to work best at peaks. Apparently at troughs, the secondary stocks, which make up most of the issues, may remain weak until the low point and keep the advance–decline figures negative.

[11]This series also has been used to evaluate non-U.S. indexes. See Linda Sandler, "Advance–Decline Line, a Popular Indicator, Warns of Correction in Tokyo Stock Market," *Wall Street Journal*, August 26, 1988, C1.

Short Interest The short interest is the cumulative number of shares that have been sold short by investors and not covered. This means the investor has not purchased the shares sold short and returned them to the investor from whom they were borrowed. Technicians compute a short-interest ratio as the outstanding short interest divided by the average daily volume of trading on the exchange. For example, if the outstanding short interest on the NYSE was 2,000 million shares and the average daily volume of trading on the exchange was 450 million shares, the short-interest ratio would be 4.44 (2,000/450). This means the outstanding short interest equals about four days' trading volume.

Technicians probably interpret this ratio contrary to your initial intuition. Because short sales reflect investors' expectations that stock prices will decline, one would typically expect an increase in the short-interest ratio to be bearish. On the contrary, technicians consider a high short-interest ratio bullish because it indicates *potential demand* for the stock by those who previously sold short and have not covered the short sale.

This is another example of a change in the decision value over time. Before 1994, the range was between 2.0 and 3.0. Based on recent experience, a technician would be bullish when the short-interest ratio approached 4.0 and bearish if it declined toward 3.0. The short-interest position is calculated by the stock exchanges and the NASD as of the twentieth of each month and is reported about two days later in the *Wall Street Journal.*

Various studies have examined the short-interest series as a predictor of stock price movements, with mixed results. For every study that supports the technique, another indicates that it should be rejected.[12] Technical analysts have pointed out that this ratio—and any ratio that involves short selling—has been affected by new techniques for short selling such as options and futures.

Stocks Above Their 200-Day Moving Average Technicians often compute moving averages of a series to determine its general trend. To examine individual stocks, the 200-day **moving average** of prices has been fairly popular. From these moving-average series for numerous stocks, Media General Financial Services calculates how many stocks currently are trading above their 200-day moving-average series, and this is used as an indicator of general investor sentiment. As shown in Figure 14.9, the market is considered to be *overbought* and bearish when more than 80 percent of the stocks are trading above their 200-day moving average. Technical analysts believe that an overbought market signals a consolidation or a negative correction. In contrast, if less than 20 percent of the stocks are selling above their 200-day moving average, the market is considered to be *oversold,* which means investors should expect a positive correction. As shown in Figure 14.9, as of mid-1998, the percent of stocks selling above their 200-day moving average is tending toward a bullish signal because it is about 50 percent, but it is at a lower level than its two previous lows.

Block Uptick–Downtick Ratio As we discussed in Chapter 4, about 50 percent of NYSE volume comes from block trading by institutions. The exchange can determine whether the price change that accompanied a particular block trade was higher or lower than the price of the prior transactions. If the block trade price is above the prior transaction price, it is referred to as an **uptick**; if the block trade price is below the prior transaction price, it is referred to as a **downtick.**

It is assumed that if the block trade was initiated by a buyer, you would expect an uptick; if it was initiated by a seller, you would expect a downtick. This led to the development of the **uptick (buyers)–downtick (sellers) ratio**, which indicates institutional investor sentiment. As shown in Figure 14.10, this ratio generally has fluctuated in the range of .70,

---

[12]See Joseph Vu and Paul Caster, "Why All the Interest in Short Interest?" *Financial Analysts Journal* 43, no. 4 (July–August 1987): 77–79.

Figure 14.9   *Percentage of NYSE Common Stocks Above Their 200-Day Moving Average*

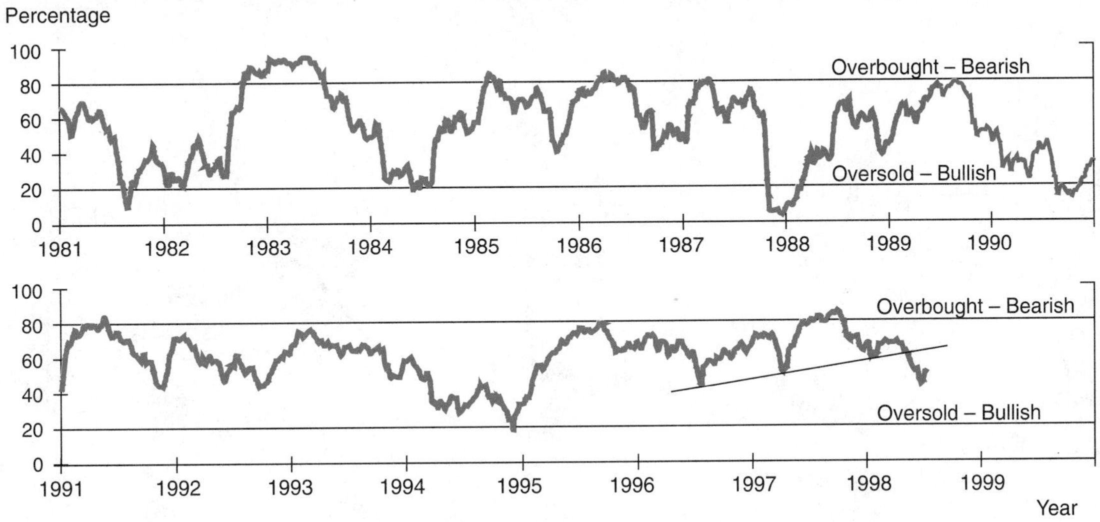

Source: *Where the Indicators Stand* (New York: Merrill Lynch, July 1998).

which indicates an oversold condition that is bullish, to about 1.10, which indicates an overbought environment and a bearish sentiment.

Stock Price and Volume Techniques

In the introduction to this chapter, we examined a hypothetical stock price chart that demonstrated the market cycle and its peaks and troughs. Also, we considered rising and declining trend channels and breakouts from channels that signal new price trends or reversals of the price trends. Although these price patterns are important, most technical trading rules for the overall market and individual stocks consider both stock price movements and corresponding volume movements. Because technicians believe that prices move in trends that persist, they seek to predict future price trends from an astute analysis of past price trends along with changes in the volume of trading.

The Dow Theory   Any discussion of technical analysis using price and volume data should begin with a consideration of the Dow Theory because it was among the earliest work on this topic and remains the basis for many technical indicators. In this section, we show how Charles Dow combined price and volume information to analyze both individual stocks and the overall stock market.

Charles Dow published the *Wall Street Journal* during the late 1800s.[13] Dow described stock prices as moving in trends analogous to the movement of water. He postulated three types of price movements over time: (1) major trends that are like tides in the ocean, (2) intermediate trends that resemble waves, and (3) short-run movements that are like ripples. Followers of the Dow Theory hope to detect the direction of the major price trend

---

[13]A study that discusses and provides support for the Dow Theory is David A. Glickstein and Rolf E. Wubbels, "Dow Theory Is Alive and Well," *Journal of Portfolio Management* 9, no. 3 (Spring 1983): 28–32. The Dow Jones Industrial Average celebrated its 100th anniversary in 1996. The *Wall Street Journal* published a special supplement on May 28, 1996, to commemorate the event.

Figure 14.10   *Time-Series Plot of Dow Jones Industrial Average and NYSE Block Uptick–Downtick Ratio (Three-Week Average.)*

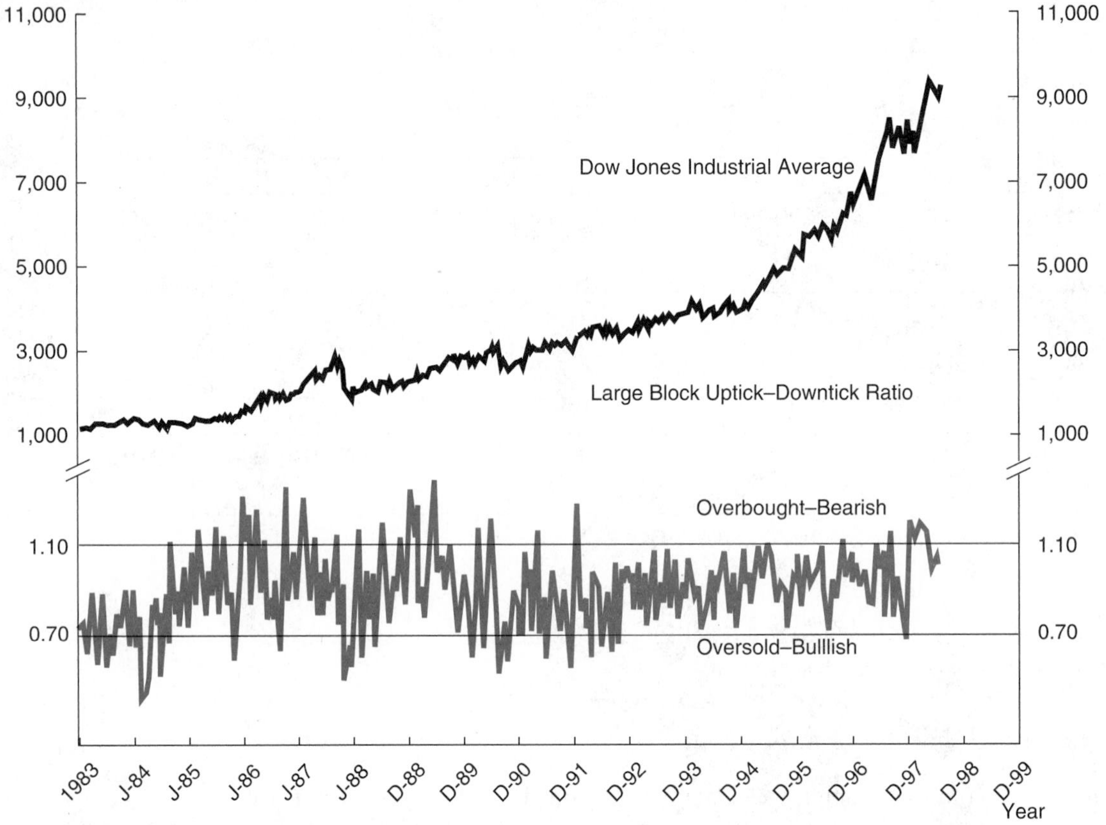

Source: *Where the Indicators Stand* (New York: Merrill Lynch, July 1996).

(tide), recognizing that intermediate movements (waves) may occasionally move in the opposite direction. They recognize that a major market advance does not go straight up, but rather includes small price declines as some investors decide to take profits.

Figure 14.11 shows the typical bullish pattern. The technician would look for every recovery to reach a new peak above the prior peak, and this price rise should be accompanied by heavy trading volume. Alternatively, each profit-taking reversal that follows an increase to a new peak should have a trough above the prior trough, with relatively light trading volume during the reversals, indicating only limited interested in profit taking at these levels. When this pattern of price and volume movements changes, the major trend may be entering a period of consolidation or a major reversal. When using the Dow Theory to analyze the overall stock market, technicians also look for confirmation of peaks and troughs in the industrial stock price series by subsequent peaks and troughs in the transportation series. Such an "echo" indicates that the change in direction and the major trend is being confirmed across the total market.

Importance of Volume   As noted in the description of the Dow Theory, technicians watch volume changes along with price movements as an indicator of changes in supply and demand for individual stocks or stocks in general. A price movement in one direc-

Figure 14.11   *Sample Bullish Price Pattern*

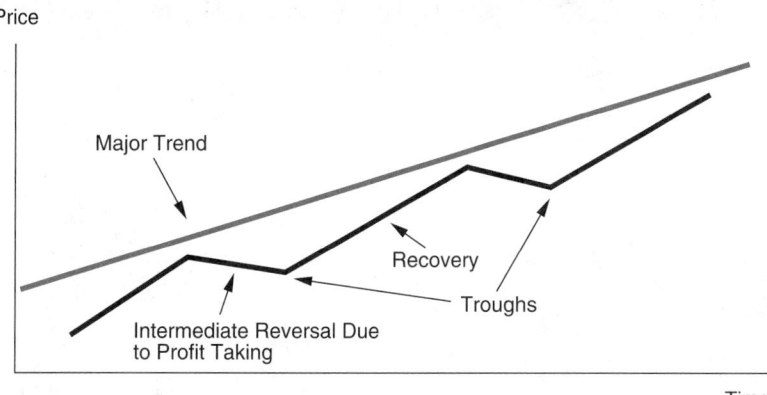

tion means that the net effect on price is in that direction, but the price change alone does not tell us how widespread the excess demand or supply is at that time. Therefore, the technician looks for a price increase on heavy volume relative to the stock's normal trading volume as an indication of bullish activity. Conversely, a price decline with heavy volume is bearish. A generally bullish pattern would be when price increases are accompanied by heavy volume and the small price reversals occur with light trading volume, indicating limited interest in selling and taking profits.

Technicians also use a ratio of upside–downside volume as an indicator of short-term momentum for the aggregate stock market. Each day the stock exchanges announce the volume of trading that occurred in stocks that experienced an increase divided by the volume of trading in stocks that declined. These data are reported daily in *Wall Street Journal* and weekly in *Barron's*. Technicians consider this ratio to be an indicator of investor sentiment and use it to pinpoint excesses. Specifically, the ratio typically ranges between a value of 0.50 and 2.00 and is upside-biased. Technicians believe that a value of 1.50 or more indicates an overbought position that is bearish because of the positive bias. Alternatively, a value of 0.75 and lower would reflect an oversold position and is considered bullish.

Support and Resistance Levels   A **support level** is the price range at which the technician would expect a substantial increase in the demand for a stock. Generally, a support level will develop after a stock has enjoyed a meaningful price increase and the stock has begun to experience profit taking. Technicians reason that, at some price below the recent peak other investors will buy who did not buy during the first price increase and have been waiting for a small reversal to get into the stock. When the price reaches this support price, demand surges and price and volume begin to increase again.

A **resistance level** is the price range at which the technician would expect an increase in the supply of stock and any price increase to reverse abruptly. A resistance level tends to develop after a stock has experienced a steady decline from a higher price level. It is reasoned that the decline in price leads some investors who acquired the stock at a higher price to look for an opportunity to sell it near their breakeven points. Therefore, the supply of stock owned by these investors is *overhanging* the market. When the price rebounds to the target price set by these investors, this overhanging supply of stock comes to the market and dramatically reverses the price increase on heavy volume. It is also possible to envision a resistance level for a stock in a rising trend wherein the

Figure 14.12   *Daily Stock Prices for Intel Corporation with Indications of Support and Resistance Levels*

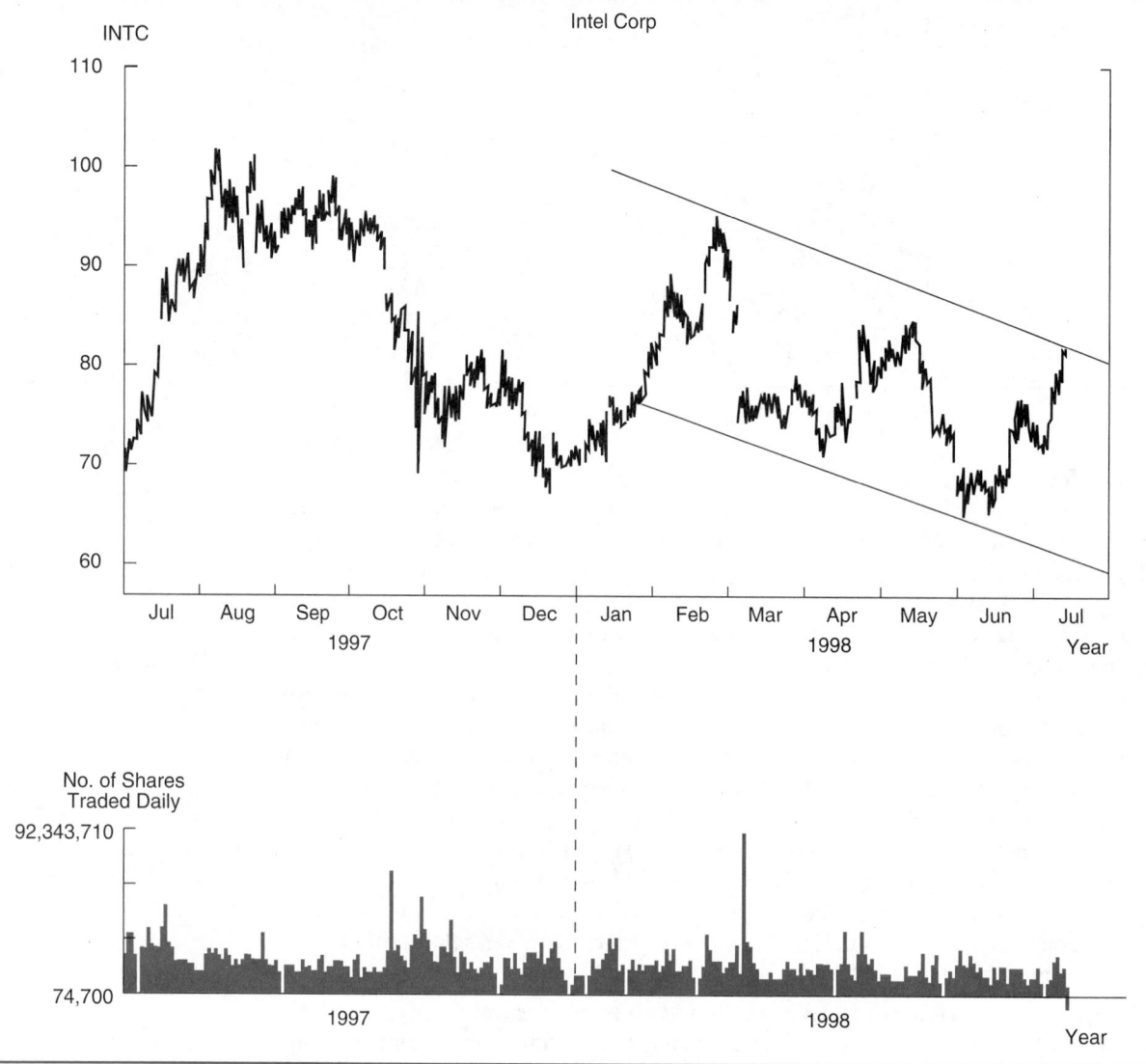

Source: Bridge Information Systems, Inc.

resistance level is a price where a number of holders feel it is appropriate to take a profit. In this latter case, there might be a succession of resistance levels over time.

Figure 14.12 shows a declining pattern of resistance values for Intel Corporation (INTC) during 1998 where each succeeding rally appears to meet a lower resistance value, which is clearly not encouraging. In addition, the support level also appears to be declining. Earlier declines in July 1997, October 1997, December 1997, and April 1998 appeared to find support at about seventy dollars, whereas the June 1998 decline went to about sixty-five dollars before a rally.

Moving-Average Lines   Earlier, we discussed how technicians use a moving average of past stock prices as an indicator of the long-run trend and how they examine current prices

Figure 14.13   *Weekly Stock Prices for Cisco Systems, Inc., with 50-Day and 200-Day Moving Average Lines*

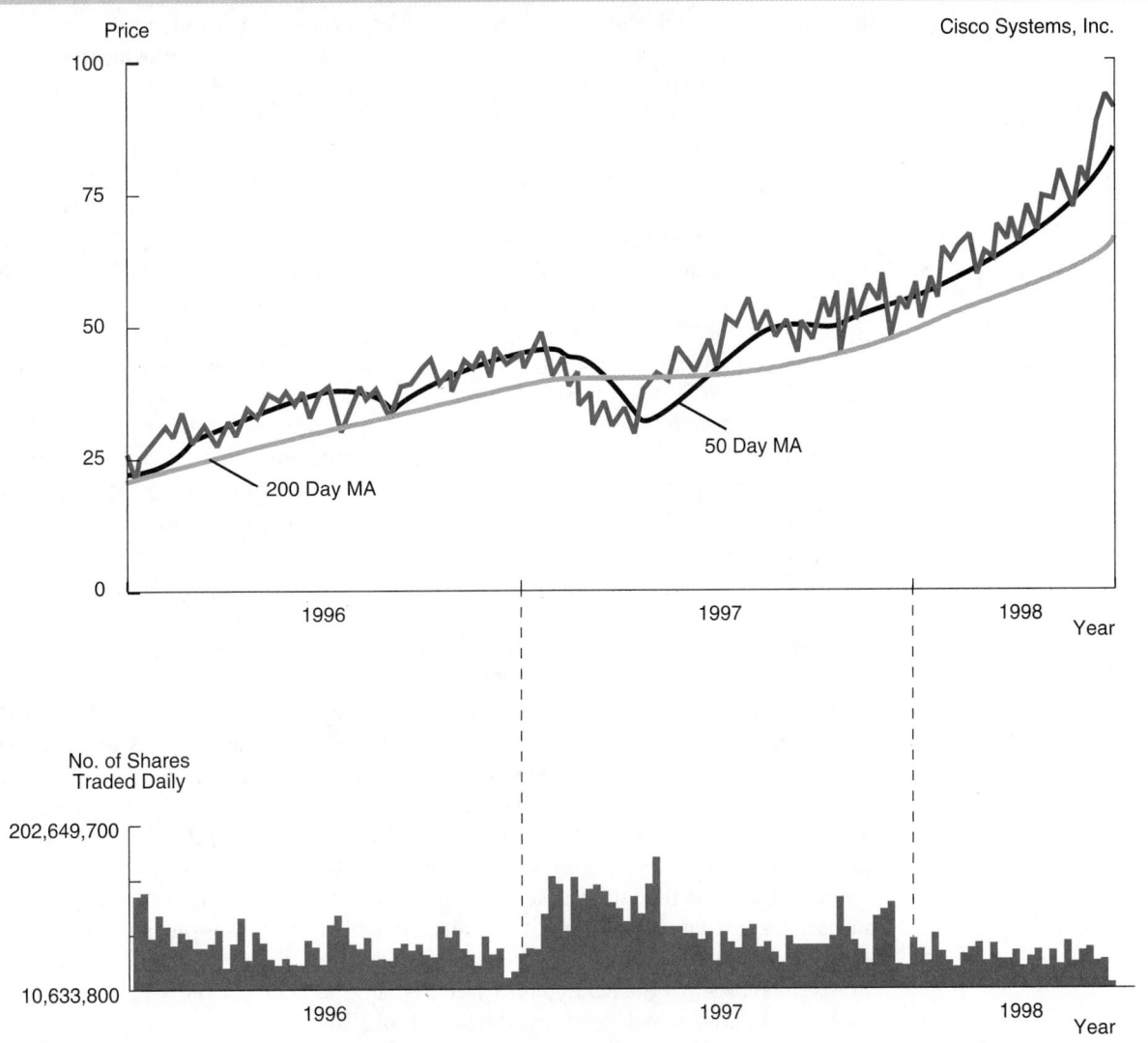

Source: Bridge Information Systems, Inc.

relative to this trend for signals of a change. We also noted that a 200-day moving average is a relatively popular measure for individual stocks and the aggregate market. In this discussion, we want to add a fifty-day moving-average price line and consider large volume.

Figure 14.13 is a weekly price and volume chart for Cisco Systems, Inc., from the Bridge System for a two and one-half year period ending in July 1998. It also contains a 50-day and 200-day moving-average (MA) line. As noted, MA lines are meant to reflect the overall trend for the price series, with the shorter MA series (50-day versus 200-day) reflecting shorter trends. Two comparisons involving the MA series are considered important. The first comparison is the specific prices to the shorter run MA series, which in this case is the fifty-day MA series. If the overall price trend of a stock or the market has been down, the moving-average price line generally would lie above current prices.

If prices reverse and break through the moving-average line *from below* accompanied by heavy trading volume, most technicians would consider this a strongly *positive* change and speculate that this breakthrough signals a reversal of the declining trend. In contrast, if the price of a stock had been rising, the moving-average line would also be rising, but it would be below current prices. If current prices broke through the moving-average line from above accompanied by heavy trading volume, this would be considered a bearish pattern that would signal a reversal of the long-run rising trend.

The second comparison is between the 50- and 200-day MA lines. Specifically, when these two lines cross, it signals a change in the overall trend. Specifically, if the 50-day MA line crosses the 200-day MA line from below on good volume, this would be a bullish indicator (buy signal) because it signals a reversal in trend from negative to positive. In contrast, when the 50-day line crosses the 200-day line from above, it signals a change to a negative trend and would be a sell signal. As shown, there was a bearish crossing in early 1997 followed by a bullish crossing in mid-1997.

Overall, for a *bullish* trend the 50-day MA line should be above the 200-day MA line as it is for Cisco Systems most of the time and since mid-1997. Notably, if this positive gap gets too large (which happens with a fast run up in price similar to what happened in mid-1998), a technician might consider this an indication that the stock is temporarily overbought. A *bearish* trend is when the 50-day MA is always below the 200-day MA line. If the gap was large on the downside, it might be considered a signal of an oversold stock, which is bullish for the short-run.

Relative Strength   Technicians believe that once a trend begins, it will continue until some major event causes a change in direction. They believe this is also true of *relative* performance. If an individual stock or an industry group is outperforming the market, technicians believe it will continue to do so.

Therefore, technicians compute weekly or monthly **relative-strength (RS) ratios** for individual stocks and industry groups as the ratio of the price of a stock or an industry index relative to the value for some stock-market series such as the S&P 500. If this ratio increases over time, it shows that the stock or industry is outperforming the market, and a technician would expect this superior performance to continue. Relative-strength ratios work during declining as well as rising markets. In a declining market, if a stock's price declines less than the market does, the stock's relative-strength ratio will continue to rise. Technicians believe that if this ratio is stable or increases during a bear market, the stock should do well during the subsequent bull market.[14] The bottom line in Figure 14.14 shows that the RS line for Cisco Systems has been generally increasing for the past nine months, which confirms the bullish MA line analysis.

Merrill Lynch publishes relative-strength charts for industry groups. Figure 14.15 describes how to read the charts.

Bar Charting   Technicians use charts that show daily, weekly, or monthly time series of stock prices. For a given interval, the technical analyst plots the high and low prices and connects the two points vertically to form a bar. Typically, he or she will also draw a small horizontal line across this vertical bar to indicate the closing price. Finally, almost all bar charts include the volume of trading at the bottom of the chart so that the technical analyst can relate the price and volume movements. A typical bar chart in Figure 14.16 shows data for the DJIA from the *Wall Street Journal* along with volume figures for the NYSE.

---

[14]A study that supports the technique is James Bohan, "Relative Strength: Further Positive Evidence," *Journal of Portfolio Management* 7, no. 1 (Fall 1981): 39–46. A study that rejects the technique is Robert D. Arnott, "Relative Strength Revisited," *Journal of Portfolio Management* 6, no. 3 (Spring 1979): 19–23. Finally, a study that combines it with modern portfolio theory is John S. Brush and Keith Boles, "The Predictive Power in Relative Strength and CAPM, " *Journal of Portfolio Management* 9, no. 4 (Summer 1983): 20–23.

Figure 14.14   *Daily Stock Prices for Cisco Systems with Moving-Average Line and Relative Strength Line*

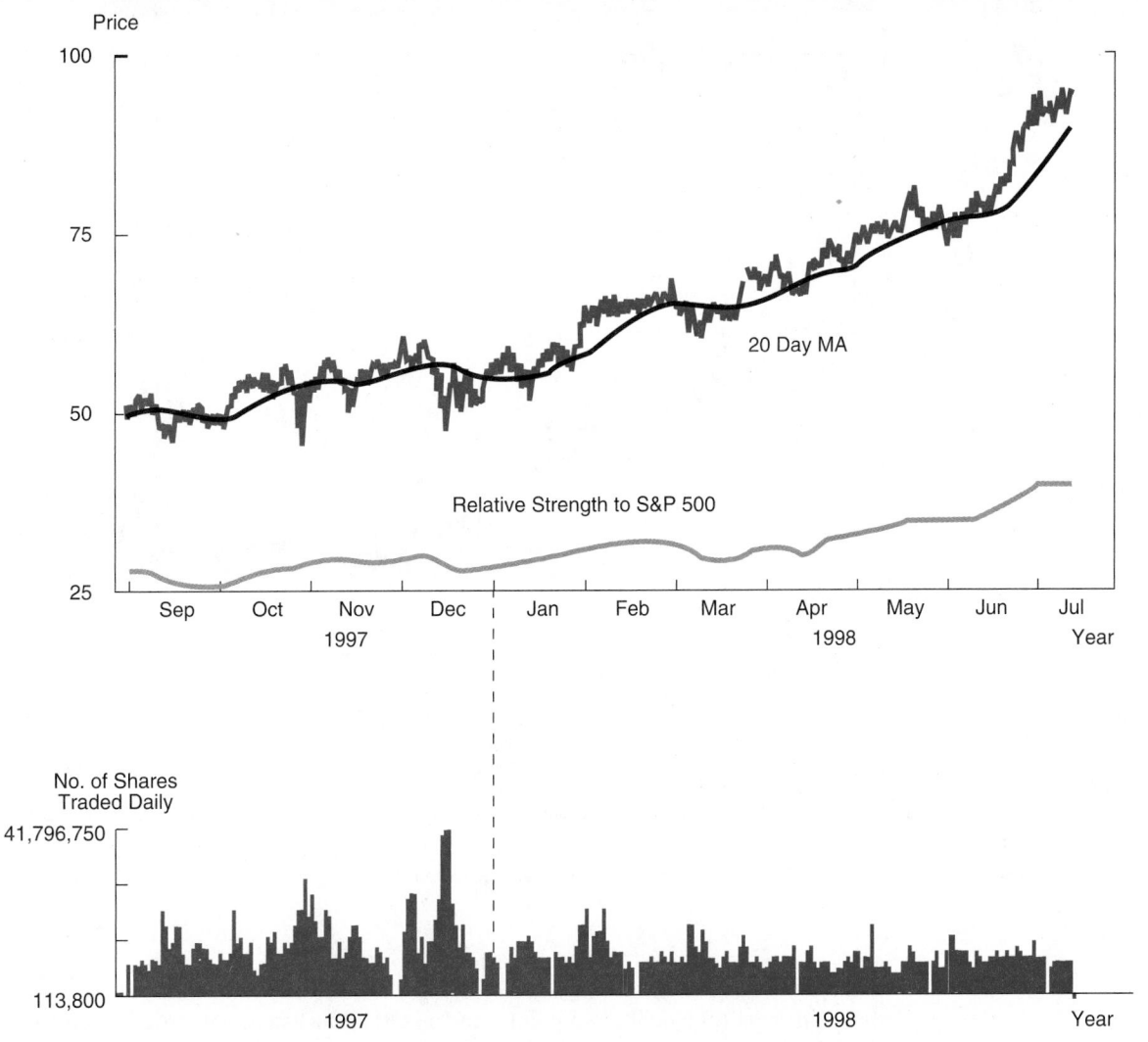

Source: Bride Information Systems, Inc.

Multiple Indicator Charts   Figure 14.14 is a fairly typical technical chart that contains several indicators that can be used together like the 20-day MA line and the RS line, which can provide added support to the analysis. Technicians include as many price and volume series as are reasonable on one chart. Notably, based on the performance of *several* technical indicators, they try to arrive at a consensus about the future movement for the stock.

Point-and-Figure Charts   Another graph that is popular with technicians is the point-and-figure chart.[15] Unlike the bar chart, which typically includes all ending prices and volumes to show a trend, the point-and-figure chart includes only significant price

[15]Daniel Seligman, "The Mystique of Point-and-Figure," *Fortune* (March 1962): 113–115.

Figure 14.15   *How to Read Industry Group Charts*

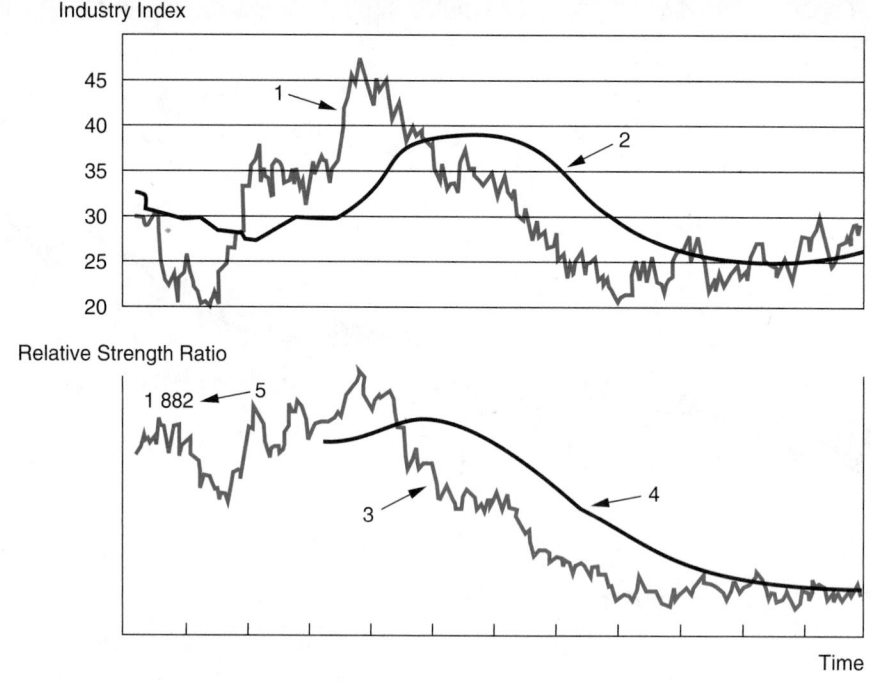

The industry group charts in this report display the following elements:

1. A line chart of the weekly close of the Standard & Poor's Industry Group Index for the past 9½ years, with the index range indicated to the left.
2. A line of the seventy-five-week moving average of the Standard & Poor's Industry Group Index.
3. A relative-strength line of the Standard & Poor's Industry Group Index compared with the New York Stock Exchange Composite Index.
4. A seventy-five-week moving average of relative strength.
5. A volatility reading that measures the maximum amount by which the index has outperformed (or underperformed) the NYSE Composite Index during the time period displayed.

Source: *Technical Analysis of Industry Groups* (New York: Merrill Lynch, monthly). Reprinted by permission of Merrill Lynch. All Rights Reserved.

changes, regardless of their timing. The technician determines what price interval to record as significant (one point, two points, and so on) and when to note price reversals.

To demonstrate how a technical analyst would use such a chart, assume you want to chart a volatile stock that is currently selling for $40 a share. Because of its volatility, you believe that anything less than a two-point price change is not significant. Also, you consider anything less than a four-point reversal, meaning a movement in the opposite direction, quite minor. Therefore, you would set up a chart similar to the one in Figure 14.17, which starts at 40 and progresses in two-point increments. If the stock moves to 42, you would place an X in the box above 40 and do nothing else until the stock rose to 44 or dropped to 38 (a four-point reversal from its high of 42). If it dropped to 38, you would move a column to the right, which indicates a reversal in direction, and begin again at 38 (fill in boxes at 42 and 40). If the stock price dropped to 34, you would enter an X at 36 and another at 34. If the stock then rose to 38 (another four-point reversal), you would move to the next column and begin at 38, going up (fill in 34 and 36). If the stock then went to 46, you would fill in more Xs as shown and wait for further increases or a reversal.

Depending on how fast the prices rise and fall, this process might take anywhere from two to six months. Given these figures, the technical analyst would attempt to determine trends just as with the bar chart.

Figure 14.16   *A Typical Bar Chart*

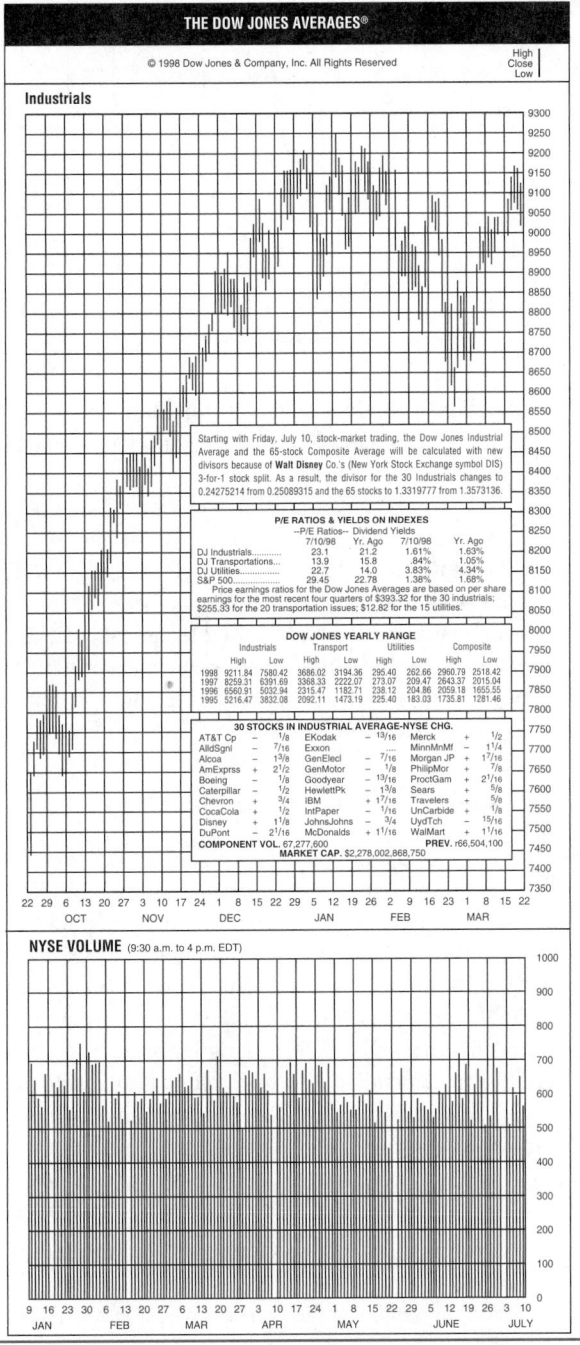

As always, you look for breakouts to either higher or lower price levels. A long horizontal movement with many reversals but no major trends up or down would be considered *a period of consolidation.* The technician would speculate that the stock is moving from buyers to sellers and back again with no strong support from either group that would indicate a consensus about its direction. Once the stock breaks out and moves up or down after

Figure 14.17   *Sample Point-and-Figure Chart*

50			
48			
46			X
44			X
42	X	X	X
40	X	X	X
38		X	X
36		X	X
34		X	X
32			
30			

a period of consolidation, analysts anticipate a major move because previous trading set the stage for it. In other words, the longer the period of consolidation, the larger the subsequent move.

Point-and-figure charts differ from bar charts by providing a compact record of movements because they only consider significant price changes for the stock being analyzed. Therefore, some technicians prefer point-and-figure charts because they are easier to work with and give more vivid pictures of price movements.

This section discussed widely used technical indicators. As noted on several occasions, technical analysts generally do not concentrate on only a few indicators or even general categories, but seek to derive an overall feel for the market or a stock based on a *consensus of numerous technical indicators*.

Technical Analysis of Foreign Markets

Our discussion thus far has concentrated on U.S. markets, but as numerous analysts and firms have discovered, these techniques apply to foreign markets as well. Merrill Lynch, for instance, prepares separate technical analysis publications for individual countries such as Japan, Germany, and the United Kingdom as well as a summary of all world markets. The examples that follow show that when analyzing non-U.S. markets, many techniques are limited to price and volume data rather than using the more detailed market information described for the U.S. market. This emphasis on price and volume data is necessary because the more detailed information that is available on the U.S. market through the SEC, the stock exchanges, the NASDAQ system, and various investment services is not always available in other countries.

Foreign Stock Market Series   Figure 14.18 contains the daily time-series plot and the fifty-day moving-average series for the German DAX Xetra Index. This chart shows the strong rising trend by the German stock market during the period September 1997 to June 1998.

In the written analysis, the market analyst at Merrill Lynch estimated support and resistance levels for the German Stock Exchange series and commented on the medium-term outlook for the German stock market.

Merrill Lynch publishes similar charts and discussions for ten other countries and a summary release that compares the countries and ranks them by stock and currency performance. The next section discusses the technical analysis of currency markets.

Technical Analysis of Foreign Exchange Rates   On numerous occasions, we have discussed the importance of changes in foreign exchange rates and their impact on the rates

Figure 14.18 *Merrill Lynch Graph and Summary Comments on the German Stock Market*

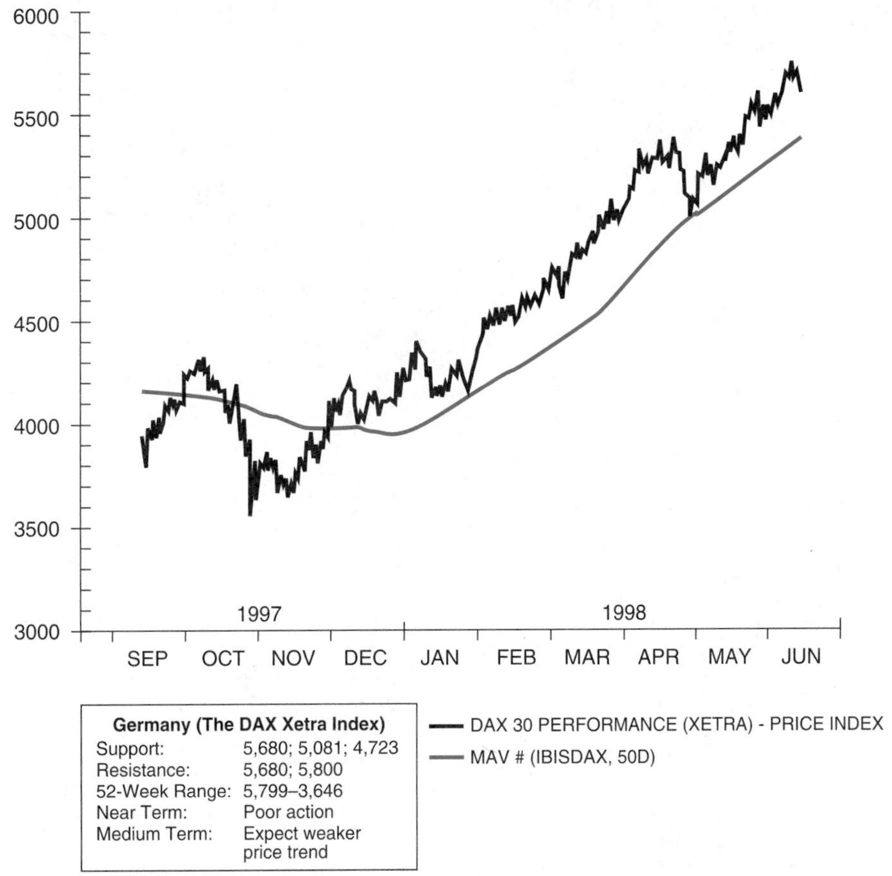
6000
5500
5000
4500
4000
3500
3000
1997
1998
SEP
OCT
NOV
DEC
JAN
FEB
MAR
APR
MAY
JUN
Germany (The DAX Xetra Index)
Support: 5,680; 5,081; 4,723
Resistance: 5,680; 5,800
52-Week Range: 5,799–3,646
Near Term: Poor action
Medium Term: Expect weaker price trend
DAX 30 PERFORMANCE (XETRA) - PRICE INDEX
MAV # (IBISDAX, 50D)

Source: *The Global Technician* (New York: Merrill Lynch, June 15, 1998).

of return on foreign securities. Because of the importance of these relationships, technicians who trade bonds and stocks in world markets examine the time-series data of various individual currencies such as the British pound. They also analyze the spread between currencies such as the difference between the Japanese yen (¥) and the German deutsche mark (DM). Finally, an analysis of the composite dollar performance over time, as shown in Figure 14.19 is useful.

Technical Analysis of Bond Markets

Thus far, we have described technical tools for the analysis of the stock market in the United States and the world. Although we have emphasized the use of technical analysis in stock markets, you should be aware that technicians also apply these techniques to the bond market. The theory and rationale for technical analysis of bonds is the same as for stocks and many of the same trading rules are used. As with stocks, the techniques apply to an individual bond, several bonds, or a bond index. A major difference is that it is generally not possible to consider the volume of trading of bonds since these data generally are not available because most bonds are traded OTC, where volume is not reported.

Figure 14.19   *Time-Series Plot of U.S. Dollar Trade-Weighted Exchange Rates*

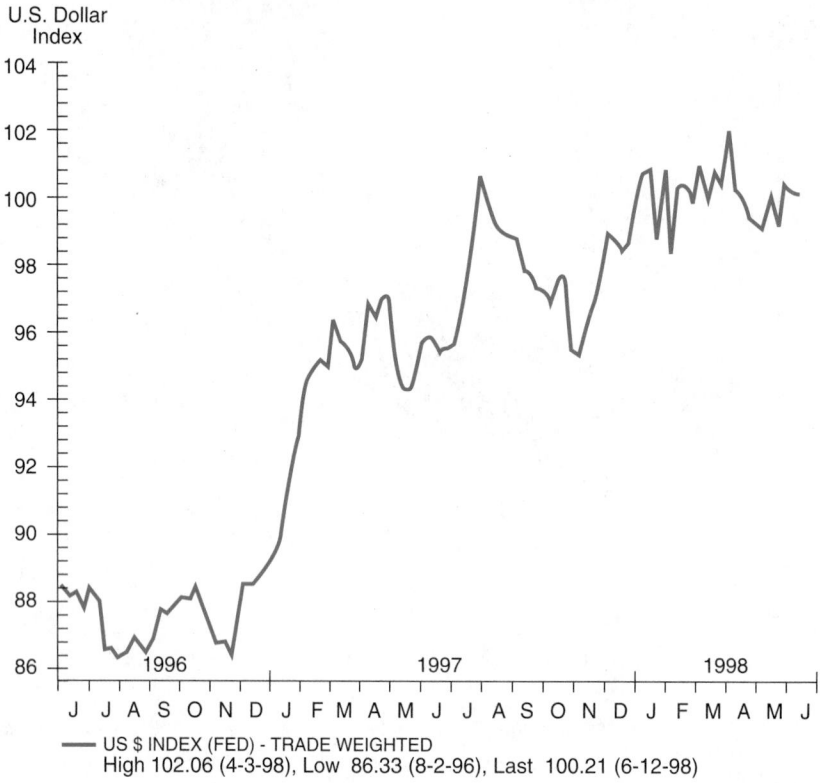

Source: *The Global Technician* (New York: Merrill Lynch, June 15, 1998).

Figure 14.20 demonstrates the use of technical analysis techniques applied to bond-yield series. Specifically, the first two graphs contain time-series plots of yields for U.S. and German ten-year bonds and a fifty-two-week moving-average line for the yields, which indicates the overall trend for the two series. Notably, both graphs indicate a declining trend in yields during late 1997 and the first half of 1998. The third graph plots the yield spread between the two bonds. In this case, the moving-average line indicates an overall rising trend in the spread with a small downturn at the end. As a result, this set of technical graphs provide important insights to a global bond portfolio manager interested in adjusting his or her portfolio mix of U.S. and German bonds. These examples show how technical analysis can be and is applied to the bond market as well as the stock market.

SUMMARY

♦ Whether you want to base your investment decisions on fundamental analysis, technical analysis, or a belief in efficient markets, you should be aware of the principles and practice of technical analysis. Numerous investors believe in and use technical analysis, the large investment houses provide extensive support for technical analysis, and a large proportion of the discussion related to securities markets in the media is based on a technical view of the market. Now that you are aware of technical analysis prin-

Figure 14.20   *Technical Analysis of U.S. and German Bond Markets Including Moving Averages of Yields and Yield Spreads*

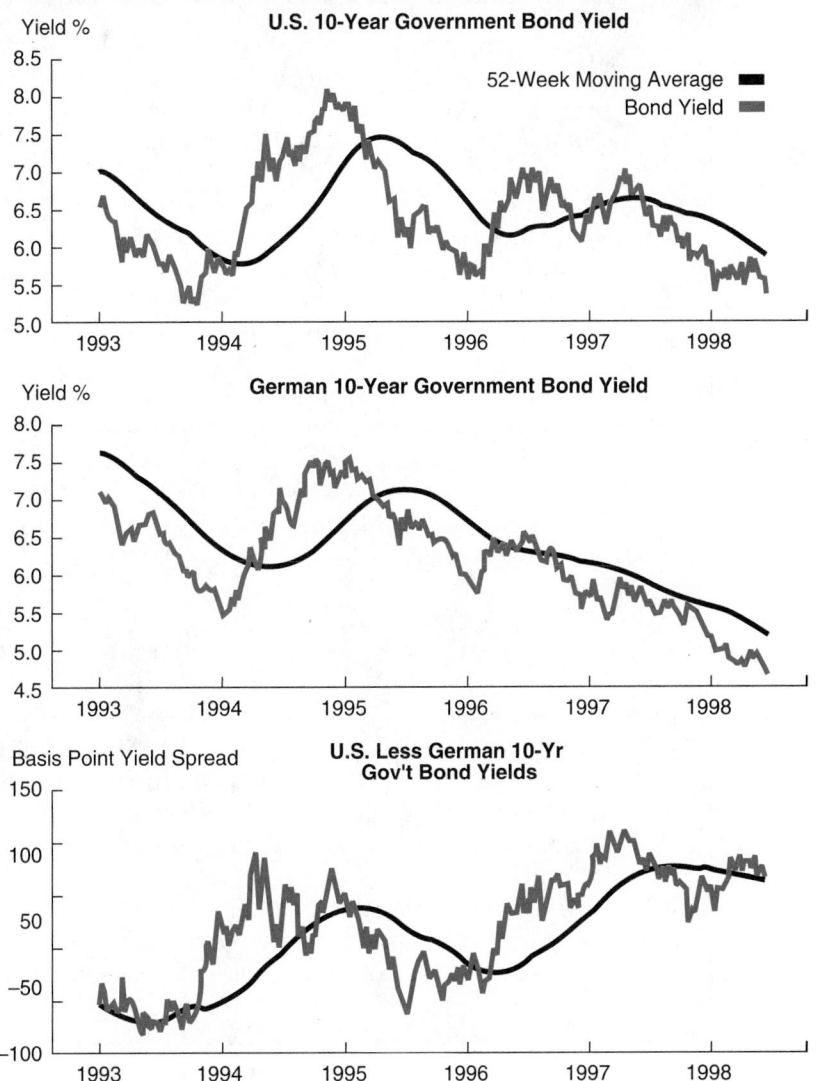

Source: *Currency and Bond Market Trends* (New York: Merrill Lynch, June 18, 1998).

ciples, techniques, and indicators, you will recognize this tendency of security market commentators.

♦ Two main differences separate technical analysts and those who believe in efficient markets. The first, related to the information dissemination process, is concerned with whether one assumes that everybody gets the information at about the same time. The second difference is concerned with how quickly investors adjust security prices to reflect new information. Technical analysts believe that the information dissemination process differs for different people. They believe that news takes time to travel from the insider and expert to the individual investor. They also believe that price adjustments are not instantaneous. As a result, they contend that security prices move in trends that persist

Investments Online

By its nature, technical analysis uses charts and graphs, and many Web sites offer them for use by investors and analysts; some are free, but some of the sites for more sophisticated users require payment for access. Here are several interesting sites:

www.mta-usa.org

The home page of the Market Technicians Association, a professional group of chartists whose goal is to enhance technical analysis and educate investors about its role. The group sponsors the Chartered Market Technician (CMT) designation. This site features news groups, investment links, training and education sources, a journal, and a variety of technical analysis charts.

www.bigcharts.com

This site offers free intraday and historical charts and price quotes. Its database includes over 24,000 stocks, mutual funds, and indexes. Users can learn which stocks have the largest percentage gain (loss) in price and volume and which stocks are hitting new 52-week highs (lows). Other features include momentum charts, stocks with the largest short interest, and a variety of other charts of interest to technicians.

www.alphachart.com

The Technical Analysis Charting site tracks over 5,000 NYSE, AMEX, and NASDAQ stocks. It offers users a sophisticated variety of charts: Bollinger bands, candlesticks, stochastic oscillators, and more.

www.investools.com

The INVESTools home page offers news, reports, data, links to a variety of charts, investment newsletter links, and insights from featured advisors.

www.stockmaster.com

A site which offers basic stock charts, including price and volume charts.

www.dbc.com

The home page of the Data Broadcasting Corporation. It has information about fixed income and equity securities, news, research resources, and market updates on indexes, currencies, futures, new high/lows, and international indexes.

and, therefore, past price trends and volume information along with other market indicators can help you determine future price trends.

♦ We discussed technical trading rules under four general categories: contrary-opinion rules, follow-the-smart-money tactics, other market indicators, and stock price and volume techniques. These techniques and trading rules also can be applied to foreign markets and to the analysis of currency exchange rates. In addition, technical analysis has been used to determine the prevailing sentiment in the bond market.

♦ Most technicians follow several indicators and decision rules at any point in time and attempt to derive a consensus decision to buy, sell, or do nothing.[16] Many technicians often conclude to do nothing.

---

[16]An analysis using numerous indicators is Jerome Baesel, George Shows, and Edward Thorp, "Can Joe Granville Time the Market?" *Journal of Portfolio Management* 8, no. 3 (Spring 1982): 5–9.

Questions

1. Technical analysts believe that one can use past price changes to predict future price changes. How do they justify this belief?
2. Technicians contend that stock prices move in trends that persist for long periods of time. What do technicians believe happens in the real world to cause these trends?
3. Briefly discuss the problems related to fundamental analysis that are considered advantages for technical analysis.
4. Discuss some disadvantages of technical analysis.
5. If the mutual fund cash position were to increase close to 12 percent, would a technician consider this cash position bullish or bearish? Give two reasons why the technical analyst would think this way.
6. Assume a significant decline in credit balances at brokerage firms. Discuss why a technician would consider this bearish.
7. If the bearish sentiment index of advisory service opinions were to increase to 61 percent, discuss why a technician would consider this bullish or bearish.
8. Suppose the ratio of specialists' short sales to total short sales increases to 70 percent. Discuss why a technician would consider this bullish or bearish.
9. Why is an increase in debit balances considered bullish?
10. Describe the Dow Theory and its three components. Which component is most important? What is the reason for an intermediate reversal?
11. Describe a bearish price and volume pattern, and discuss why it is considered bearish.
12. Discuss the logic behind the breadth of market index. How is it used to identify a peak in stock prices?
13. During a ten-day trading period, the cumulative net advance series goes from 1,572 to 1,053. During this same period of time, the DJIA goes from 8,757 to 9,120. As a technician, discuss what this set of events would mean to you.
14. Explain the reasoning behind a support level and a resistance level.
15. What is the purpose of computing a moving-average line for a stock? Describe a bullish pattern using a fifty-day moving-average line and the stock volume of trading. Discuss why this pattern is considered bullish.
16. Assuming a stock price and volume chart that also contains a 50-day and a 200-day MA line, describe a bearish pattern with the two MA lines and discuss why it is bearish.
17. Explain how you would construct a relative-strength series for an individual stock or an industry group. What would it mean to say a stock experienced good relative strength during a bear market?
18. Discuss why most technicians follow several technical rules and attempt to derive a consensus.

Problems

1. Select a stock on the NYSE and construct a daily high, low, and close bar chart for it that includes its volume of trading for ten trading days.
2. Compute the relative-strength ratio for the stock in Problem 1 relative to the S&P 500 Index. Prepare a table that includes all the data and indicates the computations as follows:

Closing Price		Relative-Strength Ratio	
Day	**Stock**	**S&P 500**	**Stock Price/S&P 500**

3. Plot the relative-strength ratio computed in Problem 2 on your bar chart. Discuss whether the stock's relative strength is bullish or bearish.
4. Currently Charlotte Art Importers is selling at $32 per share. Although you are somewhat dubious about technical analysis, you want to know how technicians who use point-and-figure charts would view this stock. You decide to note one-point movements and three-point reversals. You gather the following price information:

Date	Price	Date	Price	Date	Price
4/1	$23\frac{1}{2}$	4/18	33	5/3	27
4/4	$28\frac{1}{2}$	4/19	$35\frac{3}{8}$	5/4	$26\frac{1}{2}$
4/5	28	4/20	37	5/5	28
4/6	28	4/21	$38\frac{1}{2}$	5/6	$28\frac{1}{4}$
4/7	$29\frac{3}{4}$	4/22	36	5/9	$28\frac{1}{8}$
4/8	$30\frac{1}{2}$	4/25	35	5/10	$28\frac{1}{4}$
4/11	$30\frac{1}{2}$	4/26	$34\frac{1}{4}$	5/11	$29\frac{1}{8}$
4/12	$32\frac{1}{8}$	4/27	$33\frac{1}{8}$	5/12	$30\frac{1}{4}$
4/13	32	4/28	$32\frac{7}{8}$	5/13	$29\frac{7}{8}$

Plot the point-and-figure chart using Xs for uptrends and Os for downtrends. How would a technician evaluate these movements? Discuss why you would expect a technician to buy, sell, or hold the stock based on this chart.

5. Assume the following daily closings for the Dow Jones Industrial Average:

Day	DJIA	Day	DJIA
1	9010	7	9220
2	9100	8	9130
3	9165	9	9250
4	9080	10	9315
5	9070	11	9240
6	9150	12	9310

a. Calculate a four-day moving average for Days 4 through 12.
b. Assume that the index on Day 13 closes at 9,300. Would this signal a buy or sell decision?

6. The cumulative advance-decline line reported in *Barron's* at the end of the month is 21,240. During the first week of the following month, the daily report for the *Exchange* is as follows:

Day	1	2	3	4	5
Issues Traded	3,544	3,533	3,540	3,531	3,521
Advances	1,737	1,579	1,759	1,217	1,326
Declines	1,289	1,484	1,240	1,716	1,519
Unchanged	518	470	541	598	596

a. Compute the daily net advance-decline line for each of the five days.
b. Compute the cumulative advance-decline line for each day and the final value at the end of the week.

References

Brown, David P., and Robert H. Jennings, "On Technical Analysis," *The Review of Financial Studies* 2, no. 4 (October 1989).

Colby, Robert W. and Thomas A. Mayers. *The Encyclopedia of Technical Market Indicators.* Homewood, IL: Dow Jones–Irwin, 1988.

Dines, James. *How the Average Investor Can Use Technical Analysis for Stock Profits.* New York: Dines Chart Corporation, 1974.

Edwards, R. D. and John Magee, Jr. *Technical Analysis of Stock Trends,* 6th ed. Boston, MA: New York Institute of Finance, 1992.

Fosback, Norman G. *Stock Market Logic.* Fort Lauderdale, FL: The Institute for Economic Research, 1976.

Grant, Dwight. "Market Timing: Strategies to Consider." *Journal of Portfolio Management* 5, no. 4 (Summer 1979).

Jagadeesh, Narasimhan, "Evidence of Predictable Behavior of Security Returns," *Journal of Finance* 45, no. 3 (July 1990).

Levy, Robert A. *The Relative Strength Concept of Common Stock Price Forecasting.* Larchmont, NY: Investors Intelligence, 1968.

Meyers, Thomas A. *The Technical Analysis Course,* Chicago: Probus, 1989.

Murphy, John J. *Technical Analysis of the Futures Markets,* 2nd ed. New York: McGraw Hill, 1985.

Pring, Martin J. *Technical Analysis Explained,* 3rd ed. New York: McGraw Hill, 1991.

Shaw, Alan R. "Market Timing and Technical Analysis." In *The Financial Analysts Handbook,* 2nd ed., edited by Sumner N. Levine. Homewood, IL: Dow Jones–Irwin, 1988.

Sweeney, Richard J. "Some New Filter Rule Tests: Methods and Results." *Journal of Financial and Quantitative Analysis* 23, no. 3 (September 1988).

Zweig, Martin E. *Winning on Wall Street.* New York: Warner Books, 1986.

GLOSSARY

Declining trend channel The range defined by security prices as they move progressively lower.

Diffusion index An indicator of the number of stocks rising during a specified period of time relative to the number of stocks declining and not changing price.

Downtick A price decline in a transaction price compared to the previous transaction price.

Flat trend channel The range defined by security prices as they maintain a relatively steady level.

Group rotation The tendency for demand to shift among industry groups or other market segments.

Moving average The continually recalculated average of security prices for a period, often 200 days, to serve as an indication of the general trend of prices and also as a benchmark price.

Peak The culmination of a bull market when prices stop rising and begin declining.

Relative-strength ratio The ratio of a stock price or an industry index value to a market indicator series, indicating performance relative to the overall market.

Resistance level A price at which a technician would expect a substantial increase in the supply of a stock to reverse a rising trend.

Rising trend channel The range defined by security prices as they move progressively higher.

Support level A price at which a technician would expect a substantial increase in price and volume for a stock to reverse a declining trend that was due to profit taking.

Technical analysis Estimation of future security price movements based on past movements.

Trough The culmination of a bear market at which prices stop declining and begin rising.

Uptick An incremental movement upward in a transaction price over the previous transaction price.

Uptick–Downtick ratio A ratio of the number of uptick block transactions (indicating buyers) to the number of downtick block transactions (indicating sellers of blocks). An indicator of institutional investor sentiment.

A WORD FROM THE STREET

BY RICHARD MCCABE

Although some investors seem to believe that fundamental and technical analysis are mutually exclusive disciplines in the investment process, I believe that they can be quite compatible. Many of the most successful money managers I have met over the years have skillfully combined the two procedures in their investment selection and timing decisions. Even those who claim that they rely solely on fundamental analysis have sometimes said that they are likely to buy stocks which are "out of favor," a term which really seems to be synonymous with a technical "oversold" condition. If it can be said that the fundamental analyst provides the vehicle (i.e., an attractive stock) for a successful investment journey, then the technical analyst provides the map (i.e., an assessment of the market environment through which the stock must navigate).

Using a combination of fundamental and technical analysis can also be likened to looking into a room from windows on different sides; what is not visible through the "fundamental" window may be seen through the "technical" window. The key, however, is to realize that stock prices can go up or down, at least for a while, for reasons other than earnings trends or expectations. The role of technical analysis is to help the investor evaluate those external influences (supply–demand, investor psychology, etc.) on price movements. As such, it is an additional tool in the investment decision-making process that should not be ignored.

Richard McCabe has been a technical market analyst at Merrill Lynch for more than 35 years and is currently a first vice president, chief market analyst, and manager of the market analysis department that provides technical analysis guidance on the U.S. and foreign stock, bond, and currency markets. McCabe is a member of the Market Technician's Association and the New York Society of Security Analysts (AIMR).

PART

5

BOND ANALYSIS

For most investors, bonds are like Rodney Dangerfield—"They get no respect!" This is surprising when one considers the fact that the total market value of the bond market in the United States and in most other countries is substantially larger than the market value of the stock market. As an example, in the United States as of the end of 1996 the market value of all publicly issued bonds was more than $9.5 trillion, while the market value of all stocks was about $7 trillion. On a global basis, the market value of bonds is about $21.5 trillion. Beyond the size factor, bonds have a reputation for low, unexciting rates of return. While this may be true if one goes back fifty or sixty years, it is certainly not true during the past ten to fifteen years. There are substantial opportunities in bonds for individual and institutional investors.

The chapters in this section are intended to provide a basic understanding of bonds and the bond markets around the world as well as to provide a background on analyzing returns and risks in the bond market.

Chapter 15 on bond fundamentals describes the global bond market in terms of country participation and the makeup of the bond market in the largest countries. Also, the characteristics of bonds in categories such as government, corporate, and municipal are discussed. We also discuss the many new corporate bond instruments developed in the United States, such as asset-backed securities, zero-coupon bonds, and high-yield bonds. All of these will eventually be used around the world.

Finally, we discuss information needed by bond investors and where to get it.

Chapter 16 is concerned with the analysis of bonds including a detailed discussion of the alternative rate-of-return measures for bonds, what factors affect yields on bonds, and what influences the volatility of bond returns. This latter discussion considers the important concept of bond duration, which helps explain bond-price volatility and is also important in active and passive bond portfolio management. There is also a related consideration of the convexity of alternative bonds and the impact of convexity on bond price volatility.

In Part 7 of this text, we take another look at bonds, in the context of fixed-income portfolio management strategies.

The fact that three long chapters are devoted to the study of bonds attests to the importance of the topic and the extensive research done in this area. The fact is, during the past fifteen years, there have probably been more developments related to the valuation and portfolio management of bonds than of stocks. This growth does not detract from the importance of equities, but certainly enhances the significance of fixed-income securities. Readers of this book should keep in mind one final point. Specifically, this growth in size and sophistication of the bond market means numerous career opportunities in the bond area ranging from trading these securities, credit analysis, and portfolio management both domestically and globally.

CHAPTER

15

Bond Fundamentals

In this chapter we will answer the following questions:

♦ What are some of the basic features of bonds that affect their risk, return, and value?

♦ What is the current country structure of the world bond market and how has the makeup of this market changed in recent years?

♦ What are the major components of the world bond market and the international bond market?

♦ What are bond ratings and what is their purpose?

♦ What is the difference between investment-grade bonds and high-yield (junk) bonds?

♦ What are the characteristics of bonds in the major bond categories such as governments, agencies, municipalities, and corporates?

♦ Within each of the major bond categories, what are the differences between major countries such as the United States, Japan, the United Kingdom, and Germany?

♦ What are the important characteristics of corporate bond issues developed in the United States during the past decade, such as mortgage-backed securities, other asset-backed securities, zero coupon and deep discount bonds, and high-yield bonds?

♦ What is the basic information required by bond investors and what are the sources of this information?

♦ How do you read the quotes available for the alternative bonds categories (for example, governments, municipalities, corporates)?

The global bond market is large and diverse, and represents an important investment opportunity. This chapter is concerned with publicly issued, long-term, nonconvertible debt obligations of public and private issuers in the United States and major global

526

markets. In later chapters, we will consider preferred stock and convertible bonds. An understanding of bonds is helpful in an efficient market because U.S. and foreign bonds increase the universe of investments available for the creation of a diversified portfolio.[1]

In this chapter we review some basic features of bonds and examine the structure of the world bond market. The bulk of the chapter involves an in-depth discussion of the major fixed-income investments. The chapter ends with a brief review of the data requirements and information sources for bond investors. Chapter 16 discusses the valuation of bonds and considers several factors that influence bond value and bond price volatility. ♦

BASIC FEATURES OF A BOND

Public bonds are long-term, fixed-obligation debt securities packaged in convenient, affordable denominations, for sale to individuals and financial institutions. They differ from other debt, such as individual mortgages and privately placed debt obligations, because they are sold to the public rather than channeled directly to a single lender. Bond issues are considered fixed-income securities because they impose fixed financial obligations on the issuers. Specifically, the issuer agrees to

1. Pay a fixed amount of *interest periodically* to the holder of record.
2. Repay a fixed amount of *principal* at the date of maturity.

Normally, interest on bonds is paid every six months, although some bond issues pay in intervals as short as a month or as long as a year. The principal is due at maturity; this *par value* of the issue is rarely less than $1,000. A bond has a specified term to maturity, which defines the life of the issue. The public debt market is typically divided into three segments based on an issue's original maturity:

1. Short-term issues with maturities of one year or less. The market for these instruments is commonly known as the **money market**.
2. Intermediate-term issues with maturities in excess of one year, but less than ten years. These instruments are known as **notes**.
3. Long-term obligations with maturities in excess of ten years, called **bonds**.

The lives of debt obligations change constantly as the issues progress toward maturity. Thus, issues that have been outstanding in the secondary market for any period of time eventually move from long-term to intermediate to short-term. This change in maturity over time is important, because a major determinant of the price volatility of bonds is the remaining life (maturity) of the issue.

NOTE: Material on bonds and world bond markets in this chapter is based on information from "How Big Is the World Bond Market," 1992 update by Rosario Benavides of Salomon Brothers Inc. Copyright 1992 by Salomon Brothers Inc. Reprinted by permission.

[1]Meir Statman and Neal L. Ushman, "Bonds Versus Stocks: Another Look," *Journal of Portfolio Management* 13, no. 3 (Winter 1987): 33–38.

Bond Characteristics

A bond can be characterized based on (1) its own intrinsic features, (2) its type, or (3) its indenture provisions.

Intrinsic Features   The coupon, maturity, principal value, and the type of ownership are important intrinsic features of a bond. The **coupon** of a bond indicates the income that the bond investor will receive over the life (or holding period) of the issue. This is known as *interest income, coupon income,* or *nominal yield.*

The **term to maturity** specifies the date or the number of years before a bond matures (or expires). Bonds have two different types of maturity. The most common is a **term bond**, which has a single maturity date. Alternatively, a **serial obligation bond** issue has a series of maturity dates, perhaps twenty or twenty-five. Each maturity, although a subset of the total issue, is really a small bond issue with, generally, a different coupon. Municipalities are the main issuers of serial bonds.

The **principal**, or **par value**, of an issue represents the original value of the obligation. This is generally stated in $1,000 increments from $1,000 to $25,000 or more. Principal value is *not* the same as the bond's market value. As noted in Chapter 10, the market price of many issues rise above or fall below their principal values because of differences between their coupons and the prevailing market rate of interest. If the market interest rate is above the coupon rate, the bond will sell at a discount to par. If the market rate is below the bond's coupon, it will sell at a premium above par. If the coupon is comparable to the prevailing market interest rate, the market value of the bond will be close to its original principal value.

Finally, bonds differ in their terms of ownership. With a **bearer bond**, the holder, or bearer, is the owner, so the issuer keeps no record of ownership. Interest from a bearer bond is obtained by clipping coupons attached to the bonds and sending them to the issuer for payment. In contrast, the issuers of **registered bonds** maintain records of owners and pay the interest directly to them.

Types of Issues   In contrast to common stock, companies can have many different bond issues outstanding at the same time. Bonds can have different types of collateral and be either senior, unsecured, or subordinated (junior) securities. **Secured (senior) bonds** are backed by a legal claim on some specified property of the issuer in the case of default. For example, mortgage bonds are secured by real estate assets, and equipment trust certificates, which are used by railroads and airlines, provide a senior claim on the firm's equipment.

Unsecured bonds (debentures) are backed only by the promise of the issuer to pay interest and principal on a timely basis. As such, they are secured by the general credit of the issuer. **Subordinated (junior) debentures** possess a claim on income and assets that is subordinated to other debentures. **Income bonds** are the most junior type because interest on them is only paid if it is earned. Although income bonds are unusual in the corporate sector, they are popular municipal issues, referred to as *revenue bonds.* Finally, **refunding issues** provide funds to prematurely retire another issue. They remain outstanding after the refunding operation. A refunding bond can be either a junior or senior issue.

The type of issue has only a marginal effect on comparative yield because it is basically the credibility of the issuer that determines bond quality. A study of corporate bond price behavior found that whether the issuer pledged collateral did not become important until the bond issue approached default. The collateral and security characteristics of a bond influence yield differentials only when these factors affect the bond's quality ratings.

Indenture Provisions   The indenture is the contract between the issuer and the bondholder specifying the issuer's legal requirements. A trustee (usually a bank) acting in behalf

of the bondholders ensures that all the indenture provisions are met, including the timely payment of interest and principal.

Features Affecting a Bond's Maturity   Investors should be aware of the three alternative call features that can affect the life (maturity) of a bond. One extreme is a *freely callable* provision that allows the issuer to retire the bond at any time with a typical notification period of thirty to sixty days. The other extreme is a *noncallable* provision wherein the issuer cannot retire the bond prior to its maturity.[2] Intermediate between these is a *deferred call* provision, which means the issue cannot be called for a certain period of time after the date of issue (say, five to ten years). At the end of the deferred call period, the issue becomes freely callable. Callable bonds have a *call premium,* which is the amount above maturity value that the issuer must pay to the bondholder for prematurely retiring the bond. The call premium typically is equal to one year's coupon interest payment.

A *nonrefunding provision* prohibits a call and premature retirement of an issue from the proceeds of a lower-coupon refunding bond. This is meant to protect the bondholder from a typical refunding, but it is not foolproof. The fact is, an issue with a nonrefunding provision can be called and retired prior to maturity using other sources of funds such as excess cash from operations, the sale of assets, or proceeds from a sale of common stock. This occurred on several occasions during the 1980s and 1990s when many issuers retired previously issued high-coupon issues early because they could get the cash from one of these other sources and felt that retiring a high-coupon bond issue was a good financing decision.

Another important indenture provision that can affect a bond's maturity is the *sinking fund,* which specifies that a bond must be paid off systematically over its life rather than only at maturity. There are numerous sinking-fund arrangements, and the bondholder should recognize this as a feature that can change the stated maturity of a bond. The size of the sinking fund can be a percentage of a given issue or a percentage of the total debt outstanding, or it can be a fixed or variable sum stated on a dollar or percentage basis. Similar to a call feature, sinking-fund payments may commence at the end of the first year or may be deferred for five or ten years from the date of the issue. The point is, the amount of the issue that must be repaid before maturity from a sinking fund can range from a nominal sum to 100 percent. Like a call provision, the sinking-fund feature typically carries a nominal premium, but it is generally smaller than the straight call premium (say, 1 percent). For example, a bond issue with a twenty-year maturity might have a sinking fund that requires that 5 percent of the issue be retired every year beginning in year ten. As a result, by year twenty half of the issue has been retired and the rest is paid off at maturity. Sinking-fund provisions have a small effect on comparative yields at the time of issue, but have little subsequent impact on price behavior.

A sinking-fund provision is an obligation and must be carried out regardless of market conditions. Although a sinking-fund bond issue could be called on a random basis, most of them are retired for sinking-fund purposes through direct negotiations with institutional holders. Essentially, the trustee negotiates with an institution to buy back the necessary amount of bonds at a price slightly above the current market price.

Rates of Return on Bonds

The rate of return on a bond is computed in the same way as the rate of return on stock or any asset. It is determined by the beginning and ending price and the cash flows during the holding period. The major difference between stocks and bonds is that the

---

[2]Currently most corporate long-term bonds contain some form of call provision.

interim cash flow on bonds (the interest) is specified, whereas the dividends on stock may vary. Therefore, the holding period return (HPR) for a bond will be

15.1
$$\text{HPR}_{i,t} = \frac{P_{i,t+1} + Int_{i,t}}{P_{i,t}}$$

where:

HPR$_{i,t}$ = the holding period return for bond i during period t
$P_{i,t+1}$ = the market price of bond i at the end of period t
$P_{i,t}$ = the market price of bond i at the beginning of period t
$Int_{i,t}$ = the interest payments on bond i during period t

The holding period yield (HPY) is:

$$\text{HPY} = \text{HPR} - 1$$

Note that the only contractual factor is the amount of interest payments. The beginning and ending bond prices are determined by market forces, as discussed in Chapter 10. Notably, the ending price is determined by market forces unless the bond is held to maturity, in which case the investor will receive the par value. These price variations in bonds mean that investors in bonds can experience capital gains or losses. Interest rate volatility has increased substantially since the 1960s, and this has caused large price fluctuations in bonds.[3] As a result, capital gains or losses have become a major component of the rates of return on bonds.

THE GLOBAL BOND-MARKET STRUCTURE[4]

The market for fixed-income securities is substantially larger than the listed equity exchanges (NYSE, TSE, LSE), because corporations tend to issue bonds rather than common stock. Typically, 20 percent of all new security issues are equity, which includes preferred as well as common stock. Corporations issue less common or preferred stock because firms derive most of their equity financing from internally generated funds (that is, retained earnings). Bonds mature and are sometimes repaid by issuing new bonds; equity doesn't need to be repaid. Also, although the equity market is strictly corporations, the bond market in most countries has four noncorporate sectors: the pure government sector (such as the Treasury in the United States), government agencies (such as FNMA), state and local government bonds (municipals), and international bonds (Yankees and Eurobonds in the United States).

The size of the global bond market and the distribution among countries can be gleaned from Table 15.1, which lists the dollar value of debt outstanding and the percentage distribution for the major bond markets for the years 1992, 1994, and 1996. There has been substantial growth overall including a 36 percent increase in the total value of bonds outstanding in 1996 compared with 1992. Also, the country trends are significant. Specif-

---

[3]The analysis of bond-price volatility is discussed in detail in Chapter 16.

[4]For a further discussion of global bond markets and specific national bond markets, see *International Bond Handbook,* International Bond Research Unit, James Capel & Co., London, 1987; and Adam Greshin and Margaret Darasz Hadzima, "International Bond Investing and Portfolio Management," in *The Handbook of Fixed-Income Securities,* 5th ed., edited by Frank J. Fabozzi (Chicago, Ill.: Irwin, 1997).

Table 15.1   *Total Debt Outstanding in the 13 Major Bond Markets, by Year (U.S. Dollar Terms)*

	1996		1994		1992	
	Total Publicly Issued	**% of Total**	**Total Publicly Issued**	**% of Total**	**Total Publicly Issued**	**% of Total**
U.S. dollar	$9,583.40	44.5%	$8,592.00	43.1%	$7,350.00	46.5%
Japanese yen	$3,655.90	17.0%	$4,533.00	22.8%	$3,134.00	19.8%
Deutsche mark	$2,303.10	10.7%	$2,598.00	13.0%	$1,119.00	12.1%
Italian lira	$1,274.40	05.9%	$ 981.00	4.9%	$ 758.00	4.8%
U.K. sterling	$ 661.80	3.1%	$ 523.00	2.6%	$ 362.00	2.3%
French franc	$1,044.00	4.8%	$ 792.00	4.0%	$ 603.00	3.8%
Canadian dollar	$ 446.30	2.1%	$ 467.00	2.3%	$ 431.00	2.7%
Swedish krona	$ 253.40	1.2%	$ 203.00	1.0%	$ 189.00	1.2%
Danish krone	$ 288.00	1.3%	$ 232.00	1.2%	$ 203.00	1.3%
Swiss franc	$ 241.40	1.1%	$ 217.00	1.1%	$ 178.00	1.1%
Dutch guilder	$ 400.80	1.9%	$ 327.00	1.6%	$ 292.00	1.8%
Belgian franc	$ 386.90	1.8%	$ 335.00	1.7%	$ 296.00	1.9%
Austrian dollar	$ 163.60	0.8%	$ 124.00	0.6%	$ 85.00	0.5%

Source: "Size and Structure of the World Bond Market," successive issues, Merrill Lynch International Fixed Income Research.

ically, the U.S. market declined slightly from 1992 to 1996. In contrast, Japan went from about 20 percent to 17 percent in 1996. The German market experienced a decrease from 12.1 to 10.7 percent during the past several years, whereas the U.K. market has experienced an increase, as did the Italian and French markets.

Participating Issuers

There are generally five different issuers of bonds in a country: (1) federal governments (for example, the U.S. Treasury), (2) agencies of the federal government, (3) various state and local political subdivisions (known as municipalities), (4) corporations, and (5) international issues. The division of bonds among these five types for the three largest markets and the United Kingdom during 1992, 1994, and 1996 is contained in Table 15.2.

Government   The market for government securities is the largest sector in the United States, Japan, and the United Kingdom. It involves a variety of debt instruments issued to meet the growing needs of these governments. In Germany, the government sector was smaller than that of the other countries in Table 15.2. It grew in relative size due to deficits related to the reunification of the country in the 1990s but is now stabilizing.

Government Agencies   Agency issues have attained and maintained a major position in the U.S. market (more than 25 percent), but are a smaller proportion in other countries. It is nonexistent in the United Kingdom. These agencies represent political subdivisions of the government, although the securities are *not* typically direct obligations of the government. The U.S. agency market has two types of issuers: government-sponsored enterprises and federal agencies. The proceeds of agency bond issues are used to finance many legislative programs. In the United States many of these obligations carry government guarantees although they are not direct obligations of the government. In other countries the relationship of an agency issue to the government varies. In most countries the market yields of agency obligations generally exceed those from pure government bonds. Thus, they represent a way for investors to increase returns with only marginally higher risk.

Table 15.2 *Makeup of Bonds Outstanding in United States, Japan, Germany, United Kingdom: 1992–1996*

	1996		1994		1992	
	$ Total Value	% of Total	$ Total Value	% of Total	$ Total Value	% of Total
U.S. (dollars in billions)						
Government	2,682.3	29.0	2,392.0	27.8	2,096.0	28.5
Federal Agency	2,634.5	28.5	2,176.0	25.3	1,734.0	23.6
Municipal	1,049.6	11.4	921.0	10.7	926.0	12.6
Corporate	1,910.0	20.7	2,247.0	26.1	1,879.0	25.6
International	960.2	10.4	856.0	10.0	714.0	9.7
Total	9,236.6	100.0	8,592.0	100.0	7,350.0	100.0
Japan (yen in trillions)						
Government	226.4	44.6	195.5	43.2	168.7	43.1
Federal Agency	76.8	15.1	71.3	15.8	61.7	15.8
Municipal	40.5	8.0	30.1	6.7	21.1	5.4
Bank Debentures	76.0	15.0	78.7	17.4	76.6	19.6
Corporate	47.6	9.4	43.1	9.5	37.3	9.5
International	40.0	7.9	33.4	7.4	25.6	6.5
Total	507.3	100.0	452.1	100.0	391.0	100.0
Germany (deutsche marks in billions)						
Government	1,088.1	30.4	1,078.4	26.8	762.4	24.6
Federal Agency	86.8	2.4	198.3	4.9	128.3	4.1
State and Local	129.9	3.6	636.9	15.8	532.1	17.2
Bank	1,801.5	50.3	1,432.7	35.6	1,156.2	37.3
Corporate	3.3	0.1	3.1	0.1	3.0	0.1
International	472.2	13.2	674.2	16.8	515.1	16.6
Total	3,581.8	100.0	4,023.6	100.0	3,097.0	100.0
United Kingdom (pounds sterling in billions)						
Government	263.0	67.5	211.9	63.4	144.2	60.3
Federal Agency	0.0	0.0	0.0	0.0	0.0	0.0
Municipal	0.1	00	0.0	0.0	0.0	0.0
Corporate	19.3	4.9	18.3	5.5	14.9	6.2
International	107.5	27.6	104.2	31.2	80.1	33.5
Total	389.9	100.0	334.4	100.0	239.2	100.0

Source: "Size and Structure of the World Bond Market," successive issues, Merrill Lynch International Fixed-Income Research.

Municipalities   Municipal debt includes issues of states, school districts, cities, or other political subdivisions. Unlike government and agency issues, the interest income on them is not subject to federal income tax although capital gains is taxable. Moreover, these bonds are exempt from state and local taxes when they are issued by the investor's home state. That is, the interest income on a California issue would not be taxed to a California resident, but it would be taxable to a New York resident. The interest income of Puerto Rican issues enjoys total immunity from federal, state, and local taxes. Also, most U.S. municipal bond issues are serial obligations, which means an investor can select from a number of different maturities from short (one or two years) to fairly long (twenty years).

As shown in Table 15.2, the municipal bond market in most other countries is much smaller than in the United States. Also, although each country has unique tax laws, typically the income from a non-U.S. municipal bond would not be exempt for a U.S. investor.

Corporations   The major nongovernmental issuer of debt is the corporate sector. The importance of this sector differs dramatically among countries. It is a significant factor in the United States; a small but growing sector in Japan, where it is supplemented by bank debentures; and a small and declining proportion of the U.K. market. Finally, it is a minuscule part of the German market, because most German firms get their financing through bank loans, which explains the large percentage of bank debt in Germany.

The market for corporate bonds is commonly subdivided into several segments: industrials, public utilities, transportation, and financial issues. The specific makeup varies between countries. Most U.S. issues are industrials and utilities. Most foreign corporations do not issue public debt but borrow from the banks.

The corporate sector provides the most diverse issues in terms of type and quality. In effect, the issuer can range from the highest investment-grade firm, such as American Telephone and Telegraph or IBM, to a relatively new, high-risk firm that defaulted on previous debt securities.[5]

International   The international sector has two components: (1) foreign bonds such as Yankee bonds and Samurai bonds, and (2) Eurobonds including Eurodollar, Euroyen, Euro-deutsche mark, and Eurosterling bonds.[6] Although Eurodollar bonds have historically made up more than 50 percent of the Eurobond market, the proportion has declined as investors have attempted to diversify their Eurobond portfolios. Clearly, the desire for diversification changes with the swings in the value of the U.S. dollar.

Participating Investors

Numerous individual and institutional investors with diverse investment objectives participate in the bond market. Wealthy individual investors are a minor portion because of the market's complexity and the high minimum denominations of most issues. Institutional investors typically account for 90 to 95 percent of the trading, although different segments of the market are more institutionalized than others. For example, institutions are involved heavily in the agency market, whereas they are much less active in the corporate sector.

Individuals can invest in Treasuries through the Treasury Direct program. Forms are available at many banks or by calling 202-874-4000. In addition, a variety of institutions invest in the bond market. Life insurance companies invest in corporate bonds and, to a lesser extent, in Treasury and agency securities. Commercial banks invest in the municipal bonds and also government and agency issues. Property and liability insurance companies concentrate on municipal bonds and Treasuries. Private and government pension funds are heavily committed to corporates and also invest in Treasuries and agencies. Finally, fixed-income mutual funds have grown in size, and their demand spans the full spectrum of the market as they develop bond funds that meet the needs of individual investors. Municipal bonds funds and corporate bond funds (including high-yield bonds) have experienced significant growth.

Various institutions tend to favor different issues based on two factors: (1) the tax code applicable to the institution, and (2) the nature of the institution's liability structure. For example, because commercial banks are subject to normal taxation and have fairly short-term liability structures, they favor short- to intermediate-term municipals. Pension

---

[5]It is possible to distinguish another sector that exists in the United States but not in other countries—institutional bonds. These are corporate bonds issued by a variety of *private, nonprofit institutions* such as schools, hospitals, and churches. They are not broken out because they are only a minute part of the U.S. market and do not exist elsewhere.

[6]These bonds will be discussed in more detail later in this chapter.

funds are virtually tax-free institutions with long-term commitments, so they prefer high-yielding, long-term government or corporate bonds. Such institutional investment preferences can affect the short-run supply and demand of loanable funds and affect interest rate changes.

Bond Ratings

Bond ratings are an integral part of the bond market because most corporate and municipal bonds are rated by one or more of the rating agencies. The exceptions are very small issues and bonds from certain industries such as bank issues. These are known as *nonrated bonds.* There are four major rating agencies: (1) Duff and Phelps, (2) Fitch Investors Service, (3) Moody's, and (4) Standard & Poor's.

Bond ratings provide the fundamental analysis for thousands of issues.[7] The rating agencies analyze the issuing organization and the specific issue to determine the probability of default (credit quality), and inform the market of their analyses through their ratings.

The primary question in bond credit analysis is whether the firm can service its debt in a timely manner over the life of a given issue. Consequently, the rating agencies consider expectations over the life of the issue, along with the historical and current financial position of the company. Although the agencies have done an admirable job. mistakes happen. A study indicated that the rating services have tended to overestimate the risk of default, which has resulted in unnecessarily high risk premiums given the default probabilities. We will consider default estimation further when we discuss high-yield (junk) bonds.

Several studies have examined the relationship between bond ratings and issue quality as indicated by financial variables. The results clearly demonstrated that bond ratings were positively related to profitability, size, and cash flow coverage, and they were inversely related to financial leverage and earnings instability.[8]

The original ratings assigned to bonds affect their marketability and effective interest rate. Generally, the four agencies' ratings agree. When they do not, the issue is said to have a *split rating.* Seasoned issues are regularly reviewed to ensure that the assigned rating is still valid. If not, revisions are made either upward or downward. Revisions are usually done in increments of one rating grade.[9] The ratings are based on both the company and the issue. After an evaluation of the creditworthiness of the total company is completed, a company rating is assigned to the firm's most senior unsecured issue. All junior bonds receive lower ratings based on indenture specifications. Also, an issue could receive a higher rating than justified by its fundamentals because of credit-enhancement devices such as the attachment of bank letters of credit, surety, or indemnification bonds from insurance companies.

The agencies assign letter ratings depicting what they view as the risk of default of an obligation. The letter ratings range from AAA (Aaa) to D. Table 15.3 describes the various ratings assigned by the major services. Except for slight variations in designations,

---

[7]For a detailed listing of rating classes and a listing of factors considered in assigning ratings, see "Bond Ratings" and "Bond Rating Outlines," in *The Financial Analysts Handbook,* 2d ed., edited by Sumner N. Levine (Homewood, Ill.: Dow Jones–Irwin, 1988), 1102–1138.

[8]See, for example, Robert S. Kaplan and Gabriel Urwitz, "Statistical Models of Bond Ratings: A Methodological Inquiry," *Journal of Business* 52, no. 2 (April 1979): 231–262; Ahmed Belkaoui, "Industrial Bond Ratings: A New Look," *Financial Management* 9, no. 3 (Autumn 1980): 44–52; and James A. Gentry, David T. Whitford, and Paul Newbold, "Predicting Industrial Bond Ratings with a Probit Model and Funds Flow Components," *Financial Review* 23, no. 3 (August 1988): 269–286.

[9]Bond rating changes and bond-market efficiency are discussed in Chapter 16. Split ratings are discussed in R. Billingsley, R. Lamy, M. Marr, and T. Thompson, "Split Ratings and Bond Reoffering Yields," *Financial Management* 14, no. 2 (Summer 1985): 59–65; L. H. Ederington, "Why Split Ratings Occur," *Financial Management* 14, no. 1 (Spring 1985): 37–47.

Table 15.3 Description of Bond Ratings

	Duff and Phelps	Fitch	Moody's	Standard & Poor's	Definition
High Grade	AAA	AAA	Aaa	AAA	The highest rating assigned to a debt instrument, indicating an extremely strong capacity to pay principal and interest. Bonds in this category are often referred to as *gilt-edge securities.*
	AA	AA	Aa	AA	High-quality bonds by all standards with strong capacity to pay principal and interest. These bonds are rated lower primarily because the margins of protection are less strong than those for Aaa and AAA bonds.
Medium Grade	A	A	A	A	These bonds possess many favorable investment attributes, but elements may suggest a susceptibility to impairment given adverse economic changes.
	BBB	BBB	Baa	BBB	Bonds are regarded as having adequate capacity to pay principal and interest, but certain protective elements may be lacking in the event of adverse economic conditions that could lead to a weakened capacity for payment.
Speculative	BB	BB	Ba	BB	Bonds regarded as having only moderate protection of principal and interest payments during both good and bad times.
	B	B	B	B	Bonds that generally lack characteristics of other desirable investments. Assurance of interest and principal payments over any long period of time may be small.
Default	CCC	CCC	Caa	CCC	Poor-quality issues that may be in default or in danger of default.
	CC	CC	Ca	CC	Highly speculative issues that are often in default or possess other marked shortcomings.
	C	C			The lowest-rated class of bonds. These issues can be regarded as extremely poor in investment quality.
		C		C	Rating given to income bonds on which no interest is being paid.
		DDD DD D		D	Issues in default with principal or interest payments in arrears. Such bonds are extremely speculative and should be valued only on the basis of their value in liquidation or reorganization.

Source: *Bond Guide* (New York: Standard & Poor's Corporation, monthly), *Bond Record* (New York, Moody's Investors Services, Inc., monthly), *Rating Register* (New York: Fitch Investors Service, Inc., monthly).

the meaning and interpretation is basically the same. The agencies modify the ratings with + and − signs for Duff & Phelps, Fitch , and S&P, or with numbers (1-2-3) for Moody's. As an example, an A+ bond is at the top of the A-rated group.

The top four ratings—AAA (or Aaa), AA (or Aa), A, and BBB (or Baa)—are generally considered *investment-grade securities.* The next level of securities is known as *speculative bonds* (or high-yield or junk bonds). These include the BB and B-rated obligations. The C categories are generally either income obligations or revenue bonds, many of which

are trading "flat." A bond trading flat means the issuer is in arrears on interest payments. In the case of D-rated obligations, the issues are in outright default, and the ratings indicate the bonds' relative salvage values.

ALTERNATIVE BOND ISSUES

At this point, we have described the basic features available for all bonds and the overall structure of the global bond market in terms of the issuers of bonds and investors in bonds. In this section, we provide a detailed discussion of the bonds available from the major issuers of bonds. The presentation is longer than you would normally expect because when we discuss each issuing unit such as governments, municipalities, or corporations, we consider the bonds available in several of the major world financial centers such as Japan, Germany, and the United Kingdom.

Domestic Government Bonds

United States As shown in Table 15.2, the U.S. fixed-income market is dominated by U.S. treasury obligations. The U.S. government, with the full faith and credit of the U.S. Treasury, issues Treasury bills (T-bills), which mature in less than one year, and two forms of long-term obligations: government notes, which have maturities of ten years or less; and Treasury bonds, with maturities of ten to thirty years. Current Treasury obligations come in denominations of $1,000 and $10,000. The interest income from the U.S. government securities is subject to federal income tax but exempt from state and local levies. These bonds are popular because of their high credit quality, substantial liquidity, and the fact that those issued since 1989 are noncallable.

Short-term T-bills differ from notes and bonds because they are sold at a discount from par to provide the desired yield. The return is the difference between the purchase price and the par at maturity. In contrast, government notes and bonds carry semiannual coupons that specify the nominal yield of the obligations.

Government notes and bonds have some unusual features. First, the period specified for the deferred call feature on Treasury issues is long and is generally measured relative to the maturity date rather than from date of issue. They generally cannot be called until five years prior to their maturity date. Notably, *all* issues since 1989 have been noncallable.

A risk of bond investing is unexpected changes in inflation. An unexpected increase in inflation can cause lower real returns as the bond's fixed interest rate fails to adjust to varying inflation. In 1997 the U.S. Treasury offered a new innovation to investors in U.S. debt: inflation-protected Treasury notes.[10] Issued in $1,000 minimum denominations, the principal value of the notes change in accordance with changes in the consumer price index (CPI).[11]

Here's how they work: Interest payments are computed based upon the inflation-adjusted principal value. In times of rising consumer prices, both the principal value and interest payments rise in line with inflation. Should the CPI fall, the principal amount is reduced accordingly. As an example, suppose an inflation-indexed note with a $1,000 par value is sold at a 3 percent interest rate. If inflation over the next year is 4 percent, the

---

[10]This was an innovation for the U.S. Treasury. Inflation-adjusted bonds have been offered by other countries for some time. For example, Israel first offered these securities in 1955; the U.K. in 1981; Australia in 1985; Canada in 1991; and Sweden in 1994.

[11]Because of the initial popularity of inflation-adjusted T-notes, some federal agencies (Federal Home Loan Bank Board, TVA) have issued inflation-indexed notes as well.

principal value rises to $1,000 plus 4 percent or $1,040. The annual interest payment will be 3 percent of $1,040—0.3 × $1,040, or $31.20. With 4 percent inflation, the principal rises by 4 percent ($1,000 to $1,040) as well as the interest ($30 to $31.20).

Although the principal is not paid until the note matures, the IRS considers the year-by-year change in principal as taxable income in the year in which the change in value is made. In the above example, the investor will pay taxes on $71.20—the $31.20 in interest received and the $40 increase in principal value. This condition makes these bonds most attractive to tax-exempt or tax-deferred investors, such as pension funds and individual IRA accounts.[12]

Japan[13]   The second largest government bond market in the world is Japan's. It is controlled by the Japanese government and the Bank of Japan (Japanese Central Bank). Japanese government bonds are an attractive investment vehicle for those favoring the Japanese yen, because their quality is equal to that of U.S. Treasury securities (they are guaranteed by the government of Japan) and they are highly liquid. There are three maturity segments: medium term (two, three, or four years), long term (ten years), and super long (private placements for fifteen and twenty years). Bonds are issued in both registered and bearer form, although registered bonds can be converted to bearer bonds through the registrar at the Bank of Japan.

Medium-term bonds are issued monthly through a competitive auction system similar to that of U.S. Treasury bonds. Long-term bonds are authorized by the Ministry of Finance and issued monthly by the Bank of Japan through an underwriting syndicate consisting of major financial institutions. Most super-long bonds are sold through private placement to a few financial institutions. Government bonds, which are the most liquid of all Japanese bonds, account for more than half of the Japanese bonds outstanding and more than 80 percent of total bond trading volume in Japan.

At least 50 percent of the trading in Japanese government bonds will be in the so-called **benchmark issue** of the time. The selection of the benchmark issue is made from among ten-year coupon bonds. The designation of a benchmark issue is intended to assist smaller financial institutions in their trading of government bonds by ensuring these institutions that they would have a liquid market in this particular security. Compared to the benchmark issue, which accounts for about 50 percent of total trading in all Japanese government bonds, the comparable most active U.S. bond within a class accounts for only about 10 percent of the volume.

The yield on this benchmark bond is often as much as 50 or 60 basis points below other comparable Japanese government bonds, reflecting its superior marketability. In the U.S. market, the most liquid bond sells at a yield differential of only ten basis points. The benchmark issue changes when a designated issue matures or because of a decision by the Bank of Japan.

Germany[14]   The third largest bond market in the world is the German market, although the government segment of this market is relatively small. Table 15.2 shows that most of the domestic deutsche mark bonds are issued by the major commercial banks, whereas the Federal Republic of Germany issues the remainder through the German Central Bank.

[12]Tom Herman, "How to Decide What to Do Next Week When 'Inflation-Indexed' Bonds Debut," *Wall Street Journal,* January 24, 1997, C1, C13; David Wessel, "Treasury Plans to Sell 5-Year 'Inflation' Notes," *Wall Street Journal,* June 9, 1997, C1, C17; Michelle Clark Neely, "The Name Is Bond—Indexed Bond," *Regional Economist,* Federal Reserve Bank of St. Louis, January 1997, 10–11.

[13]For additional discussion, see "International Bond Handbook" (London: James Capel & Co., 1987); Aron Viner, *Inside Japanese Financial Markets* (Homewood, Ill.: Dow Jones–Irwin, 1988); Edwin J. Elton and Martin J. Gruber, eds., *Japanese Capital Markets* (New York: Harper & Row, 1990); and Frank J. Fabozzi, ed., *The Japanese Bond Markets* (Chicago: Probus Publishing, 1990).

[14]For additional information on the German bond market, see Graham Bishop, "Deutschemark" in *Salomon Brothers International Bond Manual,* 2d ed. (New York: Salomon Brothers, 1987); and *The European Bond Markets,* ed. by the European Bond Commission (Chicago: Probus Publishing, 1989).

The German capital market is dominated by commercial banks because Germany makes no formal distinction between investment, merchant, or commercial banks as do the United States and the United Kingdom. As a result, firms arrange their financing primarily through bank loans, and these banks in turn raise their capital through public bond issues. Therefore, industrial domestic bonds are substantially less than 1 percent of the total outstanding German bonds.

Bonds issued by the Federal Republic of Germany, referred to as *bund* bonds, are issued in amounts up to DM 4 billion (4 billion deutsche marks) with a minimum denomination of DM 100. Original maturities are normally ten or twelve years although thirty-year bonds have been issued.

Although bunds are issued as bearer bonds, individual bonds do not exist. A global bond is issued and held in safekeeping within the German Securities Clearing System (the *Kassenverein*). Contract notes confirming the terms and ownership of each issue are then distributed to individual investors. These government bunds are highly liquid because the Bundesbank makes a market at all times. They are also the highest credit quality because they are guaranteed by the German government. Although listed on the exchanges, government bonds are primarily traded over the counter and interest is paid annually.

United Kingdom[15]   The U.K. government bond market changed dramatically on October 17, 1986 (the day of the Big Bang when the trading rules and organizations in the securities business in the United Kingdom were changed). The roles of jobbers and brokers changed so that broker-dealers could act as principals or agents with negotiated commission structures. In addition, the number of primary dealers in the "gilt" market was expanded from 7 gilt jobbers to 27 primary dealers.

Maturities in this market range from short gilts (maturities of less than five years) to medium gilts (five to fifteen years) to long gilts (fifteen years and longer). Government bonds either have a fixed redemption date or a range of dates with redemption at the option of the government after giving appropriate notice. Alternatively, some bonds are redeemable on a given date or at any time afterwards at the option of the government.

Gilts are issued through the Bank of England (the British central bank) using the tender method, whereby prospective purchasers tender offering prices at which they hope to be allotted bonds. The price cannot be less than the minimum tender price stated in the prospectus. If the issue is oversubscribed, allotments are made first to those submitting the highest tenders and continue until a price is reached where only a partial allotment is required to fully subscribe the issue. All successful allottees pay the lowest allotment prices.

These issues are extremely liquid because of the size of the market and the large size of individual issues. They are also highly rated because all payments are guaranteed by the British government. Interest is paid semiannually.

Government Agency Issues

In addition to pure government bonds, the federal government in each country can establish agencies that have the authority to issue their own bonds. The size and importance of these agencies differ among countries. They are a large and growing sector of the U.S. bond market, a much smaller component of the bond markets in Japan and Germany, and nonexistent in the United Kingdom.

United States   Agency securities are obligations issued by the U.S. government through various political subdivisions, such as a government agency or a government-

[15]For further discussion, see Ian C. Collier, "An Introduction to the Gilt-Edged Market" (London: James Capel & Co., 1987); and *The European Bond Markets*.

sponsored corporation. Six government-sponsored enterprises and more than two dozen federal agencies issue these bonds. Table 15.4 lists selected characteristics of the more popular government-sponsored and federal agency obligations, including the recent size of the market, typical minimum denominations, tax features, and the availability of bond quotes.[16] The issues in the table are representative of the wide variety of different obligations that are available.

Agency issues pay interest semiannually, and the minimum denominations vary between $1,000 and $10,000. These obligations are not direct issues of the Treasury, yet they carry the full faith and credit of the U.S. government. Moreover, unlike government obligations, some of the issues are subject to state and local income tax, whereas others are exempt.[17]

One agency issue offers particularly attractive investment opportunities: GNMA ("Ginnie Mae") pass-through certificates, which are obligations of the Government National Mortgage Association.[18] These bonds represent an undivided interest in a pool of federally insured mortgages. The bondholders receive monthly payments from Ginnie Mae that include both principal and interest, because the agency "passes through" mortgage payments made by the original borrower (the mortgagee) to Ginnie Mae.

The coupons on these pass-through securities are related to the interest charged on the pool of mortgages. The portion of the cash flow that represents the repayment of the principal is tax-free, but the interest income is subject to federal, state, and local taxes. The issues have minimum denominations of $25,000 with maturities of twenty-five to thirty years but an average life of only twelve years, because as mortgages in the pool are paid off, payments and prepayments are passed through to the investor. Therefore, unlike most bond issues, the monthly payment is not fixed. In fact, the monthly payment is *extremely uncertain* because of prepayments that can vary dramatically over time when interest rates change.

These securities have prepayments in two cases. The first is when homeowners pay off their mortgages when they sell their homes. The second occurs when owners refinance their homes when mortgage interest rates decline as they did in 1992, 1993, and 1997. A major disadvantage of GNMA issues is that they can be seriously depleted by prepayments, which means that their maturities are uncertain.

The rates of return on these pass-throughs are relatively attractive compared to corporates. Also, most of the cash flow is tax-free in the later years because the tax-free part of the regular payment that is due to the return of principal is large.

Japan   The agencies in Japan, referred to as *government associate organizations*, account for about 15 percent of the total Japanese bond market. This agency market includes a substantial amount of public debt, but almost twice as much is privately placed with major financial institutions. Public agency debt is issued like government debt.

Germany   The agency market in Germany finances about 3 percent of the public debt. The major agencies are the Federal Railway, which issues *Bahn* or *Bundesbahn* bonds, and the Federal Post Office, which issues *Post* or *Bundespost* bonds. These Bahns and Posts

---

[16]We will no longer distinguish between federal agency and government-sponsored obligations; instead, the term *agency* shall apply to either type of issue.

[17]Federal National Mortgage Association ("Fannie Mae") debentures, for example, are subject to state and local income tax, whereas the interest income from Federal Home Loan Bank bonds is exempt. In fact, a few issues are even exempt from federal income tax as well (for example, public housing bonds).

[18]For a further discussion of mortgage-backed securities, see *Mortgage-Backed Bond and Pass-Through Symposium,* Charlottesville, Va. (Financial Analysts Research Foundation, 1980), Andrew S. Carron, "Collateralized Mortgage Obligations," in *The Handbook of Fixed-Income Securities,* 5th ed., edited by Frank J. Fabozzi (Chicago, Ill.: Irwin, 1997) and Amy F. Lipton, "Evolution of the Mortgage Securities Market," in *Fixed Income Management: Techniques and Practices,* edited by Dwight R. Churchill (Charlottesville, Va: Association for Investment Management and Research, 1994), pp. 26–30.

Table 15.4 *Agency Issues: Selected Characteristics*

Type of Security	Minimum Denomination	Form	Life of Issue	Tax Status		How Interest Is Earned
Government-Sponsored						
Federal Farm Credit Banks Consolidated Systemwide Notes	$ 50,000	BE	5 to 365 days	Federal: State: Local:	Taxable Exempt Exempt	Discount actual, 360-day year
Consolidated Systemwide Bonds	5,000	BE	6 and 9 months	Federal: State: Local:	Taxable Exempt Exempt	Interest payable at maturity, 360-day year
	1,000	BE	13 months to 15 years	Federal: State: Local:	Taxable Exempt Exempt	Semiannual interest
Federal Home Loan Bank						
Consolidated Discount Notes	100,000	BE	30 to 360 days	Federal: State: Local:	Taxable Exempt Exempt	Discount actual, 360-day year
Consolidated Bonds	10,000[a]	B, BE	1 to 20 years	Federal: State: Local:	Taxable Exempt Exempt	Semiannual interest, 360-day year
Federal Home Loan Mortgage						
Corporation Debentures	10,000[a]	BE	18 to 30 years	Federal: State: Local:	Taxable Taxable Taxable	Semiannual interest, 360-day year
Participation Certificates	100,000	R	30 years (12-year average life)	Federal: State: Local:	Taxable Taxable Taxable	Monthly interest and principal payments
Federal National Mortgage Association Discount Notes	50,000[a]	B	30 to 360 days	Federal: State: Local:	Taxable Taxation Taxable	Discount actual, 360-day year
Debentures	10,000[a]	B, BE	1 to 30 years	Federal: State: Local:	Taxable Taxable Taxable	Semiannual interest, 360-day year

are issued up to DM 2 billion. The issue procedure is similar to that used for regular government bonds, which involves a fixed-quota system by the Federal Bond Syndicate. Bahns and Posts are less liquid than government bunds, but the market is still quite liquid. These agency issues are implicitly, though not explicitly, guaranteed by the government.

United Kingdom   As shown in Table 15.2, the United Kingdom issues no agency bonds.

Municipal Bonds

Municipal bonds are issued by states, counties, cities, and other political subdivisions. Again, the size of the municipal bond market (referred to as *local authority* in the United Kingdom) varies substantially among countries. They comprise slightly more than 10 percent of the total U.S. market, compared to about 3 percent in Germany, and less than 1 percent in the United Kingdom. Because of the limited size of this market in other countries, we will discuss only the U.S. municipal bond market.

Municipalities in the United States issue two distinct types of bonds: general obligation bonds and revenue issues. **General obligation bonds (GOs)** are essentially backed

Table 15.4 *Agency Issues: Selected Characteristics (continued)*

Type of Security	Minimum Denomination	Form	Life of Issue	Tax Status		How Interest Is Earned
Government National Mortgage Association						
Mortgage-backed Bonds	25,000	B, R	1 to 25 years	Federal:	Taxable	Semiannual interest, 360-day year
				State:	Taxable	
				Local:	Taxable	
Modified Pass-throughs	25,000[a]	R	12 to 40 years (12-year average)	Federal:	Taxable	Monthly interest and principal payments
				State:	Taxable	
				Local:	Taxable	
Student Loan Marketing Association Discount Notes	100,000	B	Out to 1 year	Federal:	Taxable	Discount actual, 360-day year
				State:	Exempt	
				Local:	Exempt	
Notes	10,000	R	3 to 10 years	Federal:	Taxable	Semiannual interest, 360-day year
				State:	Exempt	
				Local:	Exempt	
Floating Rate Notes	10,000[a]	R	6 months to 10 years	Federal:	Taxable	Interest rate adjusted weekly to an increment over the average auction rate on 91-day Treasury bills and payable quarterly
				State:	Exempt	
				Local:	Exempt	
Tennessee Valley Authority (TVA)	**1,000**	**R, B**	**5 to 25 years**	Federal:	Taxable	Semiannual interest, 360-day year
				State:	Exempt	
				Local:	Exempt	
U.S. Postal Service	**10,000**	**R, B**	**25 years**	Federal:	Taxable	Semiannual interest, 360-day year
				State:	Exempt	
				Local:	Exempt	

Notes: Form B = Bearer; R = Registered; BE = Book entry form. Debt issues sold subsequent to December 31, 1982, must be in registered form.

[a]Minimum purchase with increments in $5,000.

Source: *United States Government Securities* (New York: Merrill Lynch Government Securities, Inc., 1985); *Handbook of Securities of the United States Government and Federal Agencies,* 31st ed. (New York: First Boston Corporation, 1984).

by the full faith and credit of the issuer and its entire taxing power. **Revenue bonds**, in turn, are serviced by the income generated from specific revenue-producing projects of the municipality, for example, bridges, toll roads, hospitals, municipal coliseums, and waterworks. Revenue bonds generally provide higher returns than GOs because of their higher default risk. Specifically, should a municipality fail to generate sufficient income from a project designated to service a revenue bond, it has absolutely no legal debt service obligation until the income becomes sufficient.

GO municipal bonds tend to be issued on a serial basis so that the issuer's cash flow requirements will be steady over the life of the obligation. Therefore, the principal portion of the total debt service requirement generally begins at a fairly low level and builds up over the life of the obligation. In contrast, most municipal revenue bonds are term issues, so the principal value is not due until the final maturity date or the last few payment dates.

The most important feature of municipal obligations is that the interest payments are exempt from federal income tax, as well as from taxes in the locality and state in which the obligation was issued. This means that their attractiveness varies with the investors' tax brackets.

You can convert the tax-free yield of a municipal bond *selling close to par* to an equivalent taxable yield (ETY) using the following equation:

15.2
$$ETY = \frac{i}{(1 - T)}$$

where:

ETY = equivalent taxable yield
**   *i* = coupon rate of the municipal obligations**
**   *T* = marginal tax rate of the investor**

An investor in the 35 percent marginal tax bracket would find that a 6 percent yield on a municipal bond selling close to its par value is equivalent to a 9.23 percent fully taxable yield according to the following calculation:

$$ETY = \frac{.06}{(1 - .35)} = .0923$$

Because the tax-free yield is the major benefit of municipal bonds, an investor's marginal tax rate is a primary concern in evaluating them. However, although the interest payment on municipals is tax-free, any capital gains are not (which is why the ETY formula is only correct for a bond selling close to its par value).

Municipal Bond Guarantees   A growing feature of the U.S. municipal bond market is **municipal bond guarantees** that provide that a bond insurance company will guarantee to make principal and interest payments in the event that the issuer of the bonds defaults. The guarantees are a form of insurance placed on the bond at date of issue and are *irrevocable* over the life of the issue. The issuer purchases the insurance for the benefit of the investor, and the municipality benefits from lower interest costs due to lower default risk, which in turn causes an increase in the rating on the bond and increased marketability.

The four private bond insurance firms are as follows: a consortium of four large insurance companies entitled the Municipal Bond Investors Assurance (MBIA), a subsidiary of a large Milwaukee-based private insurer known as American Municipal Bond Assurance Corporation (AMBAC), the Financial Security Assurance, and the Financial Guaranty Insurance Company (FGIC). These firms will insure either general obligation or revenue bonds. To qualify for private bond insurance, the issue must initially carry an S&P rating of BBB or better. Currently, the rating agencies will give an AAA (Aaa) rating to bonds insured by these firms because all of the insurance firms have AAA ratings. Issues with these private guarantees have enjoyed a more active secondary market and lower required yields.[19]

Corporate Bonds

Again, the importance of corporate bonds varies across countries. The absolute dollar value of corporate bonds in the United States is substantial and has continued to grow. At the same time, corporate debt as a percentage of total U.S. debt has declined from 26 percent to 21 percent because of the faster increase in government debt caused by large government deficits and the growth of agency (mortgage-backed) debt. The pure corporate sec-

---

[19]For a discussion of municipal bond insurance, see Sylvan Feldstein and Frank J. Fabozzi, "Municipal Bonds," in *Handbook of Fixed-Income Securities,* 5th ed., edited by Frank J. Fabozzi (Chicago, Ill.: Irwin, 1997); and D. S. Kidwell, E. H. Sorenson, and J. M. Wachowicz, "Estimating the Signalling Benefits of Debt Insurance: The Case of Municipal Bonds," *Journal of Financial and Quantitative Analysis* 22, no. 3 (September 1987): 299–313. For a discussion of a problem due to the popularity of insurance, see Constance Mitchell, "Bond Insurers Nearing Their Capacity for Backing Some Municipalities' Debt," *Wall Street Journal,* June 1, 1992, C1, C7.

tor in Japan is small, whereas bank debentures comprise a significant segment (15 percent). The pure corporate sector in Germany is almost nonexistent, whereas bank debentures used to finance corporate loans are the largest segment. Corporate debt in the United Kingdom is about 5 percent of the total.

U.S. Corporate Bond Market   Utilities dominate the U.S. corporate bond market. The other important segments include industrials (which rank second to utilities), rail and transportation issues, and financial issues. This market includes debentures, first-mortgage issues, convertible obligations, bonds with warrants, subordinated debentures, income bonds (similar to municipal revenue bonds), collateral trust bonds backed by financial assets, equipment trust certificates, and asset-backed securities (ABS), including mortgage-backed bonds.

If we ignore convertible bonds and bonds with warrants, the preceding list of obligations varies by the type of collateral behind the bond. Most bonds have semiannual interest payments, sinking funds, and a single maturity date. Maturities range from twenty-five to forty years, with public utilities generally on the longer end and industrials preferring the twenty-five- to thirty-year range. Most corporate bonds provide for deferred calls after five to ten years. The deferment period varies directly with the level of the interest rates. Specifically, during periods of higher interest rates, bond issues will typically carry a seven- to ten-year deferment, while during periods of relatively low interest rates, the deferment periods will be much shorter.

On the other hand, corporate notes, with maturities of five to seven years, are generally noncallable. Notes become popular when interest rates are high because issuing firms prefer to avoid long-term obligations during such periods. In contrast, during periods of low interest rates such as 1991 to 1993, most corporate issues did not include a call provision because corporations did not believe that they would be able to use them and did not want to pay the higher yield required to include them.

Generally, the average yields for industrial bonds will be the lowest of the three major sectors, followed by utility returns, with yields on transportation bonds generally being the highest. The difference in yield between utilities and industrials is because utilities have the largest supply of bonds, so yields on their bonds must be higher to increase the demand for these bonds.

Wall Street financial wizards are always trying to develop new securities to offer new means to spread risk among willing market participants. For example, in 1997, USAA, an insurance company, issued a bond with *tranches* or components to diversify its weather disaster risk. If the firm suffered losses of $1 billion or more from a single hurricane, interest payments would fall in one tranche and the required principal payment would fall in the other tranche. Thus, large losses would not solely be absorbed by the issuer, but by its bondholders as well.[20] The typical corporate bond has a maturity of thirty years or less; but in attempts to lock in low financing rates and to appeal to investors seeking higher yields and longer maturities, several issuers have sold 50-, 100-, and 1,000-year bonds.[21]

Some corporate bonds have unique features or security arrangements that will be discussed in the following subsections.[22]

---

[20]Leslie Scism, "Investors in USAA 'Disaster Bonds' Could Get the Wind Knocked Out of Them if Storms Strike," *Wall Street Journal,* June 18, 1997, C21.

[21]In addition to locking in low interest rates, the interest tax-deductibility gives such long-lived issues a flavor of tax-deductible equity. See the discussion in Chapter 15, "Debt Financing Choices" of C. F. Lee, J. E. Finnerty, and Edgar A. Norton, *Foundations of Financial Management,* St. Paul, Mn.: West Publishing, 1997; Craig Karmin and Charlene Lee, "First-Ever 1,000-Year Corporate Bond Is Readied As Issuer Counts on Demand for Higher Yields," *Wall Street Journal,* October 7, 1997, C25.

[22]For a further discussion of corporate bonds, see Frank J. Fabozzi, Richard S. Wilson, and Harry C. Sauvain, "Corporate Bonds," in *The Handbook of Fixed-Income Securities,* 5th ed., edited by Frank J. Fabozzi (Chicago: Irwin, 1997).

Mortgage bonds   The issuer of a mortgage bond has granted to the bondholder a first-mortgage lien on some piece of property or possibly all of the firm's property. Such a lien provides greater security to the bondholder and a lower interest rate for the issuing firm. Additional mortgage bonds can be issued, assuming certain protective covenants related to earnings or assets are met by the issuer.

Collateral trust bonds   As an alternative to pledging fixed assets or property, a borrower can pledge stocks, bonds, or notes as collateral. The bonds secured by these assets are termed **collateral trust bonds**. These pledged assets are held by a trustee for the benefit of the bondholder.

Equipment trust certificates   **Equipment trust certificates** are issued by railroads (the biggest issuers), airlines, and other transportation firms with the proceeds used to purchase equipment (freight cars, railroad engines, and airplanes) that serves as the collateral for the debt. Maturities range from one to about fifteen years. The fairly short maturities reflect the nature of the collateral, which is subject to substantial wear and tear and tends to deteriorate rapidly.

Equipment trust certificates are appealing to investors because of their attractive yields and low default record. Although they lack the visibility of other corporate bonds, they typically are fairly liquid.

Collateralized mortgage obligations (CMO) [23] Earlier we discussed mortgage bonds backed by pools of mortgages that pay bondholders proportionate shares of principal and interest paid on the mortgages in the pool. You will recall that the pass-through monthly payments necessarily contain both interest and principal and that the bondholder is subject to early retirement if the mortgagees prepay because the house is sold or the mortgage refinanced. As a result, when you acquire the typical mortgage pass-through bond, you receive monthly payments (which may not be ideal), and you would be uncertain about the size and timing of the payments.

Collateralized mortgage obligations (CMOs) were developed to offset some of the problems with the traditional mortgage pass-throughs. The main innovation of the CMO instrument is the segmentation of irregular mortgage cash flows. Specifically, CMO investors own bonds that are collateralized by a pool of mortgages or by a portfolio of mortgage-backed securities. The bonds are serviced with the cash flows from these mortgages, but rather than the straight pass-through arrangement, the CMO substitutes a *sequential distribution process* that creates a series of bonds with varying maturities to appeal to a wider range of investors.

The prioritized distribution process is as follows:

♦ Several classes of bonds are issued against a pool of mortgages, which are the collateral. As an example, if we assume a CMO issue with four classes of bonds, the first three (Class A, B, C) would pay interest at their stated rates, beginning at their issue date, and the fourth class would be an accrual bond (referred to as a *Z bond*).[24]
♦ The cash flows received from the underlying mortgages are applied first to pay the interest on the first three classes of bonds, and then to retire these bonds.
♦ The classes of bonds are retired sequentially. All principal payments are directed first to the shortest-maturity class A bonds until they are completely retired. Then all prin-

---

[23]For a detailed discussion, see Andrew S. Carron, "Collateralized Mortgage Obligations," in *The Handbook of Fixed-Income Securities,* 5th ed., edited by Frank Fabozzi (Chicago: Irwin, 1997).

[24]The four-class CMO was the typical configuration during the 1980s and is used here for demonstration purposes. CMOs are being issued with eighteen to twenty classes. More advanced CMOs are referred to as REMICs, which provide greater certainty regarding the cash-flow patterns for various components of the pool. For a discussion of REMICs, see Andrew S. Carron, "Understanding CMOs, REMICs, and Other Mortgage Derivatives," *Fixed Income Research* (New York: The First Boston Corp., 1992).

cipal payments are directed to the next shortest-maturity bonds (class B bonds). The process continues until all the classes have been paid off.

♦ During the early periods, the accrual bonds (class Z bonds) pay no interest, but the interest accrues as additional principal, and the cash flow from the mortgages that collateralize these bonds is used to pay interest on and retire the bonds in the other classes. Subsequently, all remaining cash flows are used to pay off the accrued interest, to pay any current interest, and then to retire the Z bonds.

This prioritized sequential pattern means that the A-class bonds are fairly short-term and each subsequent class is a little longer term until the Z-class bond, which is a long-term bond. It also functions like a zero-coupon bond for the initial years.

Besides creating bonds that pay interest in a more normal pattern (quarterly or semiannually) and that have more predictable maturities, these bonds are considered high-quality securities (AAA) because of the structure and quality of the collateral. To obtain an AAA rating, CMOs are structured to ensure that the underlying mortgages will always generate enough cash to support the bonds issued, even under the most conservative prepayment and reinvestment rates. The fact is, most CMOs are overcollateralized.

Further, the credit risk of the collateral is minimal, because most are backed by mortgages guaranteed by a federal agency (GNMA, FNMA) or by the FHLMC. Those mortgages that are not backed by agencies carry private insurance for principal and interest and mortgage insurance. Notably, even with this AAA rating, the yield on these CMOs has typically been higher than the yields on AA industrials. This premium yield has, of course, contributed to their popularity and growth.

Other asset-backed securities (ABS)   A rapidly expanding segment of the securities market is that of *asset-backed securities (ABS)*, which involves *securitizing debt*. This is an important concept because it allows financial institutions to bundle various types of loans and sell portions of this portfolio of loans to individual investors. This practice increases the liquidity of these individual debt instruments, whether they be individual mortgages, car loans, or credit card debt. **Certificates for automobile receivables (CARs)** are securities collateralized by loans made to individuals to finance the purchase of cars.

Auto loans are self-amortizing, with monthly payments and relatively short maturities (two to five years). These auto loans can either be direct loans from a lending institution or indirect loans that are originated by an auto dealer and sold to the ultimate lender. CARs typically have monthly or quarterly fixed interest and principal payments, and expected weighted average lives of one to three years with specified maturities of three to five years. The expected actual life of the instrument is typically shorter than the specified maturity because of early payoffs when cars are sold or traded in. The popularity of these asset-backed securities makes them important not only by themselves, but also as an indication of the potential for issuing additional collateralized securities backed by other assets and/or other debt instruments.[25]

Variable-rate notes   Introduced in the United States in the mid-1970s, **variable-rate notes** became popular during periods of high interest rates. The typical variable-rate note possesses two unique features:

1. After the first six to eighteen months of the issue's life, during which a minimum rate is often guaranteed, the coupon rate floats, so that every six months it changes to

[25]For an overview of these securities, see K. Jeanne Person, "A Review of Asset-Backed Securities" (New York: Salomon Brothers, 1987); Tracy Hudson van Eck, "Asset-Backed Securities," in *The Handbook of Fixed-Income Securities*, 5th ed., edited by Frank J. Fabozzi (Chicago: Irwin, 1997). The presentations consider not only CARs but several other asset-backed securities including debt backed by credit card obligations and boat loans.

follow some standard. Usually it is pegged 1 percent above a stipulated short-term rate. For example, the rate might be the preceding three weeks' average 90-day T-bill rate.

2. After the first year or two, the notes are redeemable at par, at the *holder's* option, usually at six-month intervals.

Such notes represent a long-term commitment on the part of the borrower, yet provide the lender with all the characteristics of a short-term obligation. They are typically available to investors in minimum denominations of $1,000. However, although the six-month redemption feature provides liquidity, the variable rates can cause the issues to experience wide swings in semiannual coupons.[26]

Zero-coupon and deep-discount bonds   The typical corporate bond has a coupon and maturity. In turn, the value of the bond is the present value of the stream of cash flows (interest and principal) discounted at the required yield to maturity (YTM). Alternatively, some bonds do not have any coupons or have coupons that are below the market rate at the time of issue. Such securities are referred to as **zero-coupon bonds** or *minicoupon bonds* or *original-issue discount (OID) bonds.* A zero-coupon discount bond promises to pay a stipulated principal amount at a future maturity date, but it does not promise to make any interim interest payments. Therefore, the price of the bond is the present value of the principal payment at the maturity date using the required discount rate for this bond. The return on the bond is the difference between what the investor pays for the bond at the time of purchase and the principal payment at maturity.

Consider a zero-coupon, $10,000 par value bond with a twenty-year maturity. If the required rate of return on bonds of equal maturity and quality is 8 percent and we assume semiannual discounting, the initial selling price would be $2,082.89, because the present-value factor at 8 percent compounded semiannually for twenty years is 0.208289. From the time of purchase to the point of maturity, the investor would not receive any cash flow from the firm. The investor must pay taxes, however, on the implied interest on the bond, although no cash is received. Because an investor subject to taxes would experience severe negative cash flows during the life of these bonds, they are primarily of interest to investment accounts not subject to taxes, such as pensions, IRAs, or Keogh accounts.

A modified form of zero-coupon bonds is the original-issue, discount (OID) bond, where the coupon is set substantially below the prevailing market rate, for example, a 4 percent coupon on a bond when market rates are 10 percent. As a result, the bond is issued at a deep discount from par value. Again, taxes must be paid on the implied 10 percent return rather than the nominal 4 percent, so the cash flow disadvantage of zero-coupon bonds, though lessened, remains.

High-yield bonds   A segment of the corporate bond market that has grown in size, importance, and controversy is **high-yield bonds**, also referred to as *speculative-grade bonds* and *junk bonds.* These are corporate bonds that have been assigned a bond rating by the rating agencies as noninvestment grade, that is, a rating below BBB or Baa.

Prior to 1980, most of the high-yield bonds were referred to as *fallen angels.* Such bonds were originally issued as investment-grade securities but because of changes in the firm over time, were downgraded into the high-yield sector (BB and below). Now, original issue high-yield bonds include those issued by (1) small firms that lack the financial strength to receive an investment-grade rating by the rating agencies, and (2) large and small firms

---

[26]For an extended discussion, see Richard S. Wilson, "Domestic Floating-Rate and Adjustable-Rate Debt Securities," in *The Handbook of Fixed-Income Securities,* 5th ed., edited by Frank J. Fabozzi (Chicago: Irwin, 1997). Adjustable-rate preferred stocks are also discussed in Richard S. Wilson, *Corporate Senior Securities* (Chicago: Probus Publishing, 1987), Chapter 6.

that issue high-yield bonds in connection with leveraged buyouts (LBOs). The high-yield bond market has gone from a residual market that included fallen angels to a new-issue market where bonds are underwritten with below-investment-grade ratings.[27]

Japanese Corporate Bond Market   The corporate bond market in Japan is made up of two components: (1) bonds issued by industrial firms or utilities and (2) bonds issued by banks to finance loans to corporations. The pure corporate bond sector has been stable over time at 9.5 percent of the total. In contrast, the amount of bank debentures is about 15 percent of the total.

Japanese corporate bonds are monitored by the *Kisaikai,* which is the council for the regulation of bond issues. The council is composed of twenty-two bond-related banks and seven major securities companies. It operates under the authority of the Ministry of Finance (MOF) and the Bank of Japan (BOJ) to determine bond-issuing procedures, including conditions for corporate debt.

Because of numerous bankruptcies during the 1930s depression, the government mandated that all corporate debt be secured, and this was enforced by the Kisaikai. During the 1970s and 1980s, corporations and securities firms were pressed to relax these requirements, which were abolished during 1988. The issuance of unsecured debt has led to the birth of bond-rating agencies, which were unneeded with completely secured debt. Currently there are five major rating agencies in Japan.

Corporate bond segments   The corporate debt market in Japan is divided into two major segments: bonds issued by electric-power companies and bonds issued by all other corporations. Because the electric-power supply firms receive preferential treatment as regulated public utilities, about 75 percent of all domestic bond issues are public utility bonds.

The Ministry of Finance specifies minimum capital requirements and issuing requirements, and it controls the issuance system that specifies who can issue bonds and when they can be issued. In addition, lead underwriting managers are rotated to ensure balance among the big-four securities firms in Japan (Nomura, Nikko, Daiwa, and Yamaichi Capital Management).

Bank bonds   The banking system in Japan is segmented into the following components:

♦ Commercial banks (thirteen big-city banks and sixty-four regional banks)
♦ Long-term credit banks (three)
♦ Mutual loan and savings banks (six)
♦ Specialized financial institutions

Currently these financial institutions sell five-year coupon debentures and one-year discount debentures directly to individual and institutional investors. The long-term credit banks are not allowed to take deposits and thus depend on the debentures to obtain funds. These bonds are traded in the OTC market. [28]

German Corporate Bond Market   Germany likewise has a combination sector in corporates that includes pure corporate bonds and bank bonds. There is a large contrast

[27]Almost everyone would acknowledge that the development of the high-yield debt market has had a positive impact on the capital-raising ability of the economy. For an analysis of this impact, see Glenn Yago, *Junk Bonds* (New York: Oxford University Press, 1991); and Kevin J. Perry and Robert A. Taggart, Jr., "The Growing Role of Junk Bonds in Corporate Finance," *Journal of Applied Corporate Finance* 1, no. 1 (Spring 1988): 37–45. An update on its characteristics and a discussion of the importance of high-yield bonds to mid-cap companies is contained in Martin S. Fridson, "The State of the High Yield Bond Market: Overshooting or Return to Normalcy," *Journal of Applied Corporate Finance* 7, no. 1 (Spring 1994): 85–97.

[28]For further discussion of this market, see Aron Viner, *Inside Japanese Financial Markets* (Homewood, Ill.: Dow Jones–Irwin, 1988), Chapters 5 and 6; and Frank J. Fabozzi, ed., *The Japanese Bond Markets* (Chicago: Probus Publishing, 1990).

because the nonbank corporate bonds are almost nonexistent, whereas the bank bonds make up more than 60 percent of the total bond market.

Bank bonds may be issued in collateralized or uncollateralized form. For the collateralized bonds the largest categories are mortgage bonds and commercial bonds.

German mortgage bonds are collateralized bonds of the issuing bank backed by mortgage loans registered with a government-appointed trustee. Due to the supervision of these bonds and the mortgage collateral, these bonds are considered of high quality. They are issued in bearer or registered form.

German commercial bonds are subject to the same regulation and collateralization as mortgage bonds. The difference is that the collateral consists of loans to or guarantees by a German public-sector entity rather than a first mortgage. Possible borrowers include the federal government, its agencies (the federal railway or the post office), federal states, and agencies of the European Economic Community (EEC). The credit quality of these loans is excellent. Mortgage and commercial bonds have identical credit standing and trade at narrow spreads.

Schuldscheindarlehen are private loan agreements between borrowers and large investors (usually a bank) who make the loan but who can (with the borrower's permission) sell them or divide the loans among several investors. These instruments are like a negotiable loan participation. These loan agreements, which come in various sizes, account for a substantial proportion of all funds raised in Germany. Because the market is not very liquid, they are typically used for the investment of large sums to maturity.

U.K. Corporate Bond Market   Corporate bonds in the United Kingdom about evenly spread among three different types: debentures, unsecured loans, and convertible bonds.

Numerous borrowers offer bonds secured by property or prior calls on the revenue of the issuers. At the same time, many large corporations and banks raise funds through unsecured borrowing and the issuance of convertible bonds.

The maturity structure of the corporate bond market is fairly wide. The coupon structure of corporate bonds features low-coupon bonds issued during the 1960s and 1970s and high-coupon bonds issued during the 1980s. Almost all U.K. corporate bonds are callable term bonds.

Corporate bonds in the United Kingdom have been issued through both public offerings underwritten by investment bankers and private placements. Early in the 1980s, the market tended toward private placements, but since 1986, the trend has been toward more public offerings through investment banking firms. Prior to the Big Bang, corporate bonds were traded on the stock exchange, whereas currently some primary dealers trade directly with each other. All corporate bonds are issued in registered form.

International Bonds

Each country's international bond market has two components. The first, *foreign bonds,* are issues sold primarily in one country and currency by a borrower of a different nationality. An example would be U.S.-dollar-denominated bonds sold in the United States by a Japanese firm. (These are referred to as *Yankee bonds.*) Second are *Eurobonds,* which are bonds underwritten by international bond syndicates and sold in several national markets. An example would be Eurodollar bonds that are securities denominated in U.S. dollars, underwritten by an international syndicate, and sold to non-U.S. investors outside the United States. The relative size of these two markets (foreign bonds versus Eurobonds) varies by country.

United States   The Eurodollar bond market has been much larger than the Yankee bond market (about $780 billion versus $175 billion). However, because the Eurodollar

bond market is heavily affected by changes in the value of the U.S. dollar, it experienced a major setback when the dollar weakened during 1986, 1987, and 1991 to 1993. Such periods have created a desire for diversification by investors.

Yankee bonds are issued by foreign firms who register with the SEC and borrow U.S. dollars, using issues underwritten by a U.S. syndicate for delivery in the United States. These bonds are traded in the United States and pay interest semiannually. More than 60 percent of Yankee bonds are issued by Canadian corporations and typically have shorter maturities and longer call protection than U.S. domestic issues, which increases their appeal.

The Eurodollar bond market is dominated by foreign investors, and the center of trading is in London. Eurodollar bonds pay interest annually, so it is necessary to adjust the standard yield calculation that assumes semiannual compounding. The Eurodollar bond market historically comprised about 40–50 percent of the total Eurobond market.

Japan   The Japanese international bond market was historically about 90 percent foreign bonds (Samurai bonds) with the balance in Euroyen bonds. In 1985 the issuance requirements for Euroyen bonds was liberalized, which caused the ratio of Samurai versus Euroyen to shift in favor of Euroyen bonds. In 1996, Euroyen bonds comprised more than two-thirds of the Japanese international bond market.

Samurai bonds are yen-denominated bonds issued by non-Japanese issuers and mainly sold in Japan, for example, a yen-denominated bond sold in Tokyo by IBM. The market is fairly small and has limited liquidity. The market has not grown in terms of yen, but has grown in U.S. dollar terms because of changes in the exchange rate.

Euroyen bonds are yen-denominated bonds sold in markets outside Japan by international syndicates. As indicated, this market has grown substantially since 1985 because of the liberal issue requirements and favorable exchange rate movements.

Germany   All deutsche mark bonds of foreign issuers can be considered Eurobonds. This is because the stability of the German currency reduces the importance of the distinction between foreign bonds (DM-denominated bonds sold in Germany by non-German firms that are underwritten by domestic institutions) and Euro-DM bonds (DM bonds sold outside Germany and underwritten by international firms). Both types of bonds share the same primary and secondary market procedures, are free of German taxes, and have similar yields.

United Kingdom   U.K. foreign bonds, referred to as *bulldog bonds,* are sterling-denominated bonds issued by non-English firms and sold in London. Eurosterling bonds are sold in markets outside London by international syndicates.

The U.K. international bond market has become dominated by the Eurosterling bonds, wherein the ratio of Eurobonds versus foreign bonds has grown to more than 25-to-one. The procedure for issuing and trading Eurosterling bonds is similar to that of other Eurobonds.

OBTAINING INFORMATION ON BONDS

As might be expected, the data needs of bond investors are considerably different from those of stockholders. For one thing, there is less emphasis on fundamental analysis because, except for speculative-grade bonds and revenue obligations, most bond investors rely on the rating agencies for credit analysis. An exception would be large institutions that employ in-house analysts to confirm assigned agency ratings or to uncover incremental-return opportunities. Because of the large investments by these institutions, the total dollar rewards from only a few basis points can be substantial. As you might expect, the institutions enjoy economies of scale in research. Finally, there are a few private research firms that concentrate on the independent appraisal of bonds.

A WORD FROM THE STREET

BY MARTIN S. FRIDSON, CFA

 High-yield bonds can enhance the income, long-term return, and diversification of an investment portfolio. During the period 1985 to 1993, the Merrill Lynch High-Yield Master Index has typically offered about 40 basis points more current yield than ten-year Treasuries. The realized rates of return during the period have been in between those of Treasuries and common stock. In addition, high-yield bonds have been an excellent diversification vehicle because the price fluctuations of high-yield bonds have tended to offset swings in Treasuries and common stock.

For most individual investors, mutual funds are the best means of capturing the benefits of the high-yield bond sector. It is advisable to hold a widely diversified portfolio of high-yield bond issues because of the comparatively high credit risk of individual issues. In addition, large odd-lot differentials (round lots are $1 million blocks) generally make it difficult for individuals to assemble well-diversified portfolios on their own. Finally, any commitment to this asset class should have a long-term horizon because high-yield bonds are necessarily subject to large annual return fluctuations. The point is, the *long-term* performance of these bonds has provided respectable returns and clear diversification benefits.

Martin S. Fridson, CFA, is managing director of High-Yield Securities Research at Merrill Lynch, Pierce, Fenner, & Smith, Inc. Fridson serves on the editorial board of the *Financial Analyst Journal* and has been a guest lecturer at the graduate business schools of Columbia, MIT, Notre Dame, and Wharton. He has been voted to the Institutional Investor All-American Fixed Income team for the high-yield bond area. Fridson is responsible for the Merrill Lynch publication titled "This Week in High Yield" and a monthly publication entitled "Extra Credit."

Required Information

In addition to information on the risk of default, bond investors need information on (1) market and economic conditions and (2) intrinsic bond features. Market and economic information allows investors to stay abreast of the general tone of the bond market, overall interest rate developments, and yield-spread behavior in different market sectors. Bond investors also require information on bond indenture provisions such as call features and sinking-fund provisions.

Some of this information is readily available in such popular publications as the *Wall Street Journal, Barron's, Business Week, Fortune,* and *Forbes,* which were discussed in Chapter 11. In addition, two popular sources of bond data are the *Federal Reserve Bulletin* and the *Survey of Current Business,* which were also described in Chapter 11.

In addition, a number of other sources of specific information are important to bond investors. The following are specifically concerned with information and analysis of bonds. Some of them were publications discussed in Chapter 11.

- *Treasury Bulletin* (monthly)
- *Standard & Poor's Bond Guide* (monthly)
- *Moody's Bond Record* (monthly)
- *Moody's Bond Survey* (weekly)
- *Fitch Rating Register* (monthly)
- *Fitch Corporate Credit Analysis* (monthly)
- *Fitch Municipal Credit Analysis* (monthly)
- *Investment Dealers Digest* (weekly)

- *Credit Markets* (weekly)
- *Duff & Phelps Credit Decisions* (weekly)
- *The Bond Buyer* (daily)

Sources of Bond Quotes

The listed information sources fill three needs of investors: evaluating the risk of default, staying abreast of bond market and interest rate conditions, and obtaining information on specific bonds. Another important data need is current bond quotes and prices.

Unfortunately, many of the prime sources of bond prices are not widely distributed. For example, *Bank and Quotation Record* is a valuable, though not widely circulated, source that provides monthly price information for government and agency bonds, listed and OTC corporate bonds, municipal bonds, and money market instruments. Current quotes on municipal bonds are available only through a fairly costly publication that is used by many financial institutions, called *The Blue List of Current Municipal Offerings.* It contains more than 100 pages of price quotes for municipal bonds, municipal notes, and industrial development and pollution-control revenue bonds.

Daily information on all publicly traded Treasury issues, most agency obligations, and numerous corporate issues is published in the *Wall Street Journal.* Similar data are available weekly in *Barron's.* Both publications include corporate bond quotes for bonds listed on the New York and American exchanges that represent a minor portion of the total corporate bond market. You will recall that the majority of corporate bond trading is on the OTC market. Finally, major bond dealers maintain firm quotes on a variety of issues for clients.

Interpreting Bond Quotes

Essentially, all bonds are quoted on the basis of either yield or price. Price quotes are always interpreted as a *percentage of par.* For example, a quote of $98^1/_2$ is not interpreted as $98.50, but $98^1/_2$ percent of par. The dollar price is derived from the quote, given the par value. If the par value is $5,000 on a municipal bond, the price of an issue quoted at $98^1/_2$ would be $4,925. Actually, the market follows three systems of bond pricing: one system for corporates, another for governments (both Treasury and agency obligations), and a third for municipals.

Corporate Bond Quotes   Figure 15.1 is a listing of NYSE corporate bond quotes that appeared in the *Wall Street Journal* on March 18, 1998. The data pertain to trading activity on March 17. Several quotes have been designated for illustrative purposes.

The first issue designated is an AT&T issue and is representative of most corporate prices. In particular, the $5^1/_8$ 01 indicates the coupon and maturity of the obligation; in this case, the AT&T issue carries a 5.125 percent coupon and matures in 2001. The next column provides the current yield of the obligation and is found by dividing the coupon by the current market price. For example, a bond with a 5.125 percent coupon selling for 97.875 would have a 5.2 percent current yield. This is *not* the YTM or even necessarily a good approximation to it. Both of these yields will be discussed in Chapter 16.

The next column gives the volume of $1,000 par value bonds traded that day (in this case, twenty bonds were traded). The next column indicates closing quotes, followed by the column for the net change in the closing price from the last day the issue was traded. In this case, AT&T closed at $97^7/_8$, which was up $^1/_8$ from the prior day.

The second bond is AlldC zr 07, which refers to an Allied Chemical zero-coupon bond ("zr") due in 2007. As discussed, zero-coupon securities pay no interest but are redeemed at par at maturity. Because there is no coupon, they sell at a deep discount, which

Figure 15.1 *Sample Corporate Bond Quotations*

NEW YORK EXCHANGE BONDS

CORPORATION BONDS
Volume, $13,466,000

	Bonds	Cur Yld	Vol	Close	Net Chg
	AMR 9s16	7.6	25	119	+ 3/8
	ATT 4³/₈99	4.5	10	98³/₈	...
	ATT 6s00	6.0	120	100	...
① →	ATT 5¹/₈01	5.2	20	97⁷/₈	+ 1/8
	ATT 7¹/₈02	6.9	165	103⁵/₈	− 3/8
	ATT 7s05	6.6	12	105⁵/₈	+ 1/4
	ATT 8.2s05	7.9	12	103⁷/₈	...
	ATT 7¹/₂06	6.9	2	109¹/₈	+ 5/8
	ATT 8¹/₈22	7.5	183	107³/₄	...
	ATT 8¹/₈24	7.6	10	107¹/₂	...
	ATT 8.35s25	7.5	30	112	+ 1/4
	ATT 8⁵/₈31	7.9	7	109⁵/₈	...
	AlldC zr2000	...	10	86¹/₈	+ 1/8
	AlldC zr01	...	100	81³/₈	− 1/8
	AlldC zr05	...	50	62¹/₂	...
② →	AlldC zr07	...	10	54¹/₈	+ 1/2
	Allwst 7¹/₄14	cv	1	91¹/₂	− 1/2
	Alza 5s06	cv	119	122³/₄	+ 3/4
	Alza zr14	...	2	53	...
	Amoco 8⁵/₈16	8.0	5	108¹/₈	− 7/8
	Amresco 10s04	9.8	10	102¹/₈	− 7/8
	Anhr 8⁵/₈16	8.3	3	103¹/₂	− 1
	Argosy 12s01	cv	131	91⁷/₈	+ 3/8
	Argosy 13¹/₄04	12.2	40	109	− 1/2
	AutDt zr12	...	1	82	...
	BkrHgh zr08	...	24	79	...
	BellPa 7¹/₈12	7.1	1	100³/₄	...
	BellPa 7¹/₂13	7.4	4	101¹/₂	− 5/8
	BellsoT 6¹/₂00	6.4	10	101³/₈	− 1/8
	BellsoT 6³/₈04	6.3	10	101¹/₄	...
	BellsoT 5⁷/₈09	5.9	65	99⁵/₈	+ 5/8
	BellsoT 8¹/₄32	7.5	21	110³/₈	...
	BellsoT 7¹/₂33	7.2	25	104⁵/₈	+ 1/8
	BellsoT 6³/₄33	6.8	40	99¹/₄	...
	BellsoT 7⁵/₈35	7.3	40	104¹/₂	− 1/8
	BstBuy 8⁵/₈00	8.4	70	102³/₈	+ 1/8
	BethSt 8³/₈01	8.2	30	102³/₈	+ 1/4
	BethSt 8.45s05	8.3	30	101³/₄	− 1/4
	Bluegrn 8¹/₄12	cv	19	100	...
	Bordn 8³/₈16	8.2	48	101⁵/₈	...
	BorgWS 9¹/₈03	8.8	10	103¹/₂	− 1/4
	CaterpInc 6s07	6.2	27	97¹/₂	− 1/2
	ChaseM 8s99	7.9	15	101¹/₂	...
	ChaseM 8s04	7.7	15	104	+ 1/2
	ChaseM 8s05	8.0	10	100³/₈	− 3/8
	CPoM 7¹/₄12	7.2	5	100³/₈	− 5/8
	ChespkE 9¹/₈06	9.0	162	101	− 1
	ChvrnC 9³/₄17	9.2	108	106	...
	ChckFul 7s12	cv	35	104¹/₂	− 1/2
	ChryF 13¹/₄99	12.0	18	110	...
	ChryF 9¹/₂99	9.0	25	105	...
	ClevEl 8³/₈11	8.2	12	102⁵/₈	...
	ClevEl 8³/₈12	8.2	10	102⁵/₈	...
	CmwE 8¹/₈07J	7.9	13	102³/₄	+ 5/8
	CompUSA 9¹/₂00	9.2	45	103¹/₈	− 1/4
	CompMgt 8s03	cv	514	99¹/₄	+ 1¹/₄
	Consec 8¹/₈03	7.6	111	107	+ 1/8
	CnEn 6⁷/₈98	6.9	10	99²⁵/₃₂	...
	ConPort 10s06	10.0	10	100³/₈	+ 3/8
	CntlHm 10s06	9.4	10	106³/₈	− 2⁵/₈
③ →	Convrse 7s04	cv	14	67	− 1
	Coty 10¹/₄05	9.6	48	106³/₄	+ 3/4
	DVI 9⁷/₈04	9.3	16	106¹/₂	− 1/2
	Datpnt 8⁷/₈06f	cv	26	71⁷/₈	− 1/8
	DelcoR 8⁵/₈07	8.3	5	104	+ 1
	duPnt dc6s01	6.0	122	100	...
	DukeEn 7s05	6.9	32	102¹/₈	+ 1/2
	DukeEn 7³/₈23	7.3	8	101³/₄	...
	DukeEn 6⁷/₈23	6.9	15	100	...
	DukeEn 7¹/₂25	7.3	20	103¹/₄	+ 1/2
	DukeEn 7s33	7.0	12	100¹/₄	− 1/2
	Exxon 6s05	6.0	1	100	− 5/8
	FedDS 8¹/₈02	7.6	20	107	− 1/8
	FldNtl zr09	...	1	82	+ 3
	FstRep 8s09	8.0	21	100	...
	FUnRE 8⁷/₈03	8.5	9	103⁷/₈	+ 3/8

Quotations as of 4 p.m. Eastern Time
Tuesday, March 17, 1998

Volume $13,583,000

SALES SINCE JANUARY 1
(000 omitted)

1998	1997	1996
$862,939	$1,367,497	$1,471,237

	Domestic		All Issues	
	Tue.	Mon.	Tue.	Mon.
Issues traded	225	233	230	239
Advances	84	122	87	125
Declines	83	68	83	69
Unchanged	58	43	60	45
New highs	14	8	14	8
New lows	2	1	2	1

Dow Jones Bond Averages

−1997− High Low	−1998− High Low		−−−1998−−− Close Chg. %Yld	−−1997−− Close Chg.
105.13 101.09	105.48 104.92	20 Bonds	104.97 −0.27 6.86	102.64 −0.16
102.89 97.64	103.02 102.19	10 Utilities	102.45 −0.07 6.97	99.49 −0.20
107.49 104.54	108.13 107.34	10 Industrials	107.49 −0.46 6.76	105.79 −0.12

Bonds	Cur Yld	Vol	Close	Net Chg
Fortune 8⁵/₈21	8.0	4	108	− 1³/₄
GPA Del 8³/₄98	8.6	15	101¹/₄	...
GMA 7¹/₈99	7.1	8	100¹/₂	− 1¹/₄
GMA 8.40s99	8.2	35	102⁷/₈	+ 1/4
GMA 5¹/₂01	5.6	114	97¹/₂	...
GMA 9⁵/₈01	8.6	5	112³/₈	+ 1⁷/₈
GMA 7s02	6.8	45	103¹/₈	− 5/8
GMA 5⁷/₈03	5.9	54	99	− 1/4
GMA dc6s11	6.4	10	94	...
GMA zr12	...	1	378³/₄	− 7/8
GMA zr15	...	11	321⁷/₈	+ 1⁷/₈
Genesc 10⁵/₈03	10.0	25	103⁵/₈	− 3/8
GrandCas 10¹/₈03	9.4	20	108	+ 1/4
Hallwd 7s00	7.3	47	96¹/₈	+ 1/8
HltRet 7¹/₂03	cv	45	111	− 2³/₄
Hlthso 9¹/₂01	9.1	4	104¹/₂	− 1/2
Hills 12¹/₂03	14.2	555	88	+ 3/8
Hilton 5s06	cv	14	114³/₄	− 1¹/₂
Hollngr 9¹/₄06	8.6	10	107³/₈	+ 7/8
HomeDpt 3¹/₄01	cv	21	155	+ 1/2
IllBel 7⁵/₈06	7.5	10	101³/₈	− 3/4
IllPwr 8s23	7.8	3	102¹/₂	− 1¹/₂
IBM 6³/₈00	6.3	30	100⁷/₈	− 1/2
IBM 7¹/₄02	6.9	15	105³/₄	+ 3/8
IBM 7¹/₂13	6.9	10	109¹/₄	+ 1³/₄
IBM 8³/₈19	7.0	18	120	+ 2¹/₈
IPap dc5¹/₈12	6.0	10	85¹/₄	...
④ → IntShip 9s03	8.8	50	102¹/₂	− 1/2
KCS En 8⁷/₈08	9.0	10	99	...
KaufB 9³/₈03	9.1	72	103¹/₂	+ 1/8
KaufB 7³/₄04	7.6	50	101⁵/₈	+ 3/4
KentE 4¹/₂04	cv	36	84¹/₂	...
Kolmrg 8³/₄09	cv	5	103¹/₂	− 1/2
LeasSol 6⁷/₈03	cv	20	103	+ 1/2
Leucadia 7³/₄13	7.5	100	103	− 1
LibPrp 8s01	cv	13	124	− 4
Loews 3¹/₈07	cv	18	92¹/₂	− 1
LgIsLt 8⁵/₈04	8.5	244	102	...
LgIsLt 7¹/₂07	7.2	20	103⁵/₈	+ 1/4
LgIsLt 9³/₄21	9.6	228	101⁵/₈	...
LgIsLt 9s22	7.9	15	114¹/₂	+ 1/4
LgIsLt 8.2s23	8.4	20	107¹/₈	− 5/8
LgIsLt 9⁵/₈24	9.5	60	101³/₈	...
Lucent 6.9s01	6.7	3	102¹/₄	− 1¹/₄
Lucent 7¹/₄06	6.7	35	107⁵/₈	− 3/8
MacNS 7⁷/₈04	cv	34	101³/₄	− 1/4
Mascotch 03	cv	11	93¹/₄	− 3/4
McDerm 9³/₈06	8.8	25	107	− 1/4
McDnl 6³/₄03	6.6	11	101⁵/₈	+ 1
MichB 7s12	6.9	5	101¹/₈	− 1/2
Mobil 7⁵/₈33	7.1	7	106³/₄	+ 1/2
Motrla zr13	...	184	75	− 2
Nabis 8.3s99	8.1	10	102	− 1¹/₈
NStl 8³/₈06	8.3	10	100³/₄	+ 1/2
Navstr 9s04	8.9	33	101⁵/₈	+ 1/4

EXPLANATORY NOTES
(For New York and American Bonds)
Yield is Current yield.
cv-Convertible bond. cf-Certificates. cld-Called. dc-Deep discount. ec-European currency units. f-Dealt in flat. ll-Italian lire. kd-Danish kroner. m-Matured bonds, negotiability impaired by maturity. na-No accrual. r-Registered. rp-Reduced principal. st, sd-Stamped. t-Floating rate. wd-When distributed. ww-With warrants. x-Ex interest. xw-Without warrants. zr-Zero coupon. vj-In bankruptcy or receivership or being reorganized under the Bankruptcy Act, or securities assumed by such companies.

implies a yield. Again, because they have no coupon payments, they do not report a current yield.

Finally, the third bond is a convertible ("cv") bond from Converse that has a 7 percent coupon and is due in 2004. The conversion feature means that the bond is convertible into the common stock of the company.

If you see a bond with "dc" before the coupon, such as the fourth bond, International Paper, $5^{1}/_{8}$ percent, due in 2012, it means "deep discount," indicating that the original coupon was set below the going rate at the time of issue. An example of such a bond would be a 5 percent coupon bond when market rates were 9 or 10 percent.

All fixed-income obligations, with the exception of preferred stock, are traded on an *accrued interest basis.* The prices pertain to the value of all *future* cash flows from the bond and exclude interest that has accrued to the holder since the last interest payment date. The actual price of the bond will exceed the quote listed because accrued interest must be added. Assume a bond with a $7^{1}/_{8}$ percent coupon. If two months have elapsed since interest was paid, the current holder of the bond is entitled to $2/_{6}$ or one-third of the bond's semiannual interest payment that will be paid in four months. More specifically, the $7^{1}/_{8}$ percent coupon provides semiannual interest income of $35.625. The investor who held the obligation for two months beyond the last interest payment date is entitled to one-third of that $35.625 in the form of accrued interest. Therefore, whatever the current price of the bond, an accrued interest value of $11.87 will be added.

Treasury and Agency Bond Quotes   Figure 15.2 illustrates the quote system for Treasury and agency issues. These quotes resemble those used for OTC securities because they contain both bid and ask prices, rather than high, low, and close. For U.S. Treasury bond quotes, "n" behind the maturity date indicates that the obligation is a Treasury *note.* A "p" indicates it is a Treasury note on which nonresident aliens are exempt from withholding taxes on the interest.

All other obligations in this section are Treasury bonds. The security identification is different because it is not necessary to list the issuer. Instead, the usual listing indicates the coupon, the month and year of maturity, and information on a call feature of the obligation.

Quote 1 is a $6^{1}/_{4}$ percent Treasury note (n) of 1999 that demonstrates the basic difference in the price system of government bonds (Treasuries and agencies). The bid quote is 100:23, and the ask is 100:25. Governments are traded in thirty-seconds of a point (rather than eighths), and the figures to the right of the colons indicate the number of thirty-seconds in the fractional bid or ask. In this case, the bid price is actually 100.71875 percent of par. These quotes are also notable in terms of the bid–ask spread, which are typically $1/_{32}$ to $4/_{32}$, which means they are typically smaller than the smallest possible spread for most stocks, which is $1/_{16}$. This reflects the outstanding liquidity and low transaction costs for Treasury securities.

For example, quote 2 is an $8^{3}/_{8}$ percent issue that carries a maturity of 2003–2008. This means that the issue has a deferred call feature until 2003 (and is thereafter freely callable), and a (final) maturity date of 2008. The bid–ask figures provided are stated as a percentage of par. The yield figure provided is yield to maturity, or *promised* yield based on the asking price. This system is used for Treasuries, agencies, and municipals.

The lower section of the first column contains quotes for U.S. Treasury securities that have been "stripped." Specifically, the typical bond that promises a series of coupon payments and its principal at maturity is divided into two separate units. One contains all the coupon interest payments and no principal and is designated as "ci" (stripped coupon interest), while the other contains only the principal payment and is designated "np" (Treasury note, stripped principal).

The securities listed next to the Treasury strip section are for U.S. Treasury bills. Notice that only dates are reported (and days to maturity) and no coupons. This is because these are pure discount securities, that is, the return is the difference between the price you pay

Figure 15.2 *Sample Quotes for Treasury Bonds, Notes, and Bills*

TREASURY BONDS, NOTES & BILLS

Tuesday, March 17, 1998

Representative and Indicative Over-the-Counter quotations based on $1 million or more.

Treasury bond, note and bill quotes are as of mid-afternoon. Colons in bond and note bid-and-asked quotes represent 32nds; 101:01 means 101 1/32. Net changes in 32nds. Treasury bill quotes in hundredths, quoted in terms of a rate discount. Days to maturity calculated from settlement date. All yields are based on a one-day settlement and calculated on the offer quote. Current 13-week and 26-week bills are boldfaced. For bonds callable prior to maturity, yields are computed to the earliest call date for issues quoted above par and to the maturity date for issues quoted below par. n-Treasury note. i-Inflation-Indexed. wi-When issued. iw-Inflation-Indexed when issued; daily change is expressed in basis points.

Source: Dow Jones/Cantor Fitzgerald.

U.S. Treasury strips as of 3 p.m. Eastern time, also based on transactions of $1 million or more. Colons in bid-and-asked quotes represent 32nds; 99:01 means 99 1/32. Net changes in 32nds. Yields calculated on the asked quotation. ci-stripped coupon interest. bp-Treasury bond, stripped principal. np-Treasury note, stripped principal. For bonds callable prior to maturity, yields are computed to the earliest call date for issues quoted above par and to the maturity date for issues below par.

Source: Bear, Stearns & Co. via Street Software Technology Inc.

GOVT. BONDS & NOTES

Rate	Maturity Mo/Yr	Bid	Asked	Chg.	Ask Yld.
5 1/8	Mar 98n	99:30	100:00	....	5.01
6 1/8	Mar 98n	99:31	100:01	....	5.10
7 7/8	Apr 98n	100:04	100:06	− 1	5.25
5 1/8	Apr 98n	99:29	99:31	....	5.29
5 7/8	Apr 98n	100:00	100:02	....	5.23
6 1/8	May 98n	100:02	100:04	....	5.23
9	May 98n	100:17	100:19	....	5.11
5 3/8	May 98n	99:30	100:00	....	5.29
6	May 98n	100:02	100:04	....	5.28
5 1/8	Jun 98n	99:29	99:31	....	5.18
6 1/4	Jun 98n	100:07	100:09	....	5.19
8 1/4	Jul 98n	100:28	100:30	− 1	5.27
5 1/4	Jul 98n	99:29	99:31	....	5.30
6 1/4	Jul 98n	100:09	100:11	....	5.27
5 7/8	Aug 98n	100:04	100:06	....	5.39
9 1/4	Aug 98n	101:16	101:18	....	5.35
4 3/4	Aug 98n	99:21	99:23	....	5.38
6 1/8	Aug 98n	100:08	100:10	....	5.40
4 3/4	Sep 98n	99:19	99:21	....	5.41
6	Sep 98n	100:08	100:10	....	5.40
7 1/8	Oct 98n	100:28	100:30	− 1	5.44
4 3/4	Oct 98n	99:15	99:17	− 1	5.52
5 7/8	Oct 98n	100:05	100:07	....	5.50
5 1/2	Nov 98n	99:30	100:00	....	5.49
8 7/8	Nov 98n	102:04	102:06	....	5.44
5 1/8	Nov 98n	99:22	99:24	− 1	5.48
5 5/8	Nov 98n	100:02	100:04	....	5.43
5 1/8	Dec 98n	99:22	99:24	....	5.44
5 3/4	Dec 98n	100:05	100:07	− 1	5.45
6 3/8	Jan 99n	100:21	100:23	....	5.46
5	Jan 99n	99:17	99:19	....	5.48
5 7/8	Jan 99n	100:08	100:10	....	5.49
5	Feb 99n	99:16	99:18	....	5.49
8 7/8	Feb 99n	102:30	103:00	....	5.46
5 1/2	Feb 99n	99:31	100:01	....	5.46
5 7/8	Feb 99n	100:09	100:11	− 1	5.50
5 7/8	Mar 99n	100:11	100:13	− 1	5.46
① → 6 1/4	Mar 99n	100:23	100:25	− 1	5.46
7	Apr 99n	101:17	101:19	....	5.45
6 3/8	Apr 99n	101:01	101:03	− 1	5.35
6 1/2	Apr 99n	101:01	101:03	− 1	5.47
6 3/8	May 99n	100:29	100:31	− 1	5.49
9 1/8	May 99n	103:31	104:01	− 1	5.48
6 1/4	May 99n	100:31	101:01	....	5.35
6 3/4	May 99n	101:13	101:15	....	5.46
6	Jun 99n	100:19	100:21	− 1	5.46
6 3/4	Jun 99n	101:17	101:19	....	5.44
6 3/8	Jul 99n	101:02	101:04	− 1	5.48
8 1/4	May 00-05	105:09	105:11	− 1	5.58
12	May 05	136:27	137:01	− 3	5.64
6 1/2	Aug 05n	105:05	105:07	− 2	5.63
10 3/4	Aug 05	130:16	130:22	....	5.63
5 7/8	Nov 05n	101:12	101:14	− 2	5.64
5 5/8	Feb 06n	99:26	99:28	− 2	5.64
9 3/8	Feb 06	123:19	123:25	− 2	5.61
6 7/8	May 06n	107:27	107:29	− 3	5.65
7	Jul 06n	108:24	108:26	− 3	5.66
6 1/2	Oct 06n	105:18	105:20	− 4	5.66
3 3/8	Jan 07i	97:13	97:14	− 1	3.72
6 1/4	Feb 07n	104:04	104:06	− 3	5.65
7 5/8	Feb 02-07	106:20	106:22	− 2	5.69
6 5/8	May 07n	106:28	106:30	− 4	5.64
6 1/8	Aug 07n	103:17	103:18	− 5	5.63
7 7/8	Nov 02-07	109:16	109:18	− 3	5.52
3 5/8	Jan 08i	99:10	99:11	....	3.70
5 1/2	Feb 08n	99:19	99:20	− 4	5.55
8 3/8	Aug 03-08	112:26	112:30	− 3	5.57 ← ②
8 3/4	Nov 03-08	114:14	114:18	− 3	5.70
9 1/8	May 04-09	117:14	117:18	− 5	5.70
10 3/8	Nov 04-09	125:14	125:20	− 4	5.70
11 3/4	Feb 05-10	134:01	134:07	− 4	5.70
10	May 05-10	124:23	124:29	− 6	5.71
12 3/4	Nov 05-10	143:00	143:06	− 5	5.71
13 7/8	May 06-11	152:12	152:18	− 7	5.72
14	Nov 06-11	155:22	155:28	− 7	5.72
10 3/8	Nov 07-12	133:16	133:22	− 10	5.77
12	Aug 08-13	147:31	148:05	− 9	5.78
13 1/4	May 09-14	160:09	160:15	− 11	5.81
12 1/2	Aug 09-14	155:00	155:06	− 12	5.82
11 3/4	Nov 09-14	149:17	149:23	− 11	5.82
11 1/4	Feb 15	157:16	157:22	− 11	5.84
10 5/8	Aug 15	151:03	151:09	− 10	5.88
9 7/8	Nov 15	143:03	143:09	− 12	5.90
9 1/4	Feb 16	136:16	136:22	− 11	5.90
7 1/4	May 16	114:22	114:26	− 10	5.91
7 1/2	Nov 16	117:15	117:19	− 11	5.93
8 3/4	May 17	131:29	132:03	− 12	5.92
8 7/8	Aug 17	133:17	133:23	− 13	5.93
9 1/8	May 18	137:02	137:08	− 14	5.93
9	Nov 18	136:00	136:06	− 14	5.94
8 7/8	Feb 19	134:23	134:29	− 14	5.94
8 1/8	Aug 19	126:01	126:07	− 13	5.94
8 1/2	Feb 20	130:27	131:01	− 15	5.95
8 3/4	May 20	134:01	134:07	− 16	5.95
8 3/4	Aug 20	134:07	134:13	− 17	5.95
7 7/8	Feb 21	123:20	123:26	− 16	5.96
8 1/8	May 21	126:27	127:01	− 15	5.96

U.S. TREASURY STRIPS

Mat.	Type	Bid	Asked	Chg.	Ask Yld.
May 98	ci	99:05	99:05	....	5.34
May 98	np	99:05	99:05	....	5.33
Aug 98	ci	97:26	97:26	....	5.46
Aug 98	np	97:26	97:26	....	5.46
Nov 98	ci	96:16	96:16	....	5.49
Nov 98	np	96:16	96:16	....	5.49
Feb 99	ci	95:06	95:06	....	5.48
Feb 99	np	95:06	95:06	....	5.48
May 99	ci	93:29	93:29	....	5.49
May 99	np	93:28	93:29	....	5.50
Aug 99	ci	92:20	92:21	− 1	5.49
Aug 99	np	92:20	92:21	− 1	5.48
Nov 99	ci	91:13	91:14	− 1	5.48
Nov 99	np	91:13	91:14	− 1	5.48
Feb 00	ci	90:04	90:05	− 1	5.49
Feb 00	np	90:05	90:06	− 1	5.48
May 00	ci	89:01	89:02	− 1	5.44
May 00	np	89:01	89:02	− 1	5.44
Aug 00	ci	87:23	87:24	− 1	5.49
Aug 00	np	87:23	87:24	− 1	5.49
Nov 00	ci	86:18	86:20	− 1	5.48
Nov 00	np	86:18	86:19	− 1	5.49
Feb 01	ci	85:12	85:14	− 1	5.48
Feb 01	np	85:12	85:14	− 1	5.48
May 01	ci	84:05	84:07	− 2	5.52
May 01	np	84:06	84:08	− 1	5.51
Aug 01	ci	82:31	83:01	− 1	5.53
Aug 01	np	83:00	83:01	− 1	5.52
Nov 01	ci	81:29	81:31	− 1	5.51
Nov 01	np	81:28	81:30	− 1	5.52
Feb 02	ci	80:23	80:25	− 1	5.54
May 02	ci	79:20	79:22	− 1	5.53
May 02	np	79:21	79:23	− 1	5.53
Aug 02	ci	78:19	78:21	− 1	5.51
Aug 02	np	78:17	78:19	− 1	5.53
Nov 02	ci	77:26	77:29	....	5.43
Feb 03	ci	76:11	76:14	− 1	5.55
Feb 03	np	76:13	76:17	− 1	5.52
May 03	ci	75:08	75:12	− 1	5.56
Aug 03	ci	74:05	74:09	− 1	5.57
Aug 03	np	74:10	74:14	− 2	5.53
Nov 03	ci	73:05	73:09	− 1	5.57
Feb 04	ci	72:01	72:05	− 2	5.60
Feb 04	np	72:11	72:15	− 2	5.52
May 04	ci	71:00	71:04	− 3	5.61
May 04	np	71:07	71:11	− 3	5.56
Aug 04	ci	70:02	70:06	− 3	5.60
Aug 04	np	70:06	70:11	− 3	5.57
Nov 04	ci	68:31	69:03	− 3	5.63
Nov 04	bp	68:30	69:02	− 3	5.64
Nov 04	np	69:04	69:08	− 3	5.59

TREASURY BILLS

Maturity	Days to Mat.	Bid	Asked	Chg.	Ask Yld.
Mar 26 '98	8	4.90	4.86	− 0.11	4.93
Apr 02 '98	15	5.13	5.09	− 0.02	5.17
Apr 09 '98	22	5.14	5.10	+ 0.02	5.19
Apr 16 '98	29	5.38	5.34	− 0.02	5.44
Apr 23 '98	36	5.39	5.35	+ 0.02	5.45
Apr 30 '98	43	5.30	5.26	+ 0.02	5.37
May 07 '98	50	5.06	5.02	+ 0.01	5.13
May 14 '98	57	5.06	5.02	+ 0.03	5.13
May 21 '98	64	5.06	5.04	+ 0.02	5.16
May 28 '98	71	5.08	5.06	+ 0.01	5.18
Jun 04 '98	78	5.02	5.00	+ 0.02	5.12
Jun 11 '98	85	4.98	4.97	+ 0.02	5.10
Jun 18 '98	92	5.00	4.98	+ 0.04	5.11
Jun 18 '98	**92**	**5.00**	**4.99**	**+ 0.01**	**5.12**
Jun 25 '98	99	5.02	5.00	+ 0.03	5.14
Jul 02 '98	106	4.98	4.96	+ 0.04	5.10
Jul 09 '98	113	4.98	4.96	+ 0.03	5.11
Jul 16 '98	120	4.97	4.95	+ 0.04	5.10
Jul 23 '98	127	4.99	4.97	+ 0.02	5.13
Jul 30 '98	134	4.88	4.86	+ 0.01	5.02
Aug 06 '98	141	4.90	4.88	+ 0.01	5.04
Aug 13 '98	148	4.92	4.90	+ 0.01	5.07
Aug 20 '98	155	5.03	5.01	+ 0.01	5.19
Aug 27 '98	162	4.92	4.90	+ 0.03	5.08
Sep 03 '98	169	4.98	4.96	+ 0.02	5.15
Sep 10 '98	176	5.01	5.00	+ 0.01	5.20
Sep 17 '98	183	5.05	5.03	+ 0.03	5.23
Sep 17 '98	**183**	**5.05**	**5.04**	**+ 0.02**	**5.24**
Oct 15 '98	211	5.04	5.02	+ 0.02	5.23
Nov 12 '98	239	5.07	5.05	+ 0.01	5.26
Dec 10 '98	267	5.06	5.04	+ 0.01	5.26
Jan 07 '99	295	5.06	5.04	+ 0.02	5.28
Feb 04 '99	323	5.08	5.06	+ 0.01	5.31
Mar 04 '99	351	5.07	5.06	+ 0.01	5.33

Source: *Wall Street Journal,* March 18, 1998, C13.

Figure 15.3   Quotes for Municipals

Indiana

100	INDIANA BD BK REV (HOOSIER EQUIP)	*B/E*	4.300	01/01/96N/C	100	NORWESMN	
550	INDIANA HEALTH FAC FING AUTH	METHODIST	5.625	09/01/02N/C	101	PRUBACG	
45	INDIANA HEALTH FAC FING AUTH	P/R @ 102	7.750	08/15/20C00	5.25	EQUITSEC	
200	INDIANA PORT COMMN PORT REV		6.750	07/01/10	993/4	NOYESDAV	
3115	INDIANA ST OFFICE BLDG COMMN	P/R @ 102	8.200	07/01/01C97	4.60	MORGANNT	
200	INDIANA ST OFFICE BLDG COMMN	MBIA	0.000	07/01/05	5.60	BEARSTER	← ①
335	INDIANA ST RECREATIONAL DEV		6.050	07/01/14	6.45	SMITHBCH	
115	INDIANA ST TOLL RD COMMN TOLL	M/S/F 11	9.000	01/01/15ETM	6.30	DRIZOS	← ②
95	INDIANA ST TOLL RD COMMN TOLL		9.000	01/01/15ETM	6.30	EMMET	
1000	INDIANA ST TOLL RD COMMN TOLL	N/C S/F 11	9.000	01/01/15ETM	6.00	WILLIAMA	
100	ELKHART CNTY IND HOSP AUTH REV (ELKHART GEN HOSP)	*B/E* RFDG	6.200	07/01/01N/C	5.40	BLAIRWM	
45	FORT WAYNE IND HOSP AUTH HOSP	S/F 97	6.875	01/01/02ETM	5.85	EMMET	
100	FORT WAYNE IND HOSP AUTH HOSP	P/R @ 102	9.125	07/01/15C95	3.80	GABRIELE	
55	GOSHEN IND CMNTY SCHS		6.600	07/01/97	4.75	NBDBKIND	
10	INDIANAPOLIS IND ARPT AUTH REV (CA @ 102.01 @ 100)	US AIR	7.500	07/01/09C97	100	HSH	← ③
15	INDIANAPOLIS IND ARPT AUTH REV	US AIR	7.500	07/01/19	8.25	STERLING	
500	INDIANAPOLIS IND GAS UTIL REV		4.300	06/01/98	5.00	CITYSEC	
60	INDIANAPOLIS IND LOC PUB IMPT		0.000	08/01/07N/C	6.10	SAPNY	
25	INDIANAPOLIS IND LOC PUB IMPT		6.750	02/01/20	100	COUGHLIN	
200	LAKE CENTRAL IND MULTI		6.000	01/15/02ETM	5.25	CREWASSC	
300	MICHIGAN CITY IND SEW WKS REV		5.200	08/01/07	5.70	NOYESDAV	

Thursday May 26, 1994   PAGE   15A

Source: *The Blue List of Current Municipal Offerings,* May 26, 1994, p. 15A. The Blue List Division of Standard & Poor's Corp., New York. Reprinted by permission of Standard & Poor's Corp.

and par at maturity. Also, the bid–ask is not the price but the promised yield if you are buying (ask) or selling (bid).[29]

Municipal Bond Quotes   Figure 15.3 contains municipal bond quotes from *The Blue List of Current Municipal Offerings.* These are ordered according to states and then alphabetically within states. Each issue gives the amount of bonds being offered (in thousands of dollars), the name of the security, the purpose or description of the issue, the coupon rate, the maturity (which includes month, day, and year), the yield or price, and finally, the dealer offering the bonds. Bond quote 1 is for $200,000 of Indiana State Office Building bonds. The MBIA indicates that the bonds are guaranteed by this firm as described earlier. These are zero- (0.000) coupon bonds due July 1, 2005. In this instance, the yield to maturity is given (5.60 percent). To determine the price you would compute the discount value or look up in a yield book the price of a zero coupon bond, due in about ten years to yield 5.60 percent. The dealer offering the bonds is Bearster. A list in the back of the publication gives the name of the firm and its phone number.

The second bond is for $115,000 of Indiana State Toll Road bonds with a 9 percent coupon. These bonds have a M/S/F (mandatory sinking fund) that becomes effective in 2011 although the bond matures in 2015. The ETM means that the sinking fund is put into "escrow till maturity." The market yield on these bonds is 6.30 percent, which means the bond would be selling at a premium.

Bond quote 3 refers to $10,000 of Indianapolis, Indiana Airport Authority revenue bonds that are backed by a contract with US Air. Although the bonds mature in 2009, they

---

[29]For a discussion on calculating yields, see Bruce D. Fielitz, "Calculating the Bond Equivalent Yield for T-Bills," *Journal of Portfolio Management* 9, no. 3 (Spring 1983): 58–60.

are callable beginning in 1997 (C97) at 102 of par. The coupon is 7.50 percent and in this case, the price of the bond is listed (100), which means its market yield is also 7.50 percent. Such bonds are called *dollar bonds.*

The "+" in the far left column indicates a new item since the prior issue of the *Blue List.* A "#" in the column prior to the yield to maturity or the price indicates that the price or yield has changed since the last issue. It is always necessary to call the dealer to determine the current yield/price, because these quotes are at least one day old when they are published.

Investments Online

This chapter discusses some of the basics of bonds—terminology, ratings, and the differences between corporate and municipal bonds. Bonds are much simpler to evaluate than stocks, since they are debt, not ownership claims, and they (usually) have a fixed time to maturity and known cash flows to the investor (barring default). But bonds are an important part of many individual and institutional portfolios, and here are some helpful Web sites for bond information:

www.bonds-online.com

This Web site covers the gamut of bonds. It offers information and price quotes on a wide variety of instruments, including treasuries, savings bonds, corporates, munis, inflation-indexed bonds, and zero coupon bonds. It features a "bond professor" to answer queries about fixed income securities, and site visitors can submit their own questions. Other information includes a capital markets commentary, a savings bond calculator, and a matrix of municipal yields by credit quality and years to maturity.

www.prusec.com/daily.htm

Prudential Securities Market Commentaries is one of the brokerage house's sites that focuses on bonds. It features eight daily market commentaries on topics such as the financial markets, munis, treasuries, and corporates, as well as the stock market. Some commentaries span the trading day, starting with pre-opening thoughts, followed by a mid-day update and after-the-close summary of what happened during the day.

Two bond ratings firms with interesting Web sites are Fitch's Investor's Service LP (**www.fitchinv.com**) and Moody's Investor Services (**www.moodys.com**). They both feature ratings, research, products, and services. Moody's includes an economic commentary, a discussion of its rating track record, and an overview of its rating process. In addition to featuring bond ratings, Moody's site also offers country sovereign risk ratings.

SUMMARY

♦ We considered the basic features of bonds: their interest, principal, and maturity. Certain key relationships affect price behavior. Price is essentially a function of coupon, maturity, and prevailing market interest rates. Bond-price volatility depends on coupon and maturity. Specifically, bonds with longer maturities and/or lower coupons respond most vigorously to a given change in market rates.

♦ Each bond has unique intrinsic characteristics and can be differentiated by type of issue and indenture provisions. Major benefits to bond investors include high returns for nominal risk, the potential to benefit from diversification with a stock portfolio, certain tax advantages, and possibly additional capital gain returns from active trading of bonds. Aggressive bond investors must consider market liquidity, investment risks, and interest rate behavior. We discussed high-yield (junk) bonds because of the continued growth in size of this segment of the bond market.

♦ The global bond market includes numerous countries. The non-U.S. markets have experienced strong relative growth, whereas the U.S. market has been stable, but constitutes less than half the world market. The four major bond markets (the United States, Japan, Germany, and the United Kingdom) have a different makeup in terms of governments, agencies, municipals, corporates, and international issues. The various market sectors are also unique in terms of liquidity, yield spreads, tax implications, and operating features.

♦ To gauge default risk, most bond investors rely on agency ratings. For additional information on the bond market, prevailing economic conditions, and intrinsic bond features, individual and institutional investors rely on a host of readily available publications. Although extensive up-to-date quotes are available on Treasury bonds and notes, trading and price information for corporates and municipals is relatively difficult to find and is expensive.

♦ The world bond market is large and continues to grow rapidly due to government deficits and the need for capital by corporations. It is also widely diverse in terms of country alternatives and issuers within countries. This chapter has provided the background fundamentals that will allow us to consider the valuation of individual bonds in Chapter 16, and to analyze the alternative bond portfolio management techniques available in Chapter 20.

Questions

1. How does a bond differ from other types of debt instruments?
2. Explain the difference between calling a bond and a bond refunding.
3. Identify the three most important determinants of the price of a bond. Describe the effect of each.
4. Given a change in the level of interest rates, what two major factors will influence the relative change in price for individual bonds? What is their impact?
5. Briefly describe two indenture provisions that can affect the maturity of a bond.
6. What factors determine whether a bond is senior or junior? Give examples of each type.
7. What is a bond indenture?
8. Explain the differences in taxation of income from municipal bonds and income from U.S. Treasury bonds and corporate bonds.
9. List several types of institutional participants in the bond market. Explain what type of bond each is likely to purchase and why.
10. Why should investors be aware of the trading volume for a bond in which they are interested?
11. What is the purpose of bond ratings? What are they supposed to indicate?
12. Based on the data in Table 15.1, which is the fastest-growing bond market in the world? Which markets are losing market share?
13. Based on the data in Table 15.2, discuss the makeup of the German bond market and how it differs from the U.S. market. Briefly discuss the reasons for this difference.
14. Discuss why an investor might consider investing in a government agency issue rather than a straight Treasury bond. What is the negative factor for such a bond relative to a Treasury?
15. Discuss the difference between a foreign bond (for example, a Samurai) and a Eurobond (such as a Euroyen issue).
16. The latter part of this chapter listed and discussed numerous sources of information on bonds. Yet the statement was made earlier that "it is almost impossible for individual investors . . . to keep abreast of the price activity of municipal holdings." Discuss this apparent paradox, explaining how such a condition might exist.

17. Using various sources of information described in the chapter, name at least five bonds rated B or better that have split ratings.
18. Select three bonds that are listed on the NYSE. Using various sources of information, prepare a brief description of each bond, including such factors as its rating, call features, sinking-fund requirements, collateral (if any), interest payment dates, and any refunding provisions.

Problems

1. An investor in the 28 percent tax bracket is trying to decide which of two bonds to purchase. One is a corporate bond carrying an 8 percent coupon and selling at par. The other is a municipal bond with a $5^1/_2$ percent coupon, and it, too, sells at par. Assuming all other relevant factors are equal, which bond should the investor select?

2. What would be the initial offering price for the following bonds (assume semiannual compounding):
   a. A fifteen-year zero coupon bond with a yield to maturity (YTM) of 12 percent.
   b. A twenty-year zero coupon bond with a YTM of 10 percent.

3. An 8.4 percent coupon bond issued by the state of Indiana sells for $1,000. What coupon rate on a corporate bond selling at its $1,000 par value would produce the same after-tax return to the investor as the municipal bond if the investor is in
   a. The 15 percent marginal tax bracket?
   b. The 25 percent marginal tax bracket?
   c. The 35 percent marginal tax bracket?

4. The Anita Corporation has just issued a $1,000 par value zero coupon bond with an 8 percent yield to maturity, due to mature fifteen years from today (assume semiannual compounding).
   a. What is the market price of the bond?
   b. If interest rates remain constant, what will be the price of the bond in three years?
   c. If interest rates rise to 10 percent, what will be the price of the bond in three years?

5. Complete the information requested for each of the following $1,000 face value, zero-coupon bonds, assuming semiannual compounding:

Bond	Maturity (Years)	Yield (Percent)	Price ($)
A	20	12	?
B	?	8	601
C	9	?	350

References

Altman, Edward I., ed., *The High Yield Debt Market.* Homewood, Ill.: Dow Jones–Irwin, 1990.

Churchill, Dwight R., ed., *Fixed Income Management: Techniques and Practices* (Charlottesville, Va: Association for Investment Management and Research, 1994).

Douglas, Livingston G. *The Fixed Income Almanac.* Chicago: Probus Publishing Co., 1993.

Elton, Edwin J., and Martin J. Gruber, eds. *Japanese Capital Markets.* New York: Harper & Row, 1990.

European Bond Commission, *European Bond Markets.* Chicago: Probus Publishing, 1989.

Fabozzi, Frank J., ed. *Advances and Innovations in the Bond and Mortgage Markets.* Chicago: Probus Publishing, 1989.

Fabozzi, Frank J., ed. *The Japanese Bond Market.* Chicago: Probus Publishing, 1990.

Fabozzi, Frank J., ed. *The New High Yield Debt Market.* New York: Harper Business, 1990.

Fabozzi, Frank J. *The Handbook of Fixed-Income Securities,* 5th ed. Chicago: Irwin, 1997.

Fridson, Martin S. *High Yield Bonds.* Chicago: Probus Publishing, 1989.

Howe, Jane Tripp. *Junk Bonds: Analysis and Portfolio Strategies.* Chicago: Probus Publishing, 1988.

Squires, Jan R., ed. *Global Bond Management.* Charlottesville, Va: Association for Investment Management and Research, 1997.

Van Horne, James C. *Financial Market Rates and Flows,* 5th ed. Englewood Cliffs, N.J.: Prentice-Hall, 1998.

Wilson, Richard S. and Frank J. Fabozzi. *The New Corporate Bond Market.* Chicago: Probus Publishing 1990.

Yago, Glenn. *Junk Bonds.* New York: Oxford University Press, 1991.

GLOSSARY

Bearer bond   An unregistered bond for which ownership is determined by possession. The holder receives interest payments by clipping coupons attached to the security and sending them to the issuer for payment.

Benchmark issue   A Japanese government bond selected to dominate trading in that market.

Certificates for automobile receivables (CARs)   Asset-backed securities backed by pools of loans to individuals for financing car purchases.

Collateral trust bond   A bond secured by financial assets held by a trustee for the benefit of the bondholders.

Collateralized mortgage obligation (CMO)   A debt security based on a pool of mortgage loans that provides a relatively stable stream of payments for a relatively predictable term.

Coupon   Indicates the interest payment on a debt security. It is the coupon rate times the par value that indicates the interest payment on a debt security.

Equipment trust certificate   A debt security issued by a transportation firm to finance the purchase of equipment (railroad rolling stock, airplanes), which serves as collateral for the debt.

Flower bond   A Treasury issue that can be redeemed at face value in payment of federal estate taxes.

General obligation bond (GO)   A municipal issue serviced from and guaranteed by the issuer's full taxing authority.

High-yield bond   A bond rated below investment grade. Also referred to as *speculative-grade bonds* or *junk bonds.*

Money market   The market for short-term debt securities with maturities of less than one year.

Municipal bond guarantees   An irrevocable insurance policy on a bond issue (paid for by the issuer) whereby a bond insurance company guarantees to make principal and interest payments on an issue in the event that the issuer of the bond defaults.

Notes   Intermediate-term debt securities with maturities longer than one year but less than ten years.

Principal (par value)   The original value of the debt underlying a bond that is payable at maturity.

Public bond   A long-term, fixed-obligation debt security in a convenient, affordable denomination for sale to individuals and financial institutions.

Refunding issue   Bonds that provide funds to prematurely retire another bond issue. These bonds can be either a junior or senior issue.

Registered bond   A bond for which ownership is registered with the issuer. The holder receives interest payments by check directly from the issuer.

Revenue bond   A bond that is serviced by the income generated from specific revenue-producing projects of the municipality.

Secured (senior) bond   A bond backed by a legal claim on specified assets of the issuer.

Serial obligation bond   A bond issue that has a series of maturity dates.

Subordinated (junior) debenture   An unsecured bond that possesses a claim on income and assets that is subordinated to other debentures.

Term bond   A bond that has a single maturity date.

Term to maturity   Specifies the date or the number of years before a bond matures or expires.

Unsecured bond (debenture)   A bond backed only by the promise of the issuer to pay interest and principal on a timely basis.

Variable-rate note   A debt security for which the interest rate changes to follow some specified short-term rate, for example, the T-bill rate.

Zero-coupon bond   A bond that pays its par value at maturity, but no periodic interest payments. Its yield is determined by the difference between its par value and its discounted purchase price. Also called a *minicoupon bond* or an *original-issue discount (OID) bond.*

16

The Valuation of Bonds

In this chapter we will answer the following questions:

♦ How do you determine the value of a bond based on the present-value formula?

♦ What various bond yields are important to investors?

♦ How do you compute the following major yields on bonds: current yield, yield to maturity, yield to call, and compound realized (horizon) yield?

♦ What factors affect the level of bond yields at a point in time?

♦ What economic forces cause changes in the yields on bonds over time?

♦ When yields change, what characteristics of a bond cause differential price changes for individual bonds?

♦ What do we mean by the duration of a bond, how do you compute it, and what factors affect it?

♦ What is modified duration and what is the relationship between a bond's modified duration and its volatility?

♦ What is the convexity for a bond, what factors affect it, and what is its effect on a bond's volatility?

♦ Under what conditions is it necessary to consider both modified duration and convexity when estimating a bond's price volatility?

In this chapter we apply the valuation principles introduced in Chapter 10 to the valuation of bonds. This chapter is concerned with how we find the value of bonds and with understanding the several measures of yields for bonds. It is also important to understand why these bond values and yields change over time. To do this, we begin with a review of value estimation for bonds using the present value model introduced in Chapter 10. This background on valuation allows us to understand and compute the

expected rates of return on bonds, which are their yields. We need to properly measure bond yields because they are important to a bond investor.

After mastering the measurement of bond yields, we consider what factors influence the level of bond yields and what economic forces cause changes in yields over time. We will discuss the effects of various characteristics and indenture provisions that affect the required returns and, therefore, the value of specific bond issues. This includes factors such as time to maturity, coupon, callability, and sinking funds.

With this background we return to the consideration of bond value and examine the characteristics that cause different changes in a bond's price. The point is, when yields change, the prices of different bonds do not change in the same way.

An understanding of the factors that affect the price changes for bonds has become more important during the past several decades because the price volatility of bonds has increased substantially. Before 1950, the yields on bonds were fairly low and both yields and prices were stable. In such an environment, bonds were considered a safe investment and most investors in bonds intended to hold them to maturity. During the past several decades, the level of interest rates has increased substantially because of inflation, and interest rates have become more volatile because of frequent changes in the rate of inflation and monetary policy. As a result, bond prices and rates of return on bonds have been much more volatile and the rates of return on bond investments have increased. Notably, given these changes, bonds are no longer as safe as they once were.   ♦

The Fundamentals of Bond Valuation

The value of bonds can be described in terms of dollar values or the rates of return that they promise under some set of assumptions. In this section, we describe both the present-value model, which computes a specific value for the bond, and the yield model, which computes the promised rate of return based on the bond's current price.

The Present-Value Model

In our introduction to valuation theory in Chapter 10, we saw that the value of a bond (or any asset) equals the present value of its expected cash flows. The cash flows from a bond are the periodic interest payments to the bondholder and the repayment of principal at the maturity of the bond. Therefore, the value of a bond is the present value of the interest payments plus the present value of the principal payment, where the discount factor is the required rate of return on the bond. We can express this in the following present value formula:

16.1
$$P = \sum_{i=1}^{n} C_t \frac{1}{(1 + i_b)^t}$$

where:

n = the number of periods in the investment horizon, or the holding period

C_t = the cash flow received in period t

i_b = the required rate of return for this bond issue.

Essentially, any fixed-income security can be valued on the basis of Equation 16.1. The value computed indicates what an investor would be willing to pay for this bond to realize a rate of return, i_b, that takes into account expectations regarding the RFR, the expected rate of inflation, and the risk of the bond. Many investors assume a holding period equal to the term to maturity of the obligation. In this case, the number of periods would be the number of years to the maturity of the bond (referred to as its *term to maturity*). In such a case, the cash flows would include all the periodic interest payments and the payment of the bond's par value at the maturity of the bond.

Aggressive bond investors, however, normally do not hold bonds to maturity. They buy bonds with the expectation that they will sell them prior to their maturity. In such a case, the length of time the investor expects to hold the bond determines the number of holding periods. This holding period can range from a few days or weeks to several years, but it would be less than the term to maturity.

Such an investor would compute the bond's value by estimating the cash flows as the periodic interest payments during the holding period and the expected selling price (SP) at the end of the holding period. Notably, the expected selling price need not be equal to the par value of the bond. The bond can sell at a **discount**, which means that its market price will be less than its par value, or it can sell at a **premium**, that is, at a market price above its par value. For example, a discount bond with a par value of $1,000 might sell for $900, whereas a premium bond with the same par value might have a market price of $1,200.[1] Therefore, when computing the value of a bond that you will sell before maturity, it is necessary to estimate both the holding period and the selling price at the end of the holding period. We will discuss how to do this in an example in the next section.

Whether you intend to hold the bond to maturity or for some shorter time period, you will discount the cash flows at your required rate of return on a bond with the given risk. As discussed in Chapter 10, your investment decision will depend on the relationship of your estimated value of the bond and its market price. If the estimated value of the bond equals or exceeds the market price, you should buy it; if your estimated value of the bond is less than its market price, you should not buy it.

The present-value formula implies that the major determinant of changes in the value of a bond is the discount rate because if the bond is held to maturity and the issuer does not default, the cash flows are known. Therefore, we will need to discuss what causes differences in discount rates between bonds and over time. That is, why do interest rates change? These questions will be considered in a subsequent section.

The Yield Model

Instead of determining the value of a bond in dollar terms, investors often price bonds in terms of **yields**, which are the promised rates of return on bonds under certain assumptions. The point is, thus far we have used cash flows and our required rate of return to compute an estimated value for the bond, which we then compared to its market price (P). To compute an expected yield, we use the current market price (P) with the expected cash flows and *compute the expected yield on the bond.* We can express this approach using the present value model as follows:

16.2

$$P = \sum_{t=i}^{n} C_t \frac{1}{(1 + i)^t}$$

---

[1]As we will see, fluctuations in market interest rates will cause bonds to sell at a discount or premium.

where:

P = the current market price of the bond

C_t = the cash flow received in period t

i = the discount rate that will discount the cash flows to equal the current market price of
   the bond

This i value gives the yield of the bond. We will discuss several different bond yields that arise from alternative assumptions of the valuation model in the next section.

Approaching the investment decision stating the bond's value as a yield figure rather than a dollar amount, you need to consider the relationship of the computed bond yield to your required rate of return on this bond. If the computed bond yield is equal to or greater than your required rate of return, you should buy the bond; if the computed yield is less than your required rate of return, you should not buy the bond.

These approaches to pricing bonds and making investment decisions are similar to the two alternative approaches by which firms make investment decisions. We referred to one approach, the net present value (NPV) method, in Chapter 10. With the NPV approach you compute the present value of the net cash flows from the proposed investment at your cost of capital and subtract the present value cost of the investment to get the net present value (NPV) of the project. If this NPV is positive, you consider accepting the investment; if it is negative, you reject it. This is basically the way we compared the value of an investment to its market price.

The second approach is to compute the **internal rate of return (IRR)** on a proposed investment project. The IRR is the discount rate that equates the present value of cash outflows for an investment with the present value of its cash inflows. You compare this discount rate, or IRR (which is also the expected rate of return on the project), to your cost of capital, and accept any investment proposal with an IRR equal to or greater than your cost of capital. We do the same thing when we price bonds on the basis of yield. If the expected yield on the bond is equal to or exceeds your required rate of return on the bond, you should invest in it; if the expected yield is less than your required rate of return on the bond, you should not invest in it.

COMPUTING BOND YIELDS

Bond investors use five alternative measures of yield for the following purposes:

Yield Measure	Purpose
Coupon rate	Measures the coupon rate or the percentage of par paid out annually as interest.
Current yield	Measures current income rate.
Promised yield to maturity	Measures expected rate of return for bond held to maturity.
Promised yield to call	Measures expected rate of return for bond held to first call date.
Realized (horizon) yield	Measures expected rate of return for a bond likely to be sold prior to maturity. It considers specific reinvestment assumptions and an estimated sales price. It can also measure the actual rate of return on a bond during some past period of time.

Coupon rate and current yields are mainly descriptive and contribute little to investment decision making. The last three yields are all derived from the present value model as described in Equation 16.2.

When we present the last three yields based on the present-value model, we consider two calculation techniques. First, we consider a fairly simple calculation to derive approximate values for each of these yields to provide reasonable estimates. Second, we use the present-value model to get accurate values. A financial calculator or spreadsheet software such as Excel or Lotus is used to determine exact returns from a series of cash flows.

To measure an expected realized yield (also referred to as the horizon yield), a bond investor must estimate a bond's future selling price. Following our presentation of bond yields, we will present the procedure for finding these prices. We conclude the section by examining the yields on tax-free bonds.

Coupon Rate

The **coupon rate** merely measures the annual income that a bond investor receives expressed as a percent of the bond's par value. It is of little use in determining a bond's actual return, as the bond's price may differ from par when purchased or capital gains or losses may occur during the holding period if the bond is sold before maturity.

Current Yield

Current yield is to bonds what dividend yield is to stocks. It is computed as

16.3
$$CY = C/P$$

where:

CY = the current yield on a bond
 C = the annual coupon payment of the bond
 P = the current market price of the bond.

Because this yield measures the current income from the bond as a percentage of its price, it is important to income-oriented investors who want current cash flow from their investment portfolios. An example of such an investor would be a retired person who lives on this investment income. Current yield has little use for most other investors who are interested in total return because it excludes the important capital gain or loss component.

Promised Yield to Maturity

Promised yield to maturity is the most widely used bond yield figure, because it indicates the fully compounded rate of return promised to an investor who buys the bond at prevailing prices, *if two assumptions hold true*. The first assumption is that the investor holds the bond to maturity. This assumption gives this yield its shortened name, *yield to maturity (YTM)*. The second assumption is implicit in the present-value method of computation, namely that all the bond's cash flows are reinvested at the computed yield to maturity. To see this, refer back to Equation 16.2. Recall that it related the current market price of the bond to the present value of all cash flows as follows:

$$P = \sum_{t=i}^{n} C_t \frac{1}{(1 + i)^t}.$$

To compute the YTM for a bond, we solve for the rate i that will equate the current price (P) to all cash flows from the bond to maturity. As noted, this resembles the computa-

tion of the internal rate of return (IRR) on an investment project. Because it is a present-value–based computation, it implies a reinvestment rate assumption because it discounts the cash flows. That is, the equation assumes that *all interim cash flows (interest payments) are reinvested at the computed YTM*. That is why this is referred to as a *promised* YTM because the bond will provide this computed YTM only *if* you meet its conditions:

1. You hold the bond to maturity.
2. You reinvest all the interim cash flows at the computed YTM rate.

If a bond promises an 8 percent nominal YTM, you must reinvest coupon income at 8 percent in order to realize that promised return. If you spend (do not reinvest) the coupon payments or if you cannot find opportunities to reinvest these coupon payments at rates as high as its promised YTM, then the actual *realized* yield you earn will be less than the promised yield to maturity. The income earned on the reinvestment of the interim interest payments is referred to as **interest-on-interest**.[2]

The impact of the reinvestment assumption (the interest-on-interest earnings) on the realized return from a bond varies directly with the bond's coupon and maturity. Higher coupons and longer terms to maturity increase the loss in value from failure to reinvest at the YTM. These conditions make the reinvestment assumption more important.

Figure 16.1 illustrates the impact of interest-on-interest for an 8 percent, twenty-five-year bond bought at par to yield 8 percent. If you invested $1,000 today at 8 percent for twenty-five years and reinvested all the coupon payments at 8 percent, you would have approximately $7,100 at the end of twenty-five years. We will refer to this money that you have at the end of your investment horizon as your **ending-wealth value**. To prove that you would have an ending-wealth value of $7,100, look up the compound interest factor for 8 percent for twenty-five years (which is 6.8493) or 4 percent for fifty periods (which assumes semiannual compounding and is 7.1073).

Figure 16.1 shows that this $7,100 is made up of $1,000 principal return, $2,000 of coupon payments over the twenty-five years ($80 a year for twenty-five years), and $4,100 in interest earned on the coupon payments reinvested at 8 percent. If you had saved but never reinvested any of the coupon payments, you would have an ending-wealth value of only $3,000. This ending-wealth value of $3,000 derived from the beginning investment of $1,000 gives you an actual (realized) yield to maturity of only 4.5 percent. That is, the rate that will discount $3,000 back to $1,000 in twenty-five years is 4.5 percent. Reinvesting the coupon payments at some rate between 0 and 8 percent would cause your ending-wealth position to be above $3,000 and below $7,100; therefore, your actual rate of return would be somewhere between 4.5 percent and 8 percent. Alternatively, if you managed to reinvest the coupon payments at rates consistently above 8 percent, your ending-wealth position would be above $7,100, and your actual realized rate of return would be above 8 percent.

Interestingly, during periods of high interest rates, you often hear investors talk about "locking in" high yields. Many of these people are subject to **yield illusion**, because they do not realize that attaining the high promised yield requires that they reinvest all the coupon payments at the same high yields. As an example, if you buy a twenty-year bond with a promised yield to maturity of 15 percent, you will actually realize the 15 percent yield *only* if you reinvest all the coupon payments at 15 percent over the next twenty years.

Computing the Promised Yield to Maturity   You can compute the promised yield to maturity in two ways: finding an approximate annual yield, or using the present-value

[2]This concept is developed in Sidney Homer and Martin L. Leibowitz, *Inside the Yield Book* (Englewood Cliffs, N.J.: Prentice-Hall, 1972), Chapter 1.

Figure 16.1 *The Effect of Interest-on-Interest on Total Realized Return*

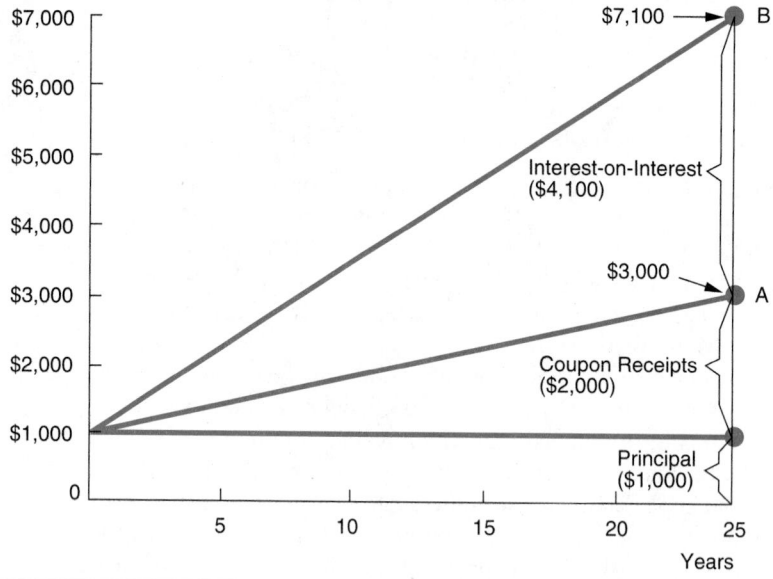

Promised yield at time of purchase: 8.00 percent.
Realized yield over the twenty-five-year investment horizon with no coupon reinvestment (A): 4.50 percent.
Realized yield over the twenty-five-year horizon with coupons reinvested at 8 percent (B): 8.00 percent.

model with semiannual compounding.[3] The present-value model gives an investor a more accurate result, and it is the technique used by investment professionals.

The approximate promised yield (APY) measure is easy to calculate as follows:

16.4

$$APY = C_t + \frac{\dfrac{par - P}{n}}{\dfrac{par + P}{2}}$$

$$= \frac{\text{Coupon} + \text{Annual Straight-Line}}{\text{Amortization of Capital Gain or Loss}}{\text{Average Investment}}$$

where:

n = number of years to maturity
C_t = the bond's *annual* coupon
P = the current market price of the bond.

This approximate value for the promised yield to maturity assumes interest is compounded annually, and it does not require the multiple computations of the present-value model. An 8 percent bond with twenty years remaining to maturity and a current price of $900 has an approximate yield of 8.95 percent:

---

[3]You can compute promised YTM assuming annual compounding, but practitioners use semiannual compounding because the interest cash flows are semiannual. Even when the cash flows are not semiannual, bond analysts use the assumption for calculating the yield. Therefore, all our calculations employ this assumption.

$$APY = \frac{80 + \dfrac{1,000 - 900}{20}}{\dfrac{1,000 + 900}{2}} = \frac{80 + 5}{950}$$

$$= 8.95\%.$$

The present-value model provides a more accurate yield to maturity value. To be consistent with actual practice, we assume semiannual compounding. Equation 16.5 shows this version of the promised yield valuation model:

16.5
$$P = \sum_{t=1}^{2n} \frac{C/2}{(1 + i)^t} + \frac{par}{(1 + i)^{2n}}.$$

All variables are as described previously except i will be the semiannual interest rate. This formula reflects the semiannual interest payments. You adjust for these semiannual payments by doubling the number of periods (two times the number of years to maturity) and dividing the annual coupon value in half.

This model is more accurate than the approximate promised yield model, but it is also more complex because the solution requires iteration. The present-value equation is a variation of the internal rate of return (IRR) calculation where we want to find the discount rate, i, that will equate the present value of the stream of coupon receipts, (C_t), and principal value, (par), with the current market price of the bond (P). Using the prior example of an 8 percent, twenty-year bond, priced at $900, the equation gives us a semiannual promised yield to maturity of 4.545 percent, which implies a nominal YTM of 9.09 percent:[4]

$$900 = 40 \sum_{t=1}^{40} \left(\frac{1}{(1.04545)^t}\right) + 1,000\left(\frac{1}{(1.04545)^{40}}\right)$$

$$= 40(18.2574) + 1,000\,(.1702)$$

$$= 900.$$

Comparing the results of Equation 16.5 with those of the approximate promised yield computation, you find a variation of 14 basis points. As a rule, the approximate promised yield tends to understate the present-value promised yield for issues selling below par value (that is, trading at a discount) and to overstate the promised yield for a bond selling at a premium. The size of the differential varies directly with the length of the holding period. Although the estimated yield value differs, the rankings of yields estimated using the APY formula (Equation 16.4) will generally be identical to those determined by the present-value method.

A Word on Yield Calculations

We quote yield to maturity for bonds paying semiannual coupons in two ways: as nominal rates or as effective rates. The yield to maturity, quoted on a nominal basis, is equal to the bond's semiannual rate of return multiplied by two:

---

[4]You will recall from your corporate finance course that you would start with one rate (for example, 9 percent or 4.5 percent semiannual) and compute the value of the stream. In this example, the value would exceed $900, so you would select a higher rate until you had a present value for the stream of cash flows of less than $900. Given the discount rates above and below the true rate, you would do further calculations or interpolate between the two rates to arrive at the correct discount rate that would give you a value of $900.

$$\text{nominal YTM} = \text{semiannual return} \times 2$$

A bond with a semiannual return of 4.545 percent has a nominal YTM of 4.545×2 or 9.09 percent.

The second method, the effective yield to maturity, considers the affect of semiannual period-by-period compounding on the annual return: interest earned in one six-month period earns interest when reinvested in subsequent periods. That is, a bond with a 4.545 percent semiannual return has an effective YTM of:

$$(1 + 0.04545)^2 - 1 - 0.0930 \text{ or } 9.30 \text{ percent.}$$

Alternatively, a bond with an effective yield to maturity of 9.30 percent has a semiannual return of

$$\sqrt{1 + 0.0930} - 1$$

which equals 0.04545 or 4.545 percent. As bond returns may be quoted using either nominal or effective returns, it is important to know how the reported rate was calculated.

YTM for a Zero-Coupon Bond   In several instances we have discussed the existence of zero-coupon bonds that only have the one cash inflow at maturity. This single cash flow means that the calculation of YTM is substantially easier as shown by the following example:

Assume a zero-coupon bond, maturing in ten years with a maturity value of $1,000 selling for $311.80. Because you are dealing with a zero-coupon bond, there is only the one cash flow from the principal payment at maturity. Therefore, you simply need to determine the discount rate that will discount $1,000 to equal the current market price of $311.80 in twenty periods (ten years of semiannual payment). The equation is as follows:

$$\$311.80 = \frac{\$1,000}{(1 + i)^{20}}$$

You will see that $i = 6$ percent, which implies a nominal rate of 12 percent.

Promised Yield to Call

Although investors use promised YTM to value most bonds, they must estimate the return on certain callable bonds with a different measure—**the promised yield to call (YTC)**. Whenever a bond with a call feature is selling for a price equal to or greater than its par value plus one year's interest, a bond investor should value the bond in terms of YTC rather than YTM. The reason is that the marketplace uses the lowest, most conservative yield measure in pricing a bond. When bonds are trading at or above a specified **crossover point**, which approximates the bond's par value plus one year's interest, the yield to call will normally provide the lowest yield measure.[5] The price at the crossover point is important because when the bond rises to this price above par, the computed YTM becomes low enough that it would be profitable for the issuer to call the bond and finance the call by selling a new bond at the prevailing market interest rate.[6] Therefore, the YTC measures the promised rate of return the

---

[5]For a discussion of the crossover point, see Homer and Leibowitz, *Inside the Yield Book*, Chapter 4.

[6]Extensive literature treats the refunding of bond issues, including W. M. Boyce and A. J. Kalotay, "Optimum Bond Calling and Refunding," *Interfaces* (November 1979): 36–49; R. S. Harris, "The Refunding of Discounted Debt: An Adjusted Present Value Analysis," *Financial Management* 9, no.4 (Winter 1980): 7–12; A. J. Kalotay, "On the Structure and Valuation of Debt Refundings," *Financial Management* 11, no. 1 (Spring 1982): 4l–42; and John D. Finnerty, "Evaluating the Economics of Refunding High-Coupon Sinking-Fund Debt," *Financial Management* 12, no. 1 (Spring 1983): 5–10.

investor will receive from holding this bond until it is retired at the first available call date, that is, at the end of the deferred call period. Investors need to consider computing the YTC for their bonds after a period when numerous high-yielding, high-coupon bonds have been issued. Following such a period, interest rates will decline, bond prices will rise, and the high-coupon bonds will subsequently have a high probability of being called.

Computing Promised Yield to Call   Again, we use two methods for computing the promised yield to call: the approximate method and the present-value method. Both methods assume that you hold the bond until the first call date. The present-value method also assumes that you reinvest all coupon payments at the YTC rate.

Yield to call is calculated using variations of Equations 16.4 and 16.5. The approximate yield to call (AYC) is computed as follows:

16.6
$$AYC = \frac{C_t + \dfrac{P_c - P}{nc}}{\dfrac{P_c + P}{2}}$$

where:

AYC = approximate yield to call (YTC)

P_c = call price of the bond (generally equal to par value plus one year's interest)

P = market price of the bond

C_t = annual coupon payment

nc = the number of years to first call date.

To find the AYC of a 12 percent, twenty-year bond that is trading at 115 ($1,150) with five years remaining to first call and a call price of 112 ($1,120), we substitute these values into Equation 16.6.

$$AYC = \frac{120 + \dfrac{1,120 - 1,150}{5}}{\dfrac{1,120 + 1,150}{2}} = 10.04\%.$$

This bond's approximate YTC is 10.04 percent, assuming the issue will be called after five years at the call price of 112. To confirm that yield to call is the more conservative and more accurate value for a bond you expect to be called in five years, you can compute the approximate promised YTM. Using Equation 16.4 indicates a promised YTM of 10.47 percent.

To compute the YTC by the present-value method, we would adjust the semiannual present-value equation (Equation 16.5) to give

16.7
$$P = \sum_{t=1}^{2nc} \frac{C_t/2}{(1 + i)^t} + \frac{P_c}{(1 + i)^{2nc}}$$

where:

P = market price of the bond

C_t = annual coupon payment

nc = number of years to first call

P_c = call price of the bond.

Following the present-value method, we solve for i, and receive an answer of 5.01 percent. The nominal yield to call will be 5.01 × 2 or 10.02 percent. The yield to call, quoted as an effective yield, will be $(1 + 0.0501)^2 - 1$ or 10.27 percent.

As with the yield to maturity, the yield to call calculation depends upon two assumptions. One is the number of years until the call occurs; the second is that all cash flows from the bond will be reinvested at the yield to call. In the above example, this means the bond's coupon cash flows of $60 will be reinvested at a semiannual rate of 5.01 percent.

Realized Yield

The final measure of bond yield, **realized yield** (or **horizon yield**) measures the expected rate of return of a bond that you expect to sell prior to its maturity. In terms of the equation, the investor has a holding period (hp) that is less than n. Realized (horizon) yield can be used to estimate rates of return attainable from various trading strategies. As such, it is a useful measure, but it also requires several additional estimates not required by the other yield measures. Specifically, the investor must estimate the expected future selling price of the bond at the end of the holding period. Also, this measure requires an explicit estimate of the reinvestment rate for the coupon flows prior to the liquidation of the bond. This technique can also be used to measure an investor's actual yields after selling bonds.

Computing Realized (Horizon) Yield The realized yields are variations on the promised yield equations (Equations 16.4 and 16.5). The approximate realized yield (ARY) is calculated as follows:

16.8
$$ARY = \frac{C_t + \dfrac{P_f - P}{hp}}{\dfrac{P_f + P}{2}}$$

where:

ARY = approximate realized yield
C_t = annual coupon payment
P_f = estimated future selling price of the bond
hp = holding period of the bond in years.

Keep in mind that P_f is not a contractual value but is *calculated* by defining the years remaining to maturity as $n - hp$ and by *estimating* a future market interest rate, i. We describe the computation of the future selling price (P_f) in the next section.

Once we determine hp and P_f, we can calculate the approximate realized yield. Assume you acquired an 8 percent, twenty-year bond for $750. Over the next two years you expect interest rates to decline. As we know, when interest rates decline, bond prices increase. Suppose you anticipate that the bond price will rise to $900. The approximate realized yield in this case for the two years would be

$$ARY = \frac{80 + \dfrac{900 - 750}{2}}{\dfrac{900 + 750}{2}} = 18.79\%.$$

The estimated high realized yield reflects your expectation of a substantial capital gains in a fairly short period of time.

Similarly, the substitution of P_f and hp into the present-value model provides the following realized-yield model:

$$\boxed{16.9} \qquad P_m = \sum_{t=1}^{2hp} \frac{C_t/2}{(1 + i)^t} + \frac{P_f}{(1 + i)^{2hp}}.$$

Again, this present-value model requires that you solve for the i that equates the expected cash flows from coupon payments and the estimated selling price to the current market price. Using a financial calculator or spreadsheet software, we find the semiannual return i is equal to 9.664 percent. This means, quoted on a nominal basis, the realized yield is 9.664×2 or 19.33 percent. Quoted as an effective yield, the realized yield will be $(1 + 0.09664)^2 - 1$ or 20.26 percent.

CALCULATING FUTURE BOND PRICES

On several occasions we have noted that a bond's price varies with the discount rate. This leads to the important concept that bond prices move inversely to interest rates. You must keep this in mind when valuing individual bonds or making bond portfolio decisions.

In two instances you will need to calculate dollar bond prices: (1) when computing realized (horizon) yield, you must determine the future selling price (P_f) of a bond, and (2) when issues are quoted on a promised-yield basis, as with municipals. You can easily convert a yield-based quote to a dollar price by using Equation 16.5, which does not require iteration. You need only solve Equation 16.5 for P. The coupon (C_t) is given, as is the par value and the nominal or effective YTM, which is used as the discount rate.

Consider a 10 percent, twenty-five-year bond with a nominal YTM of 12 percent. You would compute the current price of this issue as

$$
\begin{aligned}
P_m &= 100/2 \sum_{t=1}^{50} \frac{1}{\left(1 + \dfrac{.120}{2}\right)} + 1,000 \frac{1}{\left(1 + \dfrac{.120}{2}\right)^{50}} \\
&= .50(15.7619) + 1,000(.0543) \\
&= \$842.40.
\end{aligned}
$$

In this instance, we are determining the prevailing market price of the bond based on the market nominal YTM. These market figures indicate the consensus of all investors regarding the value of this bond. An investor who has a required rate of return on this bond that differs from the market nominal YTM would estimate a different value for the bond.

In contrast to the current market price, you will need to compute a future price (P_f) when estimating the expected realized (horizon) yield performance of different bonds. Investors or portfolio managers who consistently trade bonds for capital gains need to compute expected realized yield rather than promised yield. They would compute P_f through the following variation of the realized-yield equation:

$$\boxed{16.10} \qquad P_f = \sum_{t=1}^{2n-2hp} \frac{C_t/2}{(1 + i)^t} + \frac{\text{par}}{(1 + i)^{2n-2hp}}$$

where:

P_f = **estimated future price of the bond**
n = **number of years to maturity**
hp = **holding period of the bond in years**
C_t = **annual coupon payment**
i = **expected semiannual rate at the end of the holding period.**

Equation 16.10 is a version of the present-value model that calculates the expected price of the bond at the end of the holding period (*hp*). The term $2n - 2hp$ equals the bond's remaining term to maturity at the end of the investor's holding period, that is, the number of six-month periods remaining when the bond is sold. Therefore, the determination of P_f is based on four variables: two that are known and two that must be estimated by the investor.

Specifically. the coupon (C_t) and the par value are given. The investor must forecast the length of the holding period, and therefore the number of years remaining to maturity at the time the bond is sold ($n - hp$). The investor must also forecast the expected market YTM at the time of sale (i). With this information you can calculate the future price of the bond. The real difficulty (and the potential source of error) in estimating P_f lies in predicting *hp* and *i*.

Assume you bought the 10 percent, twenty-five-year bond just discussed at $842, giving it a nominal YTM of 12 percent. Based on an analysis of the economy and the capital market, you expect this bond's market YTM to decline to 8 percent in five years. Therefore, you want to compute its future price (P_f) at the end of year five to estimate your expected rate of return, assuming you are correct in your assessment of the decline in overall market interest rates. As noted, you estimate the holding period (five years), which implies a remaining life of twenty years, and estimate a market nominal YTM of 8 percent. Using the semiannual model in Equation 16.10 gives a future price:

$$P_f = 50 \sum_{t=1}^{40} \frac{1}{(1.04)^t} + 1,000 \frac{1}{(1.04)^{40}}$$

$$= 50(19.7928) + 1,000(.2083)$$

$$= 989.64 + 208.30$$

$$= \$1,197.94.$$

Based on this estimate of the selling price, you would estimate the approximate realized (horizon) yield on this investment on an annual basis as

$$\text{ARY} = \frac{100 + \dfrac{1,198 - 842}{5}}{\dfrac{1,198 + 842}{2}}$$

$$= \frac{100 + 71.20}{1,020}$$

$$= .1678$$

$$= 16.78\%.$$

If you want to be more accurate in your calculation, you could use the present value formula set forth in Equation 16.9.

Using yields to compare bonds and estimate potential returns is a common practice. In this section we discussed five yields, including two (coupon rate and current yield) that are used for description rather than for investment decisions. The latter three yields [promised YTM, promised YTC, and realized (horizon) yield] are all based on the present-value model and require certain assumptions about the investor's holding period and the reinvestment rate earned on coupon cash flows. These last three yields can be computed by using either an approximate method, which is fairly easy, or by using the present-value model, which is more accurate but also requires more computations.

Yield Adjustments for Tax-Exempt Bonds

Municipal bonds, Treasury issues, and many agency obligations possess one common characteristic: their interest income is partially or fully tax-exempt. This tax-exempt status affects the valuation of taxable versus nontaxable bonds. Although you could adjust each present-value equation for the tax effects, it is not necessary for our purposes. We can approximate the effect of such an adjustment, however, by computing the equivalent taxable yield, which is one of the most often cited measures of performance for municipal bonds.

Equivalent taxable yield (ETY) adjusts the promised-yield computation for the bond's tax-exempt status. To compute the ETY, we determine the promised yield on a tax-exempt bond using one of the yield formulas and adjust the computed yield to reflect the rate of return that must be earned on a fully taxable issue. It is measured as

16.11
$$\text{ETY} = \frac{\text{annual return}}{1 - T}$$

where:

T = **amount and type of tax exemption.**

The ETY equation has some limitations. It is applicable only to par bonds or current coupon obligations, such as new issues, because the measure considers only interest income and ignores capital gains. Therefore, we cannot use it for issues trading at a significant variation from par value.

WHAT DETERMINES INTEREST RATES?

Now that we have learned to calculate various yields on bonds, the question arises as to what causes differences and changes in yields over time. Market interest rates cause these effects because the interest rates reported in the media are simply the prevailing YTMs for the bonds being discussed. For example, when you hear on television that the interest rate on long-term government bonds declined from 8.40 percent to 8.32 percent, this means that the price of this particular bond increased such that the computed YTM at the former price was 8.40 percent, but the computed YTM at the new, higher price is 8.32 percent. Yields and interest rates are the same. They are different terms for the same concept.

We have discussed the inverse relationship between bond prices and interest rates. When interest rates decline, the prices of bonds increase; when interest rates rise, there is a decline in bond prices. It is natural to ask which of these is the driving force, bond prices or bond interest rates. It is a simultaneous change, and you can envision *either* factor causing it. Most practitioners probably envision the changes in interest rates as causes because they constantly use interest rates to describe changes. They use interest rates because these rates are comparable across bonds, whereas the price of a bond depends not only on the interest rate, but also on its specific characteristics including its coupon and maturity. The point is, when you change the interest rate (yield) on a bond, you simultaneously change its price in the opposite direction. Later in the chapter we will discuss the specific price–yield relationship for individual bonds and demonstrate that this price–yield relationship differs among bonds based on their particular coupon and maturity.

Understanding interest rates and what makes them change is necessary for an investor who hopes to maximize returns from investing in bonds. Therefore, in this section we will

review our prior discussion of the following topics: what causes overall market interest rates to rise and fall, why alternative bonds have different interest rates, and why the difference in rates (the yield spread) between various bonds changes over time. To accomplish this, we begin with a general discussion of the influences on interest rates, and then consider the *term structure of interest rates* (shown by yield curves), which relates the interest rates on a set of comparable bonds to their terms to maturity. The term structure is important because it reflects what investors expect to happen to interest rates in the future and it also dictates their current risk attitude. Finally, we turn to the concept of *yield spreads,* which measures the differences in yields between alternative bonds. We will describe various yield spreads and explore changes in them over time.

Forecasting Interest Rates

As discussed, the ability to forecast interest rates and changes in these rates is critical to successful bond investing. Subsequent presentations consider the major determinants of interest rates, but for now you should keep in mind that interest rates *are the price for loanable funds.* Like any price, they are determined by the supply and demand for these funds. On the one side investors are willing to provide the funds (the supply) at prices based on their required rates of return for a particular borrower. On the other side borrowers need the funds (the demand) to support budget deficits (government), to invest in capital projects (corporations), or to acquire durable goods (cars, appliances) or homes (individuals).

Although the lenders and borrowers have some fundamental factors that determine the supply and demand curves, the prices for these funds (interest rates) are also affected for short time periods by events that shift the curves. Examples include major government bond issues that affect demand, or significant changes in Federal Reserve monetary policy that affect the supply of money.

Our treatment of interest rate forecasting recognizes that you must be aware of the basic determinants of interest rates and monitor these factors. We also recognize that detailed forecasting of interest rates is a complex task that is best left to professional economists. Therefore, our goal as bond investors and bond portfolio managers is to monitor current and expected interest rate behavior. We should attempt to continuously assess the major factors that affect interest rate behavior but also rely on others, such as economic consulting firms, banks, or investment banking firms, for detailed insights on such topics as the real RFR and the expected rate of inflation.[7] This is precisely the way most bond portfolio managers operate.

Fundamental Determinants of Interest Rates

As shown in Figure 16.2, average interest rates for long-term (ten-year) U.S. government bonds during the period 1995–97 fluctuated between 6 and 8 percent. The level of U.S. interest rates remained between rates in the United Kingdom and Germany. U.K. rates remained at a level slightly above U.S. rates, while the rate on German government bonds declined from about 7.4 percent to about 5.4 percent. As a result of Japan's slow economy and troubled financial sector, Japan's bond rates fell from just over 4 percent to under 2 percent during 1995–97. As a bond investor, you need to understand *why* these differences occur, and *why* interest rates change this way. Tracking both domestic and international influences over time can provide information regarding interest-rate behavior and

---

[7]Sources of information on the bond market and interest rate forecasts would include Merrill Lynch's *Fixed Income Weekly* and *World Bond Market Monitor,* and Goldman, Sach's *Financial Market Perspectives.*

Figure 16.2 *International Long-Term Government Bond Yields*

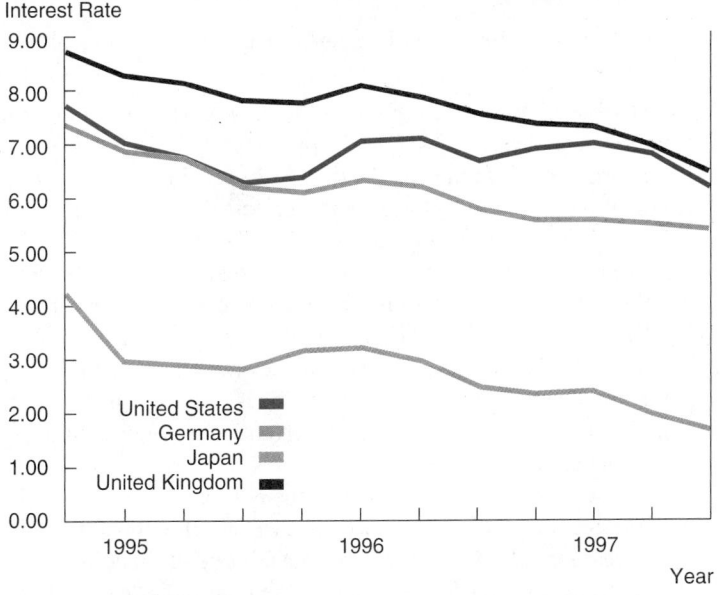

Source: Federal Reserve Bank of St. Louis, *International Economic Trends.*

expectations for future interest-rate changes. Some of these factors were discussed in Chapter 11. Additional influences will be reviewed in the rest of this section.

As you know from your knowledge of bond pricing, bond prices can increase dramatically during periods when market interest rates drop, and some bond investors experience attractive returns. In contrast, some investors have experienced substantial losses during several periods when interest rates increased. A casual analysis of Figure 16.2, which covers three years, indicates the need for monitoring interest rates. Essentially, the factors causing interest rates (*i*) to rise or fall are described by the following model:

16.12 $$i = \text{RFR} + I + \text{RP}$$

where:

RFR = real risk-free rate of interest
  I = expected rate of inflation
 RP = risk premium.

This relationship should be familiar from our presentations in Chapters 1 and 10. Equation 16.12 is a simple but complete statement of interest-rate behavior. It is a more difficult task to estimate the *future* behavior of variables such as real growth, expected inflation, and economic uncertainty. In this regard, interest rates, like stock prices, are extremely difficult to forecast with any degree of accuracy.[8] Alternatively, we can visualize the source of changes in interest rates in terms of the economic conditions and issue characteristics that determine the rate of return on a bond:

---

[8]For an overview of interest-rate forecasting, see W. David Woolford, "Forecasting Interest Rates," in *Handbook of Fixed -Income Securities,* 5th ed., edited by Frank J. Fabozzi (Chicago: Irwin, 1997).

$$i = f \, (\text{Economic Forces} + \text{Issue Characteristics})$$
$$= (\text{RFR} + I) + \text{RP}.$$

This rearranged version of Equation 16.12 helps us to isolate the determinants of interest rates.[9]

Effect of Economic Factors   The real risk-free rate of interest (RFR) is the economic cost of money, that is, the opportunity cost necessary to compensate individuals for forgoing consumption. As discussed previously, it is determined by the real growth rate of the economy with short-run effects due to ease or tightness in the capital market.

The expected rate of inflation is the other economic influence on interest rates. We add the expected level of inflation (I) to the real risk-free rate (RFR) to specify the nominal RFR, which is a market rate like the current rate on government T-bills. Given the stability of the real RFR, it is clear that the wide swings in interest rates during the 3 years covered by Figure 16.2 occurred because of changes in the expected inflation. Besides the unique country and exchange rate risk that we discuss in the section on risk premiums, differences in the rates of inflation between countries have a major impact on their level of interest rates.

To sum up, one way to estimate the nominal RFR is to begin with the real growth rate of the economy, adjust for short-run ease or tightness in the capital market, and then adjust this real rate of interest for the expected rate of inflation.

Another approach to estimating the nominal rate or changes in the rate is the macroeconomic view, where the supply and demand for loanable funds are the fundamental economic determinants of i. As the supply of loanable funds increases, the level of interest rates declines, other things being equal. Several factors influence the supply of funds. Government monetary policies imposed by the Federal Reserve have a significant impact on the supply of money. The savings pattern of U.S. and non-U.S. investors also affects the supply of funds. Non-U.S. investors have become a stronger influence on the U.S. supply of loanable funds during recent years, as shown by the significant purchases of U.S. securities by non-U.S. investors. It is widely acknowledged that this foreign addition to the supply of funds has benefited the United States in terms of reducing our interest rates and our cost of capital.

Interest rates increase when the demand for loanable funds increases. The demand for loanable funds is affected by the capital and operating needs of the U.S. government, federal agencies, state and local governments, corporations, institutions, and individuals. Federal budget deficits increase the Treasury's demand for loanable funds. Likewise, the level of consumer demand for funds to buy houses, autos, and appliances affects rates, as does corporate demand for funds to pursue investment opportunities. The total of all groups determines the aggregate demand and supply of loanable funds and the level of the nominal RFR.[10]

The Impact of Bond Characteristics   The interest rate of a specific bond issue is influenced not only by all these factors that affect the nominal RFR, but also by its unique issue characteristics. These issue characteristics influence the bond's risk premium (RP). The economic forces that determine the nominal RFR affect all securities, whereas issue characteristics are unique to individual securities (that is, these are systematic fac-

---

[9]For an extensive exploration of interest rates and interest-rate behavior, see James C. Van Horne, *Financial Market Rates and Flows,* 5th ed. (Englewood Cliffs, N.J.: Prentice-Hall, 1998).

[10]For an example of an estimate of the supply and demand for funds in the economy, see *Prospects for Financial Markets*. This annual publication of Salomon Brothers gives an estimate of the flow of funds in the economy and discusses its effect on various currencies and interest rates, making recommendations for portfolio strategy on the basis of these expectations.

tors), market sectors, or countries. Thus, the differences in the yields of corporate and Treasury bonds are not caused by economic forces but rather by different issue characteristics that cause differences in the risk premiums.

Bond investors separate the risk premium into four components:

1. The credit quality of the issue as determined by its risk of default relative to other bonds
2. The term to maturity of the issue, which can affect yield and price volatility
3. Indenture provisions, including collateral, call features, and sinking-fund provisions
4. Foreign bond risk, including exchange rate risk and country risk

Of the four factors, credit quality and maturity have the greatest impact on the risk premium for domestic bonds, while exchange rate risk and country risk are important components of risk for non-U.S. bonds.

The credit quality of a bond reflects the ability of the issuer to service outstanding debt obligations. This information is largely captured in the ratings issued by the bond-rating firms. As a result, bonds with different ratings have different yields. For example, AAA-rated obligations possess lower risk of default than BBB obligations, so they can provide lower yield.

Notably, the risk-premium differences between bonds of different quality levels have changed dramatically over time depending on prevailing economic conditions. When the economy experiences a recession or a period of economic uncertainty, the desire for quality increases, and investors bid up prices of higher-rated bonds, which reduces their yields. This is referred to as the *quality spread*. It has also been suggested by Dialynas and Edington that this spread is influenced by the volatility of interest rates.[11] This variability in the risk premium over time was demonstrated and discussed in Chapter 10.

Term to maturity also influences the risk premium because it affects an investor's level of uncertainty as well as the price volatility of the bond. In the section on the term structure of interest rates, we will discuss the typical positive relationship between the term to maturity of an issue and its interest rate.

As discussed in Chapter 15, indenture provisions indicate the collateral pledged for a bond, its callability, and its sinking-fund provisions. Collateral gives protection to the investor if the issuer defaults on the bond, because the investor has a specific claim on some set of assets in case of liquidation.

Call features indicate when an issuer can buy back the bond prior to its maturity. A bond is called by an issuer when interest rates have declined, so it is typically not to the advantage of the investor who must reinvest the proceeds at a lower interest rate. Therefore, more protection against having the bond called reduces the risk premium. The significance of call protection increases during periods of high interest rates. When you buy a bond with a high coupon, you want protection from having it called away when rates decline.[12]

A sinking fund reduces the investor's risk and causes a lower yield for several reasons. First, a sinking fund reduces default risk because it requires the issuer to reduce the outstanding issue systematically. Second, purchases of the bond by the issuer to satisfy sinking-fund requirements provide price support for the bond because of the added demand. These purchases by the issuer also contribute to a more liquid secondary market for the bond because of the increased trading. Finally, sinking-fund provisions require that the issuer

[11]Chris P. Dialynas and David H. Edington, "Bond Yield Spreads: A Postmodern View," *Journal of Portfolio Management,* 19, no. 1 (Fall 1992): 68–75.

[12]William Marshall and Jess B. Yawitz, "Optimal Terms of the Call Provision on a Corporate Bond," *Journal of Financial Research* 3, no. 3 (Fall 1980): 203–211.

retire a bond before its stated maturity, which causes a reduction in the issue's average maturity. The decline in average maturity tends to reduce the risk premium of the bond much as a shorter maturity would reduce yield.[13]

We know that foreign-currency exchange rates change over time and that this increases the risk of global investing. Differences in the variability of exchange rates among countries arise because the trade balances and rates of inflation differ among countries. More volatile trade balances and inflation rates in a country make its exchange rates more volatile, which increase the uncertainty of future exchange rates. These factors increase the exchange rate risk premium.

In addition to the ongoing changes in exchange rates, investors are always concerned with the political and economic stability of a country. If investors are unsure about the political environment or the economic system in a country, they will increase the risk premium they require to reflect this country risk.

Term Structure of Interest Rates

The **term structure of interest rates** (or the *yield curve,* as it is more popularly known) is a static function that relates the term to maturity to the yield to maturity for a sample of bonds at *a given point in time.*[14] Thus, it represents a cross section of yields for a category of bonds that are comparable in all respects but maturity. Specifically, the quality of the issues should be constant, and ideally you should have issues with similar coupons and call features. You can construct different yield curves for Treasuries, government agencies, prime-grade municipals, AAA utilities, and so on. The accuracy of the yield curve will depend on the comparability of the bonds in the sample.

As an example, Figure 16.3 shows yield curves for a sample of U.S. Treasury obligations. It is based on the yield to maturity information for a set of comparable Treasury issues from a publication such as the *Federal Reserve Bulletin* or the *Wall Street Journal.* These promised yields were plotted on the graph, and a yield curve was drawn that represents the general configuration of rates.

Not all yield curves, of course, have the same shape as those in Figure 16.3. The point of the example is that, although individual yield curves are static, their behavior over time is quite fluid. As seen in Figure 16.3, during the four-week period from February 17 to March 17, 1998, several changes occurred in the term structure. During the first three weeks, the term structure rotated around the six-month rate; that is, rates rose on securities with maturities longer than six months while shorter-term rates fell. During the last week, the process reversed and longer-term rates fell while short-term rates rose.

Also, the shape of the yield curve can undergo dramatic alterations, following one of the four patterns shown in Figure 16.4. The rising yield curve is the most common and tends to prevail when interest rates are at low or modest levels. The declining yield curve tends to occur when rates are relatively high. The flat yield curve rarely exists for any period of time. The humped yield curve prevails when extremely high rates are expected to decline to more normal levels. The slope of the curve tends to level off after fifteen years.

Why does the term structure assume different shapes? Three major theories attempt to explain this: the expectations hypothesis, the liquidity preference hypothesis, and the segmented market hypothesis.

---

[13]For a further discussion of sinking funds, see Edward A. Dyl and Michael D. Joehnk, "Sinking Funds and the Cost of Corporate Debt," *Journal of Finance* 34, no. 4 (September 1979): 887–893; and A. J. Kalotay, "Sinking Funds and the Realized Cost of Debt," *Financial Management* 11, no. 1 (Spring 1982): 43–54.

[14]For a discussion of the theory and empirical evidence, see Richard W. McEnally and James V. Jordan, "The Term Structure of Interest Rates," in *The Handbook of Fixed-Income Securities,* 4th ed., edited by Frank J. Fabozzi and T. Dessa Fabozzi (Chicago: Irwin, 1995).

Figure 16.3 *Treasury Yield Curve*

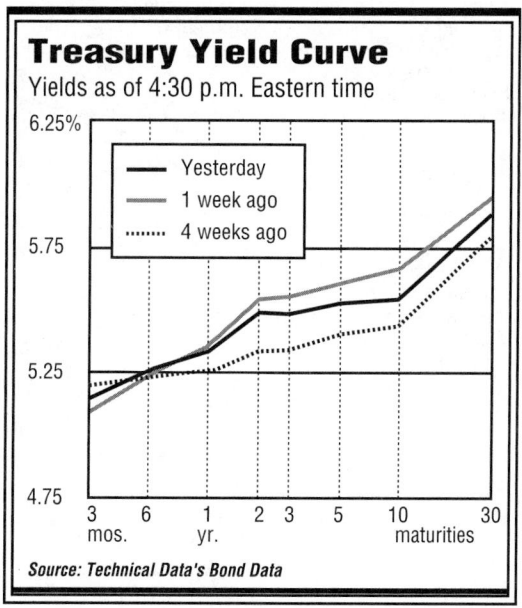

Treasury Yield Curve
Yields as of 4:30 p.m. Eastern time

Legend:
— Yesterday
— 1 week ago
...... 4 weeks ago

Y-axis: 6.25%, 5.75, 5.25, 4.75

X-axis: 3 mos., 6, 1 yr., 2, 3, 5, 10, 30 maturities

Source: Technical Data's Bond Data

Wall Street Journal, March 18, 1998, C17.

Expectations Hypothesis   According to the expectations hypothesis, the shape of the yield curve results from the interest-rate expectations of market participants. More specifically, it holds that *any long-term interest rate simply represents the geometric mean of current and future one-year interest rates expected to prevail over the maturity of the issue.* In essence, the term structure involves a series of intermediate and long-term interest rates, each of which is a reflection of the geometric average of current and expected one-year interest rates. Under such conditions, the equilibrium long-term rate is the rate the long-term bond investor would expect to earn through successive investments in short-term bonds over the term to maturity of the long-term bond.

The expectations theory can explain any shape of yield curve. Expectations for rising short-term rates in the future cause a rising yield curve; expectations for falling short-term rates in the future will cause long-term rates to lie below current short-term rates, and the yield curve will decline. Similar explanations account for flat and humped yield curves. Consider the following example using arithmetic averages:

$$_tR_1 = 5^1/_2\%$$ the 1-year rate of interest prevailing now (period t)

$$_{t+1}r_1 = 6\%$$ the 1-year rate of interest expected to prevail next year (period $t + 1$)

$$_{t+2}r_1 = 7^1/_2\%$$ the 1-year rate of interest expected to prevail 2 years from now (period $t + 2$)

$$_{t+3}r_1 = 8^1/_2\%$$ the 1-year rate of interest expected to prevail 3 years from now (period $t + 3$)

Using these values, and the known rate on a one-year bond, we compute rates on two-, three-, or four-year bonds (designated R_2, R_3, and R_4) as follows:

$$_tR_1 = 5^1/_2\%$$
$$_tR_2 = (0.055 + 0.06)/2 = 5.75\%$$

Figure 16.4   *Types of Yield Curves*

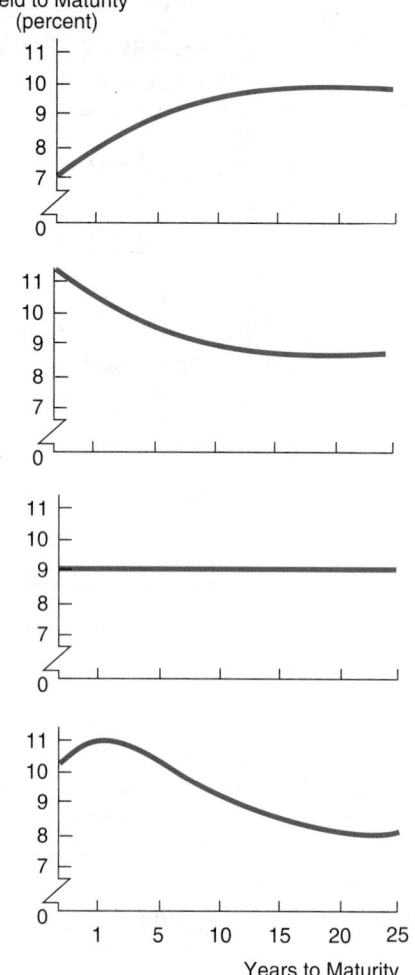

A Rising Yield Curve is formed when the yields on short-term issues are low and rise consistently with longer maturities and flatten out at the extremes.

A Declining Yield Curve is formed when the yields on short-term issues are high and yields on subsequently longer maturities decline consistently.

A Flat Yield Curve has approximately equal yields on short-term and long-term issues.

A Humped Yield Curve is formed when yields on intermediate-term issues are above those on short-term issues; and the rates on long-term issues decline to levels below those for the short-term and then level out.

$$R_3 = (0.055 + 0.06 + 0.075)/3 = 6.33\%$$
$$R_4 = (0.055 + 0.06 + 0.075 + 0.085)/4 = 6.88\%$$

In this illustration (which uses the arithmetic average as an approximation of the geometric mean), the yield curve is upward-sloping because, at present, investors expect future short-term rates to be above current short-term rates. This is not the formal method for constructing the yield curve. Rather it is constructed as demonstrated in Figure 16.3 on the basis of the prevailing promised yields for bonds with different maturities.

The expectations hypothesis attempts to explain *why* the yield curve is upward-sloping, downward-sloping, humped, or flat by explaining the expectations implicit in yield curves with different shapes. The evidence is fairly substantial and convincing that the expectations hypothesis is a workable explanation of the term structure. Because of the supporting evidence, its relative simplicity, and the intuitive appeal of the theory, the expectations hypothesis of the term structure of interest rates is rather widely accepted.

Besides the theory and empirical support, it is also possible to present a scenario wherein investor actions will cause the yield curve postulated by the theory. The expectations

hypothesis predicts a declining yield curve when interest rates are expected to fall in the future rather than rise. In such a case, long-term bonds would be considered attractive investments to buy, because investors would want to lock in prevailing higher yields (which are not expected to be as high in the future) or they would want to capture the increase in bond prices (as capital gains) that will accompany a decline in rates. By the same reasoning, investors will avoid short-term bonds or sell them and reinvest the funds in the more desirable long-term bonds. The point is, investor actions based on their expectations will reinforce the declining shape of the yield curve as they bid up the prices of long-maturity bonds (forcing yields to decline) and short-term bond issues are avoided or sold (so prices decline and yields rise). At the same time, there is confirming action by suppliers of bonds. Specifically, government or corporate issuers will avoid selling long bonds at the current high rates but would want to wait until the rates decline. In the meantime, they will issue short-term bonds if they need funds while waiting for lower long-term rates. Therefore, in the long-term market you will observe an increase in demand and a decline in the supply, which will cause an increase in the price of long bonds and a decline in yields for long-term bonds. The opposite will occur in the short-term market. These shifts between long- and short-term maturities will continue until equilibrium occurs or expectations change.

Although intuitive, using the current term structure and the expectations hypothesis does a poor job of predicting future short-term interest rates. Typically, the term structure is upward-sloped. As we've just seen, this implies that investors anticipate short-term rates to rise in the future. This does *not* agree with the observed behavior of short-term rates over time. Either investors are frequently fooled, or we need other explanations.

Liquidity Preference Hypothesis The theory of liquidity preference holds that long-term securities should provide higher returns than short-term obligations because investors are willing to accept lower yields to invest in short-maturity obligations to avoid the higher price volatility of long-maturity bonds. Another way to interpret the liquidity preference hypothesis is to say that lenders prefer short-term loans, and to induce them to lend long term, it is necessary to offer higher yields.

The liquidity preference theory contends that uncertainty causes investors to favor short-term issues over bonds with longer maturities because short-term bonds can easily be converted into predictable amounts of cash should unforeseen events occur. This theory argues that the yield curve should slope upward and that any other shape should be viewed as a temporary aberration.

This theory can be considered an extension of the expectations hypothesis because the formal liquidity preference position contends that the liquidity premium inherent in the yields for longer maturity bonds should be added to the expected future rate in arriving at long-term yields. Specifically, the liquidity premium compensates the investor in long-term bonds for the added uncertainty because of less stable prices.

Combining this risk premium perspective with the expectations hypothesis explains term-structure behavior better than the expectations hypothesis alone. The term structure should slope upward, presumably because of the liquidity preference-risk premium effect as seen in panel (a) in Figure 16.5. The term structure may become downward sloping, however, if substantial declines in future rates are expected, as shown in panel (b) of Figure 16.5.

As a matter of historical fact, the yield curve shows a definite upward bias, which implies that some combination of the expectations theory and the liquidity preference theory will more accurately explain the shape of the yield curve than either of them alone. Specifically, actual long-term rates consistently tend to be above what is envisioned from the price expectations hypothesis, which implies the existence of a liquidity premium.

Segmented-Market Hypothesis Despite meager empirical support, a third theory that attempts to explain the shape of the yield curve is the segmented-market hypothesis, which

Figure 16.5   *The Combined Effects of the Expectations and Liquidity Preference Hypotheses*

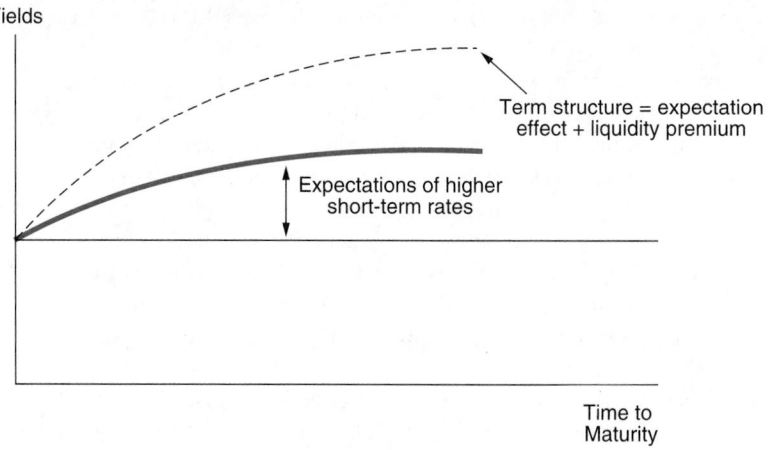

Panel (a). Upward-sloping term structure, showing the combined effects of the liquidity premium and expectations for higher future interest rates.

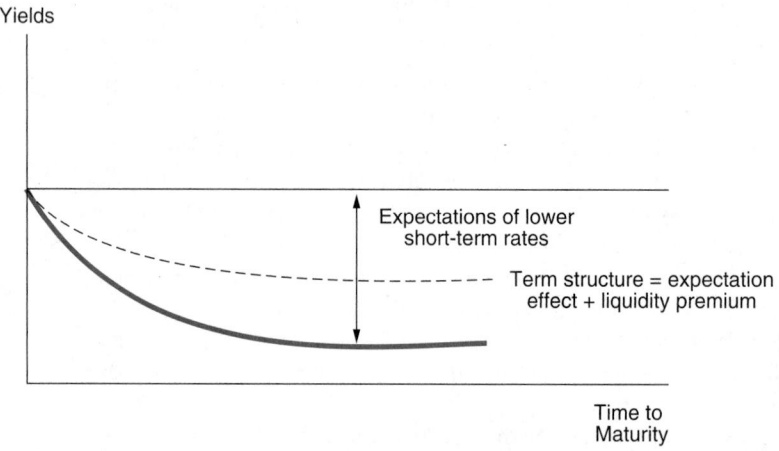

Panel (b). Downward-sloping term structure, showing the combined effects of the liquidity premium and expectations of lower future interest rates.

enjoys wide acceptance among market practitioners. Also known as the *preferred habitat,* the *institutional theory,* or the *hedging pressure theory,* it asserts that different institutional investors have different maturity needs that lead them to confine their security selections to specific maturity segments. That is, investors supposedly focus on short-term, intermediate-term, or long-term securities. This theory contends that the shape of the yield curve is ultimately a function of these investment policies of major financial institutions.

Financial institutions tend to structure their investment policies in line with factors such as their tax liabilities and the types and maturity structure of their liabilities. As an example, because commercial banks are subject to normal corporate tax rates, and their liabilities are generally short- to intermediate-term time and demand deposits, they consistently invest in short- to intermediate-term municipal bonds.

In its strongest form, the segmented-market theory holds that the maturity preferences of investors and borrowers are so strong that investors never purchase securities outside their preferred maturity range to take advantage of yield differentials. As a result, the short- and long-maturity portions of the bond market are effectively segmented, and yields for a particular maturity segment depend on the. supply and demand *within* that maturity segment.

Trading Implications of the Term Structure   Information on maturities can help you to formulate yield expectations by simply observing the shape of the yield curve. If the yield curve is declining sharply, historical evidence suggests that interest rates will probably decline. Expectations theorists would suggest that you need to examine only the prevailing yield curve to predict the direction of interest rates in the future

Based on these theories, bond investors use the prevailing yield curve to predict the shapes of future yield curves. Using this prediction and knowledge of current interest rates, investors can determine expected yield volatility by maturity sector. In turn, the maturity segments that experience the greatest yield changes give the investor the largest potential price appreciation.[15]

Yield Spreads

Another technique that can be used to help make good bond investments or profitable trades is the analysis of **yield spreads**, which are the differences in promised yields between bond issues or segments of the market at any point in time. Such differences in yield are specific to the particular issues or segments of the bond market.

There are four major yield spreads:

1. Different *segments* of the bond market may have different yields. For example, pure government bonds will have lower yields than government agency bonds; and government bonds will have much lower yields than corporate bonds.
2. Bonds in different *sectors* of the same market segment may have different yields. For example, prime-grade municipal bonds will have lower yields than good-grade municipal bonds; you will find spreads between AA utilities and BBB utilities, or between AAA industrial bonds and AAA public utility bonds.
3. Different *coupons* or *seasoning* within a given market segment or sector may cause yield spreads. Examples would include current coupon government bonds versus deep-discount governments, or recently issued AA industrials versus seasoned AA industrials.
4. Different *maturities* within a given market segment or sector also cause differences in yields. You will see yield spreads between short-term agency issues and long-term agency issues, or between three-year prime municipals and twenty-five-year prime municipals.

The differences among these bonds cause yield spreads that may be either positive or negative. More important, *the magnitude or the direction of a yield spread can change over time.* These changes in size or direction of yield spreads offer profit opportunities. We say that the spread narrows whenever the differences in yield become smaller, and it widens as the differences increase. Table 16.1 contains data on a variety of past yield spreads that demonstrates the size of these spreads and shows some large changes over time.

As a bond investor, you should evaluate yield spread changes because these changes influence bond price behavior and comparative return performance. You should attempt to identify (1) any normal yield spread that is expected to become abnormally wide or

---

[15]Gikas A. Hourdouvelis, "The Predictive Power of the Term Structure During Recent Monetary Regimes," *Journal of Finance* 43, no.2 (June 1988): 339–356.

Table 16.1 *Selected Mean Yield Spreads (Reported in Basis Points)*

Comparisons	1990	1991	1992	1993	1994	1995	1996	1997
1. Short Governments—Long Governments[a]	+48	+127	+210	+191	+114	+68	+81	+37
2. Long Governments—Long Aaa Corporates[b]	+58	+61	+62	+77	+56	+66	+57	+69
3. Long Municipals—Long Aaa Corporates[c]	+220	+185	+170	+162	+220	+179	+185	+164
4. Long Aaa Muncipals—Long Baa Municipals[d]	+104	+103	+39	+45	+40	+30	+27	+14
5. AA Utilities—AA Industrials[e]	−20	−9	−18	−7	−1	−3	−8	−9

[a]Median yield to maturity of a varying number of bonds with two to five years maturity and more than ten years, respectively.
[b]Long Aaa corporates based on yields to maturity on selected long-term bonds.
[c]Long-term municipal issues based on Bond Buyer Series, a representative list of high-quality municipal bonds with a twenty-year period to maturity being maintained.
[d]General obligation municipal bonds only.
[e]Based on a changing list of representative issues.

Source: *Federal Reserve Bulletin, Moody's Bond Record.*

narrow in response to an anticipated swing in market interest rates, or (2) an abnormally wide or narrow yield spread that is expected to become normal. A correct estimate of either change will provide profit opportunities.

Economic and market analysis would help you develop these expectations of potential for a yield spread to change. Taking advantage of these changes requires a knowledge of historical spreads and an ability to *predict* not only future changes in the overall market, but also why and when specific spreads will change.[16]

WHAT DETERMINES THE PRICE VOLATILITY FOR BONDS?

In this chapter we have learned about alternative bond yields, how to calculate them, what determines bond yields (interest rates), and what causes them to change. Now that we understand why yields change, we can logically ask, what is the effect of these yield changes on the prices and rates of return for different bonds? We have discussed the inverse relationship between changes in yields and the price of bonds, so we can now discuss *the specific factors that affect the amount of price change for a yield change* in different bonds. This section lists the specific factors that affect bond price changes for a given change in interest rates and demonstrates the effect for different bonds.

The fact is, a given change in interest rates can cause vastly different percentage price changes for alternative bonds. This section will help you understand what causes these differences between price changes. To maximize the rate of return you will receive from a correct forecast of a decline in interest rates, for example, you need to know which bonds will benefit the most from the yield change. This section will help you make this bond selection decision.

Throughout this section we will talk about bond price changes or bond price volatility interchangeably. A bond price change is measured as the percentage change in the price of the bond, computed as follows:

$$\frac{EPB}{BPB} - 1$$

---

[16]A recent article identifies four determinants of relative market spreads and suggests scenarios when they will change. See Chris P. Dialynas and David H. Edington, "Bond Yield Spreads: A Postmodern View," *Journal of Portfolio Management* 19, no. 1 (Fall 1992): 68–75.

where:

EPB = the ending price of the bond
BPB = the beginning price of the bond

Bond price volatility is also measured in terms of percentage changes in bond prices. A bond with high price volatility is one that experiences large percentage price changes for a given change in yields.

Bond price volatility is influenced by more than yield behavior alone. Malkiel used the bond valuation model to demonstrate that the market price of a bond is a function of four factors: (1) its par value, (2) its coupon, (3) the number of years to its maturity, and (4) the prevailing market interest rate.[17] Malkiel's mathematical proofs showed the following relationships between yield (interest rate) changes and bond-price behavior:

1. Bond prices move inversely to bond yields (interest rates).
2. For a given change in yields (interest rates), longer-maturity bonds post larger price changes; thus, bond price volatility is *directly* related to term to maturity.
3. Price volatility (percentage of price change) increases at a diminishing rate as term to maturity increases.
4. Price movements resulting from equal absolute increases or decreases in yield are *not* symmetrical. A decrease in yield raises bond prices by more than an increase in yield of the same amount lowers prices.
5. Higher coupon issues show smaller percentage price fluctuation for a given change in yield; thus, bond price volatility is *inversely* related to coupon.

Homer and Leibowitz showed that the absolute level of market yields also affects bond-price volatility.[18] As the level of prevailing yields rises, the price volatility of bonds increases, *assuming a constant percentage change in market yields*. It is important to note that if you assume a constant percentage change in yield, the basis-point change will be greater when rates are high. For example, a 25 percent change in interest rates when rates are at 4 percent will be 100 basis points; the same 25 percent change when rates are at 8 percent will be a 200 basis-point change. In the discussion of bond duration, we will see that this difference in basis point change is important.

The Maturity Effect

Table 16.2 demonstrates the effect of maturity on price volatility. In all four maturity classes, we assume a bond with an 8 percent coupon and assume the discount rate (nominal YTM) changes from 7 to 10 percent. The only difference among the four cases is the maturities of the bonds. The demonstration involves computing the value of each bond at a 7 percent yield and at a 10 percent yield and noting the percentage change in price. As shown, this change in yield caused the price of the one-year bond to decline by only 2.9 percent, whereas the thirty-year bond declined by almost 29 percent. Clearly, the longer-maturity bond experienced the greater price volatility.

Also, price volatility increased at a decreasing rate with maturity. When maturity doubled from ten years to twenty years, the percent change in price increased by less than 50 percent (from 18.5 percent to 25.7 percent). A similar change occurred when going from twenty years to thirty years. Therefore, this table demonstrates the first three of our

---

[17]Burton G. Malkiel. "Expectations, Bond Prices, and the Term Structure of Interest Rates," *Quarterly Journal of Economics* 76, no.2 (May 1962): 197–218.

[18]Sidney Homer and Martin L. Leibowitz, *Inside the Yield Book* (Englewood Cliffs, NJ.: Prentice-Hall, 1972).

Table 16.2 *Effect of Maturity on Bond Price Volatility*

Term to Maturity	PRESENT VALUE OF AN 8 PERCENT BOND ($1,000 PAR VALUE)							
	1 Year		10 Years		20 Years		30 Years	
Discount rate (nominal YTM)	7%	10%	7%	10%	7%	10%	7%	10%
Present value of interest	$ 75	$ 73	$ 569	$498	$ 858	$686	$1,005	$757
Present value of principal	934	907	505	377	257	142	132	54
Total value of bond	$1,009	$980	$1,074	$875	$1,115	$828	$1,137	$811
Percentage change in total value	−2.9		−18.5		−25.7		−28.7	

price–yield relationships: bond price is inversely related to yields, bond price volatility is positively related to term to maturity, and bond price volatility increases at a decreasing rate with maturity.

It is also possible to demonstrate the fourth relationship with this table. Using the twenty-year bond, if you computed the percentage change in price related to an *increase* in rates (for example, from 7 to 10 percent), you would get the answer reported—a 25.7 percent decrease. In contrast, if you computed the effect on price of a *decrease* in yields from 10 percent to 7 percent, you would get a 34.7 percent increase in price ($1,115 vs. $828). This demonstrates that prices change more in response to a decrease in rates (from 10 percent to 7 percent) than to a comparable increase in rates (from 7 percent to 10 percent).

The Coupon Effect

Table 16.3 demonstrates the coupon effect. In this set of examples, all the bonds have equal maturity (twenty years) and experience the same change in nominal YTM (from 7 percent to 10 percent). The table shows the inverse relationship between a bond's coupon rate and its price volatility: the smallest coupon bond (the zero) experienced the largest percentage price change (almost 45 percent), versus a 24 percent change for the 12 percent coupon bond.

The Yield Level Effect

Table 16.4 demonstrates the yield level effect. In these examples, all the bonds have the same twenty-year maturity and the same 4 percent coupon. In the first three cases the nominal YTM changed by a constant 33.3 percent (from 3 percent to 4 percent, from 6 percent to 8 percent, and from 9 percent to 12 percent). Note that the first change is 100 basis points, the second is 200 basis points, and the third is 300 basis points. The results in the first three columns confirm the statement that when higher yields change by a *constant percentage,* the change in the bond price is larger.

The fourth column shows that if you assume a *constant basis-point change in yields,* you get the opposite results. Specifically, a 100 basis-point change in yields from 3 percent to 4 percent provides a price change of 14.1 percent, while the same 100 basis-point change from 9 percent to 10 percent results in a price change of only 11 percent. Therefore, the yield level effect can differ depending on whether the yield change is specified as a constant percentage change or a constant basis-point change.

In summary, the price volatility of a bond for a given change in yield is affected by the bond's coupon, its term to maturity, the level of yields (depending on what kind of change in yield), and the direction of the yield change. However, although both the level and direction of change in yields affect price volatility, they cannot be used for trading strategies. When yields change, the two variables the investor or portfolio manager can control that have a dramatic effect on bond price volatility are coupon and maturity.

Table 16.3 *Effect of Coupon on Bond Price Volatility*

	PRESENT VALUE OF TWENTY-YEAR BOND ($1,000 PAR VALUE)							
	0 Percent Coupon		3 Percent Coupon		8 Percent Coupon		12 Percent Coupon	
Discount rate (nominal YTM)	7%	10%	7%	10%	7%	10%	7%	10%
Present value of interest	$ 0	$ 0	$322	$257	$ 858	$686	$1,287	$1,030
Present value of principal	257	142	257	142	257	142	257	142
Total value of bond	$257	$142	$579	$399	$1,115	$828	$1,544	$1,172
Percentage change in total value	−44.7		−31.1		−25.7		−24.1	

Table 16.4 *Effect of Yield Level on Bond Price Volatility*

	PRESENT VALUE OF A 20-YEAR, 4 PERCENT BOND ($1,000 PAR VALUE)							
	(1) Low Yield		(2) Intermediate Yields		(3) High Yields		(4) 100 Basis-Point Change at High Yields	
Discount rate (nominal YTM)	3%	4%	6%	8%	9%	12%	9%	10%
Present value of interest	$ 602	$ 547	$462	$396	$370	$301	$370	$343
Present value of principal	562	453	307	208	175	97	175	142
Total value of bond	$1,164	$1,000	$769	$604	$545	$398	$545	$485
Percentage change in total value	−14.1		−21.5		−27.0		−11.0	

Some Trading Strategies

Knowing that coupon and maturity are the major variables that influence bond price volatility, we can develop some strategies for maximizing rates of return when interest rates change. Specifically, if you expect a major *decline* in interest rates, you know that bond prices will increase, so you want a portfolio of bonds with the *maximum price volatility* so that you will enjoy maximum price changes (capital gains) from the change in interest rates. In this situation, the previous discussion regarding the effect of maturity and coupon indicates that you should attempt to build a portfolio of long-maturity bonds with low coupons (ideally a zero-coupon bond). A portfolio of such bonds should experience the maximum price appreciation for a given decline in market interest rates.

In contrast, if you expect an *increase* in market interest rates, you know that bond prices will decline, and you want a portfolio with *minimum price volatility* to minimize the capital losses caused by the increase in rates Therefore, you would want to change your portfolio to short-maturity bonds with high coupons. This combination should provide minimal price volatility for a change in market interest rates.

The Duration Measure

Because the price volatility of a bond varies inversely with its coupon and directly with its term to maturity, it is necessary to determine the best combination of these two variables to achieve your objective. This effort would benefit from a composite measure that considered both coupon and maturity. Fortunately, such a measure, the **duration** of a

security, was developed more than sixty years ago by Macaulay.[19] Macaulay showed that the duration of a bond was a more appropriate measure of time characteristics than the term to maturity of the bond, because duration considers both the repayment of capital at maturity, and the size and timing of coupon payments prior to final maturity. Duration is defined as *the weighted average time to full recovery of principal and interest payments.* Using annual compounding, duration (D) is

16.13
$$D = \frac{\sum\limits_{t=1}^{n} \dfrac{C_t(t)}{(1+i)^t}}{\sum\limits_{t=1}^{n} \dfrac{C_t}{(1+i)^t}} = \frac{\sum\limits_{t=1}^{n} t \times \mathrm{PV}(C_t)}{\text{price}}$$

where:

t = time period in which the coupon or principal payment occurs
C_t = interest or principal payment that occurs in period t
i = yield to maturity on the bond

The denominator in Equation 16.13 is the price of a bond as determined by the present value model. The numerator is the present value of all cash flows *weighted according to the time to cash receipt.* The following example, which demonstrates the specific computations for two bonds, shows the procedure and highlights some of the properties of duration. Consider the following two sample bonds:

	Bond A	Bond B
Face value	$1,000	$1,000
Maturity	10 years	10 years
Coupon	4%	8%

Assuming annual interest payments and an 8 percent effective yield to maturity on the bonds, duration is computed as shown in Table 16.5. Duration computed by discounting flows using the yield to maturity of the bond is called *Macaulay duration.* We will use Macaulay duration throughout this chapter.

Characteristics of Duration   This example illustrates several characteristics of duration. First, the duration of a bond with coupon payments will always be less than its term to maturity, because duration gives weight to these interim payments.

Second, *an inverse relationship exists between coupon and duration.* A bond with a larger coupon will have a shorter duration because more of the total cash flows come earlier in the form of interest payments. As shown in Table 16.5, the 8 percent coupon bond has a shorter duration than the 4 percent coupon bond.

A bond with no coupon payments (a zero-coupon bond or a pure-discount bond such as a Treasury bill) will have duration *equal* to its term to maturity. In Table 16.5, if you assume a single payment at maturity, you will see that duration will equal term to maturity because the only cash flow comes in the final (maturity) year.

Third, *a positive relationship generally holds between term to maturity and duration,* but duration increases at a decreasing rate with maturity. Therefore, all else being the same, a bond with longer term to maturity will almost always have a higher duration. Note that the relationship is not direct, because as maturity increases, the present value of the principal declines in value.

---

[19] Frederick R. Macaulay, *Some Theoretical Problems Suggested by the Movements of Interest Rates, Bond Yields, and Stock Prices in the United States Since 1856* (New York: National Bureau of Economic Research, 1938).

Table 16.5   *Computation of Duration (Assuming 8 Percent Market Yield)*

BOND A

(1) Year	(2) Cash Flow	(3) PV at 8%	(4) PV of Flow	(5) PV as % of Price	(6) (1) × (5)
1	$ 40	.9259	$ 37.04	.0506	.0506
2	40	.8573	34.29	.0469	.0938
3	40	.7938	31.75	.0434	.1302
4	40	.7350	29.40	.0402	.1608
5	40	.6806	27.22	.0372	.1860
6	40	.6302	25.21	.0345	.2070
7	40	.5835	23.34	.0319	.2233
8	40	.5403	21.61	.0295	.2360
9	40	.5002	20.01	.0274	.2466
10	1,040	.4632	481.73	.6585	6.5850
Sum			$731.58	1.0000	8.1193

Duration = 8.12 Years

BOND B

(1) Year	(2) Cash Flow	(3) PV at 8%	(4) PV of Flow	(5) PV as % of Price	(6) (1) × (5)
1	$ 80	.9259	$ 74.07	.0741	.0741
2	80	.8573	68.59	.0686	.1372
3	80	.7938	63.50	.0635	.1906
4	80	.7350	58.80	.0588	.1906
5	80	.6806	54.44	.0544	.2720
6	80	.6302	50.42	.0504	.3024
7	80	.5835	46.68	.0467	.3269
8	80	.5403	43.22	.0432	.3456
9	80	.5002	40.02	.0400	.3600
10	1,080	.4632	500.26	.5003	5.0030
Sum			$1,000.00	1.0000	7.2470

Duration = 7.25 Years

As shown in Figure 16.6, the shape of the duration–maturity curve depends on the coupon and the yield to maturity. The curve for a zero-coupon bond is a straight line, indicating that duration equals term to maturity. In contrast, the curve for a low-coupon bond selling at a deep discount (due to a high YTM) will turn down at long maturities, which means that under these conditions the longer-maturity bond will have lower duration.

Fourth, all else the same, there is an *inverse relationship between YTM and duration.* A higher yield to maturity of a bond reduces its duration. As an example, in Table 16.5, if the yield to maturity had been 12 percent rather than 8 percent, the durations would have been about 7.75 and 6.80 rather than 8.12 and 7.25.[20]

Finally, sinking funds and call provisions can have a dramatic effect on a bond's duration. They can accelerate the total cash flows for a bond and, therefore, significantly reduce its duration.[21] Between these two factors, the factor that causes the greatest uncertainty is the call feature because it is difficult to estimate when it will be exercised. We will consider this further in the section where we consider the effect of the call feature on the convexity of a bond.

---

[20]These properties are discussed and demonstrated in Frank K Reilly and Rupinder Sidhu, "The Many Uses of Bond Duration," *Financial Analysts Journal* 36, no.4 (July–August 1980): 58–72; and Frank J. Fabozzi, Mark Pitts, and Ravi E. Dattatreya, "Price Volatility Characteristics of Fixed Income Securities," in *The Handbook of Fixed-Income Securities,* 5th ed., edited by Frank J. Fabozzi (Chicago: Irwin, 1997).

[21]An example of the computation of duration with a sinking fund and a call feature is contained in Reilly and Sidhu, "The Many Uses of Bond Duration."

Figure 16.6 *Duration versus Maturity*

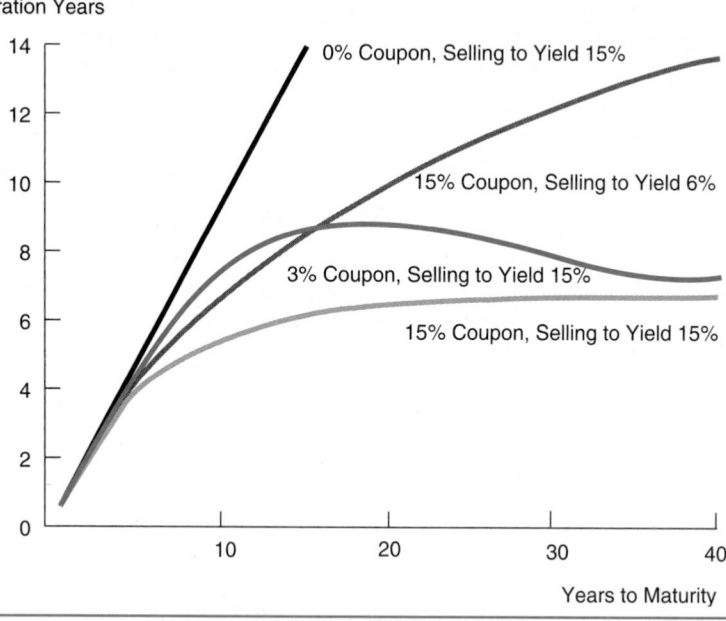

A summary of duration characteristics is as follows:

♦ The duration of a zero-coupon bond will *equal* its term to maturity.
♦ The duration of a coupon bond will always be less than its term to maturity.
♦ An *inverse* relationship exists between coupon and duration.
♦ There is generally a *positive* relationship between term to maturity and duration. Note that duration increases at a decreasing rate with maturity. Also, the duration of a deep-discount bond will decline at long maturities (over twenty years).
♦ An *inverse* relationship exists between yield to maturity and duration.
♦ Sinking funds and call provisions can cause a dramatic decline in the duration of a bond because of an early payoff (maturity). As noted, the effect of the call feature is discussed in a subsequent section.

The duration measure can be useful to you as a bond investor because it combines the properties of maturity and coupon to measure the time flow of cash from the bond. This is superior to term to maturity, which only considers when the principal will be repaid at maturity. As shown, duration is positively related to term to maturity and inversely related to coupon and to YTM.

Duration and Bond Price Volatility

Duration is more than a superior measure of the time flow of cash from the bond. An adjusted measure of duration called **modified duration** can be used to approximate the price volatility of a bond:

$$\text{modified duration} = \frac{\text{Macaulay duration}}{1 + \dfrac{\text{YTM}}{m}}$$

where:

 m = number of payments a year
YTM = nominal YTM

As an example, a bond with a Macaulay duration of ten years, a nominal yield to maturity of 8 percent, and semiannual payments would have a modified duration of

$$D_{mod} = 10/\left(1 + \frac{.08}{2}\right)$$

$$= 10/(1.04) = 9.62 \text{ years}$$

It has been shown, both theoretically and empirically, that bond price movements *will vary proportionally* with modified duration *for small changes in yields.*[22] Specifically, as shown in Equation 16.14, an estimate of the percentage change in bond price equals the change in yield times modified duration.

16.14
$$\frac{\Delta P}{P} \times 100 = -D_{mod} \times \Delta YTM$$

where:

  ΔP = change in price for the bond
   P = beginning price for the bond
  D_{mod} = the modified duration of the bond
ΔYTM = yield change in basis points divided by 100. For example, if interest rates go from
        8.00 to 8.50 percent, $\Delta YTM = 50/100 = 0.50$

The negative sign indicates that the price change is in the opposite direction of the interest rate change (i.e., when rates fall, prices rise, and vice versa).

Consider a bond with $D = 8$ years and $i = 0.10$. Assume you expect the bond's YTM to decline by 75 basis points (for example, from 10 percent to 9.25 percent). The first step is to compute the bond's modified duration as follows:

$$D_{mod} = 8/\left(1 + \frac{.10}{2}\right)$$

$$= 8/(1.05) = 7.62 \text{ years}$$

The estimated percentage change in the price of the bond using Equation 16.14 is as follows:

$$\%\Delta P = -(7.62) \times \frac{-75}{100}$$

$$= (-7.62) \times (-.75)$$

$$= 5.72$$

This indicates that the bond price should increase by approximately 5.72 percent in response to the 75 basis point decline in YTM. If the price of the bond before the

---

[22]A generalized proof of this is contained in Michael H. Hopewell and George Kaufman, "Bond Price Volatility and Term to Maturity: A Generalized Respecification," *American Economic Review* 63, no. 4 (September 1973): 749–753. The importance of the specification "for small changes in yields" will become clear when we discuss convexity in the next section.

| Table 16.6 | *Bond Duration in Years for Bond Yielding 6 Percent under Different Terms* | | | |

	COUPON RATES			
Years to Maturity	0.02	0.04	0.06	0.08
1	0.995	0.990	0.985	0.981
5	4.756	4.558	4.393	4.254
10	8.891	8.169	7.662	7.286
20	14.981	12.980	11.904	11.232
50	19.452	17.129	16.273	15.829
100	17.567	17.232	17.120	15.829
∞	17.167	17.167	17.167	17.167

Source: L. Fisher and R. L. Weil, "Coping with the Risk of Interest Rate Fluctuations: Returns to Bondholders from Naive and Optimal Strategies," *Journal of Business* 44, no. 4 (October 1971): 418. Copyright 1971. University of Chicago Press.

decline in interest rates was $900, the price after the decline in interest rates should be approximately $900 × 1.0572 = $951.48.

The modified duration is always a negative value for a noncallable bond because of the inverse relationship between yield changes and bond price changes. Also, you should remember that this formulation provides an *estimate* or *approximation* of the percentage change in the price of the bond. The following section on convexity will show that the formula that uses modified duration provides an exact estimate of the percentage price change only for small changes in yields.

Trading Strategies Using Duration   We know from the prior discussion on the relationship between modified duration and bond price volatility that the longest-duration security provides the maximum price variation. Table 16.6 demonstrates the numerous ways to achieve a given level of duration. The duration measure has become increasingly popular because it conveniently specifies the time flow of cash from a security considering both coupon and term to maturity. Therefore, the following discussion indicates that an active bond investor can use this measure to structure a portfolio to take advantage of changes in market yields.

If you expect a *decline* in interest rates, you should *increase* the average duration of your bond portfolio to experience maximum price volatility. Alternatively, if you expect an *increase* in interest rates, you should *reduce* the average duration of your portfolio to minimize your price decline. Note that the duration of your portfolio is the market-value-weighted average of the durations of the individual bonds in the portfolio.

Bond Convexity

Modified duration allows us to estimate bond price changes for a change in interest rates. Equation 16.14 is, however, accurate only for *small changes* in market yields. We will see that the accuracy of the estimate of the price change deteriorates with larger changes in yields because the modified duration calculation specified in Equation 16.14 is a *linear* approximation of a bond price change which, in fact, follows a *curvilinear* (convex) function. To understand the effect of this **convexity,** we must consider the price–yield relationship for alternative bonds.[23]

---

[23]For a further discussion of this topic, see Mark L. Dunetz and James M. Mahoney, "Using Duration and Convexity in the Analysis of Callable Bonds," *Financial Analysts Journal* 44, no. 3 (May–June 1988): 53–73.

Table 16.7 *Price–Yield Relationships for Alternative Bonds*

A. 12 PERCENT, 20-YEAR BOND		B. 12 PERCENT, 3-YEAR BOND		C. ZERO-COUPON, 30-YEAR BOND	
Yield	Price	Yield	Price	Yield	Price
1.0%	$2,989.47	1.0%	$1,324.30	1.0%	$741.37
2.0	2,641.73	2.0	1,289.77	2.0	550.45
3.0	2,346.21	3.0	1,256.37	3.0	409.30
4.0	2,094.22	4.0	1,224.06	4.0	304.78
5.0	1,878.60	5.0	1,192.78	5.0	227.28
6.0	1,693.44	6.0	1,162.52	6.0	169.73
7.0	1,533.88	7.0	1,133.21	7.0	126.93
8.0	1,395.86	8.0	1,104.84	8.0	95.06
9.0	1,276.02	9.0	1,077.37	9.0	71.29
10.0	1,171.59	10.0	1,050.76	10.0	53.54
11.0	1,080.23	11.0	1,024.98	11.0	40.26
12.0	1,000.00	12.0	1,000.00	12.0	30.31

The Price–Yield Relationship for Bonds Because the price of a bond is the present value of its cash flows at a particular discount rate, if you are given the coupon, maturity, and a yield for a bond, you can calculate its price at a point in time. The price–yield curve provides a set of prices for a specific maturity-coupon bond at a point in time using a range of yields to maturity (discount rates). As an example, Table 16.7 lists the computed prices for a 12 percent, twenty-year bond assuming nominal yields from 1 percent to 12 percent. For example, the table shows that discounting the flows from this 12 percent, twenty-year bond at a yield of 1 percent, you would get a price of $2,989.47; discounting these same flows at 10 percent gives a price of $1,171.59. The graph of these prices relative to the yields that produced them in Figure 16.7 indicates that the price–yield relationship for this bond is not a straight line but a curvilinear relationship. That is, it is convex.

Three points are important about the price–yield relationship:

1. This relationship can be applied to a single bond, a portfolio of bonds, or any stream of future cash flows.
2. The convex price–yield relationship will differ among bonds or other cash flow streams, depending on the nature of the cash flow stream, that is, its coupon and maturity. As an example, the price–yield relationship for a high-coupon, short-term security will be almost a straight line because the price does not change as much for a change in yields (for example, the 12 percent, three-year bond in Table 16.7). In contrast, the price–yield relationship for a low-coupon, long-term bond will curve radically (that is, be strongly convex), as shown by the zero-coupon, thirty-year bond in Table 16.7. These differences in convexity are shown graphically in Figure 16.8. The curved nature of the price–yield relationship is referred to as the bond's *convexity*.
3. As shown by the graph in Figure 16.7, because of the convexity of the price–yield relationship, as yield increases, the rate at which the price of the bond declines becomes slower. Similarly, when yields decline, the rate at which the price of the bond increases becomes faster. Convexity is therefore a desirable trait.

Given this price–yield curve, modified duration is the percentage change in price for a nominal change in yield as follows:[24]

---

[24]In mathematical terms, modified duration is the first differential of this price–yield relationship with respect to yield.

Figure 16.7   *Price–Yield Relationship and Modified Duration at 4-Percent Yield*

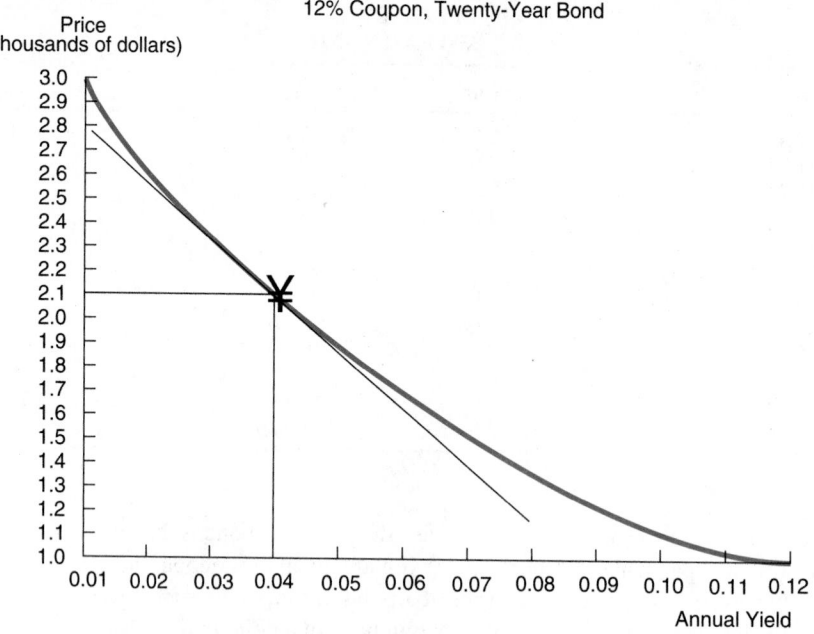

12% Coupon, Twenty-Year Bond

Price
(thousands of dollars)

Annual Yield

Figure 16.8   *Price–Yield Curves for Alternative Bonds*

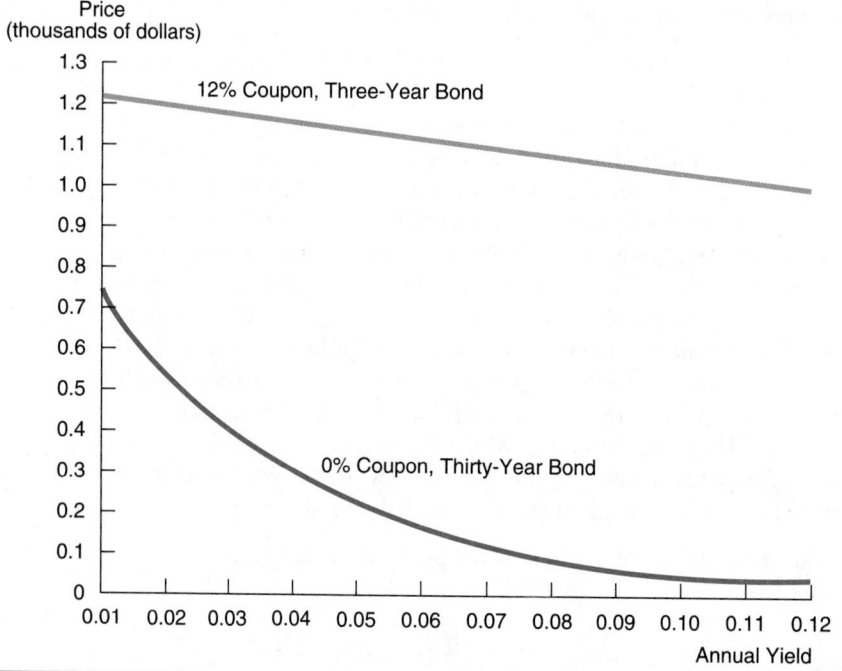

Price
(thousands of dollars)

12% Coupon, Three-Year Bond

0% Coupon, Thirty-Year Bond

Annual Yield

Figure 16.9 *Price Approximation Using Modified Duration*

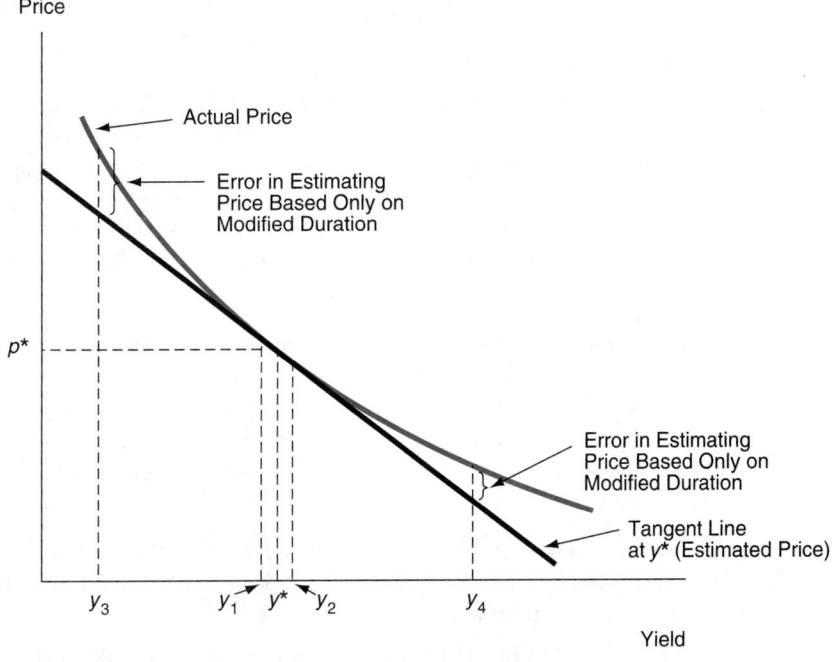

Source: Frank J. Fabozzi, Mark Pitts, and Ravi E. Dattatreya, "Price Volatility Characteristics of Fixed Income Securities," in *Handbook of Fixed Income Securities,* 5th ed., edited by Frank J. Fabozzi (Chicago: Irwin, 1997). Reprinted by permission of the publisher.

16.15
$$D_{mod} = \frac{\frac{dP}{di}}{P}$$

Notice that the *dP/di* line is tangent to the price–yield curve *at a given yield* as shown in Figure 16.9. For *small* changes in yields (i.e., from y^* to either y_1 or y_2), this tangent straight line gives a good estimate of the actual price changes. In contrast, for larger changes in yields (from y^* to either y_3 or y_4), the straight line will estimate the new price of the bond at less than the actual price shown by the price–yield curve. This misestimate arises because the modified-duration line is a linear estimate of a curvilinear relationship. Specifically, the estimate using only modified duration will *underestimate* the actual price *increase* caused by a yield decline and *overestimate* the actual price *decline* caused by an increase in yields. This graph, which demonstrates the convexity effect, also shows that price changes are *not* symmetric when yields increase or decrease. As shown, when rates decline, a larger price error occurs than when rates increase because when yields decline prices rise at an *increasing* rate, while prices decline at a *decreasing* rate when yields rise.

Determinants of Convexity   Convexity is a measure of the curvature of the price–yield relationship. Mathematically, convexity is the second derivative of price with respect to yield (d^2P/di^2) divided by price. Specifically, convexity is the percentage change in *dP/di* for a given change in yield:

| 16.16 | | $$\text{Convexity} = \frac{\dfrac{d^2P}{di^2}}{P}$$ |

Convexity is a measure of how much a bond's price–yield curve deviates from the linear approximation of that curve. As indicated by Figures 16.7 and 16.9 for *noncallable* bonds, convexity is always a positive number, implying that the price–yield curve lies above the modified duration (tangent) line. Figure 16.8 illustrates the price–yield relationship for two bonds with widely different coupons and maturities. (The yields and prices are contained in Table 16.7.)

These graphs demonstrate the following relationship between these factors and the convexity of a bond.

♦ An *inverse* relationship exists between coupon and convexity (yield and maturity constant).
♦ A *direct* relationship exists between maturity and convexity (yield and coupon constant).
♦ An *inverse* relationship exists between yield and convexity (coupon and maturity constant). This means that the price–yield curve is more convex at its lower-yield (upper left) segment.

Therefore, a short-term, high-coupon bond, such as the 12 percent coupon, three-year bond in Figure 16.8, has low convexity—it is almost a straight line. In contrast, the zero-coupon, thirty-year bond has high convexity.

The Modified Duration–Convexity Effects   In summary, the change in a bond's price resulting from a change in yield can be attributed to two sources: the bond's modified duration and its convexity. The relative effect of these two factors on the price change will depend on the characteristics of the bond (its convexity) and the size of the yield change. For example, if you are estimating the prices change for a 300 basis-point change in yield for a zero-coupon, thirty-year bond, the convexity effect would be fairly large, because this bond would have high convexity, and a 300 basis-point change in yield is relatively large. In contrast, if you are dealing with only a 10 basis-point change in yields, the convexity effect would be minimal because it is a small change in yield. Similarly, the convexity effect would be small for a larger yield change if you are concerned with a bond with small convexity (high coupon, short maturity) because its price–yield relationship is almost a straight line.

In conclusion, modified duration can help you derive an *approximate* percentage bond price change for a given change in interest rates, but you must remember that it is only a good estimate when you are considering small yield changes. You must also consider the convexity effect when you are dealing with large yield changes or when the security has high convexity. Investors see convexity as something desirable. Given two bonds with identical durations, they prefer the one with the greater convexity. The higher convexity bond will give greater price appreciation if rates fall and a smaller price loss should rates rise.

Investments Online

Bond valuation focuses on bond mathematics, the term structure, and bond features that add to the yield (such as callability) or lead to lower yields (such as putability). Bonds are normally easier to evaluate than stocks, given their stated life, cash flows, and

SUMMARY

♦ The value of a bond equals the present value of all future cash flows accruing to the investor. Cash flows for the conservative bond investor include periodic interest payments and principal return; cash flows for the aggressive investor include periodic interest payments and the capital gain or loss when the bond is sold prior to its maturity. Bond investors can maximize their rates of return by accurately estimating the level of interest rates, and more importantly, changes in interest rates and yield spreads. Similarly, they must compare coupon rates, maturities, and call features of alternative bonds.

♦ The five bond-yield measures are coupon rate, current yield, promised yield to maturity, promised yield to call, and realized (horizon) yield. The promised YTM and promised YTC equations include an implied interest-on-interest, or coupon reinvestment assumption. For the realized (horizon) yield computation, the investor estimates the reinvestment rate and may need to also estimate the future selling price for the bond. The fundamental determinants of interest rates are a real risk-free rate, the expected rate of inflation, and a risk premium.

♦ The yield curve (or the term structure of interest rates) shows the relationship between the yields on a set of comparable bonds and the term to maturity. Yield curves exhibit four basic patterns. Three theories attempt to explain the shape of the yield curve: the expectations hypothesis, the liquidity preference hypothesis, and the segmented market hypothesis.

♦ It is important to understand what causes changes in interest rates and also how these changes in rates affect the prices of bonds. We demonstrated that differences in bond price volatility are mainly a function of differences in yield, coupon, and term to maturity. The duration measure incorporates coupon, maturity, and yield in one measure that provides an estimate of the response of bond prices to changes in interest rates. Because modified duration provides a straight-line estimate of the curvilinear price–yield function, you must consider modified duration together with the convexity of a bond when estimating price changes for large changes in yields and/or when dealing with securities that have high convexity.

Questions

1. Why does the present-value equation appear to be more useful for the bond investor than for the common stock investor?

2. What are the important assumptions made when you calculate the promised yield to maturity? What are the assumptions when calculating promised YTC?

3. a. Define the variables included in the following model:

$$i = (RFR, I, RP)$$

   b. Assume the firm whose bonds you are considering is not expected to break even this year. Discuss which factor will be affected by this information.

4. We discussed three alternative hypotheses to explain the term structure of interest rates. Which one do you think best explains the alternative shapes of a yield curve? Defend your choice.

5. *CFA Examination I (June 1982)*

   a. Explain *term structure of interest rates*. Explain the theoretical basis of an upward-sloping yield curve. [8 minutes]

   b. Explain the economic circumstances under which you would expect to see the inverted yield curve prevail. [7 minutes]

   c. Define "real" rate of interest. [2 minutes]

   d. Discuss the characteristics of the market for U.S. Treasury securities. Compare it to the market for AAA corporate bonds. Discuss the opportunities that may exist in bond markets that are less than efficient. [8 minutes]

   e. Over the past several years, fairly wide yield spreads between AAA corporates and Treasuries have occasionally prevailed. Discuss the possible reasons for this. [5 minutes]

6. *CFA Examination III (June 1982)*

   As the portfolio manager for a large pension fund, you are offered the following bonds:

	Coupon	Maturity	Price	Call Price	Yield to Maturity
Edgar Corp. (new issue)	14.00%	2002	$101.3/4	$114	13.75%
Edgar Corp. (new issue)	6.00	2002	48.1/8	103	13.60
Edgar Corp. (1972 issue)	6.00	2002	48.7/8	103	13.40

   Assuming you expect a decline in interest rates over the next three years, identify and justify which of these bonds you would select. [10 minutes]

7. You expect interest rates to decline over the next six months.

   a. Given your interest rate outlook, state what kind of bonds you want in your portfolio in terms of duration and explain your reasoning for this choice.

   b. You must make a choice between the following three sets of noncallable bonds. In each case, select the bond that would be best for your portfolio given your interest rate outlook and the strategy suggested in part a. In each case, briefly discuss why you selected the bond.

		Maturity	Coupon	Yield to Maturity
Case 1:	Bond A	15 years	10%	10%
	Bond B	15 years	6%	8%
Case 2:	Bond C	15 years	6%	10%
	Bond D	10 years	8%	10%
Case 3:	Bond E	12 years	12%	12%
	Bond F	15 years	12%	8%

8. At the present time you expect a decline in interest rates and must choose between two portfolios of bonds with the following characteristics.

	Portfolio A	Portfolio B
Average maturity	10.5 years	10.0 years
Average YTM	7%	10%

	Portfolio A	Portfolio B
Modified duration	5.7 years	4.9 years
Modified convexity	125.18	40.30
Call features	Noncallable	Deferred call features that range from 1 to 3 years

Select one of the portfolios and discuss three factors that would *justify* your selection.

9. *CFA Examination 1 (1991)*

   Bill Peters is the investment officer of a $60 million pension fund. He has become concerned about the big price swings that have occurred lately in the fund's fixed-income securities. Peters has been told that such price behavior is only natural given the recent behavior of market yields. To deal with the problem, the pension fund's fixed-income money manager keeps track of exposure to price volatility by closely monitoring bond duration. The money manager believes that price volatility can be kept to a reasonable level as long as portfolio duration is maintained at approximately seven to eight years.

   Discuss the concepts of duration and convexity and explain how *each* fits into the price–yield relationship. In the situation described above, explain why the money manager should have used both duration and convexity to monitor the bond portfolio's exposure to price volatility. [15 minutes]

10. *CFA Examination I (1992)*

    A bond analyst is looking at a twenty-year, AA-rated corporate bond. The bond is noncallable and carries a coupon of 7.50 percent. The analyst computes both the standard yield to maturity and horizon return for this bond, which are as follows:

    Yield to maturity   8.00%
    Horizon return   8.96%

    Assuming the bond is held to maturity, explain why these *two* measures of return differ. [5 minutes]

11. *CFA Examination I (1993)*

    The yield to maturity on a bond is:
    a. below the coupon rate when the bond sells at a discount and above the coupon rate when the bond sells at a premium.
    b. the interest rate that makes the present value of the payments equal to the bond price.
    c. based on the assumption that all future payments received are reinvested at the coupon rate.
    d. based on the assumption that all future payments received are reinvested at future market rates.

12. *CFA Examination I (1993)*

    Which *one* of the following statements about the term structure of interest rates is *true?*
    a. The expectations hypothesis indicates a flat yield curve if anticipated future short-term rates exceed current short-term rates.
    b. The expectations hypothesis contends that the long-term rate is equal to the anticipated short-term rate.
    c. The liquidity premium theory indicates that, all else being equal, longer maturities will have lower yields.
    d. The market segmentation theory contends that borrowers and lenders prefer particular segments of the yield curve.

13. Bond-price volatility is normally highest for bonds with what coupon, duration, and maturity characteristics?

14. Under what circumstances will the yield to maturity and current yield be equal?

15. Which of the following bonds has the longest duration?
    a. nine-year maturity, 8% coupon
    b. nine-year maturity, 12% coupon
    c. sixteen-year maturity, 8% coupon
    d. sixteen-year maturity, 12% coupon

16. What is the relationship between the Macaulay duration and time to maturity of a zero-coupon bond?

Problems

1. Four years ago your firm issued $1,000 par, twenty-five-year bonds, with a 7 percent coupon rate and a 10 percent call premium.
   a. If these bonds are now called, what is the *approximate* yield to call for the investors who originally puchased them at par?
   b. If these bonds are now called, what is the *actual* yield to call for the investors who orginally purchased them at par? Quote it both on a nominal and an effective annual yield.
   c. If the current interest rate is 5 percent and the bonds were not callable, at what price would each bond sell?

2. Assume you purchased an 8 percent, twenty-year, $1,000 par, semiannual payment bond priced at $1,012.50 when it has twelve years remaining until maturity. Compute:
   a. Its approximate yield to maturity
   b. Its actual yield to maturity (nominal *and* effective)
   c. Its approximate yield to call if the bond is callable in three years with an 8 percent premium

3. Calculate the duration of an 8 percent, $1,000 par bond that matures in three years if the bond's YTM is 10 percent and interest is paid semiannually.
   a. Calculate this bond's modified duration.
   b. Assuming the bond's YTM goes from 10 percent to 9.5 percent, calculate an estimate of the price change.

4. Two years ago you acquired a ten-year zero-coupon, $1,000 par value bond at a 12 percent nominal YTM. Recently you sold this bond at an 8 percent nominal YTM. Using semiannual compounding, compute the annualized horizon return for this investment.

5. A bond for the Webster Corporation has the following characteristics:

   Maturity—12 years
   Coupon—10 percent
   Yield to Maturity—9.50 percent
   Macaulay duration—5.7 years
   Convexity—48
   Noncallable

   Calculate the approximate price change for this bond using only its duration assuming its yield to maturity increased by 150 basis points. Discuss (without calculations) the impact of including the convexity effect in the calculation.

6. *CFA Examination I (1993)*
   Philip Morris has issued bonds that pay semiannually with the following characteristics:

   Coupon—8 percent
   Yield to maturity—8 percent
   Maturity—15 years
   Macaulay duration—10 years

   a. Calculate modified duration using the information above. [5 minutes]
   b. Explain why modified duration is a better measure than maturity when calculating the bond's sensitivity to changes in interest rates. [5 minutes]
   c. Identify the direction of change in modified duration if:
      i. the coupon of the bond were 4 percent, not 8 percent.
      ii. the maturity of the bond were seven years, not fifteen years. [5 minutes]
   d. Define convexity and explain how modified duration *and* convexity are used to approximate the bond's percentage change in price, given a change in interest rates. [5 minutes]

7. *CFA Examination I (1994)*
   Bonds of Zello Corporation with a par value of $1,000 sell for $960, mature in five years, and have a 7% annual coupon rate paid semiannually.
   a. Calculate the:
      i. current yield;

   ii. yield-to-maturity (to the nearest whole percent, i.e., 3%, 4%, 5%, etc.); *and*
   iii. horizon yield (also called total return) for an investor with a three year holding period and a reinvestment rate of 6% over the period. At the end of three years the 7% coupon bonds with two years remaining will sell to yield 7%.
   Show your work. [9 minutes]
b. Cite *one* major shortcoming for *each* of the following fixed-income yield measures:
   i. current yield;
   ii. yield to maturity; *and*
   iii. horizon yield (also called total return). [6 minutes]
8. A bond with ten years to maturity has a yield to maturity of 12 percent and a modified duration of seven years. If the market yield falls by 100 basis points, what will be the bond's expected price change?

References

Dialynas, Chris P., and David H. Edington. "Bond Yield Spreads: A Postmodern View." *Journal of Portfolio Management* 19, no. 1 (Fall 1992).

Dunetz, Mark L., and James M. Mahoney. "Using Duration and Convexity in the Analysis of Callable Bonds." *Financial Analysts Journal* 44, no. 3 (May–June 1988).

Fabozzi, Frank J. "Bond Pricing and Return Measures," in Frank J. Fabozzi, ed. *The Handbook of Fixed Income Securities,* 5th ed. Chicago: Irwin, 1997.

Fabozzi, Frank J., Mark Pitts, and Ravi E. Dattatreya. "Price Volatility Characteristics of Fixed Income Securities," in Frank J. Fabozzi, ed. *The Handbook of Fixed Income Securities,* 5th ed. Chicago: Irwin, 1997.

Kritzman, Mark. "What Practitioners Need to Know about Duration and Convexity." *Financial Analysts Journal* 48, no. 6 (November–December 1992).

Macaulay, Frederick R. *Some Theoretical Problems Suggested by the Movements of Interest Rates, Bond Yields, and Stock Prices in the United States Since 1856.* New York: National Bureau of Economic Research, 1938.

Reilly, Frank K., and Rupinder Sidhu. "The Many Uses of Bond Duration." *Financial Analysts Journal* 36, no. 4 (July–August 1980).

Sundaresan, Suresh. *Fixed Income Markets and Their Derivatives.* Cincinnati, OH: South-Western Publishing, 1997.

Tuckman, Bruce. *Fixed Income Securities.* New York: John Wiley & Sons, 1995.

Van Horne, James C. *Financial Market Rates and Flows.* 5th ed. Englewood Cliffs, N.J.: Prentice-Hall, 1998.

GLOSSARY

Bond price volatility   The percentage changes in bond prices over time.

Convexity   A measure of the degree to which a bond's price–yield curve departs from a straight line. This characteristic affects estimates of a bond's price volatility.

Crossover point   The price at which it becomes profitable for an issuer to call a bond. Above this price, yield to call is the appropriate yield measure.

Current yield   A bond's yield as measured by its current income (coupon) as a percentage of its market price.

Discount   A bond selling at a price below par value due to capital market conditions.

Duration   A composite measure of the timing of a bond's cash flow characteristics taking into consideration its coupon and term to maturity.

Ending-wealth value   The total amount of money derived from investment in a bond until maturity, including principal, coupon payments, and income from reinvestment of coupon payments.

Equivalent taxable yield (ETY)   A yield on a tax-exempt bond that adjusts for its tax benefits to allow comparisons with taxable bonds.

Interest-on-interest   Bond income from reinvestment of coupon payments.

Internal rate of return (IRR)   The discount rate at which cash outflows of an investment equal cash inflows.

Modified duration   A measure of Macaulay duration adjusted to help you estimate a bond's price volatility.

Nominal yield   A bond's yield as measured by its coupon rate.

Premium A bond selling at a price above par value due to capital market conditions.

Promised yield to call (YTC) A bond's yield if held until the first available call date, with reinvestment of all coupon payments at the yield-to-call rate.

Promised yield to maturity The most widely used measure of a bond's yield that states the fully compounded rate of return on a bond bought at market price and held to maturity with reinvestment of all coupon payments at the yield to maturity (YTM) rate.

Realized (horizon) yield The expected compounded yield on a bond that is sold before it matures assuming the reinvestment of all cash flows at an explicit rate.

Term structure of interest rates The relationship between term to maturity and yield to maturity for a sample of comparable bonds at a given time. Popularly known as the *yield curve*.

Yield The promised rate of return on an investment under certain assumptions.

Yield illusion The erroneous expectation that a bond will provide its stated yield to maturity without recognizing the implicit reinvestment assumption related to coupon payments.

Yield spread The difference between the promised yields of various bond issues or market segments at a given time.

6

DERIVATIVE SECURITIES

THUS FAR WE'VE EXAMINED THE WORKINGS OF SECURITIES markets and the analysis of stocks and bonds. We've seen that equities and bonds have a value because the underlying assets they represent have value. Without the ability of real assets to generate cash flows or to promise some future cash flows, a company's stocks and bonds would have no value today. Their value is derived from the value for the company's underlying real assets.

In turn, a major development in the past 25 years has been the creation and growth of new markets and instruments beyond stocks and bonds. This growth has occurred in the area referred to as *derivatives*. These instruments create a wider range of risk-return opportunities for investors. Chapter 17 provides an initial descrip-

tion of these instruments and markets, including an understanding of the fundamental principles that determine their prices. These instruments are very useful in creating additional risk-return alternatives that can be used in your portfolio development. These instruments—known as forwards, futures, and options—are called derivatives, as they derive their value from an underlying financial security, often a company's stock.

Chapter 18 examines advanced derivative instruments, beginning with options on futures. We'll look at their characteristics, pricing, and how the pricing differs from these options compared to straight exchange-traded options. This chapter will also review warrants and convertible securities.

An Introduction to Derivative Instruments

In this chapter we will answer the following questions:

♦ What are the basic features of forward contracts, futures contracts, and options contracts?

♦ What are the similarities and differences between forward contracts and futures contracts?

♦ What terminology do we use to describe option contracts?

♦ What factors influence the price of an option?

♦ What are the relationships among the prices of puts, calls, and futures?

♦ What are some uses of derivatives in investment analysis and portfolio management? ♦

Our financial system has always demonstrated a remarkable tendency to evolve and develop new markets and instruments. In recent years, this tendency has been exhibited most clearly in the rapid development and use of derivative instruments. A **derivative instrument** has its value determined by, or derived from, the value of another investment vehicle, called the underlying asset or security. Earlier in the book we briefly described options and futures, which form the basis for much derivative trading. However, many new instruments have been created that possess some of the characteristics of options or futures and indeed some instruments that are like both options and futures. The incredible growth in the use of derivatives and the occasional controversy they engender make it all the more important that we develop an early understanding of derivatives and their role in our financial markets. This chapter introduces basic derivative instruments—forwards, futures, and options—and describes their characteristics, pricing, and some selected investment and portfolio management strategies.

Forward contracts are agreements between two parties, the buyer and seller, for the former to purchase an asset from the latter at a specific future date at a price agreed on up front. No money changes hands between the buyer and seller when the forward contract is initiated, thus, a forward contract itself is not an asset but merely an agreement. Forward contracts are created in the over-the-counter market. **Futures contracts** are somewhat like forward contracts in that they represent an agreement between a buyer and a seller to exchange a specified amount of cash for an asset at a specified future date. Unlike forward contracts, futures contracts trade on an exchange and are subject to a daily settling-up process, which will be described in more detail later. **Options** are instruments that grant to their owners the right, but not the obligation, to buy or sell something at a fixed price, either on a specific date or any time up to a specific date. Unlike a forward or futures contract, the owner of an options contract is not obliged to follow through on it if the transaction is not in his or her best interest; thus the name of "option" contract. The owner has the option to execute, or not execute, the contract.

In derivatives parlance, the buyer and seller of a contract are sometimes referred to as **counterparties** in the derivatives transaction. The buyer of a contract is said to be **long** in the contract. The seller, or writer of the contract, is **short** the contract.

Although their names are different, forwards, futures, and options have similar general characteristics. First, they all specify the asset underlying the contract and the quantity of the asset to be traded. Second, they all specify a length of time over which the contract is in force. The transaction is to be completed, or the option exercised, on or before the contract's expiration date. Third, they allow the buyer of the contract to lock in a transaction price; we call this the **exercise** or **strike price**. If the purchaser exercises his or her option, or when the forward or futures contract is fulfilled, the trade occurs at the exercise price specified in the contract. Fourth, the profit or loss on the contract depends on the relationship between the asset's *market price* (or *spot price*) and the exercise price at the time the contract is executed or when it expires. Generally, profits or losses on forward and futures contracts closely follow changes in the asset's market price. Notably, owners of option contracts can protect themselves against large losses by merely choosing not to exercise their option.

WHY DO DERIVATIVES EXIST?

Most assets that you know, such as stocks, bonds, gold, or real estate, are traded in the cash or **spot market**. The primary and secondary markets we examined earlier in the text are examples of spot markets. In these markets trades occur, and cash, along with ownership of the asset, is transferred between buyer and seller.

At times, it may be advantageous to enter into a transaction immediately with the promise that the exchange of the asset and money will take place at a future time. As an illustration, a portfolio manager may anticipate month-end cash flows from investors but she wishes to purchase attractively priced securities now, fearing their prices will rise. A corporate treasurer may want to lock in today's borrowing rates, fearing they will rise in the future. A farmer may want to lock in attractive July corn prices, although his crops won't be harvested for several months.

Such exchanges allow a transaction price to be determined today for a trade that will not occur until a mutually agreed upon future date. This can occur with two types of derivative securities, a forward contract and a futures contract. As an example, in June a wheat farmer can lock in the price at which he can sell his harvest in September by selling a September wheat contract, which means that the profits on his crop will not be affected by price swings in the wheat spot market between now and harvest time.

Others may wish to enter into an agreement that allows for a future cash transaction, but only if the contract buyer finds it in his best interest to do so. A derivative security called an option contract allows the purchaser to ultimately decide whether or not to execute the trade in the future. For example, a real estate developer may purchase an option to buy property at a fixed price during a specified time period; should property values rise, she will choose to exercise the option and purchase the land for the specified price. Alternatively, a wheat farmer may enter into an option contract to sell his harvest at a predetermined price; should the spot market price for wheat be lower at harvest, he will execute his option and receive the predetermined price. In contrast, should the spot wheat price be higher, he will choose to sell his wheat at the higher spot price and let the option contract expire. Similar option contracts exist for financial assets such as individual stocks, stock indexes, interest rates, and currencies.

Over time, derivatives such as forwards, futures, and options have evolved to fulfill desirable economic purposes. They help shift risk from those who don't want it to those who are willing to bear it; they assist in forming cash prices and provide additional information to the market. Finally, the trading mechanisms for derivatives have evolved so that in many cases it may be less costly, in terms of both commissions and required investment, to invest in derivatives rather than in the cash market. The following subsections will discuss each of these benefits in more detail.

Risk Shifting

The farmer who wants to reduce his risk can hedge by locking in now a price for wheat to be delivered at harvest. This is done by entering into a forward or futures contract with someone who is willing to bear the risk of fluctuating spot prices. The grain buyers may be speculators who believe they can gain by agreeing to buy wheat at preset prices because they think they can sell the wheat at a higher spot price in the future. Alternatively, the buyer of the contract may be a grain processor who wants to hedge the risk of fluctuating spot wheat prices by agreeing to purchase the grain in the future at a predetermined price.

The use of option contracts affects the asset's risk–return profile, because the option owner can decide not to exercise it if the transaction is disadvantageous from her perspective. Thus, options can be used to control risk by limiting losses while protecting profit opportunities.

As these illustrations show, derivative contracts can help control risk. Those wishing to reduce their exposure to a fluctuating spot price can do so by using derivatives. Similarly, an investor or speculator who is willing to increase (or "leverage") his exposure to risk can do so via appropriate derivatives trades. Later in this chapter we'll give examples of several strategies which can be used to increase or decrease exposure to risk. Additionally, Chapter 19, Equity Portfolio Management and Chapter 20, Fixed Income Portfolio Management, will illustrate how we use derivatives to modify a portfolio's risk–return profile.

Price Formation

Speculators trade in the derivative markets not only because they are willing to carry risk that others wish to hedge, but also because they believe the asset is incorrectly priced based on their analysis and information. Because speculators bring additional information into the market, the prices of the underlying assets and their corresponding futures and options contracts should more accurately reflect the intrinsic values of the assets. As shown later in this chapter, the spot, futures, and option prices are interrelated by arbitrage rela-

tionships. That means information affecting the spot market will also affect derivative prices and vice versa.

Derivative prices also provide information that can be analyzed to assist decision making. For example, some investors use futures prices as the market's best estimate for future spot prices. This can aid planning, as futures markets can provide these estimates for certain commodities, financial assets, and currency exchange rates.

Investment Cost Reduction

As the derivative markets have evolved, commissions are generally lower than in the corresponding cash market. Liquidity in this market is also enhanced as many hedgers and speculators trade derivatives. Rather than place a bet on the direction of the stock market by paying commissions and purchasing shares in each of the S&P 500 Index firms, they can purchase a single futures contract that represents the entire index. Therefore, portfolio managers can quickly adjust their portfolio's risk exposures at lower cost using futures than by using spot market trades. Unlike a spot market transaction, commodity derivative contracts do not require the purchaser to pay for storing the commodity. Additionally, margin requirements are less in futures transactions than they are on the spot market.

Though they may seem esoteric and daunting when first introduced, derivatives play an important economic role in allocating risk, forming prices, and facilitating transactions. Similar to other investment vehicles, careless or improper use of derivatives can lead to large losses. Even risk-loving speculators, when taking a large position in one market, will often hedge their risk to limit their loss by taking an offsetting position in another market.

In the following sections, we review some specifics about forwards, futures, and options contracts and the relationship between their value and that of the underlying security.

FORWARD CONTRACTS

A forward contract is an agreement between two parties to exchange an asset at a specified price at a specified date. Because it is a contract, the buyer is obligated to purchase the asset and the seller is obligated to sell at the predetermined price (the exercise price) on the specified date (the expiration date). The buyer of the contract is said to be *long forward;* the seller is said to be *short forward.*

Forward contracts are traded over the counter and are generally not standardized, meaning that as long as the buyer and seller negotiate agreeable terms, they can create their own forward contract on virtually any commodity. Notably, this flexibility has a major drawback: *forward contracts are not liquid.* Should a buyer or seller wish to get out of a forward agreement, she needs to find another party to purchase it. Another potential problem with forwards is credit risk or default risk. The contract may not be executed as planned if the buyer cannot raise the cash needed to purchase the asset, or if the seller commits fraud by not delivering the asset to be sold.

The profit or loss on a forward contract relates directly to the relationship between the actual market price of the underlying asset and the exercise price contained in the contract. The value of a forward contract is realized only at the expiration date; no payments are made at the initiation of the contract and no cash transfers are made prior to expiration.

As shown in Figure 17.1, if the market price rises above the exercise price, the buyer gains (and the seller loses, because the asset will be sold at a price below current value);

Figure 17.1   *Payoff Profiles for Long and Short Positions in a Forward Contract*

A farmer and a grain processor enter into a forward contract that obliges the farmer to sell grain to the processor at an exercise price of $3 per bushel.

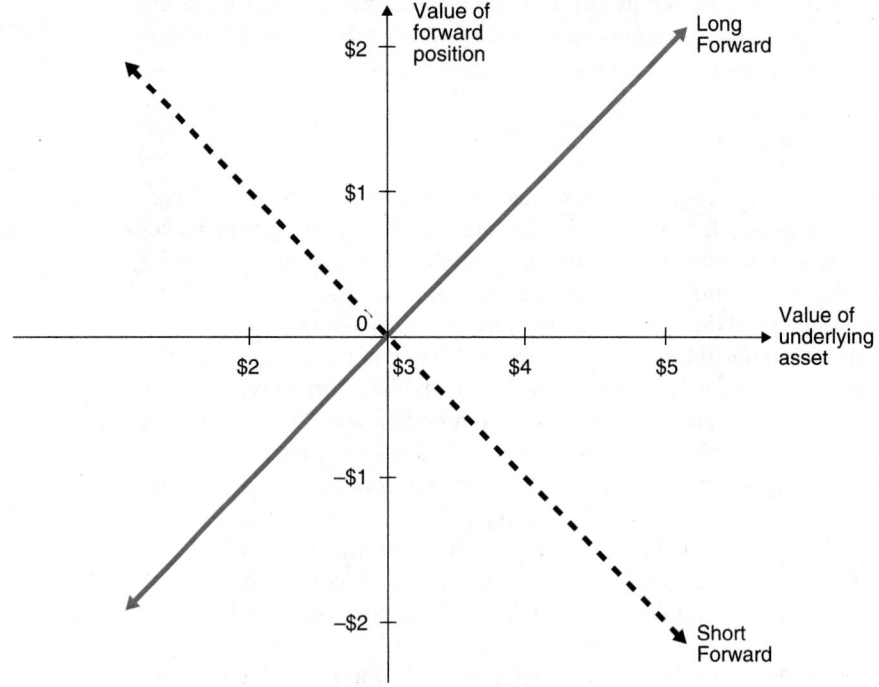

should the price fall below the exercise price, the buyer loses (and the seller gains, because the asset is sold for a price greater than its current value). Suppose a grain processor buys a forward contract from a farmer for October delivery of grain at a price of $3 a bushel. Figure 17.1 shows the grain processor's payoff profile for her long forward position (heavy arrow). Should the October spot market price be $3 a bushel, the processor breaks even as the spot price equals the previously set forward price. If the October spot price is $4 a bushel, the processor gains $1 a bushel. She is able to purchase grain which has a $4 market value at the $3 forward price. The processor's profits rise dollar for dollar as the spot price rises above the $3 forward price.

If the October spot price is only $2, the processor loses $1 per bushel; she is obligated to buy the grain for the $3 forward price, although its current spot price is $2. The processor's losses increase dollar for dollar as the spot price falls below the $3 forward price.

The situation is reversed for the farmer, who is short forward (dotted arrow). As the October spot market price rises further above $3 a bushel, the farmer suffers an opportunity loss as he is obligated to sell his grain for $3 a bushel. If the market price is $4, he has a $1-per-bushel opportunity loss. If the market price rises to $5, he has a $2-per-bushel opportunity loss. For October spot prices under $3, the forward contract generates a profit for the farmer. If the October spot price is $2, his forward contract allows him to sell his grain for $3, netting him a $1 opportunity profit.

The diagram in Figure 17.1 is called a payoff profile; it illustrates the profits and losses on an investment. The payoff profile for a long forward position is similar to that from owning the underlying asset outright; price increases make the owner wealthier. Similarly, the payoff profile for a short forward position resembles that from a short sale of the underlying asset.

Figure 17.2 *Spot and Forward Exchange Rates for January 29, 1998*

CURRENCY TRADING

EXCHANGE RATES
Thursday, January 29, 1998

The New York foreign exchange selling rates below apply to trading among banks in amounts of $1 million and more, as quoted at 4 p.m. Eastern time by Dow Jones and other sources. Retail transactions provide fewer units of foreign currency per dollar.

Country	U.S. $ equiv. Thu	U.S. $ equiv. Wed	Currency per U.S. $ Thu	Currency per U.S. $ Wed
Argentina (Peso)	1.0001	1.0001	.9999	.9999
Australia (Dollar)	.6718	.6814	1.4885	1.4676
Austria (Schilling)	.07806	.07872	12.811	12.704
Bahrain (Dinar)	2.6525	2.6525	.3770	.3770
Belgium (Franc)	.02659	.02673	37.610	37.415
Brazil (Real)	.8921	.8921	1.1210	1.1210
Britain (Pound)	1.6390	1.6425	.6101	.6088
1-month forward ...	1.6367	1.6402	.6110	.6097
3-months forward ...	1.6315	1.6349	.6129	.6117
6-months forward ...	1.6243	1.6280	.6156	.6143
Canada (Dollar)	.6826	.6859	1.4649	1.4580
1-month forward ...	.6832	.6865	1.4637	1.4566
3-months forward ...	.6843	.6877	1.4614	1.4541
6-months forward ...	.6854	.6891	1.4591	1.4511
Chile (Peso)	.002207	.002219	453.20	450.75
China (Renminbi)	.1203	.1203	8.3100	8.3100
Colombia (Peso)	.0007465	c.0007478	1339.57	c1337.30
Czech. Rep. (Koruna) ...	....	....	....	....
Commercial rate	.02859	.02875	34.977	34.778
Denmark (Krone)	.1435	.1448	6.9670	6.9050
Ecuador (Sucre)	....	....	....	....
Floating rate	.0002240	.0002240	4465.00	4465.00
Finland (Markka)	.1815	.1829	5.5104	5.4677
France (Franc)	.1633	.1646	6.1230	6.0735
1-month forward ...	.1636	.1649	6.1133	6.0637
3-months forward ...	.1641	.1655	6.0927	6.0432
6-months forward ...	.1649	.1662	6.0650	6.0153
Germany (Mark)	.5472	.5517	1.8275	1.8125
1-month forward ...	.5481	.5526	1.8246	1.8096
3-months forward ...	.5500	.5546	1.8183	1.8032
6-months forward ...	.5525	.5571	1.8100	1.7949
Greece (Drachma)	.003456	.003489	289.31	286.62
Hong Kong (Dollar)	.1292	.1293	7.7375	7.7355
Hungary (Forint)	.004847	.004859	206.33	205.82
India (Rupee)	.02580	.02584	38.760	38.700
Indonesia (Rupiah)	.00009302	.00008658	10750.00	11550.00
Ireland (Punt)	1.3725	1.3881	.7286	.7204
Israel (Shekel)	.2785	.2796	3.5912	3.5770
Italy (Lira)	.0005546	.0005593	1803.00	1788.00
Japan (Yen)	.007959	.007998	125.65	125.03
1-month forward	.007990	.008030	125.15	124.54

Country	U.S. $ equiv. Thu	U.S. $ equiv. Wed	Currency per U.S. $ Thu	Currency per U.S. $ Wed
3-months forward ...	.008062	.008105	124.03	123.38
6-months forward ...	.008160	.008204	122.55	121.89
Jordan (Dinar)	1.4134	1.4134	.7075	.7075
Kuwait (Dinar)	3.2819	3.2776	.3047	.3051
Lebanon (Pound)	.0006555	.0006555	1525.50	1525.50
Malaysia (Ringgit)	.2291	.2275	4.3653	4.3950
Malta (Lira)	2.5221	2.5349	.3965	.3945
Mexico (Peso)	....	....	....	....
Floating rate	.1179	.1190	8.4800	8.4030
Netherland (Guilder) ..	.4851	.4906	2.0614	2.0383
New Zealand (Dollar) .	.5819	.5949	1.7185	1.6810
Norway (Krone)	.1318	.1327	7.5848	7.5348
Pakistan (Rupee)	.02296	.02296	43.560	43.560
Peru (new Sol)	.3639	.3641	2.7482	2.7462
Philippines (Peso)	.02353	.02381	42.500	42.000
Poland (Zloty)	.2830	.2845	3.5340	3.5145
Portugal (Escudo)	.005343	.005390	187.17	185.54
Russia (Ruble) (a)	.1653	.1652	6.0505	6.0535
Saudi Arabia (Riyal) ...	.2666	.2666	3.7505	3.7508
Singapore (Dollar)	.5806	.5812	1.7225	1.7205
Slovak Rep. (Koruna) .	.02823	.02843	35.421	35.174
South Africa (Rand) ...	.2032	.2032	4.9205	4.9220
South Korea (Won)	.0005922	.0005922	1688.50	1688.50
Spain (Peseta)	.006446	.006507	155.14	153.67
Sweden (Krona)	.1237	.1248	8.0868	8.0105
Switzerland (Franc)	.6791	.6828	1.4725	1.4645
1-month forward ...	.6815	.6852	1.4673	1.4594
3-months forward ...	.6867	.6902	1.4563	1.4488
6-months forward ...	.6938	.6974	1.4414	1.4338
Taiwan (Dollar)	.02942	.02942	33.996	33.996
Thailand (Baht)	.01860	.01860	53.750	53.750
Turkey (Lira)	.00000466	.00000466	214705.00	214705.00
United Arab (Dirham) ..	.2723	.2723	3.6730	3.6730
Uruguay (New Peso) ..	....	....	....	....
Financial	.1002	.1002	9.9800	9.9800
Venezuela (Bolivar) ...	.001961	.001964	509.82	509.28
	---	---		
SDR	1.3526	1.3517	.7393	.7398
ECU	1.0799	1.0877	....	....

Special Drawing Rights (SDR) are based on exchange rates for the U.S., German, British, French , and Japanese currencies. Source: International Monetary Fund.

European Currency Unit (ECU) is based on a basket of community currencies.

a-fixing, c-Corrected. Moscow Interbank Currency Exchange. Ruble newly-denominated Jan. 1998.

The Wall Street Journal daily foreign exchange data for 1996 and 1997 may be purchased through the Readers' Reference Service (413) 592-3600.

Source: *Wall Street Journal*, January 30, 1998, C14

The large market for forward contracts in currencies allows corporations and financial institutions to enter into forward contracts to hedge exchange rate risks. The spot market for currencies is an informal network of financial institutions that trade large volumes of currencies by telephone or wire. Figure 17.2 illustrates the currency spot quotations that appear in the *Wall Street Journal*. Most major currencies of capitalist countries are included, although many of these currencies do not freely float with other currencies. In these cases, the exchange rates are established either by government order or by the country's central bank, which intervenes to keep the exchange rate at a given level. Note that quotes for a spot and several forward rates are included for most major trading partners of the United States.

For the example day, January 29, 1998, the spot price of the German mark was $0.5472, which means that 1 million German marks are equivalent to DM 1,000,000 ($0.5472/DM) = $547,200. In the third column the same quote is inverted, that is, expressed as units of German currency per U.S. dollar; $1 million is equivalent to $1,000,000 (DM1.8275/$) = $1,827,500. On that same day, the one-month forward rate for marks was $0.5481, which means that you could have entered into an agreement to buy DM1,000,000 in one month

at a price of $548,100. Of course, these quotations should not be interpreted as precise, because they are based on a sampling of banks and represent large transactions. Moreover, the bid–ask spread does not appear in these rates.

FUTURES CONTRACTS

A futures contract is in some ways much like a forward contract. As with a forward, a futures contract obliges the owner to purchase the underlying asset at a specified price (the exercise price or futures price) on a specified day. The payoff profile for investors that are long (short) futures is identical to the long (short) forward payoff profile shown in Figure 17.1. Futures, however, have two major distinctions that differentiate them from forwards.

First, they have *less liquidity risk* because they are traded on major futures exchanges. Futures contracts have standardized terms and conditions, such as quality and quantity of the underlying asset and expiration dates. This standardization allows futures to be bought and sold in secondary markets, just like common stocks. Someone purchasing (or selling) a futures contract can offset her obligation by selling (or purchasing) the identical type of contract.

Second, futures have *less credit risk* or default risk than forwards. Purchasers and sellers of futures are required to deposit funds, the **initial margin**, in a margin account with the exchange's clearing corporation or clearinghouse. The initial margin requirement is usually 3 percent to 6 percent of the value of the contract. Funds are added to or subtracted from the margin account daily, reflecting that day's price changes in the futures contract (at the end of each trading day, a special exchange committee determines the approximate closing price, called the **settlement price**, for each futures contract). Thus, futures are cash-settled every day through this process, known as "marking to the market." Similar to common stocks, if an investor's margin account becomes too low, the maintenance margin limit is reached and the investor must place additional funds in the margin account or have his position closed.

Thus, rather than buying or selling futures from a specific investor, the futures exchange becomes the counterparty to all transactions. Should an investor default, the exchange, rather than a specific investor, covers any losses. But the daily settling of accounts through marking to the market and the maintenance margin requirements helps to prevent an investor's deficit from growing unchecked until contract maturity.

Parties that cannot deposit the funds required on a daily basis will have their contracts liquidated. Thus, some have compared futures contracts to "a series of forward contracts [in which] each day yesterday's contract is settled and today's contract is written."[1] That is, a futures contract is like a forward contract that was purchased yesterday, expires today, and is replaced with a new one-day forward contract priced to reflect today's expectations. This contract expires tomorrow, at which time settlement occurs and a new one-day forward is created at a price reflecting tomorrow's expectations, and so on.

Although the Chicago Board of Trade is the oldest futures exchange, many other futures exchanges operate in the United States and in the rest of the world. Table 17.1 lists the U.S. futures exchanges and provides a few details about them.

The Chicago Board of Trade (CBOT) remains the largest futures exchange, but it is rivaled by the Chicago Mercantile Exchange (CME). Although the CBOT specializes in

---

[1]Fischer Black, "The Pricing of Commodity Contracts," *Journal of Financial Economics* 3, nos. 1, 2 (January–March 1976): 167–179.

Table 17.1 *U.S. Futures Exchanges*

Chicago Board of Trade (CBOT) Referred to as "The Board of Trade." The world's oldest and largest futures exchange. The primary exchange for futures on agricultural commodities and a major market for trading in financial futures, particularly on intermediate and long-term Treasury securities.

Chicago Mercantile Exchange (CME) Referred to as "The Merc." The second largest futures exchange. Originally specialized in livestock futures, but now most trading is in stock index, interest rate, and foreign currency futures through its subsidiaries the Index and Option Market and the International Monetary Market.

Commodity Exchange (COMEX) Referred to as "Comex." The primary market for metal futures.

Coffee, Sugar, and Cocoa Exchange (CSCE) Located in New York. Specializes in coffee, sugar, and cocoa.

Kansas City Board of Trade (KCBT) Specializes in grain and has a small volume in stock index futures. It was the first exchange to offer trading in stock index futures.

MidAmerica Commodity Exchange (MCE) Referred to as "The MidAm." Trades scaled-down versions of many of the contracts on the Chicago Board of Trade and Chicago Mercantile Exchange.

Minneapolis Grain Exchange (MGE) Small volume of trading in grain futures.

New York Cotton Exchange (NYCTN) Specializes in cotton and orange juice, which trades on its subsidiary the Citrus Associates and has a small volume of trading in currency and financial futures on its subsidiary the Financial Instruments Exchange (FINEX).

New York Futures Exchange (NYFE) Referred to as "NYFE" (pronounced "Nife"). Created out of the New York Stock Exchange. Specializes in stock index futures and has a small volume of trading in a commodity futures index and in Treasury bond futures.

New York Mercantile Exchange (NYMEX) Referred to as "NYMEX." The primary market for energy futures.

Philadelphia Board of Trade (PBT) Created out of the Philadelphia Stock Exchange. Has a small volume of trading in currency futures. In June 1998 it agreed to a merger with the American and NASDAQ exchanges, to occur during a five-year transition period.

Twin Cities Board of Trade (TCBT) Created out of the Minneapolis Grain Exchange. Has a small volume of trading in currency futures.

---

grains, its biggest contract is its highly successful U.S. Treasury bond futures, which was launched in 1977 and has traditionally experienced the largest volume of any futures contract. The CME originally specialized in livestock futures, but most of its current volume comes from numerous successful futures contracts on foreign currencies, stock indexes, and the Eurodollar. The third largest exchange is the New York Mercantile Exchange (NYMEX), which specializes in futures on energy products such as crude oil, gasoline, and heating oil. Trading in these contracts has exploded in recent years, because NYMEX's contracts have enabled firms to hedge the extremely volatile energy market. A listing of some of the more popular contracts with their exchanges is provided in Table 17.2

How do futures contracts develop? As part of their marketing function, the futures exchanges develop futures contracts for outstanding assets (for example, commodities, bonds) that they believe will meet the needs of various traders and investors. In late 1997, futures trading began on two new futures contracts that may be of interest to individual and institutional investors. One, called the "mini" S&P 500 futures, allows futures trading on a contract that is one-tenth the value of the regular S&P 500 futures contract. The second allows futures trading on the value of the Dow Jones Industrial Average, one of the world's best-known stock-market indexes and one with which most individual investors are familiar.

Figure 17.3 presents an example of the futures quotation page from the *Wall Street Journal.* Suppose you were considering buying a corn futures contract. The listing shows that the contract trades at the Chicago Board of Trade (CBT, using the *Wall Street Journal's* abbreviation) and trades in units of 5,000 bushels. The price quoted is in cents per bushel. The

Table 17.2 *Popular Futures Contracts and Exchanges*

Underlying Asset	Exchange
A. Physical Commodities	
Corn, soybeans, soybean meal, soybean oil, wheat	Chicago Board of Trade
Cattle—feeder, cattle—live, hogs, pork bellies	Chicago Mercantile Exchange
Lumber	
Heating oil	
Cocoa, coffee, sugar—world, sugar—domestic	Cocoa, Sugar, and Coffee
	Exchange
Copper, gold, silver	New York Commodity Exchange
Crude oil, heating oil, gasoline, natural gas	New York Mercantile Exchange
Platinum	
B. Financial Securities	
Yen, deutsche mark, Canadian dollar, Swiss franc,	International Monetary Market
British pound, Mexican peso, Australian dollar,	(Chicago Mercantile Exchange)
Treasury bills, Eurodollar (LIBOR), mini	
S&P 500, S&P 500 Index, Nikkei 225 Index,	
Russell 2000 Index	
Treasury bonds, Treasury notes, Municipal bond index,	Chicago Board of Trade
federal funds, Dow Jones Industrial Avg	
Major Market Index	
Eurodollar, British gilt, German bunds	London International Financial
Euromarks, Eurofrancs, Eurolira	Futures Exchange
FT-SE 100 Index	

September contract on the fourth line opened at 285 cents per bushel, had a high of 286 cents per bushel, and a low of $284\frac{1}{4}$ cents per bushel. The settlement price, which is roughly the closing price and is the price at which contracts are marked to market, was $284\frac{3}{4}$ cents per bushel. The settlement price was down by $\frac{1}{2}$ cent per bushel from the previous day. During the lifetime of the September 1998 contract, its high was 301 and its low was 244. The open interest, the number of contracts currently outstanding, was 9,369. At the bottom of each commodity listing is summary information on the overall volume, the volume the previous day, and the overall open interest for this commodity.

The right column of the figure contains the stock-index futures contracts. If you were interested in the S&P 500 futures, you would see that it trades at the Chicago Mercantile Exchange (CME) and its price is 250 times the index. The September contract opened at 1017, which means the value of the contract was actually 250×1017 or $254,250. The high during the day was 1018.00, the low was 1000.00, and the settlement price was 1006.90, up 5.20 from the previous day. During its lifetime, the September contract had a high of 1022.95 and a low of 884.00. Its open interest was 3,006 contracts. At the bottom of the S&P 500 listing is information on volume and open interest and information about the actual S&P 500 Index, which closed at 985.49 on January 29, 1998.

The lower column of the figure contains information on interest rate futures. The Treasury bond contract on the Chicago Board of Trade is for $100,000 face value of Treasury bonds and the price quote is in $\frac{1}{32}$ of 100 percent of face value. For example, the settlement price of the September 1998 contract is $121\frac{5}{32}$, up $\frac{41}{32}$, or $1\frac{9}{32}$, from the previous day. This is an actual price of $(121\frac{5}{32}) \times \$100,000$ or $121,156.25. The final column contains the open interest and the bottom line below the Treasury bond futures listing contains volume and open interest information on all contracts.

Figure 17.3   *Selected Futures Prices for January 29, 1998*

Thursday, January 29, 1998.
Open Interest Reflects Previous Trading Day.

GRAINS AND OILSEEDS

	Open	High	Low	Settle	Change	Lifetime High	Low	Open Interest
CORN (CBT) 5,000 bu.; cents per bu.								
Mar	277¼	278	275	275½	− 2	305	236	143,284
May	284½	285	282¼	282¾	− 1¾	310	241¾	64,637
July	290	290½	287½	288	− 1¾	315½	245	69,430
Sept	285	286	284¼	284¾	− ½	301	244	9,369
Dec	285¼	286	284	285¼	− ½	299½	247	44,871
Mr99	291	291¼	289½	291¼	− ¼	305	277½	2,727
July	....	....	....	298	− ½	312	256¼	612
Dec	279½	279½	279½	279½	− 1	291½	265	808
Est vol 46,000; vol Wed 42,890; open int 335,775, +1,926.								
OATS (CBT) 5,000 bu.; cents per bu.								
Mar	149	149	148	148½	− ½	180	146½	7,658
May	153½	153¾	153	153¼	− ½	182½	151	3,024
July	157	157¾	157	157¼	− ¼	184	153	1,834
Sept	159½	160	159½	159½	....	177	155	741
Dec	162	162	162	162	....	177½	161½	861
Est vol 650; vol Wed 1,053; open int 14,119, +34.								
SOYBEANS (CBT) 5,000 bu.; cents per bu.								
Mar	680½	683	675	679½	− 1¾	749½	593	55,369
May	685	685	677½	682¼	− 1¼	752	601	29,559
July	687¼	688	680½	685½	− ¾	753	611½	32,934
Aug	684	687	681	684½	− 1	745	631	5,255
Sept	673	673	670	670	− 3	723	637	617
Nov	668	670½	664¼	667¼	− 2½	717	597	13,239
Est vol 38,000; vol Wed 39,613; open int 137,505, −604.								

INDEX

	Open	High	Low	Settle	Chg	High	Low	Open Interest
DJ INDUSTRIAL AVERAGE (CBOT) $10 times average								
Mar	7935.0	8052.0	7917.0	7975.0	+ 33.0	8335.0	6970.0	14,532
June	8015.0	8125.0	7990.0	8052.0	+ 34.0	8346.0	7070.0	1,144
Sept	8085.0	8200.0	8075.0	8128.0	+ 34.0	8455.0	7150.0	293
Est vol 15,000; vol Wd 12,868 ; open int 16,034, −207.								
The index: High 8015.12; Low 7883.09; Close 7973.02 +57.55								
S&P 500 INDEX (CME) $250 times index								
Mar	981.80	999.40	979.50	987.10	+ 5.00	100260	854.40	385,660
June	991.00	100900	990.30	997.10	+ 5.10	101200	864.25	12,550
Sept	101700	101800	100000	100690	+ 5.20	102295	884.00	3,006
Dec	....	....		101660	+ 4.90	103625	890.85	1,914
Ju99	....	....		103800	+ 5.00	106115	959.35	216
Dec	107000	107170	105470	106070	+ 5.00	106870	101490	262
Est vol 130,869; vol Wd 107,939; open int 403,722, −57.								
Indx prelim High 992.65; Low 975.21; Close 985.49 +8.03								
MINI S&P 500 (CME) $50 times index								
Mar	982.00	999.00	979.75	987.00	+ 5.00	100100	854.50	10,946
Est vol 13,775; vol Wd 13,167; open int 11,071, +125.								
S&P MIDCAP 400 (CME) $500 times index								
Mar	327.00	331.80	326.75	328.00	+ .75	346.70	257.05	13,143
Est vol 667; vol Wd 611; open int 13,146, +196.								
The index: High 329.40; Low 325.11; Close 327.13 +1.89								
NIKKEI 225 STOCK AVERAGE (CME)-$5 times index								
Mar	17110.	17240.	16960.	17005.	− 245	20955.	14540.	16,958
Est vol 1,209; vol Wd 1,286; open int 17,075, +252.								
The index: High 17106.69; Low 16926.17; Close 17014.59 +40.76								
NASDAQ 100 (CME)-$100 times index								
Mar	108000	109100	106550	107300	+ 1.75	118600	944.00	7,330
June	....	....		108710	+ 1.75	119275	963.75	202
Est vol 2,747; vol Wd 2,305; open int 7,532, +197.								
The index: High 1082.08; Low 1059.60; Close 1069.00 +5.78								
GSCI (CME)-$250 times nearby index								
Feb	175.30	177.70	175.20	177.00	+ 2.70	208.40	167.90	24,871
Est vol 833; vol Wd 732; open int 24,932, +28.								
The index: High 177.62; Low 175.10; Close 176.87 +2.73								
RUSSELL 2000 (CME)-500 times index								
Mar	431.50	436.30	431.50	433.00	+ 1.10	475.50	345.00	9,893
Est vol 581; vol Wd 713; open int 9,898, −116.								
The index: High 432.09; Low 428.50; Close 431.99 +3.39								

INTEREST RATE

	Open	High	Low	Settle	Change	Lifetime High	Low	Open Interest
TREASURY BONDS (CBT)-$100,000; pts. 32nds of 100%								
Mar	120-17	122-00	120-13	121-28	+ 42	124-09	104-21	652,982
June	120-04	121-20	120-03	121-16	+ 41	123-28	104-03	52,081
Sept	120-08	121-06	120-08	121-05	+ 41	123-10	103-22	10,911
Dec	....	....		120-26	+ 41	122-30	103-13	5,131
Mr99	120-19	120-19	120-16	120-16	+ 41	121-26	103-04	80
Est vol 600,000; vol Wed 361,939; open int 721,189, −4,507.								
TREASURY BONDS (MCE)-$50,000; pts. 32nds of 100%								
Mar	120-19	122-00	120-14	121-29	+ 45	124-09	111-27	15,843
Est vol 7,000; vol Wed 5,540; open int 15,910, −454.								
TREASURY NOTES (CBT)-$100,000; pts. 32nds of 100%								
Mar	112-23	113-19	112-20	113-15	+ 24	115-08	105-24	411,943
June	112-21	113-18	112-20	113-14	+ 24	115-06	106-26	72,710
Est vol 133,337; vol Wed 96,960; open int 487,628, −3,385.								
5 YR TREAS NOTES (CBT)-$100,000; pts. 32nds of 100%								
Mar	09-085	09-295	09-045	109-27	+ 18.5	11-075	106-07	254,875
June	109-05	109-30	109-05	09-275	+ 19.0	110-25	107-28	3,107
Est vol 94,207; vol Wed 58,426; open int 257,982, +888.								
2 YR TREAS NOTES (CBT)-$200,000; pts. 32nds of 100%								
Mar	104-06	04-147	04-047	04-132	+ 7.2	105-01	103-08	36,587
Est vol 3,600; vol Wed 2,088; open int 36,614, −208.								
30-DAY FEDERAL FUNDS (CBT)-$5 million; pts. of 100%								
Jan	94.445	94.445	94.440	94.440	− .005	94.480	93.970	4,932
Feb	94.52	94.54	94.52	94.53	....	94.63	93.84	7,778
Mar	94.50	94.52	94.50	94.51	+ .01	95.30	94.13	4,646
May	94.57	94.65	94.56	94.61	+ .04	94.76	94.15	1,145
Est vol 3,333; vol Wed 1,722; open int 22,180, +800.								
MUNI BOND INDEX (CBT)-$1,000; times Bond Buyer MBI								
Mar	123-02	124-08	122-29	124-03	+ 35	126-21	116-29	15,862
Est vol 4,800; vol Wed 3,114; open int 15,963, +182.								
The index: Close 124-06; Yield 5.32.								

	Open	High	Low	Settle	Chg	Discount Settle	Chg	Open Interest
TREASURY BILLS (CME)-$1 mil.; pts. of 100%								
Mar	95.12	95.16	95.09	95.14	+ .04	4.86	− .04	8,701
June	95.14	95.22	95.09	95.19	+ .07	4.81	− .07	2,431
Est vol 820; vol Wed 573; open int 11,216, +176.								

Source: *Wall Street Journal*, January 30, 1998, C14

Figure 17.4 *Currency Futures Prices for January 29, 1998*

CURRENCY

	Open	High	Low	Settle	Change	Lifetime High	Lifetime Low	Open Interest
JAPAN YEN (CME)-12.5 million yen; $ per yen (.00)								
Mar	.8052	.8072	.7992	.8011	− .0061	.9375	.7512	93,316
June	.8139	.8160	.8104	.8113	− .0062	.9090	.7637	2,602
Sept	.8250	.8250	.8215	.8215	− .0063	.8695	.7735	518
Est vol 19,113; vol Wd 27,806; open int 96,440, +5,071.								
DEUTSCHEMARK (CME)-125,000 marks; $ per mark								
Mar	.5533	.5554	.5480	.5484	− .0050	.6160	.5383	73,949
June	.5571	.5571	.5510	.5511	− .0050	.5995	.5470	3,436
Sept	.5564	.5564	.5540	.5535	− .0050	.5944	.5540	1,648
Est vol 27,064; vol Wd 27,914; open int 79,039, +4,190.								
CANADIAN DOLLAR (CME)-100,000 dlrs.; $ per Can $								
Mar	.6882	.6882	.6815	.6825	− .0053	.7670	.6807	57,369
June	.6898	.6908	.6825	.6840	− .0056	.7470	.6825	5,370
Sept	.6900	.6905	.6845	.6853	− .0057	.7463	.6845	1,555
Dec	.6895	.6895	.6860	.6865	− .0059	.7400	.6860	782
Mr99	.6900	.6900	.6875	.6876	− .0061	.7247	.6875	258
Est vol 13,547; vol Wd 8,050; open int 65,336, +917.								
BRITISH POUND (CME)-62,500 pds.; $ per pound								
Mar	1.6398	1.6412	1.6326	1.6364	− .0016	1.7020	1.5680	29,531
June	1.6290	1.6320	1.6250	1.6286	− .0018	1.6940	1.5610	1,534
Est vol 5,460; vol Wd 6,899; open int 31,070, −145.								
SWISS FRANC (CME)-125,000 francs; $ per franc								
Mar	.6870	.6898	.6815	.6825	− .0048	.7450	.6687	49,470
June	.6945	.6965	.6890	.6897	− .0048	.7304	.6750	1,235
Sept	....	....	....	.6967	− .0048	.7310	.6840	1,113
Est vol 17,339; vol Wd 13,800; open int 51,824, +1,227.								
AUSTRALIAN DOLLAR (CME)-100,000 dlrs.; $ per A.$								
Mar	.6796	.6824	.6713	.6731	− .0095	.7590	.6328	15,645
Est vol 926; vol Wd 2,867; open int 15,695, +5.								
MEXICAN PESO (CME)-500,000 new Mex. peso, $ per MP								
Mar	.11670	.11705	.11550	.11592	− 00110	.12340	.09700	21,171
June	.11280	.11285	.11170	.11195	− 00107	.11985	09200	4,812
Sept	.10850	.10880	.10810	.10832	− 00105	.11680	.08000	5,024
Dec	.10570	.10580	.10470	.10492	− 00105	.11440	.08000	7,261
Est vol 7,711; vol Wd 8,224; open int 38,268, +1,188.								

Source: *Wall Street Journal*, January 30, 1998, C14

In 1972, the Chicago Mercantile Exchange began trading futures based on the currencies of the leading trading partners of the United States. The currency futures market is quite active, although it is smaller than the over-the-counter currency forward market. Figure 17.4 presents a sample of the quotations from the *Wall Street Journal* for currency futures. Current trading is in the Japanese yen, German mark, Canadian dollar, British pound, Swiss franc, Australian dollar, and the Mexican peso. In addition, there is a contract based on an index of the U.S. dollar. The most active trading is in the yen and mark contracts.

For example, a yen contract is for 12.5 million yen, with the current settlement price of the September yen contract equal to 0.8215. However, because there are so many yen in a dollar, it is understood that two decimal places precede the price. Thus, the actual price is $.008215 per yen. For a full contract, the price is equal to ¥12,500,000($.008215/¥) or $102,687.50.

OPTIONS

As described earlier, an option grants an investor the right to buy or sell an asset at a fixed price on or before a specific point in time. An option to buy an asset is referred to as a *call option,* whereas an option to sell an asset is called a *put option.* Buyers of options (either calls or puts) are said to be "long" and sellers are said to be "short."

The price paid for the option itself is called the **option premium.** The price at which the asset can be acquired or sold is the *exercise price* or *strike price.* For example, if a stock call option has an exercise price of $45, it means that this call option permits the owner of the option to buy the stock for $45 a share. If the underlying stock's current market price is $50, the call option has an intrinsic value of $5, as it allows the holder to pay $45 for

something that has a market value of $50. If the underlying stock's price is $40, the call option's intrinsic value is $0; it is worthless, and the holder will choose not to exercise the option, as it makes little sense to pay $45 (the exercise price) for something that has a spot market value of $40.

Similarly, suppose a put option permits its owner to sell the stock for $45 a share. If the underlying stock's current market price is $40, the put option has an intrinsic value of $5, as it allows the holder to sell for $45 an asset that has a market value of only $40. If the underlying stock's price is $50, the put option's intrinsic value is $0; it is worthless, and the holder will choose not to exercise the option, as it makes little sense to sell an asset for $45 (the exercise price) when he can go to the spot market and sell it for $50.

The date on which the option expires, or the last date on which it can be exercised, is the *expiration date*. For options trading on exchanges, the expiration dates are typically specified in terms of a given month and the time within the month is likewise specified as the Saturday following the third Friday. A July option would expire the Saturday following the third Friday in July. However, off the exchanges, options can be created by any two parties and can have any expiration date desired. Options that trade on exchanges are generally fairly liquid so that they can be sold before expiration. Few options are exercised; in-the-money options are usually closed out before the expiration date, giving the holder a profit on the difference between the premium paid for the option and the premium he or she receives when selling it.

Some options permit the holder to exercise them only on the expiration day. These are called **European options**. Those that permit the holder to exercise any time up to and including the expiration day are called **American options**. These names have no relationship to geography; both European and American options trade extensively on exchanges and in over-the-counter (OTC) markets in both the United States and Europe as well as other parts of the world.

For both puts and calls, **at the money** means that the stock price is approximately equal to the exercise price. An **in-the-money option** has some intrinsic value in and of itself; the exercise price allows the holder to purchase an asset below current market value or sell an asset at a price above its current market value. An **out-of-the-money option** has no intrinsic value and will not be exercised because the holder can buy the stock for less in the market (out-of-the-money call) or sell it for more (out-of-the-money put). However, an out-of-the-money option can subsequently become in the money and vice versa prior to expiration.

Table 17.3 summarizes some option-contract terminology. Table 17.4 summarizes some of the major distinctions between forwards, futures, and options contracts.

Option Exchanges

Until 1973, option trading took place exclusively through private contracts involving individuals or institutions. In other words, if an individual wanted to buy a call on General Motors stock that would expire in exactly thirty-seven days at an exercise price of 60 the individual would have to find another individual or institution willing to write, or sell, that particular option. The Put and Call Brokers and Dealers Association existed for the purpose of finding a party willing to take the opposite side of such an option contract. Its member firms worked as brokers, arranging trades between parties. If no counterparty could be found, a member firm might write the option itself, thereby acting as a dealer. Thus, at any given time there might be hundreds, perhaps thousands, of outstanding options, each with potentially different terms. The options were meant to be held to expiration because of the limited secondary market. What existed was an over-the-counter options market.

Table 17.3   *Important Options Terminology*

Call Option	right to purchase an asset at a specific price on or before a specific date
Put Option	right to sell an asset at a specific price on or before a specific date
Option Premium	price paid by the investor to purchase the option contract
Exercise or Strike Price	price at which the underlying asset can be bought or sold
Expiration date	date on which the option to exercise the contract expires
Write an option	sell at option contract
At the money	exercise price is the same as the underlying asset spot price
In the money	the option has some positive intrinsic value; trading at the exercise price is more attractive to the option holder rather than trading at the market price for the underlying asset. For calls, asset spot price exceeds exercise price; it is cheaper to buy the asset at the exercise price. For puts, asset spot price is less than exercise price; gain more by selling the asset at the exercise price
Out of the money	the option has no intrinsic value; trading at the spot price is more attractive to the option holder rather than trading at the exercise price. For calls, asset spot price is less than exercise price; it is cheaper to buy the asset at the spot price. For puts, asset spot price exceeds exercise price; gain more by selling the asset at the spot price

Table 17.4   *Differences between Forwards, Futures, and Options*

Forward Contract	Futures Contract	Option Contract
obligation to trade at time T at a specified price	obligation to trade at time T at a specified price	option to trade at time T at a specified price
traded OTC	exchange traded	exchange traded
terms are not standardized	standardized terms	standardized terms
poor secondary market (not liquid)	liquid (varies among contracts)	liquid (varies among contracts)
settlement occurs at expiration	daily settlement (marking to the market)	daily settlement
Close long position by selling identical contract to another party or the original seller	Close long position by selling the contract on the exchange	Close long position by selling the contract on the exchange
Exposed to credit/default risk by the counterparty	No credit/default risk	No credit/default risk
Can earn a profit or loss in a long position	Can earn a profit or loss in a long position	Can limit losses by choosing not to exercise the option

Everything changed dramatically in 1973, when the Chicago Board of Trade (CBOT), the largest futures exchange, created a separate exchange called the Chicago Board Options Exchange (CBOE). The CBOE became a centralized facility for trading standardized options contracts. Specifically, the CBOE offered the following features:

1. A central marketplace with regulatory, surveillance, disclosure, and price dissemination capabilities.
2. The Clearing Corporation as the guarantor of every CBOE option. Standing as the opposite party to every trade, the Clearing Corporation enables buyers and sellers of options to terminate their positions in the market at any time by making an offsetting transaction.
3. Standardized expiration dates. CBOE options have specific expirations. All stocks are classified into one of three cycles: the January cycle (January, April, July, and October), the February cycle (February, May, August, and November), and the March cycle (March, June, September, and December). Each stock's options have an expiration in the current month, the next month, and the next two months in one of these three cycles. The options expire on the Saturday following the third Friday

Table 17.5 *Popular Option Contracts and Exchanges*

Underlying Asset	Exchange
A. Financial Securities	
Individual Equities S&P 100 Index, Dow Jones Industrial Average	Chicago Board Options Exchange
Yen, deutsche mark, Canadian dollar, Swiss franc, British pound, Australian dollar S&P 500 Index, mini S&P 500	International Monetary Market (Chicago Mercantile Exchange)
B. Futures Options	
Cattle—feeder, cattle—live, hogs, pork bellies	Chicago Mercantile Exchange
Yen, deutsche mark, Canadian dollar, Swiss franc, British pound Eurodollar (LIBOR), 2 year Eurodollar S&P 500 Index	International Monetary Market (Chicago Mercantile Exchange)
Corn, soybeans, soybean meal, soybean oil, wheat	Chicago Board of Trade
Treasury bonds, Treasury notes	
Major Market Index	
British gilt, German bunds Euromark FT-SE 100 Index	London International Financial Futures Exchange
Crude oil, heating oil, gasoline, natural gas	New York Mercantile Exchange
Copper, gold, silver	New York Commodity Exchange

of the month. In recent years, the CBOE has added some long-term options, called LEAPS, that have expirations of two to three years. Options on stock indexes follow a pattern of having expiration dates over the next several consecutive months.

4. Standardized exercise prices. Options are available with exercise prices that bracket the current stock price. Exercise prices are generally set in five-dollar intervals. As a stock price moves, additional options with new exercise prices are added.

5. Standardized contract size. Options are traded in units, called contracts, which are standardized at 100. Thus, buying one option contract is actually buying options on 100 shares. Adjustments are made for stock splits and stock dividends, which can create odd-lot option contracts.

6. A secondary market. As a result of the standardization of expirations and exercise prices, a secondary market for options became feasible. Before option exchanges were established, the buyers and sellers of OTC options were essentially committed to their positions until the expiration date.

Exchange-traded options on individual stocks are generally American options (that is, they are exercisable on any day up to and including the expiration day). However, some index options are European-style, meaning that they can be exercised only on the expiration day.

The CBOE started with options on sixteen stocks, a number that gradually increased until today the CBOE offers options on almost 1,400 stocks. Table 17.5 provides a description of the index options that also trade on the various exchanges. Index options have special appeal because they involve taking a position on the market as a whole, rather than on individual stocks.

Figure 17.5 presents an example of the option quotation page from the *Wall Street Journal.* Suppose you were considering buying a call option on Chrysler. Under Chrysler's name is the prior day's closing price on Chrysler stock: $34^{13}/_{16}$. Next to Chrysler's name, in the

Figure 17.5 *Stock Option Quotations*

Option	Strike	Exp.	Call Vol.	Call Last	Put Vol.	Put Last
CalGlf	25	Feb	256	$2\frac{1}{2}$	274	$\frac{3}{8}$
$27\frac{1}{8}$	30	Feb	406	$\frac{9}{16}$	400	3
$27\frac{1}{8}$	30	Mar	210	$1\frac{1}{16}$	85	$3\frac{3}{8}$
$27\frac{1}{8}$	30	May	549	$1\frac{3}{8}$	103	$4\frac{1}{4}$
CambTc	35	Mar	400	$9\frac{1}{2}$	...	...
CapsPhm	$12\frac{1}{2}$	Mar	300	$\frac{3}{4}$	...	...
CardnlHl	75	Mar	390	$5\frac{3}{8}$	...	...
Cellstar	$17\frac{1}{2}$	Feb	275	$3\frac{1}{4}$	202	$\frac{3}{4}$
20	$22\frac{1}{2}$	Feb	284	$\frac{3}{4}$	20	$4\frac{1}{4}$
Cendant	30	Feb	1018	$3\frac{3}{4}$	...	...
$33\frac{11}{16}$	35	Aug	500	$3\frac{1}{4}$	15	$3\frac{1}{2}$
Centocor	40	Feb	1133	$1\frac{1}{2}$	168	3
$38\frac{3}{8}$	40	Mar	474	$2\frac{3}{4}$	124	4
Chase n	95	Jun	...	...	320	$2\frac{7}{8}$
$106\frac{13}{16}$	100	Feb	776	$7\frac{1}{2}$	163	$\frac{7}{8}$
$106\frac{13}{16}$	100	Mar	...	...	2213	$1\frac{7}{8}$
$106\frac{13}{16}$	105	Feb	232	$4\frac{1}{8}$	345	$2\frac{1}{16}$
$106\frac{13}{16}$	105	Mar	91	$5\frac{3}{4}$	247	$3\frac{1}{4}$
$106\frac{13}{16}$	115	Feb	489	$\frac{1}{2}$	1	$7\frac{1}{4}$
$106\frac{13}{16}$	115	Mar	287	$1\frac{15}{16}$	...	...
ChesEng	$7\frac{1}{2}$	Feb	533	$\frac{3}{16}$	...	...
$5\frac{15}{16}$	$7\frac{1}{2}$	Jun	16	$\frac{3}{4}$	2150	$2\frac{1}{16}$
ChinaTlc	35	Mar	221	$1\frac{1}{16}$	...	...
Chryslr	30	Apr	10	$5\frac{1}{8}$	529	$\frac{1}{4}$
$34\frac{13}{16}$	35	Feb	467	$\frac{13}{16}$	20	$\frac{5}{8}$
$34\frac{13}{16}$	35	Apr	324	$1\frac{3}{8}$	30	$1\frac{5}{8}$
$34\frac{13}{16}$	$37\frac{1}{2}$	Apr	358	$1\frac{1}{16}$	...	...
CienaCp	55	Feb	780	$2\frac{1}{4}$	109	$3\frac{1}{8}$
Circus	$22\frac{1}{2}$	Mar	34	$2\frac{1}{4}$	219	$1\frac{1}{16}$
$23\frac{1}{2}$	25	Feb	1343	$1\frac{5}{8}$	10	$2\frac{1}{2}$
$23\frac{1}{2}$	25	Mar	241	$1\frac{3}{4}$	10	$2\frac{3}{4}$
Cisco	55	Feb	303	$9\frac{1}{2}$	545	$\frac{7}{16}$
$63\frac{3}{4}$	55	Mar	73	$10\frac{3}{4}$	207	$1\frac{5}{16}$
$63\frac{3}{4}$	60	Feb	2110	$4\frac{7}{8}$	1928	$1\frac{1}{8}$
$63\frac{3}{4}$	60	Mar	297	6	943	$1\frac{7}{8}$
$63\frac{3}{4}$	60	Apr	319	$7\frac{1}{4}$	3147	$2\frac{15}{16}$
$63\frac{3}{4}$	65	Feb	3309	$1\frac{13}{16}$	1123	$2\frac{13}{16}$
$63\frac{3}{4}$	65	Mar	1914	$2\frac{7}{8}$	522	4
$63\frac{3}{4}$	65	Apr	710	$4\frac{1}{8}$	88	$4\frac{5}{8}$
$63\frac{3}{4}$	65	Jul	221	7	6	$6\frac{3}{4}$
$63\frac{3}{4}$	70	Feb	638	$\frac{5}{16}$	85	$6\frac{5}{8}$
$63\frac{3}{4}$	70	Mar	1380	$1\frac{5}{16}$	26	7
$63\frac{3}{4}$	70	Apr	558	$2\frac{1}{8}$	75	$7\frac{1}{2}$
$63\frac{3}{4}$	70	Jul	972	$4\frac{1}{2}$	...	...
Cisco o	$66\frac{5}{8}$	Apr	620	$3\frac{1}{2}$	...	...
Citicp	110	Feb	10	11	417	$\frac{7}{8}$
$118\frac{7}{16}$	115	Feb	383	6	403	$2\frac{3}{4}$
$118\frac{7}{16}$	120	Feb	948	3	205	$4\frac{1}{2}$
$118\frac{7}{16}$	125	Feb	279	$1\frac{1}{4}$	...	...
CitrixS	70	Feb	340	$3\frac{5}{8}$	22	$5\frac{1}{4}$
Coke	65	Feb	1089	$1\frac{5}{8}$	744	$1\frac{11}{16}$
$64\frac{3}{4}$	65	May	347	$4\frac{1}{2}$	260	$3\frac{1}{2}$
$64\frac{3}{4}$	70	Feb	298	$\frac{3}{8}$	10	$5\frac{3}{4}$
$64\frac{3}{4}$	70	Mar	1483	$\frac{3}{4}$	2	$5\frac{1}{2}$
$64\frac{3}{4}$	70	May	361	$.2$	105	$6\frac{5}{8}$

Source: *Wall Street Journal,* January 30, 1998, C17

second and third column, you'll find exercise (or strike) prices and expiration dates on Chrysler option contracts. The fourth and fifth columns give the day's trading volume and the last price (or premium) for a call-option contract trade; the sixth and seventh columns present the trading volume and last price (or premium) for a put-option trade. If "...". appears under the call or put columns, it indicates that the option contract did not trade that day. If you had done the last trade on the Chrysler February 35 call, the option premium would have been $\frac{13}{16}$ or $0.8125 per share. Because each contract is for 100 calls, the total option premium cost would have been $81.25. Notably, there are two potentially misleading facts about these prices. First, the closing stock price of $34\frac{13}{16}$ and the closing option prices are not necessarily synchronized. The last trade of the day for the stock and the last trade of the day for an option on the stock may have occurred at different times.[2] In addition, the prices are not identified as bid or ask prices. Thus, even if the stock and option prices were synchronized and no additional information had affected prices since the last trade, you might have to pay more than $81.25. This is because the option price you see may have represented a trade in which an investor sold an option to the CBOE

---

[2]In fact, the New York Stock Exchange closes at 4:00 P.M. Eastern time, whereas the CBOE closes at 4:15 P.M. Eastern time.

market maker, which means that it would have been the bid price. Thus, if you had wanted to purchase an option from a market maker, you would have to pay the ask price, which would be higher.

The fact that option premiums are small, in comparison to the stock's market price, can lead to rather large percentage gains (or losses) on the option buyer's invested capital. This is called leverage by option investors. Let's look at what happens when the price of the underlying stock rises before the option expires. Suppose you purchase the above-mentioned February 35 call option for $0.8125 per share and Chrysler's stock rises to $40 by the option expiration date, an increase of 14.9 percent. The shareholder's return would be the same as this increase, 14.9 percent. But the call option's intrinsic value on the expiration date will be $5, namely $40 less the exercise price of $35. Your investment of $0.8125 per share grew to a value of $5 per share, a percentage return of ($5 − $0.8125)/$0.8125 = 515 percent, far above the stockholder's percentage return.

What if Chrysler's stock price fell 10 percent, so by the expiration date the call option is out of the money? The shareholder faces a 10 percent loss on her investment. But the option holder faces a 100 percent loss, as his option expires, out-of-the money, worthless.[3] The option's leverage is clear: because a relatively small premium controls much value, small percentage changes in the value of the stock can result in large percentage changes for an option position. For this reason, option trading is not for the novice investor. Option trading strategies exist that help reduce an investor's risk; these will be discussed later in the chapter.

Figure 17.6 presents an example of the *Wall Street Journal*'s index option quotations. If, for example, you had done the last trade of the day on the February 460 call on the S&P 100 (calls are designated with a "c," puts with a "p"), the price would have been $16\frac{1}{4}$, which is a premium of $1,625.00 per contract. The information in the table "Ranges for Underlying Indexes" tells us the underlying index closed at 471.38, which means that this option is in the money and has an intrinsic value of 11.38.

Figure 17.7 presents the sample quotations for currency options from the *Wall Street Journal.* Foreign currency options are traded on the Philadelphia Stock Exchange. Contracts trade on the Australian dollar, British pound, Canadian dollar, German mark, Japanese yen, French franc, and Swiss franc. Note both European and American versions of these options; the European options are labeled as "European Style." The American versions are more actively traded because they provide more flexibility.

The price quotations are laid out much like those of options on stocks. Let us consider the German marks (American option) March call 56 option, which grants the right to buy 62,500 German marks by the expiration day in March at a price of $0.56/DM. Because the price of the call option is 0.59 cents per mark, or $0.0059, this contract would cost DM62,500 × ($0.0059/DM) or $368.75.

Option Payoff Diagrams

Forwards and futures carry an *obligation* to execute the contract (unless offset by another contract so the investor's net position is zero). An option contract is just that—it gives the owner the *option* to purchase (call option) or sell (put option) an asset. Thus, if exercising the option will cause the owner to lose wealth, the option can expire unexercised and have a value of zero. Whereas losses on futures and forwards can grow as a result of adverse moves in the value of the underlying asset, losses on option contracts can be truncated by merely choosing not to exercise them. In this case, the pre-tax loss is limited to the premium paid to purchase the option plus commission.

---

[3]We ignore commissions and taxes for simplicity in this example.

Figure 17.6 *Quotations for Options on Selected Indexes*

INDEX OPTIONS TRADING

Thursday, January 29, 1998

Volume, last, net change and open interest for all contracts. Volume figures are unofficial. Open interest reflects previous trading day. p-Put c-Call

CHICAGO

Strike		Vol.	Last	Net Chg.	Open Int.
CB MEXICO INDEX(MEX)					
Mar	100p	15	1⅜	− ½	78
Sep	100p	3	6⅞	...	...
Feb	110c	25	3⅛	− 1⅝	20
Mar	110c	11	5½	− 1⅝	78
Sep	140c	5	2¾	...	...
Call Vol.		41	Open Int.		506
Put Vol.		18	Open Int.		684
CB TECHNOLOGY(TXX)					
Feb	210p	10	2 1/16	− 6 9/16	10
Call Vol.		0	Open Int.		155
Put Vol.		10	Open Int.		60
DJ INDUS AVG(DJX)					
Feb	64p	20	1/16	− 1/16	1,359
Mar	64p	20	3/16	− 3/16	4,439
Mar	68c	3	12¼	+ 1¼	131
Mar	68p	153	5/16	− ⅜	1,496
Feb	72c	2	7¾	+ 1⅛	17
Feb	72p	105	3/16	− 1/16	2,018
Mar	72p	80	⅝	− 1/16	4,005
Jun	72p	5	1⅝	− ¼	1,293
Sep	72p	40	2 7/16	− ⅜	269
Feb	73p	120	3/16	− ⅛	1,222
Feb	74c	202	6⅛	+ ⅝	449
Feb	74p	20	¼	− ⅛	2,379
Mar	74c	29	6½	+ ½	372
Feb	75c	21	5⅛	+ ⅝	413
Feb	75p	190	⅜	− 1/16	1,452
Mar	75p	91	1 1/16	− 1/16	818
Feb	76c	111	3⅞	+ ¼	2,248
Feb	76p	578	7/16	− 3/16	4,050
Mar	76c	416	4⅞	+ ⅜	16,038
Mar	76p	96	1 3/16	− 1/16	13,766
Jun	76c	64	7⅜	+ ⅝	2,126
Jun	76p	60	2 7/16	− 5/16	2,107
Sep	76c	20	8½	+ 1⅛	316
Sep	76p	25	3⅜	− ¼	1,632
Feb	77c	177	3¼	+ 5/16	1,013
Feb	77p	85	⅝	− ⅛	1,831
Mar	77c	5	4¾	+ 1	291
Mar	77p	20	1 5/16	− 7/16	754
Feb	78c	558	2½	+ ¼	3,543
Feb	78p	513	⅞	− 3/16	4,796
Mar	78c	202	3⅜	+ ¼	5,563
Mar	78p	161	1 11/16	− ¼	5,908
Feb	79c	184	2	+ ½	1,762
Feb	79p	598	1 3/16	− 3/16	1,031
Mar	79c	123	3¼	+ 11/16	3,984
Mar	79p	103	1 15/16	− 5/16	763
Feb	80c	337	1¼	+ ¼	2,995
Feb	80p	1,023	1⅝	− 3/16	1,483
Mar	80c	276	2 7/16	+ 7/16	12,785
Mar	80p	629	2 7/16	− ⅛	17,592
Jun	80c	25	4⅞	+ 1¼	4,543
Jun	80p	18	3¾	− ¼	5,343
Sep	80c	17	6	+ ½	10,343
Sep	80p	80	4½	− ½	11,187
Feb	81c	381	⅞	+ ¼	7,398
Feb	81p	201	2¼	− 3/16	1,169
Mar	81c	7	1⅞	+ 1	5
Feb	82c	142	9/16	+ 3/16	6,591
Feb	82p	23	2 13/16	− 7/16	700
Mar	82c	6	1 5/16	+ 5/16	18,866
Mar	82p	114	3¼	− 1¾	1,118
Feb	83c	175	5/16	+ ⅛	1,584
Mar	83c	25	1	+ 9/16	100
Feb	84c	100	3/16	+ 1/16	296
Mar	84c	5	11/16	+ ⅛	3,001
Jun	84c	2	2⅝	+ 5/16	2,195
Jun	84p	10	5⅞	− 1	32
Feb	86c	100	1/16	...	368
Feb	86p	5	6	− 2	5
Mar	86c	250	¼	...	2,445
Mar	88c	50	⅛	− 1/16	428
Jun	88c	30	1	+ ¼	208
Jun	88p	30	8	− ⅞	1,002
Mar	95c	4	1/16	...	471
Call Vol.		4,090	Open Int.		140,674
Put-Vol.		5,706	Open Int.		160,082

RANGES FOR UNDERLYING INDEXES

Thursday, January 29, 1998

	High	Low	Close	Net Chg.	From Dec. 31	% Chg.
DJ Indus (DJX)	80.15	78.83	79.73	+ 0.58	+ 0.65	+ 0.8
DJ Trans (DTX)	335.78	331.00	334.02	+ 2.76	+ 8.37	+ 2.6
DJ Util (DUX)	265.70	263.15	263.90	0.00	− 9.17	− 3.4
S&P 100 (OEX)	474.86	466.48	471.38	+ 4.15	+ 11.44	+ 2.5
S&P 500 -A.M.(SPX)	992.65	975.21	985.49	+ 8.03	+ 15.06	+ 1.6
CB-Tech (TXX)	226.28	221.54	222.54	− 0.31	+ 6.75	+ 3.1
CB-Mexico (MEX)	111.31	109.02	109.28	− 2.03	− 17.70	− 13.9
CB-Lps Mex (VEX)	11.13	10.90	10.93	− 0.20	− 1.77	− 13.9
MS Multintl (NFT)	552.12	542.74	548.86	+ 4.55	+ 17.31	+ 3.3
GSTI Comp (GTC)	152.59	149.17	150.59	+ 0.78	+ 7.13	+ 5.0
Nasdaq 100 (NDX)	1082.08	1059.60	1069.00	+ 5.78	+ 78.20	+ 7.9
NYSE (NYA)	516.09	508.44	513.13	+ 3.91	+ 1.94	+ 0.4
Russell 2000 (RUT)	432.09	428.50	431.99	+ 3.39	− 5.03	− 1.2
Lps S&P 100 (OEX)	94.97	93.30	94.28	+ 0.83	+ 2.29	+ 2.5
Lps S&P 500 (SPX)	99.27	97.52	98.55	+ 0.80	+ 1.51	+ 1.6
S&P Midcap (MID)	329.40	325.11	327.17	+ 1.93	− 6.20	− 1.9
Major Mkt (XMI)	844.71	832.39	840.51	+ 5.38	+ 3.66	+ 0.4
HK Fltg (HKO)	183.93	183.91	183.93	+ 0.02	− 30.63	− 14.3
HK Fixed (HKD)	....	....	184.04	0.00	− 31.00	− 14.4
IW Internet (IIX)	280.62	273.22	275.99	+ 1.99	+ 15.74	+ 6.1
AM-Mexico (MXY)	122.24	119.84	120.08	− 2.16	− 21.45	− 15.2
Institut'l -A.M.(XII)	1090.58	1070.91	1083.15	+ 9.28	+ 32.99	+ 3.1
Japan (JPN)	....	....	175.22	+ 0.49	+ 17.58	+ 11.2
MS Cyclical (CYC)	487.22	478.89	484.57	+ 4.19	+ 9.56	+ 2.0
MS Consumr (CMR)	460.97	452.58	456.67	+ 2.31	+ 11.03	+ 2.5
MS Hi Tech (MSH)	472.77	460.71	465.17	+ 1.52	+ 17.65	+ 3.9
Pharma (DRG)	591.07	581.72	588.24	+ 4.26	+ 54.50	+ 10.2
Biotech (BTK)	161.46	154.00	155.21	− 6.25	− 7.21	− 4.4
Comp Tech (XCI)	483.52	471.80	476.38	+ 2.46	+ 37.39	+ 8.5
Gold/Silver (XAU)	78.31	75.41	75.41	− 3.56	+ 1.22	+ 1.6
OTC (XOC)	792.01	776.28	783.25	+ 4.93	+ 45.30	+ 6.1
Utility (UTY)	301.72	298.79	299.86	− 0.09	− 10.17	− 3.3
Value Line (VLE)	874.47	865.88	870.77	+ 4.23	− 6.07	− 0.7
Bank (BKX)	732.92	716.81	725.74	+ 8.52	− 29.61	− 3.9
Semicond (SOX)	294.56	285.14	287.73	− 0.78	+ 24.10	+ 9.1
Top 100 (TPX)	939.48	923.10	933.60	+ 8.19	+ 23.98	+ 2.6
Oil Service (OSX)	103.32	99.27	101.86	+ 3.92	− 12.51	− 10.9
PSE Tech (PSE)	303.81	297.73	300.16	+ 1.40	+ 9.60	+ 3.3

Strike		Vol.	Last	Net Chg.	Open Int.
Mar	990p	8	15	− 8	1,398
Feb	1010p	132	9	+ ⅛	692
Mar	1010c	9	89	+ 6⅜	24
Feb	1020c	2	69⅛	+ 11⅛	668
Feb	1020p	5	9¾	− 2⅛	194
Feb	1030c	119	53	+ 2	444
Feb	1030p	41	13	− ½	599
Feb	1040c	11	45¾	+ 4¾	996
Feb	1040p	8	14	− 3½	199
Apr	1040c	3	74	+ 12	3
Apr	1040p	3	36½	...	...
Feb	1050c	425	43¾	+ 8	281
Feb	1050p	1,540	18⅜	− ⅞	842
Mar	1050p	7	31	+ ⅝	121
Feb	1060c	90	33½	+ 4	185
Feb	1060p	38	22	− ⅜	118
Mar	1060c	2	53	+ 13	25
Feb	1070c	24	26½	+ 13⅝	416
Feb	1070p	13	24½	− 29½	2
Mar	1070c	6	50½	+ 12	181
Mar	1070p	1	40	− 68	30
Feb	1080c	166	21½	+ 2½	1,036
Feb	1080p	1,262	30	− 3	504
Mar	1080c	2	45¾	+ 25¼	856
Mar	1080p	5	42	− 51½	507

Strike		Vol.	Last	Net Chg.	Open Int.
Feb	440c	12	3¾	+ 1⅜	240
Mar	440c	11	9⅞	+ 1¼	145
Feb	445c	1	2½	+ 1 3/16	47
Feb	455c	5	¾	− 5⅞	40
Mar	455c	1	3½	+ ⅜	100
Call Vol.		771	Open Int.		18,002
Put Vol.		850	Open Int.		17,146
S & P 100 INDEX(OEX)					
Feb	380p	1,162	¼	− 1/16	13,830
Feb	390p	325	⅜	− 1/16	3,234
Mar	390p	455	1⅜	− 3/16	321
Apr	390p	30	2½	− ½	704
Feb	400p	563	½	− ⅛	9,089
Mar	400p	53	1 11/16	− 5/16	2,641
Apr	400p	2	3⅜	− ⅝	930
Feb	410c	2	59¾	+ ¾	30
Feb	410p	926	11/16	− ⅛	6,845
Mar	410c	2	67¼	+ 8¾	31
Mar	410p	26	2⅛	− ¾	2,519
Apr	410p	17	4⅜	− ½	2,042
May	410p	1	6	− 1	817
Feb	415p	518	13/16	− 3/16	3,453
Mar	415p	15	2⅝	− ⅜	1,562
Feb	420c	49	52⅜	+ 2⅜	894

Strike		Vol.	Last	Net Chg.	Open Int.
Feb	455p	3,499	3⅞	− ¾	15,773
Mar	455c	13	27¼	+ 5¼	571
Mar	455p	289	8⅛	− 1⅜	4,126
Apr	455p	6	11	− 6¼	332
Feb	460c	3,651	16¼	+ 2½	17,073
Feb	460p	8,261	5	− 1	16,725
Mar	460c	2,244	22½	+ 2½	4,632
Mar	460p	2,463	9½	− 1½	4,473
Apr	460c	1	26½	+ 1⅜	498
Apr	460p	11	12½	− 2½	879
Feb	465c	4,689	11¾	+ 1¼	10,493
Feb	465p	8,477	6½	− 1¼	8,072
Mar	465c	322	19⅛	+ 1⅞	3,947
Mar	465p	63	11½	− 1	3,118
Apr	465c	60	25⅞	+ 8⅝	11
Apr	465p	39	14½	− 1⅝	136
Feb	470c	9,441	8¾	+ 1⅛	13,541
Feb	470p	8,741	8⅝	− 1⅛	5,447
Mar	470c	809	16	+ 2⅜	5,292
Mar	470p	812	13⅛	− 1⅜	6,346
Apr	470c	226	20½	+ 1½	2,261
Apr	470p	8	15½	− 1¾	133
May	470p	3	19⅞	− 1⅞	590
Feb	475c	8,033	6⅛	+ ⅞	9,928
Feb	475p	1,535	10¾	− 2⅜	1,082
Mar	475c	64	14½	+ 3⅜	1,649
Mar	475p	14	15	− 1½	14
Apr	475c	250	20	+ 6⅛	2,304
Apr	475p	250	18½	...	...
Feb	480c	7,575	4⅛	+ ¾	12,557
Feb	480p	315	13½	− 2¼	328
Mar	480c	127	10¾	+ 2⅛	5,027
Mar	480p	43	15¾	− 9⅛	518
Apr	480c	63	16¾	+ 3¼	6,549
Apr	480p	24	19	− 4	63
May	480c	200	20⅞	+ 3¼	91
May	480p	577	24⅛	− 8⅝	82
Feb	485c	6,269	2⅝	+ ⅜	10,805
Feb	485p	37	16¾	− 4	58
Mar	485c	86	7⅛	+ ¾	1,461
Apr	485c	1	14⅜	+ 4⅛	3,980
Apr	485p	2	23½	...	...
Feb	490c	4,488	1 11/16	+ 5/16	12,357
Feb	490p	49	21¾	− 2	51
Mar	490c	32	6⅛	+ 1⅜	6,172
Mar	490p	2	22⅜	− 3⅛	40
Apr	490c	12	11⅛	+ 2⅛	4,091
Apr	490p	10	25¼	...	...
May	490c	50	15½	+ 4	1,058
Feb	495c	2,636	1⅛	+ 5/16	4,407
Feb	495p	20	24	− 8⅜	7
Mar	495c	47	4¼	+ ⅝	1,127
Apr	495c	532	8⅜	+ 2¼	2,630
Apr	495p	3	28½	...	3
Feb	500c	3,759	11/16	+ ⅛	7,560
Mar	500c	47	3¾	+ 1	4,762
Apr	500c	412	7¼	+ 2⅛	279
Apr	500p	5	32¾	− 2⅞	36
May	500c	319	9½	+ 4⅛	7
Feb	505c	1,135	7/16	+ ⅛	6,931
Mar	505c	185	3¼	+ 1 9/16	864
Feb	510c	1,988	5/16	+ 3/16	5,656
Mar	510c	123	1¾	+ ½	1,789
Apr	510c	48	4⅛	+ ⅞	285
Call Vol.		67,703	Open Int.		212,505
Put Vol.		58,719	Open Int.		218,627
S & P 500 INDEX-AM(SPX)					
Mar	40c	324	6¾	+ 1½	2,406
Mar	60p	7,650	68½	...	7,400
Mar	650p	5	⅜	− 1/16	6,007
Mar	700p	123	⅝	− ⅛	11,224
Feb	720p	110	⅛	− 3/16	353
Mar	725p	100	⅞	...	8,640
Feb	750p	12	¼	...	3,428
Mar	750p	328	1⅛	− ½	16,222
Feb	760p	10	¼	− ¾	127
Mar	775p	120	1¾	− ⅛	15,121
Feb	800p	1,685	7/16	− ⅛	14,834
Mar	800p	19	2	− ⅞	17,395
Feb	825p	127	½	− ⅜	3,451
Mar	825c	535	171	+ 29	6,359
Mar	825p	22	3	− 1	11,136
Apr	825p	72	5¼	− 1¼	195
Feb	840p	120	1	− ¼	2,525
Feb	850p	180	1	− ¼	8,647
Mar	850c	350	145	+ 6¾	7,563
Mar	850p	30	4	− ¾	21,085
Apr	850p	120	7	− 1	108
Feb	855p	5	1 1/16	− 1 3/16	153
Feb	860p	10	⅞	− 1	2,011

Source: *Wall Street Journal,* January 30, 1998, C17

Figure 17.7 *Quotations on Currency Options*

PHILADELPHIA OPTIONS

Thursday, January 29, 1998

		Calls Vol.	Calls Last	Puts Vol.	Puts Last
SFranc					67.86
62,500 Swiss Franc EOM-European style.					
67	Jan	...	...	200	0.04
68½	Jan	40	0.19	100	0.40
69	Feb	...	...	10	1.04
Australian Dollar					67.33
50,000 Australian Dollars-cents per unit.					
64	Jun	...	...	1	0.48
65	Mar	...	...	20	0.26
66	Feb	...	...	20	0.18
66	Jun	1	2.60	...	...
67	Jun	1	1.93	...	...
68	Mar	2	0.78	...	...
68	Jun	55	1.46	...	...
69	Feb	13	0.26	...	...
70	Jun	1	0.73	...	...
British Pound					163.84
31,250 Brit. Pounds-European Style.					
162	Feb	...	...	32	0.50
31,250 Brit. Pounds-cents per unit.					
165	Feb	9	0.77	...	...
166	Mar	...	...	9	3.58
Canadian Dollar					68.13
50,000 Canadian Dollars-European Style.					
68½	Mar	200	0.58	...	...
50,000 Canadian Dollars-cents per unit.					
70½	Feb	...	...	16	2.06
50,000 Canadian Dollars-cents per unit.					
68½	Jun	5	1.00	...	...
69	Mar	...	...	20	0.85
French Franc					163.23
250,000 French Francs-European Style					
16½	Jun	2	4.64	...	...
German Mark					54.68
62,500 German Mark EOM-European style.					
55	Jan	...	...	25	0.20
62,500 German Marks EOM-European style.					
55½	Jan	...	...	200	0.57
62,500 German Marks EOM-cents per unit.					
55½	Jan	100	0.08	...	...
62,500 German Marks-European Style.					
55½	Feb	300	0.34	...	...
56	Jun	14	1.04	...	...
62,500 German Marks-cents per unit.					
54	Feb	...	...	50	0.19
54	Mar	...	...	120	0.50
54½	Feb	...	...	50	0.27
55	Feb	...	...	28	0.62
55	Mar	1	0.90	...	...
56	Mar	70	0.59	14	1.50
57	Feb	8	0.08	...	...
57	Mar	...	...	2	2.20
57	Jun	25	0.87	...	...
Japanese Yen					79.56
6,250,000 J.Yen EOM-European style.					
79	Feb	20	2.00	...	...
6,250,000J.Yen EOM 100ths of a cent per unit.					
80½	Jan	150	0.11	...	...
6,250,000J.Yen EOM 100ths of a cent per unit.					
79	Jan	...	...	400	0.15
79	Feb	...	...	2	0.80
80	Jan	...	...	50	0.36
6,250,000J.Yen-100ths of a cent per unit.					
75	Mar	5	5.36	...	...
76	Jun	...	...	23	0.99
76½	Mar	...	...	1	0.46
77	Jun	...	...	27	1.24
79	Mar	...	...	5	1.08
80	Mar	20	1.85	...	...
80	Jun	...	...	50	2.22
82	Mar	...	...	4	2.58
83	Jun	10	2.07	...	...
83½	Mar	1	0.50	...	...
85	Jun	200	1.30	...	...
89	Jun	1	0.58	...	...
90	Mar	...	...	20	0.87
Swiss Franc					67.86
62,500 Swiss Francs-European Style.					
64	Mar	...	...	40	0.09
65	Feb	4	3.72	...	...
66	Feb	52	2.20	...	...
66	Mar	30	2.78	...	...
67	Feb	104	1.34	12	0.25
67	Mar	10	1.96	...	...
67½	Mar	...	...	50	0.65
68	Feb	...	...	50	0.50
68	Mar	26	1.21	10	0.80
69	Feb	12	0.31	10	1.10
69	Mar	65	1.02	5	1.34
69½	Mar	...	...	4	1.72
70	Mar	30	0.46	38	1.90
72	Mar	...	...	4	3.36
74	Mar	230	0.05	...	...
62,500 Swiss Francs-cents per unit.					
69½	Mar	5	0.61	...	...
70	Mar	33	0.64	...	...
Call Vol 3,221			Open Int ... 94,704		
Put Vol 2,940			Open Int ... 119,258		

Source: *Wall Street Journal,* January 30, 1998, C14

At expiration, the intrinsic value of a call option will be either the asset's value minus the exercise price (if the asset's value exceeds the exercise price) or zero (if the asset's value is less than the strike price). If we let V denote the market value of the underlying asset and X denote the option's exercise price, the value of an option just prior to expiration will be the maximum of V − X or 0; this can be written Max [0, V − X]. Panel A in Figure 17.8 graphically illustrates the payoff diagram for a call option with an exercise price of $50. The value of the call option is zero should the asset value fall below $50. If the asset's value rises above the exercise price, say to $60, the intrinsic value of the call option rises dollar for dollar. In this case, the call option is valuable; the holder can buy a stock at $50 when it has a current market value of $60.

If this were not the case, arbitrage operations would make it so. For example, suppose the exercise price on a stock's call option is $50 and the stock is selling for $60. The call option has an intrinsic value of V − X = $60 − $50 or $10. If the call option's price were only $8, arbitrageurs would buy the option for $8, immediately exercise it and pay $50 to purchase the stock; they would then sell the stock at its market price of $60 and receive a profit of $2, ignoring commissions and taxes. In other words, they paid a total of $8 (option) plus $50 (exercise price) or $58; selling the stock for $60 results in a $2 profit. The buying pressure in the options market and selling pressure in the stock market would cause the option and stock prices or both to change and eliminate the risk-free profit opportunity.

Panel B of Figure 17.8 shows the payoff diagram for the seller or writer of the call option. Whereas increases in the asset's value above X are beneficial to the call purchaser, they harm the call seller. This is so because the call option allows the buyer to purchase the higher-priced asset at the lower exercise price. As the asset's value climbs, the call writer faces a larger loss. If the option is exercised and the call writer does not own the underlying asset, she may have to purchase the asset at price V and sell it to the call buyer at price X, suffering the loss (X − V). For example, if the exercise price is $50 and the stock's price rises

Figure 17.8   *Payoff Profiles for Call and Put Options at Expiration*

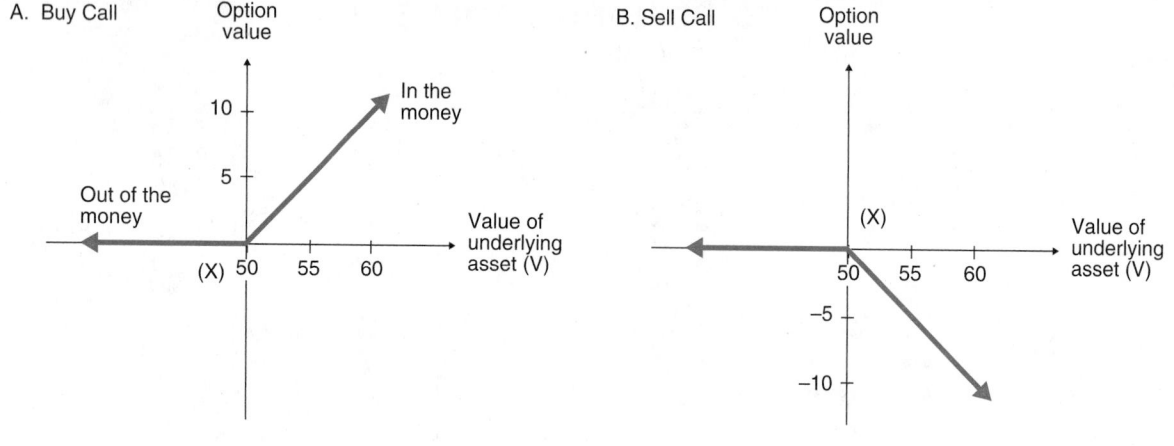

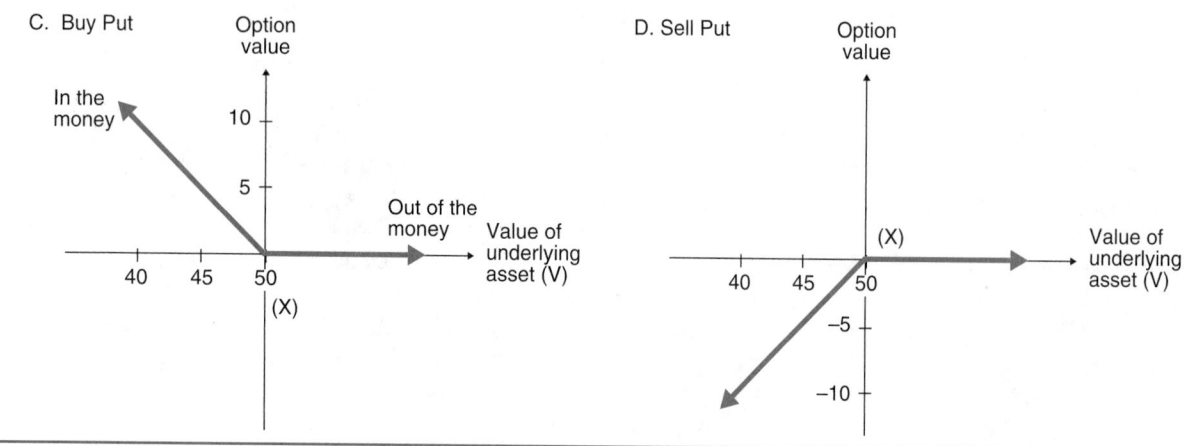

to $60, the call writer may have to purchase the stock in the open market at $60 and sell it to the owner of the call option for $50, thus losing $10. If the call writer already owns the stock, she suffers an opportunity loss of $10; instead of selling the stock at its spot price of $60, she must sell it to the option holder at the exercise price of $50.

Panels C and D in Figure 17.8 show payoff diagrams for put option buyers and writers. As the put option allows the owner to sell the underlying asset at the exercise price X, the put option becomes more valuable to the buyer as the value V of the asset falls below X. On the other hand, the option to sell an asset for X when the asset's value is greater than X will cause the put option to have no intrinsic value. Thus, the intrinsic value of the option at expiration is the maximum of X − V or zero, or Max [0, X − V]. As the asset's value falls below the exercise price X, the option becomes more in the money and the value of the put option rises in correspondence with the fall of the asset's value, as seen in panel C.

Table 17.6 *Call and Put Intrinsic Values*

Assume: Exercise price of $50

Call Option

Current Stock Price	Exercise Price	Intrinsic Value	Comment
(V)	(X)	Max [0, V − X]	
$45	$50	$0	out of the money
50	50	0	at the money
55	50	0	in the money

Put Option

Current Stock Price	Exercise Price	Intrinsic Value	Comment
(V)	(X)	Max [0, X − V]	
$45	$50	$5	in the money
50	50	0	at the money
55	50	0	out of the money

For example, if a put option has an exercise price of $50, the option is worthless if the stock's current market value is $60; anyone wanting to sell the stock will choose to do so in the stock market and will receive $60. If the stock's price is only $40, however, the put option has an intrinsic value of $50 − $40 or $10, because it allows the owner of the put option to sell the stock for $50 when the stock's market value is only $40. Similar to the call option, arbitrage will ensure that this put option's price will be at least $10. For example, should the put's price be $7, arbitrageurs will buy the put for $7 and buy the stock for $40; they will then immediately exercise the put, forcing the put writer to purchase their stock at the exercise price of $50. The arbitrageurs will gain a risk-free profit of $3: $7 (put option) + $40 (stock's market value) or $47; selling the stock by exercising the put gains them $50, for a profit of $50 − $47 = $3.

The situation is reversed for the writer or seller of the put option. The payoff diagram for the writer of the put appears in panel D of Figure 17.8. As the asset's value falls below X, the writer will be forced to purchase the asset for more than the asset's current market value and suffer a loss of V − X. For example, if the put's exercise price is $50 and the stock's market value is $40, the put writer may have to purchase the stock at the $50 exercise price, thereby paying $10 more than the stock is currently worth. Should the asset's value rise above X, the put option loses its intrinsic value, because the asset can be sold in the open market for a price exceeding the put's exercise price.

Table 17.6 summarizes some intrinsic values for these put and call relationships.

Thus far, we have reviewed the intrinsic value of options to provide the basic concepts. In reality, the option's market value will equal its intrinsic value only at expiration; at all other times, the option's market price will exceed its intrinsic value. The major reason for this differential between intrinsic value and market price is *time*. As long as the option has time remaining until expiration, the option buyer is purchasing both the option's intrinsic value *and* its time value. The remaining time to expiration on the option is important, because the longer the time to expiration, the greater the chance of the option becoming in-the-money (if it was originally at the money or out of the money), or even more in the money than it originally was. Several factors affect the current market price of an option including the option's exercise price, its time to expiration, the underlying asset's current price and price volatility, and the current market interest rate. In the following section we discuss each of these factors in more detail.

VALUATION OF CALL AND PUT OPTIONS

We use five factors to calculate the value of an American call or put option, assuming the stock does not pay a dividend: (1) the stock price, (2) the exercise price, (3) the time to maturity, (4) the interest rate, and (5) the volatility of the underlying stock. You can allow for dividends through an additional calculation. The following discussion will relate each of the factors to the value of a call option. After this, we will note how they relate to the value of a put option.

Stock Price

The value of a call option is positively related to the price of the underlying stock. With a given exercise price, the price of the stock determines whether the option is in the money, and therefore has an intrinsic value, or out of the money, with only speculative or time value.

Exercise Price

The value of a call option is inversely related to its exercise price. For a given stock price, a lower exercise price raises the value of a call on the stock. As an example, consider a stock selling at $70 a share. A call option with an exercise price of $50 would certainly be worth more than a call option with an exercise price of $60. The first option is in the money by $20, the second by only $10.

Time to Expiration

The value of an option depends to a great extent on its time to expiration. All other factors being equal, a longer time to expiration increases the value of the option because it lengthens the span of time during which gains are possible. The longer option allows investors to reap all the benefits of a shorter option for a longer time.

Interest Rate

An investor who acquires an option buys control of the underlying stock for a period of time, with downside risk limited to the cost of the option. The option gives upside potential that grows because of its leverage. Therefore, the option resembles buying on margin, except that the interest charge is implicit. A higher market interest rate increases the saving from using options, and therefore the value of the option. This creates a *positive* relationship between the market interest rate and the value of the call option.

Volatility of Underlying Stock Price

When determining the value of most investments, a high level of price volatility indicates greater risk, which reduces value, all other factors being equal. For call options on a stock, however, the opposite is true; an option's value has a positive relationship with the volatility of the underlying stock. This is because greater volatility implies greater upside potential, and the downside protection of the option, which limits the maximum loss, is also worth more.[4]

---

[4]For an article that discusses how to estimate volatility, see Galen Burghardt and Morton Lane, "How to Tell If Options Are Cheap," *Journal of Portfolio Management* 16, no. 2 (Winter 1990): 72–78.

Table 17.7 *Option Pricing Relationships*	Call Option	Put Option
Stock price	+	−
Exercise price	−	+
Time to expiration	+	+
Interest rate	+	−
Volatility of underlying stock	+	+

Valuation Factors and Put Options

As noted, the same five factors determine the value of put options, although several of the relationships differ. First, the value of put options relates *inversely* to the price of the underlying stock, all else remaining the same. This is because the intrinsic value of a put option is the difference between the exercise price and the stock price; the exercise price of an in-the-money put option exceeds the stock price. Following from this, the value of the put option relates *positively* to the exercise price.

The relationship of put option value to the third factor, time to expiration, is positive, as for a call option. Again, the reasoning is that the longer maturity provides more time for the put option to increase in value. The effect of the interest-rate factor on the value of a put option also differs. The interest rate effect on the value of a put option is *negative* because buying a put option is like deferring the *sale* of stock because you receive the proceeds of the sale in the future. Therefore, we are dealing with the present value of the future proceeds, and a higher interest rate reduces the present value of those proceeds. Finally, the effect of the volatility of the stock price on the value of the put option is the same as for the call option. Higher price volatility increases the value of the put option because it increases the probability of the put option being in the money. These relationships are summarized in Table 17.7.

Derivation of the Valuation Formula

Black and Scholes developed a formula for determining the value of American call options in a classic article published in 1973.[5] Merton later refined this formula under less restrictive assumptions.[6] The resulting formula is set forth and demonstrated in the Chapter 17 Appendix. For their work in option-pricing theory, Scholes and Merton received the 1997 Nobel Prize in Economics. Black's untimely death in 1995 prevented him from joining his colleagues in receiving this honor as the Nobel Prize is awarded only to living persons.

---

[5]Fischer Black and Myron Scholes, "The Pricing of Options and Corporate Liabilities," *Journal of Political Economy* 81, no. 2 (May–June 1973): 637–654. For a background discussion, see Fischer Black, "How We Came up with the Option Formula," *Journal of Portfolio Management* 15, no. 2 (Winter 1989): 4–8.

[6]Robert C. Merton, "The Theory of Rational Option Pricing," *Bell Journal of Economics and Management Science* 4, no. 3 (August 1973): 141–183.

As discussed in the appendix, although the formula appears rather forbidding, one can observe almost all the required inputs directly in the market. Further, although the calculations are rather difficult, numerous computer programs can expedite the process, as can programs available for hand-held calculators.

OPTION TRADING STRATEGIES

Investors quickly learned that option trading greatly increases the number and complexity of investment strategies. In this section, we will not attempt to cover all the strategies, but will limit our discussion to the major alternatives. Also, to understand the more sophisticated strategies, you must understand the basic techniques because the more advanced methods build on these. Some of the end-of-chapter references describe the more sophisticated techniques. In this section we explicitly take option premiums into consideration as we consider profits and losses from various option positions.

For the option strategies we shall examine, let us assume that the following options are available for trading:

Exercise Price (per share)	Call Premium (per share)	Put Premium
70	6 $^1/_8$	2 $^1/_4$
75	3 $^1/_2$	4 $^3/_4$

We'll assume the stock price is $73.25, and, for simplicity, we will ignore taxes and commissions and treat the options as European options. In addition, we will assume all strategies are held to expiration. Although this is not required and usually is not done, we cannot understand how to evaluate option strategies closed out before expiration without a better grasp of option-pricing theory.

Buying Call Options

Investors buy call options because they expect the price of the underlying stock to increase during the period prior to the expiration of the option. If this expectation comes true, the purchase of an option will yield a large return on a small dollar investment. Investors may have the choice of purchasing an out-of-the-money option, an at-the-money option, or an in-the-money option. An out-of-the-money option costs the least but offers the lowest potential return. An in-the-money option costs the most but offers the highest potential return.

Consider the purchase of the call option with a $70 exercise price (we will refer to this as the 70 call). You would pay 100 × $6.125 or $612.50 for this call. The overall profit from the call-option transaction can be stated as:

$$\text{Max } [0, V - X] - \text{call premium.}$$

Assume the stock price ends up at $68. The profit is Max [0, (68 − 70)] − 6.125; this equals −6.125, or a loss of $6.125 per option. If the stock price ends up at $75, the profit is Max [0, (75 − 70)] − 6.125, which is −1.125, or a loss of $1.125 per option. You would break even if the stock price at expiration is $70 (the exercise price) + $6.125 (the call premium), or $76.125.

Figure 17.9 illustrates these results in the form of a payoff diagram that reflects the initial cost of the option premium. You can see that the call-buying strategy has a limited loss of the option premium, which in this case is $612.50 per contract. No limit exists on the upside because the stock price can rise without limit. The leverage inherent in

Figure 17.9   *Profits to Buyer of Call Option*

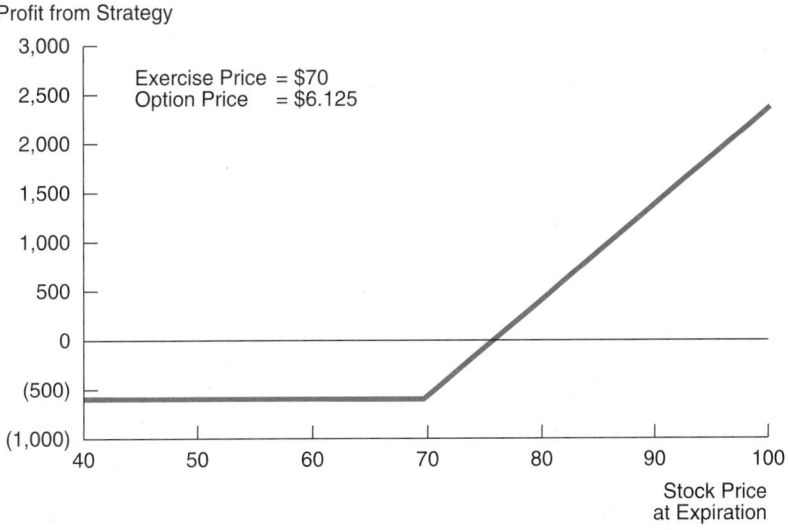

options is quite tempting. For example, assume the stock price rises 20 percent over the life of the option, going from $73.25 to $87.90. At expiration, the option would end up being worth $17.90 [Max (0, 87.90 − 70)], or $1790 per 100-share contract. Thus, a 20 percent stock price increase led to a 192 percent increase in the option premium [(17.90 − 6.125)/6.125]. On the other hand, if the stock price fell from $73.25 to 65 by expiration, which is an 11.3 percent decline, the option value would fall to zero, a 100 percent loss. Although the loss is 100 percent of the option value, the dollar loss of $6.125 a share is fairly small relative to the stock price (about 8.4 percent). Investors need to be careful about interpreting potential option profits and losses. The lure of potentially large profits with limited dollar losses must be tempered with the fact that the large profits occur quite rarely, whereas small losses occur quite frequently.

You could have chosen the out-of-the-money option with the $75 exercise price and paid a call premium of only $3.50. This option would have limited your overall loss to $350. However, the stock price would have had to rise to $78.50 ($75 exercise price + $3.50 call premium) at expiration before you would have made money.

Selling Call Options

Now let us look at the profits for the individual who sold, or wrote, the 70 call. When a call is sold, the writer receives the premium, which in this case is $6.125 (or, more properly, $6.125 × 100 shares or $612.50). If we assume the seller does not own the stock, this transaction is referred to as an **uncovered** or **naked call**, for reasons that will become apparent.

Recall that the seller of the call will *owe* the value Max [0, V − X] at expiration, because the seller may have to buy the stock at its market price, V, and sell it at X. If the stock price is substantially greater than the exercise price, the seller of the option can incur a large loss. As we saw above, the seller's profits are simply −1 multiplied by the buyer's profits.

Figure 17.10 graphs the seller's profits, which you should recognize as simply Figure 17.9 inverted. The seller of the option can earn a maximum amount equal to the

Figure 17.10   *Profits to Seller of Uncovered Call Option*

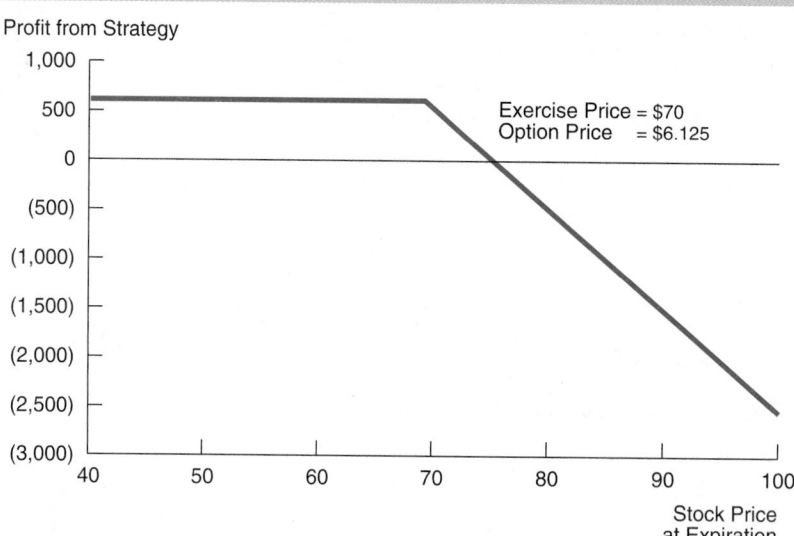

premium of $612.50, which is retained if the option ends up out of the money. The seller's loss is potentially unlimited.[7]

The risk of unlimited losses explains why we refer to this option writing strategy as uncovered or naked. If, however, the writer owns the stock, this is a **covered call**. In this case, if the call option is exercised, the covered call writer need not buy the stock in the market. He or she simply delivers the stock held, effectively selling it for the exercise price. Thus out-of-pocket losses are minimal, aside from an opportunity cost if the option expires in the money (the writer of the call option sells the stock at a price below current market value).

The profit to the call writer from a covered call can be broken down into two components: the profit from writing the call and the profit on the stock held. The profit from writing the call is $-\text{Max}[0, V - X] + \text{call premium}$; the profit on the stock is either the current value V minus the original price the investor paid for the stock if the call expires out of the money, or the exercise price minus the original stock purchase price should the call expire in the money.

Figure 17.11 shows the profits of the writer of the covered call; graphically as well as arithmetically it equals the combined profits of its component strategies, the long position in the stock plus an uncovered call. If the stock falls, the covered call writer keeps the premium and the stock, while the premium received cushions against the loss in value of the stock. On the upside, however, the covered call writer's gains are limited because the stock must be sold for the exercise price regardless of how much it is worth in the market.

Covered call writers are considered to be smart option traders because they make money by capitalizing on the public's excessive optimism about potential stock price moves. If the public is indeed overly optimistic, a covered call writer can collect the premiums, knowing that the stock is unlikely to move high enough to justify the premium. Many covered call writers view this as an opportunity to generate income off of a slow-moving stock.

---

[7]Clearly, the seller can be literally "wiped out." For that reason, the seller's broker will generally require the seller to post margin money. Another way to reduce the risk of disaster is for the seller to own the stock, a strategy we shall examine next.

Figure 17.11   *Profits to Seller of Covered Call Option*

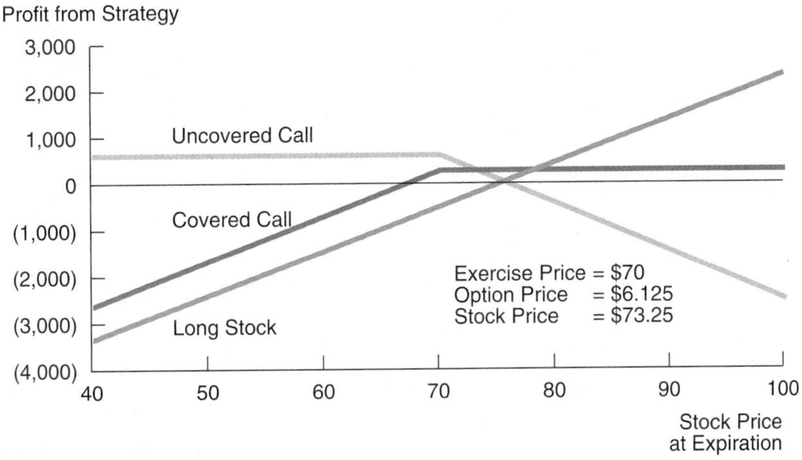

Exercise Price = $70
Option Price = $6.125
Stock Price   = $73.25

Buying Put Options

Several major reasons exist for acquiring a put option on a stock. The most obvious is that you expect a particular stock to decline in price and you want to profit from this decline. As will be shown, buying a put option allows you to do this with the benefits of leverage while limiting the potential loss if your expectation regarding a price decline in the stock is wrong. Buying put options offers two advantages over selling the stock short: (1) the losses are limited to the put premium and (2) costly short sale margin requirements are avoided. In addition, put options can serve as a hedge if you own a stock and do not want to sell it at the present time, although you believe it might decline in the near term. In this case, you can buy a put option on the stock you own as a hedge against the decline; if the stock declines, you will offset the decline in the stock with an increase in the value of the put option.

Consider the strategy of purchasing the 70 put for $2.25. The put will be worth $Max[0, X - V]$ at expiration. Thus, the profit from buying the put can be expressed as:

$$Max[0, X - V] - \text{put option premium.}$$

If the put expires in the money, the put owner can effectively buy the stock in the market for V and sell it to the put writer for the higher exercise price X. The profit on the transaction is this trading profit minus the put premium paid up front. If the put expires out of the money, the put's intrinsic value is zero (no trading profit) and the put holder simply loses the put premium that was paid up front.

Suppose the stock price ends up at $60. The $60 stock can be sold for $70, netting a profit of $10 − $2.25 or $7.75 per share, or $775 per contract. If the stock price ends up at $80, the option expires worthless and the put holder loses the $225 premium. Figure 17.12 illustrates the profits for the put buyer. As you can see, the put buyer's loss is limited to the premium of $225. The gains are limited because the stock price can never fall below zero. If the company went bankrupt, the stock could theoretically fall to zero and the put buyer would make $70 − $2.25 or $67.75 per option or $6,775 overall. Of course, this extreme case is quite unlikely.

Puts, like calls, also offer enormous leverage. As before, assume the stock is currently priced at $73.25. If the stock price falls 20 percent to $58.60, the put price will rise 406.7 percent to $11.40. Because the put is currently out of the money ($73.25 exceeds the

Figure 17.12   *Profits to Buyer of Put Option*

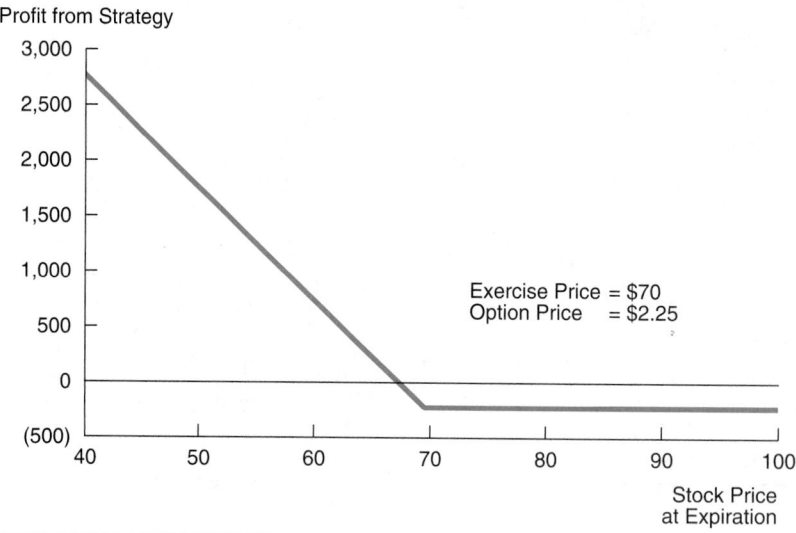

exercise price of $70), should the price fall 4.44 percent, to $70, the put option will expire worthless and its loss will be 100 percent.

One of the more attractive strategies employing puts is called the **protective put**. This involves the purchase of a put accompanied by a long position in the stock. Should the price of the stock decline below the exercise price, the rising value of the put option will offset the decline in the stock price. Similar to the covered call, the profit from this strategy can be broken down into the profit from the stock plus the profit from the put option.

Figure 17.13 graphically illustrates the returns on a protective put by combining the payoff diagrams for a stock purchase with those of a long put position. Notice that the protective put payoff diagram resembles that of the long call in Figure 17.9. In fact, it is sometimes referred to as a **synthetic call** because the holder of the protective put has limited losses and unlimited gains. Thus, two different options strategies result in similar payoffs regardless of the stock's price at expiration. We will return to this interesting point in our discussion of put/call parity later in this chapter.

The protective put is also a classic example of how to insure (hedge) a stock position. The holder of the stock can be viewed as someone holding an asset at risk of losing value. Some investors might be interested in purchasing insurance that would limit the losses on the asset. The put serves as this insurance. By paying the premium up front, the insurer (the put writer) promises to absorb all stock price decreases below the exercise price. If the stock price rises, the put expires worthless, which is equivalent to an insurance policy expiring without having had a claim.

Selling Put Options

The seller or writer of the put option, like the seller of the call option, has a profit that can be expressed as simply −1 times the put-option buyer's profit. The seller of the put is accepting the premium up front for his willingness to purchase the stock at expiration at the exercise price. The put seller's gains are limited, however his losses, like the put buyer's gains, although limited, can be quite large if the stock price experiences a dramatic decline.

Figure 17.13 *Profits to Buyer of Protective Put Option*

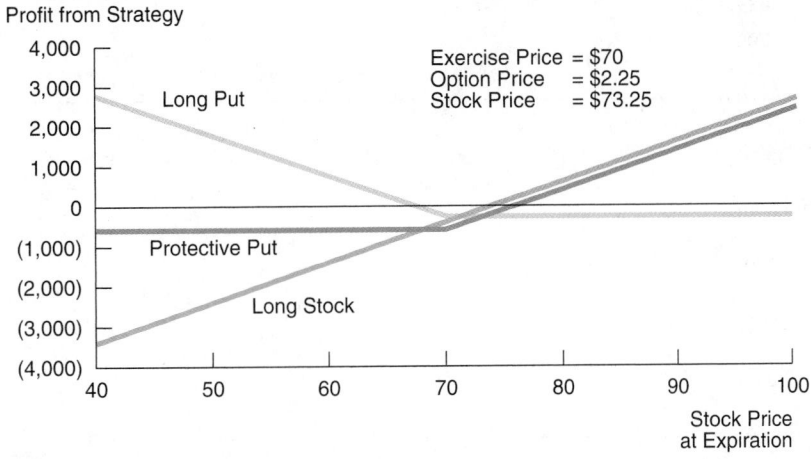

Figure 17.14 illustrates the profits to the seller of the put option. Comparing Figure 17.14 with Figure 17.12, which shows the profits to the put buyer, we can see that these two figures are mirror images of each other.

Option Spreads

Rather than simply buying or selling a call option, you can do both by entering into a spread. There are two basic types of spreads. First, a **price spread** (also called a *vertical spread*), involves buying the call option for a given stock, expiration date, and strike price, and selling a call option for the same stock and expiration date, but at a different strike price. For example, buying a Ford October 35 and selling a Ford October 40. The second type, a **time spread** (also called a *horizontal* or *calendar spread*), involves both buying and selling options for the same stock and strike price, but with different expiration dates. An example would be buying a Ford October 40 and selling a Ford January 40. Option spreads can serve a variety of investment goals.

Bullish Spreads   You might consider a bullish spread strategy if you were generally bullish on the underlying stock, but you wanted to be conservative. Assume you are optimistic on the outlook for Ford stock, which is currently selling for $35, and want to enter into a price spread. A Ford October 30 option is currently priced at 7, whereas a Ford October 40 option is priced at 2.

Because you are bullish you would buy the higher-priced Ford October 30 option and sell the lower-priced Ford October 40 option. The net cost of 5 ($500) is your maximum loss. If your expectations were correct, and the stock rose from $35 to $45, the October 30 option would be worth about 15, its intrinsic value, whereas the October 40 would sell for about 5. Closing out both positions would give you a $500 gain as follows:

October 30: Bought at 7, Sold at 15	= Gain 8
October 40: Sold at 2, Bought at 5	= Loss 3
Overall	= Gain 5

If the stock were to decline dramatically, your maximum loss would be $500 (your initial cost), even though both options would expire worthless. Your maximum gain would

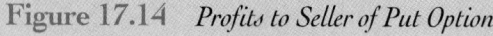

Figure 17.14 *Profits to Seller of Put Option*

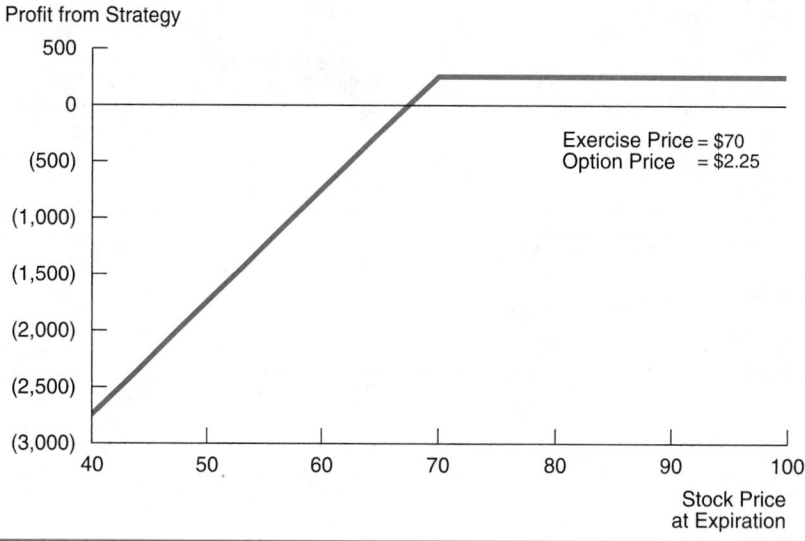

also be $500. At some high stock price, the value of the options will differ by 10, which would give you a gross profit of $1,000 less the $500 initial cost. The payoff diagram for this option strategy is shown in Figure 17.15.

Bearish Spreads   Assume, on the other hand, that you are generally bearish on a stock or the market and want to act using a conservative strategy. You could enter into a bearish spread, selling the higher-priced option and buying the lower-priced option. You would sell the Ford October 30 at 7, and buy the Ford October 40 at 2, generating an immediate gain of $500.

If you are correct and Ford stock declines below 30, both options will expire worthless and you will have the $500 profit. In contrast, if the stock rises to 45, the results would be as follows:

October 30: Sold at 7, Bought at 15	= Loss 8
October 40: Bought at 2, Sold at 5	= Gain 3
Overall	= Loss 5

The loss of $500 compares favorably with the potential loss of $800 or more if the spread did not partially offset the adverse movement. At a high stock price, the two options will differ in price by 10, so your maximum loss is $500, or a gross loss of $1,000 less a $500 gain on the original transaction. The payoff diagram is shown in Figure 17.16.

Option spreads allow numerous other potential transactions to meet almost any possible set of risk–return conditions.[8]

PUT/CALL PARITY

As it turns out, the prices of calls and puts are not completely independent of one another. They are related to each other through a concept known as **put/call parity**. The

---

[8]A more extensive discussion appears in M. J. Gombola, R. Roenfeldt, and P. L. Cooley, "Spreading Strategies in CBOE Options: Evidence on Market Performance," *Journal of Financial Research* 1, no. 1 (Winter 1978): 35–44.

Figure 17.15 *Payoff Diagram for a Bullish Price Spread*

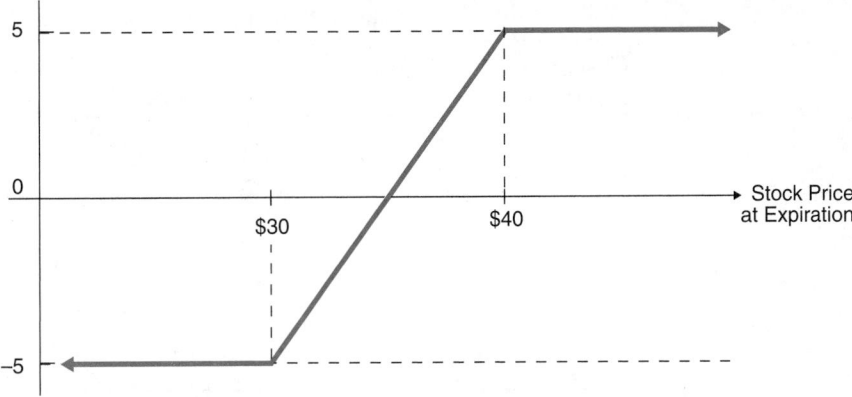

Figure 17.16 *Payoff Diagram for a Bearish Price Spread*

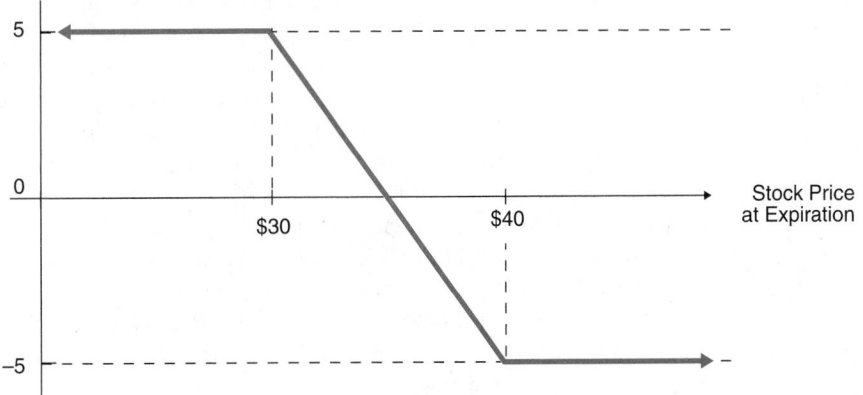

basic intuition behind this concept is that if two portfolios will have the same value at some future time T, the prices of the two portfolios should be the same today. If this is not true arbitrage will result, because investors will buy the underpriced portfolio and sell the over-priced one until their prices are equivalent.

Consider four securities: one call and one put option, each with the same exercise price $50, on one share of the same stock; one share of the stock; and one risk-free zero-coupon bond with par value of $50. The two options and the bond mature or expire on the same day, T. Suppose we construct Portfolio A consisting of the share of stock and the put option. We also construct Portfolio B consisting of the call option and the risk-free discount bond with a par value of $50.

We know the values of the options depend on the stock's value, V, at expiration and the option's exercise price. Let us examine these two portfolios under two situations: first with the stock's price V less than the exercise price X, $50 at expiration, and second with V exceeding X, $50, at expiration. These results are shown in Table 17.8.

In the first case, V (say, $40) is less than or equal to X (say, $50), so the call option expires worthless, out of the money. The value of Portfolio B will be 0 (value of call option) + $50 (par value of the matured bond), which sums to $50. For Portfolio A, the put option expires in the money and will have a value equal to $X - V$; the stock itself has a price of V. The value of Portfolio A at option expiration is $50 − $40 (value of the put option)

Table 17.8 *Values of Portfolios A and B on the Option Expiration Date, Time T*

Portfolio	Value at Expiration, Time T			
	Stock Price < Strike Price		Stock Price > Strike Price	
A				
One share of stock	V		V	
One put option	X − V		0	
	X		V	
B				
One call option	0		V − X	
Risk-free discount bond	X		X	
	X		V	

+ V ($40 value of the stock), this sums to $50. Thus, if the stock's price is less than $50 when the options expire, the values of Portfolios A and B both equal $50.

In the second case, V (say, $60) is greater than the $50 exercise price (X) so the call option expires in the money, with a value of $60 − $50. The value of Portfolio B will then be $60 − $50 (value of call option) + $50 (par value of matured bond), which sums to V or $60. The put option expires out of the money and so has a value equal to 0. The stock itself has a price of V. The value of Portfolio A at option expiration is 0 (value of the put option) + V ($60 value of the stock); this sums to $60. Thus, if the stock's price is greater than $50 when the options expire, the values of Portfolios A and B both equal $60.

So we see that Portfolios A and B will have the same value when the options expire under each possibility. If the stock's price is less than the exercise price, both portfolios have a value of X or $50; if the stock's price is greater than the exercise price, both portfolios will have a value of V, or $60 in this example. Because they both have the same value at time T, both portfolios must have the same price today. Thus, the value of Portfolio A must equal the value of Portfolio B, or:

Stock Price + Put Premium = Call Premium + Risk-Free Discount Bond Price

This result is not really all that surprising. Recall that earlier we saw that the payoff diagrams of Figure 17.13 (protective put) and Figure 17.9 (call option) are identical. That is what the above relationship expresses algebraically! The left-hand side of the equation is the protective put strategy: long on the stock and long on a put option. The right-hand side represents a long call position, with the extra cash invested in a risk-free security (the extra cash represents the difference between the stock's price and the call premium). Arbitrage will ensure that the value of a protective put strategy will be in parity with that of a long call position.

By rearranging the above equation in numerous ways, we can determine the appropriate price of a put option as a function of the call price, stock price, and the price of risk-free discount bonds:

put premium = call premium + risk-free discount bond − stock price

Sketching a payoff diagram of a combination of a long call and a short stock position will result in payoff resembling that of a long put position; buying a call and shorting the stock is a **synthetic put**. Similarly, we can determine the call's price from the values of the other

three assets. We can also estimate the stock's price using information about the prices of
call and put options and risk-free discount bonds:

$$\text{Stock price} = \text{call premium} - \text{put premium} + \text{risk-free discount bond}$$

This shows that the payoff diagram for a long stock position results from combining the
payoffs of a long call and short put position.

    Futures prices are also related to call and put option prices. To see this intuitively, recall
that the payoff diagram for a long futures position is identical to that of a long position
in the underlying asset. The same applies to a short futures position and its underlying
asset. Conceptually, similar to the above situation, a portfolio containing a futures contract and put option will have the same value as a portfolio containing a call option and
a risk-free discount bond.

SUMMARY

♦ Derivative securities are rising in importance and popularity. Forwards, futures, and options are used in a variety of ways, both by investors and corporations. They can be used to control risk through hedging, generate income through writing puts and calls, or used with the goal of earning capital gains.

♦ Forward contracts are the oldest derivative; a forward contract represents an obligation by the owner to buy the underlying asset before a specified date (the expiration date) at a specified price (the exercise or strike price). The gain or loss on a forward contract is transmitted on the contract's expiration date. The value of a forward contract rises and falls with increases and decreases in the value of the underlying asset. Currencies are the underlying asset for many forward contracts.

♦ Futures contracts are similar to forwards, because they also represent an obligation by the owner to purchase the underlying asset on a specified day and at a specified price. Notably, the futures' liquidity is enhanced by standardized contracts. Credit risk is also reduced, because buyers and sellers of futures must post a margin account. Through the process of "marking to the market," the daily change in the value of an investor's position is added to or subtracted from the margin accounts. If the balance in the margin account becomes too low, a margin call will be issued.

♦ A major distinction between options contracts and futures is that the option provides the owner with the *right,* rather than an obligation, to buy an asset (call options) or sell an asset (put options). This feature allows option buyers to limit their losses if the price of the underlying asset moves adversely to their position. Various trading strategies are available to option investors, including buying and selling calls and puts, writing covered calls, and using protective puts.

♦ Puts, calls, and futures with the same underlying asset will have prices that are related to each other; this is called put/call parity. Arbitrage between the spot market, futures market, and options market will ensure that put/call parity holds rather closely over time. Chapter 18 discusses more sophisticated derivative strategies.

Questions

1. How are options like forward contracts? How are they different?
2. How do forward contracts differ from futures contracts? How are they similar?
3. Identify the maximum and minimum prices of puts and calls and explain why they are the maximum and minimum.
4. If the price of a stock and a put option exceeded the price of a call option and a risk-free bond with a face value equal to the exercise price, what kind of transaction should you make? Explain.
5. What is a derivative security? Why would an investor want to own or sell a derivative instead of the underlying asset?
6. What factors affect the price of an option contract? Explain how each affects the option premium.
7. Why do futures contracts have less credit or default risk than forward contracts?
8. Why are futures and options contracts available on only a limited set of assets?
9. For options written on the same stock and at the same exercise price, would the price of an American option be greater than, less than, or equal to the price of a European option? Explain.
10. Is it riskier to write covered or uncovered calls? Explain.
11. If a stock's standard deviation of returns rises, what happens to the value of its call and put options? If the stock's beta rises, what happens to the value of its call and put options?

12. *CFA Level II Exam (1997)*

Current equity call prices for Furniture City are contained in the table below. In reviewing these prices Jim Smith, CFA, notices discrepancies between several option prices and basic option pricing relationships.

Closing Prices Furniture City Equity Call Options
May 30, 1998

		Expiration Month			
Close	Strike	June	July	August	September
$119\frac{1}{2}$	110	$8\frac{7}{8}$	$12\frac{1}{2}$	15	18
$119\frac{1}{2}$	120	$1\frac{1}{2}$	$3\frac{3}{4}$	3	$4\frac{1}{4}$
$119\frac{1}{2}$	130	1	$2\frac{1}{4}$	$2\frac{7}{8}$	5

Identify *three different* apparent pricing discrepancies in the above table. Identify which of the basic option-pricing relationships *each* discrepancy violates.

[Note: The fact that option contracts do not always trade at the same time as the underlying stock should *not* be identified as a discrepancy.]

13. *CFA Level I Exam (1993)*

Michelle Industries issued a Swiss franc–denominated five-year discount note for SFr200 million. The proceeds were converted to U.S. dollars to purchase capital equipment in the United States. The company wants to hedge this currency exposure and is considering the following alternatives:

   i. At-the-money Swiss franc call options
   ii. Swiss franc forwards
   iii. Swiss franc futures

Contrast the essential characteristics of *each* of these *three* derivative instruments. Evaluate the suitability of *each* in relation to Michelle's hedging objective, including both advantages and disadvantages.

Problems

1. The current stock price is 56. Find the lower bound of the option prices assuming the following exercise prices:
   a. 55 call
   b. 60 call
   c. 55 put
   d. 60 put
2. Find the value at expiration of the following options if the stock price at expiration is 41.
   a. 40 call
   b. 45 call
   c. 40 put
   d. 45 put
3. Using the information in Figure 17.2, how much more or less expensive is it to buy French francs with a one-month forward contract rather than purchase francs in the spot market? In the three-month forward market? In the six-month forward market? Redo these calculations, this time using the Japanese yen.
4. Answer the following using the futures price data in Figure 17.3.
   a. What is the dollar value of the July corn futures contract at the settlement price?
   b. Suppose the initial margin requirement is 5 percent of the contract value. How much must you deposit in a margin account on this contract if you purchase it at the settlement price?
   c. Suppose the contract expires at a price of 275 cents per bushel. What is your percentage return?

5. Answer the following using the futures price data in Figure 17.3
   a. The notation by the future price quotation for the S&P Midcap 400 Index states the value of the contract is $500 times the index. Suppose the initial margin is 10 percent. How much must you deposit in the margin account if you buy the March contract at the settlement price?
   b. Compare the return on your futures investment to the return on a cash investment in the index if the March contract expires at 340. The cash market value of the index is listed in the last line of the Midcap Index quotes.
   c. Compare the return on your futures investment to the return on a cash investment in the index if the March contract expires at 320.
6. Chase's options listing appears in Figure 17.5
   a. What was the closing price of Chase stock?
   b. Which options are in the money? Out of the money?
   c. What is the dollar return on the March 105 call option if you purchased it and the expiration date price of Chase stock is $100? $105? $110?
   d. What is the dollar return on the February 115 put option if you purchased it and the expiration date price of Chase stock is $110? $115? $120?
7. Answer the following using the data for Chrysler's options appearing in Figure 17.5
   a. What is the value of the time premium between the February and April 35 call options? Put options?
   b. What is the intrinsic value of the April 30 call and put options? The April $37\frac{1}{2}$ call and put options?
   c. What arbitrage would investors do if the April 30 call was priced at $1\frac{1}{4}$?
   d. What arbitrage would investors do if the April $37\frac{1}{2}$ put was priced at $1\frac{1}{2}$?
8. Do the following using the data for Chrysler's options appearing in Figure 17.5.
   a. Draw the payoff diagram if an April 30 call is purchased.
   b. Draw the payoff diagram for writing an uncovered call using the April 30 call option.
   c. Draw the payoff diagram for writing a covered call using the April 30 call option.
9. Do the following using the data for Chrysler's options appearing in Figure 17.5.
   a. Draw the payoff diagram if an April 35 put is purchased.
   b. Draw the payoff diagram for a protective put strategy using the April 35 put option.
   c. Draw the payoff diagram for writing the April 35 put option.
10. Using the data from Figure 17.5, compute the following:
   a. The dollar return from a bullish spread of buying the Chase February 105 call and selling the February 115 call if the expiration price is $95; $105; $115; $125.
   b. The dollar return from a bearish spread of buying the Chase February 115 call and selling the February 105 call if the expiration price is $95; $105; $115; $125.
11. Illustrate put/call parity in the case of stock options with an exercise price of $100 (that is, replicate Table 17.8 using appropriate numerical values).
12. Using the stock price, call premium, and put premium data for Chase's March 105 options, use put/call parity to estimate the price of a risk-free discount bond.
13. Assume the appropriate risk-free discount bond has a par value of 114.24. Using the stock price and call premium for the Chase March 115 option, what should be the premium for the March 115 put option?
14. A put option on a stock has an exercise price of $35 and is priced at $2 a share. A call option with the same exercise price is priced at $4. What is the maximum loss per share to a writer of an uncovered put and the maximum profit per share to a writer of an uncovered call?
15. An investor buys 200 shares of stock for $43 per share and sells call options for all this stock, with an exercise price of $45, for a premium of $3 per share. Ignoring dividends and transaction costs, what is the maximum profit the investor can earn if this position is held to expiration?

References

Chance, Don M. *An Introduction to Options and Futures.* 3d ed. Fort Worth: The Dryden Press, 1995.

Clarke, Roger C., *Options and Futures: A Tutorial.* Charlottesville, VA: The Research Foundation of the Institute of Chartered Financial Analysts, 1992.

Dubosky, David A. *Options and Financial Futures: Valuation and Uses.* New York: McGraw-Hill, 1992.

Stoll, Hans R., and Robert E. Whaley. *Futures and Options: Theory and Applications.* Cincinnati: South-Western Publishing, 1993.

GLOSSARY

American option An option that allows the holder to exercise the option any time up to and including the expiration day.

At-the-money option An option with an exercise price approximately equal to the stock's market price.

Counterparty The name used for investors in derivative security positions.

Covered call option Selling an option contract against stock that you own.

Derivative instrument An investment that has its value determined by, or derived from, the value of another investment vehicle called the underlying asset or security.

European option An option that allows the holder to exercise the option only on the expiration day.

Exercise price or strike price The transaction price specified in an option contract.

Forward contract An agreement between two traders for delivery of an asset at a fixed time in the future for a specified price.

Futures contract An agreement between a trader and an exchange clearinghouse for the exchange of an asset at a fixed, standardized time in the future for a specified price.

Initial margin The funds buyers and sellers of futures are required to deposit in a margin account with an exchange's clearing corporation or clearinghouse.

In-the-money option An option with a favorable exercise price in relation to the stock's market price.

Option An investment instrument that grants to the owner the right to buy or sell something at a fixed price,

either on a specific date or any time up to a specific date.

Option premium The price paid for an option.

Out-of-the-money option An option with an unfavorable exercise price in relation to the stock's market price.

Price spread Simultaneously buying and selling options that are identical except for their exercise prices.

Protective put A put option strategy that involves the purchase of a put accompanied by a long position in the stock.

Put/call parity The relationship between put and call options on the same underlying asset with the same exercise price.

Settlement price The approximate closing price of the futures contract determined by a special exchange committee at the end of each trading day.

Spot market The trading market in which cash and asset ownership are transferred between the buyer and the seller.

Synthetic call Another name for a protective put; so called because the payoff diagram for a protective put resembles that of a call option.

Synthetic put A put-like position that arises from having a short stock position together with a long call position in the same stock.

Time spread Simultaneously buying and selling options that are identical except for their expiration dates.

Uncovered (naked) call option Selling an option contract on a stock that you do not own; you would have to acquire it if the option owner called for the stock.

A P P E N D I X *17*   *Black–Scholes Option Pricing Formula*

In this appendix we present the Black–Scholes (B–S) valuation formula and identify the variables involved. Subsequently, we discuss how to implement the formula and conclude with an example of its application.

The basic B–S and Merton valuation formula is:[9]

$$P_0 = P_s[N(d_1)] - X[e^{-rt}][N(d_2)]$$

---

[9]Fischer Black and Myron Scholes, "The Pricing of Options and Corporate Liabilities," *Journal of Political Economy* 81, no. 2 (May–June 1973): 637–654; Robert C. Merton, "The Theory of Rational Option Pricing," *Bell Journal of Economics and Management Science* 4, no. 3 (August 1973): 141–183.

where:

P_0 = market value of call option
P_s = current market price of underlying common stock
$N(d_1)$ = cumulative density function of $d1$ as defined below
X = exercise price of call option
r = current annualized market interest rate for prime commercial paper
t = time remaining before expiration in years (90 days 50.25)
$N(d_2)$ = cumulative density function of $d2$ as defined below

The cumulative density functions are defined as:

$$d_1 = \left[\frac{\ln(P_s/X + (r + 0.5\sigma^2)t}{\sigma(t)^{1/2}} \right]$$

$$d_2 = d_1 - [\sigma(t)^{1/2}]$$

where:

$\ln(Ps/X)$ = natural logarithm of (Ps/X)
s = standard deviation of annual rate of return on underlying stock

Implementing the Option Pricing Formula

Although the formula appears quite forbidding, almost all the required data are observable. The major inputs are current stock price (P_s), exercise price (X), market interest rate (r), time to expiration (t), and standard deviation of annual returns (σ). The only variable that is not observable, the volatility of price changes as measured by the standard deviation of returns (σ), becomes the major variable that you must estimate. It is also the variable that will cause differences in the estimates of market value for the option.

In a subsequent article, Black made several observations regarding how an investor goes about making this estimate.[10] First, he noted that knowledge of past price volatility should be helpful, but more is needed because the volatility of an individual stock changes over time. Therefore, in addition to a historical measure of the stock's volatility, you need to consider factors that would make its volatility increase or decrease during the period before expiration. This could include industry factors or internal corporate variables; do you expect any changes in business risk, financial risk, or liquidity risk?

One other variable requires some attention: the interest rate. You should use a rate that corresponds to the term of the option. The most obvious, the interest rate on prime commercial paper, is quoted daily in the *Wall Street Journal* for maturities of 30, 60, 90, and 240 days.

To demonstrate the application of the formula, consider an example with the following variables:

P_s = $36
X = $40
r = 0.10 (the rate on 90-day prime commercial paper)
t = 90 days (0.25 year)

---

[10]Fischer Black, "Fact and Fantasy in the Use of Options," *Financial Analysts Journal* 31, no. 4 (July–August 1975): 36–41. Also see Galen Burghardt and Morton Lane, "How to Tell If Options Are Cheap," *Journal of Portfolio Management* 16, no. 2 (Winter 1990): 72–78.

Table 17A.1 *Calculation of Option Value ($\sigma = 0.40$)*

$$d_1 = \left[\frac{\ln(36/40) + [0.10 + 0.5(0.4)^2]0.25}{0.4(0.25)^{1/2}} \right]$$

$$= \left[\frac{-0.1054 + 0.045}{0.2} \right]$$

$$= -0.302$$

$$d_2 = -0.302 - [0.4(0.25)^{1/2}]$$

$$= -0.302 - 0.2$$

$$= -0.502$$

$$N(d_1) = 0.3814$$

$$N(d_2) = 0.3079$$

$$P_0 = P_s[N(d_1)] - X[e^{-rt}][N(d_2)]$$

$$= [36][0.3814] - [40][e^{-0.025}][0.3079]$$

$$= 13.7304 - [40][0.9753][0.3079]$$

$$= 13.7304 - 12.0118$$

$$= 1.7186$$

Table 17A.2 *Calculation of Option Value ($\sigma = 0.50$)*

$$d_1 = \left[\frac{\ln(36/40) + [0.10 + 0.5(0.5)^2]0.25}{0.5(0.25)^{1/2}} \right]$$

$$= \frac{-0.1054 + 0.05625}{0.25}$$

$$= -0.1966$$

$$d_2 = -0.1966 - [0.5(0.25)^{1/2}]$$

$$= -0.1966 - 0.25$$

$$= -0.4466$$

$$N(d_1) = 0.4199$$

$$N(d_2) = 0.3275$$

$$P_0 = [36][0.4199] - [40][e^{-0.025}(-0.025)][0.3275]$$

$$= 15.1164 - [40][0.9753][0.3275]$$

$$= 15.1164 - 12.7764$$

$$= 2.34$$

Historical $\sigma = 0.40$

Expected $\sigma = 0.50$ (analysts expect an increase in the stock's beta because of a new debt issue)

All the values except stock price volatility are observable. A historical measure of volatility is given, but the analyst expects the stock's volatility to increase.

Table 17A.1 details the calculations for the option, assuming the historical volatility ($\sigma = 0.40$). Table 17A.2 shows the same calculations, assuming the higher volatility ($\sigma = 0.50$).

These results indicate the importance of estimating stock price volatility. A 25 percent increase in volatility (0.50 versus 0.40) causes a 36 percent increase in the value of the option. Because everything else is observable, this variable will differentiate estimates.

A WORD FROM THE STREET

BY MARK KRITZMAN, CFA

Windham Capital management offers three investment services: equity management, currency management, and tactical asset allocation. The currency management and tactical asset allocation strategies are implemented using futures and forward contracts. The following are examples of how this is done.

Many institutional investors allocate a fraction of their portfolios to foreign assets. The foreign asset exposures are equivalent to exposures to the domestic returns of the foreign assets together with exposures to respective currencies. If we expected favorable domestic performance from a foreign asset but depreciation of the foreign currency, we could sell currency futures and forward contracts to eliminate the currency risk while preserving the desired exposure to the foreign assets' domestic returns.

We also attempt to generate profits by trading currency futures and forward contracts independently of our clients' exposures to foreign assets. For example, purchasing currency futures or forward contracts in an amount equal to an underlying Treasury bill portfolio, we effectively convert an investment in U.S. Treasury bills into an investment in foreign short-term securities. We also employ financial futures contracts to manage the allocation of our clients' portfolios to stocks, bonds, and Treasury bills. For example, if we wanted to reduce the stock and bond components of a portfolio and increase the allocation to U.S. Treasury bills, we would sell futures contracts on the S&P 500 Index and on Treasury bonds in an amount equal to the desired percent change of the stock and bond portfolios. If the underlying portfolio is invested in the same asset as the asset upon which the futures contract is based, combining it with an equivalent short futures position produces Treasury bill exposure.

The use of futures contracts to effect asset mix shifts carries two significant advantages. First, the desired changes can be implemented without sacrificing the value that the manager of the underlying portfolios is expected to add, because the value of the portfolio does not change. Second, the asset mix changes can be implemented at a lower cost with futures contracts than by trading the portfolio in the cash market.

Mark Kritzman, CFA, is a founding partner of Windham Capital Management, an investment advisory firm specializing in currency hedging, equity management, and tactical asset allocation. Previously, he held investment positions at the Equitable, AT&T, and Bankers Trust Company. Mr. Kritzman serves on the Prize Committee of the Institute for Quantitative Research in Finance and on the Review Board of the Institute of Chartered Financial Analysts' Research Foundation. He is on the editorial boards of the *Journal of Derivatives,* the *Journal of Financial Engineering,* and the *Financial Analysts Journal,* to which he contributes a column entitled, "What Practitioners Need to Know." He has published more than forty articles and is the author of the *Portable Financial Analyst; Asset Allocation for Institutional Portfolios;* and *Quantitative Methods for Financial Analysis.*

CHAPTER

18

Advanced Derivatives, Warrants, and Convertible Securities

In this chapter we will answer the following questions:

♦ What is an option on a future?

♦ How do profit and loss factors differ for a futures contract, an option , and an option on a future?

♦ Why would investors want to invest in an option on a future?

♦ What is a warrant and how does it differ from a listed call option?

♦ What factors determine the value of a fixed-income warrant, and how is this valuation related to the Black–Scholes option pricing model?

♦ What are currency exchange warrants?

♦ What is a convertible security, and what are the main characteristics of convertible bonds?

♦ What are the main advantages of a convertible bond to the issuing firm?

♦ What are the main disadvantages of a convertible bond to investors?

♦ How do you determine the value of a convertible bond?

♦ What do we mean by the terms *conversion premium* and *payback (breakeven) period*, and how do we compute these values?

♦ How does a firm go about forcing the conversion of a convertible bond?

♦ What are the unique characteristics of convertible preferred stock, and what determines its value?

In Chapter 17, we introduced derivative instruments and discussed the basics of options, forwards, and futures. In Chapter 19 we'll consider how these instruments can be used to modify risk for equity portfolios, and in Chapter 20 we'll consider how they can be used in portfolio management. In this chapter our discussion focuses on the use of options on futures, which are growing in popularity because they are a combination

of the other securities. In addition, we examine three option securities that have been trading for years, that is, warrants, convertible bonds, and convertible preferred stock. Although they have been in existence for many years, the growth in knowledge and popularity of pure options has enhanced the use and valuation of these securities and led to further innovations.   ♦

OPTIONS ON FUTURES

An important innovation in the financial markets during 1982 was the reintroduction of **options on futures**, which are called *futures options* and *commodity options*. These instruments had existed in this country previously but were banned due to some scandals. Thus, when the Commodity Futures Trading Commission (CFTC) allowed them to be traded again, it was done on a limited basis. Originally, only a few contracts were permitted, but the program was a complete success, and many more contracts have been added.

The owner of a call or put on a futures has the right, but not the obligation, to buy or sell a futures contract at a fixed price. These options can be European or American, though most are American and are based on specific underlying futures contracts. For example, assume an option exists to buy an S&P 500 Index futures with an exercise price of 1080. If the option is exercised, the owner of the call establishes a long position in the March futures contract at 1080, which is equivalent to buying the futures at a price of 1080. If we assume that when the option is exercised the futures price is 1085, the call holder receives a long position in the futures at 1080, and this futures contract is immediately marked to market at 1085, which gives the call holder a credit of 5. Margin on the futures must be deposited as usual. The writer of the call establishes a short futures position at 1080 that is marked to 1085 and the writer is charged 5. The exercise of a put establishes a short futures position for the owner and a long futures position for the writer.

Some of the contracts have the options expire at the same time the futures expires; others have the options expire as much as a month earlier than the futures. The options and the underlying futures contract trade side by side on a futures exchange in contrast to options on stocks, which do *not* trade side by side with the underlying stocks. This side-by-side trading makes it easy to execute arbitrage transactions between the options and the futures, which makes the market more efficient. In addition, because there are options on commodity futures, but not options on commodities themselves, these options allow investors to take option positions based on expected price movements in commodities.

Sample Quotations and Trades

Figure 18.1 contains a sample of the price quotations for options on futures taken from the *Wall Street Journal.* The quotes are grouped by type of instrument (agricultural, interest rate, and index). Below the name of the underlying asset is an indication of the size of the contract.

Stock Index   For example, one S&P 500 contract is priced at $250 times the premium. The premium of the March 1070 call is shown as 14.50. Thus, the total price paid for this call option contract is: $14.50 (250) = $3,625. This call option contract permits the purchase of the March S&P 500 futures at a price of 1070. The futures price is not indicated but can be found on the pages containing futures prices, which are usually located near the

Figure 18.1 *Options on Futures Quotations*

FUTURES OPTIONS PRICES

Tuesday, March 17, 1998.

AGRICULTURAL

CORN (CBT)
5,000 bu.; cents per bu.

Strike Price	May	Calls-Settle Jly	Sep	May	Puts-Settle Jly	Sep
250	22½	30¾	....	⅜	2½	6¼
260	13⅞	23½	29¾	1⅝	5½	10
270	7¼	18	24¾	4¾	9¾	14¾
280	3⅜	13½	21	11	15	20½
290	1½	10¼	17½	19	21½	27
300	⅞	7⅞	15	28¼	29	34¼

Est vol 14,000 Mn 11,866 calls 5,151 puts
Op int Mon 188,631 calls 102,005 puts

SOYBEANS (CBT)
5,000 bu.; cents per bu.

Strike Price	May	Calls-Settle Jly	Aug	May	Puts-Settle Jly	Aug
600	57⅜	64	....	⅞	5¾	11
625	34⅞	46½	....	3¼	12½	19½
650	17¼	32	40½	10½	23	33
675	7	22	31	25⅛	38¼	48
700	2⅝	15½	24¼	45⅝	56	65½
725	⅞	11	19¼	68⅞	76	85½

Est vol 14,000 Mn 6,965 calls 7,555 puts
Op int Mon 109,169 calls 62,085 puts

SOYBEAN MEAL (CBT)
100 tons; $ per ton

Strike Price	May	Calls-Settle Jly	Aug	May	Puts-Settle Jly	Aug
160	12.65	....	....	.65	1.90	3.00
165	....	12.75	....	1.50	3.25	....
170	5.00	9.75	....	3.00	5.25	6.50
175	3.00	7.50	....	5.75	7.75	9.00
180	1.65	5.50	8.25	9.40	10.75	12.00
185	.80	4.25	....	13.70	14.35	....

Est vol 2,000 Mn 1,855 calls 984 puts
Op int Mon 30,838 calls 23,675 puts

SOYBEAN OIL (CBT)
60,000 lbs.; cents per lb.

Strike Price	May	Calls-Settle Jly	Aug	May	Puts-Settle Jly	Aug
2650	1.100	1.700	....	.200	.580	.960
2700	.800	1.420	1.680	.360	.790	1.220
2750	.530	1.180	1.500	.610	1.050	....
2800	.350	.980	1.320	.930	1.350	....
2850	.230	.800	1.140	....	1.670	....
2900	.140	.650	.990	....	2.030	....

Est vol 6,000 Mn 1,506 calls 1,039 puts
Op int Mon 43,192 calls 37,026 puts

WHEAT (CBT)
5,000 bu.; cents per bu.

Strike Price	May	Calls-Settle Jly	Sep	May	Puts-Settle Jly	Sep
320	22¼	35	44¾	1¾	5⅞	7⅞
330	14½	27½	38	4½	8½	11
340	9	22½	31¾	8¾	13¼	14½
350	5½	17½	26½	15¼	18¼	19
360	3¾	13¾	22	23¾	24½	24¼
370	2¼	10¾	18¼	32¼	31½	....

Est vol 3,000 Mn 2,164 calls 422 puts
Op int Mon 59,281 calls 35,766 puts

INTEREST RATE

T-BONDS (CBT)
$100,000; points and 64ths of 100%

Strike Price	Apr	Calls-Settle May	Jun	Apr	Puts-Settle May	Jun
119	2-02	2-25	....	0-02	0-25	....
120	1-07	1-43	2-06	0-07	0-43	1-07
121	0-25	0-24	....	0-26	1-07	....
122	0-06	0-13	1-06	1-06	1-43	2-06
123	0-01	0-07	....	2-01	2-24	....
124	0-01	0-03	0-32	3-00	3-12	3-31

Est. vol. 165,000;
Mn vol. 59,351 calls; 41,939 puts
Op. int. Mon 485,986 calls; 476,588 puts

T-NOTES (CBT)
$100,000; points and 64ths of 100%

Strike Price	Apr	Calls-Settle May	Jun	Apr	Puts-Settle May	Jun
111	....	2-16	....	0-01	0-06	0-15
112	1-03	1-18	1-32	0-01	0-16	0-30
113	0-14	0-40	0-56	0-12	0-39	0-55
114	0-02	0-16	0-31	1-00	....	1-29
115	0-01	0-06	0-15	....	....	2-12
116	0-01	0-02	0-07	....	....	3-03

Est vol 36,000 Mn   11,281 calls 10,-770 puts
Op int Mon 223,727 calls 171,282 puts

5 YR TREAS NOTES (CBT)
$100,000; points and 64ths of 100%

Strike Price	Apr	Calls-Settle May	Jun	Apr	Puts-Settle May	Jun
10800	....	....	....	0-01	0-03	0-08
10850	1-00	1-06	1-14	0-01	0-07	0-14
10900	0-33	....	0-55	0-02	0-14	0-24
10950	0-09	....	0-36	0-10	0-27	0-37
11000	0-01	0-14	0-23	0-34	....	0-56
11050	0-01	....	0-14	....	....	1-14

Est vol 18,000 Mn 5,844 calls 9,116 puts
Op int Mon 66,095 calls 63,162 puts

MUNI BOND INDEX (CBT)
$1,000; times Bond Buyer MBI

Strike Price	Mar	Calls-Settle Apr	Jun	Mar	Puts-Settle Apr	Jun
122	1-36	....	....	....	....	....
123	0-42	0-56	....	0-07	....	....
124	0-08	....	....	0-38	....	....
125	....	....	....	....	....	....
126	0-01	....	....	....	....	....
127	0-01	....	....	....	....	....

Est vol 1,000 Mn 0 calls 0 puts
Op int Mon 1,756 calls 15,298 puts

EURODOLLAR (CME)
$ million; pts. of 100%

Strike Price	Apr	Calls-Settle May	Jun	Apr	Puts-Settle May	Jun
9375	....	....	0.62	....	....	0.00
9400	....	....	0.38	0.00	....	0.01
9425	0.13	0.14	0.15	0.01	0.02	0.03
9450	0.01	0.02	0.03	0.14	0.15	0.16
9475	0.00	0.00	0.01	....	....	0.38
9500	0.00	....	0.00	....	....	0.62

Est. vol. 55,734;
Mon vol. 57,322 calls; 23,608 puts
Op. int. Mon 1,308,909 calls; 821,915 puts

INDEX

DJ INDUSTRIAL AVG (CBOT)
$100 times premium

Strike Price	Mar	Calls-Settle Apr	May	Mar	Puts-Settle Apr	May
86	16.65	33.40	41.65	1.60	9.70	18.10
87	8.55	26.20	....	3.00	12.45	....
88	3.30	20.10	29.55	....	16.35	....
89	.90	14.05	24.10	....	20.30	....
90	.15	10.35	19.35	....	....	....
91	.10	6.95	15.45	....	....	....

Est vol 1,000 Mn 525 calls 275 puts
Op int Mon 29,380 calls 23,789 puts

S&P 500 STOCK INDEX (CME)
$250 times premium

Strike Price	Mar	Calls-Settle Apr	May	Mar	Puts-Settle Apr	May
1070	14.50	36.00	44.90	2.10	11.90	20.90
1075	10.40	32.30	41.50	3.00	13.20	22.50
1080	6.90	28.90	38.30	4.50	14.80	24.20
1085	4.10	25.60	35.10	6.70	16.40	26.00
1090	2.10	22.60	32.20	9.70	18.40	28.00
1095	.90	19.70	29.30	....	20.50	....

Est vol 13,567 Mn 14,501 calls 8,513 puts
Op int Mon 115,125 calls 221,083 puts

Source: *Wall Street Journal*, March 18, 1998, C15.

futures options quotes. In this example, the March S&P futures was selling for 1082.4, which meant that this call option on this futures contract was in-the-money. Notably, the range for the S&P 500 Index during the life of this March 1070 option was 762.20 to 1083.00.

To demonstrate the advantages of options on futures, the second example will discuss an option on a Treasury bond futures similar to the futures contracts considered in Chapter 17.

Treasury Bonds   Treasury bond futures as traded by the Chicago Board of Trade are based on an "assumed" underlying twenty-year Treasury bond with an 8 percent coupon. Many Treasury bonds of varying maturities and coupons are actually deliverable, though,

Figure 18.2   *Treasury Bond Futures Factor Computation*

Treasury: $7^{1}/_{2}$% due Aug. 2016
Delivery month: June 1998
Years from 6/98 to 11/16: round down to 18
Price of 18-year Treasury $7^{1}/_{2}$% to yield 8%: $952.73
Divided by 100 = 0.9527 (the bond's factor)

because Treasury bond futures provide an example of "basket delivery." A contract summary for U.S. Treasury bond futures is as follows:

Exchange	Chicago Board of Trade
Contract unit	U.S. Treasury bond, $100,000 par value, nominal 8 percent coupon.
Good delivery	Any U.S. Treasury bond with a minimum of fifteen years remaining to call date or maturity date, whichever is shorter.
Settlement	Upon delivery of $100,000 par amount of eligible Treasury bonds, the seller receives the contract settlement price times a delivery factor for the bonds delivered, plus any accrued interest.
Daily price change limit	2 points ($2,000 per contract)
Delivery months	March, June, September, December

Treasury bond futures have a maximum price change or "limit move" of 2 points per day, which represents $2,000 per contract. Should the futures price increase or decrease by more than 2 points, trading is halted and no transactions beyond the limit can be completed. Futures transactions also require margin on both sides of the market, buy and sell, requiring initial deposits when each transaction is executed, and maintenance margin should adverse market changes cause the margin to fall below a maintenance level.

To be eligible for delivery, a Treasury bond must have at least fifteen years remaining before it is callable or it matures, whichever is sooner. The Treasury bonds delivered must have a par value of $100,000.

To determine the price on the Treasury bond that corresponds to a given futures price, an investor must determine the "factor" for the Treasury bond. The factor for a specific Treasury is based on the price of that bond at an 8 percent yield to maturity or yield to call (whichever is earlier). The contract expiration month is used to determine the eligibility of a particular bond as well as the maturity to use in the price calculation. Specifically, the number of years from the first day of the delivery month to the maturity (or call) date is rounded down to the nearest number of complete quarter years. Figure 18.2 provides an example using the Treasury $7^{1}/_{2}$ percent bond due in August 2016.

The price of this bond to yield 8 percent to call on delivery in June 1998 is 957.23. This price divided by 100 provides the ratio of 0.9572, which is the delivery factor. Note that the factor depends on both the bond used and the contract delivery month; the factor for Treasury $7^{1}/_{2}$ for other futures delivery months will be different.

Just as options on Treasury bonds may be used as an alternative to the underlying fixed-income security, options on futures provide an alternative to the underlying financial futures contract. Figure 18.3 illustrates the purchase of a Treasury bond futures contract.

An investor purchasing the June 1998 Treasury bond futures contract at 120 would obtain the return pattern displayed in Figure 18.3. We will consider this Alternative A. The possible level of the June Treasury bond futures price is displayed on the horizontal axis; the investor's profit or loss is displayed on the vertical axis. If the market were unchanged, an investor would break even. An investor would make a point for every point

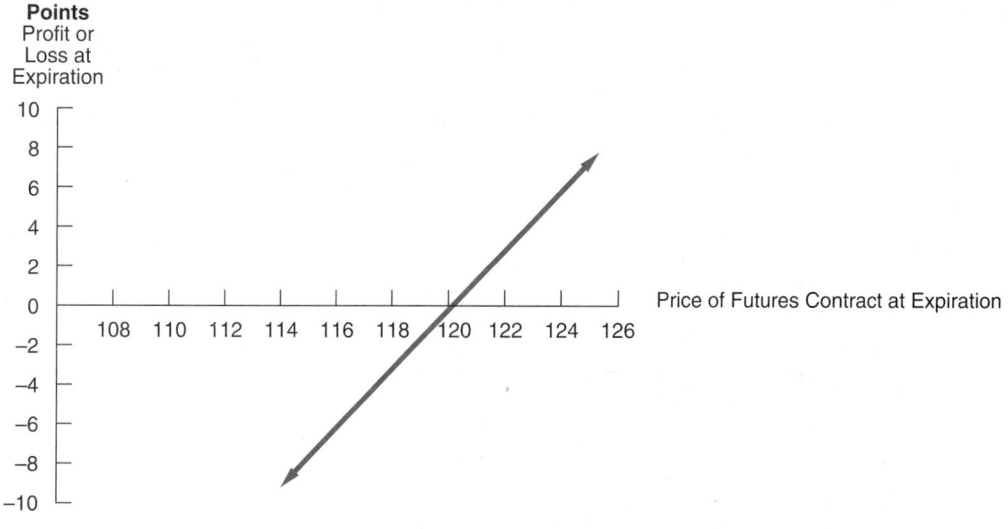

the futures contract increased while losing as the price of the futures contract decreased. Because the Treasury bond futures contract is not an interest-bearing security, the breakeven level is the initial transaction price.

Now let us suppose that instead of purchasing the June 1998 Treasury bond futures contract at 120, the investor purchases a call on the contract for 2 points. If the market is unchanged or declines, the investor forfeits the option premium, losing 2 points. This is the investor's worst case, a loss of 2 points. For every point the price of the futures contract rises, the investor makes a point. If the futures contract rises to 122, the investor breaks even, as the 2-point gain in price appreciation offsets the 2-point option premium. As the price rises further, the investor profits point for point. Figure 18.4 displays this strategy graphically. We will refer to this as Alternative B.

The comparison of Alternatives A and B is straightforward and is displayed in Figure 18.5. In addition, the profit and loss of each of these alternatives at various ending market levels are displayed in Table 18.1.

Alternative A (buy-and-hold Treasury bond futures contract) provides a higher return if the price remains unchanged or increases. Both alternatives provide participation in a favorable market. If prices decline below 118, Alternative B (the call option on the Treasury bond future) provides superior performance by providing greater downside protection. At a price of 114, for example, the call option does 4 points better than the outright purchase of the futures contract.

Another benefit of the call option as opposed to the actual financial futures contract is that no maintenance margin is required. Once the option premium is paid, no matter how far the price of the futures contract moves adversely, the option holder has the chance that the price will rebound and will potentially provide a profit. There is no need to provide additional capital under adverse circumstances. This is not the case with the holder of the futures contract. Additional margin is constantly required as the price moves adversely. If sufficient capital were not available, a position might be forced to be closed. If the price were to subsequently rebound, the financial futures investor could be in the unfortunate position of having been correct on the ultimate price move and still

Figure 18.4   *Profit–Loss Graph if Investor Buys June 1998 T-Bond Future 120 Call at 2*

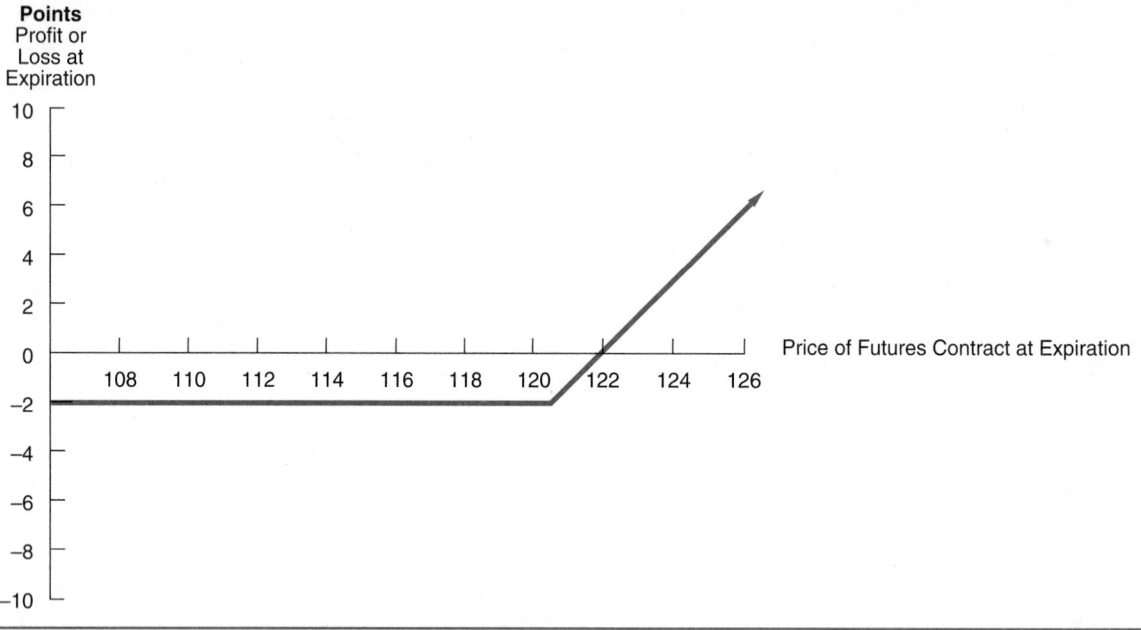

Figure 18.5   *Comparative Profit–Loss Graphs for Alternative Strategies*

Alternative A: Investor buys June 1998 T-bond future at 120
Alternative B: Investor buys June 1998 T-bond future 120 call option at 2

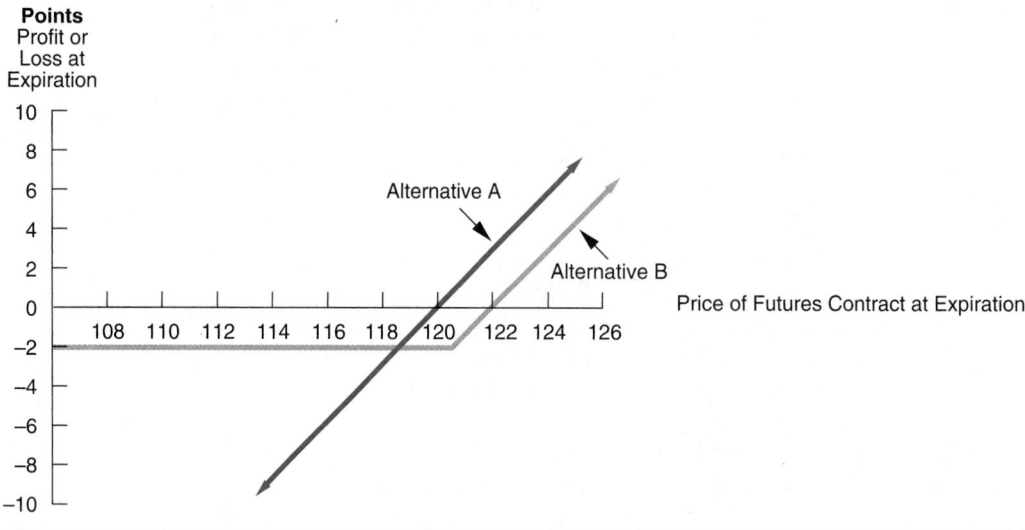

having lost money. This margin requirement of a long futures position becomes particularly onerous during limit moves. These may preclude the financial futures investor from covering the outstanding position. The holder of an option on the financial futures contract (just as the holder of an option on a fixed-income security) is in a position of limited liability. The maximum loss is limited to the initial option premium.

Table 18.1 *Profit or Loss at Expiration*

Ending Price	Alternative A	Alternative B	Difference
114	−6	−2	+4
116	−4	−2	+2
118	−2	−2	0
120	0	−2	−2
122	+2	0	−2
124	+4	+2	−2
126	+6	+4	−2
128	+8	+6	−2

WARRANTS

A **warrant** is an option to buy a stated number of shares of common stock at a specified price at any time during the life of the warrant. Although this definition is quite similar to the description of a call option, it has several important differences. First, when originally issued, the life of a warrant is usually much longer than that of a call option. Although the listed options markets have recently introduced long-term options, the typical exchange-traded call option has a term to expiration that ranges from three to nine months. In contrast, a warrant generally has an original term to maturity of at least two years, and most are between five and ten years. Some are much longer, including a few perpetual warrants.

A second major difference is that warrants are usually issued by the company on whose stock the warrant is written. As a result, when the warrant is exercised, the investor buys the stock from the company, and the proceeds from the sale are new capital to the issuing firm.[1]

Because these options could have value if the stock price increases as expected, warrants often are used by companies as sweeteners to make new issues of debt or equity more attractive. When offering a new stock or bond issue, the warrant is often attached, and, after the initial purchase, it can be detached and traded on the stock exchange or the OTC market. At the same time, whenever the warrant is exercised, it provides a major source of new equity capital for the company.

Investors are generally interested in warrants because of the leverage possibilities, as we will discuss. Also, investors should be aware that warrants do not pay dividends, and the warrant holder has no voting rights. Further, the investor should be sure that a warrant offers protection to the warrant holder against dilution in the case of stock dividends or stock splits whereby either the exercise price is reduced or the number of shares that can be acquired is increased.

Example of Warrants

Consider the following hypothetical example. The Bourke Corporation is going to issue $10 million in bonds but knows that within the next five years it will also need an additional $5 million in new external equity beyond the expected retained earnings. One way to make the bond issue more attractive, and also possibly sell the required stock, is to attach warrants to the bonds. To keep things simple, we shall assume the warrants are

[1]Although most warrants outstanding have been issued in this manner, in recent years an increasing number of warrants issued by firms and foreign governments are written on other securities or indexes.

European-style, that is, they cannot be exercised before the expiration.[2] If Bourke common stock is currently selling at $45 a share, the firm may decide to issue five-year warrants that will allow the holder to acquire the company's common stock at an exercise price of $50. Because the firm wants to raise $5 million in equity, it must issue warrants for 100,000 shares ($5 million/$50). How many bonds will the firm sell and how many warrants will be attached to each bond? To raise $10 million in debt, the firm will need to sell 10,000 bonds (at $1,000 par value). If each warrant allows the holder to purchase one share (that is, the **conversion ratio** is one), the number of warrants attached to each bond will be: (100,000 shares/10,000 bonds) = 10. Ten warrants will be attached to each bond. Assume the bond sale is successful, and the market price on the firm's common stock reaches $55 a share at the expiration of the warrants. At this point, the warrants will have an intrinsic value of $5 each ($55 − $50), and all the warrants will be exercised. As a result, the company will sell 100,000 shares of new common stock at $50 a share. The company pays no explicit commission cost but does have administrative costs.

Valuation of Warrants

The value of a warrant is determined much like that of a call option. The major difference is the longer term of the warrant. As an investor, you do not care whether the option allows you to buy the stock from another investor or directly from the firm. You should consider the two components of the value of a warrant, which are similar to those of a call option: its intrinsic value and its speculative (or time) value. We will discuss each of these components.

Intrinsic Value   The intrinsic value of a warrant is the difference between the market price of the common stock and the warrant exercise price, as follows:

$$\text{Intrinsic value} = (\text{Market Price of Common Stock} - \text{Warrant Exercise Price}) \times \text{Number of Shares Specified by the Warrant}$$

If the market price of the stock exceeds the warrant exercise price, the warrant has a positive intrinsic value. If the stock price is less than the exercise price, the equation would give a negative value and we would say that the warrant is zero intrinsic value. As an example, consider the following company that has outstanding warrants that expire in 2000, which allow the holder of the warrant to buy two shares of stock at $17 a share. The common stock is currently selling for $21, and the warrant is priced at $10. The warrant therefore has an intrinsic value of $8 as follows: [($21.00 − $17.00) × 2]. This is because the warrant allows the holder to buy the stock at a price below its market price. Note that the market price of the warrant ($10) is above its intrinsic value ($8). This excess market value relative to the intrinsic value is its speculative value, as we discuss next.

Speculative Value   Similar to a call option, a warrant's leverage, which causes the value of the warrant to increase and decline by larger percentages than the value of the underlying stock, is important. As an example, assume a stock is selling for $48, and a warrant for the stock with an exercise price of $50 is selling for $3 on the basis of its speculative value. This warrant would have no intrinsic value because its exercise price is above the market price. If the stock were to increase 15 percent to $55 the warrant would rise to at least $5, its new intrinsic value. Thus, a stock price increase of about 15 percent would cause the price of the warrant to increase by at least 67 percent, from $3 to $5. Any speculative value would boost the price of the warrant even higher.

---

[2]Most warrants issued by firms on their own shares are American-style and will be exercised early only if sufficiently high dividends are paid.

Table 18.2   *Warrant Leverage and Ratio of Stock Price to Warrant Price*

	Time				
	T	**T+1**	**T+2**	**T+3**	**T+4**
Stock price	$22	$30	$40	$50	$60
Warrant price*	$2	$10	$20	$30	$40
Ratio of stock price to warrant price (SP/WP)	11.00	3.00	2.00	1.67	1.50
Percentage change in stock price	—	36.40	33.30	25.00	20.00
Percentage change in warrant price	—	400.00	100.00	50.00	33.30

*Strike price, $20 per share.

You can evaluate leverage involved in a warrant by examining the *ratio of the stock price to the warrant price.* A larger ratio of stock price to warrant price means greater leverage. We can demonstrate this relationship with the example in Table 18.2, which assumes that the warrant has an exercise price of $20 and sells at its theoretical value over time. The example demonstrates the effect on the stock price to warrant price (SP/WP) ratio of different percentage changes in the price of the stock and the price of the warrant. A higher SP/WP ratio increases the leverage of the warrant, that is, there is a larger percentage change in the warrant price for a given percentage change in the stock price. At a beginning SP/WP ratio of 11, a 36 percent stock price increase brings a warrant price increase of 400 percent. After this change, when the SP/WP ratio was 3, a 33 percent stock price increase boosted the warrant price by 100 percent.

Note that this leverage works both ways; a decline in the stock price would cause a larger decline in the warrant price. Because investors in warrants typically consider this leverage a positive attribute, a greater SP/WP ratio increases the speculative value of the warrant.

A major factor in the price of a warrant, as in the price of a call option, is the time to maturity. A longer term to maturity increases the value of the warrant. Because warrants typically possess long terms to expiration, they typically have speculative value even when they are deeply out-of-the-money. A three-year warrant with an exercise price of $50 would have time value even when the stock was selling for $40. As noted, this difference in the original time to maturity is a major factor distinguishing warrants from call options, which typically cover less than nine months.

Another important factor in warrant valuation is the volatility of the stock's price. Higher volatility in the stock price makes a positive move above the exercise price more probable and boosts the value of the warrant. Again, this effect is similar for call options. This volatility factor would matter little in the valuation of a warrant on a relatively stable stock, but it could affect the speculative value for stocks with high price volatility.

The value of the warrant would suffer if the firm paid a dividend on the underlying stock. The dividend payment would reduce the total value of the firm and therefore the stock price, but the warrant holder would not receive any dividend.

To summarize, the value of the warrant is determined by the following factors:

1. Intrinsic value of the warrant, which is based on the difference between the market price of the stock and the exercise price of the warrant times the number of shares per warrant.
2. Speculative value of the warrant, sometimes referred to as its *premium value* or *time value,* which is a function of the following factors:
   a. Potential leverage, which is a function of the ratio of the stock price to the warrant price (SP/WP). More potential leverage means a larger speculative value.
   b. Time to maturity. A longer time to maturity increases speculative (time) value.

Figure 18.6 *Graph of Maximum, Minimum, and Actual Warrant Prices*

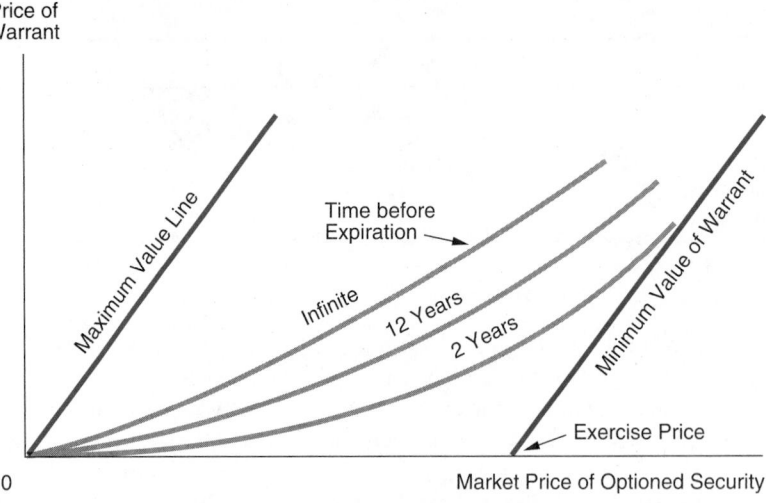

c. Price volatility of the underlying stock. More price volatility increases the premium value.

d. Dividend paid by the stock. A larger dividend reduces premium value.

Based on these valuation factors, the graph in Figure 18.6 indicates the maximum theoretical value the warrant could have, which equals the share price (no one will pay more for the warrant than they would for the underlying stock). It also shows the warrant's minimum value, which is its intrinsic value. Finally, the graph shows how the likely market value for a warrant is affected by the time remaining before expiration. You could envision multiple curves for each maturity to represent different levels of price volatility for the underlying security.

Warrant Strategies

A basic investment philosophy should guide your use of warrants. Once you have analyzed a stock and decided that it would be a good investment over the next several years, you should find out whether the firm has any warrants outstanding. These warrants would allow you to control a large amount of the stock for a fairly long period (possibly several years) for a modest investment.[3] Several considerations influence investment in warrants as part of the overall program:

1. The ultimate performance of the warrant depends on the performance of the stock. Remember that the leverage factor works both ways. You should consider buying a warrant only if you are bullish on the stock. The warrant gives you a means to maximize the return from a good stock.

---

[3]For a further discussion on warrant pricing, see Michael G. Ferri, Joseph W. Kremer, and H. Dennis Oberhelman, "An Analysis of the Pricing of Corporate Warrants," *Advances in Futures and Options Research* 1 (1986): 201–225; Michael G. Ferri, Scott B. Moore, and David C. Schirm, "Investor Expectations about Callable Warrants," *Journal of Portfolio Management* 14, no. 3 (Spring 1988): 84–86. For an analysis of hedging with warrants, see Moon K. Kim and Allan Young, "Rewards and Risks from Warrant Hedging," *Journal of Portfolio Management* 6, no. 4 (Summer 1980): 65–68.

2. Diversification is as important with warrants as with other investments. If you decide to invest in warrants, you should probably consider acquiring a number of them on several desirable stocks.

3. Once you own a diversified portfolio of warrants with high-leverage characteristics, be sure to cut your losses short and let the profits run. This strategy governs any leveraged investment, including options or commodities. Successful warrant investing combines inevitable small losses with a few big winners. Returns in excess of 100 percent from three warrants can easily compensate for losses on five or six warrant positions of 25 to 30 percent.

4. The most desirable warrants generally have little intrinsic value, and therefore large SP/WP ratios, and high leverage. In addition, you probably want a minimum of two years remaining to maturity, and preferably three or four years. Also, look for highly volatile stock prices. In these recommendations we assume the warrants have standard protective features against dilution and calls.

Based on these characteristics, you determine whether the speculative or premium value of a warrant is reasonable. This requires comparing alternative warrants to their underlying stocks. As stated initially, when you buy a warrant, you ultimately invest in the underlying stock.

Other Types of Warrants

Recently, a number of other innovative warrants have been introduced, including **currency exchange warrants** that allow investors to acquire a specific number of U.S. dollars at specified exchange rates for a non-U.S. currency. For example, the Student Loan Marketing Association (Sallie Mae) has issued warrants that allow the holder to purchase $50 for a specific number of Japanese yen. If the dollar strengthens against the yen, the warrants would increase in value. These instruments, like index options, usually are exercised by means of a cash settlement. Sallie Mae will be obligated to provide U.S. dollars and receive yen in payment. Obviously, Sallie Mae faces some risk, and it usually hedges that risk by trading in the currency futures or options market.[4]

CONVERTIBLE SECURITIES

A **convertible security** gives the holder the right to convert one type of security into a stipulated amount of another type at the investor's discretion. Typically, but not invariably, the security is convertible into common stock, but it could be converted into preferred stock or into a special class of common stock. The most popular convertible securities are convertible bonds and convertible preferred stock. Convertibles exhibit some characteristics of a bond and other characteristics of the security they are convertible into. Convertible issues generally are subordinated to the firm's other debt.

In 1998, more than 930 issues of convertible securities were traded in the United States with a market value of more than $140 billion. The market value of the global convertibles market was more than $380 billion. Some convertible issuing firms are small and mid-cap firms; others are large, well-established firms such as Ford, Chrysler, and Motorola.

Like warrants, convertibles are usually offered to attract investors to a bond issue. For example, many firms can issue straight debt, that is, bonds that are not convertible. Adding the convertible feature makes the debt more attractive. Many years ago it was thought that

---

[4]For a case study of the Sallie Mae currency-exchange warrants, see Richard J. Rogalski and James K. Seward, "Corporate Issues of Foreign Currency Warrants," *Journal of Financial Economics* 30, no. 2 (December 1991): 347–366.

firms that issued convertibles were generally lower-quality firms that made their bonds convertible to make them more attractive. In recent years, the popularity of derivative securities has made convertible debt financing attractive to many high-quality firms.

Characteristics of Convertible Bonds

As an example of a typical convertible bond, consider an issue offered by Amoco that matures in the year 2013, carries a coupon of $7\frac{3}{8}$ percent, with interest paid semiannually on March 1 and September 1. It has a face value of $1,000 and can be converted into 19.048 shares of Amoco Corporation common stock. This value, 19.048, is the conversion ratio. Alternatively, when the face value of $1,000 is divided by the conversion ratio of 19.048, it gives $52.50, which is called the **conversion price**. A convertible can be thought of as an ordinary bond with a call option attached, which allows the bondholder to buy 19.048 shares of stock by simply tendering the bond.

Advantages to Issuing Firms

Issuing convertible bonds is considered attractive for a company for several reasons. By attaching the convertible feature, a firm can often get a *lower interest rate* on its debt. The bondholders are, in effect, substituting the certain stream of interest payments for the uncertainty of the growth prospects of the firm. If a firm performs well after the issuance of the convertibles, holders of convertible bonds will be able to gain by converting their bonds into the now-more-valuable stock.

Another advantage of convertibles is that they represent *potential common stock.* The bondholder may decide to convert the bond, or the firm can make it possible to force conversion in the future by including a call feature on the bonds. This future common stock feature may be desirable for a firm that currently needs equity capital for an investment but does not want to issue common stock immediately because of the potential dilution before the investment begins generating earnings. After the investment begins generating earnings, the stock price should rise above the conversion value, and the firm can force conversion by calling the bond. We will discuss forced conversion later.

Advantages to Investors

As noted, convertible bonds have special features that typically allow them to have coupon rates below what you would expect on the basis of the quality of the issue. The fact is, *they provide the upside potential of common stock and the downside protection of a bond.* The upside potential occurs because the convertible contains an option to buy the stock by simply surrendering the bond. If the stock price increases, the convertible bond gains in value due to the increased value of the stock into which it can be converted.

The convertible bond has downside protection because, irrespective of what happens to the stock, the price of the bond will not decline below what it would be worth as a straight bond. In other words, if the firm's performance deteriorated somewhat and the stock price fell, the convertible would fall in price, but unless it became likely that the firm could not make the interest payments, the convertible's price would not fall as much. Thus, it has downside protection because in the worst case, it will act like an ordinary bond.

Another plus is that the convertible usually has a higher current yield than the underlying common stock. Assume Amoco pays a dividend of $2.20/share. The Amoco bond is convertible into 19.048 shares of stock, which means that the total dividends on the stock would be 19.048 ($2.20) = $41.91. In contrast, the bond pays $7\frac{3}{8}$ percent interest, which is $73.75.

An advantage that has been lost is the potential for leverage on convertible bonds. Prior to the 1970s, investors could buy convertibles on margin at about the same rate at which they could borrow on straight debt (about 80 percent). This capability made it possible to invest in convertibles with little cash and use the interest on the bond to offset part of the interest on the loan. Currently, however, the margin on convertible bonds is the same as the margin on common stocks.

Valuation of Convertible Bonds

Because a convertible bond is actually a combination of a bond and a call option on the common stock, it is necessary to consider both aspects of the security. First, as a straight bond, what should be its yield and implied price? This analysis will indicate your *downside risk* if the stock were to decline to the point where the security had value only as a straight bond.

The value of the convertible as a bond is called its **bond** or **investment value**. To determine the bond value, you must determine the bond's required yield if it had no conversion feature attached. A simple but not always feasible way to do this is to identify a nonconvertible bond with similar characteristics issued by the company. The most comparable straight issue of Amoco is its $8^5/_8$s of 2016. These bonds are priced at 110 for a yield of 7.72 percent. Let us round this off and assume the convertible as a straight bond would yield 7.70 percent and have a maturity of twenty years. Using these assumptions, the bond value of the Amoco convertible bond with a $7^3/_8$ coupon would be about $950. At the present time, the convertible as a straight bond would not sell for less than $950. You should compare this bond value to the current market price of the convertible (which is $1,215) to determine the downside price risk of the bond (also referred to as the *investment premium*). In this case this is

$$\frac{1,215.00 - 950.00}{1,215.00} = 21.81\%$$

This is a measure of your downside risk assuming the bond's yield would not change if the firm's performance deteriorated. This is probably true over a range of stock prices. If, however, the stock price fell substantially because of a perceived threat of bankruptcy, the bond's required yield would rise and its investment value would fall.

Next we need to compute the bond's **conversion** or **equity value**, which is the value of the common stock the investor will receive if she converts the bond. The conversion value equals the conversion ratio of 19.048 multiplied by the current stock price. If Amoco was trading at 57, the conversion value would be: $19.048 \times \$57 = \$1,085.74$. Obviously, the conversion value is linearly related to the stock price. The value of the convertible bond must exceed the conversion value or the bond value, whichever is larger. Thus, as a minimum, we can say that

$$\text{Minimum Price of Convertible} = \text{Max (Bond Value, Conversion Value)}$$

In this case, the minimum value is the conversion value of $1,085.74, which exceeds the bond value of $950.

The market value of the convertible will typically be higher than its minimum value except at maturity. This premium exists because of the option to convert the bond into stock. The difference between the market value of the convertible and its minimum value is the value of the option to convert. This premium over its minimum value (conversion value) is called the **conversion premium** and is calculated as

$$\text{Conversion Premium} = \frac{\text{Market Price} - \text{Minimum (Conversion) Value}}{\text{Minimum (Conversion) Value}}$$

If the Amoco convertible was selling at $1,215, the conversion premium would be

$$\frac{\$1,215.00 - \$1,085.74}{\$1,085.74} = 11.91\%$$

This indicates that the option value adds about 12 percent to the minimum value of the bond.

Another useful measure for a convertible bond is the **conversion parity price**. This is defined as

$$\text{Conversion Parity Price} = \frac{\text{Market Price of Convertible Bond}}{\text{Conversion Ratio}}$$

For our bond, this is

$$\frac{\$1,215.00}{19.048} = \$63.79$$

The conversion parity price indicates that if the bond were purchased and immediately converted, the effective price paid for the common stock would be $63.79 compared to the current stock price of $57. Obviously, this is fairly far from the current stock price. When it gets closer, conversion may be imminent. Of course, the conversion parity price should never be below the current stock price or someone could buy the convertible, immediately convert it, and sell the stock for a risk-free profit.

Another factor that is considered to be important when evaluating convertible bonds is the **payback** or **breakeven time**, which measures how long the higher-interest income from the convertible bond compared to the dividend income from the common stock must persist to make up for the market price of the bond relative to its conversion value (the conversion premium). The calculation is as follows:

$$\text{Payback} = \frac{\text{Convertible Bond Market Price} - \text{Conversion Value}}{\text{Bond Income} - \text{Income from Equal Investment in Common Stock}}$$

The dividend yield on the stock is $2.20/$57.00 = .0386. If you invested the current cost of the bond, you would receive dividends of $1,215.00 (.0386) = $46.90 per year. Thus, the payback would be

$$\frac{\$1,215.00 - \$1,085.74}{\$73.75 - \$46.90} = \frac{\$129.26}{\$26.85} = 4.81 \text{ years}[5]$$

Like its counterpart in capital budgeting analysis, the payback is not a discounted cash-flow method, so it does not properly incorporate the time value of money. However, it can serve as a useful indicator of the relative attractiveness of a convertible along with other characteristics. Generally, it is preferable to have a short payback.

---

[5]As noted, this calculation assumes you would use the $1,215 to buy 21.316 shares of stock at $57 a share. An alternative assumption is that your choice is to convert the bond into 19.048 shares of stock and receive dividends of $41.91 (19.048 × $2.20). In this case, the estimated breakeven time would be: $129.26/31.84 = 4.06 years.

Figure 18.7   *Value of Convertible Bond*

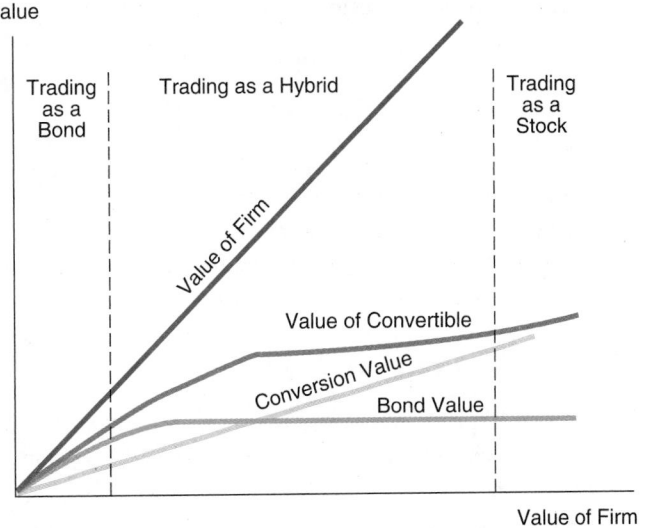

Figure 18.7 illustrates the factors involved in the value of a convertible bond. There is an upper bound for the value of a convertible; it cannot sell for more than the firm's assets. Thus, the value of the convertible must be below the forty-five-degree line. Note that the line for the bond value is relatively flat for a wide range of firm values because higher firm values do not increase the value of the bond because the bondholders receive only their promised payments. In contrast, at fairly low firm values the value of the convertible drops off as bankruptcy becomes more likely. Conversion value rises directly with the value of the firm. This graph shows that for low firm values, the bond value will be the minimum value of the convertible, and for high firm values, the conversion value will be the minimum value of the convertible. Finally, the line for the value of the convertible shows that when the firm value is low, the convertible will act more like a bond, trading for only a slight premium over the bond value. Alternatively, when firm values are high, the convertible will act more like a stock, selling for only a slight premium over the conversion value. In the fairly wide middle range, the convertible will trade as a hybrid security that acts somewhat like a bond and somewhat like a stock.

Forcing Conversion

Although most convertible bonds are callable, the firm will never call a bond selling for less than its call price. After the conversion value of the bond reaches its call price, the firm should consider calling the bond. Under these conditions, investors will have an incentive, as noted earlier, to convert the bond into stock that is worth more than what they would receive from the call price. In the case of Amoco, if we assume a call price of 107, when the conversion value reaches about 110 ($1,100), the firm could call the bond and force bondholders to convert.

Some convertibles even have stepped-up conversion prices that provide greater incentive to convert. With a stepped-up conversion price, the number of shares obtainable upon conversion (the conversion ratio) decreases according to a specific schedule.

With this feature, it may be advisable to convert just before the conversion price increases. Firms may also encourage conversion by increasing the dividends on the stock because one reason investors defer conversion is the higher income from interest than from dividends.

Sources of Information on Convertibles

Information on many convertible bonds is available in reference books on ordinary bonds such as *Standard & Poor's Bond Guide* and *Moody's Bond Record.* Merrill Lynch publishes a monthly statistical report, *Convertible Securities,* which contains extensive data on many convertible bonds and preferred stocks. You can also obtain information on convertibles as well as warrants from *Value Line Convertibles.*

Convertible Preferred Stock

Convertible preferred stock is similar to convertible bonds; it is a combination of preferred stock and common stock. Beyond the conversion privilege, however, these issues typically have the following characteristics:

1.   They are cumulative but not participating (the dividend accumulates if it is not paid, but the holders do not participate in earnings beyond the dividend).
2.   They have no sinking fund or purchase fund.
3.   They have a fixed conversion rate.
4.   A waiting period is usually not required before conversion can take place.
5.   The conversion privilege does not expire.[6]

Most convertible preferred stock is issued in connection with mergers as a way of providing income and yet not diluting the common equity of the acquiring firm. Although preferred stock and convertible preferred stock have not been a major source of new financing, some convertible preferred issues remain available for the interested investor.

Because convertible preferred stock is a hybrid security involving both preferred and common stock, the valuation analysis involves two steps. Consider a convertible preferred stock issue from GATX Corp., a rail car leasing and equipment financing firm. The issue is a $2.50 cumulative convertible preferred, indicating that it pays an annual dividend of $2.50. It is listed on the New York Stock Exchange and is convertible into 2.50 shares of the firm's common stock. Suppose the common stock is selling for $40.50 and the convertible preferred stock is $103 a share.

In terms of a pure preferred stock issue, it has substantial downside risk. Currently, most straight preferred-stock issues are yielding 8 percent to 9 percent, whereas the yield on the GATX convertible preferred issue is 2.43 percent. Using the conservative 9 percent figure indicates that the price of the stock as a straight preferred stock issue should be about $27.78 ($2.50/.09). This is about 72 percent lower than its current market price of $103. This preferred-stock value, which is significantly below the market value of the preferred stock, is a measure of the stock's downside risk. Clearly in this example the convertible preferred stock is selling on the basis of its conversion (option) value with a slight conversion premium. Specifically, the conversion value of the stock is $101.25 (2.50 × $40.50), compared to the market price of the convertible preferred

[6]George E. Pinches, "Financing with Convertible Preferred Stock, 1960–1967" *Journal of Finance* 25, no. 1 (March 1970): 53–63; Ronald W. Melicher, "A Comment on Financing with Convertible Preferred Stock, 1960–1967, *Journal of Finance* 26, no. 1 (March 1971): 148–149; and George E. Pinches, "Financing with Convertible Preferred Stock: 1960–1967: Reply," *Journal of Finance* 26, no. 1 (March 1971): 150–151.

stock of $103. This implies about a 2 percent conversion premium. You can also derive a conversion parity price for the convertible preferred stock by dividing the current market price of the convertible preferred stock by the conversion ratio. In this case, the conversion parity is $41.20 ($103/2.50).

You should examine the income relationship between the common stock and the preferred stock. If the common stock was paying an annual dividend of $1.50 a share, it would have a dividend yield of 3.70 percent ($1.50/$40.50). In contrast, the preferred stock pays an annual dividend of $2.50, indicating a 2.43 percent yield ($2.50/$103).

Investments Online

Bonds, a relatively simple financing and investing instrument, can become as complex as an equity to value when they contain imbedded options such as convertibility, warrants, or callability. Several Web sites can help students and investors learn more about these advanced applications of derivatives.

www.alternativeinvestment.com

We first saw this home page in Chapter 6. The Alternative Investment Corporation seeks to encourage investors to use convertible securities and "convertible arbitrage" in their portfolios (convertible arbitrage, as explained on this site, involves going long in a convertible security while shorting shares of the underlying equity). The site contains examples of how the use of convertible securities can enhance a portfolio's return without affecting its risk.

www.calamos.com

Calamos Asset Management, Inc., specializes in research, investment, and management of convertible securities. This site features descriptions of convertibles, their uses and characteristics, and their benefits to issuers and investors. A chart shows the relative performance of convertibles compared to a variety of other bonds. In addition, news, analysis, and market updates are available here, as are several good FAQs (frequently asked questions) about convertibles and their place in a portfolio.

www.optionscentral.com

The Options Clearing Corporation is the issuer and guarantor of all exchange-traded options contracts in the U.S. This, their home page, allows users to download free software and videos. It features a "Strategy of the Month" for options trading and has a number of resource links to exchanges which trade options.

www.optionsanalysis.com

The home page of Options Analysis offers free and purchased information to visitors, including price and volume analysis for many different options on futures contracts, including currencies, interest rates, indices, commodities, energy, and metals. It features an options primer and calculated value of options' implied volatilities over different time frames.

Several other sites may be of interest to those interested in advanced derivative techniques:

SUMMARY

♦ The richness of option pricing theory manifests itself in this chapter as we saw that many securities have the characteristics of options. Having considered options and futures in Chapter 17, along with the application of these instruments in portfolio management, we began this chapter by discussing options on futures. These options are useful for investors who want to participate in the futures market but want the downside protection of options where the loss is limited to the price (premium) for the option and the investor is not subject to marking to market every day.

♦ We examined warrants, which are options written by firms and are similar to ordinary calls, except that they tend to have longer original maturities, and when they are exercised the number of firms' shares increases.

♦ We examined convertible bonds, which can be exchanged for a certain number of shares of common stock, so these securities can be viewed as ordinary debt plus options to buy common stock. It was demonstrated that they will behave like a bond when the firm is performing poorly, and somewhat like a stock when the firm is performing well. Convertibles can be priced using some principles derived from option theory. In addition, convertible preferred stock is preferred stock that likewise has a call option so that it can be converted into common stock.

♦ All of these investment instruments provide additional investment opportunities. The analysis and valuation of these instruments are complex, but they add the potential for an improved risk–return profile and should not be ignored when constructing diversified global portfolios.

Questions

1. Briefly explain an option on a futures contract.
2. Assuming the underlying asset for a futures contract goes up in value by 15 percent, would you be better off owning a futures contract or an option on the future? Which instrument would you want if the asset declined by 20 percent?
3. What are the major differences between a warrant and a call option?
4. Identify the factors that influence the value of a warrant.

5. What condition must exist at expiration for the holder of a warrant to decide to exercise it?
6. The Baron Corporation debentures are rated Aa by Moody's and are selling to yield 9.30 percent. The firm's subordinated convertible bonds are rated A by Moody's and are selling to yield 8.20 percent. Explain how this phenomenon could exist.
7. Describe what we mean by the upside potential of convertible bonds. Why do convertible bonds also provide downside protection?
8. Assume a convertible bond's conversion value is substantially above par. Why would the bondholder continue holding the bond rather than converting?
9. Describe how a firm forces conversion. What conditions must exist?
10. Explain what is meant by the payback period or breakeven time for a convertible bond. Why would you want a high or low payback value?

Problems

1. A firm has 100,000 shares of stock outstanding priced at $40. It has no debt. The firm issues 10,000 warrants, each allowing the purchase of one share of stock at a price of $50. The warrants expire in five years and currently are priced at $2.
   a. Estimate the intrinsic value of the warrants.
   b. Determine the speculative value of the warrant and discuss the justification for this value.
   c. Assume the stock price increases by 50 percent. What will be the minimum increase in the value of the warrant?
2. The Harley Corporation has an 8 percent subordinated convertible debenture outstanding that is due in ten years. The current yield to maturity on this A-rated bond is 5 percent. The current yield on nonconvertible A-rated bonds is 10 percent. This bond is convertible into twenty-one shares of common stock and is callable at 106 of par, which is $1,000. The company's $10 par-value common stock is currently selling for $54.
   a. What is the straight-debt value of this convertible bond, assuming semiannual interest payments?
   b. What is the conversion value of this bond?
   c. At present, what would be the minimum value of this bond?
   d. At present, could the Harley Corporation get rid of this convertible debenture? If it can, discuss specifically how it would do so.
3. Extractive Industries has debentures outstanding (par value $1,000) that are convertible into the company's common stock at a price of $25. The convertibles have a coupon interest rate of 11 percent and mature ten years from today. Interest is payable semiannually, and the convertible debenture is callable with a one-year interest premium.
   a. Calculate the conversion value if the stock price is $20 per share.
   b. Calculate the conversion value if the stock price is $28 per share.
   c. Calculate the straight-bond value, assuming that nonconvertible bonds of equivalent risk and maturity are yielding 12 percent per year compounded semiannually.
   d. Assume the stock price is $28. The convertible is selling for $1,225. Calculate the conversion parity price.
   e. Using the information in part d, calculate the conversion premium.
   f. Using the information in part d and the fact that the stock is paying a dividend of $1.25, calculate the payback for the convertible bond.
4. Sitting next to Dan at a business luncheon, Rachel explained, "I bought American Desk at $20 a share and it's gone to $40." Dan said, "You would have done better to buy American's warrants, as I did."
   a. Why did Dan say this?
   b. The exercise price of American Desk warrants is $18. Dan purchased the warrants for $4 each when American Desk's stock price was $20 a share. Each warrant entitles Dan to purchase one share of American stock. Assuming the original $2 time value of the warrant dropped to $1, what is the current price of the warrant?
   c. Calculate Rachel's percentage gain.
   d. Calculate Dan's percentage gain when the stock price is $40 and the time value of the warrant is $1.

5. The common stock of Apex Corporation is currently selling at $12 per share, whereas Apex's warrants, which have five years until expiration, are selling at $3 and permit the purchase of a share of common stock at $11 per share. By the end of the year you expect the time value on the warrants to have decreased by 20 percent and the following probability distribution to exist for the stock:

Probability	Price
.10	10
.30	13
.40	16
.15	19
.05	25

a. Given the probability distribution, what is the expected stock price?
b. Given the probability distribution, what is the expected warrant price?
c. If average expectations are met, what would be your annual return from an investment in the stock?
d. If average expectations are met, what would be your annual return from an investment in the warrants?

6. The Anita Bank issues a hybrid security called Market Index Notes (called MINs) based on the performance of the S&P 500 index but which also pay off a promised amount as a minimum. The notes have a one-year maturity and promise to pay off $100 plus one-half the difference between the S&P 500 at the end of the year and 1100.

a. Calculate the value of this note at expiration if the S&P 500 ends up at 1120.
b. Calculate the value of this note at expiration if the S&P 500 ends up at 1080.

References

Bhattacharya, Mihir and Yu Zhu. "Valuation and Analysis of Convertible Securities." In *The Handbook of Fixed Income Securities,* 4th ed., edited by Frank J. Fabozzi and T. Dessa Fabozzi. Chicago, IL: Irwin, 1995.

Black, Fischer, and Myron Scholes. "The Pricing of Options and Corporate Liabilities." *Journal of Political Economy* 81, no. 2 (May–June 1973).

Brennan, Michael J., and Eduardo S. Schwartz. "Analyzing Convertible Bonds." *Journal of Financial and Quantitative Analysis* 15, no. 4 (November 1980).

Burns, Terence E. *Derivatives in Portfolio Management.* Charlottesville, VA: Association for Investment Management and Research, 1998.

Chen, K. C., R. Stephan Sears, and Manuchehr Shahrokhi. "Pricing Nikkei Put Warrants: Some Empirical Evidence." *Journal of Futures Markets* 15, no. 3 (Fall 1992).

Galai, Dan, and Meir I. Schneller. "Pricing Warrants and the Value of the Firm." *Journal of Finance* 33, no. 5 (December 1978).

Hull, John. *Options, Futures and Other Derivative Instruments,* 2nd ed. Englewood Cliffs, N.J.: Prentice-Hall, 1993.

Ingersoll, Jonathan E., Jr. "A Contingent Claims Valuation of Convertible Securities." *Journal of Financial Economics* 4, no. 4 (May 1977).

Kim, Moon, and Allan Young. "Rewards and Risk from Warrant Hedging." *Journal of Portfolio Management* 6, no. 4 (Summer 1980).

Merton, Robert C. "Financial Innovation and Economic Performance." *Journal of Applied Corporate Finance* 4, no. 4 (Winter 1992).

Miller, Merton H. "Financial Innovation: Achievements and Prospects." *Journal of Applied Corporate Finance* 4, no. 4 (Winter 1992).

Pinches, George E. "Financing with Convertible Preferred Stock, 1960–1967." *Journal of Finance* 25, no. 1 (March 1970).

Ritchie, J. C., Jr. "Convertible Securities." In *The Handbook of Fixed Income Securities*, 4th ed., edited by Frank J. Fabozzi. Chicago, Ill.: Irwin, 1995.

Ritchken, Peter. *Options: Theory, Strategy, Applications.* Glenview, Ill.: Scott, Foresman, 1989.

Rogalski, Richard J., and James K. Seward. "Corporate Issues of Foreign Currency Exchange Warrants." *Journal of Financial Economics* 30, no. 2 (December 1991).

APPENDIX 18 *Convertibles Glossary*

Bond equivalent *See* Fixed income equivalent.

Bond value *See* Investment value.

Breakeven time The time required for the added income from the convertible relative to the stock to offset the conversion premium. Also referred to as *payback period.*

"Busted" convertibles *See* Fixed income equivalent.

Call provisions Indenture provisions describing the date, price, and other circumstances under which the issuer may redeem a convertible.

Conditional call *See* Provisional call.

Conversion parity price The market value of a convertible bond divided by the number of shares into which it can be converted (its conversion ratio).

Conversion premium The excess of the market value of the convertible over its equity value if immediately converted into common stock. Typically expressed as a percentage of the equity value.

Conversion (or exercise price) The price at which common stock can be obtained by surrendering the convertible instrument at par value.

Conversion ratio The number of shares of common stock for which a convertible security may be exchanged.

Conversion value *See* Equity value.

Convertible preferred stock A preferred stock issue that the holder can exchange for a stated number of shares of common stock.

Convertible security A security that gives the holder the right to convert one type of security into a stipulated amount of another security at the investor's discretion.

Currency exchange warrant A warrant contract that allows investors to acquire a specific number of U.S. dollars at a specified exchange rate of a non-U.S. currency.

Equity equivalent A convertible with price behavior dominated by changes in the common stock price, with relatively little sensitivity to changes in interest rates.

Equity value The value of the convertible security if converted into common stock at the stock's current market price. Also referred to as *parity* or *conversion value.*

Fixed income equivalent A convertible with price behavior dominated by changes in interest rates, with relatively little sensitivity to changes in common stock price.

Floor value *See* Investment value.

Forced conversion If an issuer attempts to redeem a convertible for cash by issuing a call, and if the equity value exceeds the exemption price, the investor is "forced" to convert the bond into common stock in order to obtain the higher equity value.

Hard call A convertible that does not have any provisional call feature is said to have *hard call* protection.

Initial premium The conversion premium at the time a new convertible security is offered.

Investment premium The difference between a convertible's market price and its investment value, expressed as a percentage of market price (also called *downside risk*).

Investment value The price at which a debenture would have to sell as a straight debt instrument. Also referred to as *bond value* or *floor value.*

Options on Futures An options contract where the underlying security is a futures contract.

Parity (or conversion parity) *See* Equity value.

Payback *See* Breakeven time.

Provisional call Indenture provision that permits the company to call a convertible security prior to the stated call date if the common stock price rises above a preset level. Typically expressed as a percentage (such as 140 percent or 150 percent) of the specified conversion price.

Unit offering A combination of notes and warrants that is issued as a unit but may subsequently be traded either separately or as a unit. Also referred to as *synthetic convertibles.*

Warrant An option to buy a stated number of shares of common stock from the company at a specified price at any time during the life of the warrant.

Warrant conversion ratio The number of shares of stock that can be purchased for each warrant.

Yield advantage The difference between the current yield of the convertible bond and the current yield of the common stock.

Yield to first call Rate of return at the current price, assuming the issue is called at the first call date and at its call price.

Yield to first put Rate of return at the current price, assuming the issue is called at the first put date and at its put price.

Source: Adapted from Luke D. Knecht and Michael L. McCowin, "Valuing Convertible Securities," Harris Trust and Savings Bank (1986).

PART

7

PORTFOLIO MANAGEMENT: PRACTICE AND APPLICATION

KNOWING THE WORKINGS OF SECURITIES MARKETS. IDENtifying an investor's risk preferences, and analyzing stocks and bonds are of little use unless they are combined to construct and maintain an efficient portfolio. In Part 7 we review techniques for constructing and managing portfolios of stocks and bonds. Since equity and fixed income portfolio management are usually done by full-time professionals, this part of the book reviews the small investor's portfolio management team, namely mutual fund and investment companies used as a means of achieving a well-diversified, professionally managed portfolio. We conclude with a review of how to analyze the risk-adjusted performance of a portfolio.

Chapter 19 contains a discussion of equity portfolio management. Methods of active and passive management are reviewed. Since equity is usually just one component of an investor's overall portfolio, we discuss several asset allocation strategies. The chapter reviews the use of investing styles such as "growth" and "value" and discusses the use of futures and options contracts in managing an equity portfolio.

Chapter 20 considers how to employ our background in bond fundamentals and analysis to create and manage a bond portfolio. There are three major portfolio strategies; each of these is considered in detail. The first set is passive strategies, which include either a simple buy-and-hold strategy or an indexing strategy. The second is active management strategies, which can involve one of five alternatives: interest rate anticipation, valuation analysis, credit analysis, yield spread analysis, or bond swaps. The third set is matched funding strategies, which includes constructing dedicated portfolios, classical immunization portfolios, or horizon matching. We review the use of derivatives to help manage fixed income portfolios.

Chapter 21 considers an alternative to analyzing securities and managing your own portfolio: investment companies. After a basic explanation of the concept of investment companies and a description of the major forms, we examine the numerous types of funds available. Almost any investment objective can be met by investing in one or several investment companies. A review of studies that have examined the performance of funds indicates that generally they are not able to outperform the aggregate market, but they are capable of fulfilling a number of other functions that are important to investors.

We conclude the book with Chapter 22, which deals with the evaluation of portfolio performance. After a discussion of what is required of a portfolio manager and a benchmark portfolio, we review in detail the major risk-adjusted portfolio performance models and consider how they relate to each other. This is followed by a demonstration of their use with a sample of mutual funds. We also review performance attribution analysis, which allows us to determine why a portfolio's overperformance (or underperformance) occurred.

As always, it is important to understand potential problems with a technique or model. Therefore, we consider potential problems with the portfolio performance measures including a review of Roll's benchmark problem and its effect on these performance models. We demonstrate that this problem has become more significant with the growth of global investing. We also review techniques used to evaluate the performance of bond portfolios.

CHAPTER 19

Equity Portfolio Management

In this chapter we will answer the following questions:

♦ What are the two generic equity portfolio management styles?

♦ What three generic strategies can active equity portfolio managers use?

♦ What are three techniques for constructing a passive index portfolio?

♦ How does the goal of a passive equity portfolio manager differ from the goal of an active manager?

♦ What techniques do active managers use in an attempt to outperform their benchmark?

♦ What investment styles may portfolio managers follow?

♦ In what ways can investors use information about a portfolio manager's style?

♦ What skills should a good "value" portfolio manager possess? A good "growth" portfolio manager?

♦ How can futures and options be useful in managing an equity portfolio?

♦ What are four asset allocation strategies?   ♦

Recent chapters have reviewed how to analyze industries and companies, how to estimate a stock's intrinsic value, and how technical analysis can assist in stockpicking. Some equity portfolios are constructed one stock at a time. Research staffs analyze the economy, industries, and companies, evaluate firms' strategies and competitive advantages, and recommend individual stocks for purchase or for sale.

Other equity portfolios are constructed using a computer-intensive, rather than analyst-intensive, method. Computers analyze relationships between stocks and market sectors in an attempt to identify undervalued stocks. Quantitative "screens" and factor models help construct portfolios of stocks with certain attributes, such as low P/E

668

ratios, low price/book value ratios, or stocks whose returns are strongly correlated with economic variables such as interest rates. Computer programs help detect trading patterns and place buy and sell orders depending on past price movements. Computers examine pricing relationships between the stock, options, and futures markets and place orders across these markets to arbitrage small price differences.

Portfolio managers modify equity portfolio return profiles through use of futures and options. They can trade futures contracts on major indexes, as well as options on indexes, on selected industry groups, and on individual stocks. These derivative securities help portfolio managers shift a portfolio's exposure to systematic and unsystematic risk.

PASSIVE VERSUS ACTIVE MANAGEMENT

Equity portfolio management styles fall into one of two categories: passive or active. Some argue that "hybrid" active/passive equity portfolio management styles exist, but such styles actually reflect active management philosophies. As with traditional active management, "hybrid"-style managers invest to find undervalued sectors or securities. The following discussion reviews the traditional definitions of *passive* and *active* portfolio management.

Passive equity portfolio management is a long-term buy-and-hold strategy. Usually the manager purchases stocks so that the portfolio's returns track those of an index over time. Occasional rebalancing occurs as dividends are reinvested and because stocks merge or drop out of the target index and other stocks are added. Notably, the portfolio is designed not to "beat" the target index, but to match its performance. A manager of an index portfolio is judged on how well he or she tracks the target index.

Active equity portfolio management attempts to outperform, on a risk-adjusted basis, a passive benchmark portfolio.[1] A *benchmark portfolio* is a passive portfolio whose average characteristics (in terms of beta, dividend yield, industry weighting, firm size, and so on) match the risk–return objectives of the client and serves as a basis for evaluating the performance of an active manager.

In the next sections we will examine more closely the mechanics of passive and active equity portfolio management.

AN OVERVIEW OF PASSIVE EQUITY PORTFOLIO MANAGEMENT STRATEGIES

Passive equity management attempts to design a portfolio to replicate the performance of an index. The key word here is *replicate*. As we learned in Chapter 2, the portfolio manager who earns higher returns by violating the client's policy statement should be fired; a passive manager who isn't really passive should likewise be dismissed. A true passive manager earns his or her fee by constructing a portfolio that closely tracks the performance of a specified index that meets the client's needs and objectives. Any attempts by the manager to do better than the index selected violate the passive premise of the portfolio. In actuality, a passive index portfolio may slightly underperform the target index after fees and commissions are deducted from the gross returns.

In Chapter 8, we presented several reasons for investing in a passive equity portfolio. Strong evidence indicates that the stock market is fairly efficient. For most active managers, the costs of actively managing a portfolio (1 to 2 percent of the portfolio's assets)

---

[1]Evaluating the risk-adjusted performance of a portfolio is the subject of Chapter 22.

are difficult to overcome. Typically, the S&P 500 index outperforms most equity mutual funds on an annual basis. Note that, although the S&P 500 is the most popular index to track, a client can choose from among about thirty different indexes.

Chapter 5 described many different market indexes. Domestic U.S. indexes include the S&P 500, 400, and 100; the Value Line index; and the Wilshire 5000. The *Wall Street Journal* publishes the daily values of indexes for the organized exchanges, the OTC market, and various industry groups. Indexes exist for small capitalization stocks (Russell 2000), for value- or growth-oriented stocks (Russell Growth index and the Russell Value index), for numerous world regions (such as the EAFE index), as well as for smaller regions and individual countries. As passive investing has grown in popularity, money managers have created an index fund for virtually every broad market category.

The goal of a passive portfolio is to track the index as closely as possible. But the incursions of cash inflows and outflows and company mergers and bankruptcies and securities that must be bought and sold mean that this ideal can only be approximated, not reached. Certainly, substantial or prolonged deviations of the portfolio's returns from the index's returns would be a cause for concern.

The three basic techniques for constructing a passive index portfolio are full replication, sampling, and quadratic optimization or programming. The first, and most obvious, technique is **full replication**. With this technique, all the securities in the index are purchased in proportion to their weights in the index. This technique helps ensure close tracking, but it may backfire for two reasons. First, buying many securities increases transaction costs, which detracts from performance. Second, dividend reinvestment also results in high commissions when many firms pay small dividends at different times in the year.

The second technique, **sampling**, addresses the problem of numerous stock issues. Statisticians have taught us that we need not ask everyone in the United States for their opinion to determine who may win an election. Opinion pollsters query only a small sample of the population to gauge public sentiment. This sampling technique can also be applied to passive portfolio management. With sampling, a portfolio manager attempts to buy a representative sample of stocks that comprise the benchmark index. Stocks with larger index weights are purchased according to their weight in the index; smaller issues are purchased so that their aggregate characteristics (industry distribution, dividend yield, and so on) approximate the rest of the underlying benchmark. With fewer stocks to purchase, the buyer can take larger positions in the issues acquired, which should incur proportionately lower commissions. Reinvestment of dividend cash flows becomes less problematic because fewer securities must be purchased to rebalance the portfolio. The disadvantage of sampling is that portfolio returns will not track the index as closely as with full replication; there will be some **tracking error**.

Figure 19.1 estimates the tracking error that occurs from sampling.[2] For example, full replication of the S&P 500 would (in theory) have no tracking error. As smaller samples are used to replicate the S&P's performance, the potential tracking error increases (note that tracking error can be positive or negative—the sample may overperform or underperform the index over any period of time). There must be an analysis of the costs (tracking error) and the benefits (easier management, lower trading commissions) of using smaller samples.

Rather than obtaining a sample based on industry or security characteristics, managers can use **quadratic optimization or programming** techniques to construct a passive portfolio. With quadratic programming, historical information on price changes and correlations between securities are input to a computer program that determines the composition

---

[2]When a portfolio's goal is to mimic an index, the portfolio's returns should closely follow or "track" those of the index. The quality of an index portfolio is not measured by the magnitude of its returns; rather, it is measured by its tracking error, or the degree to which the portfolio's returns deviate from those of the actual index.

Figure 19.1   *Expected Tracking Error between the S&P 500 Index and Portfolios Comprising Samples of Less Than 500 Stocks*

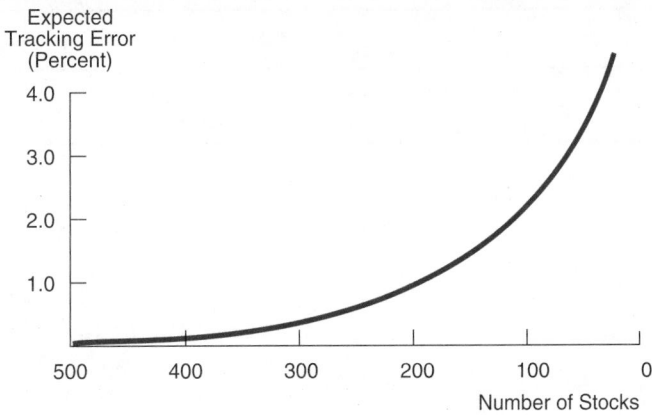

of a portfolio that will minimize tracking error with the benchmark. The drawback of this technique is that it relies on *historical* correlations, and if these change over time, portfolio performance may fail to track the index.

Some passive portfolios are not based on a published index. "Customized" passive portfolios, called **completeness funds**, can be constructed to complement active portfolios that do not cover the entire market. For example, a large pension fund may allocate some of its holdings to active managers who it believes can outperform the market. Many times these active portfolios are overweighted in certain market sectors or stock types. In this case, the pension fund manager may want the remaining funds to be invested passively to "fill the holes" of market sectors that are underweighted by the active managers. The manager compares the performance of the completeness fund to a specialized benchmark that incorporates the characteristics of the stocks not covered by the active managers.

For example, suppose a pension fund hires three active managers to invest part of the fund's money. One manager emphasizes small-capitalization U.S. stocks; the second invests only in Pacific Rim countries, and the third invests in U.S. stocks with low P/E ratios. To ensure adequate diversification, the pension fund may want to passively invest the remaining funds in a completeness fund. In this case, the completeness fund's specialized benchmark will include large- and mid-capitalization U.S. stocks, U.S. stocks with normal to high P/E ratios, and international stocks outside the Pacific Rim.

Still other passive portfolios and benchmarks exist for investors with certain unique needs and preferences.[3] Some investors may want their funds to be invested only in stocks that pay dividends or in companies that produce products or services that the investor deems socially responsible. The benchmarks produced reflect these desired attributes, and passive portfolios track the performance of the customized benchmark over time to satisfy investors' special needs.

Dollar-cost averaging is an investment method popular with many who passively invest. Rather than try to predict the time of market highs and lows, this strategy invests an equal amount of funds each period. With dollar-cost averaging, the manager purchases fewer shares with the fixed-dollar investment when stock prices are high and purchases more shares when the stock price falls. This disciplined approach to investing prevents

---

[3]Recall our discussion in Chapter 2 on investors' objectives and constraints; two of the constraints were legal and regulatory requirements and unique needs and preferences.

Table 19.1   *Dollar-Cost Averaging vs. Lump Sum Investing*

	DOLLAR-COST AVERAGING					LUMP SUM	
$1000 INVESTED AT t = 1, 2, 3						$3000 INVESTED AT t = 1	
	t=1	t=2	t=3	Total number of shares	Market Value at t=3	Number of shares	Market Value at t=3
Scenario 1: Rising stock price							
Stock Price	$10	$15	$20			300	
Number of Shares	100	66.67	50	216.67	216.67 × $20 = $4,333.40		300 × 20 = $6,000
Scenario 2: Falling stock price							
Stock Price	$10	$7	$5			300	
Number of Shares	100	142.86	200	442.86	442.86 × $5 = $2,214.30		300 × 5 = 1,500
Scenario 3: Rising, then falling, stock price							
Stock Price	$10	$15	$10			300	
Number of Shares	100	66.67	100	266.67	266.67 × $10 = $2,666.70		300 × 10 = 3,000
Scenario 4: Falling, then rising, stock price							
Stock Price	$10	$5	$10			300	
Number of Shares	100	200	100	400	400 × $10 = $4,000		300 × 10 = 3,000

investors from buying too many shares when they may be overly optimistic after prices have risen. On the other hand, buying more shares when prices are low will position the portfolio for attractive gains if prices rebound.

As a simple example, suppose you can invest $3,000 all at once in a stock or $1,000 a month over the next three months. If the price of the index is $10, your $3,000 will purchase 300 shares. Table 19.1 presents the effects of dollar-cost averaging in four scenarios. In the first scenario, prices rise; in the second scenario, prices fall. In scenarios 3 and 4, prices rise or fall before returning to their original level. Dollar-cost averaging causes more shares to be purchased over time in scenarios 2 and 4 and the performance of the dollar-cost averaged portfolio outperforms the lump-sum investment. In a rising market (scenarios 1 and 3) dollar-cost averaging underperforms the lump-sum strategy.

Dollar-cost averaging is an attractive strategy to prevent attempts to time the market or to prevent investing a large sum at an inopportune time. It performs best when the market declines sometime after the initial investment. Because the market never continually rises, dollar-cost averaging is a favored investment strategy of many individual investors.[4]

AN OVERVIEW OF ACTIVE EQUITY PORTFOLIO MANAGEMENT STRATEGIES

The goal of active management is to earn a portfolio return that exceeds the return of a passive benchmark portfolio, net of transaction costs, on a risk-adjusted basis. An important issue for active managers and their clients to resolve is the selection of an appropriate benchmark (sometimes called a "normal" portfolio).[5] The benchmark should

[4]Persons who have money deducted from their paycheck and invested in insurance products, variable annuities, 401(k) and other retirement plans are automatic dollar-cost averagers; their fixed-amount funds are invested on a periodic basis, every pay period.

[5]The construction of benchmark portfolios is discussed in Chapter 22.

incorporate the average qualities of the client's portfolio strategy. Thus, an active portfolio manager who invests mainly in small-capitalization stocks with low P/E ratios because the client specified this strategy should not have his performance compared to a broad market index such as the S&P 500. A better strategy is to construct a specialized benchmark portfolio that reflects the average characteristics of the actively managed portfolio and the client's risk tolerance. For example, a first step in constructing the normal benchmark portfolio may be to include, on an equally weighted basis, all stocks with market capitalizations under $1 billion and P/E ratios less than 80 percent of the S&P 500 P/E ratio. Computerized databases allow managers to construct such passive benchmarks and monitor returns over time. This example benchmark may be chosen as the standard by which a small-stock, low-P/E manager is evaluated.

Practical Difficulties of Active Management

The job of an active equity manager is not easy. If transaction costs total 1.5 percent of the portfolio's assets annually, the portfolio has to earn a return 1.5 percentage points above the passive benchmark just to keep pace with it. If the manager's strategy involves overweighting market sectors in anticipation of price increases, the risk of the active portfolio will exceed that of the passive benchmark, so the active portfolio's return will have to exceed the benchmark by an even wider margin to compensate for its higher risk.

Thus, active managers must overcome two difficulties relative to the benchmark. First, an actively managed portfolio will have higher transaction costs. Second, in all likelihood, it will have higher risk than the passive benchmark.

One key to success is for managers to be consistent in their area of expertise. Market gyrations occur and investment styles go in and out of favor. Successful long-term investing requires that you maintain your investment philosophy and composure while others are panicking.

Another key to success is to minimize the trading activity of the portfolio. Attempts to time price movements over short horizons will result in profits disappearing because of growing commissions.

Three Strategies

Managers use three generic themes in their attempts to time the market and add value to their portfolios in comparison to the benchmark:

♦ Trying to time the equity market by shifting funds into and out of stocks, bonds, and T-bills depending on broad market forecasts and estimated risk premiums.
♦ Shifting funds among different equity sectors and industries (financial stocks, consumer cyclicals, durable goods, and so on) or among investment styles (large capitalization, small capitalization, value, growth, and so on) to catch the next "hot" concept or theme before the rest of the market does.
♦ Stockpicking—look at individual issues in an attempt to buy low and sell high.

They use some specific strategies to implement these themes.

Global Investing

Global portfolios can apply the economic analysis discussed in Chapter 11 to identify different countries whose equity markets are potentially undervalued or overvalued. The global portfolio can then overweight or underweight those countries relative to a global benchmark portfolio based upon the active manager's forecast of their return potential.

A second global portfolio strategy is to manage the portfolio from an industry perspective rather than from a country perspective.[6] As competition becomes more global, more analysts are examining industries and firms and disregarding country boundaries. For example, Caterpillar and Komatsu compete globally in the heavy-equipment industry, and Boeing, McDonnell Douglas, and Airbus compete globally in the airline manufacturing industry. Evidence of the global automobile market is on every street.

Global portfolio managers focus on global economic trends, industry competitive forces, and company strengths and strategies. Their analyses of financial statements (Chapter 10), industries (Chapter 12), and companies (Chapter 13) are applied in a global, rather than a national, setting in order to identify undervalued industrial sectors and firms.

Sector Rotation

A **sector rotation strategy**, used by managers who invest in domestic equities, involves positioning the portfolio to take advantage of the market's next move. Often this means emphasizing or overweighting (relative to the benchmark portfolio) certain economic sectors or industries in response to the next expected phase of the business cycle. Figure 12.2, on page 416, contains suggestions on how sector rotators may position their portfolios to take advantage of stock market trends during the economic cycle.

"Sector" can also include different stock attributes. Because the market seems to favor some attributes more than others, sector rotation can also involve overweighting stocks with certain characteristics, such as small- or large-capitalization stocks, high- or low-P/E stocks, or stocks classified as "value" or "growth" stocks.

The existence of computer databases has encouraged the use of computer screening and other quantitatively based methods of evaluating stocks. These screening methods tend to invest in portfolios of stocks with certain characteristics rather than examining individual stocks to determine whether they are underpriced.

The simplest computer screens identify groups of stocks based on a set of attributes. Screens also narrow the list of thousands of stocks to a manageable few that can then be evaluated using more traditional analytical means. Stocks can be screened on many company and stock price characteristics. For example, programs can generate a list of "value" stocks with at least a 20 percent return on equity and stable or growing dividends over the past ten years.

Some more complicated quantitative strategies are similar to sector rotation. Factor models, similar to those used in the APT, can identify stocks whose earnings or prices are sensitive to economic variables such as exchange rates, inflation, interest rates, or consumer sentiment. With this information, managers can "tilt" portfolios by trading those stocks most sensitive to the analyst's economic forecast. The manager can try to improve the portfolio's relative performance in a recession by purchasing stocks that are *least* sensitive to the analyst's pessimistic forecast.

Some quantitatively oriented portfolio managers use what is called a "long–short" approach to investing.[7] In the long–short approach, stocks are passed through a number of screens and assigned a rank. Stocks at the top of the ranking are purchased; stocks at the bottom are sold short. Such a strategy can be neutral on the overall market, because the value of the long position can approximate that of the short position. The performance

---

[6]For example, see Robert Steiner, "Stock Pickers Slice Up Asia by Sector," *Wall Street Journal*, October 21, 1993, C1, C23.

[7]James A. White, "How Jacobs and Levy Crunch Stocks for Buying—and Selling," *Wall Street Journal*, March 20, 1991, C1, C8.

of the top-ranked stocks is expected to exceed that of the lower-ranked stocks, regardless of whether the overall stock market rises, falls, or trades in a narrow range.

How do managers know that these and other quantitative models have the potential to offer above-average risk-adjusted returns? The answer is that they hope the future will resemble the past because these quantitative strategies have been **backtested**. This involves using computers to examine the composition and returns of portfolios based on historical data to determine if the strategy would have worked successfully in the past. The risk of this testing is that relationships that existed in the past are not guaranteed to hold in the future.

Some managers let the computers do all the work. Neural networks are computer programs that attempt to imitate the thinking patterns of the human brain. They use vast databases and artificial intelligence capabilities to find cause-and-effect patterns in stock returns.[8] The computer attempts to discover undervalued securities by identifying such patterns and "learning" what stock attributes drive the market.

Active managers also use quadratic programming to solve the efficient frontier optimization problem of Markowitz. The optimizer uses the manager's expectations about returns, risk, and correlations to select portfolios that offer the optimal risk–return trade-off. Linear programming techniques help construct portfolios that maximize an objective (such as expected return) while satisfying linear constraints dealing with items such as the portfolio's beta, dividend yield, and diversification.

Styles

Most equity managers follow an investing style. **Style investing** involves constructing portfolios in such a way as to capture one or more of the characteristics of equity securities. Though it has been around in a variety of forms for many years, style investing has had its most recent endorsement in the efficient markets anomaly literature. Research studies purporting to show above-average risk-adjusted returns to small-capitalization stocks, low-P/E stocks, and the like lead some investment managers to focus on segments of the market, hoping to capture extra return.

A variety of investing styles exist. Some investment managers favor "large cap" stocks, those on the higher tiers of market capitalization. These managers may focus on the stocks that comprise the S&P 500 index and seek to outperform the index by overweighting its various industries and sectors that they anticipate will do well and underweighting the expected poorer performing sectors. Other managers favor "small-cap" stocks, those on the lower tier of market capitalization. They believe that small firms are less analyzed than larger firms, so the market may not be as efficient for small firms. Or they may focus on small-capitalization firms in order to take advantage of the "small-firm effect" anomaly, which finds small firms' returns have been overcompensated for their beta risk over time. Still others may focus on "mid-cap" stocks, whose market values place them neither among the large nor small. These managers hope that inefficiencies exist in the neglected mid-range as large- and small-cap styles are now well recognized and have attracted many investors in search of higher returns.

Still others place themselves in the "value" or "growth" camp. **Value stocks** are those that appear to be underpriced because their price/book or price/earnings ratio is

---

[8]Robert McGough, "Fidelity's Bradford Lewis Takes Aim at Indexes with His 'Neural Network' Computer Program," *Wall Street Journal,* October 27, 1992, C1, C23; Delvin D. Hawley, John D. Johnson and Dijjotam Raina, "Artificial Neural Systems: A New Tool for Financial Decision-Making," *Financial Analysts Journal* (November 1990): 63–72; George S. Swales, Jr., and Young Yoon, "Applying Artificial Neural Networks to Investment Analysis," *Financial Analysts Journal* (September 1992): 78–80.

low, or their dividend yield is high, compared to the rest of the market. **Growth stocks**, according to popular terminology, are stocks of firms enjoying above-average earnings per share increases and usually have above-average ratios of price/book and price/earnings. This is related to the **earnings momentum** and **price momentum** strategies. The market at times seems to reward the stocks of companies whose earnings have steady, above-average growth, or whose prices are rising because of market optimism.

Some managers combine styles along the large-cap–small-cap and value-growth continuums, creating many possible mixes: large-cap value, large-cap growth, small-cap value, small-cap growth, mid-cap value, and mid-cap growth. Not every manager falls into one of these categories; their portfolio's exposure to small or large, value or growth may change over time. Some managers may emphasize one style, while others may tilt or bias a portfolio only slightly toward one style. Many indexes exist that can form the basis for judging the performance of these varied investment styles.[9]

Table 19.2 illustrates the characteristics of the four main investment styles. Value stocks generally have smaller capitalizations than growth stocks (columns 1 and 2), although their profile is much different from that of the typical small-stock fund (columns 1 and 4). Value stocks have P/E and P/B ratios significantly lower than those of growth stocks while their dividend yield is much higher. Growth and level of earnings is higher in growth stocks, and the growth stocks favor industries such as technology and discretionary consumer (such as retail outlets and restaurants). Value stocks were more likely to involve firms in the energy section, materials and processing, and financial services.

Distinctions between large- and small-cap stocks are obvious in the size category. Small-cap stocks had some growth-stock characteristics in terms of P/E, P/B, and dividend yield, but their sector weightings were not all that markedly different than larger-capitalization stocks. Small-cap stocks tended to favor the technology, health care, and discretionary consumer categories. Thus, a growth or value portfolio, or any style portfolio, is not as well diversified as the market portfolio. A style portfolio will contain some unsystematic risk that will not be diversified away. A style investor must be willing to take on this risk exposure and the investment policy statement should reflect it.

Does Style Matter?

Money managers used to focus on broad categories such as "equities" or "fixed income." Now many specializations appear among investment managers. Investing according to a certain style (generally, large cap, small cap, value, or growth) has several implications for portfolio managers and their clients.[10]

First, a manager's choice to align with an investment style communicates information to potential and actual clients about the investor's focus, area of expertise, and stock evaluation methods. The operations and systems of a growth manager should focus on whether past profit trends are sustainable and can be surpassed. Those of the value manager will focus mainly on stocks whose prices appear to be unfairly depressed by an unknowing or overly pessimistic market.

Second, determining an investment manager's style is useful for measuring his or her performance relative to a benchmark. The S&P 500 index or the NYSE index, so pop-

---

[9]Melissa R. Brown and Claudia E. Mott, "Understanding the Differences and Similarities of Equity Style Indexes," in T. Daniel Coggin, Frank J. Fabozzi, and Robert D. Arnott, ed., *The Handbook of Equity Style Management,* 2nd ed. (New Hope, PA: Frank J. Fabozzi Associates, 1997), pp. 21–53.

[10]For a fuller discussion, see Charles Trzcinka, "Is Equity Style Management Worth the Effort? Some Critical Issues for Plan Sponsors," in T. Daniel Coggin, Frank J. Fabozzi, and Robert D. Arnott, ed., *The Handbook of Equity Style Management,* 2nd ed. (New Hope, PA: Frank J. Fabozzi Associates, 1997), pp. 301–312.

Table 19.2   *Comparison of Value, Growth, Large-Cap, and Small-Cap Portfolios as of December 31, 1993*

Characteristic	Value	Growth	Market-Oriented	Small-Cap
Capitalization Distribution				
% Large (Top 50 stocks)	16.2	30.9	26.6	0.0
% Medium/Large (51 to 200)	25.4	25.0	38.9	1.4
% Medium (201 to 500)	22.9	37.3	21.0	3.7
% Medium/Small (501 to 1,000)	24.3	5.9	11.0	33.6
% Small (1,000+)	11.2	0.9	2.5	61.4
Valuation Characteristics				
P/E on Normalized EPS	12.9	22.8	17.3	28.6
Price/Book	1.43	5.32	2.54	3.44
Dividend Yield	2.70	0.62	2.09	0.35
Growth Characteristics				
Long-Term Forecast				
I/B/E/S Growth	9.8	20.6	12.9	19.3
Return on Equity	12.7	25.5	17.2	12.7
Earnings Variability	88.8	62.4	56.5	84.5
Economic Sectors				
% Technology	6.2	25.8	13.7	18.3
% Health Care	8.2	9.8	6.1	11.2
% Consumer Discretionary	7.2	29.2	19.9	23.4
% Consumer Staples	3.5	0.0	7.3	0.0
% Integrated Oils	4.9	0.0	6.5	1.0
% Other Energy	6.2	3.6	3.8	2.7
% Materials and Processing	21.8	6.5	7.6	4.7
% Producer Durables	2.3	0.0	6.1	9.9
% Autos and Transportation	1.5	3.4	3.5	4.4
% Financial Services	29.6	15.6	18.7	16.1
% Utilities	7.5	6.1	6.7	6.4
% Sector Deviation	24	25	12	19

Source: Jon A. Christopherson and C. Nola Williams, "Equity Style: What It Is and Why It Matters" in T. Daniel Coggin, Frank J. Fabozzi, and Robert D. Arnott, ed., *The Handbook of Equity Style Management,* 2nd ed. (New Hope, PA: Frank J. Fabozzi Associates, 1997), pp. 1–19. This table is adapted from their Exhibit 3, p. 7.

ular in research studies, are poor comparison portfolios if a manager believes she can add value by focusing on a particular style. Style benchmarks show the characteristics of an unmanaged style portfolio in terms of risk and return performance. A manager who emphasizes small stocks should be judged relative to the performance of a small-stock index or benchmark. A value manager's performance similarly needs to be compared to an index of stocks that meet the "value" criteria. More will be said on this performance measurement issue in Chapter 22.

Third, style identification allows an investor to select investment managers that allow his overall portfolio to be properly diversified. Identifying managers' styles allows investors to diversify their portfolio by, for example, choosing one manager from the growth, value, large-cap, and small-cap styles. Completeness funds can remove any unwanted bias or style tilts from the resulting portfolio. If the investor does not pay attention to style when choosing managers, she may find her portfolio overweighted toward one style over another.

Finally, style investing allows control of the total portfolio to be shared between the investment managers and a knowledgeable sponsor (such as a pension fund manager or wealthy investor) who hires investment managers. If the sponsor chooses to try to time styles, they can shift funds to managers whose style is expected to outperform from managers whose style is expected to underperform. For example, if an investor believes small

stocks will outperform large stocks in the late 1990s, she can remove funds from her large cap managers and give them to her small-cap managers to invest. Control over the portfolio is shared in that the sponsor makes the macro allocation among different styles while the hired managers make the specific stock selections.

Timing between Styles

Does it make economic sense for sponsors to try to "time" between different styles? Examining historical returns from investing in different styles leads to an affirmative answer. One study found that $1 invested in the best-performing asset class (switching monthly between stocks, bonds, or T-bills over the period 1982–93) would have grown to $85. But $1 invested in each month's best performer from the S&P 500's ten economic sector groups would have grown to $4,170! One dollar invested in a simple buy-and-hold strategy in the S&P 500 would have grown to "only" $5.90 over this eleven-year period. Another study focused on the returns from four different equity styles (small value, large value, small growth, and small value) and four asset classes (stocks, bonds, T-bills, and real estate). They found the average return differential between the best- and worst-performing equity style, 23.5 percent, exceeded the average return differential between the best- and worst-performing asset class.[11] A study by Nobel laureate William Sharpe found that even within stock mutual funds, 90 percent of the variation in returns among the mutual funds could be attributed to differences in their investment style.[12]

Still other studies indicate that large- and small-stock returns move in cycles, as do value and growth stocks. Over time one style overperforms, then underperforms. Attempts to time styles may rely upon forecasting stages of the business cycle. Firms whose earnings growth mirrors the cycles of the economy may comprise many of the "value" stocks. The ideal time to purchase value stocks is when the economy is nearing a business cycle trough and preparing for the next expansion phase.

Growth stocks, on the other hand, have earnings growth patterns that arise from these firms' ability to generate their own demand, irrespective of the overall state of the economy. With little sensitivity to the state of the business cycle, portfolio managers may consider selling value stocks and buying growth stocks as the economy nears the peak of an expansion and a downturn is likely in the near future.[13] This is similar to our discussion of the economy-industry-firm top-down approach to equity investing discussed in Chapter 11.

Other models of equity style timing exist. As an example, one method relies mainly on a technical analysis of stock market trends to predict whether growth or value stocks will overperform. After considering long-term trend analysis, short-term trends, and seasonality factors, the model issues a probability that value will outperform growth in the coming quarter. Based upon this probability, the manager will increase, maintain, or decrease her commitment to value stocks relative to growth stocks. In terms of long-term trend analysis, the model assumes the greater the deviation of returns from a long-term trend line, the greater the probability that the direction of the deviation will soon reverse. Intermediate-term influences are examined by counting how many consecutive quarters one style has outperformed the other; the longer the period of overperformance, the greater

---

[11]These studies are reported in Douglas W. Case and Steven Cusimano, "Historical Tendencies of Equity Style Returns and the Prospects for Tactical Style Allocation," in Robert A. Klein and Jess Lederman, ed., *Equity Style Management* (Chicago: Irwin, 1995), pp. 259–287.

[12]William F. Sharpe, "Asset Allocation: Management Style and Performance Measurement," *Journal of Portfolio Management* 18, no. 2 (Winter 1992): 7–19.

[13]A business-cycle discussion of switching between value and growth stocks appears in Case and Cusimano, ibid.

the likelihood of a reversal. Finally, seasonalities are included in the analysis as some studies indicate value stocks do well in the first quarter of the year while growth stocks typically overperform in the fourth quarter.[14]

Value versus Growth

At times growth stocks outperform value stocks and at times the opposite occurs. Over the long run, studies indicate, on average, that value stocks offer somewhat higher returns than growth stocks.[15] Several reasons can be offered for this empirical finding. First, studies have focused on before-tax returns of value and growth stocks. If investors are concerned with after-tax returns, they will demand a return premium from value stocks, which typically have higher dividends and lower expected capital gains than growth stocks. Second, the typical value stock may have a low comfort level with investors. Bad news, disappointments, or an uncertain future lead investors to perceive them to be riskier and less desirable. This results in a higher risk premium for value stocks. Investor's negative perceptions about a value stock can lead to pessimism about the firm's future sales and earnings, which can itself lead to positive earnings surprises and superior stock returns when better times arrive. The apparent superior risk–return tradeoff for value stocks compared to growth stocks is a subject of on-going research and investigation.

IMKAV and Value/Growth Investing

A portfolio consists of any number of individual stock investments. Analysts recommending stocks to a portfolio manager need to identify and monitor key assumptions and variables (IMKAV) related to their suggested stocks. IMKAV analysis has implications for portfolio management and style investing, too. Value investors focus on one set of key assumptions and variables, whereas growth investors focus on another. To more closely examine growth and value, let's look at Figure 19.2, which represents the cycle of rising and falling expectations about a firm's earnings over time. This is a stylistic drawing; it tells nothing about the relative length of its various stages. Indeed, the length of the stages is firm-specific. It is the job of the analyst and portfolio manager to make decisions regarding where firms are in this cycle and how long they may stay in their current position.

Investors known as "contrarians" (1) invest in beaten-down stocks that usually have poor consensus earnings forecasts. These stocks are unattractive and are generally thought of as risky and poor investment selections. Some of these firms really are down and out; but others eventually show signs of renewal and start to experience good news about their markets, sales, and earnings. After some initial good news, investors who used to ignore the firm start paying attention to it. Quantitative analysts who focus on positive earnings surprises begin to examine the firm as well (2). If earnings continue to rise, more and more investors pay attention to it and consider it for their portfolios. Soon, investors begin to feel optimistic about the firm and its future. In time, analysts revise earnings estimates upward (3). Earnings surprises continue. The momentum of earnings increases attracts the attentions of still more investors and analysts, who proclaim the stock as a "growth" stock (4).

---

[14]Geoffrey Gerber, "Equity Style Allocations: Timing Between Growth and Value," in Jess Lederman and Robert A. Klein, ed., *Global Asset Allocation* (New York: Wiley, 1994), pp. 108–122.

[15]Carlo Capaul, Ian Rowley, and William F. Sharpe, "International Value and Growth Stock Returns," *Financial Analysts Journal* (January/February 1993): 27–36; David Umstead, "International Equity Style Management," in Robert A. Klein and Jess Lederman, ed., *Equity Style Management* (Chicago, IL: Irwin Professional Publishing, 1995), pp. 118–140; and J. Lakonishok, A. Shleifer, and R. Vishny, "Contrarian Investment, Extrapolation, and Risk," Working paper presented to The Berkeley Program in Finance, Spring 1994.

Figure 19.2 *Earnings Expectation Cycle*

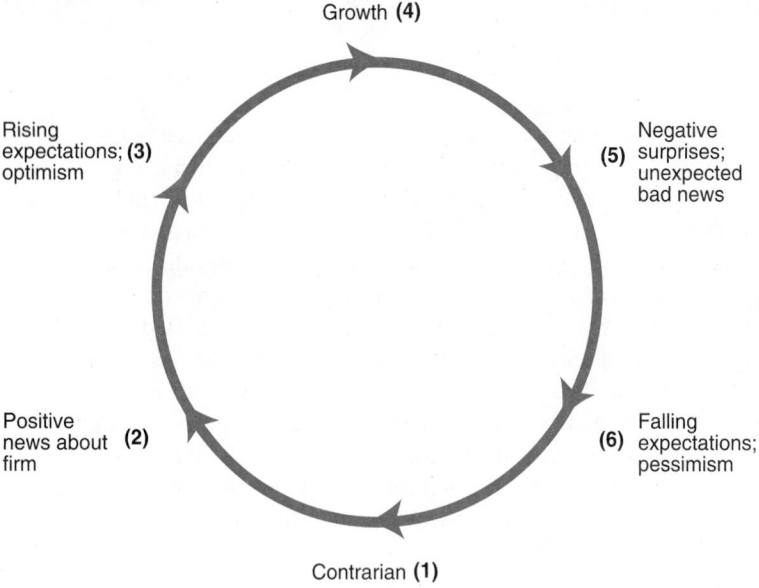

Source: Adapted from Richard Bernstein, "The Earnings Expectations Life Cycle," *Financial Analysts Journal,* March/April 1993, pp. 90–93; Figure A.

But all good things come to an end; at some time the firm's stock will be "torpedoed" by an earnings disappointment. Earnings may still be up, but maybe not as high as analysts expected, or earnings may decline (5). Some investors will sell the stock. In the future, the earnings may recover and such investors look foolish. Or the firm may continue in the cycle, but now on the downside. Negative surprises continue; the firm's upward trend in earnings starts to level off or to become a downward trend. Problems develop within the firm, its strategy, or its markets. After a time, pessimism about the firm grows and the stock price continues to fall (6). Fewer and fewer investors hold the stock in high regard, and many direct their attention to other companies. Soon, the neglected stock once again becomes the kind that is owned by contrarians (1), who hope for a recovery that may or may not come.

The expectational perspective illustrated in Figure 19.3 has implications for the kinds of stocks that make those with a value or growth tilt successful over time. One skill that separates a bad value portfolio manager from a good one is knowing when to buy a stock. Buying a stock too early results in poor stock performance as bad or disappointing news continues. A value manager who picks the right time to buy enjoys benefits from a growing collection of good news about a firm and from a rising stock price as other investors jump on the bandwagon and buy into the stock.

One skill that separates a good growth portfolio manager from a bad one is knowing when to sell. The bad growth manager remains optimistic about the firm or believes that any bad news will soon be replaced by good news. They characteristically hold onto their stocks so long that previously earned returns shrink or disappear. Portfolio managers who consider themselves "growth" or "value" investors need to have systems or processes in place to monitor their key variables about their holdings and potential investments so they can, on average, buy in and sell out at appropriate times.

Figure 19.3 *Earnings Expectation Cycle and Style Investing*

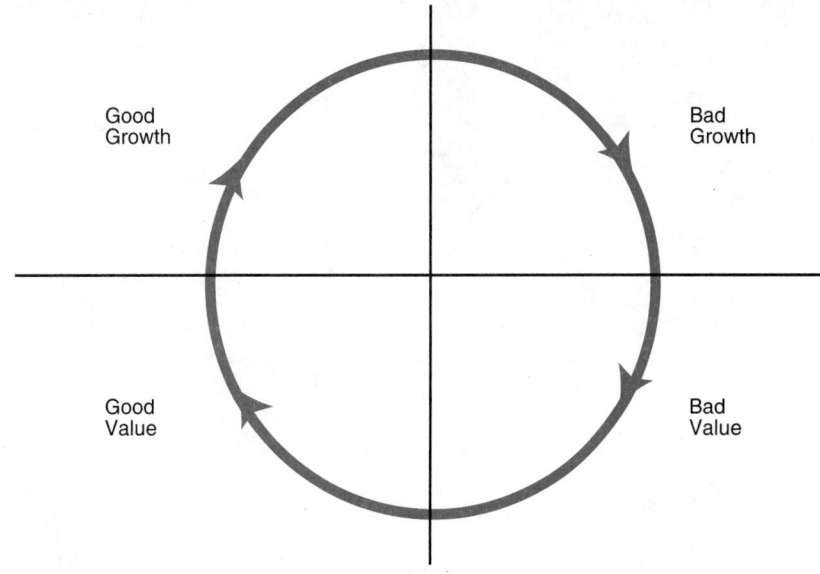

Good
Growth

Bad
Growth

Good
Value

Bad
Value

Source: Adapted from Richard Bernstein, Figure B, p. 92, in "The Earnings Expectations Life Cycle," *Financial Analysts Journal,* March/April 1993, pp. 90–93.

FUTURES AND OPTIONS IN EQUITY PORTFOLIO MANAGEMENT

The systematic and unsystematic risk of equity portfolios can be modified by using futures and options derivatives. The portfolio mix between equities and other assets can be adjusted by the use of equity derivatives as well. In addition, cash inflows and outflows can be hedged through appropriate derivative strategies. Due to the cost, risk, and restrictions of short selling, selling futures contracts or purchasing puts are attractive alternatives to short selling for long–short managers.

Modifying Portfolio Risk and Return: A Review

As discussed in Chapter 17, futures and options can affect the risk and return distribution for a portfolio. In general, a dollar-for-dollar relationship exists between changes in the price of the underlying security and the price of the corresponding futures contract. In effect, buying (selling) futures is identical to subtracting (adding) cash from or to the portfolio. Purchasing futures has the effect of increasing the exposure to the asset; selling futures decreases the portfolio's exposure. Suppose Figure 19.4A represents a portfolio's probability distribution of returns. Buying futures on the portfolio's underlying asset increases the portfolio's exposure (or sensitivity) to price changes of the asset. As shown in Figure 19.4B, the return distribution widens, indicating a larger return variance. Selling futures has the effect of decreasing the portfolio's sensitivity to the underlying asset. Figure 19.4C shows the effect on the portfolio if futures are sold; the variance of returns declines, causing a "narrower" return distribution.

Figure 19.4 illustrates that futures have a symmetrical impact on portfolio returns, because their impact on the portfolio's upside and downside return potential is the same.

Figure 19.4   *Return Distributions Are Modified When Futures Contracts Are Purchased or Sold*

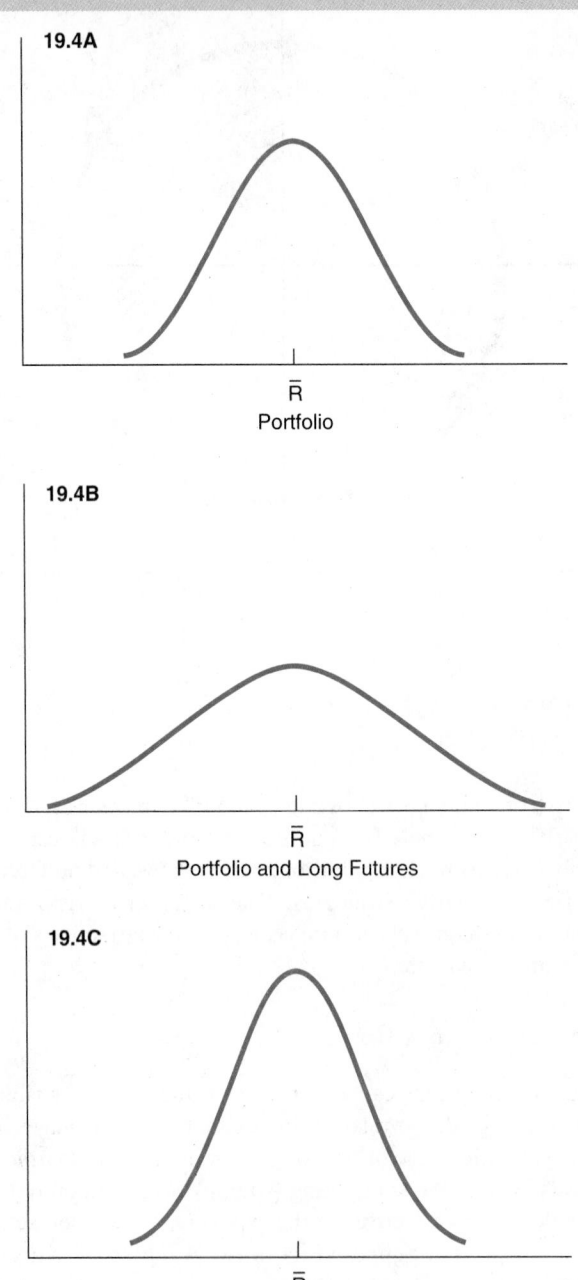

19.4A

$\bar{R}$
Portfolio

19.4B

$\bar{R}$
Portfolio and Long Futures

19.4C

$\bar{R}$
Portfolio and Short Futures

This is because of the close relationship between changes in the futures price and changes in the price of the underlying asset.

A futures contract represents an obligation to buy or sell the underlying asset unless canceled by an offsetting transaction. In contrast, options give their owner the right (but not the obligation) to buy or sell the underlying asset. This choice of whether to exercise or not

Figure 19.5 *Examples of Truncated Return Distributions When Options Are Used to Modify Portfolio Risk*

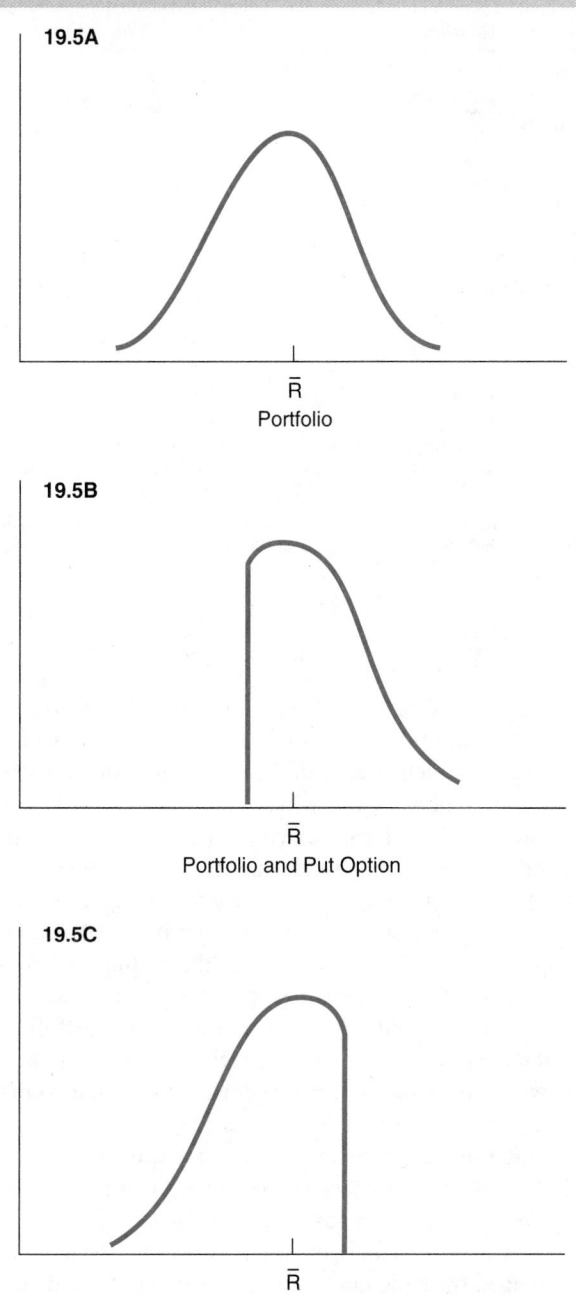

19.5A

$\bar{R}$
Portfolio

19.5B

$\bar{R}$
Portfolio and Put Option

19.5C

$\bar{R}$
Portfolio and Written Call Option

exercise the option means that options do not have a symmetrical impact on returns. For example, as shown in Chapter 17, buying a call option limits losses; buying a put when the investor owns the underlying security has the effect of controlling downside risk, as shown in Figure 19.5B. Writing a covered call, on the other hand, limits upside returns while not affecting loss potential, as seen in Figure 19.5C; writing a put option has the same effect.

Table 19.3   *List of Countries with Stock Index Futures*

Country	Percent of FT-Actuaries World Index
Australia	1.3%
Canada[a]	1.8
Denmark	0.3
France[a]	3.3
Germany	3.3
Hong Kong	1.4
Japan[a]	25.4
Netherlands	1.5
New Zealand	0.1
Spain	0.9
Sweden	0.7
Switzerland	2.0
United Kingdom[a]	10.5
United States[a]	42.8
Total as of December 31, 1992	95.3%

[a]Approved for use by U.S. investors.

Source: Roger G. Clarke, "Application of Derivative Strategies in Managing Global Portfolios." Reprinted with permission, from *Derivative Strategies for Managing Portfolio Risk.* Copyright 1993, Association for Investment Management and Research, Charlottesville, Va. All Rights Reserved.

The Use of Futures in Asset Allocation

In times of changing market conditions, shifting a portfolio's asset allocation must be done quickly to take advantage of the manager's forecast. Such changes are costly because securities must be identified and then sold and bought to facilitate the reallocation. Commissions and the market impact of large trades can harm the portfolio's return potential.

Rather than identifying specific securities for sale and purchase and issuing large buy-and-sell orders, the portfolio manager can use futures. Buying and selling appropriate futures contracts can quickly and easily change the portfolio's asset mix at lower transaction costs than trading large quantities of securities. Over time, the manager can identify specific assets to buy and sell so the trading will not have an adverse market impact.

Futures can help achieve a proper stock/bond mix in a multiple-manager environment. In many medium and large pension funds, the portfolio is divided among different individual managers to exploit their specialized expertise in managing different asset classes. The overall pension fund manager can use futures to maintain the desired asset allocation; otherwise he or she would have to disrupt the specialized managers by adding or removing funds from them because of reallocation.

Futures can also be used to gain exposure to international markets. As listed in Table 19.3, many major stock markets have futures traded where the value of the futures contract is based on a major stock price index. Exposure to different currencies can also be managed by using currency futures contracts and currency options.

The Use of Derivatives in Equity Portfolios

Regardless of whether the equity portfolio is passively or actively managed, futures and options can help control cash inflows and outflows from the portfolio. In reality, most options used to modify portfolio risk are options whose underlying "security" is another derivative security—a futures contract. These options are called future options or options on futures, which are discussed in Chapter 18.

Hedging Portfolio Inflows

When a large sum of money is deposited with a manager, the fund's asset composition changes; the lump sum cash inflow has the effect of reducing the portfolio's exposure to equities because a larger proportion of the portfolio's assets are currently in cash. The portfolio manager who makes hurried investments in the market runs a greater chance of purchasing inappropriate securities. Also, large purchases can lead to sizable commissions and a price-pressure influence on the stocks purchased.

A better strategy is to use part of the cash inflow to purchase stock-index futures contracts so that the total contract value approximates the size of the inflow. Alternatively, you could purchase call options. In doing so, the money is immediately invested with lower commissions and the price impact is less than if stocks had been purchased outright. Once the futures are purchased, the manager has time to decide what assets to buy, and the smaller purchases over time will reduce the price pressure. As these purchases are made, the futures contracts can be sold.

Hedging Portfolio Outflows

A large planned withdrawal from a portfolio is usually accomplished by selling securities over time so that when the withdrawal date occurs, the needed funds are available for transfer. Similar to a cash deposit, the sale of securities causes an increase in cash holdings, thus reducing the portfolio's equity exposure. A possible strategy to counterbalance the effect of a larger cash position is to buy futures contracts or call options as securities are sold. The net effect is to maintain the portfolio's overall exposure to stocks while accumulating cash. On the cash withdrawal date, the futures contracts can be sold and the portfolio's operations have not been disrupted.

The Standard & Poor's 500 Index Futures Contract

We will include futures contracts in this initial review of derivative securities in equity portfolio management because futures, and options on the futures, are the derivative tools that portfolio managers typically use.[16]

Table 19.4 lists the various exchange-traded financial futures contracts. Although a complete review of the numerous futures contracts is beyond our current discussion, we will use the Chicago Mercantile Exchange's S&P 500 index futures contract as an illustration.

Purchasers of futures contracts must place funds in a margin account. Initial margin requirements are $6,000 for those buying futures for speculative purposes and $2,500 for investors buying futures for hedging purposes. Hedgers must show current ownership of an equity portfolio whose market value approximates that of the futures traded.

The value of the S&P 500 futures contract is equal to $250 times the value of the index, so each one-point change in the index leads to a $250 change in the value of the contract. When the S&P 500 futures contract expires, delivery or settlement of the contract is *not* made in the shares of 500 different stocks, but in cash. Every day, the contract is marked to market, which means its change in value is added to or subtracted from the investors' margin account. When investors close out their position, or when the futures contract expires, they receive the funds in their margin accounts. The difference between the funds in their account when it is closed and their initial margin deposit represents their profit or loss, which equals the change in value of the futures contract over the holding period.

---

[16]In addition to futures, options, and options on futures, swaps are another derivative security useful in portfolio management.

Table 19.4   *Financial Futures Contracts Available on U.S. Exchanges (as of January 1998)*

Treasury bonds (CBOT, MCE)
Six and one half- to ten-year Treasury notes (CBOT)
Five-year Treasury notes (CBOT)
Two-year Treasury notes (CBOT)
Thirty-day Federal funds rate (CBOT)
Treasury bills (CME)
One-month Eurodollars (CME)
One-month LIBOR (CME)
Euroyen (CME)
Municipal Bond Index (CBOT)
Dow Jones Industrial Average (CBOT)
S&P 500 Index (CME)
Mini-S&P 500 Index (CME)
Nikkei 225 Stock Average (CME)
NASDAQ 100 (CME)
Russell 2000 (CME)
NYSE Composite Index (NYFE)
Value Line Stock Index (KCBT)
S&P 400 MidCap Index (CME)

There is one exception to this. Should the funds in the investors' margin account become too low because of adverse price movements, investors will receive a margin call. Maintenance margin requires that the account balance be increased to at least $2,500 for speculators and $1,500 for hedgers using the Chicago Mercantile Exchange's S&P 500 index futures contract.

Prior to discussing how portfolio managers buy and sell S&P 500 futures, it is necessary to discuss how managers determine the appropriate number of S&P 500 futures to buy or sell—that is, the hedge ratio. We'll examine two examples.

Determining How Many Contracts to Trade to Hedge a Deposit or a Withdrawal   As discussed, futures can help maintain the desired exposure to stocks when the portfolio experiences a cash inflow or outflow. The number of futures contracts to be traded will equal

$$\frac{\text{Cash Flow}}{\text{Value of 1 contract}} \times \text{Portfolio Beta}$$

The value of one contract is the price times $250. If the price of the S&P 500 futures contract is quoted as 1006.90, the value of the contract will be $251,725.

The beta of the underlying futures index is taken to be 1.0. To determine the portfolio's beta to be used in the hedge ratio formula, portfolio returns are regressed on those of the underlying index:

19.1 $R_{\text{portfolio}} = \text{alpha} + \text{beta} \, (R_{\text{index}})$

The resulting slope estimate is the relative volatility of the portfolio's returns compared to those of the underlying index. We multiply the number of contracts by beta so the value of the futures position will change in value with the value of the portfolio.

Given the existence of several stock-index futures contracts, a way to determine which contract is best for a particular portfolio is to examine the coefficient of determination (R^2) from estimating Equation 19.1 with different indexes. The index with the highest R^2 is the

one that best follows the variations in the portfolio over time, which indicates it may be the most appropriate index. Generally, R^2 will be higher for well-diversified portfolios.

For example, to determine the appropriate number of futures contracts, assume an equity portfolio manager will receive a $5 million cash inflow today. The beta of the portfolio, measured against the S&P 500, is 1.15. The value of the contract is $251,725. The number of S&P 500 futures contracts that should be purchased to hedge this cash inflow is equal to

$$(\$5 \text{ million}/\$251,725) \times 1.15 = 22.84 \text{ contracts}$$

Because fractional contracts do not exist, managers typically round this number to the nearest integer and would purchase twenty-three contracts to hedge the cash inflow. These twenty-three contracts will be sold over time as the $5 million in cash is invested in stocks.

Determining How Many Contracts to Trade to Adjust Portfolio Beta   In Chapter 7, we learned the beta of a stock portfolio equals the weighted average of its components' betas. This concept also serves to determine how many futures contracts to buy or sell to increase or decrease a portfolio's beta.

Suppose a $25 million equity portfolio has $22.5 million invested in stocks and $2.5 million is invested in Treasury bills. The equity component of the portfolio has a beta of 0.95. Assume that the manager expects rising stock prices, so he or she wants to increase the overall portfolio's beta to 1.10. As above, we'll assume the value of a futures contract is $251,725. The beta of the cash or T-bill component of a portfolio is usually assumed to be zero and thus is ignored in the analysis.

Currently, the weight of the equity component of the portfolio is $22.5 million/$25 million or 0.90; the beta of the equity component is 0.95. The beta of the futures contract is 1.0. The weight of the futures component of the portfolio will be $(F \times \$251,725)/\$25$ million, where F represents the number of futures contracts to be traded. Because the target beta for the entire portfolio is 1.10, the weighted average of the portfolio's components must equal 1.10:

$$\underset{\text{Target Beta}}{1.10 =} \quad \underset{\substack{\text{Contribution of Common} \\ \text{Stock Portfolio}}}{0.90 \times 0.95\ +} \quad \underset{\substack{\text{Contribution of the} \\ \text{futures component}}}{\frac{F \times \$251,725}{\$25 \text{ million}} \times 1.0}$$

Solving for F, we find that 24.33 contracts must be purchased to attain the target beta. Rounding to the nearest integer, the manager will buy twenty-four contracts.

If the manager forecasts a falling market and wants to reduce the beta of the portfolio to 0.80, the number of futures contracts required is determined as follows:

$$\underset{\text{Target Beta}}{0.80 =} \quad \underset{\substack{\text{Contribution of Common} \\ \text{Stock Portfolio}}}{0.90 \times 0.95\ +} \quad \underset{\substack{\text{Contribution of the} \\ \text{futures component}}}{\frac{F \times \$251,725}{\$25 \text{ million}} \times 1.0}$$

Solving for F, we find the answer is -5.46. The negative sign indicates that futures contracts must be sold to reduce the portfolio beta to 0.80. Rounding to the nearest integer, the manager will sell five contracts in order to attain the desired portfolio. Note that options contracts *cannot* be used to adjust a portfolio's beta because they have an asymmetrical effect on a portfolio's return distribution.

Using Futures in Passive Equity Portfolio Management

A passive investment strategy generally seeks to buy and hold a portfolio of equity securities. A popular passive portfolio strategy is to replicate a stock-market index, such as those described in Chapter 5. A passive strategy will not try to change a portfolio's beta based upon an economic forecast.

With a passive investment strategy, the manager is expected to manage cash inflows and outflows without harming the ability of the portfolio to track its target index. The prior example on hedging a cash inflow or outflow is directly applicable to passive portfolio management. Instead of investing all cash inflows in the index or a subsample of the index, the manager can purchase an appropriate number of futures contracts to maintain the portfolio's structure and reduce the portfolio's tracking error relative to the index while the manager determines where to invest the funds. Similarly, anticipated cash outflows can be hedged by liquidating part of the portfolio over time while maintaining the portfolio's exposure to the market through the use of futures contracts.

Options can be used to a limited extent in passive management. When cash rebalancing is imperfect and an index fund becomes overweighted in a sector or in individual stocks relative to its index, it is possible to sell call options on firms or industry groups to correct the portfolio's weights.

Using Futures in Active Equity Portfolio Management

Active management often attempts to adjust the portfolio's systematic risk, unsystematic risk, or both. Systematic risk is a portfolio's exposure to price fluctuations caused by changes in the overall stock market. Unsystematic risk includes the portfolio's exposure to industries, sectors, or firms different from the benchmark.

Modifying Systematic Risk   An equity portfolio's systematic risk is the sensitivity of the portfolio's value to changes in the benchmark index as measured by the portfolio's beta. If a rising market is expected, active portfolio managers will want to increase their portfolio's beta whereas expectations of a falling market will invite managers to reduce their portfolio's betas.

Traditionally, when the market was expected to rise, active managers would sell low-beta stocks and buy high-beta stocks to raise the portfolio's weighted average beta. Alternatively, the use of futures provides a quicker and cheaper way to do this with less disruption to the traits of the portfolio.[17] As discussed previously, buying or selling futures allows the manager to increase or decrease a portfolio's beta.

It is possible to sell futures so the value of the overall portfolio will be unaffected by market changes over the length of the futures contract. This is accomplished by selling a sufficient number of futures so the portfolio's beta becomes zero. To illustrate, assume a $25 million portfolio with $22.5 million invested in stocks and the rest in T-bills. The equity portfolio has a beta of 0.95 and T-bills have zero beta. The beta of the futures contract is 1.0, and the value of a futures contract is $251,725. To determine the required number of futures to sell to make the beta of the portfolio zero, we need to solve the following equation:

---

[17]This is an important advantage; should the active managers believe they have expertise in identifying mispriced or undervalued securities, they may want to continue holding them in spite of predictions of an adverse market move.

$$0.00 = \quad 0.90 \times 0.95 + \quad \frac{F \times \$251{,}725}{\$25 \text{ million}} \times 1.0$$

| Target Beta | Contribution of Common Stock Portfolio | Contribution of the futures component |

We find that F equals -84.91, which means that to make the portfolio market-neutral, it is necessary to sell eighty-five futures contracts. By setting the portfolio beta equal to zero, the return earned on the portfolio should approximate that of a risk-free asset such as short-term T-bills. An active manager who has the ability to identify mispriced or under-valued securities may generate an extra return component.

Modifying Unsystematic Risk   Opportunities exist for controlling the unsystematic risk in an equity portfolio. Futures and options on futures exist for a limited number of sectors, whereas options exist for numerous components of the equity market. Option contracts are also available on market indexes such as the S&P 100 and S&P 500; for stock groups such as consumer goods and cyclicals; and for selected industries such as banks, utilities, pharmaceuticals, and semiconductors. Options can be had on over 1,400 individual stocks. Thus, even when industry option contracts don't exist, portfolio managers can buy or sell individual stock options for the industry to modify their exposure.

Unfortunately, we cannot determine the number of option contracts to be traded for a given effect because options truncate the return profile, which affects the portfolio's beta and its responsiveness to market changes.

Options trading can take advantage of the portfolio manager's forecasts for certain sectors and industries, by trading either sector options or options of firms in the industry. Options on index futures can also exploit anticipated market changes. Because of their truncation effect on return distributions, options on index futures can affect both a portfolio's systematic and unsystematic risk.

For example, a manager can buy call options when anticipating a rise in the market, in a sector or industry, or in a group of individual stocks. The lower call premiums can provide more leverage than buying futures, and options contracts can allow greater precision in targeting sectors of the market rather than an entire index. The maximum loss for such strategies is limited to the call premium.

Similarly, investors can buy put options on an index futures, a sector, or group of stocks in anticipation of a decline in value. Calls can be written on the market and subsets of the market when declining or stable values are forecast. Writing put options on the market and its subsectors can generate income when the portfolio managers expect their values to be stable or to rise.

Modifying the Characteristics of an International Equity Portfolio

Futures and options can help modify or hedge positions in international equity portfolios. As noted, international portfolios represent positions in both securities and currencies. Futures and options contracts on major currencies allow the portfolio manager to manage the risks of each of these separately. Currency futures and options on currency futures can help modify the currency exposure of an international stock portfolio without affecting the actual holdings of the portfolios. For example, a portfolio manager may be bullish on German stocks but believe that the deutsche mark is currently overvalued relative to the U.S. dollar. He can purchase the German securities and then adjust the overall currency exposure of the portfolio through the use of currency options and futures.

Consider the following example. Assume a stock portfolio has the equivalent of $30 million invested: $9 million in the United States; $12 million in Germany; the remainder in the United Kingdom. Thus, the current allocation across countries and currencies is: 30 percent United States, 40 percent Germany, and 30 percent United Kingdom. Assume the manager believes that the deutsche mark is overvalued and expects a strengthening pound. Given this outlook, the manager wishes to reduce her exposure to the deutsche mark by $4.5 million (or −15 percent of the portfolio) while increasing her exposure to the pound by $4.5 million (or +15 percentage points). In other words, the desired *currency* allocation is: 30 percent U.S. dollar, 25 percent German deutsche mark, and 45 percent U.K. pound.

Traditional currency rebalancing would require rebalancing the country allocation whereby the manager would lose the chance to participate in security markets she thinks are undervalued. Also, such security rebalancing would be costly and time consuming. Such a rebalancing scenario would cause the portfolio manager to ignore what presumably she does best, namely identifying undervalued markets and securities. The point is, she would be forced to make decisions based on currency forecasts.

Currently, the manager can maintain the country exposure while modifying the currency exposure. Assume the futures dollar/pound exchange rate is £1 = $1.62. Because the pound futures contract calls for the delivery of £62,500, the value of one contract is 1.62 $/£ × £62,500 = $101,250. If the deutsche mark/dollar futures exchange rate is DM 1 = $0.55 and the deutsche mark contract calls for the delivery of DM 125,000, the value of the deutsche mark futures contract is 0.55 $/DM × DM 125,000 = $68,750.

If our manager wants to reduce the deutsche mark exposure of the portfolio by $4.5 million, she accomplishes this by selling $4,500,000/$68,750 = 65.45 (rounded off to 65) futures contracts on the deutsche mark. The portfolio's exposure to the pound can be increased by $4.5 million, by purchasing $4,500,000/$101,250 = 44.44 (or 44) British pound futures contracts.

Following these transactions, the security allocation across these countries remains as before: 30 percent United States, 40 percent Germany, 30 percent United Kingdom. Alternatively, through the use of currency hedging, the portfolio's exposure to the (presumably overvalued) deutsche mark is only 25 percent, whereas exposure to the (presumably undervalued) pound is 45 percent. The use of derivatives allows the portfolio manager to shift currency exposures in a quicker, less costly manner than reallocating stocks across countries, while allowing the manager to maintain the desired exposure to undervalued securities.

ASSET ALLOCATION STRATEGIES

An equity portfolio does not stand in isolation; rather it is part of an investor's overall investment portfolio. Many times the equity portfolio is part of a balanced portfolio that contains holdings in various long-term and short-term debt securities (such as bonds and Treasury bills) in addition to equities.

In such situations, the portfolio manager must consider more than just the composition of the equity or the bond component of the portfolio. The manager must also determine the appropriate mix of asset categories in the entire portfolio. Managers follow one of four general strategies for determining the asset mix of a portfolio: the integrated, strategic, tactical, or insured asset allocation method.

Integrated Asset Allocation

Integrated asset allocation separately examines: (1) capital market conditions, and (2) the investor's objectives and constraints. They are then combined as inputs to an optimizer

(such as that used to derive the Markowitz efficient frontier), which determines the portfolio asset mix that offers the best opportunity for meeting the investor's needs given the capital market forecast. The actual returns from the portfolio are then used as inputs to an iterative process in which changes over time in the investor's objectives and constraints are noted along with changes in capital market expectations. The optimizer selects a new asset mix based on this update of investor needs and capital market expectations.

Strategic Asset Allocation

Strategic asset allocation determines the long-term policy asset weights in a portfolio. Typically, long-term average asset returns, risk, and covariances are used as estimates of future capital market results. Efficient frontiers are generated using this historical return information and the investor decides which asset mix is appropriate for his or her needs during the planning horizon. This results in a constant-mix asset allocation with periodic rebalancing to adjust the portfolio to the specified asset weights.

For example, assume an investor determines his stock/bond portfolio should have a 50/50 mix. Subsequently, stocks rise 10 percent in value while bonds fall 10 percent, making the mix 55/45. To adjust the portfolio mix back to the desired level, some stocks will have to be sold and the proceeds used to purchase bonds.

Tactical Asset Allocation

In tactical asset allocation, the investor's risk tolerance and constraints are assumed to be constant over time and it is changing capital market conditions that lead to changes in the portfolio's stock–bond mix. Tactical asset allocation models sometimes are driven by risk premium estimates; the proportion of equity in the overall portfolio rises when the equity risk premium appears large relative to the bond risk premium or falls when the equity risk premium appears small relative to the bond risk premium. As such, tactical asset allocation strategies are somewhat contrarian in nature.

Insured Asset Allocation

Insured asset allocation likewise results in continual adjustments in the portfolio allocation. Insured asset allocation assumes that expected market returns and risks are constant over time, whereas the investor's objectives and constraints change as her wealth position changes. For example, rising portfolio values increase the investor's wealth and consequently her ability to handle risk, which means the investor can increase her exposure to risky assets. Declines in the portfolio's value lowers the investor's wealth, consequently decreasing her ability to handle risk, which means the portfolio's exposure to risky assets must decline. Often, insured asset allocation involves only two assets, such as common stocks and T-bills. As stock prices rise, the asset allocation increases the stock component. As stock prices fall, the stock component of the mix falls while the T-bill component increases. This is opposite of what would happen under tactical asset allocation.

Selecting an Allocation Method

Which asset allocation strategy is used depends on the perceptions of the variability in the client's objectives and constraints and the perceived relationship between past and future capital market conditions. If you believe that capital market conditions are relatively constant over time, you would use strategic or insured asset allocation. If you believe that the client's goals, risk preferences, and constraints are constant, you would likewise use tactical or strategic asset allocation. Integrated asset allocation assumes that both the

investor's needs and capital market conditions are variable and therefore must be constantly monitored. Under these conditions the portfolio mix must be constantly updated to reflect current changes in these parameters.

Investments Online

Equity portfolio management is the "how-to"—it combines what we know of stock selection and portfolio theory with the practice of constructing, monitoring, and updating equity portfolios to meet the needs of individual or institutional clients. Several professional money managers describe their services on the Internet, and here's a sampling of some of them:

www.russell.com
The home page of Frank Russell and Company contains descriptions of Russell's many services. Of special interest to us here are the links to Russell's indexes, including its various style indexes, for the U.S. and several other countries.

www.seic.com/iag/portfolios/portfolios.html
This is a page from the Web site of SEI Investments. It shows the asset allocation policies of different portfolios along with a description of their current allocations in pie-chart format. Assets are allocated in the portfolios across different markets and styles. By clicking on a piece of the pie chart, the site links us to a page of information on the manager and the fund's strategy. On other pages, this site offers news and analysis by SEI portfolio managers.

www.fquadrant.com
First Quadrant is a leader in the application of quantitative investment techniques to equity portfolio management. The product section of this site features a description of its quantitative perspective of style management. Other sections allow users to order copies of research monographs and published articles by First Quadrant personnel.

www.wilshire.com
Wilshire Associates, Inc., offers indexes, consulting, and other services to investors. This home page offers links to a market environment commentary and to information about its indexes (the Wilshire 5000 is a widely used benchmark to represent the total equity market in the United States). The site offers a description of each Wilshire index, including such helpful information as the fundamental characteristics of each index and their exposure to different stock market sectors.

SUMMARY

♦ Passive equity portfolios attempt to track the returns of an established benchmark such as the S&P 500 or some other benchmark that meets the investor's needs. Active portfolios attempt to add value relative to their benchmark by market timing and/or by seeking to buy undervalued stocks.

♦ Managers use several methods for constructing and managing a passive portfolio, including full replication and sampling. Active management strategies include sector rotation, the use of factor models, quantitative screens, and linear programming methods.

- Investment styles include small cap, large cap, value, and growth. Style investing tries to take advantage of possible anomalies or strengths of the portfolio manager. Identifying with a certain style conveys information to potential clients and helps identify appropriate benchmark portfolios. Just as asset-allocation models exist, some have tried to develop models to predict when one style will outperform another. A value manager will focus on the best time to buy undervalued securities; a growth manager focuses on determining appropriate times to sell securities before they are harmed by bad or disappointing news.

- We also examined the use of derivative securities in equity portfolio management. Futures can hedge against portfolio cash inflows and outflows; keep a passive portfolio fully invested and help minimize tracking error; and to change an actively managed portfolio's beta. Alternatively, options can be employed to modify a portfolio's unsystematic risk. Finally, derivatives can be used in managing currency exposures in international equity portfolios.

- Because equity portfolios are typically used with other assets in an investor's overall portfolio, we reviewed several common asset-allocation strategies, including integrated asset allocation, strategic asset allocation, tactical asset allocation, and insured asset allocation. The basic difference between these strategies is whether they rely on current market expectations or long-run projections, and whether the investor's objectives and constraints remain constant over the planning horizon or change with market conditions.

Questions

1. Why have passive portfolio management strategies increased in use over time?
2. What do we mean by an indexing portfolio strategy, and what is the justification for this strategy? How might it differ from another passive portfolio?
3. Briefly describe four techniques that are considered active equity portfolio management strategies.
4. Describe several techniques for constructing a passive portfolio.
5. Discuss three strategies active managers can use to add value to their portfolios.
6. How do trading costs and market efficiencies affect the active manager? How may an active manager try to overcome these obstacles to success?
7. What is meant by an investment style? How do value stocks differ from growth stocks?
8. Explain how style identification is an important component of the client–portfolio manager relationship.
9. Some studies suggest that value investors earn higher risk-adjusted returns than growth investors. Does this mean investors should focus on value investing and not on other styles?
10. What are the characteristics of a good value-stock portfolio manager? A good growth-stock portfolio manager?
11. How are completeness funds used with style investing?
12. Describe four asset-allocation strategies. In what ways do they differ from each other?
13. List and describe the two components of risk in an equity portfolio.
14. What is a hedge ratio? Why is it useful?
15. Is it possible to "immunize" an equity portfolio so its value is not affected by changes in the overall market? Why or why not?
16. Why might it be easier to construct a bond-market index than a stock-market index portfolio?
17. What trade-offs are involved when constructing a portfolio using a full replication or a sampling method?
18. Because of inflationary expectations, you expect natural-resource stocks such as mining companies and oil firms to perform well over the next three to six months. As an active portfolio manager, describe the various methods available to take advantage of this forecast.

Problems

1. You have a portfolio with a market value of $50 million and a beta (measured against the S&P 500) of 1.2. If the market rises 10 percent, what value would you expect your portfolio to have?

2. Given the monthly returns below, how well did the passive portfolio track the S&P 500 benchmark? Find the R^2, alpha, and beta of the portfolio.

Month	Portfolio Return	S&P 500 Return
January	5.0%	5.2%
February	−2.3	−3.0
March	−1.8	−1.6
April	2.2	1.9
May	0.4	0.1
June	−0.8	−0.5
July	0.0	0.2
August	1.5	1.6
September	−0.3	−0.1
October	−3.7	−4.0
November	2.4	2.0
December	0.3	0.2

3. Using the Ibbotson data on asset returns from Chapter 3, what percentage of the equity risk premium is consumed by trading costs of 1.5 percent? Assuming a normal distribution of returns, what is the probability that an active manager can earn a return that will overcome these trading costs?

4. Assume you actively manage a $100 million portfolio, 95 percent invested in equities, with a portfolio beta of 1.05. Your passive benchmark is the S&P 500. The current S&P 500 index value is 1010.50.

   a. You anticipate a $3 million cash inflow from a pension fund next week. How many futures contracts should you buy or sell to mitigate the effect of this inflow on the portfolio's performance?

   b. Rather than a cash inflow, suppose you expected a cash outflow of $8 million. How many futures contracts should you buy or sell to mitigate the effect of this outflow on the portfolio's performance?

5. You manage the portfolio described in Problem 4. How many S&P 500 futures contracts must you buy or sell to

   a. Increase the portfolio beta to 1.15?

   b. Increase the portfolio beta to 1.30?

   c. Reduce the portfolio beta to 0.95?

   d. Reduce the portfolio beta to zero?

6. You own a stock portfolio worth $1.5 million with a beta of 1.3. The current value of the S&P 500 index is 985.37.

   a. What is the value of one S&P 500 futures contract traded on the Chicago Mercantile Exchange?

   b. How many futures contracts must you buy or sell to completely hedge the value of the portfolio against an expected market decline?

   c. Suppose the market, as measured by the S&P 500, drops 10 percent over the course of the next several months. Given the answer to part (b),

      i. What is the profit or loss on your futures position?

      ii. What is the expected profit or loss for your stock portfolio (unhedged)?

      iii. What is the overall impact of the market decline on your hedged portfolio?

   d. Suppose the market, as measured by the S&P 500, increases 10 percent over the course of the next several months. Given the answer to part (b),

      i. What is the profit or loss on your futures position?

      ii. What is the expected profit or loss for your stock portfolio (unhedged)?

      iii. What is the overall impact of the market rise on your hedged portfolio?

7. You own a stock portfolio worth $2.3 million with a beta of 1.1. The current value of the S&P 500 index is 1051.73.

   a. What is the value of one S&P 500 futures contract traded on the Chicago Mercantile Exchange?

b. How many futures contracts must you buy or sell to hedge the portfolio against an expected market decline?

c. Suppose the market, as measured by the S&P 500, drops 10 percent over the course of the next several months, but your portfolio, because of unsystematic risk, falls 13 percent in value. Given the answer to part (b),

    i. What is the profit or loss on your futures position?

    ii. What is the profit or loss for your stock portfolio (unhedged)?

    iii. What is the overall impact of the market decline on your hedged portfolio? Why is this number not closer to zero?

d. Suppose the market, as measured by the S&P 500, increases 10 percent over the course of the next several months while your stock portfolio rises 15 percent. Given the answer to part (b),

    i. What is the profit or loss on your futures position?

    ii. What is the profit or loss for your stock portfolio (unhedged)?

    iii. What is the overall impact of the market rise on your hedged portfolio? Why is this number not closer to zero?

References

Bhatia, Sanjiv, ed. *Global Equity Investing.* Charlottesville, VA: Association for Investment Management and Research, May 1996.

Brown, Keith C., ed. *Derivative Strategies for Managing Portfolio Risk.* Charlottesville, Va.: Association for Investment Management and Research, 1993.

Coggin, Daniel T., Frank J. Fabozzi, and Robert D. Arnott, eds. *The Handbook of Equity Style Management,* 2nd ed. New Hope, PA: Frank J. Fabozzi Associates, 1997.

Klein, Robert A., and Jess Lederman, eds. *Equity Style Management.* Chicago: Irwin Professional Publishing, 1995.

Levine, Sumner N., ed. *The Financial Analysts Handbook.* 2nd ed. Homewood, Ill.: Dow Jones–Irwin, 1988.

Maginn, John L., and Donald L. Tuttle, eds. *Managing Investment Portfolios.* 2nd ed. Boston, Mass.: Warren, Gorham, and Lamont, 1990.

GLOSSARY

Active equity portfolio management An attempt by the manager to outperform, on a risk-adjusted basis, a passive benchmark portfolio.

Backtest A method of testing a quantitative model in which computers are used to examine the composition and returns of portfolios based on historical data to determine if the selected strategy would have worked in the past.

Benchmark portfolio A passive portfolio whose average characteristics (in terms of beta, dividend yield, industry weighting, firm size, and so on) match the risk–return objectives of the client and serves as a basis for evaluating the performance of an active manager.

Completeness fund A specialized index used to form the basis of a passive portfolio whose purpose is to provide diversification to a client's total portfolio by excluding those segments in which the client's active managers invest.

Earnings momentum A strategy in which portfolios are constructed of stocks of firms with rising earnings.

Full replication A technique for constructing a passive index portfolio in which all securities in an index are purchased in proportion to their weights in the index.

Growth stocks Stocks of firms enjoying above-average earnings-per-share increases and that usually have above-average ratios of price/book and price/earnings.

Passive equity portfolio management A long-term buy-and-hold strategy so that returns will track those of an index over time.

Price momentum A portfolio strategy in which you acquire stocks that have enjoyed above-market stock price increases.

Quadratic optimization A technique that relies on historical correlations in order to construct a portfolio that seeks to minimize tracking error with an index.

Sampling A technique for constructing a passive index portfolio in which the portfolio manager buys a representative sample of stocks that comprise the benchmark index.

Sector rotation strategy An active strategy that involves purchasing stocks in specific industries or stocks with specific characteristics (low P/E, growth, value) that are anticipated to rise in value more than the overall market.

Style investing Involves constructing portfolios in such a way to capture one or more of the characteristics of equity securities.

Tracking error The difference between a passively managed portfolio's returns and that of the index it seeks to imitate.

Value stocks Stocks that appear to be underpriced because their price/book or price/earning ratio is low, or their dividend yield is high, compared to the rest of the market.

CHAPTER

20

Fixed Income Portfolio Management Strategies

In this chapter we will answer the following questions:

♦ What are three major bond portfolio management strategies?

♦ What are the two specific strategies for passive portfolio management?

♦ What are the five strategies available for active portfolio management?

♦ What do we mean by matched-funding techniques, and what are the four specific strategies for these techniques?

♦ How can futures and options aid bond portfolio management?

Successful bond portfolio management involves far more than mastering vast amounts of technical information. Such information is useful only to the extent that it helps generate higher risk-adjusted returns. In this chapter, we shift attention from the technical dimensions of bond portfolio management to the equally important strategic dimension. We first discuss several alternative portfolio management strategies. Then we examine how the use of derivative securities can assist fixed-income portfolio managers.

ALTERNATIVE BOND PORTFOLIO STRATEGIES

Bond portfolio management strategies can be divided into three groups:[1]

1. Passive portfolio strategies
   a. Buy and hold
   b. Indexing

---

[1]This breakdown benefited from the discussion of Martin L. Leibowitz, "The Dedicated Bond Portfolio in Pension Funds—Part I: Motivations and Basics," in *Financial Analysts Journal* 42, no. 1 (January–February 1986): 61–75.

2. Active management strategies
    a. Interest-rate anticipation
    b. Valuation analysis
    c. Credit analysis
    d. Yield-spread analysis
    e. Bond swaps
3. Matched-funding techniques
    a. Classical ("pure") immunization
    b. Dedicated portfolio, exact cash match
    c. Dedicated portfolio, optimal cash match, and reinvestment
    d. Horizon matching

We will discuss each of these alternatives because they are all viable for certain portfolios with different needs and risk profiles. Prior to the 1960s, only the passive and active strategies were available, and most bond portfolios were managed on a buy-and-hold basis. The 1960s and early 1970s saw growing interest in alternative active bond portfolio management strategies. The investment environment since the late 1970s has been characterized by periods of record-breaking inflation and interest rates, declining inflation and interest rates, extremely volatile rates of return in bond markets, the introduction of many new financial instruments in response to the increase in return volatility, and the development of several new funding techniques or contingent portfolio management techniques to meet the emerging needs of institutional clients. Several of these new portfolio management techniques have become possible because of the "rediscovery" of the concept of duration in the early 1970s.

Passive Bond Portfolio Strategies

Managers employ two specific passive portfolio strategies. First is a **buy-and-hold strategy** in which a manager selects a portfolio of bonds based on the objectives and constraints of the client with the intent of holding these bonds to maturity. In the second passive strategy, **indexing**, the objective is to construct a portfolio of bonds that will equal the performance of a specified bond index such as the Lehman Brothers Government Bond Index.

Buy-and-Hold Strategy   The simplest portfolio management strategy is to buy and hold the securities until maturity. Well known to bond investors, buy and hold involves finding issues with desired quality, coupon levels, term to maturity, and important indenture provisions, such as a call feature. Buy-and-hold investors do not consider active trading to achieve attractive returns, but rather look for vehicles whose maturities (or duration) approximate their stipulated investment horizon in order to reduce price and reinvestment risk. Many successful bond investors and institutional portfolio managers follow a modified buy-and-hold strategy wherein they invest in an issue with the intention of holding it until the end of the investment horizon, but they still actively look for opportunities to trade into more desirable positions.[2]

Whether the investor follows a strict or modified buy-and-hold approach, the key ingredient is finding investment vehicles that possess attractive maturity and yield features. The strategy does not restrict the investor to accept whatever the market has to offer, nor does it imply that selectivity is unimportant. The investor actively seeks attractive high-yielding issues with desirable features and quality standards. As an example, these investors recognize that agency issues generally provide incremental returns relative to

---

[2]If the strategy became too modified, it would become one of the active strategies.

Treasuries with little sacrifice in quality, that utilities provide higher returns than comparably rated industrials, and that various call features affect the risk and realized yield of an issue. Thus, successful buy-and-hold investors use their knowledge of markets and issue characteristics to seek out attractive realized yields.

Indexing Strategy   As discussed in Chapter 8, Efficient Capital Markets, numerous empirical studies have demonstrated that the majority of money managers fail to match the risk–return performance of common stock or bond indexes. As a result, many clients opt to have some part of their bond portfolios indexed, which means that the portfolio manager builds a portfolio that will match the performance of a selected bond-market index such as the Lehman Brothers Index, Merrill Lynch Index, or Salomon Brothers Index. In such a case, the portfolio manager is not judged on the basis of risk and return compared to an index, but by how closely the portfolio tracks the index. Specifically, the analysis of performance involves examining the **tracking error**, which equals the difference between the rate of return for the portfolio and the rate of return for the index. For example, if the portfolio experienced an annual rate of return of 8.2 percent during a period when the index had a rate of return of 8.3 percent, the tracking error would be ten basis points.

When the manager initiates an indexing strategy, selection of the appropriate market index is critical to meeting the need for consistency with the client's risk–return preferences and the investment policy statement. This requires the manager to be familiar with all the characteristics of the index.[3] The characteristics of indexes can change over time; for example, studies have shown that the market has experienced significant changes in composition, maturity, and duration during the period 1975 to 1991.[4]

Active Management Strategies[5]

Managers have available five active management strategies that range from interest-rate anticipation, which involves economic forecasting, to valuation analysis and credit analysis, which require detailed bond and company analysis. Finally, yield-spread analysis and bond swaps require economic and market analysis.

Interest Rate Anticipation   **Interest rate anticipation** is perhaps the riskiest active management strategy because it involves relying on uncertain forecasts of future interest rates. The idea is to preserve capital by reducing portfolio duration when interest rates are expected to increase and achieve attractive capital gains by increasing portfolio duration when a decline in yields is anticipated.

For example, consider two bonds, Short and Long. Bond Short has a modified duration of 2.5 years; Bond Long has a modified duration of 10 years. Suppose we anticipate a decline in interest rates. For every one percentage point decline in market rates, the price of Long will rise about 10 percent (modified duration of ten times the one percentage

[3]An article that briefly discusses the indexes is F. Hawthorne, "The Battle of the Bond Indexes," *Institutional Investor* (April 1986). An article that describes a couple of the indexes and discusses how their characteristics affect their performance in different interest rate environments is Chris P. Dialynas, "The Active Decisions in the Selection of Passive Management and Performance Bogeys," in *The Handbook of Fixed-Income Securities,* 3d ed., ed. Frank J. Fabozzi (Burr Ridge, Ill.: Business One–Irwin, 1991).

[4]An article that describes the major indexes, analyzes the relationship among them, and also examines how the aggregate bond market has changed is Frank K. Reilly, Wenchi Kao, and David J. Wright, "Alternative Bond Market Indexes," *Financial Analysts Journal* 48, no. 3 (May–June 1992): 44–58.

[5]For further discussion on this topic, see H. Gifford Fong, "Active Strategies for Managing Bond Portfolios," in *The Revolution in Techniques for Managing Bond Portfolios,* ed. Donald Tuttle (Charlottesville, Va.: The Institute of Chartered Financial Analysts, 1983), 21–38. Another interesting source is Dwight D. Churchill, ed., *Fixed-Income Management: Techniques and Practices,* Charlottesville, VA: Association for Investment Management and Research, 1994.

Figure 20.1   *Ladder and Barbell Strategies*

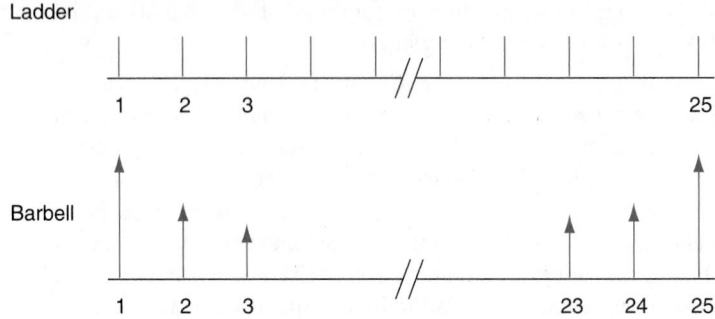

point change in market rates) while Short rises only about 2.5 percent. Thus, investors anticipating a decrease in rates will want to lengthen the durations of their portfolios by selling shorter-duration bonds and buying longer-duration bonds.

Should we anticipate a rise in interest rates, we would want to pursue the opposite strategy to protect the value of our holdings. For every one percentage point rise in interest rates, the value of Short falls only about 2.5 percent, but the value of Long falls about 10 percent.

When you expect a rate decline, portfolio liquidity is important because you must be able to close out the position quickly when the drop in rates is complete. Therefore, you would prefer high-grade securities such as Treasuries, agencies, or corporates rated AAA through Baa. Another reason for using these securities is that the higher the quality of an obligation, the more sensitive its value to interest rate changes. Your portfolios should include noncallable issues or those with strong call protection because of the substantial call risk discussed in Chapter 16 that arises should rates decline as predicted.

Obviously, shifting portfolio duration in anticipation of rate changes incurs risk. When durations are shortened in the face of an expected rate increase, one risk is that the rate forecast turns out to be incorrect and the portfolio will be poorly positioned to earn capital gains should rates fall. In addition, income returns are generally lower for shorter-term bonds, so a strategy to lower duration also leads to lower portfolio coupon income.

Similarly risky are portfolio shifts prompted by the anticipation of declining rates. By lengthening duration, the portfolio's value could sharply decline should rates rise rather than fall as anticipated. And, if rates are forecast to fall at a time when the yield curve is inverted, you will sacrifice current income by shifting from high-coupon short bonds to longer-duration bonds.

To avoid the risks of having an all-short or all-long duration portfolio built to take advantage of a specific rate forecast, some managers prefer to take a more neutral stance toward anticipating interest rates changes. They do this by spreading the maturities of their holdings across many years. These "ladder" and "barbell" strategies are illustrated in Figure 20.1.

The **ladder strategy** places an equal amount of the portfolio's holdings in a wide range of maturities. Maturing bonds are reinvested in the longest-term bonds. To reduce reinvestment risk, coupon income is reinvested across the maturity spectrum. With this strategy, the increases and declines in interest rates are averaged out over the business cycle, leading to less risky returns when compared to the all-short or all-long strategy.

In the **barbell strategy**, about one-half of the funds are invested in short duration securities and the remainder are invested in long duration securities. This combines the

high return, high income potential of long-term bonds with the lower risk, high liquidity aspects of shorter-term securities. This strategy is especially appropriate for times when short-term rates are expected to rise and long-term rates are expected to be stable or decline (that is, when the term structure of interest rates is expected to flatten).

Valuation Analysis   With **valuation analysis**, the portfolio manager attempts to select bonds based on their intrinsic value. In turn, a bond's value is based on its coupon cash flows, market interest rates, and its characteristics such as callability, the existence of a sinking fund, and credit rating. The average value placed on these characteristics in the marketplace can be estimated by examining bond market data or by running multiple regression models. As an example, a bond's rating will dictate a certain spread, or yield differential, relative to comparable Treasury bonds; long maturity might be worth additional basis points relative to short maturity (that is, the maturity spread); a given deferred call feature might require a lower yield compared to a callable bond. Given all the characteristics of the bond and their average impact on a bond's yield, you can determine the required yield, and therefore, the bond's implicit intrinsic value. After you have done this for a number of bonds, you would compare these derived bond values to the prevailing market prices to determine which bonds are undervalued or overvalued; next, you would buy the undervalued issues and ignore or sell the overvalued issues. Success in valuation analysis arises from understanding the characteristics that are important in valuation and being able to accurately estimate the value of these characteristics over time.

A difficulty in implementing valuation analysis is that the price the market is willing to pay for certain characteristics varies across time. For example, bonds with strong put provisions offered yields twenty to forty basis points below that of comparable bonds in 1989 (due to bondholder fears subsequent to the large RJR–Nabisco leveraged buyout); but a year later such issues were not priced significantly different from nonputable issues.[6]

Credit Analysis   A **credit analysis** strategy involves detailed analysis of the bond issuer to determine expected changes in its default risk. As such, it is similar in scope and detail to equity analysis. Credit analysis involves attempts to project changes in the quality ratings assigned to bonds by the four rating agencies discussed in Chapter 15. These rating changes are affected by internal changes in the entity (for example, changes in important financial ratios) and also by changes in the external environment (changes in the firm's industry and the economy). During periods of strong economic expansion, even financially weak firms may be able to survive and perhaps prosper. In contrast, during severe economic contractions, normally strong firms may find it difficult or impossible to meet financial obligations. Therefore, historically rating changes have shown a strong cyclical pattern—typically, downgradings increase during economic contractions and decline during economic expansions.

To employ credit analysis as a management strategy, you must project rating changes prior to the announcement by the rating agencies. Studies have found that the bond market adjusts rather quickly to bond rating changes—especially downgradings. Therefore, you should acquire bond issues *expected* to experience upgradings and sell or avoid those *expected* to be downgraded.

Table 20.1 lists the results for one study that considers the full spectrum of bonds. It shows substantial differences in cumulative default rates for bonds with different ratings for the periods five, ten, and fifteen years after issue. Over ten years, the default rate for

[6]Evidence on this is seen in L. Crabbe, "Event Risk: An Analysis of Losses to Bondholders and 'Super Poison Put' Bond Covenants," *Journal of Finance* (June 1991): 689–706.

Table 20.1	*Average Cumulative Default Rates for Corporate Bonds: 1971–1994*		

		Years Since Issue	
Ratings	5	10	
AAA	0.08%	0.08%	
AA	1.20	1.3	
A	0.53	0.98	
BBB	2.39	3.66	
BB	10.79	15.21	
B	23.71	35.91	
CCC	45.63	57.39	

Source: K. Scott Douglass and Douglas J. Lucas, "Historical Default Rates of Corporate Bond Issuers, 1971–1994" (New York: Moody's Investors Services, July 1995). Copyright by Moody's Investors Service, Inc. Reprinted by permission.

BBB investment-grade bonds is only 3.7 percent, but the default rate increases to more than 15 percent for BB and to 35.9 percent for B-rated bonds. CCC-rated issues would have even higher default rates.

These default rates do not mean that investors should avoid high-yield bonds (sometimes called junk bonds), but they do indicate that extensive credit analysis is a critical component for success within this sector. If you can avoid defaults and downgrades, you can earn substantial rates of return from high-yield bonds due to their substantial average yield spreads over Treasuries. The route to avoiding such bond issues is through rigorous, enlightened credit analysis.

The credit analysis of these bonds can employ a statistical model or a basic fundamental analysis that recognizes some of the unique characteristics of these bonds. Altman's Z-score model, first used to predict firm bankruptcies, has been adapted for predicting bond rating changes.[7] The Z-score model combines traditional financial measures with a multivariate technique known as multiple discriminant analysis to derive a set of weights for the specified variables. The result is an overall credit score (zeta score) for each firm. The original Altman Z-score model is[8]

$$\text{zeta} = 0.012\,X1 + 0.014\,X2 + 0.033\,X3 + 0.006\,X4 + 0.999\,X5$$

where:

zeta = overall credit score
X1 = net working capital/total assets (expressed in percentage terms)
X2 = retained earnings/total assets (expressed as a percentage)
X3 = EBIT/total assets (expressed as a percentage)
X4 = market value of common and preferred equity/book value of total liabilities
**   (expressed as a percentage)**
X5 = sales/total assets

In his original model, Altman's critical zeta value was 2.67. It was hypothesized that firms with scores less than this were likely to go bankrupt.

---

[7]Edward I. Altman and Scott A. Nammacher, *Investing in Junk Bonds* (New York: Wiley, 1987).

[8]Edward I. Altman, "Financial Ratios, Discriminant Analysis, and the Prediction of Corporate Bankruptcy," *Journal of Finance* 23, no. 4 (September 1968): 589–609.

In contrast to using a model that provides a composite credit score, most analysts and investment houses simply adapt their basic corporate bond analysis techniques to the unique needs of high-yield bonds, which are considered low-quality credits that have characteristics of common stock. It is suggested that analysis of high-yield bonds should include in-depth analysis in five areas:[9]

♦ The firm's competitive position in terms of cost and pricing
♦ The firm's borrowing capacity and cash flow relative to cash requirements for interest payments, research, and growth, during periods of economic decline
♦ The liquidity value of the firm's assets and whether these assets are available for liquidation (that is, are there any claims against them?)
♦ The competence of the total management team, including general administration, finance, marketing, and production. Are they committed and capable of operating in the firm's high-risk environment?
♦ The firm's financial leverage on an absolute basis and also on a market-adjusted basis (using market value for equity and debt)

In summary, the substantial increase in high-yield bonds issued and outstanding has been matched by an increase in research and credit analysis. An in-depth analysis of these bonds is critical because of the number of such issues, the wide diversity of quality within the junk bond universe ("quality" junk versus "junk" junk), and the growing complexity of these issues.

Yield-Spread Analysis   As discussed in Chapter 16, spread analysis assumes normal relationships between the yields for bonds in alternative sectors (for example, the spread between high-grade versus low-grade industrial or between industrial versus utility bonds). Therefore, a bond portfolio manager would monitor these relationships and, when an abnormal relationship occurs, would execute various sector swaps. The crucial factor is developing the background to know the normal yield relationship and evaluate the liquidity necessary to buy or sell the required issues quickly enough to take advantage of the supposedly temporary abnormality. Yield spread analysis differs from valuation analysis in that valuation analysis examines many issue-specific influences on yield; yield spread analysis focuses only on the difference in yield between sectors.

Changes in yield spreads are related to the economic environment. Specifically, the spreads widen during periods of economic uncertainty and recession because investors require larger risk premiums (that is, larger spreads) on riskier issues. In contrast, spreads decline during periods of economic confidence and expansion.

Bond Swaps   **Bond swaps** involve selling a bond (frequently called the *S bond,* as it may be sold) and simultaneously buying a different issue (called the *P bond,* as it may be purchased) with similar attributes but a chance for improved return.[10] Swaps can be executed to increase current yield, to increase yield to maturity, to take advantage of shifts in interest rates or the realignment of yield spreads, to improve the quality of a portfolio, or for tax purposes. Some are highly sophisticated and require a computer for the necessary calculations. Most, however, are fairly simple transactions, with obvious goals and risk. They go by such names as profit takeouts, substitution swaps, intermarket spread swaps, or tax swaps. Although many of these swaps involve low risk (such as the pure yield

---

[9]Jane Tripp Howe, "Credit Considerations in Evaluating High-Yield Bonds," in *The Handbook of Fixed-Income Securities,* 3d ed., ed. Frank J. Fabozzi (Burr Ridge, Ill.: Business One–Irwin, 1991); Jane Tripp Howe, *Junk Bonds: Analysis and Portfolio Strategies* (Chicago: Probus Publishing, 1988).

[10]The bond swaps we are discussing here should not be confused with interest-rate swaps. Interest-rate swaps involve an agreement in which two parties agree to exchange interest cash flows, typically one based on a fixed-interest rate and the other based on a variable or floating rate.

pickup swap), others entail substantial risk (the rate-anticipation swap). Regardless of the risk involved, all swaps have one basic purpose: portfolio improvement.

Inputs to the swap analysis include current interest rates and prices on the S and P bonds as well as predictions for future interest rates. These predictions may be based on a belief that the market level of rates will rise or fall, that the yield curve may become steeper or flatten, or that sector spreads will increase or decrease. The input to the analysis also includes a time horizon, called the work-out time, over which the forecasted interest rate change will occur. Typical work-out times are six months or one year. Swap analysis examines the three components of bond return (coupon income, interest earned on reinvested bond income, and the change in the bond's price) over the work-out time to determine whether the S or P bond offers better returns given the interest rate forecast. Of course, commissions and taxes paid from selling one bond and buying another should also figure in the analysis by using prices net of commissions.

The analysis must also examine the several different types of risk to which swaps are exposed. One obvious risk is that the market will move against you while the swap is outstanding. In other words, interest rates may behave differently than forecasted by moving up when they were expected to fall, or yield spreads may fail to respond as anticipated.

Another risk is that the P bond may not be a true substitute for the S bond; for example, the S bond may receive a credit rating upgrade while the P bond's rating remains unchanged. In this case, even if the expectations and interest rate formulations are correct, the swap may be unsatisfactory because the wrong issue was selected.

Finally, a problem can occur if the work-out time is longer than anticipated, in which case the realized return from selling the S bond and buying the P bond might be less than expected. Such risks can be evaluated by using a variety of interest rate assumptions and work-out times to compare the sensitivity of the swap's incremental return to its risk.

The following subsections consider three of the more popular bond swaps.[11]

Pure yield pickup swap   The pure yield pickup involves swapping out of a low-coupon bond into a comparable higher-coupon bond to realize an automatic and instantaneous increase in current yield and yield to maturity. One risk inherent in this type of swap is that the market may be pricing the issues differently because of an anticipated credit rating change for one of the issues. Another risk is the higher probability that the higher-coupon bond will be called in the event of a future interest rate decline.

An example of a pure yield pickup swap would be an investor who currently holds a thirty-year, Aa-rated, 10 percent issue that is trading at an 11.50 percent yield. Assume a comparable thirty-year, Aa-rated obligation bearing a 12 percent coupon priced to yield 12 percent becomes available. The investor would report (and realize) some book loss if the original issue was bought at par but is able to improve current yield and yield to maturity simultaneously if the new obligation is held to maturity as shown in Table 20.2.

The investor need not predict rate changes, and the swap is not based on any imbalance in yield spread. The object is simply to seek higher yields. Quality and maturity stay the same, as do all other factors except coupon.

As an example of the risk of this swap, consider the situation in which the 12 percent yield on the candidate bond is correct because the market anticipates the Aa candidate bond will be downgraded to an A rating. Suppose this occurs, and by the end of the one-year time frame the candidate bond has an A rating and is selling to yield 12.5 percent. In this case, the return calculations for the candidate bond are as follows:

---

[11]For additional information on these and other types of bond swaps, see Sidney Homer and Martin L. Leibowitz, *Inside the Yield Book* (Englewood Cliffs, N.J.: Prentice-Hall, 1972).

Table 20.2 *A Pure Yield Pickup Swap*

Pure yield pickup swap: A bond swap that involves a switch from a low-coupon bond to a higher-coupon bond of similar quality and maturity in order to pick up higher current yield and a better yield to maturity.

Example:

Currently hold: thirty-year. Aa, 10.0 percent coupon priced at 874.12 to yield 11.5 percent.

Swap candidate: thirty-year, Aa 12 percent coupon priced at $1,000 to yield 12.0 percent.

The analysis for a one-year time frame appears below. For simplicity, we assume the next semiannual coupon payment occurs in six months.

	S Bond	P Bond
Dollar investment	$874.12	$1,000.00
Coupon income	100.00	120.00
Interest from reinvesting one coupon	3.00	3.60
Principal value at year-end	874.66	1,000.00
Total accrued value at year-end	977.66	1,123.60
Realized compound yield	11.85%	12.36%

Value of swap: 51.0 basis points in one year (using above interest rate assumptions).

The rewards for a pure yield pickup swap are automatic and instantaneous in that both a higher-coupon yield and a higher yield to maturity are realized from the swap. Other advantages include the following:

1. No specific work-out period needed because the investor is assumed to hold the new bond to maturity
2. No need for interest rate speculation
3. No need to analyze prices for overvaluation or undervaluation

A major disadvantage of the pure yield pickup swap is the book loss involved in the swap. In this example, if the current bond was originally bought at par, the book loss would be ($1,000 − 874.12) = $125.88. Other risks involved in the pure yield pickup swap include the following:

1. Increased risk of call in the event interest rates decline
2. Reinvestment risk is greater with higher-coupon bonds
3. The two bonds have different yields because the market anticipates a credit rating change for one of them

Swap evaluation procedure is patterned after a technique suggested by Sidney Homer and Martin L. Leibowitz.

Source: Adapted from Sidney Homer and Martin L. Leibowitz, *Inside the Yield Book* (Englewood Cliffs, N.J.: Prentice-Hall, and New York Institute of Finance, New York, 1972).

	P Bond
Dollar investment	$1,000.00
Coupon income	120.00
Interest from reinvesting one coupon	3.60
Principal value at year-end (selling at a 12.5% yield)	961.15
Total accrued value at year-end	$1,084.65
Realized compound yield	8.47%

The 8.47 percent realized compound yield is far below that expected on the S bond shown in Table 20.2. Some credit analysis should be undertaken before swaps are completed to ensure the quality of the bonds is similar.

Substitution swap The substitution swap is done to exploit an apparent short-term mispricing between two bond issues that are identical with respect to coupon rate, credit

Table 20.3   A Substitution Swap

Substitution swap: A swap executed to take advantage of temporary market anomalies in yield spreads between issues that are equivalent with respect to coupon, quality, and maturity.

Example:

Currently hold: thirty-year, Aa 12 percent coupon priced at $1,000 to yield 12 percent.

Swap candidate: thirty-year, Aa 12 percent coupon priced at $984.08 to yield 12.2 percent, which we believe will fall to equal the 12 percent yield of the currently held bond.

Assumed work-out period: one year; Reinvested at 12 percent.

	S Bond	P Bond
Dollar investment	$1,000.00	$984.08
Coupon income	120.00	120.00
Interest from reinvesting one coupon	3.60	3.60
Principal value at year-end	1,000.00	1,000.00
Total accrued value at year-end	1,123.60	1,123.60
Realized compound yield (one year work-out period)	12.36%	14.18%

Value of swap: 182 basis points in one year.

Swap evaluation procedure is patterned after a technique suggested by Sidney Homer and Martin L. Leibowitz.

Source: Adapted from Sidney Homer and Martin L. Leibowitz, *Inside the Yield Book* (Englewood Cliffs, N.J.: Prentice-Hall, and New York Institute of Finance, New York, 1972).

rating, and time to maturity. It is subject to considerably more risk than the pure yield pickup swap, as the apparent mispricing may persist because of quality differences which the market perceived before the bond-rating agencies.

For example, an investor might hold a thirty-year, 12 percent issue that is yielding 12 percent (the S bond) and be offered a comparable thirty-year, 12 percent bond that is yielding 12.20 percent (the P bond). Because it has a higher yield but the same coupon and maturity, the P bond will sell for a lower price than the current value of the S bond.

Ideally, the yield spread imbalance would be corrected over a short period of time as the yield on the P bond declines to 12 percent and the P bond rises in value. But the yield difference may persist if, despite their credit ratings, the quality of the bonds is not really identical. The work-out time will have an important effect on the differential realized return. Even if the yield is not corrected until maturity, thirty years hence, you will still experience a small increase in realized yield (about ten basis points). In contrast, if the correction takes place within one year, the differential realized return is much greater, as shown in Table 20.3.

Another possibility is that the value of the P bond may remain constant while the 12 percent yield on the S bond *rises* to 12.2 percent. In this case, a loss in the value of the S bond is avoided if the swap is completed. Table 20.3 shows a basic analysis, but a more complete analysis would consider different scenarios to gauge the risk and return potential of the transaction.

Tax swap   The tax swap is popular with individual investors because it is a relatively simple procedure that involves no interest-rate projections and few risks. Investors' reasons for entering into tax swaps often include tax law provisions and realized capital gains in their portfolios. Assume you acquired $100,000 worth of corporate bonds and after two years sold the securities for $150,000, implying a capital gain of $50,000. One way to eliminate the tax liability of that capital gain is to sell an issue that has a comparable long-term

Table 20.4   *A Tax Swap*

Tax swap: A swap you undertake when you wish to offset capital gains through the sale of a bond currently held and selling at a discount from the price paid at purchase. By swapping into a bond with as nearly identical features as possible, you can use the capital loss on the sale of the bond for tax purposes and still maintain your current position in the market.

Example: You currently hold two sets of bonds. One set is corporate bonds purchased for $100,000; their current market value is $150,000. The second set is municipal bonds (New York, twenty-year, 7 percent coupon) purchased for $100,000 with a current market value of $50,000. The swap candidate is $50,000 in New York twenty-year, 7.1 percent bonds.

A. Corporate bonds sold and long-term capital gains profit established	$50,000
Capital gains tax liability, assuming a 20% capital gains tax rate	($50,000 × .20) = $10,000
B. N.Y. 7s sold and long-term capital *loss* established	($50,000)
Reduction in capital gains tax liability	(loss of $50,000 × .20 = $10,000)
Net capital gains tax liability	$0
Tax savings realized	$10,000
C. Complete tax swap by buying New York 7.1s from proceeds of New York 7s sale	
(therefore, amount invested remains largely the same)[a]	
Annual tax-free interest income—New York 7s	$7,000
Annual tax-free interest income—New York 7.1s	$7,100
Net increase in annual tax-free interest income	$100

[a]New York 7.1s will show a substantial price rise when liquidated at maturity (because they were bought at deep discounts) and, therefore, will be subject to future tax liability. The swap is designed to use the capital loss resulting from the swap to offset capital gains from other investments. At the same time, your funds remain in a security almost identical to your previous holding while you receive a slight increase in both current income and YTM. Because the tax swap involves no projections in terms of work-out period, interest rate changes, and so on, it has minimal risk. Your major concern should be to avoid potential wash sales.

capital loss.[12] If you had a long-term investment of $100,000 with a current market value of $50,000, you could execute a tax swap to establish the $50,000 capital loss. By offsetting this capital loss and the comparable capital gain, you would reduce your income taxes.

Municipal bonds are considered particularly attractive tax swap candidates, because you can increase your tax-free income and use the capital loss (which is subject to normal federal and state taxation) to reduce capital gains tax liability. To continue our illustration, assume that, in addition to the above-mentioned corporate bonds, you also own $100,000 worth of New York City, twenty-year, 7 percent bonds that you bought at par, but they have a current market value of $50,000. Given this tax loss, you need a comparable bond swap candidate. Suppose you find a twenty-year New York City bond with a 7.1 percent coupon and a market value of 50. By selling your New York 7s and instantaneously reinvesting in the New York 7.1s, you would eliminate the capital gains tax from the corporate bond transaction. In effect, you have $50,000 of tax-free capital gains, and you have increased your current tax-free yield. You can use the money saved by avoiding the tax liability to increase the portfolio's yield, as shown in Table 20.4.

An important caveat is that *you cannot swap identical issues,* such as selling the New York 7s to establish a loss and then buying back the same New York 7s. If the same issue is purchased within thirty days, the IRS considers the transaction a **wash sale** and does not allow the loss. It is easier to avoid wash sales in the bond market than it is in the stock market, because every bond issue, even with identical coupons and maturities, is considered distinct. Likewise, it is easier to find comparable bond issues with only modest differences in coupon, maturity, and quality. Tax swaps are common at year-end as investors establish capital losses, because the capital loss must occur in the same taxable

---

[12]Although this discussion deals with tax swaps that involve bonds, comparable strategies apply to other types of investments.

year as the capital gain. This procedure differs from other swap transactions in that it exists because of tax statutes rather than temporary market anomalies.

Strategies and market efficiency   What does market efficiency imply regarding specific bond-market strategies, such as bond swaps and trading on the basis of yield spreads? By their very nature, bond swaps suggest some market inefficiency by implying temporary anomalies within or between market segments that afford alert investors the opportunity for above-average returns. The existence of numerous profitable swap opportunities would suggest that underlying price irregularities are neither rare nor random events. Such opportunities may be caused by the institutional nature of the market, which could lead to market segmentation. In effect, this would imply that artificial constraints, regulations, and statutes are mostly responsible for opportunities to execute profitable bond swaps. Lack of data for individual firms makes it difficult to conduct an empirical study, and so we have no rigorous empirical evidence on the success of these strategies.

Bond portfolio styles   Just as managers employ various investment styles in the equity markets (as we saw in Chapter 19), managers have various investing styles in the fixed-income markets. Although valuation analysis, taking advantage of yield spreads, and bond swaps can add incremental return to a bond portfolio, the two main determinants of a portfolio's return are duration and overall credit quality. The term structure of interest rates illustrates the effect of time to maturity and duration on overall yield to maturity; generally, longer duration securities offer higher yields to maturity. Credit quality reflects a default risk premium on a bond; higher quality bonds have lower default risk premiums and therefore have lower yields than lower quality issues.

Comparing a bond manager's performance or selecting a bond manager requires sharing information regarding the portfolio style characteristics of duration and credit quality characteristics. It makes little sense to judge a small-capitalization stock portfolio on the basis of the S&P 500. Neither is it appropriate to compare the performance of a manager investing in low-quality securities to a high-quality corporate bond index, nor the performance of a manager who focuses on the short-end of the term structure with a long-duration benchmark.

A Global Fixed-Income Investment Strategy   An active management strategy that considers one or several of the techniques we have discussed should apply these techniques to a global portfolio. The optimum global fixed-income asset allocation must consider three interrelated factors: (1) the local economy in each country, including the effect of domestic and international demand; (2) the impact of total demand and domestic monetary policy on inflation and interest rates; and (3) the effect of the economy, inflation, and interest rates on the exchange rates among countries. Based on evaluating these factors using the tools discussed in Chapter 11, a portfolio manager must decide the relative weight for each country (that is, the proportion of the bond portfolio invested in a country). In addition, one might consider an allocation within each country among government, municipal, and corporate bonds.

Matched-Funding Techniques[13]

As discussed previously, an increase in interest rate volatility and the needs of many institutional investors has led to growth in the use of matched-funding techniques ranging from pure cash-matched dedicated portfolios to portfolios that employ immunization.

[13]An overview of these alternative strategies is contained in Martin L. Leibowitz, "The Dedicated Bond Portfolio in Pension Funds—Part I: Motivation and Basics," *Financial Analysts Journal* 42, no. 1 (January–February 1986): 68–75; and Martin L. Leibowitz, "The Dedicated Bond Portfolio in Pension Funds—Part II: Immunization, Horizon Matching, and Contingent Procedures," *Financial Analysts Journal* 42, no. 2 (March–April 1986): 47–57.

Immunization Strategies   Immunization attempts to earn a specified rate of return (generally quite close to the current market rate) over a given investment horizon regardless of what happens to market interest rates. Whether market rates rise or fall, the value of the portfolio at the end of the time horizon (that is, the ending wealth value) should be close to its target value in an immunized portfolio. Portfolio immunization attempts to balance the two components of interest rate risk: price risk and reinvestment risk.

Components of interest-rate risk   If the term structure of interest rates were flat and market rates never changed between the time of purchase and the horizon date when funds were required, you could acquire a bond with a term to maturity equal to the desired **investment horizon**, and the ending wealth from the bond would equal the promised wealth position implied by the promised yield to maturity. As an example, assume you acquired at par a ten-year, $1 million bond with an 8 percent coupon. If conditions were as specified (a flat yield curve and no changes in the curve), your wealth position at the end of your ten-year investment horizon (assuming semiannual compounding) would be: $1,000,000 $\times (1.04)^{20} = \$1,000,000 \times 2.1911 = \$2,191,100$. This is the same as taking the $40,000 interest payment you receive every six months and compounding them to the end of the period at an 4 percent nominal rate every six months and adding the $1,000,000 principal at maturity.

Unfortunately, in the real world, the term structure of interest rates is not typically flat and the level of interest rates is constantly changing. Consequently, the bond portfolio manager faces **interest rate risk** between the time of investment and the future target date. Interest rate risk is the uncertainty regarding the ending-wealth value of the portfolio due to changes in market interest rates between the time of purchase and the target date. It involves two component risks in turn: price risk and coupon-reinvestment risk.

Price risk occurs because varying interest rates may cause the market price for the bond to change over time. If rates were to increase after the time of purchase, the market price for the bond would fall, whereas if rates declined, the realized price would rise. The point is, because you do not know whether rates will increase or decrease, you are uncertain about the bond's future price.

The **reinvestment risk** arises because the yield-to-maturity computation implicitly assumes all coupon cash flows will be reinvested at the promised yield to maturity. If, after the purchase of the bond, interest rates decline, the coupon cash flows will be reinvested at rates below the promised YTM, and the ending wealth will be below expectations. In contrast, if interest rates increase, the coupon cash flows will be reinvested at rates above expectations, and the ending wealth will be above expectations. Again, because you are uncertain about future rates, you are uncertain about these reinvestment rates.

Classical immunization and interest rate risk   The price risk and the reinvestment risk caused by a change in interest rates have opposite effects on the ending-wealth position. An increase in interest rates will cause an ending price below expectations (if the bond is sold before maturity), but the reinvestment rate for interim cash flows will be above expectations. A decline in market interest rates will cause the reverse situation. Clearly, a bond portfolio manager with a specific target date (investment horizon) will attempt to balance these two effects. The process intended to eliminate interest rate risk is referred to as immunization.

Assuming a flat yield curve and parallel shifts in the yield curve as interest rates change, *a portfolio of bonds is immunized from interest rate risk if the modified duration of the portfolio is always equal to the desired investment horizon.* As an example, if the investment horizon of a bond portfolio is eight years, in order to immunize the portfolio, the *modified duration* of the bond portfolio should equal eight years. To attain a given modified duration, the weighted-average modified duration (with weights equal to the proportion of value) is set at the desired length and all subsequent cash flows are invested

Table 20.5   *An Example of the Effect of a Change in Market Rates on a Bond (Portfolio)*
That Uses the Maturity Strategy versus the Duration Strategy

	Results with Maturity Strategy			Results with Duration Strategy		
Year	Cash Flow	Reinvestment Rate	End Value	Cash Flow	Reinvestment Rate	End Value
1	80	.08	$ 80.00	80	.08	$ 80.00
2	80	.08	166.40	80	.08	166.40
3	80	.08	259.71	80	.08	259.71
4	80	.08	360.49	80	.08	360.49
5	80	.06	462.12	80	.06	462.12
6	80	.06	596.85	80	.06	596.85
7	80	.06	684.04	80	.06	684.04
8	$1,080	.06	$1,805.08	$1,120.64[a]	.06	$1,845.72

Expected Wealth Ratio = 1.8509 or $1,850.90.

[a]The bond could be sold at its market value of $1,040.64, which is the value for an 8 percent bond with two years to maturity priced to yield 6 percent.

in securities to keep the portfolio modified duration equal to the remaining investment horizon.[14]

Example of classical immunization   Table 20.5 shows the effect of attempting to immunize a portfolio by matching the investment horizon and the duration of a bond portfolio using a single bond. The portfolio manager's investment horizon is eight years, and the current yield to maturity for eight-year bonds is 8 percent. Therefore, if we assumed no change in yields, the ending-wealth ratio for an investor should be $(1.08)^8$ or 1.8509 with annual compounding.[15] As noted, this should also be the ending-wealth ratio for a completely immunized portfolio.

The example considers two portfolio strategies: (1) the **maturity strategy**, where the portfolio manager would acquire a bond with a term to maturity of eight years, and (2) the **duration strategy**, where the portfolio manager sets the duration of the portfolio at eight years. For the maturity strategy, the portfolio manager acquires an eight-year, 8 percent bond; for the duration strategy, the manager acquires a ten-year, 8 percent bond that has approximately an eight-year duration (8.12 years), assuming an 8 percent YTM. We assume a single shock to the interest rate structure at the end of year four, when rates go from 8 percent to 6 percent and stay there through year eight.

Although the maturity strategy eliminates price risk (because the bond matures at the end of year eight), the wealth ratio for the maturity strategy bond is below the desired wealth ratio because of the shortfall in the reinvestment cash flow after year four.

The duration strategy portfolio performed much better in terms of attaining the desired ending wealth ratio. Although it suffered a shortfall in reinvestment cash flow because of the change in market rates, this shortfall was partially offset by an increase in the ending value for the bond because of the decline in market rates. Under the dura-

---

[14]Some researchers have pointed out several specifications of the duration measure. The Macaulay duration measure, which is used throughout this book, discounts all flows by the prevailing yield to maturity on the bond being measured. Alternatively, some have defined duration using future one-period interest rates (forward rates) to discount the future flows. Depending on the shape of the yield curve, the two definitions could give different answers. If the yield curve is flat, the two definitions will compute equal durations. It has been discovered that, except at high coupons and long maturities, the values of the alternative definitions are similar, and the Macaulay definition is preferable because it is a function of the yield to maturity of the bond. This means you do not need a forecast of one-period forward rates over the maturity of the bond.

[15]We use annual compounding to compute the ending-wealth ratio because the example uses annual observations.

tion strategy the original ten-year bond is sold at the end of year eight for $1,040.64, which is the price of an 8 percent coupon bond with two years to maturity selling to yield 6 percent. Because the price increase helped to offset the reinvestment shortfall, the duration strategy had an ending-wealth value ($1,845.72) much closer to the expected-wealth ratio ($1,850.90) than the maturity strategy had ($1,805.08).

Had market interest rates increased, the maturity strategy portfolio would have experienced an excess of reinvestment income compared to the expected cash flow, and the ending-wealth ratio for this strategy would have been above expectations. In contrast, in the duration portfolio, the excess cash flow from reinvestment under this assumption would have been partially offset by a decline in the ending price for the bond (that is, it would have sold at a small discount to par value). Although the ending-wealth ratio for the duration strategy would have been lower than the maturity strategy, it would have been closer to the expected-wealth ratio. The point is that the whole purpose of immunization is to *eliminate uncertainty* due to interest rate changes by having the realized-wealth position equal the expected-wealth position. As shown, this is what is accomplished with the duration-matched strategy.

Another view of immunization The previous example assumed both bonds were acquired and held to the end of the investment horizon. An alternative way to envision what is expected to happen with an immunized portfolio is to concentrate on the specific growth path from the beginning-wealth position to the ending-wealth position and examine what happens when interest rates change. Assume the initial-wealth position is $1 million, your investment horizon is ten years, and the coupon and current nominal YTM is 8 percent. We know from an earlier computation that this implies the expected ending-wealth value is $2,191,100 (with semiannual compounding). Figure 20.2A shows the compound growth rate path from $1 million to the expected ending value at $2,191,100. In Figure 20.2B, it is assumed that at the end of year two, interest rates increase by 2 percent (10 percent). We know that with no prior rate changes, at the end of year two the value of the portfolio would have grown at an 8 percent compound rate to $1,169,900 [$1.04^4 =$ 1.1699]. Given the rate change, we can foresee two changes for this portfolio: (1) the price (value of the portfolio) will decline to reflect the higher interest rate—the new value will be $1,003,743[16]; and (2) the reinvestment rate, which is the growth rate, will increase to 10 percent. If this new wealth value grows at 10 percent a year for eight years, the ending-wealth value will be

$$\$1,003,743 \times 2.1829 \ (5\% \text{ for } 16 \text{ periods}) = \$2,191,070$$

The difference between the expected value and projected value is due to rounding. This example shows that the price decline is almost exactly offset by the higher reinvestment rate—assuming that the modified duration of the portfolio at the time of the rate change was equal to the remaining horizon.

What happens if the portfolio is not properly matched? If the modified duration is greater than the remaining horizon, the price change will be greater. Thus, if interest rates increase, the value of the portfolio after the rate change will be less than $1,003,743. In this case, even if the new value of the portfolio grew at a nominal rate of 10 percent a year,

---

[16]An important question is, how much will the portfolio value decline? The answer depends on the modified duration of the portfolio when rates change. If the modified duration is equal to the remaining horizon, the price change will be such that at the new growth rate (10 percent), the new portfolio value will grow to the expected-wealth position. You can approximate the change in portfolio value using the modified duration and the change in market rates. Here, the approximate change in price is 16 percent based on a modified duration of 8 years and a 200 basis-point change. The actual change in price (between $1,169,900 and $1,003,743) is 14.2 percent.

Figure 20.2 *The Growth Path to the Expected Ending-Wealth Value and the Effect of Immunization*

A. Constant 8% Growth Rate

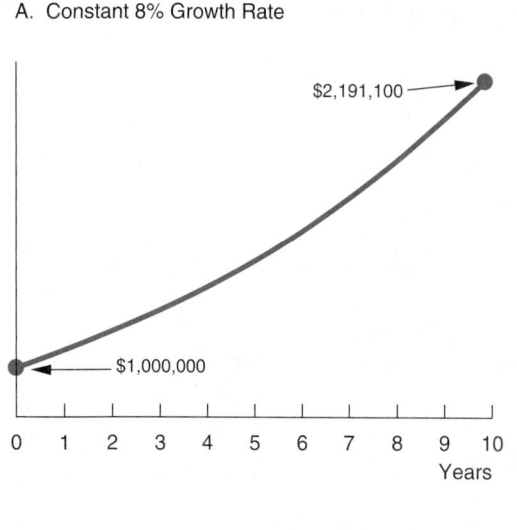

B. Effect of Interest Rate Increase after Two Years with Duration Equal to Investment Horizon

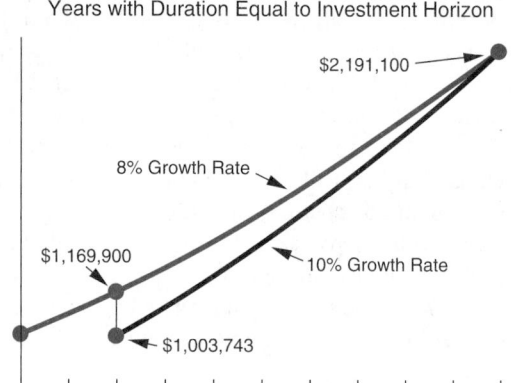

C. Effect of Interest Rate Increase with Duration Greater than Investment Horizon

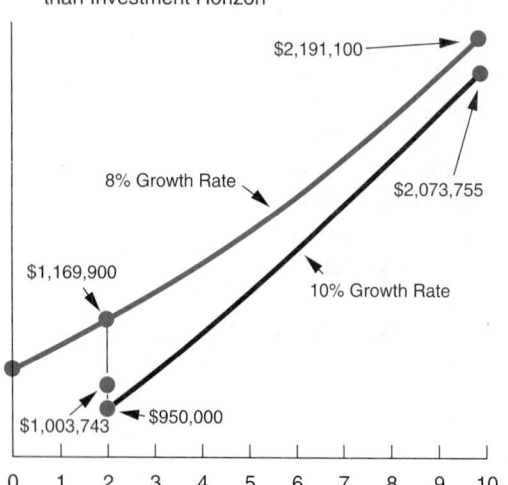

D. Effect of Interest Rate Decline with Duration Greater than Investment Horizon

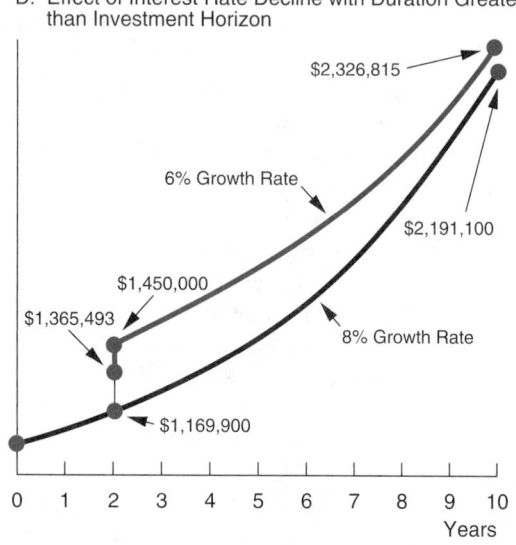

it would not reach the expected ending-wealth value. This scenario is shown in Figure 20.2C where it is assumed that the portfolio value declined to $950,000. If this new value grew at 10 percent a year for the remaining eight years, its ending value would be

$$950,000 \times 2.1829 \ (5\% \text{ for 16 periods}) = \$2,073,755$$

Therefore, the shortfall of $118,000 between the expected-wealth value and the realized-wealth value is because the portfolio was not properly duration matched (immunized) when interest rates changed.

Alternatively, if interest rates had declined, and the modified duration had been longer than eight years, the new portfolio value would have been greater than the

required value of $1,003,743. Figure 20.2D shows what can happen if the portfolio is not properly matched and interest rates decline by 200 basis points to 6 percent. First, if the portfolio is properly matched, the value will increase to $1,365,493. If this new portfolio value grows at 6 percent for eight years, its ending value will be:

$$\$1,365,493 \times 1.6047 \ (3\% \text{ for 16 periods}) = \$2,191,207$$

Again, this deviates slightly from the expected ending-wealth value ($2,191,100) due to rounding. If the modified duration had been above eight years, the new portfolio value would have been greater than the required value of $1,365,493. Assuming the portfolio value increased to $1,450,000, the ending value would be

$$\$1,450,000 \times 1.6047 \ (3\% \text{ for 16 periods}) = \$2,326,815$$

In this example, the ending-wealth value would have been greater than the expected-wealth value because you were mismatched and interest rates went in the right direction. The important point is that, when you are not duration matched, you are speculating on interest rate changes, and the result can be terrific or dismal. The purpose of immunization is to avoid these uncertainties and ensure the expected ending-wealth value ($2,191,100) irrespective of interest rate changes.

Application of classical immunization   Once you understand the reasoning behind immunization (that it is meant to offset the components of interest rate risk) and the general principle (that you need to match modified duration and the investment horizon), you might conclude that this strategy is fairly simple to apply. You might even consider it a passive strategy; simply match modified duration and the investment horizon, and you can ignore the portfolio until the end of the horizon period. The following discussion will show that immunization is neither a simple nor a passive strategy.

Except for the case of a zero-coupon bond, *an immunized portfolio requires frequent rebalancing;* bonds with various modified durations must be sold and bought in order to keep the portfolio's weighted average duration approximately equal to the remaining time horizon. The zero-coupon bond is unique because it is a pure discount bond. As such, it incurs *no reinvestment risk* because it has no intermediate cash flows. It incurs *no price risk* if you set the duration at your time horizon, because you will receive the face value of the bond at maturity. Also, recall that the duration of a zero-coupon bond is always equal to its term to maturity. In summary, if you immunize by matching your investment horizon with a zero-coupon bond of equal maturity and duration, you need not rebalance.

In contrast, if you immunize a portfolio using coupon bonds, several characteristics of duration make it impossible to set a modified duration equal to the remaining investment horizon at the initiation of the portfolio and ignore it thereafter. First, assuming no change in market interest rates, *duration declines more slowly than term to maturity.* As an example, assume you have a security with a computed modified duration of five years at a 10 percent market yield. A year later, at a 10 percent market rate, its modified duration will be approximately 4.2 years; that is, although the term to maturity has declined by a year, the modified duration has declined by only 0.8 years. This means that, assuming no change in market rates, the portfolio manager must rebalance the portfolio to reduce its modified duration to four years. Typically, this is not too difficult because cash flows from the portfolio can be invested in short-term T-bills to shorten the modified duration.

Second, *modified duration changes with a change in market interest rates.* In Chapter 16 we discussed the inverse relationship between market rates and duration—higher market rates lead to lower duration and vice versa. Therefore, a portfolio that has the appropriate modified duration at a point in time can have its modified duration changed

immediately if market rates change. If this occurs, a portfolio manager would have to rebalance the portfolio if the deviation from the required modified duration becomes too large.

Third, the assumption that when market rates change, they all will change by the same amount and in the same direction (a parallel shift of the yield curve) is frequently violated. Nonparallel shifts in the yield curve will work to move a portfolio away from immunization. As an example, assume you own a portfolio of long- and short-term bonds with a weighted-average six-year duration (say, one-half two-year duration bonds and one-half ten-year duration bonds). Suppose short-term rates decline and long-term rates rise (an increase in the slope of the yield curve). In such a case, you would experience a major price decline in the long-term bonds, but you would also be penalized on reinvestment, assuming you generally reinvest the cash flow in short-term securities. This potential problem suggests that you should bunch your portfolio selections close to the desired modified duration. For example, an eight-year duration portfolio should be made up of seven- to nine-year duration securities to avoid this term structure risk.

Finally, a problem can arise in acquiring the bonds you select as optimum for your portfolio. For instance, can you buy long-duration bonds at the price you consider acceptable? In summary, it is important to recognize that classical immunization is not a passive strategy because it is subject to all of these potential problems.[17]

Dedicated Portfolios   Dedication refers to bond portfolio management techniques used to service a prescribed set of liabilities. The idea is that a pension fund has a set of future liabilities, and those responsible for administering these liabilities want a money manager to construct a portfolio of assets with cash flows that will match this liability stream. Such a "dedicated" portfolio can be created in several ways. We will discuss two alternatives.

A **pure cash-matched dedicated portfolio** is the most conservative strategy. Specifically, the objective of pure cash-matching is to develop a portfolio of bonds that will provide a stream of payments from coupons, sinking funds, and maturing principal payments that will exactly match the specified liability schedules.

The goal is to build a portfolio that will generate sufficient funds in advance of each scheduled payment to ensure that the payment will be met. One alternative is to find zero-coupon Treasury securities that will exactly cash-match each liability. Such an exact cash-match is referred to as a *total passive portfolio,* because it is designed so that any prior receipts would not be reinvested (that is, it assumes a zero reinvestment rate).

Dedication with reinvestment is the same as the pure cash-matched technique except it is assumed that the bonds and other cash flows do not have to exactly match the liability stream. Specifically, any inflows that precede liability claims can be reinvested at some reasonably conservative rate. This assumption allows the portfolio manager to consider a substantially wider set of bonds that may have higher return characteristics. In addition, the assumption of reinvestment within each period and between periods will also generate a higher return for the asset portfolio. As a result, the net cost of the portfolio will be lower, with almost equal safety, assuming the reinvestment rate assumption is conservative. An example would be to assume a reinvestment rate of 3 percent in an environment where market interest rates are currently ranging from 4 to 6 percent.

Potential problems exist with both of these dedicated portfolio strategies. For example, when you select potential bonds for these dedicated portfolios, it is critical to be aware of call and prepayment possibilities (refundings, calls, sinking funds) with specific bonds or mortgage-backed securities.

---

[17]Several of these problems are discussed in William L. Nemerever, "Managing Bond Portfolios through Immunization Strategies," *The Revolution in Techniques for Managing Bond Portfolios* (Charlottesville, Va.: The Institute of Chartered Financial Analysts, 1983), 39–65.

Figure 20.3   *The Concept of Horizon Matching*

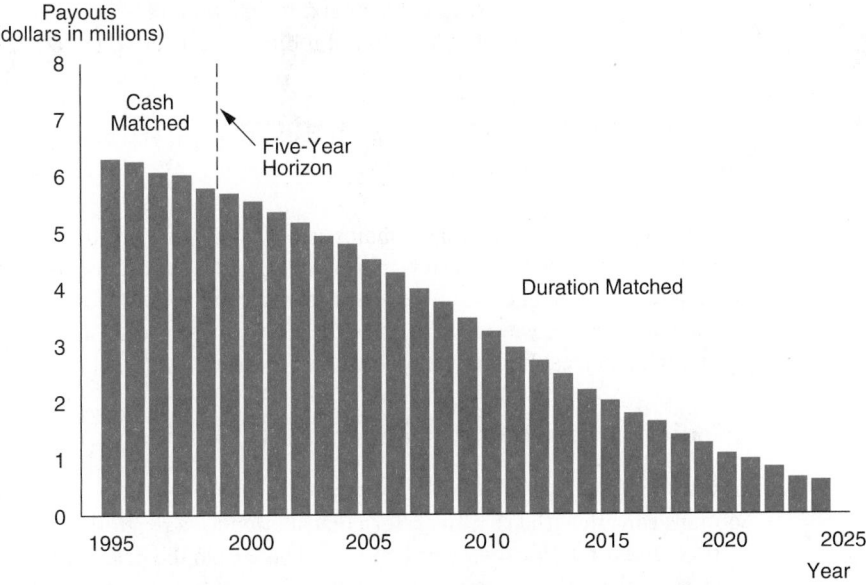

Source: Martin L. Leibowitz, Thomas E. Klaffky, Steven Mandel, and Alfred Weinberger, *Horizon Matching: A New Generalized Approach for Developing Minimum-Cost Dedicated Portfolios* (New York: Salomon Brothers, 1983). Copyright 1983 by Salomon Brothers Inc. Reprinted by permission of the authors and Salomon Brothers Inc.

Although quality is also a legitimate concern, it is probably not necessary to invest only in Treasury bonds if the portfolio manager diversifies across industries and sectors. A diversified portfolio of AA or A industrial bonds can provide a current and total annual return of forty to sixty basis points above Treasuries. This differential over a thirty-year period can significantly affect the net cost of funding a liability stream.

Horizon Matching   Horizon matching is a combination of two techniques discussed—cash-matching dedication and immunization. As shown in Figure 20.3, the liability stream is divided into two segments. In the first segment the portfolio is constructed to provide a cash match for the liabilities during this horizon period (say, the first five years). The second segment is the remaining liability stream following the end of the horizon period—in the example, it is the twenty-five years after the horizon period. During this second time period, the liabilities are covered by a duration-matched strategy based on immunization principles. As a result, the client receives the certainty of cash matching during the early years and the cost saving and flexibility of duration-matched flows thereafter.

The combination technique also helps alleviate one of the problems with classical immunization—the potential for nonparallel shifts in the yield curve. Most of the problems related to nonparallel shifts are concentrated in the short end of the yield curve because this is where the most severe curve reshaping occurs. Because the short end is taken care of by the cash matching, these are not of concern and we know that the long end of the yield curve tends toward parallel shifts.

An important decision when using horizon matching is the length of the horizon period. The trade-off when making this decision is between the safety and certainty of cash matching and the cost and flexibility of duration-based immunization. The portfolio manager should provide the client with a set of horizon alternatives, and the costs and benefits of each of them, and allow the client to make the decision.

It is also possible to consider rolling out the cash-matched segment over time. Specifically, after the first year the portfolio manager would restructure the portfolio to provide a cash match during the original year six, which would mean that you would still have a five-year horizon. The ability and cost of rolling out depends on movements in interest rates.

USING DERIVATIVE SECURITIES IN FIXED-INCOME PORTFOLIO MANAGEMENT

Derivative securities can play a major role in managing fixed-income portfolios. Their use can modify a portfolio's risk–return profile and change a portfolio's sensitivity to overall interest rate changes or to those of broad sectors. In addition, portfolio managers use them in a variety of ways to lower the cost of trading, to shift asset allocations, and to maintain a fund's investment exposure following a large cash inflow.

Modifying Portfolio Risk and Return: A Review

As we first saw in Chapter 17 in our introduction to derivative instruments, futures and options can affect the risk and return distribution for a portfolio. For the most part, a dollar-for-dollar relationship exists between changes in the price of the underlying security and the price of the corresponding futures contract. In effect, the act of purchasing futures is identical to that of subtracting cash from the portfolio, and selling futures is identical to adding cash to the portfolio. Buying futures increases exposure to the asset; selling futures decreases the portfolio's exposure. Suppose Figure 20.4A represents a portfolio's probability distribution for its returns. Buying futures on the portfolio's underlying asset increases the portfolio's exposure (or sensitivity) to price changes of the asset. As shown in Figure 20.4B, when you buy futures, the return distribution widens, showing a larger return variance. Selling futures on the portfolio's underlying asset has the effect of decreasing the portfolio's sensitivity to the underlying asset. Figure 20.4C shows the effect on the portfolio if futures are sold. In this case the variance of the returns for the portfolio declines, making for a "narrower" return distribution.

Figure 20.4 also illustrates that futures have a symmetrical impact on portfolio returns, because their impact on the portfolio's upside and downside return potential is the same. This occurs due to the close relationship between changes in the price of the futures contract and changes in the price of the underlying asset.

Futures represent an obligation to buy or sell the underlying asset unless canceled by an offsetting transaction. Options, however, give their owner the right to buy or sell the underlying asset. Because of the owner's choice to exercise or not to exercise the option, options do *not* have a symmetrical impact on returns. For example, as shown in Chapter 17, buying a call option limits losses; buying a put when you are long the underlying security has the effect of controlling downside risk. Writing a covered call, on the other hand, limits upside returns while not affecting loss potential (except that the premium is an offset to a loss); writing a put option has the same effect. Figure 20.5 shows the truncated return distributions that arise from various strategies that combine the use of options and their underlying asset.

Using Derivatives for Asset Allocation

In times of changing market conditions or in the face of large inflows or expected outflows of cash, shifting a portfolio's asset allocation must be done quickly to take advantage of the manager's forecast. The problem is, such changes are costly because securities must

Figure 20.4   *Demonstration of How Return Distributions Are Modified When Futures Contracts Are Purchased or Sold*

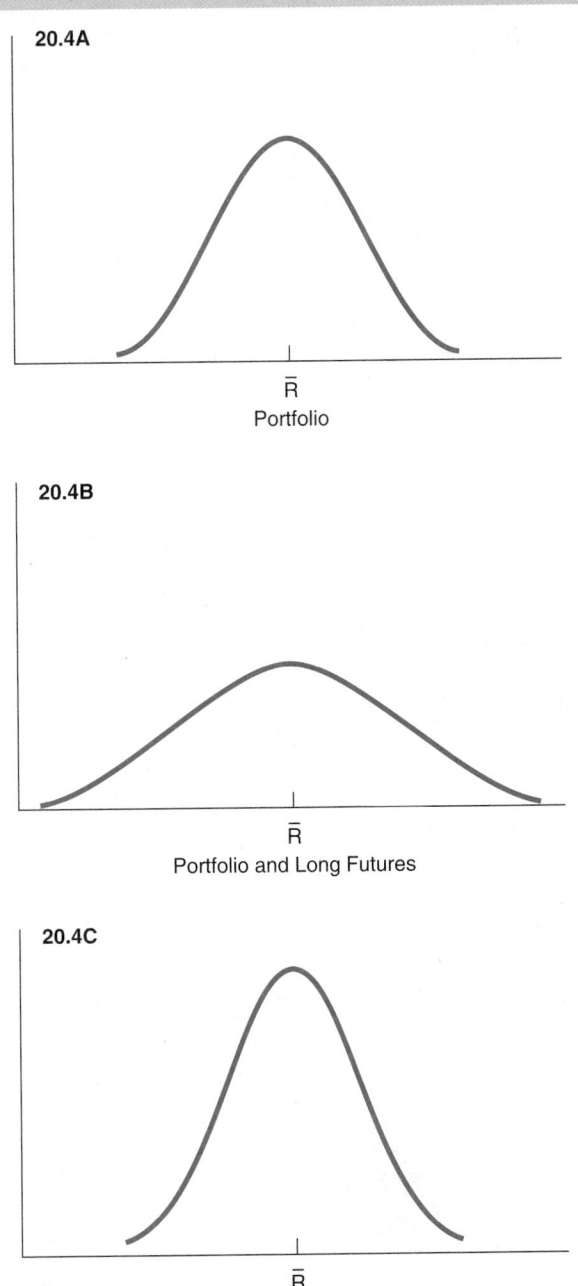

20.4A

$\bar{R}$
Portfolio

20.4B

$\bar{R}$
Portfolio and Long Futures

20.4C

$\bar{R}$
Portfolio and Short Futures

be sold and bought to facilitate the reallocation; attractive securities must be identified for purchase and specific securities in the portfolio must be tagged for sale. Commissions and the market impact of large trades can detract from the portfolio's return potential.

Rather than identifying specific securities for sale and purchase, and rather than issue large buy-and-sell orders, the portfolio manager can use futures. Buying and selling

Figure 20.5   *Examples of Truncated Return Distributions When Options Are Used to Modify Portfolio Risk*

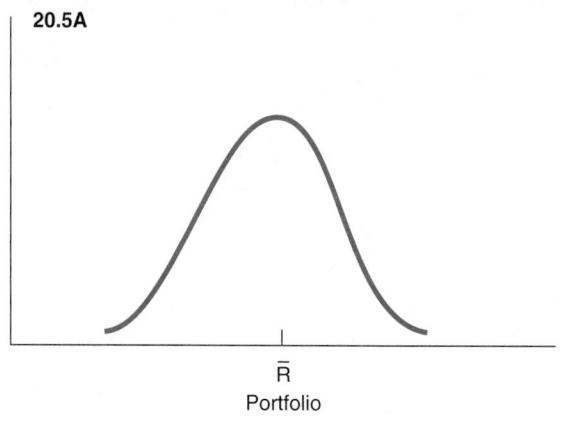

20.5A

$\bar{R}$
Portfolio

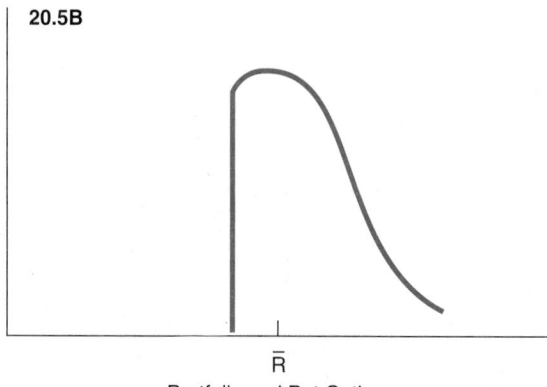

20.5B

$\bar{R}$
Portfolio and Put Option

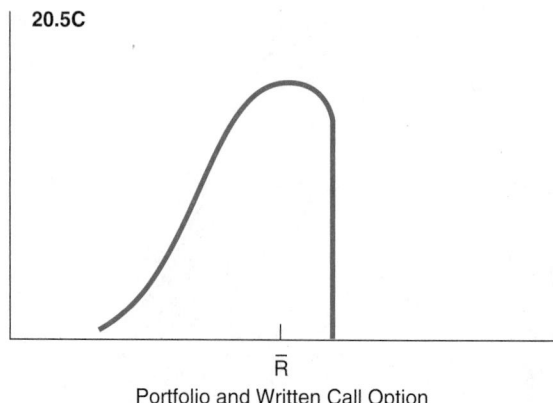

20.5C

$\bar{R}$
Portfolio and Written Call Option

appropriate futures contracts can quickly and easily change the portfolio's asset mix at lower transaction cost than trading large quantities of securities. Over time, the manager can identify specific assets to buy and sell, and times trading to avoid adverse market impacts.

Futures can also be used to achieve a desired mix of stocks and bonds in a multiple-manager environment. Many medium and large pension funds divide their portfolios among

different individual managers to exploit the specialized asset expertise of each. The overall pension-fund manager can use futures to maintain the desired asset allocation rather than disrupt the specialized managers by adding or removing large sums of cash from their funds for reallocation purposes.

Using Derivatives to Control Portfolio Cash Flows

Regardless of whether the fixed-income portfolio is passively or actively managed, futures and options can help control cash inflows and outflows from the portfolio. In reality, the most frequent use of options to modify portfolio risk is to use options whose underlying "security" is another derivative security—a futures contract. These options are called future options or **options on futures** and were discussed in Chapter 18.

Hedging Portfolio Cash Inflows   When a large sum of money is deposited with a manager, the fund's asset composition changes; the lump sum inflow of cash reduces the portfolio's exposure to fixed-income investment because a larger proportion of the portfolio's assets are in cash. Also, the desire to quickly invest the funds may cause the manager to purchase securities that he or she otherwise would not. Finally, large purchases can lead to sizable commissions and a price pressure impact on the bonds acquired.

A better strategy would be to use part of the cash inflow to purchase appropriate bond futures contracts that have a value equal to the deposit; purchasing call options may be another possibility. The effect is that the money is immediately invested with lower commissions and less price impact than an outright purchase of bonds. Once the futures are purchased, the manager has time to decide on the specific assets to be purchased. Smaller purchases over time should eliminate or substantially reduce price pressure. As bond purchases are made, the futures contracts can be sold.

Hedging Portfolio Cash Outflows   A large, planned withdrawal from a portfolio is accomplished by selling securities to generate cash prior to the withdrawal date. Similar to a cash deposit, the sale of securities causes an increase in cash holdings, which reduces the portfolio's exposure to bonds. A possible strategy to counterbalance the cash increase is to buy an appropriate number of futures contracts or call options as bonds are sold. The net effect will be to maintain the portfolio's overall exposure to bonds while accumulating cash. When the cash is paid out the futures contracts can be sold and the portfolio's characteristics have not been disrupted.

The Treasury Bond Futures Contract

To illustrate the use of derivative securities in bond portfolio management we will focus on futures contracts in this review. Futures, and options on futures, are the derivative tool portfolio managers typically use.[18]

Table 19.4 (see page 684) listed the various financial futures contracts traded on an exchange. To illustrate our examples, we will use the Treasury bond futures contract.

When the Treasury bond (or T-bond) futures contract expires, **delivery** or settlement of the contract is made in the actual underlying security—a T-bond. Bonds with a par value of $100,000 must be delivered to settle the contract. With the variety of Treasury bonds available, the futures contract has to be written with a specific Treasury bond in mind. The contract specifies the underlying security is an 8 percent coupon Treasury bond with at least fifteen years until maturity or first call. The fact is, only rarely does such a bond actually

---

[18]In addition to futures, options, and options on futures, swaps are another derivative security useful in portfolio management.

exist! How can delivery occur in a nonexistent bond? More importantly, why would anyone trade a futures contract based upon a fictitious underlying security?

The answer is that a T-bond is delivered to settle the contract, but another T-bond can be substituted for the 8 percent coupon, fifteen-years-to-maturity bond. The contract allows for any bond with fifteen years until maturity or first call to be delivered. If a bond is delivered with a coupon rate above (or below) 8 percent, the person accepting delivery pays a higher (or lower) price. The bond delivered by the seller of the futures contract will be the **cheapest-to-deliver (CTD)** Treasury bond that satisfies the contract's specifications. In other words, the seller will deliver the lowest-price bond possible to satisfy the terms of the futures contract. At any point in time, the CTD bond will be known to both buyers and sellers of the futures contract, and the price of the contract will be set using the known CTD bond as the underlying asset. Over time, the effects of changing market interest rates on the duration and convexity of bonds will cause the CTD bond to change. For example, as interest rates rise, longer-duration bonds become CTD. Whenever a new bond becomes CTD, the futures price follows that bond until it is replaced by another as CTD.

Portfolio managers will buy and sell T-bond futures in a variety of ways that we will review. Prior to that we will discuss how managers determine the appropriate number of T-bond futures to buy or sell. This number is also known as the **hedge ratio**. We'll examine two situations.

Determining How Many Contracts to Trade to Hedge a Deposit or Withdrawal As discussed previously, futures can be used to maintain the desired exposure to bonds while the portfolio receives or distributes a cash flow. The number of futures contracts to be traded will equal:[19]

$$\frac{\text{Cash Flow}}{\text{Value of 1 Contract}} \times \text{Conversion Factor} \times \text{Duration Adjustment Factor}$$

The value of one contract is the price times $1,000. T-bond futures price quotes are always in terms of thirty-seconds. If the price of the T-bond futures contract is quoted as 114-26, the price is 114 26/32, or 114.8125. The value of the contract will be $114,812.50.

The **conversion factor** is necessary because the deliverable bond will probably *not* have an 8 percent coupon. The conversion factor adjusts the current CTD bond to reflect the fact that $100,000 par value of the CTD bond will not cost the same to deliver as an 8 percent coupon, fifteen-year T-bond. Tables listing conversion factors for bonds of different coupons and maturities are available from the futures exchanges and many financial institutions.

The **duration adjustment factor** reflects the difference in interest rate sensitivity between the portfolio and the CTD bond. It equals the ratio of the portfolio duration divided by the duration of the CTD bond.[20]

An important caveat is necessary: because we are using durations to find the hedge ratio, our analysis is subject to the duration assumptions. Namely, we are assuming a flat yield curve and that all yield curve shifts are parallel.

Consider the following example of how to find the number of futures contracts. Assume a bond portfolio manager will receive a $5 million cash inflow today when the current conversion factor is .90. The bond portfolio under management has a duration of 7.5 years; the

[19]This relationship is identical to the "basis-point value" (BPV) method that appears in Chicago Board of Trade materials on the use of bond futures.

[20]Those who manage corporate bond portfolios have no corporate bond futures contract with which to hedge; thus, they are forced to use the T-bond futures contract. In this case, the ratio of durations does not measure the different price sensitivities to interest rate changes between Treasury and corporate bonds. An alternative method is to use the slope from a regression that uses the portfolio's value as the dependent variable and the price of the CTD bond as the independent variable.

duration of the CTD bond is 6.5 years. The value of the contract is $114,812.50. The number of T-bond futures contracts required to hedge this cash inflow is equal to

$$\frac{\$5 \text{ million}}{\$114,812.50} \times 0.90 \times \frac{7.5 \text{ years}}{6.5 \text{ years}} = 45.22 \text{ contracts}$$

Because fractional contracts do not exist, the manager will round this number to the nearest integer and purchase forty-five contracts to hedge the cash inflow. These forty-five contracts will be sold over time as the $5 million in cash is invested in bonds.

As a simplifying assumption, in the rest of this chapter we will assume no adjustment for a conversion factor is needed.

Determining How Many Contracts to Trade to Adjust Portfolio Duration

In Chapter 16 we learned that the duration of a bond portfolio equals the weighted average of its component durations. This concept is used to determine how many futures contracts must be bought or sold to increase or decrease a portfolio's duration. This is called the **weighted-average-durations approach**.[21]

Suppose a $25 million bond portfolio has $22.5 million invested in bonds and the remainder invested in T-bills. The duration of the bond component of the portfolio is 5.5 years. Because the manager expects falling interest rates, he wants to lengthen the portfolio's duration to 7.5 years. Again we'll assume the value of a futures contract is $114,812.50. The duration of the futures contract is seven years. The duration of the cash or T-bill component of a portfolio is usually assumed to be zero.

Currently the weight of the bond component of the portfolio is $22.5 million/$25 million or 0.90. The duration of the bond component is 5.5 years and the duration of the futures contract is 7.0 years. The weight of the futures component of the portfolio will be $(F \times \$114,812.50)/\$25$ million, where F represents the number of futures contracts. Assuming a target portfolio duration of 7.5, the weighted average of the portfolio's components must equal 7.5:

7.5	=	$0.90 \times 5.5 +$	$\dfrac{F \times \$114,812.50}{\$25 \text{ million}} \times 7.0$
Target Duration		Contribution of Current Bond Portfolio	Contribution of the Futures Component

Solving for F, we find that 79.32 contracts must be purchased to accomplish this increase in portfolio duration. Rounding to the nearest integer, seventy-nine contracts will be bought.

Suppose the manager forecasts a sharp increase in interest rates and wants to shorten the duration of the portfolio to two years. To find the required number of futures to be traded, we need to solve the following for F:

2.0	=	$0.90 \times 5.5 +$	$\dfrac{F \times \$114,812.50}{\$25 \text{ million}} \times 7.0$
Target Duration		Contribution of Current Bond Portfolio	Contribution of the Futures Component

---

[21]This is identical to the BPV method used in Chicago Board of Trade materials.

Solving for F indicates the answer is -91.76. The negative sign indicates that futures contracts must be *sold* to shorten the duration to two years. Rounding to the nearest integer, the manager will sell ninety-two futures contracts to attain the desired portfolio position.

Using Futures in Passive Fixed-Income Portfolio Management

A passive investment strategy generally seeks to buy and hold a portfolio of fixed-income securities. Many times the portfolio manager attempts to replicate a bond-market index, such as those described in Chapter 5. A passive strategy will not actively try to lengthen or shorten portfolio duration in the light of an interest rate forecast; nor will it involve swapping bonds to take advantage of expected changes in sector yield spreads.

With a passive investment strategy, the manager attempts to manage deposits and withdrawals without harming the ability of the portfolio to achieve its stated goal. Therefore, the prior example on hedging a cash deposit or withdrawal is relevant for passive management. Instead of investing all cash inflows immediately in the specified index, the manager can purchase an appropriate number of futures contracts. This will maintain the portfolio structure and reduce index-tracking error while the manager determines how to invest the funds.[22] Similarly, anticipated cash withdrawals can be hedged by liquidating part of the portfolio while maintaining the portfolio's exposure to the bond market by using futures contracts.

Using Futures in Active Fixed-Income Portfolio Management

Active management may focus on adjusting the portfolio's systematic risk, unsystematic risk, or both. Systematic risk in the fixed-income arena involves a portfolio's exposure to price fluctuations caused by changes in interest rates. Unsystematic risk includes the portfolio's exposure to changes in sector or maturity spreads. It is difficult to control a portfolio's unsystematic risk beyond diversification, but there are well-developed tools available to modify systematic risk.

Modifying Systematic Risk   In a fixed-income portfolio, market or systematic risk arises from the sensitivity of the portfolio's value to changes in interest rates. The tool for measuring this sensitivity is the portfolio's duration. Thus, adjusting the portfolio's duration allows us to change the portfolio's exposure to systematic (interest rate) risk. If forecasters predict rising interest rates, active portfolio managers may want to shorten their portfolios' durations. Predictions of falling interest rates will cause managers to lengthen the duration of their portfolios.

Traditionally, when rates were expected to fall, active managers would identify short-term duration bonds to sell and long-term duration bonds to purchase in order to raise the portfolio's weighted-average duration. The fact is, the use of futures gives managers a quicker and less costly means of accomplishing this, with less disruption to the portfolio's characteristics.[23] Buying futures allows the manager to lengthen portfolio duration as discussed and illustrated earlier. We also discussed how to determine how many futures contracts should be sold to shorten portfolio duration if you expected an increase in interest rates.

It is possible to sell futures so the overall portfolio will be unaffected by interest rate changes over the length of the futures contract. This is accomplished by selling a spec-

[22]When a portfolio's goal is to mimic an index, the portfolio's returns should closely follow or "track" those of the index. An index fund's quality is not measured by the magnitude of its returns but by its tracking error, or the degree to which the portfolio's returns deviated from those of the actual index.

[23]This is an important advantage; the active manager who has expertise in identifying mispriced or undervalued securities may want to continue holding these specific securities in spite of predictions of an adverse interest-rate move.

Table 20.7	*Hedging a Long Position in Treasury Bonds*

Intent: Sell futures contracts against a long position in Treasury bonds to hedge an unexpected increase in interest rates.

	Spot	**Futures**
Nov. 1:	You own $1 million of 21-year, 8 3/8 percent Treasury bonds priced at 82–17, yielding 10.45 percent. Your portfolio value is $825,312.50.	Sell ten March Treasury bond futures at a price of 80–09. The basis is 2 8/32 (82 17/32 − 80 9/32).
Mar. 3:	You sell the 8 3/8 percent bonds at 70–26 to yield 12.31 percent. Your portfolio value is $708,125. This is a loss of 11 23/32 per bond or $117,187.50 overall.	Buy ten March Treasury bond futures at 66–29. This is a gain of 13 12/32 per contract or $133,750. The basis is now 3 29/32 (70 26/32 − 66 29/32).

Conclusion: The overall transaction resulted in a portfolio value gain. The loss of $117,187.50 was offset by a gain on the futures transaction of $133,750 for a net gain of $16,562.50. Another way of looking at the gain is the strengthening of the basis of 3 29/32 that resulted from the futures price decreasing more than the spot price. Because the position is long spot and short futures, the overall position benefits from the stronger basis. The basis went from 2 8/32 to 3 29/32 for an increase of 1 21/32, which is $16,562.50, the overall gain.

ified number of futures so the portfolio's duration becomes zero.[24] To illustrate, assume we manage a $25 million portfolio that currently has $22.5 million invested in bonds; the remainder is in T-bills. The bond component of the portfolio has a duration of 5.5 years; T-bills are assumed to have zero duration. The duration of the futures contract is seven years, and the value of a futures contract is $114,812.50. The goal is to sell an appropriate number of futures, to bring the duration of the portfolio to zero. Using the weighted-average-of-durations approach, we have:

$$0.0 \quad = \quad 0.90 \times 5.5 + \quad \frac{F \times \$114,812.50}{\$25 \text{ million}} \times 7.0$$

Target Duration	Contribution of Current Bond Portfolio	Contribution of the Futures Component

Solving this, we find that F equals -153.98. Therefore, to make the portfolio rate-neutral, 154 futures contracts would have to be sold. By setting the portfolio duration equal to zero, the return earned on the portfolio should approximate those of a risk-free asset such as short-term T-bills. If the active manager can identify mispriced or undervalued securities, an extra return component may be earned if she were successful in identifying such bonds.

As an example of a hedge, consider the example in Table 20.7. Assume that to hedge a $1 million portfolio of Treasury bonds against an interest rate increase you decide to sell 10 Treasury bond futures contracts. Table 20.7 shows that a potential loss of $117,187.50 in the portfolio is offset by a gain of $133,750 on the futures position. Fortuitously, your hedged portfolio had an overall gain of $16,562.50 following the rise in rates.

Modifying Unsystematic Risk   Unlike the situation with equities, few opportunities exist for controlling the unsystematic risk in a fixed-income portfolio. Futures

---

[24]Note: this is *not* the same as immunizing a portfolio. Immunization is a carefully planned asset-allocation strategy wherein the portfolio is constructed to earn a target rate of return that will not be affected by changing interest rates over a known time horizon. Immunization by active managers would be frowned upon by their clients who hired them for their active investment expertise. Constructing an interest-rate-neutral active portfolio would be a *temporary* defensive measure during a period of interest rate uncertainty or volatility. Also, some managers may use it as part of a strategy to take advantage of mispricing between the futures and cash markets, or to create "synthetic" securities.

and options exist only in a limited number of broad sectors and maturities. Sectors include Treasury bonds, mortgage-backed securities, and municipal bonds. Different maturity sectors include short-term (Treasury bills, Eurodollars), intermediate-term (Treasury notes), and long-term (Treasury bonds) maturities approximated by the noted futures contracts.

By buying or selling an appropriate number of futures or option contracts, active managers can increase or decrease their portfolios' exposure to these sectors or yield curve maturities to take advantage of expected sector yield shifts. Changes in portfolio asset allocation among alternative sectors can be accomplished faster and at lower cost by using futures contracts.

For example, assume a Treasury portfolio currently has a duration of five years, which the manager wishes to maintain although he expects the shape of the yield curve to change: intermediate rates are expected to increase, but long-term rates are expected to fall. To take advantage of these fluctuations, the manager will want to decrease the portfolio's exposure to intermediate-term notes while increasing its exposure to long-term bonds, while maintaining a duration of five years. He can accomplish this by selling Treasury note futures and purchasing an appropriate number of T-bond futures.

Because the portfolio duration remains unchanged, the changes in interest-rate sensitivity from these transactions must be offsetting. In other words, the change in portfolio duration from selling T-note futures must be offset by the change in portfolio duration arising from buying T-bond futures. This means the following must be true:

$$
\begin{array}{c}
\text{Number of T-Note} \\ \text{Contracts Traded}
\end{array} \times
\begin{array}{c}
\text{Value of} \\ \text{T-Note Contract}
\end{array} \times
\begin{array}{c}
\text{Duration of} \\ \text{T-Note Contract}
\end{array} =
$$

$$
\begin{array}{c}
\text{Number of T-Bond} \\ \text{Contracts Traded}
\end{array} \times
\begin{array}{c}
\text{Value of} \\ \text{T-Bond Contract}
\end{array} \times
\begin{array}{c}
\text{Duration of} \\ \text{T-Bond Contract}
\end{array}
$$

As an example, assume that the value of a T-bond contract is \$114,812.50 and its duration is seven years. A Treasury-note futures contract has a value of \$112,437.50 and a duration of 2.8 years. To offset the impact of selling T-note futures and buying T-bond futures, it must be true that:

$$
\begin{array}{c}
F_{\text{T-notes}} \\ \text{Number of T-Note} \\ \text{Contracts Traded}
\end{array} \times
\begin{array}{c}
\$112,437.50 \\ \text{Value of} \\ \text{T-Note Contract}
\end{array} \times
\begin{array}{c}
2.8 \text{ years} \\ \text{Duration of} \\ \text{T-Note Contract}
\end{array} =
$$

$$
\begin{array}{c}
F_{\text{T-bonds}} \\ \text{Number of T-Note} \\ \text{Contracts Traded}
\end{array} \times
\begin{array}{c}
\$114,812.50 \\ \text{Value of} \\ \text{T-Note Contract}
\end{array} \times
\begin{array}{c}
7.0 \text{ years} \\ \text{Duration of} \\ \text{T-Note Contract}
\end{array} =
$$

Solving for the ratio of T-bond contracts to T-note contracts indicates the following:

$$
\frac{F_{\text{T-notes}}}{F_{\text{T-notes}}} = 0.392
$$

which means that for every T-note futures contract sold, .392 T-bond contracts should be purchased. Because fractional contracts are not traded, the portfolio manager will round his purchase of T-bond contracts to the nearest integer. For example, should 100 T-note contracts be sold, 39 T-bond contracts would be purchased.

Because no corporate-bond futures currently exist, strategies involving corporate bonds can be implemented using T-bond futures. We generally determine the number of

T-bond futures to be traded as shown in our prior examples, but it is not always appropriate to use durations in the calculation. The problem arises because the prices of default-free Treasury securities change in response to changes in interest rates, whereas the value of corporate bonds is affected by both interest rates and fluctuations in the yield spread between corporate and Treasury bonds. Rather than rely solely on durations, some managers will regress the price changes of their corporate bond portfolio to the price changes of the T-bond contract:

Price of Corporate Bond Portfolio = Alpha + Beta × (Price of Futures Contract)

The slope of this equation is used to determine the hedge ratio. Taking the number of futures as computed in previous examples and multiplying it by the slope estimate will tell the manager the appropriate number of T-bond futures to trade to cross-hedge the corporate bond portfolio.

For example, previously we showed that 91.76 (rounded to 92) futures contracts must be sold to reduce a portfolio's duration from 5.5 years to 2.0 years when (1) the value of a T-bond futures contract is $114,812.50, (2) the portfolio has a value of $25 million, and (3) $22.5 million of the portfolio is in bonds. Assume that this is a *corporate* bond portfolio. Historical regression analysis finds that a one-dollar change in the value of the futures contract is associated with an eighty-eight-cent change in the value of the corporate bond portfolio. Given this result, the appropriate number of T-bond futures that need to be sold to reduce the duration of this corporate bond portfolio is: 91.76 × 0.88 or 80.75. With rounding, this implies that eighty-one T-bond contracts need to be sold.

Modifying the Characteristics of an International Bond Portfolio

Futures and options can be used to modify positions or to hedge positions in international bond portfolios. For example, if a manager believes that German bonds are attractive investments, she can purchase them directly or be exposed to them through a German government bond-futures contract (traded on LIFFE). Similarly, positions in British gilts or long-term British government bonds can be established by purchasing the specific securities, by purchasing long gilt futures, or by buying an option where the long gilt futures contract is the underlying security.

International bond portfolios generally represent positions in both securities and currencies. The existence of futures and option contracts on major currencies allows the portfolio manager to manage the risks of the security and the currency separately. Currency futures and options on currency futures serve to modify the currency exposure of an international bond portfolio without affecting the actual holdings of the portfolios. For example, a portfolio manager may be bullish on German bonds because of expectations of falling German interest rates, but may also believe that the deutsche mark is currently overvalued relative to the U.S. dollar. She can purchase the German securities and then adjust the currency exposure of the portfolio through use of currency options and futures.

For illustrative purposes, assume that a bond portfolio has the equivalent of $30 million invested; $9 million is invested in the United States; $12 million is invested in Germany; the remainder is invested in the United Kingdom. Thus, the allocation across countries and currencies is currently 30 percent United States, 40 percent Germany, and 30 percent United Kingdom. Because of fears that the mark is overvalued and a forecast of a strengthening pound, the manager wishes to reduce his exposure to the deutsche mark by $4.5 million (or −15 percentage points) while increasing his exposure to the pound by $4.5 million (or +15 percentage points). In other words, the manager's *desired currency* allocation is 30 percent U.S. dollar, 25 percent German mark, and 45 percent British pound.

Investments Online

Fixed-income management analytics and software are typically proprietary. The sites listed below offer some additional information about the techniques discussed in the text and will give you insight into the use of various analytical and portfolio management techniques.

www.ryanlabs.com

Ryan Labs is a leader in the construction and analysis of fixed-income indexes. Their site offers information on their research, data, indexing, consulting, and asset/liability management skills (this latter feature is of particular importance to portfolios that must meet a stream of cash outflows, such as a pension fund). The site discusses the quantitative nature of bond-portfolio management, fixed-income index construction, and the variety of risk and reward measures used for bond investment analysis.

www.bondbasics.com

BondBasics home page offers daily analysis for institutional fixed income investors. Their information and analysis is for subscribers only, but a sample site gives visitors a flavor of some of their analytical products, including an analysis of the U.S. Treasury market, yield-curve projections, and computed present values from the current term structure.

www.cms-info.com

The home page of Capital Management Sciences allows users to move to sites featuring CMS's various products. CMS sells fixed-income analytical software to institutional investment managers. Research papers on fixed income security analysis are offered free of charge to users who fill out an on-line form. BondEdge is a product offering "what-if" simulations, volatility appraisals, and other analytics to fixed-income portfolio managers. BondVu does single-security analysis, including valuation, horizon-return analysis, swap analysis, and price/yield calculations, among others.

Several brokerage houses offer fixed-income portfolio information and strategies with an orientation to the individual investor. Two such sites are:

www.prusec.com/ladder.htm Prudential Securities' site, which presents an overview of the bond laddering strategy; and

www.deanwitter.com/tfi/milp.html Dean Witter's site discusses laddering strategies as well. It presents several hypothetical examples for retirement, college funding, and monthly income laddering strategies.

Traditional currency rebalancing meant rebalancing the country allocation, too, thus preventing the manager from fully participating in security markets that were thought to be undervalued. Such security rebalancing would also be costly and time consuming. Rather than letting portfolio managers do what they do best, which is identifying undervalued markets and securities, portfolio managers would have to make decisions based on currency forecasts.

The derivatives market helps the manager maintain the country exposure while modifying the currency exposure. If we assume that the futures dollar/pound exchange rate is £1 = \$1.62 and the pound futures contract calls for the delivery of £62,500, the value of

one contract is 1.62 \$/£ × £62,500 = \$101,250. If the mark/dollar futures exchange rate is DM 1 = \$0.55 and the deutsche mark contract calls for the delivery of DM 125,000, the value of the deutsche mark futures contract is 0.55 \$/DM × DM 125,000 = \$68,750.

If our manager wants to reduce his deutsche mark exposure by \$4.5 million, he accomplishes this by selling \$4,500,000/\$68,750 = 65.45 (rounded off to 65) futures contracts on the deutsche mark. To increase the portfolio's exposure to the pound by \$4.5 million, he must purchase \$4,500,000/\$101,250 = 44.44 (or 44) British pound futures contracts.

Once these transactions are completed, the allocation of the securities across these countries remains as before: 30 percent United States, 40 percent Germany, 30 percent United Kingdom. Through the use of currency hedging, the manager's portfolio's exposure to the (presumably overvalued) deutsche mark is only 25 percent while his exposure to the (presumably undervalued) pound is 45 percent. The use of derivatives allows the portfolio manager to shift currency exposures faster and at less cost than reallocating bonds across countries. These techniques allow the manager to maintain the desired exposure to securities he believes are undervalued.

SUMMARY

♦ The past decade has seen a significant increase in the number and range of available bond-portfolio management strategies. Bond-portfolio management strategies include the relatively straightforward buy-and-hold and bond-indexing strategies, several alternative active portfolio strategies, dedicated cash matching, classical immunization, and horizon matching. It is important to understand the alternatives available and how to implement them, but you should also recognize that the choice of a specific strategy is based on the needs and desires of the client. In turn, the success of any strategy will depend on the background and talents of the portfolio manager.

♦ We examined the use of derivative securities in bond portfolio management. Futures and options can help hedge against portfolio cash inflows and outflows. They can help keep passive portfolios fully invested and help minimize tracking error. In active portfolios they can help change duration and provide limited control of the portfolio's unsystematic risk. Portfolios with combinations of active and passive management, such as immunized portfolios, can make use of derivatives to help keep portfolio duration equal to the remaining time horizon.

♦ Finally, we examined the use of derivatives in managing currency exposures in international fixed-income portfolios.

Questions

1. Explain the difference between a pure buy-and-hold strategy and a modified buy-and-hold strategy.
2. What is an indexing portfolio strategy, and what is the justification for using this strategy?
3. Briefly define the following bond swaps: pure yield pickup swap, substitution swap, and tax swap.
4. What are two primary reasons for investing in deeply discounted bonds?
5. Briefly describe three active bond-portfolio management strategies.
6. Discuss two variables that you would examine carefully if you were analyzing a junk bond and indicate why they are important.
7. What are the advantages of a cash-matched dedicated portfolio? Discuss the difficulties of developing such a portfolio and the added costs.

8. Identify and describe the two components of interest rate risk.
9. What is bond portfolio immunization?
10. If the yield curve were flat and did not change, how would you immunize your portfolio?
11. You begin with an investment horizon of four years and a portfolio with a duration of four years with a market interest rate of 10 percent. A year later, what is your investment horizon? Assuming no change in interest rates, what is the duration of your portfolio relative to your investment horizon? What does this imply about your ability to immunize your portfolio?
12. It has been contended that a zero-coupon bond is the ideal financial instrument to use for immunizing a portfolio. Discuss the reasoning for this statement in terms of the objective of immunization (that is, the elimination of interest rate risk).
13. During a conference with a client, the subject of classical immunization is introduced. The client questions the fee charged for developing and managing an immunized portfolio. The client believes that it is basically a passive investment strategy, so the management fee should be substantially lower. What would you tell the client to show that it is not a passive policy and that it requires more time and talent than a buy-and-hold policy?
14. *CFA Examination III (June 1983)*
    The ability to immunize a bond portfolio is desirable for bond portfolio managers in some instances.
    a. Discuss the components of interest rate risk—assuming a change in interest rates over time, explain the two risks faced by the holder of a bond.
    b. Define immunization and discuss why a bond manager would immunize a portfolio.
    c. Explain why a duration-matching strategy is a superior technique to a maturity-matching strategy for the minimization of interest rate risk.
    d. Explain in specific terms how you would use a zero-coupon bond to immunize a bond portfolio. Discuss why a zero-coupon bond is an ideal instrument in this regard.
15. *CFA Examination III (June 1988)*
    After you have constructed a structured fixed-income portfolio (one that is dedicated, indexed, or immunized), it may be possible over time to improve on the initial optimal portfolio while continuing to meet the primary goal. Discuss three conditions that would be considered favorable for a restructuring, assuming no change in objectives for the investor, and cite an example of each condition.
16. *CFA Examination III (June 1988)*
    The use of bond-index funds has grown dramatically in recent years.
    a. Discuss the reasons you would expect it to be easier or more difficult to construct a bond-market index than a stock-market index.
    b. It is contended that the operational process of managing a corporate-bond–index fund is more difficult than managing an equity index fund. Discuss three examples that support this contention.
17. *CFA Examination III (June 1986)—adapted*
    During the past several years substantial growth has occurred in the dollar amount of portfolios managed using immunization and dedication techniques. Assume a client wants to know the basic differences between (1) classical immunization, (2) cash-matched dedication, and (3) duration-matched dedication.
    a. Briefly describe each of these three techniques.
    b. Briefly discuss the ongoing investment action you would have to carry out if managing an immunized portfolio.
    c. Briefly discuss three of the major considerations involved in creating a cash-matched dedicated portfolio.
    d. Select one of the three alternative techniques that you believe requires the least degree of active management and justify your selection.
18. How does the use of futures affect a portfolio's return distribution? How does the use of options affect a portfolio's return distribution?
19. How can you use futures to hedge portfolio cash inflows? Portfolio cash outflow?
20. Describe the characteristics of the Treasury-bond futures contract.
21. What is systematic risk in a bond portfolio? What is unsystematic risk? How can you use futures and options to modify a bond portfolio's systematic and unsystematic risk exposure?

22. How is it possible to modify a bond portfolio's currency exposure without buying or selling the bonds of different countries?

23. *CFA Examination II (1996)*

    The shape of the U.S. Treasury yield curve appears to reflect two expected Federal Reserve reductions in the Federal Funds rate. The first reduction of approximately fifty basis points (bp) is expected six months from now, and the second reduction of approximately fifty bp is expected one year from now. The current U.S. Treasury term premiums are ten bp per year for each of the next three years (throughout the three-year benchmark).

    You agree that the two Federal Reserve reductions described above will occur. However, you believe that they will be reversed in a single 100 bp increase in the Federal Funds rate 2½ years from now. You expect term premiums to remain ten bp per year for each of the next three years (throughout the three-year benchmark).

    a. Describe or draw the shape of the Treasury yield curve out through the three-year benchmark.

    b. State which term structure theory supports the shape of the U.S. Treasury yield curve described in Part a. Justify your choice.

    Kent Lewis, an economist, also expects two Federal Reserve reductions in the Federal Funds rate, but believes that the market is too optimistic about how soon they will occur. Lewis believes that the first fifty bp reduction will be made 1 year from now and that the second fifty bp reduction will be made 1 1/2 years from now. He expects these reductions to be reversed by a single 100 bp increase 21/2 years from now. He believes that the market will adjust to reflect his beliefs when new economic data are released over the next two weeks.

    Assume you are convinced by Lewis's argument, and are authorized to purchase either the two-year benchmark U.S. Treasury or a cash/three-year benchmark U.S. Treasury barbell weighted to have the same duration as the U.S. Treasury

    c. Select an investment in *either* the two-year benchmark U.S. Treasury (bullet) or the cash/three-year benchmark U.S. Treasury barbell. Justify your choice.

24. *CFA Examination II (1997)*

    Mike Lane will have $5 million to invest in five-year U.S. Treasury bonds three months from now. Lane believes interest rates will fall during the next three months and wants to take advantage of prevailing interest rates by hedging against a decline in interest rates. Lane has sufficient funds to pay the costs of entering into and maintaining a futures position.

    a. Describe what action Lane should take using five-year U.S. Treasury note futures contracts to protect against declining interest rates.

    Assume three months have gone by and, despite Lane's expectations, five-year cash and forward markets interest rates have increased by 100 basis points compared with the five-year forward market interest rates of three months ago.

    b. Discuss the effect of higher interest rates on the value of the futures position that Lane entered into in Part a.

    c. Discuss how the return from Lane's hedged position differs from the return he could now earn if he had not hedged in Part a.

25. (1998 CFA Level I sample exam) What two sources of bond risk have offsetting effects.

    a. default risk and interest rate risk
    b. reinvestment risk and default risk
    c. Interest rate risk and reinvestment risk
    d. none of the above

Problems

1. You have a portfolio with a market value of $50 million and a Macaulay duration of seven years (assuming a market interest rate of 10 percent). If interest rates jump to 12 percent, what would be the estimated value of your portfolio using duration? Show all your computations.

2. Answer the following questions, assuming that at the initiation of an investment account, the market value of your portfolio is $200 million, and you immunize the portfolio at 12 percent for six years. During the first year, interest rates are constant at 12 percent.

a. What is the market value of the portfolio at the end of year one?

b. Immediately after the end of the year, interest rates decline to 10 percent. Estimate the new value of the portfolio assuming you did the required rebalancing (use only modified duration).

3. Compute the Macaulay duration under the following conditions:

a. A bond with a five-year term to maturity, a 12 percent coupon (annual payments), and a market yield of 10 percent

b. A bond with a four-year term to maturity, a 12 percent coupon (annual payments), and a market yield of 10 percent

c. Compare your answers to Parts a and b, and discuss the implications of this for classical immunization.

4. Compute the Macaulay duration under the following conditions:

a. A bond with a four-year term to maturity, a 10 percent coupon (annual payments), and a market yield of 8 percent

b. A bond with a four-year term to maturity, a 10 percent coupon (annual payments), and a market yield of 12 percent

c. Compare your answers to Parts a and b. Assuming it was an immediate shift in yields, discuss the implications of this for classical immunization.

5. Answer the following questions about a zero-coupon bond with a term to maturity at issue of ten years (assume semiannual compounding):

a. What is the duration of the bond at issue assuming a market yield of 10 percent? What is its duration if the market yield is 14 percent? Discuss these two answers.

b. Compute the initial issue price of this bond at a market yield of 14 percent.

c. Compute the initial issue price of this bond at a market yield of 10 percent.

d. A year after issue, the bond in Part c is selling to yield 12 percent. What is its current market price? Assuming you owned this bond during this year, what is your rate of return?

6. Evaluate the following pure yield pickup swap: You currently hold a twenty-year, Aa-rated, 9 percent coupon bond priced to yield 11 percent. As a swap candidate, you are considering a twenty-year, Aa-rated, 11 percent coupon bond priced to yield 11.5 percent. (Assume reinvestment at 11.5 percent.)

	Current Bond	Candidate Bond
Dollar investment		
Coupon		
i on one coupon		
Principal value at year-end		
Total accrued		
Realized compound yield		

Value of swap: basis points in one year

7. Evaluate the following substitution swap: You currently hold a twenty-five-year, 9.0 percent coupon bond priced to yield 10.5 percent. As a swap candidate, you are considering a twenty-five-year, Aa-rated, 9.0 percent coupon bond priced to yield 10.75 percent. (Assume a one-year work-out period and reinvestment at 10.5 percent.)

	Current Bond	Candidate Bond
Dollar investment		
Coupon		
i on one coupon		
Principal value at year-end		
Total accrued		
Realized compound yield		

Value of swap: basis points in one year

8. *CFA Examination III (June, 1984)*

   Reinvestment risk is a major factor for bond managers to consider when determining the most appropriate or optimal strategy for a fixed-income portfolio. Briefly describe each of the following bond-portfolio management strategies, and explain how each deals with reinvestment risk:

   a. Active management
   b. Classical immunization
   c. Dedicated portfolio

9. "The risks involved in implementing an interest rate anticipation strategy are not equal. Shortening durations when an interest rate rise is expected is much less risky than lengthening durations when a decline in rates is anticipated." Is this statement true? Why or why not?

10. Having attracted a large pension fund as a new client, you are expecting a rather large cash deposit of $25 million into your bond portfolio next month. If the conversion factor between the current CTD bond and the 8 percent coupon, fifteen-years-to-maturity bond specified in the Treasury bond futures contract is 1.05, the duration of the CTD bond is 6.0 years, and your portfolio has a duration of 8.5 years, how many T-bond futures contracts should you purchase or sell to hedge this cash flow? Assume the T-bond futures contract value is $121,156.25.

11. Assume all the information in Problem 10 still holds, except that you manage a corporate bond portfolio. Regression analysis gives you this additional information:

    price of corporate bond portfolio = 980 + 0.92 × (price of the futures contract)

    How many T-bond futures contracts should you buy or sell to hedge this expected cash inflow?

12. Your $50 million bond portfolio is currently 95 percent invested in bonds and has a 5 percent cash reserve. The bond component of the portfolio has a duration of 4.3 years. If the T-bond futures contract has a duration of 8.0 years, a value of $105,000 per contract, and the conversion factor is 0.95, how many futures contracts must you buy or sell to change your portfolio's duration

    a. to 5 years?
    b. to 8 years?
    c. to 3 years?
    d. to make the portfolio insensitive to changes in interest rates?

13. A $100 million international bond portfolio has 25 percent of its assets in U.S. bonds, 30 percent in German bonds, 15 percent in U.K. gilts, and 35 percent in Japanese bonds. Let's assume the current futures prices are $1 = ¥100, $1 = £0.75, $1 = DM 1.65. What must you do in order to change your currency exposure to those given below? Note: look in the financial section of a newspaper such as the *Wall Street Journal* to determine the characteristics of the currency future contracts.

	U.S.	Germany	U.K.	Japan
a.	25%	25%	25%	25%
b.	20%	50%	25%	5%
c.	30%	10%	20%	40%

References

Altman, Edward I., ed. *The High Yield Debt Market.* Homewood, Ill. Dow Jones–Irwin, 1990.

Brown, Keith C., ed. *Derivative Strategies for Managing Portfolio Risk.* Charlottesville, Va.: Association for Investment Management and Research, 1993.

Fabozzi, Frank J., T. Dessa Fabozzi, and Irving M. Pollack, eds. *Handbook of Fixed Income Securities,* 3d ed. Burr Ridge Ill.: Business One–Irwin, 1991.

Homer, Sidney, and Martin L. Leibowitz. *Inside the Yield Book.* Englewood Cliffs, N.J.: Prentice-Hall, 1972.

Maginn, John L., and Donald L. Tuttle, eds. *Managing Investment Portfolios,* 2nd ed. Boston, Mass.: Warren, Gorham, and Lamont, 1990.

The Chicago Board of Trade has a great wealth of educational materials, brochures, and booklets about its listed futures contracts and options on futures. For more information, write to:

Chicago Board of Trade
Education and Marketing Services Department
LaSalle at Jackson
Chicago, IL 60604
or call 1-800-THE-CBOT or 1-312-435-3558

GLOSSARY

Barbell strategy   With this bond portfolio strategy, about one-half of the funds are invested in short-duration securities and the remainder are invested in long-duration securities. This combines the high return, high income potential of long-term bonds with the lower risk, high liquidity aspects of shorter-term securities.

Bond swap   An active bond portfolio management strategy that exchanges one position for another to take advantage of some difference between them.

Buy-and-hold strategy   A passive bond portfolio management strategy in which bonds are bought and held to maturity.

Cheapest-to-deliver (CTD) bond   The bond the seller of a Treasury bond futures contract will deliver to the buyer to settle the futures contract, because the bond specified in the futures contract (8 percent coupon, fifteen years to maturity or first call) rarely exists.

Conversion factor   Used to adjust the value of the CTD bond to reflect the cost to deliver the 8 percent coupon, fifteen-years-to-maturity Treasury bond specified in the T-bond futures contract.

Credit analysis   An active bond portfolio management strategy designed to identify bonds expected to experience changes in rating. This strategy is critical when investing in high-yield bonds.

Dedication   A portfolio management technique in which the portfolio's cash flows are used to retire a set of liabilities over time.

Dedication with reinvestment   A dedication strategy in which portfolio cash flows may precede their corresponding liabilities. Such cash flows can be reinvested to earn a return until the date the liability is due to be paid.

Delivery   The settlement of a Treasury-bond futures contract made in the actual underlying security, a T-bond.

Duration adjustment factor   A factor that reflects the difference in interest rate sensitivity between the bond portfolio and the cheapest-to-deliver Treasury bond.

Duration strategy   A portfolio management strategy employed to reduce the interest rate risk of a bond portfolio by matching the modified duration of the portfolio with its investment horizon. For example, if the investment horizon is ten years, the portfolio manager would construct a portfolio that has a modified duration of ten years. This strategy is referred to as *immunization of the portfolio*.

Hedge ratio   The appropriate number of futures to buy or sell to hedge against a position.

Portfolio immunization   A bond portfolio management technique of matching modified duration to the investment horizon of the portfolio to eliminate interest rate risk.

Indexing   A passive bond portfolio management strategy that seeks to match the composition, and therefore the performance, of a selected market index.

Interest rate anticipation   An active bond portfolio management strategy designed to preserve capital or take advantage of capital gains opportunities by predicting interest rates and their effects on bond prices.

Interest rate risk   The uncertainty of returns on an investment due to possible changes in interest rates over time.

Investment horizon   The time period used for planning and forecasting purposes or the future time at which the investor requires the invested funds.

Ladder strategy   This portfolio strategy places an equal amount of the portfolio's holdings in a wide range of maturities. Maturing bonds are reinvested in the longest-term bonds. To reduce reinvestment risk, coupon income is reinvested across the maturity spectrum.

Maturity strategy   A portfolio management strategy employed to reduce the interest rate risk of a bond portfolio by matching the maturity of the portfolio with its investment horizon. For example, if the investment horizon is ten years, the portfolio manager would construct a portfolio that will mature in ten years.

Price risk   The component of interest rate risk due to the uncertainty of the market price of a bond caused by possible changes in market interest rates.

Pure cash-matched dedicated portfolio   A conservative dedicated portfolio management technique aimed at developing a bond portfolio that will provide payments exactly matching the specified liability schedules.

Reinvestment risk   The component of interest rate risk due to the uncertainty of the rate at which coupon payments will be reinvested.

Tracking error   The difference between the return of a portfolio that is constructed to replicate an index and the return on the index itself.

Valuation analysis   An active bond portfolio management strategy designed to capitalize on expected price increases in temporarily undervalued issues.

Wash sale   The term for selling an issue for a capital loss and repurchasing it within thirty days. In such cases the IRS does not allow the loss.

Weighted-average-durations approach   An approach used to determine how many futures contracts should be bought or sold to quickly increase or decrease a portfolio's duration.

A Word from the Street

By Martin L. Leibowitz

Several decades ago, bonds typically were purchased on a buy-and-hold basis. During the past twenty-five years, institutional bond investment has evolved into a highly active search for improved performance relative to a well-defined benchmark.

The development of active bond management coincided with the introduction of performance measurement in the fixed-income markets. As managers began to compete more aggressively on the basis of their short-term returns, they became subject to the same intensive scrutiny that had long characterized the equity market.

The first bond-performance index was developed in 1972, and was restricted to long-term, high-grade corporates. The bond market's expansion in both sectors and maturities created a need for more comprehensive indices that reflected the entire domestic market: Treasuries, agencies, corporates, and mortgaged securities in all maturity ranges. By the early 1980s several such indices had appeared. The widespread use of these broad indices for performance measurement has caused managers' results to be in a narrow range around the overall market returns.

A bond portfolio's duration is the primary determinant of its short-term return. A natural consequence of performance measurement is that managers tend to match their portfolio durations to that of the market as a whole. Managers must now assess investment opportunities on a duration-adjusted basis; that is, the antici-

pated rewards of a bond investment decision must be balanced against its duration risk relative to the benchmark.

In summary, the past twenty-five years have witnessed the transformation of fixed-income management from a yield-obsessed, buy-and-hold mentality into an intensely active pursuit of short-term returns relative to a well-defined market benchmark. It is envisioned that in the future, more attention will be directed to important questions about the appropriate role of the fixed-income component within the overall portfolio.

Martin Leibowitz is the director of research at Salomon Brothers Inc. and a member of the firm's executive committee. He joined Salomon Brothers in 1969 to form the first research unit directed toward fixed-income portfolio analysis.

Dr. Leibowitz coauthored with Sidney Homer a classic book in the fixed-income area entitled *Inside the Yield Book*. He has written or coauthored more than one hundred articles on such topics as immunization techniques, total portfolio duration, and surplus management for pension funds. Dr. Leibowitz has been president of the Board of Trustees for the New York Academy of Sciences. He also serves on the Board of Overseers for NYU's Stern School of Business and on the Board of Directors of the Institute for Quantitative Research in Finance.

Portfolio Management Using Investment Companies

In this chapter we will answer the following questions:

♦ What is an investment company?

♦ How do you compute the net asset value (NAV) for an investment company?

♦ What is the difference between a closed-end and an open-end investment company?

♦ Why is there usually a difference between the NAV and market price for a closed-end fund?

♦ What is the difference between a load and a no-load open-end fund?

♦ What is a 12b-1 plan fund and how does this feature affect an investor in such a fund?

♦ How well have fund managers succeeded in correctly timing the market and performing in a consistent manner?

♦ What does research on mutual fund performance tell us about fund expenses, portfolio turnover, and returns?

♦ Is it a good strategy to buy the types of mutual funds that other investors are purchasing?

♦ What is a good procedure for determining which mutual funds to purchase?

♦ When might it be appropriate to sell your shares in a mutual fund?

♦ What are some major sources of information on current and historical performance of funds and costs associated with buying and owning investment companies? ♦

Up to this point in the book, we have discussed how to analyze the aggregate market, various industries, and individual companies as well as their stocks and bonds in order to build a portfolio consistent with your investment objectives. We have also reviewed different instruments such as options, convertibles, and futures that provide additional

risk–return possibilities beyond those available from a straight stock–bond portfolio. This chapter introduces another investment opportunity: investment companies that sell shares in portfolios of stocks, bonds, or some combination of securities. Investment companies can make up part of a larger portfolio along with investments in individual stocks and bonds, or your total portfolio can be composed of investment companies.

Studies of efficient capital markets have indicated that few individual investors outperform the aggregate market averages. This makes managed investment companies an appealing alternative to direct investments because they provide several services. Many different types of investment companies offer a wide variety of alternative investment instruments with a range of risk and return characteristics.

The initial sections in this chapter explain investment companies and discuss the management organizations for investment company groups. The second section breaks investment companies into major types (closed-end and open-end) based on how they are traded in the secondary market, and how they charge for their services (load vs. no-load). Open-end investment companies, also known as mutual funds, are most prevalent, and so most of our discussion focuses on them. We also review several sources of information that are helpful to fund investors.

To choose among more than *seven thousand* investment companies available, you need to understand how to evaluate their performance. After discussing some major studies of what features are important and how to examine them, we consider the implications of these results for investors, including when to sell a fund.

WHAT IS AN INVESTMENT COMPANY?

An **investment company** invests a pool of funds belonging to many individuals in a portfolio of individual investments such as stocks and bonds. As an example, an investment company might sell 10 million shares to the public at $10 a share for a total of $100 million. If this common stock fund emphasized blue-chip stocks, the manager would invest the proceeds of the sale ($100 million less any commissions) in the stock of such companies as AT&T, Exxon, IBM, Xerox, and General Electric. Therefore, each individual who bought shares of the investment company would own a percentage of the investment company's total portfolio.

The value of these shares depends on what happens to the investment company's portfolio of stocks. With no further transactions, if the total market value of the stocks in the portfolio increased to $105 million (net of any liabilities, such as borrowing on margin), then each original share of the investment company would be worth $10.50 ($105 million/10 million shares). This per share value is the **net asset value (NAV)** of the investment company. It equals the total market value of all its assets (net of liabilities) divided by the number of fund shares outstanding.

The investment company is typically a corporation that has as its major assets the portfolio of marketable securities referred to as a fund. The management of the portfolio of securities and most of the other administrative duties are handled by a separate **investment management company** hired by the board of directors of the investment company.

To achieve economies of scale, many management companies start numerous funds with different characteristics. The variety of funds allows the management group to appeal to many investors with different risk– return preferences. In addition, it allows investors to switch among funds at low or no cost as economic or personal conditions change. This "family of funds" promotes flexibility and also increases the total capital the investment firm manages. Fidelity Investments, the nation's largest investment company, offers more than two hundred mutual funds.

CLOSED-END VERSUS OPEN-END INVESTMENT COMPANIES

Investment companies begin like any other company—someone sells an issue of common stock to a group of investors. An investment company, however, uses the proceeds to purchase the securities of other publicly held companies rather than buildings and equipment. A closed-end investment company (typically referred to as a *closed-end fund*) differs from an open-end investment company (often referred to as a *mutual fund*) in the way each operates *after* the initial public offering.

Closed-End Investment Companies

A **closed-end investment company** operates like any other public firm. Its stock trades on the regular secondary market, and the market price of its shares is determined by supply and demand. Such an investment company typically offers no further shares and does not repurchase the shares on demand. Thus, if you want to buy or sell shares in a closed-end fund, you make transactions in the public secondary market. The shares of many of these funds are listed on the NYSE. No new investment dollars are available for the investment company unless it makes another public sale of securities. Similarly, no funds are withdrawn unless the investment company decides to repurchase its stock, which is quite unusual.

The closed-end investment company's net asset value (NAV) is computed twice daily based on prevailing market prices for the securities in the portfolio. The market price of the investment company shares is determined by the relative supply and demand for the investment company stock in the public, secondary market. When you buy or sell shares of a closed-end fund, you pay or receive this market price plus or minus a regular trading commission. You should recognize that the NAV and the market price of a closed-end fund are almost never the same! Over the long run, the market price of these shares have historically been from 5 to 20 percent below the NAV (that is, they sell at a discount to NAV). Figure 21.1 is a list of closed-end stock funds, including general equity funds, specialized equity funds, world equity funds, convertible security funds, and dual-purpose funds, quoted in *Barron's*. *Barron's* also contains a listing of closed-end bond funds, including world income funds, national municipal bond funds, and single-state municipal bond funds.

Besides the long-run discount of market price to NAV, these funds seem to suffer short-run discounts following their initial public offerings (IPOs). As discussed in Chapter 8, numerous studies have shown that prices of most individual stock IPOs experience positive abnormal returns within a day after the offering. In contrast, studies of closed-end fund IPOs show fairly stable prices initially, which then drift to a discount over a four-month period. This unusual pattern prompted an SEC study of the question.[1]

At the time of the quotes in Figure 21.1, most of the funds were selling at discounts to their NAV. This typical relationship has prompted the following questions from investors: Why do these funds sell at a discount? Why do the discounts differ between funds? What are the returns available to investors from funds that sell at large discounts? This final question arises because an investor who acquires a portfolio at a price below market value (that is, below NAV) expects a dividend yield above the average. Still, the total rate of return on the fund depends on what happens to the discount during the

---

[1]Michael Siconolfi, "SEC Studies Closed-End Fund 'Mystery,'" *Wall Street Journal,* May 23, 1988, 31; and Kathleen Weiss, "The Post Offering Performance of Closed-End Funds," *Financial Management* 18, no. 3 (Autumn 1989): 57–67.

Figure 21.1 *Closed-End Stock and Bond Funds*

CLOSED-END FUNDS

Friday, February 13, 1998

Fund Name (Symbol)	Stock Exch	NAV	Market Price	Prem /Disc	52 week Market Return
General Equity Funds					
Adams Express (ADX)	♣N	29.99	25 5/8	− 14.6	32.0
Alliance All-Mkt (AMO)	N	33.98	32 11/16	− 3.8	62.0
Avalon Capital (MIST)	O	16.15	N/A	N/A	N/A
Baker Fentress (BKF)	♣N	22.31	19	− 14.8	21.8
Bergstrom Cap (BEM)	A	163.79	145	− 11.5	32.7
Blue Chip Value (BLU)	♣N	10.08	10 5/8	+ 5.4	39.4
Central Secs (CET)	A	29.40	30 3/4	+ 4.6	18.5
Corp Renaissance (CREN)-c	O	8.76	6 5/16	− 27.9	− 15.8
Engex (EGX)	A	12.25	8 7/8	− 27.6	− 22.8
Equus II (EQS)	♣A	30.13	25 7/8	− 14.1	55.2
Gabelli Equity (GAB)	N	11.92	11 13/16	− 0.9	39.0
General American (GAM)	♣N	30.13	26 5/8	− 11.6	36.9
Librty AllStr Eq (USA)	♣N	13.96	13 5/8	− 2.4	29.0
Librty AllStr Gr (ASG)	♣N	13.60	12 13/16	− 5.8	37.4
MFS Special Val (MFV)	N	14.89	19 1/4	+ 29.3	16.6
Morgan FunShares (MFUN)-c	O	13.63	12	− 12.0	34.1
Morgan Gr Sm Cap (MGC)	♣N	11.87	10 3/4	− 9.4	22.9
NAIC Growth (GRF)-c	C	11.45	15 1/8	+ 32.1	37.7
Royce Value (RVT)	♣N	17.37	15 13/16	− 9.0	37.6
Royce,5.75 '04Cv-w	N	N/A	N/A	N/A	N/A
Salomon SBF (SBF)	N	19.06	17 3/4	− 6.9	24.6
Source Capital (SOR)	N	52.61	54 5/8	+ 3.8	33.4
Tri-Continental (TY)	♣N	33.64	27 7/8	− 17.1	24.0
Zweig (ZF)	♣N	12.50	13 1/8	+ 5.0	27.6
Specialized Equity Funds					
C&S Realty (RIF)	♣A	N/A	N/A	N/A	N/A
C&S Total Rtn (RFI)-a	♣N	17.36	17 5/8	+ 1.5	15.3
Centrl Fd Canada (CEF)-c	♣A	4.75	4 1/2	− 5.3	3.3
Delaware Gr Div (DDF)-a	N	17.90	18 13/16	+ 5.1	21.2
Delaware Grp Gl (DGF)-a	N	16.95	18 3/8	+ 8.4	18.7
Duff&Ph Util Inc (DNP)	N	9.82	10 5/8	+ 8.2	26.4
Emer Mkts Infra (EMG)	♣N	13.92	11 5/16	− 18.7	− 9.2
Emer Mkts Tel (ETF)	♣N	15.87	13 5/16	− 16.1	− 0.6
First Financial (FF)	N	17.14	17 15/16	+ 4.7	25.8
Gabelli Gl Media (GGT)	N	10.32	9	− 12.8	40.7
H&Q Health Inv (HQH)	♣N	19.87	17 1/8	− 13.8	8.4
H&Q Life Sci Inv (HQL)	♣N	16.38	13 15/16	− 14.9	0.4
INVESCO Gl Hlth (GHS)	♣N	20.31	18 3/16	− 10.5	25.6
J Han Bank (BTO)	♣N	12.79	13	+ 1.6	65.7
J Han Pat Globl (PGD)	♣N	15.20	13 5/8	− 10.4	17.4
J Han Pat Sel (DIV)	♣N	16.82	15 11/16	− 6.7	11.9
Nations Bal Tgt (NBM)-a	N	10.44	9 1/2	− 9.0	25.3
Petroleum & Res (PEO)	♣N	40.37	37	− 8.3	13.7
Royce Micro-Cap (OTCM)	♣O	11.03	10 1/4	− 7.1	40.6
SthEastrn Thrift (STBF)	♣O	27.42	29	+ 5.8	61.0
Thermo Opprtunty (TMF)	A	11.83	10 7/16	− 11.8	− 12.1
Preferred Stock Funds					
J Han Pat Pref (PPF)	♣N	14.32	14 3/4	+ 3.0	16.7
J Han Pat Prm (PDF)-a	♣N	10.52	10 3/16	− 3.2	11.1
J Han Pat Prm II (PDT)	♣N	13.22	12 3/16	− 7.8	14.6
Preferred Inc Op (PFO)	♣N	13.57	12 3/4	− 6.0	15.6
Preferred IncMgt (PFM)	♣N	16.28	15 1/2	− 4.8	18.7
Preferred Income (PFD)	♣N	16.60	15 13/16	− 4.7	14.8
Putnam Divd Inc (PDI)	N	11.84	10 5/8	− 10.3	13.8
Convertible Sec's. Funds					
Bancroft Conv (BCV)	♣A	28.00	25 1/8	− 10.3	26.1
Castle Conv (CVF)	A	28.39	25 1/4	− 11.1	12.2
Ellsworth Conv (ECF)	♣A	11.88	10 5/8	− 10.6	25.0
Gabelli Conv Sec (GCV)	N	11.67	10 1/4	− 12.2	29.6
Lincoln Conv (LNV)-c	♣N	18.80	18 1/8	− 3.6	10.3
Putnam Conv Opp (PCV)	N	27.63	27 1/8	− 1.8	23.3
Putnam Hi Inc Cv (PCF)	N	10.04	10 11/16	+ 6.4	14.4
TCW Conv Secs (CVT)	♣N	9.61	9 15/16	+ 3.4	9.4
VKAC Cv Sec (ACS)	N	25.13	21 7/8	− 13.0	19.9
U.S. Mortgage Bond Funds					
2002 Target Term (TTR)-c	N	15.30	13 13/16	− 9.7	6.2
Amer Oppty Inc (OIF)-c	♣N	6.74	6 3/16	− 8.2	7.1
Amer Sel Port (SLA)-c	♣N	12.95	12 3/16	− 5.9	9.0
Amer Str Inc II (BSP)-c	♣N	13.06	11 15/16	− 8.6	8.2
Amer Str Inc III (CSP)-c	♣N	12.46	11 13/16	− 5.2	9.0
Amer Str Income (ASP)-c	♣N	13.00	11 13/16	− 9.1	8.1
BlckRk 1998 Term (BBT)-ac	N	9.96	9 3/4	− 2.1	5.1
BlckRk 1999 Term (BNN)-ac	N	9.90	9 7/16	− 4.7	4.3
BlckRk 2001 Term (BLK)-ac	N	9.42	8 11/16	− 7.8	4.6
BlckRk Adv Term (BAT)-ac	N	10.79	9 9/16	− 11.4	6.4
BlckRk Income (BKT)-ac	N	8.17	7 1/8	− 12.8	7.9

Fund Name (Symbol)	Stock Exch	NAV	Market Price	Prem /Disc	12 Mo. Yield 1/30/98
U.S. Gov't. Bond Funds					
ACM Govt Inc (ACG)	N	10.58	11 7/16	+ 8.1	7.9
ACM Govt Oppty (AOF)	N	8.70	8 1/8	− 6.6	7.7
ACM Govt Secs (GSF)	N	10.49	10 1/8	− 3.5	9.0
ACM Govt Spec (SI)	N	7.27	6 11/16	− 8.0	9.0
Amer Govt Income (AGF)-c	♣N	5.88	5 7/16	− 7.5	6.7
Amer Govt Port (AAF)-c	♣N	7.00	6 7/16	− 8.0	6.5
Bull&Bear US Gvt Sec (BBG)	♣A	15.10	13 3/4	− 8.9	6.6
Investment Grade Bond Funds					
1838 Bd-Deb (BDF)	N	22.60	21	− 7.1	7.4
All-American Tm (AAT)-c	N	15.14	13 7/8	− 8.4	7.2
Circle Income (CINS)-c	O	11.97	11 1/2	− 3.9	7.3
Current Inc Shs (CUR)	N	13.58	12 7/16	− 8.4	6.9
Fortis Secs (FOR)	N	9.69	9 1/2	− 2.0	7.8
Ft Dearborn Inc (FTD)	♣N	16.89	15 7/8	− 6.0	6.9
Hatteras Income (HAT)-a	N	16.19	15 3/16	− 6.2	7.5
INA Investments (IIS)	N	19.41	17 9/16	− 9.5	7.0
Independence Sq (ISIS)	O	18.51	17 3/8	− 6.1	7.9
InterCap Income (ICB)	♣N	18.81	17 9/16	− 6.6	7.4
Montgomery St (MTS)	N	20.58	20	− 2.8	7.2
Pac Amer Income (PAI)	N	16.40	16 3/8	− 0.2	8.9
Pioneer Int Shs (MUO)	N	13.95	15	+ 7.5	7.3
Transam Income (TAI)	N	25.53	25 5/8	+ 0.4	7.4
VKAC Bd Fd (ACB)	N	21.25	21 1/8	− 0.6	7.4
Vestaur Secs (VES)-c	N	14.87	14 7/8	0.0	7.2

Fund Name (Symbol)	Stock Exch	NAV	Market Price	Prem /Disc	52 week Market Return
World Equity Funds					
ASA Limited (ASA)-cv	N	20.78	23 3/16	+ 11.6	− 31.8
Anchor Gold&Curr (GCT)	C	4.77	4 9/16	− 4.4	− 27.0
Argentina (AF)	N	15.69	12 7/8	− 17.9	− 2.8
Asia Pacific (APB)	N	8.51	8 13/16	+ 3.6	− 24.0
Asia Tigers (GRR)	N	8.87	8 3/8	− 5.6	− 22.9
Austria (OST)	♣N	12.32	10 15/16	− 11.2	28.0
BGR Prec Metals (BPT.A)-cy	T	15.64	12 1/4	− 21.7	− 29.0
Brazil (BZF)	N	25.80	20 15/16	− 18.8	− 5.5
Brazilian Equity (BZL)	♣N	9.47	8 1/8	− 14.2	− 15.5
Cdn Genl Inv (CGI)-yd	♣T	18.14	16 11/32	− 9.9	36.6
Cdn Wrld Fd Ltd (CWF)-cy	♣T	6.23	4 3/4	− 23.8	1.1
Central Eur Eqty (CEE)	♣N	21.57	18 1/2	− 14.2	9.6
Chile (CH)	♣N	18.87	15 7/8	− 15.9	− 20.1
China (CHN)	N	13.14	11 11/16	− 11.1	− 8.9
China, Greater (GCH)	♣N	12.33	10 7/8	− 11.8	− 6.5
Clemente Global (CLM)-c	N	12.13	10 1/2	− 13.4	38.0
Czech Republic (CRF)	N	14.70	12 1/16	− 17.9	− 21.3
Dessauer Glbl Eq (DGE)	N	12.25	11 11/16	− 4.6	N/A
Economic Inv Tr (EVT)-cy	T	156.00	115	− 26.3	60.5
Emer Mkts Grow (N/A)	z	53.94	N/A	N/A	N/A
Emerging Mexico (MEF)-c	N	11.64	9 1/2	− 18.4	16.9
Europe (EF)	♣N	20.02	17 5/8	− 12.0	18.0
European Warrant (EWF)-c	N	19.24	17 7/16	− 9.4	64.7
F&C Middle East (EME)-c	N	17.99	16 1/2	− 8.3	5.3
Fidelity Em Asia (FAE)	♣N	10.85	10	− 7.8	− 29.0
Fidelty Ad Korea (FAK)	♣N	4.23	5 1/4	+ 24.1	− 44.0
First Australia (IAF)	A	9.33	8 1/8	− 12.9	− 4.8
First Israel (ISL)	♣N	15.41	12 15/16	− 16.0	0.5
First Philippine (FPF)	N	7.96	8	+ 0.5	− 51.9
France Growth (FRF)	N	13.63	11 5/16	− 17.0	20.8
GT Glbl Estn Eur (GTF)	N	12.80	11 9/16	− 9.7	− 1.0
Germany Fund (GER)	♣N	16.62	14 5/8	− 12.0	39.5
Germany, Emer (FRG)	♣N	13.20	11 1/2	− 12.9	48.9
Germany, New (GF)	♣N	17.37	14 1/2	− 16.5	23.5
Global Small Cap (GSG)	A	17.31	14 9/16	− 15.9	18.9
Growth Fd Spain (GSP)	♣N	19.46	18	− 7.5	55.8
Herzfeld Caribb (CUBA)	O	6.31	5 31/32	− 5.4	7.9
India Fund (IFN)	N	7.43	6 7/8	− 7.5	− 16.7
India Growth (IGF)-d	N	9.57	9 3/8	− 2.0	− 24.2
Indonesia (IF)	♣N	2.73	5 3/8	+ 96.9	− 50.0
Irish Inv (IRL)	N	21.31	17 7/8	− 16.1	26.4
Italy (ITA)	N	14.94	12 5/8	− 15.5	28.1
Jakarta Growth (JGF)	N	2.06	3 3/4	+ 82.0	− 59.2
Japan Equity (JEQ)	♣N	6.49	8 3/16	+ 26.2	− 16.0
Japan OTC Equity (JOF)	N	4.95	5 13/16	+ 17.4	− 14.3
Jardine Fl China (JFC)	♣N	10.98	9 1/2	− 13.5	− 18.8
Jardine Fl India (JFI)-gc	♣N	7.50	6 7/8	− 8.3	− 14.1
Korea (KF)	N	6.29	8 1/16	+ 28.2	− 48.6
Korea Equity (KEF)	N	2.81	3 11/16	+ 31.2	− 46.4
Korean Inv (KIF)	N	3.57	4 13/16	+ 34.8	− 39.8
Latin Amer Disc (LDF)	N	11.89	11 5/8	− 2.2	20.5
Latin Amer Eq (LAQ)	♣N	15.74	12 15/16	− 17.8	− 12.2
Latin Amer Growth (LLF)	♣N	10.83	9 1/4	− 14.6	− 15.0
Latin Amer Inv (LAM)	♣N	16.92	13 15/16	− 17.6	− 9.8
Malaysia (MF)	N	5.50	8	+ 45.5	− 53.7
Mexico (MXF)-c	N	22.69	18 1/4	− 19.6	14.7
Mexico Eqty&Inc (MXE)-c	N	11.95	9 7/8	− 17.4	28.0
Morgan St Africa (AFF)	N	15.00	12 7/16	− 17.1	− 6.3
Morgan St Asia (APF)	N	8.91	8 1/16	− 9.5	− 18.1
Morgan St Em (MSF)	N	13.00	12 1/8	− 6.7	− 13.2
Morgan St India (IIF)	N	7.80	8 1/2	+ 9.0	− 17.1
Morgan St Russia (RNE)	N	24.25	22 9/16	− 7.0	2.4
New South Africa (NSA)	♣N	15.80	13 1/16	− 17.3	1.8
Pakistan Inv (PKF)	N	5.71	4 3/4	− 16.8	− 15.4
Portugal (PGF)	♣N	21.91	18 1/8	− 17.3	46.0
ROC Taiwan (ROC)	N	10.28	9 1/4	− 10.0	10.7
Royce Global Trust (FUND)	♣O	6.22	5 3/8	− 13.6	29.4
Schroder Asian (SHF)-c	N	8.72	8 5/16	− 4.7	− 31.4
Scud Spain & Por (IBF)	N	16.05	14 7/8	− 7.3	57.8
Scudder New Asia (SAF)	N	11.78	11	− 6.6	− 15.1
Scudder New Eur (NEF)	N	20.01	17 1/4	− 13.8	29.6
Singapore (SGF)-c	♣N	7.59	8 3/8	+ 10.3	− 35.0
Southern Africa (SOA)	N	16.77	14	− 16.5	6.3
Spain (SNF)	N	17.98	15 13/16	− 12.1	56.4
Swiss Helvetia (SWZ)	♣N	35.97	29 5/8	− 17.6	49.6
Taiwan (TWN)-c	N	20.95	18 15/16	− 9.6	− 2.9
Taiwan Equity (TYW)-c	♣N	15.92	13 1/4	− 16.8	21.8
Templeton China (TCH)-c	N	10.01	8 7/16	− 15.7	− 35.7
Templeton Dragon (TDF)	N	12.50	11 1/8	− 11.0	− 19.5
Templeton Em App (TEA)-c	N	12.61	12 11/16	+ 0.6	6.9
Templeton Em Mkt (EMF)	N	14.90	17 7/8	+ 20.0	− 6.1
Templeton Russia (TRF)-c	N	25.82	34 3/8	+ 33.1	0.1
Templeton Vietnm (TVF)	N	9.07	9 3/16	+ 1.3	− 20.3
Thai (TTF)	N	4.71	8 9/16	+ 81.8	− 43.3
Thai Capital (TC)	♣N	3.81	5 9/16	+ 46.0	− 40.7
Third Canadian (THD)-cy	T	23.99	19 3/4	− 17.7	5.5
Turkish Inv (TKF)	N	7.07	6 3/8	− 9.8	− 5.3
United Corps Ltd (UNC)-cy	T	75.80	55 3/32	− 27.3	40.1
United Kingdom (UKM)	♣N	16.33	14 5/16	− 12.4	16.6
Z-Seven (ZSEV)	O	8.20	8 3/16	− 0.2	5.1

Fund Name (Symbol)	Stock Exch	NAV	Market Price	Prem /Disc	12 Mo. Yield 1/30/98
U.S. Gov't. Bond Funds					
ACM Govt Inc (ACG)	N	10.58	11 7/16	+ 8.1	7.9
ACM Govt Oppty (AOF)	N	8.70	8 1/8	− 6.6	7.7
ACM Govt Secs (GSF)	N	10.49	10 1/8	− 3.5	9.0
ACM Govt Spec (SI)	N	7.27	6 11/16	− 8.0	9.0
Amer Govt Income (AGF)-c	♣N	5.88	5 7/16	− 7.5	6.7
Amer Govt Port (AAF)-c	♣N	7.00	6 7/16	− 8.0	6.5
Bull&Bear US Gvt Sec (BBG)	♣A	15.10	13 3/4	− 8.9	6.6

Source: Portions from "Closed-End Funds," *Barron's*, February 16, 1998. Reprinted by permission of *Barron's*, © 1998 Dow Jones & Company, Inc. All Rights Reserved Worldwide.

holding period. If the discount relative to the NAV declines, the investment should generate positive excess returns. If the discount increases, the investor will likely experience negative excess returns.

Some studies find evidence that the size of the discount changes according to the level of the fund's undistributed capital gains, which are taxable to the investor. Others argue that, because small investors typically purchase closed-end investment company shares, the relative size of the discount or premium measures small investor optimism or pessimism of the market. The analysis of these discounts remains a major question of modern finance.[2]

The uncertainty about discounts is both a blessing and a bane to investors. Some investors view the discounts favorably, because they can purchase a portfolio of assets for less than market value. Some closed-end investors focus more on the discount than the investment manager; such investors seek to buy shares in funds selling at a large discount in the hope of selling them when the discount narrows. A closed-end fund investor can earn attractive returns two ways: one, when the fund performs well, and two, when the discount to NAV narrows and the shares can be sold for a capital gain despite lackluster manager investment performance. Another fact in favor of closed-end funds is that for many investors they are the only means to invest in selected overseas markets. Emerging markets are risky; the risk of buying a few shares of a few stocks in a small developing country—with the concomitant difficulties of settlement, taxes, and so on—makes investing in such markets unattractive to many. But if a closed-end investment company focuses on such a market, the small investor can use the professionally managed fund as a means of acquiring a diversified portfolio of stock in an emerging market. Closed-end funds are the only means whereby investors can have a diversified stake in markets such as Russia, Turkey, Czechoslovakia, Mexico, and a variety of other small and emerging markets.

But the discount puzzle is a bane to many closed-end investors who, although favorable to the idea of buying shares below NAV, now are unhappy with shares that remain priced below NAV. Or they made the mistake of buying a closed-end fund IPO, after which the fund's price dipped below the IPO price in the secondary market and remained at a discount below NAV. Investors have become smarter about not buying into a closed-end IPO. From 101 closed-end IPOs in 1992 and 121 in 1993, new closed-end IPOs have fallen to 41 in 1994 and 5 each in 1995, 1996, and 1997. The equity closed-end fund IPO in 1997 for the Dessauer Global Equity Fund contained a new twist: a feature that will convert it automatically to an open-end fund should its price trade at a discount to NAV of 5 percent or more for fifteen consecutive days, unless 80 percent of its shareholders vote to maintain its closed-end status.[3] Other closed-end investment funds, in an effort to placate shareholders who are unhappy with their shares selling at a discount, have taken a cue from their corporate counterparts and have initiated stock-buyback programs in an attempt to reduce their share's discount.[4]

---

[2]Studies throughout the years include Charles Lee, Andrei Shleifer, and Richard Thaler, "Investor Sentiment and the Closed-End Fund Puzzle," *Journal of Finance* 46, no. 1 (March 1991): 76–110; and Michael Barclay, Clifford Holderness, and Jeffrey Pontiff, "Private Benefits from Block Ownership and Discounts on Closed-End Funds," *Journal of Financial Economics* 33, no. 3 (June 1993): 263–292. For a discussion of bond funds, see Malcolm Richards, Donald Fraser, and John Groth, "The Attractions of Closed-End Bond Funds," *Journal of Portfolio Management* 8, no. 2 (Winter 1982): 56–61. For a discussion of performance and opportunities in closed-end funds, see Thomas J. Herzfeld, "Battered Beauties?" *Barron's,* August 13, 1990; Thomas J. Herzfeld, "Finding Value in Closed-End Funds," *Investment Advisor,* July, 1990.

[3]Alok K. Jha, "Year's Sole Closed-End Stock Fund Has Automatic 'Open End' Trigger," *Wall Street Journal,* July 3, 1997, page R16.

[4]Kathryn Haines, "Closed-End Funds Are Taking Steps to Address Their Discount Problems," *Wall Street Journal,* September 26, 1996, B10I.

Figure 21.2 *Herzfeld Closed-End Average*

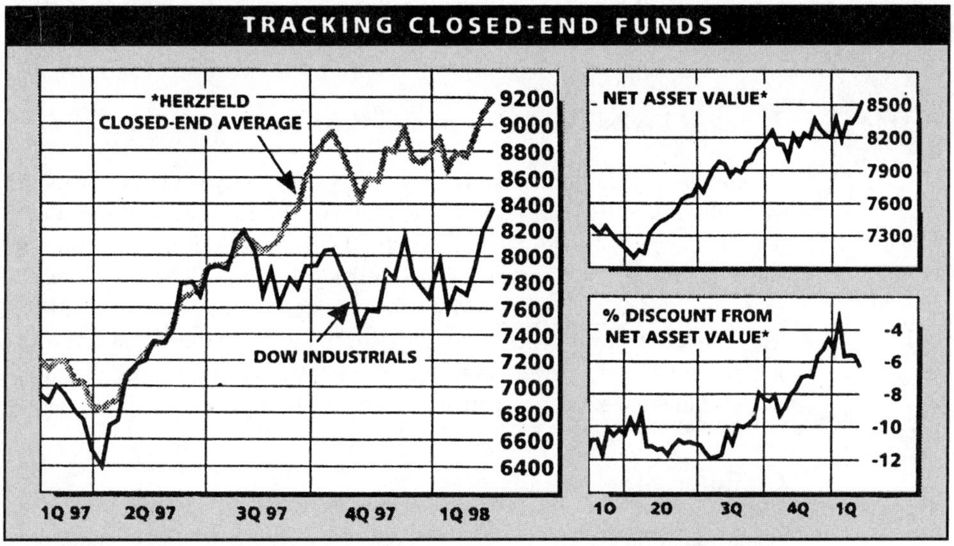

TRACKING CLOSED-END FUNDS

Closed-End Fund Index

The interest in closed-end funds has led a firm that specializes in these funds (Thomas J. Herzfeld Advisors) to create an index that tracks the market price performance of seventeen U.S. closed-end funds that invest principally in U.S. equities. This price-weighted index is based on the fund's secondary market prices rather than their NAVs. In addition to its market price index, Herzfeld also computes the average discount from NAV. The graph in Figure 21.2, which is updated weekly in *Barron's,* indicates that the average discount from NAV changes over time and these changes have major effects on the market performance of the index. As an example, during the third quarter of 1997 the average discount started to rise from a low of 12 percent. As a result, the performance of the Herzfeld closed-end average was good during a period when the DJIA was relatively flat.

Open-End Investment Companies

Open-end investment companies are funds that continue to sell and repurchase shares after their initial public offerings. They stand ready to sell additional shares of the fund at the NAV, with or without a sales charge, or to buy back (redeem) shares of the fund at the NAV, with or without a redemption fee. As of 1997, investments in mutual fund accounts totaled more than $3.5 trillion dollars. More than 30 percent of U.S. households own mutual funds. Including money market funds, investors choose among 7,600 mutual funds.

As we shall soon examine, not all the money placed in a mutual fund is invested and earns returns. The fact is, some of the funds are used to pay expenses of marketing the funds, hiring investment advisers, and paying commissions. One of the mutual fund investor's best aids to understanding these costs is the fund's prospectus. Before committing funds, an investor must receive, by law, a copy of the fund's prospectus. A **prospectus**

provides information about the fund, including the fund's objectives, historical and forecast expenses, historical returns, investment strategy, risks, information about how to buy and sell fund shares, and when dividends and capital gains are distributed to fund shareholders.

Types of Investment Companies Based on Portfolio Objectives

We classify mutual funds in a variety of ways. One way is to classify them by their investment objectives. Figure 21.3 is a list of mutual fund categories used by the *Wall Street Journal*. It lists four broad categories: stock funds, taxable bond funds, municipal bond funds, and funds that invest in both stocks and bonds. The *Wall Street Journal* records money market mutual funds in a separate listing, so they are not mentioned in Figure 21.3. These asset categories include a variety of funds, from those that invest in the broad asset market to those that invest in narrow segments, and from those that invest aggressively to those that have a conservative focus. Let's briefly review the variety of funds.

Common Stock Funds

Some funds invest almost solely in common stocks, whereas others invest in preferred stocks and bonds. Within the category of common stock funds, you find wide differences in emphasis, including funds that focus on growth companies, small-cap stocks, companies in specific industries or sectors (for example, Chemical Fund, Oceanography Fund) or even geographic areas (such as the Northeast Fund). International equity funds invest only in non-U.S. securities; global equity funds invest worldwide, both in U.S. and non-U.S. stocks. Conservative equity funds have equity income as their primary objective; more aggressive funds include some of the sector funds, small company funds, and those whose main objective is capital appreciation. Index funds also are available, in which the manager tries to replicate the performance over time of a stock market index, such as the S&P 500.

Taxable Bond Funds

Bond funds generally seek to generate current income with minimal risk, although several aggressive bond funds exist. Investors can choose funds that invest in a certain segment of the yield curve (short-term, intermediate-term, or long-term maturities), in different sectors (governments, corporates, mortgage-backed, or high yield), and in funds that focus on domestic or global securities. Management strategies of these funds can range from buy and hold to extensive trading of the bonds in the portfolio in an attempt to earn high total returns (income plus capital gains). Index funds also are available, in which the manager tries to replicate the performance over time of a bond-market index, such as the Salomon Brothers Broad Investment Grade (BIG) bond index.

Municipal Bond Funds

A change in the tax law in 1976 caused the creation of numerous municipal bond funds. These funds provide investors with monthly interest payments that are exempt from federal income taxes, although some of the interest may be subject to state and local taxes. To avoid the state tax, some municipal bond funds concentrate on bonds from specific states, such as the New York Municipal Bond Fund, which allows New York residents to avoid most state taxes on the interest income. As with taxable bonds, investors can find funds that concentrate on short-, intermediate-, or long-term bonds.

Figure 21.3 *Mutual Fund Objectives*

MUTUAL FUND OBJECTIVES

Categories compiled by The Wall Street Journal, based on classifications by Lipper Analytical Services Inc.

STOCK FUNDS

Capital Appreciation (CP): Seeks rapid capital growth, often through high portfolio turnover.
Growth (GR): Invests in companies expecting higher than average revenue and earnings growth.
Growth & Income (GI): Pursues both price and dividend growth. Category includes S&P 500 Index funds.
Equity Income (EI): Tends to favor stock with the highest dividends.
Small Cap (SC): Stocks of lesser-known, small companies.
MidCap (MC): Shares of middle-sized companies.
Sector (SE): Environmental; Financial Services; Real Estate; Specialty & Miscellaneous.
Global Stock (GL): Includes small cap global. Can invest in U.S.
International Stock (IL) (non-U.S.): Canadian; International; International Small Cap.
European Region (EU): European markets or operations concentrated in Europe.
Latin America (LT): Markets or operations concentrated in Latin America.
Pacific Region (PR): Japanese; Pacific Ex-Japan; Pacific Region; China Region.
Emerging Markets (EM): Emerging market equity securities (based on economic measures such as a country's GNP per capita).
Science & Technology (TK): Science, technology and telecommunications stocks.
Health & Biotechnology (HB): Health care, medicine and biotechnology.
Natural Resources (NR): Natural resources stocks.
Gold (AU): Gold mines, gold-oriented mining finance houses, gold coins or bullion.
Utility (UT): Utility stocks.

TAXABLE BOND FUNDS

Short-Term (SB): Ultrashort obligation and short, short-intermediate investment grade corporate debt.
Short-Term U.S. (SG): Short-term U.S. Treasury; Short, short-intermediate U.S. government funds.
Intermediate (IB): Investment grade corporate debt of up to 10-year maturity.
Intermediate U.S. (IG): U.S. Treasury and government agency debt.
Long-Term (AB): Corporate A-rated; Corporate BBB-rated.
Long-Term U.S. (LG): U.S. Treasury; U.S. government; zero coupon.
General U.S. Taxable (GT): Can invest in different types of bonds.
High Yield Taxable (HC): High yield high-risk bonds.
Mortgage (MG): Ginnie Mae and general mortgage; Adjustable-Rate Mortgage.
World (WB): Short world multi-market; short world single-market; global income; international income; Emerging-Markets debt.

MUNICIPAL BOND FUNDS

Short-Term Muni (SM): Short, short-intermediate municipal debt; Short-intermediate term California; Single states short-intermediate municipal debt.
Intermediate Muni (IM): Intermediate-term municipal debt including single-state funds.
General Muni (GM): A variety of municipal debt.
Single-State Municipal (SS): Funds that invest in debt of individual states.
High Yield Municipal (HM): High yield low credit quality.
Insured (NM): California insured, New York insured, Florida insured, all other insured.

STOCK & BOND FUNDS

Balanced (BL): A balanced portfolio of both stocks and bonds with the primary objective of conserving principal.
Stock/Bond Blend (MP): Multi-purpose funds such as balanced target; convertible; flexible income; flexible portfolio; global flexible and income funds that invest in both stocks and bonds.

Source: *Wall Street Journal*, January 30, 1998, C18.

Stock and Bond Funds

These are known by a variety of names, such as balanced funds, blended funds, or flexible funds. Their objective is to maximize return or income by combining common stock with fixed-income securities, including government bonds, corporate bonds, convertible bonds, or preferred stock. The ratio of stocks to fixed-income securities will vary by fund, as stated in each fund's prospectus.

Money Market Funds

Money market funds first appeared during 1973 when short-term interest rates were at then-record levels. These funds attempt to provide current income, safety of principal, and liquidity by investing in a diversified portfolio of short-term securities such as Treasury bills, bank certificates of deposit, bank acceptances, and commercial paper. They

are typically no-load funds and, unlike bank CDs, impose no penalty for withdrawal at any time. They typically allow holders to write checks against their account.[5] Their NAV is a constant one dollar; any income earned is returned to the investor or is reinvested in additional shares. Notably, money invested in money market mutual funds is *not* government insured.[6] Yields on money market mutual funds generally exceed those of interest-bearing bank checking accounts.

Not all money market funds are alike. Although they all hope to invest investors' funds in short-term securities and to offer higher yields than those available in bank CDs, strategies differ on how to do that. The risk of money market mutual funds depends upon the securities they purchase. Some purchase mainly federal government and federal agency short-term paper; others seek higher yields (and higher risk) by investing in commercial paper issued by corporations. With an upward-sloping yield curve, a fund seeking higher yields may increase the average maturity of its securities by purchasing securities that, though still short-term, mature in several months rather than several weeks. A fund's yield depends on its risk exposure and average maturity, as well as the fund's expenses and fee absorption or waiver by the fund's parent (many new funds, in order to attract investors, will waive fees for a time in order to offer investors higher returns).

Table 21.1 lists some of the attributes of mutual fund investing and compares them with closed-end investment companies and shares of common stock. Overall, closed-end funds are like any other stock issue, except that instead of buying one share of one company, each closed-end share represents part ownership in a pool of equity or fixed-income securities. Mutual funds generally offer investors greater liquidity. They also offer a package of attributes for the individual investor: diversification, professional management, flexibility, accessibility, and investment choices.

In the past few years, two innovations arose in the mutual fund industry: life-stage funds and mutual fund "supermarkets." Rather than require investors to apply the asset allocation process discussed in Chapter 2 to select appropriate funds (or pay a financial adviser to do so), life-stage funds (sometimes called life-cycle funds or date-definite funds) offer the investor automatic asset allocation and diversification. Such funds take investors' money and allocate it among three to five mutual funds. The allocations between cash, bond, and stock funds reflect expert views of how money should be allocated across asset classes given the objectives and constraints of an "average" aggressive, growth, income, or conservative investor. Rather than focusing on investor labels, other life-stage funds allocate funds from the perspective of the "average" thirty-, forty-, fifty-, or sixty-year-old, or from the perspective of someone who wants to withdraw his or her funds ten, twenty, or thirty or more years in the future. Such funds are useful in that they can allocate assets for investors automatically. But, like "one-size-fits-all" programs, proper asset allocation depends upon a careful study of influences reviewed in Chapter 2: an investor's specific objectives and constraints. Some lifestyle funds offer higher expenses than their

---

[5]For a list of names and addresses of money market funds, write to Investment Company Institute, 1775 K St. NW, Washington, DC 20006. A service that concentrates on money market funds is *Donoghue's Money Letter,* 770 Washington St., Holliston, MA 01746.

[6]Losses could occur if overly aggressive managers invest funds in risky assets, such as derivative securities or low-rated commercial paper of an issuer that later defaulted. Known as "breaking the buck" (that is, dipping below the one-dollar NAV), mutual fund families have at times pumped money into their money market fund to cover such losses to protect their investors and the reputation of their funds. Stricter SEC regulations following a commercial paper panic in the early 1990s have helped to reduce risk in money market mutual funds. Despite this, a default in 1997 on commercial paper issued by Mercury Finance Company caused Strong Capital Management to purchase Mercury's paper from three of its money-market funds to prevent the loss on the defaulted paper from causing the funds to "break the buck." See Julie Creswel and Robert McGough, "Money-Market Funds Nearly 'Break the Buck,' " *Wall Street Journal,* February 4, 1997, C1; Charles Gasparino, "Mercury Lights Up Money-Fund Flaw," *Wall Street Journal,* February 7, 1997, C25.

Table 21.1 *Attributes of Investment Companies and Common Stock Shares*

Attributes	Mutual Fund	Closed-End Investment Company	Share of Common Stock
Liquidity	Yes; buy, sell from mutual fund	Perhaps; depends on secondary market liquidity; Frequently, price is less than NAV	Perhaps; depends on secondary market liquidity
Diversification	Yes; offers partial ownership in a pool of securities	Yes; offers partial ownership in a pool of securities	No
Choice of investment objectives	Yes	Yes	Yes
Professional management	Yes	Yes	No
Flexibility	Yes; exchange privileges allow investor to shift money among the "family" of funds	No	No
Accessibility	Frequently via telephone, otherwise via a broker; some offer check-writing services, automatic deposit and withdrawal	Limited; some funds offer automatic reinvestment of dividends and capital gains	Via broker or firm's investor relations department

component parts; investors may be able to save some money by allocating investment dollars themselves among stock, bond, and cash funds. Of course, they must periodically rebalance their allocations themselves, too; such rebalancing occurs automatically in a life-stage fund.

Fund "supermarkets" are somewhat more controversial. Offered by firms such as Charles Schwab, Fidelity Investments, and others, the supermarket concept allows investors one-stop fund shopping. They can invest in a broad array of funds, not just the sponsoring firm's own "in-house" funds. Investors can transfer money between funds of different families without paying fees that would ordinarily occur when money is withdrawn from one fund and reinvested in another firm's funds. Such convenience comes at a price: higher fees for investors. In addition to paying regular mutual fund fees (to be described in the following section), supermarkets require the funds to pay twenty-five to forty cents for every \$100 (or 0.25–0.40 percent) invested through the supermarket; some require an additional up-front fee when a new fund joins the supermarket.[7]

MUTUAL FUND COSTS

Mutual funds offer liquidity, diversification, and professional management to the small investor. But such services are not free! This section discusses some of the expenses associated with mutual fund investing.

Load versus No-Load Open-End Funds Some open-end funds charge a load, or commission, when an investor buys the fund. The stated purpose of the load is to pay a commission to the financial planner or broker selling the fund. The offering price for a share of a load fund equals the NAV of the share plus a sales charge, which can be

---

[7]Ellen E. Schultz and Vanessa O'Connell, "No Free Lunch: 'Supermarket' Fees Lift Costs," *Wall Street Journal*, September 18, 1996, C1, C25; David Whitford, "The Mutual Fund Revolution: Is It Good for You?," *Fortune*, February 3, 1997, pp. 136–140.

as high as 8.5 percent of the NAV. If a fund had an 8 percent sales charge (**load**), an individual who invested $1,000 would receive shares that are worth $920. Such funds generally charge no redemption fee, which means the shares can be redeemed at their NAV. These funds are typically quoted with an NAV and an offering price. The NAV price is the redemption (bid) price, and the offering price equals the NAV divided by 1.0 minus the load percentage. As an example, if the NAV of a load fund with an 8 percent load is $8.50 a share, the offering price would be $9.24 ($8.50/0.92). The seventy-four-cent differential is really 8.7 percent of the NAV. The load percentage typically declines with the size of the order.

A **no-load fund** imposes no initial sales charge, so it sells shares at their NAV. Some of these funds may charge a small redemption fee of about one-half of 1 percent. In the *Wall Street Journal,* quotes for these no-load funds list bid prices as the NAV with the designation "NL" (no-load) for the offering price.

Between the full-load fund and the pure no-load fund, you can find several important variations. The first is the **low-load fund**, which imposes a front-end sales charge when you buy the fund, typically in the 3 percent range rather than in the 7 to 8 percent range. Generally, low-load funds are bond funds or equity funds offered by management companies that also offer no-load funds. Competitive pressure has led some funds that previously charged full loads to reduce their loads.

Other Marketing Expenses: 12b-1 Fees, Rear-End Loads   A second cost that mutual fund investors should be aware of is 12b-1 fees, named after the 1980 SEC rule that permits it. This plan permits funds to deduct as much as 0.75 percent of average net assets *per year* to cover distribution costs, such as advertising, commissions paid to brokers, and general marketing expenses.[8] Thus, rather than have investors pay an up-front load, 12b-1 fees allow a fund to collect money to pay marketing expenses over time. A growing number of no-load funds are adopting these plans, as are a few low-load funds. You can determine if a fund has a 12b-1 plan by reading the prospectus, by using an investment service that reports charges in substantial detail, or look to see if the fund's listing in the *Wall Street Journal* has a "p" following the fund's name.

Finally, some funds have instituted **contingent deferred sales loads**, also called redemption charges or "rear-end loads." Rather than charge an initial commission, this charge requires that investors pay when they sell or redeem their shares. Often these sales charges are steep—7 percent—if shares are sold within a year of their purchase, but the charges decline over time, usually at a rate of one percentage point a year. Thus, an investor who holds the shares for a long period of time may pay no rear-end load. Funds with such deferred sales charges have an "r" following the fund's name in its listing in the *Wall Street Journal.* Funds with both 12b-1 fees and rear-end loads have a "t" following their name.

It is important to note that none of these sales charges—loads, 12b-1 fees, or contingent deferred sales charges—relate to fund performance. These charges do not reward the fund's management for superior investment performance. Their sole purpose is to pay commissions, finance telemarketing phone banks and 800 phone numbers, fund supermarket fees, and pay for advertising material (print, radio, and TV).

The details regarding a fund's charges are found in the fund's prospectus. Some no-load funds advertise the fact that their investors pay no front-end loads or redemption charges, but most no-load funds cover their marketing expenses by charging 12b-1 fees. Thus, investors often face a tradeoff when investing: pay a load (or commission) up front

[8]Under SEC rules, mutual funds can charge no more than 0.75 percent for 12b-1 fees and 0.25 percent in "service" fees, which are used to compensate brokers for maintaining records of your investments. Prior to these SEC ceilings, many funds charged up to 1.25 percent for 12b-1 fees.

and have only part of your investment invested for you, or have all your money go to work for you in a no-load fund and pay yearly 12b-1 fees.

The idea of having all your money invested up front appeals to investors. Although load funds still constitute about 60 percent of fund assets under management, investments of no-load fund shares have been rising while purchases of load fund shares have fallen over time.

As a marketing tool, some load mutual funds offer investors a choice regarding how commissions and marketing expenses can be paid; they offer investors the choice of "A," "B," or "C" fund shares. "A" shares pay the usual front-end load charge. "B" shares do not have an initial load, but have an annual 12b-1 charge and a contingent deferred sales charge should shareholders sell their shares after only a few years. After a specified number of years, during which the equivalent of the front-end load fee has been paid, the "B" shares convert into "A" shares, which means that the 12b-1 fee and the redemption charge are canceled. "C" shares have no front-end or redemption charge, but they do have a 12b-1 fee which is never canceled.

Merrill Lynch's Class D shares have front-end loads and a modest 12b-1 fee of 0.25 percent. Fidelity offers Class I shares; they have no loads or 12b-1 fees, but an investor will be charged an annual fee of at least 0.50 percent of his assets by his broker or financial adviser. A new share class that is under consideration by the SEC is the installment load. An installment load is similar to a front-end load that is paid in installments over time. The size of the charge is a fixed percentage, say 5 percent, of the investor's investment in the fund. But rather than paying the load up-front and reducing the net investment, the installment load would be paid over a set number of years.[9]

Sophisticated investors will compare the impact of front-end loads versus 12b-1 fees over their investment horizon to determine which is the less expensive alternative. Typically, investors who anticipate redeeming their investment in the near future are better off with a 12b-1 fee. Due to the cumulative nature of 12b-1 fees, long-term investors who plan on buying a fund's shares and holding them into the foreseeable future may be better off paying only an up-front load. The installment load, if approved by the SEC, may be an attractive choice to many who have been paying front-end loads. Some investors clarify the confusing array of choices by constructing a spreadsheet that incorporates average returns, loads, and all fees over the investor's assumed time horizon to see which alternative results in the highest returns.

Fund Management Fees   The contract between the investment company and the investment management company indicates the duties and compensation of the management company. The major duties of the investment management company include investment research, the management of the portfolio, and administrative duties such as issuing securities and handling redemptions and dividends. For these management and operational duties, the management company charges an annual **management fee**. This fee is generally stated as a percentage of the total value of the fund and typically ranges from one-quarter of 1 percent to 1 percent, with a sliding scale as the size of the fund increases. For example, a fund with assets under $1 billion might charge 1 percent, whereas one with assets over $1 billion might charge 0.50 percent.

Portfolio Turnover   Another cost component from investing in mutual funds does not explicitly appear in the prospectus, but its effect is reflected in shareholder returns. Similar to any investor, the mutual fund's managers must pay commissions whenever they

---

[9]Thomas D. Lauricella, "New Mutual-Fund Share Class on the Way," *Wall Street Journal,* August 25, 1997, C21; Ellen E. Schultz, "Bewildering Class Structure Is Lurking in the Shadows of Mutual Fund Investing," *Wall Street Journal,* February 21, 1996, C1.

Table 21.2   *Annual Average Expense Ratios for Mutual Funds*

Fund Category	Asset-Weighted Expense Ratio (1997)
Value	0.80%
Growth	1.09
International/Sector	1.35
Taxable Bond	0.86
Tax-Exempt Bond	0.74

Source: Robert McGough, "Investors Acquire Taste for Cheaper Funds," *Wall Street Journal,* July 3, 1997, R1. Reprinted by permission of the Wall Street Journal, © 1997 Dow Jones & Company, Inc. All rights reserved worldwide.

purchase or sell securities for the fund. In the prospectus, mutual funds must report portfolio turnover. A portfolio turnover of 100 percent implies that, on average, the securities owned by the mutual fund "turned over" once, or were bought and sold once during the year. Another way to view this is that a turnover of 100 percent implies that all the securities owned in January were sold and replaced by another set of securities by December. It is possible to see a prospectus reporting portfolio turnover rates of 150 percent, 200 percent, or higher. Because commissions are paid with every stock or bond purchase and sale, higher turnover rates result in higher brokerage commission, and, all else equal, lower returns to the investor. A fund's turnover rates are higher when the purpose of the fund is to aggressively seek capital gains, when the financial markets are particularly volatile, or when the fund experiences unusually high cash inflows and outflows from sales and redemptions of mutual fund shares.

Expense Ratios   Operating expenses are paid out of each fund's assets and therefore lower the fund's returns to shareholders. Expenses include management fees, 12b-1 fees, costs of record keeping, accounting, processing shareholder transactions, transaction costs of trading the fund's securities, legal and audit fees. Fund investors should always review a fund's expense ratio, which represents the fund's annual expenses expressed as a percentage of the fund's assets. Later in this chapter, we will review evidence that funds with low expense ratios, on average, earn higher shareholder returns than high-expense-ratio funds.

A fund's expense ratios will depend on the fund's objectives and management philosophy. All else equal, a passively managed index fund has a lower expense ratio than an actively managed fund; an aggressive growth equity fund generally has a higher expense ratio than a more conservative equity income fund. Table 21.2 shows the average expense ratios for funds with different objectives. For example, an expense ratio of 1.1 percent is quite good for an international fund, would be high for an equity income fund, and about average for a growth fund.

SOURCES OF INFORMATION ABOUT MUTUAL FUNDS

Because a wide variety of types of funds are available, you should examine the performance of various funds over time to derive some understanding of their goals and management philosophies. Daily quotations for numerous open-end funds appear in the *Wall Street Journal.* A description of what is provided is shown in Figure 21.4. The *Wall Street Journal* provides information on a fund's objective, NAV, offer price, load, expense ratio, and historical returns ranked on a five-point scale.

A comprehensive weekly list of quotations with data on dividend income and capital gain for the previous twelve months is carried in *Barron's.* In addition, *Barron's* publishes quarterly updates on the performance of various funds during the previous ten years. As

Figure 21.4 *Description of Daily Mutual Fund Quotations in the* Wall Street Journal

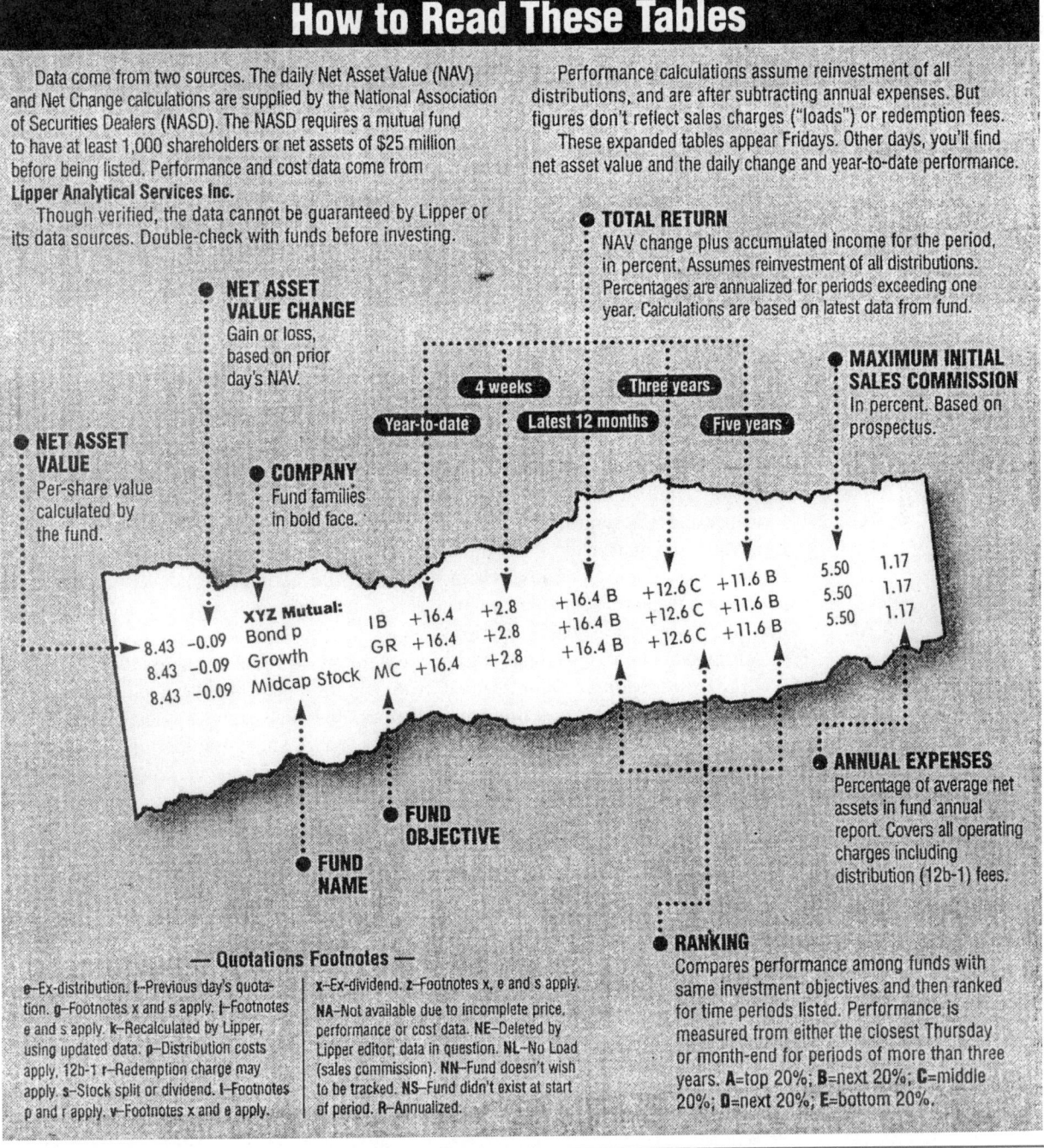

Source: "Mutual Fund Quotations," *Wall Street Journal,* January 30, 1998, C18.

shown earlier in Figure 21.1, *Barron's* lists closed-end stock and bond funds with their current net asset values, current market quotes, and the percentage of difference between the two figures.

A major source of comprehensive historical information is an annual publication issued by Arthur Wiesenberger Services entitled *Investment Companies.* This book

contains statistics for more than six hundred mutual funds arranged alphabetically. It describes each major fund, including a brief history, investment objectives and portfolio analysis, statistical history, special services available, personnel, advisers and distributors, sales charges, and a chart of the value of a hypothetical $10,000 investment over ten years. Figure 21.5 shows a sample page for the Fidelity Growth and Income fund. The Wiesenberger book also contains a summary list with annual rates of return and price volatility measures for a number of additional funds.

Wiesenberger has two other services. Every three months the firm publishes *Management Results,* which updates the long-term performance of more than four hundred mutual funds, arranged alphabetically and grouped by investment objective. The firm's monthly publication, *Current Performance and Dividend Record,* reports the dividend and short-run performance of more than four hundred funds.

Another source of analytical historical information on funds is *Forbes.* This biweekly financial publication typically discusses individual companies and their investment potential. In addition, the magazine's August issue contains an annual survey of mutual funds. A sample page in Figure 21.6 demonstrates the survey reports on annual average ten-year returns and past-three-year returns. The survey also provides information regarding each fund's sales charge and its annual expense ratio.

Business Week publishes a "Mutual Fund Scoreboard." Figure 21.7 contains a sample of this scoreboard. The magazine publishes a comparable one for closed-end, fixed-income funds and equity funds. Besides information on performance (both risk-adjusted performance and total return), sales charges (including those for 12b-1 plans), expenses, portfolio yield and maturity, an accompanying table contains telephone numbers for all the funds. The *Business Week* stock listings contain information on funds' after-tax returns, ten-year trend analysis, and investment style (for example, growth versus value, small capitalization versus large capitalization).

Morningstar provides a number of services for mutual fund investors. Its basic service is *Morningstar Mutual Funds,* which evaluates the performance of more than 1,300 open-end mutual funds and provides an informative one-page sheet on each fund. An example sheet for a fund is shown in Figure 21.8. This sheet provides up-to-date information on the fund's objective and its risk-adjusted performance relative to the risk-adjusted performance of all other funds in the same class or investment style. There is also an analysis of performance and a discussion of the fund's investment strategy based on an interview with the fund manager.

In addition, the firm publishes an annual source book that provides a year-end profile of 2,400 open-end funds, a source book for 370 closed-end funds, a monthly performance report (similar to the stock guide) on 2,500 mutual funds, and an annual reference publication of the elite 500 open- and closed-end funds.

The most recent new service for mutual funds is "The Value Line Mutual Fund Survey." The service, which is modeled after Value Line's well-regarded company analysis service, covers 2,000 funds—1,500 established funds and 500 newer, smaller funds. Each fund survey contains performance data, portfolio data, and tax data. Notably, the report considers what happened during the latest bull and bear markets.

PERFORMANCE OF INVESTMENT COMPANIES

Studies have examined the historical performance of mutual funds because these funds reflect the performance of professional money managers and data on the funds are available for a long period. The basic result of these studies parallels what we discovered in the efficient capital markets chapter: It is difficult for mutual funds to outperform their

Figure 21.5 Sample Page from Investment Companies

Fidelity Growth & Income (FGRIX)
Family: Fidelity Investment

	Category	Data As of
	Growth and Current Income	12/31/1996

Total Returns	NAV	Load Adj.
Year-To-Date	20.02%	-
1 Month	-0.99%	-
3 Month	6.93%	-
1 Year	20.02%	20.02%
3 Year Avg	18.45%	18.45%
5 Year Avg	17.24%	17.24%
10 Year Avg	17.31%	17.31%
15 Year Avg	-	-
20 Year Avg	-	-
Since Inception	18.81%	18.79%

Growth of $10,000 (Ending Value = $66,611)

Yearly Total Returns (NAV)

Year	Return
1996	20.02%
1995	35.38%
1994	2.27%
1993	19.53%
1992	11.54%
1991	41.84%
1990	-6.80%
1989	29.60%
1988	22.98%
1987	5.77%

Top Equity Holdings of 07/1996 / % of Equity Holdings

Holding	%
PHILIP MORRIS COS INC	4.26%
GENERAL ELEC CO	3.73%
ROYAL DUTCH PETE CO	2.24%
BRITISH PETE PLC	2.23%
AMERICAN EXPRESS CO	2.20%
FEDERAL NATL MTG ASSN	2.16%
BRISTOL MYERS SQUIBB CO	1.53%
TYCO INTL LTD	1.47%
LOCKHEED MARTIN CORP	1.35%
STUDENT LN MARKETING ASSN	1.32%

MPT Statistics

	3 Yr.	5 Yr.	10 Yr.
Std Dev	8.62	7.65	14.02
Alpha(%)	0.86	3.84	2.73
Beta	0.87	0.81	0.90
R Sq(%)	94	83	92
Sharpe	1.55	1.68	0.83
Treynor	1.21	1.25	1.02

Portfolio Composition 12/1996

■ Stocks	92.8%
☐ Bonds	1.0%
■ Preferreds	0.0%
▨ Convertibles	0.7%
▧ Cash	5.5%

Sector Weighting 07/1996

Sector	%
Basic Industries	4.4%
Cap. Goods & Tech.	21.4%
Consumer Cyclicals	14.3%
Consumer Non-Cyclical	28.4%
Energy	8.4%
Finance	15.1%
Transportation	1.2%
Utilities	4.3%
Miscellaneous	2.3%

Tot. Rtn. % w/in Category

1 Year	275/536 = 51%
3 Year	80/366 = 22%
5 Year	19/225 = 9%
10 Year	1/143 = 1%
15 Year	

Fund Description

The Fund seeks high total return through a combination of current income and capital appreciation. The Fund invests mainly in equity securities of companies that pay current dividends and offer potential growth of earnings.

Operations

NAV:	$30.73
Inception:	12/30/1985
Net Assets (12/31/1996):	$23896.5 Mil
Phone:	(800) 544-8888
Mgr1 (01/14/1993):	Steve Kaye
Mgr2 (N/A):	
Closed?	N
Turnover (09/30/1996):	41%

CUSIP:	316389204
Min Initial Inv:	$2500
Min Sub Inv:	$250
Min IRA:	$500
CDA Rating:	16
30-Day Dist Rate:	1.82%
Last Inc Div (12/20/1996):	$0.140
Last Cap Gain (12/20/1996):	$0.120

Fees & Expenses

Total Expense Ratio:	0.74%
12b1 Fee:	0.00%
Max Front End Sales Charge:	0.00%
Max Deferred Sales Charge:	0.00%

Source: Courtesy of Wiesenberger Investment Companies Service, *Investment Companies Yearbook 1997*, p. 79.

Figure 21.6 *Sample Fund Rating Page from* Forbes

▲▼ FUND SURVEY

Stock funds

We rate stock funds through four up-and-down market cycles; to be graded, a fund must have been in existence for at least three full cycles, or since May 31, 1990. You should pay as much attention to the cost of owning a fund as to its past performance. The variations in the cost column are as wide as those in the results column. The Vanguard Index 500 portfolio is hard to beat in efficien-cy, with an annual cost burden of only 20 cents per $100 of assets. At the other end of the spectrum is Van Kampen American Capital Real Estate Securities, with a cost of $2.60. It is not entirely a coincidence that the index fund is hard to beat in performance, too. Only 67 of the 789 U.S. stock funds shown here have beaten it over the past three years.

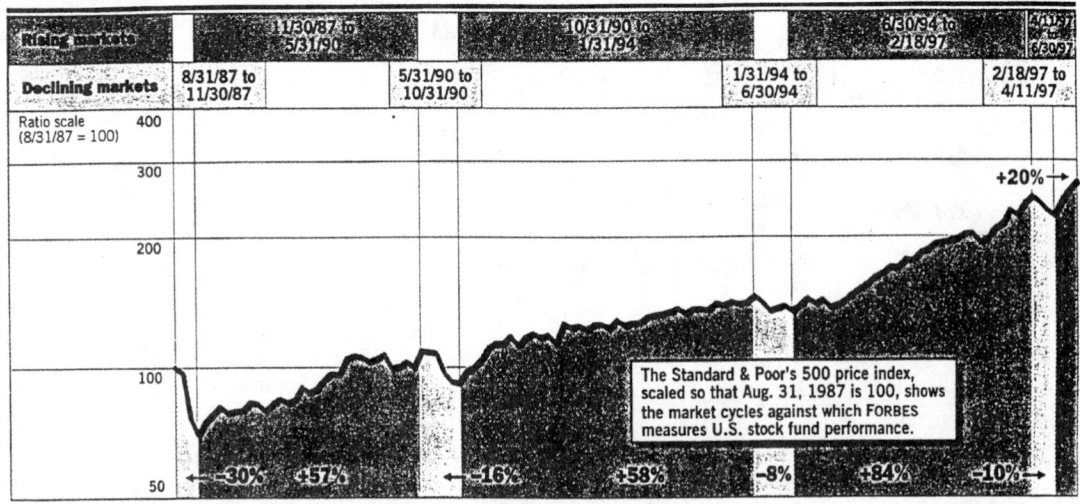

MARKET PERFORMANCE Up ▲ Down ▼		Fund/distributor	Annualized total return 8/31/87 to 6/30/97	3-year	$10,000 grew to (aftertax)[1]	Assets 6/30/97 ($mil)	Weighted average P/E	Median market cap ($bil)	Maximum sales charge	Annual expenses per $100
		STANDARD & POOR'S 500 STOCK AVERAGE	**13.8%**	**28.7%**						
		FORBES STOCK FUND COMPOSITE	**12.5%**	**22.9%**			**21.9**	**$12.5**		**$1.16**
D ■ B		AAL Capital Growth Fund-A/AAL	—*	25.5%	$18,925	$2,028	26.5	$19.4	4.00%	$1.06
		AAL Mid Cap Stock-A/AAL	—*	25.1	18,657	539	27.8	2.3	4.00	1.35
		AAL Utilities Fund-A/AAL	—*	12.9	13,923	144	15.8	14.2	4.00	1.15
B	D	AARP Growth–Capital Growth/Scudder	12.6%	25.7	19,075	1,095	20.1	24.1	none	0.90
D	A	AARP Growth–Growth & Income/Scudder	13.6	25.2	18,611	5,899	15.4	14.0	none	0.69
		Accessor Growth Fund/Bennington	—*	28.6	20,124	84	19.7	24.0	none	0.91
		Accessor Small to Mid Cap/Bennington	—*	24.5	18,153	126	18.9	1.8	none	1.12
		Accessor Value & Income/Bennington	—*	25.3	18,501	65	15.3	22.7	none	1.06
A	C	Acorn Fund/Acorn	14.2	18.6	15,571	3,221	27.5	0.5	none	0.57
C	C	Addison Capital Shares/Janney	11.9	26.3	18,667	67	16.0	6.1	none	1.87
C	C	Advantus Horizon Fund-A/Mimlic	11.3	23.3	17,202	50	25.7	22.5	5.00	1.44
C	B	AIM Advisor–Equity Portfolio-A[2]/AIM	12.4	24.2	18,339	161	18.1	27.3	5.50	1.56

Three-year return 6/30/94 through 6/30/97. ■ Fund rated for three periods only; maximum allowable grade A. *Fund not in operation or did not meet asset minimum for full period. [1]Hypothetical three-year return for upper-middle-income investor after federal tax on distributions; no deduction for load or for tax on unrealized gains. [2]Formerly Invesco Advisor–Equity.
Sources: Forbes; Lipper Analytical Services; Morningstar, Inc.

Rules, page 162. Distributor table, page 257.

Figure 21.7 Mutual Fund Scoreboard

FUND	OVERALL RATING (COMPARES RISK-ADJUSTED PERFORMANCE OF EACH FUND AGAINST ALL FUNDS)	CATEGORY (COMPARES RISK-ADJUSTED PERFORMANCE OF FUND WITHIN CATEGORY)	RATING	SIZE ASSETS $MIL	% CHG. 1996-97	FEES SALES CHARGE (%)	EXPENSE RATIO (%)	1997 RETURNS (%) PRE-TAX	1997 RETURNS (%) AFTER-TAX	1997 RETURNS (%) YIELD
AARP BALANCED STOCK & BOND		Domestic Hybrid		635.7	43	No load	0.88	21.9	19.5	3.3
AARP CAPITAL GROWTH	C–	Large-cap Blend	D	1174.7	34	No load	0.90	35.1	32.8	0.6
AARP GROWTH & INCOME	A	Large-cap Blend	A	6404.6	39	No load	0.69	31.0	27.9	2.0
ACORN	C	Small-cap Blend	B	3618.5	27	No load	0.57	25.0	22.4	0.9
ACORN INTERNATIONAL	C	Foreign	B+	1690.1	–5	No load	1.17	0.2	–1.3	2.0
ACORN USA		Small-cap Blend		176.0	234	No load	1.79	32.3	31.6	0.0
AIM ADVISOR FLEX C (a)	B+	Domestic Hybrid	B+	602.8	23	1.00**	2.26†	23.6	22.4	1.4
AIM ADVISOR LARGE CAP VALUE C (b)	B	Large-cap Blend	C	172.1	25	1.00**	2.26†	30.7	27.8	0.0
AIM ADVISOR MULTIFLEX C (c)		Mid-cap Value		376.8	41	1.00**	2.45†	18.5	16.1	0.7
AIM AGGRESSIVE GROWTH	D	Small-cap Growth	B	3679.9	35	5.50‡	1.10†	12.2	11.4	0.0
AIM BALANCED A	B	Domestic Hybrid	C	683.8	105	4.75	1.15†	24.4	22.6	2.1
AIM BLUE CHIP A	C	Large-cap Growth	B+	569.9	261	5.50	1.26†	31.9	31.3	0.2
AIM CAPITAL DEVELOPMENT A		Small-cap Growth		590.4	86	5.50	1.35†	23.7	23.7	0.0
AIM CHARTER A	C	Large-cap Blend	C–	3531.6	26	5.50	1.12†	24.7	21.1	0.9
AIM CONSTELLATION A	D	Mid-cap Growth	C	13990.8	17	5.50	1.14†	12.9	11.2	0.0
AIM GLOBAL AGGRESSIVE GROWTH B		World		1198.6	29	5.00**	2.37†	3.5	3.5	0.0
AIM GLOBAL GROWTH B		World		228.2	60	5.00**	2.48†	13.3	12.6	0.0
AIM GLOBAL UTILITIES A	C	Utilities	C–	179.6	10	5.50	1.17†	23.7	22.6	2.5
AIM GROWTH B		Mid-cap Growth		356.3	27	5.00**	2.03†	18.5	15.6	0.0
AIM INTERNATIONAL EQUITY A	C–	Foreign	B	1601.7	31	5.50	1.57†	5.7	5.6	0.4
AIM SUMMIT	C–	Mid-cap Growth	B	1656.0	27	8.50	0.70	24.2	21.5	0.1
AIM VALUE B		Large-cap Blend		6828.9	40	5.00**	1.94†	23.0	19.7	0.0
AIM WEINGARTEN A	C–	Mid-cap Growth	C–	5896.7	15	5.50	1.12†	26.0	21.5	0.0
ALGER CAPITAL APPRECIATION B (d)		Large-cap Growth		215.3	38	5.00**	2.45†	20.2	18.0	0.0
ALGER GROWTH B (e)	D	Large-cap Growth	C–	283.2	–2	5.00**	2.07†	23.1	18.7	0.0
ALGER SMALL CAPITALIZATION B (f)	D	Mid-cap Growth	D	571.2	–2	5.00**	2.13†	9.2	7.8	0.0
ALLIANCE A	C	Large-cap Blend	D	1159.2	21	4.25	1.04†	36.0	26.4	0.0
ALLIANCE GROWTH & INCOME A	B	Large-cap Blend	C	821.5	40	4.25	0.97†	28.9	23.8	1.4
ALLIANCE GROWTH B	B	Large-cap Blend	C	3758.3	38	4.00**	1.99†	26.2	24.2	0.0
ALLIANCE PREMIER GROWTH B	C–	Large-cap Blend	F	910.5	124	4.00**	2.32†	31.8	29.6	0.0
ALLIANCE QUASAR B	C–	Small-cap Growth	B+	550.6	239	4.00**	2.51†	16.3	14.8	0.0
ALLIANCE REAL ESTATE INVESTMENT B		Real Estate		293.2	778	4.00**	2.44†	22.2	20.9	3.1
ALLIANCE TECHNOLOGY B		Technology		1023.2	54	4.00**	2.44†	3.8	3.6	0.0
ALLIANCE WORLDWIDE PRIVATIZATION A		Foreign		480.2	–9	4.25	1.71†	13.2	9.9	1.4
AMCAP	C	Large-cap Growth	B	4536.6	20	5.75	0.69†	30.6	26.3	0.6
AMCORE VINTAGE EQUITY	B	Large-cap Blend	C	381.6	51	No load	1.33†	30.1	27.4	0.1
AMERICAN BALANCED	B+	Domestic Hybrid	B+	5035.9	28	5.75	0.67†	21.0	17.7	3.3
AMERICAN CENT. BALANCED (g)	C	Domestic Hybrid	D	925.3	5	No load	0.99	16.9	14.3	2.0
AMERICAN CENT. EQUITY GROWTH (h)	A	Large-cap Value	B+	702.6	156	No load	0.63	36.1	31.2	1.1
AMERICAN CENT. EQUITY INCOME (i)		Mid-cap Value		287.7	54	No load	1.00	28.3	21.1	3.3
AMERICAN CENT. GLOBAL GOLD (j)	F	Precious Metals	D	225.3	–48	No load	0.62	–41.5	–42.2	1.4
AMERICAN CENT. INCOME & GROWTH (k)	A	Large-cap Value	B+	1680.1	135	No load	0.62	34.3	30.3	1.4
AMERICAN CENT. STRAT. ALLOC.: MOD. (l)		Domestic Hybrid		201.1	201	No load	1.10	15.2	13.3	2.3
AMERICAN CENT. VALUE (m)		Mid-cap Value		2342.9	51	No load	1.00	26.0	19.8	1.5
AMERICAN CENT.-20THC. GIFTRUST (n)	F	Small-cap Growth	D	2342.9	168	No load	0.98	–1.2	–2.0	0.0

*Includes redemption fee. **Includes deferred sales charge. †12(b)-1 plan in effect. ‡Not currently accepting new accounts. §Less than 0.5% of assets. NA=Not available. NM=Not meaning'ul. (a) Formerly Invesco Adv. Flex C. (b) Formerly Invesco Adv. Eq. C. (c) Formerly Invesco Adv. MultiFlex C. (d) Formerly Alger Cap. Apprec. (e) Formerly Alger Growth. (f) Formerly Alger Sm.

Source: "Mutual Fund Scoreboard," Business Week, February 2, 1998, 90, 91.

Figure 21.7 Mutual Fund Scoreboard (continued)

LARGEST HOLDING Company (% Assets)	3 YR Pretax	3 YR Aftertax	5 YR Pretax	5 YR Aftertax	10 YR Pretax	10 YR Aftertax	HISTORY Results vs. All Funds	Untaxed Gains %	P-E Ratio	Foreign %	Cash %	Turnover	Risk Level	Best QTR	Best %Ret	Worst QTR	Worst %Ret	Telephone
Xerox (2)	19.6	17.6	NA	NA	NA	NA	3	22	21	16	9	Low		NA	NA	NA	NA	800-322-2282
Compaq Computer (3)	28.6	26.3	17.3	15.3	16.7	14.7	1 3 3 1	39	23	8	5	Average	High	II 97	20.8	I 94	-8.1	800-322-2282
Xerox (3)	28.1	25.5	20.2	18.0	16.9	14.9	3 2 2 1	37	22	20	3	Low	Low	II 97	15.5	I 94	-3.3	800-322-2282
AES (3)	22.8	19.7	17.8	15.3	18.2	15.8	1 1 1 2	48	29	15	9	Low	Average	III 97	13.7	I 94	-5.5	800-922-6769
TT Tieto Cl. B (3)	9.6	8.8	13.6	13.0	NA	NA	1 4	25	27	96	12	Low	Average	IV 93	14.6	IV 94	-7.0	800-922-6769
CalEnergy (5)	NA	NA	NA	NA	NA	NA	2 3 3	19	27	NA	8	Low		NA	NA	NA	NA	800-922-6769
First Chicago NBD (2)	21.4	19.8	14.7	13.0	NA	NA	3 3 2	33	22	11	2	Low	Very low	II 97	11.5	I 94	-3.9	800-554-1156
Textron (3)	25.9	24.5	17.5	15.0	15.3	12.5	2 1 1	46	24	6	2	Low	Average	II 97	16.4	I 94	-3.0	800-554-1156
Patriot American Hospitality (1)	19.1	17.5	NA	NA	NA	NA		24	23	27	6	Average		NA	NA	NA	NA	800-554-1156
Brightpoint (1)	22.0	20.7	23.0	22.2	21.7	20.2	1 1 3	30	32	5	4	Average	High	II 97	21.2	I 97	-13.9	800-347-4246
Compaq Computer (1)	26.0	24.5	17.0	15.6	15.4	14.1	4 1 1 3 2	20	29	7	4	Average	Low	II 97	13.2	I 94	-3.8	800-347-4246
Philip Morris (2)	29.2	26.1	18.7	16.4	16.1	14.7	3 3 3 1	20	28	3	4	Average	Average	II 97	18.2	I 94	-3.4	800-347-4246
Medical Manager (1)	NA	NA	NA	NA	NA	NA		23	31	5	8	High		NA	NA	NA	NA	800-347-4246
Philip Morris (2)	26.5	23.0	16.2	13.6	16.5	14.2	2 2 3 2	31	28	7	0	High		II 97	17.6	IV 94	-3.1	800-347-4246
Dell Computer (1)	21.2	19.7	16.1	15.1	20.4	18.9	1 1 1 1	19	31	5	5	Average	Average	II 97	15.6	IV 97	-8.7	800-347-4246
Fomento Econ. Mexicana B (1)	18.6	18.6	NA	NA	NA	NA	3	14	29	63	8	Average		NA	NA	NA	NA	800-347-4246
Rohm (1)	20.5	20.0	NA	NA	NA	NA	3	17	28	68	6	Average		NA	NA	NA	NA	800-347-4246
El Paso Natural Gas (3)	21.7	20.4	12.4	10.9	NA	NA	2 4 2	28	30	34	2	Average	Average	II 97	10.5	I 94	-7.8	800-347-4246
Compuware (1)	22.8	20.5	NA	NA	NA	NA		30	30	5	8	High		IV 93	13.9	IV 97	-7.9	800-347-4246
Philips Electronics (1)	13.6	12.8	15.6	14.9	NA	NA	1 4	18	27	99	5	Average	High	II 97	17.3	II 94	-5.3	800-347-4246
Dell Computer (2)	26.3	23.2	16.2	13.6	17.3	14.9	1 1 1 3 2	37	28	4	5	High	High	NA	NA	NA	NA	800-347-4246
WorldCom (5)	23.1	20.8	NA	NA	NA	NA	3	27	25	15	10	High		II 97	16.8	II 94	-4.4	800-347-4246
Service International (1)	25.9	21.2	15.1	11.5	16.7	14.5	1 2 3 2	35	28	10	3	High	High	NA	NA	NA	NA	800-992-3863
Texas Instruments (3)	34.7	33.4	NA	NA	NA	NA	2 3	23	31	4	4	High		II 95	17.5	II 94	-6.4	800-992-3863
Texas Instruments (3)	24.2	21.5	17.8	15.3	18.1	16.3	1 1 1 3	34	29	3	2	High	High	II 95	22.8	I 97	-11.6	800-992-3863
USA Waste Services (3)	19.2	16.0	12.8	10.2	19.7	17.2	1 1 1 4	25	33	8	4	High	Very high	II 97	20.8	I 94	-3.8	800-992-3863
Republic Industries (6)	29.2	22.3	19.2	13.4	17.7	13.1	2 1 2 1	40	30	5	0	Average	High	III 97	12.4	I 94	-3.8	800-227-4618
Chase Manhattan (5)	30.2	25.5	18.4	14.6	16.1	11.7	1 2 3 1	30	23	2	3	Average	Low	II 97	17.2	I 97	-4.4	800-227-4618
CUC International (6)	25.7	24.3	20.1	18.4	20.4	18.0	1 1 1 2	33	28	8	1	Average	Average	II 97	21.3	I 94	-3.7	800-227-4618
MBNA (5)	33.3	30.6	19.5	17.5	NA	NA	2 1 1	27	29	7	5	High	High	I 96	18.7	II 94	-8.0	800-227-4618
Parker Drilling (3)	30.9	25.5	18.9	14.3	NA	NA	3 1	14	30	7	12	High	High	NA	NA	NA	NA	800-227-4618
Starwood Lodging Trust (5)	NA	NA	NA	NA	NA	NA		12	33	NA	3	Low		NA	NA	NA	NA	800-227-4618
Compaq Computer (7)	21.3	20.4	NA	NA	NA	NA	4	25	33	6	6	Low		NA	NA	NA	NA	800-227-4618
Deutsche Telekom (2)	13.3	10.8	NA	NA	NA	NA	3	25	20	98	3	Average		NA	NA	NA	NA	800-227-4618
Medtronic (4)	24.3	20.5	16.3	12.5	15.3	12.2	2 2 3 2	42	30	2	12	Low	Average	I 97	14.7	I 94	-3.0	800-421-4120
Warner-Lambert (3)	28.9	27.2	18.2	17.0	NA	NA	3 1	48	29	0	0	Low	Average	II 97	18.1	I 94	-3.2	800-438-6375
Alcoa (2)	20.3	17.1	14.2	11.5	13.6	10.8	3 2 3 3	22	33	7	16	Average	Very low	II 97	10.0	I 94	-4.5	800-421-4120
Tyco Intl. (4)	16.9	13.8	11.4	9.1	NA	NA	3 4 3	25	28	7	5	High	Average	II 97	12.3	I 97	-2.6	800-345-2021
Ford Motor (4)	32.6	28.2	21.0	17.7	NA	NA	2 1	23	22	1	1	High	Low	II 97	15.3	I 94	-4.6	800-345-2021
Giant Food Cl. A (5)	27.0	21.8	NA	NA	NA	NA	1	20	21	1	2	High		NA	NA	I 97	-3.7	800-345-2021
Barrick Gold (15)	-14.7	-15.5	-1.3	-1.9	NA	NA	4 1 4	-35	33	70	2	Average	Very high	II 93	34.3	IV 97	-31.4	800-345-2021
Merck (3)	31.7	28.2	20.4	17.6	NA	NA	2 1 1	23	22	4	1	Average	Low	II 97	15.7	I 94	-4.5	800-345-2021
Merrill Lynch (2)	NA	NA	NA	NA	NA	NA		7	28	33	2	High		NA	NA	NA	NA	800-345-2021
Giant Food Cl. A (5)	27.6	22.9	NA	NA	NA	NA	1	21		1	2	High		NA	NA	NA	NA	800-345-2021
Jabil Circuit (3)	13.1	11.4	16.6	14.4	20.6	18.5	1 1 1 1	21	37	9	11	High	Very high	III 97	21.2	I 97	-20.8	800-345-2021

Cap. (g) Formerly 20th Cent. Balanced. (h) Formerly 20th Cent. Eq. Growth. (i) Formerly 20th Cent. Eq.-Inc. (j) Formerly Benham Inc. & Gr. (k) Formerly Benham Global Gold. (l) Formerly 20th Cent. Strat. Alloc.: Moder. (m) Formerly 20th Cent. Value. (n) Formerly 20th Century Giftrust.

DATA: MORNINGSTAR, INC., CHICAGO, IL.

Source: "Mutual Fund Scoreboard," Business Week, February 2, 1998, 90, 91.

Figure 21.8   *Example Page from Morningstar Mutual Funds*

Vanguard Index 500

	Ticker	Load	NAV	Yield	SEC Yield	Total Assets	Mstar Category
	VFINX	None	$84.31	1.6%	1.63%	$43,927.1 mil	Large Blend

Prospectus Objective: Growth and Income

Vanguard Index Trust 500 Portfolio seeks investment results that correspond with the price and yield performance of the S&P 500 index.

The fund allocates the percentage of net assets each company receives on the basis of the stock's relative total-market value: its market price per share multiplied by the number of shares outstanding.

Shareholders are charged an annual account-maintenance fee of $10 for accounts with less than $10,000. Prior to Dec. 21, 1987, the fund was named Vanguard Index Trust. Prior to 1980, it was named First Index Investment Trust.

Historical Profile

Return	Above Avg
Risk	Average
Rating	★★★★ Above Avg

Investment Style
Equity
Average Stock %

Growth of $10,000
- Investment Value $000 of Fund
- Investment Value $000 S&P 500

▼ Manager Change
▽ Partial Manager Change
► Mgr Unknown After
◄ Mgr Unknown Before

Performance Quartile (within Category)

	1986	1987	1988	1989	1990	1991	1992	1993	1994	1995	1996	09-97	History
	24.27	24.65	27.18	33.64	31.24	39.32	40.97	43.83	42.97	57.60	69.16	84.31	NAV
	18.06	4.71	16.22	31.37	-3.33	30.22	7.42	9.89	1.18	37.45	22.86	22.82	Total Return %
	-0.62	-0.55	-0.39	-0.32	-0.21	-0.26	-0.20	-0.17	-0.14	-0.09	-0.09	-0.09	+/- S&P 500
	0.64	0.60	-0.98	-0.06	0.76	-2.25	-0.78	0.16	3.53	-0.21	1.31	0.08	+/- Wilshire Top 750
	3.69	2.42	4.56	4.33	3.54	3.87	2.96	2.83	2.69	3.02	2.29	0.83	Income Return %
	14.37	2.28	11.66	27.04	-6.86	26.35	4.46	7.06	-1.52	34.42	20.57	21.98	Capital Return %
	.35	.38	.38	.71	.54	.50	.43	.48	.19	8	72	22	Total Rtn % Rank Cat
	0.89	0.69	1.10	1.20	1.17	1.15	1.12	1.13	1.17	1.22	1.28	0.54	Income $
	2.02	0.17	0.32	0.75	0.10	0.12	0.10	0.03	0.20	0.13	0.25	0.04	Capital Gains $
	0.28	0.26	0.22	0.21	0.22	0.20	0.19	0.19	0.19	0.20	0.20	—	Expense Ratio %
	3.40	3.15	4.08	3.62	3.60	3.07	2.81	2.65	2.72	2.38	2.04	—	Income Ratio %
	29	15	10	8	23	5	4	6	1	4	4	—	Turnover Rate %
	485.1	826.3	1,055.1	1,803.8	2,173.0	4,345.3	6,517.7	8,272.7	9,356.4	17,371.8	30,331.9	43,927.1	Net Assets $mil

Portfolio Manager(s)

George U. Sauter. Since 10-87. BA'76 Dartmouth C.; MBA'80 U. of Chicago. Sauter joined Vanguard in 1987. As vice president of core management, he is responsible for the management of all Vanguard's index funds. He previously spent two years as a trust-investment officer with FNB Ohio.

Performance 08-31-97

	1st Qtr	2nd Qtr	3rd Qtr	4th Qtr	Total
1993	4.33	0.43	2.52	2.30	9.89
1994	-3.84	0.40	4.86	-0.05	1.18
1995	9.71	9.49	7.94	6.01	37.45
1996	5.36	4.44	3.05	8.35	22.86
1997	2.64	17.41	—	—	—

Trailing	Total Return%	+/- S&P 500	+/- Wil Top 750	%Rank All	%Rank Cat	Growth of $10,000
3 Mo	6.45	-0.02	-0.86	31	61	10,645
6 Mo	14.71	-0.07	-0.47	20	41	11,471
1 Yr	40.53	-0.10	0.97	6	17	14,053
3 Yr Avg	26.46	-0.10	0.46	4	8	20,222
5 Yr Avg	19.62	-0.13	0.82	11	17	24,495
10 Yr Avg	13.65	-0.23	0.17	13	18	35,958
15 Yr Avg	17.91	-0.37	0.28	9	7	118,430

Tax Analysis	Tax-Adj Return %	% Pretax Return
3 Yr Avg	25.25	95.4
5 Yr Avg	18.44	94.0
10 Yr Avg	12.30	90.1

Potential Capital Gain Exposure: 31% of assets

Risk Analysis

Time Period	Load-Adj Return %	Risk %Rank¹ All	%Rank¹ Cat	Morningstar Return	Morningstar Risk	Morningstar Risk-Adj Rating
1 Yr	40.53					
3 Yr	26.46	68	48	1.52	0.83	★★★★★
5 Yr	19.62	66	37	1.27	0.83	★★★★
10 Yr	13.65	67	49	1.27	0.91	★★★★

Average Historical Rating (141 months): 4.0★s

¹1=low, 100=high

Category Rating (3 Yr) ① ② ③ ④ ⑤   Worst — Best   Return High   Risk Average

Other Measures	Standard Index S&P 500	Best Fit Index S&P 500
Alpha	-0.1	-0.1
Beta	1.00	1.00
R-Squared	100	100
Standard Deviation	14.08	
Mean	24.33	
Sharpe Ratio	1.71	

Analysis by Kevin McDevitt 09-12-97

Vanguard Index Trust 500 Portfolio has given up ground to its smaller-cap rivals, but that doesn't diminish its long-term appeal.

After several years of outperformance, this fund's blue-chip stocks have finally slowed their advance in recent months relative to the rest of the market. Its portfolio is heavily concentrated in the giant-cap stocks that have dominated the market, but some of these issues have fallen hard in recent weeks. Top-10 holding Coca-Cola gave back 16% in August alone as investors punished the stock for its uncertain earnings. On the other hand, smaller energy and retail stocks with lower multiples recorded respectable gains. In fact, the small-cap Russell 2000 index rose 2.3% in August while this fund lost nearly 5%.

Indeed, although the fund has been almost unbeatable over the long term, there have been significant stretches when it has lagged its smaller-cap peers. In the late 1970s and early 1980s, when small-cap stocks ruled the market, the fund logged mostly subpar calendar-year returns. Currently, with a median market cap that's two thirds larger than the category average, the fund has minimal exposure to mid-caps and only a trace of small caps. Consequently, the fund is at a considerable disadvantage when these stocks rally. This also points out the fund's inadequacy as a proxy for the overall market.

However, regardless of what sector leads the market, this fund should continue to compare favorably with its large-blend peers over the long term. Its trailing returns show the power of its huge cost advantage over its average rival. Further, with no more than 15% of its assets in any one sector, its broad diversification has led to moderate volatility.

The legions of new investors that have piled into this fund shouldn't expect its top-quartile finishes to be the norm. Its benefits should persist over the long term, but there will be periods of underperformance as well.

Portfolio Analysis 08-31-97

Share Chg (07-97)000	Amount 000	Total Stocks 516 Total Fixed-Income 0	Value $000	% Net Assets
217	20,274	General Electric	1,267,135	2.88
79	7,406	Microsoft	979,014	2.23
165	15,346	Exxon	938,998	2.14
109	10,124	Intel	930,743	2.12
164	15,322	Coca-Cola	878,114	2.00
80	7,460	Merck	684,965	1.56
142	13,253	Royal Dutch Petroleum (ADR)	672,525	1.53
161	15,011	Philip Morris	654,856	1.49
66	6,138	IBM	619,183	1.41
45	4,186	Procter & Gamble	557,051	1.27
150	14,002	Wal-Mart Stores	497,073	1.13
66	6,180	Bristol-Myers Squibb	469,656	1.07
88	8,232	Johnson & Johnson	466,637	1.06
86	7,980	Pfizer	441,919	1.01
75	6,977	El duPont de Nemours	434,781	0.99
47	4,353	American International Group	410,832	0.94
108	10,042	AT&T	391,633	0.89
67	6,280	Hewlett-Packard	385,070	0.88
31	2,863	Citicorp	365,377	0.83
37	3,433	Eli Lilly	359,127	0.82
52	4,863	Mobil	353,760	0.81
2,119	4,795	Bell Atlantic	347,071	0.79
102	9,471	PepsiCo	340,946	0.78
1,735	6,142	Boeing	334,342	0.76
45	4,172	Walt Disney	320,497	0.73

Current Investment Style

Style: Value Blend Growth / Size: Large Med Small

	Stock Port Avg	Relative S&P 500 Current	Hist	Rel Cat
Price/Earnings Ratio	25.0	1.00	1.0	1.00
Price/Book Ratio	5.7	1.00	1.0	1.08
Price/Cash Flow	16.4	1.00	1.0	1.03
3 Yr Earnings Gr%	21.8	1.00	1.0	0.98
1 Yr Earnings Est%	15.2	1.00	—	0.96
Debt % Total Cap	43.3	1.00	1.0	1.03
Med Mkt Cap $mil	31,689	1.0	1.0	1.52
Foreign %	3.1		—	0.47

Special Securities % of assets 08-31-97	
○ Restricted/Illiquid Secs	0
○ Emerging-Markets Secs	0
○ Options/Futures/Warrants	No

Composition % of assets 08-31-97		Market Cap	
		Giant	55.1
Cash	1.9	Large	36.7
Stocks	98.2	Medium	8.0
Bonds	0.0	Small	0.2
Other	0.0	Micro	0.0

Sector Weightings	% of Stocks	Rel S&P	5-Year High	Low
Utilities	2.7	1.0	9	3
Energy	8.3	1.0	11	8
Financials	15.8	1.0	16	8
Ind Cycls	15.6	1.0	19	15
Cons Dur	4.0	1.0	6	3
Cons Stpls	10.6	1.0	15	10
Services	11.9	1.0	18	10
Retail	5.3	1.0	9	5
Health	10.4	1.0	13	8
Tech	14.3	1.0	14	5

Address:	Vanguard Financial Ctr. P.O. Box 2600 Valley Forge, PA 19482 800-662-7447 / 610-669-1000
Advisor:	Vanguard Core Management Group
Subadvisor:	None
Distributor:	Vanguard Group
States Available:	All plus PR,VI,GU
Report Grade:	A+
NTF Plans:	N/A

Minimum Purchase:	$3000	Add: $100	IRA: $1000
Min Auto Inv Plan:	$3000	Systematic Inv: $50	
Date of Inception:	08-31-76		
Sales Fees:	No-load		
Management Fee:	Provided at cost., at cost%A		
Actual Fees:	Mgt: 0.00%	Dist: —	
Expense Projections:	3Yr: $36	5Yr: $61	10Yr: $124
Annual Brokerage Cost:	—	Income Distrib: Quarterly	
Total Cost (relative to category):		Below Avg	

M○**RNINGSTAR** Mutual Funds   369

Source: *Morningstar Mutual Funds,* Morningstar, Inc., September 26, 1997.

benchmark indexes. Numerous studies, both in the academic and popular press, have found below-average returns on actively managed equity and bond funds.

Do a Fund's Objectives Matter?

An investor considering buying a fund needs to know whether the fund's performance is consistent with its stated objective. For example, does the performance of a balanced fund reflect less risk and lower return than an aggressive growth fund? To answer this question, several studies have examined the relationship between funds' stated objectives and their measures of risk and return.

Their results show a positive relationship between the funds' stated objectives and risk measures, with risk measures increasing as objectives become more aggressive. The studies have also found a positive relationship between return and risk.[10] Thus, it is worthwhile for investors to seek mutual funds with objectives and risk levels similar to their own risk tolerance.

Do Managers Generally Buy Low and Sell High?

As noted on several occasions, one way to achieve superior performance is through market timing wherein you invest aggressively prior to strong markets and restructure into strongly conservative portfolios prior to weak or declining markets. Can mutual fund managers do this on your behalf? Several studies have examined the ability of mutual funds to time market cycles and react accordingly. That is, can fund portfolio managers increase the relative volatility of their portfolios in anticipation of a bull market and reduce volatility prior to a bear market?

Studies have found that funds were not able to time market changes and change risk levels accordingly.[11] Kon and Jen examined the ability of mutual funds to change portfolio composition to take advantage of market cycles and the ability to select undervalued securities.[12] Although many of the funds experienced a significant change in risk during the test period, implying superior timing ability, no individual fund was able to *consistently* generate superior results.

Two studies examined the overall market forecasting and the specific stock selection ability of fund managers. Chang and Lewellen tested for market timing ability and found little market forecasting going on, or, if any was being done, it was overwhelmed by other portfolio decisions.[13] They found neither skillful market timing nor clever security selection. The authors concurred with the conclusion of prior studies that mutual funds generally did not outperform a passive investment strategy.

Henriksson considered a total period and two subperiods to test the ability of funds to enjoy consistent success.[14] The results showed little evidence of market timing ability, and the results for individual funds for the two periods were independent. They found that managers could not forecast large changes, and those who were good at stock selection appar-

[10]John D. Martin, Arthur J. Keown, Jr., and James L. Farrell, "Do Fund Objectives Affect Diversification Policies?" *Journal of Portfolio Management* 8, no. 2 (Winter 1982): 19–28.

[11]Frank J. Fabozzi and Jack C. Francis, "Mutual Fund Systematic Risk for Bull and Bear Markets," *Journal of Finance* 34, no. 5 (December 1979): 1243–1250.

[12]Stanley J. Kon and Frank C. Jen, "The Investment Performance of Mutual Funds: An Empirical Investigation of Timing, Selectivity, and Market Efficiency," *Journal of Business* 52, no. 2 (April 1979): 263–289.

[13]Eric C. Chang and Wilbur G. Lewellen, "Market Timing and Mutual Fund Investment Performance," *Journal of Business* 57, no. 1, part 1 (January 1984): 57–72.

[14]Roy D. Henriksson, "Market Timing and Mutual Fund Performance: An Empirical Investigation," *Journal of Business* 57, no. 1, part 1 (January 1984): 73–96.

ently had negative market timing ability. A study that analyzed the timing performance of nineteen mutual funds designated asset-allocation funds found no evidence that these funds demonstrated market timing abilities.[15] Also, an analysis of the total performance of these funds suggested relatively poor performance compared to the benchmark portfolio.

Can We Do Better than the Market Averages?

Some studies have found that mutual funds can outperform market averages based on the funds' *gross* returns. But once the expenses of investing and managing the fund are included, the funds' *net* returns, on average, fail to outperform broad stock-market averages for equity funds and broad bond-market averages for fixed-income funds. Numerous studies on mutual fund performance have generally agreed on the following findings: On a risk-adjusted basis, the average mutual fund underperforms the market averages; better performance is related to low expense ratios; and past performance of a mutual fund is not strongly related to future performance. Similar results have been found for international equity mutual funds and for bond mutual funds.[16]

The average equity fund has an expense ratio of 1.42 percent. S&P 500 index funds' average expense ratio is 0.45 percent (one of the lowest-expense index funds has an expense ratio of only 0.20 percent) or about one percentage point below that of the actively managed funds. This means the average equity fund has to earn gross returns one percentage point above the S&P 500 just to earn the same net return as the index fund after subtracting expenses. Studies have shown that it is difficult for active managers to do this on a risk-adjusted basis. That's why indexing of both equities and bond funds has attracted an increasing number of investors and their money. By 1997 more than 120 index funds, combined, held nearly $100 billion in assets. Vanguard's Index 500 fund, which seeks to index the performance of the S&P 500, was catching up with Fidelity's actively managed Magellan Fund as the nation's largest mutual fund.

Do Fees Matter?

As we stated earlier, fees such as the front-end load, contingent deferred sales charge, and 12b-1 fees are related to marketing expenses, not fund manager compensation. Studies have compared the risk-adjusted performance[17] of load and no-load funds and the result is clear: The average load fund offers investors no better performance than the average no-load fund.[18]

What about Expenses and Portfolio Turnover?

The level of coupon income and changes in market interest rates are the main driving forces determining the returns on bonds and bond mutual funds. Lower expenses in managing

[15]Anthony Chan and Carl R. Chen, "How Well Do Asset Allocation Mutual Fund Managers Allocate Assets?" *Journal of Portfolio Management* 18, no. 3 (Spring 1992): 81–91.

[16]Bruce N. Lehmann and David M. Modest, "Mutual Fund Performance Evaluations: A Comparison of Benchmarks and Benchmark Comparisons," *Journal of Finance* 42, no. 2 (June 1987): 233–265; Robert E. Cumby and Jack D. Glen, "Evaluating the Performance of International Mutual Funds," *Journal of Finance* 45, no. 2 (June 1990): 497–522; Warren Bailey and Joseph Lim, "Evaluating the Diversification Benefits of the New Country Funds," *Journal of Portfolio Management* 18, no. 3 (Spring 1992): 74–80; Christopher R. Blake, Edwin J. Elton, and Martin J. Gruber, "The Performance of Bond Mutual Funds," *Journal of Business* 66, no. 3 (July 1993): 371–403.

[17]The details of adjusting portfolio returns for risk differences will be discussed in Chapter 22.

[18]See, for example, Jonathan Clements, "Taking the First Step in Picking Your Fund," *Wall Street Journal*, July 22, 1991, C1, C21.

Table 21.3 *Expenses and Returns: Ten-Year Data, July 1981–1991*

	Bond Funds		Equity Funds	
	Average Expense Ratio	**Average Return**	**Average Expense Ratio**	**Average Return**
High Expense Ratio	1.21%	12.0%	1.83%	10.8%
Low Expense Ratio	0.60	12.7	0.67	13.8

Source: Jonathan Clements, "Selecting a Fund? Expenses Can Be Crucial," *Wall Street Journal,* July 24, 1991, C1, C9. Reprinted by permission of the Wall Street Journal, © 1991 Dow Jones & Company, Inc. All rights reserved worldwide.

a bond fund directly translate into higher investor return. Between July 1989 and July 1992, low-expense bond funds (those with expenses less than 0.37 percent of NAV) had an average return of 10.38 percent controlling for differences in fund objectives; the average bond fund returned 9.62 percent. High-expense-ratio bond funds (expenses exceeded 2.00 percent of NAV) averaged an 8.00 percent return; controlling for differences in fund objectives, the average bond fund returned 9.35 percent.[19]

Data for a ten-year study ending in July 1991 are reported in Table 21.3. The evidence is clear: On average, high-expense-ratio bond and equity funds have lower returns; lower-expense-ratio funds average higher returns.[20] It is interesting that the difference in average returns between high- and low-expense-ratio bond funds is almost entirely explained by the difference in their average expense ratio. The average taxable bond fund has an expense ratio of about 0.9 percent; the average diversified stock mutual fund has an expense ratio of about 1.3 percent during this period.

Mutual fund portfolio turnover affects shareholders' returns. A study of equity mutual funds over ten years found higher turnover to be associated with higher brokerage fees and lower mutual fund shareholder returns. Those funds with the lowest portfolio turnover had an average return about 0.7 percent higher than the highest turnover portfolios.[21] If high portfolio turnover is more likely for an aggressive, risk-taking mutual fund, the difference in average returns on a risk-adjusted basis is apt to be even greater.

Taxes Portfolio turnover in a mutual fund has another implication for investors; it affects their tax obligations.[22] Higher portfolio turnover leads to higher levels of realized capital gains for fund shareholders. A year-end statement from a mutual fund showing a large capital-gain distribution can wreak havoc on a carefully planned strategy that sought to minimize taxes.

A fund's prospectus will inform you of when the fund distributes its accumulated capital gains. If you buy the fund just prior to such distributions, the IRS considers the capital gains distribution a taxable event, and you will be liable for capital gains taxes on the funds you receive. For example, assume a fund distributes its realized capital gains on December 15 and you invest $1,000 to purchase fifty shares at their NAV of $20 on December 12. This

[19]Barbara Donnelly, "Bond Fund's Expense Ratios Can Spell Difference between High and Low Yields," *Wall Street Journal,* August 21, 1992, C1, C11.

[20]Jonathan Clements, "Selecting a Fund? Expenses Can Be Crucial," *The Wall Street Journal,* July 24, 1991, C1, C9. Some updated information, which replicates this analysis for the ten years ending in December 1993, finds the 25 percent of U.S. equity funds with the lowest expense ratios earned an average return of 13.4 percent a year, with the 25 percent of funds with the highest expense ratio had average annual returns of 11.5 percent. See Robert McGough, "Use Yardsticks to Weed Through Fees," *Wall Street Journal,* July 7, 1994, R8.

[21]Jonathan Clements, "Mutual Funds with Low Turnover Find Penny Saved Is Penny Earned," *Wall Street Journal,* May 17, 1990, C1, C10.

[22]This is not the case for mutual funds that are part of a tax-deferred investment plan, such as an individual retirement account (IRA) or 401(k) plan.

year's realized capital gain distribution is $2 a share. After this distribution, the NAV will be $18 a share (as $2 in value has been paid in cash to shareholders). Although you have not benefited from this $2 in realized capital gains during the past year, the IRS considers the $2 you've received as capital gains; at a 20 percent tax rate, you will now owe $2 × 50 shares × 0.20 or $20 in tax on your investment of a few days ago. After taxes, this means you've received a capital gain distribution of $100 − $20 or $80. And the market value of your investment is now only $900 ($1,000 initial investment less the $100 pre-tax capital gain distribution). Your $1,000 investment has become $980 because of mutual fund regulations and the tax laws. And more commission may need to be paid to reinvest the $80 after-tax distribution you thought you invested just a few days prior!

This aspect of portfolio turnover, combined with dividend and bond income generated by a fund's investments, can also lead to misleading mutual fund promotional material. Most mutual funds advertise (and their prospectuses report) before-tax returns. But an investor's after-tax returns may be 30–40 percent less than this, depending on their tax bracket and the quantity of income generated and realized capital gains taken by the fund's managers.[23] The "tax-efficiency" of a fund (the tax-adjusted return as a percentage of the pre-tax return of a fund) is even more important now given the tax code changes described in Chapter 2. There is a substantial difference in the top federal tax rate of 39.6 percent for ordinary income and short-term capital gains, the 20 percent rate for capital gains on investments held longer than eighteen months, and the 18 percent capital gains rate (starting in the year 2001) for assets held longer than five years. *Business Week* and *Fortune* are two publications that provide pre-tax and estimated after-tax returns on mutual fund investments.

All else equal, higher turnover funds will generate more realized capital gains and more realized short-term capital gains than lower turnover funds. Thus, if a high-turnover and a low-turnover fund have the same pre-tax return, investors in the lower turnover fund will likely have a higher after-tax return. Index funds, where active trading is discouraged and turnovers are traditionally low, will likely have higher tax-efficiency than most actively managed funds.

Strategies to increase tax efficiency   A mutual fund can implement several strategies to lower shareholders taxes. The fund can use the same tax-wise strategies that individual investors use when they manage their own investments. First, funds can identify which stocks they are selling rather than using a "first-in, first-out" method. Under first-in, first-out, if a fund owns 500,000 shares of IBM and wishes to sell 200,000 shares, the first shares purchased are assumed to be the first shares sold. The specific identification method, on the other hand, allows the fund to specify which of the 500,000 shares are sold. For tax efficiency, it will want to specify the 200,000 shares with the highest cost basis to minimize capital gains. For this reason, specific identification is sometimes called HIFO, meaning "highest-in, first-out."

Second, a fund can tax-manage its portfolio by seeking to sell stocks that have depreciated in price to offset the capital gains from appreciated shares. By combining this with HIFO, a fund's realized capital gains can be substantially reduced.

Third, if the fund's charter allows, managers can try to reduce portfolio turnover and seek to invest in lower-dividend-yielding stocks, as turnover and income from dividends lead to higher potential taxes.

Investors can examine the tax-efficiency records of funds listed in publications such as *Business Week* and *Fortune*. Reading the prospectus can provide insight into whether

---

[23]Barbara Donnelly, "Beware Tax Consequences of Mutual Funds," *Wall Street Journal,* February 20, 1992, C1, C13; Robert McGough, "Tax Bite Is Worse for Some Funds than Others," *Wall Street Journal,* April 30, 1993, C1, C16. *Business Week* and *Fortune* provide pre-tax and estimated after-tax returns on mutual funds.

tax management is important to the fund's managers. But studies have found that tax efficiency is enhanced when a fund attracts many new investors. The fastest-growing funds
often are highly tax-efficient. New money pouring in represents new shares, so the
year-end tax bill is diluted; it is spread across many new shares and shareholders. If a fund
distributes gains in December, someone buying shares in August gets a capital gains distribution that reflects year-long gains, although they have only directly participated in
the gains that have occurred since August.

Without new funds coming in, a portfolio manager may decide to sell some stock to
raise cash in order to take advantage of newly identified attractive investments. But if new
money pours into a fund, the manager need not sell investments to raise cash; she can fun-
nel the new shareholder money into the recently identified opportunities. Similarly,
rather than having to sell investments to satisfy shareholder redemptions, the manager can
satisfy the needs of investors selling fund shares by paying out the newly arriving cash
from new shareholder investments.

Investors who make asset allocation decisions that involve taxable accounts should focus
on after-tax rather than advertised pre-tax returns. Table 21.4 illustrates the importance
of tax-wise investing for taxable investors. For IRA and other tax-deferred accounts, focusing on pre-tax returns is appropriate and portfolio B is the preferred choice, as its pre-
tax expected return is 9.0 percent versus portfolio A's pre-tax expected return of
8.6 percent.

But the story changes for a taxable investment. Portfolio A's emphasis on tax-exempt
income (municipal bonds), passive investing (large-cap stock index), and capital gains
potential (international stocks, emerging market stocks, and small-cap stocks) lowers its
tax bill. Portfolio A's estimated after-tax return of 6.5 percent is preferred to B's 5.8 percent anticipated after-tax return.

With the tax code changes in 1997, tax-wise investing has become even more important. Tax-efficient mutual funds are preferable to inefficient ones and asset allocation in
taxable accounts needs to carefully incorporate after-tax returns.

Consistency of Performance

Although several studies have considered consistency along with overall performance, some
studies have concentrated on it. Dunn and Theisen examined institutional portfolios over
a ten-year period to determine what proportion of managers were consistently successful, that is, their funds' returns were frequently in the top 25 percent for their type of fund.[24]
A test of whether managers remained in the same quartile over time concluded that historical results give little help in explaining future results. The authors concluded that historical performance should be given little weight when selecting a manager.[25]

Should Mutual Fund Investors Follow the Crowd?

The studies we have reviewed here and many others show that it is difficult to identify
a mutual fund that will provide above-average, risk-adjusted returns. If individuals have
a difficult time identifying attractive funds, maybe investors as a group are smart enough
to find successful funds. What happens if we buy the types of funds others are buying,
and redeem our shares when others are selling?

[24]Patricia C. Dunn and Rolf D. Theisen, "How Consistently Do Active Managers Win?" *Journal of Portfolio Man-agement* 9, no. 4 (Summer 1983): 47–50.

[25]James S. Ang and Jess H. Chua, "Mutual Funds: Different Strokes for Different Folks?" *Journal of Portfolio Management* 8, no. 2 (Winter 1982): 43–47.

Table 21.4 *Comparing Tax Implications of Two Portfolios*	
Investor wants to allocate 40 percent in bonds, 60 percent in equities.	
Portfolio A	**Portfolio B**
40% municipal bonds	40% taxable bonds
32% index of U.S. large-cap stocks	50% actively managed U.S. stocks
12% international stocks	5% international stocks
6% emerging market stocks	5% U.S. small-cap stocks
5% U.S. small-cap growth stocks	
5% U.S. small-cap value stocks	
PRE-TAX RETURN: 8.6%	PRE-TAX RETURN: 9.0%
AFTER-TAX RETURN: 6.5%	AFTER-TAX RETURN: 5.8%

Source: "Which Is Your Portfolio?," *Fortune,* March 18, 1996, 88.

This strategy of following the crowd often leads the mutual fund investor down the wrong path. One study examined mutual fund performance between late 1986 and mid-1992.[26] During this total time period, crowd followers who bought the mutual funds that others were buying earned a 19.4 percent average return. During this same time, investors in bond funds earned 55.8 percent, stock fund investors received an average return of 70.4 percent, and money market fund investors earned a return of 42.4 percent (these returns do not include taxes or loads).

On the other hand, contrarians who bought the types of mutual funds the crowd was selling earned an average return of 74.8 percent over that $5^{1}/_{2}$ years. Similar to individual stock research, it may be more profitable to go against the crowd when selecting mutual funds.

Follow the High-Returning Fund

Future performance of a mutual fund may relate to recent performance. Thus, rather than seek funds with stunning long-term records, some studies suggest investing in funds with stunning short-term records.

One study examined the 1970 to 1992 period to see what would have happened if an investor purchased mutual funds in the top 25 percent based on previous one-year, five-year, and ten-year returns; the funds thus selected were held for a five-year period.[27] Table 21.5 reports the study's results. Funds with a top 25 percent one-year performance record had an average total return of 95.6 percent over the subsequent five years. Those funds with longer track records of success earned lower total returns over the next five years, showing average returns below those of the average equity mutual fund. The good short-term performer had a better subsequent five-year average performance than those with better longer-term records.

Good performance leads to higher inflows for cash for the winning mutual fund. Gruber finds that new money flows into recently high-performing funds and this new money earns higher returns than those earned by the average mutual fund investor.[28]

---

[26]Jonathan Clements, "Following the Herd Can Lead Investor In Mutual Funds Down the Wrong Path," *Wall Street Journal,* July 15, 1992, C1, C11.

[27]Jonathan Clements, "Word to the Wise: Buy Last Year's Hot Funds," *Wall Street Journal,* December 8, 1992, C1, C23; see also Darryll Hendricks, Jayendu Patel, and Richard Zeckhauser, "Hot Hands in Mutual Funds: Short-Run Persistence of Relative Performance, 1974–1988," *Journal of Finance* 48, no. 1, (March 1993): 93–130.

[28]Martin J. Gruber, "Another Puzzle: The Growth in Actively Managed Mutual Funds," *Journal of Finance,* July 1996, 783–810.

Table 21.5	*Following the Hot Fund*

Study period: 1970–1992; purchase the top 25 percent of funds based on past one-year, five-year, and ten-year performance.

Top 25 Percent of Past Year(s)	Average Gain, Next 5 Years	Number of Times the Average Equity Fund Had a Lower Return than a Historical Top Performer
1 year	95.6%	12 out of 19 periods
5 years	80.7	6 out of 19 periods
10 years	82.6	8 out of 19 periods
Average five-year return on a general equity fund: 84 percent.		

Why Is the Future Performance of Good Past Performers So Poor?

The results of these studies may seem counterintuitive; one would imagine a good long-term track record would be a good predictor of future success, but, on average, this is not the case. This result can be attributed to several influences and can give us information that is helpful to the prospective mutual fund investor.

One influence explaining the inferior future performance of well-performing five- and ten-year funds is that they are victims of their own success. Good returns attract investors' money; large inflows of cash are difficult to invest wisely and quickly, and thus may harm future returns. Also, continued superior performance requires the fund manager to identify additional securities with good return potential. As a result larger funds own many different securities, sometimes hundreds or thousands, each stock representing a small part of the overall portfolio. In essence, by owning so many securities, they are buying the market. Thus, their returns will tend to more closely resemble the market over time. As a result, they become a *de facto* index fund with active management fees.

Second, a fund with an attractive five- or ten-year record may have the record because of performance in one or two exceptionally good (or exceptionally lucky) years. Because occasional blips on a fund's record are no guarantee of future skill (or luck), future returns are more modest than the past record may predict.

Third, investment returns seem to run in cycles. For example, although small-capitalization stocks have higher long-run returns than large-capitalization stocks, this is *not* true over shorter timespans. Sometimes small-cap stocks outperform large-cap stocks (as in the early 1990s); sometimes larger stocks have higher returns (as was the case during most of the 1980s and the latter part of the 1990s). Thus, mutual funds focusing on large stocks did well in the 1980s; mutual funds focusing on small stocks outperformed in the early 1990s. Similarly, sometimes "growth" stocks (those with high earnings growth rates) become popular, and other times "value" stocks (those with prices apparently below their intrinsic values; typically such stocks have high dividend yields or low P/Es) outperform other stocks. This implies that mutual funds with, for example, good five-year performance records may have done well because their particular "style" of investing was in favor. Over the next five years, some other style may offer better returns. The funds with good one-year records, as seen in Table 21.5, may reflect the currently favored investment style, while those with attractive five- and ten-year records indicate styles going out of favor.

More recent academic studies have incorporated style analysis in their examination of mutual fund returns. This is important, as style cycles can lead to perceptions of over-performance merely because a certain style (small cap, large cap, growth, value) is in vogue, not because of superior manager performance. After controlling for style, Kahn

and Rudd found that above-average risk-adjusted returns did not persist for a sample of equity mutual funds over the 1983–93 time period. The average impact of trying to invest in above-median fixed income mutual funds also led to below-average performance over time.[29] Another study compared equity mutual fund performance to fund-specific benchmarks created on the basis of the size, book/market ratio, and prior-year return of the average stock held by the mutual fund. Excess returns were not large enough to compensate for the fees and expenses of active management from 1975 to 1994. No evidence was found of managers' ability to time different styles by switching into a style that was coming into favor as another one was going out of favor.[30]

Some Suggested Mutual Fund Investment Strategies

Based on what we have learned from prior chapters as well as this chapter's discussion of mutual funds, we can construct the following suggestions for investing in mutual funds.

1. Choose only those mutual funds consistent with your objectives and constraints. Remember from our Chapter 2 discussion that over the long run, only equity funds have offered positive real returns on an after-tax, after-cost basis. For taxable investment accounts, municipal bonds offer positive after-tax, after-cost real returns as well, but at a lower return level than stock funds.
2. Consider index funds for a large portion of your fund portfolio. Your index funds will never be featured as the quarter's or the year's top performer, but over longer periods of time, most actively managed funds underperform the market averages. A variety of equity, bond, and international no-load funds that seek to replicate both broad and narrow indexes are available for the small investor.
3. Whenever possible, invest in no-load funds, particularly those that do not have front-end loads, rear-end loads, and 12b-1 fees. Information sources discussed earlier can help you identify these funds. Try to find funds with below average expense ratios for their investment objective.
4. Invest at least 10 percent to 20 percent of your mutual fund portfolio in international or global funds to diversify and to participate in the high return potential of non-U.S. securities.
5. Own mutual funds in several asset classes in order to diversify and participate in the different investment cycles. For example, you may want to purchase shares in both value- and growth-oriented equity funds, in large- and small-capitalization funds, and in high-grade and low-grade bond funds.
6. If you want to actively manage your mutual fund portfolio, consider investing in the past year's "hot" funds because of investment cycle considerations.
7. Don't attempt to "time" the market by aggressively entering and exiting the stock market. Timing strategies appear to add little value, and they can increase risk considerably. During 1926 to 1993 the average annual S&P 500 return was 9.44 percent. Notably, if an investor was out of the market for the fifty best months, the average return would have been 0 percent. Missing the market's best twenty-six months would have earned the stock portfolio an average return equal to that of T-bills.
8. To help avoid market timing, use a dollar-cost average strategy of investing a set dollar amount every month. Most mutual funds have plans that accept regular deposits;

[29]R. N. Kahn and A. Rudd, "Does Historical Performance Predict Future Performance?" *Financial Analysts Journal,* Nov.–Dec. 1995, pp. 43–52.
[30]Kent Daniel, Mark Grinblatt, Sheridan Titman, and Russ Wermers, "Measuring Mutual Fund Performance with Characteristic-Based Benchmarks," *Journal of Finance,* July 1997, pp. 1035–1058.

many will assist you to make arrangements to automatically withdraw funds from a bank account.

9. Many mutual funds distribute capital gains around December; to avoid paying taxes on capital gains shortly after you've purchased a fund's shares, read the prospectus and avoid investing money shortly before the capital gains distribution dates.

10. Don't own too many funds. Diversifying holdings across too many actively managed funds leads to performance that will likely follow the indexes but at the cost of active management. Studies indicate that the diversification benefits of owning more than seven to ten funds is practically nil.[31]

When to Sell a Fund's Shares

Careful research can help identify appropriate index funds and actively managed funds to meet your needs. If, however, an investment choice sours, when should you sell a mutual fund investment and reinvest the proceeds elsewhere?

Generally, when your objectives and constraints change, it may be appropriate to rebalance or rearrange your portfolio. As people age, asset allocation gradually shifts from equities to bonds. As big bills, such as a child's college tuition, approach, funds are transferred into short-term, low-risk investments. Aside from such policy changes, the following considerations should help you determine when it may be time to sell a fund's shares.

First, two warnings. Beware of the "quick trigger," and be aware of any capital gains tax obligations based on increases in your shares' net asset value. The quick trigger occurs when disappointing short-term performance leads investors to sell their shares and switch to another fund. Most fund investing should be part of a longer-run strategy. Assuming that fund investors know that market cycles occur, reductions in fund value may reflect opportunities to purchase additional shares to prepare for the next cyclical upswing.

If you purchased the shares some time ago and are now thinking of selling, the difference between the purchase price and the selling price has tax implications. Disappointing current performance on a fund that has performed well over a longer period of time may require that you pay a large capital gains tax if you sell the shares.

With those warnings, the following are some events that may cause you to sell your shares. First, it may be time to sell when the fund's portfolio manager changes and the new manager lacks an attractive track record. Typically, when the manager of a fund leaves, the investment company will attempt to replace him or her with a manager who has successfully run another fund within the fund family. For example, when Peter Lynch departed the phenomenally successful Fidelity Magellan Fund, he was replaced by Morris Smith, who had proved himself with above-average returns at another Fidelity fund. When Morris Smith stepped down, Jeff Vinik, another successful manager of several Fidelity funds, took his place; Bob Stansky was managing several good performing Fidelity mutual funds when he replaced Jeff Vinik. Replacing a successful fund manager with an unknown may indicate that it is time to reduce or close out one's position in the fund.

As of July 1, 1993, the Securities and Exchange Commission has required mutual funds to identify their managers in their prospectus. Fund shareholders must be informed of any changes in managers. However, this requirement has a loophole: funds whose investment decisions are made by committees need not have a single manager named in the prospectus; in fact, none of the committee members need to be publicly disclosed. Of the funds it tracks, Morningstar reports that 15 percent were managed by committees in 1989; after

---

[31]Kevin J. Delaney, "Overkill: Risks of Piling on Mutual Funds," *Wall Street Journal,* September 9, 1997, C1, C29.

the SEC requirement came into effect in 1994, more than 30 percent of the funds indicated they are run by committees.[32]

Second, it may be time to sell when the fund's portfolio manager changes his or her investment style or philosophy. Changes in a fund can occur when an experienced manager appears to be straying from a past successful investment pattern. This may be a sign of a panicking manager. When a growth manager starts seeking value stocks or when a low P/E manager starts investing in stocks with average P/Es, it may be time to invest elsewhere to maintain your overall portfolio's balance.

Beware of fund managers bailing out of their investment philosophy or style because it is cyclically out of favor. Recall that small-stock mutual funds generally underperformed the overall market during the 1980s, but managers who stuck with this investment style earned sizable returns during the early 1990s.

Information sources are available for letting fund investors know of managerial style changes. The fund's quarterly report and comments from the manager, in sources such as Morningstar, are useful for determining changes in a fund's investment philosophy. The Morningstar reports are especially helpful, as Morningstar classifies a fund's equity investments as value, blend, or growth, and as favoring small-, medium-, or large-capitalization stocks. Changes in these classifications may signal it is time to consider selling a fund's shares.

Third, with Fidelity Magellan as a well-known exception (although it has had inconsistent returns in the mid-1990s), a fund that is becoming "too large" or growing "too rapidly" may have inferior future performance. Managers typically have difficulties in wisely investing continuously large cash infusions from investors. Also, large funds may start to look and act like index funds.

Fourth, it may be time to sell a fund when it underperforms similar funds for three or more years. The key word here is "similar." The performance of a small-capitalization fund should be compared to other small-cap funds, not to the S&P 500. A small-cap fund that averages 15 percent when the S&P 500 averages 10 percent and other small-cap funds average 20 percent is an underperformer.

Circumstances differ over time and between investors. Because of this, except for the last point, we have avoided recommending specific conditions for selling a fund's shares. A change to an unproven manager, a change in investment style, a fund that is growing quickly due to investor deposits, a large fund, and an underperforming fund are several signals to watch for when deciding to sell.

Investments Online

As mutual funds have grown in popularity as a means to gain instant diversification and professional management, so have the number of Web sites devoted to some aspect of mutual fund investing. Any of the major fund companies (Fidelity, T. Rowe Price, Vanguard, Scudder, and so on) will have interesting Web sites to visit. Here are some others:

www.cefd.com
This is the *Closed-End Fund Digest* site, a newsletter. This site offers descriptions of the newsletter's features. A sample copy can be viewed online.

---

[32]Robert McGough, "Names of Managers Are Hidden to Avert Sudden Investor Flight," *Wall Street Journal*, April 7, 1994, R9.

Investments Online *(cont.)*

www.cda.com/wiesenberger/welcome.html
The home page of CDA/Wiesenberger offers an overview of their firm's various investment products. Both closed-end and open-end investment company data, analysis, and software can be purchased, hard copy or on-line, from this firm. This site has a page with links to many mutual fund sites, including mutual fund families and variable annuity firms.

www.fundsinteractive.com/index.shtml
The Mutual Funds Interactive Web site offers basic information about mutual fund investing: quotes of fund prices, charts, and market commentary. Its education features include discussions of investing topics, the different type of mutual funds, a Q&A section, and a manager profile.

www.mfea.com
A good place to start if you want to learn more about mutual funds is this home page for the Mutual Fund Education Alliance. This site, called the Mutual Fund Investor's Center, offers a great deal of information. The News Center features information, economic analysis and market commentary from mutual fund analysts. The Fund Center allows users to research, track, and customize their own fund portfolio from a list of more than one thousand funds. Investors can search by a specific fund's name or search for funds that have certain characteristics, including investment category, level of 12b-1 fee, expense ratio, sales charge, and so on. Investors can also discover the three top-performing funds year-to-date in different investment categories and find the lowest cost fund by investment category. The Learn page deals with the basics of mutual fund investing, and the Research/Plan page covers information and investment strategies for retirement, future college, and children. The site has links to various fund families.

www.investorguide.com/MutualFunds.html
The InvestorGuide Web site was reviewed in Chapter 1. This page from that Web site focuses on mutual fund investing and has links to a variety of mutual fund–related sites. Topics include learning about mutual funds, getting performance data and ratings, screening mutual funds, and obtaining a mutual fund prospectus.

quest.stocksmart.com/questprojects/stocksmart/wizard.html
www.stocksmart.com/mutualfunds.html
These two related sites help users find mutual funds in which to invest. The first site, the Stock Smart Fund Wizard, has users answer questions about their mutual fund preferences. The "Wizard" will find funds that best match these criteria. The second site ranks the current performance of more than 6,900 mutual funds and compares their relative performance to that of the S&P 500 and to a peer comparison group.

www.mfcafe.com
The Mutual Fund Cafe site is designed for mutual fund business and marketing professionals. It includes information and updates on legal issues, the SEC, accounting issues, industry news, and interviews.

www.morningstar.net
Morningstar is a leading provider of mutual fund information. The site features much information and many links of interest to mutual fund investors. Items on

Investments Online *(cont.)*

the Web site include news, analysis, personal investor case studies, columns by several Morningstar writers, and an interview with a fund manager. Past articles are available in an archive. The site also features sections dealing with learning, planning, and researching about mutual funds. A mutual fund screen allows users to find funds from Morningstar's database that meet certain investment category, return, rating, and volatility criteria.

www.mfmag.com
The Web site of Mutual Funds Online is a subscription service offering fund price quotes, a variety of performance rankings, profiles on more than nine thousand funds, and the ability to apply a variety of screens to find funds that best suit your needs.

www.indexfund.com
This site advertises a book about on-line mutual fund investing. Included in the site are links to mutual fund–related sites that update and expand those found in the book.

SUMMARY

♦ An investment company can be defined as a pool of funds from many sources that is invested in a collection of individual investments such as stocks, bonds, and other publicly traded securities. Investment companies can be classified as closed-end or open-end; the latter can include either load or no-load funds. A wide variety of funds are available, so you can find one to match almost any investment objective or combination of objectives.

♦ Numerous studies have examined the historical performance of mutual funds. Most studies have found that fewer than half the funds matched the risk-adjusted net returns of the aggregate market. The results with gross returns generally indicated average risk-adjusted returns about equal to the market's, with about half of the funds outperforming the market.

♦ The performances of actively managed mutual funds are hurt somewhat by their higher expenses and brokerage commissions from high portfolio turnover. Several studies have found that index funds are above-average, long-term performers among mutual funds, in part because their passive investment strategy limits their expenses and portfolio turnover.

♦ Investors should not necessarily invest in mutual funds with above-average, longer-term performance records without first doing some research. The fund's superior performance may be because the fund's investment style (for example, small stocks) was cyclically in favor in recent years. Alternatively, a good five-year or ten-year record may arise from just one or two years of outstanding returns, which may not be repeatable in the future.

♦ Although the returns received by the average individual investor on funds managed by investment companies will probably be inferior to the average results for a specific U.S. or international market, several other important services such as diversification, reinvestment, and recordkeeping are provided by investment companies. Therefore, you should give serious consideration to these funds as an important alternative to investing in individual stocks and bonds in the United States or worldwide.

Questions

1. How do you compute the net asset value of an investment company?

2. Discuss the difference between an open-end investment company and a closed-end investment company.

3. What two prices are provided for a closed-end investment company? What is the typical relationship between these prices?

4. What is the difference between a load fund and a no-load fund?

5. What are the differences between a common stock fund and a balanced fund? How would you expect their risk and return characteristics to compare?

6. Why might you buy a money market fund? What would you want from this investment?

7. Do you care about how well a mutual fund is diversified? Why or why not?

8. Discuss why the stability of a risk measure for a mutual fund is important to an investor. Are mutual funds' risk measure generally stable?

9. Should the performance of mutual funds be judged on the basis of return alone or on a risk-adjusted basis? Discuss why, using examples.

10. Define the net return and gross return for a mutual fund. Discuss how you would compute each.

11. As an investor in a mutual fund, discuss why net returns or gross returns are relevant to you.

12. As an investigator evaluating how well mutual fund managers select undervalued stocks or project market returns, discuss whether net or gross returns are more relevant.

13. Based on the numerous tests of mutual fund performance, you are convinced that only about half of the funds do better than a naive buy-and-hold policy. Does this mean you would forget about investing in investment companies? Why or why not?

14. You are told that Fund X experienced above-average performance over the past two years. Do you think it will continue over the next two years? Why or why not?

15. You are told that Fund Y experienced consistently above-average performance over the past six years. Do you think it will continue over the next six years? Why or why not?

16. You see advertisements for two mutual funds indicating that they have investment objectives consistent with yours.

    a. How would you get a quick view of these two funds' performance over the past two or three years?

    b. Where would you find more in-depth information on the funds, including addresses so you can write for prospectuses?

17. Why would an individual investor consider purchasing shares of a mutual fund?

18. Why would an individual investor consider purchasing shares of a closed-end fund?

19. Why should index funds be a part of most investors' mutual fund investment strategy?

20. Why might a fund with a good one- or two-year performance record be a better investment selection than one with a good five-year performance record?

21. What are some characteristics investors should look for in a mutual fund before investing?

22. A mutual fund that you own performed well over several years but has had below average returns this year. What factors should you consider before selling your fund shares?

23. Considering each of the events below separately, explain why or why not it is an indicator that it is time to sell your position in a mutual fund.

    a. There is a change in the fund's manager.

    b. A small-cap fund has underperformed the S&P 500 for three years in a row.

    c. According to Morningstar, the fund's style has changed from mid-cap value to small-cap growth.

Problems

1. Suppose ABC Mutual Fund had no liabilities and owned only four stocks as follows:

Stock	Shares	Price	Market Value
W	1,000	12	$12,000
X	1,200	15	$18,000
Y	1,500	22	$33,000
Z	1,800	16	$12,800
			$75,800

The fund began by selling $50,000 of stock at $8 per share. What is its NAV?

2. Suppose you are considering investing one thousand dollars in a load fund that charges a fee of 8 percent, and you expect your investment to earn 15 percent over the next year. Alternatively, you could invest in a no-load fund with similar risk that charges a 1 percent redemption fee. You estimate that this no-load fund will earn 12 percent. Given your expectations, which is the better investment and by how much?

3. In *Barron's,* look up the NAVs and market prices for five closed-end funds. Compute the difference between the two values for each fund. How many are selling at a premium to NAV? How many are selling at a discount to NAV? What is the overall average premium or discount? How does this compare to the Herzfeld chart published in *Barron's* that tracks the average discount on these funds over time?

4. Compute the offer prices for the following mutual funds:

Fund	NAV	Load Fee
HBJ	$19.67	8%
ICFB	$41.23	3%
EAN	$17.59	6%
FKR	$75.90	NL

5. Given the fees and return expectations below for each pair, which is the better investment?

	E(Return)	Load	12b-1 fee	Rear-end load	# years to be held
Pair I					
a.	10%	3%	1.00%	0%	5
b.	9%	6%	0.25%	0%	5
Pair II					
a.	13%	6%	0%	0%	8
b.	15%	NL	1%	0%	8
Pair III					
a.	8%	0%	1%	6% (reduces by 1% per year)	3
b.	10%	6%	0%	0%	3

References

Blake, Christopher, Edwin J. Elton, and Martin J. Gruber. "The Performance of Bond Mutual Funds." *Journal of Business* 66, no. 3 (July 1993).

Bogle, John C. "Selecting Equity Mutual Funds." *Journal of Portfolio Management* (Winter 1992): 94–100.

Bogle, John C. *Bogle on Mutual Funds.* Burr Ridge, Ill: Irwin Professional Publishing, 1994.

The Investment Company Institute is the industry trade association for investment companies. They publish helpful pamphlets and an annual book on the mutual fund industry. Many of their brochures are available at little or no charge for classroom purposes. They can be contacted at

Investment Company Institute, 1600 M Street, NW, Washington, DC 20036. Phone: (202) 293-7700.

A P P E N D I X   21   *Mutual Funds Glossary*

This glossary is divided into three parts: (A) general terms used in the mutual funds industry, (B) specific terms for types of mutual funds, and (C) a description of alternative retirement plans, each of which can include mutual funds.

A. GENERAL TERMS

Accumulation (periodic payment) plan   An arrangement through which an investor can purchase mutual fund shares periodically in large or small amounts, usually with provisions for the reinvestment of income dividends and capital gains distributions in additional shares.

Adviser   The organization employed by a mutual fund to give professional advice on the management of its assets.

Asked (offering) price   The price at which you can purchase a mutual fund's shares equal to the net asset value per share plus, at times, a sales charge.

Automatic reinvestment   *See* Reinvestment privilege.

Bid (redemption) price   The price at which a mutual fund redeems (buys back) its shares, usually equal to the net asset value per share.

Bookshares   A modern share recording system that eliminates the need for share certificates, but gives fund shareowners records of their holdings.

Broker–dealer (dealer)   A firm that retails mutual fund shares and other securities to the public.

Capital gains distributions   Payments, usually annual, to mutual fund shareholders for gains realized on the sale of the fund's portfolio securities.

Capital growth   An increase in the market value of a mutual fund's securities that is reflected in the NAV of its shares. Maximizing this factor is a long-term objective of many mutual funds.

Closed-end investment company   An investment company that issues only a limited number of shares, which it does not redeem (buy back). Instead, closed-end shares are traded in securities markets at prices determined by supply and demand.

Contingent deferred sales load   A mutual fund that imposes a sales charge when the investor sells or redeems shares. Also referred to as *rear-end load* or *redemption charge*.

Contractual plan   A program for the accumulation of mutual fund shares in which the investor agrees to invest a fixed amount on a regular basis for a specified number of years. A substantial portion of the sales charge applicable to the total investment is usually deducted from early payments.

Conversion (exchange) privilege   A provision that enables a mutual fund shareholder to transfer an investment, if needs or objectives change, from one fund to another within the same fund group, sometimes with a small transaction charge.

Custodian   The organization (usually a bank) that holds the securities and other assets of a mutual fund in custody and safekeeping.

Dollar-cost averaging   Investing equal amounts of money at regular intervals regardless of whether the stock market is moving upward or downward. This reduces the average share

costs in periods of lower securities prices, and the number of shares purchased in periods of higher prices.

Exchange privilege   *See* Conversion privilege.

Income dividends   Payments to mutual fund shareholders of dividends, interest, and short-term capital gains earned on the fund's portfolio after deduction of operating expenses.

Investment adviser   *See* Adviser.

Investment company   A corporation, trust, or partnership in which investors pool their money to obtain professional management and portfolio diversification. Mutual funds are the most popular type of investment company.

Investment objective   The goal, such as long-term capital growth or current income, that an investor or a mutual fund pursues.

Investment management company   A company, separate from the investment company, that manages the portfolio and performs administrative functions.

Load   *See* Sales charge.

Low-load fund   A mutual fund that imposes a moderate front-end sales charge when the investor buys the fund, typically about 3 to 4 percent.

Management fee   The compensation an investment company pays to the investment management company for its services. The average annual fee is about .5 percent of fund assets.

Mutual fund   An investment company that pools money from shareholders and invests in a variety of securities, including stocks, bonds, and money market securities. A mutual fund ordinarily stands ready to buy back (redeem) its shares at their current net asset value, which depends on the market value of the fund's portfolio of securities at the time. Mutual funds generally continuously offer new shares to investors.

Net asset value (NAV) per share   The market value of an investment company's assets (securities, cash, and any accrued earnings) after deducting liabilities, divided by the number of shares outstanding.

No-load fund   A mutual fund that sells its shares at net asset value without adding sales charges.

Open-end investment company   The more formal name for a mutual fund, which derives from the fact that it continuously offers new shares to investors and redeems them (buys them back) on demand.

Payroll deduction plan   An arrangement offered by some employers through which an employee may accumulate shares in a mutual fund. Employees authorize the employer to deduct specified amounts from their salaries at stated times and transfer the proceeds to the designated fund or funds.

Periodic payment plan   *See* Contractual plan.

Prospectus   A booklet that describes a mutual fund and offers its shares for sale. It contains information required by the Securities and Exchange Commission on such subjects as the fund's investment objective and policies, services, investment restrictions, officers and directors, procedures for buying or redeeming shares, charges, and financial statements.

Redemption price   *See* Bid price.

Reinvestment privilege   A provision of most mutual funds by which the investor can automatically reinvest income dividends and capital gains distributions in additional shares.

Sales charge   An amount charged to purchase shares in most mutual funds that are sold by brokers or other members of a sales force. Typical charges range from 4 to 8.5 percent of the initial investment. The charge is added to the net asset value per share to determine the offering price. *See also* No-load fund.

Short-term fund   An industry designation for money market and short-term municipal bond funds.

Transfer agent   The organization employed by a mutual fund to prepare and maintain records relating to the accounts of fund shareholders.

12b-1 fee   A fee charged by some funds, named after the SEC rule that permits it. Such fees pay for distribution costs, such as advertising, or for brokers' commissions. The fund's prospectus details any 12b-1 charges that apply.

Underwriter (principal underwriter)   The organization that acts as the distributor of a mutual fund's shares to broker-dealers and the public.

Unit investment trust   An investment company that purchases a fixed portfolio of income-producing securities to create a trust and sells units in the trust to investors through brokers.

Variable annuity   A contract under which an annuity is purchased with a fixed amount of money that is converted into a varying number of accumulation units. At retirement, the annuitant is paid a fixed number of monthly units, which are converted into varying amounts of money. The value of both accumulation and annuity units varies with the performance of a portfolio of equity securities.

Variable life insurance   An equity-based life insurance policy the reserves of which may be invested in common stocks. The death benefit is guaranteed never to fall below the face value, but it would increase if the value of the securities were to increase. This kind of policy may have no guaranteed cash-surrender value.

Voluntary plan   A flexible accumulation plan that states no definite time period or total amount to be invested.

Withdrawal plan   A mutual fund provision that allows shareholders to receive payments from their investments at regular intervals. These payments typically are drawn from the fund's dividends and capital gains distributions, if any, and from principal, as needed. Many mutual funds offer these plans.

B. Types of Mutual Funds

Aggressive growth fund   A fund that seeks maximum capital gains as its investment objective. Current income is not a significant factor. Some may invest in stocks on the fringes of the mainstream, such as those of fledgling companies, new industries, companies fallen on hard times, or industries temporarily out of favor. They may also use specialized investment techniques such as option writing. The risks are obvious, but the potential for handsome rewards should accompany them.

Balanced fund   A fund with, generally, a three-part investment objective: (1) to conserve the investors' principal, (2) to pay current income, and (3) to increase both principal and income. The fund aims to achieve this by owning a mixture of bonds, preferred stocks, and common stocks.

Corporate bond fund   Like an income fund, this type of fund seeks a high level of income. It does this by buying bonds of corporations for the majority of the portfolio. Some part of the portfolio may be in U.S. Treasury and other government bonds.

Flexible portfolio fund   A fund that invests in common stocks, bonds, money market securities, and other types of debt securities. The portfolio may hold up to 100 percent of any one of these types of securities or any combination of them, depending on market conditions.

Global bond fund   A fund that invests in bonds issued by companies from countries worldwide, including the United States.

Global equity fund   A fund that invests in the stock of both U.S. and foreign companies.

GNMA (Ginnie Mae) fund   A fund that invests in the government-backed mortgage securities of the Government National Mortgage Association. To qualify for this category, the majority of a fund's portfolio must always be invested in mortgage-backed securities.

Growth and income fund   A fund that invests mainly in the common stock of companies with longer track records—companies that combine the expectation of higher share values and solid records of paying dividends.

Growth fund   A fund that invests in the common stock of more settled companies, but again, with the primary aim of building the value of its investments through capital gains rather than a steady flow of dividends.

High-yield bond fund   A corporate bond fund that invests predominantly in bonds rated below investment grade. In return for a generally higher yield, investors bear greater risk than more highly rated bonds require.

Income equity fund   A fund that invests primarily in stocks of companies with good dividend-paying records.

Income-bond fund   A fund that invests in a combination of government and corporate bonds to generate income.

Income-mixed fund   A fund that seeks a high level of current income, often by investing in the common stock of companies that have good dividend-paying records. Often corporate and government bonds are also part of the portfolio.

International stock fund   A fund that invests in the stocks of companies located outside the United States.

Long-term municipal bond fund   A fund that invests in bonds issued by local governments, such as cities and states, which use the money to build schools, highways, libraries, and the like. Because the federal government does not tax the income earned on most of these securities, the fund can pass the tax-free income through to shareholders.

Long-term state municipal bond fund   A fund that invests predominantly in long-term municipal bonds issued within a single state. These issues are exempt from both federal income tax and state taxes for residents of the same state.

Money market mutual fund   A fund that invests in short-term securities sold in the money market. (Large companies, banks, and other institutions also invest their surplus cash in the money market for short periods of time.) In the entire investment spectrum, these are generally the safest, most stable securities available. They include Treasury bills, certificates of deposit of large banks, and commercial paper (short-term IOUs of large corporations).

Option/income fund   A fund that seeks a high current return by investing primarily in dividend-paying common stocks on which call options are traded on national securities exchanges. Current returns generally consist of dividends and premiums from writing call options, but other sources include short-term gains from asset sales, often to satisfy exercised options, and profits from closing purchase transactions.

Short-term municipal bond fund   A fund that invests in municipal securities with relatively short maturities, also known as a *tax-exempt money market fund.*

Short-term state municipal bond fund   A fund that invests in municipal securities with relatively short maturities issued in a single state. Such issues are exempt from state taxes for residents of the same state.

U.S. Government Income Fund   A fund that invests in a variety of government securities, including U.S. Treasury bonds, federally guaranteed mortgage-backed securities, and other government issues.

C. RETIREMENT PLANS

Federal income tax laws permit the establishment of various tax-deferred retirement plans, each of which may be funded with mutual fund shares.

Corporate and self-employed retirement plan   A tax-qualified pension and profit-sharing plan that can be established by corporations or self-employed individuals. Changes in the tax laws have made retirement plans for corporate employees essentially comparable to those for self-employed individuals. Contributions to a plan are tax deductible and earnings accumulate on a tax-deferred basis. The maximum annual

amount that may be contributed to such a plan on behalf of an individual is limited to the lesser of 25 percent of the individual's compensation or $30,000.

Individual retirement account   Any wage earner under the age of $70\frac{1}{2}$ may set up an individual retirement account (IRA) and may contribute as much as 100 percent of his or her compensation each year up to $2,000. For additional details, see the Chapter 2 discussion of IRAs.

Qualified retirement plan   A private retirement plan that meets the rules and regulations of the Internal Revenue Service. In almost all cases, contributions to a qualified retirement plan are tax deductible and earnings on such contributions are always exempt from taxes until the investor retires.

Simplified employee pension (SEP)   An employer-sponsored plan that may be viewed as an aggregation of separate IRAs. In a SEP, the employer contributes up to $30,000 or 15 percent of compensation, whichever is less, to an individual retirement account maintained for the employee.

Section 403(b) plan   Section 403(b) of the Internal Revenue Code permits employees of certain charitable organizations and public school systems to establish tax-sheltered retirement programs. These plans may be invested in either annuity contracts or mutual fund shares.

Section 401(k) plan   A particularly popular type of plan that may be offered by either corporate or noncorporate entities. A 401(k) plan is a tax-qualified profit-sharing plan that includes a "cash or deferred" arrangement, which permits employees to have a portion of their compensation contributed to a tax-sheltered plan on their behalf or paid to them directly as additional taxable compensation. An employee may elect to reduce his or her other taxable compensation with contributions to a 401(k) plan, where those amounts will accumulate tax-free. The Tax Reform Act of 1986 established new, tighter antidiscrimination requirements for 401(k) plans and curtailed the amount of elective deferrals that may be made by all employees. Nevertheless, 401(k) plans remain excellent and popular retirement savings vehicles.

CHAPTER

22

Evaluation of Portfolio Management

In this chapter we will answer the following questions:

♦ What are clients' major requirements of their portfolio managers?

♦ What important characteristics should any benchmark possess?

♦ What is the Treynor portfolio performance measure?

♦ What is the Sharpe portfolio performance measure?

♦ What is the critical difference between the Treynor and Sharpe portfolio performance measures?

♦ What is the Jensen portfolio performance measure, and how does it relate to the Treynor measure?

♦ How do you determine if a portfolio being evaluated is above or below the SML when using the Treynor measure?

♦ When you evaluate a sample of portfolios, how do you determine how well diversified they are?

♦ What is the bias found regarding the composite performance measures?

♦ How do the various performance measures relate to each other in terms of rankings?

♦ What is the Roll "benchmark error" problem, and what two factors are affected when computing portfolio performance measures?

♦ What impact has global investing on the significance of the benchmark error problem?

♦ What two methods can you use to determine a portfolio's style exposure over time?

♦ What is portfolio performance attribution analysis? How does it assist the process of analyzing a manager's performance?

♦ How do bond portfolio performance measures differ from equity portfolio performance measures?

♦ What measure of risk is used in the Wagner and Tito bond portfolio performance measure?

♦ What are the components of the Dietz, Fogler, and Hardy bond portfolio performance measure?   ♦

Investors are always interested in evaluating the performance of their portfolios. Because it is both expensive and time-consuming to analyze and select securities for a portfolio, an individual, company, or institution must determine whether this effort was worth the time and money invested in it. Investors who manage their own portfolios should evaluate their own performance just as those who pay one or several professional money managers must. In the latter case, it is imperative to determine whether the investment performance justifies the cost of the service.

This chapter outlines the theory and practice of evaluating the investment portfolio performance. In the initial sections, we consider what is required of portfolio managers and the benchmark portfolio that will be used to evaluate their performance.

Second, we discuss basic portfolio performance evaluation techniques and issues. We review performance measures that evaluate a portfolio's risk-adjusted return. We demonstrate these measures by applying them to gauge the performance of a selected sample of mutual funds.

Third, we discuss factors to consider when applying these performance measures. This includes consideration of the work of Roll that questioned any evaluation technique that depends on the CAPM and the use of a market portfolio. This controversy is referred to as the *benchmark problem*. We examine how to determine, *ex post*, a manager's style exposure. We also discuss why this benchmark problem becomes more significant when you begin investing globally.

The fourth section reviews performance attribution analysis. Attribution analysis seeks to discover why a particular portfolio strategy resulted in returns that were higher (or lower) than the benchmark portfolio. In the final section we recognize that the factors that determine the performance of a bond portfolio differ from those that affect common stocks. Therefore, we consider several models developed to evaluate the performance of bond portfolios.

WHAT IS REQUIRED OF A PORTFOLIO MANAGER?

Portfolio managers face three major requirements:

1. Follow the client's policy statement
2. Earn above-average returns for a given risk class
3. Diversify the portfolio to eliminate unsystematic risk

In Chapter 2 we learned that the portfolio manager should assist clients in their understanding of capital market risks and reasonable return expectations. Once the client develops a portfolio policy statement, it is the manager's duty to follow it. A review of the portfolio's risks, returns, and performance relative to an appropriate benchmark or index can help determine if a portfolio manager satisfied the first criterion.

In terms of the second requirement, the return objective is obvious, but the necessity of considering *risk* in this context was not generally apparent prior to the 1960s, when work in portfolio theory showed its significance.

Figure 22.1   *Return Patterns of a Successful Equity Market Timer*

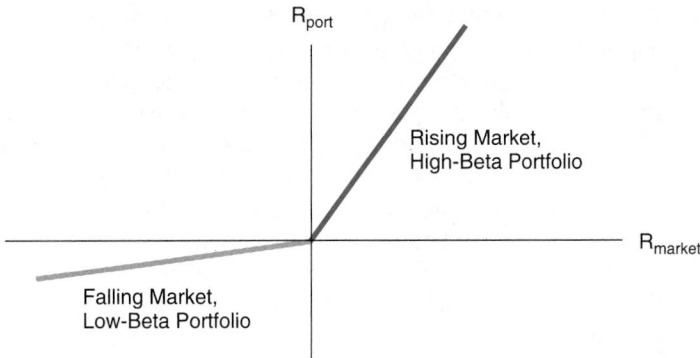

In modern theory, superior risk-adjusted returns can be derived through *either* superior timing or superior security selection. An equity portfolio manager who can do a superior job of predicting the peaks or troughs of the equity market can adjust the portfolio's composition to anticipate market trends, holding a completely diversified portfolio of high-beta stocks through rising markets and favoring low-beta stocks and money market instruments during declining markets. Bigger gains in rising markets and smaller losses in declining markets would give the portfolio manager above-average, risk-adjusted returns. The portfolio returns of a successful market timer will resemble those of Figure 22.1. In bull markets, a high-beta portfolio earns returns above the market's returns; in bear markets, a shift to a low-beta portfolio causes returns to be less negative than the overall market.

A fixed-income portfolio manager with superior timing ability would change the portfolio's duration in anticipation of interest rate changes. Specifically, the manager would increase the duration of the portfolio in anticipation of falling interest rates and reduce the duration of the portfolio when rates are expected to rise. If properly executed, this bond portfolio management strategy would likewise provide superior risk-adjusted returns.

As an alternative strategy, a portfolio manager and his or her analysts could try to consistently select undervalued stocks or bonds. Even without superior market timing, such a strategy, if successfully implemented, would generate above-average, risk-adjusted returns.

A third factor to consider when evaluating a portfolio manager is the ability to diversify completely. As noted in Chapter 7, the market rewards investors only for bearing systematic (market) risk. Unsystematic risk is not considered when determining required returns because it can be eliminated in a diversified market portfolio. Investors consequently want their portfolios completely diversified, which means that they want the portfolio manager to completely eliminate unsystematic risk. The level of diversification can be judged on the basis of the correlation between the portfolio returns and the returns for a market portfolio. A completely diversified portfolio is perfectly correlated with the fully diversified market portfolio.

These three requirements of a portfolio manager are important because some portfolio evaluation techniques take into account one requirement but not the others (for example, some evaluations consider returns only). Other techniques implicitly consider the factors but do not differentiate between them.

BENCHMARK PORTFOLIOS

A **benchmark portfolio** represents the performance evaluation standard for a portfolio manager. The benchmark portfolio is usually a passive index or portfolio. For example, the benchmark for many actively managed broad equity funds is the well-known S&P 500 Index. Portfolio managers, by earning an active management fee, will be evaluated based on whether they are able to add value relative to the benchmark. One reason for the proliferation of indexes over the years (recall the market indexes from Chapter 5) is the need for different types of benchmarks to meet the needs of clients who want to invest funds in equities and bonds and internationally.

For clients who hire several money managers benchmarks present special challenges; this is a particularly critical need of pension plans and endowments that hire multiple managers with widely divergent investment styles.[1] For example, a pension fund may hire several specialized managers to manage the equity portion of the fund while others manage the bond component, and still others invest funds in venture capital or emerging markets. Because of a desire not only to evaluate aggregate portfolio performance but also to identify what factors and managers contributed to superior or inferior performance, such funds need two levels of benchmarks. One benchmark must reflect the composition of the entire portfolio; that is, a benchmark that contains the broadest mixture of risky assets available from around the world. A second set of benchmarks serve at a fairly specific level to evaluate the management style of each individual money manager.[2]

Specialized or customized benchmarks, sometimes called **normal portfolios**, are constructed to evaluate a manager's unique investment style or philosophy (for example, investing in small stocks with high earnings momentum). To use a broad market index rather than a specific benchmark portfolio would imply that the portfolio manager lacks an investment style, which is quite unrealistic. Specialized benchmarks allow the client to determine if the money manager is being consistent with his or her stated investment style.

Required Characteristics of Benchmarks

Any useful benchmark should have the following basic characteristics:

♦ *Unambiguous.* The names and weights of securities composing the benchmark are clearly defined.
♦ *Investable.* The client can always choose to forego active management and simply hold the benchmark.
♦ *Measurable.* It is possible to calculate the return on the benchmark on a reasonably frequent basis.
♦ *Appropriate.* The benchmark is consistent with the manager's investment style or biases; the returns of the actively managed portfolio should be highly correlated with those of the benchmark.
♦ *Reflective of current investment opinions.* The manager has current investment knowledge (be it positive, negative, or neutral) of the securities that make up the benchmark.
♦ *Specified in advance.* The benchmark is constructed before an evaluation period begins.

---

[1]Jeffrey V. Bailey, Thomas M. Richards, and David E. Tierney, "Benchmark Portfolios and the Manager/Plan Sponsor Relationship," *Current Topics in Investment Management* (New York: Harper & Row, 1990). For a discussion of who should construct a customized benchmark, see Jeffrey V. Bailey and David E. Tierney, "Gaming Manager Benchmarks," *Journal of Portfolio Management* 19, no. 4 (Summer 1993): 37–40.

[2]For a discussion of how to use appropriate benchmarks to determine management style, see William F. Sharpe, "Asset Allocation: Management Style and Performance Measurement," *Journal of Portfolio Management* 18, no. 2 (Winter 1992): 7–19.

If a benchmark does not possess all of these properties, it is ineffective as a management tool. One example of a flawed benchmark is to compare an active manager's performance with that of the median manager (that is, 50 percent of managers did worse, 50 percent did better) from a universe of managers. Comparing performance against the manager universe does not satisfy many of the above-specified characteristics of a benchmark.[3] For example, such a benchmark would be ambiguous, as different managers in the universe may focus on different sets of stocks or sectors. It is hard to frequently measure returns, as the median manager changes over time because of differing relative performances of their portfolios. Such a benchmark is also not investable, because no one knows beforehand who the median manager will be.

Building a Benchmark

A benchmark may be a well-known market index, such as the S&P 500, the Russell 2000, or the Merrill Lynch Corporate Bond Index. Alternatively, many clients require a specialized index. Similarly, a manager who believes she has specialized expertise will want to be evaluated on the basis of a specialized index. Such an index may be constructed by taking a broad, well-known index and eliminating some issues, adding others, and reweighting it in order to reflect the manager's specialized expertise. For example, consider the following benchmark:

> The Tuttle Group Index is weighted 90 percent equities, 10 percent ninety-day Treasury bills. The benchmark return on the Treasury bill component is the actual ninety-day Treasury bill return. The equity benchmark is constructed as follows: The equities are based on the S&P 500. Stocks will be deleted from the index if their debt/equity ratios exceed a multiple of 1.5 of their industry mean. Stocks with low earnings growth (those with growth rates in the bottom 10 percent of the S&P 500 stocks) are also omitted. The remaining issues will be weighted as follows:
>
> 1. Firms with market values above $2.5 billion will be equally weighted.
> 2. Firms with market values of $2.5 billion or less will be value weighted.

Such a benchmark includes cash reserves because the normal asset allocation is 90 percent stocks, 10 percent cash. The equity benchmark portfolio includes stocks in the S&P 500 that lack excessively high financial risk or poor earnings prospects. It is well known that small stocks have higher historical average returns than large stocks. In order to reflect this effect, small-capitalization stocks are value weighted whereas large-capitalization stocks are equally weighted. As a result, smaller firms will have a larger proportionate share in this benchmark than in the S&P 500.

To protect the client from a portfolio manager who seeks to earn returns higher than the benchmark's returns by taking on higher levels of risk, the portfolio's investments may be limited in composition, risk, and diversification, as follows:

> Equities not specifically included in the benchmark index may be purchased for the actual portfolio under management. The portfolio's median characteristics of capitalization distribution and P/E ratio should represent the average characteristics of the Tuttle Equity Benchmark over the course of a market cycle. The Tuttle Equity Benchmark has had a historical beta, relative to the S&P 500, of 1.05. The allowable range for the portfolio beta is 0.88 to 1.25. The portfolio returns are expected to have an R^2 (coefficient of determination) in the range of 0.85 to 0.95 when regressed on the returns of the S&P 500.

---

[3]Jeffrey V. Bailey, "Are Manager Universes Acceptable Performance Benchmarks?" *Journal of Portfolio Management* 18, no. 3 (Spring 1992): 9–13. For a general discussion of what to look for in a benchmark, see Jeffrey V. Bailey, "Evaluating Benchmark Quality," *Financial Analysts Journal* 48, no. 3 (May–June 1992): 33–39.

These constraints prohibit the portfolio manager from "gaming" the benchmark by constructing an actual portfolio that is measurably different from the benchmark. The actual portfolio should reflect the size distribution and P/E characteristics of the benchmark. The portfolio's betas and R^2 values are limited to prescribed ranges. Deviations from these constraints are grounds for the dismissal of the manager unless extenuating circumstances exist.

Note that the Tuttle Group Index satisfies the six desirable benchmark characteristics above. It is unambiguous, because securities that belong in the benchmark are explicitly noted. The benchmark is investable, because funds can be placed in a specified passive index of 10 percent Treasury bills and 90 percent equities. Also, the benchmark's returns are measurable and it reflects current investment opinions regarding small stock returns, the disfavor of high financial risk and low-growth stocks. Such a benchmark should only be constructed after the manager and client discuss the client's objectives and constraints and together draft a mutually agreeable policy statement. Should the client determine that the manager's abilities or style are inconsistent with the benchmark, that manager should be replaced with one whose skills and style match the benchmark.

COMPOSITE (RISK-ADJUSTED) PORTFOLIO PERFORMANCE MEASURES

This section describes in detail the three major composite equity portfolio performance measures that combine risk and return performance into a single value. We describe each measure and what it is meant to do and demonstrate how to compute it and interpret the results. We also compare the measures and discuss how they differ and why they might rank portfolios differently.

Sharpe Portfolio Performance Measure

Sharpe developed a composite measure to evaluate the performance of mutual funds, but it can be used to evaluate any portfolio.[4] The measure follows closely his earlier work on the capital asset pricing model (CAPM), dealing specifically with the capital market line (CML).

From our discussion in Chapter 7 of asset pricing models, we saw how the CML is derived. By introducing a risk-free asset, investors can choose between placing funds in the risk-free asset and in risky portfolios along the Markowitz efficient frontier. Rational investors will seek to earn the highest return possible given their risk preferences; they will shift their allocations between the risk-free asset and risky portfolios until they do so. In essence, investors seek to maximize the slope of the line connecting the risk-free return to the Markowitz efficient frontier, or equivalently, they seek the Markowitz efficient portfolio that allows them to maximize their expected excess return-to-risk ratio:

$$\text{Maximize Slope of the Capital Market Line} =$$

$$\text{Maximize } \frac{\text{Expected Excess Return}}{\sigma_{port}} =$$

$$\text{Maximize } \frac{E(R_p - RFR)}{\sigma_{port}}$$

[4]William F. Sharpe, "Mutual Fund Performance," *Journal of Business* 39, no. 1, part 2 (January 1966): 119–138.

The Sharpe measure for risk-adjusted return is based on this relationship. It is the ratio of the portfolio's actual excess return divided by its standard deviation:

$$\text{Sharpe Measure} = S = \frac{(R_{port} - RFR)}{\sigma_{port}}$$

From Chapter 7 we know the slope of the CML is the excess return on the market portfolio $(R_m - RFR)$ divided by the standard deviation of the market's returns. That is, the Sharpe measure for the risk-adjusted performance of the market portfolio is simply the slope of the CML.

This composite measure of portfolio performance seeks to measure the *total risk* of the portfolio by including the standard deviation of returns rather than considering only the systematic risk by using beta. Because the numerator is the portfolio's risk premium, this measure indicates the *risk premium return earned per unit of total risk.* In terms of capital market theory, this portfolio performance measure uses total risk to compare portfolios to the CML. Portfolios with Sharpe measures higher than the Sharpe measure for the market lie above the CML; portfolios with Sharpe measures below those of the market lie below the CML.

Demonstration of Composite Sharpe Measure   The following example computes the Sharpe measure of performance for several portfolios. We'll assume the risk-free rate during our period of analysis was 8 percent, the return on the market portfolio during the period was 14 percent, and that the standard deviation of the market's annual returns over this period was 20 percent. We want to examine the performance of the following portfolios:

Portfolio	Average Annual Rate of Return	Standard Deviation of Return
D	0.13	0.18
E	0.17	0.22
F	0.16	0.23

The Sharpe measures for these portfolios are as follows:

$$S_{market} = \frac{(0.14 - 0.08)}{0.20} = 0.300$$

$$S_D = \frac{(0.13 - 0.08)}{0.18} = 0.278$$

$$S_E = \frac{(0.17 - 0.08)}{0.22} = 0.409$$

$$S_F = \frac{(0.16 - 0.08)}{0.23} = 0.348$$

The D portfolio had the lowest risk-adjusted return, or lowest excess return per unit of total risk, failing to perform as well as the aggregate market portfolio. In contrast, Portfolios E and F performed better than the aggregate market; Portfolio E had the best risk-adjusted return.

Because we know the return and standard deviation for the market portfolio during this period, we can draw the CML. We can also plot the results for Portfolios D, E, and F on this graph, as shown in Figure 22.2. Portfolio D plots below the line, showing poor risk-adjusted performance. Portfolios E and F lie above the line, indicating superior risk-adjusted performance.

Figure 22.2   *Plot of Performance on the Capital Market Line*

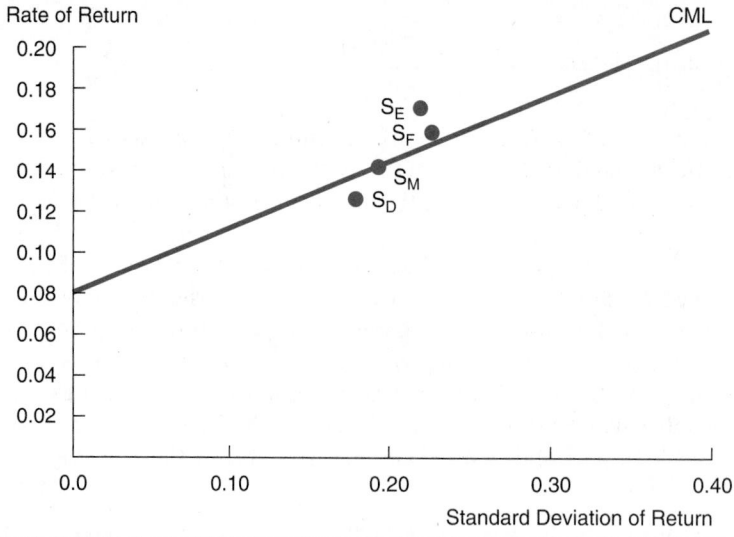

Sharpe has recently suggested a more general performance measure that relates performance to any benchmark for a portfolio as follows.[5]

Let R_{pt} = the return on a portfolio in period t.
$\quad R_{Bt}$ = the return on the benchmark portfolio in period t.
$\quad D_t$ = the differential return in period t.
$\quad D_t = R_{pt} - R_{Bt}$
$\quad \bar{D}$ = the average value of D_t over the period being examined.

$$\bar{D} = \frac{\sum_{t=1}^{T} D_t}{N}$$

$\quad \sigma_D$ = the standard deviation of the differential return during the period.

Therefore, the historic (*ex post*) Sharpe Ratio (S) is:

$$S = \frac{\bar{D}}{\sigma_D}$$

This ratio indicates the historic average differential return (relative to a specified benchmark) per unit of historic variability of the differential return. Notably, the emphasis is on a differential return relative to a *specific benchmark* that coincides with the objectives of the portfolio.

Treynor Portfolio Performance Measure

Treynor recognized two components of risk: risk produced by general market fluctuations, and risk resulting from unique fluctuations in the securities in the portfolio.[6] He recog-

[5]William F. Sharpe, "The Sharpe Ratio." This copyright material is reprinted with permission from the *Journal of Portfolio Management,* 488 Madison Avenue, New York, NY 10022.

[6]Jack L. Treynor, "How to Rate Management of Investment Funds," *Harvard Business Review* 43, no. 1 (January–February 1965): 63–75.

nized that in a completely diversified portfolio, the unique returns for individual stocks should cancel out. His measure of risk-adjusted performance focuses on the portfolio's undiversifiable risk, which we also know as market risk or systematic risk. This risk, which represents the relative volatility of the portfolio's returns compared to the market's returns, is measured by beta (β). Treynor developed a measure that incorporated a portfolio's excess returns and its level of systematic risk. The Treynor measure, designated as *T*, is equal to:

$$T = \frac{(R_{port} - RFR)}{\beta_{port}}$$

Because the numerator of this ratio ($R_{port} - RFR$) is the *risk premium* and the denominator is a measure of risk, the total expression indicates the portfolio's *risk premium return per unit of risk*. All risk-averse investors would prefer to maximize this value.

Note that the risk variable beta measures systematic risk and indicates nothing about the diversification of the portfolio. It *implicitly assumes* a completely diversified portfolio, which means that systematic risk is the relevant risk measure.

Comparing a portfolio's *T* value to a similar measure for the market portfolio indicates whether the portfolio would plot above the SML. You calculate the *T* value for the aggregate market as follows:

$$T = \frac{(R_{market} - RFR)}{\beta_{market}} = \frac{(R_{market} - RFR)}{1.0} = R_{market} - RFR$$

Because the beta of the market portfolio always equals 1.00, the Treynor measure for the market portfolio reduces to $R_{market} - RFR$, the market risk premium, which, as we first saw in Chapter 7, equals the slope of the security market line (SML). Therefore, a portfolio with a *T* value higher than the market risk premium would plot above the SML, indicating superior risk-adjusted performance. A portfolio with a *T* value lower than the market risk premium would plot below the SML, showing poor risk-adjusted performance.

Demonstration of Comparative Treynor Measures   As before, let's assume that during a most recent period the average annual total rate of return (including dividends) on the S&P 500 was 14 percent and the average nominal rate of return on government T-bills was 8 percent. You wish to evaluate the performance of three equity managers:

Investment Manager	Average Annual Rate of Return	Beta
W	0.12	0.90
X	0.16	1.05
Y	0.18	1.20

On the basis of this information, we can compute T values for the market portfolio and for each of the individual portfolio managers as follows:

$$T_{market} = \frac{(0.14 - 0.08)}{1.00} = 0.060$$

$$T_W = \frac{(0.13 - 0.08)}{0.90} = 0.044$$

Figure 22.3   *Plot of Performance on the Security Market Line*

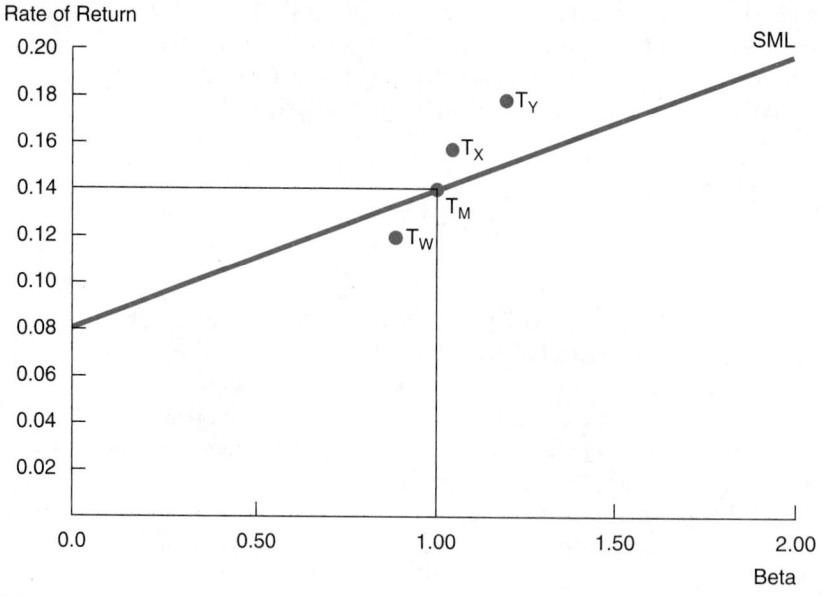

$$T_X = \frac{(0.17 - 0.08)}{1.05} = 0.076$$

$$T_Y = \frac{(0.16 - 0.08)}{1.20} = 0.083$$

These results indicate that investment manager W not only ranked the lowest of the three managers, he performed worse than the aggregate market. In contrast, both X and Y beat the market portfolio, and manager Y performed somewhat better than manager X on a risk-adjusted basis. In terms of the SML, both of their portfolios plotted above the line, as shown in Figure 22.3.

Poor performance or excellent performance with low risk can yield negative *T* values. An example of poor performance would be a portfolio with both an average rate of return below the risk-free rate and a positive beta. As an example, assume a fourth portfolio manager, Z, had a portfolio beta of 0.50 and an average rate of return of 7.00 percent. The *T* value would be

$$T_Z = \frac{(0.07 - 0.08)}{0.50} = -0.020$$

Obviously, this performance would plot below the SML in Figure 22.3. A portfolio with a *negative* beta and an average rate of return above the risk-free rate of return would likewise have a negative *T* value. In this case, however, it would indicate exemplary performance. As an example, assume portfolio manager G invested heavily in gold mining stocks during a period of great political and economic uncertainty. Because gold typically has a negative correlation with most stocks, this portfolio's beta could be negative. If you were examining this portfolio after gold prices increased in value, you might find excellent returns. Assume our gold bug portfolio G had a beta of -0.20 and yet experienced an average rate of return of 10 percent. The *T* value for this portfolio would then be

$$T_G = \frac{(0.10 - 0.08)}{-0.20} = -0.010$$

Although the T value is -0.010, you can see that if you plotted these results on the graph, it would indicate a position substantially above the SML in Figure 22.3.

Because negative betas can yield T values that give confusing results, it is preferable either to plot the portfolio on an SML graph or to compute the expected return for this portfolio using the SML equation and compare this expected return to the actual return. This comparison will tell you whether the actual return was above or below expectations. In the preceding example for portfolio G, the expected return would be

$$\begin{aligned}
E(R_G) &= RFR + \beta_G(R_m - RFR) \\
&= 0.08 + (-0.20)(0.14 - 0.08) \\
&= 0.08 - 0.012 \\
&= 0.068
\end{aligned}$$

Comparing this expected (required) rate of return of 6.8 percent to the actual return of 10 percent shows that portfolio manager G has done a superior job.

Jensen Portfolio Performance Measure

The Jensen measure is similar to the measures already discussed in that it is based on the capital asset pricing model (CAPM).[7] All versions of the CAPM calculate the expected one-period return on any security or portfolio by the following expression:

$$E(R_j) = RFR + \beta_j[E(R_m) - RFR]$$

where:

$E(R_j)$ = the expected return on security or portfolio j
RFR = the one-period risk-free interest rate
β_j = the systematic risk (beta) for security or portfolio j
$E(R_m)$ = the expected return on the market portfolio of risky assets

Assuming the asset pricing model is empirically valid, we can express the expectations formula in terms of *realized* rates of return over time period t as follows:

$$R_{jt} = RFR_t + \beta_j[R_{mt} - RFR_t] + U_{jt}$$

That is, the realized rate of return on a security or portfolio during a given time period is a linear function of the risk-free rate of return during the period plus a risk premium that depends on the systematic risk of the security or portfolio during the period plus a random error term.

Subtracting the risk-free return from both sides, we have

$$R_{jt} - RFR_t = \beta_j[R_{mt} - RFR_t] + U_{jt}$$

This indicates that, according to the security market line, the risk premium earned on the jth security or portfolio j is equal to β_j times a market risk premium plus a random error term.

---

[7]Michael C. Jensen, "The Performance of Mutual Funds in the Period 1945–1964," *Journal of Finance* 23, no. 2 (May 1968): 389–416.

But superior portfolio managers who can forecast market turns or consistently select undervalued securities will earn higher risk premiums than those implied by this model. Similarly, inferior portfolio managers will earn lower risk premiums. Specifically, superior portfolio managers would have consistently positive random error terms because the actual returns for their portfolios would consistently exceed the expected returns implied by this model, and inferior managers would have negative terms because returns for their portfolios would fall below the implied expected returns.

To detect and measure for superior or inferior performance, we need to allow for an intercept (a nonzero constant) that measures any positive or negative difference from the model. Consistent positive differences would cause a positive intercept, whereas consistent negative differences (inferior performance) would cause a negative intercept. With an intercept or nonzero constant, the earlier equation becomes

22.1
$$R_{jt} - RFR_t = a_j + \beta_j[R_{mt} - RFR_t] + U_{jt}$$

In this equation, the a_j value (or "alpha") indicates whether the portfolio manager is superior or inferior in market timing and stock selection or both. The alpha represents how much of the rate of return on the portfolio is attributable to the manager's ability to derive above-average returns adjusted for risk. A superior manager will have a significant positive a_j; an inferior manager's returns will have a significant negative value for a_j. A portfolio manager who basically matched the market on a risk-adjusted basis will have a value for alpha that will not be significantly different from zero. Groups of investors and the financial press many times discuss a manager's alpha or seek information about positive alpha managers; they are discussing this a_j intercept term.

Manager alphas can be computed two different ways. Period-by-period alphas can be computed using Equation 22.1, assuming a zero residual (Ujt) term. That is, we rearrange Equation 22.1 to solve for alpha:

22.2
$$a_j = [R_{jt} - RFR_t] + \beta_j[R_{mt} - RFR_t]$$

Second, time-series data on a portfolio's returns, the risk-free rate, and the market return can be gathered and Equation 22.1 can be estimated using simple linear regression. The constant or intercept term from the regression is the estimate of the manager's alpha. Most regression packages will also report the standard error of the alpha estimate, so a statistical t-test can be done to determine if the alpha value is significantly positive (superior performance), significantly negative (inferior performance), or not different from zero (average performance).

We can use the first method to compute the alphas for portfolio managers W, X, and Y. Assume during the past year the actual market return was 14 percent and the risk-free rate was 8 percent. The results for the three portfolio managers were as follows:

	Rate of Return	Beta
Manager W	0.12	0.90
Manager X	0.16	1.05
Manager Y	0.18	1.20

Using Equation 22.2, we can find each manager's alpha over the past year.

$$a_W = [0.12 - 0.08] - 0.90[0.14 - 0.08] = -0.014$$
$$a_X = [0.16 - 0.08] - 1.05[0.14 - 0.08] = +0.017$$
$$a_Y = [0.18 - 0.08] - 1.20[0.14 - 0.08] = +0.028$$

This analysis confirms what the Treynor analysis told us; after adjusting for systematic risk differences, manager W underperformed the market while managers X and Y outperformed it. Of the three managers, manager Y has the best risk-adjusted performance as measured by the Jensen measure.

Sharpe versus the Treynor and Jensen Measures

The Sharpe portfolio performance measure uses the standard deviation of returns as the measure of risk, whereas both the Treynor and Jensen performance measures use beta (systematic risk). The Sharpe measure, therefore, evaluates the portfolio manager on the basis of both rate of return performance and diversification.

When examining completely diversified portfolios, that is, portfolios without any unsystematic risk, the Sharpe, Treynor, and Jensen measures will agree on how managers should be ranked, from best risk-adjusted performance to the worst. The ranks will agree because the total variance of a completely diversified portfolio is its systematic variance.

But when both diversified and undiversified portfolios are under review, a poorly diversified portfolio could have a high ranking on the basis of the Treynor or Jensen performance measure but a much lower ranking on the basis of the Sharpe performance measure. The difference in ranks occurs because of the difference in diversification. The Sharpe measure examines total risk, which for an undiversified portfolio includes both systematic and unsystematic components; the Treynor and Jensen measures only include systematic risk when adjusting portfolio returns for risk differences.

The Sharpe and Treynor measures do not examine period-by-period returns over time; rather, they are calculated using the *average* returns over time for the portfolios, the market, and the risk-free asset. The Jensen and new Sharpe measures, however, require a different risk-free rate, market (or benchmark) return, and portfolio return for each time interval in the sample period. For example, to examine the performance of a fund manager over a ten-year period using yearly intervals, you must examine the fund's annual returns less the return on risk-free assets for each year, and relate this to the annual return on the market portfolio less the same risk-free rate. That is, Equation 22.2 must be computed ten times using annual data, or ten observations on the returns must be used as input to estimate Equation 22.1 by regression.

When we use the Sharpe, Treynor, and Jensen measures to evaluate the performance of fairly well-diversified portfolios such as broad-market mutual funds, these performance measures will be highly correlated. Studies routinely find their correlations exceeding 0.90.

Application of Portfolio Performance Measures

To demonstrate how to apply these measures, we selected twenty open-end mutual funds and used monthly data for the five-year period from 1988 to 1992. The monthly rates of return for the first fund (Aim Constellation Fund) and the S&P 500 are contained in Table 22.1.[8] The total rate of return for each month is computed as follows:

$$R_{it} = \frac{EP_{it} + Div_{it} + Cap.\ Dist_{it} - BP_{it}}{BP_{it}}$$

---

[8]For illustrative purposes, we assume the S&P 500 is an appropriate benchmark for the funds analyzed in this section. In reality, more detailed benchmark analysis may be needed. For specialized managers, the assumptions of complete diversification for the Treynor and Jensen measures may not be appropriate; in such cases, the Sharpe measure will give a better measure of risk-adjusted return.

Table 22.1   *Example of Computation of Portfolio Evaluation Measures Using Aim Constellation Fund, Inc.*

	R_{it}	R_{mt}	RFR_t	$R_{it} - RFR_t$	$R_{mt} - RFR_t$
Jan. 1988	−1.00	4.27	0.49	−1.49	3.78
Feb. 1988	9.50	4.70	0.47	9.03	4.23
Mar. 1988	0.60	−3.02	0.47	0.13	−3.49
Apr. 1988	3.50	1.08	0.49	3.01	0.59
May 1988	−2.00	0.78	0.52	−2.52	0.26
June 1988	12.00	4.64	0.54	11.46	4.10
July 1988	−3.00	−0.40	0.50	−3.50	−0.90
Aug. 1988	−5.00	−3.31	0.53	−5.53	−3.84
Sep. 1988	4.50	4.24	0.54	3.96	3.70
Oct. 1988	0.00	2.73	0.61	−0.61	2.12
Nov. 1988	−3.00	−1.42	0.64	−3.64	−2.06
Dec. 1988	3.80	1.81	0.67	3.13	1.14
⋮	⋮	⋮	⋮	⋮	⋮
⋮	⋮	⋮	⋮	⋮	⋮
Jan. 1992	2.10	−1.86	0.32	1.78	−2.18
Feb. 1992	1.60	1.28	0.32	1.28	0.96
Mar. 1992	−3.00	−1.96	0.34	−3.34	−2.30
Apr. 1992	−5.00	2.91	0.32	−5.32	2.59
May 1992	0.70	0.54	0.31	0.39	0.24
June 1992	−5.00	−1.45	0.31	−5.31	−1.76
July 1992	6.00	4.03	0.27	5.73	3.76
Aug. 1992	−3.00	−2.02	0.26	−3.26	−2.28
Sep. 1992	3.70	1.15	0.25	3.45	0.90
Oct. 1992	6.20	0.36	0.24	5.96	0.12
Nov. 1992	8.20	3.37	0.26	7.94	3.11
Dec. 1992	4.00	1.31	0.27	3.73	1.04
Mean (annual)	26.40	15.71	6.20		
Standard Deviation (annual)	20.67	13.25	0.50		
Beta	1.351				
S_i	0.977				
S_m	0.717				
T_i	14.949				
T_m	9.508				
Jensen Intercept	0.610				
$Beta_j$	1.351				
R^2	0.752				

where:

R_{it} = the total rate of return on fund i during month t
EP_{it} = the ending price for fund i during month t
$Cap.\ Dist_{it}$ = the capital gain distributions made by fund i during month t
Div_{it} = the dividend payments made by fund i during month t
BP_{it} = the beginning price for fund i during month t

These return computations do not take into account any sales charges by the funds. Given the monthly results for the fund and the aggregate market (as represented by the S&P 500), you can compute the composite performance measures presented in Table 22.2.

The arithmetic average annual rate of return for Aim Constellation Fund was 26.40 percent versus 15.71 percent for the market, and the fund's beta of 1.351 exceeds that of the market. Using the average rate of T-bills of 6.20 percent as the RFR, the Treynor mea-

sure for the Aim Constellation Fund is substantially greater than the comparable measure for the market (14.949 versus 9.508). Likewise, the standard deviation of returns for Aim Constellation was greater than the market's (20.67 versus 13.25). Even with the higher standard deviation, the Sharpe measure for the fund was larger than the measure for the market (0.977 versus 0.717).

Finally, a regression of the fund's annual risk premium ($R_{it} - RFR_t$) and the market's annual risk premium ($R_{mt} - RFR_t$) indicated a positive intercept (constant) value of 0.610, but it was not statistically significant. If this intercept value had been significant, it would have indicated that Aim Constellation's risk-adjusted annual rate of return averaged about .61 percent above the market.

Total Sample Results   Analysis of the overall results in Table 22.2 indicate that they are generally consistent with the findings of earlier studies. Our sample was rather casually selected because we intended it for demonstration purposes only. The mean annual return for all the funds was quite close to the market return (15.45 versus 15.71). Considering only the rate of return, seven of the twenty funds outperformed the market.

The R^2 for a portfolio with the market can serve as a measure of diversification. The closer the R^2 is to 1.00, the more completely diversified the portfolio is. The average R^2 for our sample was fairly low at 0.766, and the range was quite large, from 0.285 to 0.948. This indicates that many of the funds were poorly diversified. Of the twenty funds, eleven had values less than 0.80.

The two risk measures (standard deviation and beta) likewise show a wide range, but are generally consistent with expectations. Specifically, eight of the twenty funds had larger standard deviations than the market, and the mean standard deviation was smaller (12.12 versus 13.25). Only six funds had a beta above 1.00; the average beta was 0.799.

Alternative measures ranked the performance of individual funds consistently. Using the Sharpe or the Treynor measure, eleven of the twenty funds had a value better than the market. The Jensen measure indicated that eleven of the twenty had positive intercepts, but only five of the positive intercepts were statistically significant (none of the negative intercepts was significant). The mean values for the Sharpe and Treynor measures were greater than the figure for the aggregate market. These results indicate that, on average, and without considering transaction costs, this sample of funds yielded results slightly better than the market during this time period.

You should analyze the individual funds and consider each of the components: rate of return, risk (both standard deviation and beta), and the R^2 as a measure of diversification. One might expect the best performance by funds with low diversification, because these funds are apparently attempting to beat the market by being unique in their selection or timing. This is apparently true for the top-performing funds such as Lindner Dividend Fund and Gabelli Asset Fund and also for some unsuccessful funds that had poor diversification but unfortunately low returns such as the Value Line Special Situations Fund.

Relationship among Performance Measures   Analysis of the rankings using the three measures generally confirms that they provide similar rankings. A rank correlation that related ranks rather than exact values can provide a more exact measure. The rank correlations for the funds in Table 22.2 are

Sharpe–Treynor:	0.97
Sharpe–Jensen:	0.94
Treynor–Jensen:	0.96

Because the alternative measures give similar, but not identical, rankings, we recommend that you employ all three measures. Each provides somewhat different information about risk-adjusted return and diversification.

Table 22.2   *Performance Measures for Twenty Selected Mutual Funds, Based on Monthly Total Returns*

	Average Annual Rate of Return	Standard Deviation	Beta	R^2	Treynor	Sharpe	Jensen
Aim Constellation Fund, Inc.	26.40	20.67	1.351	0.751	14.949 (6)	0.977 (7)	0.610 (2)
Dean Witter Developing Growth Fund	13.72	9.51	0.594	0.605	5.650 (19)	0.332 (19)	-0.430 (20)
Dreyfus Growth Opportunity Fund	13.22	14.20	0.905	0.713	7.764 (15)	0.495 (16)	-0.134 (15)
Fasciano Fund, Inc.	17.66	12.53	0.757	0.641	15.144 (5)	0.915 (8)	0.355 (5)
Fidelity Magellan Fund	18.46	14.32	1.048	0.941	11.699 (10)	0.856 (9)	0.192 (9)
Fidelity Puritan Fund	15.24	9.12	0.645	0.878	14.029 (7)	0.992 (6)	0.240 (8)
Gabelli Asset Fund	17.42	9.51	0.594	0.686	18.888 (2)	1.180 (4)	0.463* (4)
Guardian Park Avenue Fund	16.04	12.91	0.828	0.723	11.883 (9)	0.762 (11)	0.160 (10)
IDS Mutual Fund	11.88	9.17	0.662	0.916	8.584 (13)	0.620 (13)	-0.053 (12)
Income Fund of America, Inc.	14.68	6.98	0.458	0.758	18.504 (3)	1.216 (2)	0.342* (6)
Investment Company of America Fund	16.88	10.68	0.785	0.948	13.615 (8)	1.000 (5)	0.296* (7)
Janus Venture Fund	22.54	13.45	0.889	0.768	18.374 (4)	1.215 (3)	0.657* (1)
Kemper Technology Fund	13.70	17.05	1.106	0.739	6.780 (17)	0.440 (18)	-0.253 (17)
Lindner Dividend Fund	15.06	5.64	0.227	0.285	39.064 (1)	1.573 (1)	0.555* (3)
Oppenheimer Fund	12.42	12.32	0.818	0.818	7.603 (16)	0.505 (15)	-0.149 (16)
Putnam Fund for Growth and Income A	14.26	9.77	0.700	0.902	11.514 (11)	0.825 (10)	0.117 (11)
Templeton World Fund	12.86	12.32	0.810	0.810	8.224 (14)	0.541 (14)	-0.100 (14)
T. Rowe Price Growth Stock Fund	12.94	14.49	1.033	0.893	6.525 (18)	0.465 (17)	-0.258 (18)
Value Line Special Situations Fund	11.00	17.53	1.033	0.609	4.651 (20)	0.274 (20)	-0.481 (19)
Vanguard Wellington Fund	12.66	10.20	0.745	0.939	8.668 (12)	0.634 (12)	-0.053 (13)
Mean	15.45	12.12	0.799	0.766	12.606	0.791	0.107
S&P 500	15.71	13.25	1.000	1.000	9.508	0.717	0.000
90-Day T-Bill Rate	6.20	0.50					

*Significant.

FACTORS THAT AFFECT USE OF PERFORMANCE MEASURES

These performance measures are only as good as their data input. You need to be careful when computing the rates of return to take proper account of all inflows and outflows. More importantly, you should use judgment and be patient in the evaluation process. It is not possible to evaluate a portfolio manager on the basis of a quarter or even a year. Your evaluation should extend over several years and cover at least a full market cycle. This will allow you to determine whether the manager's performance differs during rising and declining markets.[9] Beyond these general considerations, you should consider several specific factors when using these measures.

The Market Portfolio Problem

All of the equity portfolio performance measures we have discussed are derived from the CAPM, which assumes the existence of a market portfolio at the point of tangency on the Markowitz efficient frontier. Theoretically, the market portfolio is an efficient, diversified portfolio that contains all risky assets in the economy, weighted by their market values.

The problem arises in finding a real-world proxy for this theoretical market portfolio. As noted previously, analysts typically use the Standard & Poor's 500 Index as the proxy for the market portfolio because it contains a fairly diversified portfolio of stocks, and the sample is market-value-weighted. Unfortunately, the S&P 500 Index does not represent the true composition of the market portfolio. Specifically, it includes *only* common stocks, and most of them are listed on the NYSE. Notably, it *excludes* many other risky assets that theoretically should be included, such as AMEX and OTC stocks, foreign stocks, foreign and domestic bonds, real estate, coins, precious metals, stamps, and antiques.

This lack of completeness has always been recognized, but it was not rigorously evaluated until several articles by Roll detailed the problem with the market proxy and pointed out its implications for measuring portfolio performance.[10] Although a detailed discussion of Roll's critique is not appropriate, we need to consider his concern with the measurement of the market portfolio, which he refers to as a **benchmark error**.

Various portfolio performance techniques employ the market portfolio as the benchmark. In addition, we use the market portfolio to derive our risk measures (betas). Roll showed that if the proxy for the market portfolio is not a truly efficient portfolio, the SML using this proxy may not be the true SML; the true SML could have a higher slope. In such a case, a portfolio that plotted above the SML derived using a poor benchmark could actually plot below the SML that uses the true market portfolio. An example would be Portfolio A in Figure 22.4.

A second problem is that the beta derived using this market proxy could differ from that computed using the true market portfolio. For example, if the "true" beta were larger than the beta computed using the proxy, the true position of the portfolio would shift to the right.

---

[9]For a formal presentation related to the importance of the time element, see Mark Kritzman, "How to Detect Skill in Management Performance," *Journal of Portfolio Management* 12, no. 2 (Winter 1986): 16–20.

[10]Richard Roll, "A Critique of the Asset Pricing Theory's Tests," *Journal of Financial Economics* 4, no. 4 (March 1977): 129–176; Richard Roll, "Ambiguity When Performance Is Measured by the Securities Market Line," *Journal of Finance* 33, no. 4 (September 1978): 1051–1069; Richard Roll, "Performance Evaluation and Benchmark Error I," *Journal of Portfolio Management* 6, no. 4 (Summer 1980): 5–12; and Richard Roll, "Performance Evaluation and Benchmark Error II," *Journal of Portfolio Management* 7, no. 2 (Winter 1981): 17–22.

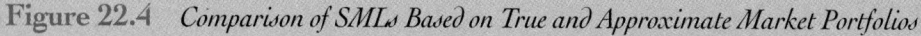

Figure 22.4   *Comparison of SMLs Based on True and Approximate Market Portfolios*

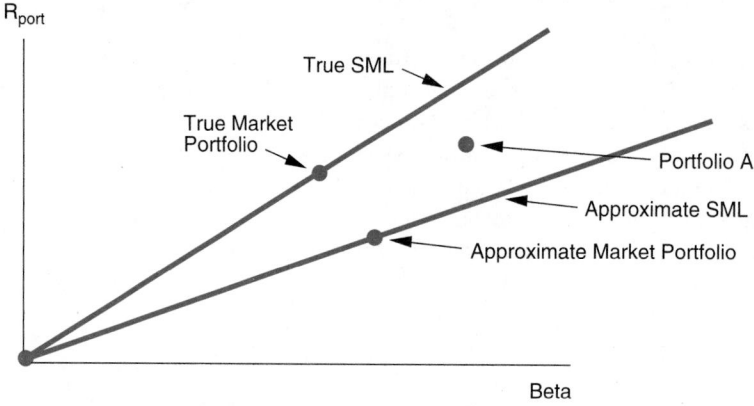

Benchmark Errors and Global Investing

Concern with the benchmark error increases with global investing. The studies on international diversification discussed in Chapters 3 and 7 state clearly that adding non-U.S. securities to the portfolio universe almost certainly will move the efficient frontier to the left because including foreign securities reduces risk. You will recall that this reduction in risk continues as you add countries that have less economic interaction with the United States, such as some Asian and third-world countries. Also, some of these additions increase the expected returns of the universe, which means that the efficient frontier would move up as well as to the left. The point is, the efficient frontier will almost certainly change when you invest in foreign securities.

The extent of the shift in the efficient frontier depends on the relationships among countries, and these relationships will change dramatically in the coming decade. Because our trade with European and Asian countries will continue its rapid growth of recent years, the interdependence of our economies and the correlation of our financial markets should increase. Also, following the creation of the European Economic Community (EEC) in 1992, individual European countries have become more interdependent because numerous barriers to trade and travel in the EEC were eliminated.

A Demonstration of the Global Benchmark Problem   Let us examine the impact of the benchmark problem in an environment of global capital markets. The following analysis considers what happens to the individual measures of risk (beta) and to the SML when the world equity market is used as the proxy for the market portfolio.[11] Table 22.3 contains estimates of the characteristic line intercept and slope (beta) and R^2 for the thirty stocks in the Dow Jones Industrial Average (DJIA) using the S&P 500, which is the typical market proxy, and the Morgan Stanley World Stock Index, which is a market-value-weighted index that contains stocks from around the world. The major differences are reflected in the betas and the R^2 of the regression lines. Specifically, in all thirty cases, the beta was *smaller* when measured against the world index than against the S&P 500 Index. In fact, the average beta (0.991 vs. 0.581) was about 40 percent lower. The effect is also reflected in the R^2, which was almost always lower with the world index. Specif-

---

[11]Frank K. Reilly and Rashid A. Akhtar, "The Benchmark Error Problem with Global Capital Markets" *Journal of Portfolio Management* 22, no. 1 (Fall 1995): 33–52.

Table 22.3 *Parameters of the Characteristic Lines for the Stocks in the Dow Jones Industrial Average, Monthly Data: 1989–94*

Stock	Standard Deviation	S&P 500			World		
		Intercept	Beta	R^2	Intercept	Beta	R^2
Alcoa	0.066	−0.004	1.115	0.394	0.007	0.411	0.056
Allied Signal	0.067	0.002	0.984	0.277	0.011	0.439	0.066
American Express	0.089	−0.006	1.104	0.191	0.003	0.546	0.055
AT&T	0.062	0.000	0.944	0.292	0.007	0.671	0.199
Bethlehem Steel	0.111	−0.013	1.531	0.241	−0.001	0.872	0.101
Boeing	0.068	0.001	0.917	0.227	0.007	0.679	0.168
Chevron	0.054	0.005	0.514	0.105	0.009	0.384	0.077
Coca-Cola	0.061	0.012	1.048	0.401	0.021	0.786	0.307
DuPont	0.065	0.001	0.941	0.263	0.009	0.576	0.129
Eastman Kodak	0.062	0.000	0.582	0.104	0.004	0.366	0.051
Exxon	0.036	0.000	0.507	0.251	0.003	0.406	0.221
General Electric	0.059	0.001	1.227	0.571	0.011	0.721	0.263
General Motors	0.081	−0.004	0.718	0.093	0.001	0.479	0.051
Goodyear	0.098	−0.012	1.067	0.142	−0.003	0.448	0.024
IBM	0.075	−0.009	0.512	0.047	−0.005	0.321	0.019
International Paper	0.066	−0.003	1.124	0.369	0.006	0.651	0.163
McDonald's	0.071	0.005	0.942	0.227	0.012	0.628	0.133
Merck	0.075	0.000	1.182	0.318	0.009	0.732	0.161
Minnesota M&M	0.044	0.001	0.809	0.430	0.007	0.488	0.208
Navistar	0.126	−0.022	1.136	0.095	−0.011	0.378	0.002
Philip Morris	0.073	0.003	1.041	0.258	0.011	0.644	0.131
PA	0.096	−0.009	1.814	0.458	0.006	0.931	0.157
Procter & Gamble	0.065	0.006	1.002	0.304	0.014	0.548	0.117
Sears	0.068	−0.006	0.988	0.266	0.001	0.617	0.136
Texaco	0.046	−0.002	0.488	0.136	0.001	0.472	0.181
USX	0.094	−0.004	1.028	0.146	0.005	0.559	0.051
Union Carbide	0.111	0.008	0.925	0.079	0.014	0.695	0.059
United Technologies	0.081	−0.002	1.079	0.231	0.006	0.719	0.136
Westinghouse	0.079	−0.018	1.071	0.228	−0.009	0.471	0.051
Woolworth	0.085	−0.018	1.344	0.319	−0.007	0.805	0.151
Mean	0.074	−0.003	0.991	0.249	0.005	0.581	0.121

ically, the average R^2 (0.249 vs. 0.121) was 51 percent smaller. These results imply a fairly significant impact on the individual measures of risk with a clear tendency for a decline in the systematic risk measure. You will recall from Chapter 7 that beta is equal to the covariance between an asset and the market portfolio divided by the variance of the market portfolio. The world portfolio has a lower variance than the S&P 500, which is what we would expect because of the international diversification. At the same time, the covariance between these U.S. stocks and a world stock index was much lower, which caused the decline in beta in Table 22.3.

Implications of the Benchmark Problem Several points are significant regarding this benchmark criticism. First, the benchmark problems noted by Roll, which are increased with global investing, do *not* negate the value of the CAPM as a *normative* model of equilibrium pricing; the theory is still viable. The problem is one of *measurement* when using the theory to evaluate portfolio performance.

Assuming a measurement problem related to a proxy for the market portfolio, it is necessary to find a better proxy for the market portfolio or to adjust any measure of

performance for benchmark errors. In fact, Roll made several suggestions to help overcome this problem.[12] From Chapter 5 we know that new comprehensive stock-market and bond-market series are being developed as market portfolio proxies. Finally, a multiple markets index (MMI) has been developed by Brinson, Diermeier, and Schlarbaum that includes foreign and domestic stocks and bonds as well as real estate and venture capital. This index, which is maintained monthly by Brinson Partners, Inc., is a major step toward a truly comprehensive world market portfolio.[13]

Alternatively, you might consider giving greater weight to the Sharpe portfolio performance measure because it does not depend so heavily on the market portfolio. Recall that this performance measure relates excess return to the *standard deviation* of return, that is, to the total risk of the portfolio being evaluated. Although this evaluation process generally uses a benchmark portfolio as an example of an unmanaged portfolio for comparison purposes, the risk measure for the portfolio being evaluated does not directly depend on a market portfolio. Also recall that the new Sharpe Ratio evaluates performance based upon differential return relative to a specified benchmark portfolio, and the risk measure is the standard deviation of this differential return.

BENCHMARKING AND PORTFOLIO STYLE

How can we tell if a portfolio manager who claims to follow a certain style really does adhere to it? Such information is important. An investor who desires to put money into "value" stocks will not be pleased if he later discovers the portfolio manager was following a growth strategy. An investment policy statement may place some constraints on investment choices; the client needs some way of assessing if his instructions were followed. As we discussed earlier, we need to identify appropriate benchmarks or indexes with which to judge a portfolio's risk and return performance. We are comparing apples to oranges if a small-stock mutual fund's performance is judged against the S&P 500; similar problems arise if a growth-stock fund is judged by a value-stock index.

Here we focus on two methods for determining a portfolio manager's style. Although the focus of our discussion will be on equities, these methods apply to fixed-income and balanced (containing some equity and some fixed income) portfolios as well.

One means of determining style is to use **returns-based analysis** or **effective mix analysis**, developed by William F. Sharpe.[14] Returns-based analysis uses the historical return pattern of the portfolio in question and compares this to the historical returns of various well-specified indexes. The analysis uses sophisticated quadratic programming techniques to indicate what styles or style combinations were most similar to the portfolio's actual historical returns. Today many pension fund and investment management consultants use software based upon Sharpe's technique to identify investment styles and to evaluate manager performance over time.

---

[12]Richard Roll, "Performance Evaluation and Benchmark Error II," *Journal of Portfolio Management* 7, no. 2 (Winter 1981): 17–22. Several more recent papers on this topic include Jeffrey V. Bailey, "Are Manager Universes Acceptable Performance Benchmarks?" *Journal of Portfolio Management* 18, no. 3 (Spring 1992): 9–13; and Richard C. Grinwold, "Are Benchmark Portfolios Efficient?" *Journal of Portfolio Management* 19, no. 1 (Fall 1992): 34–40.

[13]The multiple markets index (MMI) is described in Gary P. Brinson, Jeffrey J. Diermeier, and G. G. Schlarbaum, "A Composite Portfolio Benchmark for Pension Plans," *Financial Analysts Journal* 42, no. 2 (March–April, 1986): 15–24. This index is also discussed with changes in asset weights in Roger G. Ibbotson and Gary P. Brinson, *Global Investing* (New York: McGraw-Hill, 1993) pp. 18–19.

[14]William F. Sharpe, "Asset Allocation: Management Style and Performance Measurement," *Journal of Portfolio Management* (Winter 1992): 7–19.

Figure 22.5   *Example of a Style Benchmark and Performance Attribution*

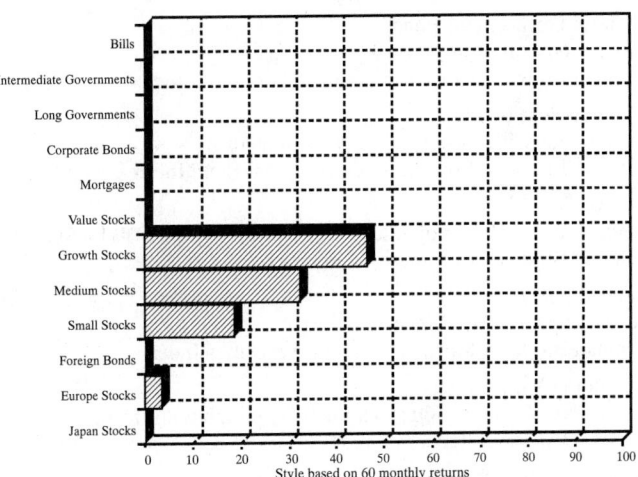

FIDELITY MAGELLAN FUND
JANUARY 1985-DECEMBER 1989

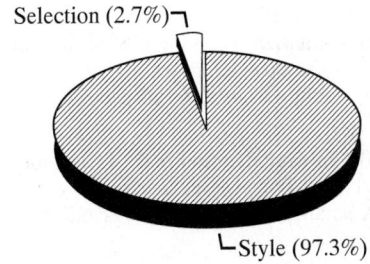

Source: In William F. Sharpe, "Asset Allocation: Management Style and Performance Measurement," *Journal of Portfolio Management* (Winter 1992): 12, Figure 5.

To illustrate, Table 22.4 shows the asset classes and indexes that Sharpe used in his initial study. He used twelve different indexes to represent a variety of investment styles, including cash (T-bills), bond indexes of various maturities and sources (government, corporate, mortgage-backed, and non-U.S.); and various stock indexes, including large-, medium-, and small-capitalization stocks; large value and large growth stocks; and European and Japanese stocks. Although Sharpe used only these asset classes in his initial study, continued use of his mathematical procedure by others has expanded the number and type of indexes used. In his study, Sharpe used sixty monthly observations of returns from these indexes and several test portfolios to illustrate his method.

For example, the top of Figure 22.5 illustrates Sharpe's analysis of the Fidelity Magellan Fund, a growth stock fund, using the indexes in Table 22.4. During the sixty-month period from January 1985 to December 1989, Magellan's returns were similar to a passive benchmark portfolio with 47 percent invested in a growth stock index, 32 percent in a medium-capitalization stock index, 19 percent in a small-capitalization stock index, and the remainder in a European-stock index.

In the pie chart underneath Sharpe shows that these indexes and allocations explain 97.3 percent of the monthly variation in Magellan's returns. In other words, in terms of

Table 22.4   *Asset Class Indices Used in Sharpe's Return-Based Analysis*

Bills
 Cash-equivalents with less than 3 months to maturity
 Index: Salomon Brothers' 90-day Treasury Bill Index

Intermediate-Term Government Bonds
 Government bonds with less than 10 years to maturity
 Index: Lehman Brothers' Long-Term Government Bond Index

Long-Term Government Bonds
 Government bonds with more than 10 years to maturity
 Index: Lehman Brothers' Long-Term Government Bond Index

Corporate Bonds
 Corporate bonds with ratings of at least Baa by Moody's or BBB by Standard & Poor's
 Index: Lehman Brothers' Corporate Bond Index

Mortgage-Related Securities
 Mortgage-backed and related securities
 Index: Lehman Brothers' Mortgage-Backed Securities Index

Large-Capitalization Value Stocks
 Stocks in Standard & Poor's 500 stock index with high book-to-price ratios
 Index: Sharpe/BARRA Value Stock Index

Large-Capitalization Growth Stocks
 Stocks in Standard & Poor's 500 stock index with low book-to-price ratios
 Index: Sharpe/BARRA Growth Stock Index

Medium-Capitalization Stocks
 Stocks in the top 80% of capitalization in the U.S. equity universe after the exclusion of
  stocks in Standard & Poor's 500 stock index
 Index: Sharpe/BARRA Medium Capitalization Stock Index

Small-Capitalization Stocks
 Stocks in the bottom 20% of capitalization in the U.S. equity universe after the exclu-
  sion of stocks in Standard & Poor's stock index
 Index: Sharpe/BARRA Small Capitalization Stock Index

Non-U.S. Bonds
 Bonds outside the U.S. and Canada
 Index: Salomon Brothers' Non-U.S. Government Bond Index

European Stocks
 European and non-Japanese Pacific Basin stocks
 Index: FTA Euro-Pacific Ex Japan Index

Japanese Stocks
 Japanese stocks
 Index: FTA Japan Index

Source: William F. Sharpe, "Asset Allocation: Management Style and Performance Measurement," *Journal of Portfolio Management* (Winter 1992): 9, Table 1.

performance attribution, 97.3 percent of the monthly variation in Magellan's returns can be explained by a passive benchmark portfolio comprised of the above specified indexes and percentage allocations. The unexplained variation in Magellan's return, presumably due to stock selection skill, is only 2.7 percent.

This analysis can be replicated on a "rolling basis" in which, as new monthly returns become available, the new month's data are added to the sixty monthly returns and the oldest observation is dropped. This allows analysts and managers to see how a fund's investment strategy or style changes over time. Figure 22.6 shows the results of rolling analysis on Magellan's returns from the late 1980s. Its style exposures changed during these

Figure 22.6 *Rolling Analysis Shows Trends in Style Exposure*

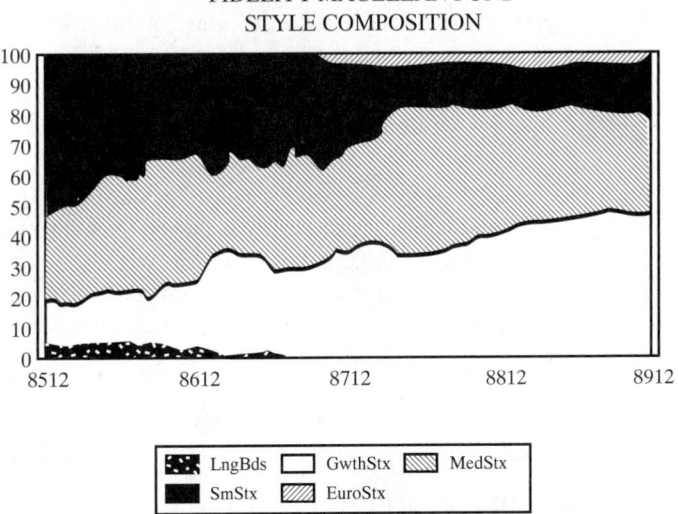

FIDELITY MAGELLAN FUND
STYLE COMPOSITION

Legend: LngBds · GwthStx · MedStx · SmStx · EuroStx

Source: William F. Sharpe, "Asset Allocation: Management Style and Performance Measurement," *Journal of Portfolio Management* (Winter 1992): 12, Figure 6.

five years. Peter Lynch, the fund's manager at the time, emphasized large growth stocks relatively more and small stocks relatively less.

A second method for determining style is to analyze the characteristics of the securities that currently compose a manager's portfolio. Rather than using historical returns, **characteristic analysis** is based on the belief that the portfolio's current make-up will be a good predictor for the next period's returns.[15]

The method classifies a portfolio manager into four basic equity styles: value, growth, market-oriented, and small-capitalization. The methodology uses a complex decision-tree approach to classify a portfolio's stocks relative to fundamental characteristics of indexes created by the Frank Russell Company, the consulting firm that developed characteristic analysis. The manager's portfolio is examined on the basis of its small-stock exposure, price/book ratio, dividend yield, price/earnings ratio, and return on equity of its constituent stocks. Finally, Russell's analysts develop a "sector deviation measure" to compare the portfolio's economic sector weightings (consumer, capital goods, technology, and so on) to those of the Russell 3000 Index, an overall market index. The results of these analyses are combined to determine the portfolio's style.

The effective mix and characteristic analysis approaches have advantages and disadvantages, some of which are discussed in the references in footnote 15. The detailed characteristic analysis method is likely to be most useful for forecasting a portfolio's near-term future returns, given its current style composition and a set of forecasts for style index returns. It is useful as well for determining whether a manager's current style is in line with her past investing patterns. Sharpe's effective mix method may be the best for the historical evaluation of a manager. Using software to which many consultants and investment

---

[15]Developed by analysts at the Frank Russell Company in Tacoma, Washington, this approach is described in Jon A. Christopherson and Dennis Trittin, "Equity Style Classification System," in T. Daniel Coggin and Frank J. Fabozzi, ed., *The Handbook of Equity Style Management* (New Hope, PA: Frank J. Fabozzi Associates Publishing, 1995), pp. 69–98; and Jon A. Christopherson, "Equity Style Classifications," *Journal of Portfolio Management* (Spring 1995): 32–43.

managers have access, the effective mix method shows past allocations and trends in a manager's style exposure.

Sharpe's method is also more useful for performance attribution. A benchmark portfolio can be constructed, using the outcomes of the effective mix analysis. A regression analysis can be done, using the form of Equation 22.3:

22.3

$$\text{Return}_{\text{portfolio}} = \text{alpha} + \text{beta}\,(\text{Return}_{\text{benchmark}})$$

By using regression analysis, we can determine variation in the portfolio's actual returns that can be explained by the passively managed benchmark. This allows us to see what percentage of the managed portfolio's returns were because of style (the R^2 measure or coefficient of determination of the regression) and how much occurred because of stock selection skill $(1 - R^2)$. The alpha of the regression is Jensen's alpha, which gives us a measure of the manager's ability to earn above-average risk-adjusted returns.

DETERMINING THE REASONS FOR SUPERIOR (OR INFERIOR) PERFORMANCE

In addition to examining historical returns, determining style, and adjusting them for risk, portfolio evaluation also involves identifying why a manager did better or worse than the benchmark. For example, a manager's superior returns could have been the result of (1) an insightful asset allocation strategy that overweighted an asset class that earned high returns; (2) investing in undervalued sectors; (3) selecting individual securities that earned above average returns; or (4) some combination of these reasons. Of course, poor returns can likewise arise from a combination of inappropriate strategies.

Performance attribution seeks to discover what went right or wrong and why. The post-mortem, coupled with a review of economic and industry conditions existing at the time that portfolio decisions were made, can be useful in determining what key variables drove portfolio returns.

Another key component of performance attribution is the client's policy statement. Performance attribution begins with the policy statement and the portfolio's normal weights (or asset allocation) and benchmark returns. These allow us to determine what the portfolio returns would have been had the manager invested funds according to the normal weights in the benchmark indexes. By comparing this with the portfolio's actual asset weights and actual returns, the sources of superior or inferior return can be pinpointed.

Performance attribution analysis begins with an overall view, focusing on major portfolio decisions that affected returns, and then examines more detailed aspects of how the portfolio was constructed. Because of this, the first step of performance attribution examines the impact of the *asset-allocation decision* on portfolio returns. In other words, we seek first to determine the difference in the policy portfolio and actual portfolio returns that occurs because the actual portfolio weights differ from the client's normal policy levels.

The effects of asset allocation are examined by comparing the impact of policy weights and actual asset weights on portfolio returns. Specifically, you would compare the policy portfolio returns (assets weighted according to policy, earning the index's returns) and the return on a portfolio that purchased the asset indexes in the same proportion as the actual portfolio weights.

The second phase of the analysis involves determining the impact of *sector and security selection*. This analysis compares the return components of the actual portfolio (actual weights, actual asset returns) with those of the portfolio invested in the asset indexes

Table 22.5 *Return Attribution Analysis*

Portfolio Weights

Policy weights	Actual weights
60% stock	70% stock
40% bond	30% bond

Component Returns

Index returns	Actual returns
15% stock index	14% stock component
10% bond index	12% bond component

in the same proportion as the actual portfolio weights. This comparison allows us to determine the effect of sector selection and security selection on portfolio returns as it focuses on the difference between portfolio returns versus index returns.

In other words, how much of the return in our portfolio occurred from overweighting good-performing sectors and underweighting poor performers, and how much of the extra return arose from selecting superior individual securities in the different sectors? We can measure the impact of sector selection by comparing sector weights in the index with the portfolio's sector weightings.

Here's an example. Suppose a portfolio that invested in both stocks and bonds returned 13.4 percent last year. During the year, the portfolio was 70 percent invested in stocks and 30 percent invested in bonds. Table 22.5 reports the relevant data on the policy portfolio stock and bond allocation, the actual portfolio allocation, the stock and bond index returns last year, and the actual returns on the portfolio's stock and bond components.

The first step of the process is to examine the asset allocation decision. Here, we assume the funds were invested in indexes and we compare the return that would have occurred (a) if the funds were invested using the policy weights and (b) if the funds were invested using the actual weights:

	Stock	Bond
Policy allocation, index returns:	$.6 \times 15\%$ +	$.4 \times 10\% = 13\%$
Actual allocation, index returns:	$.7 \times 15\%$ +	$.3 \times 10\% = 13.5\%$

The manager earned an extra $+0.5$ percent return because of a shift in allocation to the equity market during a time period when the equity market outperformed the bond market.

The second step of the process seeks to determine the role of superior (or inferior) sector or security selection on portfolio returns:

	Stock	Bond
Actual allocation, actual returns:	$.7 \times 14\%$ +	$.3 \times 12\% = 13.4\%$
Actual allocation, index returns:	$.7 \times 15\%$ +	$.3 \times 10\% = 13.5\%$

Sector/security selection hurt the portfolio's performance; returns were a 0.1 percentage point less than if the manager invested the funds in the stock and bond indexes. Overall, the manager made a good allocation decision (which increased returns 0.5 percent) but poor sector/security selection (which lowered returns by 0.1 percent).

EVALUATION OF BOND PORTFOLIO PERFORMANCE

The analysis of risk-adjusted performance for equity portfolios started in the late 1960s following the development of portfolio theory and the capital asset pricing model (CAPM). The common stock risk measures have been fairly simple—either total risk (the standard deviation of returns) or systematic risk (betas). No such development has simplified analysis for the bond market, where numerous and complex factors can influence portfolio returns. One reason for this lack of development of bond portfolio performance measures was that prior to the 1970s most bond portfolio managers followed buy-and-hold strategies, so their performance probably did not differ much. A reason for this buy-and-hold strategy is that interest rates were stable, active bond portfolios management provided little gain.

The environment in the bond market changed dramatically in the 1970s, and especially in the 1980s, when interest rates increased dramatically and became more volatile. This new environment created an incentive to trade bonds, and this trend toward more active management led to substantially greater dispersion in the performance by alternative bond portfolio managers. In turn, this dispersion in performance created a demand for techniques that would help investors evaluate manager performance.

As with the equity market, critical questions are: (1) How did performance compare among portfolio managers relative to the overall bond market or specific benchmarks? and (2) What factors explain or contribute to superior or inferior bond-portfolio performance? In this section, we present several attempts to develop bond-portfolio performance evaluation systems that consider multiple-risk factors.[16]

A Bond Market Line

A prime factor needed to evaluate performance properly is a measure of risk such as the beta coefficient for equities. This is difficult to achieve because a bond's maturity and coupon have a significant effect on the volatility of its prices.

You know from our discussion in Chapter 15 that an appropriate composite risk measure that indicates the relative price volatility for a bond compared to interest rate changes is the bond's *duration.* Using this as a measure of risk, Wagner and Tito derived a bond market line that is similar in concept to the security market line used to evaluate equity performance.[17] Duration simply replaces beta as the risk variable. The bond market line in Figure 22.7 is drawn from points defined by returns on Treasury bills to the Lehman Brothers Government–Corporate Bond Index rather than the S&P 500.[18] The Lehman Brothers Index gives the market's average annual rate of return during some common period, and the duration for the index is the value-weighted duration for the individual bonds in the index.

Given the bond market line, this technique divides the portfolio return that differs from the return on the Lehman Brothers Index into four components: (1) a policy effect, (2) a rate anticipation effect, (3) an analysis effect, and (4) a trading effect. When the latter three effects are combined, they are referred to as the **management effect.**

[16]An overview of this area and a discussion of the historical development is contained in H. Gifford Fong, "Bond Management: Past, Current, and Future," in *The Handbook of Fixed-Income Securities,* 3d ed., edited by Frank Fabozzi (Homewood, Ill.: Business One–Irwin, 1991).

[17]Wayne H. Wagner and Dennis A. Tito, "Definitive New Measures of Bond Performance and Risk," *Pension World* (May 1977): 17–26; and Dennis A. Tito and Wayne H. Wagner, "Is Your Bond Manager Skillful?" *Pension World* (June 1977): 10–16.

[18]As you know from the presentation in Chapter 5, it would be equally reasonable to use a comparable bond-market index series from Merrill Lynch, Salomon Brothers, or the Ryan Index.

Figure 22.7   *Specification of Bond Market Line Using the Lehman Brothers Bond Index*

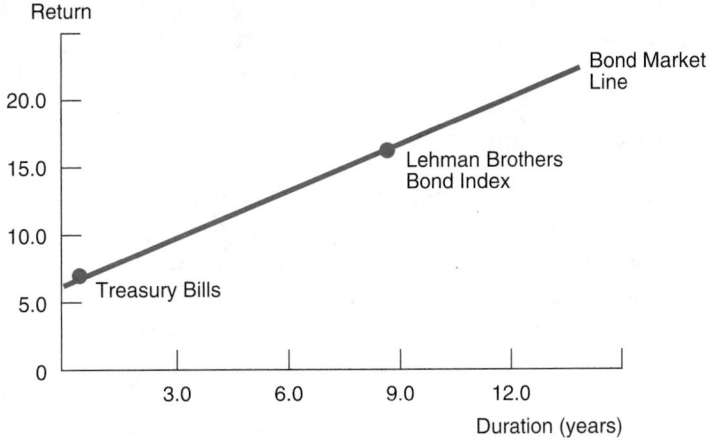

Source: Dennis A. Tito and Wayne H. Wagner, "Definitive New Measures of Bond Performance and Risk," *Pension World* (June 1977).

The **policy effect** measures the difference in the expected return for a given portfolio because of a difference in the portfolio's long-term policy duration target compared to that of the Lehman Brothers Index. This assumes that the policy duration of an unmanaged portfolio would equal the Lehman Brothers Index. A difference between a portfolio's policy duration and that of the index indicates a decision regarding relative risk. Therefore, given a difference in duration (that is, a difference in interest rate risk), expected returns should be different.

The **interest rate anticipation effect** attempts to measure the differential return from *changing* the duration of the portfolio during this period compared to the portfolio's long-term policy duration. You would hope that the manager would increase the duration of the portfolio if declining interest rates are expected and reduce the duration if rising interest rates are anticipated. The interest rate anticipation effect is determined by comparing the portfolio's duration over a period to the long-term policy duration of the portfolio. The difference in expected return for these two durations can be determined using the bond market line.

The difference between the *expected* return based on the portfolio's duration and the *actual* return for the portfolio during this period is a combination of an analysis effect and a trading effect. The **analysis effect** is the extra return attributable to acquiring bonds that are temporarily mispriced relative to their risk. To measure the analysis effect, you compare the *expected* return for the portfolio held at the beginning of the period (using the bond market line) to the *actual* return of this same portfolio *if it were passively managed* (that is, a buy-and-hold policy). If the actual passive return is greater than the expected return, it implies that the portfolio manager acquired some underpriced issues that became properly priced and provided excess returns during the period.

Finally, the **trading effect** occurs due to short-run changes in the portfolio during the period. It is measured by subtracting the analysis effect from the total excess return based on duration.

This technique examines the return based on the duration, which is used as a comprehensive risk measure. The only concern is that *duration does not consider differences in the risk of default*. Specifically, the technique does not differentiate between an AAA bond with a duration of eight years and a BBB bond with the same duration. This could

clearly affect the performance. A portfolio manager who invested in BBB bonds, for example, could experience a positive analysis effect simply because the bonds were lower quality than the average quality implicit in the Lehman Brothers Index. The only way to avoid this would be to construct differential market lines for alternative ratings or construct a benchmark line that matches the quality makeup of the portfolio being evaluated.[19]

Decomposing Portfolio Returns

Dietz, Fogler, and Hardy set forth a technique to decompose the bond portfolio returns into maturity, sector, and quality effects.[20] The total return for a bond during a period of time is composed of a known **income effect** (caused by normal yield-to-maturity factors) and an unknown **price change effect** (caused by an interest rate effect, a sector/quality effect, and a residual effect). It is diagrammed as follows:

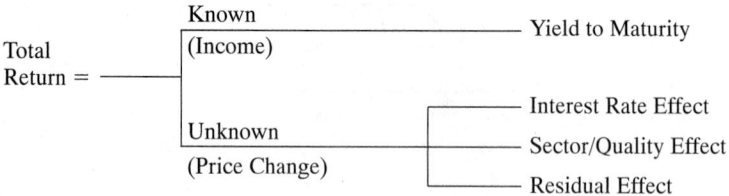

The **income** (or yield-to-maturity) **effect** is the return an investor would receive if the shape and position of the yield curve remained constant during the period. That is, the investor would receive the interest income, and any price change due to the passage of time and the shape of the yield curve.

The **interest rate effect** measures what happened to each issue because of changes in the term structure of interest rates during the period. Each bond is valued based on the Treasury yield curve at its maturity and takes account of its normal premium relative to Treasury yields. For example, assume a normal risk premium spread of thirty basis points and also assume that yields on Treasury bonds with the maturity of your bond go from 8.50 percent to 9.25 percent. To determine the interest rate effect, you would compute the value of your bond at 8.80 percent (8.50 + 0.30) and at 9.55 percent (9.25 + 0.30) and then compute the price change. This is the price change caused by a change in market interest rates.

The **sector/quality effect** measures the expected impact on the returns because of changing yield spreads between bonds in different sectors (for example, corporates, utilities, financial, GNMA) and ratings (AAA, AA, A, BBB). As an example, during a given period you might find that an average AA-rated utility bond had negative excess returns of −0.50 percent after taking account of the yield to maturity and the interest rate effect. Alternatively, an average A-rated corporate bond based upon a comparable analysis experienced a positive excess return of 0.30 percent. Therefore, the sector/quality effect would be −0.50 and 0.30 for these sets of bonds.

The **residual effect** is what remains after taking account of the three prior factors— yield to maturity, interest rate effect, and the sector/quality effect. The presence of a consistently large positive residual would indicate superior bond selection capabilities. Specifically, a positive residual indicates that after taking account of all market effects

[19]This problem is briefly discussed in Frank K. Reilly and Rupinder Sidhu, "The Many Uses of Bond Duration," *Financial Analysts Journal* 36, no. 4 (July–August 1980): 58–72.

[20]Peter D. Dietz, H. Russell Fogler, and Donald J. Hardy, "The Challenge of Analyzing Bond Portfolio Returns," *Journal of Portfolio Management* 6, no. 3 (Spring 1980): 53–58.

from interest rate changes and sector/quality, it is still possible the bond manager has helped provide positive returns due to bond selection.

For a given portfolio, you should prepare a time-series plot of these alternative effects to determine the strengths and weaknesses of your bond portfolio manager. Also, these results net of transaction costs and taxes should be compared to the results for a static portfolio (that is, assume you buy and hold the beginning portfolio). Finally, these results should be compared to the performance of a broad bond-market index, which would be considered an unmanaged portfolio.

Investments Online

Mutual fund performance is a matter of public knowledge, but performance for the vast variety of pension funds, endowments, insurance company portfolios, trust portfolios, and other private investment pools may not be public. Investors will have to use the tools discussed in this chapter to evaluate the performance of nonpublic portfolios. Many investor consultants and software firms have proprietary databases and products, and they try to sell their services to individual and institutional investors as a means of evaluating portfolio performance. Consultants who evaluate money managers for clients will not offer the proprietary results of that research for free on the Internet. Nonetheless, some sites are helpful in showing applications of the material covered in this chapter.

www.nelnet.com
The Web site of the Nelson Investment Manager database calls itself the "World's Best Money Managers" page. Nelson has a database of more than 1,700 investment managers and more than 6,000 investment styles and strategies. After registering at the site, users can specify investment categories and obtain ranking performance data in a variety of formats. The site offers links to industry analysis and news as well as to investment managers' home pages and to sites of institutional investment managers.

www.first-rate.com
The First Rate, Inc., Web site offers sample portfolio evaluation reports that can be viewed on-line. Users pay to receive actual reports.

www.styleadvisor.com
Zephyr Associates, Inc.'s, Web site features information about StyleADVISOR. StyleADVISOR is a returns-based style and performance analysis software package. It uses Sharpe's techniques of performance analysis and attribution. Pages offer visitors the chance to learn about StyleADVISOR and to view sample reports, some of whose formats are similar to those shown in this chapter (for example, Figure 22.5). Past newsletters are available for viewing; they give analysis and insights into portfolio performance attribution issues.

www.fundstyle.com
After visitors register for free, Advisor Software, Inc., offers free style analyses on more than 6,300 mutual funds.

www.morningstar.net
This site, mentioned in Chapter 21, allows users to obtain summary reports on funds. These "Quicktake" reports offer information on returns, volatility statistics, Morningstar rating, and MPT (modern portfolio theory) statistics such as alpha and

Investments Online *(cont.)*

beta. The report gives the fund's style, as well, using
Morningstar's 3x3 style box.
www.valueline.com
Subscribers can obtain useful mutual fund performance information, including
charts, both absolute and relative-to-peer-group return performance, and the
fund's style, using Value Line's style box.
www.aimr.org
First referred to in Chapter 2, the Association for Investment Management and
Research's home page offers a link to information about the AIMR Performance
Presentation Standards. These are a set of ethical principles and guidelines to
help ensure fair representation, full disclosure, and comparability in reported
portfolio performance results. The site provides links to resources for training
and for library information on the standards.

SUMMARY

◆ The first major goal of portfolio management is to follow the client's policy statement
to meet his or her objectives and satisfy his or her constraints. A second goal of portfolio management is to derive rates of return that equal or exceed the returns on a naively
selected portfolio with equal risk. The third goal is to attain complete diversification.
An initial step to ensure good client–manager relations and fair manager appraisal is to
select or construct an appropriate benchmark portfolio. The performance of the actively
managed portfolio will be judged relative to the passive benchmark.

◆ Several measures have been developed to evaluate equity portfolios in terms of both risk
and return (composite measures). The original Sharpe measure indicates the excess return
relative to the risk-free return per unit of total risk. The new Sharpe Ratio examines the
average differential return relative to the portfolio's benchmark divided by the standard
deviation of the differential return. The Treynor measure considers the excess return
earned per unit of systematic risk. The Jensen alpha also evaluates performance in terms
of the systematic risk and shows how to determine whether the difference in risk-
adjusted performance (good or bad) is statistically significant. Methods of performance attribution, which examined the impact of asset allocation and selection on a
portfolio's returns relative to their benchmark, were also reviewed.

◆ Roll challenged the validity of all techniques that assume a "market portfolio" that theoretically includes all risky assets, when investigators typically use a proxy such as the
S&P 500 that is limited to U.S. common stocks. This criticism does not invalidate the
normative asset pricing model, only its application because of measurement problems
related to the proxy used for the market portfolio. We discussed how the benchmark measurement problem is increased in an environment where global investing is the norm.
The good news is that more comprehensive indexes are feasible, and one has been developed by Brinson Partners.

◆ The performance of portfolio managers who follow a specific style must be compared
to appropriate benchmarks. Two main techniques help determine a manager's style.
Returns-based or effective mix analysis uses quadratic programming to determine

what subset and percentage allocations from a group of indexes most closely resembles the portfolio's performance over time. Characteristic analysis examines the characteristics of the securities held in the portfolio to judge the manager's style.

♦ Although the techniques for evaluating equity portfolio performance have been in existence for almost thirty-five years, comparable techniques for examining bond portfolio performance were initiated only about fifteen years ago. Notably, the evaluation models for bonds typically consider separately the several important decision variables related to bonds: the overall market factor, the impact of maturity–duration decisions, the influence of sector and quality factors, and the impact of individual bond selection.

♦ In conclusion, investors need to evaluate their own performance and the performance of hired managers. The various techniques discussed provide theoretically justifiable measures that differ slightly. Although correlation was high among the various measures, *all the measures should be used* because each provides different insights regarding the performance of managers. Finally, a portfolio manager should be evaluated many times and in a variety of *market environments* before a final judgment is reached regarding his or her strengths and weaknesses.

Questions

1. Assuming you are managing your own portfolio, discuss whether you should evaluate your own performance. What would you compare your performance against?
2. What are the three major factors to consider when evaluating a portfolio manager?
3. How can a portfolio manager earn superior risk-adjusted returns?
4. What is the purpose of diversification according to the CAPM?
5. How can you measure whether a portfolio is completely diversified? Explain why this measure makes sense.
6. Define and discuss the Treynor measure of portfolio performance.
7. Define and discuss the original Sharpe measure of portfolio performance.
8. Why is it suggested that an evaluation employ both the Treynor and Sharpe measures of performance? What additional information do we gather when we compare the rankings achieved using the two measures?
9. Define the new Sharpe Ratio and discuss how it differs from the original Sharpe measure.
10. Define the Jensen measure of performance, and discuss whether it should produce results similar to those from the Treynor or the Sharpe methods.
11. Assuming the proxy used for the market portfolio is not a good proxy, discuss the potential problem with the measurement of portfolio beta. Show by an example the effect on a portfolio evaluation graph if the measured beta is significantly lower than the true beta.
12. Assuming the market proxy is a poor proxy, show an example of the potential impact on the security market line (SML) and demonstrate with an example how a portfolio that was superior relative to the proxy SML line could be inferior when compared to the true SML.
13. Show with a graph the effect global investing should have on the aggregate efficient frontier. Discuss the effect of this on the world SML and individual betas.
14. Why is it important to determine a portfolio manager's style?
15. What is returns-based analysis? Describe the value of its result to a portfolio manager's client or potential client.
16. What is characteristic analysis? What advantage(s) does it have over returns-based analysis?
17. It is contended that the derivation of an appropriate model for evaluating the performance of a bond portfolio manager is more difficult than an equity portfolio evaluation model because the former requires more decisions. Discuss some of the specific decisions you must consider when evaluating the performance of a bond portfolio manager.
18. Briefly describe what you are trying to measure in the following cases:
    a. The interest rate effect (that is, market effect)
    b. The maturity effect (duration)

    c. The sector/quality effect

    d. The selection effect

19. Which of the effects in Question 18 are under the control of the bond portfolio manager?

20. *CFA Examination III (1981)*

    Richard Roll, in an article on using the capital asset pricing model (CAPM) to evaluate portfolio performance, indicated that it may not be possible to evaluate portfolio management ability if there is an error in the benchmark used.

    a. In evaluating portfolio performance, describe the general procedure, with emphasis on the benchmark employed. [5 minutes]

    b. Explain what Roll meant by the benchmark error and identify the specific problem with this benchmark. [5 minutes]

    c. Draw a graph that shows how a portfolio that has been judged as superior relative to a "measured" security market line (SML) can be inferior relative to the "true" SML. [10 minutes]

    d. Assume you are informed that a given portfolio manager has been evaluated as superior when compared to the DJIA, the S&P 500, and the NYSE Composite Index. Explain whether this consensus would make you feel more comfortable regarding the portfolio manager's true ability. [5 minutes]

    e. While conceding the possible problem with benchmark errors as set forth by Roll, some contend this does not mean the CAPM is incorrect, but only that there is a measurement problem when implementing the theory. Others contend that because of benchmark errors, the whole technique should be scrapped. Take and defend one of these positions. [5 minutes]

21. *CFA Examination III (1982)*

    During a quarterly review session, a client of Fixed Income Investors, a pension fund advisory firm, asks Fred Raymond, the portfolio manager for the company's account, if he could provide a more detailed analysis of their portfolio performance than simply total return. Specifically, the client had recently seen a copy of an article by Dietz, Fogler, and Hardy on the analysis of bond portfolio returns that attempted to decompose the total return into the following four components:

    a. Yield-to-maturity effect

    b. Interest rate effect

    c. Sector/quality effect

    d. Residual

    Although he does not expect you to be able to provide such an analysis this year, he asks you to explain each of these components to him so he will be better prepared to understand such an analysis when you do it for his company's portfolio next year. Explain each of these components. [20 minutes]

22. What are the attributes of a good benchmark?

23. "If an equity portfolio manager can't do better than the S&P 500 over two or three years, I fire them!" says I. M. Quick, who oversees several external managers of his company's pension fund. Do you agree that Mr. Quick has a good policy? Why or why not?

24. Using the Bond Market Line, is it possible for a manager to have a negative policy effect but a positive interest rate anticipation effect? Can the analysis effect be negative while the trading effect is positive? Explain.

Problems

1. Assume during the past 10-year period the risk-free rate was 8 percent, and three portfolios had the following characteristics:

Portfolio	Return (%)	Beta	σ
A	13	1.10	14
B	11	0.90	10
C	17	1.20	20

Compute the Treynor value for each portfolio, and indicate which portfolio had the best performance. Assume the market return during this period was 12 percent; how did these managers fare relative to the market?

2. Given the standard deviations specified in Problem 1, compute the Sharpe measure of performance for the three portfolios. Is there any difference in the ranking achieved using the Treynor versus the Sharpe measure? Discuss the probable cause.

3. Assume that instead of covering ten years, the information in Problem 1 covers a one-year time period. Compute Jensen's alpha measures for portfolios A, B, and C.

4. The portfolios identified below are being considered for investment; some statistics for the most recent year are presented. During this time the risk-free rate was 7 percent.

Portfolio	Return	Beta	σ
P	15	1.0	5
Q	20	1.5	10
R	10	1.6	3
S	17	1.1	6
Market	13	1.0	4

a. Compute the Sharpe measure of each portfolio and the market portfolio.
b. Compute the Treynor measure of each portfolio and the market portfolio.
c. Compute the Jensen measure for each portfolio and the market portfolio.
d. Rank the portfolios using each measure.

5. You have decided to undertake an evaluation of the performance of the Cirrus International Fund (CIF) for your Investment Club. You've collected the following data: Return on CIF = 15%; RFR = 5%; β for CIF = 1.20; market return = 10%.
a. Draw the security market line.
b. Compute a risk-adjusted return measure for CIF. How does CIF compare to the market portfolio?

6. Below are some approximate data on the returns and risks of several assets. Rank them based on their Sharpe and Treynor measures. Which measure provides the most relevant rankings in this case?

Asset	Average Return	Standard Deviation	Beta (Based on the S&P 500)
Small-company stocks	18%	36%	1.34
Large-company stocks	12	21	1.00
Long-term Treasury bonds	9	8	0.70
Intermediate-term Treasury bonds	8	7	0.60
Treasury bills	4	4	0.10

7. What were the actual returns on the portfolios of manager A and manager B? What was the source of the over- or underperformance by managers A and B?

Weights

Manager A	Policy	Actual
	50% stocks	55% stocks
	50% bonds	45% bonds

Returns

	Index	Actual
	10% stocks	8% stocks
	6% bonds	8% bonds

Weights		
Manager B	**Policy**	**Actual**
	60% stocks	50% stocks
	30% bonds	30% bonds
	10% cash	20% cash

Returns		
	Index	**Actual**
	−5% stocks	−2% stocks
	7% bonds	8% bonds
	3% cash	3.5% cash

References

Brinson, Gary P., and Nimrod Fachler. "Measuring Non-U.S. Equity Portfolio Performance." *Journal of Portfolio Management* 11, no. 3 (Spring 1985).

T. Daniel Coggin and Frank J. Fabozzi, ed. *The Handbook of Equity Style Management,* 2nd ed. New Hope, PA: Frank J. Fabozzi Associates Publishing, 1997.

Dietz, Peter O., and Jeannette R. Kirschman. "Evaluating Portfolio Performance." In *Managing Investment Portfolios,* 2nd ed., ed. John L. Maginn and Donald L. Tuttle. Boston: Warren Gorham and Lamont, 1990.

Fama, Eugene. "Components of Investment Performance." *Journal of Finance* 27, no. 3 (June 1972).

Fong, Gifford, Charles Pearson, Oldrich Vasicek, and Theresa Conroy. "Fixed-Income Portfolio Performance: Analyzing Sources of Return." In *The Handbook of Fixed-Income Securities,* 3d ed., edited by Frank J. Fabozzi. Homewood, Ill.: Business One–Irwin, 1991.

Kahn, Ronald N. "Bond Performance Analysis: A Multi-Factor Approach." *Journal of Portfolio Management* 18, no. 1 (Fall 1991).

Klein, Robert A., and Jess Lederman, ed. *Equity Style Management.* Chicago: Irwin Professional Publishing, 1995.

Leibowitz, Martin L., Lawrence Bader, and Stanley Koselman. "Optimal Portfolios Relative to Benchmark Allocations," *Journal of Portfolio Management* 19, no. 4 (Summer 1993).

Shulka, Ray, and Charles Trzcinka. "Performance Measurement of Managed Portfolios." In *Financial Markets, Institutions and Investments.* Vol. 1, no. 4. New York: New York University Salomon Center, 1992.

GLOSSARY

Analysis effect   The difference in performance of a bond portfolio from that of a chosen index due to acquisition of temporarily mispriced issues that then move to their correct prices.

Benchmark error   An inaccuracy in evaluation of portfolio performance due to poor representation of market performance because of the market indicator series chosen as a proxy for the market portfolio.

Benchmark portfolio   A portfolio that represents the performance evaluation standard for a portfolio manager. The benchmark portfolio is usually a passive index or portfolio with an asset allocation equal to that specified in the investor's policy statement.

Characteristic analysis   Characteristic analysis is based on the belief that the portfolio's current make-up will be a good predictor for the next period's returns. The methodology uses a complex decision-tree approach to classify a portfolio's stocks relative to fundamental characteristics of indexes.

Income effect   The known component of the total return for a bond during a period of time if the shape and position of the yield curve did not change. Also known as the *yield-to-maturity effect.*

Interest rate anticipation effect   The difference in return caused by changing the duration of the portfolio during a period as compared with the portfolio's long-term policy duration.

Interest rate effect The return on a bond portfolio caused by changes in the term structure of interest rates during a period.

Management effect A combination of the interest rate anticipation effect, the analysis effect, and the trading effect.

Normal portfolio A specialized or customized benchmark constructed to evaluate a specific manager's investment style or philosophy.

Policy effect The difference in performance of a bond portfolio from that of a chosen index due to differences in duration, which result from a fund's investment policy.

Price change effect The unknown component of the total return for a bond portfolio during a period of time due to the interest rate effect, sector/quality effect, and residual effect.

Residual effect The return on a bond portfolio not caused by the yield-to-maturity, interest rate, and sector/quality effects.

Returns-based analysis or **effective mix analysis** Returns-based analysis compares the historical return pattern of the portfolio in question to the historical returns of various well-specified indexes. The analysis uses sophisticated quadratic programming techniques to indicate what styles or style combinations were most similar to the portfolio's actual historical returns.

Sector/quality effect The return on a bond portfolio caused by changing yield spreads between bonds in different sectors and with different quality ratings.

Trading effect The difference in performance of a bond portfolio from that of a chosen index due to short-run changes in the composition of the portfolio.

APPENDIX 22 *Computing Portfolio Returns*

Before we can evaluate portfolio performance, we need to measure it. In Chapter 1 we learned how to calculate a holding period yield, which equals the change in portfolio value plus income divided by beginning portfolio value, or:

$$\text{HPY} = \frac{(\text{Ending Value} - \text{Beginning Value}) + \text{Income}}{\text{Beginning Value}}$$

Depending on the length of the holding period, it is possible to convert the holding period yield into an annualized return (if the holding period was less than one year) or an average annual return (if the holding period exceeded one year).

This calculation is not appropriate for many portfolios that experience cash inflows or cash outflows over time, such as a pension fund or mutual fund. The portfolio's ending value may be contaminated by the net effect of the periodic cash flows. We can use two basic approaches to account for intermittent cash flows: the dollar-weighted rate of return or the time-weighted rate of return.

To illustrate how to compute these two measures, we'll use the following scenario: at time 0 we invest $1,000 in Unbelievable Mutual Fund (a no-load fund). The fund shares have a NAV of $20, so we are purchasing fifty shares. At time 1, the fund pays a $1 per share income distribution, so we receive $1 × 50 shares or $50 in income. Also, the value of the fund increases by 25 percent to a NAV of $25, which means our holdings are worth $1,300 (50 shares × $25/share NAV + $50 income distribution). The fund has returned 30 percent during this first period.

At time 1 we invest another $1,000 in Unbelievable by purchasing another forty shares ($1,000/$25 NAV). Our share total is now ninety shares, At time 2, Unbelievable pays an income distribution of $1 per share (we receive $90) and the NAV has risen 40 percent to

$35. The value of our holdings is now 90 shares × $35 + $90 (income distribution) = $3,240.

What has been our return over this time period? It depends on whether you compute a dollar-weighted rate of return or a time-weighted rate of return.

Dollar-Weighted Rate of Return

The dollar-weighted rate of return (DWRR) is simply the internal rate of return on the portfolio's cash flows. It is the rate of return that sets the present value of the cash outflows equal to the present value of the cash inflows. In other words, it is the return earned on the invested funds that allow them to grow to the end-of-period value. To determine the DWRR, our cash outflows to the portfolio were:

$1,000 at time 0
$1,000 at time 1

The cash inflows from our investment were:

$50 at time 1
$90 at time 2
$3,150 worth of mutual fund shares at time 2

Setting the present values of the inflows and outflows equal to each other, we have:

$$\$1,000 + \frac{\$1,000}{(1+r)} = \frac{\$50}{(1+r)} + \frac{(\$90 + \$3,150)}{(1+r)^2}$$

Solving for r, the internal rate of return or DWRR is 38.66 percent. Our average annual return over these two periods was 38.66 percent.

Time-Weighted Rate of Return

The time-weighted rate of return (TWRR) is simply the geometric average return. The TWRR is computed by finding the product of the holding period returns (which equals 1 + HPY) for the n periods of time, raising it to the power of $1/n$, and then subtracting 1 from it:

$$\text{TWRR} = [(\text{HPR}_1)(\text{HPR}_2)(\text{HPR}_3)\dots(\text{HPR}_n)]^{1/n} - 1.$$

The history of our Unbelievable investment was:

Time	Market Value before Cash Flow	Cash In (Out)	Market Value after Cash Flow	Return
0	$0	$1,000	$1,000	Not applicable

(NAV is $20/share; we purchase 50 shares)

1	$1,300	($50) + $1,000	$2,250	$1,300/$1,000 − 1 = 30%

(NAV is now 25% higher, or $25/share; we purchase an additional 40 shares; we now own a total of 90 shares)

2	$3,240	($90)	$3,150	$3,240/$2,250 − 1 = 44%

Thus, the first period's return was 30 percent; the second period's return was 44 percent. The time-weighted rate of return is:

$$\text{TWRR} = [(1 + .30)(1 + .44)]^{1/2} - 1 = 0.3682,$$

or the average annual return is 36.82 percent.

So we've computed our returns two different ways and we have two different answers. The DWRR is 38.66 percent; the TWRR is 36.82 percent. Which of these is the correct return?

Why the Time-Weighted Rate of Return Is Superior

The TWRR is generally acknowledged as the best way to compute returns; in fact, the portfolio performance standards adopted by the Association for Investment Management and Research require that returns be computed using the TWRR approach.[21] The TWRR is regarded as the better method because it considers only the actual period-by-period portfolio returns. As such, the TWRR has no size bias whereas the dollar-weighted rate of return does. The DWRR's size bias is inappropriate because portfolio managers generally have little control over the cash flows into or out of their portfolios. New pension fund clients depositing funds, retiree withdrawals, IRA deposits, heavy cash inflows due to a mutual fund's investment success—all of these cash flows will affect the DWRR and will therefore cause the DWRR to present a biased picture of overall fund returns.

This size bias was evident in our example. The first period's return was 30 percent; after more funds were invested, the second period's return was 44 percent. The DWRR of 38.66 is higher than the TWRR of 36.82 percent because the fund was larger when it had a higher return in period 2.

We can easily show that, had the periodic returns been reversed, the DWRR would be less than the TWRR since the fund's large 44 percent return would occur during a period when less funds were invested in it. The following table represents the cash flows and market values assuming a 44 percent first-period return and a 30 percent second-period return. As before, we assume an annual income distribution of $1 a share, and the initial NAV is $20 a share.

Time	Market Value before Cash Flow	Cash In (Out)	Market Value after Cash Flow	Return
0	$0	$1,000	$1,000	Not applicable

(NAV is $20 per share; we purchase fifty shares)

Time	Market Value before Cash Flow	Cash In (Out)	Market Value after Cash Flow	Return
1	$1,440	($50) + 1,000	$2,390	$1,440/$1,000 − 1 = 44%

(NAV is now 39 percent higher, or $27.8 per share; we purchase an additional 35.97 shares; we now own a total of 85.97 shares)

Time	Market Value before Cash Flow	Cash In (Out)	Market Value after Cash Flow	Return
2	$3,107	($85.97)	$3,021.03	$3,107/$2,390 − 1 = 30%

It is straightforward to see the TWRR remains the same at 36.82 percent:

$$\text{TWRR} = [(1 + .44)(1 + .30)]^{1/2} - 1 = 0.3682.$$

---

[21]*Performance Presentation Standards,* Association for Investment Management and Research, Charlottesville, Va., 1993.

Again, the dollar-weighted rate of return is found by equating the present values of the cash inflows and outflows:

$$\$1,000 + \frac{\$1,000}{(1 + r)} = \frac{\$50}{(1 + r)} + \frac{(\$85.97 + \$3,021.03)}{(1 + r)^2}$$

Solving for r, we see the dollar-weighted rate of return is now 35.05 percent. It is lower than the TWRR now because Unbelievable's returns were lower in the second period when the fund size was larger. This illustrates the DWRR's size bias and indicates that a more accurate picture of a fund's returns is generated by using the TWRR.

For simplicity, our examples here assumed annual cash flows. Real-world managers deal with fund cash inflows and outflows daily that result from dividends, bond coupons, and investor deposits and withdrawals. They must make day-by-day accountings of cash flows and portfolio market values. The time-weighted rate of return is a daily average return; the annual return is derived by compounding the daily return over 365 days.

Once portfolio returns have been measured, they can be compared to those of the benchmark. Portfolio returns should be adjusted for the level of portfolio risk to determine if higher returns were earned solely because the manager invested in higher risk securities.

APPENDIX A

How to Become a Chartered Financial Analyst

As mentioned in the section on career opportunities, the professional designation of Chartered Financial Analyst (CFA) is becoming a significant requirement for a career in investment analysis and/or portfolio management. For that reason, this section presents the history and objectives of the Institute of Chartered Financial Analysts and general guidelines for acquiring the CFA designation. If you are interested in the program, you can write to the Institute for more information.

The Institute of Chartered Financial Analysts (ICFA) was formed in 1959 in Charlottesville, Virginia. The CFA candidate examinations were first offered in 1963. The ICFA, along with the Financial Analysts Federation, form the Association for Investment Management and Research (AIMR).

The Institute of Chartered Financial Analysts (ICFA) was organized to enhance the professionalism of those involved in various aspects of the investment decision-making process and to recognize those who achieve a high level of professionalism by awarding the designation of Chartered Financial Analyst (CFA).

The basic missions and purposes of the AIMR/ICFA are

■ To develop and keep current a "body of knowledge" applicable to the investment decision-making process. The principal components of this knowledge are financial accounting, economics, both fixed-income and equity securities analysis, portfolio management, ethical and professional standards, and quantitative techniques.

■ To administer a study and examination program for eligible candidates, the primary objectives of which are to assist the candidate in mastering and applying the body of knowledge and to test the candidate's competency in the knowledge gained.

■ To award the professional CFA designation to those candidates who have passed three examination levels (encompassing a total of 18 hours of testing over a minimum of three years), who meet stipulated standards of professional conduct, and who otherwise are eligible for membership in the ICFA.

■ To provide a useful and informative program of continuing education through seminars, publications, and other formats that enable members, candidates, and others in the investment constituency to be more aware of and to better utilize the changing and expanding body of knowledge.

■ To sponsor and enforce a *Code of Ethics and Standards of Professional Conduct* that apply to enrolled candidates and to all members.

A college degree is necessary to enter the program. A candidate may sit for all three examinations without having had investment experience *per se* or having joined a constituent Society of the Financial Analysts Federation. However, after passing the three examination levels, the CFA Charter will not be awarded unless or until the candidate

■ has at least three years of experience as a financial analyst, which is defined as a person who has spent and/or is spending a substantial portion of his/her professional time collecting, evaluating, and applying financial, economic, and related data to the investment decision-making process, and

■ has applied for membership or is a member of a constituent Society of the Financial Analysts Federation, if such a Society exists within 50 miles of the candidate's principal place of business.

The curriculum of the CFA study program covers:

1. Ethical and Professional Standards
2. Financial Accounting
3. Economics
4. Fixed-Income Securities Analysis
5. Equity Securities Analysis
6. Portfolio Management
7. Quantitative Techniques

Members and candidates are typically employed in the investment field. From 1963 to 1991, over 13,000 charters have been awarded. More than 13,000 individuals currently are registered in the CFA Candidate Program. If you are interested in learning more about the CFA program, the Institute has a booklet that describes the program and includes an application form. The address is Institute of Chartered Financial Analysts, P.O. Box 3668, Charlottesville, Virginia 22903.

Source: Reprinted with permission from The Financial Analysts Federation and The Institute of Chartered Financial Analysts, Charlottesville, Virginia.

APPENDIX B

Code of Ethics and Standards of Professional Conduct

THE STANDARDS OF PROFESSIONAL CONDUCT

I. **Obligation to Inform Employer of Code and Standards**
The financial analyst shall inform his employer, through his direct supervisor, that the analyst is obligated to comply with the Code of Ethics and Standards of Professional Conduct, and is subject to disciplinary sanctions for violations thereof. He shall deliver a copy of the Code and Standards to his employer if the employer does not have a copy.

II. **Compliance with Governing Laws and Regulations and the Code and Standards**

A. **Required Knowledge and Compliance**
The financial analyst shall maintain knowledge of and shall comply with all applicable laws, rules, and regulations of any government, governmental agency, and regulatory organization governing his professional, financial, or business activities, as well as with these Standards of Professional Conduct and the accompanying Code of Ethics.

B. **Prohibition Against Assisting Legal and Ethical Violations**
The financial analyst shall not knowingly participate in, or assist, any acts in violation of any applicable law, rule, or regulation of any government, governmental agency, or regulatory organization governing his professional, financial, or business activities, nor any act which would violate any provision of these Standards of Professional Conduct or the accompanying Code of Ethics.

C. **Prohibition Against Use of Material Nonpublic Information**
The financial analyst shall comply with all laws and regulations relating to the use and communication of material nonpublic information. The financial analyst's duty is generally defined as to not trade while in possession of, nor communicate, material nonpublic information in breach of a duty, or if the information is misappropriated.

Duties under the Standard include the following: (1) If the analyst acquires such information as a result of a special or confidential relationship with the issuer or others, he shall not communicate the information (other than within the relationship), or take investment action on the basis of such information, if it violates that relationship. (2) If the analyst is not in a special or confidential relationship with the issuer or others, he shall not communicate or act on material nonpublic information if he knows, or should have known, that such information (a) was disclosed to him, or would result in a breach of a duty, or (b) was misappropriated.

If such a breach of duty exists, the analyst shall make reasonable efforts to achieve public dissemination of such information.

D. **Responsibilities of Supervisors**
A financial analyst with supervisory responsibility shall exercise reasonable supervision over those subordinate employees subject to his control, to prevent any violation by such persons

*Masculine personal pronouns, used throughout the Code and Standards to simplify sentence structure, shall apply to all persons, regardless of sex.

of applicable statutes, regulations, or provisions of the Code of Ethics or Standards of Professional Conduct. In so doing the analyst is entitled to rely upon reasonable procedures established by his employer.

III. **Research Reports, Investment Recommendations and Actions**

A. **Reasonable Basis and Representations**
1. The financial analyst shall exercise diligence and thoroughness in making an investment recommendation to others or in taking an investment action for others.
2. The financial analyst shall have a reasonable and adequate basis for such recommendations and actions, supported by appropriate research and investigation.
3. The financial analyst shall make reasonable and diligent efforts to avoid any material misrepresentation in any research report or investment recommendation.
4. The financial analyst shall maintain appropriate records to support the reasonableness of such recommendations and actions.

B. **Research Reports**
1. The financial analyst shall use reasonable judgment as to the inclusion of relevant factors in research reports.
2. The financial analyst shall distinguish between facts and opinions in research reports.
3. The financial analyst shall indicate the basic characteristics of the investment involved when preparing for general public distribution a research report that is not directly related to a specific portfolio or client.

C. **Portfolio Investment Recommendations and Actions**
1. The financial analyst shall, when making an investment recommendation or taking an investment action for a specific portfolio or client, consider its appropriateness and suitability for such portfolio or client. In considering such matters, the financial analyst shall take into account (a) the needs and circumstances of the client, (b) the basic characteristics of the investment involved, and (c) the basic characteristics of the total portfolio. The financial analyst shall use reasonable judgment to determine the applicable relevant factors.
2. The financial analyst shall distinguish between facts and opinions in the presentation of investment recommendations.
3. The financial analyst shall disclose to clients and prospective clients the basic format and general principles of the investment processes by which securities are selected and portfolios are constructed and shall promptly disclose to clients any changes that might significantly affect those processes.

D. **Prohibition Against Plagiarism**
The financial analyst shall not, when presenting material to his employer, associates, customers, clients, or the general public, copy or use in substantially the same form material prepared by other persons without acknowledging its use and identifying the name of the author or publisher of such material. The analyst may, however, use without acknowledgement factual information published by recognized financial and statistical reporting services or similar sources.

E. **Prohibition Against Misrepresentation of Services**
The financial analyst shall not make any statements, orally or in writing, which misrepresent (1) the services that the analyst

or his firm is capable of performing for the client, (2) the qualifications of such analyst or his firm, or (3) the expected performance of any investment.

The financial analyst shall not make, orally or in writing, explicitly or implicitly, any assurances about or guarantees of any investment or its return except communication of accurate information as to the terms of the investment instrument and the issuer's obligations under the instrument.

F.   Performance Presentation Standards

1. The financial analyst shall not make any statements, oral or written, which misrepresent the investment performance that the analyst or his firm has accomplished or can reasonably be expected to achieve.

2. If an analyst communicates directly or indirectly individual or firm performance information to a client or prospective client, or in a manner intended to be received by a client or prospective client ("Performance Information"), the analyst shall make every reasonable effort to assure that such performance information is a fair, accurate and complete presentation of such performance.

3. The financial analyst shall inform his employer about the existence and content of the Association for Investment Management and Research's Performance Presentation Standards, and this Standard III F, and shall encourage his employer to adopt and use the Performance Presentation Standards.

4. If Performance Information complies with the Performance Presentation Standards, the analyst shall be presumed to be in compliance with III F 2 above.

5. An analyst presenting Performance Information may use the following legend on the Performance Information presentation, but only if the analyst has made every reasonable effort to assure that such presentation is in compliance with the Performance Presentation Standards in all material respects:

> This Report has been prepared and presented in compliance with the Performance Presentation Standards of the Association for Investment Management and Research.

This Standard shall take effect January 1, 1993.

G.   Fair Dealing with Customers and Clients

The financial analyst shall act in a manner consistent with his obligation to deal fairly with all customers and clients when (1) disseminating investment recommendations, (2) disseminating material changes in prior investment advice, and (3) taking investment action.

IV.   Priority of Transactions

The financial analyst shall conduct himself in such a manner that transactions for his customers, clients, and employer have priority over transactions in securities or other investments of which he is the beneficial owner, and so that transactions in securities or other investments in which he has such beneficial ownership do not operate adversely to their interests. If an analyst decides to make a recommendation about the purchase or sale of a security or other investment, he shall give his customers, clients, and employer adequate opportunity to act on this recommendation before acting on his own behalf.

For purposes of these Standards of Professional Conduct, a financial analyst is a "beneficial owner" if he directly or indirectly, through any contract, arrangement, understanding, relationship or otherwise, has or shares a direct of indirect pecuniary interest in the securities or the investment.

V.   Disclosure of Conflicts

The financial analyst, when making investment recommendations, or taking investment actions, shall disclose to his customers and clients any material conflict of interest relating to him and any material beneficial ownership of the securities or other investments involved that could reasonably be expected to impair his ability to render unbiased and objective advice.

The financial analyst shall disclose to his employer all matters that could reasonably be expected to interfere with his duty to the employer, or with his ability to render unbiased and objective advice.

The financial analyst shall also comply with all requirements as to disclosure of conflicts of interest imposed by law and by rules and regulations of organizations governing his activities and shall comply with any prohibitions on his activities if a conflict of interest exists.

VI.   Compensation

A.   Disclosure of Additional Compensation Arrangements

The financial analyst shall inform his customers, clients, and employer of compensation or other benefit arrangements in connection with his services to them which are in addition to compensation from them for such services.

B.   Disclosure of Referral Fees

The financial analyst shall make appropriate disclosure to a prospective client or customer of any consideration paid or other benefit delivered to others for recommending his services to that prospective client or customer.

C.   Duty to Employer

The financial analyst shall not undertake independent practice which could result in compensation or other benefit in competition with his employer unless he has received written consent from both his employer and the person for whom he undertakes independent employment.

VII.   Relationships with Others

A.   Preservation of Confidentiality

A financial analyst shall preserve the confidentiality of information communicated by the client concerning matters within the scope of the confidential relationship, unless the financial analyst receives information concerning illegal activities on the part of the client.

B.   Maintenance of Independence and Objectivity

The financial analyst, in relationships and contacts with an issuer of securities, whether individually or as a member of a group, shall use particular care and good judgment to achieve and maintain independence and objectivity.

C.   Fiduciary Duties

The financial analyst, in relationships with clients, shall use particular care in determining applicable fiduciary duty and shall comply with such duty as to those persons and interests to whom it is owed.

VIII.   Use of Professional Designation

The qualified financial analyst may use, as applicable, the professional designation "Member of the Association for Investment Management and Research", "Member of the Financial Analysts Federation", and "Member of the Institute of Chartered Financial Analysts", and is encouraged to do so, but only in a dignified and judicious manner. The use of the designations may be accompanied by an accurate explanation (1) of the requirements that have been met to obtain the designation, and (2) of the Association for Investment Management and Research, the Financial Analysts Federation, and the Institute of Chartered Financial Analysts, as applicable.

The Chartered Financial Analyst may use the professional designation "Chartered Financial Analyst", or the abbreviation "CFA", and is encouraged to do so, but only in a dignified and judicious manner. The use of the designation may be accompanied by an accurate explanation (1) of the requirements that have been met to obtain the designation, and (2) of the Association for Investment Management and Research, and the Institute of Chartered Financial Analysts.

IX.   Professional Misconduct

The financial analyst shall not (1) commit a criminal act that upon conviction materially reflects adversely on his honesty, trustworthiness or fitness as a financial analyst in other respects, or (2) engage in conduct involving dishonesty, fraud, deceit or misrepresentation.

Amended - May 2, 1992, Standard III C, E, G, IV and VI C revised
Amended - May 2, 1992, Standard III F added

APPENDIX C

Interest Tables

TABLE C.1   Present Value of $1: PVIF $= 1/(1 + k)^t$

Period	1%	2%	3%	4%	5%	6%	7%	8%	9%	10%	12%	14%	15%	16%	18%	20%	24%	28%	32%	36%
1	.9901	.9804	.9709	.9615	.9524	.9434	.9346	.9259	.9174	.9091	.8929	.8772	.8696	.8621	.8475	.8333	.8065	.7813	.7576	.7353
2	.9803	.9612	.9426	.9246	.9070	.8900	.8734	.8573	.8417	.8264	.7972	.7695	.7561	.7432	.7182	.6944	.6504	.6104	.5739	.5407
3	.9706	.9423	.9151	.8890	.8638	.8396	.8163	.7938	.7722	.7513	.7118	.6750	.6575	.6407	.6086	.5787	.5245	.4768	.4348	.3975
4	.9610	.9238	.8885	.8548	.8227	.7921	.7629	.7350	.7084	.6830	.6355	.5921	.5718	.5523	.5158	.4823	.4230	.3725	.3294	.2923
5	.9515	.9057	.8626	.8219	.7835	.7473	.7130	.6806	.6499	.6209	.5674	.5194	.4972	.4761	.4371	.4019	.3411	.2910	.2495	.2149
6	.9420	.8880	.8375	.7903	.7462	.7050	.6663	.6302	.5963	.5645	.5066	.4556	.4323	.4104	.3704	.3349	.2751	.2274	.1890	.1580
7	.9327	.8706	.8131	.7599	.7107	.6651	.6227	.5835	.5470	.5132	.4523	.3996	.3759	.3538	.3139	.2791	.2218	.1776	.1432	.1162
8	.9235	.8535	.7894	.7307	.6768	.6274	.5820	.5403	.5019	.4665	.4039	.3506	.3269	.3050	.2660	.2326	.1789	.1388	.1085	.0854
9	.9143	.8368	.7664	.7026	.6446	.5919	.5439	.5002	.4604	.4241	.3606	.3075	.2843	.2630	.2255	.1938	.1443	.1084	.0822	.0628
10	.9053	.8203	.7441	.6756	.6139	.5584	.5083	.4632	.4224	.3855	.3220	.2697	.2472	.2267	.1911	.1615	.1164	.0847	.0623	.0462
11	.8963	.8043	.7224	.6496	.5847	.5268	.4751	.4289	.3875	.3505	.2875	.2366	.2149	.1954	.1619	.1346	.0938	.0662	.0472	.0340
12	.8874	.7885	.7014	.6246	.5568	.4970	.4440	.3971	.3555	.3186	.2567	.2076	.1869	.1685	.1372	.1122	.0757	.0517	.0357	.0250
13	.8787	.7730	.6810	.6006	.5303	.4688	.4150	.3677	.3262	.2897	.2292	.1821	.1625	.1452	.1163	.0935	.0610	.0404	.0271	.0184
14	.8700	.7579	.6611	.5775	.5051	.4423	.3878	.3405	.2992	.2633	.2046	.1597	.1413	.1252	.0985	.0779	.0492	.0316	.0205	.0135
15	.8613	.7430	.6419	.5553	.4810	.4173	.3624	.3152	.2745	.2394	.1827	.1401	.1229	.1079	.0835	.0649	.0397	.0247	.0155	.0099
16	.8528	.7284	.6232	.5339	.4581	.3936	.3387	.2919	.2519	.2176	.1631	.1229	.1069	.0930	.0708	.0541	.0320	.0193	.0118	.0073
17	.8444	.7142	.6050	.5134	.4363	.3714	.3166	.2703	.2311	.1978	.1456	.1078	.0929	.0802	.0600	.0451	.0258	.0150	.0089	.0054
18	.8360	.7002	.5874	.4936	.4155	.3503	.2959	.2502	.2120	.1799	.1300	.0946	.0808	.0691	.0508	.0376	.0208	.0118	.0068	.0039
19	.8277	.6864	.5703	.4746	.3957	.3305	.2765	.2317	.1945	.1635	.1161	.0829	.0703	.0596	.0431	.0313	.0168	.0092	.0051	.0029
20	.8195	.6730	.5537	.4564	.3769	.3118	.2584	.2145	.1784	.1486	.1037	.0728	.0611	.0514	.0365	.0261	.0135	.0072	.0039	.0021
25	.7798	.6095	.4776	.3751	.2953	.2330	.1842	.1460	.1160	.0923	.0588	.0378	.0304	.0245	.0160	.0105	.0046	.0021	.0010	.0005
30	.7419	.5521	.4120	.3083	.2314	.1741	.1314	.0994	.0754	.0573	.0334	.0196	.0151	.0116	.0070	.0042	.0016	.0006	.0002	.0001
40	.6717	.4529	.3066	.2083	.1420	.0972	.0668	.0460	.0318	.0221	.0107	.0053	.0037	.0026	.0013	.0007	.0002	.0001	*	*
50	.6080	.3715	.2281	.1407	.0872	.0543	.0339	.0213	.0134	.0085	.0035	.0014	.0009	.0006	.0003	.0001	*	*	*	*
60	.5504	.3048	.1697	.0951	.0535	.0303	.0173	.0099	.0057	.0033	.0011	.0004	.0002	.0001	*	*	*	*	*	*

*The factor is zero to four decimal places.

TABLE C.2

Present Value of an Annuity of $1 Per Period for *n* Periods:

$$PVIFA = \sum_{t=1}^{n} \frac{1}{(1+k)^t} = \frac{1 - \dfrac{1}{(1+k)^n}}{k}$$

Number of Payments	1%	2%	3%	4%	5%	6%	7%	8%	9%	10%	12%	14%	15%	16%	18%	20%	24%	28%	32%
1	0.9901	0.9804	0.9709	0.9615	0.9524	0.9434	0.9346	0.9259	0.9174	0.9091	0.8929	0.8772	0.8696	0.8621	0.8475	0.8333	0.8065	0.7813	0.7576
2	1.9704	1.9416	1.9135	1.8861	1.8594	1.8334	1.8080	1.7833	1.7591	1.7355	1.6901	1.6467	1.6257	1.6052	1.5656	1.5278	1.4568	1.3916	1.3315
3	2.9410	2.8839	2.8286	2.7751	2.7232	2.6730	2.6243	2.5771	2.5313	2.4869	2.4018	2.3216	2.2832	2.2459	2.1743	2.1065	1.9813	1.8684	1.7663
4	3.9020	3.8077	3.7171	3.6299	3.5460	3.4651	3.3872	3.3121	3.2397	3.1699	3.0373	2.9137	2.8550	2.7982	2.6901	2.5887	2.4043	2.2410	2.0957
5	4.8534	4.7135	4.5797	4.4518	4.3295	4.2124	4.1002	3.9927	3.8897	3.7908	3.6048	3.4331	3.3522	3.2743	3.1272	2.9906	2.7454	2.5320	2.3452
6	5.7955	5.6014	5.4172	5.2421	5.0757	4.9173	4.7665	4.6229	4.4859	4.3553	4.1114	3.8887	3.7845	3.6847	3.4976	3.3255	3.0205	2.7594	2.5342
7	6.7282	6.4720	6.2303	6.0021	5.7864	5.5824	5.3893	5.2064	5.0330	4.8684	4.5638	4.2883	4.1604	4.0386	3.8115	3.6046	3.2423	2.9370	2.6775
8	7.6517	7.3255	7.0197	6.7327	6.4632	6.2098	5.9713	5.7466	5.5348	5.3349	4.9676	4.6389	4.4873	4.3436	4.0776	3.8372	3.4212	3.0758	2.7860
9	8.5660	8.1622	7.7861	7.4353	7.1078	6.8017	6.5152	6.2469	5.9952	5.7590	5.3282	4.9464	4.7716	4.6065	4.3030	4.0310	3.5655	3.1842	2.8681
10	9.4713	8.9826	8.5302	8.1109	7.7217	7.3601	7.0236	6.7101	6.4177	6.1446	5.6502	5.2161	5.0188	4.8332	4.4941	4.1925	3.6819	3.2689	2.9304
11	10.3676	9.7868	9.2526	8.7605	8.3064	7.8869	7.4987	7.1390	6.8052	6.4951	5.9377	5.4527	5.2337	5.0286	4.6560	4.3271	3.7757	3.3351	2.9776
12	11.2551	10.5753	9.9540	9.3851	8.8633	8.3838	7.9427	7.5361	7.1607	6.8137	6.1944	5.6603	5.4206	5.1971	4.7932	4.4392	3.8514	3.3868	3.0133
13	12.1337	11.3484	10.6350	9.9856	9.3936	8.8527	8.3577	7.9038	7.4869	7.1034	6.4235	5.8424	5.5831	5.3423	4.9095	4.5327	3.9124	3.4272	3.0404
14	13.0037	12.1062	11.2961	10.5631	9.8986	9.2950	8.7455	8.2442	7.7862	7.3667	6.6282	6.0021	5.7245	5.4675	5.0081	4.6106	3.9616	3.4587	3.0609
15	13.8651	12.8493	11.9379	11.1184	10.3797	9.7122	9.1079	8.5595	8.0607	7.6061	6.8109	6.1422	5.8474	5.5755	5.0916	4.6755	4.0013	3.4834	3.0764
16	14.7179	13.5777	12.5611	11.6523	10.8378	10.1059	9.4466	8.8514	8.3126	7.8237	6.9740	6.2651	5.9542	5.6685	5.1624	4.7296	4.0333	3.5026	3.0882
17	15.5623	14.2919	13.1661	12.1657	11.2741	10.4773	9.7632	9.1216	8.5436	8.0216	7.1196	6.3729	6.0472	5.7487	5.2223	4.7746	4.0591	3.5177	3.0971
18	16.3983	14.9920	13.7535	12.6593	11.6896	10.8276	10.0591	9.3719	8.7556	8.2014	7.2497	6.4674	6.1280	5.8178	5.2732	4.8122	4.0799	3.5294	3.1039
19	17.2260	15.6785	14.3238	13.1339	12.0853	11.1581	10.3356	9.6036	8.9501	8.3649	7.3658	6.5504	6.1982	5.8775	5.3162	4.8435	4.0967	3.5386	3.1090
20	18.0456	16.3514	14.8775	13.5903	12.4622	11.4699	10.5940	9.8181	9.1285	8.5136	7.4694	6.6231	6.2593	5.9288	5.3527	4.8696	4.1103	3.5458	3.1129
25	22.0232	19.5235	17.4131	15.6221	14.0939	12.7834	11.6536	10.6748	9.8226	9.0770	7.8431	6.8729	6.4641	6.0971	5.4669	4.9476	4.1474	3.5640	3.1220
30	25.8077	22.3965	19.6004	17.2920	15.3725	13.7648	12.4090	11.2578	10.2737	9.4269	8.0552	7.0027	6.5660	6.1772	5.5168	4.9789	4.1601	3.5693	3.1242
40	32.8347	27.3555	23.1148	19.7928	17.1591	15.0463	13.3317	11.9246	10.7574	9.7791	8.2438	7.1050	6.6418	6.2335	5.5482	4.9966	4.1659	3.5712	3.1250
50	39.1961	31.4236	25.7298	21.4822	18.2559	15.7619	13.8007	12.2335	10.9617	9.9148	8.3045	7.1327	6.6605	6.2463	5.5541	4.9995	4.1666	3.5714	3.1250
60	44.9550	34.7609	27.6756	22.6235	18.9293	16.1614	14.0392	12.3766	11.0480	9.9672	8.3240	7.1401	6.6651	6.2402	5.5553	4.9999	4.1667	3.5714	3.1250

TABLE C.3 Future Value of $1 at the End of *n* Periods: $FVIF_{k,n} = (1 + k)^n$

Period	1%	2%	3%	4%	5%	6%	7%	8%	9%	10%	12%	14%	15%	16%	18%	20%	24%	28%	32%	36%
1	1.0100	1.0200	1.0300	1.0400	1.0500	1.0600	1.0700	1.0800	1.0900	1.1000	1.1200	1.1400	1.1500	1.1600	1.1800	1.2000	1.2400	1.2800	1.3200	1.3600
2	1.0201	1.0404	1.0609	1.0816	1.1025	1.1236	1.1449	1.1664	1.1881	1.2100	1.2544	1.2996	1.3225	1.3456	1.3924	1.4400	1.5376	1.6384	1.7424	1.8496
3	1.0303	1.0612	1.0927	1.1249	1.1576	1.1910	1.2250	1.2597	1.2950	1.3310	1.4049	1.4815	1.5209	1.5609	1.6430	1.7280	1.9066	2.0972	2.3000	2.5155
4	1.0406	1.0824	1.1255	1.1699	1.2155	1.2625	1.3108	1.3605	1.4116	1.4641	1.5735	1.6890	1.7490	1.8106	1.9388	2.0736	2.3642	2.6844	3.0360	3.4210
5	1.0510	1.1041	1.1593	1.2167	1.2763	1.3382	1.4026	1.4693	1.5386	1.6105	1.7623	1.9254	2.0114	2.1003	2.2878	2.4883	2.9316	3.4360	4.0075	4.6526
6	1.0615	1.1262	1.1941	1.2653	1.3401	1.4185	1.5007	1.5869	1.6771	1.7716	1.9738	2.1950	2.3131	2.4364	2.6996	2.9860	3.6352	4.3980	5.2899	6.3275
7	1.0721	1.1487	1.2299	1.3159	1.4071	1.5036	1.6058	1.7138	1.8280	1.9487	2.2107	2.5023	2.6600	2.8262	3.1855	3.5832	4.5077	5.6295	6.9826	8.6054
8	1.0829	1.1717	1.2668	1.3686	1.4775	1.5938	1.7182	1.8509	1.9926	2.1436	2.4760	2.8526	3.0590	3.2784	3.7589	4.2998	5.5895	7.2058	9.2170	11.703
9	1.0937	1.1951	1.3048	1.4233	1.5513	1.6895	1.8385	1.9990	2.1719	2.3579	2.7731	3.2519	3.5179	3.8030	4.4355	5.1598	6.9310	9.2234	12.166	15.916
10	1.1046	1.2190	1.3439	1.4802	1.6289	1.7908	1.9672	2.1589	2.3674	2.5937	3.1058	3.7072	4.0456	4.4114	5.2338	6.1917	8.5944	11.805	16.059	21.646
11	1.1157	1.2434	1.3842	1.5395	1.7103	1.8983	2.1049	2.3316	2.5804	2.8531	3.4785	4.2262	4.6524	5.1173	6.1759	7.4301	10.657	15.111	21.198	29.439
12	1.1268	1.2682	1.4258	1.6010	1.7959	2.0122	2.2522	2.5182	2.8127	3.1384	3.8960	4.8179	5.3502	5.9360	7.2876	8.9161	13.214	19.342	27.982	40.037
13	1.1381	1.2936	1.4685	1.6651	1.8856	2.1329	2.4098	2.7196	3.0658	3.4523	4.3635	5.4924	6.1528	6.8858	8.5994	10.699	16.386	24.758	36.937	54.451
14	1.1495	1.3195	1.5126	1.7317	1.9799	2.2609	2.5785	2.9372	3.3417	3.7975	4.8871	6.2613	7.0757	7.9875	10.147	12.839	20.319	31.691	48.756	74.053
15	1.1610	1.3459	1.5580	1.8009	2.0789	2.3966	2.7590	3.1722	3.6425	4.1772	5.4736	7.1379	8.1371	9.2655	11.973	15.407	25.195	40.564	64.358	100.71
16	1.1726	1.3728	1.6047	1.8730	2.1829	2.5404	2.9522	3.4259	3.9703	4.5950	6.1304	8.1372	9.3576	10.748	14.129	18.488	31.242	51.923	84.953	136.96
17	1.1843	1.4002	1.6528	1.9479	2.2920	2.6928	3.1588	3.7000	4.3276	5.0545	6.8660	9.2765	10.761	12.467	16.672	22.186	38.740	66.461	112.13	186.27
18	1.1961	1.4282	1.7024	2.0258	2.4066	2.8543	3.3799	3.9960	4.7171	5.5599	7.6900	10.575	12.375	14.462	19.673	26.623	48.038	85.070	148.02	253.33
19	1.2081	1.4568	1.7535	2.1068	2.5270	3.0256	3.6165	4.3157	5.1417	6.1159	8.6128	12.055	14.231	16.776	23.214	31.948	59.567	108.89	195.39	344.53
20	1.2202	1.4859	1.8061	2.1911	2.6533	3.2071	3.8697	4.6610	5.6044	6.7275	9.6463	13.743	16.366	19.460	27.393	38.337	73.864	139.37	257.91	468.57
21	1.2324	1.5157	1.8603	2.2788	2.7860	3.3996	4.1406	5.0338	6.1088	7.4002	10.803	15.667	18.821	22.574	32.323	46.005	91.591	178.40	340.44	637.26
22	1.2447	1.5460	1.9161	2.3699	2.9253	3.6035	4.4304	5.4365	6.6586	8.1403	12.100	17.861	21.644	26.186	38.142	55.206	113.57	228.35	449.39	866.67
23	1.2572	1.5769	1.9736	2.4647	3.0715	3.8197	4.7405	5.8715	7.2579	8.9543	13.552	20.361	24.891	30.376	45.007	66.247	140.83	292.30	593.19	1178.6
24	1.2697	1.6084	2.0328	2.5633	3.2251	4.0489	5.0724	6.3412	7.9111	9.8497	15.178	23.212	28.625	35.236	53.108	79.496	174.63	374.14	783.02	1602.9
25	1.2824	1.6406	2.0938	2.6658	3.3864	4.2919	5.4274	6.8485	8.6231	10.834	17.000	26.461	32.918	40.874	62.668	95.396	216.54	478.90	1033.5	2180.0
26	1.2953	1.6734	2.1566	2.7725	3.5557	4.5494	5.8074	7.3964	9.3992	11.918	19.040	30.166	37.856	47.414	73.948	114.47	268.51	612.99	1364.3	2964.9
27	1.3082	1.7069	2.2213	2.8834	3.7335	4.8223	6.2139	7.9881	10.245	13.110	21.324	34.389	43.535	55.000	87.259	137.37	332.95	784.63	1800.9	4032.2
28	1.3213	1.7410	2.2879	2.9987	3.9201	5.1117	6.6488	8.6271	11.167	14.421	23.883	39.204	50.065	63.800	102.96	164.84	412.86	1004.3	2377.2	5483.8
29	1.3345	1.7758	2.3566	3.1187	4.1161	5.4184	7.1143	9.3173	12.172	15.863	26.749	44.693	57.575	74.008	121.50	197.81	511.95	1285.5	3137.9	7458.0
30	1.3478	1.8114	2.4273	3.2434	4.3219	5.7435	7.6123	10.062	13.267	17.449	29.959	50.950	66.211	85.849	143.37	237.37	634.81	1645.5	4142.0	10143.
40	1.4889	2.2080	3.2620	4.8010	7.0400	10.285	14.974	21.724	31.409	45.259	93.050	188.88	267.86	378.72	750.37	1469.7	5455.9	19426.	66520.	•
50	1.6446	2.6916	4.3839	7.1067	11.467	18.420	29.457	46.901	74.357	117.39	289.00	700.23	1083.6	1670.7	3927.3	9100.4	46890.	•	•	•
60	1.8167	3.2810	5.8916	10.519	18.679	32.987	57.946	101.25	176.03	304.48	897.59	2595.9	4383.9	7370.1	20555.	56347.	•	•	•	•

*FVIFA > 99.999

TABLE C.4 Sum of an Annuity of $1 Per Period for n Periods:

$$FVIFA_{k,n} = \sum_{t=1}^{n}(1+k)^{t-1} = \frac{(1+k)^n - 1}{k}$$

Number of Periods	1%	2%	3%	4%	5%	6%	7%	8%	9%	10%	12%	14%	15%	16%	18%	20%	24%	28%	32%	36%
1	1.0000	1.0000	1.0000	1.0000	1.0000	1.0000	1.0000	1.0000	1.0000	1.0000	1.0000	1.0000	1.0000	1.0000	1.0000	1.0000	1.0000	1.0000	1.0000	1.0000
2	2.0100	2.0200	2.0300	2.0400	2.0500	2.0600	2.0700	2.0800	2.0900	2.1000	2.1200	2.1400	2.1500	2.1600	2.1800	2.2000	2.2400	2.2800	2.3200	2.3600
3	3.0301	3.0604	3.0909	3.1216	3.1525	3.1836	3.2149	3.2464	3.2781	3.3100	3.3744	3.4396	3.4725	3.5056	3.5724	3.6400	3.7776	3.9184	4.0624	4.2096
4	4.0604	4.1216	4.1836	4.2465	4.3101	4.3746	4.4399	4.5061	4.5731	4.6410	4.7793	4.9211	4.9934	5.0665	5.2154	5.3680	5.6842	6.0156	6.3624	6.7251
5	5.1010	5.2040	5.3091	5.4163	5.5256	5.6371	5.7507	5.8666	5.9847	6.1051	6.3528	6.6101	6.7424	6.8771	7.1542	7.4416	8.0484	8.6999	9.3983	10.146
6	6.1520	6.3081	6.4684	6.6330	6.8019	6.9753	7.1533	7.3359	7.5233	7.7156	8.1152	8.5355	8.7537	8.9775	9.4420	9.9299	10.980	12.135	13.405	14.798
7	7.2135	7.4343	7.6625	7.8983	8.1420	8.3938	8.6540	8.9228	9.2004	9.4872	10.089	10.730	11.066	11.413	12.141	12.915	14.615	16.533	18.695	21.126
8	8.2857	8.5830	8.8923	9.2142	9.5491	9.8975	10.259	10.636	11.028	11.435	12.299	13.232	13.726	14.240	15.327	16.499	19.122	22.163	25.678	29.731
9	9.3685	9.7546	10.159	10.582	11.026	11.491	11.978	12.487	13.021	13.579	14.775	16.085	16.785	17.518	19.085	20.798	24.712	29.369	34.895	41.435
10	10.462	10.949	11.463	12.006	12.577	13.180	13.816	14.486	15.192	15.937	17.548	19.337	20.303	21.321	23.521	25.958	31.643	38.592	47.061	57.351
11	11.566	12.168	12.807	13.486	14.206	14.971	15.783	16.645	17.560	18.531	20.654	23.044	24.349	25.732	28.755	32.150	40.237	50.398	63.121	78.998
12	12.682	13.412	14.192	15.025	15.917	16.869	17.888	18.977	20.140	21.384	24.133	27.270	29.001	30.850	34.931	39.580	50.894	65.510	84.320	108.43
13	13.809	14.680	15.617	16.626	17.713	18.882	20.140	21.495	22.953	24.522	28.029	32.088	34.351	36.786	42.218	48.496	64.109	84.852	112.30	148.47
14	14.947	15.973	17.086	18.291	19.598	21.015	22.550	24.214	26.019	27.975	32.392	37.581	40.504	43.672	50.818	59.195	80.496	109.61	149.23	202.92
15	16.096	17.293	18.598	20.023	21.578	23.276	25.129	27.152	29.360	31.772	37.279	43.842	47.580	51.659	60.965	72.035	100.81	141.30	197.99	276.97
16	17.257	18.639	20.156	21.824	23.657	25.672	27.888	30.324	33.003	35.949	42.753	50.980	55.717	60.925	72.939	87.442	126.01	181.86	262.35	377.69
17	18.430	20.012	21.761	23.697	25.840	28.212	30.840	33.750	36.973	40.544	48.883	59.117	65.075	71.673	87.068	105.93	157.25	233.79	347.30	514.66
18	19.614	21.412	23.414	25.645	28.132	30.905	33.999	37.450	41.301	45.599	55.749	68.394	75.836	84.140	103.74	128.11	195.99	300.25	459.44	700.93
19	20.810	22.840	25.116	27.671	30.539	33.760	37.379	41.446	46.018	51.159	63.439	78.969	88.211	98.603	123.41	154.74	244.03	385.32	607.47	954.27
20	22.019	24.297	26.870	29.778	33.066	36.785	40.995	45.762	51.160	57.275	72.052	91.024	102.44	115.37	146.62	186.68	303.60	494.21	802.86	1298.8
21	23.239	25.783	28.676	31.969	35.719	39.992	44.865	50.422	56.764	64.002	81.698	104.76	118.81	134.84	174.02	225.02	377.46	633.59	1060.7	1767.3
22	24.471	27.299	30.536	34.248	38.505	43.392	49.005	55.456	62.873	71.402	92.502	120.43	137.63	157.41	206.34	271.03	469.05	811.99	1401.2	2404.6
23	25.716	28.845	32.452	36.617	41.430	46.995	53.436	60.893	69.531	79.543	104.60	138.29	159.27	183.60	244.48	326.23	582.62	1040.3	1850.6	3271.3
24	26.973	30.421	34.426	39.082	44.502	50.815	58.176	66.764	76.789	88.497	118.15	158.65	184.16	213.97	289.49	392.48	723.46	1332.6	2443.8	4449.9
25	28.243	32.030	36.459	41.645	47.727	54.864	63.249	73.105	84.700	98.347	133.33	181.87	212.79	249.21	342.60	471.98	898.09	1706.8	3226.8	6052.9
26	29.525	33.670	38.553	44.311	51.113	59.156	68.676	79.954	93.323	109.18	150.33	208.33	245.71	290.08	405.27	567.37	1114.6	2185.7	4260.4	8233.0
27	30.820	35.344	40.709	47.084	54.669	63.705	74.483	87.350	102.72	121.09	169.37	238.49	283.56	337.50	479.22	681.85	1383.1	2798.7	5624.7	11197.9
28	32.129	37.051	42.930	49.967	58.402	68.528	80.697	95.338	112.96	134.20	190.69	272.88	327.10	392.50	566.48	819.22	1716.0	3583.3	7425.6	15230.2
29	33.450	38.792	45.218	52.966	62.322	73.639	87.346	103.96	124.13	148.63	214.58	312.09	377.16	456.30	669.44	984.06	2128.9	4587.6	9802.9	20714.1
30	34.784	40.568	47.575	56.084	66.438	79.058	94.460	113.28	136.30	164.49	241.33	356.78	434.74	530.31	790.94	1181.8	2640.9	5873.2	12940.	28172.2
40	48.886	60.402	75.401	95.025	120.79	154.76	199.63	259.05	337.88	442.59	767.09	1342.0	1779.0	2360.7	4163.2	7343.8	22728.	69377.	•	•
50	64.463	84.579	112.79	152.66	209.34	290.33	406.52	573.76	815.08	1163.9	2400.0	4994.5	7217.7	10435.	21813.	45497.	•	•	•	•
60	81.669	114.05	163.05	237.99	353.58	533.12	813.52	1253.2	1944.7	3034.8	7471.6	18535.	29219.	46057.	•	•	•	•	•	•

*FVIF > 99.999

APPENDIX D

Standard Normal Probabilities

z	0.00	0.01	0.02	0.03	0.04	0.05	0.06	0.07	0.08	0.09
0.0	.5000	.5040	.5080	.5120	.5160	.5199	.5239	.5279	.5219	.5359
0.1	.5398	.5438	.5478	.5517	.5557	.5596	.5636	.5675	.5714	.5753
0.2	.5793	.5832	.5871	.5910	.5948	.5987	.6026	.6064	.6103	.6141
0.3	.6179	.6217	.6255	.6293	.6331	.6368	.6406	.6443	.6480	.6517
0.4	.6554	.6591	.6628	.6664	.6700	.6736	.6772	.6808	.6844	.6879
0.5	.6915	.6950	.6985	.7019	.7054	.7088	.7123	.7157	.7190	.7224
0.6	.7257	.7291	.7324	.7357	.7389	.7422	.7454	.7486	.7517	.7549
0.7	.7580	.7611	.7642	.7673	.7704	.7734	.7764	.7794	.7823	.7852
0.8	.7881	.7910	.7939	.7967	.7995	.8023	.8051	.8078	.8106	.8133
0.9	.8159	.8186	.8212	.8238	.8264	.8289	.8315	.8340	.8365	.8389
1.0	.8413	.8438	.8461	.8485	.8508	.8531	.8554	.8577	.8599	.8621
1.1	.8643	.8665	.8686	.8708	.8729	.8749	.8770	.8790	.8810	.8830
1.2	.8849	.8860	.8888	.8907	.8925	.8943	.8962	.8980	.8997	.9015
1.3	.9032	.9049	.9066	.9082	.9099	.9115	.9131	.9147	.9162	.9177
1.4	.9192	.9207	.9222	.9236	.9251	.9265	.9279	.9292	.9306	.9319
1.5	.9332	.9345	.9357	.9370	.9382	.9394	.9406	.9418	.9429	.9441
1.6	.9452	.9463	.9474	.9484	.9495	.9505	.9515	.9525	.9535	.9545
1.7	.9554	.9564	.9573	.9582	.9591	.9599	.9608	.9616	.9625	.9633
1.8	.9641	.9649	.9656	.9664	.9671	.9678	.9686	.9693	.9699	.9706
1.9	.9713	.9719	.9726	.9732	.9738	.9744	.9750	.9756	.9761	.9767
2.0	.9772	.9778	.9783	.9788	.9793	.9798	.9803	.9808	.9812	.9817
2.1	.9821	.9826	.9830	.9834	.9838	.9842	.9846	.9850	.9854	.9857
2.2	.9861	.9864	.9868	.9871	.9875	.9878	.9881	.9884	.9887	.9890
2.3	.9893	.9896	.9898	.9901	.9904	.9906	.9909	.9911	.9913	.9916
2.4	.9918	.9920	.9922	.9925	.9927	.9929	.9931	.9932	.9934	.9936
2.5	.9938	.9940	.9941	.9943	.9945	.9946	.9948	.9949	.9951	.9952
2.6	.9953	.9955	.9956	.9957	.9959	.9960	.9961	.9962	.9963	.9964
2.7	.9965	.9966	.9967	.9968	.9969	.9970	.9971	.9972	.9973	.9974
2.8	.9974	.9975	.9976	.9977	.9977	.9978	.9979	.9979	.9980	.9981
2.9	.9981	.9982	.9982	.9983	.9984	.9984	.9985	.9985	.9986	.9986
3.0	.9987	.9987	.9987	.9988	.9988	.9989	.9989	.9989	.9990	.9990

PERMISSIONS

Figure 21.7 "Mutual Fund Scoreboard," reprinted from February 2, 1998 issue of BUSINESS WEEK, by special permission, © 1998 by The McGraw-Hill Companies, Inc.

Figure 21.8 "Vanguard Index 500," from MORNINGSTAR, INC., September 26, 1997. Reprinted by permission.

Table 22.4 From "Asset Allocation: Management Style and Performance Measurement," by William F. Sharpe, in *Journal Of Portfolio Management*, Winter 1992. Reprinted by permission of Institutional Investor Journals, a Division of Institutional Investor, Inc.

Figure 22.5 From "Asset Allocation: Management Style and Performance Measurement," by William F. Sharpe, in *Journal Of Portfolio Management*, Winter 1992. Reprinted by permission of Institutional Investor Journals, a Division of Institutional Investor, Inc.

Figure 22.6 From "Asset Allocation: Management Style and Performance Measurement," by William F. Sharpe, in *Journal Of Portfolio Management*, Winter 1992. Reprinted by permission of Institutional Investor Journals, a Division of Institutional Investor, Inc.

Figure 22.7 "Definitive New Measures of Bond Performance and Risk," by D.A. Tito and W.H. Wagner, from *Pension World*, June 1977. Reprinted by permission.